AF865278

PRENTICE HALL 2002–2003

Economics Faculty Directory

Compiled by

James R. Hasselback

Pearson Education

PRENTICE HALL, Upper Saddle River, NJ 07458

Editor-in-Chief: *PJ Boardman*
Executive Marketing Manager: *Kathleen McLellan*
Executive Editor: *Rod Banister*
Managing Editor: *Gladys Soto*
Assistant Editor: *Marie McHale*
Editorial Assistant: *Lisa Amato*
Manager, Print Production: *Christy Mahon*
Production Editor: *Carol Zaino*
Cover Design: *Michael Fruhbeis*
Manufacturer: *Victor Graphics, Inc.*

Pearson Education LTD.
Pearson Education Australia PTY, Limited
Pearson Education Singapore, Pte. Ltd
Pearson Education North Asia Ltd
Pearson Education, Canada, Ltd
Pearson Educación de Mexico, S.A. de C.V.
Pearson Education–Japan
Pearson Education Malaysia, Pte. Ltd

Prentice Hall

10 9 8 7 6 5 4 3 2 1
ISBN 0-13-009055-7

table of contents

Principles of Economics

NEW! O'Sullivan/Sheffrin, *Economics: Principles and Tools wth Active Learing CD-ROM 3/e* 1

Case/Fair, *Principles of Economics with ActiveEcon CD-ROM 6/e* 2

Principles of Microeconomics

Case/Fair, *Principles of MicroEconomics* activebook 3

Princples of Macroeconomics

Case/Fair, *Principles of Macroeconomics* activebook 4

One-Semester Survey of Economics

NEW! O'Sullivan/Sheffrin, *Survey of Economics: Principles and Tools* 6

Heyne/Boettke/Prychitko, *The Economic Way of Thinking 10/e* 6

Collinge/Ayers, *Economics by Design: Principles and Issues 2/e* 7

Economic History – Freshman-Level Survey

Heilbroner/Milberg, *The Making of Economic Society 11/e* 8

Intermediate Macroeconomics

NEW! Colander/Gamber, *Macroeconomics* 8

Blanchard, *Macroeconomics 3/e* 9

NEW! Froyen, *Macroeconomics: Theories and Policies 7/e* 10

Intermediate Microeconomics

Pindyck/Rubinfeld, *Microeconomics 5/e* 11

NEW! Mathis/Koscianski, *Microeconomics: An Integrated Approach* 11

Eaton/Allen, *Microeconomics 5/e* 12

Managerial Economics

Keat/Young, *Managerial Economics; Economics Tools for Today's Decision Makers 4/e* 13

Milgrom/Roberts, *The Economics, Organization, and Management* 14

Industrial Organization

Adams/Brock, *The Structure of American Industry 10/e* 14

Caves, *American Industry: Structure, Conduct, Performance 7/e* 15

Labor Economics

Blau/Ferber/Winkler, *The Economics of Women, Men, and Work 4/e* 15

Reynolds/Masters/Moser, *Labor Economics and Labor Relations 11/e* 16

International Economics

Roberts, *The Choice: A Fable of Free Trade and Protectionism* 16

Sawyer/Sprinkle, *International Economics* 17

Developmental Economics

NEW! Lynn, *Economic Development: Theory and Practice for a Divided World* 17

The Economics of Poverty and Discrimination

Schiller, *The Ecoonomics of Poverty and Discrimination 8/e* 18

Cost-Benefit Analysis

Boardman/Greenburg/Vining/Weimer, *Cost-Benefit Analysis: Concepts and Practice 2/e* 18

Government and Business

Weidenbaum, *Business and Government in the Global Marketplace 6/e* 19

Urban Economics

Bogart, *The Economics of Cities and Suburbs* 19

DiPasquale/Wheaton, *Urban Economics and Real Estate Markets* 20

Health Economics

Folland/Goodman/Stano, *The Economics of Health and Health Care 3/e* 20

Econometrics

NEW! Greene, *Econometric Analysis 5/e* 21

Mathematical Economics

NEW! Hess, *Using Mathematics in Economic Analysis* 22

Sports Economics

NEW! Fort, *Sports Economics* 23

Economics of E-Business

NEW! Singh, *Electronic Commerce: Economics and Strategy* 23

Special Offers

The Wall Street Journal 25
Financial Times 26
Economist.com 27

Prentice Hall Technology

Internet and Online Solutions 28
Text-Specific Web sites 29
Companion Website 30
Online and Web-Enhanced Courses 31
Blackboard 32
CourseCompass 33
CourseCompass with ebook 33
WebCT 34
activebooks 35
Software Solutions
Mastering Economics 37

Principles of Economics

Two Semester Principles of Economics

Economics: Principles and Tools with Active Learning CD-ROM

Third Edition

Arthur O'Sullivan, Lewis and Clark College
Steven M. Sheffrin, University of California, Davis

© 2003, 704 pp., Cloth Package w/ CD,
0-13-008151-5

BASIC APPROACH

This modern principles text has a strong foundation in demand and supply, the most important topic in learning and teaching principles of economics. Its improved coverage of change in demand vs. change in quantity demanded (also in supply coverage) enables students to better visualize and truly understand the difference between these two fundamental concepts. Early coverage of comparative advantage and externalities reflects a more modern approach to teaching and understanding the underpinnings of microeconomics. In macroeconomics, a balanced presentation between long run and short run topics allow professors to cover the important issues of growth early, and gives them the flexibility to cover Keynesian material when they feel it is important.

CONTENTS

I. INTRODUCTION AND KEY PRINCIPLES.
1. Introduction: What Is Economics?
2. Key Principles of Economics.
3. Markets and Government in the Global Economy.
4. Supply, Demand, and Market Equilibrium.

II. A CLOSER LOOK AT SUPPLY AND DEMAND.
5. Elasticity: A Measure of Responsiveness.
6. Market Efficiency and Government Intervention.
7. Consumer Choice.

III. MARKET STRUCTURES AND PRICING.
8. Production and Cost.
9. Perfect Competition: Short Run and Long Run.
10. Monopoly.
11. Entry and Monopolistic Competition.
12. Oligopoly and Strategic Behavior.
13. Using Market Power: Price Discrimination and Advertising.
14. Controlling Market Power: Antitrust Policy and Deregulation.

IV. SPILLOVERS AND INFORMATION.
15. Imperfect Information and Disappearing Markets
16. Public Goods, Taxes, and Public Choice.
17. Environmental Policy.

V. THE LABOR MARKET AND ECONOMIC CHALLENGES.
18. The Labor Market.
19. Economic Challenges: Poverty, Aging, Health Care.

VI. THE BASIC CONCEPTS IN MACROECONOMICS.
20. Measuring a Nation's Production and Income.
21. Unemployment and Inflation.

VII. THE ECONOMY IN THE LONG RUN.
22. Classical Economics: The Economy at Full Employment.
23. Why Do Economies Grow?

VIII. ECONOMIC FLUCTUATIONS.
24. Aggregate Demand and Aggregate Supply.
25. Keynesian Economics and Fiscal Policy.
26. Investment and Financial Intermediation.

IX. MONEY, BANKING, AND MONETARY POLICY.
27. Money, the Banking System, and the Federal Reserve.
28. Monetary Policy in the Short Run.

X. INFLATION, UNEMPLOYMENT, AND ECONOMIC POLICY.
29. From the Short Run to the Long Run.
30. The Dynamics of Inflation and Unemployment.
31. Current Issues in Macroeconomic Policy.

XI. THE INTERNATIONAL ECONOMY.
32. International Trade and Public Policy.
33. The World of International Finance.

Macroeconomics: Principles and Tools with Active Learning CD-ROM

© 2003, 384 pp., Paper (0-13-035811-8)

Microeconomics: Principles and Tools with Active Learning CD-ROM

© 2003, 448 pp., Paper (0-13-035812-6)

SUPPLEMENTS

- Review Copy
- Study Guide
- Micro Study Guide
- Macro Study Guide
- Active Learning CD-ROM
- Macro Test Item File
- Micro Test Item File
- Macro Test Item File #2
- Micro Test Item File #2
- Instructor's Resource CD with CTB and PowerPoint Slides
- Instructor's Manual
- Transparency Acetates
- Companion Website
- WebCT
- Blackboard
- CourseCompass
- Course Compass with E/book

Generic supplements

- Prentice Hall Guide to Economist.com
- Using Economic Experiments and Cases in the Classroom
- Prentice Hall's Guide to E-Business for Economics
- Prentice Hall Guide to The Wall Street Journal
- Prentice Hall Guide to the Financial Times
- The Choice: A Fable of Free Trade and Protectionism, Updated and Revised Edition

Ask your Prentice Hall representative about Value-saving text and supplement packages!

Principles of Economics and ActiveEcon CD

Sixth Edition

Karl E. Case, Wellesley College
Ray C. Fair, Yale University

© 2002, 743 pp., Cloth Bound w/CD-ROM, 0-13-073772-0

BASIC APPROACH

Written by two highly respected economists and educators, the text uses the "Stories, Graphs, and Equations" approach to make economic concepts accessible and relevant to students with various learning styles.

Known for its unified and logical structure, lively writing style, clear explanations and unparalleled supplements packages, the text supports both the instructor and the student through this first, often challenging, economics course. Case/Fair is one of the most widely adopted texts in this market, nationwide!

CONTENTS

I. INTRODUCTION TO ECONOMICS.
1. The Scope and Method of Economics.
2. The Economic Problem: Scarcity and Choice.
3. Demand, Supply, and Market Equilibrium.
4. The Price System, Demand and Supply, and Elasticity.

II. FOUNDATIONS OF MICROECONOMICS: CONSUMERS AND FIRMS.
5. Household Behavior and Consumer Choice.
6. The Production Process: The Behavior of Profit Maximizing Firms.
7. Short-Run Costs and Output Decisions.
8. Costs and Output Decisions in the Long Run.
9. Input Demand: The Labor and Land Markets.
10. Input Demand: The Capital Market and the Investment Decision.
11. General Equilibrium and the Efficiency of Perfect Competition.

III. MARKET IMPERFECTIONS AND THE ROLE OF GOVERNMENT.
12. Monopoly and Antitrust Policy.
13. Monopolistic Competition and Oligopoly.

14. Externalities, Public Goods, Imperfect Information, and Social Choice.
15. Income Distribution and Poverty.

IV. CONCEPTS AND PROBLEMS IN MACROECONOMICS.

16. Introduction to Macroeconomics.
17. Measuring National Output and National Income.
18. Long-Run and Short-Run Concerns: Growth, Productivity, Unemployment, and Inflation.

V. THE GOODS AND MONEY MARKETS.

19. Aggregate Expenditure and Equilibrium Output.
20. The Government and Fiscal Policy.
21. The Money Supply and the Federal Reserve System.
22. Money Demand, the Equilibrium Interest Rate, and Monetary Policy.

VI. MACROECONOMIC ANALYSIS.

23. Money, the Interest Rate, and Output: Analysis and Policy.
24. Aggregate Demand, Aggregate Supply, and Inflation.
25. The Labor Market, Unemployment, and Inflation.
26. Macroeconomic Issues and Policy.
27. Household and Firm Behavior in the Macroeconomy: A Further Look.
28. Long-Run Growth.
29. Debates in Macroeconomics: Monetarism, New Classical Theory, and Supply Side Economics.

VII. THE WORLD ECONOMY.

30. International Trade, Comparative Advantage, and Protectionism.
31. Open Economy Macroeconomics: The Balance of Payments and Exchange Rates.
32. Economic Growth in Developing and Transitional Economies.

Glossary of Terms.
Solutions to Even-Numbered Problems.

Principles of Macroeconomics with Active Econ CD-ROM, 6/e

©2002, 457pp., Paper (0-13-074645-2)

Principles of Microeconomics with Active Econ CD-ROM, 6/e

©2002, 423pp., Paper (0-13-074643-6)

SUPPLEMENTS

- Review Copy
- Study Guide
- Macro Study Guide
- Micro Study Guide
- ActiveEcon CD-ROM
- ABC Video Library 2001
- Instructor's Manual with Video Guide
- Micro Test Item File #1
- Micro Test Item File #2
- Micro Test Item File #3
- Macro Test Item File #1
- Macro Test Item File #2
- Macro Test Item File #3
- IRCD with PowerPoints & Test Managers
- Transparency Acetates
- WebCT
- Blackboard
- CourseCompass
- Companion Website - www.prenhall.com/casefair

Generic Supplements

- Student Guide to the Financial Times
- Prentice Hall Guide to the Wall Street Journal
- Prentice Hall Guide to Economist.com
- Prentice Hall's Guide to E-Business for Economics
- Mastering Economics Interactive CD-ROM

PRINCIPLES OF MICROECONOMICS

Principles of Microeconomics activebook

Karl E. Case, Wellesley College
Ray C. Fair, Yale University

© 2002, Paper, 0-13-064847-7

BASIC APPROACH

Case/Fair's Microeconomics activebook is an interactive, online, digital book that completely integrates multimedia resources with the textbook to greatly enhance the student learning experience. The activebook experience:

- Uses the web for what it's good at!-An activebook takes full advantage of the online environment. Gearing Up sections highlight the chapter's central concepts. Active Examples and Active Exercises help students explore the chapter's most important points through video, audio, and text. Concept Checks allow students to test their understanding of the material at the end of every major section, with links back to appropriate coverage. Chapter Wrap-Ups include a practice quiz, which gives students a chance to test their knowledge. Dynamic content is updated as often as needed.

- Lets students learn the way they learn best!-An activebook engages students of all learning styles through online print, audio, and video resources. The activebook experience is customizable by faculty and students. Students can annotate their activebook and customize their view of the book's dynamic resources.
- Gives you more for less!-Despite the increased amount of multimedia and interactive content, activebooks cost less than traditional textbooks. Even though the core text is retained in print, the print component of an activebook is shorter than a traditional text. All boxed material, chapter summaries, exercises, and other content that can be made dynamic reside in the online component of the activebook.
- Active examples and Active exercises use video, audio, and additional tools, such as Active graphs to bring the text to life! For example, graphs come to life when studetns click on Active Examples, embedded thoughout the activebook. Students can change the value of a variable and look at the effects on the equilibrium.

Log on to www.prenhall.com/myactivebook for a demo chapter.

CONTENTS

I. INTRODUCTION TO ECONOMICS.
1. The Scope and Method of Economics.
2. The Economic Problem: Scarcity and Choice.
3. Demand, Supply, and Market Equilibrium.
4. The Price System, Demand and Supply, and Elasticity.

II. FOUNDATIONS OF MICROECONOMICS: CONSUMERS AND FIRMS.
5. Household Behavior and Consumer Choice.
6. The Production Process: The Behavior of Profit Maximizing Firms.
7. Short-Run Costs and Output Decisions.
8. Costs and Output Decisions in the Long Run.
9. Input Demand: The Labor and Land Markets.
10. Input Demand: The Capital Market and the Investment Decision.
11. General Equilibrium and the Efficiency of Perfect Competition.

III. MARKET IMPERFECTIONS AND THE ROLE OF GOVERNMENT.
12. Monopoly and Antitrust Policy.
13. Monopolistic Competition and Oligopoly.
14. Externalities, Public Goods, Imperfect Information, and Social Choice.
15. Income Distribution and Poverty.

IV. THE WORLD ECONOMY.
16. International Trade, Comparative Advantage, and Protectionism.
17. Economic Growth in Developing and Transitional Economies.

Glossary of Terms.

Solutions to Even-Numbered Problems.

SUPPLEMENTS

- Instructor's Resource CD
- Prentice Hall Guide to the Wall Street Journal
- Online Course Solutions are available in Blackboard, CourseCompass, and WebCT.

Generic Supplements

- Prentice Hall's Guide to E-Business for Economics

PRINCIPLES OF MACROECONOMICS

Principles of Macroeconomics, activebook

Karl E. Case, Wellesley College

Ray C. Fair, Yale University

© 2002, Paper, 0-13-066339-5

BASIC APPROACH

Case/Fair's Macroeconomics activebook is an interactive, online, digital book that completely integrates multimedia resources with the textbook to greatly enhance the student learning experience. The activebook experience:

- Uses the web for what it's good at! -An activebook takes full advantage of the online environment. Gearing Up sections highlight the chapter's central concepts. Active Examples and Active Exercises help students explore the chapter's most important points through video, audio, and text. Concept Checks allow students to test their understanding of the material at the end of every major section, with links back to appropriate coverage. Chapter Wrap-Ups include a practice quiz, which gives students a chance to test their knowledge.
- Lets students learn the way they learn best!-An activebook engages students of all learning styles through online print, audio, and video resources. The activebook experience is customizable by faculty and students. Students can annotate their activebook and customize their view of the book's dynamic resources.
- Gives you more for less!-Despite the increased amount of multimedia and interactive content, activebooks cost less than traditional textbooks. Even though the core text is retained in print, the print component of an activebook is shorter than a traditional text. All boxed material, chapter summaries, exercises, and other content that can be made dynamic reside in the online component of the activebook.
- Active examples and Active exercises use video, audio, and additional tools, such as Active graphs to bring the text to life! For example, graphs come to life when studetns click on Active Examples, embedded thoughout the activebook. Students can change the value of a variable and look at the effects on the equilibrium.

CONTENTS

I. INTRODUCTION TO ECONOMICS.
1. The Scope and Method of Economics.
2. The Economic Problem: Scarcity and Choice.
3. Demand, Supply, and Market Equilibrium.
4. The Price System and Demand and Supply.

II. CONCEPTS AND PROBLEMS IN MACROECONOMICS.
5. Introduction to Macroeconomics.
6. Measuring National Output and National Income.
7. Long-Run and Short-Run Concerns: Growth, Productivity, Unemployment, and Inflation.

III. THE GOODS AND MONEY MARKETS.
8. Aggregate Expenditure and Equilibrium Output.
9. The Government and Fiscal Policy.
10. The Money Supply and the Federal Reserve System.
11. Money Demand, the Equilibrium Interest Rate, and Monetary Policy.

IV. MACROECONOMIC ANALYSIS.
12. Money, the Interest Rate, and Output: Analysis and Policy.
13. Aggregate Demand, Aggregate Supply, and Inflation.
14. The Labor Market, Unemployment, and Inflation.
15. Macroeconomic Issues and Policy.
16. Household and Firm Behavior in the Macroeconomy: A Further Look.
17. Long-Run Growth.
18. Debates in Macroeconomics: Monetarism, New Classical Theory, and Supply Side Economics.

V. THE WORLD ECONOMY.
19. International Trade, Comparative Advantage, and Protectionism.
20. Open Economy Macroeconomics: The Balance of Payments and Exchange Rates.
21. Economic Growth in Developing and Transitional Economies.

Glossary of Terms.
Solutions to Even-Numbered Problems.

SUPPLEMENTS

- Instructor's Resource CD
- Prentice Hall Guide to the Wall Street Journal
- Online Course Solutions are available in Blackboard, CourseCompass, and WebCT.

Generic Supplements

- Prentice Hall's Guide to E-Business for Economics

One-Semester Survey of Economics

New Title!

Survey of Economics: Principles and Tools

Arthur O'Sullivan, Lewis and Clark College
Steven M. Sheffrin, University of California, Davis

© 2002, 0-13-060143-8, Paper

BASIC APPROACH

For one-semester or one-quarter survey or introductory courses in economics.

By focusing on five key principles and reinforcing them throughout the text, students see how various topics in this first course fit together. This text teaches students how to think like economists by showing them how to use economic concepts in their everyday lives and careers. By using key concepts repeatedly, illustrating them with compelling real-world examples, and giving students lots of practice at "Active Learning," students will learn how to apply and use the principles and tools. Covers both Micro and Macroeconomics in one concise paperback volume.

CONTENTS

1. Principles of Economics.
2. Supply, Demand, and Market Equilibrium.
3. Elasticity: A Measure of Responsiveness.
4. Production and Cost.
5. Perfect Competition: Short Run and Long Run.
6. Monopoly.
7. Monopolistic Competition, Oligopoly, and Antitrust.
8. Public Goods, Spillovers, and Imperfect Information.
9. The Labor Market.
10. Measuring a Nation's Production and Income.
11. Unemployment and Inflation.
12. Why Do Economies Grow?
13. Aggregate Demand and Aggregate Supply.
14. Keynesian Economics and Fiscal Policy.
15. Money, the Banking System, and the Federal Reserve.
16. Monetary Policy and Inflation.
17. International Trade and Finance.

SUPPLEMENTS

- Review Copy
- Instructor's Manual
- Test Item File
- Computerized Test Item File
- PowerPoint on Web
- Using Experiments, Cases, and Activities in the Classroom
- Companion Website - www.prenhall.com/osullivan
- Study Guide
- Active Learning CD-ROM
- Standard WebCT
- Standard Blackboard
- Standard CourseCompass
- Course Compass with E-book

Generic Supplements

- Mastering Economics (CD): Universal CD-ROM Edition, Version 1.0
- Prentice Hall's Guide to E-Business for Economics
- Prentice Hall Guide to Economist.com
- Prentice Hall Guide to Financial Times
- Prentice Hall Guide to the Wall Street Journal

The Economic Way of Thinking

Tenth Edition

Paul Heyne, University of Washington
Peter J. Boettke, George Mason University
David L. Prychitko, Northern Michigan University

©2003, 568 pages, Paper, 0-13-060810-6

BASIC APPROACH

For one-term Principles/Survey of Economics courses.

Noted for its clear and informative style, this text provides an in-depth discussion of a limited, but crucial set of economic principles and concepts, then applies these tools of analysis to a wide variety of familiar situations. It presents conceptually demanding material in a lively, often witty fashion that is both accessible and pertinent for beginning students.

The two new co-authors will remain loyal to Paul Heyne's philosophy and writing style. This edition includes improvements to the coverage of growth theory, additional historical figures, and updated examples including recent public policy disputes.

CONTENTS

1. The Economic Way of Thinking
2. Efficiency, Exchange, and Comparative Advantage
3. Substitutes Everywhere: The Concept of Demand
4. Opportunity Cost and the Supply of Goods
5. Supply and Demand: A Process of Cooperation
6. Supply and Demand: Issues and Applications
7. Information, Middlemen, and Speculators
8. Profit and Loss
9. Competition and Monopoly
10. Price Searching
11. Competition and Government Policy
12. The Distribution of Income
13. Externalities and Conflicting Rights
14. Markets and Government
15. The Overall Performance of Economic Systems
16. The Supply of Money
17. Monetary and Fiscal Policies
18. National Policies and International Exchange
19. Employment and Unemployment
20. Promoting Economic Growth
21. Economic Performance and Political Economy
22. The Limitations of Economics

SUPPLEMENTS

- Instructor's Manual
- Study Guide
- Test Item File
- Test Manager
- Companion Website - www.prenhall.com/heyne
- PowerPoint (web only)

Economics by Design: Principles and Issues

Second Edition

Robert A. Collinge
Ronald M. Ayers, both of the University of Texas at San Antonio

© 2000, 509 pp., Paper 0-13-013298-5

BASIC APPROACH

Known for its flexibility, this text can be used in a one-term survey of economics, or an economics issues course.

This text is ideal for issues-oriented courses that teach essential economic principles. Current issues and core principles of mainstream economics are presented in an intuitive manner that captures and holds student interest. The text systematically combines this presentation with a wealth of relevant, up-to-date applications that students can relate to.

CONTENTS

I. THE ECONOMIC JOURNEY.
1. Roadmap for Economics.
2. Production, Growth, and Trade.

II. THE POWER OF PRICES.
3. Market Prices: Supply and Demand.
4. Price Changes: Political Prices and Elasticity.
5. Into the International Marketplace.

III. THE ENERGY OF THE MARKETPLACE.
6. The Firm.
7. Market Models.
8. Income from Labor and Human Capital.

IV. PROBING THE PUBLIC SECTOR.
9. Market Failure.
10. Taxation and Public Choice.

V. AGGREGATES FOR THE BIG PICTURE.
11. Measuring the Macroeconomy.
12. Policy for Long-Run Growth.

SUPPLEMENTS

- Instructor's Manual
- Test Item File
- Coputerized Test Item File
- PowerPoint's (on Web)
- Traparency Masters (on web)
- Companion Website - www.prenhall.com/collinge

Economic History: Freshman-Level Survey

The Making of Economic Society

Eleventh Edition

Robert L. Heilbroner
William Milberg, both of New School for Social Research

© 2002, 201 pp., Paper, 0-13-091050-3

BASIC APPROACH

For courses in U.S. Economic History, Principles of Economics, and American Business History.

With its roots in history and eyes on the future, this text traces the development of our economic society from the Middle Ages to the present, offering a balanced perspective of why our economy is the way it is and where it may be headed.The Eleventh Edition includes two new chapters (one on socialism and one on developing economies), as well as end-of-chapter cirtical thinking boxes.

CONTENTS

1. The Economic Problem.
2. The Premarket Economy.
3. The Emergence of Market Society.
4. The Industrial Revolution.
5. The Impact of Industrial Technology.
6. The Great Depression.
7. The Rise of the Public Sector.
8. Modern Capitalism Emerges in Europe.
9. The Golden Age of Capitalism.
10. The Golden Age Comes to an End.
11. The Rise and Fall of Socialism.
12. The Globalization of Economic Life.
13. Why Some Nations Remain Poor.
14. Problems and Possibilities.

Intermediate Macroeconomics

New Title!

Macroeconomics

David Colander, Middlebury College
Edward Gamber, Lafayette College

© 2002, 550 pp., Cloth, 0-13-030372-0

BASIC APPROACH

The authors recognize that the economy is a complex system and that economists do not have all the answers; basic economic models do not hold true under all circumstances. The text provides students with a framework for discussing complicated questions and the tools to think about models and the economy in the way that macroeconomists and policy makers do. Theory is developed as needed to understand policy, rather than presenting theory first and then adding policy, and is presented with a minimum of technical detail. The authors present modern macroeconomic concepts and issues in a lively, accessible and entertaining style.

CONTENTS

I. INTRODUCTION TO MACROECONOMICS.

1. Introduction to Macroeconomics.
2. Measuring the Economy.
3. Grappling with Inflation, Unemployment, and Growth.
4. Understanding Policy for the Long Run and the Short Run.

II. GROWTH AND THE LONG RUN.

5. The Neoclassical Growth Model.
6. Beyond the Solow Growth Model.
7. Money, Inflation, and Exchange Rates in the Long Run.

III. FLUCTUATIONS AND THE SHORT RUN.

8. The Determination of Output in the Short Run.
9. Policy Analysis with the IS/LM Model.
10. Short-run Fluctuations in an Open Economy.
11. Aggregate Supply and Aggregate Demand.
12. Microfoundations of Consumption and Investment.

IV. THE NUTS AND BOLTS OF MACRO POLICY.

13. The Nuts and Bolts of Monetary Policy.
14. The Nuts and Bolts of Fiscal Policy.
15. The Art of Macroeconomic Policy.

SUPPLEMENTS

- Review Copy
- Study Guide
- Instructor's Manual
- Test Item File
- Computerized Test Item File
- Transparency Masters on Web
- PowerPoints on Web
- Companion Website - www.prenhall.com/colander
- Standard WebCT
- Standard Blackboard
- CourseCompass with E-book

Generic Supplements

- Prentice Hall Guide to Economist.com
- Student Guide to the Financial Times
- Prenctice Hall Guide to the Wall Street Journal

Macroeconomics

Third Edition

Olivier Jean Blanchard, Massachussetts Institute of Technology

© 2003, Cloth Package, 0-13-067100-2

BASIC APPROACH

The fundamental goals of this text are to provide an integrated view of macroeconomics, and to make close contact with current macroeconomic events. Theoretical material is always presented within the context of a real world application in three ways: in words, in graphs, and with algebra.

This text has been widely adopted both in the U.S. and internationally. The text has been translated into four foreign language editions.

CONTENTS

1. A Tour of the World.
2. A Tour of the Book.

THE CORE.

The Short Run (IS-LM).

3. The Goods Market.
4. Financial Markets.
5. Goods and Financial Markets: The IS-LM Model.

The Medium Run (AS-AD).

6. The Labor Market.
7. Putting All Markets Together: The AS-AD Model.
8. The Phillips Curve.
9. Inflation, Activity, and Money Growth

The Long Run.

10. The Facts of Growth.
11. Saving, Capital Accumulation, and Output.
12. Technological Progress and Growth.
13. Technological Progress, Wages, and Unemployment.

Expectations.

14. Expectations: The Basic Tools.
15. Financial Markets and Expectations.
16. Expectations, Consumption, and Investment.
17. Expectations, Output, and Policy.

The Open Economy.

18. Openness in Goods and Financial Markets.
19. The Goods Market in an Open Economy.
20. Output, The Interest Rate, and the Exchange Rate.
21. Exchange Rate Regimes.

Pathologies.

22. Pathologies I: High Unemployment.
23. Pathologies II: High Inflation.
24. Pathologies III: Transition in Eastern Europe, the Asian Crisis, and the slump in Japan.

BACK TO POLICY.

Policy.

25. Should Policy Makers Be Restrained?
26. Monetary Policy: A Summing Up.
27. Fiscal Policy: A Summing Up.
28. Epilogue: The Story of Macroeconomics.

Appendix 1: An Introduction to National Income and Product Accounts.

Appendix 2: A Math Refresher.
Appendix 3: An Introduction to Econometrics.

SUPPLEMENTS

- Instructor's Manual
- Study Guide and Tutorial
- Active Graphs CD-ROM
- Companion Website - www.prenhall.com/blanchard
- Test Item File
- Test Manager
- PowerPoints (on web)
- Transparency Masters (on web)

Generic Supplements

- Using Economic Experiments in the Classroom
- Prentice Hall's Guide to E-Business for Economics
- Prentice Hall Guide to Economist.com
- Prentice Hall Guide to Financial Times
- Prentice Hall Guide to the Wall Street Journal

Macroeconomics: Theories and Policies

Seventh Edition

Richard T. Froyen, University of North Carolina at Chapel Hill

© 2002, 512 pp., Cloth, 0-13-032859-6

BASIC APPROACH

This text traces the history of macroeconomics, the evolution of macroeconomic thought, and the resulting theory and policy. The book places the various macroeconomic theories in the order in which they developed, and illustrates the similarities and differences of all economic modelss. The result is a comprehensive, detailed, unbiased view of modern macroeconomic theory. The Seventh Edition includes a Web site with critical thinking questions and concept checks.

CONTENTS

I. INTRODUCTION AND MEASUREMENT.

1. Introduction.
2. Measurement of Macroeconomic Variables.

II. MACROECONOMICS MODELS.

3. Classical Macroeconomics (I): Equilibrium Output and Employment.
4. Classical Macroeconomics (II): Money, Prices, and Interest.
5. The Keynesian System (I): The Role of Aggregate Demand.
6. The Keynesian System (II): Money, Interest, and Income.
7. The Keynesian System (III): Policy Effects in the IS-LM Model.
8. The Keynesian System (IV): Aggregate Supply and Demand.
9. The Monetarist Counterrevolution.
10. Output, Inflation and Unemployment: Monetarist and Keynesian Views.
11. New Classical Economics.
12. Real Business Cycles and New Keynesian Economics.
13. Macroeconomic Models: A Summary.

III. OPEN ECONOMY MACROECONOMICS.

14. Exchange Rates and the International Monetary System.
15. Monetary and Fiscal Policy in the Open Economy.

IV. ECONOMIC POLICY.

16. The Money Supply Process.
17. Monetary Policy.
18. Fiscal Policy.

V. EXTENSIONS OF THE MODELS.

19. Long- and Intermediate-Term Economic Growth.
20. Consumption and Investment.
21. Money Demand.

SUPPLEMENTS

- Study Guide
- Instructor's Manual with Testbank
- PH Custom Test
- Website - www.prenhall.com/froyen

Generic Supplements

- Prentice Hall's Guide to e-Business for Economics
- Prentice Hall Guide to Economist.com
- Prentice Hall Guide to Financial Times
- Prentice Hall Guide to the Wall Street Journal

Intermediate Microeconomics

Microeconomics

Fifth Edition

Robert S. Pindyck,
Massachusetts Institute of Technology
Daniel L. Rubinfeld,
University of California, Berkeley

© 2001, 700 pp., Cloth, 0-13-016583-2

BASIC APPROACH

The market leader in Intermediate Microeconomics, the book is well known for its coverage of modern topics (Game theory, Economics of Information), clarity of its writing style and graphs, and integrated use of real world examples. The book is used in both economics departments and business schools and is well received for its applied nature. The emphasis on relevance and application to both managerial and public-policy decision making are focused goals of the book. It succeeds in showing how microeconomics can be used as a tool for decision making.

CONTENTS

I. INTRODUCTION: MARKETS AND PRICES.
1. Preliminaries.
2. The Basics of Supply and Demand.

II. PRODUCERS, CONSUMERS, AND COMPETITIVE MARKETS.
3. Consumer Behavior.
4. Individual and Market Demand.
5. Choice under Uncertainty.
6. Production.
7. The Cost of Production.
8. Profit Maximization and Competitive Supply.
9. The Analysis of Competitive Markets.

III. MARKET STRUCTURE AND COMPETITIVE STRATEGY.
10. Market Power: Monopoly and Monopsony.
11. Pricing with Market Power.
12. Monopolistic Competition and Oligopoly.
13. Game Theory and Competitive Strategy.
14. Markets for Factor Inputs.
15. Investment, Time, Capital Markets.

IV. INFORMATION, MARKET FAILURE, AND THE ROLE OF GOVERNMENT.
16. General Equilibrium and Economic Efficiency.
17. Markets with Asymmetric Information.
18. Externalities and Public Goods.

SUPPLEMENTS

- Review Copy
- Study Guide
- PH Custom Test
- Instructor's Manual
- Test Item File
- Transparency Acetates
- PowerPoint Slides (WEB)
- Companion Website - www.prenhall.com/pindyck
- WebCT
- Blackboard

Generic Supplements

- Using Economic Experiments in the Classroom
- eBiz: The Prentice Hall Guide to E-Business in Economics

New Title!

Microeconomics: An Integrated Approach

Stephen Mathis, Ph.D.
Janet Koscianski, Ph.D., both of Shippensburg University

©2003, 738 Pages, Cloth, 0-13-011418-9

BASIC APPROACH

This text presents microeconomics using an approach that focuses on constructing and analyzing fundamental models. The text covers the fundamental concepts while at the same time integrating calculus throughout. The authors believe full and broad understanding of microeconomics is greatly facilitated by applying several tools of analysis. Accordingly, the text develops theoretical microeconomic concepts with words, graphs, mathematics, and real-world examples.

CONTENTS

I. Preliminaries
1. Review of Basic Calculus Techniques
2. Unconstrained and Constrained Optimization of Multivariate Functions

II. Theory of the Consumer
3. Utility Theory
4. Consumer Optimization
5. Individual Demand Functions and Other Related Topics
6. Market Demand Curves
7. Demand Related Elasticities

III. Theory of the Firm
8. Production in the Short Run
9. Production in the Long Run
10. Long Run Optimization for the Firm
11. Costs of Production in the Long Run
12. Costs of Production in the Short Run

IV. Market Structures
13. Perfect Competition in the Short Run
14. Perfect Competition in the Long Run
15. Monopoly
16. Additional Topics Related to Monopoly
17. Oligopoly
18. Applications of Game Theory to Oligopolistic Firm Behavior
19. Monopolistic Competition

V. Input Markets
20. Demand for Labor
21. Supply of Labor
22. Capital Markets

VI. General Equilibrium Analysis
23. General Equilibrium Analysis In An Exchange Economy
24. General Equilibrium Analysis In An Economy with Production and Exchange

SUPPLEMENTS

- Study Guide
- Instructor's Manual with Testbank
- Companion Website - www.prenhall.com/mathis

New Title!

Microeconomics

Fifth Edition

B. Curtis Eaton, Diane F. Eaton,
Douglas W. Allen, Simon Fraser University

© 2002, 704 pp. Cloth, 0-13-033011-6

BASIC APPROACH

This fifth edition is appropriate for second-year university courses in intermediate microeconomics. It teaches microeconomics as a way of looking at the world, using plenty of new applications and examples to demonstrate the theory. Because it uses calculus (only in footnotes), this text is considered to be in the upper mid-range in its mathematical rigor.

CONTENTS

Preface.

I. AN INTRODUCTION TO MICROECONOMICS.
1. Microeconomics: A Working Methodology.
   Appendix A1: Model Building.

II. INDIVIDUAL CHOICE.
2. A Theory of Preferences.
3. Demand Theory.
   Appendix 3A: Composite Commodities.
4. More Demand Theory.
5. Intertemporal Decision Making and Capital Values.

III. PRODUCTION AND COST.
6. Production and Cost: One Variable Input.
7. Production and Cost: Many Variable Inputs.

IV. MARKETS FOR GOODS.
8. The Theory of Perfect Competition.
9. Applications of the Competitive Model.
10. Monopoly.

V. RESOURCE MARKETS AND GENERAL EQUILIBRIUM.
11. Input Markets and the Allocation of Resources.
12. The Distribution of Income.

13. Competitive General Equilibrium.
    Appendix 13A: Efficiency.

VI. IMPERFECT COMPETITION.

14. Price Discrimination and Monopoly Practices.
15. Game Theory and Oligopoly.
16. Product Differentiation.

VII. UNCERTAINTY AND ASYMMETRIC INFORMATION.

17. Choice Making Under Uncertainty.
18. Asymmetric Information, the Rules of the Game, and Externalities.
19. The Theory of the Firm.
20. Asymmetric Information and Market Behaviour.
    Answers to Problems.

SUPPLEMENTS

- Computerized Test Item File
- Instructor's Resource Manual
- Test Item File
- Electronic PowerPoint Transparencies
- Problem Solving in Microeconomics

MANAGERIAL ECONOMICS

Managerial Economics: Economic Tools for Today's Decision Makers

Fourth Edition

Paul G. Keat, Thunderbird, American Graduate School
Philip K.Y. Young, Pace University

© 2003, 750 pp., Cloth, 0-13-013538-0

BASIC APPROACH

For undergraduate courses in Managerial Economics and first-year MBA students in departments of Economics and Finance.

Written with a strong focus on the "managerial". A unifying business case used in every chapter involves hypothetical challenges for managers in various functions and levels of responsibility. Actual business examples from the popular press—with emphasis on international examples—are incorporated into the chapters. A new chapter on information technology will cover the dotcoms, e-business/e-commerce, globalism and new business models.

CONTENTS

1. Introduction.
2. The Firm and Its Goals.
   Appendix 2A: Review of Mathematical Concepts Used in Managerial Economics.
3. Supply and Demand.
   Appendix 3A: The Mathematics of Supply and Demand.
4. Demand Elasticity.
   Appendix 4A: Applications of Supply and Demand.
5. Demand Estimation.
6. Forecasting.
   Appendix 6A: Forecasting and the Computer.
7. The Theory and Estimation of Production.
   Appendix 7A: The Multiple-Input Case.
   Appendix 7B: Expressing the Production Function with the Use of Calculus.
8. The Theory and Estimation of Cost.
   Appendix 8A: A Mathematical Restatement of the Short-Run Cost Function.
   Appendix 8B: The Estimation of Cost.
9. Pricing and Output Decisions: Perfect Competition, Monopolistic Competition, and Monopoly.
   Appendix 9A: The Use of Calculus in Pricing and Output Decisions.
   Appendix 9B: Break-Even Analysis (Volume-Cost-Profit).
10. Oligopoly.
11. Special Pricing Practices.
12. New Economy
13. Capital Budgeting.
    Appendix 13A: Calculations for Time Value of Money.
14. Risk and Uncertainty.

15. Government and Industry: Challenges and Opportunities for Today's Manager.
16. Managerial Economics in Action: The Case of the Semiconductor Industry.

Appendix A: Linear Programming.
Appendix B: Statistical and Financial Tables.

SUPPLEMENTS

- Excel Templates downloadable from www.prenhall.com/keat
- Instructor's Manual/Test Item File
- WIN PH Test Manager
- Companion Website - www.prenhall.com/keat
- Transparency Masters (on web)
- PowerPoint Lecture Presentation (on web)

The Economics, Organization and Management

Paul Milgrom and John Roberts, both of Stanford University

© 1992, 600 pp., cloth, 0-13-224650-3

BASIC APPROACH

A systematic treatment of the economics of the modern firm, this book draws on the insights of a variety of areas in modern economics and other disciplines, but presents a coherent, consistent, innovative treatment of the central problems in organizations of motivating people and coordinating their activities.

CONTENTS

I. THE CONCEPTUAL FRAMEWORK.

1. Does Organization Matter?
2. Economic Organization and Efficiency.

II. THEORIES OF COORDINATION AND MOTIVATION.

3. Using Prices for Coordination and Motivation.
4. Coordinating Plans and Actions.
5. Incentives and Motivation.
6. Moral Hazard.
7. Risk Sharing and Incentive Contracts.
8. Rents and Efficiency.

III. COORDINATION, MOTIVATION, AND MANAGEMENT.

9. Ownership and Property Rights.
10. Employment Policy and Human-Resource Management.
11. Internal Labor Markets, Job Assignments, and Promotions.
12. Compensation and Motivation.
13. Executive and Managerial Compensation.

IV. DESIGNING AND CHOOSING ORGANIZATIONAL FORMS.

14. The Classical Theory of Investments and Finance.
15. Financial Structure, Ownership, and Corporate Control.
16. The Boundaries and Structure of the Firm.

Glossary.
Author and Subject Indexes.

INDUSTRIAL ORGANIZATION

The Structure of American Industry

Tenth Edition

Walter Adams, Deceased, Michigan State University & Trinity University, Texas
James W. Brock, Miami University, Ohio

© 2001, 384 pp., Paper, 0-13-017916-7

BASIC APPROACH

The tenth edition of this widely used industry casebook continues to offer the leading "real-world" survey of contemporary American industries. Providing a sound new treatment of the role of public policy in a free enterprise economy, this text illustrates the broadest possible range of American market structures through a series of carefully chosen and well-developed case studies of specific industries, all written by leading authorities in their field.

CONTENTS

1. Agriculture, Daniel B. Suits.
2. Petroleum, Stephen Martin.
3. Cigarettes, Adam B. Jaffe.
4. Beer, Kenneth G. Elzinga.
5. Automobiles, James W. Brock.
6. Computers, Don E. Waldman.
7. Motion Picture Entertainment, Barry R. Litman.
8. Airlines, William G. Shepherd.

9. Commercial Banking, Steven J. Pilloff.
10. Health Care, John Goddeeris.
11. Telecommunications, Manley R. Irwin & James McConnaughey.
12. College Sports, John L. Fizel & Randall W. Bennett.
13. Public Policy in a Free Enterprise Economy, James W. Brock.

American Industry: Structure, Conduct, Performance

Seventh Edition

Richard Caves, Harvard University

© 1992, 144 pp., paper, 0-13-029893-X

BASIC APPROACH

This popular volume provides a compact account of the core concepts of the field of industrial organization and their application to American industry.

CONTENTS

1. The Business Sector and Its Organization.
2. Elements of Market Structure.
3. The Large Corporation.
4. Market Conduct.
5. Market Performance.
6. The Promotion of Competition and the Control of Monopoly.
7. Public Policy: Regulation and Public Enterprise.

Selected Readings.

LABOR ECONOMICS

The Economics of Women, Men, and Work

Fourth Edition

Francine D. Blau, Cornell University
Marianne A. Ferber, University of Illinois at Urbana-Champaign
Anne E. Winkler, University of Missouri-St. Louis

© 2002, 496 pp., Paper, 0-13-090922-X

BASIC APPROACH

For courses concerned with the economic status of women, economics of gender, and economics of the family, but also applicable to interdisciplinary women's studies courses, introductory-level courses in economic problems, and as a supplement to general labor economics courses.

This text draws into a single, highly accessible volume the most current summary and synthesis of research and data from economics and other social sciences on women, men, and work in the labor market and household.

CONTENTS

1. Introduction.
2. Women and Men: Changing Roles in a Changing Economy.
3. The Family as an Economic Unit.
4. The Allocation of Time between the Household and the Labor Market.
5. Differences in Occupations and Earnings: Overview.
6. Differences in Occupations and Earnings: The Human Capital Model.
7. Differences in Occupations and Earnings: The Role of Labor Market Discrimination.
8. Recent Developments in the Labor Market: Their Impact on Women and Men.
9. Changing Work Roles and the Family.
10. Policies Affecting Paid Work and Family.

11. Gender Differences in Other Countries.
    Author Index.
    Subject Index.

SUPPLEMENTS

- Transparency Masters (on web)
- Answers to Discussion Questions (on web)

Labor Economics and Labor Relations

Eleventh Edition

Lloyd G. Reynolds, Yale University
Stanley H. Masters, SUNY at Binghamton
Colletta H. Moser, Michigan State University

© 1998, 581 pp., Cloth, 0-13-263310-8

BASIC APPROACH

A classic exploration of how labor markets are influenced by economic forces and the legal and institutional framework as well as an analysis of their interactions.

CONTENTS

1. Labor Economics: Institutions and the Market.
2. A First Look at Labor Markets.
3. Labor Supply Decisions.
4. Labor Demand.
5. Human Capital: Education and Job Training.
6. Real Wage Rates, Productivity, and Inequality.
7. Inequality and Discrimination.
8. Equal Employment Opportunity: Policies and Controversies.
9. Unemployment.
10. American Workers in a World Economy.
11. The Changing Workplace: Comparisons Across Countries.
12. Internal Labor Markets.
13. Compensation.
14. An Introduction to Unions.
15. Unions, Politics, and the Law.
16. Bargaining.
17. Union Effects.
18. Labor Issues: Past, Present, and Future.

INTERNATIONAL ECONOMICS (INTERNATIONAL TRADE)

The Choice: A Fable of Free Trade and Protectionism

Updated and Revised Edition

Russell Roberts, Washington University in Saint Louis

© 2001, 116 pp., Paper, 0-13-087052-8

BASIC APPROACH

Written as a novel, the book makes the complex concepts, issues and terminology of international trade understandable for students.

The fictional element brings these topics to life so that students gain the intuition and understanding of how trade changes the lives of people and the industries they work in. The fundamental intuition of how international markets function, including general equilibrium effects and policy analysis, is provided.

CONTENTS

1. Minutes of the Heavenly Court: Soul of David Ricardo.
2. The Challenge of Foreign Competition.
3. The Roundabout Way to Wealth.
4. Is Trade Good for America?
5. The New Generation of American Know-How.
6. Do Tariffs Protect American Jobs?
7. Tariffs vs. Quotas.
8. Road Trip.
9. The Case for Protection.
10. Do Trade Deficits Hurt America?
11. Fair Trade vs. Free Trade.
12. Should America Trade Freely with Low-Wage Nations?
13. Self-Sufficiency Is the Road to Poverty.
14. The Choice.
15. A Final Word from David Ricardo.
16. Explanations, Sources, and Further Reading.

International Economics

W. Charles Sawyer, University of Southern Mississippi
Richard L. Sprinkle, University of Texas

© 2003, Paper, 0-13-017276-6

BASIC APPROACH

For one semester courses in International Economics.

Addressing the changing face of economics education, Sawyer and Sprinkle's international economics text is a thoroughly modern approach to the subject. Providing a discussion of international economics that is more accessible to a wider range of students than is currently available anywhere else, the text incorporates a modern approach to open economy macroeconomics, and shifts the emphasis from pure theory to the applications of basic theory that use basic tools of analysis.

CONTENTS

1. Introduction: An Overview of the World Economy.
2. Why Nations Trade.
3. Factor Endowments and The Commodity Composition of Trade.
4. Intraindustry Trade.
5. International Factor Movements.
6. Tariffs.
7. Nontariff Distortions to Trade.
8. International Trade Policy.
9. Regional Economic Issues.
10. National Income Accounting & The Balance of Payments.
11. International Transactions and Capital Markets.
12. Exchange Rates and Their Determination: A Basic Analysis.
13. Money, Interest Rates, and The Exchange Rate.
14. Price Levels and Exchange Rates in The Long Run.
15. Output and The Exchange Rate in The Short Run.
16. Macroeconomic Policy and Floating Exchange Rates.
17. Fixed Exchange Rates and Optimum Currency Areas.
18. International Monetary Arrangements.

SUPPLEMENTS

- Instructor's Manual with testbank
- Computerized testbank
- Transparency Masters (on web)
- PowerPoint (on web)
- Companion Website

DEVELOPMENTAL ECONOMICS

New Title!

Economic Development: Theory and Practice for a Divided World

Stuart R. Lynn, Assumption College

©2003, 650 Pages, Paper, 0130141615

BASIC APPROACH

The text presents contemporary coverage of key development topics such as human capital, technology, the environment, and population growth. The book highlights the role of market system and government policy in the gap between rich and poor countries, the controversies surrounding the topic of economic development and the resulting changes in its approach, and the application of development theory in real-world situations. 36 Cases Studies present economic issues being faced by developing countries such as Taiwan, Brazil, India, China, Ghana, Mexico, and Thailand. 24 Development Spotlight boxes illustrate and apply key theoretical concepts to real-world situations.

CONTENTS

1. The Idea Of Economic Development
2. Measuring Economic Development
3. The Evolution Of Development Thought
4. Financial Resources For Development
5. Natural Building Blocks Of Development. Resources And The Environment
6. Population Growth And Migration
7. Human Capital. Health And Education
8. The Key Role Of Agriculture In Development
9. Industry, Technology, And Employment
10. The Ambiguous Role Of The State In Development

11. Macroeconomic Policy, Inflation, And Stabilization
12. Foreign Trade And Development Strategy
13. Foreign Aid And Direct Investment
14. Debt And Adjustment
15. Global Capital Markets And The East Asian Development Model
16. Lessons Learned And Open Questions

SUPPLEMENTS

- Instructor's Manual (on web) at http://www.prenhall.com/lynn

Economics of Poverty and Discrimination

The Economics of Poverty and Discrimination

Eighth Edition

Bradley R. Schiller, The American University

© 2001, 302 pp., Paper, 0-13-017322-3

BASIC APPROACH

This text has been the leading college text in this field for over twenty years. From the beginning, the text has been distinguished by its coverage, tight organization, multidisciplinary perspective, and timeliness. The forthcoming eighth edition preserves these qualities while incorporating new material.

CONTENTS

I. THE DIMENSIONS OF POVERTY.
1. Views of Inequality and Poverty.
2. Counting the Poor.

II. CAUSES OF POVERTY.
3. Labor Force Participation.
4. The Working Poor.
5. Age and Health.
6. Family Size and Structure.
7. The Underclass: Culture and Race.
8. Education and Ability.
9. Discrimination in Education.
10. Discrimination in the Labor Market.

III. POLICY OPTIONS.
11. Welfare Programs.
12. Social Insurance Programs.
13. Employment Policies.
14. Equal Opportunity Policies.
15. Directions and Prospects.

Index.

SUPPLEMENTS

- Instructor's Manual: www.prenhall.com/schiller

Cost-Benefit Analysis

Cost-Benefit Analysis: Concepts and Practice

Second Edition

Anthony E. Boardman, University of British Columbia
David H. Greenberg, University of Maryland, Baltimore County
Aidan R. Vining, Simon Fraser University
David L. Weimer, University of Wisconsin, Madison

© 2001, 526 pp., Cloth, 0-13-087178-8

BASIC APPROACH

This text uses numerous up-to-date illustrations and examples to show students how theories and techniques are applied to real world situations. Students are provided with a practical orientation and introduction to cost-benefit analysis through problem solving.

CONTENTS

I. OVERVIEW.
1. Introduction to Cost-Benefit Analysis.
2. Conceptual Foundations of Cost-Benefit Analysis.

II. FUNDAMENTALS OF CBA.
3. Basic Microeconomic Foundations of Cost Benefit Analysis.
4. Valuing Benefits and Costs in Primary Markets.
5. Valuing Benefits and Costs in Secondary Markets.
6. Discounting Future Benefits and Costs.
7. Dealing with Uncertainty: Expected Value, Sensitivity Analysis, and the Value of Information.
8. Option Price and Option Value.

9. Existence Value.
10. The Social Discount Rate.

III. VALUATION OF IMPACTS.

11. Valuing Impacts from Observed Behavior: Demonstrations.
12. Valuing Impacts from Observed Behavior: Direct Estimation of Demand Curves.
13. Valuing Impacts from Observed Behavior: Other Revealed Preference Methods.
14. Valuing Impacts through Surveys: Contingent Valuation.
15. Shadow Prices from Secondary Sources.
16. Shadow Prices: Applications to Developing Countries.

IV. RELATED METHODS AND ACCURACY.

17. Cost-Effectiveness Analysis and Cost-Utility Analysis.
18. Distributionally Weighted Cost-Benefit Analysis.
19. How Accurate Is CBA?

A Selected Cost-Benefit Analysis Bibliography.
Name Index.
Subject Index.

SUPPLEMENTS

- Solutions Manual (Web only) www.prenhall.com/boardman
- Extended Bibliography (Web only)
- Instructor's Manual (Web only)
- Transparency Masters (on Web)

GOVERNMENT AND BUSINESS

Business and Government in the Global Marketplace

Sixth Edition

Murray L. Weidenbaum, Washington University

© 1999, 397 pp., Paper, 0-13-080625-0

BASIC APPROACH

This book addresses the intricate relationship between the public and the private sector, covering why and how government intervenes in the economy and how business can respond. It provides analysis from both perspectives, presenting the ways that government policy affects the activities of the modern corporation and the key responses on the part of business.

CONTENTS

I. SETTING THE FRAMEWORK.

1. The Powers of Government and Business.

II. GOVERNMENT REGULATION OF BUSINESS.

2. The Rationale for Regulation.
3. Government and the Consumer.
4. Protecting the Environment.
5. Achieving Equal Employment Opportunity.
6. Government and the Work Place.
7. Traditional Economic Regulation.
8. Economic Deregulation.
9. Reforming Government Regulation.

III. THE GLOBAL MARKETPLACE.

10. Business and Government in the World Economy.
11. Government and International Commerce.
12. Promoting Global Competitiveness.

IV. GOVERNMENT PROMOTION OF BUSINESS.

13. Business and Tax Policy.
14. Government Credits and Bailouts.
15. Government as a Market.

V. THE BUSINESS RESPONSE.

16. Business-Government Relations.
17. Issues Management.
18. Business Participation in Politics.

VI. THE FUTURE OF THE CORPORATION.

19. Corporate Activists and Corporate Governance.
20. The Outlook for Private Enterprise.

URBAN ECONOMICS

The Economics of Cities and Suburbs

William Thomas Bogart, Case Western Reserve University

©1998, 366 pp., Cloth, 0-13-569971-1

BASIC APPROACH

Designed to convey the excitement of studying cities while developing a set of formal tools for analyzing their economies. Attempts to remove the division between "urban" economics and "regional" economics by demonstrating that the traditional intermetropolitan models of specialization and trade can also be extended to intrametropolitan analysis, thus unifying their treatment.

CONTENTS

I. INTRODUCTION TO URBAN ECONOMICS.

1. What Is a City?
2. Cities in History.
3. Market Areas and Central Place Theory.
4. Location of Economic Activity.

II. AGGREGATE ANALYSIS OF METROPOLITAN AREAS.

5. Intermetropolitan Trade.
6. Factor Abundance and Specialization.
7. Agglomeration and Metropolitan Growth.
8. Government Policy and Metropolitan Growth.

III. INTRAMETROPOLITAN ANALYSIS.

9. Clusters and Urban Form: Business Districts, Suburbs, and "Edge Cities."
10. Land-Use Controls.
11. Intrametropolitan Competition and Economic Development Policy.
12. Urban Labor Markets and Poverty.
13. Housing Markets.
14. Housing Problems and Policies.
15. Transportation.

Urban Economics and Real Estate Markets

Denise DiPasquale, Harvard University
William C. Wheaton, Massachusetts Institute of Technology

© 1996, 378 pp., cloth, 0-13-225244-9

BASIC APPROACH

This text presents a unique combination of both economic theory and real estate applications, providing students with the tools and techniques needed to understand the operation of urban real estate markets. It examines residential and non-residential real estate markets-from the perspectives of both macro- and micro- economics-as well as the role of government in real estate markets.

CONTENTS

I. INTRODUCTION TO REAL ESTATE MARKETS.

1. The Property and Capital Markets.
2. The Operation of Property Markets: A Micro and Macro Approach.

II. MICROECONOMIC ANALYSIS OF PROPERTY MARKETS.

Residential Real Estate.

3. The Urban Land Market: Rents and Prices.
4. The Urban Housing Market: Structural Attributes and Density.

Non-Residential Property Markets.

5. Firm Site Selection, Employment Decentralization and Multi-Centered Cities.
6. Retail Location and Market Competition.

III. MACROECONOMIC ANALYSIS OF PROPERTY MARKETS.

7. Economic Growth and Metropolitan Real Estate Markets.

Residential Real Estate.

8. The Market for Housing Units: Households, Prices, and Financing.
9. The Market for Housing Services: Moving, Sales and Vacancy.
10. The Cyclical Behavior of Metropolitan Housing Markets.

Non-Residential Property Markets.

11. The Operation of Non-Residential Property Markets.
12. Econometric Analysis of Metropolitan Office and Industrial Markets.

IV. THE IMPACT OF LOCAL GOVERNMENTS ON REAL ESTATE MARKETS.

13. Local Governments, Property Taxes and Real Estate Markets.
14. Public Goods, Externalities and Development

HEALTH ECONOMICS

The Economics of Health and Health Care

Third Edition

Sherman Folland, Oakland University
Allen C. Goodman, Wayne State University
Miron Stano, Oakland University

© 2001, 667 pp., Cloth, 0-13-012215-7

BASIC APPROACH

Core text for courses in health care economics found in Departments of Economics, Health Administration, Public Health, nursing and medical programs.

This best-selling comprehensive introduction to the economics of health and health care thoroughly develops and explains economic ideas and models and reflects the full spectrum of the most current health economics literature. It provides students with a solid working knowledge of the analytical tools of economics and econometrics as applied to contemporary health care issues.

CONTENTS

I. BASIC ECONOMIC TOOLS.

1. Introduction.
2. Microeconomic Tools.
3. Statistical Tools.
4. Cost-Benefit Analysis and Other Tools of Economic Evaluation.

II. SUPPLY AND DEMAND.

5. The Production of Health.
6. Demand for Health Capital.
7. Insurance.
8. Consumer Choice and Demand.

III. INFORMATION.

9. Asymmetric Information and Agency.
10. Imperfect Information: SID and SAV.

IV. INSURANCE AND ORGANIZATION OF HEALTH PROVIDERS.

11. The Organization of Health Insurance Markets.
12. Managed Care.

V. TECHNOLOGY.

13. The Production and Cost of Health Care.
14. Technology.

VI. LABOR.

15. Labor Markets and Professional Training.
16. The Training and Practice of Physicians.

VII. HOSPITALS AND NURSING HOMES.

17. Nonprofit Firms.
18. Hospitals and Long Term Care.

VIII. SOCIAL INSURANCE AND HEALTH SYSTEM REFORM.

19. Equity, Efficiency and Need.
20. Government Intervention.
21. Government Regulation.
22. Social Insurance.
23. Comparative Health Care Systems.

IX. POLICY ISSUES AND ANALYSES.

24. Health Systems Reform.
25. Advertising, Health Goods and Bads.
26. The Pharmaceutical Industry.

SUPPLEMENTS

- Instructor's Manual - www.prenhall.com/folland
- Using Economic Experiments in the Classroom
- eBiz: The Prentice Hall Guide to E-Business in Economics

ECONOMETRICS

Econometric Analysis

Fifth Edition

William H. Greene, New York University, Stern School of Business

© 2003, 1,004 pp., Cloth Bound, 0-13-066189-9

BASIC APPROACH

A standard text/reference in courses that include basic techniques in regression analysis and extensions used when linear models prove inadequate or inappropriate. Areas of application include Economics, Sociology, Political Science, Medical Research, Transport Research, and Environmental Economics. This book introduces students to the broad field of applied econometrics. An effective bridge to both on-the-job problems and to the professional literature, it features extensive applications and presents sufficient theoretical background to enable students to recognize new variants of the models that they learn about here as merely natural extensions that fit within a common body of principles.

CONTENTS

1. Introduction.
2. Matrix Algebra.
3. Probability and Distribution Theory.
4. Statistical Inference.
5. Computation and Optimization.
6. The Classical Multiple Linear Regression Model: Specification and Estimation.
7. Inference and Prediction.
8. Functional Form, Nonlinearity, and Specification.
9. Large-Sample Results and Alternative Estimators for the Classical Regression Model.
10. Nonlinear Regression Models.
11. Nonspherical Disturbances, Generalized Regression, and GMM Estimation.
12. Heteroscedasticity.
13. Autocorrelated Disturbances.
14. Models for Panel Data.
15. Systems of Regression Equations.
16. Simultaneous Equations Models.
17. Regressions with Lagged Variables.
18. Time-Series Models.
19. Models with Discrete Dependent Variables.
20. Limited Dependent Variable and Duration Models.
Appendix A. Data Sets Used in Applications.
Appendix B. Statistical Tables.
References.
Author Index.
Subject Index.

SUPPLEMENTS

- Solutions Manual
- LIMDEP Software

MATHEMATICAL ECONOMICS

New Title!

Using Mathematics in Economic Analysis

Peter N. Hess, Davidson College

© 2002, 450 pp., Cloth, 0-13-020026-3

BASIC APPROACH

For undergraduate courses in mathematical economics where students have completed a first course in calculus and intermediate microeconomic theory and/or intermediate macroeconomic theory. Also serves as a supplement to the standard intermediate microeconomic and macroeconomic theory courses, graduate programs in economics, and Master's programs in business and public policy.

This text is designed to help students develop mathematical skills that will open up a new dimension of economic analysis, thereby enhancing their understanding of economic theories.

CONTENTS

1. Introduction to Economic Models.
2. A Review of Some Basic Mathematics.

I. ANALYSIS OF MARKETS.

3. Perfectly Competitive Markets: Static Analysis.
4. Perfectly Competitive Markets: Dynamic Analysis.
5. Systems of Linear Equations and General Equilibrium.

II. OPTIMIZATION.

6. Theory of the Firm: Short-Run Decision Rules.
7. Competition Among Many: Perfectly Competitive Firms and Monopolistically Competitive Firms.
8. Monopolies and Monopsonies.

9. Duopolies and Oligopolies.
10. Theory of the Firm: Constrained Optimization.
11. Theory of the Firm: Inequality Constraints.
12. Theory of Consumer Behavior.

III. MACROECONOMIC ANALYSIS.

13. Basic Macroeconomic Models: Input-Output Analysis and a Simple Keynesian Model.
14. IS-LM and Aggregate Demand-Aggregate Supply Models.
15. Growth Rates and Growth Models.

SUPPLEMENTS

- Instructor's Manual–Provides answers to all end-of-chapter problems.

SPORTS ECONOMICS

Sports Economics

New Title!

Rodney Fort, Washington State University

©2003, 472 Pages, Cloth, 0-13-085091-8

BASIC APPROACH

To meet the growing interest in the business side of sports, this text will look at the underlying economic implications of both college and professional team sports. Designed for undergraduate level courses in the following departments: economics, business (especially sport management programs, recreation and physical education). It will require basic understanding of economics at a Principles level and will look at demand, supply, input markets, equilibrium of markets and business and government issues. The primary approach to the theory will be graphical but the math will also be included in boxes. Learning Highlights boxes spotlight important people and moments in sports history.

CONTENTS

1. Warm Up: The Business of Sports
2. Demand and Sports Revenue
3. The Market for Sports Broadcast Rights
4. Team Cost, Profit, and Winning
5. Sports Market Outcomes
6. The Value of Sports Talent
7. The History of Player Pay
8. Labor Relations in Pro Sports
9. Subsidies and Economic Impact Analysis
10. The Stadium
11. Taxes, Antitrust, and Competition Policy
12. College Sports

SUPPLEMENTS

- Instructor's Manual (on the web)
- PowerPoint Lecture Presentation (on the web)

ECONOMICS OF E-BUSINESS

Electronic Commerce: Economics and Strategy

New Title!

Nirvikar Singh, University of California, Santa Cruz

©2003, Paper, 0-13-091150-X

BASIC APPROACH

This text is designed for a Junior or Senior level undergraduate course in the Economics of E-Business. The text looks at the new economy from an economic perspective. The book describes what electronic commerce is, then examines how economic principles govern its operation, and finally explains what those economic principles imply for business strategy.

CONTENTS

I. Basics

1. Introduction
2. Technology Overview
3. Law Overview
3. Law Overview

II. More Economics

5. Firms and Industries
6. Households
7. The Organization of Markets
8. Intermediaries

III. Economics of E-Commerce
9. New Types of Products and Services
10. New Types of Firms
11. The Changing Nature of Firms
12. Changing Organization of Markets and Payments

IV. E-commerce Strategy—Topics
13. Customization and Bundling
14. Pricing
15. Marketing and Selling
16. Achieving Customer Lock-In
17. Managing Intellectual Property Rights

V. E-commerce—Industries
18. Physical Products Online
19. Digital Products Online
20. Financial Services Online
21. Skills Online

VI. Wrap-up
22. Government Policies
23. Global E-commerce
24. The Crystal Ball

SUPPLEMENTS

- Instructor's Manual
- PowerPoint Lecture Presentation (on Web)
- Companion Website: www.prenhall.com/singh

SPECIAL OFFERS

THE WALL STREET JOURNAL

PRINT AND INTERACTIVE EDITIONS!

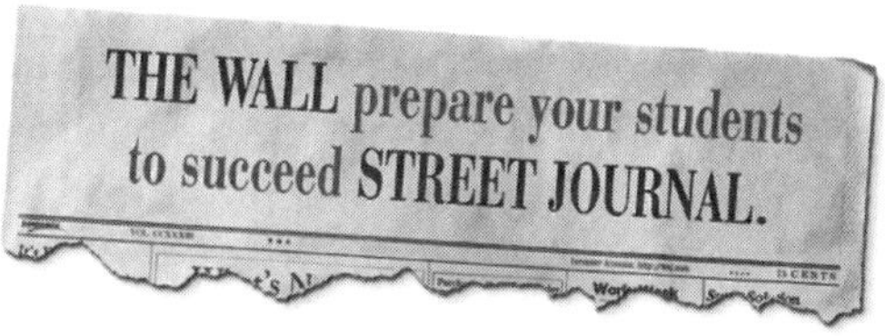

You are preparing tomorrow's business leaders. You want to expose them to the most pressing and timely business and economic issues. The most respected and trusted daily source for business information is The Wall Street Journal.

To ensure that your students are sufficiently prepared, Prentice Hall has formed a strategic alliance with The Wall Street Journal. With selected accounting, economics, and finance titles, your students can receive a 10-week subscription to both The Wall Street Journal newspaper and The Wall Street Journal Interactive Edition for a nominal charge. And, as an adopting professor, you'll receive a free subscription of both the print and interactive editions as well as weekly subject-specific Wall Street Journal lesson plans.

With this alliance, not only will your students receive the benefit of The Wall Street Journal newspaper, which provides great stories that apply to your students' studies and new perspectives from business and financial leaders, but also the added benefit of The Wall Street Journal Interactive Edition subscription!

As an Interactive Journal subscriber, you will receive:

- All the news from The Wall Street Journal–plus 24-hour-a-day updates.
- The ability to search for past Journal articles.
- Detailed Briefing Books providing background, historical and financial information, news articles and press releases on over 9,000 companies.
- Exclusive access to Barron's Online.
- Powerful personalization features, including online portfolios.
- In-depth coverage of technology and much more!

Package the Wall Street Journal for only $10.00 over the cost of the following Prentice Hall texts:

Blanchard, Macroeconomics, 3/e
Case & Fair, Principles of Economics with Active Econ CD, 6e
Case & Fair, Principles of Microeconomics with Active Econ CD, 6e
Case & Fair, Principles of Macroeconomics with Active Econ CD, 6e
Colander/Gamber, Macroeconomics
Collinge/Ayers, Economics by Design, 2e
Froyen, Macroeconomics, 7e
Heilbroner/Milberg, The Making of Economic Society 11/e
O'Sullivan & Sheffrin, Economics with Active Learning CD, 3e
O'Sullivan & Sheffrin, Microeconomics with Active Learning CD, 3e
O'Sullivan/Sheffrin, Macroeconomics with Active Learning CD, 3e
O'Sullivan/Sheffrin, Survey of Economics: Principles and Tools
Pindyck/Rubinfeld, Microeconomics, 5e

Special Offers

Financial Times

Special Rates with Select Prentice Hall Economics Texts!

Prepare your students to be tomorrow's business leaders by using the Financial Times in your economics classroom.

FINANCIAL TIMES
World business newspaper.

Free subscriptions for professors who use the FT/Prentice Hall text value pack!
Participating professors will qualify for a **complimentary one-year personal subscription to the *Financial Times*.** (Value: $298 at regular subscription rates; $99 at our education program rates.)

$10 subscriptions for students!
Participating students qualify for a **$10.00 net, 15-week subscriptions to the *Financial Times***, value: $29.

How it works:
The Prentice Hall textbook + subscription package will contain a 16-page, full-color Financial Times Student Guide, shrink-wrapped to the textbook. Bound inside the Student Guide will be a postcard, which entitles the student to claim a pre-paid 15-week subscription to the Financial Times. The student mails in the reply card and the subscription should begin in 5 to 7 business days of receipt of the card.

Professor Subscription:
Please point your browser to **www.ftsubs.com/prenhallprofs** and provide the password. Please contact your Prentice Hall Representative for the password. Delivery should begin within 5 to 7 business days.

Financial Times Contacts
Please direct all questions to the Financial Times Customer Service dept: **Tel: 800-628-0007; email: useducation@ft.com**

Ask your Prentice hall representative for other options.

Blanchard, Macroeconomics, 2e
Case & Fair, Principles of Economics with Active Econ CD, 6e
Case & Fair, Principles of Microeconomics with Active Econ CD, 6e
Case & Fair, Principles of Macroeconomics with Active Econ CD, 6e
Colander/Gamber, Macroeconomics
Froyen, Macroeconomics, 7e
Heilbroner/Milberg, The Making of Economic Society, 11e
O'Sullivan & Sheffrin, Economics with Active Learning CD, 3e
O'Sullivan & Sheffrin, Microeconomics with Active Learning CD, 3e
O'Sullivan/Sheffrin, Macroeconomics with Active Learning CD, 3e
O'Sullivan & Sheffrin, Survey of Economics
Pindyck/Rubinfeld, Microeconomics, 5e

SPECIAL OFFERS

ECONOMIST.COM

SPECIAL RATES WITH SELECT PRENTICE HALL ECONOMICS TEXTS!

Economist.com

With unmatched content, concise analysis and authoritative insight,Economist.com is one of the most powerful tools you can give your students. They'll have access to the same distinct resources that have made *The Economist* a leading news source for business and political leaders worldwide. Your students will delve inside the world's markets, governments,industry, and other news-making organizations anytime, anywhere through a wealth of exclusive online services for a fraction of the retail cost.

Immediate access to Economist.com is in their hands - and yours! (And for instructors it's FREE.)

When you adopt Prentice Hall textbooks, your students can take advantage of these online services for a full 12 weeks for only $7.50. Plus, you can enjoy the same privileges free for six months!

Unlimited access to all premium articles on Economist.com.

- **The ADVANCED SEARCH** feature retrieves archives of over 30,000 Economist articles and renowned surveys published since May 1997. CURRENT ARTICLES onsubjects ranging from Science & Technology to Finance & Economics are availableaspremium (E+) content every Thursday after 10 p.m. London time.
- **THE GLOBAL AGENDA** offers analysis of the international issues and events that matter most.
- **The CITIES GUIDE** provides concise insider information on major international cities: essential facts; news; tips on hotels and entertainment; etiquette; weather; street maps; and currency converters.
- **COUNTRY BRIEFINGS** offers continuously updated reports, forecasts, economic statistics, news and analysis on 60 countries around the world.
- **MARKETS & DATA** features global market data and charting, economic indicators from The Economist, stock quotes, foreign exchange graphs for 164 countries, and our annual favorite: The Big Mac Index.

Activate Your Subscription NOW!

Access Codes will be provided to instructors by their Prentice Hall sales representative upon adoption of any Prentice Hall Business Publishingvalue-pack. See the list below for current value-pack options. For more details, or for more value pack options, please contact your local Prentice Hall sale representative.

Blanchard, Macroeconomics, 2e 0-13-076053-6
Blau/et al., The Economics of Men, Women and Work, 4e 0-13-074733-5
Case/Fair, Principles of Economics, 6e 0-13-074660-6
Case/Fair, Principles of Microeconomics 0-13-074671-1
Case/Fair, Principles of Macroeconomics, 6e 0-13-074672-X
Colander/Gamber, Macroeconomics 0-13-074665-7
Froyen, Macroeconomics, 7e 0-13-074676-2
Heilbroner, The Making of Economic Society, 11e 0-13-074857-9
O'Sullivan/Sheffrin, Economics: Principles and Tools, 2e 0-13-074669-X
O'Sullivan/Sheffrin, Microeconomics: Principles and Tools, 2e 0-13-074668-1
O'Sullivan/Sheffrin, Macroeconomics: Principles and Tools, 2e 0-13-074667-3
O'Sullivan/Sheffrin, Survey of Economics: Principles and Tools 0-13-076052-8
Pindyck/Rubinfeld. Microeconomics, 5e 0-13-074675-4

Prentice Hall Technology

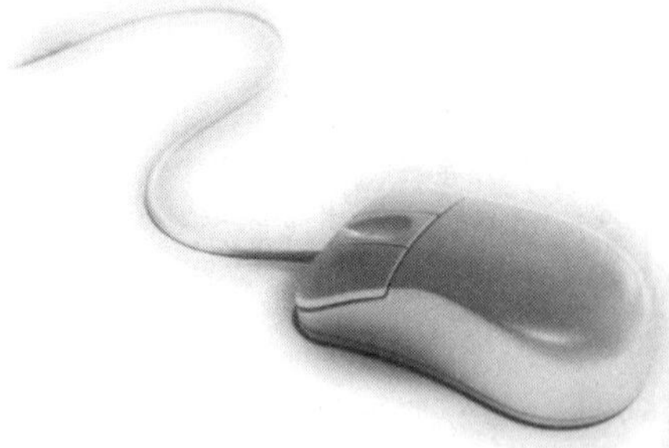

Internet and Online Solutions

Text-Specific Web sites
Companion Websites
Online Courses:
- Blackboard
- CourseCompass
- CourseCompass with ebook
- WebCT

activebooks

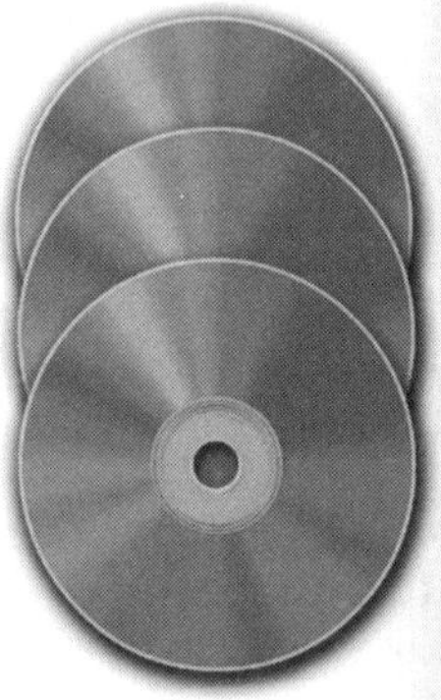

Software Solutions

Case/Fair Active Economics CD
O'Sullivan/Sheffrin Active Learning CD
Blanchard Active Graph CD-ROM
Colander Active Graph CD-ROM
Instructor's Resource CD/Course Organizer
PH Test Manager

Video Solutions

ABC Video Library 2001
activebooks
Mastering Economics

Internet and Online Solutions

Text-Specific Websites

Companion Websites

Author	Title	Web Site Address
Blanchard	Macroeconomics, 3e	www.prenhall.com/blanchard
Case/Fair	Principles of Economics, 6e	www.prenhall.com/casefair
Colander/Gamber	Macroeconomics	www.prenhall.com/colander
Heyne	The Economic Way of Thinking, 9e	www.prenhall.com/heyne
O'Sullivan/Sheffrin	Economics: Principles and Tools, 3e	www.prenhall.com/osullivan
O'Sullivan/Sheffrin	Survey of Economics, 2e	www.prenhall.com/osullivan
Pindyck	Microeconomics, 5e	www.prenhall.com.pindyck

See the following page for a complete description of the resources available on Companion Websites.

Web sites

Author	Title	Web Site Address
Blau/Ferber/Winkler	The Economics of Men, Women, and Work, 4e	www.prenhall.com/blau
Boardman/Greenberg/ Vining/Weimer	Cost-Benefit Analysis, 2e	www.prenhall.com/boardman
Collinge/Ayers	Economics by Design: Principles and Issues, 2e	www.prenhall.com/collinge
Folland/Goodman/Stano	The Economics of Health and Health Care, 3e	www.prenhall.com/folland
Froyen	Macroeconomics: Theories and Policies, 7e	www.prenhall.com/froyen
Heyne/Prychitko/Boethke	The Economic Way of Thinking 10e	www.prenhall.com/heyne
Keat/Young	Managerial Economics, 3e	www.prenhall.com/keat
Lynn	Economic Development: Theory and Practice	www.prenhall.com/lynn
Mathis/Koscianski	Microeconomic Theory: An Integrated Approach	www.prenhall.com/mathis
Petersen/Lewis	Managerial Economics, 4e	www.prenhall.com/petersen
Schiller	The Economics of Poverty and Discrimination, 8e	www.prenhall.com/schiller
Fort	Sports Economics	www.prenhall.com/fort

Internet and Online Solutions

Companion Websites

STUDENTS LEARN BETTER WITH COMPANION WEBSITES!

- **Online Quizzes** for each chapter enable students to test their skills and get immediate scoring and feedback
- **Bulletin Board** enables students and faculty to post messages
- **Ask the Tutor** provides students with an additional resource to provide coaching
- **Current Events** articles help students see the relevance of text topics to today's news
- **Downloadable Resources** include tutorial software, PowerPoints, and much more!

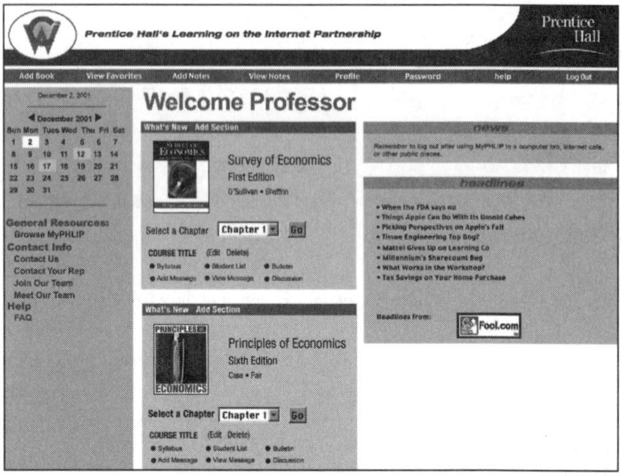

OTHER SPECIAL FEATURES INCLUDE

- **Individual homepages, for students and faculty,** provide easy, one-click navigation to our vast, dynamic database of online teaching and learning resources. Faculty and students can organize the online resources for all of their classes on this single, customizable homepage.
- **A powerful new point-and-click syllabus creation tool** can be usedby faculty for each course and section they teach. Additionally, faculty can annotate and link each resource on a companion website to their syllabi.
- **Faculty can even upload their own personal resources to our site** and have these resources available to their students via their personalized syllabus.

Please visit a companion website at **www.prenhall.com/economics**.
For more information on this, and other Prentice Hall Economics texts, please visit our Web site at www.prenhall.com/economics.

Internet and Online Solutions

Online and Web-Enhanced Courses

Blackboard, CourseCompass, or WebCT

Do you plan to offer a distance learning course or would you like to enhance your traditional classroom with a wealth of Internet-based resources? Prentice Hall has the answers to all of your needs in your choice of platforms: Blackboard, CourseCompass, and WebCT!

Ask your Prentice Hall Representative for an up-to-the-minute list of available courses!

Courses include many of the following features:

- Online Testing
- Course Management and Page Tracking
- Gradebook
- Course Information
- Multiple-Section Chat Rooms
- Bulletin Board Conferencing
- Syllabus and Calendar Functions
- E-mail Capability

INTERNET AND ONLINE SOLUTIONS

BLACKBOARD

Blackboard's simple templates and tools make it easy to create, manage, and use online materials. Prentice Hall's class-tested online content is now available in Blackboard's products, with its easy-to-use interface.

Course Management System

Course management tools include progress tracking, class and student management, gradebook, communication, assignments, and reporting tools.

Communication Tools

Blackboard offers communication tools such as the Virtual Classroom™ (chat rooms, whiteboard, slides), document sharing, and bulletin boards.

Testing

Testing programs include the capability for instructors to create online quizzes and tests, and automatically grade and track results. All tests can be entered into the gradebook for easy course management.

Hosting

Blackboard courses can be hosted at your institution (Blackboard site license required) or by Prentice Hall (for a nominal fee).

To view a Blackboard demonstration, visit **www.prenhall.com/blackboard**

Internet and Online Solutions

COURSE COMPASS

With the highest level of service, support, and training available today, CourseCompass combines tested, quality online course resources with easy-to-use online tools. CourseCompass is designed to address the needs of instructors who want to create an online course in less than 15 minutes–without any special technical skills or training.

The combination of the unique CourseCompass software platform with Prentice Hall's unparalleled content helps us give you and your students the easiest-to-use course management system available.

Comprehensive Support and Hosting
CourseCompass courses are hosted on the Prentice Hall server, which offers a fully-supported system that relieves individuals and institutions of the burdens of trouble-shooting and maintenance.

Greater Ease of Use
Unlike other course management systems, you will be able to create an online course in 15 minutes or less.

High Flexibility
Professors can adapt Prentice Hall content to match their own teaching goals, with little or no outside assistance needed.

Tools
CourseCompass offers assessment, customization, class administration, and communication tools.

Point-and-Click Access
Prentice Hall's vast educational resources are available to instructors at a click of the mouse.

Testing
Testing programs include the capability for instructors to create online quizzes and tests, and automatically grade and track results. All tests can be entered into the gradebook for easy course management.

To preview a CourseCompass course, visit **www.prenhall.com/coursecompass**

PREMIUM COURSECOMPASS WITH eBOOK

Now you get even more when you team up with CourseCompass to teach your Economics courses! All the quality course content and easy-to-use management tools of CourseCompass–plus a searchable, Web-based e-book:

- **One integrated study experience for students.** With one click, students have access to all course materials (text, quizzes, research links), all in one place.
- **Easy-to-use, anytime, anywhere.** As easy as a book, students can gain access from any computer online.
- **Affordable, searchable e-textbook.** Prentice Hall and MetaText have partnered to provide a unique Web-based study experience which, when combined with the online study guide and tools of CourseCompass,provides a value for students.

Internet and Online Solutions

WEBCT

WebCT offers a powerful set of tools that enables you to create practical Web-based educational programs–the ideal resources to enhance a campus course or to construct one entirely online. The WebCT shell and tools, integrated with Prentice Hall's superior content, result in a versatile, course-enhancing teaching and learning system.

Course Management System

Robust course management tools make it easy for you to manage your course online. Tools include page tracking, progress tracking, class and student management, gradebook, an interactive calendar, reporting tools, and more.

Communication Tools

One of the most powerful features of WebCT is its communication system. Communication tools include three levels of chat rooms, bulleting boards, private e-mail, and whiteboard.

Testing

Testing tools help you create and administer online quizzes and tests that can be timed, selectively released, and that feature multiple choice, short answer, and essay questions. Quiz questions can be scrambled, and algorithmically-generated questions are included in the content provided by Prentice Hall.

Hosting

WebCT courses can be hosted at your institution (WebCT site license required) or by Prentice Hall (for a nominal fee).

To view a WebCT demonstration, visit **www.prenhall.com/webct**

INTERNET AND ONLINE SOLUTIONS

INTRODUCING activebooks

A NEW Web-enabled learning tool is now at your fingertips. Welcome to a new way to learn.

What is an activebook?
activebooks connect the conceptual flow of a text with a dynamic array of online resources including print, audio, and video components to create a completely integrated live learning environment.

Leveraging the Power of Print and Technology
An activebook consists of two components:

- The print component looks exactly like the online component and indicates when the user needs to go online to work with a multimedia component.
- The online component includes the core text plus the multimedia component. The common look of the print and online components simplifies navigation.

activebooks vs. Traditional Books
activebooks are all about integration. Static text material comes alive in real time through the integration of printed word and media. Students and instructors can easily access all media supplements with the click of a mouse to enhance the learning experience.

INTERNET AND ONLINE SOLUTIONS

activebooks **are:**

Interactive and Web-enabled:
activebooks allow each student to participate in a web-enabled environment. Online "Concept Checks," for example, help students keep track of their progress while polls and discussions spark critical thinking. Media components reach students of all learning styles through print, audio, and video resources–delivered via links embedded in the online text–to ensure a positive learning experience for everyone.

Up-To-The-Minute:
In an activebook, dynamic content is moved online and updated as often as needed. Examples remain fresh, numbers stay current, and links are always active.

Customizable:
An activebook provides students and instructors with greater levels of customization than traditional texts. Professors can reorder chapters in the text, annotate sections of the text for their students, and track each student's progress through the material. Students can annotate their activebook and customize their view of the book's resources.

Price-Friendly:
activebooks cost less than traditional textbooks. Even though the core text is retained, the print component of an activebook is shorter than a traditional text. All boxed material, chapter summaries, exercises, and other dynamic content reside in the online component of the activebook.

DON'T JUST READ. LEARN.

ENHANCING THE TEXTBOOK TO ENGAGE LEARNERS

An activebook puts students in control–empowering them to fully harness the power of the media resources that accompany their text. The result is a truly dynamic learning experience.

activebooks **are now available for:**
- Case/Fair, Principles of Microeconomics
- Case/Fair, Principles of Macroeconomics
- O'Sullivan/Sheffrin, Microeconomics: Principles and Tools
- O'Sullivan/Sheffrin, Macroeconomics: Principles and Tools

Note: More titles and subsequent editions may also include this special offer. Contact your Prentice Hall Representative with questions.

www.prenhall.com/myactivebook

Software Solutions

Mastering Economics

Part of the Mastering Business Series

Mastering Economics is an interactive multimedia CD-ROM that uses video and interactive exercises to help students link the theory they learn in class with realistic business situations. The episodes and interactive exercises on the CD are based on CanGo, a fictional e-commerce startup that sells a variety of entertainment products and services online. The episodes show students how all the functional areas of business work together to ensure the growth of the company as well as how to apply business theories to CanGo's daily operations.

Features include:

- **Integrates the business curriculum**—Shows how the various functional areas in business work together to resolve business problems.
- **Bridges theory and practice**—Starts with realistic business situations and then explains how theories apply to them.
- **Makes business interesting and interactive.**
  - Videos engage students in dramatic business situations and corresponding interactive exercises get them to actively participate in the learning process.
- **Academically rigorous**—All content in the series was created and reviewed by university professors and experts in interactive instructional design.
- **Self-paced design**—Each of the 12 episodes takes 30-45 minutes of student time outside of class, leaving class time for discussing relevant topics in the Mastering Economics situations.

TOPICS

1. Economic Way of Thinking.
2. Supply and Demand.
3. Price Determination.
4. Market Intervention.
5. Costs and Input Markets.
6. Marginal Analysis and Perfect Competition.
7. Imperfect Competition.
8. National Income (Measurement of Key Economic Data).
9. Business Cycles.
10. Fiscal Policy (Federal Government "Tax and Spend" Policy).
11. Monetary Policy.
12. International Trade

Software Solutions

Mastering Economics

Part of the Mastering Business Series

You can put the power of Mastering Economics in your students' hands for only $5 net with new Prentice Hall texts by ordering the following ISBNs. Please contact your Prentice Hall representative for more information and additional value-pack ISBNs.

The entire Mastering Business Series (Strategy, Management, Accounting, Finance, Economics, Marketing, Operations Management, and Introduction to Business) can also be shrink-wrapped to our textbooks for an additional charge. Contact your local sales representative for more information.

Blanchard, Macroeconomics, 2e	0-13-076137-0
Case & Fair, Principles of Economics with Active Econ CD, 6e	0-13-076142-7
Case & Fair, Principles of Microeconomics with Active Econ CD, 6e	0-13-076130-3
Case & Fair, Principles of Macroeconomics with Active Econ CD, 6e	0-13-076139-7
Colander/Gamber, Macroeconomics	0-13-076135-4
Froyen, Macroeconomics, 7e	0-13-076138-9
Heilbroner/Milberg, The Making of Economic Society, 11e	0-13-076134-6
Hess, Using Mathematics in Economic Analysis	0-13-076136-2
O'Sullivan & Sheffrin, Economics with Active Learning CD, 3e	0-13-072341-X
O'Sullivan & Sheffrin, Microeconomics with Active Learning CD, 3e	0-13-072342-8
O'Sullivan/Sheffrin, Macroeconomics with Active Learning CD, 3e	0-13-072343-6
O'Sullivan/Sheffrin, Survey of Economics	0-13-076132-X
Pindyck/Rubinfeld, Microeconomics, 5e	0-13-076143-5

Contact your local Prentice Hall sales rep for more information.

THE 2001-2002 PRENTICE HALL GUIDE TO ECONOMICS FACULTY

Compiled by
James R. Hasselback
Professor of Taxation
6753 Thomasville Rd, PMB 108-321
Tallahassee, Florida 32312
850-894-2244 Phone/Recorder/Fax
E-Mail: jhassel@cob.fsu.edu

Prentice Hall Inc. is publishing the fifth Guide to Economics Faculty. The Directory includes a listing of the Dean, Department Chairpersons, and full-time Economics faculty from almost 850 schools. It is compiled from information provided by the respective schools. The Directory is for the academic year 2001-2002. Only United States schools plus five foreign schools were included in the survey. The Directory is published every two years.

Updated information is provided on almost 85 percent of the schools. Typically at least three requests went to any school listed as not responding. Only that information received by August 29, 2001, is included in the Directory.

The department phone number follows the area code in the first line of each school. At the right side of the first line is the school's electronic-mail code. The fax number is shown in the second line. The department secretary/administration assistant is included at the end of the second line.

The columns are as follows:

Name Rank School-Phone Electronic-Mail Area Degr/Date/School Start

$ next to a Dean or Chairman indicates "Acting"

For the Chairperson, the title and rank are:

C	Chairman	D	Director	H	Head
Pr	Professor	Ac	Associate	As	Assistant

The electronic-mail column includes the individual's address. The individual address must be combined with the school electronic-mail address; for instance, jim@fsu. When an individual address includes an "@", that individual has a different school address from the school address listed in the first line of the school; the individual's complete electronic-mail address is included in the electronic-mail column. However, if an individual electronic-mail address ends with a "." then the school's address must be added to the individual address provided. Additional school addresses may be shown in a third line for the school. In some cases, an individual address was too long to fit in the column and was truncated with a "+" or was included in a line following the individual. Use the Super Computer to decipher this paragraph.

The degree column represents the highest earned degree or "all but dissertation," date received, and school.

The start column is for the year of beginning full-time employment at that school.

The teaching/research column is as follows:

A General Economics & Teaching
B Methodology & History of Econ Thought
C Mathematical & Quantitative Methods
D Microeconomics
E Macroeconomics & Monetary Economics
F International Economics
G Financial Economics
H Public Economics
I Health, Education, & Welfare
J Labor Economics
K Law & Economics
L Industrial Organization
M Business Adm & Business Economics
N Economic History
O Economic Development, Technological Change, & Growth
P Economic Systems
Q Agricultural & Natural Resource Economics
R Urban, Rural, & Regional Economics
T Demographic Economics

adapted from Journal of Economic Literature listing

In the second part of the Directory, individuals are listed in alphabetical order. The phone and electronic-mail columns are replaced with the individual's school.

Any mistakes in the Directory are my responsibility. However, some of the misinformation belongs to schools not providing complete information.

Any corrections, additional information, and new schools should be sent directly to me. If your school is not included, please send me a listing in a format similar to that provided in the Directory.

James R. Hasselback

JAMES R. HASSELBACK

James R. Hasselback is a Professor of Taxation at Florida State University and has previously taught at Eastern Michigan University, the University of Florida, and Texas A&M University. A member of the American Accounting Association and the American Taxation Association, he has published over 150 papers in professional and academic journals, including *The Accounting Review*, *The Tax Adviser*, *Financial Management*, *Journal of Real Estate Taxation*, and the *American Business Law Journal*.

Dr. Hasselback has presented papers at numerous national and regional professional meetings, and served as chairman at tax sessions of professional conferences. He regularly presents continuing education seminars for Certified Public Accountants. He is co-author and technical editor on a two-volume introductory taxation series published by CCH Inc. for the past eighteen years. Jim has also served as technical editor on several publications by CCH Inc. and Harper-Collins Inc. He is a contributing author on *2001 U.S. Master Accounting Guide*, by CCH Incorporated. Jim is co-author with Irvin Gleim on the *Eleventh Edition of Federal Tax Exam Questions and Explanations* and also co-author of the third edition of a four-volume *EA Review for the IRS Special Enrollment Exam*.

In addition to the *Guide to Economics Faculty*, Jim Hasselback compiles the *Accounting Faculty Directory* published by Prentice Hall. Published each year for 28 years, the *Accounting Faculty Directory* may be the most cited reference in the Accounting field. The other Directories in the business field include: a Directory of Management Faculty, a Directory of Finance Faculty, a Directory of Marketing Faculty, and a Directory of Business Law Faculty. An Engineering Faculty Directory was published in 1992 and 1995. A Computer Science Faculty Directory was published in 1994 and 1996. The Nursing Faculty Directory was published in January 1995. The last three directories are in the process of being updated.

Dr. Hasselback teaches two courses, Income Tax Planning and Estate Planning, in Florida State University's Certificate in Financial Planning Program, both on campus and through the internet. He taught for several years in the Florida State University's CPA Review Course.

2001-2002 ECONOMICS FACULTY DIRECTORY
ALPHABETICAL BY SCHOOL

NAME	RANK	PHONE	Electronic-Mail	AREA	Degr/Date/School			START
Adams State College	Alamosa, CO		81102	(719) 587-7161			adams.edu	
Department of Economics	School of Business		Fax=587-7603				Ms. Dolly Maestas	
Weston, Rafael R.	Dean	587-7161	rrweston		PHD	72	Harvard	1988
Ellis, Theodore	Prof	587-7511	tjellis		PHD	72	Colo St	1967
Keiser, Kurt J.	Asst	587-7303	kjkeiser		ABD		Colo St	
Lyell, Ed	Asst	587-7751	ehlyell		PHD		Colorado	
Adelphi University	Garden City, NY		11530	(516) 877-4690			adelphi.edu	
Department of Economics	School of Business		Fax=877-4607					
Libertella, Anthony F.	Dean	877-4690			PHD	72	Ohio St	2000
Gleicher, David	Assoc	877-4971		BJ	PHD	84	Columbia	1981
Machlis, David	Assoc	877-4972		E	PHD	71	Rutgers	1968
Heinowitz, Harvey	Asst	877-4668			MBA		Adelphi	
Mariano, Torras	Asst	877-4644			PHD		Mass	
Adrian College	Adrian, MI		49221-2575	(517) Ext 4432			adrian.edu	
Economics Faculty	Dept of Accounting & Econ		Fax=264-3331				Pat Husband	
phone: 265-5161								
Bachman, William	C-Pr	264-3939	wbachman	Mgt	ABD	73	Kentucky	8-81
Habib, Ahsan M.	Prof	Ext 3945	ahabib		PHD	80	McMaster	1981
University of Akron	Akron, OH		44325-1908	(330) 972-7546			uakron.edu	
Department of Economics	Buchtel Col Arts & Sci		Fax=972-5356				Jeanette Quinn	
Homepage: uakron.edu/econ								
Creel, Roger	Dean	972-7881	rcreel		PHD	69	Iowa St	1970
Nelson, Michael A.	C-Pr	972-7939	manelson	AH	PHD	80	Purdue	2000
Garofalo, Gasper A.	Prof	972-7548	ggarofalo	ADR	PHD	74	Pittsburgh	1979
Malhotra, Devinder	Prof	972-7937	dmalhotra	ADR	PHD	79	Kansas St	1979
McGuire, Robert A.	Prof	972-7521	rmcguire	AKN	PHD	78	U Wash	1990
Erickson, Elizabeth L.	Assoc	972-7973	eerickson	AOQ	PHD	72	Illinois	1969
King, Randall H.	Assoc	972-7975	king	ADJ	PHD	78	Ohio St	1978
Myers, Steven	Assoc	972-7421	smyers	ACJ	PHD	80	Ohio St	1979
Stratton, Richard	Assoc	972-7440	dickstratton	ADJ	PHD	77	Conn	1978
Ghosh, Sucharita	Asst	972-7549	sghosh	AEF	PHD	93	Kansas	1993
University of Alabama	Tuscaloosa, AL		35487-0224	(205) 348-7842			cba.ua.edu	
Dept Econ, Fnce & Legal Stds	Col Commerce & Bus Adm		Fax=348-0590				Sheila Smith, Prog Asst	
Mason, J. Barry	Dean	348-7443	jbmason	Mktg	PHD	67	Alabama	1967
Russell Professor of Business Administration								
Helms, Billy P.	H-Pr	348-7842	bhelms	Fnce	PHD	73	Tennessee	1973
Cover, James P.	Prof	348-8977	jcover		PHD	82	Virginia	1982
Elder, Harold W.	Prof	348-7842	helder		PHD	82	Va Tech	1981
Formby, John P.	Prof	348-8667	jformby		PHD	65	Colorado	1982
Hayes Professor of Economics								
Leathers, Charles G.	Prof	348-7842	cleather		PHD	68	Oklahoma	1968
Misiolek, Walter S.	Prof	348-8900	wmisiole		PHD	76	Cornell	1975
Senior Associate Dean & Director of Graduate Programs								
Pecorino, Paul	Prof	348-0379	ppecorin		PHD	90	Duke	1994
Schlesinger, Harris	Prof	348-7842	hsclesi		PHD	80	Illinois	1987
Hooks, Donald L.	Assoc	348-7842	dhooks		PHD	71	Tx A&M	1971
Silver, J. Lew	Assoc	348-7842	jsilver		PHD	80	Duke	1990
Dakhlia, Sami F.	Asst	348-2927	sdakhlia		PHD	98	Wash U	1999
Heung, C. James	Asst	348-8971	chueng		PHD	97	Wisconsin	1997
Hoover, Gary A.	Asst	348-6033	ghoover		PHD	98	Wash U	1998
Temimi, Akram	Asst	348-8961	atemimi		PHD	96	Illinois	1996
U of Alabama at Birmingham	Birmingham, AL		35294-4460	(205) 934-8830			uab.edu	
Department of Economics	School of Business		Fax=975-6234				Rose McCoy	
email: @1=mail.business.uab.edu								
Holmes, Robert E.	Dean	934-0055		Mgt	PHD	71	Arkansas	1-99
Burns, Richard M.	C-Ac	934-8830	rburns	Fnce	PHD	86	Georgia	9-87
Bos, Theodore	Prof	934-8830	tedbos	CG	PHD	82	Illinois	1982
Lee, Seung-Dong	Prof	934-8830	sdlee	CDFQ	PHD	79	So Meth	1979
Stanford, Robert	Prof	934-8830	stanford	C	PHD	71	Berkeley	1982
VanMatre, Joe G.	Prof	934-8830	jgv	C	PHD	70	Alabama	1971
Culver, Sarah E.	Assoc	934-8830	sculver	CEFG	PHD	93	Houston	1993
Dasgupta, Manabendra	Assoc	934-8830	dasgupta@1	CDHL	PHD	89	So Meth	1992
Ignatin, George	Assoc	934-8830	gig@1	AJK	PHD	69	Tx-Austin	1969
Wilson, Bradley	Asst	934-8830		CEF	PHD	97	Kansas	1997

U of Alabama in Huntsville — Huntsville, AL 35899 (256) 890-6590 — uah.edu
Dept Economics & Finance — Col of Admin Science Fax=890-6328 — Ms. Liz Patillo

Billings, C. David	Dean	890-6735		H	PHD	69	Missouri	1981
Wilhite, Allen W.	C-Pr	890-6694		DK	PHD	81	Illinois	1988
Schnell, John F.	Prof	890-6590		J	PHD	84	Illinois	1990
Schoening, Niles C.	Prof	890-6782		R	PHD	83	Tennessee	1983
Allen, W. David	Assoc	890-6105		J	PHD	94	Arkansas	1994

Alabama A&M University — Normal, AL 35762 (256) 851-5085 — asnaam.aamu.edu
Dept of Economics & Finance — School of Business Fax=851-5874 — Sibyl Moore

Jones, Barbara A. P.	Dean	851-5092		AP	PHD	73	Geo St	1997
Rahimian, Eric N.	C-Pr	851-5085		ADOF	PHD	75	Indiana	1975
Alexander, James	Prof	858-4794		EAOH	PHD	89	Tx-Austin	1983
Elike, Uchenna I.	Asst	858-8487		AOF	PHD	85	Alabama	1985
Robbani, Mohammad G.	Asst	851-5095	aammgr01	GO	PHD	94	Fla Intl	9-94
Yousif, Salah A.	Asst	858-4788		AJ	MA		Howard	1976
Adcock, Marvin	Inst	858-4792						
Briggs, Charles	Inst	858-4787		A	MS	90	Alab A&M	1990
Gebremikael, Fesseha	Inst	858-4795		A	MS	97	Alab A&M	1996
McGuire, Wanda	Exec	858-5083						

Alabama State University — Montgomery, AL 36101-0271 (334) 229-4142 — alasu.edu
Department of Business Adm — Col of Business Admin Fax=265-9144 — Ms. Jenette Williams

Vaughn, Percy J. Jr.	Dean	229-4124		Mktg	DBA	75	Tx Tech	1974
Yeh, Chiou-Nan	C-Pr	229-4127			PHD	74	Mass	1974
Bakir, Saad T.	Assoc	229-6805	sbakir	CM	PHD	77	Va Tech	1-93
Suwanakul, Sontachai	Assoc	293-6962			PHD	86	Arkansas	1989

Univ of Alaska Anchorage — Anchorage, AK 99508-8244 (907) 786-1770 — uaa.alaska.edu
Department of Economics — Col of Bus & Public Affairs Fax=786-7739 — Janet Burton

Green, G. Hayden	Dean	786-4126	afhg	Bus	PHD	74	Arkansas	1974
Johnson, Paul R.	C-Ac	786-4311	afprj		PHD	85	Rochester	1989
Huskey, Lee	Prof	786-1905	aflh	AJR	PHD	77	Wash U	1977
Jackstadt, Stephen L.	Prof	786-1901	aycee	AEH	EDD	81	Indiana	1985
Ross, Larry L.	Prof	786-1613	afllr	ADE	MS	71	Oregon	1971
Hill, Pershing J.	Assoc	786-1763	afpjh	EFH	PHD	76	Wash St	1975

Univ of Alaska Fairbanks — Fairbanks, AK 99775-6080 (907) 474-7119 — som.uaf.edu
Department of Economics — School of Management Fax=474-5219

Collins, James M.	D-As$	474-7119	ffjmc	Mgt	PHD	91	Tx-Austin	1991
Pippenger, Michael	H-As	474-6530	ffmkp		PHD	90	Purdue	1991
Goering, Gregory	Assoc	474-5572	ffgeg		PHD	90	Purdue	1990
Hermann, Mark	Assoc	474-7116	ffmlh		PHD	90	Wash St	1990
Logan, Robert	Assoc	474-6783	ffrrl		PHD	86	Iowa	1986
Read, Colin	Assoc	474-5975	ffclri		PHD	88	Queen's	1989
Reynolds, Douglas	Asst	474-6531	ffdmr		PHD			

Univ of Alaska Southeast — Juneau, AK 99801-8671 (907) 465-6405 — alaska.edu
Economics Faculty — Academic Programs Fax=465-6406 — Lisa Ward

Madden, Mary Lou	Dean	465-6417						
Ahrens, Ashley	Asst	465-6397			PHD			

Albany State University — Albany, GA 31705 (229) 430-4772 — asurams.edu
Economics Faculty — School of Business Adm Fax=430-5119 — Kathy Dawsey
Homepage: www.asurams.edu

Ojemakinde, Abiodun	Dean	430-2749	aojemaki	M	PHD	89	LSU	9-89
Norton, Virgil	Prof	430-4084	vjnorton	QI	PHD	63	Oregon St	1-01
Rogers, Michael	Prof	430-4784	mrogers	L	PHD	88	Tennessee	9-89
Ansari, Mohammed	Assoc	430-4611	mansari	F	PHD	89	Simon Fr	8-01
Norton, Nancy	Assoc	430-2952	nanorton	Q	PHD	94	W Virginia	1-01
Kuforiji, John	Asst	430-1746	jkuforij	J	PHD	87	Pittsburgh	8-00

Albion College — Albion, MI 49224-1899 (517) 629-0419 — albion.edu
Economics Faculty — Dept of Economics & Mgt Fax=629-0428 — Becky Ketchum
Homepage: www.albion.edu/econ

Christiansen, Daniel S.	C-Pr	629-0425	christiansen	CD	PHD	75	Stanford	1981
Hooks, Jon A.	Prof	629-0530	jhooks	G	PHD	89	Mich St	1989
McCarley, James F.	Prof	629-0294	jmccarley	J	PHD	70	Mich St	1965
Saltzman, Gregory M.	Prof	629-0422	gsaltzman	J	PHD	82	Wisconsin	1982
Steinhauer, Larry	Prof	629-0423	lsteinauer	E	PHD	74	Chicago	1968

Albright College — Reading, PA 19612-5234 (610) 921-7538 — alb.edu
Economics Faculty — Dept of Econ & Business Fax=921-7883 — Mrs. Linda Reinhart

Bell, Christine A.	C-As	921-7701	MBA	77	Temple	1989
Martin, David A.	Prof	921-7888	DA	80	Lehigh	1983
Moyer, James T.	Prof	921-7781	PHD	76	Lehigh	9-68
Lever, Jacqueline	Assoc	921-7704	PHD	82	Pittsburgh	1990
Saboori, Farhad	Assoc	921-7884	PHD	85	Indiana	1986
Wilder, Lisa A.	Asst	921-7538	PHD	95	Va Tech	2001

Alcorn State University — Alcorn State, MS 39096-7500 (601) 877-6411 — lorman.alcorn.edu
Dept of Social Sciences — Sch of Arts & Sciences Fax=877-6256 — Mrs. Rogena Jones
Homepage: www.alcorn.edu/academic/academ/social.htm

Cotton, Bernard	Dean$	877-6120	bcotton	PolS	PHD	78	Wash St	1971
Morris, Alpha	C-Ac	877-6411		Soc	PHD	77	Miss St	
Gau, Carolina	Prof	877-6416			PHD		Missouri	
Gau, Paul K.	Prof	877-6417			PHD	71	Illinois	1972

Coordinator, Economics

Alfred University — Alfred, NY 14802 (607) 871-2124 — alfred.edu
Economics Program — College of Business Fax=871-2114
Homepage: econ.alfred.edu

Duserick, Frank	Dean$	871-2124	fduserick	MBA	72	Harvard	1978
Booker, James F.	C-Ac	871-2685	fbooker	PHD	90	Colo St	1993
Mapalad, Claret	Asst	871-2687	mapalad	PHD	94	Ca-Rivers	7-99
Ozsoy, Onur	VAsst	871-2685	fozsoy	PHD	98	SUNY-Bin	2000

Allegheny College — Meadville, PA 16335-3902 (814) 332-3358 — alleg.edu
Economics Faculty — Department of Economics Fax=332-2789 — Ms. Linda Maurd

Adams, Earl W. Jr.	C-Pr	332-3331	eadams	AEGH	PHD	71	MIT	1972
Andrew Wells Robertson Professor of Economics								
Casler, Stephen D.	Prof	332-3337	scasler	ACEQ	PHD	83	Illinois	1988
Cupper, Robert Dean	Prof	332-2881	bcupper	ACD	PHD	74	Pittsburgh	1977
Afrasiabi, Ahmad	Assoc	332-3334	bafrasia	BCQR	PHD	85	W Virginia	1985
Baskan, Asuman	Assoc	332-3336	abaskan	CDFE	PHD	88	Lehigh	1987
Goldstein, Donald	Assoc	332-3340	dgoldste	ABG	PHD	91	Mass	1989
Moskwa, Antoni	Assoc	332-3339	amoskwa	AFCP	PHD	75	Warsaw	1982
Nonnenmacher, Tomas	Asst	332-3820	tnonnenm	DKLN	PHD	96	Illinois	1996
Onyeiwu, Stephen Z.	Asst	332-3338		ADLM	PHD	97	Conn	2001

Alma College — Alma, MI 48801-1599 (517) 463-7183 — alma.edu
Economics Faculty — Department of Economics Fax=463-7277

Mueller, James V.	C-Ac	463-7183	mueller	ABEH	ABD		Ca-Irvine	1976
Choksy, George Dorian	Assoc	463-7390	choksy	DNRC	PHD	86	Tennessee	1989
Cunningham, Robert	Asst	463-7015	cunningham		PHD		SUNY-Bin	1999

American University — Washington, DC 20016-8029 (202) 885-3770 — american.edu
Department of Economics — Col of Arts & Sciences Fax=885-3790 — Sheila Budnyj

Mussell, Kay	Dean	885-2446	mussell		PHD	74	Iowa	1999
Sawers, Larry	C-Pr	885-3766	lsawers		PHD	69	Michigan	1969
Blecker, Robert A.	Prof	885-3767	blecker		PHD	87	Stanford	1985
Bradford, Colin	Prof	885-3784	cbrad		PHD	70	Columbia	1998
Broder, Ivy E.	Prof	885-2125	ibroder		PHD	74	SUNY-SBr	1975
Feinberg, Robert M.	Prof	885-3788	feinberg		PHD	76	Virginia	1989
Golan, Amos	Prof	885-3784	agolan		PHD	88	Berkeley	1996
Hahnel, Robin E.	Prof	885-2712	rhahnel		PHD	79	American	1976
Lane, Julia I.	Prof	885-3781	jilane		PHD	82	Missouri	1990
Lerman, Robert I.	Prof	885-3770	rlerman		PHD	70	MIT	1989
Muller, Ronald E.	Prof	527-0990			PHD		American	1970
Schydlowsky, Daniel M.	Prof	885-2521	dschyd		PHD	66	Harvard	1990
Wachtel, Howard M.	Prof	885-3784			PHD	69	Michigan	1969
Wisman, Jon D.	Prof	885-3158	jdwisma		PHD	74	American	1971
Ayittey, George B. N.	VAsoc	885-3779			PHD	81	Manitoba	1994
Floro, Maria Sagrario	Assoc	885-3139	mfloro	OGDQ	PHD	87	Stanford	1988
Graham, Fred C.	Assoc	885-3782	fgraham		PHD	85	Virginia	1988
Hazilla, Michael	Assoc	885-3148	hazilla		PHD	78	SUNY-Bin	1988
Husted, Thomas A.	Assoc	885-3773	husted		PHD	86	N Carol	1986
Isaac, Alan G.	Assoc	885-3785			PHD	86	Ca-Davis	1987
Meurs, Mieke E.	Assoc	885-3776	mmeurs		PHD	88	Mass	1989
Park, Walter G.	Assoc	885-3774	wgp		PHD	91	Yale	1991
Willoughby, John A.	Assoc	885-3759	jwillou		PHD	79	Berkeley	1979
Carey, Kevin	Asst	885-3747	kcarey	E	PHD	95	Princeton	1997

American International Coll Springfield, MA 01109-3189 (413) 205-3306 aic.edu
Department of Economics Sch Bus Adm/Sch Arts &S Fax=205-3943

Somers, Trudy L.	Dean	203-3230	tsomers	Hrm	PHD	88	Michigan	1999
Orcutt, Bonnie	C-As	205-3943		ADJH	PHD	93	Clark	1992
Smolowitz, Ira E.	Prof	747-6369			PHD	84	Rensselaer	1988

Director, Center for Economic Education; Dean, Bureau of Business Research

Amherst College Amherst, MA 01002-5000 (413) 542-2249 amherst.edu
Economics Faculty Department of Economics Fax=542-2090 Jeanne E. Reinle
Homepage: www.amherst.edu/econ/

Woglom, Geoffrey R.	C-Pr	542-2433	grwoglom	AEG	PHD	74	Yale	1978
Richard S. Volpergt '56 Professor in Economics								
Barbezat, Daniel P.	Prof	542-7948	dpbarbezat	ANO	PHD	88	Illinois	1988
Beals, Ralph E.	Prof	542-2570	rebeals	ACO	PHD	70	MIT	1966
Clarence Francis Professor of Economics								
Kohler, Heinz	Emer	542-2083	hkohler	APCD	PHD	61	Michigan	1961
Willard Long Thorp Professor of Economics								
Nicholson, Walter E.	Prof	542-2191	wenicholson	ACDK	PHD	70	MIT	1968
Ward H. Patton, Jr. Professor of Economics								
Westhoff, Frank H.	Prof	542-2190	fwesthoff	ADHC	PHD	74	Yale	1973
Yarbrough, Beth V.	Prof	542-2429	bvyarbrough	ADF	PHD	83	U Wash	1982
Willard Long Thorp Professor of Economics								
Rivkin, Steven G.	Assoc	542-2106	sgrivkin	AIJ	PHD	91	UCLA	1993
Irons, John S.	Asst	542-8422	jsirons	AEH	PHD	99	MIT	1999
Kingston, Christopher G.	Asst	542-2249	cgkingston	AFOP	PHD	01	Stanford	2001
Takeyama, Lisa N.	Asst	542-2271	lntakeyama	ADLQ	PHD	92	Stanford	1994

Anderson University Anderson, IN 46012-3462 (765) 641-4358 anderson.edu
Department of Business Falls Sch of Business Fax=641-4356 Chris Smith/Carol Whetsel
Homepage: www.anderson.edu/falls

Armstrong, Ken D.	Dean	641-4364	kdarmstrong		PHD	85	Nrthwstrn	1990
Ritchey, Barry	Prof	641-4357	bcritchey	DHR	PHD	88	Syracuse	1991
Heberling, Gregory Dean	Assoc	641-4363	gdherberling		MBA		Ball St	1978
Truitt, Terry C.	Assoc	641-4354	tctruitt	G	PHD	96	Miss St	1995

Andrews University Berrien Spr, MI 49104-0024 (616) 471-3429 andrews.edu
Economics Department School of Business Fax=471-6158 Ruth Tidwell

Gibson, Ann	Dean	471-3102	gibson	Atg	PHD	92	Wash St	1992
Gashugi, Leonard K.	C-Pr	471-3581	gashugi	CF	PHD	92	Boston U	1979
Chuak, Sam	Prof	471-3453	chuahki	CD	PHD	92	Wash St	1998
Russell, Malcolm B.	Prof	471-3104	russell	EN	PHD	78	J Hopkins	1979
Shepard, Delynne	Asst	471-3429	shepard	EJ	PHD	95	Purdue	1995

Angelo State University San Angelo, TX 76909 (915) 942-2046 mailserv.angelo.edu
Dept Acct, Economics & Fnce Col Bus & Prof Studies Fax=942-2285

Butler, Michael W.	Dean	942-2337		P	PHD	74	Iowa	2001
Sunderman, Norman A.	H-Pr	Ext 248	norman.sund+	Atg	DMA	69	Michigan	1987
Dane, Andrew J.	Prof	Ext 259	andy.dane	P	PHD	75	Oklahoma	1973
Maddox, D. Pat	Assoc	Ext 251	pat.maddox	PI	PHD	82	Tx Tech	1988
Owens, Gerald P.	Assoc	Ext 238	gerry.owens	PI	PHD	65	Ohio St	1996
Kara, S. Murat	Asst	Ext 254	murat.kara	PM	PHD	83	Tx Tech	2000
Murat, Kara S.	Asst	Ext 254	murat.kara	PM	PHD	93	Tx Tech	2000

Appalachian State Univ Boone, NC 28608-2051 (828) 262-2148 appstate.edu
Department of Economics Walker College of Bus Fax=262-6105 Beth Haymore
Homepage: www.eco.appstate.edu

Peacock, Kenneth E.	Dean	262-2058	peacockke	Atg	PHD	79	LSU	1983
Schieren, George A.	C-Pr	262-4033	schierenga	CDE	PHD	75	N Carol	1977
Combs, J. Paul	Prof	262-6161	compsjp	MR	PHD	73	N Car St	1971
Courbois, Jean-Pierre	Prof	262-2117	courboisjp	F	PHD	68	American	1968
Durden, Gary C.	Prof	262-6077	durdengc	EH	PHD	71	Fla St	1982
Elledge, Barry	Prof	262-6121	elledgebw	IM	PHD	70	N Car St	1969
Ellis, Larry V.	Prof	262-6123	ellislv	E	PHD	78	Missouri	1978
Gaynor, Patricia E.	Prof	262-6129	gaynorpe	C	PHD	73	U Miami	1976
Millsaps, Steven	Prof	262-6080	millsapssw	CDQ	PHD	73	N Car St	1973
Perri, Timothy J.	Prof	262-2251	perritj	DJ	PHD	78	Ohio St	1980
Kirkpatrick, Rickey C.	Assoc	262-6127	kirkpatrickrc	FM	PHD	78	Tulane	1980
McRae, Larry T.	Assoc	262-6125	mcraelt	CDE	PHD	78	N Carol	1977
Cherry, Todd	Asst	261-6081	cherrytl	DQ	PHD	98	Wyoming	2001
Dawson, John	Asst	262-6128	dawsonjw	E	PHD	97	N Car St	2000
Maske, Kellie	Asst	262-6555	maskekl	DF	PHD	98	N Carol	2000

Aquinas College Grand Rapids, MI 49506-1799 (616) 459-8281 aquinas.edu
Economics Faculty Economics Department Fax=732-4487
phone: 459-8281

Beversluis, Eric H.	C-Ac	Ext 3602	bevereri		PHD	70	Nrthwstrn	1988
Chaffee, Donald M. Jr.	Prof	Ext 4626	chaffdon		PHD	70	Ca-Davis	1992
Robertson, Gary L.	Assoc	Ext 4458	robergar		MA		Detroit	1969
Yamazaki, Masato	Asst	Ext 4466	yamaemas		PHD	84	Duke	1987

Arcadia University Glenside, PA 19038-3295 (215) 572-2891 arcadia.edu
Economics Faculty Dept of Bus Adm & Econ Fax=572-4489 Lisa C. Scholly

Biggs, William D.	C-Pr	572-2937	biggs	Mgt	PHD	74	Penn St	8-80
Morra, Wayne A.	Assoc	572-2125	morra	ALR	PHD	84	Temple	8-81
Palugod, Paul	Asst	572-2881	palugod	AFM	PHD	93	Pittsburgh	9-99

University of Arizona Tucson, AZ 85721-0108 (520) 621-6224 bpavms.bpa.arizona.edu
Department of Economics Col Business & Pub Adm Fax=621-8450 Lanna Miller, Adm Asst
Homepage: w3.arizona.edu/~econ
email @1=u.arizona.edu

Zupan, Mark	Dean	621-2165			PHD	87	MIT	1996
Fishback, Price V.	H-Pr	621-4421	pfishback		PHD	83	U Wash	1990
Block, Michael K.	Prof	621-2854			PHD	72	Stanford	1981
Cox, James C.	Prof	621-2164	jcox		PHD	71	Harvard	1977
Kantor, Shawn E.	Prof	621-6230	skantor		PHD	90	Cal Tech	1990
Libecap, Gary D.	Prof	621-4821	glibecap		PHD	76	Penn	1984
Director Karl Eller Center								
Marshall, Robert H.	Emer	621-5831			PHD	57	Ohio St	1957
Oaxaca, Ronald L.	Prof	621-4135	rlo@1		PHD	71	Princeton	1976
Reynolds, Stanley	Prof	621-6251	reynolds		PHD	83	Nrthwstrn	1982
Rieber, Michael	Prof	621-4281			PHD	63	MIT	1978
Smith, Kenneth R.	Prof	621-6224	ksmith		PHD	68	Nrthwstrn	1980
Smith, Vernon L.	Emer	621-4747			PHD	55	Harvard	1975
Taylor, Lester D.	Prof	621-6222	ltaylor		PHD	63	Harvard	1972
Tullock, Gordon	Emer	621-2640			JD	47	Chicago	1987
Walker, Mark A.	Prof	621-6155	mwalker		PHD	70	Purdue	1990
Wells, Donald A.	Emer	621-6240			PHD	61	Oregon	1969
Zajac, Edward E.	Emer	621-2192	ezajac		PHD	54	Stanford	1983
Drabicki, John Z.	Assoc	621-4221	jdrabicki		PHD	73	Purdue	1970
Heckerman, Donald G.	Assoc	621-6065			PHD	67	MIT	1971
Lucking-Reiley, David	Assoc	621-6224	reiley		PHD	96	MIT	2001
McBearty, James C.	Assoc	621-1639			PHD	68	Illinois	1968
Sands, Barbara N.	Assoc	621-2166	bsands		PHD	85	U Wash	1985
Swanson, Gerald	Assoc	621-6220	swansong		PHD	72	Illinois	1970
Wooders, John C.	Assoc	621-6231	jwooders		PHD	91	Cornell	1991
Flores-lagunes, Alfonso	Asst	621-6224			PHD	01	Ohio St	2001
Horrace, William	Asst	62-6230	whorrace		PHD	96	Mich St	1996
Houser, Daniel	Asst	621-6223	dhouser		PHD	97	Minnesota	1997
Sundaram, Ramya	Asst	6216224			PHD	01	Penn	2001

Arizona State University Tempe, AZ 85287-3806 (480) 965-3531 asu.edu
Department of Economics College of Business Fax=965-0748

Penley, Larry E.	Dean	965-5516	larry.penley	Mgt	PHD	76	Georgia	1985
Blakemore, Arthur E.	C-Pr	965-3531	arthur.blakem+		PHD	77	S Illinois	1979
Boyes, William J.	Prof	965-5504	william.boyes		PHD	74	Claremont	1969
Brada, Josef C.	Prof	965-6524	josef.brada		PHD	71	Minnesota	1978
Burgess, Paul L.	Prof	965-8432	paul.burgess		PHD	69	Colorado	1969
DeSerpa, Allan C.	Prof	965-6192	allen.deserpa		PHD	70	Ca-SnBarb	1975
Faith, Roger L.	Prof	965-6244	roger.faith		PHD	73	UCLA	1981
Gooding, Elmer R.	Prof	965-5596	elmer.gooding		PHD	69	Kansas	1988
Happel, Stephen K.	Prof	965-5001	stephen.happel		PHD	76	Duke	1975
Hoffman, Dennis L.	Prof	965-3531	dennis.hoffman		PHD	78	Mich St	1979
Associate Dean								
Hogan, Timothy D.	Prof	965-3961	timothy.hogan		PHD	71	Va Tech	1970
Director of Center for Business Research								
Kingston, Jerry L.	Prof	965-7457	jerry.kingston		PHD	69	Penn St	1969
Low, Stuart A.	Prof	965-5498	stuart.low		PHD	79	Illinois	1979
Manelli, Alejandro	Prof	965-4682	alejandro.man+		PHD	88	Berkeley	1997
McDowell, John M.	Prof	965-7109	john.mcdowell		PHD	79	UCLA	1978
McPheters, Lee R.	Prof	965-3961	lee.mcpheters		PHD	72	Va Tech	1976
Associate Dean, Graduate Program								
Melvin, Michael T.	Prof	965-6860	michael.melvin		PHD	80	UCLA	1980
Mendez, Jose A.	Prof	965-2723	jose.mendez		PHD	80	So Meth	1980
Ormiston, Michael B.	Prof	965-7350	michael.ormis+		PHD	77	J Hopkins	1984
Rogerson, Richard D.	Prof	965-3531			PHD	84	Minnesota	2001
Edward Rondthaler Professor								
Santos, Manuel	Prof	965-6335	manuel.santos		PHD	84	Chicago	1999
Bank One Professor								
Schlee, Edward E.	Prof	965-5745	edward.schlee		PHD	88	Illinois	1990

Zhou, Lin	Prof	965-3531		CF	PHD	89	Princeton	2001
Lincoln Professor								
Ahn, Seung C.	Assoc	965-6574	seung.ahn		PHD	90	Mich St	1990
Cogley, Timothy	Assoc	727-7977	timothy.cogley		PHD	88	Berkeley	1999
Reffett, Kevin	Assoc	965-3531	kevin.reffett		PHD	90	Purdue	1995
Winkelman, Richard D.	Assoc	965-2128	richard.wink+		PHD	66	Illinois	1965
Chade, Hector	Asst	965-4714	hector.chade		PHD	96	Illinois	1997
Datta, Manjira	Asst	965-6433	manjira.datta		PHD	92	Cornell	1995
Hendricks, Lutz	Asst	965-1462	lutz.hendricks		PHD	96	Penn	1996

University of Arkansas Fayetteville, AR 72701-1201 (501) 575-ECON walton.uark.edu
Department of Economics Walton Coll of Bus Adm Fax=575-7687 Susan Yell

Williams, Doyle Z.	Dean	575-5949		Atg	PHD	65	LSU	1993
Ziegler, Joseph A.	H-Pr	575-3266		R	PHD	71	Notre Dm	1980
Britton, Charles R.	Prof			E	PHD	71	Iowa	1978
Curington, William P.	Prof			J	PHD	79	Syracuse	1989
Dixon, Bruce	Prof			TQ	PHD	76	Ca-Davis	1986
Gay, David E.	Prof			H	PHD	73	Tx A&M	1983
McKinnon, Thomas	Prof			NA	PHD	72	Miss	1981
Murray, Tracy W.	Prof			F	PHD	69	Mich St	1978
Distinguished Professor & Chairholder, Phillips Petroleum Company Chair/IEB								
Farmer, Amy F.	Assoc			DK	PHD	91	Duke	1999
Ferrier, Gary D.	Assoc			DC	PHD	88	N Carol	1993
Horowitz, Andrew W.	Assoc			OFD	PHD	89	Wisconsin	1998
Kali, Raja	Asst			LOFD	PHD	96	Maryland	1999
Kuester, Dan	VAsst				PHD	00	Missouri	2000
Peck, Cary	Asst				PHD	01	Arizona	2001
Stapp, Robert	VAsst				PHD		Okla St	1996

U of Arkansas at Little Rock Little Rock, AR 72204-1099 (501) 569-3354 ualr.edu
Dept of Economics & Finance College of Business Adm Fax=569-8898 Karen Wisdom 569-3354

Goolsby, William C.	Dean	569-3356	wcgoolsby	Fnce	PHD	74	Wi-Milwa	7-96
Terry, Andy	C-Ac	569-8872	haterry		PHD	89	Michigan	1989
Chisholm, Roger K.	Prof	569-8894	rkchisholm		PHD	67	Chicago	1985
Ford, Richard	Prof	569-8876	rkford		PHD	79	Arkansas	1981
Galchus, Kenneth	Prof	569-8893	kegalchus		PHD	70	Wash U	1976
Associate Dean								
Lindeman, Bruce	Prof	569-8870			PHD	68	Duke	1975
Pickett, John C.	Prof	569-3354			PHD	70	Missouri	1986
Holland, Larry C.	Assoc	569-3042	lcholland		PHD	96	Okla St	1995
Elder, Erick	Asst	569-8879	emelder		PHD	97	Pittsburgh	8-96
Hall, John R. Jr.	Asst	569-3355	jrhall		PHD	92	Indiana	
Keller, Anita	Inst	569-8873	apkeller		MBA	76	Ark St	1991

U of Arkansas at Pine Bluff Pine Bluff, AR 71601 (870) 543-8575 vx4500.uapb.edu
Economics Faculty Sch of Business & Mgt Fax=543-8574

Grayson, Barbara A.	Dean$	543-8577			EDD	83	Okla St	1987
Shahjahan, Mirza	C-Pr	543-8575			PHD		Bonn	
Burkett, Evelyn	Asst	543-8575			MA		Houston	
Diagne, Assane	Asst	575-8904			PHD	96	LSU	

Arkansas State University State Univ, AR 72467-0239 (870) 972-3416 cherokee.astate.edu
Dept of Economics & Dec Sys College of Business Fax= Ms. Jeanette Gatlin

Duggar, Jan W.	Dean	972-3035	jduggar		PHD	67	Fla St	2000
Brown, Christopher R.	C-Ac	972-3416	crbrown	AEKM	PHD	89	Tennessee	1990
Crawford, Jerry L.	Prof	972-3416	crawford	ADTM	PHD	69	Arkansas	1966
Dale, Lawrence Raymond	Prof	972-3810	dalex	ABPQ	PHD	79	Ohio U	1986
Kesselring, Randall G.	Prof	972-3416	randyk	ACJF	PHD	80	Oklahoma	1984
Latanich, Gary A.	Assoc	972-3416	latanich	AREM	PHD	78	Nebraska	1981
Marburger, Daniel R.	Assoc	972-3416	marburge	AJMD	PHD	89	Ariz St	1989
Guha, Gauri-Shankar	Asst	972-3416			PHD			

Arkansas Tech University Russellville, AR 72801-2222 (501) 968-0354 mail.atu.edu
Dept of Business & Economics School of Business Fax=968-0677

Tyler, Thomas P.	Dean	968-0490	tom.tyler		PHD	80	Arkansas	1967
Roach, David W.	H-Pr	968-0613	david.roach	Mgt	PHD	91	Arkansas	8-83
Cole, Raymond E.	Prof	968-0491	gene.cole		PHD	76	Arkansas	1970
Moore, Joseph L.	Prof	968-0688	joe.moore		PHD	75	Arkansas	1988
Smith, Richard S.	Assoc	968-0492	richard.smith		PHD	74	Tx-Austin	1991
Benefield, Michael E.	Asst	968-0264	mike.benefield		PHD	89	Purdue	1995

Armstromg Atlantic St Univ — Savannah, GA 31419-1997 (912) 961-3171 — mail.armstrong.edu
Economics Faculty — Col of Arts & Sciences Fax=921-3782 — Kimberly Ashley

Wheeler, Ed R.	Dean	927-5279	wheeleed	Math	PHD	73	Virginia	1987
Saadatmand, Yassaman	H-Ac	927-3171	saadatya	FO	PHD	88	NewHamp	1989
Cebula, Richard J.	Prof	921-3781	cebulari	EDR	PHD	71	Geo St	1999
Eminent Scholar in Economics								
McGrath, Richard	Asst	927-5525	mcgrathri	DHG	PHD	97	Virginia	1997
Mizak, Patrick	Asst	921-3172	mizakpat		MA	98	Clev St	2000
Toma, Michael	Asst	927-5527	tomamich	RE	PHD	96	GeoMason	1997

Ashland University — Ashland, OH 44805 (419) 289-5912 — ashland.edu
Department of Economics — College of Bus & Econ Fax=289-5949 — Linda Braun

Sears, Paul A.	Dean	289-5212	psears		PHD	90	Case Wes	8-97
Nadler, Mark A.	C-Ac	289-5912	mnadler		PHD	83	Iowa St	1989
A. L. Garber Family Chair of Economics								
Rafeld, Frederick J.	Prof	289-5746	rrafeld		PHD	68	Ohio St	9-70
Garcia, Javier F.	Assoc	289-5734	jgarcia		JD		Akron	1980
Rogers, Robert P.	Assoc	289-5739	rrogers1		PHD	83	Geo Wash	1993
Wasnich, Wendy S.	Asst	289-5735	wwasnich		MA		Ohio St	1985

Assumption College — Worcester, MA 01615-0005 (508) 767-7379 — eve.assumption.edu
Economic Faculty — Dept Econ & Global Stu Fax=799-4502 — Janet Truscott

Lynn, Stuart R.	C-Ac	767-7565	slynn	DBFO	PHD	71	N Carol	1987
Doyle, George A.	Emer	767-7579	gdoyle	FBOP	PHD	51	Fordham	1961
Fahy, Colleen A.	Assoc	767-7558	cfahey	HLCD	PHD	89	SUNY-Bin	1994
Hickey, Kevin L.	Assoc	767-7296	khickey		MLA	76	Harvard	1972
Kantarelis, Demetrius	Assoc	767-7557	dkantar	DCKL	PHD	83	Clark	1983
White, Thomas J.	Assoc	767-7556	twhite	EGQ	PHD	89	SUNY-Bin	1995
Charlebois, Cecile M.	Lect	767-7004		AHJ	ABD		Clark	1980
Moser, William	Lect				ABD		Clark	

Athens State University — Athens, AL 35611 (205) 233-8211 — athens.edu
Economics Faculty — School of Business Fax=233-8164 — Donna Thomas

Gulbro, Robert	Dean	233-8116		Mgt	DBA	91	Miss St	1994
Wilkes, William	Asst	233-8191	bwilkes	AF	DA	98	Mid Tenn	1996

Auburn University — Auburn, AL 36849-5242 (334) 844-4910 — business.auburn.edu
Department of Economics — College of Business Fax=844-4615 — Lola Burnett 844-2901

Jahera, John S. Jr.	Dean$	844-4030		Fnce	PHD	81	Georgia	9-80
Long, James E.	H-Pr$	844-2911	jlong		PHD	74	Fla St	1974
Caudill, Steven B.	Prof	844-2907	scaudill		PHD	82	Florida	1981
Ekelund, Robert B. Jr.	Prof	844-2929	rekelund		PHD	67	LSU	1979
Lowder Eminent Scholar								
Garrison, Roger W.	Prof	844-2920	rgarrisn		PHD	81	Virginia	1983
Jackson, John D.	Prof	844-2906	jjackson		PHD	77	Claremont	1984
Kaserman, David L.	Prof	844-2905	kaserman		PHD	76	Florida	1986
Torohmark Professor								
Whitten, David O.	Prof	844-2928	dwhitten		PHD	70	Tulane	1968
Ault, Richard W.	Assoc	844-2919	rault		PHD	83	Virginia	1983
Beard, Thomas Randolph	Assoc	844-2918	rbeard		PHD	88	Vanderbilt	1988
Beil, Richard O.	Assoc	844-2921	rbeil		PHD	88	Tx A&M	1988
Gropper, Daniel M.	Assoc	844-2908	dgropper		PHD	89	Fla St	1988
Saba, Richard P.	Assoc	844-2922	rsaba		PHD	74	Tx A&M	1974

Auburn U at Montgomery — Montgomery, AL 36117-3596 (334) 244-3454 — monk.aum.edu
Department of Economics — School of Business Fax=244-3792

Lantz, Keith W.	Dean	224-3478	klantz	Atg	PHD	75	Iowa	1995
Gregorowicz, Phillip	H-Pr	244-3575	pgregorwic	EFGJ	PHD	82	N Illinois	1980
Deravi, M. Keivan	Prof	244-3555	dkeravi	DFGJ	PHD	85	Okla St	1985
Director of Center for Government & Public Affairs								
Hegji, Charles E.	Prof	244-3563	chegji	DFMJ	PHD	80	Wash U	1985
Lacy, Allen W.	Emer	244-3511	alacy	ETIH	PHD	71	Iowa St	1976
Chiles, Ted W.	Assoc	244-3512	tchiles	ADJM	PHD	90	Penn St	1990
Clark, Joy	Assoc	244-3561	jclark	APQB	PHD	88	Tx A&M	1988
Sollars, David L.	Assoc	244-3486	dsollars	KHAE	PHD	91	Fla St	1990
Assistant Dean								
Schneider, Lynn	Asst		lschneider		PHD	96	Houston	1998
Lucy-Bouler, Tink	Inst	244-3310	tink					

Augsburg College Minneapolis, MN 55454 (612) 330-1320 augsburg.edu
Economics Faculty Department of Economics Fax=330-1649 Heather Olson
Homepage: www.augsburg.edu

Kimball, Chris	Dean	330-1024	kimball		PHD		Chicago	1991
Boeh, Jeanne	C-Ac	330-1760	boeh	I	PHD	89	Il-Chicago	1990
Gilsdorf, Keith F.	Asst	330-1320		FE	PHD	90	Nebraska	2001
Hofrenning, Stella	Asst	330-1320		I	PHD	92	Il-Chicago	2001

Augusta State University Augusta, GA 30904-2200 (706) 737-1560 admin.ac.edu
Economics Faculty College of Business Adm Fax=667-4064 Ettie Westjohn

Widener, Jack K.	Dean	737-1418			MBA			
Brauer, Jurgen	Assoc	737-1560	jbrauer	AFIT	PHD	89	Notre Dm	1991
Leightner, Jonathan E.	Assoc	737-1560	jleightn	DTOP	PHD	89	N Carol	1989

Augustana College IL Rock Island, IL 61201-2296 (309) 794-7457 augustana.edu
Department of Economics Div of Business & Educa Fax=794-7605 Georgia Moreno

Jurasek, Richard T.	Dean	794-7311	adcrj		PHD	75	Ohio St	9-98
Ballman, Richard J. Jr.	C-Pr	794-7517	ecballman	ABDE	PHD	77	Iowa	1972
Marme, Christopher B.	Asst	794-7514	ecmarme	ACEO	PHD	94	Illinois	1988
Short, Joanna	Inst	794-7268	ecshort	ANHD	ABD		Indiana	2001

Augustana College SD Sioux Falls, SD 57197 (605) 274-5226 inst.augie.edu
Department of Economics Div of Social Sciences Fax=274-5229

Eggleston, Brian D.	C-Ac	274-5307	egglesto	ABQ	PHD	91	Wash St	1988
Nesiba, Reynold F.	Asst	274-5310	nesiba	EG	PHD	95	Notre Dm	1995
Sorenson, David	Asst	274-5223	dsorenso	RG	PHD	97	W Virginia	1997

Austin Peay State University Clarksville, TN 37044 (931) 221-7788 apsu01.apsu.edu
Department of Economics College of Business Fax=221-5985 Ms. Penny Howard

Newport, Stephanie	Dean$	221-7674	newports	Mgt	PHD	90	Tx-Arlin	1993
Meadows, Tommy C.	C-Pr	221-7747	meadowst	HJ	PHD	79	Clemson	1977
Kim, Kil-Joong	Prof	221-7788	kimk	FO	PHD	80	Cincinnati	1980
Langston, Vicky	Assoc	221-7851	langstonv	RM	PHD	83	Tx-Austin	1997

Azusa Pacific University Azusa, CA 91702-7000 (626) 812-3085 apu.edu
Economics Faculty School of Bus & Mgt Fax=815-3802 Beverly Castle
Homepage: www.apu.edu:8080/sbm/

Bezjian, Ilene L.	Dean	812-3085		Mgt	DBA	86	US Intl	1-93
Conover, Roger B.	C-As	815-3823			MA	82	Ca-SnDgo	9-90
Verdugo, Paul R.	Asst	812-3091			MA	76	Ca Poly	9-80

Babson College Babson Park, MA 02457-0901 (781) 239-4580 babson.edu
Division of Economics School of Management Fax=239-5239 Linda Katz

Jones, Kent A.	C-Pr	239-4477	kjones	F	PHD	81	Geneva	1982
Bayer, Arthur A.	Prof	239-4321	bayer	AH	PHD	68	Mich St	1978
Casey, William L. Jr.	Prof	239-4244	casey	F	PHD	63	Boston C	1964
Marthinsen, John E.	Prof	239-4324	martinsen	FD	PHD	74	Conn	1974
Moss, Laurence S.	Prof	239-5573	lmos@a	K	PHD	71	Columbia	1977
Carliner, Geoffrey	VAsoc	239-4580		F				
McAuliffe, Robert E. Jr.	Assoc	239-4515	mcauliffe	EL	PHD	82	Virginia	1982
Ricciardi, Joseph M.	Assoc	239-4530	ricciardi	EO	PHD	85	Tx-Austin	1985
Axarloglou, Kostas	Asst	239-5512	axarloglou	F	PHD	93	Michigan	1994
Han, Hsiang-Ling	Asst	239-5851	han	CE	PHD	92	Rochester	1997
Minniti, Maria	Asst	239-4296	minniti	E	PHD	97	NYU	1997
Polutnik, Lidija	Asst	239-4211	polutnik	HJ	PHD	94	Geo St	1991
Evans, Stacey	VInst	239-4580	sevans	AE				
Kafi, Farhoud	VInst	239-4580	kafi	D	MA		Northeas	

Baldwin-Wallace College Berea, OH 44017-2088 (440) 826-2113 baldwinw.edu
Department of Economics Div of Social Sciences Fax=826-3835 Sandara Wojtolewicz

Rolleston, Barbara Sherman	C-Ac	826-2003	brollest	HR	PHD	83	Cornell	1983
Ebert, Robert R.	Prof	826-2033	rebert	DFP	PHD	74	Case Wes	1967
Heinicke, Craig W.	Assoc	826-2419	cheinicke	NOE	PHD	91	Toronto	1991
Miller, Dennis D.	Assoc	826-2002	dmiller	OQ	PHD	85	Colorado	1987
Peart, Sandra Joan	Assoc	826-2120	speart	BD	PHD	89	Toronto	1989
Ross, Thomas A.	Assoc	826-2118	tross	CG	MS		Bowl Gr	
Sage, Lewis C.	Assoc	826-2119	lsage	CIJ	PHD	85	Maryland	1985

Ball State University Muncie, IN 47306-0340 (765) 285-5360 bsu.edu
Department of Economics College of Business Fax=285-8024 Ms. Rita Disher
Homepage: www.bsu.edu/econ/

Richardson, Lynne D.	Dean	285-8192	lrichard	Mktg	PHD	89	Alabama	7-01
Flowers, Marilyn	C-Pr	285-5360		H	PHD	74	Va Tech	1990
Bohanon, Cecil E.	Prof	285-5363		H	PHD	81	Va Tech	1980
Cheng, Chu-Yuan	Prof	285-5366		OP	PHD	64	Geotown	1971
Coehlo, Philip R. P.	Prof	285-5376		NT	PHD	69	U Wash	1986
Deitsch, Clarence R.	Prof	285-5368		J	PHD	74	NewHamp	1974
Santoni, Gary J.	Prof	285-5365		E	PHD	72	New Mex	1988
Stone, Courtney C.	Prof	285-5378		EM	PHD	73	UCLA	1991
Van Cott, T. Norman	Prof	285-5370		FH	PHD	69	U Wash	1977
Green, Jeffery	Assoc	285-2056		C	PHD	72	Cornell	1972
Horowitz, John B.	Assoc	285-1436		HJ	PHD	88	Tx A&M	1989
Keil, Stanley R.	Assoc	285-5360		QR	PHD	73	Oregon	1973
Liu, Tung	Assoc	285-5360		C	PHD	90	Ca-SnDgo	1990
McClure, James Edward	Assoc	285-5375		J	PHD	83	Purdue	1982
Spector, Lee C.	Assoc	285-5360		E	PHD	85	Iowa	1985
Yoho, Devon L.	Assoc	285-8020		A	PHD	74	Missouri	1978
Director of Center for Economic Education								
Zegeye, Abera	Assoc	285-5379		A	PHD	77	Indiana	1974
Shupp, Robert	Asst	285-3724						

University of Baltimore Baltimore, MD 21201-5779 (410) 837-4994 ubmail.ubalt.edu
Dept of Economics & Finance Merrick Sch of Business Fax=837-5722 Cindy Tannebaum

Gerlowski, Daniel A.	Dean$	837-4455	dgerlowski	ALM	PHD	87	Pittsburgh	8-87
Acs, Zoltan J.	Prof	837-5012	zacs		PHD	80	New Sch	1989
Levy, David T.	Prof	837-5026	dlevy		PHD		N Carol	
Sawhney, Bansi L.	Prof	837-5049	bsawhney		PHD	75	Geo Wash	1971
Stevens, David W.	Prof	837-4727	dstevens		PHD	65	Colorado	
Executive Director of Jacob France Center								
Brownstein, Barry	Assoc	837-4960	bbrownstein		PHD	77	Rutgers	

Barnard College New York, NY 10027-6598 (212) 854-3454 barnard.columbia.edu
Economics Faculty Department of Economics Fax=854-8947
Homepage: www.econ.barnard.columbia.edu

Mehrling, Perry G.	C-Pr	854-4369	pmehrling	EGB	PHD	88	Harvard	1987
Burgstaller, Andre C.	Prof	854-3167	aburgstaller	EOBF	PHD	79	Columbia	1977
Macunovich, Diane J.	Prof	854-9150	dmacunovich	JT	PHD	89	S Calif	1999
Weiman, David F.	Prof	854-5755	dweiman	NL	PHD	84	Stanford	2001
Sethi, Rajiv	Assoc	854-5140	rsethi	DQ	PHD	93	New Sch	1995
Dye, Alan	Asst	854-3868	adye	NOL	PHD	91	Illinois	1995
Harrison, Sharon	Asst	854-3333	sharrison	EC	PHD	97	Nrthwstrn	1997
Munasinghe, Lalith	Asst	854-5652	lmunasinghe	JC	PHD	95	Columbia	1997
Reddy, Sanjay	Asst	854-3790	sreddy	NO	PHD	00	Harvard	2001

Barry University Miami Shores, FL 33161-6695 (305) 899-3500 mail.barry.edu
Dept Economics & Finance Andreas Sch of Business Fax=892-6412

Scarborough, Jack W.	Dean	899-3500	jscarborough	Mgt	PHD	88	Maryland	8-89
Duchatelet, Martine	Prof	899-3510	mduchatelet		PHD	77	Stanford	1989
Associate Dean								
Hervitz, Hugo M.	Prof	894-3514	hhorvitz		PHD	83	Indiana	1982
Morrell, Stephen O.	Prof	899-3513	smorrell		PHD	77	Va Tech	1990
Payne, Bruce C.	Prof	899-3519	bpayne		PHD	77	LSU	8-98
Cruz, Robert D.	Assoc	899-3522	rcryz		PHD	85	Penn	1993
Daghestani, Eddie	Assoc	899-3509	edaghestani		PHD	71	Colo St	1988

Barton College Wilson, NC 27893 (252) 399-6422 e-mail.barton.edu
Economics Faculty School of Business Fax=399-6571 Jennifer Jones

Bethune, John J.	Dean	399-6422	jbethune		PHD	87	Fla St	8-00
Edmondson, Robert	Asst	399-6429	redmonds		MBA	87	Wake For	8-91

Bates College Lewiston, ME 04240 (207) 786-6193 abacus.bates.edu
Economics Faculty Department of Economics Fax=786-8338

Hughes, James W.	C-As	786-6193	jhughes	J	PHD	87	Michigan	1982
Aschauer, David Alan	Prof	786-6099		E	PHD	84	Rochester	1990
Elmer W. Campbell Professor of Economics								
Murray, Michael P.	Prof	786-6085	mmurray	RH	PHD	74	Iowa St	1986
Phillips Professor of Economics								
Walther, Theodore	Prof	786-6088		FG	PHD	64	New Sch	1958
Williams, Anne D.	Prof	786-6091		O	PHD	76	Chicago	1981
Lewis, Lynne	Assoc	786-6089			PHD	94	Colorado	2000
Maurer-Fazio, Margaret	Assoc	786-6087		O	PHD	94	Pittsburgh	1994
Oliver, Michael	Assoc	786-6047			PHD	95	Manchest	2001
Schwinn, Carl R.	Assoc	786-6090		IO	PHD	78	Cornell	1975
Mechnet, Emily	Asst	786-6195			PHD	98	Harvard	1998

Baylor University Waco, TX 76798-8003 (254) 710-2263 baylor.edu
Department of Economics Hankamer Sch Busines Fax=710-1092 Susan Armstrong
Homepage: hsb.baylor.edu/htm/eco

Maness, Terry S.	Dean	710-3411	terry_maness	Fnce	PHD	77	Indiana	1977
Green, Steven L.	C-Pr	710-4543	steve_green		PHD	84	Brown	1986
Gardner, H. Stephen	Prof	710-6147	steve_gardner	FP	PHD	78	Berkeley	1978
Herman Brown Professor of Economics								
Gilbreath, L. Kent	Prof	710-3535	kent_gilbreath	GN	PHD	71	Florida	1973
Stevens Professor of Private Enterprise								
Henderson, James W.	Prof	710-4139	jim_henderson	IJ	PHD	81	So Meth	1981
Ben H. Williams Professor of Economics								
Kelly, Thomas M.	Prof	710-4146	tom_kelly	R	PHD	70	Okla St	1969
Director Center for Economic Analysis								
McKinney, Joseph A.	Prof	710-6141	joe_mckinney	F	PHD	70	Mich St	1976
Truitt, W. James	Prof	710-2263	jim_truitt	D	PHD	68	Illinois	1968
Director Cntr/Priv Entrp								
VanHoose, David D.	Prof	710-6206	david_vanhoose	EF	PHD	84	N Carol	2001
Herman W. Lay Professor of Private Enterprise								
Pisciotta, John L.	Assoc	710-6224	john_pisciotta		PHD	71	Tx-Austin	1980
Gwin, Carl	Asst	710-6251	carl_gwin	DL	PHD	97	Indiana	2001
North, Charles	Asst	710-6229	charles_north	K	PHD	99	Tx-Austin	1998
Taylor, Beck	Asst	710-4549	beck_taylor	D	PHD	97	Purdue	1997
Bowman, Judy C.	Lect	710-6174	judy_bowman		MS	74	Baylor	1974
Johnson, Karen R.	Lect	710-6149	karen_johnson		MIM		Baylor	1979
Newsome, Heather	Lect	710-6466	heather_news+		MS	96	Baylor	1996
Odegaard, Thomas A.	Lect	710-4892	tom_odegaard		MA	70	Rice	1985

Belhaven College Jackson, MS 39202-1789 (601) 968-5965 belhaven.edu
Economics Faculty Div of Business Adm Fax=968-9998

Penn, William M.	Prof	968-5966		AM	PHD	68	Duke	1981

Bellarmine University Louisville, KY 40205-0671 (502) 452-8240 bellarmine.edu
Department of Economics Rubel Sch of Business Fax=456-1844 Ms. Carol Huff

Bauer, Daniel L.	Dean$	452-8240	dbauer	Fnce	DBA	96	Miss St	9-95
McCrickard, Myra J.	C-Pr	452-8240	mmcrickard	AL	PHD	89	N Car St	1989
Slesnick, Frank L.	Prof	452-8240	fslesnick	AIKJ	PHD	72	Minnesota	1975
Eller, Eric P.	Asst	452-8240	eller	AEFO	PHD	98	Virginia	9-98
Raymond, Frank	Asst	452-8240	fraymond	AFOR	PHD	97	Indiana	2000

Belmont University Nashville, TN 37212-3757 (615) 460-6175 mail.belmont.edu
Economics Faculty College of Business Adm Fax=460-6455 Sue Kinzer

Clapper, James M.	Dean	460-5511	clapperj	Mgt	PHD	74	Mass	1997
Cochran, Howard H. Jr.	Assoc	460-6477	cochran	AFM	DA	94	Mid Tenn	1989
Hodgin, Gary L.	Assoc	460-6333	hodging		PHD	85	Tennessee	1983
Thompson, Mary M.	Asst	460-6318	thompsonm		MA		Notre Dm	1983

Bemidji State University Bemidji, MN 56601-2699 (218) 755-2907 bemidji.msus.edu
Department of Economics Col of Social & Nat Sci Fax=755-4100 Tammy Mayer
Did Not Respond--1999-2000 Listing

Ley, Robert D.	C-Pr	755-2730			PHD	77	Wash St	1977
Johnson, Lowell E.	Prof	755-3709			PHD	75	Cornell	1976
Welle, Patrick G.	Prof	755-3873			PHD	86	Wisconsin	1982

Benedict College Columbia, SC 29204 (803) 253-5187
Business Adm & Econ Dept Sch Professional Prgms Fax=253-5225 Ms. Marlese Hodge

Cole, John A.	Dean	253-5212			PHD	80	Michigan	
Mahdi, Syed I.	C-Pr	253-5187			PHD	76	Mass	1975
Candley, William	Prof	253-5189			PHD	76	Pittsburgh	1999
Lee, Raymond	Prof	253-5191			PHD	95	Cincinnati	1998
Njoku, Anthanasius O.	Prof	253-5406			PHD	71	Illinois	1971

Benedictine University Lisle, IL 60532-0900 (630) Ext 6460 eagle.ibc.edu
Dept of Econ & Intl Bus Div of Social Science Fax=960-1126 Ms. Kathie Carter
phone: 829-6460

Thornburg, Jack	H	Ext 6460						
Lee, Soyon	Prof	Ext 6463		GO	PHD	77	N Illinois	1974
Lobo, Isobel	Asst			FAO	PHD	98	Notre Dm	2001

Bentley College Waltham, MA 02154-4705 (781) 891-3183 bentley.edu
Economics Faculty College of Business Fax=891-2896 Terry Lesanto

Schlorff, H. Lee	Dean	891-2113	hschlorff	Atg	PHD	73	Missouri	1978
Clarke, William A.	C-Pr	891-2143	wclarke	AD	PHD	73	Rutgers	1972
Callan, Scott J.	Prof	891-2024	scallan	CDQ	PHD	85	Tx A&M	1987

Grubaugh, Stephen G.	Prof	891-2539	sgrubaugh	CF	PHD	82	Chicago	1981
Kuntz, Dale F.	Prof	891-2237	dkuntz	AEO	PHD	79	Conn	1975
Leeth, John D.	Prof	891-2029	jleeth	GCJ	PHD	83	N Carol	1987
Santerre, Rexford E.	Prof	891-2938	rsanterre	DHI	PHD	83	Conn	1983
Stollar, Andrew J.	Prof	891-2268	astollar	CFP	PHD	73	Boston C	1976
Sumner, Scott B.	Prof	891-2945	ssumner	EN	PHD	84	Chicago	1982
Thomas, Janet M.	Prof	891-2053	jthomas	DHQ	PHD	87	Boston C	1987
Zampieron, Alexander Alg	Prof	891-2126	azampieron	ABF	PHD	72	Fletcher	1965
Gulley, O. David	Assoc	891-2355	dgulley	EG	MA	89	Kentucky	1990
Mukerjee, Swati	Assoc	891-2956	smukerjee	DFI	PHD	86	Boston U	1989
Peregon, Michael	Asst	891-3183	mperegon	AJ	MA	76	Wayne St	2001
Rhodus, W. Gregory	Asst	891-3483		ACG	MA	75	Conn	1992

Berea College — Berea, KY 40404 (859) 985-9341 — berea.edu
Economics Faculty — Dept of Business & Econ Fax=985-3912 — Becky Grandgeorge
Did Not Respond--1999-2000 Listing; phone: 986-9341

Bolin, John	Dean	985-9341		Engl	PHD	70	Michigan	1970
Kazura, Martie	C-As	985-3149			MBA	90	Montana	1991
Sowell, Clifford	Prof	985-9341			PHD	78	Georgia	1981
Spears, Philip V.	Prof	985-9341			PHD	71	Kentucky	1968
Isaacs, Patricia	Assoc	985-9341			DBA	94	Kentucky	1989
Tolliver, R. Wayne	Assoc	985-9341			DBA	87	Kentucky	1975
Best, Michael	Asst	985-9341			PHD	94	Kentucky	1996
McCormack, Edward	Asst	985-9341			MBA	80	Estrn Ky	1985

Berry College — Mt. Berry, GA 30149 (706) 290-2679 — berry.edu
Economics Faculty — Campbell Sch Business Fax=238-7854 — Linda Eden

Dhir, Krishna S.	Dean	236-2233	kdhir	Mgt	PHD	75	Colorado	8-01
Mixon, J. Wilson	Prof	290-2679	wmixon	N	PHD	74	U Wash	1986
Sockwell, William D.	Assoc	290-2685	bsockwell	B	PHD	89	Vanderbilt	1988
Roseman, Gary	Asst	238-7945	ghhroseman	G	PHD	97	Emory	2000
Stephenson, E. Frank	Asst	238-7878	efstephenson	EH	PHD	97	N Carol	1997
Tohamy, Soumaya	Asst	238-7979	stohamy	FH	PHD	94	Emory	1997

Bethel College-MN — St. Paul, MN 55112-6999 (651) 638-6320 — bethel.edu
Economics Faculty — Business & Economics Fax=635-8712 — Sheila Werder

Olsen, Bruce	C	638-6320						
Essenburg, Timothy J.	Prof	638-6296	esstim	AI	PHD	91	Tennessee	1989
Cabrera, Glenn	Asst	638-6293		CF	PHD	98	Rice	2001

Bethune-Cookman College — Daytona Bch, FL 32015 (904) Ext 339 — cookman.edu
Economics Faculty — Division of Business Fax=255-3989
phone 255-1401

Long, Aubrey E.	C-Pr	Ext 355	longa	Bus	PHD	80	Ohio St	1988
Dimkpah, Young	Asst	Ext 527	dimkpahy		PHD	97	Howard	2001

Biola University — LaMirada, CA 90639-0001 (562) 903-4770 — biola.edu
Economics Faculty — School of Business Fax=906-4545 — Karen Dirks

Strand, Larry D.	Dean	903-4770			MBA	69	S Calif	1986
Rundle, Steve	Asst	903-4770		DEFN	PHD	97	Claremont	1998

Birmingham-Southern Coll — Birmingham AL 35254 (205) 226-4820 — bsc.edu
Economics Faculty — Div of Econ & Bus Admin Fax=226-3080 — Dea Green/Nancy Parsons

Blanshan, Sue A.	D	226-4820						
Cleveland, Paul	Assoc	226-4817	pclevela		PHD	85	Tx A&M	1995
Morrow, Bert	Asst	226-4827	bmorrow		PHD		Tx A&M	2001
Rossman, Kathleen	Asst	226-4820	krossman		PHD	99	Colorado	1999

Bloomsburg Univ of Penn — Bloomsburg, PA 17815-1301 (570) 389-4335 — planetx.bloomu.edu
Department of Economics — College of Liberal Arts Fax=389-4338
Homepage: deparatments.bloomu.edu/econ

Liu, Hsien-Tung	Dean	389-4410						
Khan, Saleem M.	C-Pr	389-4681	skhan	AEOP	PHD	67	J Gutenb	1-78
Bohling, Peter H.	Prof	389-4343			PHD	77	Mass	1978
Haririan, Mehdi	Prof	389-4682			PHD	87	New Sch	1982
Lee, Woo Bong	Prof	389-4335			PHD	72	Rutgers	1977
Mohindru, Rajesh K.	Prof	389-4341			PHD	69	Penn	
Obutelewicz, Robert S.	Assoc	389-4342			PHD	71	Mass	
Patch, Elizabeth P.	Assoc	389-4737			PHD	90	Lehigh	
Ross, Robert P.	Assoc	389-4335			MA	58	Wash U	1967
Bagi, Sukhwinder	Asst	389-4839			PHD	87	Vanderbilt	

Boise State University | Boise, ID 83725 (208) 426-3351 | cobfac.boisestate.edu
Department of Economics | Col of Bus & Economics Fax=426-2071 | Lea Tibbs

Lathen, William C.	Dean	426-1125	blathen	Atg	PHD	82	Ariz St	9-84
Holley, Don	C-Vis	426-1158	dholley	DMR	PHD	71	Ca-Rivers	1999
Lichtenstein, Peter M.	Prof	426-1471	reclicht	PEF	PHD	74	Colorado	1975
Loucks, Christine	Prof	426-1468	reclouck	ELH	PHD	83	Wash St	1989
Payne, Richard D.	Prof	426-1477	recpayne	HEA	PHD	70	S Calif	1970
Reynolds, R. Larry	Prof	426-1469	recreyno	BID	PHD	77	Wash St	1979
Twight, Charlotte	Prof	426-1335	rectwigh	HKN	PHD	83	U Wash	1986
Church, John	SpLec	426-3465	jchurch	ART	MS	80	Idaho	2000

Boston College | Chestnut Hl, MA 02467-3806 (617) 552-3670 | bc.edu
Department of Economics | College of Arts & Sci Fax=552-2308 | Donna Meltale
Homepage: http://www.bc.edu/ec/

Quinn, Joseph F.	Dean	552-2393	joseph.quinn	DJ	PHD	75	MIT	1975
Ireland, Peter N.	C-Ac	552-3687	peter.ireland	E	PHD	91	Chicago	1998
Anderson, James E.	Prof	552-3691	james.anderson	DFN	PHD	69	Wisconsin	1969
Arnott, Richard J.	Prof	662-3674	richard.arnott	DHR	PHD	75	Yale	1988
Bai, Jushan J.	Prof	552-3689	jushan.bai	CE	PHD	92	Berkeley	1998
Belsley, David A.	Prof	552-3676	david.belsley	CD	PHD	65	MIT	1966
Cox, Donald C.	Prof	552-3677	donald.cox	DJ	PHD	80	Brown	1987
Gollop, Frank M.	Prof	552-3693	frank.gollop	DL	PHD	74	Harvard	1979
Gottschalk, Peter	Prof	552-4517	peter.gottschalk	DIJ	PHD	73	Penn	1987
Kraus, Marvin C.	Prof	552-3692	marvin.kraus	DR	PHD	73	Minnesota	1972
Lewbel, Arthur	Prof	552-3678	arthur.lewbel	CD	PHD	84	MIT	1998
Schiantarelli, Fabio	Prof	552-4512	fabio.schiant+	CEF	PHD	81	LondonEc	1992
Baum, Christopher F.	Assoc	552-3673	christopher.baum	CE	PHD	77	Michigan	1977
Konishi, Hideo	Assoc	552-1209	hideo.konishi	DHL	PHD	94	Rochester	1999
Marcouiller, Douglas	Assoc	552-3685	douglas.marc+	FO	PHD	94	Tx-Austin	1994
McLaughlin, Francis M.	Assoc	552-3675	francis.mclau+	JN	PHD	64	MIT	1961
Assistant Chairperson, Department of Economics								
Murphy, Robert G.	Assoc	552-3688	robert.murphy	EF	PHD	84	MIT	1984
Ng, Serena	Assoc	552-2182	serena.ng	CE	PHD	93	Princeton	1996
Petersen, Harold A.	Assoc	552-4550	harold.petersen	G	PHD	63	Brown	1960
Tresch, Richard W.	Assoc	552-3670	richard.tresch	H	PHD	73	MIT	1969
Alger, I.	Asst	552-1589	i.alger	DL	PHD	97	Toulouse	1999
Butcher, Kristin F.	Asst		kristin.butcher	DJ	PHD	93	Princeton	1995
on leave								
Ghironi, F.	Asst	552-3686	f.ghironi	CE	PHD	99	Berkeley	2001
Konya, Istvan	Asst	552-3690	istvan.konya	FJ	PHD	01	Nrthwstrn	2001
Monacelli, T.	Asst		t.monacelli	EF	PHD	99	NYU	1999
on leave								

Boston University | Boston, MA 02215 (617) 353-4389 | bu.edu
Department of Economics | College of Arts & Sci Fax=353-4449 | Gloria Murray
Homepage: econ.bu.edu

Berkey, Dennis	Dean			Math	PHD	74	Cincinnati	
Kotlikoff, Laurence J.	C-Pr	353-4002	kotlikof	EH	PHD	77	Harvard	
Chamley, Christophe	Prof	353-4250	chamley	HEO	PHD	77	Harvard	
Cooper, Russell W.	Prof	353-7082	rcooper	CDE	PHD	79	Penn	
Associate Chair								
Doeringer, Peter B.	Prof	353-4438	doeringe	JL	PHD	66	Harvard	1974
Eaton, Jonathan	Prof	353-4142	eaton	FG	PHD	76	Yale	
Ellis, Randall P.	Prof	353-2741	ellisrp	CILQ	PHD	81	MIT	1981
Harris, John R.	Prof	353-8903	harrisjr	ER	PHD	67	Nrthwstrn	1975
Jones, Leroy P.	Prof	353-4123	jones	HLO	PHD	74	Harvard	1976
Director of Public Enterprise								
Kyn, Oldrich	Prof	353-4539	okyn	CEP	PHD		Charles	1971
Lang, Kevin	Prof	353-5694	lang	JC	PHD	82	MIT	1987
Director of Undergraduate Studies								
Loury, Glenn C.	Prof	353-5662	gloury	DJ	PHD	76	MIT	1991
Lucas, Robert E. B.	Prof	353-4147	rlucas	CFJO	PHD	72	MIT	1976
Manove, Michael	Prof	353-3299	manove	D	PHD	70	MIT	1975
Miron, Jeffrey A.	Prof	353-4442	jmiron	EKN	PHD	84	MIT	1990
Mookherjee, Dilip M.	Prof	353-4392	dilipm	HLO	PHD	82	LondonEc	1995
Director, Institute for Economic Development								
Perron, Pierre	Prof			C	PHD	86	Yale	1997
Director of Graduate Studies								
Rosenthal, Robert W.	Prof	353-2742	rosentha	CD	PHD	71	Stanford	1987
Vogelsang, Ingo	Prof	353-2996	vogelsan	HL	PHD	69	Heidelbe	1981
Weiss, Andrew M.	Prof	353-3086	aweiss	DGJ	PHD	76	Stanford	1987
Leahy, John V.	Assoc			E	PHD	90	Princeton	1997
Ma, Ching-to Albert	Assoc	353-4010	ma	DIL	PHD	88	LondonEc	1987
Director, Industry Studies Program								
Tandon, Pankaj	Assoc	353-3089	ptandon	DO	PHD	79	Harvard	1978
Berman, Eli	Asst	353-6324	eli	CJ	PHD	93	Harvard	1993
Botticini, Maristella	Asst			N	ABD		Nrthwstrn	1997
Bui, Linda T.	Asst	353-4140	ltbui	HLQ	PHD	93	MIT	1993

Cati, Regina C.	Asst			C	PHD	95	Sao Paulo	1997
Gilchrist, Simon	Asst	353-6824	sgilchrist	C	PHD	90	Wisconsin	1995
Kortum, Sam	Asst	353-4822	kortum	ELO	PHD	92	Yale	1991
Minehart, Deborah	Asst	353-4436	minehart	CDL	PHD	94	Berkeley	1994
Neeman, Zvika	Asst	353-3184	zvika	CD	PHD	95	Nrthwstrn	1995
Olnetti, Claudia	Asst	353-4389		CJ	PHD	01	Penn	2001

Bowdoin College Brunswick, ME 04011 (207) 725-3340 bowdoin.edu
Economic Faculty Department of Economics Fax=725-3691 Ms. Elizabeth Hernandez

Goldstein, Jonathan Paul	C-Pr$	725-3595	jgoldste	EC	PHD	82	Mass	1979
Fitzgerald, John M.	Prof	725-3593	jfitzger	HC	PHD	83	Wisconsin	1983
Freeman, Albert Myrick III	Prof	725-3597	rfreeman	QD	PHD	65	U Wash	1965
William Shipman Professor of Economics								
Vail, David Jeremiah	Prof	725-3596	dvail	OQ	PHD	71	Yale	1970
Adams-Catlin Professor of Economics								
Connelly, Rachel E.	Assoc	725-3790	connelly	JT	PHD	85	Michigan	1985
DeCoster, Gregory Paul	Assoc	725-3726	gdecoste	ER	PHD	85	Tx-Austin	1985
Jones, Michael	Assoc	725-3598	mjones	F	PHD	79	Yale	1987
DeGraff, Deborah S.	Asst	725-3591	ddegraff	OT	PHD	89	Michigan	1991
Herreiner, Dorothea K.	Asst	725-3340		L	PHD	00	Florence	2001
Hornsten, James	Asst	725-3907	jhornste	L	ABD		Nrthwstrn	1999
Khan, B. Zorina	Asst	725-3841	bhkan	GN	PHD	91	UCLA	1996
Pannell, Kerry E.	Asst	725-3549	kpannell	NOF	PHD	88	Colorado	2000

Bowling Green State Univ Bowling Gr, OH 43403-0268 (419) 372-2646 cba.bgsu.edu
Department of Economics College of Business Fax=372-2875 Kelly M. Dove
Homepage: www.cba.bgsu.edu/econ/

Sullivan, James A.	Dean	372-2747	jsulliv	Stat	PHD	71	Ohio St	1971
Hoag, John H.	C-Pr	372-8231	jhoag		PHD	72	Kansas	1972
Browne, M. Neil	Prof	372-8060	nbrown2		PHD	69	Tx-Austin	1968
Distinguished Teaching Professor								
Haas, Paul F.	Prof	372-2649	phaas		PHD	70	Boston C	1967
Kim, Kyoo H.	Prof	372-2735	kkim		PHD	78	Wisconsin	1978
Reed, J. David	Emer	372-2647	dreed		PHD	70	Kansas St	1968
Benedict, Mary Ellen	Assoc	372-8221	mbenedi		PHD	91	Car Mellon	1991
Douglas, Richard W. Jr.	Assoc	372-2648	rdougla		PHD	75	Iowa	1976
Fuerst, Timothy S.	Assoc	372-6868	tfuerst		PHD	90	Chicago	1993
Haight, Alan D.	Assoc	372-8111	ahaight		PHD	90	Wisconsin	1991
Quinn, J. Kevin	Assoc	372-8652	kquinn		PHD	89	American	1990
Vanderhart, Peter G.	Assoc	372-8070	pvander		PHD	91	Wisconsin	1991
Carroll, Michael	Asst	372-2646			PHD	97	Colo St	2001
Ziliak, Stephen T.	Asst	372-8055	ziliak		PHD	96	Iowa	1996

Bradley University Peoria, IL 61625-0254 (309) 677-2296 bradley.bradley.edu
Department of Economics College of Business Adm Fax=677-3374 Karla Layne

Baer, Robert B.	Dean	677-2255	rbb	SocP	PHD	81	Miami U	8-84
Scott, Robert C.	C-Pr	677-2297			PHD	75	Iowa	1975
Goldberg, Kalman	Prof	677-2301			PHD	54	Cornell	1952
Highfill, Jannett K.	Prof	677-2304			PHD	85	Kansas	1985
Sattler, Edward L.	Prof	677-2303			PHD	79	Illinois	1977
Wojcikewych, Raymond	Prof	677-2296			PHD	80	Penn St	1977
Felder, Joseph	Assoc	677-2302			PHD	79	UCLA	1981
O'Brien, Kevin M.	Assoc	677-2299			PHD	88	Illinois	1992
Polley, William	Asst	677-2298			PHD	99	Iowa	1999

Brandeis University Waltham, MA 02254-9110 (781) 736-2240 binah.cc.brandeis.edu
Department of Economics Faculty of Arts & Sci Fax=736-2269 Claire Cincotta
Homepage: www.brandeis.edu/departments/economics/econ.html

Owens, Jessie Ann	Dean	736-3451	owens		PHD		Princeton	
Jaffe, Adam B.	C-Pr	736-2251	afaffe		PHD	85	Harvard	1994
Carter, Anne P.	Prof	736-3446	carter		PHD	49	Harvard	1971
Fred C. Hecht Professor of Economics								
Dolbear, F. Treanery Jr.	Prof	736-2244	dolbear		PHD	63	Yale	1968
Jefferson, Gary H.	Prof	736-2253	jefferson		PHD	86	Yale	1984
LeBaron, Blake	Prof	736-2258	blebaron		PHD	88	Chicago	1999
McCulloch, Rachel	Prof	736-2245	mcculloch		PHD	73	Chicago	1987
Coiner, H. Michael	Assoc	736-2239	coiner		PHD	79	Yale	1980
Gomes-Casseres, Benjamin	Assoc	736-2264	bgc		DBA	85	Harvard	1995
Harrison, Paul	Assoc	736-2255	pharrison		PHD	94	Duke	1995
Bown, Chad B.	Asst	736-3823	cbown		PHD	99	Wisconsin	1999
Bulan, Laarni	Asst	736-2240			PHD	01	Columbia	2001
Kose, Ayham	Asst	736-2266	akose		PHD	97	Iowa	1997
Menon, Nidhiya	Asst	736-2240			PHD	01	Brown	2001
Sanyal, Paroma	Asst	736-2240			PHD	01	Ca-Irvine	2001
Shih-Fen, Chen	Asst	736-2257	shihfen		PHD	96	Illinois	1999
Subramanian, Narayanan	Asst	736-2261	nsubra		PHD	99	Brown	1999
Villanueva, Miguel	Asst	736-2249	mvillanu		PHD	99	Ohio St	1999
Stout, Eric	Lect	736-4826	esout		PHD		Stanford	1999

Brescia University Owensboro, KY 42301-3023 (270) 686-4217 brescia.edu
Economic Faculty Wm Thompson Sch of Bus Fax=686-4266 Nancy Rhodes
Did Not Respond--1999-2000 Listing

Asefa, Sally Ann	C-Pr	686-4264	sallya		PHD	78	Iowa St	8-80

University of Bridgeport Bridgeport, CT 06601-2449 (203) 576-4383 bridgeport.edu
Dept of Business Economics School of Business Fax=576-4388

Bassett, Glenn A.	Dean	576-4384		Mgt	PHD	78	Yale	1979
Kim, Gew-Rae	Assoc	576-4372			PHD	92	CUNY	
Maine, Robert	Asst	576-4373			PHD	78	Conn	1996

Brigham Young University Provo, UT 84602-2363 (801) 378-2859 byu.edu
Department of Economics Col Family,Home &SocSci Fax=378-2844 Andrea Sneed
Homepage: http://fhss.byu.edu/econ/

McDonald, James B.	C-Pr	378-3463	james_mcdonald	C	PHD	70	Purdue	1972
Butler, Richard J.	Prof	378-1372	richard_butler	J	PHD	79	Chicago	1982
Jensen, Farrell E.	Prof	378-4057	fejensen	QG	PHD	72	Kansas St	1982
Kearl, James R.	Prof	378-5812	j_r_kearl	KD	PHD	75	MIT	1975
Lambson, Val E.	Prof	378-7765	val_lambson	L	PHD	83	Rochester	1989
Pope, C. Arden III	Prof	378-2157	arden_pope		PHD	81	Iowa St	1984
Pope, Clayne L.	Prof	378-4740	clayne_pope	N	PHD	72	Chicago	1970
Pope, Rulon D.	Prof	378-3178	rulon_pope	QD	PHD	76	Berkeley	1982
Ransom, Michael R.	Prof	378-4736	ransom	J	PHD	83	Princeton	1988
Spencer, David E.	Prof	378-7277	david_spencer	EC	PHD	74	Tx A&M	1986
Wimmer, Larry T.	Prof	378-3354	larry_wimmer	NT	PHD	68	Chicago	1963
Jensen, Mark J.	Assoc	378-3182	mark_jensen	EC	PHD	94	Wash U	2001
Phillips, Kerk	Assoc	378-5928	kerk_phillips	EFO	PHD	91	Rochester	1992
Showalter, Mark H.	Assoc	378-4645	showalter	LC	PHD	91	MIT	1991
Bradford, Scott	Asst	378-8358	bradford	F	PHD	98	Harvard	1998
Cardon, James H.	Asst	378-5735	cardon	LC	PHD	96	Princeton	1996
Eide, Eric	Asst	378-5169	eide	JC	PHD	93	Ca-SnBarb	1993
Lefgren, Lars	Asst	378-5169	lars_lefgren		PHD	01	Chicago	2001
Mackay, Bret P.	Asst	378-2253	bret_mackay	CG	PHD	99	U Wash	2001
Thurston, Norman K.	Asst	378-4883	norm_thurston	HIJ	PHD	95	Princeton	1995

Brigham Young Univ-Hawaii Laie, HI 96762-1294 (808) 293-3580 byuh.edu
Economics Faculty School of Business Fax=293-3582

Wilson, Brent	Dean	293-3580	wilsonb	Mgt	PHD	79	Harvard	2001
Haynes, C. Beth	Prof	293-3587	haynesb	DAO	PHD	81	Purdue	1994
Kimzey, Bruce W.	Prof	293-3585	kimzeyb		PHD	70	Wash St	1989

Brown University Providence, RI 02912 (401) 863-3836 brown.edu
Economic Faculty Department of Economics Fax=863-1970
Homepage: http://econ.pstc.brown.edu

Lancaster, Anthony	C-Pr	863-2112	tony.lancaster		PHD	64	Cambridge	1986
Herbert H. Goldberger Professor of Economics								
Borts, George H.	Prof	863-2458	george_borts		PHD	53	Chicago	1964
George S. and Nancy B. Parker Professor of Economics								
Buchinsky, Moshe	Prof	863-2951	buchins@pste3.	CJ	PHD	91	Harvard	
Director of the Graduate Program								
Grossman, Herschel I.	Prof	863-2606	herschel_gross+		PHD	65	J Hopkins	1973
Merton P. Stolz Professor in the Social Sciences								
Henderson, J. Vernon	Prof	863-2886	j_henderson		PHD	72	Chicago	1974
Eastman Professor of Political Economy								
Howitt, Peter	Prof	863-2145	peter_howitt	E	PHD	73	Nrthwstrn	2000
Lumsdaine, Robin	Prof	863-3836			PHD	91	Harvard	
Page, Talbot	Prof	863-1988	talbot_page		PHD	72	Cornell	
Pitt, Mark M.	Prof	963-2970	mark_pitt		PHD	77	Berkeley	
Polemarchakis, Hereakles	Prof	863-9828	herakles_pole+		PHD	78	Harvard	2000
Putterman, Louis G.	Prof	863-3837	ec424000		PHD	80	Yale	1980
Ryder, Harl E.	Prof	863-2179	ec415000		PHD	67	Stanford	1965
Schupack, Mark B.	Emer	863-3836	ec40500		PHD	60	Princeton	1970
Serrano, Roberto	Prof	860-2764	rserrano		PHD	92	Harvard	
Vohra, Rajiv	Prof	863-3030	rajiv_vohra		PHD	83	J Hopkins	
Weil, David	Prof	863-1754	dnweil		PHD	90	Harvard	
Replacement Officer								
Feldman, Allan M.	Assoc	863-2415	allan_feldman		PHD	72	J Hopkins	1977
Director of Undergraduate Programs								
Hahn, Jinyong	Assoc	863-3883	jinyong_hahn		PHD	93	Harvard	2000
Driscoll, John	Asst	863-1584	john_driscoll		PHD	95	Harvard	1995
Elul, Ronel	Asst	863-2953	ronel_elul		PHD	95	Yale	
Hansen, Peter	Asst	863-9864	peter_hansen		PHD	00	Ca-SnDgo	2000
Ito, Harumi	Asst	863-2887	harumi_ito		PHD	97	Stanford	
Krebs, Tom	Asst	863-2097	tom_krebs		PHD	95	Columbia	1999
Krishna, Pravin	Asst	863-2170	pk@econ.pstc.		PHD	95	Columbia	1995
Nakajami, Tomoyuki	Asst	863-3836			PHD	99	Chicago	1999
Palacios-Huercta, Ignacid	Asst	863-2691	ipalacios		PHD	95	Chicago	
Spolaore, Enrico	Asst	863-2697	enrico_spolaore		PHD	93	Harvard	
Friedberg, Rachel	Lect	863-7578	rachel_friedberg		PHD	93	MIT	

Bryant College — Smithfield, RI 02917-1284 (401) 232-6338 — bryant.edu
Department of Economics — College of Business — Fax=232-6319
Homepage: www.bryant.edu/~economix

Briden, Earl	Dean	232-6440	ebriden		PHD	70	Brown	8-80
Mirmirani, Sam	C-Pr	232-6338	smirmira	IMO	PHD	85	Clark	1982
Ilacqua, Joseph A.	Prof	232-6098	jllacqua	AJ	EDD	93	Boston U	1968
Shaanan, Joseph	Prof	232-6340	jshaanan	FL	PHD	79	Cornell	
Sweeney, William B. Jr.	Prof	232-6097	wsweeney	AE	PHD	73	Sarasota	
Bates, Laurie	Assoc	232-6459	lbates	HD	PHD	89	Conn	
Mini, Peter S.	Assoc	232-6226	pmini	BN	PHD	65	Tulane	
Kim, Jongsung	Asst	232-6129	jkim	AJ	PHD	98	J Hopkins	1998

Bryn Mawr College — Bryn Mawr, PA 19010-2899 (610) 526-5038 — brynmawr.edu
Economics Faculty — Department of Economics — Fax=526-5331 — Lorraine Kirschner
Homepage: www.brynmawr.edu/acads/econ/

Ross, David R.	C-Ac$	526-5180	dross		PHD	84	Nrthwstrn	1992
Farley, Noel J. J.	Prof	526-5179	nfarley		PHD	65	Yale	1971
Ceglowski, Janet E.	Assoc	526-5182	jceglows		PHD	86	Berkeley	1990
Newburger, Harriet B.	Assoc	526-5181	hnewburg		PHD	84	Wisconsin	1987
Redenius, Scott	Lect	526-5398	sredeniu		PHD	01	Yale	2000

Bucknell University — Lewisburg, PA 17837 (570) 577-1476 — bucknell.edu
Department of Economics — College of Arts & Sci — Fax=577-3451 — Alice VanBuskirk
Homepage: www.departments.bucknell.edu/economics/

Padilla, Mark	Dean	577-3292	mpadilla		PHD			
Sackrey, Charles Melvin	C-Ac	577-1476	sackrey	A	PHD	65	Tx-Austin	1980
Griffith, Winston Harold	Prof	577-1476	wgrif	FOD	PHD	81	Howard	1987
Kresl, Peter K.	Prof	577-1478	kresl	FO	PHD	70	Tx-Austin	1969
Shackelford, Jean A.	Prof	577-1476	jshackel	ABE	PHD	74	Kentucky	1975
Ge, Wei	Assoc	577-3452	weige	DFOR	PHD	93	Penn	9-95
Kinnaman, Thomas	Assoc	577-1476	kinnaman	HQ	PHD	94	Virginia	9-94
Knoedler, Janet T.	Assoc	577-1476	knoedler	LNO	PHD	91	Tennessee	9-92
Krohn, Gregory A.	Assoc	577-3448	krohn	EGA	PHD	85	Wisconsin	1983
Moohr, Michael	Assoc	577-1476	moohr	FNO	PHD	71	Cambridge	1975
White, Nancy E.	Assoc	577-1476	nwhite	RH	PHD	87	Colorado	1986
Banks, Nina	Asst	577-1476	nbanks	JNR	PHD	99	Mass	9-01
Magee, Chris	Asst	577-1476	cmagee	F	PHD	98	Wisconsin	9-01
O'Connor, Catherine	Asst	577-3442	cmoconnr	DJC	PHD	96	Virginia	9-96
Schneider, Geoffrey	Asst	577-1476	gschedr	NOBA	ABD	97	N Carol	9-96
Wolaver, Amy	Asst	577-1476	awolaver	IJH	PHD	98	Wisconsin	9-98

Buena Vista University — Storm Lake, IA 50588-1798 (712) 749-2410 — bvu.edu
Economics Faculty — School of Business — Fax=749-1462

Polson, Houston	Dean	749-2410		Law	JD	80	Creighton	2001
Ullerich, Stan	Prof	749-2419	ullerich	AQMA	PHD	95	Purdue	9-94

Butler University — Indianapolis, IN 46208-3485 (317) 940-9221 — butler.edu
Department of Economics — College of Business Adm — Fax=940-9455 — Sharon Bratcher

Fetter, Richard E. Jr.	Dean	940-9221	rfetter	Mktg	PHD	93	Indiana	8-92
Main, Robert S.	C-Pr	940-9528	rmain	HQ	PHD	73	UCLA	1981
Rieber, William J.	Prof	940-9846	wrieber	F	PHD	79	Pittsburgh	1989
Grossman, Peter Z.	Assoc	940-9727	pgrossma	NL	PHD	92	Wash U	1994
Efroymson Chair in Economics								
Gjerde, Kathy A. Paulson	Asst	940-8413	kpaulson	LJ	PHD	93	Purdue	1997
Meister, J. Patrick	VAsst	940-9761	pmeister	L	PHD	92	Michigan	1996

Calif Univ of Pennsylvania — California, PA 15419-1394 (724) 938-4371 — cup.edu
Dept of Business & Economics — Eberly Col Sci & Tech — Fax=938-5908 — Shirley Elnikar
Did Not Respond--1999-2000 Listing

Colelli, Len	Dean	938-4169						
Brown, Burrell	C-Pr	938-4371		Mgt	JD	73	Pittsburgh	1989
Chawdhry, M. Arshad	Prof	938-5990			PHD	74	Illinois	1976
Cole, Ismail	Prof				PHD	86	Pittsburgh	1984
Omarzai, Mahmood	Prof				PHD	76	Indiana	1979
Park, Young J.	Prof	938-4371			PHD	74	Temple	1977
Tarullo, P. Ronald	Prof				PHD	76	Pittsburgh	1978
Mongell, Susan	Assoc				PHD		Pittsburgh	1990

U of California at Berkeley — Berkeley, CA 94720-3880 (510) 642-3581 — econ.berkeley.edu
Department of Economics — Col of Letters & Sci — Fax=642-6615 — Casey Gardner
Homepage: http://elsa.berkeley.edu/econ/
Did Not Respond--1999-2000 Listing; email @1=uclink.berkeley.edu @2=haas.berkeley.edu

Tyson, Laura D.	Dean	643-2027	tyson		PHD	74	MIT	1977
Auerbach, Alan J.	C-Pr	643-0711	auerbach	GEH	PHD	78	Harvard	1994

Akerlof, George A.	Prof	642-5837	akerlof		PHD	66	MIT	1966
Anderson, Robert M.	Prof	642-5248			PHD	77	Yale	
Bardhan, Pranab K.	Prof	642-4527	bardhan		PHD		Cambridge	
Brown, R. Clair	Prof	643-7090	cbrown@1	J	PHD	73	Maryland	9-73
Card, David E.	Prof	643-2767	card		PHD	83	Princeton	
Craine, Roger	Prof	642-3021			PHD	72	Maryland	1977
Debreu, Gerard	Emer	642-7284	debreu		DSC	56	Paris	1962
DeLong, J. Bradford	Prof	643-4027	delong		PHD	87	Harvard	1995
DeVries, Jan	Prof	642-2813			PHD	70	Yale	
Edlin, Aaron	Prof	642-4719	edlin		PHD	93	Stanford	1995
Eichengreen, Barry	Prof	642-2772	eichengr		PHD	79	Yale	1987
Farrell, Joseph V.	Prof	642-9854			PHD	81	Oxford	
Gilbert, Richard J.	Prof	642-1507	gilbert		PHD	76	Stanford	1976
Goldman, Steven M.	Prof	642-2787	goldman		PHD	66	Stanford	1979
Grossman, Gregory	Emer	642-4631	grossman		PHD	53	Harvard	1953
Hall, Bronwyn H.	Prof	642-3878	bhhall		PHD	88	Stanford	1987
Hermalin, Benjamin E.	Prof	642-7575	hermalin@2		PHD	88	MIT	1988
Katz, Michael	Prof	643-0661	katz@2		PHD		Oxford	
Keeler, Theodore E.	Prof	642-4411	keeler		PHD	71	MIT	1977
Lee, Ronald D.	Prof	642-4535			PHD	71	Harvard	1979
McFadden, Daniel L.	Prof	643-8428	mcfadden		PHD	62	Minnesota	1963
Obstfeld, Maurice	Prof	643-3581	obstfeld		PHD	79	MIT	
Pierce, James L.	Emer	642-4321	pierce		PHD	64	Berkeley	1976
Power, James	Prof	643-0709	powell		PHD	82	Stanford	1995
Quigley, John M.	Prof	643-7411	quigley		PHD	72	Harvard	1979
Rabin, Matthew J.	Prof	643-8622	rabin		PHD	89	MIT	
Reich, Michael	Prof	642-3647	mreich		PHD	74	Harvard	1974
Romer, Christina D.	Prof	642-1955	cromer		PHD	85	MIT	1988
Romer, David H.	Prof	642-1955	dromer		PHD	85	MIT	1988
Rothenburg, Thomas J.	Prof	642-5843	rothenbe		PHD	66	MIT	1966
Rubinfeld, Daniel L.	Prof	642-1959	rubinfld		PHD	72	MIT	1983
Ruud, Paul A.	Prof	642-6709	ruud		PHD	81	MIT	1981
Smale, Stephen	Emer	642-4367			PHD	57	Michigan	
Williamson, Oliver E.	Prof	642-8697	owilliams@2		PHD	63	Car Mellon	1988
Yellen, Janet L.	Prof	643-1397	yellen@2		PHD	71	Yale	1980
Eissa, Nada	Asst	643-0708	eissa		PHD	95	Harvard	1995

Univ of California, Davis Davis, CA 95616-8578 (530) 752-0741 ucdavis.edu
Department of Economics Col of Letters & Sci Fax=752-9382 Gerri Refsland
Homepage: http://www.econ.ucdavis.edu

Sheffrin, Steven M.	Dean	752-1576	smsheffrin	EH	PHD	76	MIT	1976
Hoover, Kevin D.	C-Pr	752-2129	kdhoover	BE	DPHI	85	Oxford	1985
Bonanno, Giacomo F.	Prof	752-1574	gfbonanno	CD	PHD	75	LondonEc	1987
Brzeski, Andrzej	Emer	752-8491	abrzeski	AP	PHD	64	Berkeley	1963
Clark, Gregory	Prof	752-9242	gclark	NO	PHD	85	Harvard	1990
Feenstra, Robert	Prof	752-7022	rcfeenstra	F	PHD	81	MIT	1986
Jorda, Oscar	Prof	752-7021	ojorda	E	PHD	97	Ca-SnDgo	1997
Kaneda, Hiromitsu	Emer			AFOQ	PHD	64	Stanford	1973
Lindert, Peter H.	Prof	752-1983	phlindert	FN	PHD	67	Cornell	1978
Makowski, Louis	Prof	752-6142	lmakowski	DE	PHD	75	UCLA	1985
Mayer, Thomas	Emer	752-1550		BE	PHD	53	Columbia	1962
Olmstead, Alan L.	Prof	752-2043	alolmstead	HN	PHD	70	Wisconsin	1969
Quinzii, Martine	Prof	752-1567	mmquinzii	CDG	PHD	74	U Paris	1991
Shen, T. Y.	Emer			L	PHD	56	Yale	7-63
Silvestre, Joaquim	Prof	752-1570	jbsilvestre	D	PHD	73	Minnesota	1983
Tuma, Elias H.	Emer	752-1550	tuma@vfv.net	ANO	PHD	62	Berkeley	1967
Walton, Gary M.	Prof	757-4630	fte4efl@a	ADN	PHD	66	U Wash	1981
Wegge, Leon L.	Emer	752-1550	llwegge	F	PHD	63	MIT	1966
Woo, Wing T.	Prof	752-3035	wtwoo	EFOP	PHD	82	Harvard	1985
Helms, L. Jay	Assoc	752-2094	ljhelms	DHI	PHD	79	MIT	1985
Hoynes, Hilary	Assoc	752-3225	hoynes@ssds.	D	PHD	92	Stanford	
Nehring, Klaus D.	Assoc	752-3379	kdnehring	DG	PHD	91	Harvard	1992
Salyer, Kevin D.	Assoc	752-8359	kdsalyer	EG	PHD	85	Ca-SnBarb	1990
Swenson, Deborah	Assoc	752-1569	deswenson	FH	PHD	91	MIT	1993
Taylor, Alan M.	Assoc	752-1572	amtaylor	FNO	PHD	92	Harvard	1987
Bergin, Paul	Asst	752-8398	prbergin	EF	PHD	96	Yale	1996
Branstetter, Lee	Asst	752-3033	branstet@polar.	FL	PH	96	Harvard	1996
Cameron, Colin	Asst	752-8376	accameron	CIJ	PHD	88	Stanford	1989
Page, Marianne E.	Asst	752-1551	mepage	HJ	PHD	95	Michigan	1996
Pieger, Jim	Asst	752-8727	jeprieger	LD	PHD	99	Ca-SnBarb	1993
Gustafson, W. Eric	Emer		egustaf652@a	AO	PHD	59	Harvard	1978

Univ of Calif, Irvine Irvine, CA 92697-5100 (949) 824-5788 uci.edu
Department of Economics Sch of Social Sciences Fax=824-2182 Hein Park/Nancy Carter-Fields

Schonfeld, William R.	Dean	824-6801	wrschonf	PolS	PHD	70	Princeton	
Garfinkel, Michelle	C-Ac	824-3190	mgarfink		PHD	88	Brown	1991
Bell, Duran	Prof	824-7053	dbell		PHD	65	Berkeley	1965
Brownstone, David	Prof	824-6231	dbrownstone		PHD	80	Berkeley	1984

Cohen, Linda	Prof	824-5189	lrcohen		PHD	79	Cal Tech	1988
DeVany, Arthur S.	Prof	824-5269	asdevany		PHD	70	UCLA	1984
DiNardo, John	Prof	824-3191	jdinardo		PHD	90	Princeton	1991
Fielding, Gordon J.	Emer	824-5448	gjfieldi		PHD	62	UCLA	1965
Glazer, Amihai	Prof	824-5974	aglazer		PHD	78	Yale	1978
Johnston, John	Emer	824-5581	jjohnsto		PHD	57	Wales	1978
Kassouf, Sheen T.	Emer	824-7161	rpellegr		PHD	65	Columbia	1965
Lave, Charles	Emer	824-6502	calave		PHD	68	Stanford	1964
Lilien, David M.	Prof	824-6232	dmlilien		PHD	77	MIT	1984
Luce, Ducan	Emer	824-6239	rdluce		PHD	50	MIT	1988
Margolis, Julius	Emer	824-7003	jmargoli		PHD	49	Harvard	1976
McGuire, Martin C.	Prof	824-6190	mcmcguir		PHD	64	Harvard	1992
Poirier, Dale	Prof	824-3186	dpoirier		PHD	73	Wisconsin	1999
Small, Kenneth A.	Prof	824-5658	ksmall		PHD	76	Berkeley	1983
Skaperdas, Stergios	Assoc	824-4167	sskapero		PHD	88	J Hopkins	1988
Black, Duncan	Asst	824-5788			PHD	99	Brown	1999
Genicot, Garance	Asst	824-5788			PHD	99	Cornell	1999
Moore, M.	Asst	824-4221	mpmoore		PHD	97	MIT	1997
Naito, Hisahiro	Asst	824-5788			PHD	98	Michigan	1999
Ranjan, Priya	Asst	824-1926	pranjan		PHD	97	Columbia	1997
Richardson, Gary	Asst	824-5788			PHD	99	Berkeley	1999
Tobias, Justin	Asst	824-5788			PHD	99	Chicago	1999

Univ of Calif, Los Angeles Los Angeles, CA 90024-1447 (310) 825-1011 ucla.edu
Department of Economics Col of Letters & Sci Fax=206-2313
Did Not Respond Again--1997-98 Listing; email @1=econ.sscnet.ucla.edu

Ellickson, Bryan C.	C-Pr	825-4556			PHD	70	MIT	1973
Aoki, Masanao	Emer	825-2360			PHD	65	Tokyo In	1983
Azariadis, Constantine C.	Prof	825-6682			PHD	75	Car Mellon	
Currie, Janet	Prof	206-8380			PHD	88	Princeton	1988
Demsetz, Harold	Emer	825-3651			PHD	59	Nrthwstrn	1971
Edwards, Sebastian	Prof	825-1011			PHD	81	Chicago	1985
Farmer, Roger E. A.	Prof	825-2523			PHD	82	W Ontario	1988
Hansen, Gary D.	Prof	825-3847			PHD	86	Minnesota	1987
Harberger, Arnold C.	Prof	825-7520			PHD	50	Chicago	
Intriligator, Michael D.	Emer	825-4144			PHD	63	MIT	1972
Klein, Benjamin	Prof	825-6547			PHD	70	Chicago	1978
Lal, Deepak	Prof	825-4521			PHD	65	Oxford	
Lamoreaux, Naomi	Prof	825-0225			PHD	79	J Hopkins	
Leamer, Edward E.	Prof	825-3557			PHD	70	Michigan	1975
Leijonhufvud, Axel S. B.	Emer	825-4126			PHD	87	Nrthwstrn	
Levine, David K.	Prof	825-3810			PHD	81	MIT	1981
McCall, John J.	Emer	825-1849			PHD	59	Chicago	
Ostroy, Joseph M.	Prof	825-4627			PHD	70	Nrthwstrn	
Riley, John G.	Prof	825-1541			PHD	72	MIT	1973
Rosenthal, Jean-Laurent	Prof	825-2490			PHD	88	Cal Tech	1988
Shapley, Lloyd S.	Emer	825-3723			PHD	53	Princeton	
Sokoloff, Kenneth L.	Prof	825-4249			PHD	82	Harvard	1980
Thomas, Duncan	Prof	825-5304			PHD	86	Princeton	
Thompson, Earl A.	Prof	825-4387			PHD	61	Harvard	1965
Zame, William	Prof	206-9463			PHD	70	Tulane	
Murphy, George G. S.	Emer	825-9397			PHD	57	U Wash	
Ozler, Sule	Assoc	825-2997			PHD	86	Stanford	1985
Vegh, Carlos	Assoc	825-7371			PHD	87	Chicago	
Asea, Patrick	Asst	206-6869			PHD	93	J Hopkins	
Hu, Wei-Yin	Asst	825-6838			PHD	94	Stanford	
Hubbard, Thomas	Asst	826-7652			PHD	96	Stanford	
Hyslop, Dean	Asst	826-9665			PHD	95	Princeton	
Lahiri, Amartya	Asst	825-8018			PHD	95	Maryland	
Lambertini, Luisa	Asst	206-1256			PHD	95	Berkeley	
McGarry, Kathleen	Asst	826-2833			PHD	92	SUNY-SBr	
Potter, Simon M.	Asst	206-6732			PHD	90	Wisconsin	1990
Williams, Darrell L.	Asst	206-2794	williams@1	GKL	PHD	91	Wash U	F-90

Univ of Calif, Riverside Riverside, CA 92521-0427 (909) Ext 1474 ucr.edu
Department of Economics Col Human, Arts & SocSc Fax=787-5685 Jayne Gales
Homepage: www.ucr.edu/chss/depts/econ/econhome.htm
phone 787-5037

O'Brien, Patricia	Dean	878-3594	patricia.obrien		PHD		Columbia	1999
Cullenberg, Stephen E.	C-Pr	Ext 1573	stephen.cullenbe	ABCP	PHD	87	Mass	1988
Bandyopadhayay, Taradas	Prof	Ext 1586	taradas.bandy+	AD	PHD	80	So Meth	1987
Carter, Susan B.	Prof	Ext 1589	susan.carter	AJNT	PHD	81	Stanford	1990
Chilcote, Ronald H.	Prof	Ext 1571	ronald.chilcote.	P	PHD	65	Stanford	1963
Dymski, Gary A.	Prof	Ext 1570	gary.dymski	AEHP	PHD	87	Mass	1991
Gaffney, Mason	Prof	Ext 1574	mason.gaffney	AHR	PHD	56	Berkeley	1976
Griffin, Keith B.	Prof	787-4108	keith.griffin	AOP	DPHI	65	Oxford	1988
Khan, Azizur Rahman	Prof	Ext 1581	azizur.khan	FOPR	PHD	66	Cambridge	1988
Lippit, Victor D.	Prof	Ext 1582	victor.lippit	AOP	PHD	71	Yale	1971
Pattanaik, Prasanta	Prof	Ext 1592	prasanta.pattana	AO	PHD	68	Delhi	1991

Russell, R. Robert	Prof	Ext 1585	robert.russell	ADH	PHD	65	Harvard	1986
Sutch, Richard C.	Prof	Ext 1501	richard.sutch	AN	PHD	68	MIT	1998
Ullah, Aman	Prof	Ext 1591	aman.ullah	C	PHD	71	Delhi	1989
Fairris, David H.	Assoc	Ext 1578	david.fairris	AJP	PHD	84	Duke	1989
Gonzalez-Rivera, Gloria	Assoc	Ext 1590	gloria.gonzalez	CG	PHD	91	Ca-SnDgo	1991
Guo, Jang-Ting	Assoc	Ext 1588	jangting.guo	AC	PHD	93	UCLA	1993
Lee, Tae-Hwy	Assoc	Ext 1509	tae.lee	ACG	PHD	90	Ca-SnDgo	1995
Chauvet, Marcelle	Asst	Ext 1587	marcelle.chauvet	AE	PHD	95	Penn	1995
Cheng, Xu	Asst	Ext 1502	xu.cheng	CFO	PHD	99	Columbia	1998
Helfand, Steven	Asst	Ext 1572	steven.helfand	AOQ	PHD	94	Berkeley	1995

Univ of Calif, San Diego La Jolla, CA 92093-0508 (858) 534-3383 ucsd.edu
Department of Economics Thurgood Marshall Col Fax=534-7040 Beverly Applequist
Homepage: //econ.ucsd.edu

Hamilton, James D.	C-Pr	534-1055	jhamilto	D	PHD	83	Berkeley	1992
Attiyeh, Richard E.	Prof	534-6654		EI	PHD	66	Yale	1982
Vice Chancellor of Research and Dean, OGSR								
Bear, Donald V. T.	Emer	534-3383		AE	PHD	63	Stanford	1965
Betts, Julian R.	Prof	534-3369	jbetts	CJ	PHD	90	Queen's	1990
Carson, Richard T.	Prof	534-6319	rcarson	CQ	PHD	85	Berkeley	1985
Conlisk, John	Emer	534-3383	jconlisk	ET	PHD	65	Stanford	1968
Crawford, Vincent	Prof	534-3952	vcrawfor	D	PHD	76	MIT	1976
denHaan, Wouter	Prof	543-0762	wdenhaan	AE	PHD	91	Car Mellon	1991
Engle, Robert F.	Prof	534-4553	rengle	CGR	PHD	66	Cornell	1975
Chancellor's Associates Chair in Econometrics								
Gordon, Roger H.	Prof	534-4828	rogordon	H	PHD	76	MIT	2001
Granger, Clive W. J.	Prof	534-3856	cgranger	C	PHD	74	Nottinghm	1974
Chancellor's Associates Chair in Economics								
Groves, Theodore	Prof	534-2818	tgroves	DHM	PHD	70	Berkeley	1978
Machina, Mark J.	Prof	534-2391	mmachina	D	PHD	79	MIT	1979
Ramanathan, Ramu	Emer	534-3383	rramanat	CFO	PHD	67	Minnesota	1967
Ramey, Garey	Prof	534-5721	gramey	D	PHD	87	Stanford	1987
Ramey, Valerie	Prof	543-2388	vramey	E	PHD	87	Stanford	1987
Rauch, James E.	Prof	534-2405	jrauch	FO	PHD	85	Yale	1986
Sobel, Joel	Prof	534-4367	jsobel	D	PHD	78	Berkeley	1978
Starr, Ross	Prof	534-3879	rstarr	DE	PHD	72	Stanford	1980
Timmermann, Allan	Prof	534-3383	atimmerm	CG	PHD	92	Cambridge	1994
White, Halbert L.	Prof	534-3502	hwhite	C	PHD	76	MIT	1979
White, Michelle J.	Prof	534-2783	miwhitee	RK	PHD	73	Princeton	2001
Elliott, Graham	Assoc	534-3383	gelliott	CEF	PHD	94	Harvard	1994
Flavin, Marjorie A.	Assoc	534-4649	mflavin	E	PHD	81	MIT	1992
Watson, Joel	Assoc	534-3383	jwatson	CF	PHD	92	Stanford	1994
Antonovics, Kate	Asst	534-2973	kantonov	JIH	PHD	00	Wisconsin	2000
Sorensen, Alan	Asst	534-4479	asorense	LH	PHD	99	MIT	1999

U of Calif, Santa Barbara Santa Barbara CA 93106-9210 (805) 893-3670 econ.ucsb.edu
Department of Economics Col of Letters & Sci Fax=893-8830 Kate Carver
Homepage: www.econ.ucsb.edu

Mehra, Rajnish	C-Pr	893-3238	mehra	GF	PHD	78	Car Mellon	1988
Bergstrom, Theodore C.	Prof	893-3744	tedb		PHD	67	Stanford	
Bohn, Henning	Prof	893-4532	bohn	EF	PHD	86	Stanford	1992
Comanor, William S.	Prof	893-2287	eomanor	LD	PHD	64	Harvard	1975
Crouch, Robert L.	Prof	893-2152	rlcc	A	PHD	67	Essex	1973
Deacon, Robert T.	Prof	893-3569	deacon	QH	PHD	72	U Wash	1972
DeCanio, Stephen J.	Prof	893-3130	decanio	NCD	PHD	72	MIT	1978
Frech, H. E. III	Prof	893-3569	frech	LAI	PHD	74	UCLA	1973
Kolstad, Charles	Prof	893-2108	kolstad	QLD	PHD	82	Stanford	1992
Krouse, Clement G.	Prof	893-3804	krouse	D	PHD	69	UCLA	1979
LeRoy, Stephen F.	Prof	893-2438	sleroy	GE	PHD	71	Penn	1997
Marshall, John M.	Prof	893-3670	marshall	A	PHD	69	MIT	1972
Mercer, Lloyd J.	Prof	893-2895	mercer	ND	PHD	67	U Wash	1966
Morgan, W. Douglas	Prof	893-2653	dmorgan	HDE	PHD	69	Berkeley	1973
Phillips, Llad	Prof	893-2023	llad	JC	PHD	69	Harvard	1972
Sengupta, Jati K.	Prof	893-3797	sengupta	CO	PHD	62	Iowa St	1976
Shapiro, Perry	Prof	893-2253	pxshap	DH	PHD	67	Berkeley	1969
Sonstelie, Jon C.	Prof	893-2242	jon	HR	PHD	75	Nrthwstrn	1977
Stuart, Charles	Prof	893-3216	stuart	HKD	PHD	75	Lunds	1980
Qin, Cheng-Zhong	Assoc	893-2753	qin	D	PHD	89	Iowa	1989
Steigerwald, Douglas G.	Assoc	893-3151	doug	C	PHD	89	Berkeley	1988
Bedard, Kelly	Asst	893-5571	kelly		PHD	96	Queen's	
Charness, Gary	Asst	893-7309		D	PHD	96	Berkeley	2001
Deschenes, Olivier	Asst	893-7309		JD	ABD			2001
Garratt, Rodney J.	Asst	893-2849	garratt	AEH	PHD	91	Cornell	1991
McAusland, Carol	Asst	893-4823	mcauslan		PHD		Michigan	
Proulx, Christopher	Asst	893-5572	rabbit	D	PHD	98	Michigan	1998
Troger, Thomas	Asst	893-7309		D	PHD	99	Bonn	2001
Nisbet, Mary J.	SLect	893-2284	nisbet	G	PHD	91	Glasgow	1991
Academic Coordinator								
Funkhouser, Ed	Lect	893-3490	funkhous	OJ	PHD	90	Harvard	1992

Univ of Calif, Santa Cruz Santa Cruz, CA 95064 (408) 459-2743 cats.ucsc.edu
Department of Economics Social Sciences Fax=459-5077 Kim Tyler

Hutchison, Michael M.	C-Pr	459-2600	hutch	EFG	PHD	83	Oregon	1985
Aizeuman, Joshua	Prof	459-2743		EFH	PHD	81	Chicago	2001
Dooley, Michael	Prof	459-3662	mpd	F	PHD	71	Penn	1992
Friedman, Daniel	Prof	459-4981	dan	CDGL	PHD	77	Ca-SanCrz	1979
Grieson, Ronald E.	Prof	459-2968	grieson	RHD	PHD	72	Rochester	1980
Ibister, John W.	Prof	459-2246	isbister	O	PHD	69	Princeton	1968
Provost Merrill College								
Kaun, David E.	Prof	459-4745	nuclear	J	PHD	64	Stanford	1966
Kletzer, Kenneth M.	Prof	459-3407	kkletzer	FDOH	PHD	82	Berkeley	1992
Singh, Nirvikar	Prof	459-4093	boxjenk	DLOM	PHD	82	Berkeley	1982
Walsh, Carl E.	Prof	459-4082	walshc	E	PHD	76	Berkeley	1987
Wittman, Donald A.	Prof	459-4445	wittman	KD	PHD	70	Berkeley	1969
Cheung, Yin-Wong	Assoc	459-4247	cheung	CFG	PHD	90	Penn	1990
Elbaum, Bernard	Assoc	459-4248	elbaum	N	PHD	82	Harvard	1986
Fung, Kwok-Chiu	Assoc	459-3273	kcfung	F	PHD	70	Wisconsin	1989
Brooks, Eileen	Asst	459-2743		FL	PHD	01	Harvard	2001
Chinn, Menzie	Asst	459-2079	chinn	FCE	PHD	91	Berkeley	1991
Fairlie, Robert	Asst	459-3332	rfairlie	J	PHD	94	Nrthwstrn	1994
Guo, Binbin	Asst	459-4453	guo	CG	PHD	98	Yale	2000
Kletzer, Lori Gladstein	Asst	459-3596	lketzer	J	PHD	86	Berkeley	1993
McCalman, Philip	Asst	459-4381	mccalman	FL	PHD	98	Wisconsin	2000
Ravenna, Federico	Asst	459-2743		EFG	PHD	01	NYU	2001
Yan, Huibih	Asst	459-2743		CD	PHD	01	Wash U	2001
Shepherd, Robert J.	Lect	459-5080	shep	M	MSA	70	S Calif	1990

California Institute of Tech Pasadena, CA 91125 (626) 395-4065 caltech.edu
Economics Faculty Div of Human & Soc Sci Fax=405-9841 Susan G. Davis, Div Adm
Homepage: http://www.hss.caltech.edu

Ledyard, John O.	C-Pr	395-8482			PHD	67	Purdue	1985
Camerer, Colin	Prof	395-4054			PHD	81	Chicago	1994
Rea A. & Lela G. Axline Professor of Business Economics								
Davis, Lance E.	Prof	395-4092		N	PHD	56	J Hopkins	1968
Mary Stillman Harkness Professor of Social Science								
Grether, David M.	Prof	395-4068			PHD	69	Stanford	1970
Jackson, Matthew O.	Prof	395-4022			PHD	88	Stanford	1997
Palfrey, Thomas R.	Prof	395-4088			PHD	81	Cal Tech	1986
Plott, Charles R.	Prof	395-4209			PHD	65	Virginia	1971
Edward S. Harkness Professor of Economics and Political Science								
Border, Kim Christian	Assoc	395-4218		C	PHD	79	Minnesota	1979
Bossaerts, Peter	Assoc	395-4028		G	PHD	86	UCLA	1990
Dubin, Jeffrey A.	Assoc	395-4059			PHD	82	MIT	1982
Fohlin, Caroline	Asst	395-4401		NFL	PHD	94	Berkeley	1994
Ghirardato, Paolo	Asst	395-4094		D	PHD	95	Berkeley	1995
Sherman, Robert P.	Asst	395-4337			PHD	91	Yale	1996
Wilkie, Simon	Asst	395-4216		L	PHD	90	Rochester	1995

California Lutheran Univ Thousand OaksCA 91360-2787 (805) 493-3360 clunet.edu
Economics Faculty School of Business Fax=493-3719 Joan Rensch

Maxey, Charles	Dean	493-3360	maxey	Soc	PHD	82	Illinois	1991
Akbari, Ali	Prof	493-3379	akbari		PHD	85	S Calif	1984
Damooei, Jamshid	Assoc	493-3357	damooei		PHD		Surrey	1987

Cal Polytechnic State U-SLO S Luis Obispo CA 93407 (805) 756-2783 cymbal.calpol
Economics Department School of Business Fax=756-1473 Sharon Leib 756-2783

Pendergast, William	Dean	756-2705	wpenderg		PHD		Columbia	9-00
Shiers, Alden F.	C-Prc	756-2564			PHD	77	Ca-SnBarb	1975
Beardsley, George L.	Prof	756-2356			PHD	74	Penn	1975
Fanchon, Phillip F.	Prof	756-1766			PHD	82	Ca-SnBarb	
Kersten, Timothy W.	Prof	756-2555			PHD	73	Oregon	1971
Marlow, Michael L.	Prof	756-1764			PHD	78	Va Tech	1988
Papakyriazis, Panagiotis A.	Prof	756-7176			PHD	74	Ca-SnDgo	1971
Williamson, Daniel P.	Prof	756-1768			PHD	73	Ca-SnDgo	1970
Villegas, Daniel J.	Assoc	756-1767			PHD	79	Stanford	1987

Calif State Poly U-Pomona Pomona, CA 91768-4082 (909) 869-3842 csupomona.edu
Economics Department Cl Letters, Arts & SocS Fax=869-6987 Rosie Pasos

Rush, Lynda M.	C-Pr	869-3857	lmrush		PHD	84	Ca-Davis	1986
Al-Sabea, Taha H.	Prof	869-3855	thalsabea		PHD	68	S Calif	1968
Bray, Robert T.	Prof	869-3847	rtbray		PHD	72	UCLA	1965
Bresnock, Anne E.	Prof	869-4593	aebresnock		PHD	81	Colorado	1990
Burton, Maureen	Prof	869-3853	mburton		PHD	86	Ca-Rivers	1988
Ho, Franklin Y. H.	Prof	869-3854	fho		PHD	57	S Calif	1961
Jaques, David G.	Prof	869-3851	dgjaques		PHD	73	Claremont	1965
Safarzadeh, Mohammad R.	Prof	869-3852	mssafarzadeh		PHD	84	Claremont	1987

Shute, Laurence	Prof	869-3850	lshute		PHD	73	Columbia	1988
Sutton, James E.	Prof	869-3846	jesutton		BS	55	Wisconsin	1964
Ruiz, Nestor M.	Assoc	869-3972	nmruiz		PHD	89	Ca-Davis	1990
Brown, Bruce	Asst	869-5074	bbrown		PHD		UCLA	

Calif State U., Bakersfield Bakersfield, CA 93311-1099 (661) 664-2460 csubak.edu
Economics Department Sch of Arts & Sciences Fax=664-2049 Dawn Carlon

Iyasere, Marla M.	Dean	664-2221	miyasere	Engl	PHD	73	SUNY-Bin	1974
Grammy, Abbas P.	C-Pr	664-2466	agrammy	ACOR	PHD	82	Colorado	1989
Evans, Mark O.	Prof	664-2496	mevans	AIQR	PHD	77	New Mex	1978
Malixi, Margaret M.	Prof	664-2464	mmalixi	ACFP	PHD	88	Wisconsin	1988
Oswald, Donald J.	Assoc	664-2465	doswald	ABKN	PHD	74	Wash St	1961
VanGilder, Jennifer A.	Asst	664-2026	jvangilder	JDT	PHD	00	SUNY-Bin	2000
Khe, Sriram	Lect	664-2095	skhe	RO	PHD	93	S Calif	2000

Calif State Univ, Chico Chico, CA 95929-0430 (530) 898-6141 oavax.csuchico.edu
Department of Economics Col of Behav & Soc Sci Fax=898-5901 Annette Schmidt

Adams, Ronald G.	Prof	898-6141		ACKR	PHD	75	Kansas St	1971
Eckalbar, John C.	Prof	898-5808		CE	PHD	75	Colorado	1978
Fisher, Robert B.	Prof	895-5808		H	PHD		Oregon	1968
Francis, Gary E.	Prof	898-6141		ABGH	PHD	72	Colorado	1967
Gallo, David E.	Prof	898-5232		AEHQ	PHD	74	Oregon	1970
James, Robert G.	Prof	898-5997		EFG	PHD	78	Oregon	1981
Morlock, Mark J.	Prof	898-4784		J	PHD	78	Wash St	1980
O'Toole, James K.	Prof	898-5759		ADR	PHD	83	Va Tech	1984
Perelman, Michael A.	Prof	898-5321		N	PHD	71	Berkeley	1971
Shockley, Frederica	Prof	898-6141		HMOR	PHD	78	Geo St	1978
Coolidge, Cathleen J.	Assoc	898-6141		AHKL	PHD	83	Va Tech	1984

Calif St U-Dominguez Hills Carson, CA 90747 (310) 243-3446 csudh.edu
Economics Department Col of Arts & Sciences Fax=
email @1=dhvx20.csudh.edu

Palmer, Richard L.	Dean	243-3490	rpalmer@1	PolS	PHD	73	Claremont	1972
Billes, Frank V.	C-Pr	243-3446	fbilles@1	AENP	PHD	74	UCLA	1972
Freed, Rodney Alan	Prof	243-3497		ACR	PHD	77	Virginia	1979
Harris, James G.	Prof	243-3303	jharris	AEDH	PHD	70	Oregon	1969
Kidane, Abraham Z.	Prof	243-3507	akidane	AFOI	PHD	71	UCLA	1971
Moite, Leonard M.	Assoc	243-3492	lmoite@1	AEDJ	PHD	84	UCLA	1980

Calif State Univ-Fresno Fresno, CA 93740-0020 (559) 278-3916 csufresno.edu
Department of Economics Sch of Social Sciences Fax=278-7234 Sherry McCulloch

Gruenbaum, Ellen R.	Dean	278-3013	elleng	Anth	PHD	82	Conn	
Shaffer, Linda J.	C-Pr	278-4936	linda_shaffer	JIC	PHD	78	Nrthwstrn	1984
Allison, Robert J.	Prof		robert_allison	B	PHD	66	Colorado	1967
Cypher, James M.	Prof	278-4935	james_cypher	OP	PHD	73	Ca-Rivers	1967
Leet, Don R.	Prof	278-4045	don_leet	TNA	PHD	72	Penn	1969
Shaw, John A. Jr.	Prof	278-2673	john_shaw	DNF	PHD	69	Purdue	1965
Houser, Scott	Assoc	278-3045	scott_houser	HRI	PHD	96	Wisconsin	1996
Fayazmanesh, Sasan	Asst	278-2672		BCE	PHD	84	Ca-Rivers	1990
Hays, Sally	Asst	278-4932	salley_hays	QLC	PHD	99	Oregon	2000
Iwasa, Jeanette	Asst	278-4933	jeanette_iwasa	E	ABD		Nebraska	2001

Calif State Univ, Fullerton Fullerton, CA 92834-6848 (714) 278-2228 fullerton.edu
Department of Economics School of Bus Adm & Ec Fax=278-3097 Shelley Drath
Did Not Respond--1999-2000 Listing

Puri, Anil K.	Dean	278-3817	apuri	HR	PHD	77	Minnesota	1977
Wong, David C.	C-Pr	278-2228	dwong	CO	PHD	84	Ca-SnBarb	1981
Chu, Kwang-Wen	Prof	278-3841	kchu	D	PHD	72	UCLA	1970
Dietz, James L.	Prof	278-3810	jdietz	O	PHD	74	Ca-Rivers	1973
Gill, Andrew M.	Prof	278-3076	agill	J	PHD	85	Wash St	1984
Hall, Jane V.	Prof	278-2236	jhall	Q	PHD	77	Berkeley	1981
Hettich, Walter	Prof	278-3756	whettich	H	PHD	67	Yale	1983
Long, Stewart L.	Prof	278-2243	slong	N	PHD	74	Illinois	1973
Michaels, Robert J.	Prof	278-2588	rmichaels	L	PHD	72	UCLA	1968
Naish, Howard F.	Prof	278-2241	hnaish	E	PHD	83	S Calif	1988
Rahmatian, Morteza	Prof	278-3859	mrahmatian	Q	PHD	82	Wyoming	1988
Solberg, Eric J.	Prof	278-2237	esolberg	J	PHD	74	Claremont	1973
Wolfson, Murray	Prof	278-3816	mwolfson	BC	PHD	63	Wisconsin	1986
Brajer, Victor	Assoc	278-3818	vbrajer	DQ	PHD	83	New Mex	1987
Flessig, Adrian	Assoc	278-2228	aflessig	EF	PHD	93	N Car St	1999
Purkayastha, Dipankar	Assoc	278-3151	dpurkayastha	O	PHD	90	Wash St	1990
Battacharya, Radha S.	Asst	278-3652	rbattacharya	E	PHD	90	Penn St	1990
Dropsy, Vincent	Asst	278-3307	vdropsy	FE	PHD	90	S Calif	1989
Roy, Suddhasatwa	Asst	2778-381	9sroy	LF	PHD	96	Purdue	1998

Calif State Univ, Hayward Hayward, CA 94542-3068 (510) 885-3331 csuhayward.edu
Department of Economics Sch of Business & Econ Fax=885-4796

Tontz, Jay L.	Dean	885-3291	jtonz	EGM	PHD	66	N Carol	9-69
Baird, Charles W.	C-Pr	885-3275	cbaird	BHJ	PHD	68	Berkeley	1972
Ahiakpor, James C.	Prof	885-3330	jahiakop	BEO	PHD	81	Toronto	1991
Cassuto, Alexander E.	Prof	885-3922	acassuto	CEGM	PHD	73	UCLA	1971
Christiansen, Gregory B.	Prof	885-3301	gchrista	BEHO	PHD	81	Wisconsin	1983
Kamath, Shyam J.	Prof	885-4275	skamath	BFMO	PHD	87	Simon Fr	1986
Leube, Kurt R.	Prof	885-3368	kleube	DBHK	DLE	71	Salzburg	1985
Lima, Anthony K.	Prof	885-3889	tlima	CEGM	PHD	80	Stanford	1979
Maxwell, Nan L.	Prof	885-3191	nmaxwell	ADJT	PHD	83	Fla St	1985
Paringer, Lynn C.	Prof	885-3986	lparinge	CDI	PHD	78	Wisconsin	1981
Shmanske, Steven	Prof	885-3334	sshmansk	CDHL	PHD	82	UCLA	1979
St. Clair, David J.	Prof	885-3327	dstclair	BENP	PHD	79	Utah	1979
Kahane, Leo H.	Assoc	885-3369	lkahane	CFL	PHD	91	Columbia	1991
Lopus, Jane S.	Assoc	885-3140	jlopus	AEH	PHD	90	Ca-Davis	1979

Humboldt State University Arcata, CA 95521-8299 (707) 826-3224 humboldt.edu
Sch of Business & Economics Col of Professional Std Fax=826-6666 Kristin Nelson

Costello, John A.	Dean	826-3961	costello	PE	EDD	77	Columbia	1997
Kenyon, Peter B.	C-Pr	826-4762	pbk1	Atg	PHD	85	Santa Cl	1984
Hackett, Steven C.	Assoc	826-3237	sh2		PHD	89	Tx A&M	1994
Eschker, Erik	Asst	826-3216	ee3		PHD	97	Ca-Davis	1998
Wilson, Beth	Asst	826-3224	baw21		PHD	95	Oregon	2001

Calif State Univ, Long Beach Long Beach, CA 90840-4607 (562) 985-5061 csulb.edu
Department of Economics College of Liberal Arts Fax=985-5804 Karen Fawson
Homepage: www.cuslb.edu/~econ

Abrahamse, Dorothy Z.	Dean	985-5381			PHD	67	Michigan	1967
Magaddino, Joseph P.	C-Pr	985-5061			PHD	72	Va Tech	1973
Anderson, Roy C.	Prof	985-5078			PHD	65	Tulane	1965
Beaumont, Marion S.	Prof	985-5078			PHD	67	Claremont	1967
Cole, Charles L.	Prof	985-5078			PHD	63	S Calif	1967
Crowther, Simeon J.	Prof	985-4634			PHD	70	Penn	1968
Edwards, Alejandra C.	Prof	985-5969			PHD	84	Chicago	1966
Farrell, Michael J.	Prof	985-5060			PHD	69	Stanford	1969
Glezakos, Constantine	Prof	985-5079			PHD	70	S Calif	1968
Grobar, Lisa M.	Prof	985-1652			PHD	89	Michigan	1989
Hall, Darwin C.	Prof	985-5045			PHD	77	Berkeley	1986
Hou, Jack W.	Prof	985-4710			PHD	89	Yale	1989
Ishimine, Tomotaka	Prof	985-5065			PHD	71	Wisconsin	1967
Medoff, Marshall H.	Prof	985-5077			PHD	73	Berkeley	1979
Muraoka, Dennis D.	Prof	985-5078			PHD	81	Ca-SnBarb	1982
Rooney, Robert F.	Prof	985-5086			PHD	65	Stanford	1970
Singh, Davinder	Prof	985-5071			PHD	78	S Carol	1983
Skov, Iva L.	Prof	985-5087			PHD	76	S Calif	1972
Stern, Andrew	Prof	985-5083			PHD	67	Columbia	1967
Monaco, Kristen	Assoc	985-5076		LJ	PHD	98	Wi-Milwa	1998
Radsich, Aleksander	Asst	985-8513			PHD	99	Princeton	1999
Yamashiro, Guy	Asst	985-5054			PHD	01	Ca-SnDgo	2001

Calif State U, Los Angeles Los Angeles, CA 90032-8124 (323) 343-2930 calstatela.edu
Dept of Economics & Stat School of Bus & Econ Fax=343-5462 Pat Tom
Homepage: www.calstate.edu/academic/business/economics/index

Haight, G. Timothy	Dean	343-2800	thaight	Fnce	DBA	80	Geo Wash	9-90
Hsieh, Edward W.	C-Pr	343-2939	ehsieh		PHD	88	Houston	1989
Canarella, Giorgio	Prof	343-2933	gcanare		PHD	73	Virginia	1973
Garston, Neil H.	Prof	343-2934	ngarsto		PHD	73	Brown	1975
Kim, Sun K.	Prof	343-2944			PHD	66	S Calif	1964
Lai, Kon Sun	Prof	343-2930	klai		PHD	87	Penn	1987
Larson, Tom Edward	Prof	343-2938	tlarson		PHD	86	Berkeley	1987
Mohanty, Madhu	Prof	343-2935	mmohant		PHD	90	Wi-Milwa	1990
Sapra, Sunil	Prof	343-2941	ssapra		PHD	83	Columbia	1991
Tran, Dang	Prof	343-2949	dtran		PHD	77	Syracuse	1987
Carrington, Samantha	Assoc	343-2946	scarrin		PHD	85	Ca-SnBarb	1986
Finney, Miles	Assoc	343-2937	mfinney		PHD	92	Houston	1991
Pulchritudoff, Nikolai	Assoc	343-2943	npulchr		PHD	71	Ca-Davis	1972
Vaidya, Ashish K.	Assoc	343-2980	avaidya		PHD	90	Ca-Davis	1991
Yoon, Mann	Assoc	343-2936	myoon		PHD	91	Illinois	1991
Chen, Li Hsueh	Asst	343-2934	lchen4		PHD	98	Michigan	1998

Calif State Univ, Northridge Northridge, CA 91330-8245 (818) 885-2462 csun.edu
Department of Economics Sch of Bus Adm & Econ Fax=885-4903 Lucy Larson

Hosek, William R.	Dean	677-2455	william.hosek		PHD	67	Ca-SnBarb	1988
Gifford, Adam Jr.	C-Pr	677-2462	adam.gifford		PHD	72	Ca-SnDgo	1975
Anderson, Gary M.	Prof	677-2462	gary.anderson	GLTR	PHD	87	GeoMason	1987

Blake, Daniel R.	Prof	677-2447	daniel.blake		PHD	71	Oregon	1971
Brown, William W.	Prof	677-2462	william.brown		MA	66	UCLA	1975
Chapman, Kenneth S.	Prof	677-2462	kenneth.chapman	IG	PHD	86	Minnesota	1991
Johnson, Ivan C.	Prof	677-2462	ivan.johnson		PHD	71	W Ontario	1973
Krol, Robert	Prof	677-2462	robert.krol	FGT	PHD	82	S Illinois	1983
Lowenberg, Tony	Prof	677-2462	tony.lowenberg	GH	PHD	84	Simon Fr	1984
Roberts, William W.	Prof	677-2462	william.roberts		PHD	74	Ca-SnDgo	1973
Associate Dean								
Svorny, Shirley V.	Prof	677-2462	shirley.svorny	IG	PHD	79	UCLA	1978
Yu, Ben T.	Prof	677-2462	ben.yu		PHD	78	U Wash	1984
Halcoussis, Dennis	Assoc	677-2462	dennis.halcous+	C	PHD	92	Penn	1991
Ng, Kenneth	Assoc	677-2462	kenneth.ng	N	PHD	88	Rochester	1986
Tchakerian, Viken	Assoc	677-2434	viken.tchakerian	N	PHD	91	UCLA	1991
Virts, Nancy L.	Assoc	677-2434	nancy.virts	N	PHD	85	UCLA	1985
Marcal, Leah	Asst	677-4245	leah.marcal		PHD	96	Wisconsin	1996
Nadenichek, Jon	Asst	677-4571	jon.nadenichek		PHD	96	Rochester	1996
Whitman, D. Glen	Asst	677-4542	glen.whitman		PHD	00	Wyoming	2000

Calif State Univ, Sacramento — Sacramento, CA 95819-6082 (916) 278-6223 — csus.edu
Department of Economics — Sch Social Sci & Int Ds Fax=278-5768 — Nancy L. Carrillo

Sheley, Joseph	Dean	278-6504	sheleyj					
Sexton, Terri A.	C-Pr	278-6223	sextont		PHD	81	Minnesota	1987
Calandri, Kevin	Prof	278-6131	calandrikv		PHD	85	Ca-Davis	1986
Gutowsky, Albert R.	Prof	278-5588	arg		PHD	65	Oregon	1967
Henry, John F.	Prof	278-6193	henryjf		PHD	74	McGill	1970
Kerby, William C.	Prof	278-7112	kerbywc		PHD	71	Oregon	1967
Director, Economic Education Center								
Lund, Peter B.	Prof	278-7078	pblund		PHD	67	Berkeley	1970
McGowan, Susan	Prof	278-6504	susan.mcgowan		PHD	77	Ca-Davis	1974
Associate Dean								
Polkinghorn, Bette A.	Prof	278-7080	bapolkinghorn		PHD	72	Ca-Davis	1971
Yang, Yung Y.	Prof	278-6264	yangyy		PHD	74	Oregon	1974
Dube, Smile W.	Assoc	278-7519	dubes		PHD	89	Tx-Austin	1989
Gallet, Craig	Asst	278-6223		CDL	PHD	95	Iowa St	2001
O'Keefe, Suzanne	Asst	278-6223			PHD	00	Berkeley	2001
Perez, Stephen J.	Asst	278-6223			PHD	95	Ca-Davis	2001

Calif St U, San Bernardino — S Bernardino, CA 92407-2397 (909) 880-5511 — csusb.edu
Department of Economics — Sch of Soc & Behave Sci Fax=880-7025 — Parne Jonest

Conley, John	Dean	880-5500	jconley	SocS	PHD		Mich St	1977
Rose, Nancy E.	C-Pr	880-5516	nrose	IN	PHD	85	Miss	1985
Asheghian, Par	Prof	880-5499	pasheghi	F	PHD	80	Geo St	1991
Charkins, Ralph James	Prof	880-5518	rcharkin	A	PHD	70	N Carol	1976
Nilsson, Eric A.	Prof	880-5564	enilsson	FJ	PHD	89	Mass	1989
Pierce, Thomas J.	Prof	880-5515	tpierce	E	PHD	76	Notre Dm	1976
Toruno, Mayo C.	Prof	880-5517	mtoruno	B	PHD	83	Ca-Rivers	1983
Aldana, Carolyn	Assoc	880-7315	cbrod	E	PHD	95	Ca-Rivers	1995
Konyar, Kazim	Assoc	880-5514	kkonyar	CQ	PHD	85	Ca-Rivers	1991

Calif State U - San Marcos — San Marcos, CA 92069-1477 (760) 750-4152 — csusm.edu
Department of Economics — Col of Arts & Sciences Fax=750-4111 — Cara Goger

Ghiara, Ranjetta	C-Ac	750-4176	ghiara		PHD	94	Ca-Rivers	1994
Arnold, Roger A.	Prof	750-4077	rarnold		PHD	79	Va Tech	
Brown, Robert W.	Assoc	750-4196	rbrown	GIKH	PHD	91	Ca-SnBarb	1997
Rider, Robert L.	Assoc	750-4140	rrider	CDHK	PHD	89	S Calif	1992

Calif State U, Stanislaus — Turlock, CA 95382 (209) 667-3181 — toto.csustan.edu
Department of Economics — Col Arts, Letters & Sci Fax=667-3588 — Laura Riddell
Homepage: http://www.csustan.edu/econ/dept/

Elmmallah, Amin A.	Dean	667-3287	elmallah	Atg	PHD	74	Illinois	7-00
Erickson, Edward C.	C-Pr	633-3338			PHD	70	S Calif	1970
Crist, William D.	Prof	667-3500	crist		PHD	72	Nebraska	1969
Director of PERS								
Lee, Albert Yin-Po	Emer	667-3339	aylee		PHD	70	S Illinois	1970
Renning, H. Dieter	Emer	667-3327			DR	61	Freiburg	1970
Jasek-Rysdahl, Kelvin	Assoc	667-3182	kjasekry		PHD	96	Colo St	1996
Kim, Eungsuk	Asst	667-3339	ekime		PHD	99	Indiana	2000
Peterson, Elaine J.	Asst	667-3327	epeterso		PHD	96	Wisconsin	1996

Calvin College — Grand Rapids, MI 49546 (616) 957-7191 — calvin.edu
Dept of Economics & Business — Division of Social Sci Fax=957-6501 — Susan Camp

Diephouse, David	Dean	957-6203	ddiephou		PHD	74	Princeton	1974
Hoksbergen, Roland G.	C-Pr	957-6188	hoksro		PHD	86	Notre Dm	1983
Monsma, George N. Jr.	Prof	957-6191	gmonsma		PHD	69	Princeton	1969
Schaefer, Kurt C.	Prof	957-6368	schk		PHD	84	Michigan	1987

Tiemstra, John P.	Prof	957-6192	tmst		PHD	75	MIT	1975
Van Der Heide, Evert M.	Prof	957-6099	evheide		PHD	82	Wayne St	1982
Vander Linde, Scott H.	Prof	957-6477	vdls		PHD	89	Notre Dm	
Abadeer, Adel	Assoc	957-6199	aabadeer		PHD	92	Boston U	1999
DeVries, Rick	Asst	957-6247	redevrie		PHD	99	Notre Dm	1995

Cameron University Lawton, OK 73505-6377 (580) 581-2267 cameron.edu
Economics Faculty Department of Business Fax=581-2253

Burgess, Sylvia	Dean$	581-2267	sylviab	Law	JD	82	Oklahoma	1995
Amyx, Jack F.	AcDn	581-2267		Atg	EDD	72	Okla St	1964
Courington, John M.	Prof	581-2266			PHD	87	Okla St	1979
Horner, James	Prof	581-2269			PHD	85	Tx-Dallas	1976
Sukar, Abdul Hamid	Prof	581-2845			PHD	89	Tx Tech	1987

Campbell University Buies Creek, NC 27506 (910) 893-1390
Dept Bus Adm & Econ Box218 Lundy-Fetterman Sch Bus Fax=893-1424 Sandra McLeod
phone 893-1383

Zinkhan, F. Christian	Dean	Ext 1380			DBA	86	Miss St	1987
Mostashari, Shahriar	C-Pr	Ext-1390			PHD	78	N Car St	1982
Hsiao, Yu-Mong	Prof				PHD	85	N Car St	1984
Sikes, Ellen	Assoc				MS		N Carol	1966
Cwik, Paul F.	Asst				ABD		Auburn	1998
Paleisek, Karen Y.	Inst				PHD		GeoMason	1993

Canisius College Buffalo, NY 14208-1098 (716) 888-2670 canisius.edu
Dept of Economics & Finance Wehle Sch of Business Fax=888-2525 Nancy Muenzner/Karen Armenia

Shick, Richard A.	Dean	888-2160	shick	G	PHD	73	SUNY-Buf	1978
Palumbo, George M.	C-Pr	888-2667	palumbo	RT	PHD	77	Syracuse	1978
Bosshardt, Donald I.	Prof	888-2676	bosshard	G	PHD	77	Wisconsin	1987
Hutton, Patricia A.	Prof	888-2673	hutton	EC	PHD	80	Wisconsin	1981
Pfaff, Philip	Prof	888-2675	pfaff	G	PHD	73	Mich St	1979
Wall, Richard A.	Prof	888-2666	wall	EG	PHD	84	SUNY-Buf	1980
Wilson, F. Scott	Prof	888-2674	wilson	C	PHD	76	Minnesota	1977
Zaporowski, Mark P.	Prof	888-2679	zaporowsk	EC	PHD	85	SUNY-Alb	1983
Falkowski, Daniel C.	Assoc	888-2668	falkow	F	PHD	72	NYU	1975
Lichtenstein, Larry	Assoc	888-2677	lichten	DRH	PHD	81	SUNY-Bin	1981
Reiber, Ronald R.	Assoc	888-2665	reiber	G	PHD	74	Arizona	1971
Eisenhauer, Joseph G.	Asst	888-2676	eisenhauer	EI	PHD	91	SUNY-Buf	1986
Rogers, Craig	Asst	888-3264	rogersc	RT	MA	94	SUNY-Buf	1998

Capital University Columbus, OH 43209-2394 (614) 236-6595 capital.edu
Dept of Business & Economics College of Arts & Sci Fax=236-6540

Raabe, William A.	Dean	236-6510		Atg	PHD	79	Illinois	2001
Mellum, Steven D.	C-Ac	236-6132		Atg	MBA		Ohio St	1991
Baker, Stephen A.	Prof	236-6136			PHD	82	York UK	1987
Lawson, Robert	Asst	236-6138			PHD		Fla St	1996

Carleton College Northfield, MN 55057 (507) 646-4109 carleton.edu
Economics Faculty Department of Economics Fax=646-4044 Susan Quay

Hemesath, Michael	C-Ac	646-4105	mhemesat	AFP	PHD	88	Harvard	1989
Bierman, H. Scott	Prof	646-4108	sbierman	DHL	PHD	85	Virginia	1982
Ada M. Harrison Professor of Social Sciences								
Lamson, George H.	Prof	646-4107	glamson	EF	PHD	71	Nrthwstrn	1969
Wadsworth W. Williams Professor of Economics								
Lewis, Stephen R. Jr.	Prof	646-4305		FO	PHD	63	Stanford	1987
President								
Paas, Martha W.	Prof	646-4103	mpaas	BNO	PHD	79	Bryn Mawr	1975
Strand, Stephen H.	Prof	646-4104	sstrand	DL	PHD	76	Vanderbilt	1981
Raymond Plank Professor of Economics								
Kanazawa, Mark T.	Assoc	646-4106	mkanazaw	DKNQ	PHD	87	Stanford	1985
Gibbons, Donna M.	Asst	646-5239	dgibbons	DOR	PHD	95	Brown	1993
Grawe, Nathan	Asst	646-5239	ngrawe	IJ	PHD	01	Chicago	1999
Wahl, Jenny Bourne	Asst	646-4007	jwahl	JKN	PHD	86	Chicago	1998

Carnegie Mellon University Pittsburgh, PA 15213-3890 (412) 268-2294 andrew.cmu.edu
Department of Economics Col of Human & Soc Sci Fax=268-7357 Marian Lee 268-2874
Homepage: http://bighurt.gsia.cmu.edu/economics/contents.htm

Lehoczky, John P.	Dean	268-2832			PHD	69	Stanford	1969
Thomas Lord Professor of Statistics								
Zin, Stanley E.	H-Pr	268-3700	sz0h		PHD	87	Toronto	1988
Richard M. Cyert and Morris H. DeGroot Professor of Economics and Finance								

Name	Rank	Phone	E-mail	Fields	Degree	Yr	Institution	Year
Epple, Dennis N.	Prof	268-1536	epple		PHD	74	Princeton	1974
Green, Richard	Prof	268-2302	rg0b		PHD	82	Wisconsin	
Richard M. and Margaret S. Cyert Professor of Economics and Management								
Klepper, Steven I.	Prof	268-3235	sk3f		PHD	75	Cornell	1980
Kydland, Finn	Prof	268-3691	kydland		PHD	73	Car Mellon	1977
Lave, Lester B.	Prof	268-8837	1101		PHD	63	Harvard	1963
Harry B. & James H. Higgins University Professor of Economics								
McCallum, Bennett T.	Prof	268-2347	bm05		PHD	69	Rice	1981
H. J. Heinz Professor of Economics								
Meltzer, Allan H.	Prof	268-2282	am05		PHD	58	UCLA	1957
The Allan H. Meltzer University Professor of Political Economy								
Seppi, Duane J.	Prof	268-2298	ds65		PHD	88	Chicago	1986
Spatt, Chester S.	Prof	268-8834	cspatt		PHD	79	Penn	1979
Mellon Bank Professor of Finance								
Spear, Stephen E.	Prof	268-8831	ss1f		PHD	82	Penn	1982
Srivastava, Sanjay	Prof	268-3703	sslg		PHD	82	MIT	1982
Alumni Professor of Economics and Finance								
Dammon, Robert	Assoc	268-3696	re19		PHD	84	Wisconsin	
Hollifield, Burton	Assoc	268-6505	burtonh		PHD	92	Car Mellon	
Miller, Robert A.	Assoc	268-3701	ramiller		PHD	82	Chicago	1982
Rajan, Uday	Assoc	268-5744	urajan		PHD	95	Stanford	1995
Sieg, Holger	Assoc	268-6564	holgers		PHD	96	Car Mellon	
Smith, Anthony A.	Assoc	368-7583	smithaa		PHD	91	Duke	1992
Sowell, Fallaw B.	Assoc	268-3769	fs0v		PHD	86	Duke	1988
Telmer, Chris I.	Assoc	268-8838	telmerc		PHD	92	Queen's	1992
Wang, Cheng	Assoc	268-2289	chewang		PHD	94	W Ontario	1994
Cleminti, Gian Luca	Asst	268-6892	clem		PHD	00	Rochester	2000
Coen-Pirani, Daniele	Asst	268-6143	coenp		PHD	00	Rochester	2000
Goettler, Ronald	Asst	268-7058	rong		PHD	99	Yale	
Manuszak, Mark	Asst	268-5993	manuszak		PHD	00	Nrthwstrn	
Parlour, Christine	Asst	268-5806	parlourc		PHD	95	Queen's	1995
Routledge, Bryan	Asst	268-7588	rout		PHD	95	Brit Colum	1995
Tallarini, Thomas	Asst	268-5805	tomjr		PHD	95	Chicago	1995
Dalton, W. Robert	SrLec	268-2726	wd0d		PHD	72	Missouri	1985
Lerrick, Adam	SrLec	268-9027	alerrick		PHD	81	MIT	
Friends of Allan H. Meltzer Chair								
Sileo, Patrick	SrLec	268-5867	ps37		PHD	94	Car Mellon	

Carroll College Waukesha, WI 53186 (262) 547-1211 carroll1.cc.edu
Dept of Business & Economics Col of Arts & Sciences Fax=524-7139

Name	Rank	Phone	E-mail	Fields	Degree	Yr	Institution	Year
Moody, Merlene A.	C-Pr	514-7160	mmoody	Mgt	MBA	78	W Mich	1992
Debrecht, Dennis M.	Asst	524-7163			PHD	81	Iowa St	1984

Carson-Newman College Jefferson Cy, TN 37760-9061 (865) 471-3316 cn.edu
Dept of Business & Economics Division of Business Fax=471-3599 Rebecca Dinkins

Name	Rank	Phone	E-mail	Fields	Degree	Yr	Institution	Year
Young, Gary F.	Dean	471-3316	gyoung	LMQR	PHD	77	La Tech	2000
Sites, Millicent M.	C-Ac	471-3433	taylorm	EFGO	PHD	85	Tennessee	8-95
Knight, Tori H.	Asst	471-4803	tknight	CDHI	PHD			2000

Carthage College Kenosha, WI 53140-1994 (262) 551-5831 cns.carthage.edu
Economics Faculty Department of Economics Fax=551-6208 Sandy Fredericks
Did Not Respond--1999-2000 Listing

Name	Rank	Phone	E-mail	Fields	Degree	Yr	Institution	Year
Schlack, Robert F.	C-Pr	551-5831	rfs	FPRC	PHD	77	Wayne St	1975
Maltsev, Yuri N.	Assoc	551-5880	yuri	DFJP	PHD	80	Inst Labor	1991
McClintock, Brent	Assoc	551-5852	btm	EFG	PHD	90	Colo St	1991

Case Western Reserve Univ Cleveland, OH 44106-7206 (216) 368-2970 po.cwru.edu
Economics Department Weatherhead Sch of Mgt Fax=368-5039 Lenora Mitchell

Name	Rank	Phone	E-mail	Fields	Degree	Yr	Institution	Year
Anvari, Mohsen	Dean	368-2046		Fnce	PHD	79	Case Wes	8-01
Bogart, William T.	C-Ac	368-4296	wtb	HRDA	PHD	90	Princeton	1990
Carlsson, Bo A.	Prof	368-4112	bxc4	DFMO	PHD	72	Stanford	1984
DeWindt Professor of Industrial Economics; Assoc Dean								
Erdilek, Asim	Prof	368-4110	axe3	F	PHD	72	Harvard	1971
Peirce, William S.	Prof	368-4131	wsp	HOQ	PHD	66	Princeton	1966
Rebitzer, James B.	Prof	368-5537	jbr	J	PHD	85	Mass	1997
Rosegger, Gerhard	Emer	368-4295	gxr2	OFND	DIUR	53	Austria	1965
Frank Tracy Carlton Professor Emeritus of Economics								
Shatten, Richard	Prof	368-5535	rxs90	HR	MBA	80	Harvard	1997
Professor for the Practice of Public Policy & Mgt; Director, Center Regional								
Dor, Avi	Assoc	368-0208	axd9	I	PHD	86	CUNY	1995
John R. Mannix Blue Cross & Blue Shield Professor of Health Care Economics								
Dubin, Robin A.	Assoc	368-3981	rad4	RCD	PHD	82	J Hopkins	1988
Helper, Susan	Assoc	368-5541	sxh23	ONM	PHD	87	Harvard	1990
Bettinger, Eric	Asst	368-2184	epb4	IS	PHD	00	MIT	2000
Cooper, David J.	Asst	368-1818		CD	PHD	92	Princeton	1999
Slonim, Robert L.	Asst	368-5811	rls18	CD	PHD	95	Duke	1998
Stanky, Marius	Asst	368-8844	mms24	IS	PHD	00	Harvard	2000

Catawba College	Salisbury, NC		28144-2488 (704) 637-4405				catawba.edu	
Economic Faculty	Ketner School of Bus		Fax=637-4422				Dorothy Earle	
Tseng, S. C.	Prof	637-4407			PHD	72	Oklahoma	
Carter, J. Alvin	Assoc	637-4406		Mgt	MBA		Geo St	1968

Catholic Univ of America	Washington, DC		20064 (202) 319-5236				cua.edu	
Dept of Economics & Business	Sch of Arts & Sciences		Fax=319-4426				Ms. Brenda Nichols	
Suziedelis, Antanas	Dean	319-5115		Psy	PHD	57	Catholic	
Forbes, Kevin F.	C-Ac	319-4794	forbes	DHLQ	PHD	82	Maryland	1983
Piedra, Alberto M.	Prof	319-5235	piedra	BNO	PHD	62	Geotown	
Aguirre, Sophia	Assoc	319-4957	aguirre	FG	PHD	92	Notre Dm	1993
Zampelli, Ernest M.	Assoc	319-6683	zampelli	DHQ	PHD	82	Maryland	9-85
Aka, Arsene A.	Asst	319-5238	aka		PHD		Pittsburgh	8-00
Leon, Jean-Claude	Asst	319-5239	leon		PHD		Geo Wash	

Cedarville College	Cedarville, OH		45314-0601 (937) 766-7910				cedarville.edu	
Economic Faculty	Dept of Business Admin		Fax=766-2760				Vicki Edem	
Hazen, Marinus	C-Ac	766-7924	hazenm	Atg	PHD	97	Clev St	1983
Smith, Galen	Prof	766-7923	smithg	ABFH	DMIN	98	Trinity	1981
Wheeler, Bert	Assoc	766-7714	wheelerb	AFOP	PHD	85	Tennessee	1992

Centenary College	Hackettstown, NJ		07840-9989 (908) Ext 2241				centenarycollege.edu	
Economics Faculty	Division of Business		Fax=813-1984					
phone 852-1400								
Quade, Robert	C-Ac	852-1400	rquade	Mktg	MBA	53	Iowa	8-86
Dunham, Heather	Prof	852-1400	hdunham	ADEM	EDD	99	St Johns	8-84
Schomaker, Charles	Asst	852-1400	cschomaker	ADEM	MSBA		Indiana	8-00

Univ of Central Arkansas	Conway, AR		72035-0001 (501) 450-3109				mail.uca.edu	
Dept of Economics & Finance	College of Business Adm		Fax=450-5302				Barbara Hopp	
Cantrell, Pat	C-Ac	450-5333	pat		PHD	83	So Meth	8-84
Horton, Joseph J.	C-Pr	450-3106			PHD	68	So Meth	7-96
Bell, Jim	Prof	450-3109						
Johnson, W. Clint	Prof	450-3019			PHD	75	Tx Tech	1975
Kordsmeier, William F.	Assoc	350-3109			PHD	86	Tx A&M	
McGarrity, Joseph	Assoc	450-3109			PHD	94	GeoMason	8-95
Weller, Jim	Asst	450-3109						

Central Connecticut St Univ	New Britain, CT		06050-4010 (860) 832-2725				ccsu.edu	
Department of Economics	School of Arts & Sci		Fax=832-2730					
Higgins, June B.	Dean	832-2600	jhiggins	Psy	PHD	70	Rochester	1970
Pae, Ki-Tai	C-Pr	832-2725	pae	C	PHD	71	Conn	1971
Altieri, Paul L.	Prof	832-2735	altieri	E	PHD	76	Boston C	1975
Daigle, Ronald R.	Prof	832-2726	daigle	EG	PHD	75	Clark	1976
Kim, Ki Hoon	Prof	832-2727	kimk	FO	PHD	68	Conn	1967
Loughlin, James C.	Prof	832-2731	loughlin	DH	PHD	65	Clark	1968
Papathanasis, Anastasios	Prof	832-2733	papathanasis	LK	PHD	79	Ca-Davis	1984
Zottola, Armand J.	Prof	832-2732	zottola	JRT	PHD	70	Catholic	1970

Univ of Central Florida	Orlando, FL		32816-1400 (407) 823-3266				bus.ucf.edu	
Department of Economics	College of Business Adm		Fax=823-3269				Mrs. Frances Percival	
Homepage: www.bus.ucf.edu/economics								
Keon, Thomas L.	Dean	823-2181	tkeon	Mgt	PHD	79	Mich St	8-97
Hosni, Djehane	C-Ac	823-2069	djehane.hosni	O	PHD	78	Arkansas	1978
Dickie, Mark T.	Prof	823-4730	mark.dickie	Q	PHD	89	Wyoming	2001
Gerking, Shelby D.	Prof	823-4729	shelby.gerking	R	PHD	75	Indiana	2001
Hofler, Richard A.	Prof	823-2606	richard.hofler	CIJ	PHD	82	N Carol	1989
McHone, W. Warren	Prof	823-2629	warren.mchone	R	PHD	80	Penn	1982
Milon, J. Witter	Prof	823-1881	wmilon	Q	PHD	78	Fla St	2000
Rungeling, Brian S.	Prof	275-2592	brian.rungeling	J	PHD	69	Kentucky	1981
Braun, Bradley M.	Assoc	823-2343	brad.braun	D	PHD	86	Tulane	1986
Day, A. Edward	Assoc	823-2620	edward.day	D	PHD	76	Purdue	1983
Gibbs, W. Ernest	Assoc	823-5818	ernst.gibbs	D	PHD	87	Rutgers	1987
Hamilton, Steve	Assoc	823-4728	shamilton	Q	PHD	96	Berkeley	2001
Martin, Thomas L.	Assoc	823-5681	thomas.martin	B	PHD	81	Rice	1983
Pennington, Robert L.	Assoc	823-2886	robert.penning+	D	PHD	77	Tx A&M	1983
Soskin, Mark D.	Assoc	823-3266	mark.soskin	C	PHD	79	Penn St	1988
White, Kenneth R.	Assoc	823-5656	kenneth.white	C	PHD	71	Oklahoma	1968
Xander, James A.	Assoc	823-5657	james.xander	D	PHD	74	Georgia	1969
Anton, Wilma	Asst	823-4446	wilma.anton	Q	PHD	01	Illinois	2001
Bisakha, Sen	Asst	823-2232	bisakha.sen	J	PHD	98	Ohio St	1998
Elston, Julie Ann	Asst	823-2078	jelston	G	PHD	92	U Wash	1998
Finoff, David	Asst	823-4731	david.finoff	Q	PHD	91	Wyoming	2001
Lee, Junsoo	Asst	823-2070	jlee	E	PHD	91	Mich St	1998
Mikhail, Ossama	Asst	823-4258	ossama.mikhail	E	ABD		McGill	2001

Scrogin, David	Asst	823-4129	david.scrogin	Q	PHD	99	New Mex	2000
Tomlin, KaSaundra	Asst	823-2601	ktomlin	F	PHD	98	Oregon	1998
Euzent, Patricia	Inst	823-6075	peuzent	A	MA	82	Clemson	1991
Moore, Barbara	Inst	823-5256	bmoore	A	MAAE	97	Cen Fla	1988

Central College of Iowa Pella, IA 50219 (515) 628-5307 central.edu
Economics Faculty Dept Econ, Atg & Mgt Fax=628-5375

Iverson, Thomas	Prov	628-5175	iversont	Math	PHD	75	Claremont	1976
Vruwink, Carol J.	C-Pr	628-5258	vruwinkc		MS	82	Drake	1979
Glendening, Richard N.	Prof	628-5120	glendeningr	EFHO	PHD	93	Iowa St	1966
Wallace, Suzanne	Assoc	628-5318	wallaces	DJE	PHD	91	Georgia	1991

Central Michigan University Mt. Pleasant, MI 48859-2372 (517) 774-3870 cmich.edu
Department of Economics College of Business Adm Fax=774-2040 Debbie Clearwater

Schleede, John M.	Dean	774-7412	john.schleede	Mktg	PHD	78	Mich St	8-99
Shields, Michael P.	C-Pr	774-6460	michael.p.shi+	OJR	PHD	75	Utah	1993
Basu, Bharati	Prof	774-3730	b.basu	FODJ	PHD	82	Rochester	1990
Cecen, A. Aydin	Prof	774-3677	a.cecen		PHD	86	Indiana	1987
Chakraborty, Debasish	Prof	774-3678	d.chakraborty		PHD	87	Pittsburgh	1988
Falls, Gregory A.	Prof	774-3655	g.falls		PHD	82	Purdue	1981
Natke, Paul A.	Prof	774-3653	p.natke		PHD	82	Notre Dm	1981
Brunner, Lawrence P.	Assoc	774-3638	l.brunner		PHD	81	J Hopkins	1982
Clemmer, Richard B.	Assoc	774-3908	r.clemmer		PHD	81	Chicago	1982
Hill, James Richard	Assoc	774-3706	j.r.hill		PHD	80	Kentucky	1981
Barbour, G. Jeffrey	Asst	774-3380	j.barbour		PHD	73	Fla St	1971
Irwin, James R.	Asst	774-3697	j.irwin		PHD	86	Rochester	1989
McDevitt, Catherine L.	Asst	774-3648	c.mcdevitt		PHD	86	Rochester	1989
Youngil, Seon	Asst	774-3870	yongil.seon		PHD		Ca-SnDgo	2000
Zimmer, Basil G.	Asst	774-3600	b.zimmer		PHD	72	Rutgers	1969

Central Missouri State Univ Warrensburg, MO 64093-5074 (660) 543-4246 cmsu1.cmsu.edu
Dept of Economics & Finance Harmon College Bus Adm Fax=543-8465 Mrs. Nancy Dyer

Wilson, George W.	Dean	543-4560	gwilson		PHD	76	Okla St	1972
Engelmann, Paul H.	C-Pr	543-4246	engelmann		PHD	76	Okla St	1972
Brock, Baird A.	Prof	543-8614	brock		PHD	77	Arkansas	1969
Chambers, Paul	Prof	543-8610	pchambers		PHD	89	Kentucky	1990
Karscig, Mark P.	Prof	543-4817	karscig		PHD	87	Pittsburgh	1981
Andrews, Kim	Assoc	543-8597	andrews		PHD	94	Okla St	1990
Chambers, Catherine M.	Assoc	543-8605	chambers		PHD	90	Kentucky	1990
Swanson, James A.	Assoc	543-8580	swanson		PHD	87	Wash St	1986
Kugler, Penny L.	Inst	543-8570	kugler		MA	88	Cen Mo St	1988

Univ of Central Oklahoma Edmond, OK 73034-5209 (405) 974-5843 ucok.edu
Department of Economics College of Business Adm Fax=974-3853 Ofelia Tovar
Homepage: www.busn.ucok.edu/econ/

Metzger, Michael R.	C-Pr	974-5257	mmetzger	DIL	PHD	78	Stanford	1991
Maxwell, Don P.	Prof	974-5261	dmaxwell	ADEH	PHD	82	Okla St	1981
Shaaf, Mohammad	Prof	974-5326	mshaaf	BDEG	PHD	82	Tx Tech	1980
De los Santos, Tomas	Assoc	974-5256	tdelossantos	AEFO	PHD	88	Clark	1991
Hepner, Mickey A.	Asst	974-2829		HDJI				
Johnson, Joseph T.	Asst	974-5838	jjohnson	AMR	PHD	80	Chicago	1992
Zhu, Zhen	Asst	974-5287	zzhu	CFG	PHD	94	Michigan	1994

Central State Univ-Ohio Wilberforce, OH 45384 (937) 376-6441 csu.ccs.edu
Dept of Atg & Economics Col Business & Industry Fax=376-6206

Showell, Charles H. Jr.	Dean	376-6441		BAdm	PHD	75	Ohio St	9-88
Vafaie, Massie S.	C-As	376-6421			PHD	79	Cincinnati	1991
Iwomi, Peter O.	Assoc	376-6446			EDD		Cincinnati	1981

Central Washington Univ Ellensburg, WA 98926-7486 (509) 963-2664 cwu.edu
Department of Economics Sch of Business & Econ Fax=963-1992 Barbara Cook

Savoian, Roy T.	Dean	963-1955			PHD	79	Ca-SnBarb	1998
Carbaugh, Robert John	Prof	963-3443		AFEK	PHD	74	Colo St	1985
Cocheba, Donald John	Prof	963-2411		QR	PHD	71	Wash St	1970
Distinguished Professor, Research (1992)								
Mack, Richard Stanley	Prof	963-2663		RQP	PHD	72	Colo St	1972
Distinguished Professor, Research (1988)								
Saunders, Peter J.	Prof	963-1266		EHQ	PHD	81	Colorado	1988
Ghosh, Koushik	Assoc	963-1014			PHD		Wash St	
Hedrick, David W.	Assoc	963-2664		AIO	PHD	84	Oregon	1987
Elkins, Ron	Inst	963-1043						1996

Centre College — Danville, KY 40422-1394 (606) 238-5231 — centre.edu
Department of Economics — Div of Social Studies Fax=236-7925 — Shayne Jarman

Anderson, David A.	C-Ac	238-5260	david	ACHK	PHD	92	Duke	1992
Blazer Associate Professor of Economics								
Brownlee, Robert J.	Prof	238-5245	brownlee	AER	PHD	73	Syracuse	1978
Johnson, Bruce K.	Prof	238-5242	johnsonb	AD	PHD	85	Virginia	1987
James Graham Brown Professor of Economics								
Martin, Robert E.	Prof	238-5260	bmart	CD	PHD	79	So Meth	1996
Ewing T. Boles Professor of Economics								
Winrich, J. Steven	Prof	238-5237	winrich	APN	PHD	78	Kentucky	1981
Director of Institutional Research								
Michos, Leon	VAsst	238-5403			PHD	00	Clemson	2001
Edwards, Dennis	VInst	238-5256		AF	ABD		LSU	2000

Chadron State College — Chadron, NE 69337-2690 (308) 432-6290
Department Business & Econ — Sch Bus & Applied Sci Fax=432-6430 — Debby McDowell

Crouse, Margaret	Dean	432-6365		HEc	PHD	84	Okla St	1979
Anderson, Tim	C-Pr	432-6290			EDD		Nebraska	1977
Burke, Ronald L.	Prof	432-6290		MQE	PHD	70	Minnesota	1987
Swanke, Thomas A.	Asst	432-6290		B	PHD	93	Colorado	2001

Chaminade University — Honolulu, HI 96816-1578 (808) 735-6744 — chaminade.edu
Department of Economics — College of Business Fax=735-4734 — James Moses

Schroeder, Scott	Dean	739-4600			PHD			
Street, Barbara P.	Prof	377-5865		ACEI	PHD	86	Virginia	1981
Director, Master of Business Adminstration Program								

Chapman University — Orange, CA 92866 (714) 997-6684 — nexus.chapman.edu
Economics Faculty — Argyros Sch of Bus &Eco Fax=532-6081 — Donna Myers/Jennifer Freebury

Butler, Henry	Dean	997-6576		Fnce	PHD	82	Va Tech	7-01
Adibi, Esmael	Prof	997-6693	adibi	AEFC	PHD	80	Claremont	1978
Director, A. Gary Anderson Center for Economic Research; Anderson Chair								
Booth, Donald R.	Prof	997-6804	booth	AD	PHD	70	UCLA	1959
Broughton, John B.	Prof	997-6852	broughto	G	PHD	89	Va Tech	1993
Associate Dean								
Doti, James L.	Prof	997-6611	doti	AEC	PHD	76	Chicago	1974
President of the University								
Pierson, Lynne M.	Prof	997-6805	pierson	NE	PHD	78	Ca-Rivers	1972
Sfeir, Raymond	Prof	997-6551	sfeir	AC	PHD	82	Ca-SnBarb	1985

College of Charleston — Charleston, SC 29424-0001 (843) — cofc.edu
Dept of Economics & Finance — Sch of Business & Econ Fax=953-5697 — Ms. Barbara Green

Condon, Clarence M. III	Dean	953-5627	condonc		PHD	78	S Carol	1980
Morgan, J. Michael	C-Pr	953-8100	morganm		PHD	77	S Carol	1967
Clary, Betsy Jane	Prof	953-8107	claryb		PHD	81	Miss	1984
Hefner, Frank L.	Assoc	953-8100	hefnerf		PHD	88	Kansas	1995
Balaban, Rita	Asst	953-7166	balabanr	AI	PHD	00	Pittsburgh	2000
Blackwell, Calvin	Asst	953-7836	blackwellc		PHD	01	New Mex	2001
Snyder, Marcia	Inst	953-8100	snyderm		MA	95	London	1999

University of Chicago — Chicago, IL 60637-1561 (773) 702-9016 — chicago.edu
Economics Faculty — Department of Economics Fax=702-8490 — Marda J. Gross

Lucas, Robert E. Jr.	D-Pr	702-8179			PHD	64	Chicago	1974
John Dewey Distinguished Service Professor; 1995 Nobel Prize								
Hansen, Lars Peter	C-Pr	702-8170			PHD	78	Minnesota	1982
Homer J. Livingston Distinguished Service Professor								
Becker, Gary S.	Prof	702-8168			PHD	55	Chicago	1970
Nobel Prize 1992								
Bowman, Mary Jean	Emer				PHD	38	Harvard	1958
Chiappori, Pierre Andre	Prof				PHD	81	Paris	1997
Fogel, Robert W.	Prof	702-7709			PHD	63	J Hopkins	1981
Charles R. Walgreen Professor/Director, Center for Population Economics								
Friedman, Milton	Emer				PHD	46	Columbia	1946
Paul Snowden Russell Distinguished Service Professor Emeritus								
Galenson, David W.	Prof	702-8258			PHD	79	Harvard	1978
Haile, Philip	VProf				PHD	96	Nrthwstrn	2001
visiting from University of Wisconsin								
Harberger, Arnold C.	Emer				PHD	50	Chicago	1953
Gustavus F. and Ann M. Swift Distinguished Service Professor								
Heckman, James J.	Prof	702-0634			PHD	71	Princeton	1973
Henry Schultz Professor of Economics & Soc Sciences; 2000 Nobel Prize								
Johnson, D. Gale	Emer	702-8251			PHD	45	Iowa St	1944
Eliakim Hastings Moore Distinguished Service Professor								
Levitt, Steven D.	Prof	834-1862			PHD	94	MIT	1997
Myerson, Roger B.	Prof	834-9071			PHD	76	Harvard	2001

Sjaastad, Larry A.	Prof	702-8172			PHD	61	Chicago	1965
Sonnenschein, Hugo F.	Prof	834-5960			PHD	64	Purdue	
Charles L. Hutchinson Distringushed Service Professor								
Stokey, Nancy	Prof	702-0915			PHD	78	Harvard	1990
Frederick Henry Prince Professor								
Telser, Lester G.	Emer	702-8193		1-98	PHD	56	Chicago	1958
Tolley, George S.	Emer	702-8199			PHD	55	Chicago	1966
Townsend, Robert M.	Prof	702-8178			PHD	75	Minnesota	1985
Charles E. Merriam Professor								
Alvarez, Fernando	Assoc	702-4412			PHD	94	Minnesota	1996
Mulligan, Casey	Assoc	702-9017			PHD	93	Chicago	1993
Neal, Derek A.	VAsoc				PHD	92	Virginia	2001
visiting from University of Wisconsin								
Philipson, Tomas J.	Assoc	702-9128			PHD	89	Penn	1996
Campbell, Jeffrey	Asst	702-9014			PHD	95	Nrthwstrn	1999
Ghatak, Maintreesh	Asst	834-0887			PHD	96	Harvard	1996
Heller, Dana	Asst	834-3056			PHD	98	Stanford	1998
on leave 7-01 to 6-02								
Hortascu, Ali	Asst				PHD	01	Maryland	2001
Syvelson, Chad	Asst				PHD	01	Stanford	2001
Vissing-Jorgensen,	Asst	702-9127			PHD		MIT	1998
Yorukoglu, Mehmet	Asst	702-9015			PHD	96	Rochester	1996
Sanderson, Allen	SLect	702-9459			MA	70	Chicago	
Tsiang, Grace	SLect	702-3410			PHD	91	Chicago	1990

Chicago State University	Chicago, IL		60628-1598	(773) 995-2186				csu.edu
Dept Geog, Econ & Anthrop	Col of Arts & Sciences		Fax=995-2030					Janie Davis
Lindsey, Rachel L.	Dean	995-2105		Psyc	PHD	84	Chicago	1976
Bouman, Mark	C-Pr	995-2187	m-bouman		PHD	84	Minnesota	1984
Leach, Elroy M.	Prof	995-2173			PHD	85	Il-Chicago	1985
Pingkarawat, Nampeang	Prof	995-2340	man-ing		PHD	83	Il-Chicago	1982
Johnson, Mark A.	Assoc	995-2373	ma-johnson	J	PHD	85	Stanford	1995

Christian Brothers Univ	Memphis, TN		38104-5581	(901) 321-4222				cbu.edu
Dept of Economics & Finance	School of Business		Fax=321-3566					
Dukes, Thomas A.	Dean	321-3316	tdukes	Mktg	PHD	83	La Tech	2000
Kugele, Lynn P.	C-As	321-4222	lkugele	Fnce	PHD	98	Memphis	1998
Brittingham, Robert L.	Prof	321-3489	rbrittin	AD	PHD	73	St Louis	1989
Kamery, Rob H.	Prof	321-3414	rkamery	ABJ	MS	81	Arkansas	1987
Papachristou, Patricia T.	Prof	321-3301	ppapachr	TI	MBA	79	Memphis	1980
Bails, Dale G.	Assoc	321-3564	dbails		PHD	78	S Dakota	1995

Christopher Newport Univ	Newport News VA		23606-2988	(757) 594-7176				cnu.edu
Dept Econonics & Finance	School of Business		Fax=594-7808					Ms. Iris Price
Mottilla, Donna T.	Dean	594-7184	mottilla	Mgt	DBA	83	Kent St	1999
Booker, H. Marshall	Prof	594-7174	mbooker	AFMO	PHD	65	Virginia	1971
Park, Sang O.	Prof	594-7265	spark	DFOR	PHD	63	N Carol	1982
Colonna, Carl M.	Assoc	594-7144	ccolona	AEIR	MA		Old Dom	1970
Rahim, Niazur	Assoc	594-7727	nrahim		PHD	94	Va Comm	1998
Sen, Swapan	Assoc	594-7148	swap		PHD	91	Nebraska	1998
Vachris, Michelle A.	Assoc	594-7719	mvachris	DFHK	PHD	92	GeoMason	1994
Winder, Robert C.	Assoc	594-7176	rwinder		PHD	81	Rutgers	1991
Zestos, George K.	Assoc	594-7067	gzestos	CFHO	PHD	91	Indiana	1993

University of Cincinnati	Cincinnati, OH		45221-0371	(513) 556-2600				uc.edu
Department of Economics	McMicken Col Arts & Sci		Fax=556-2669					Geri Kirchner
Caruso, Joseph A.	Dean	556-5860	joseph.caruso	Chem	PHD	67	Mich St	
Herman, E. Edward	H-Pr$	556-2611	edward.herman	J	PHD	65	McGill	1966
Berry, Charles A.	Prof	556-2624	charles.berry	O	PHD	68	Cincinnati	1961
Gallo, Joseph C.	Prof	556-2605	joseph.gallo	L	PHD	69	Missouri	1967
Leftwich, Howard M.	Prof	556-2615	howard.leftw+	J	PHD	65	Illinois	1964
Coordinator of Labor & Employment Relations Program								
Mayer, Wolfgang	Prof	556-2618	wolfgang.mayer	FD	PHD	71	SUNY-Buf	1970
David Sinton Professor								
Vredeveld, George	Prof	556-2948	george.vrede+		PHD	73	Indiana	1977
Wellington, Donald C.	Prof	556-2607		D	PHD	66	Chicago	
Whitmore, Harland W. Jr.	Prof	556-2622	harland.whit+	E	PHD	69	Mich St	1967
Escoe, Gisela Meyer	Assoc	556-3023	gisela.escoe	O	PHD	91	Ohio St	1991
Goddard, Haynes C.	Assoc	556-2621	haynes.goddard	H	PHD	70	Indiana	
Kelton, Christina	Assoc	556-0525	chris.kelton		PHD	79	Wisconsin	1996
Director of Graduate Studies								
Mills, Jeffrey A.	Assoc	556-2619	jeffrey.mills	C	PHD	89	Wash U	1992
Pal, Debashis	Assoc	556-2630	debashis.pal	L	PHD	90	Florida	1994
Powers, John A.	Assoc	556-2616	john.powers	C	PHD	66	Purdue	1965
Way, Philip K.	Assoc	556-2613	philip.way	J	PHD	86	Warwick	1985
Williams, Nicolas	Assoc	556-2390	nicolas.will+	J	PHD	89	Nrthwstrn	1990
Zandvakili, Sourushe	Assoc	556-2629	sourushe.zand+	J	PHD	87	Indiana	1987

The Citadel Charleston, SC 29409-0215 (843) 953-5056 citadel.edu
Economics Faculty Dept of Business Adm Fax=953-6764 Ms. Georgeann Pringle
Did Not Respond--1999-2000 Listing; Mark rarely responds

Bebensee, Mark A.	H-Ac	953-5056	bebenseem		PHD	77	Duke	8-77
Sparks, Donald L.	Prof	953-5159	sparksd		PHD	85	London	8-86
Silver, Stephen J.	Assoc	953-5163	silvers		PHD	83	Maryland	8-90
Woolsey, W. William	Assoc	953-5161	woolseyw		PHD	86	GeoMason	8-86

CUNY-Baruch College New York, NY 10010 (212) 802-6350 cunyvm.cuny.edu
Dept of Economics & Finance Zicklin School of Bus Fax=802-6353 Sylvia Clark/Allison Davis

Lirtzman, Sidney I.	Dean	802-6550	Mgt	PHD	55	Columbia	1973
Wolf, Avner S.	C-Pr	802-6350		PHD	83	Columbia	
Gutmann, Peter M.	Prof	802-6366	EF	PHD	57	Harvard	1963
Joyce, Theodore	Prof	802-6964		PHD	85	CUNY	1986
Lustgarten, Steven	Prof	802-6420		PHD	71	UCLA	
Marty, Alvin L.	Prof	802-5726		PHD	55	Berkeley	1960
O'Neill, June E.	Prof			PHD	70	Columbia	1987
Director, Center for the Study of Business and Government							
Ross, Howard N.	Prof	802-6365		PHD	64	Columbia	1964
Stone, Irving	Prof	802-6369		PHD	62	Columbia	1962
Su, Vincent	Prof	802-6364		PHD	70	Rutgers	1971
Kleinberg, Norman L.	Assoc	802-6368		PHD	77	MIT	
Lee, Jae Won	Assoc	802-6360		PHD	69	CUNY	1972
Weiss, Jeffrey H.	Assoc	802-6357		PHD	81	Wisconsin	1981
Huckins, Larry E.	Asst	802-6381		PHD	83	Chicago	1980
Ma, Barry K.	Asst	802-6386		PHD	86	Stanford	1989
Pasupathy, Meenakshi	Asst	802-6378		PHD	96	Wash U	1996
Tansey, Francis B.	Lect	802-6356		MBA	65	CUNY	1967

CUNY-Brooklyn College Brooklyn, NY 11210-2889 (718) 951-5317 cunyvm.cuny.edu
Department of Economics College of Liberal Arts Fax=951-4867 Alycen Bray-Hughes

Arcadi, Antony	C-Ac	951-5317			MA	86	CUNY	1985
Bell, Robert	Prof	951-5686		M	PHD	72	Brunel	1986
Cherry, Robert D.	Prof	951-5264		AJ	PHD	69	Kansas	1977
Friedman, Hershey H.	Prof	951-5119		M	PHD	77	CUNY	1986
Laibman, David	Prof	951-5317		AP	PHD	73	New Sch	1967
Minars, David	Prof	951-5097			JD	70	NYU	1971
Sardy, Hyman	Prof	951-5326		C	PHD	63	New Sch	1957
Shoenthal, Edward R.	Prof	951-5568	edwards		PHD	85	NYU	1973
Solomon, Howard	Prof	951-5266			LLM	67	Brooklyn	1967
Arenberg, Yuri	Assoc	951-5245		D	PHD	86	NYU	1985
Davidoff, Howard	Assoc	951-5037			LLM	87	NYU	1986
Fox, Mark	Assoc	951-5569			PHD	98	Harvard	1989
Goldberg, Paul A.	Assoc	951-5101		HP	PHD	84	Columbia	1978
Klein, Yehuda L.	Assoc	951-4159		CDQ	PHD	85	Berkeley	1989
Lachman, Teddy	Assoc	951-5037			MBA	74	CUNY	1980
McTague, Edward	Assoc	951-5037			MBA	75	Fairl Dick	1982
Testa, Gary	Assoc	951-5548			MBA	78	St Johns	1978
Widman, Robert	Assoc	951-5266			MBA	73	Rutgers	1978
Zelcer, Moishe	Assoc	951-5245		G	PHD	91	Baruch	1977
Amoo, Taiwoo	Asst	951-5219			PHD	92	Exeter	1999
Bhattacharya, Anindya	Asst	951-5219			PHD	71	Columbia	1998
Giladi, Kroindal C	Asst	951-5264			MA	81	CUNY	1981
Langbert, Mitchell	Asst	951-5101			PHD	91	Columbia	1998
Thorne, Emanuel D.	Asst	951-5317		A	PHD	94	Yale	1989
Uctum, Merih	Asst	951-5097			PHD	89	Queens	1996

CUNY-City College New York, NY 10031 (212) 650-5404 cunyvm.cuny.edu
Economics Faculty Department of Economics Fax=650-6341
Did Not Respond--1999-2000 Listing

Farrell, Ronald A.	Dean	650-8156			PHD	72	Cincinnati	1997
Friedlander, Stanley	C-Pr	650-5403		DJ	PHD	64	MIT	1964
Chow, Peter	Prof	650-6206		O	PHD	76	S Illinois	1986
Galatin, Malcolm	Prof	650-6208		CE	PHD	65	MIT	1967
Greenwald, William	Prof	650-6211		CE	PHD	50	NYU	1946
Kellman, Mitchell	Prof	650-6203		DEF	PHD	72	Penn	1982
Klebaner, Benjamim	Prof	650-6212		E	PHD	52	Columbia	1947
Cakici, Nusret	Assoc	650-6204		G	PHD	89	Baruch	1997
Shachmurove, Yochanan	Assoc	650-6202		CEFG	PHD	83	Minnesota	1997
David, Byron	Asst	650-6210	bydcc	LM	PHD	90	CUNY	1994
Foster, Kevin	Asst	650-					Yale	1998
Louisy-Louis, Valerie	Asst	650-6207		MG	PHD	97	CUNY	
Weiner, Ross	Asst	650-6213		ADJL	PHD	99	Mass	1999
Jelen, Jonathan	Adj	650-6213		AM	PHD	92	PAU France	1977
Odoom, Charles	Adj	650-6201		AM			New Sch	1990
Portera, Kenneth	Adj	650-6213		AM			Pace	1979
Silver, Morris	Adj	650-6209		E	PHD	64	Columbia	1961
Weistock, Mark	Adj	650-6201		AM				

CUNY-Lehman College Bronx, NY 10468-1589 (718) 960-8297 cunyvm.cuny.edu
Economics Faculty Dept of Economics & Atg Fax=960-1173 Kim Pierce
Did Not Respond--1999-2000 Listing

Shreiber, Chanoch	C-Pr	960-8297		PHD	73	Columbia	
Cirace, John	Prof	960-8388		PHD	75	Columbia	
Sharav, Itzhak	Prof	960-8388		PHD	71	CUNY	9-67
Kayaalp, Orhan	Assoc	960-8598		PHD	84	CUNY	1979
Alexanderson, Peter	Asst	960-8598		JD			
Chatha, Jaspal	Asst	960-8461		PHD	85	New Sch	
DiLiberto, Maryann	Asst	960-8461		PHD	84	Columbia	
Fields, Judith M.	Asst	960-8384		PHD	84	NYU	1984
Honig, Susan	Asst	960-8389		MS		Pace	
Kamen, Michelle	Asst	960-8384		MBA		St Johns	
Kraus, James A.	Asst	960-8159		JD		Columbia	
Ratowsky, Henry	Asst	960-8507		PHD	76	CUNY	1988
Rios, Roberto J.	Asst	960-8461		PHD	87	Columbia	1979
Tauber, Linda	Asst	960-8389		MBA			
Chung, Kuk-Soo	Lect	960-8386		MA		Yale	
Rodriguez, Ada	Lect	960-8389		MBA			

CUNY-Hunter College New York, NY 10021 (212) 772-5400 cunyvm.cuny.edu
Department of Economics Sch of Arts & Sciences Fax=772-5398 J. Tyson/B. Saunders

Cohen, Ann H.	Dean	772-5121		PHD			8-98
Honig, Marjorie	C-Pr	772-5400	mahhc	PHD	71	Columbia	
Agbeyegbe, Terence	Prof	772-5405		PHD	83	Essex	1994
Chernick, Howard	Prof	772-5400		PHD	76	Penn	1982
Reimers, Cordella W.	Prof	772-5400		PHD	77	Columbia	1982
Filer, Randall K.	Assoc	772-5399		PHD	79	Princeton	1986
Golbe, Devra L.	Assoc	772-5408		PHD	79	NYU	1987
Goodspeed, Timothy J.	Assoc	772-5434		PHD	86	Maryland	9-94
McLaughlin, Kenneth J.	Assoc	772-5439		PHD	87	Chicago	9-94
Liveson, Avi O.	Asst	772-5394		LLM	75	NYU	9-86
Osborne, Theresa	Asst	772-5400		PHD	97	Princeton	9-97

CUNY-Queens College Flushing, NY 11367-0904 (718) 997-5440 qc1.qc.edu
Department of Economics School of Gen Studies Fax=997-5466 Ms. Barbara Crohn
email @1=qcvaxa.acc.qc.edu @2=cunyvm.cuny.edu @3=qc.edu

Scott, Donald	Dean							
Hill, M. Anne	C-Pr	997-5440	mah$econ	JC	PHD	80	Duke	1989
Edelstein, Michael	Prof	997-5455		NOF	PHD	70	Penn	1974
Franklin, Raymond S.	Emer	997-5204		JBP	PHD	66	Berkeley	1966
Gram, Harvey H.	Prof	997-5448	har$econ	FCE	PHD	73	Wisconsin	1974
Kaufmann, Hugo M.	Prof	997-5449	kaufmann@1	FE	PHD	68	Columbia	1967
Levenson, Albert M.	Emer	997-5444	albert_leve+@3	DFC	PHD	59	Columbia	1961
Lipsey, Robert E.	Emer	997-5443	relqc@2	FC	PHD	61	Columbia	1967
Riskin, Carl A.	Prof	997-5454	riskin@1	POQ	PHD	69	Berkeley	1974
Roistacher, Elizabeth A.	Prof	997-5453	elizabeth_ro+@3	RH	PHD	72	Penn	1974
Tabb, William K.	Prof	997-5451	wta$econ	RO	PHD	68	Wisconsin	1971
Thurston, Thom B.	Prof	997-5457	tbt$econ	EC	PHD	70	Berkeley	1971
Devereux, John J.	Assoc	997-5446	jdevereu	DFO	PHD	89	Chicago	1998
Dohan, Michael R.	Assoc	997-5464	dohan@1	PQ	PHD	69	MIT	1971
Field-Hendrey, Elizabeth	Assoc	997-5456	efh$econ	NJC	PHD	85	Duke	1989
Gabel, David J.	Assoc	997-5452	davidgabel@a	DNC	PHD	87	Wisconsin	1987
Nix, Joan	Assoc	997-5447	nix$econ	DG	PHD	89	NYU	1988
Solon, Babette S.	Emer	997-5445	sbo$econ	DJ	PHD	58	MIT	1961
Feliciano, Zadia M.	Asst	997-5440	zadia_felic+@3	JFN	PHD	95	Harvard	1994
Chiremba, Daniel S.	Lect	997-3142		O	MA	69	New Sch	1969

CUNY-Col of Staten Island Staten Isl, NY 10314 (718) 982-2900 postbox.csi.cuny.edu
Economics Faculty Dept Pol Sci,Econ &Phil Fax=982-2888 Patricia Burmmeister

Petratos, Vasilios	C-Ac	982-2903	BF	PHD	70	NYU	1974
Schwarz, Samuel	Prof	982-2897	KC	PHD	78	Columbia	1986
Meltzer, Yale L.	Asst	982-2896	EG	MBA	66	NYU	1983
Osakue, John U.	Asst	982-2898	FO	PHD	80	Nebraska	1991
Wegge, Simone	Asst	982-2897	JN	PHD	97	Nrthwstrn	
White, Mark D.	Asst	982-3193	C	PHD	97	Cincinnati	1993

Claremont McKenna College Claremont, CA 91711-6400 (909) 607-9597 claremontmckenna.edu
Economics Faculty Department of Economics Fax=621-8249 Polly Baker

Ascher, William	Dean	621-8117	wascher	PHD	75	Yale	2000
Smith, Janet K.	C-Pr	607-3276	janet.smith	PHD	80	UCLA	1996
Arndt, Sven W.	Prof	621-8012	sven.arndt	PHD	64	Berkeley	1990
Charles M. Stone Professor of Money, Credit & Trade							
Bjork, Gordon C.	Prof	607-3625	gordon.bjork	PHD	63	U Wash	1975
Jonathan B. Lovelace Professor							
Burdekin, Richard C. K.	Prof	607-2884	richard.burdekin	PHD	85	Houston	1989

Mulherin, Harold	Prof	607-3141	harold.mulherin		PHD	84	UCLA	2001
Stubblebine, William Craig	Prof	621-8012			PHD	63	Virginia	1966
Teeples, Ronald K.	Prof	607-2964	ron.teeples		PHD	70	UCLA	1969
Boswell Professor of Economics								
Willett, Thomas D.	Prof	621-8012	tom.willett		PHD	67	Virginia	1977
Horton Professor of Economics								
Wright, Colin	Prof	607-3003	colin.wright		PHD	66	Chicago	1977
Norwood and Frances Berger Professor of Business & Soc								
Brown, William O.	Assoc	607-3064	william.brown		PHD	93	Clemson	1994
Helland, Eric	Assoc	607-2654	eric.helland		PHD	95	U Wash	1998
Keil, Manfred W.	Assoc	607-3899	manfred.keil	ECJA	PHD	85	LondonEc	7-95
Antecol, Heather	Asst	607-7140	heather.antecol	JIG	PHD	99	McMaster	
Harbaugh, Richard	Asst	607-7363	rick.harbaugh		PHD	97	Pittsburgh	1999
Ward-Batts, Jennifer	Asst	607-2800	jennifer.ward+		PHD	99	U Wash	
Weidenmier, Marc	Asst	607-8497	marc.weidenmier		PHD	99	Illinois	1999

Clarion Univ of Pennsylvania — Clarion, PA 16214-1232 (814) 393-2627 — clarion.edu
Department of Economics — College of Business Fax=393-1910 — Sharon Bauer
Homepage: www.clarion.edu/econ

Pesek, James G.	Dean$	393-2600	pesek	AdSc	PHD	84	Pittsburgh	8-80
Balough, Robert S.	C-Pr	393-2627	balough		PHD	81	N Illinois	1981
Haggerty, Mark E.	Prof	393-2614	haggerty		PHD	88	Wash St	1989
Sanders, William V.	Prof	393-2623	sanders		PHD	81	Penn St	1981
Sohng, Soong Nark	Prof	393-2632	sohng		PHD	82	Wayne St	1981
Stine, William F.	Prof	393-2612	stine		PHD	83	Fordham	1981
Yang, Chin-Wei	Prof	393-2609	yang	DFHR	PHD	79	W Virginia	1981
Raehsler, Rod D.	Assoc	393-2630	raehsler		PHD	93	Iowa	
Smith, Lynn A.	Assoc	393-2633	lsmith		PHD	85	Pittsburgh	1989
Woodburne, Paul	Asst	1965	pwoodburne		PHD	99	Ca-Rivers	1998

Clark University — Worcester, MA 01610-1477 (508) 793-7226 — vax.clarku.edu
Economics Faculty — Department of Economics Fax=793-8849 — Ms. Cindy Rice
Homepage: www.clarku.edu/departments/econ

Gray, Wayne B.	C-Ac	793-7693	wgray		PHD	83	Harvard	1984
Hsu, Robert C.	Prof	793-7281	rhsu		PHD	70	Berkeley	1971
Ott, Attiat F.	Prof	793-7447	aott		PHD	62	Michigan	1969
Director, Institute for Economic Studies								
Puffer, Frank W.	Prof	793-7228	fpuffer		PHD	68	Brown	1968
Veendorp, Emiel C.	Prof	793-7101			PHD	63	Rice	1976
Weinrobe, Maurice D.	Prof	793-7248	mweinrobe		PHD	69	Cornell	1976
Bernhofen, Daniel	Assoc	793-7185	dbernhofen		PHD	94	Syracuse	1994
Brown, John C.	Assoc	793-7390	jbrown		PHD	86	Michigan	1986
Geoghegan, Jacqueline	Asst	793-7709	jgeoghegan		PHD	95	Berkeley	1996

Clark Atlanta University — Atlanta, GA 30314-4391 (404) 880-6273 — sbus.cau.edu
Department of Economics — School of Business Fax=880-6276 — Gwen Donaway

Davis, Edward L.	Dean	880-8454	edavis	Mgt	PHD	77	N Car St	9-80
Bezuneh, Mesfin	C-Ac	880-6274			PHD	85	Va Tech	
Carter, Charlie	Assoc	880-6288			PHD	75	Illinois	
Nyomba, Ajamu	Asst	880-6286			PHD	91	Tx-Austin	
Yiheyis, Zelealm	Asst	880 6289			PHD			
Dadzie, Frank	Lect	880-6287			MA			

Clarkson University — Potsdam, NY 13699-5785 (315) 268-2300 — clarkson.edu
Faculty of Economics — School of Business Fax=268-3810 — Fran Nelson
Homepage: www.som.clarkson.edu

Sugrue, Timothy F.	Dean	268-2300	tsugrue	Fnce	PHD	85	Mass	2000
Atesoglu, H. Sonmez	Prof	268-7981		EFO	PHD	72	Pittsburgh	1977
Menz, Fredric C.	Prof	268-6427		HQD	PHD	70	Virginia	1974
Mullen, John K.	Prof	268-4283		GHR	PHD	78	SUNY-Bin	1977
Frascatore, Mark	Assoc	268-3850		DL	PHD	94	Va Tech	1994
Boyer, Carol	Asst	268-3890		GM	PHD	00	Fla St	2000
MacDonald, John A.	Asst	268-3870		GM	PHD	87	Va Tech	1995
Siqueira, Kevin	Asst	268-6609		HD	PHD	98	Iowa St	1999

Clayton College & St Univ — Morrow, GA 30260-0285 (770) 961-3410 — mail.clayton.edu
Economics Faculty — School of Business Fax=961-0801 — Carol Leavell

Miller, Ernest M. (Bud)	Dean	961-3410	ernestmiller		MBA	70	Harvard	1998
Arjomand, H. Lari	Prof	961-3417	lariarjomand		PHD	80	Oklahoma	1980
Haberland, Chris	Asst	961-3729	chrishaberland		MBA	76	Geo St	1987

Clemson University Clemson, SC 29634-1309 (864) 656-3481 clemson.edu
Department of Economics Col Business & Beh Sci Fax=656-4192 Laura Cobb
Homepage: www.clemson.edu/economics

Trapnell, Jerry E.	Dean	656-3177	trapnel	Atg	PHD	77	Georgia	1986
Dougan, William R.	C-Pr	656-3497	douganw	HDEL	PHD	81	Chicago	1988
Benjamin, Daniel K.	Prof	656-3964	wahoo	DEGJ	PHD	75	UCLA	1985
Lindsay, Cotton M.	Prof	656-3955	lindsay	DHJK	PHD	68	Virginia	1984
J. Wilson Newman Professor								
Maloney, Michael T.	Prof	656-3430	maloney	DGKL	PHD	78	LSU	1974
McCormick, Robert E.	Prof	656-3441	sixmile	DGKH	PHD	78	Tx A&M	1982
Thompson, G. Richard	Prof	656-0946	tg	HLM	PHD	72	Virginia	1983
Wallace, Myles S.	Prof	656-3965	myles	EFC	PHD	76	Colorado	1980
Warner, John T.	Prof	656-3967	jtwarne	DJE	PHD	76	N Car St	1980
Gordon, David B.	Assoc	656-3956	gd	DE	PHD	95	Chicago	1992
Placone, Dennis L.	Assoc	656-3951	dlplc	FPH	PHD	82	Pittsburgh	1976
Simon, Curtis J.	Assoc	656-3966	cjsmn	JOR	PHD	85	SUNY-Bin	1985
Tamura, Robert F.	Assoc	656-1242	rtamura	IJO	PHD	88	Chicago	1996
Baier, Scott L.	Asst	656-3481	sbaier	FED	PHD	96	Mich St	2001
Hakes, Jahn K.	Asst	656-3481	jhakes	HQC	PHD	96	Duke	1999

Cleveland State University Cleveland, OH 44115 (216) 687-4520 csuohio.edu
Department of Economics College of Arts & Sci Fax=687-9206 Mrs. Joan A. Tucker

Steckol, Karen F.	Dean	687-3660	k.steckol		PHD	78	Memphis	1996
Harford, Jon D.	C-Ac	687-4524	j.harford	DHKQ	PHD	74	Stanford	1982
Mathur, Vijay K.	Prof	687-4526	v.mathur	DR	PHD	69	Wayne St	1968
Bell, Edward B.	Assoc	687-4519	e.bell	DHJ	PHD	73	Ohio St	1971
Chang, Myong-Hun	Assoc	687-4523	m.chang	LDMN	PHD	89	J Hopkins	1988
Stein, Sheldon H.	Assoc	687-4537	s.stein	CER	PHD	78	J Hopkins	1976
Stewart, Douglas O.	Assoc	687-4515	d.o.stewart	DH	PHD	74	Michigan	1972
Taub, Allan J.	Assoc	687-4528	a.taub	CD	PHD	73	Nrthwstrn	1971

Coe College Cedar Rapids, IA 52402 (319) 399-8619 coe.edu
Economics Faculty Dept of Bus Adm & Econ Fax=399-8030 Ms. Ann Zeal

Carstens, Pamela J.	C-Pr	399-8690	pcarsten		PHD	93	Iowa	1985
Wu, Mickey Tai Chuen	Prof	359-8727	mwu	ACEF	PHD	79	Kentucky	1979
George R. Baker Professor of Economics and Business Administration								
Berri, David	Asst	399-8714		BD	PHD	97	Colo St	1998
Eichhorn, Richard	Asst	399-8862	eichhorn	CE	PHD	99	Colo St	2000

Colby College Waterville, ME 04901-8852 (207) 872-3564 colby.edu
Economics Faculty Economic Department Fax=872-3263 Dianne Labrec
Homepage: www.colby.edu/economics

Donihue, Michael R.	C-Ac	872-3115	mrdonihu	CEA	PHD	89	Michigan	1989
Findlay, David W.	Prof	872-3153	dwfindla	EGA	PHD	86	Purdue	1985
Dana Professor								
Franko, Patrice	Prof	872-3347	pmfranko	FAO	PHD	86	Notre Dm	1986
Gemery, Henry A.	Prof	878-3137	hagemery	NAB	PHD	67	Penn	1961
Pugh Family Professor of Economics								
Hogendorn, Jan S.	Prof	872-3142	jshogend	FOA	PHD	66	London	1966
Grossman Professor of Economics								
Meehan, James W.	Prof	872-3136	jwmeehan	DM	PHD	67	Boston C	1973
Herbert E. Wadsworth Professor of Economics								
Nelson, Randy A.	Prof	872-3567	ranelson	GM	PHD	79	Illinois	1987
Douglas Professor of Economics								
Reid, Clifford E.	Prof	872-3116	cereid	DCHR	PHD	73	Princeton	1987
Dana Professor								
Tietenberg, Thomas H.	Prof	872-3143	thtieten	QK	PHD	71	Wisconsin	1977
Mitchell Family Professor of Economics								
Barbezat, Debra A.	Assoc	872-3154	dabarbez	JIA	PHD	85	Michigan	1992
Mansori, Kashif	Asst	872-3563	kmansori	EF	PHD	97	Princeton	1997

Colgate University Hamilton, NY 13346 (315) 228-7533 mail.colgate.edu
Economics Faculty Economics Department Fax=228-7033 Ginger Irwin

Tiefenthaler, Jill M.	C-Ac	228-7523	tiefenthaler	TO	PHD	91	Duke	1991
Haines, Michael R.	Prof	228-7536	mhaines	TN	PHD	71	Penn	1990
Banfi Vintners Professor of Economics								
Kato, Takao	Prof	228-7562	tkato	J	PHD	86	Queen's	1986
Mandle, Jay R.	Prof	228-7540	jmandle	ON	PHD	69	Penn	
W. Bradford Wiley Professor of Economics								
Michl, Thomas R.	Prof	228-7526	tmichl	EJ	PHD	84	New Sch	1983
Pinchin, Hugh M.	Prof	228-7539	hpinchin	F	PHD	70	Yale	1965
Turner, Robert W.	Prof	228-7529	rturner	CH	PHD	84	MIT	1983
Waldman, Don E.	Prof	228-7535	dwaldman	L	PHD	76	Cornell	1981
Richard M. Kessler Professor of Economic Studies								
Baldani, Jeffrey P.	Assoc	228-7519	jbaldani	CD	PHD	83	Cornell	1982
Grapard, Ulla A.	Assoc	228-7538	ugrapard	AB	PHD	90	Cornell	1985

Khanna, Jyoti	Assoc	228-7527	jkhanna	H	PHD	90	Iowa	1992
Rask, Kevin N.	Assoc	228-7524	krask	QI	PHD	91	Duke	1991
Ghosh, Sudeep	VAsst	228-7241	sghosh	D	PHD	01	Iowa	2001
Jubinski, Dan	Asst	228-7541	djubinski	G	PHD	01	Virginia	2001
Long, Cheryl	Asst	228-7955	clong	K	PHD	01	Wash U	2001
Simpson, Nicole B.	Asst	228-7991	nsimpson	E	PHD	01	Iowa	2001
Sturges, David M.	Asst	228-8795	dsturges	EG	PHD	94	Yale	1995
Tomljanovich, Marc	Asst	228-7537	mtomljanovich	E	PHD	00	Cornell	2000

The Colorado College Colorado Spr, CO 80903 (719) 389-6407 cc.colorado.edu
Economics Faculty Economics Department Fax=389-6927 C. Antonuccio/S. Fuller

Redmount, Esther R.	C-Ac	389-6412	eredmount		PHD	85	Virginia	1987
Bird, Michael C.	Prof	389-6445	mbird		PHD	68	Colorado	1968
Griffiths, L. Christopher	Prof	389-6417	cgriffiths		PHD	70	Colorado	1967
Hecox, Walter E.	Prof	389-6413	whecox		PHD	69	Syracuse	1970
Rittenberg, Libby T.	Prof	389-6410	lrittenberg		PHD	80	Rutgers	1989
Weida, William J.	Prof	389-6409			DBA	75	Colorado	1985
Anna, Alexandra	Assoc	389-6654	aaanna		PHD	95	Utah	2001
Kapuria-Foreman, Vibha	Assoc	389-6419	vkapuria		PHD	87	Pittsburgh	1989
Smith, Mark G.	Assoc	389-6411	msmith		PHD	87	Duke	1988

Univ of Colorado at Boulder Boulder, CO 80309-0256 (303) 735-5500 colorado.edu
Department of Economics College of Arts & Sci Fax=492-8960 Lenora Oliva 492-5168
Homepage: www.colorado.edu/economics

Spear, Petear	Dean	492-7294	peter.spear	Psy	PHD	70	Yale	1996
Maskus, Keith E.	C-Pr	492-7588	keith.maskus		PHD	81	Michigan	1981
Carlos, Ann M.	Prof	492-8737	ann.carlos		PHD	80	W Ontario	1990
Glahe, Fred R.	Prof	492-5186	fred.glahe		PHD	64	Purdue	1965
Greenwood, Michael J.	Prof	492-7413	michael.greenw+		PHD	67	Nrthwstrn	1980
Howe, Charles W.	Prof	492-7245	charles.howe		PHD	59	Stanford	1970
Hsiao, Frank S. T.	Prof	492-7908	frank.hsiao		PHD	67	Rochester	1975
Kaempfer, William H.	Prof	492-4486	william.kaempfer		PHD	79	Duke	1981
Lillydahl, Jane H.	Prof	492-4599	jane.lillydahl		PHD	76	Duke	1976
Markusen, James R.	Prof	492-0748	james.markusen		PHD	73	Boston C	1990
Director, Carl McGuire Center for International Studies								
McNown, Robert F.	Prof	492-8295	robert.mcnown		PHD	71	Ca-SnDgo	1971
Morey, Edward R.	Prof	492-6898	edward.morey		PHD	78	Brit Colum	1980
Poulson, Barry W.	Prof	492-7414	barry.poulson		PHD	65	Ohio St	1965
Roper, Don E.	Prof	492-7466	donald.roper		PHD	70	Chicago	1985
Singell, Larry D.	Prof	492-1809	larry.singell		PHD	65	Wayne St	1968
Waldman, Donald M.	Prof	492-6781	donald.waldman		PHD	79	Wisconsin	1984
Zax, Jeffrey S.	Prof	492-8268	jeffrey.zax		PHD	84	Harvard	1990
deBartolome, Charles	Assoc	492-4464	charles.debar+		PHD	85	Penn	1993
Rutherford, Thomas F.	Assoc	492-5169			PHD	87	Stanford	1995
Boileau, Martin	Asst	492-2108	martin.bioleau		PHD	94	Queen's	1998
Canals-Cerda, Jose	Asst	492-7869	jose.canals-c+		PHD	98	Virginia	
Chen, Yongmin	Asst	491-8736	yongmin.chen		PHD	92	Boston U	1996
Flores, Nicholas E.	Asst	492-8145	nicholas.flores		PHD	95	Ca-SnDgo	1995
Iyigun, Murat	Asst	492-6653	murat.iyigun		PHD	95	Brown	2000
Janeba, Eckhard	Asst	492-3021	edkhard.janeba		PHD	94	Bonn	
Robles, Jack	Asst	492-7407	jack.robles		PHD	96	Ca-SnDgo	1996
Rubinchik-Pessarh, Anna	Asst	735-0220			PHD	01	Penn	2001
Walsh, Randall	Asst	492-4599	randall.walsh		PHD	01	Duke	2001

U of Colorado at Co Springs Colorado Spr, CO 80933-7150 (719) 262-4018 mail.uccs.edu
Department of Economics Letters, Arts, & Sci Fax=262-4558 Petrina Mazza
Homepage: www.uccs.edu/~economics/index.html

Grobsmith, Elizabeth	Dean	262-4550		Antr	PHD			1986
DeBoer, Dale	C-Ac	262-4032		DFO	PHD	93	Ca-Davis	1993
Ballantyne, A. Paul	Prof	262-4002		ABEO	PHD	65	Stanford	1967
Greenwood, Daphne T.	Prof	262-4031		HJT	PHD	80	Oklahoma	1980
Brock, John R. Jr.	VAsoc	262-4033		DHKL	PHD	88	Cornell	1998
Eubanks, Larry S.	Assoc	262-4003		DHQ	PHD	80	Wyoming	1986

Univ of Colorado at Denver Denver, CO 80217-3364 (303) 556-4413 carbon.cudenver.edu
Dept of Economics, CB 181 Col Liberal Arts & Sci Fax=556-3547 Lynn Ferguson, Prof Asst
Homepage: econ.cudenver.edu

Smith, W. James	Dean	556-2557	jsmith		PHD	76	Colorado	
Mocan, Naci H.	C-Pr	556-8540	nmocan	CJI	PHD	89	CUNY	1990
Helburn, Suzanne W.	Emer	556-8305		BI	PHD	61	Indiana	1970
Hsiao, Mei-chu W.	Prof	556-8322	mhsiao	OC	PHD	67	Rochester	1981
Medema, Steven G.	Prof	556-8511	smedema	BHDK	PHD	89	Mich St	1989
Morris, John R. Jr.	Emer	556-2570		BI	PHD	66	Purdue	1970
Argys, Laura M.	Assoc	556-3949	largys	IOCD	PHD	93	Colorado	1990
Beckman, Steven R.	Assoc	556-3048	sbeckman	F	PHD	82	Ca-Davis	1988
Bramhall, David F.	Emer				PHD	61	Penn	

Rees, Daniel I.	Assoc	556-3348	drees	J	PHD	92	Cornell	1993
Zheng, Buhong	Assoc	556-8375	bzheng	O	PHD	93	W Virginia	1995
Duncan, Brian	Asst	556-6763	bduncan	HC	PHD	98	Ca-SnBarb	1998
Emerson, Patrick	Asst	556-3950	pemerson		PHD	00	Cornell	
Knabb, Shawn	Asst	352-3697			PHD	01	Ca-SnBarb	

Colorado State University Fort Collins, CO 80523-1771 (970) 491-6566 colostate.edu
Department of Economics Col of Liberal Arts Fax=491-2925 Barbara Alldredge
Homepage: www.colostate.edu/depts/econ

Hoffert, Robert	Dean$	451-5421	robert.hoffert	PolS	PHD	74	Cornell	
Phillips, Ronnie J.	C-Pr	491-6079	ronnie.phillips	GB	PHD	80	Tx-Austin	1983
Cochrane, Harold	Prof	491-6653	harold.cochrane	EA	PHD	75	Colorado	1975
Cutler, Harvey	Prof	491-5704	harvey.cutler	EC	PHD	85	U Wash	1980
Fan, Chuen-mel	Prof	491-5438	chuenmel.fan	HD	PHD	72	Minnesota	1978
Fan, Liang-Shing	Prof	491-5336	liangshing.fan	AOF	PHD	65	Minnesota	1968
Keller, Robert R.	Prof	491-5679	robert.keller	EN	PHD	71	Wisconsin	1974
Driector, Honor's Program								
Ozawa, Terutomo	Prof	491-6076	terutomo.ozawa	FO	PHD	66	Columbia	1974
Shulman, Steven J.	Prof	491-6940	steven.shulman	JKEI	PHD	84	Mass	1984
Stanfield, James Ronald	Prof	491-6891	ronald.stanfield	BA	PHD	72	Oklahoma	1976
Bernasek, Alexandra	Assoc	491-6856	alexandra.ber+	DA	PHD	92	Michigan	1992
Jianakoplos, Nancy A.	Assoc	491-6537	nancy.jianak+	CE	PHD	83	Ohio St	1990
Kling, Robert W.	Assoc	491-6566	robert.kling	DQ	PHD	85	Kansas	1984
Nickerson, David	Assoc	491-5249	david.nickerson	G	PHD	81	Nrthwstrn	2001
Revier, Charles F.	Assoc	491-2929	charles.revier	EH	PHD	78	MIT	1974
Weiler, Stephan	Assoc	491-3883	stephen.weiler	RO	PHD	94	Berkeley	1996
Mushinski, David	Asst	491-3911	david.mushinski	CHO	PHD	96	Wisconsin	1997

Columbia University New York, NY 10027-6989 (212) 854-8057 columbia.edu
Div of Finance & Economics School of Business Fax=316-9219 Shawn M. Patenaude
Homepage: www.columbia.edu/cu/economics

Feldberg, Meyer	Dean	854-6083			PHD	69	Capetown	1989
Edwards, Franklin R.	C-Pr	854-4202	fre1		PHD	64	Harvard	1966
Arthur F. Burns Professor of Free and Competitive Enterprise								
Bagwell, Kyle W.	Prof	854-5890	kwb8	LF	PHD	86	Stanford	1996
Bartel, Ann	Prof	854-4419	apb2		PHD	74	Columbia	1976
A. Barton Hepbum Professor of Economics								
Donaldson, John B.	Prof	854-4436	jd34		PHD	76	Car Mellon	1977
Mario J. Gabelli Professor of Finance								
Greenwald, Bruce C. N.	Prof	854-3491	bg7		PHD	78	MIT	1991
Robert Heilbrunn Professo of Finance and Asset Management								
Heal, Geoffrey M.	Prof	854-6084	gmh1		PHD	68	Cambridge	1983
Paul Garett Professor of Public Policy and Business Responsibility								
Hodrick, Robert	Prof	854-3492	rh169		PHD	96	Chicago	1996
Nomure Professor of International Finance								
Hubbard, R. Glenn	Prof	854-3493	rgh1	HEG	PHD	83	Harvard	1988
Russell L. Carson Professor of Finance and Economics								
Lichtenberg, Frank R.	Prof	854-4408	frl1		PHD	82	Penn	1983
Courtney C. Brown Professor of Business								
Mishkin, Frederic S.	Prof	854-3488	fsm3		PHD	76	MIT	1983
Alfred Lerner Professor of Banking and Financial Institutions								
Noam, Eli	Prof	854-4596	emn1		PHD	75	Harvard	1976
Patrick, Hugh T.	Prof	854-3497	hp1		PHD	60	Michigan	1984
R. D. Calkins Professor of International Business								
Riordan, Michael H.	Prof	854-9152	mhr21	DLG	PHD	81	Berkeley	1999
Sicherman, Nachum	Prof	854-4464	ns38		PHD	87	Columbia	1991
Siconolfi, Paolo	Prof	854-3474	ps17		PHD	87	Penn	1989
Wilkinson, Maurice	Prof	854-4481	mw16		PHD	65	Harvard	1965
Zeldes, Stephen P.	Prof	854-2492	spz1		PHD	84	Brown	1996
Benjamin Rosen Professor of Finance and Economics								
Gentry, William M.	Assoc	854-5092	wmg6		PHD	91	Princeton	1995
Himmelberg, Charles P.	Assoc	854-2622	cph15	DEL	PHD	90	Nrthwstrn	1995
Boivin, Jean	Asst	854-9091	jb903		PHD	99	Princeton	1999
Carrillo, Juan	Asst	854-8057			PHD			2001
Fisman, Raymond	Asst	854-9157	rf250		PHD	98	Harvard	1999
Thomadsen, Raphael	Asst	854-4708	rct27		PHD		Stanford	2000
Willard, Kristen L.	Asst	854-4438	klw12	DFH	PHD	94	Princeton	9-94

Columbia University New York, NY 10027-6989 (212) 854-3680 columbia.edu
Department of Economics College of Arts & Sci Fax=854-8059 Angela Reid
Homepage: www.columbia.edu/cu/economics

Clarida, Richard	C-Pr	854-3682	rhc2	FE	PHD	83	Harvard	1988
Bhagwati, Jagdish	Prof	854-6297	jb38	F	PHD	67	MIT	1980
Casella, Alessandra	Prof	854-2459	ac186	EF	PHD	88	MIT	1983
Davis, Donald R.	Prof	854-4037	drd28	F	PHD	92	Columbia	1999
Desai, Padma	Prof	854-2266	pd5	O	PHD	60	Harvard	1980
Dhrymes, Phoebus	Prof	854-4459	pjd1	B	PHD	61	MIT	1973

Dutta, Prajit	Prof	854-4742	pkd1	DLG	PHD	87	Cornell	1992
Ericson, Richard	Prof	854-5124	ree3	O	PHD	79	Berkeley	1985
Findlay, Ronald	Prof	854-3674	ref2	FB	PHD	60	MIT	1970
Mundell, Robert	Prof	854-3669	ram15	EF	PHD	56	MIT	1974
Phelps, Edmund	Prof	854-2060	esp2	EG	PHD	59	Yale	1971
Sala-i-Martin, Xavier	Prof	854-7055	xs23	OE	PHD	90	Harvard	1996
Weinstein, David E.	Prof	854-6880	dew35	F	PHD	91	Michigan	1999
Wellisz, Stanislaw	Prof	854-8033	sw11	O	PHD	54	Harvard	1964
Idson, Todd	Assoc	854-4067	ti18	CJ	PHD	86	Columbia	1990
O'Flaherty, Brendan	Assoc	854-2449	bo2	RA	PHD	80	Harvard	1987
Rivera-Batiz, Francisco L.	Assoc	854-4478	flr9	FOJ	PHD	79	MIT	1991
Abdulkadiroglu, Atila	Asst	854-3680			PHD	01	Rochester	2001
Amarante, Massimiliano	Asst	854-5488	ma734	C	PHD	99	MIT	1999
Cameron, Stephen	Asst	854-4818	sc337	JC	PHD	93	Chicago	1994
Chaudhuri, Shubham	Asst	854-4661	sc301	HOD	PHD	93	Princeton	1994
Das, Mitali	Asst	854-4641	md448	CIG	PHD	98	MIT	1998
Dehijia, Rajeev	Asst	854-4659	rd247	JCD	PHD	97	Harvard	1998
Edlund, Lena	Asst	854-4513	le93	HIT	PHD	96	Stockholm	1999
Henry, Marc	Asst	854-3690	mh530	CIG	PHD	98	LondonEc	1998
Kockesen, Levent	Asst	854-2512	lk290	DB	PHD	99	NYU	1999
Leonard, Kenneth	Asst	854-4092	kl206	9D	PHD	97	Berkeley	1997
Madajewicz, Margaret	Asst	854-4561	mm1174	BOM	PHD	99	Harvard	1999
Miller, Ronald	Asst	854-5713	rm170	EO	PHD	94	Princeton	1994
Miyagawa, Eiichi	Asst	854-3926	em347	DH	PHD	92	Rochester	1998
Onatski, Alexei	Asst	854-3680			PHD	01	Harvard	2001
Pande, Rohini	Asst	854-5712	rp461	OH	PHD	99	London	1999
Pfaff, Alexander	Asst	854-4190	ap196	DQ	PHD	95	MIT	1995
Tay, Abigail	Asst	854-8277	at436	LI	PHD	99	Stanford	1999

Columbus State University Columbus, GA 31907-5645 (706) 568-2280 colstate.edu
Dept of Business Adm Turner College of Bus Fax=568-2184
Did Not Respond--1999-2000 Listing

Johnson, Robert S.	Dean	568-2044	johnson_robert		PHD	64	Virginia	1993
Bill Heard Chair of Business Administration								
Daniels, Michael J.	Prof		daniels_michael	JKR	PHD	79	Geo St	1980
Associate Dean								

Concordia College MN Moorhead, MN 56562 (218) 299-4411 gloria.cord.edu
Economics Faculty Dept of Bus, Atg & Econ Fax=299-4277 Leslie Hartford

Stradley, Scot A.	C-Pr	299-3115	NAB	PHD	77	Utah	2001
Moewes, David S.	Prof	299-3488	EH	PHD	82	Utah	1968
Hiestand, Thomas W.	Assoc	299-3483	CD	PHD	74	Kansas St	1972

Connecticut College New London, CT 06320-4196 (860) 439-2248 conncoll.edu
Economics Faculty Department of Economics Fax=439-5332 Gina Foster
Did Not Respond--1999-2000 Listing

Cruz-Saco, Maria A.	C-Ac	447-1911	macru	O	PHD	83	Pittsburgh	1990
Pack, Spencer J.	Prof	447-1911	sjpac	B	PHD	83	NewHamp	1981
Peppard, Donald M. Jr.	Prof	447-1911	dmpep	R	PHD	75	Mich St	
Visgilio, Gerald R.	Prof	447-1911	grvis	K	PHD	73	Rhode Isl	
Howes, Candance	Assoc	447-1911	chow	DF	PHD	91	Berkeley	1995
Jensen, Rolf W.	Assoc	447-1911	rwjen	O	PHD	81	Mass	
McKenna, Edward J.	Assoc	774-1911	ejmck	E	PHD	81	SUNY-SBr	

University of Connecticut Storrs, CT 06269-1063 (860) 486-3022 uconnvm.uconn.edu
Department of Economics Col of Lib Arts & Scien Fax=486-4463 Sharon Syrene
Homepage: www.econ.unconn.edu/
Did Not Respond--1999-2000 Listing

Mackinnon, Ross D.	Dean	486-4447	mackinn	Geog	PHD	68	Nrthwstrn	1996
Allen, Polly R.	Prof	486-3955	pallen	FE	PHD	70	Brown	1976
Barth, Peter S.	Prof	486-3023	barth	J	PHD	65	Michigan	1973
Carstensen, Fred V.	Prof	486-0614	carsten	N	PHD	76	Yale	1982
Hallwood, C. Paul	Prof	445-3478	hallwood	F	PHD	88	Aberdeen	1986
Heffley, Dennis R.	Prof	486-4669	dheffley	RI	PHD	75	Ca-SnBarb	193
Langlois, Richard N.	Prof	486-3472	langlois	B	PHD	81	Stanford	1983
McEachern, William A.	Prof	486-3272	mceacher	H	PHD	75	Virginia	1978
Miceli, Thomas J.	Prof	486-5810	miceli	KR	PHD	88	Brown	1987
Ray, Subhash C.	Prof	486-3967	ray	CD	PHD	81	Ca-SnBarb	1982
Sacks, Stephen R.	Prof	486-4859	sacks	H	PHD	71	Berkeley	1971
Segerson, Kathleen	Prof	486-4567	segerson	QD	PHD	84	Cornell	1986
Wright, Arthur W.	Prof	486-3773	wright	KD	PHD	69	MIT	1979
Ahking, Francis W.	Assoc	486-3026	anking	EF	PHD	81	Va Tech	1980
Alpert, William T.	Assoc	322-3466	alpert	J	PHD	79	Columbia	1983
Cosgel, Metin M.	Assoc	486-4662	cosgel	N	PHD	89	Iowa	1989
Cunningham, Steven R.	Assoc	486-3550	cunning	EB	PHD	89	Fla St	1989
Harmon, Oskar R.	Assoc	322-3466	harmon	H	PHD	80	Rutgers	1982

Kimenyi, Samson M.	Assoc	486-3027	kimenyi	HI	PHD	86	GeoMason	1991
Landau, Daniel L.	Assoc	596-4080	lanau	O	PHD	74	Chicago	1981
Lott, William F.	Assoc	486-3885	wlott	C	PHD	69	N Car St	1969
Minkler, Alanson P.	Assoc	486-4070	minkler	DK	PHD	88	Ca-Davis	1989
Randolph, Susan M.	Assoc	486-4171	randolph	O	PHD	83	Cornell	1984
Sazama, Gerald W.	Assoc	486-3366	shazam	H	PHD	67	Wisconsin	1966
Couch, Kenneth A.	Asst	486-4570	couchch	J	PHD	92	Wisconsin	1995
Lin, Emily	Asst	486-4752	lin	HJ	PHD	98	Michigan	1998
Morand, Oliver	Asst	486-6546	morand	DO	PHD	97	Ariz St	1997
Ross, Stephen	Asst	486-3533	ross	R	PHD	94	Syracuse	1994

Converse College Spartanburg, SC 29302-0006 (803) 596-9603 converse.edu
Dept of Economics & Business Col of Arts & Sciences Fax=596-9202

Lever, Joe Ann	Dean	596-9091		Biol	MA			1962
Hughes, Woodrow W. Jr.	C-As	596-9089	woodyhughes		PHD	89	S Carol	1986
Young, Madelyn V.	Asst	596-909	madelyn.young		PHD	91	Geo St	1991

Cornell University Ithaca, NY 14853-7601 (607) 255-4254 cornell.edu
Department of Economics Col of Arts & Sciences Fax=255-2818

Mitra, Tapan	C-Pr	255-4062	tm19		PHD	75	Rochester	
Basu, Kaushik	Prof	255-2525	kb40	DHLO	PHD	76	LondonEc	
on leave to MIT								
Blume, Lawrence E.	Prof	255-9530	lb19		PHD	77	Berkeley	
Coate, Stephen	Prof	255-1912	sc163		PHD	88	Nrthwstrn	
Davis, Tom E.	Prof	255-5007			PHD	56	J Hopkins	
Easley, David A.	Prof	255-6283	dae3	DGC	PHD	79	Nrthwstrn	9-79
Henry Scarborough Professor of Social Sciences								
Ehrenberg, Ronald G.	Prof	225-3026	rg2		PHD	70	Nrthwstrn	1985
Irving M. Ives Professor of Industrial & Labor Relations and Economics								
Hay, George A.	Prof	256-3378	ghay@law.mail.		PHD	69	Nrthwstrn	1979
Edward Cornell Professor Law and Professor of Economics								
Hong, Youngmaio	Prof	255-5130	yh20		PHD	93	Ca-SnDgo	7-93
Kanbur, Sanjiv	Prof	255-6209	sk145		PHD	81	Oxford	
Lee Teng-hui Professor of World Arts								
Kiefer, Nicholas M.	Prof	255-6315	nmk		PHD	76	Princeton	1980
Ta-Chung Liu Professor of Economics								
Lyons, Thomas P.	Prof	255-9534	tp14		PHD	83	Cornell	1988
Majumdar, Mukul K.	Prof	255-3640	mkm5		PHD	70	Berkeley	
H.T. & R.I. Warshow Professor of Economics								
Masson, Robert T.	Prof	255-6288	rtm2		PHD	69	Berkeley	1976
McClelland, Peter D.	Prof	256-6285			PHD	67	Harvard	1968
Possen, Uri M.	Prof	255-6367	ump1		PHD	71	Yale	1971
Razin, Assaf	Prof	255-9665	az156		PHD	69	Chicago	7-01
Friedman Professor of International Economics								
Schuler, Richard E.	Prof	255-7579	res1	Engr	PHD	72	Brown	1972
Shell, Karl	Prof	255-5277	ks22		PHD	65	Stanford	1986
Robert Julius Thorne Professor of Economics								
Staller, George J.	Prof	255-4955	gjs3		PHD	59	Cornell	1960
Wan, Henry Y. Jr.	Prof	255-6211	hyw1		PHD	61	MIT	
Vogelsang, Timothy	Assoc	255-5108	tjv2		PHD	93	Princeton	9-83
Melnikov, Oleg	Asst	255-6314	om32		PHD	00	Yale	7-01
O'Donoghue, Ted	Asst	255-6287	edo1		PHD	96	Berkeley	
Park, K.	Asst	255-6337	kp78		PHD	01	UCLA	7-01
Subramanian, Shankar	Asst	255-2355	ss55	OQ	PHD	88	Berkeley	8-93
Wen, Yi	Asst	255-6338	yw57		PHD	96	Iowa	9-99

Creighton University Omaha, NE 68178-0130 (402) 280-2612 creighton.edu
Dept of Economics & Finance College of Business Adm Fax=280-2172 Ms. Shirley Gust
Homepage: cobweb.creighton.edu/ecofin/

Pitts, Robert E.	Dean	280-2852	rpitts		PHD	77	S Carol	1997
Wingender, John R.	C-Pr	280-2612	jwings	Fnce	PHD	85	Nebraska	
Associate Dean								
Allen, Robert F.	Prof	280-2442	rallen	DKL	PHD	69	Mich St	1986
Goss, Ernest P.	Prof	280-4757	ernieg	RC	PHD	83	Tennessee	1992
MacAllister Chair in Regional Economics								
Murthy, N. R. Vasudeva	Prof	280-2128	vmurthy	CDH	PHD	75	SUNY-Bin	1979
Nitsch, Thomas O.	Emer	280-2887	tnitsch	ENP	PHD	63	Ohio St	1969
Fitzsimmons, Edward L.	Assoc	280-2170	efitzsimmons	AD	PHD	84	Nebraska	1984
Coordintor of Economics and International Business								
Funk, Herbert J.	Emer			AC	PHD	64	Iowa St	1967
Knudsen, James J.	Asst	280-2281	jimknu	CHJ	PHD	89	Iowa St	1989

Cumberland College Williamsburg, KY 40769-7984 (606) 539-4254 cc.cumber.edu
Economics Faculty Dept of Business Admin Fax=

Hubbard, Harold F.	C-Pr	539-4254	hhubbard	BAdm	MBA	60	Kentucky	7-60
Carter, Jane	Assoc	539-4274	jcarter		MBA	85	Kentucky	1985
Tan, Chinteck	Assoc	539 4457	ctans		MBA	88	Tenn Tech	1988
Briley, James	Asst	539-4305	jbriley		PHD	98	Tx Tech	1985

University of Dallas Irving, TX 75062-4736 (972) 721-5308 acad.udallas.edu
Department of Economics Constantin C of Lib Art Fax=721-4034 Kate Hohlt
Homepage: www.udallas.edu/econdept/econ.html

Lindsay, Thomas K.	Dean	721-5242	lindsay		PHD	89	Chicago	1999
Bostaph, Samuel H.	C-Ac	721-5308	bostaph	BNP	PHD	76	S Illinois	1981
Doyle, William	Assoc	721-5054	bdoyle	GN	PHD	91	Tennessee	1991
Kpakol, Mahnus L.	VAsst	721-4071	mlkpakol	CFJO	PHD	88	Tx-Dallas	2000
Weston, Samuel C.	Asst	721-5238	sweston	B	PHD	87	Pittsburgh	1987

Dallas Baptist University Dallas, TX 75211-9299 (214) 333-5244 dbu.edu
Department of Economics College of Business Fax=333-5293 Shirtly Mitchell

Smiles, Ronald	C-Pr	333-5253	rons	R	PHD	87	Tx-Arlin	1987
Kakoli, Philip	Asst	333-5218	philip	F	PHD	01	Niarobi	1988

Dartmouth College Hanover, NH 03755-3514 (603) 646-2617 dartmouth.edu
Department of Economics Col of Arts & Sciences Fax=646-2122 Julie Guillette/Karen Pelletie
Homepage: http://www.dartmough.edu/artsci/economics/

Bharucha, Jamshed	Dean	646-3999						
Fischel, William Alan	C-Pr	646-2538			PHD	73	Princeton	1973
Blanchflower, David Graham	Prof	646-2536			PHD	85	London	1989
Gustman, Alan Leslie	Prof	646-2641			PHD	69	Michigan	1969
Loren M. Berry Professor								
Irwin, Douglas A.	Prof	646-2942			PHD	88	Columbia	1997
Kohn, Meir G.	Prof	646-2648			PHD	73	MIT	1978
Marion, Nancy P.	Prof	646-2511			PHD	77	Princeton	1976
Samwick, Andrew A.	Prof	646-2893			PHD	93	MIT	1994
Scott, John T.	Prof	646-2941			PHD	76	Harvard	1977
Skinner, Jonathan	Prof	646-2535			PHD	83	UCLA	1995
John French Professor								
Venti, Steven F.	Prof	646-2526			PHD	82	Harvard	1982
Anderson, Patricia Mary	Assoc	646-2532			PHD	91	Princeton	1991
Lusardi, Annamaria	Assoc	646-2099			PHD	92	Princeton	1993
Slaughter, Matthew J.	Assoc	646-2939			PHD	94	MIT	1994
Staiger, Douglas O.	Assoc	646-2979			PHD	90	MIT	1998
Baicker, Katherine	Asst	646-2943			PHD	98	Harvard	1998
Chandra, Amitabh	Asst	646-0642			PHD	00	Kentucky	2000
Durell, Alan	Asst	646-0075			PHD	99	Harvard	1999
Edmonds, Eric V.	Asst	646-2944			PHD	99	Princeton	1999
Feyrer, James	Asst	646-2533			PHD	01	Brown	2001
Hastings, Justine	Asst	646-2531			PHD	01	Berkeley	2001
Pavcnik, Nina	Asst	646-2537			PHD	99	Princeton	1999
Sacerdote, Bruce I.	Asst	646-2121			PHD	98	Harvard	1998

Davidson College Davidson, NC 28036-1719 (704) 894-2398 davidson.edu
Economics Faculty Department of Economics Fax=894-2874 Barbara M. Carmack

Appleyard, Dennis R.	C-Pr	894-2456	deappleyard	F	PHD	66	Michigan	1990
James B. Duke Professor of International Studies								
Hess, Peter N.	Prof	894-2249	pehess	OT	PHD	82	N Carol	1980
Gail M. and Ernst G. Doe Professor of Economics								
Martin, David W.	Prof	894-2253	damartin	GQ	PHD	84	Illinois	1984
Ross, Clark G.	Prof	894-2204	clross	P	PHD	76	Boston C	1979
Frontis Johnston Professor of Economics								
Baker, Ben	Assoc	894-2397	bebaker	G	MA	83	S Carol	1997
Kumar, Vikram	Assoc	894-2265	vikumar	E	PHD	87	Vanderbilt	1986
Chaston, Kelly	Asst	894-2574	kechaston	DL	PHD	97	Boston C	1997
Foley, Mark	Asst	894-2248	mafoley	JP	PHD	97	Yale	2000
Smith, Fred	Asst	894-2023	frsmith	RN	PHD	01	Vanderbilt	2000

University of Dayton Dayton, OH 45469-2251 (937) 229-2416 udayton.edu
Dept of Economics & Finance School of Business Adm Fax=229-2477 Ms. Sandy L. Murphy
Homepage: www.sba.udayton.edu/ecofin

Gould, Sam B.	Dean	229-3731	gould	Mgt	PHD	75	Mich St	1985
Gustafson, Elizabeth F.	C-Ac	229-2406	gustafso	C	PHD	74	N Carol	1983
Beladi, Hamid	Prof	229-2407	beladi	F	PHD	83	Utah St	1988
Frasca, Ralph R.	Prof	229-2405	frasca	A	PHD	75	Indiana	1972
Hadley, Lawrence H.	Assoc	229-2403	hadleyla	J	PHD	75	Conn	1977
Ruggiero, John	Assoc	229-2550	ruggiero	R	PHD	95	Syracuse	1995
Oladi, Gholamreza	Asst	229-5422	oladi	D	PHD	00	McGill	2000
Poitras, Marc	Asst	229-2419	poitras	A	PHD	95	GeoMason	1998

University of Delaware Newark, DE 19716-2720 (302) 831-2563 be.udel.edu
Department of Economics Col of Business & Econ Fax=831-6968 Gail E. Walford, Off Coor
Homepage: http://www.be.udel.edu/econ_site/econhp.html

Ginzberg, Michael J.	Dean	831-2551	ginzberg	Mgt	PHD	75	MIT	2000
Hoffman, Saul D.	C-Pr	831-1907	hoffmans	TJ	PHD	77	Michigan	1977

Abrams, Burton A.	Prof	831-1900	abramsb	EH	PHD	74	Ohio St	1974
Anderson, Lee G.	Prof	831-2650		Q	PHD	70	U Wash	1974
Professor, College of Marine Studies								
Butkiewicz, James L.	Prof	831-1891	butkiewj	E	PHD	77	Virginia	1976
Grubb, Farley	Prof	831-1905	grubbf	N	PHD	84	Chicago	1983
Koford, Kenneth	Prof	831-1909	kofordk	H	PHD	77	UCLA	1979
Lewis, Kenneth A.	Prof	831-1912	lewisk	CE	PHD	69	Princeton	1973
Associate Chair, Economics								
Link, Charles R.	Prof	831-1921	linkc	J	PHD	71	Wisconsin	1701
Miller, Jeffrey B.	Prof	831-1911	millerj	EP	PHD	76	Penn	1976
Mulligan, James G.	Prof	831-1918	mulligaj	L	PHD	80	Minnesota	1980
O'Neill, James B.	Prof	831-2559	oneillj	A	PHD	71	Purdue	1971
Director, Center for Economic Education								
Seidman, Laurence S.	Prof	831-1917	seidmanl	H	PHD	74	Berkeley	1982
Settle, Russell F.	Prof	831-1914	settler	H	PHD	74	Wisconsin	1974
Agnello, Richard J.	Assoc	831-1901	agnellor	C	PHD	70	J Hopkins	1968
Arnold, Michael	Assoc	831-1916	arnoldm	LD	PHD	92	UCLA	1992
Associate Chair								
Beck, Stacie E.	Assoc	831-1915	becks	GEF	PHD	87	Penn	1986
Black, David E.	Assoc	831-1902	blackd	HO	PHD	69	MIT	1975
Craig, Eleanor D.	Assoc	831-1904	craige	H	MA	61	Penn	1962
Daniel, Joseph	Assoc	831-1913	danielj	L	PHD	92	Minnesota	1991
Donnelley, Lawrence P.	Assoc	831-1908		O	PHD	70	Brown	1968
Falaris, Evangelos M.	Assoc	831-1768	falarise	O	PHD	79	Minnesota	1986
Harris, William	Assoc	831-1923	harrisw	H	PHD	79	Va Tech	1983
Latham, William R. III	Assoc	831-6846	lathamw	RC	PHD	73	Illinois	1971
Thornton, James R.	Assoc	831-1919	thorntoj	P	PHD	74	Cornell	1973
Ying, John S.	Assoc	831-1903	yingj	L	PHD	87	Berkeley	1987
Parsons, George R.	Asst	831-6792		Q	PHD	85	Wisconsin	1985
College of Marine Studies								
Stockman, David	Asst	831-1903	stockmad	CE	PHD	97	Chicago	1998
Wang, Sivan	Asst	831-1924	wangs	CF	PHD	01	S Calif	2001
Yatawara, Ravi	Asst	831-1906	yatawarr	FO	PHD	01	Columbia	2000

Delaware State University	Dover, DE		19901-2277	(302) 739-2705				dsc.edu
Dept of Accounting & Finance	School of Management		Fax=739-3517				Ms. Claudia L. Daniels	
Williamson, Joan W.	C-Ac	857-6928		Atg	PHD	97	Delaware	
Bieker, Richard F.	Prof	857-6912			PHD	70	Kentucky	
Christopher, Jan E.	Assoc	857-6938		CDMR	PHD	93	Howard	1994
Ikein, Augustine A.	Assoc	857-6920		Soc	PHD	88	Atlanta	
Kwak, Young-sik	Assoc	857-6913			PHD	94	Miss	1993

Delta State University	Cleveland, MS		38733	(662) 846-4185				dsu.deltast.edu
Division of Econ & Finance	School of Business		Fax=846-4215				Cathy Conico	
Stewart, William S.	Dean	846-4200		Mgt	PHD	77	Miss	8-97
Moore, Billy C.	C-Pr	846-4185	bmoore	AG	PHD	95	Miss	8-86
Wagoner, Charles B.	Asst	846-4188		ACFG	PHD	93	Tulane	8-95
Matthews, Michelle	Inst	846-4189			ABD		Miss	8-01

Denison University	Granville, OH		43023	(614) 587-6245				cc.denison.edu
Economics Faculty	Department of Economics		Fax=587-6348				Judy Thompson	
Did Not Respond--1999-2000 Listing								
LaRoe, Ross M.	C-Ac	587-6473	laroe	AHQ	PHD	82	American	1985
Bartlett, Robin L.	Prof	587-6574	barlett	AJ	PHD	74	Mich St	1973
Laura C. Harris Chair								
Behdad, Sohrab	Prof	587-6404	behdad	BF	PHD	73	Mich St	1985
King, Paul G.	Prof	587-6314	king	OAQ	PHD	71	Illinois	1967
John Harris Chair								
Lucier, Richard L.	Prof	587-6462	lucier	ADF	PHD	72	Claremont	1971
Miller, Timothy I.	Prof	587-6403	millert	CE	PHD	79	S Illinois	1978
Boyd, David W.	Assoc	587-6317	boyd	KLD	PHD	91	Ohio St	1991
Boyd, Laura A.	Assoc	587-6316	boydl	JI	PHD	91	Ohio St	1991
Ziegert, Andrea	Asst	587-6575	ziegert		PHD	85	N Carol	1997

University of Denver	Denver, CO		80208-2685	(303) 871-2685				du.edu
Department of Economics	Arts, Humanities & SocS		Fax=871-2605				Cheryl O'Leary	
Ho, Peter S.	C-Ac	871-2259	pho	FO	PHD	89	Stanford	1987
Freeman, Katherine	Assoc	871-2151	kafreema	AD	PHD	78	Fla St	1983
Mott, Tracy L.	Assoc	871-2569	tmott	BE	PHD	82	Stanford	1991
Urquhart, Robert	Assoc	871-2258	rurquhar	BN	PHD	88	New Sch	1988
Johnson, Laurie	Asst	871-2146	lauriejo	DHQ	PHD	98	U Wash	2000
Wilson, Matthew	Asst	871-2260		HR	PHD	00	Tx-Austin	2001

DePaul University Chicago, IL 60604-2287 (312) 362-8781 wppost.depaul.edu
Department of Economics Col Arts & Sci/Cl Comm Fax=362-5452 Kelly Burda

Miller, Michael S.	C-Ac	362-8477	E	PHD	80	Pittsburgh	1980
Batavia, Bala	Prof	362-5766	CD	PHD	74	N Car St	1976
Ciecka, James E.	Prof	362-8831	CD	PHD	70	Purdue	1970
Diamond, James J.	Emer		EC	PHD	62	Nrthwstrn	9-55
Ghoshal, Animesh	Prof	362-8008	DE	PHD	74	Michigan	1981
Krautmann, Anthony C.	Prof	362-6176	DL	PHD	85	Iowa	1985
Mark, Adolph E.	Emer		A	PHD	63	Illinois	9-61
Mondschean, Thomas H.	Prof	362-5210	EG	PHD	89	Wisconsin	1987
Oppenheimer, Margaret M.	Prof	362-8651	JDK	PHD	74	Nrthwstrn	9-76
Sander, William III	Prof	362-5240	RD	PHD	78	Cornell	1989
Wiltgen, Richard J.	Prof	362-8016	B	PHD	74	Illinois	1973
Berdell, John	Assoc	362-5247	NE	PHD	91	Cambridge	1991
Bucci, Gabriella A.	Assoc	362-6787	DH	PHD	88	J Hopkins	1989
Choi, Jin	Assoc	362-8842	GMC	PHD	82	Iowa St	8-88
Donley, Thomas D.	Assoc	362-8887	C	PHD	93	Wisconsin	8-90
Epstein, Seth	Assoc	362-8112	D	PHD	88	Arizona	1992
Opiela, Timothy P.	Assoc	362-5584	EG	PHD	87	Tx A&M	2000
Owen, Laura J.	Assoc	362-8771	NJ	PHD	91	Yale	1990
Tenorio, Rafael	Assoc	362-8309	EDA	PHD	88	J Hopkins	1999
Dill, Floyd R.	Emer		N	PHD	73	Cornell	1975
Woo, Jaejoon	Asst	362-8781	EC	PHD	97	Harvard	2000

DePauw University Greencastle, IN 46135-0037 (765) 658-4878 depauw.edu
Dept of Economics & Mgt College of Liberal Arts Fax=658-4764 Jayne Williams

Wachter, Daniel R.	C-Ac	658-4879	dwachter	PHD	82	Purdue	1979
Catanese, Anthony V.	Prof	658-4884		PHD	72	S Illinois	1979
Field, William J.	Prof	658-4886		PHD	80	Michigan	1979
Lemon, Gary D.	Prof	658-4882	garylemon	PHD	82	Kansas	1976
English, Mary P.	Assoc	658-4355		PHD	89	So Meth	1988
Associate Dean of Academic Affairs							
Goma, Ophelia							
Gropp, Jeffrey							
Musser, Thomas							
Villinski, Michele							

University of Detroit Mercy Detroit, MI 48219-0900 (313) 993-1238 udmercy.edu
Department of Economics Col of Liberal Arts Fax=993-1166
Did Not Respond--1999-2000 Listing

Shen, Raphael	Prof	993-1148	PHD	75	Mich St	1977
Byrne, Donald R.	Prof	993-3391	PHD	71	Notre Dm	1966
Pemberton, Donald K.	Prof	993-1097	PHD	70	Kansas	1969
Song, Yoon K.	Prof	993-1095	PHD	69	Illinois	1969
Brorby, Bruce M.	Asst	993-1600	MA	67	Detroit	1971
Assistant Dean						
Mosby, James B.	Asst	993-1096	MA	70	Detroit	1972
Schad, Tom	Asst					

Dickinson College Carlisle, PA 17013-2896 (717) 245-1381 dickinson.edu
Economics Faculty Department of Economics Fax=245-1854 Isabel L. Houston
Did Not Respond Again--1997-98 Listing

Koont, Sinan	C-As	245-1381	koont	CFE	PHD	87	Mass	1986
Barone, Charles A.	Assoc		barnone	AO	PHD	78	American	1975
Bergsten, Gordon S.	Assoc	245-1529	bergsten	BNDE	PHD	77	Berkeley	1984
Bellinger, William K.	Asst	245-1358	bellinger_w	JE	PHD	85	Nrthwstrn	1981
Burczak, Ted A.	Asst	245-1264	burczak	ELF	PHD	94	Mass	
Skrabis, Kristin	Asst	245-1596	skrabis	QD				

Dillard University New Orleans, LA 70122 (504) 816-4699 dillard.edu
Economics/Finance Area Division of Business Fax=816-4851 Helen Bougere 816-4698
Homepage: http://www.dillard.edu

Chase, Edgar L. III	Dean	816-4697	echase	Atg	JD		Loyola
Fugar, Christian V.	C-Ac	816-4699	cfugar		PHD	89	Howard
Mengistu, Tadessa	Assoc	816-4698	tmengistu		PHD	86	Indiana
Sheriff, Mohamed A.	Assoc	816-4698	msheriff		PHD	91	Howard

Univ of District of Columbia Washington, DC 20008 (202) 274-7002 udc.edu
Dept Atg, Fnce, & Economics Sch of Bus & Prof Stds Fax=274-7105 Ms. Sarah G. Hardeman
Homepage: www.udc.edu

Quigley, Herbert G.	Dean	274-7048		DBA	77	Geo Wash	1969
Goyal, Tarsiam L.	C-Pr	274-7049		DSC	70	Geo Wash	1967
Ezeani, Eboh	Prof	274-7053	O	PHD	76	American	1976
Boland, Dennis	Assoc	274-7051	BA	PHD	70	Illinois	1976
Omar, Hanai	Assoc	274-7064	AH	PHD	96	Am World	1976
Samhan, Muhammad	Assoc	274-7055	OP	PHD	82	American	1976

Dowling College — Oakdale, NY 11769-1999 (516) 244-3155 — dowling.edu
Department of Economics — Sch of Arts & Sciences Fax=589-6644 — Patti Zarataotz

Greer, Mark	C-As	244-3239	greerm		PHD	90	Michigan	1994
Raji, Seyed	Prof	244-3118			PHD	72	NYU	
Gullason, Edward T.	Assoc	244-3167			PHD	86	Penn	
Sonny, Jacob	Assoc	244-3117			PHD	71	New Sch	

Drake University — Des Moines, IA 50311-4505 (515) 271-3122 — drake.edu
Dept of Economics & Finance — College of Arts & Sci Fax=271-2055 — Nancy A. Smith

Hosseinzadeh, Esmail	Prof	271-4026	ismael.zadeh		PHD	87	New Sch	1988
Boal, William M.	Assoc	271-3129	william.boal		PHD	85	Stanford	1995
Hewett, Roger S.	Assoc	271-3834	roger.hewett		PHD	84	Illinois	1981
Weaver, Janice E.	Assoc	271-2898	janice.weaver		PHD	76	Illinois	1983

Drew University — Madison, NJ 07940-4037 (201) 408-3434 — drew.edu
Department of Economics — College of Liberal Arts Fax=408-3142 — Lydia Feldman

Cucchi, Paolo M.	Dean				PHD	72	Princeton	1984
Isenberg, Dorene L.	C-Pr	408-3435		E	PHD	86	Ca-Rivers	1989
Cole, Donald P.	Prof	408-3429		AH	PHD	68	Ohio St	1966
Curtis, Fred	Prof	408-3432		BJO	PHD	83	Mass	1978
Seneca, Rosalind S.	Prof	408-3433		DL	PHD	71	Penn	1981
Colton, Nora Ann	Assoc	408-3665		FPT	DPHL	92	Oxford	1994
Smith, Bernard	Assoc	408-3595		HOP	PHD	89	Yale	1986
Dickens, Edwin T.	Asst	408-3024		EG	PHD	90	New Sch	1996

Drexel University — Philadelphia, PA 19104-2875 (215) 895-2123 — duvm.ocs.drexel.edu
Economics & Intl Business — College of Business Adm Fax=895-6975

Harral, William	Dean$	895-2111	william.harral	Mgt	MBA		MIT	2000
Madan, Vibhas	C-Ac	895-2124	madanv		PHD	89	Mich St	1989
Koziara, Edward C.	Prof	895-6994	koziarec		PHD	65	Wisconsin	1966
McCain, Roger A. III	Prof	895-2176	mccainra		PHD	71	LSU	1988
Yan, Chiou-shuang	Prof	895-6972	yancsj		PHD	66	Purdue	1967
Hammoudeh, Shawka M.	Assoc	895-6673	hammousm		PHD	80	Kansas	1990
Jeon, Bang Nam	Assoc	895-2125	jeonbana		PHD	87	Indiana	1988
Lester, Bijou	Assoc	895-6973	lesterby		PHD	81	Penn	1988
Jensen, Paul	Asst	895-2123			PHD	97	Penn St	1997
Lybecker, Kristina	Asst	895-6990			PHD	00	Berkeley	2000
Soller, Elizabeth	Asst	895-2123			PHD	97	Indiana	1997
Tang, Linghui	Asst	895-1034			PHD	98	Syracuse	1998

Drury University — Springfield, MO 65802 (417) 873-7509 — lib.drury.edu
Economics Faculty — Breech S Bus Adm & Econ Fax=873-7537 — Judy Gibson

Zimmerer, Thomas W.	D-Pr	873-7509		Mgt	PHD	71	Arkansas	
Rohlf, William D. Jr.	Prof	865-8731			PHD	72	Kansas St	1972
Mullins, Steven	Assoc				PHD	83	Okla St	1982

Duke University — Durham, NC 27708-0097 (919) 660-1800 — econ.duke.edu
Economics Department — College of Arts & Sci Fax=684-8974 — Betty Henderson 660-1852

McElroy, Marjorie B.	C-Pr	660-1815	mcelroy	J	PHD	69	Nrthwstrn	1976
Bollerslev, Tim	Prof	660-1846	bauer	CG	PHD	86	Ca-SnDgo	1999
Director of Graduate Studies								
DeMarchi, Neil B.	Prof	660-1834	demarchi	EB	PHD	70	Austr Natl	1983
Goodwin, Craufurd	Prof	684-3936	goodwin	ABFN	PHD	58	Duke	9-62
James D. Duke Professor								
Grabowski, Henry G.	Prof	660-1839	grabow		PHD	67	Princeton	1972
Graham, D. A.	Prof	660-1802	dag		PHD	69	Duke	1969
Kelley, Allen C.	Prof	660-1825	kelley	O	PHD	64	Stanford	1972
James D. Duke Professor								
Kimbrough, Kent P.	Prof	660-1811	kent	F	PHD	80	Chicago	1980
Mendoza, Enrique	Prof	660-1814	mendozae	FO	PHD	89	W Ontario	1997
Sloan, Frank A.	Prof	660-1820	fsloan	I	PHD	69	Harvard	1993
Alexander McMahon Professor								
Tauchen, George	Prof	660-1812	get	CG	PHD	78	Minnesota	1977
Tower, Edward	Prof	660-1818	tower	EF	PHD	71	Harvard	1974
Treml, Vladimir G.	Emer		treml		PHD	63	N Carol	1967
Vernon, John M.	Prof	660-1829	vernon	L	PHD	66	MIT	1969
Wallace, T. Dudley	Emer	660-1855	wallace					
James D. Duke Professor								
Weintraub, E. Roy	Prof	660-1838	erw	N	PHD	69	Penn	1970
Yohe, William P.	Emer		yohe		PHD	59	Michigan	1958
Peretto, Pietro	Assoc	660-1807	peretto	EFLM	PHD	94	Yale	9-94
Connolly, Michelle	Asst	660-1819	connolly	FG	PHD	96	Yale	1997
Coppejans, Mark	Asst	660-1804	mtc	CG	PHD	96	Nrthwstrn	1996
Crawford, Gregory	Asst	660-1828	gsc	CL	PHD	98	Stanford	1996
Burmeister, Edwin	Resr	660-1849	eb	GC	PHD	65	MIT	
Toniolo, Gianni	Resr	660-1855	giannit	FB	LAUR	66	Venice	

Duquesne University

Economics	Pittsburgh, PA 15282-0104 (412) 396-5831							duq.edu
	School of Bus & Admin Fax=396-4764							Karyn Plack
Stalder, James	Dean	396-1849	stalder		BS	62	Penn St	2000
Bober, Stanley	Prof	396-6263			PHD	62	NYU	1964
Bond, Richard E.	Assoc	396-6262			PHD	69	Maryland	1969
Marlin, Matthew R.	Assoc	396-6250			PHD	81	Fla St	1987
Hettler, Paul	Asst	396-6246			PHD	98	Pittsburgh	1999
Wagner, Gary	Asst	396-6268			PHD	99	W Virginia	2001

Earlham College

Economics Faculty	Richmond, IN 47374-4095 (765) 983-1525							earlham.edu
Did Not Respond--1999-2000 Listing	Department of Economics Fax=983-1207							Cheri Gaddis
Diskin, Jonathan	C-Ac	983-1427	jond		PHD	89	Mass	1988
Klose, Gilbert	Prof	983-1206	gilk		MA		Nrthwstrn	1960

East Carolina University

Department of Economics	Greenville, NC 27858-4353 (252) 328-6006							mail.ecu.edu
	College of Arts & Sci Fax=328-6743							Mrs. Kimberly Moore
Sparrow, Keats	Dean	328-6249	sparrowk		PHD		Kentucky	
Bays, Carson W.	C-Pr	328-6006	baysc	IKL	PHD	74	Michigan	1982
Baldwin, Marjorie L.	Prof	328-6383	baldwinm	DIJ	PHD	88	Syracuse	1989
Bishop, John A.	Prof	328-6756	bishopj	DHI	PHD	87	Alabama	1988
Parker, Randall E.	Assoc	328-6755	parkerr	EN	PHD	86	Kentucky	1986
Rothman, Philip	Assoc	328-6151	rothmanp	CE	PHD	90	NYU	1992
Zeager, Lester A.	Assoc	328-6408	zeagerl	DIJ	PHD	87	Pittsburgh	1986
Bin, Oxmuung	Asst	328-6006	bino	CQ	PHD	98	Oregon St	2001
DeSimone, Jeffrey	Asst	328-6742	desimonej	DIJ	PHD	98	Yale	1999
Holmes, George M.	Asst	328-4165	holmesg	CIJ	PHD	99	N Carol	1999
Li, Dong	Asst	328-6820	lid	CDG	PHD	98	Tx A&M	1999
Rupp, Nicholas	Asst	328-6006	ruppn	LQ	PHD	98	Tx A&M	2001
Schumacher, Edward	Asst	328-1083	schumachere	DIJ	PHD	94	Fla St	1994
Zinn, Gary	VAsst	328-6751	zinng	A	PHD	77	Syracuse	2000

East Central University

Dept of Business Admin	Ada, OK 74820-6899 (580) Ext 274							ecok.edu
phone: 332-8000	School of Business Fax=							
Mitchusson, Linda C.	Dean	Ext 649		Atg	PHD	75	Arkansas	1996
Steger, Eric K.	Prof	Ext 267			PHD	80	La Tech	1970

East Stroudsburg University

Department of Economics	E Stroudsburg PA 18301-2999 (570) 422-3251							esu.edu
	Sch of Arts & Sciences Fax=422-3777							Melanie Deuerlein
Newmann, Bonnie	Dean	422-3494			PHD	72	New Mex	1992
Hartman, Harrison G.	C-Pr	422-3251		J	PHD	76	NYU	1964
Bunjun, Seewoonundun	Prof	422-3240		D	PHD	79	Penn St	1979
Christofides, Constantinos A	Prof	422-3329		CRT	PHD	77	Lehigh	1971
Kidman, Peter N.	Prof	422-3830		K	PHD	71	W Virginia	1977
DeCosmo, Michael C.	Assoc	422-3108			MBA	84	Lehigh	1984
Kane, Mamadou	Assoc	422-3279		EFN	MA	72	NYU	1973
Kercsmar, John	Assoc	422-3829		M	PHD	85	Houston	
Nyamwange, Richard	Assoc	422-3404		D	MBA	82	Long Isl	1987
Behr, Todd	Asst	422-3831		EH	MBA	78	Lehigh	1989
Neelakantan, P.	Asst	422-3002		D	PHD	92	SUNY-Buf	1992

East Tennessee State Univ

Dept of Econ, Fnce & Urban S	Johnson City, TN 37614-0686 (423) 439-4202							etsu.edu
	College of Business Fax=439-8583							Ms. Mimi Mick
Garceau, Linda R.	Dean	439-5489	garceau	Atg	DBA	86	Boston U	2000
Alavi, Jafar	C-Pr	439-4202	drjalavi		PHD	86	Tennessee	1985
Dotterweich, Douglas P.	Prof	439-4202	dotterwe		PHD	78	Delaware	1984
Hipple, F. Steb	Prof	439-4202	hipples		PHD	72	So Meth	1982
Everett, Michael David	Assoc	439-4202	everettm		PHD	67	Wash U	1977
Mackara, W. Frederick	Assoc	439-4202	mackara		PHD	76	Tx A&M	1975
Smith, Jon L.	Assoc	439-4202	smitj01		PHD	82	S Carol	1980
Warren, J. Harold	Assoc	439-4202	warrenh		PHD	69	Okla St	1969
Jennings, Donna	Asst	439-4202	jenningd		PHD	95	Vanderbilt	1994
Trogen, Paul	Asst	439-4202	trogenp		PHD	95	Fla St	1995

Eastern Conn State Univ

Economics Faculty	Willimantic, CT 06226-2295 (860) 465-5239							easternct.edu
	Department of Economics Fax=456-2231							Ms. Jean Stencil
Horrocks, Robert	Dean	456-5293						
Parzych, Kenneth M.	C-Pr	456-5239	parzych		PHD	70	Conn	
Lombard, John	Prof				PHD	78	Conn	
Free, Rhona C.	Assoc	456-2231			PHD	83	Notre Dm	1983
Mann, Prem S.	Assoc	456-5216			PHD	88	UCLA	1980
Pachis, Dimitrios S.	Assoc				PHD	82	Mass	
Associate Vice President for Academic Affairs								
Roy, Tapan K.	Assoc	456-5502			PHD	80	Temple	1977

Eastern Illinois Univ Charleston, IL 61920-3099 (217) 581-2719 eiu.edu
Department of Economics College of Sciences Fax=581-5997 Lois Luallen

Wall, Lida	Dean	581-3328		Comm	PHD		Ohio St	1995
Karbassioon, Ebrahim	C-Pr	581-5429	cfexk		PHD	81	Nebraska	1980
Corley, Edward M.	Prof	581-2378	efemc		PHD	64	Okla St	1967
Dao, Minh Quang	Prof	581-6329	cfmqd		PHD	87	Illinois	1987
Thompson, William F.	Prof	581-2927			PHD	79	Arkansas	1981
Bates, Lawrence W.	Assoc	581-2710	cflwb		PHD	75	Tx-Austin	1970
Brodsky, Noel	Assoc	581-6334	cfnb		PHD	88	Illinois	1988
Bruehler, James	Assoc	581-2719	cfjrb		PHD	93	Illinois	1993
Champlin, Dell	Assoc	581-2719	cfdpc		PHD	90	Utah	1995
Fahy, Paul R.	Assoc	581-6332	cfprf		PHD	76	Conn	1976
Grant, Alan	Assoc	581-7794	cfapq		PHD	96	Kansas St	1997
Mason, Timothy I.	Assoc	581-6966	cftim		PHD	87	Indiana	1989
Moshtagh, Ali R.	Assoc	581-6967	cfam1		PHD	88	Arkansas	1987
Ghent, Linda	Asst	581-6331	cflsgl	DJ	PHD	94	N Car St	
Hake, Eric	Asst	581-6333	cfernz		PHD	94	Tennessee	
Upadhyay, Mukti	Asst	581-3812	cfmpu		PHD	95	J Hopkins	

Eastern Kentucky University Richmond, KY 40475-3176 (859) 622-1769 eku.edu
Department of Economics Col of Arts & Sciences Fax=622-5065 Mrs. Laura A. Weitkamp

Hart, Dominick J.	Dean$	622-1405			PHD	70	S Carol	1970
Wade, John A.	C-Ac	622-1767	john.wade		PHD	82	Purdue	2000
O'Connor, J. Francis	Prof	622-1769	frank.oconnor		PHD	74	Minnesota	1989
Watkins, Thomas G.	Prof	622-4980	tom.watkins		PHD	79	Iowa St	1984
Dickey, Steven W.	Assoc	622-4987	steve.dickey		PHD	85	S Illinois	1983
Ruppel, Fred J.	Assoc	622-2411	fred.ruppel		PHD	84	Maryland	1997
Harter, John F. R.	Asst	622-1773	john.harter		PHD	92	Purdue	1999
Houston, Robert G.	Asst	622-2160	bob.houston		ABD	99	Kentucky	1998

Eastern Michigan University Ypsilanti, MI 48197 (734) 487-3395 online.emich.edu
Department of Economics Col of Arts & Science Fax=481-9666 Ms. Annetta Green
Homepage: http://www.emich.edu
email @1=emich.edu

Fish, Barry A.	Dean	487-4345	barry.fish@1		PHD	71	Wayne St	1970
Hanna, Raouf S.	H-Pr	487-3395	raouf.hanna@1		PHD	73	Indiana	1977
Abdullah, Dewan A.	Prof	487-0072	eco_abdullah		PHD	84	Kentucky	1988
Chung, Young-Iob	Prof	487-6833	eco_chung		PHD	65	Columbia	1966
Edgren, John A.	Prof	487-3068	eco_edgren		PHD	79	Michigan	1979
Erenburg, Sharon J.	Prof	487-0385	eco_erenburg		PHD	86	Illinois	1987
Esposto, Alfredo G.	Prof	487-0004	eco_esposto		PHD	83	Temple	1990
Moreland, Kemper W.	Prof	487-0279	eco_moreland		PHD	80	Wisconsin	1980
Pearson, Donald W.	Prof	487-0008	eco_pearson		PHD	70	Tx-Austin	1969
Thornton, James	Prof	487-0080	eco_thornton		PHD	91	Oregon	1991
Vogt, Michael G.	Prof	487-0006	eco_vogt		PHD	76	Wisconsin	1978
Woodland, Bill M.	Prof	487-0269	eco_woodland		PHD	81	Purdue	1981
Crary, David B.	Assoc	487-0001	eco_crary		PHD	82	Maryland	1980
Hayworth, Steve	Assoc	487-0009	eco_hayworth		PHD	87	MIT	1977

Eastern New Mexico Univ Portales, NM 88130 (505) emnu.edu
Department of Economics College of Business Fax=562-2252
Did Not Respond--1999-2000 Listing

Huybregts, Gerry	Dean	562-2343	gerry.huybregts	Mgt	PHD	88	UCLA	1988
Brunsen, William H.	C-Pr	562-2744	brunsenb	GHMA	PHD	76	Virginia	1987
Bice, Douglas	Asst	562-2342			PHD	96	Kentucky	1997
McFerrin, Randy	Asst	562-2369			PHD	95	Tx A&M	1995

Eastern Oregon University LaGrande, OR 97850-2899 (541) 962-3508 eou.edu
Department of Economics School of Arts & Sci Fax=962-3893 Dawna Flanagan

Swzuger, Dennis	Dean$	962-3555	dswzuger		PHD	74	Idaho	9-78
Johnson, Jeffery	C	962-3578	jjohnson		PHD	78	Ca-Rivers	9-82
Johnson, Colleen	Prof	962-3340	johnsonc	AEJM	PHD	88	Wash St	9-86
Steenstra, Alex	Asst	962-3371	steensa	ABDQ	PHD	97	Utah	9-97

College of Eastern Utah Price, UT 84501 (435) 613-5218 ceu.edu
Economics Faculty Dept of Social Science Fax=613-4102 Linda Jensen 613-5642

Hekmat, Ali	C-Pr	613-5218	ahekmat	E	PHD	93	Wi-Milwa	1994

Eastern Washington Univ Cheney, WA 99004-2431 (509) 359-2281 ewu.edu
Department of Economics Social & Behavioral Sci Fax=359-6583 Nancy Millard

Chertox, Jeffers	Dean	359-2287		Soc	PHD	73	Oregon	
Trulove, William T.	C-Pr	359-2332			PHD	73	Oregon	1969
Bunting, David C.	Prof	359-7947			PHD	72	Oregon	1971
Karier, Thomas M.	Prof	623-4387			PHD	85	Berkeley	1981

Kiser, Larry L.	Prof	359-4307			PHD	73	Rutgers	1971
Liu, Tsung-Hua	Prof	359-2430			PHD	69	Toronto	1970
Brown, Lisa Jo	Assoc	359-2838			PHD	86	Colorado	1981
Orr, Douglas V.	Assoc	359-2424			PHD	82	Colorado	1991
Bownds, Lynne	Asst	359-2422			PHD	98	Tennessee	1999
Forsyth, Grant	Asst	359-6517			PHD	96	Wash St	1999

Edinboro University of PA — Edinboro, PA 16444 (814) 732-2407 — vax.edinboro.edu
Dept of Business Adm & Econ — Sch of Sci, Mgt & Tech Fax=732-1610 — Ms. Kathleen Schruers

Randall, Eric	Dean	732-2400	erandall		PHD			1977
Hannan, Michael J.	C-Pr	732-2407	hannan		PHD	88	W Virginia	1988
Dunn, James R.	Prof	732-1540	dunn		PHD	81	SUNY-Bin	1974
Adams, Robert J.	Assoc	732-2895	adamsr		PHD	71	Penn St	1977
Hannes, Lance E.	Assoc	732-2419	hannes		MBA	87	SUNY-Buf	1978
Morris, Gayle A.	Asst	732-1527	gmoris	FGOQ	PHD	81	Penn St	1999

Elizabethtown College — Elizabethtown PA 17022-2298 (717) 361-1270 — etown.edu
Economics Faculty — Department of Business Fax=361-1487 — Ms. Eunice Ginder
phone: 361-1270

Evans, Hugh G. Jr.	C-Ac	Ext 1276	evanshg		MA	66	Penn St	1968
Hoppie, Maurice R.	Assoc	Ext 1277	hoppiemr		PHD	85	Tennessee	1980

Elmhurst College — Elmhurst, IL 60126-3296 (630) 617-3122 — elmhcx9.elmhurst.edu
Center for Bus & Economics — Div of Social Sciences Fax=617-6497 — Gail Herff

Heiney, Joseph N.	D-Pr	279-4100	josephh		PHD	83	Chicago	1977
Coleman Foundation Distinguished Chair in Business								
Thoma, George A. Jr.	Prof	617-3098	georget		PHD	73	N Illinois	1970
Schmitz, Suzanne	Asst	617-3115	susans		PHD	89	Kentucky	1990
Wan, Siaw-Peng	Asst	617-3112	siawpeng		PHD	94	Illinois	1995

Elmira College — Elmire, NY 14901 (607) 735-1942 — elmira.edu
Economics Faculty — Department of Economics Fax=735-1701 — Dawn Haupt

Hoffman, Naphtali	C-Ac	735-1942	nhoffman		PHD	80	Case Wes	1976
Kahwar, Mariam	Asst	735-4930	mkahwar		PHD	97	J Hopkins	1997

Elon University — Elon College, NC 27244-2020 (336) 278-6000 — elon.edu
Department of Economics — Love School of Business Fax=278-5952 — Mrs. Teresa Walker
Homepage: elon.edu/econ

Burbridge, John J. Jr.	Dean	278-6000	burbridg	Mgt	PHD	70	Lehigh	1996
Lilly, Gregory A.	C-Ac	278-5944	lillyg	CDA	PHD	88	Duke	1990
Tiemann, Thomas K.	Prof	278-5957	tiemann	RC	PHD	75	Vanderbilt	1984
Barbour, James L.	Assoc	278-5945	barbour	AB	PHD	87	Kentucky	1990
Das, Jayoti	Asst	278-5941	dastina	FL	PHD	93	Cincinnati	1996
DeLoach, Stephen B.	Asst	278-5943	deloach	EF	PHD	93	Mich St	1996
King, Amanda	Asst	278-5949	aking	EJ	PHD	00	Vanderbilt	2000
Redington, Douglas B.	Asst	278-5948	redingto	Q	PHD	89	Wyoming	1995

Embry-Riddle Aeronautical U — Daytona Bch, FL 32114-3900 (386) 226-6694 — db.erau.edu
Economics Faculty — Business Administration Fax=226-6696 — Linda Larkin
Homepage: www.db.erau.edu
email @1=cts.db.erau.edu

Petree, Daniel L.	C-Pr	226-4967	petreed	JT	PHD	00	Kansas	2001
Harraf, Abe	Prof	226-6493	harraf		PHD	84	Utah St	
Vasigh, Bijan	Prof	226-6722	vasighb@1		PHD	84	SUNY-Bin	
Knabe, Rudolph	Assoc	226-6731	knaber@1		MA	76	Tennessee	
Tacker, Thomas L.	Assoc	226-6701	tackert@1		PHD	87	N Carol	
Kornecki, Lucyna	Asst	226-4963	korneckl@1		PHD	80	Krakow	
Marett, Pamela	Asst	226-6721	marlettp@1		PHD	82	Tennessee	

Emory University — Atlanta, GA 30322-2240 (404) 727-6364 — emory.edu
Economics Faculty — Department of Economics Fax=727-4639 — Susan Lee/L. Bassel/L. McNutt
Did Not Respond--1999-2000 Listing

Sanderson, Steve	Dean	727-6062						
Chirinko, Robert	C-Ac$	727-6645	rchirin	EGH	PHD	82	Nrthwstrn	1994
Aranson, Peter H.	Prof	727-6648	paranso	HKL	PHD	72	Rochester	1981
Benston, George J.	Prof	727-7831		GKLM	PHD	63	Chicago	9-87
John H. Harland Professor of Finance, Economics, and Accounting								
Muth, Richard F.	Prof	727-0328	rmuth	N	PHD	58	Chicago	1983
Fuller E. Callaway Professor of Economics								
Rubin, Paul	Prof	727-6365	prubin	K	PHD	70	Purdue	1991
Schaffer, Beverly K.	Prof	727-6361	bschaff	D	PHD	67	Duke	1965
Carlson, Leonard	Assoc	727-6375	econlac	DJN	PHD	77	Stanford	1975
Chakravorty, Ujjayant	Assoc	727-1381	unc	QRH	PHD	89	Hawaii	1999

Curran, Christopher	Assoc	727-6355	econcc	CDK	PHD	72	Purdue	1970
Dezhbakhsh, Hashem	Assoc	727-4679	econhd	CG	PHD	89	Ohio St	1992
Levy, Daniel	Assoc	727-2941	econdl	EC	PHD	90	Ca-Irvine	1992
Arbatskaya, Maria	Asst			DL	ABD		Indiana	9-99
Beelders, Owen	Asst	727-6650	obeelde	CG	PHD	98	Rochester	1997
Carpenter, Robert	Asst	727-2770	econrc	EL	PHD	92	Wash U	1992
Islam, Nazrul	Asst	727-8643	nislam	ECO	PHD	93	Harvard	1997
Mazumdar, Joy	Asst	727-7833	jmazumd	FEO	PHD	96	Michigan	1996
Ozden, Caglar	Asst	727-0355	cozden	FL	PHD	98	Stanford	1998
Schrag, Joel	Asst	727-6363	jschrag	DKL	PHD	93	Berkeley	1993
Emory and Henry College	Emory, VA	24327-0947	(540) 944-4121					ehc.edu
Economics Faculty	Dept of Econ & Business Fax=944-6223							
Did Not Respond--1999-2000 Listing								
Love, Barry A.	C-Ac	944-4121			PHD	78	Virginia	1984
Holbert L. Harris Professorship in Free Enterprise								
Dobkins, Linda H.	Asst	944-6194	lhdobkin	ROF	PHD	95	Va Tech	1996
Emporia State University	Emporia, KS	66801-5087	(620) 341-5346					esumail.emporia.edu
Dept of Accounting & CIS	School of Business Fax=341-6346							Jennifer Werly
Hashmi, Sajjad A.	Dean	341-5274			PHD	66	Penn	8-83
Jones Distinguished Professor								
Hindi, Nitham	C-Pr	341-5346	hinginit	Atg	DBA	91	Miss St	6-97
Catlett, Robert B.	Asst	341-5678			MA	75	Nebraska	1976
Chakraborhy, L.	Asst	341-5913			PHD	98	Utah St	2000
Ghosh, Dipak	Asst	341-5891			PHD	94	Tulane	1997
Janssen, Arthur J.	Asst	341-5401			MA		Missouri	1976
University of Evansville	Evansville, IN	47722	(812) 479-2851					evansville.edu
Dept of Accounting & Bus Adm	School of Business Adm Fax=479-2872							Sherry Hawkins
phone 1-800-423-8633 ext 2851								
Reeder, David B.	Dean	479-2866	dr4	Atg	MBA	80	Kentucky	1968
Blalock, M. Gale	C-Ac	479-2868	gb3		PHD	80	Okla St	1977
Zimmer, Michael A.	Prof	479-2864	mz3		PHD	77	Tennessee	1976
Evergreen State College	Olympia, WA	98505	(360) Ext 6513					
Economics Faculty	Pol Economy & Soc Chg Fax=							
Did Not Respond--1999-2000 Listing								
Hahn, Jeanne	C	866-6000		PolS	ABD	68	Chicago	1972
Bohmer, Peter G.		866-6000			PHD	85	Mass	1987
Bowerman, Priscilla V.		866-6000			MPHI	71	Yale	1973
Academic Dean								
Bruner, Bill		866-6000			BA	67	W Wash	1981
Nasser, Alan		866-6000			PHD	71	Indiana	1975
Weeks, Gregory C.		866-6000			PHD	78	Wash St	1981
Womeldorf, Thomas		866-8600			PHD	89	American	1991
Fairfield Universiy	Fairfield, CT	06430-5195	(203) Ext 2279					fairi.fairfield.edu
Department of Economics	Col of Arts & Sciences Fax=254-4074							Joan Huave
phone: 254-4000								
Lane, Philip J.	C-Ac	254-4000	lane	EGR	PHD	83	Tufts	1981
Buss, James A.	Prof	254-4000	jabuss	EOP	PHD	72	Conn	1975
Deak, Edward J.	Prof	254-4000	deak	LRK	PHD	74	Conn	1970
LeClair, Mark S.	Assoc	254-4000	mleclair	FGC	PHD	87	Rutgers	1988
Miners, Laurence A.	Assoc	254-4000	miners	CIJA	PHD	79	N Carol	1981
Nantz, Kathryn A.	Assoc	254-4000	nantz	JDPA	PHD	87	Purdue	1986
Franceschi, Dina	Asst	254-4000	dfrancheschi	QPO	PHD		Tennessee	1999
Kelly, Robert A.	Asst	254-4000	rakelly	HKC	PHD	71	Geotown	1978
Miners, Cathy	VAsst	254-4000	cminers	EG	PHD	81	N Carol	1998
Fairleigh Dickinson Univ	Madison, NJ	07940	(973) 443-8721					www.fdu.edu
Dept of Social Sci & Hist	Becton C of Arts & Sci Fax=443-8799							Grethe Zarnitz
Salmore, Barbara	Dean	443-8750	salmore	SSci	PHD	71	Rutgers	2000
Woolley, Peter J.	C	443-8721	woolley	DS	PHD	89	Pittsburgh	1987
Englander, Frederick	Prof	443-8832	englander	DE	PHD	75	Rutgers	9-87
Greenfield, Robert L.	Prof	443-8846		GP	PHD	79	Rutgers	8-79
Jonnard, Claude	Prof	443-8810	jonnard	A	PHD	63	NYU	9-65
Koppl, Roger	Assoc	443-8800	koppl	BEG	PHD	88	Auburn	1988
Fairleigh Dickinson Univ	Teaneck, NJ	07666-1914	(201) 692-7215					alpha.fdu.edu
Atg, Ec, Fn, Tx Lw, Intl Bus	Silbermann Col of Bus Fax=692-7219							Mrs. Eileen Kerrigan
Rogers, Leo	Dean$	692-7201			MA	63	Temple	
Oseghale, Braimoh	C-Ac	692-7221		F	PHD	89	Temple	1994

Djimopoulos, Evangelos S. Prof 692-7292 ADEF PHD 69 Columbia
Anastasopoulos, Petros Assoc 692-7268 ADE PHD 84 New Sch 1986
Kessler, Adam Assoc 692-7214 ACDE PHD 78 NYU
Kjetsaa, Richard W. Assoc 692-7295 AEG PHD 85 Fordham
Kiernan, Joseph J. Asst 692-7298 AEG PHD 80 Fordham

Fairmont State College Fairmont, WV 26554-2470 (304) 367-4261 mail.fscwv.edu
Department of Economics Sch of Business & Econ Fax=366-4870 Joyce Rose
Schaupp, Rebecca C-Pr 367-4261 ras EDD W Virginia 1984
Khalil, Mohamad C-Pr 367-4727 mak CF PHD 88 W Virginia 1988
Alshallah, Mohamed Assoc 367-4750 mha AD MBA Bridgepr 1988
Laughlin, William Assoc 367-4726 wml AE MA Cincinnati 1966
Potter, William Assoc 367-4724 potter AJ MA Memphis 1970

Fayetteville State Univ Fayetteville, NC 28301-4298 (910) 672-1617 sbel.uncfsu.edu
Dept of Mgr Econ & Finance Sch of Business & Econ Fax=672-2065 Ms. Tracey Burns
Davis, Charles H. Dean 486-1267 cdavis Mktg PHD 81 Tennessee 1993
Nijhawan, Inder P. C-Pr 486-1618 nijhawan PHD 71 N Carol
Jonsson, Petur O. Prof 486-1984 jonsson PHD 86 Penn St
Okpala, Amon O. Prof 486-1594 okpala PHD 84 LSU 1984
Roayaei, A. Jean Prof 486-1592 roayaei PHD 84 Fla St

Ferris State University Big Rapids, MI 49307-2284 (231) 591-2431 ferris.edu
Atg, Economics & Stat Dept College of Business Fax=591-3521 Kay Anderson
Nicol, David M. Dean 591-2422 Mgt PHD 94 Houston 2001
El-Saidi, Mohammed A. C-Pr 591-2479 mo+_el-saidi Mgt PHD 86 Memphis 1986
Afifi, Ashraf S. Prof 591-2766 aafifi ADH PHD 83 Kansas 1980
Ferdowsi, Abdollah Prof 591-2738 ferdowsa PHD 82 Mich St 1984
Teferra, Daniel Prof 591-2767 dteferra PHD 79 Wisconsin 1980

University of Findlay Findlay, OH 45840-3695 (419) 424-4539 lucy.findlay.edu
Economics Faculty College of Business Fax=424-6781 Ms. Kathy Bradford
Did Not Respond--1999-2000 Listing
Mathern, Dennis C. D-Ac 424-4546 mathern Mktg PHD 98 Bowl Gr
Gupta, Shiv K. Prof 424-4548 AJ DBA 83 London 1983
Gamba, Maria V. Asst 424-4718 AD MS Wright St 1988

Fisk University Nashville, TN 37208-3051 (615) 329-8570
Economics Faculty Div of Business Admin Fax=329-8758 Mrs. Eula Black
Did Not Respond--1999-2000 Listing
Cambronero, Alfredo C-As 329-8698 DOE PHD 92 Vanderbilt 1992

Fitchburg State College Fitchburg, MA 01420-2697 (978) 665-3397 fsc.edu
Economics Faculty Social Sciences Dept Fax=665-4530
Did Not Respond--1999-2000 Listing
Micciche, Pasquale E. C-Pr 665-3429 Hst PHD 76 Boston U 1969
Wiegersma, Nancy A. Prof 665-3088 PHD 76 Maryland 1979
Lwamugira, Pirudas L. Assoc 665-3281 PHD 90 Temple 1991
Turk, Michael Assoc 665-3731 PHD 76 Harvard 1982

University of Florida Gainesville, FL 32611-7140 (352) 392-0151 dale.cba.ufl.edu
Department of Economics College of Business Adm Fax=392-7860 Dian Studstill
Homepage: http://www.cba.ufl.edu/eco/index.html
Kraft, John L. Dean 392-2397 kraftj PHD 71 Pittsburgh 1990
West, Carol Taylor C-Pr 392-0171 ctwest RQC PHD 74 Michigan 1989
Director, Forcasting Program Bureau of Economics and Business Research
Adams, James D. Prof 392-0124 adams OJ PHD 76 Chicago 1979
Berg, Sanford V. Prof 392-0132 berg T PHD 70 Yale 1971
Exec Dir Public Utility Research Ctr;Public Utilities & Distinguished Serv Pr
Blair, Roger Duncan Prof 392-0179 rblair KT PHD 68 Mich St 1970
Huber Hurst Professor of Business and Legal Studies
Denslow, David A. Jr. Prof 392-0171 denslow EH PHD 74 Yale 1970
Distinguished Service Professor
Dinopoulos, Elias Prof 392-8150 dinopoe FO PHD 85 Columbia 1988
Hamilton, Johnathan H. Prof 392-2999 hamilton HRD PHD 82 MIT 1984
Kenny, Lawrence W. Prof 392-0151 kenny DHJ PHD 77 Chicago 1975
Lewis, Tracy R. Prof 392-7489 TDQ PHD 75 Ca-SnDgo 1991
James Walter Eminent Scholar in Economics
Romano, Richard E. Prof 392-4812 romano THOD PHD 82 Pittsburgh 1982
Gerald L. Gunter Professor
Rush, Mark Prof 392-0318 rush EF PHD 82 Rochester 1982
Sappington, David A. Prof 392-3904 sapping TD PHD 80 Princeton 1989
Lanzillotti-McKethan Eminent Scholar; Dir Public Policy Research Center

Slutsky, Steven M.	Prof	392-8106	slutsky	DH	PHD	75	Yale	1984
Smith, Stanley K.	Prof	392-0171	stans	J	PHD	76	Michigan	1976
Director, Bureau of Economic and Business Research								
Bomberger, William A.	Assoc	392-0135	billb		PHD	73	Brown	1977
Waldo, Douglas G.	Assoc	392-1370	waldo	EFO	PHD	80	N Carol	1981
Ai, Chunrong	Asst	392-7859	aic	CT	PHD	90	MIT	1994
Beckert, W.	Asst	392-0113	beckert	C	PHD	00	Berkeley	2000
Werner, Megan	Asst	392-0475	wernermj	CHQ	PHD	94	Ca-SnDgo	1994
Xu, Bin	Asst	392-0122	xub	FO	PHD	95	Columbia	1995

Florida A&M University Tallahassee, FL 32307-4800 (850) 599-3138 famu.edu
Department of Economics Coll of Arts & Sciences Fax=561-2050 Ms. Shequita Corker

Washington, Arthur	Dean	599-3430			PHD			
Oguledo, Victor I.	C-Pr	599-3138		FL	PHD	89	Nebraska	1990
Burggraf, Shirley	Prof	599-3126		CE	PHD	68	Case Wes	1968
Daniels, Rudolph	Prof	561-2052		DJQ	PHD	80	Fla St	1977
Bierhanzl, Elwood	Assoc	501-2055						
Auzenne, George R.	Lect	561-2057		LM	MS	63	Boston	1976

Florida Atlantic Univ Boca Raton, FL 33431-0991 (561) 297-3220 fau.edu
Department of Economics Col of Social Sciences Fax=297-2542 Patricia Spitale

Register, Charles A.	C-Pr	297-3222	cregister	JL	PHD	84	Okla St	1997
Hung, Chao-shun	Prof	297-3223	chung	D	PHD	82	Tx A&M	1982
Stronge, William B.	Prof	297-2833	strongew		PHD	71	Iowa St	1971
Bosshardt, William D.	Assoc		wbosshar	F	PHD	91	Purdue	1995
Director of Center for Economic Education								
Manage, Neela D.	Assoc	297-3226	manage	FE	PHD	81	Geo Wash	1981
Rhodd, Rupert	Assoc	236-1296	rhodd	FO	PHD	84	Fordham	1985
Scott, Gerald E.	Assoc	297-3225	scott	DF	PHD	87	Maryland	1993
Yuhn, Ky-hyang	Assoc	297-3224	yuhn	ECG	PHD	85	N Illinois	8-93
Benchekroun, Hassan	Asst	762-3222	benchekr	DL	PHD	98	Laval	1999
Gupta, Srabana	Asst	762-5251	sgupta	DL	PHD	95	Florida	1995
McCown, James	Asst	296-8502	jmccown	FE	PHD	97	Ohio St	1997
Vishwasrao, Sharmila	Asst	297-3229	svishwas	F	PHD	94	Purdue	1995

Florida Institute of Tech Melbourne, FL 32901-6975 (321) 674-7167 fit.edu
Dept of Economics School of Business Fax=674-8896 S. Farinella

Hollingsworth, A. Thomas	Dean	674-7327	aholling	Mgt	PHD	69	Mich St	1990
Turner, Craig	C-As	674-7392	cturner	Mgt	PHD	99	Tennessee	1999
Cahill, Gerard	Assoc	674-7495	gcahill	AG	PHD	73	NYU	1987
Slotkin, M.	Asst	674-7267	mslotkin	AFQ	PHD	95	N Carol	1996
Vamosi, Alexander R.	Asst	674-7497	avamosi	AEC	PHD	95	N Carol	2001

Florida International Univ Miami, FL 33199 (305) 348-2316 fiu.edu
Department of Economics College of Arts & Sci Fax=348-1524 Deuixieme Maison #314/316

Herriott, Arthur	Dean	348-2866	herriott	Chem	PHD	67	Florida	1993
Liossatos, Panagis S.	C-Pr	348-3288	liossato	CODR	PHD	68	Penn	1981
Alonso, Irma T. de	Prof	348-2318	alonsoi	OCFI	PHD	69	York-Eng	1981
Carvajal, Manuel J.	Prof	348-3290	carvajal	JITQ	PHD	74	Florida	1981
Jorge, Antonio	Prof	348-2072		BPO	PHD		Villanova	
Salazar-Carrillo, Jorge	Prof	348-3283	salazar	OFA	PHD	67	Berkeley	
Director, Center of Economic Research & Education								
Wilkins, Mira	Prof	348-3352	wilkinsm	NF	PHD	57	Cambridge	1974
Anbarci, Nejat M.	Assoc	348-2735	anbarcin	DC	PHD	88	Iowa	1995
Bhat, Mahadev G.	Assoc	348-1210	bhatm	Q	PHD	91	Tennessee	1994
Boyd, John H. III	Assoc	348-3287	boydj	DC	PHD	86	Indiana	1998
Karayalcin, Ali Cem	Assoc	348-3285	karayalc	EF	PHD	89	Columbia	1989
Lipner, Kenneth	Assoc	919-5859	lipnerk	RJA	PHD	77	Rutgers	1981
Roy, Santanu	Assoc	348-6362	roys	DLQF	PHD	91	Cornell	1998
Syropoulos, Constantinos	Assoc	348-2592	syropoul	FLO	PHD	89	Yale	1996
Willumsen, Maria Jose	Assoc	348-3400	willumse	RO	PHD	84	Cornell	1984
Chisik, Richard	Asst	348-3286	chisikr	DFL	PHD	97	Nrthwstrn	2000
Ciliberto, Federico	Asst	348-1070		DL	ABD		Nrthwstrn	2001
Lemke, Robert J.	Asst	348-6031	lemker	DJ	PHD	97	Wisconsin	1997
Mitra, Devashish	Asst	348-3893	mitrad	FLO	PHD	96	Columbia	1996
Thomakos, Dimitrios	Asst	348-6639	thomakos	CEO	PHD	98	Columbia	1998
Wang, Tao	Asst	348-2682	wangtao	EFG	PHD	00	J Hopkins	1999
Chuderewicz, Russell	VLect	348-3733	chudere	AEFG	PHD	97	Penn St	2000
Gummerson, A.	Lect	348-2381	gummerso	AEF	PHD	71	Wisconsin	1989

Florida Southern College Lakeland, FL 33801-5698 (863) 680-4280 flsouthern.edu
Dept of Bus & Economics Division of Bus Adm Fax=680-4126 Linda C. Murray

Brown, Carl C.	C-Pr	680-4280	cbrown	EFHL	PHD	79	Okla St	1980
William F. Chatlos Professorship in Business & Economics								
Buccino, Joan G.	Prof	680-4277		A	PHD	90	S Fla	1980
Dorotha Tanner Chair in Ethics in Business & Economics								
Lebrenz, Eugene R.	Prof	680-4274		J	EDD		N Illinois	1987
Bias, Peter V.	Assoc	680-4282		ER	PHD	89	Cincinnati	1988

Florida State University Tallahassee, FL 32306-2180 (850) 644-5001 garnet.acns.fsu.edu
Department of Economics College of Soc Sciences Fax=644-4535 Fran Loeb 644-7089
email @1=mailer.fsu.edu @2=coss.fsu.edu

Cowart, Marie	Dean	644-5488	mcowart@1		PHD			
Cobbe, James H.	C-Pr	644-7091	jcobbe@2	O	PHD	77	Yale	1976
Adamovich, Ljubisa S.	Prof	644-7097	ladamov	E	PHD	61	Belgrade	1967
Benson, Bruce L.	Prof	644-7094	bbenson@2	K	PHD	78	Tx A&M	1987
VeDoe Moore Distinguished Research Professor								
Canterbery, E. Ray	Prof	644-7209	rcanterb	F	PHD	66	Wash U	1970
Fournier, Gary M.	Prof	644-7080	gfournie@2	L	PHD	81	Virginia	1980
Gwartney, James D.	Prof	644-7645	jgwartne	A	PHD	69	U Wash	1968
Holcombe, Randall G.	Prof	644-7095	holcombe@2	H	PHD	76	Va Tech	1988
DeVoe Moore Professor								
Ihlanfeldt, Keith R.	Prof	644-0075	kihlanfe@1	HR	PHD	78	Wash U	2000
DeVoe Moore Eminent Scholar Chair								
Isaac, R. Mark	Prof	644-7081	misaac@1		PHD	81	Cal Tech	2001
Quinn Eminent Scholar Chair								
Koo, Anthony Y.	VProf	644-7086	ykoo	F	PHD	46	Harvard	
Macesich, George	Prof	644-7079	gmacesic	E	PHD	58	Chicago	1959
Macpherson, David A.	Prof	644-3586	dmacpher@2	J	PHD	87	Penn St	1992
Research Director, Pepper Institute on Aging & Public Policy								
Marquis, Milton H.	Prof	644-7204	mmarquis	E	PHD	85	Indiana	1986
on leave								
Norrbin, Stefan C.	Prof	644-7206	snorrbin	F	PHD	86	Ariz St	1990
Rasmussen, David W.	Prof	644-7659	drasmuss@2	K	PHD	69	Wash U	1968
Director, DeVoe Moore Center								
Schlagenhauf, Don E.	Prof	644-3817	dschlage@1	E	PHD	77	Illinois	1998
Brim Eminent Scholar Chair								
Serow, William J.	Prof	644-1762	wserow@2	T	PHD	72	Duke	1981
Director, Center for Study of Population								
Sliger, Bernard F.	Prof	644-4772	sliger@1	A	PHD	55	Mich St	1972
Beaumont, Paul M.	Assoc	644-7085		C	PHD	84	Penn	1988
on leave								
Mason, Patrick L.	Assoc		pmason	J	PHD	91	New Sch	1999
McCaleb, Thomas S.	Assoc	644-1816	tmccaleb@1		PHD	75	N Carol	1980
Prasad, Kislaya	Assoc	644-7083	kprasad@2	D	PHD	88	Syracuse	1988
Sass, Tim R.	Assoc	644-7087	tsass@2	L	PHD	84	U Wash	1990
Schmertmann, Carl P.	Assoc	644-7100	schmert@2	C	PHD	88	Berkeley	1990
Zuehlke, Thomas W.	Assoc	644-7208	tzuehlke	C	PHD	83	Florida	1983
Graduate Director								
Burke, Mary A.	Asst	644-5003	mburke@1	D	PHD	98	J Hopkins	1997
Garriga, Carlos	Asst	644-7208			PHD	99	Barcelona	2001
Lee, Susan		644-4557	slee		PHD	00	Wisconsin	2000
Salmon, Tim		644-7207	tsalmon		PHD	99	J Hopkins	2000
Young, Eric		644-7088	eyoung		PHD	01	Car Mellon	2001

Fordham University New York, NY 10458 (212) 817-4048 murray.fordham.edu
Department of Economics Col of Arts & Sciences Fax=817-3518 Angela Bates
Did Not Respond--1999-2000 Listing

Himmelberg, Robert	Dean			Hist	PHD	63	Penn St	
Salvatore, Dominick	C-Pr	817-4048			PHD	71	CUNY	1970
Cammarosano, Joseph R.	Prof	817-4057			PHD	56	Fordham	1955
Dowling, Edward T.	Prof	817-4062			PHD	73	Cornell	1973
Vinod, Hrishinesh D.	Prof	817-4065			PHD	65	Harvard	1982
Basu, Parantap	Assoc	817-4061			PHD	85	Ca-SnBarb	1988
Brent, Robert J.	Assoc	817-4058			PHD	76	Manchest	1980
Diulio, Eugene A.	Assoc	817-4055			PHD	66	Columbia	1963
Assistant Chair, Undergraduate Education								
Leighton, Linda S.	Assoc	817-4054			PHD	78	Columbia	1979
Champ, Bruce	Asst	817-4056			PHD	90	Minnesota	1994
Geddes, Raymond R.	Asst	817-4049			PHD	91	Chicago	1991
James, Duncan	Asst	817-4066			PHD	98	Arizona	1999
McLeod, Darryl L.	Asst	817-4063			PHD	82	Berkeley	1984
Reagle, Derrick	Asst	817-3866			PHD	98	Vanderbilt	1998
Rowland, Patrick	Asst	817-4051			PHD	98	Ca-SnBarb	1996
Schwalbenberg, Henry M.	Asst	817-4059			PHD	88	Columbia	1988
Assistant Chair, Graduate Education								
Winczewski, Greg A.	Asst	817-4050			PHD	92	Fordham	1995

Fort Hays State University Hays, KS 67601-4099 (785) 628-5805 fhsu.edu
Dept of Economics & Finance Col of Bus & Leadership Fax=628-4418 Linda Kepka
Homepage: www.fhsu.edu/econ

Parker, Carl D.	C-Pr	628-5805	cparker	DIJM	PHD	71	Okla St	1976
Director, Employee Relations								
Gamble, Ralph C. Jr.	Prof	628-5325	rgamble	AEG	PHD	89	Okla St	1984
Rickman, Bill D.	Prof	628-5318	brickman	DEJ	PHD	82	Okla St	1972
Gilson, Preston	Assoc	628-4107	pgilson	F	PHD	93	St Louis	1988
Johansen, Thomas C.	Assoc	628-5867	tjohanse	GE	PHD	90	Okla St	1989
Terry, Rory L.	Asst	628-5337	rterry	GE	PHD	92	Utah	1997
Toulaboe, Dosse	Asst	628-5868	dtoulabo	DEFL	PHD	98	Okla St	2000

Fort Lewis College Durango, CO 81301-3999 (970) 247-7294 fortlewis.edu
Department of Economics School of Business Adm Fax=247-7623 Rose Clay
Homepage: http://ww.fortlewis.edu/soba/soba.html

Cave, John E. Jr.	Dean	247-7294	cave_s	BusA	PHD	75	Minnesota	1990
Atencio, Leonard D.	Prof	247-7589	anencio_l		PHD	69	Kansas St	1968
Clay, James P.	Prof	247-7591	clay_j		PHD	74	Kansas St	1982
Lynch, Vernon E. Jr.	Prof	247-7404	lynch_v		PHD	76	Arizona	1972
Lehman, Dale E.	Assoc	247-7494	lehman_d		PHD	81	Rochester	1983
Hai, Wen	Asst	247-7494	wai_w		PHD	91	Ca-Davis	1992

Fort Valley State University Fort Valley, GA 31030-3298 (478) 825-6270 mail.fvsu.edu
Dept of Business Adm & Econ Col of Arts & Sciences Fax=825-6394 Shuri Rand

Jenkins, Wilsie	Dean	825-6454			PHD			
Givens, Norma N.	C-Pr	825-6270	givens	Mgt	EDD	77	Georgia	8-79
Yasin, Jehad	Assoc	825-6270	jyasin	ETAC	PHD	87	Fla St	9-88

Framingham State College Framingham, MA 01701-9101 (508) 626-4850 sagan.frc.mass.edu
Economics Faculty Dept of Econ & Bus Adm Fax=626-4040 Dori Pedroli

White, Charles E.	C-Pr	626-4892	cwhite		PHD	81	Chicago	9-85
Dunne, Maureen E.	Prof	626-4861	mdunne		MBA		Detroit	
Krier, Donald F.	Prof	626-4884	dkrier		PHD	69	Boston C	1973
McKinney, Marie M.	Prof	626-4853	mmckinn		PHD	83	SUNY-Bin	1985
Meaney, Martha M.	Prof	626-4889	mmeaney		MA		Boston C	
Wallace, Robert	Prof	626-4888	rwallac		PHD	72	Nrthwstrn	
Doyle-Burke, Christine	Assoc	626-4886	cdoyle		MA		Boston C	
MacRitchie, Donald R.	Assoc	626-4881	dmacrit		MA	85	Boston C	1987
Devine, Robert	Asst	626-4882	rdevine		MA		Northeas	
Ryan, Peter C.	Asst	626-4844	pryan		PHD	77	Mass	

Francis Marion University Florence, SC 29501-0547 (843) 661-1432 fmarion.edu
Economics Faculty School of Business Fax=661-1165 Carol Austin
Did Not Respond--1999-2000 Listing

Goebel, E. L. (Jack)	Dean	661-1430		Mgt	PHD	68	Georgia	8-95
Rinehart, James R.	C-Pr	661-1426			PHD	62	Virginia	
Phillip N. Truluck Professor of Economics and Public Policy								
Kyer, Ben L.	Prof	661-1436			PHD	84	W Virginia	
Marcis, John G.	Assoc	661-1412			PHD		Missouri	
O'Brien, M. Barry	Assoc	661-1437			PHD	86	S Carol	
Pompe, Jeffrey	Assoc	661-1438			PHD	90	Fla St	

Franklin University Columbus, OH 43215-5399 (614) 341-6330 franklin.edu
Div Atg, Fnce & Intl Bus Col of Business & Tech Fax=228-8478
Did Not Respond--1999-2000 Listing

Newton, James E.	C-Pr	341-6330	newtonj		PHD	97	Ohio St	
Assistant Dean								

Franklin and Marshall Coll Lancaster, PA 17604-3003 (717) 291-3916 acad.fandm.edu
Economics Faculty Department of Economics Fax=291-4369 Maryfrances Mason
Homepage: www.famdm.edu/departments/economics/economics.html

Callari, Antonio	C-Pr	291-3947	a_callari		PHD	81	Mass	1979
Caniglia, Alan S.	Prof	291-3945	a_caniglia		PHD	83	Virginia	1982
The Sigmund M. and Mary B. Hyman Professor of Economics								
Flaherty, Sean	Prof	291-3940	s_flaherty	J	PHD	81	Berkeley	1980
Whitesell, William E.	Prof	291-3938	w_whitesell		PHD	63	Tx-Austin	1965
Henry P. & Mary B. Stager Professor of Economics								
Zein-Elabdin, Eiman	Assoc	291-4045	e_zein-elabdin		PHD	93	Tennessee	1995
A'Hearn, Brian	Asst	291-3990	b_ahearn		PHD	94	Berkeley	1999
Brennan, David	Asst	291-3926	d_brennan		PHD	00	Notre Dm	1998
Maynard, Raymond	Asst	394-7155	r_maynard		PHD	00	Tennessee	2000
Mulder, Cathy	Inst	291-3920	c_mulder		ABD		Mass	1999

Freed Hardeman University Henderson, TN 38340-2399 (731) 989-6091 fhu.edu
Economics Faculty School of Business Fax=989-6757 Mrs. Estelle Maxwell

Wilson, Dwayne H.	Dean	989-6091	dwilson	CDEQ	PHD	91	Miss	8-75
Director of the Free Enterprise Center								
Perkins, Garey B.	Assoc	989-6983	gperkins	DEQ	PHD	71	Tennessee	8-98
Brooks, Rickey A.	Asst	989-6054	rbrooks	DEF	MBA	91	Miss	8-92

Frostburg State University Frostburg, MD 21532-1099 (301) 687-4386 fre.fsu.umd.edu
Department of Economics School of Business Fax=687-4760 Ms. Yvonne R. Beal
Did Not Respond--1999-2000 Listing

Wilkinson, Steven P.	Dean	687-4089			PHD	77	S Illinois	8-87
Stair, Anthony G.	C-Ac	687-4788			PHD	93	W Virginia	1984

Dalton, Margaret M.	Prof	687-4386			PHD	86	W Virginia	1981
Mizak, Daniel A.	Prof	687-4096			PHD	84	Pittsburgh	1977
McLellan, Jacquelynne W.	Assoc	687-4394			PHD	93	Wayne St	1994
Neral, John A.	Assoc	687-4265			PHD	89	Pittsburgh	1986
Rossi, Armond A.	Asst	687-4407			PHD	93	W Virginia	1988
Kiriazis, David M.	Lect	687-4390			PHD	97	Wayne St	

Furman University — Greenville, SC 29613-1130 (864) 294-2132 — furman.edu
Economics Faculty — Dept of Econ & Bus Adm Fax=294-2990 — Brenda Chandler

Patterson, Cheryl C.	C-Ac	294-3311	cheryl.pat+	Mgt	PHD	87	Clemson	9-86
Horney, Mary Jean	Prof	294-3315			PHD	77	Duke	1979
Frederick W. Symmes Professor of Economics								
Roe, R. David	Prof	294-3320			PHD	78	Duke	1977
Stanford, Richard A.	Prof	294-3322			PHD	71	Georgia	1968
David C Garrett Jr. Professor of Economics								
Khandke, Kailash	Assoc	294-3316			PHD	93	Ca-Davis	1995
Peterson, Kenneth D.	Assoc	294-3043			PHD	91	SUNY-SBr	1990

Gallaudet University — Washington DC 20002-3695 (202) 651-5040 — gallaudet.edu
Department of Business — Grad & Prof Studies Sch Fax=651-5516

Allen, Thomas E.	Dean	651-5576	thomas.allen	EdPs	PHD	78	Minnesota	
Chaikind, Stephen B.	C-Pr	651-5040	steve.chaikin		PHD	78	CUNY	1989
Cook, Laura	Fell	651-5040			MA	01		

Gannon University — Erie, PA 16541-0001 (814) 871-7585 — gannon.edu
Business Administration — Dahlkemper Sch of Bus Fax=871-7210

Doan, William	Dean	874-7549	doan001	FArt	PHD	99	Case Wes	
Prokop, Duane R.	C	871-7576	prokopool	Mktg	MBA	78	Youngstwn	1-81
Aburachis, Abdelrahman E.	Prof	871-7584	aburachidol	G	PHD	72	Pittsburgh	
Brooker, Robert F.	Assoc	871-7586	brookercol	C	PHD	85	N Car St	1982
Mahan, Gary P.	Assoc	871-7588	mahancon		PHD	78	N Car St	1977
Bennett, Charles A.	Asst	871-7585	bennett	A	MA	68	Fordham	1968

Gardner-Webb University — Boiling Spr, NC 28017 (704) 406-4375 — gardner-webb.edu
Economics Faculty — Broyhill Sch of Mgt Fax=406-4738 — Sharon Webb

Honts, Arlen K.	Dean	406-2361	ahonts	Mgt	PHD	97	Vanderbilt	1993
Bottoms, I. Glenn	Prof	406-4377	gbottoms		PHD	81	Geo St	1983
Negbenebor, Anthony I.	Prof	406-3820	anegbenebor		PHD	88	Miss St	1989

Geneva College — Beaver Falls, PA 15010-3599 (724) 847-6615 — geneva.edu
Economics Faculty — Dept of Bus, Atg & Mgt Fax=847-6696 — B. Dawson
Homepage: www.geneva.edu

Nutter, J. Randall	C-Pr	847-6613	jrn	Mgt	DBA	91	Nova SE	1992
Fong, Tat P.	Asst	847-6615	tfong	F	PHD	91	Pittsburgh	1996

George Fox University — Newberg, OR 97132-2697 (503) Ext 2811 — georgefox.edu
Economics Faculty — Dept of Business & Econ Fax=554-2829 — Cheri Hampton Ext 2810
phone 544-2811

Head, Tom	C-Pr	Ext 2811	thead		MA	80	Berkeley	
Dykema, Eugene R.	Prof	Ext 2812	edykema		PHD	83	Notre Dm	
Worden, Debra	Asst	Ext 2816	dworden		PHD	84	Purdue	

George Mason University — Fairfax, VA 22030-4444 (703) 993-1130 — gmu.edu
Department of Economics — College of Arts & Sci Fax=993-1133 — Keri Finkenbinder
Homepage: www.gmu.edu/departmens/economics

Bondreaux, Donald	C-Pr	993-1131	dbondrea		PHD	86	Auburn	
Bennett, James T.	Prof	993-1155	jbennett		PHD	70	Case Wes	1975
William P. Snavely Professor of Economics								
Buchanan, James M.	Emer	993-2327			PHD	48	Chicago	1983
University Professor of Economics Emeritus								
Congleton, Roger D.	Prof	993-2328	congleto		PHD	78	Va Tech	1988
Cowen, Tyler	Prof	993-1136	tcowen		PHD	87	Harvard	
Crain, W. Mark	Prof	993-2325	mcrain		PHD	76	Tx A&M	
Heiner, Ronald A.	Prof	993-2322	rheiner		PHD	75	UCLA	1989
Rowley, Charles K.	Prof	993-4026	crowley		PHD	64	Nottinghm	1984
Vaughn, Karen I.	Prof	993-1146	kvaughn		PHD	71	Duke	1978
Wagner, Richard E.	Prof	993-2324	rwagner		PHD	66	Virginia	1988
Holbert L. Harris Professor of Economics								
Williams, Walter E.	Prof	993-1148	wwilliams		PHD	72	UCLA	1981
John M. Olin Distinguished Professor of Economics								
Levy, David M.	Assoc	993-2319	dlevy		PHD	79	Chicago	1983
Meyer, Carrie A.	Assoc	993-1143	cmeyer		PHD	88	Illinois	1988
Reid, Joseph D.	Assoc	993-1159	jreid		PHD	74	Chicago	1983

Thorbecke, Willem	Assoc	993-1150	wthorbec		PHD	88	Berkeley	
Wiest, Philip Ray	Assoc	993-1130	pwiest		PHD	76	Pittsburgh	
Caplan, Bryan	Asst	993-1124	bcaplan		PHD	97	Princeton	1997
Hanson, Robin	Asst	993-2826	rhanson		PHD	99	Cal Tech	1999
Menes, Rebecca	Asst	993-1156	rmenes		PHD	97	Harvard	1999
Ramirez, Carlos D.	Asst	993-1145	cramirez		PHD	93	Harvard	

George Washington Univ	Washington, DC		20052	(202) 994-6150			gwu.edu	
Department of Economics	Columbian C Arts & Sci		Fax=994-6147				Julie Schumakes	
Lefton, Lester A.	Dean	994-6210			PHD			
Watson, Harry S.	C-Pr	994-6685	hsw	H	PHD	81	Indiana	1980
Boulier, Bryan L.	Prof	994-8088	mortile	JT	PHD	74	Princeton	1981
Bradley, Michael D.	Prof	994-8089	mbrad	E	PHD	82	N Carol	1987
Brock, Gerald W.	Prof	994-3989	gbrock	L	PHD	73	Harvard	1990
Cordes, Joseph J.	Prof	994-6151	cordes	H	PHD	77	Wisconsin	1975
Dunn, Robert M. Jr.	Prof	994-7379	rmdunn	F	PHD	67	Stanford	1978
Goldfarb, Robert S.	Prof	994-7581	gldfrb	BJ	PHD	68	Yale	1980
Kaminsky, Graciela	Prof	994-6686	graciela	F	PHD	83	MIT	1998
Kwoka, John E. Jr.	Prof	994-6922	kwoka	L	PHD	72	Penn	1981
Labadie, Pamela A.	Prof	994-7068	labadie	E	PHD	84	Chicago	1996
Millar, James R.	Prof	994-6342	millar	P	PHD	65	Cornell	1989
Parsons, Donald O.	Prof	994-3984	dopars	J	PHD	70	Chicago	1997
Pelzman, Joseph	Prof	994-7108	jpelz	F	PHD	76	Boston C	1980
Trost, Robert P.	Prof	994-9011	trost	C	PHD	77	Florida	1981
Yezer, Anthony M.	Prof	994-6755	yezer	R	PHD	74	MIT	1972
Joshi, Sumit	Assoc	994-6154	sumjos	CD	PHD	91	Indiana	1992
Joutz, Frederick L.	Assoc	994-4899	bmark	EC	PHD	87	U Wash	1988
Malik, Arun	Assoc	994-5471	amalik	Q	PHD	84	J Hopkins	1992
Moore, Michael Owen	Assoc	994-6157	mom	F	PHD	88	Wisconsin	1988
Phillips, Robert F.	Assoc	994-8619	rphil	C	PHD	85	Columbia	1985
Ribar, David	Assoc	994-7608	dcr7	J	PHD	93	Brown	1996
Smith, Stephen C.	Assoc	994-8086	scsmith	O	PHD	83	Cornell	1983
Snyder, Christopher	Assoc	994-6581	csnyder	L	PHD	94	MIT	1994
Suranovic, Steven M.	Assoc	994-7579	smsuan	F	PHD	87	Cornell	1988
Vonortas, Nicholas S.	Assoc	994-6458	vonortas	OL	PHD	89	NYU	
Fon, Vincy	Asst	994-7580	vfon	CD	PHD	81	Kansas	1979
Soares, Jorge	Asst	994-0192	jsoares	E	PHD	96	Rochester	1998
Bailey, Mary Ann	Adj	994-5838	mabaily	I	PHD	74	MIT	1983
Solomon, Elinor H.	Adj	994-6581	esolomon	E	PHD	48	Harvard	1982

Georgetown University	Washington, DC		20057-1036	(202) 687-5830			georgetown.edu	
Department of Economics	College of Arts & Sci		Fax=687-6102					
Cuddington, John T.	C-Pr	687-6103	duddingj	FO	PHD	78	Wisconsin	1986
Albrecht, James W.	Prof	687-6105	albrecht	DJ	PHD	76	Berkeley	1992
Anderlini, Luca	Prof	687-5601	la2	D	PHD	97	Cambridge	2001
Canzoneri, Matthew B.	Prof	687-5911	canzonem	EFG	PHD	75	Minnesota	1985
Cumby, Robert	Prof	687-2990	cumbyr	FG	PHD	82	MIT	1994
Evans, Martin D. D.	Prof	687-1570	evansm12	EFG	PHD	87	Princeton	1996
Gale, Ian L.	Prof	687-5732	galei	L	PHD	86	Princeton	1995
McNelis, Paul D.	Prof	687-5573	mcnelisp	EFG	PHD	74	J Hopkins	1977
Rogers, Carol Ann	Prof	687-5816	rogersc	EH	PHD	83	Princeton	1984
Schwartz, Marius	Prof	687-6112	schwarm2	DL	PHD	82	UCLA	1982
Viksnins, George J.	Prof	687-5890	viksning	GP	PHD	64	Geotown	1968
Vroman, Susan	Prof	687-6024	vromans	DJ	PHD	77	J Hopkins	1978
Brown, Douglas M.	Assoc	687-5772	browndm	DIR	PHD	69	W Virginia	1972
Collins, Susan M.	Assoc	687-5781	collins1	FO	PHD	84	MIT	1992
Diba, Behzad T.	Assoc	687-5682	dibab	EFG	PHD	84	Brown	1988
Lagunoff, Roger D.	Assoc	687-1510	lagunoffr	DLH	PHD	89	Minnesota	1996
Lennson, Arik M.	Assoc	687-5571	aml6	HQ	PHD	93	Columbia	2000
Oweiss, Ibrahim M.	Assoc	687-5582	oweissi	OF	PHD	69	Minnesota	1967
Chaudhuri, Adhrp	Asst	687-6113	chaudhur	IFB	PHD	79	Columbia	1979
Cross, Phil	Asst	687-8202		HD	PHD	01	Wisconsin	2001
Huggett, Mark	Asst	687-6683	mh5	O	PHD	91	Minnesota	1999
Kaneda, Mitch	Asst	687-5894	kanedam	F	PHD	94	Penn	1994
Ludema, Rodney	Asst	687-1429	ludemar	F	PHD	90	Columbia	1995
Olley, G. Steven	Asst	687-7144	olleys	L	PHD	92	Wisconsin	1997
Westbrook, M. Daniel	Asst	687-5880	westbrom	D	PHD	78	Ohio St	1978
Yousef, Tarek M.	Asst	687-0347	youseft	OB	PHD	97	Harvard	1999

University of Georgia	Athens, GA		30602-6252	(706) 542-1311			terry.uga.edu	
Department of Economics	Terry College of Bus		Fax=542-3376				Cindy Owensby	
Benson, P. George	Dean	542-8100		Stat	PHD	77	Florida	1998
DeLorme, Charles D. Jr.	H-Pr	542-3682	delorme	EH	PHD	66	LSU	1968
Atkinson, Scott E.	Prof	542-3691	atknsn	CQK	PHD	72	Colorado	1985
Bateman, Fred	Prof	542-3692	bateman	N	PHD	65	Tulane	1991
Nicholas A. Beadles Professor								
Danielsen, Albert L.	Prof	542-3807	daniel	MH	PHD	66	Duke	1963

Kamerschen, David R.	Prof	542-3681	davidk	DK	PHD	64	Mich St	1974
Jasper N. Dorsey Professor								
Keenan, Donald C.	Prof	542-3668	keenan	CHR	DSC	78	Wash U	1978
Lee, Dwight R.	Prof	542-3970	lee	DHM	PHD	72	Ca-SnDgo	1985
Bernard B. & Eugenia A. Ramsey Professor								
Lovell, Knox	Prof	542-3689	knox	D	PHD	66	Duke	1994
Herman & Mary Virginia Terry Professor								
Cornwell, Christopher M.	Assoc	542-3670	cornwl	CHJ	PHD	85	Mich St	1988
Lastrapes, William D.	Assoc	542-3569	last	CEF	PHD	86	N Carol	1990
Selgin, George A.	Assoc	542-2734	selgin	EN	PHD	86	NYU	1989
Snow, Arthur	Assoc	542-3752	snow	DH	PHD	79	Wisconsin	1989
Trandel, Gregory A.	Assoc	542-3673	trandel	GK	PHD	92	Princeton	1989
Warren, Ronald S.	Assoc	542-3693	warren	JC	PHD	76	N Carol	1985
Chatterjee, Santanu	Asst	542-3696	schatt		PHD	01	U Wash	2001
Klein, Peter G.	Asst	542-3697	klein	GKL	PHD	95	Berkeley	1995
Mustard, David B.	Asst	542-1311	mustard	DJK	PHD	97	Chicago	1997

Georgia College Milledgeville GA 31061-4090 (478) 453-4210 mail.gcsu.edu
Dept of Econ, Finance & Mktg School of Business Fax=445-1535 Virginia Simmons

Jones, Jo Ann	Dean	453-5497			PHD	77	La Tech	1976
Sarkar, Amin U.	C-Pr	445-1807		OQ	PHD	88	Berkeley	
Jones, Kenneth D.	Prof	471-2063			PHD	77	La Tech	1987
Dean, Graduate School								
Samprone, Joseph C. Jr.	Prof	454-2596		AD	PHD	75	Ca-SnBarb	1983
Farr, William Kendrick	Assoc	454-2593		ADQ	PHD	85	Georgia	1985
Arias, James J.		445-2085		E	PHD	96	Tx A&M	
Butler, Doug		445-2414			ABD			
Walker, Doug		445-2596			PHD			
Xu, Zhenhui		445-2592			PHD	93	Virginia	

Georgia Institute Tech Atlanta, GA 30318-6015 (404) 894-4919 econ.gatech.edu
School of Economics Allen Col Mgt, Plcy & I Fax=894-1890 Carolyn Stephens/M. Johnson
Did Not Respond--1999-2000 Listing

Hawkins, Robert G.	Dean	894-2601			PHD	66	NYU	1993
email: robert.hawkins@iac.gatech.edu								
Ries, Christine P.	C-Pr	894-4919	christine.ries		PHD	77	Chicago	1997
Biven, W. Carl	Prof	894-1885	carl.biven	EB	PHD	56	St Louis	1958
Boston, Thomas D.	Prof	894-5020	thomas.boston	JN	PHD	76	Cornell	1985
Chu, Kong	Prof	894-1886	kong.chu	OC	PHD	64	Tulane	1968
Schaffer, William A.	Prof	894-4915	william.schaffer	R	PHD	63	Duke	1963
Belton, Willie J. Jr.	Assoc	894-4388	willie.belton	E	PHD	86	Penn St	1987
McCarty, Marilu H.	Assoc	894-2621	marilu.mccarty	EH	PHD	72	Geo St	1972
Li, Haizheng C.	Asst	894-3542	clifford.li	C	PHD	97	Colorado	1997
McCabe, Mark J.	Asst	385-0512	mccabe.mark	L	PHD	91	MIT	1998
Nair, Usha C.	Asst	894-4903	usha.nair	F	PHD	95	Purdue	1996

Georgia Southern University Statesboro, GA 30460-8151 (912) 681-5161 gsvms2.cc.gasou.edu
Dept of Finance & Economics College of Business Adm Fax=871-1835 Barbara Focht, Kaye Brammen

Byington, J. Ralph	Dean	681-5106	byington	Atg	PHD	85	Arkansas	1995
Paul, Chris W.	C-Pr	681-5161	cpaul	K	PHD	79	Tx A&M	2000
White, John B.	C-Pr	681-5161	jwhite	Fnce	PHD	85	Virginia	1989
Davis, Elynor G.	Prof	681-5020	edavis		PHD	78	Tx A&M	1979
Isley, Phyllis	Assoc	681-0213	pisley		PHD	86	NewHamp	1998
Levernier, William B.	Assoc	681-5227	sofinbl		PHD	88	W Virginia	1989
Barilla, Anthony	Asst	681-0894	barilla		PHD	01	Kansas St	2001
Brock, Greg J.	Asst	681-5161	gbrock	PO	PHD	89	Ohio St	1999
Brown, John H.	Asst	681-0896	jbrown		PHD	89	Mich St	1994
Koch, S.	Asst	681-5161	skoch		PHD	97	Penn St	1998
Ogloblin, Constantin	Asst	681-7561	costya@msn.com		PHD	99	Kent	2000
Yang, Bill	Asst	681-5727	byand	LG	PHD	93	Iowa	2000
Yanochik, Mark	Asst	681-5020	myanochi		PHD	97	Auburn	2000

Georgia Southwestern Coll Americus, GA 31709-4693 (912) 931-2079 business.gsw.edu
Economic Faculty Div of History & Pol Sc Fax=
Did Not Respond Again--1997-98 Listing

Baringer, Richard L.	C-Pr	931-2079		Hst	PHD	69	G Peabdy	
Huddleston, Kenneth M.	Asst	931-2079			MBA		Geo St	

Georgia State University Atlanta, GA 30303-3083 (404) 651-2626 gsuvm1.gsu.edu
Department of Economics Andrew Young Sch Policy Fax=651-4985 Caroline Patton Griffin

Bahl, Roy W. Jr.	Dean	651-3993	prcrwb	HR	PHD	65	Kentucky	1988
Alm, James R.	C-Pr	651-0420	prcjra	DHO	PHD	80	Wisconsin	1999
Cummings, Ronald G.	Prof	651-1888	prcrgc	Q	PHD	68	Kansas	1993
Noah Langdale Jr. Eminent Scholar Chair of Environmental Policy								
Kaufman, Bruce E.	Prof	651-2922	ecobek	JN	PHD	78	Wisconsin	1977

Martinez, Jorge L.	Prof	651-3989	prcjlm	DF	PHD	78	Wash U	1977
Sjoquist, David L.	Prof	651-3995	prcdls	DR	PHD	71	Minnesota	1970
Stephan, Paula E.	Prof	651-3988	prcpes	JO	PHD	71	Michigan	1971
Turnbull, Geoffrey K.	Prof	651-2626	prcgkt	R	PHD	83	Wi-Milwa	2001
Farnham, Paul G.	Assoc	651-2624	ecopgf	DHI	PHD	78	Berkeley	1977
Gurmu, Shiferaw	Assoc	651-1907	prcsg	CI	PHD	92	Indiana	1998
Hotchkiss, Julie L.	Assoc	651-3986	prcjlh	CJ	PHD	89	Cornell	1989
Mansfield, Jon	Assoc	651-2626	ecojxm	AM	PHD	92	Geo St	1996
Moore, Robert E.	Assoc	651-3756	prcrem	FO	PHD	88	Cornell	1989
Associate Dean								
Seaman, Bruce A.	Assoc	651-2775	ecobas	DL	PHD	78	Chicago	1978
Taylor, Laura L.	Assoc	651-2873	prclot	C	PHD	94	N Car St	1994
Walker, Mary Beth	Assoc	651-3751	prcmbw	DC	PHD	86	Rice	1991
Wallace, Sally	Assoc	651-3959	prcskw	GH	PHD	88	Syracuse	1991
Xu, Yongsheng	Assoc	651-2626		DHC	PHD	92	Tulane	1999
Bae, Jay	Asst	651-4967	prcjbp	I	PHD	93	UCLA	2000
Edmiston, Kelly D.	Asst	651-3519	prckde	EGHR	PHD	98	Tennessee	1998
Ferraro, Paul	Asst	651-2626	prcpjf	C	PHD	01	Cornell	2001
Laury, Susan K.	Asst	651-2626		HC	PHD	96	Indiana	1999
Pitts, M. Melinda	Asst	651-4979	prcmmp	IJ	PHD	97	N Car St	1998
Rioja, Felix K.	Asst	651-0417	prcfkr	EFG	PHD	97	Ariz St	1997
Scafidi, Benjamin P.	Asst	651-2977	prcbps	HIR	PHD	97	Virginia	1998
Tekin, Erdal	Asst	651-2626	prcete	I	PHD	01	N Carol	2001
Valev, Neven T.	Asst	651-0418	prcntv	EF	PHD	97	Purdue	1998

Gettysburg College — Gettysburg, PA 17325-1486 (717) 337-6670 — cc.gettysburg.edu
Economics Faculty — Department of Economics Fax=337-6638 — Ms. Susan Holz

Fletcher, Jean W.	C-Ac	337-6674	fletcher	AJD	PHD	83	Wash U	1986
Fender, Ann Harper	Prof	337-6671	fendera	ADNL	PHD	76	J Hopkins	1978
Gondwe, Derrick K.	Prof	337-6673	dgondwe	ABEO	PHD	78	Manitoba	1977
Railing, William F.	Prof	337-6678	wrailing	AHP	PHD	58	Cornell	1964
Nirro, Katsuyuki	Assoc	337-6676	niirok	AC	PHD	75	Pittsburgh	1972
Kaiser, Brooks	Asst	337-6668	bkaiser	ADNQ	PHD	98	Nrthwstrn	2000
Stillwaggon, Eileen	Asst	337-6675	estillwa	AFQO	PHD	79	American	1995
Weise, Charles	Asst	337-6672	cweis	ABEF	PHD	93	Wisconsin	2000

Gonzaga University — Spokane, WA 99258-0009 (509) 323-3403 — jepson.gonzaga.edu
Department of Economics — Sch of Business Adm Fax=323-5811 — Stacey Chatman

Barnes, Clarence H.	Dean	323-3402	barnes		PHD	73	Tennessee	9-73
Beck, John H.	D-Ac	323-3429	beck	BH	PHD	76	Mich St	1988
Bennett, Randall W.	Prof	323-3411	bennett	HL	PHD	84	Mich St	1988
Wiseman, A. Clark	Prof	323-3432	wiseman	AFQ	PHD	68	U Wash	1981

Gordon College — Wenham, MA 01984-1899 (978) 927-2300 — gordon. edu
Economics Faculty — Dept of Economics & Bus Fax=524-3704

Webb, Bruce G.	C-Pr	Ext 4391	webb	BGE	PHD	78	Clark	1977
Mason, John D.	Prof	Ext 4390	mason	AJR	PHD	69	Mich St	1968
Smith, Stephen L. S.	Prof	Ext 4421	ssmith	FO	PHD	88	Stanford	1987

Goshen College — Goshen, IN 46526 (219) — goshen.edu
Economics Faculty — Dept of Atg, Bus & Econ Fax=535-7660

Stalter, Anita	Dean	535-7503	dean		PHD	96	Mich St	7-01
Kaufman, Cheryl	C-Ac	535-7192	cheryldk	Mktg	MBA	90	Villanova	9-96
Good, Delmar	Prof	535-7452	delgg	AH	PHD	70	Illinois	2-67
Gunden, Randal G.	Assoc	535-7454	randygg	EIO	ABD		Notre Dm	1984

Graceland College — Lamoni, IA 50140-1699 (641) 784-5170 — graceland.edu
Economics Faculty — Division of Soc Sc-Econ Fax=784-5410

Anders, Steven L.	C-Pr	784-5175	anders	ARD	PHD	88	Kansas St	1978
Vice Provost of Faculty								
Peterson, Rebecca	C	784-5170						
Beck, Paul	Assoc	784-5176	beck	AFJE	PHD	94	Missouri	1992

Grambling State University — Grambling, LA 71245 (318) 274-6290 — alpha0.gram.edu
Economics Department — College of Business Fax=274-2191 — Ms. Ollie Pruitt

Wilkie, Macil C. Jr.	Dean$	274-2275	wilkie	Atg	PHD	68	LSU	7-85
Bashir, Abdel H.	H-As	274-6289	bashirah		PHD	90	Wisconsin	1990
Cadet, Marc	Assoc	274-2794	cadet		PHD	91	Kansas St	9-68
Ghebreyesus, Ghirmay	Assoc	274-2779	ghebreg	EFJO	PHD	88	Strathcl	1990
Ghebreyohannes, Keleta	Assoc	274-2795	keleta		PHD		Colo St	9-81
Haj, Mahmoud	Asst	274-3825			PHD	00	N Orleans	8-99

Grand Valley State Univ Allendale, MI 49401 (616) 895-2535 gvsu.edu
Department of Economics Seidman Sch Bus & Adm Fax=895-3286 Thelma Cathey
Homepage: gvsu.edu/~econ.index.htm
Did Not Respond--1999-2000 Listing

Mielke, David E.	Dean	895-2163	mielked	Atg	PHD	81	Wisconsin	1999
Singh, Harinder	C-Pr	895-2545	singhh		PHD	85	Il-Chicago	1995
Gonce, Richard A.	Prof	895-2540		ABDK	PHD	66	Wisconsin	1972
Reifel, John W.	Prof	895-2541	reifelj	AHOR	PHD	72	Mich St	1971
Dalmia, Sonia	Asst	895-2535	dalmias		PHD	99	Iowa	1999
Isely, Paul N.	Asst	895-2499	iselyp		PHD	95	Purdue	1997
Sicilian, Paul	Asst	895-2542	siciliap	ACDJ	PHD	91	Illinois	1987
Simons, Gerald P.	Asst	895-2538	simonsg		PHD	95	Kansas	1995
Thorsnes, Paul E.	Asst	895-2539	thorsnep		PHD	94	Oregon	1995

Greensboro College Greensboro, NC 27401-1875 (336) 272-7102 gborocollege.edu
Economics Faculty Div of Business Adm Fax=271-6634
phone 272-7102

Jones, Thomas O. Jr.	C-Pr	272-7102		BAdm	DBA	72	Geo Wash	1986
Fred L. Proctor Sr. Professor of Business Administration								
Oerther, Frederick J.	Prof	272-7102		EH	PHD	89	GeoMason	1990
Kondeas, Alexander G.	Asst	272-7102		EG	PHD	98	Auburn	1999

Grinnell College Grinnell, IA 50112-0806 (641) grinnell.edu
Department of Economics Div of Social Studies Fax=269-4985

Montgomery, Mark	C-Pr	269-3146	montgome	JQH	PHD	82	Wisconsin	1989
Bateman, Bradley W.	Prof	269-3145	bateman	B	PHD	84	Kentucky	1987
Mutti, John	Prof	269-3143	mutti	FHQ	PHD	74	Wisconsin	1987
Sydney Meyer Professor of International Economics								
Ferguson, William D.	Assoc	269-3132	ferguso1	JE	PHD	89	Mass	1989
Munyon, Paul G.	Assoc	269-3142	munyon	L	PHD	75	Harvard	1982
Powell, Irene	Assoc	269-3125	powelli	IL	PHD	85	Wisconsin	1989
Seiz, Janet A.	Assoc	269-4868	seiz	BO	PHD	85	Duke	1989

Grove City College Grove City, PA 16127-2104 (724) 458-2010 moses.gcc.edu
Economics Faculty Dept of Social Sciences Fax=458-3852
email @1=gcc.edu

Ayers, David J.	C-Pr	458-2010						
Herbener, Jeffrey M.	Prof	458-2204	jmherbener@1		PHD	82	Okla St	1997
Miller, Tracy C.	Assoc	458-2013	millertc		PHD	86	Chicago	1995
Ritenour, Shawn	Asst	458-2000	srritenour		PHD	98	Auburn	2001

Guilford College Greensboro, NC 27410 (336) 316-2282 guilford.edu
Economics Faculty Department of Economics Fax=316-2950
Did Not Respond--1999-2000 Listing

Williams, Robert G.	C-Pr	316-2282		POFE	PHD	78	Stanford	1978
Williams, Robert B.	Assoc	316-2218		HQRL	PHD	84	N Carol	1987

Gustavus Adolphus College Saint Peter, MN 56082-1498 (507) 933-7414 gac.edu
Economics Faculty Dept of Economics & Mgt Fax=933-6032 Connie Baum

Johnson, Bruce H.	C-Ac	933-7011			PHD	79	Houston	1986
Bungum, John L.	Assoc	933-7406			PHD	77	Nebraska	1979
Reese, David A.	Assoc	933-7405			PHD	80	Va Tech	1979
Abraham, Elizabeth	Asst	933-6273			ABD		Arizona	1997
Estenson, Paul	Asst	933-7408			PHD	86	Nebraska	1986
Misdzar, Sujetlana	Asst	933-7409			PHD	96	Minnesota	1994
Rauch, James	Asst	933-7420			PHD	94	Nebraska	1998

Hamilton College Clinton, NY 13323 (315) 859-4450 hamilton.edu
Economics Faculty Department of Economics Fax=859-4477 Dawn Woodward

Balkan, Erol M.	C-Pr	859-4180	ebalkan	OF	PHD	88	SUNY-Bin	1987
Bradfield, James	Prof	859-4190	jbradfie	GD	PHD	73	Rochester	1976
Jensen, Elizabeth J.	Prof	859-4437	ejensen	LN	PHD	84	MIT	1983
Jones, Derek C.	Prof	859-4381	djones	PJ	PHD	74	Cornell	1972
Georges, Christophre	Assoc	859-4472	cgeorges	EJB	PHD	89	Michigan	1989
Hagstrom, Paul Alan	Assoc	859-4146	phagstro	JHI	PHD	91	Wisconsin	1991
Pliskin, Jeffrey L.	Assoc	859-4143	jpliskin	CF	PHD	85	Michigan	1982
Owen, Ann	Asst	859-4419	aowen	EO	PHD	95	Brown	1997
Wu, Stephen	Asst	859-4645	swu	IJ	PHD	00	Princeton	2000

Hamline University St. Paul, MN 55104-1284 (651) 523-2295 piper.hamline.edu
Economics Faculty Dept of Mgmt and Econ Fax=523-2956 Katina Krull 523-2295
Did Not Respond--1999-2000 Listing; email @1=gw.hamline.edu

Aziz, Fahima	C-As	523-2262	fazia@1	DJ	PHD	95	Minnesota	1994

Jessup, Paul F.	Prof	523-2261	pjessup	G	PHD	66	Nrthwstrn	1988
William Kahlert Professor								
Akhavi-Pour, Hossein	Assoc	523-2223	hakhavi	FO	PHD	79	Kansas	1988
Bochnak, Mary	Assoc	523-2377	mbochnak	M	PHD	82	Minnesota	1990
Gunderson, Elizabeth W.	Assoc	523-2263	egunders	C	PHD	91	Union In	1980

Hampton University Hampton, VA 23668 (757) 727-5036 unixvax.hampton.edu
Dept of Econ & Entrepreneur School of Business Fax=727-5048

Credle, Sid H.	Dean	727-5361	sid.credle	Atg	PHD	89	Tx-Austin	9-99
Rolle, JoAnn	C-Ac	727-5036			PHD		Howard	1996
Sarki, Ayuba J.	Assoc	727-5860			PHD	84	Georgia	1982
Ferdnance, Tyrone	Asst	727-5134		OCFN	PHD	94	Notre Dm	1998

Hardin-Simmons University Abilene, TX 79698-6220 (915) 670-1357 hsutx.edu
Department of Economics School of Business Fax=670-1573 Clara Stovall

Monhollon, Jimmie R.	Dean	670-1508			PHD	61	Vanderbilt	1995
Distinguished Professor								
Hill, John A.	Asst	670-5871			PHD	95	Tennessee	1998
Monhollon, Michael	VAsst	670-5870			JD	84	Virginia	1998

Harding University Searcy, AR 72149-0001 (501) 279-4470 harding.edu
Economics Faculty School of Business Fax=279-4195 Debi Adcock

McLeod, Randall M.	Dean	279-4201	rmmcleod	Mktg	JD	74	Memphis	8-88
Diffine, Donald P.	Prof	279-4470	d.diffine		PHD	75	Miss	1971
Robertson, Marvin H.	Prof	279-4307	robertson	EDK	JD	73	Arkansas	8-79

University of Hartford W Hartford, CT 06117-1599 (860) 768-4581 mail.hartford.edu
Dept of Econ, Fnce & Ins Barney School of Bus Fax=768-4911 Alice Schoenrock

Norgaard, Corine T.	Dean	768-4243	norgaard	Atg	PHD	65	Tx-Austin	1996
Kolluri, Bharat R.	C-Pr	768-4581	kollur	CEGH	PHD	77	SUNY-Buf	1976
Giannoros, Demetrios	Prof	768-4835	giannaros	AEMP	PHD	81	Boston U	
Panik, Michael J.	Prof	768-4836	panik	CDHO	PHD	70	Boston C	1968
Rassekh, Farhad	Prof	768-5007	rassekh	ADFO	PHD	83	Houston	1989
Singamsetti, Nageswara Rao	Assoc	768-4779	singamset	CDLM	PHD	73	SUNY-Buf	1974
Cohen, Jeffrey P.	Asst	768-4834	jcohen	CDER	PHD	98	Maryland	2000

Hartwick College Oneonta, NY 13820 (607) 431-4940 hartwick.edu
Department of Economics Div Social & Behav Sci Fax=431-4954

Gotsch, Susan	Dean		gotschs					
Malone, Laurence J.	C-Ac	431-4943	malonel	ABFN	PHD	91	New Sch	1986
Alexander, Peter	Assoc		alexanderp	ACDL	PHD	90	Mass	1997
Cochi Ficano, Carlena	Asst		cochificanoc	ACDJ	PHD	97	Cornell	1997

Harvard University Cambridge, MA 02138 (617) 495-2144 harvard.edu
Department of Economics Faculty of Arts & Sci Fax=495-7730 Patricia Shanahan 495-2185
Homepage: http://www.economics.harvard.edu

Knowles, Jeremy R.	Dean							
Hart, Oliver D'Arcy	C-Pr	496-3461	ohart		PHD	74	Princeton	1993
Andrew Turner Professor of Economics								
Aghion, Philippe	Prof	495-6675	p_aghian		PHD		Harvard	
Alesina, Alberto F.	Prof	495-8388	aalesina		PHD	86	Harvard	1988
Paul Sack Associate Professor of Political Economy								
Barro, Robert J.	Prof	495-3203	vbarro		PHD	70	Harvard	1987
Campbell, John	Prof	496-6448	john_campbell	GE	PHD	84	Yale	7-94
Otto Eckstein Professor of Applied Economics								
Caves, Richard E.	Prof	495-2127	rcaves		PHD	58	Harvard	1962
Nathaniel Ropes Professor of Political Economy								
Chamberlain, Gary	Prof	495-1869	gchamberlain		PHD	75	Harvard	1987
Director of Graduate Studies								
Cooper, Richard N.	Prof	495-5076	rcooper		PHD	62	Harvard	1981
Maurits C. Boas Professor ofInternational Economics								
Cutler, David M.	Prof	496-5216	dcutler		PHD	91	MIT	
Feldstein, Martin S.	Prof	495-2167	mfeldstein		DPHL	67	Oxford	1969
George F. Baker Professor of Economics								
Freeman, Richard B.	Prof	868-3900	freeman		PHD	68	Harvard	
Herbert S. Ascherman Professor of Economics								
Friedman, Benjamin M.	Prof	495-4246	bfriedman		PHD	71	Harvard	1972
William Joseph Maier Professor of Political Economy								
Fudenberg, Drew D.	Prof	496-5895	dfudenberg		PHD	81	MIT	1987
Goldin, Claudia D.	Prof	495-3934	cgoldin		PHD	72	Chicago	1990
Green, Jerry R.	Prof	495-3950	jgreen@hbs.edu		PHD	70	Rochester	1973
David A. Wells Professor of Political Economy								
Helpman, Eihanen	Prof	495-4690	ehelpman		PHD		Harvard	1974

Jorgenson, Dale W.	Prof	495-4661	djorgenson		PHD	59	Harvard	1969
Frederick E. Abbe Professor of Economics								
Katz, Lawrence F.	Prof	495-5148	lkatz		PHD	85	MIT	1986
on leave 2002-2002								
Kornai, Janos	Prof	495-1236	jkornai		DSC	66	Hungaria	1986
on leave Fall 2001								
Kremer, Michael R.	Prof	495-9045	mkremer	E	PHD	92	Harvard	1985
Mankiw, N. Gregory	Prof	495-4301	ngmankiw		PHD	84	MIT	1985
Marglin, Stephen A.	Prof	495-3759	smarglin		PHD	65	Harvard	
Walter S. Barker Professor of Economics								
Maskin, Eric S.	Prof	495-4167	emaskin		PHD	76	Harvard	
Medoff, James L.	Prof	495-4209	jmedoff		PHD	75	Harvard	
Meyer Kestnbaum Professor of Labor & Industry								
Pakes, Ariel	Prof	495-5320		CL	PHD	79	Harvard	
Perkins, Dwight H.	Prof	495-2164	dwight_perkins		PHD	64	Harvard	1963
Harold Hitchings Burbank Professor of Political Economy								
Rogoff, Kenneth S.	Prof	495-4022	krogoff		PHD	80	MIT	2001
Rosovsky, Henry	Emer	495-4151			PHD	59	Harvard	1965
Lewis P. and Linda L. Geyser University Professor, Emeritus								
Roth, Alvin E.	Prof	495-6009	al-roth		PHD	74	Stanford	
Sachs, Jeffrey D.	Prof	495-4112	jsachs		PHD	80	Harvard	1983
Galen L. Stone Professor of International Trade								
Shleifer, Andrei	Prof	495-5046	ashleifer		PHD	86	MIT	1991
Stein, Jeremy	Prof	496-6455	jeremy_stein		PHD	86	MIT	
Weitzman, Martin L.	Prof	495-5133	mweitzman		PHD	67	MIT	1989
Ernest E. Monrad Professor of Economics								
Williamson, Jeffrey G.	Prof	495-2438	jwilliam		PHD	61	Stanford	1983
Laird Bell Professor of Economics								
Glaeser, Edward L.	Assoc	495-0575			PHD	92	Chicago	
Hoxby, Caroline Minter	Assoc	496-3588	choxby	JH	PHD	94	MIT	7-94
Calvet, Laurent E.	Asst	495-4129	lavrent_calvet		PHD		Yale	
Caselli, Franesco	Asst	496-7081	caselli_		PHD		Harvard	
Foote, Chris	Asst	495-0968	clfoote		PHD	96	Michigan	
Laibson, David	Asst	496-3402	dlaibson	DE	PHD	94	MIT	7-94
LaPorta, Rafael	Asst	495-2144	rlaporta		PHD	94	Harvard	
Li, Judith	Asst	495-8823	judith_li		PHD		Harvard	
Melitz, Marc J.	Asst	495-8297			PHD		Michigan	
Metrick, Andrew P.	Asst	496-7081	ametrick		PHD	94	Harvard	
Mobius, M.	Asst	496-3419	mobius		PHD		MIT	
Mortimer, Julie	Asst	496-2442	jmortimer		PHD	01	UCLA	2001
Porter, Jack	Asst	495-2896	jporter		PHD	96	MIT	
Saez, Emmanuel	Asst				PHD		MIT	
on leave 2001-2002								
Schwarz, Michael	Asst	496-0832	mschwarz		PHD		Stanford	
Thompson, Samuel	Asst	496-1526	sthompson		PHD		Berkeley	
Vuolteenaho, Tuomo	Asst	496-6284	vuolteen		PHD		Chicago	
Wolcowitz, Jeffrey	SLect	495-2109	j_wolcowitz	HDRJ	PHD	82	Harvard	7-78

University of Hawaii-Hilo	Hilo, HI		96720-4091 (808) 974-7400				hawaii.edu	
Bus Adm & Economics Div	School of Business		Fax=974-7685				Mitzi Hennessey	
Worchel, Stephen	Dean	974-7300	worchel	Soc	PHD	71	Duke	2000
Sakai, Marcia	C-Pr	974-7400	marcias		PHD	85	Hi-Manoa	1991
Cauley, Jon	Prof	974-7384	jcaualey@1		PHD	71	Colorado	
Hahn, Youngki	Prof	974-7767	yhahn		PHD	71	Ca-Rivers	
Hammes, David L.	Prof	974-7523	hammes		PHD	85	Simon Fr	1988
Im, Eric I.	Prof	974-7462	eim		PHD	82	HI-Manoa	
Bhandari, Ravi	Asst	974-7766			PHD	01	Amherst	2001

Univ of Hawaii at Manoa	Honolulu, HI		96822-2223 (808) 956-8496				hawaii.edu	
Department of Economics	Col of Social Sciences		Fax=956-4347		Irene Uemoto/Shirley Pang			
Dubanoski, Richard A.	Dean	956-6570	dickd	Psyc	PHD	66	Minnesota	
La Croix, Sumner J.	C-Pr	956-7061	lacroix		PHD	81	U Wash	1981
Lee, Chung H.	Prof	956-8427	lchung		PHD	66	Berkeley	1980
Mak, James	Prof	956-8280	jmak		PHD	70	Purdue	1970
Mason, Andrew	Prof	956-8730	amason		PHD	75	Michigan	1975
Moncur, James E. T.	Prof	956-7143	jmoncur		PHD	71	Wash St	1969
Naya, Seiji	Prof	586-2355	naya		PHD	66	Wisconsin	1961
Roumasset, James A.	Prof	956-7496	jimr		PHD	73	Wisconsin	1976
Yeh, Yeong-Her	Prof	956-7749	yeongher		PHD	66	Minnesota	1965
Bonham, Carl S.	Assoc	956-7605	bonham		PHD	89	Tx-Austin	1989
Gangnes, Byron S.	Assoc	956-7285	gangnes		PHD	90	Penn	1990
Russo, Gorard G.	Assoc	956-7065	russo		PHD	89	Nrthwstrn	1987
Sherstyuk, Ekaterina	Assoc	956-7851	katya		PHD	95	Cal Tech	2000
Cheong, Kwang-Soo	Asst	956-7653	kscheong		PHD	94	Stanford	1994
Greaney, Theresa M.	Asst	956-7285	greaney	F	PHD	94	Michigan	2000
Konan, Denise	Asst	956-6310	konan		PHD	93	Colorado	1993
Wang, Xiaojun	Asst	956-7721	xiaojun		PHD	01	Ohio St	2001

Hawaii Pacific University	Honolulu, HI	96813	(808) 544-0283					hpu.edu
Economics Faculty	Department of Economics	Fax=566-2403					Jeannie Manzauo	
Romig, Rodney	Dean	544-0283	rromig		PHD	75	Nebraska	8-87
Drabkin, Eric	C-Ac	544-9393	edrabkin	MCEF	PHD	93	UCLA	1994
Abrams, Eric	Assoc	544-0816	eabrams		PHD	97	Iowa	1997
Mardfin, Ward	Assoc	233-3213			PHD	79	Hi-Manoa	1992
Saraniti, Brett	Assoc	544-0826	basaranit		PHD	97	Nrthwstrn	1997
Scholland, Ken	Assoc	544-1177		MLFB	MSFB		Geotown	1991
Espiritu, Antonina	Asst	544-0892	aesprit		PHD	98	Nebraska	1998
Lucas, Eruesto	Asst	544-0842	elucas		PHD	69	Hi-Manoa	1993

Heidelberg College	Tiffin, OH	44883	(419) 448-2280					heidelberg.edu
Economics Faculty	Dept of Bus Adm & Econ	Fax=448-2236						
Tucker, Barbara L.	C-Pr	448-2307	btucker	Atg	MSA	83	Jms Mad	1989
Rennie, Henry	Prof	448-2221	hrennie	CFG	PHD	73	Ohio St	9-92
Cook, John P. Jr.	Asst	448-2205	jcook	AG	PHD	94	Kentucky	1995

Hendrix College	Conway, AR	72032-3080	(501) 329-6811					mercury.hendrix.edu
Economics Faculty	Dept of Econ & Business	Fax=450-1200						
Rupert, Lyle M.	C-Ac	450-1237	rupert	G	MBA	85	Chicago	1987
Scott, Ralph D.	Prof	450-1306		EF	PHD	83	Tulane	1979
Berry, Stanley Keith	Assoc	450-1233		DL	PHD	79	Vanderbilt	1989
Stanley, Tom D.	Assoc	450-1276		CN	PHD	82	Purdue	1986

Hillsdale College	Hillsdale, MI	49242-1298	(517) 437-7341					
Economics Faculty	Dept Econ, Bus Adm, Atg	Fax=437-3923						
Did Not Respond--1999-2000 Listing; phone: 437-7341								
Ebeling, Richard M.	C-Ac				MA	80	Rutgers	1988
Ludwig von Mises Chair								
Wolfram, Gary	Assoc				PHD	76	Berkeley	1989
Coppock, Lee	Asst				PHD	94	GeoMason	1994

Hofstra University	Hempstead, NY	11550-1090	(516) 463-5592					hofstra.edu
Dept Economics & Geography	Col Liberal Arts & Sci	Fax=463-6519					Rosemarie Augustine	
Firestone, Bernie	Dean	463-5441						
Guttmann, Robert P.	Prof	463-5602	ecorpg	F	PHD	79	London	
Moghadam, Fatemeh	Prof	463-5598	ecofzm	NOQ	PHD	79	Oxford	
Christensen, Paul P.	Assoc	463-6024	ecoppc	B	PHD	76	Wisconsin	
DeFreitas, Gregory E.	Assoc	463-5040	ecoged	J	PHD	79	Columbia	
Kozlov, Nicholas N.	Assoc	463-6954	econnk	P	PHD	88	NewHamp	
Melkoneam, Martin	Asst	463-5595	ecomzm		MA	64	New Sch	

College of the Holy Cross	Worcester, MA	01610-2395	(508) 793-3362					holycross.edu
Economics Faculty	Department of Economics	Fax=793-3708					Mrs. Beverly Bylund	
Anderton, Charles H.	C-Pr	793-3441	canderto	ACDF	PHD	86	Cornell	1986
Carter, John R.	Prof	793-2676	jcarter	CDL	PHD	76	Cornell	1976
O'Connell, John F.	Prof	793-2680	joconnel	CDIJ	PHD	70	Wisconsin	1974
Schap, David J.	Prof	793-2688	dschap	CDK	PHD	82	Wash U	1981
Gottschang, Thomas R.	Assoc	793-2678	tgottsch	AOP	PHD	82	Michigan	1979
Perkins, George M.	Assoc	793-3879	gperkins	AH	PHD	76	Boston C	2000
Rask, Kolleen J.	Assoc	793-2768	krask	EFOP	PHD	89	Yale	1989
Sanchez, Nicolas	Assoc	793-3362	nsanchez	DENO	PHD	72	S Calif	1977
Cahill, Miles B.	Asst	793-2682	mcahill	AEJ	PHD	95	Purdue	1995
Dupree, Jill L.	Asst	793-2334	jvanston	FNT	PHD	96	Colorado	1996
Kiel, Katherine A.	Asst	793-2743	kkiel	CDQR	PHD	89	Ca-SnDgo	1998

Holy Family College	Philadelphia, PA	19114-2094	(215) Ext 3274					hfc.edu
Economics Faculty	School of Business Adm	Fax=637-5937						
phone: 637-7700								
DiPrimio, Anthony	Dean	Ext 3415			PHD			7-98
Tokar, Bette L.	Prof	Ext 3274	btokar	AFED	EDD	93	Temple	9-75
Mazzarella, James	Asst	Ext 3404			PHD	87	Columbia	

Hood College	Frederick, MD	21701-8575	(301) 696-3685					hood.edu
Economics Faculty	Dept of Economics & Mgt	Fax=696-3771					Colette Cooney	
Dahms, Joseph E.	C-Ac	696-3687	dahms	NOP	PHD	83	American	1978
Rock, Michael	C-Pr	696-3756	rock		PHD	72	Pittsburgh	1999
Kim, Sang	Asst	696-3693	kim		PHD	95	Penn St	2001

Hope College Holland, MI 49422-9000 (616) hope.cit.hope.edu
Economics Faculty Dept of Econ & Bus Adm Fax=395-7922 Joy Forgwe
Did Not Respond--1999-2000 Listing

Heisler, James B.	C-Pr	395-7915		PD	PHD	75	Nebraska	1981
Lunn, John E.	Prof	395-7931		LD	PHD	80	UCLA	1992
Gentenaar, Robert	Assoc	395-7579		EC	PHD	77	Mich St	1977
Klay, Robin	Assoc	395-7581		BO	PHD	73	Princeton	1979
Steen, Todd P.	Assoc	395-7582		JT	PHD	93	Harvard	1988

University of Houston Houston, TX 77204-5019 (713) 743-3800 uh.edu
Department of Economics Col Lib Arts & Soc Sci Fax=743-3798

Achsenbaum, Andrew	Dean	743-2994						
Antel, John J.	C-Pr	743-3808	antel	J	PHD	82	UCLA	1981
Bhargava, Alok	Prof	743-3837		C	PHD	82	London	1989
Craig, Steven C.	Prof	743-3812	econ30	HR	PHD	81	Penn	1989
Dechert, W. Davis	Prof	743-3800		C	PHD	77	Cornell	
DeGregori, Thomas R.	Prof	743-3838	econ1m	O	PHD	65	Tx-Austin	1967
Gregory, Paul R.	Prof	743-3828		P	PHD	69	Harvard	1972
Mayor, Thomas H.	Prof	743-3801		AK	PHD	65	Maryland	1969
Papell, David H.	Prof	743-3807	econh	E	PHD	81	Columbia	1984
Ruffin, Roy J.	Prof	743-3827		F	PHD	67	Nrthwstrn	1976
Smith, Barton A.	Prof	743-3834		ADR	PHD	74	Chicago	1973
Steele, Henry B.	Prof	743-3835		A	PHD	57	MIT	
Bean, Richard N.	Assoc	743-3831		N	PHD	71	U Wash	1970
Juhn, Chinhui	Assoc	743-3823		J	PHD	91	Chicago	1992
Kohlhase, Janet E.	Assoc	743-3799		RHD	PHD	80	Penn	1983
Wilcox, Nathaniel	Assoc	743-3840		D	PHD	92	Chicago	1991
Chin, Aimee	Asst	743-3800		OJ	PHD	01	MIT	2001
Dinlersoz, Emin	Asst	743-3839		L	PHD	00	Rochester	2000
Kalemli-Ozcan, Sebnem	Asst	743-3824		FO	PHD	00	Brown	2000
Murray, Chris	Asst	743-3835		E	PHD	98	U Wash	1998
Thompson, Peter	Asst	743-3841			PHD	94	Florida	1996

Univ of Houston-Clear Lake Houston, TX 77058-1098 (281) 283-3185 cl.uh.edu
Economics Faculty Sch of Bus & Public Adm Fax=283-3951 Noel Turner

Cummings, W. Theodore	Dean	283-3100	ted	Mktg	PHD	78	Ariz St	1980
McCormack, Joseph P.	C-Ac	283-3217		Fnce	PHD	82	Tx A&M	9-90
Cloninger, Dale O.	Prof	283-3210			DBA	73	Fla St	9-74
Hodgin, Robert F.	Assoc	283-3211			DA	80	Illin St	9-81
Halil, Kiymaz	Asst	283-3208			PHD	94	N Orleans	1-97

Univ of Houston-Downtown Houston, TX 77002-1001 (713) 221-8903 dt.uh.edu
Finance, Atg, & Comp Inf Sys College of Business Fax=226-5238 Ms. Marie Cepeda

Bizzell, Bobby G.	Dean	221-8179		Mgt	PHD	71	Tx-Austin	1989
Nazemzadah, Asghar	C-Pr	221-8631	nazemzadah		PHD	83	Fla St	1989
Islam, Anisul	Prof	221-8903			PHD	84	Alberta	1990
Marvasti, Akbar B.	Assoc	221-8903			PHD	85	LSU	1990

Houston Baptist University Houston, TX 77074-3298 (281) 649-3325 hbu.edu
Economics Area Col of Business & Econ Fax=649-3436
Homepage: www.hbu.edu
Did Not Respond--1999-2000 Listing

Gillette, Lynn G.	Dean	649-3325			PHD	81	Tx A&M	1998

Howard University Washington, DC 20059 (202) 806-1568 howard.edu
Dept Fnce, Intl Bus & Insur School of Business Fax=986-4409 Tiffini McMillian

Harvey, Barron H.	Dean	806-1507	bharvey	Atg	PHD	77	Nebraska	1982
Lee, Youngho	C-Ac	806-1597	ylee	Fnce	PHD	81	Geo Wash	1986
Lindsey, Debra A.	Assoc	806-1638	dlindsey		PHD	83	Howard	
Aiyegoro, Ademola	Asst	806-1658	aaiyegoro		PHD	90	GeoMason	
Ekanem, Frank	Asst	806-1639	fekanem	EGHR	PHD	74	Geo Wash	1987
Hull, Everson W.	Asst	806-1542	ehull		PHD	77	Howard	
Straight, Ronald L.	Asst	806-1531	rstraight		DBA	79	Geo Wash	1988

Howard University Washington, DC 20059 (202) 806-6717 fac.howard.edu
Department of Economics College of Arts & Sci Fax=806-5262 Santina Merchant Huff

Donaldson, James	Dean	806-6700	jdonaldson		PHD			
Palmer, Ransford W.	C-Pr	806-6717	palmer	HO	PHD	66	Clark	1973
Betsey, Charles L.	Prof	806-6717	cbetsey	J	PHD	76	Michigan	1990
Green, Rodney D.	Prof	806-6717	alaec06@a	R	PHD	80	American	1977
Hung, Gregory	Prof	806-6717	ghung	O	PHD	65	Virginia	
Kwack, Sung Y.	Prof	806-6717	skwack	E	PHD	68	Berkeley	
McDonald, Vincent R.	Prof	806-6717	vmcdonald		PHD	68	Maryland	
Wadhawan, Satish C.	Prof	806-6717	swadhawan	FO	PHD		Nehru	

Blank, Emily	Assoc	806-6717	eblank	J	PHD	85	Boston C	1985
Dompere, Kofi	Assoc	806-6717	kdompere	HEC	PHD	80	Temple	1977
Lee, Byung	Assoc	806-6717	blee	CDH	PHD	73	Catholic	8-73
Perkins, Mary	Assoc	806-6717		D	PHD	82	American	
Dorsainvil, Kathleen	Asst	806-6717	kdorsainvil	CEO	PHD	97	Penn St	1995
Hunte, C. Kenrick	Asst	806-6717		OF	PHD		Ohio St	
email=kenjacks@errols.com								
Kurban, Haydar	Asst	806-6717	hkurban	R	PHD	99	Il-Chicago	2001
Meepagaia, Gaminie	Asst	806-6717	gmeepagala	C	PHD	86	SUNY-Alb	1988

Howard Payne University Brownwood, TX 76801-2794 (915) 649-8704 hputx.edu
Department of Business School of Business Adm Fax=649-8928 Mary Hill

Plagens, Les	Dean	649-8705	lplagens		EDD	86	Tx A&M	1997
Spraberry, Hubert O.	Prof	649-8704	hspraber		PHD	85	Tx Tech	1986

University of Idaho Moscow, ID 83844-3240 (208) 885-6294 uidaho.edu
Department of Economics Col of Business & Econ Fax=885-8939 Cheryll R. Means
Homepage: http://www.uidaho.edu/~econ

Dangerfield, Byron J.	Dean	885-6478	bdange	Mgt	PHD	85	U Wash	1987
Ghazanfar, Shaikh M.	H-Pr	885-7144	ghazi	HOB	PHD	69	Wash St	1968
DiNoto, Michael J.	Prof	885-7148	dnt@crow.csrv.	JR	PHD	73	SUNY-Buf	1970
Miller, Jon R.	Prof	885-7506	jrmecon	BQ	PHD	74	Wash U	1989
Coffman, Richard B.	Assoc	885-7155	richardc	DL	PHD	72	U Wash	1978
Lyman, R. Ashley	Assoc	885-7145	alyman	DC	PHD	72	Nrthwstrn	1976
Genc, Ismail H.	Asst	885-7147		ACG	PHD	99	Tx A&M	1999

Idaho State University Pocatello, ID 83209-8053 (208) 282-2346 isu.edu
Department of Economics Col of Arts & Sciences Fax=282-3186 Sue Ann Bowman

Swanson, Merwin "Bob"	Dean$	282-3053	swanmerw	Hst	PHD	72	Minnesota	1972
Stegner, Tesa	C-Ac	282-2346	stegtesa	AHQ	PHD	89	Wash St	1992
Norman, Lee	Prof	282-2385	normlee	ALN	PHD	80	Utah	1981
Tokle, Robert J.	Prof	282-3835	toklrobe	AGL	PHD	86	Iowa St	1986
Benson, C. Scott	Assoc	282-2860	bensscot	ABEF	PHD	88	Ca-Davis	1990
Green, Gregory G.	Asst	282-2943	greegreg	ACEF	PHD	97	Temple	1997
Hill, Cynthia D.	Asst	282-4945	hillcynt	AIJQ	PHD	97	Wash St	1998

University of Illinois Champaign, IL 61820 (217) 333-0120 uiuc.edu
Department of Economics Col of Comm & Bus Admin Fax=244-6678 Marsha Davis-Hubert
email: @1=igpa.uiuc.edu @2=srwilliams.econ.uiuc.edu

Ghosh, Avijit	Dean	333-2747		Mktg	PHD	79	Iowa	2001
Arnould, Richard J.	H-Pr	333-0120	rarnould	DIKL	PHD	68	Iowa St	1967
Alston, Lee	Prof	333-7664	l-alston	NQ	PHD	78	U Wash	1988
Baer, Werner	Prof	333-8388	w-baer	EFO	PHD	58	Harvard	1974
Bera, Anil K.	Prof	333-4596	a-bera	C	PHD	83	Austr Natl	1983
Bernhardt, Dan	Prof	244-5708	danber	DGJL	PHD	86	Car Mellon	1998
Brueckner, Jan K.	Prof	333-4557	jbrueckn	DHR	PHD	76	Stanford	1976
Cho, In-Koo	Prof	333-4579	inkoocho	CDE	PHD	86	Princeton	1998
Conley, John	Prof	333-4590	jpconley	DGH	PHD	90	Rochester	1990
DeBrock, Lawrence	Prof	333-4553	ldebrock	DIL	PHD	80	Cornell	1979
Gahvari, Firouz	Prof	333-7651	fgahvari	DH	PHD	81	UCLA	1994
Giertz, J. Fred	Prof	244-4822	fredg@1	HO	PHD	70	Nrthwstrn	1980
Gottheil, Fred	Prof	333-4591	fgotthei	AB	PHD	59	Duke	1959
Grinols, Earl L.	Prof	333-4595	grinols	DFO	PHD	77	MIT	1984
Koenker, Roger	Prof	333-4558	rkoenker	CL	PHD	74	Michigan	1983
Krasa, Stefan	Prof	333-7698	skrasa	DG	PHD	87	Vienna	1990
Neal, Larry	Prof	333-4678	l-neal	EGN	PHD	68	Berkeley	1967
Rashid, Salim	Prof	333-7388	s-rashid	BGO	PHD	76	Yale	1981
Resek, Robert W.	Prof	244-4827	r-resek	CR	PHD	61	Harvard	1961
Shafer, Wayne	Prof	333-0645	w-shafer	CD	PHD	72	Ca-SnBarb	1990
Taub, Bart	Prof	333-3467	b-taub	E	PHD	81	Chicago	1989
Villamil, Anne P.	Prof	244-6330	avillami	EG	PHD	88	Minnesota	1988
Williams, Steven R.	Prof	333-4516	srw@2	CD	PHD	82	Nrthwstrn	1992
Yannelis, Nicholas C.	Prof	333-4584	nyannelis	D	PHD	83	Rochester	1988
Arvan, Lanny D.	Assoc	333-4587	l-arvan	CD	PHD	81	Nrthwstrn	1980
Esfahani, Hadi S.	Assoc	333-2681	esfahani	EFLO	PHD	84	Berkeley	1984
Hallock, Kevin F.	Assoc	333-4842	hallock	HJ	PHD	95	Princeton	1995
Parente, Stephen	Assoc	244-3625	parente	DG	PHD	90	Minnesota	1999
Williamson, H. F. Jr.	Assoc	333-4511	billw	AR	PHD	69	Yale	1964
Capps, Cory	Asst	333-4260	cscapps	IL	ABD		Nrthwstrn	1998
Che, Jiahua	Asst	333-4680	che	DG	PHD	96	Stanford	2001
Deltas, George M.	Asst	333-4586	deltas	CDKL	PHD	96	Yale	1995
Kim, Soyoung	Asst	265-0682	kim11	EF	PHD	96	Yale	1997
Powers, Elizabeth	Asst	244-4828	epowers	IJR	PHD	94	Penn	1996
Seppala, Juhh	Asst	244-9506	seppala	DG	PHD	00	Chicago	2000
Xiao, Zhijie	Asst	333-4520	zxiao	CL	PHD	97	Yale	1997

Univ of Illinois at Chicago Chicago, IL 60607-7121 (312) 996-2684 uic.edu
Department of Economics Col of Business Admin Fax=996-3344 Ms. Carol Martell
Homepage: www.uic.edu/cba/cba-depts/economics/

Wiewel, Wim	Dean	996-2671	win	R	PHD	84	Nrthwstrn	1979
Chiswick, Barry R.	H-Pr	996-2683	brchris	J	PHD	67	Columbia	1978
Ayal, Eliezer B.	Emer	355-0505	eayal	O	PHD	61	Cornell	1970
Bassett, Gilbert W.	Prof	996-5777	gib	C	PHD	73	Michigan	1973
Camacho, Antonio	Prof	996-8651	acamacho	D	PHD	65	Minnesota	1973
Chaloupka, Frank J. IV	Prof	413-2367	fjc	I	PHD	88	CUNY	1988
Chiswick, Carmel U.	Prof	996-8721	cchis	JT	PHD	72	Columbia	1978
Karras, Georgios	Prof	996-2321	gkarras	E	PHD	90	Ohio St	1990
Kosobud, Richard F.	Prof	996-2266	kosobud	D	PHD	63	Penn	1966
Lehrer, Evelyn L.	Prof	996-2363	elehrer	T	PHD	78	Nrthwstrn	1980
Director, Undergraduate Studies								
McCloskey, Deirdre N.	Prof	355-4380	deirdre2	B	PHD	70	Harvard	2000
McDonald, John F.	Prof	413-2360	mcdonald	R	PHD	71	Yale	1971
McMillen, Daniel P.	Prof	413-2100	mcmillen	R	PHD	87	Nrthwstrn	1999
Miller, Oscar	Emer	996-2683	omiller	A	MA	46	Chicago	1948
Officer, Lawrence H.	Prof	413-9342	lofficer	F	PHD	65	Harvard	1987
Persky, Joseph J.	Prof	996-2687	jpersky	R	PHD	71	Harvard	1974
Stokes, Houston H.	Prof	996-0971	hhstokes	D	PHD	69	Chicago	1967
Tam, Mo-Yin S.	Prof	413-9448	moyintam	P	PHD	74	SUNY-SBr	1974
Peck, Richard M.	Assoc	996-2365	rmpeck	D	PHD	83	Princeton	1981
Pieper, Paul J.	Assoc	996-5214	pieper	E	PHD	84	Nrthwstrn	1982
Director of Graduate Studies								
Stanford, William G.	Assoc	996-0970	wgstan	C	PHD	84	Nrthwstrn	1983
Adsera, Alicia	Asst	413-9442	adsera	EF	PHD	96	Boston U	1999
Ierulli, Kathryn	Asst	996-3913	kierulli	D	PHD	94	Chicago	1993
Liang, Lan	Asst	413-9444	liang	I	PHD	96	Duke	1999
Roberts, Helen	Asst	995-0378	hroberts	E	PHD	95	Chicago	1995
Tauras, John M.	Asst	413-3289	tauras	I	PHD	98	Il-Chicago	2000
Akarca, Ali	Lect	996-1416	akarca	E	MS	72	Nrthwstrn	1985
Lee, Jin Man	ResSp	996-8785	jmlee	C	PHD	00	Il-Chicago	2000

Univ Illinois at Springfield Springfield, IL 62794-9243 (217) 206-7174 uis.edu
Department of Economics Col of Business & Mgt Fax=206-7543 Ruth Mullenix
Homepage: www.uis.edu/economics

McDevitt, Paul K.	Dean$	206-6533	pmcde1	Mktg	PHD	74	Tulane	8-83
Siddiquee, Baker A.	H-Ac	206-7174	bsidd1	EFO	PHD	88	Manitoba	1987
Mouhammed, Adil	Assoc	786-6299	amouh1	FP	PHD	85	Nebraska	1988
Scannell, Nancy J.	Asst	206-7174	nscan1	AG	PHD	92	Il-Chicago	1996

Illinois Institute of Tech Chicago, IL 60661-3691 (312) 906-6500 stuart.iit.edu
Department of Business Adm Stuart Grad Sch of Bus Fax=906-6549

Hassan, M. Zia	Dean	906-6515		Mgt	PHD	65	Ill Tech	1960
Tourk, Khairy A.	Assoc	906-6537			PHD	71	Berkeley	

Illinois State University Normal, IL 61790-4200 (309) 438-8625 ilstu.edu
Dept of Economics Box 4200 Col of Arts & Sciences Fax=438-5228 Janice Pritchett

Ramsey, David D.	C-Ac	438-8625	ddramsey	DEH	PHD	67	Minnesota	1973
Chizmar, John F.	Prof	438-7301	jfchizmar	CM	PHD	71	Boston C	1971
Cohn, Raymond L.	Prof	438-7892	rlcohn	DN	PHD	77	Oregon	1983
Hiebert, L. Dean	Prof	438-7509	dhieber	ADE	PHD	72	Wisconsin	1973
Ostrosky, Anthony L. Jr.	Prof	438-7071	alostros	ADEC	PHD	73	Pittsburgh	1973
Ram, Rati	Prof	438-7101	rram		PHD	76	Chicago	1982
Distinguished Professor								
Skaggs, Neil T.	Prof	438-7204	ntskaggs	BDE	PHD	80	Duke	1979
Carlson, J. Lon	Assoc	438-8625	lcarlson	PQ	PHD	84	Illinois	1986
Goel, Rajeev Kumar	Assoc	438-2360	rkgoel	CO	PHD	87	Houston	1989
Mohammadi, Hassan	Assoc	438-7777	hmohamma	E	PHD	88	Wash St	1988
Rich, Daniel P.	Assoc	438-7647	dprich	DJ	PHD	87	Houston	1987
Walbert, Mark S.	Assoc	438-3935	mswalber	CDE	PHD	84	New Mex	1984
Loomis, David	Asst	438-7979	dloomis	OE	PHD	95	Temple	8-96
Toole, Andrew	Asst	438-3935		CILO	PHD	98	Michigan	8-01
Zhang, Kevin	Asst	438-8928	khzhang	F	PHD	96	Colorado	8-97

Illinois Wesleyan University Bloomington, IL 61702-2900 (309) 556-3266 titan.iwu.edu
Department of Economics Business & Econ Div Fax=556-3719 Sue Olson

Seeborg, Michael C.	C-Pr	556-3184	mseeborg	J	PHD	76	Utah	1989
Robert S. Eckley Distinguished Professor of Economics								
Chapman, Margaret L.	Prof	556-3191	mchapman	L	PHD	77	Illinois	1977
Leekley, Robert M.	Assoc	556-3266	bleekley	H	PHD	74	Mich St	1974
Mendez-Carbajo, Diego	Asst	556-3826	dmindez	E	PHD	00	Fla Intl	2000
Ossella-Durbal, Ilaria	Asst	556-3906	iossella	O	PHD	99	Cornell	1999

Immaculata College	Immaculata, PA 19345-0901 (610) Ext 3472						immaculata.edu	
Economics Faculty	Dept of Econ, Atg & Bus Fax=251-1668							
phone: 647-4400								
Assumpta, Sister Virginia A	C-Ac	Ext 3147	vassumpta		MA		Catholic	9-68
Coyle, Sister Ann	Assoc	Ext 3470	coyle		MA		Temple	1978
Bull, Jacqueline Henry	Asst	Ext 3031	jhenry		MA		Cen Mich	1998
Ryan, Julie	Asst	Ext 3463	jryan		PHD			1999
Pugh, Joseph	Inst	Ext 3461	jpugh		MBA		Averett	
Zwaan, Thomas	Inst	Ext 3472	tzwaan		MBA		Delaware	

Indiana University	Bloomington, IN 47405-5301 (812) 855-1021						indiana.edu	
Department of Economics	Col of Arts & Sciences Fax=855-3736						Harriet Kenny	
Homepage: http://www.indiana.edu/~econweb/								
Subbaswamy, Kumble R.	Dean	855-2392	swamy		PHD	76	Indiana	2000
Becker, Robert	C-Pr	855-3014	becker		PHD	78	Rochester	1978
Alexeev, Michael	Prof	855-7103	malexeev		PHD	84	Duke	1992
Becker, William	Prof	855-3577	beckerw		PHD	73	Pittsburgh	1979
Buffie, Edward F.	Prof	855-9566	ebuffie		PHD	82	Yale	1992
Gardner, Roy J.	Prof	855-6383	gardner		PHD	75	Cornell	1983
Chancellor Professor								
Glomm, Gerhard	Prof	855-7256	gglomm		PHD	88	Minnesota	2000
Shi, Shouyong	Prof	855-4764	shski		PHD	91	Toronto	2000
Trivedi, Pravin K.	Prof	855-3567	trivedi		PHD	70	LondonEc	1987
Rudy Professor of Economics								
von Furstenberg, George	Prof	855-4764	vonfurst		PHD	66	Princeton	1970
Walker, James M.	Prof	855-2760	walkerj		PHD	78	Tx A&M	1984
Williams, Arlington W.	Prof	855-4564	williama		PHD	78	Arizona	1979
Chang, Fwu-Ranq	Assoc	855-6070	changf		PHD	85	Chicago	1983
Kaganovich, M.	Assoc	855-6967	mkaganov		PHD	85	USSR	1991
Leeper, Eric M.	Assoc	855-9157	eleeper		PHD	89	Minnesota	1995
Rotella, Elyce J.	Assoc	885-7858	rotella		PHD	77	Penn	1981
Witte, Willard E.	Assoc	855-2080	witte		PHD	75	Wisconsin	1981
Kelley, Hugh E.	Asst	855-7928	kukelley		PHD	98	Calif	2000
Li, Tong	Asst	855-2363	toli		PHD	93	Ca-SnDgo	1999
Ming, Xing	Asst	855-1021	xming		PHD	95	Rice	1995
Pedroni, Peter	Asst	855-7925	ppedroni		PHD	93	Columbia	1993

Indiana University	Bloomington, IN 47405-5301 (812) 855-9219						indiana.edu	
Dept Bus Econ & Pub & Policy	Kelley Sch of Business Fax=855-3354						Rosie Glaze	
Dalton, Daniel R.	Dean	855-8489	dalton	Mgt	PHD	79	Ca-Irvine	1979
Fratianni, Michele	C-Pr	855-9219	fratiann		PHD	71	Ohio St	1971
Baye, Michael R.	Prof	855-9219	mbaye	DIO	PHD	83	Purdue	1997
Davidson, Larry	Prof	855-9219	davidso		PHD	77	N Carol	1990
Green, Jeffery	Prof	855-8924	green		PHD	67	Illinois	1985
Jaffee, Bruce	Prof	855-8796	jaffee		PHD	71	J Hopkins	1971
Kang, Keejoon	Prof	855-9219	kang		PHD	80	U Wash	1980
Rasmusen, Eric	Prof	855-9219	erasmuse		PHD	84	MIT	1992
VonHagen, Jurgen	Prof	855-9219	vonhagen		PHD	86	Bonn	1987
Lyon, Tom	Assoc	855-9219	tlyon		PHD	89	Stanford	1989
Maxwell, John	Asst	855-9219	jwmax		PHD	93	Queen's	1992
Marcus, Morton	Lect	855-5507	marcus		MA	63	Wash U	1973

Indiana U-Purdue U/Indy	Indianapolis IN 46202-5140 (317) 274-4756						iupui.edu	
Department of Economics	School of Liberal Arts Fax=274-0097						Jeannette Rowe	
Homepage: www.iupui.edu/~econ								
Sandy, Robert	C-Ac	274-2176	icjz100	J	PHD	77	Mich St	1974
Chakrabarti, Subir	Prof	274-2412	imxl100	C	PHD	85	Iowa	1985
Harris, Robert	Prof	274-0095	rharris	A	PHD	79	Ohio St	1981
Director, Center for Economic Education								
Rangazas, Peter	Prof	274-8641	prangaza	EH	PHD	83	Indiana	1989
Spechler, Martin	Prof	274-7379	mspechle	BFNP	PHD	71	Harvard	1986
Steinberg, Richard	Prof	274-8671	rsteinbe	HL	PHD	84	Penn	1991
Bilodeau, Marc	Assoc	274-5684	mbilodea	HL	PHD	90	W Ontario	1996
Bivin, David	Assoc	274-7207	dbivin	E	PHD	80	Purdue	1985
Burke, Jonathan L.	Assoc		jolburke	C	PHD	85	MIT	1998
Carlin, Paul S.	Assoc	274-3998	pcarlin	J	PHD	85	Pittsburgh	1985
Deb, Partha	Assoc	274-5216	pdeb	C	PHD	91	Rutgers	1991
Rooney, Patrick	Assoc	348-7203	rooney	JH	PHD	87	Notre Dm	1987
Russell, Steven	Assoc	274-0420	shrusse		PHD	89	Minnesota	1993
Wilhelm, Mark	Assoc	274-8130	mowilhel	CH	PHD	90	NYU	1998
Morrison, Gwendolyn	Asst	274-4756		I	PHD	96	York	2001
Osili, Una O.	Asst	274-4755	uosili	O	PHD	97	Nrthwstrn	1999
Royalty, Anne B.	Asst	274-7941	royalty	J	PHD	93	Yale	1999
Warner, Geoffrey	Asst		gwarner	I	PHD	94	CUNY	1998
Askari, Ammar	Lect	348-7290	aaskari		PHD	95	Indiana	1989
Kaviani, Mohammad	Lect	274-0096	mkaviani		MA	85	Indiana	1986
Associate Director, Center for Economic Education								

Indiana Univ at Kokomo Kokomo, IN 46904-9003 (317) iuk.indiana.edu
Economics Faculty Div of Business & Econ Fax=

Von der Embse, Thomas J.	Dean	455-9446		Mgt	PHD	68	Ohio St	1990
Parkison, Kathy	Assoc	455-9462			PHD	83	Purdue	1993
Pendse, Dilip C.	Assoc	455-9279			PHD	71	Oregon St	
Pulikonda, Naga	Assoc	455-9282			PHD	77	Illinois	

Indiana Univ South Bend South Bend, IN 46634-7111 (219) 237-4346 iusb.edu
Economics Faculty Sch of Business & Econ Fax=237-4866 Catherine Coleman

Schwartz, Bill N.	Dean	237-4292	bschwart	Atg	PHD	78	UCLA	2001
Agbetsiafa, Douglas K.	Prof	237-4208	dagbetsiafa	AGO	PHD	80	Notre Dm	1980
Bartholomew, A. Wayne	Prof	237-4397	wbarthol	AET	PHD	72	Cornell	1972
Herschede, Alfred J.	Prof	237-4303	aherschede	ADP	PHD	76	Illinois	1976
Joray, Paul A.	Prof	237-4227	pjoray	ADJ	PHD	71	Illinois	1971
Kochanowski, Paul S.	Prof	237-4243	pkochanowski	CDR	DBA	72	Indiana	1972
Konzelmann, Suzanne	Assoc	237-4142	skonzelmann	ADJ	PHD	91	Notre Dm	1989

Indiana Univ Northwest Gary, IN 46408-1197 (219) 980-6633 iunbus1.iun.indiana.edu
Economics Faculty Div of Business & Econ Fax=980-6579 Karen Peterson

Rominger, Anna	Dean$	980-6633	arominge	Mgt	JD	72	Boston U	1992
Lynch, Gary	Prof	980-6907	gary	RTE	PHD	70	Wash St	1981
Bhatia, Shyam L.	Assoc	980-6634	bhatia	FDEL	PHD	76	Indiana	1976

Indiana Univ Southeast New Albany, IN 47150-6405 (812) 941-2362 iusmail.ius.indiana.edu
Department of Economics School of Business Fax=941-2672 Mrs. Lydia Brainard

Dufrene, Uric B.	Dean	941-2325	udufrene	Fnce	PHD	92	Miss	1992
Altmann, James L.	Prof	941-2307	jaltmann	DM	PHD	78	Wisconsin	1978
Alse, Jahardhanan	Asst	941-2520	jalse	FE	PHD	93	Wisconsin	1992
Faulk, Dagney	Asst	941-2362	dfaulk	R	PHD	99	Geo St	1999
Schansberg, D. Eric	Asst	941-2527	dshansb	HJC	PHD	91	Tx A&M	1992

Indiana U of Pennsylvania Indiana, PA 15705-1087 (724) 357-2640 grove.iup.edu
Economics Faculty Humanities & Social Sci Fax=357-6485 Mrs. Mary Anne Lupinetti

Carter, Brenda	Dean	357-2280	brenda_carter		PHD			
Karatjas, Nicholas	C-Pr	357-4855	karatjas	ADI	PHD	76	SUNY-SBr	1978
Asamoah, Yaw	Prof	357-2641	osebo	FO	PHD	85	Wash U	1984
Dyal, James A.	Prof	357-4856	jimdyal	JR	PHD	75	Illinois	1977
Martel, Arthur H.	Prof	357-4775	amartel	JK	PHD	74	Mass	1970
Radell, Willard W.	Prof	357-4776	willard_radell	NP	PHD	80	Illinois	1981
Cross, John W.	Assoc	357-4781	jwcross	EG	MA	68	Mass	1969
Radakovic, George	Assoc	357-4826	georad	JR	PHD	79	Pittsburgh	1986
Brewer, Stephanie M.	Asst	357-2642	smbrewer	DHF	PHD	99	Indiana	1999
Jozefowicz, James J.	Asst	357-4774	jimjozef	CEL	PHD	99	SUNY-Alb	1999

Indiana State University Terre Haute, IN 47809 (812) 237-2160 isugw.indstate.edu
Department of Economics College of Arts & Sci Fax=237-4349 Kelly Halldges
Homepage: www.indstate.edu/econ/

Conant, John L.	C-Pr	237-2163	econjlc	DJB	PHD	84	Tennessee	1981
Burkett, Paul G.	Prof	237-2164	ecburke	EO	PHD	84	Syracuse	1991
Parks, Terrance C.	Prof	237-2173	ecparks	OED	PHD	74	Illinois	1966
Richards, Donald G.	Prof	237-2179	ecdrich	FO	PHD	83	Conn	1985
Chen, Aimin	Assoc	237-2175	ecchen	PD	PHD	90	Penn St	1991
Guell, Robert	Assoc	237-2169	ecguell	HC	PHD	91	Syracuse	1991
Lotspeich, Richard	Assoc	237-2176	eclotsp	PQ	PHD	86	New Mex	1990
Israel, Debra	Asst	237-2160	ecissrael		PHD	99	Wisconsin	2001
Owen, Jeff	Asst	237-2160	ecowen		PHD	00	Iowa	2000

Indiana Wesleyan Marion, IN 46953-4999 (765) 677-2145 indwes.edu
Department of Economics Div of History & Soc Sc Fax=677-2380

Martin, Glenn R.	C-Pr	677-2300	gmartin	Hist	PHD	73	Ball St	1967
Pongracic, Ivan	C-As	677-2145	ipongrac	AEFP	MA	68	Zagreb	1987

University of Indianapolis Indianapolis, IN 46227-3697 (317) 788-3378 gandlf.uindy.edu
Department of Economics School of Business Fax=788-3300
Did Not Respond--1999-2000 Listing

Conrad, James M.	Dean	788-3370	conrad		PHD	70	Kentucky	1979
Gurtunca, Esen Z.	Prof	788-3287			PHD	73	Purdue	1974

Donald W. Tanselle Professor of Economics

Iona College New Rochelle, NY 10801-1890 (914) 633-2216 iona.edu
Dept of Economics Col of Arts & Science Fax=633-2608

Rosenberg, Warren	Dean			Bio	PHD	82	NYU	1981
Pescatrice, Donn R.	C-Pr	637-2729		CDE	PHD	75	Purdue	1983
Jantzen, Robert H.	Prof	637-2731	rhj1	CIJ	PHD	82	Northeas	1982
Lesser, Mary H.	Assoc	633-2215	mhal	FG	PHD	82	Fordham	1982
Spagnolo, John A.	Assoc	637-2730		R	PHD	82	Fordham	1978

University of Iowa Iowa City, IA 52242-1000 (319) 335-0829 uiowa.edu
Department of Economics Henry B. Tippie Col Bus Fax=335-1956 Shari Tolander

Fethke, Gary C.	Dean	335-0868	gary-fethke		PHD	68	Iowa	1974
Williamson, Stephen D.	C-Pr	335-0831	stephen.will+		PHD	84	Wisconsin	1992
Albrecht, William P.	Prof	335-3125	william-albrecht		PHD	65	Yale	1965
Fethke, Carol C.	Prof	335-0504	carol-fethke		PHD	71	Iowa	1975
Forsythe, Robert Associate Dean	Prof	335-0865	robert-forsythe		PHD	75	Car Mellon	1981
Joseph, Hyman	Prof	335-0837	hyman-joseph		PHD	69	Nrthwstrn	1966
Nelson, Forrest D.	Prof	335-0854	forrest-nelson		PHD	75	Rochester	1980
Neumann, George R.	Prof	335-0850	george-neumann		PHD	74	Nrthwstrn	1984
Nordquist, Gerald L.	Emer	335-0833	gerald-nordquist		PHD	60	Iowa	1968
Pogue, Thomas F.	Prof	335-0843	thomas-pogue		PHD	68	Yale	1965
Riezman, Raymond G.	Prof	335-0829	raymond-riezman		PHD	77	Minnesota	
Savin, Nathan E.	Prof	335-0855	gene-savin		PHD	69	Berkeley	1986
Sgontz, Larry G.	Emer	r35-0852	larry-sgontz		PHD	64	Illinois	1964
Siebert, Calvin D.	Emer	335-0851	calvin-siebert		PHD	66	Berkeley	1965
Whiteman, Charles H.	Prof	335-0834	whiteman		PHD	81	Minnesota	1980
Wu, Shih-Yen	Emer	335-0846	shih-yen-wu		PHD	60	Nrthwstrn	1964
Balch, Michael S.	Assoc	335-0847	michael-balch		PHD	65	NYU	1971
Ingram, Marlynne B. F.	Assoc	335-0897	beth-ingram		PHD	86	Iowa	1988
Paarsch, Harry	Assoc	335-0936	harry-paarsch		PHD	87	Stanford	1996
Solow, John L.	Assoc	335-0845	john-solow		PHD	83	Stanford	1981
Franco, April	Asst	335-0961	april.tranco		PHD	99	Rochester	1999
Sleet, Christopher	Asst	335-1015	christopher.s+	E	PHD	98	Stanford	2000
Temzelides, Ted	Asst	335-0272	ted.tenzelides		PHD	95	Minnesota	1997

Iowa State University Ames, IA 50011-1070 (515) 294-6740 iastate.edu
Department of Economics Col Liberal Arts & Sci Fax=294-0221 Diana McLaughlin

Hira, Labh	Dean$	294-2422	lhira	Atg	PHD	75	Missouri	1982
Hallam, Arne	C-Pr	294-5861	ahallam	D	PHD	83	Berkeley	1983
Adams, Jean W.	Prof	294-5886	jwadams	L	PHD	73	Illinois	1972
Adams, Roy Dean	Prof	294-5886	radams	HE	PHD	72	Illinois	1972
Fletcher, Lehman B.	Prof	294-5820	lbf	O	PHD	69	Berkeley	1960
Harl, Neil E.	Prof	294-6354	harl	QK	PHD	65	Iowa St	1964
Huffman, Wallace E.	Prof	294-6359	whuffman	J	PHD	72	Chicago	1974
Lapan, Harvey E.	Prof	294-5917	hlapan	DF	PHD	71	MIT	1972
Mattila, John Peter	Prof	294-5813	jpm	J	PHD	69	Wisconsin	1973
Orazem, Peter F.	Prof	294-5827	pfo	J	PHD	83	Yale	1982
Tesfatsion, Leigh S.	Prof	294-0138	tesfatsi	E	PHD	75	Minnesota	1990
Vandewetering, Hylke	Prof	294-5888	hivdw	O	PHD	64	Iowa St	1964
Falk, Barry L.	Assoc	294-5875	bfalk	E	PHD	82	Minnesota	1980
Quirmbach, Herman C.	Assoc	294-6221	hcqbach	L	PHD	83	Princeton	1990
Schroeter, John R.	Assoc	294-5876	johns	L	PHD	81	Minnesota	1983
Volij, Oscar	Assoc	274-6740		H	PHD	94	Hebrew	2001
Wang, Chena	Assoc	294-6740		E	PHD	94	W Ontario	2001
Bhatacharya, Joydeep	Asst	294-5886	joydeep	E	PHD	96	Cornell	1999
Bose, Subir	Asst	294-5860	bose	D	PHD	96	Yale	1996
Bunzel, Helle	Asst	294-6163	hbunzel	C	PHD	99	Cornell	1999
Doyle, Matthew	Asst	294-6740		D	PHD	01	Brit Colum	2001
Kreider, Brent	Asst	294-6740		J	PHD	94	Wisconsin	2001
Singh, Rajesh	Asst	294-6740		F	PHD	01	UCLA	2001

Ithaca College Ithaca, NY 14850 (607) 274-3200 ithaca.edu
Department of Economics Sch of Humanities & Sci Fax=274-3474 Tina Bennett
Homepage: www.ithaca.edu/economics

Erlich, Howard	Dean	274-3102		Comm	PHD	75	Mass	
Kacapyr, Elia W.	C-Ac	274-3274	kacapyr	CE	PHD	78	Geo St	1985
Musgrave, Frank W.	Prof	274-3613		IJ	PHD	68	Rutgers	1968
Hinderliter, Roger H.	Assoc	274-3582		BE	PHD	70	Wash U	1986
Kolberg, William	Assoc	274-3609		AQ	PHD	84	Rhode Isl	1984
Christianson, Kenneth	Asst	274-3200			ABD		Syracuse	2000
Warren, Shainne	Asst				PHD		Utah	2000

Jackson State University — Jackson, MS 39217-0560 (601) 968-2531 — ccaix.jsums.edu
Dept Econ, Finance & Gen Bus — Sch Business Box 17760 Fax=968-2690 — Ella King

Glover, Glenda	Dean	968-2411		Atg	PHD	90	Geo Wash	1994
Hurley, John F.	C-Ac	968-2531	jhurley		PHD	71	Illinois	1972
Freeman, Patricia A.	Assoc	968-2610	pfreeman		PHD	88	LSU	1998
Grass, R. Gail	Assoc	968-2028	ggrass		PHD	89	Harvard	1989
Anyamele, Dennis	Asst	968-2608	danyame		PHD	92	Howard	
Assad, Jean-Claud	Asst	968-2604	jassad		PHD	87	Howard	1991
Didia, Dal	Asst	968-2606	jdidia		PHD	93	LSU	1997
Jeffries, Christopher N.	Asst	968-2607	cjeffrie		PHD	88	Fla St	1992
McGill-Tillman, Patricia	Inst	968-2605			MA	65	Atlanta	1968
Opara-Nadi, Gregory	Inst	968-2679	goparana		MBA	77	Rust	

Jacksonville University — Jacksonville, FL 32211-3394 (904) 745-7432 — mail.ju.edu
Economics Faculty — College of Business Fax=745-7467 — Nicole Hipp

Mullins, Terry W.	Dean	Ext 7431	tmullin	Mgt	PHD	78	Houston	1998
Brady, James J.	Prof	Ext 7442	jbrady		PHD	69	Notre Dm	
Jessie Ball duPont Professor of Economics								
Pordeli, Hassan	Prof	Ext 7450	hpordel		PHD	83	Nebraska	1983
Hugh F. Culverhouse Professor of Economics								
Buck, John	Asst	745-7431	jbuck		PHD	89	Wisconsin	1994

Jacksonville State Univ — Jacksonville, AL 36265-1602 (256) 782-5776 — succ.jsu.edu
Finance, Econ & Accounting — Col Commerce & Bus Adm Fax=782-5312 — Ms. Pat Upton

Fielding, William T.	Dean	782-5505	fielding		PHD	76	S Carol	1968
Scroggins, William A.	H-Pr	782-5388	scroggin	Fnce	DBA	85	Miss St	8-79
Bennett, Doris S.	Prof	782-5514	dbennett		PHD	79	Alabama	1986
McCarty, Cynthia S.	Assoc	782-5777	cmccarty		PHD	94	N Carol	1990
Carter, Shawn	Asst	792-5199	scarter		PHD	97	Tx A&M	1998

James Madison University — Harrisonburg, VA 22807 (540) 568-3216 — jmu.edu
Economics Program — Col of Business MSC0204 Fax=568-3010 — Mrs. Loretta Grunewald
Did Not Respond--1999-2000 Listing

Reid, Robert D.	Dean	568-3252	reidrd	Mkgt	EDD	85	Va Tech	9-86
Ahmed, Ehsan	D-Pr	586-3214	ahmedex	EC	PHD	83	Mich St	1984
Director Office of Economic Services								
Carrier, Ronald E.	Prof	568-6241		A	PHD	60	Illinois	1971
President								
Fields, T. Windsor	Prof	568-3097	fieldstw	EC	PHD	78	Virginia	1990
Horn, Robert N.	Prof	568-3219	hornrn	JD	PHD	78	NewHamp	1978
Kohen, Andrew I.	Prof	568-3220	kohenai	JD	PHD	73	Ohio St	1976
Rosser, J. Barkley Jr.	Prof	568-3212	rosserjb	R	PHD	76	Wisconsin	1977
Varghese, K. Thomas	Prof	568-3206	varghekt	E	PHD	71	Wayne St	1970
Wood, William C.	Prof	568-3243	woodwc	DA	PHD	80	Virginia	1989
Director, Center for Economic Education								
Jerome, Robert T. Jr.	Assoc	568-3029	jeromert	DF	PHD	82	Virginia	1981
Kreutzer, David W.	Assoc	568-3218	kreutzdw	FH	PHD	84	GeoMason	1984
Milliman, Scott R.	Assoc	568-3213	millimsr	DQ	PHD	85	Wisconsin	1986
Rosser, Marina V.	Assoc	568-3094	rossermv	FP	PHD	79	MoscowSt	1987
Smith, Vardaman Russell	Assoc	568-3221	smithvr	B	PHD	80	Penn St	1979
Brunton, Bruce G.	Asst	581-3211	bruntobg	FNO	PHD	89	Utah	1984
Doyle, Joanne M.	Asst	568-3030	doylejm	DC	PHD	93	Boston C	1993
Elwood, S. Kirk	Asst	568-3098	elwoodsk	FFC	PHD	93	Ca-Davis	1992

John Carroll University — Cleveland, OH 44118 (216) 397-4508 — jcu.edu
Dept of Economics & Finance — School of Business Fax=397-1728 — Tina Frabotta

Navratil, Frank J.	Dean	397-4521	navratil	G	PHD	74	Notre Dm	1973
Zlatoper, Thomas J.	C-Pr	397-4583	zlatoper	ACD	PHD	80	Nrthwstrn	1984
Soper, John C.	Prof	397-3027	jsoper	ENA	PHD	70	Mass	1982
Calkins, Lindsay Noble	Assoc	397-4467	calkins	ADH	PHD	86	Michigan	1986
Cima, Lawrence R.	Assoc	397-4534	lrcima	ADEF	PHD	82	W Virginia	1971
Kahai, Simran K.	Asst	397-4655		CDFL	PHD	95	Auburn	2001
Simmons, Walter O.	Asst	397-4659	wsimmons	JKNO	PHD	94	Wayne St	1995
Welki, Andrew M.	Asst	397-4550	welki	HR	PHD	83	Penn St	1982

Johns Hopkins University — Baltimore, MD 21218-2685 (410) 516-7601 — jhu.edu
Department of Economics — Sch of Arts & Sciences Fax=516-7600 — Donna Althoff 516-7677
email @1=jhunix.hcf.jhu.edu

McCarty, Richard C.	Dean	516-8212					
Maccini, Louis J.	C-Pr	516-7607	maccini	PHD	70	Nrthwstrn	1969
Ball, Laurence M.	Prof	516-7605	ball	PHD	80	MIT	1994
Carroll, Christopher D.	Prof	516-7602	carroll	PHD	90	MIT	1995
Gersovitz, Mark	Prof	516-7612		PHD	75	Yale	1994
Hamilton, Bruce W.	Prof	516-7613	hamilba	PHD	72	Princeton	1973
Harrington, Joseph E.	Prof	516-7615	harringt@1	PHD	84	Duke	1983

Karni, Edi	Prof	516-7608	karni@1		PHD	71	Chicago	1981
Khan, M. Ali	Prof	516-8545	akhan		PHD	73	Yale	1988
Moffitt, Robert A.	Prof	516-7611	moffitt		PHD	75	Brown	1995
Young, H. Peyton	Prof	516-6118	pyoung		PHD	70	Michigan	1994
Chan, Jimmy	Asst	516-7610	chan@1		PHD	98	Berkeley	1998
Lubik, Thomas	Asst	516-5564						
Shum, Matthew	Asst	516-8828						

Kalamazoo College Kalamazoo, MI 49006-3295 (616) 337-7028 kzoo.edu
Dept of Economics & Business Liberal Arts Education Fax=337-5733 Sandy Rook 337-7053

McKinney, Hannah J.	C-As	337-7024	mckinney	HJR	PHD	84	Penn	1988
Hussen, Ahmed M.	Prof	337-7025	hussen	DQ	PHD	78	Oregon St	1985
Moffit, Tim	Asst	337-7031	moffit	M	MBA	84	Dartmouth	1994
Rochon, Louis-Phillip	Asst	337-7023	lprochon		PHD	98	New Sch	1999
Vernengo, Matias	Asst	337-7027			PHD		New Sch	2001
Stull, Charles	Inst	337-7053	cstull		ABD		Wisconsin	

University of Kansas Lawrence, KS 66045-7589 (785) 864-3501 ukans.edu
Department of Economics Col Liberal Arts & Sci Fax=864-5270 Leanea Wales

Sicilian, Joseph M.	C-Ac	864-3501	jsic	D	PHD	77	Purdue	1977
El-Hodiri, Mohamed A.	Prof	864-2838			PHD	66	Minnesota	1966
Rosenbloom, Joshua L.	Prof	864-2839	jrosenbloom	NJ	PHD	88	Stanford	1988
Weiss, Thomas J.	Prof	864-2840	t-weiss	NF	PHD	67	N Carol	1967
Bhattacharya, Gautam	Assoc	864-2869	gbhattacharya	LDO	PHD	80	Rochester	1980
Comolli, Paul M.	Assoc	864-2863	pcomolli	QF	PHD	75	Purdue	1975
Faurot, David J.	Assoc	864-2865	dfaurot	J	PHD	75	Nrthwstrn	1975
Iwata, Shigeru	Assoc	864-2867	shigeru	EJ	PHD	88	UCLA	1988
Zhang, Jianbo	Assoc	864-2861		D	PHD	90	Penn St	1990
Asiedu, Elizabeth	Asst	864-2843	asiedu	F	PHD	98	Illinois	1998
Earnhart, Dietrich	Asst	864-2866	earnhart	QK	PHD	95	Wisconsin	8-97
Jin, Yi	Asst	864-3501		E	PHD	01	Iowa	2001
Ju, Biung-Ghi	Asst	864-3501		D	PHD	01	Rochester	2001
Juhl, Ted	Asst	864-2849		E	PHD	99	Illinois	1999
Keating, John W.	Asst	864-3501	keating	E	PHD	89	Nrthwstrn	8-97
Larudee, Mehrene	Asst	864-2837	mehrene	F	ABD		Mass	1984
Wu, Shu	Asst	864-2868		EG	PHD	00	Stanford	2000

Kansas State University Manhattan, KS 66506-4001 (785) 532-7357 ksu.edu
Department of Economics Col of Arts & Sciences Fax=532-6919 Susan Koch
Homepage: www.ksu.edu/economics

Nicholls, Peter	Dean	532-6900	nicholls	Math	PHD		Cambridge	1991
Ragan, James F. Jr.	H-Pr	532-7357	jfrjr	JA	PHD	75	Wash U	1977
Babcock, Michael W.	Prof	532-4571	mwb	RQ	PHD	73	Illinois	1972
Bratsberg, Bernt	Prof	532-4572	bernt	JD	PHD	91	Ca-SnBarb	1991
Nafziger, E. Wayne	Prof	532-4579	nafwayne	OPF	PHD	67	Illinois	1966
Thomas, Lloyd B. Jr.	Prof	532-4584	lbt	EA	PHD	70	Nrthwstrn	1968
Weisman, Dennis	Prof	532-4588	weisman	LKD	PHD	93	Florida	1993
Akkina, Krishna Rao	Assoc	532-4570	krishna	ECO	PHD	72	Minnesota	1972
Cassou, Steven P.	Assoc	532-6342	scassou	EC	PHD	89	Minnesota	1996
Chang, Yang-Ming	Assoc	532-4573	ymchang	DCF	PHD	84	SUNY-Buf	1984
Gormely, Patrick J.	Assoc	532-4576	gormely	OF	PHD	67	Duke	1967
Oldfather, Michael	Assoc	532-4580	mon812	EJ	PHD	80	Ohio	1983
Bidarkota, Prasad V.	Asst	532-4578	pbidarko	CEG	PHD	96	Ohio St	1999
Blankenau, William F.	Asst	532-7357	blankenw	EC	PHD	97	Iowa	2001
Lu, Xiaohua	Asst	532-4575	xlu	LDC	PHD	95	Tx-Austin	1997
Turner, Tracy M.	Asst	532-4583	turner	HD	PHD	00	Ca-Davis	2000
Trenary, Roger C.	Inst	532-4585	trenary	A	MA	72	Wayne St	1977

Kean University Union, NJ 07083 (908) 527-2238 kean.edu
Dept Econ, Fnce & Geography Sch Bus, Govt & Tech Fax=353-8656 Elaine Mahon
Did Not Respond--1999-2000 Listing

Anderson, Charles E.	Dean	527-2531			PHD	75	Stanford	7-88
Kempey, William M.	C-Pr	527-2390			PHD	70	NYU	9-78
Kim, Youn Suk	Prof	527-2489			PHD	73	New Sch	9-74
Carreno, Eufronio	Assoc	527-2374		DEFO	PHD	80	Rutgers	9-88
Jackson, Peter	Assoc	527-2429			PHD		Harvard	
Saffer, Henry	Assoc	527-2400			PHD	77	CUNY	9-85
Yamoah, David A.	Assoc	527-2794			PHD	90	Rutgers	9-87
Associate Dean								
Condon, Carol M.	Asst	527-2391			PHD	78	Columbia	9-85
Griffith, Jacqueline	Asst	527-3210			MBA			
Skoorka, Bruce	Asst	527-2429			PHD	92	NYU	
Tully, Cathyann	Asst	527-2428						

Keene State College — Keene, NH 03431-4183 (603) 358-2544 — keene.edu
Department of Economics — Sciences & Soc Sciences Fax=358-2257 — Mary Ann Williams

Leversee, Gordon J.	Dean	358-2544	gleverse		PHD	73	Duke	1981
Duston, Thomas E.	Assoc	358-2625	tduston		PHD	72	Brown	1984
Sherry, Robert L.	Assoc	358-2626	rsherry		PHD	79	Yale	1984

Kennesaw State University — Kennesaw, GA 30144-5591 (770) 423-6091 — coles2.kennesaw.edu
Dept of Economics & Finance — Coles College of Bus Fax=499-3209 — Rommy Lane

Mescon, Timothy S.	Dean	423-6342	tim_mescon		PHD	79	Georgia	1990
Tutterow, Roger C.	C-Pr	423-6091	roger_tuterow	CDGM	PHD	90	Geo St	1991
Ackert, Lucy F.	Prof	423-6111	lucy_ackert	GM	PHD	90	Emory	2000
Brotman, Billie Ann	Prof	423-6496	billie_brotman	AGIM	PHD	78	Notre Dm	1989
Bumgarner, Mary	Prof	423-6341	mary_bumgarner	AERH	PHD	84	Geo St	1985
Curley, Michael D.	Prof	423-6091	michael_curley	ADMG	PHD	74	Kentucky	1984
Gilliam, Kenneth P.	Prof	423-6319	ken_gilliam	ACD	PHD	76	Lehigh	1984
Park, Jong-Heum	Prof	423-6429	jong_park	ADFO	PHD	74	Okla St	1988
Prime, Penelope B.	Prof	423-6579	penelope_prime	ADFO	PHD	87	Michigan	1991
Goodwin, Randall B.	Assoc	423-6101	randall_goodwin	ADM	PHD	82	Georgia	1982
Rider, Mark	Assoc	423-6583	mark_rider	CDHJ	PHD	92	Geo St	1999
Sabbarese, Donald M.	Assoc	423-6094	don_sabbare	AEM	PHD	84	Geo St	1978
Terrebonne, Peter	Assoc	420-4371	pete_terrebonne	DMQ	PHD	92	Emory	2000
Tiwari, Kashi N.	Assoc	423-6086	kashi_tiwari	CEG	PHD	81	So Meth	1988
Doral, Murat	Inst	423-6605	murat_doral	AHG	MBA	90	W Virginia	1999
Lucas, Terry	Inst	423-6720	terry_lucas	AF	MS	69	USCG	1999

Kent State University — Kent, OH 44242-0001 (330) 672-2366 — bsa3.kent.edu
Department of Economics — College of Business Adm Fax=672-9808 — Diane Williams
Homepage: http://business.kent.edu/academic/econ/

Stevens, George E.	Dean	672-2772	gstevens	ADMS	DBA	79	Kent St	1995
Kent, Richard J.	C-Ac	672-1092	rkent	E	PHD	76	Berkeley	1983
Casper, Cheryl A.	Prof	672-1087	ccasper	D	PHD	75	Case Wes	1973
McKee, David L.	Prof	672-1096	dmckee	OR	PHD	66	Notre Dm	1967
Mount, Randall I.	Prof	672-1086	rmount	CD	PHD	69	Purdue	1966
Upton, Charles W.	Prof	672-1089	cupton	EQ	PHD	69	Car Mellon	8-89
Williams, Donald R.	Prof	672-1095	dwilliams	J	PHD	84	Nrthwstrn	1983
Butler, Alison	Assoc	672-1097	abutler	FEO	PHD	89	Oregon	1999
Ellis, Michael A.	Assoc	672-1091	mellis	EF	PHD	91	Tx A&M	1990
Metzgar, Matthew	Asst		mmetzgar	H	ABD		Tennessee	2001
Qi, Min	Asst	672-1088	mqi	CDFG	PHD	96	Ohio St	1996
Wilson, Kathryn S.	Asst	672-1093	kwilson	DHIJ	PHD	96	Wisconsin	1996

University of Kentucky — Lexington, KY 40506-0034 (859) 257-3626 — pop.uky.edu
Department of Economics — Gatton Col Bus & Econ Fax=323-1920 — Debbie Wheeler
Homepage: //gatton.uky.edu/academic/economics/economics.html

Furst, Richard W.	Dean	257-8939	furst	Fnce	DBA	68	Wash U	1981
Blomquist, Glenn C.	C-Pr	257-3924	gcblom	IHQ	PHD	77	Chicago	1980
Pollard Professor								
Ali, Mukhtar M.	Prof	257-7636	mmali	C	PHD	69	Wisconsin	1969
Berger, Mark C.	Prof	257-1282	mberger	J	PHD	81	Ohio St	1981
Stugill Professor								
Fackler, James S.	Prof	257-7649	eco134	E	PHD	77	Indiana	1982
Garen, John E.	Prof	257-3581	jgaren	J	PHD	82	Ohio St	1982
Gatton Professor								
Gift, Richard E.	Prof	257-7640	regift01	FB	PHD	65	Duke	1965
Hoyt, William H.	Prof	257-2518	whoyt	RHG	PHD	86	Wisconsin	1986
Gatton Professor								
Scott, Frank A. Jr.	Prof	257-7643	fscott	GH	PHD	79	Virginia	1979
Gatton Professor								
Waller, Christopher J.	Prof	257-0226	cjwall	E	PHD	86	Wash St	1998
Gatton Chair								
Bollinger, Christopher R.	Assoc	257-9524	crboll	CDJ	PHD	93	Wisconsin	1998
Gillette, J. Robert	Assoc	257-1411	jrgill01	A	PHD	86	Tx A&M	1994
Hoyt, Gail Mitchell	Assoc	257-2517	ghoyt	A	PHD	92	Kentucky	1994
Kim, Yoonbai	Assoc	257-2838	ykim01	EFG	PHD	87	Stanford	1991
Thompson, Eric	Assoc	257-1386	ecthom1	R	PHD	92	Wisconsin	1995
Toma, Mark	Assoc	268-4966	mtoma	E	PHD	77	Va Tech	1989
Yelowitz, Aaron	Assoc	257-7634		HI	PHD	94	MIT	2001
Castaneda, Marco	Asst	257-1266		LD	PHD	00	Wash U	2001
Newlon, Elizabeth H.	Asst	257-7641	enewlon	H	PHD	01	Car Mellon	2000
Reed, Robert R. III	Asst	257-5975	rrreedd	E	PHD	98	Penn St	2000
Trask, Kathleen	Asst	257-9681	katrask	FO	PHD	98	Penn St	1998

Kentucky State University — Frankfort, KY 40601 (502) 597-6708 — gwmail.kysu.edu
Dept of Bus Adm-Economics — School of Business Fax=597-6404 — Monique Roberts

Okonkwo, C. Valentine	Dean	597-6708	vokonkwo		PHD	85	Fla St	2000
Assibey-Mensah, Albert	Asst	597-6284	aassibeymensah	AG	PHD	94	Cincinnati	1994
Sokoloff, Joel J.	Asst	597-6914	jsokoloff	ACE	MA	67	Mass	1974

Kenyon College | Gambier, OH 43022-9623 (740) 427-5657 | kenyon.edu
Economics Faculty | Department of Economics Fax=427-5276 | April Farmer

Keeler, James	C-Pr	427-5285	keeler	CEB	PHD	81	Indiana	1984
Gensemer, Bruce L.	Prof	427-5283	gensemer	HPDI	PHD	66	Michigan	1966
Trethewey, Richard L.	Prof	427-5270	trethewe	NFKB	PHD	71	U Wash	1969
Harrington, David E.	Assoc	427-5393	harrington	QRHC	PHD	84	Wisconsin	1986
Himmelright Associate Professor in Economics								
Kynski, Kathy	Assoc	427-5328	krynski	CDIJ	PHD	86	Wisconsin	7-86
Himmelright Associate Professor of Economics								
Melick, William R.	Assoc	427-5291	melickw	EGCF	PHD	87	Ohio St	7-98
Rodriguez, Gustavo	VAsst	427-5657	rodriguezg	DCL	PHD	94	NYU	7-01
Xu, Jian	VAsst	427-5657	xuj	FEC	PHD	99	U Wash	7-01

Kettering University | Flint, MI 48504-4898 (810) 762-7952 | kettering.edu
Economics Faculty | Management Department Fax=762-9944
Did Not Respond--1999-2000 Listing

Pouck, David W.	C	762-7959						
Ioannatos, Petros	Asst	762-1955			PHD	89	Wayne St	
Wing, Martin M.	Asst	762-7986			PHD	89	Wayne St	

King's College | Wilkes-Barre, PA 18711 (570) Ext 5972 | kings.edu
Dept of Economics & Finance | McGowan Sch of Business Fax=208-5989 | Janet Meade
phone 208-5900

Martin, David G.	Dir	208-5932	dgmartin	Fnce	PHD	91	St Louis	7-01
Singer, Russell	C-As$	208-5900	rjsinger		BS	58	Wilkes	9-67
Hosseini, Hamid S.	Prof	208-5900	hshossei	BEFO	PHD	77	Oregon	9-86
John S. Davis Distinguished Service Professor								
Heahigh, David J.	Assoc	208-5900	djleahig		PHD	79	Geotown	9-90
Rose, Margarita M.	Assoc	208-5900	mmrose	AO	PHD	89	Notre Dm	9-90

Kutztown University of PA | Kutztown, PA 19530-0730 (610) 683-4584 | kutztown.edu
Department of Economics | College of Business Fax=683-4573 | Mrs. Donna DeLong

Hartz, Theodore A.	Dean	683-4575	hartz	Fnce	MBA		Lehigh	1977
Hvidding, James M.	C-Pr	683-4593	hvidding	EB	PHD	76	Maryland	1986
Daneshyar, Arifeen M.	Prof	683-4592	daneshya	AE	PHD	76	S Illinois	1984
Margolis, H. Albert	Prof	683-1372	margolis	NC	PHD	69	Purdue	1976
Luizer, James C.	Assoc	683-4595		JC	PHD	84	Lehigh	1984
Sraiheen, Abdulwahab	Assoc	683-4597	sraiheen	CM	PHD	86	Penn St	1990
Zelleke, Girma	Assoc	683-4598	zelleke	FO	PHD	84	Colorado	1986

Lafayette College | Easton, PA 18042-1776 (610) 330-5298 | lafayette.edu
Economics Faculty | Dept of Econ & Business Fax=330-5715 | Mrs. Carol Riffert/Carolyn Lee

Heavey, Jerome F.	C-Pr	330-5300	heaveyj	DHP	PHD	76	Penn St	1973
Chambers, Donald R.	Prof	330-5303	chambers	MG	PHD	81	N Carol	1992
Walter E. Hanson/KPMG Professor of Business & Finance								
Hochman, Harold M.	Prof	330-5315	hochmanh	HIK	PHD	65	Yale	1992
Wm. E. Simon Professor of Political Economics								
Seifried, Edmond J.	Prof	330-5314	seifried	JM	PHD	71	W Virginia	1978
Ahene, Rexford A.	Assoc	330-5305	ahener	OR	PHD	83	Wisconsin	1982
on leave 2001-2002								
Averett, Susan	Assoc	330-5307	averetts	CJI	PHD	91	Colorado	1991
Beckman, Mary P.	Assoc	330-5301	beckmanm	OP	PHD	86	Notre Dm	1985
on leave 2001-2002								
Bodenhorn, Howard	Assoc	330-5308	bodenhoh	AN	PHD	90	Rutgers	1993
Bruggink, Thomas H.	Assoc	330-5307	bruggint	CQ	PHD	79	Illinois	1978
DeVault, James M.	Assoc	330-5312	devaultj	EFQ	PHD	90	Wisconsin	1989
Gamber, Edward N.	Assoc	330-5310	gambere	EC	PHD	86	Va Tech	1992
Hutchinson, Gladstone	Assoc	330-5304	hutchins	AO	PHD	90	Clark	1992
on leave 2001-2002								
Shively, Philip	Asst	330-5313	shivelp	CG	PHD	97	Michigan	1997

Lake Superior State Univ | Sault S Marie MI 49783-1626 (906) 635-2426 | lakers.lssu.edu
Economics Faculty | Col of Business & Econ Fax=635-2821 | Ms. Kathy Danielkiewicz

Titus, Varkey K.	Dean	635-7560	vtitus	Mgt	PHD	80	Wash St	7-00
Erkkila, John	Prof	635-2108	jerkkila	ADEF	PHD	87	W Ontario	9-90
Harger, Bruce T.	Prof	635-2421	bharger	A	PHD	91	Mich St	9-67

Lakeland College | Sheboygan, WI 53082-0359 (414) 565-1543 | lakeland.edu
Economics Faculty | Dept of Business Admin Fax=565-1206

Schilcutt, J. Garland	C-Pr	565-1271		M	LLD		Marian	1958
Kudek, James F.	Assoc	565-1273		ABCD	MBA		Wi-Milwa	1982
Qastin, Abdul Masesh	Assoc	565-1269		DGNP	PHD		Kennedy W	1985
Schwartz, Adina Tzur	Assoc	565-1296		AEFG	MA		Wi-Milwa	1986
Botana, Joseph D.	Asst	565-1336		AFND	MBA		Roosevelt	1990

Lamar University Beaumont, TX 77710 (409) 880-8647 lamar.edu
Dept of Economics & Finance College of Business Fax=880-1752 Mrs. Cloris Moser

Moore, Gary A.	Dean$	880-8603	moore	J	PHD	74	Nebraska	1998
Hawkins, Charles F.	C-Pr	880-8647		RK	PHD	80	LSU	1966
Regents' Professor of Economics								
Allen, Charles L.	Prof	880-8656		RC	PHD	78	Arkansas	1979
Bacdayan, Andrew W.	Prof	880-8657		AE	PHD	73	Utah St	
Choi, Jai-Young	Prof	880-8062		DF	PHD	82	Oklahoma	1982
Montano, Carl B.	Prof	880-8651		OQ	PHD	82	Mich St	1981

Lander University Greenwood, SC 29649 (864) 388-8232 lander.edu
Economic Faculty School of Business Adm Fax=388-8890 Joyce Shelton

Grider, Douglas T.	Dean	388-8232	dgrider	Mgt	PHD	72	Geo St	1999
Caines, W. Royce	Prof	388-8359		ALPQ	PHD	88	Clemson	1988
Dickes, Lori	Asst	38-8355			MA	96	Cen Fla	1998

La Salle University Philadelphia, PA 19141-1108 (215) 951-1178 lasalle.edu
Department of Economics College of Arts & Sci Fax=951-1488 Sister Betty McDonald
Homepage: http://www.lasalle.edu/academ/econ/main.htm

Ratkus, Mark J.	C-As	951-1178	ratkus	O	PHD	76	Notre Dm	1973
George, David L.	Assoc	951-1185	george	ABN	PHD	84	Temple	1979
Grady, John	Assoc	951-1360	grady	BE	MA		Temple	1960
Paulin, Elizabeth	Assoc	951-1181	paulin	J	PHD	87	Tx-Austin	1988
Robison, H. David	Assoc	951-1184	robison	LQC	PHD	83	Maryland	1988
Cairo, Joseph P.	Asst	951-1177	cairo	BE	MA		Penn	1963
Mshomba, Richard	Asst	951-1116	mshomba	FO	PHD	92	Illinois	1991

La Sierra University Riverside, CA 92515-8247 (909) 785-2064 lasierra.edu
Economics Faculty Sch of Business & Mgt Fax=785-2700 Vernell Kaufholtz

Thomas, Johnny	Dean	785-2085	jthomas	C	PHD	01	Claremont	1989
Selivanoff, George A.	C-Pr	785-2313	gselivan	AFM	PHD	64	American	1984
Ogum, George	Assoc	785-2314	gogum	CFGM	DBA	90	Memphis	1997

University of LaVerne LaVerne, CA 91750 (909) 593-3511 ulv.edu
School of Bus & Global Study College of Grad & Prof Fax=392-2704 Barbara Buchanan

Orr, Verne	Dean	539-3511	orrv		MBA	39	Stanford	1999
Ispahani, Ahmed S.	C-Pr	593-3511	ispahani		PHD	66	S Calif	1964
Park, Gon Yung	Prof	593-3511	parkg		PHD	93	Brown	1995
Thakur, Rita	Prof	593-4206	thakur		MBA		NW Mo St	1978

Lawrence Technological Univ Southfield, MI 48075-1058 (248) 204-3520 ltu.edu
Dept of Humanities Col of Arts & Sciences Fax=204-3518 Joyce McKissen

Rodgers, James	Dean	204-3500	rodgers	Engl	PHD	79	E Anglia	1968
Munevar, Gonzalo	C-Pr	204-3520	munevar	Phil	PHD	75	Berkeley	1999
Stevens, Flumo Y.	Prof	204-3508	stevens	G	PHD	74	Nebraska	1987
Hotelling, Harold	Assoc	204-3530	hotelling	KL	PHD	82	Duke	9-89

Lebanon Valley College Annville, PA 17003 (717) 867 6327 lvc.edu
Dept of Pol Sci & Econ Fax=867-6124

Hey, Jeanne C.	C Ac	867-6327	hey		PHD	90	Lehigh	1989
Heise, Paul A.	Assoc	867-6328	heise		PHD	91	New Sch	1991

Lehigh University Bethlehem, PA 18015-3117 (610) 758-3420 lehigh.edu
Department of Economics College of Bus & Econ Fax=758-4677 Diane Oechsle

Durand, Richard M.	Dean	758-3400	rmd6	Mktg	PHD	75	Florida	1999
Hyclak, Thomas J.	C-Pr	758-3425	tjh7	JR	PHD	76	Notre Dm	1979
Aronson, J. Richard	Prof	758-3411	jra1	HG	PHD	64	Clark	1965
William L. Clayton Professor of Business and Economics								
Innes, Jon T.	Prof	758-3417	jti1	EB	PHD	67	Oregon	1987
King, Arthur E.	Prof	758-4451	aek0	FP	PHD	76	Ohio St	1976
Munley, Vincent G.	Prof	758-3428	vgm0	HI	PHD	79	SUNY-Bin	1980
Lee Iacocca Professor of Business & Economics								
Thornton, Robert J.	Prof	758-3460	rjt1	JI	PHD	70	Illinois	1970
Charles W. MacFarlane Professor of Economics								
Dearden, James A.	Assoc	758-5129	jad8	DH	PHD	87	Penn St	1989
Deily, Mary E.	Assoc	758-4951	med4	LQ	PHD	85	Harvard	1991
Gunter, Frank R.	Assoc	758-4540	frg2	FK	PHD	85	J Hopkins	1984
McDonald, Judith Ann	Assoc	758-5345	djm0	FE	PHD	86	Princeton	1990
O'Brien, Anthony P.	Assoc	758-3442	ao01	NE	PHD	86	Berkeley	1987
Taylor, Larry W.	Assoc	758-3416	lwt0	CE	PHD	84	N Carol	1984
Francis, Neville	Asst	758-3420			PHD	01	Ca-SnDgo	2001
Watkins, Todd A.	Asst	758-4954	taw4	LO	PHD	95	Harvard	1992
Weng, Wenlong	Asst	758-3420			PHD	01	Stanford	2001

LeMoyne College Syracuse, NY 13214-1399 (315) 445-4465 maple.lemoyne
Economics Faculty Department of Economics Fax=445-4540
Did Not Respond--1999-2000 Listing

Ruwe, Marcia	Dean	445-4310	ruweml		DBA	82	Kentucky	1995
Shepard, Edward M.	C-Ac	445-4465	shepard	HJL	PHD	87	Boston C	1990
Arora, Harjit K.	Prof	445-4436	arora	EFH	PHD	84	Wi-Milwa	1987
Blackley, Dixie M.	Prof	445-4437	black_d	DRC	PHD	84	Syracuse	1982
Blackley, Paul R.	Prof	445-4465	black_p	HR	PHD	82	Syracuse	1982
Saunders, Kent T.	Asst	445-4488	sanuders	ADG	PHD	95	Clemson	1998

Lenoir-Rhyne College Hickory, NC 28603 (828) 328-7218 lrc.edu
Dept of Economics & Pol Sci Div of Social & Beh Sci Fax=328-7338 Dottie Crafton

Mauney, William M.	C-Pr	328-7218	mauneyw	AE	MA	76	Appalach	1967
Centennial Professor of Economics - Director Broyhill Institute								
Ashman, H. Lowell	Prof	328-7213	l_ashman		PHD	73	Utah	1975
Wright, Jeffrey J.	Prof	328-7217	wright_jj	AFK	PHD	87	Conn	1989

Lewis & Clark College Portland, OR 97219-7899 (503) 768-7606 lclark.edu
Department of Economics Col of Arts & Sciences Fax=768-7611 Kathy Anderson

Goodstein, Eban	C-Ac	768-7626	eban	QDGL	PHD	89	Michigan	1995
Hart-Landsberg, Martin	Prof	768-7624	marty	POFA	PHD	74	Wisconsin	1978
O'Sullivan, Arthur M.	Prof	768-7606		RKHQ	PHD	81	Princeton	2001
Schleef, Harold J.	Prof	768-7603	schleef	Fnce	PHD	77	Chicago	
Bekar, Clifford T.	Asst	768-7612	bekar	HPIL	ABD		Simon Fr	1998
Grant, James H.	Asst	768-7623	grant	CDJA	PHD	79	Mich St	1987
Zahrt Geib, Elizabeth	Asst	768-7605	zahrt	GEBJ	PHD	97	Calif	1997

Liberty University Lynchburg, VA 24502-2269 (804) 582-2480 liberty.edu
Dept Econ & Finance & MIS School of Bus & Govt Fax=582-2366 Sharon Woods
Did Not Respond--1999-2000 Listing

Adkins, Robert T.	Dean	582-2480		Mktg	PHD	77	Arkansas	1991
Mateer, Robert N.	C-Pr	582-2338			MBA	64	Tulane	1984
Lai, T. H.	Assoc	582-2910		AEFG	PHD	84	Ohio St	9-85
Rencher, Robert	Assoc	582-7743			MBA	81	Fairl Dick	1991
Terrell, Timothy	Asst	582-2338		ACPQ	PHD	98	Auburn	1998

Lincoln University-MO Jefferson Cty MO 65101-0029 (573) 681-5489 lincolnu.edu
Dept of Bus & Economics Col Bus & Prof Studies Fax=681-6074

Quartey, Kojo A.	Dean	651-5489	quarteyk		PHD	87	Miss St	8-99
Linhardt, Wayne C.	H	681-5487	linhardt		ABD		Nova SE	1965
LePage, James	Assoc	681-6081			PHD		Kansas	1984
Arabian, Ghodratollah	Asst	681-6077			PHD	85	Indiana	1984

Lincoln University-PA Lincoln Univ, PA 19352 (610) Ext 3394 lu.lincoln.edu
Dept of Economics & Bus Adm Div of Social Sciences Fax=932-1079 Melanie Murray Ext 3394
Homepage: 1570 Balimore Pike
phone 932-8300

Dadson, William K.	C-Pr	Ext 6191	dadson		PHD	83	Denver	
Ramdas, Ganga P.	Asst	Ext 3376	gramdas		PHD	87	Temple	

Lindenwood University St. Charles, MO 63301-1695 (636) 949-2000 lc.lindenwood.edu
Economics Faculty Div Management & LCIE Fax=949-4910

Hardman, Jay	Dean	949-2000						
Kamm, Judy	Asst	949-4833	jkamm		MS		Mo-StLou	8-96
Najjar, Annette	Asst	949-4876	anajjar		MBA	95	Millsaps	4-01

Linfield College McMinnville, OR 97128-6894 (503) 434-2405 linfield.edu
Economics Faculty Economics Fax=434-2402 Jean Claus

Grant, Randy R.	C-Ac	434-2402	rgrant		PHD	96	Nebraska	1993
Bull, Vivian A.	Prof	434-2408	bull		PHD	74	NYU	1992
President								
Hansen, David	Prof	434-2253	dhansen		MS		Portland	1969
Summers, Jeffrey A.	Assoc	434-2297	jsummer		PHD	87	Purdue	1992
Bathgate, James	VAsst				PHD	01	Conn	2001

Lock Haven U of Pennsylvania Lock Haven, PA 17745 (570) 893-2163 lhup.edu
Dept Hist, Pol S & Economics College of Arts & Sci Fax=893-2830 Gale Spangler

Johnson, Roger	Dean	893-2136	rjohnson		PHD	68	Illinois	1998
Harvey, Karen	C	893-2646	kharvey		PHD	84	Penn St	1989
Carroll, Richard R.	Prof	893-2447	rcarroll		PHD	73	Kentucky	1977
Chatterton, R. Edward	Prof	893-2222	rchatter		PHD	80	Wash St	1982
Wion, Douglas A.	Assoc	893-2217	dwion		PHD	80	Penn St	1980

Long Isl U, Brooklyn Campus — Brooklyn, NY 11201-5372 (718) 488-1025 — liunet.edu
Department of Economics — Conolly C Liberal A & S Fax=780-4106 — Ms. Mina Pacheco
Did Not Respond--1999-2000 Listing

Cohen, David B.	Dean			Biol	PHD	73	NYU	
Varma, Ranbir	C-Pr	834-1025		AFOP	PHD	57	New Sch	1959
Lombardi, Waldo J.	Prof			ACD	PHD	70	Columbia	
Zewail, Amin A.	Assoc			AEHR	PHD	75	Fordham	

Long Island U.-C.W. Post — Brookville, NY 11548-0570 (516) 299-2321 — eagle.liunet.edu
Department of Economics — College of Liberal Arts Fax=299-4169 — Rhonda Pereira
Did Not Respond--1999-2000 Listing

Sherwin, Paul	Dean	299-2236			PHD		Yale	
Gafar, John S.	C-Pr	299-2371			PHD	79	W Indies	1980
Mourdoukoutas, Panos	Prof	299-2322			PHD	83	SUNY-SBr	1984
Solar, Donald	Prof	299-2321			PHD	63	Columbia	1965
Roy, Udayan	Assoc	299-2405			PHD	91	SUNY-SBr	
Zeineldin, Aly	Assoc	299-2370			PHD	79	NYU	
Lu, Laura	Asst	299-2369			PHD	89	SUNY-SBr	

Longwood College — Farmville, VA 23909 (804) 395-2042 — lwcnet.lwc.edu
Dept of Economics & Finance — School of Bus & Econ Fax=395-2203 — Ms. Janet Evans
Did Not Respond--1999-2000 Listing

Flanigan, Mary A.	C-Ac	395-2042	mflaniga	Atg	PHD	95	Va Comm	1989
Shaw, Sue O.	Prof	395-2371	sshaw		PHD	67	Harvard	1986
Adusei, Edward O.	Assoc	395-2459	eadusei		PHD	88	Va Tech	1992
Brastow, Raymond T.	Assoc	395-2370	rbrastow	J	PHD	87	U Wash	1987
Marks, Melanie B.	Assoc	395-2372	mmerrell		PHD	93	Tx A&M	1993

Loras College — Dubuque, IA 52004-0178 (319) — loras.edu
Department of Economics — Div Soc Sci & Beh Stds Fax=
Did Not Respond--1999-2000 Listing

Simon, Peter J.	C-Ac	588-7915	psimon		PHD	89	N Illinois	1989
Giannakouros, George	Prof	588-7646	ggiannak		PHD	74	Iowa	1966
O'Connor, Dennis A.	Prof	588-7519	doconnor		PHD	84	Notre Dm	1983
Sula, Laddie J.	Prof	588-7507	lsula		PHD	76	Geo St	1983

U of Louisiana at Lafayette — Lafayette, LA 70504-4570 (337) 482-6662 — louisiana.edu
Dept of Economics & Finance — Col of Business Admin Fax=482-6195 — Sandy Latham

Fronmueller, Michael	Dean	482-6491	mfronm	Mgt	PHD	91	Wash St	1999
Greco, Anthony J.	H-Pr	482-6669		ADL	PHD	78	Tennessee	8-84
Heath, W. Cary	Assoc	482-5728			PHD	82	LSU	
Gale, Louis	Asst	482-6663			PHD	94	Ariz St	1995
La Point, James	Asst	482-6671						
Ressler, Rand W.	Asst	482-6666	rwr5011	DJ	PHD	93	Auburn	8-93
Waters, Melissa S.	Asst	482-6082	msw9633	CJT	PHD	89	LSU	8-90
Watson, J. Keith	Asst	482-5727			PHD	83	Tx A&M	
Rumore, Nancy C.	Inst	482-6667			MS	80	LSU	

Univ of Louisiana at Monroe — Monroe, LA 71209-0130 (318) 342-1150 — ulm.edu
Dept of Economics & Finance — College of Business Adm Fax=342-1209 — Juanita Hyatt

Eisenstadt, Robert C.	H-Acc	342-1150	eceisenstadt	JI	PHD	91	Geo St	
Kogut, Carl A.	Assoc	342-1154	eckogut	DLJ	PHD	84	Tx A&M	1992
Nelson, Paul S.	Assoc	342-1162	ecnelson	DL	PHD	85	Tx A&M	1989
Scott, John L.	Assoc	342-1160	ecscott	DC	PHD	90	S Carol	1989
Futayyeh, Mohamed-Amin	Asst	342-1163	ecfutayyeh		PHD	70	Oklahoma	
Parker, Tommy R.	Asst	342-1162						

Louisiana State University — Baton Rouge, LA 70803-6306 (225) 578-5211 — lsu.edu
Department of Economics — College of Business Adm Fax=578-3807 — Mary Jo Neathery

Clark, Thomas D. Jr.	Dean	578-3211			DBA	77	Fla St	8-95
Hill, R. Carter	C-Pr	578-1490	eohill	C	PHD	75	Missouri	
Marjory B. Ourso Excellence in Teaching Professor								
Beard, Thomas R.	Emer	578-3789	trbreard	E	PHD	63	Duke	1961
LSU Alumni Professor Emeritus								
Culbertson, W. Patton Jr.	Prof	578-3784	wculber	F	PHD	72	Tx-Austin	
Jones, Lamar B.	Prof	578-3803	bajone	J	PHD	65	Tx-Austin	1967
Associate Director of EMBA								
Koray, Faik A.	Prof	578-3801	eokora	EF	PHD	84	Duke	1984
Director Graduate Studies								
McMillin, W. Douglas	Prof	578-3798	eodoug	E	PHD	79	LSU	1985
South Central Bell Business Partnership Professor								
Moore, William J.	Prof	578-3792	eomoore	IJ	PHD	70	Tx-Austin	
Gulf Coast Coca Cola Business Partnership Professor								

Newman, Robert J.	Prof	578-3794	eonewm	IJ	PHD	80	UCLA	1983
South Central Bell Business Partnership Professor								
Rice, G. Randolph	Emer	578-3799	rrice		PHD	70	Kentucky	1969
Richardson, James A.	Prof	578-6743	parich	H	PHD	71	Michigan	1970
Alumni Professor of Economics; Director Public Administration Institute								
Scott, Loren C.	Emer	578-3779	lscott	J	PHD	69	Okla St	1969
Miyagiwa, Kaz	Assoc	578-3793	kmiyagi	FO	PHD	85	Tx-Austin	8-95
Palivos, Theodore	Assoc	578-3791	eopali	F	PHD	92	Penn St	1992
Mack Hornbeak Business Partnership Professor								
Terrell, Dek	Assoc	578-3785	mdterre	C	PHD	91	Duke	8-96
Freeport McMoran Endowed Chair; Director Center for Econ Dev & Forecasting								
Okten, Cagla	Asst	578-5211		L	PHD	99	Nrthwstrn	8-99
Papageorgio, Chris	Asst	578-3790	cpapa	E	PHD	96	Pittsburgh	8-97
Sarangi, Sudipta	Asst	578-7193	sarangi	L	PHD	00	Virginia	8-00
Zachariadis, Marios	Asst	578-3787	zachariadis	E	PHD	00	Ohio St	8-00

Louisiana St in Shreveport — Shreveport, LA 71115-2399 (318) 797-5241 — lsuvm.sncc.lsu.edu
Dept of Economics & Finance — College of Business Adm Fax=797-5208 — Marlin Hadley

Harju, Melvin W.	Dean	797-5027			PHD	72	Florida	8-77
Bible, Douglas S.	C-Pr	797-5241	dbible	Insu	PHD	77	Ohio St	8-85
Austin, John A.	Prof	797-5022			PHD	72	Ariz St	1983
Brendler, Michael D.	Prof	797-5019			PHD	77	Tx A&M	1977
Jones, Charlotte A.	Prof	797-5383			DBA	85	La Tech	1984
Hsieh, Chengho	Assoc	797-5145			PHD		LSU	1989

Louisiana Tech University — Ruston, LA 71272-0001 (318) 257-4149 — cab.latech.edu
Dept of Economics & Finance — College of Admin & Bus Fax=257-4253 — Brenda Sanderson

Anderson, Dwight C.	H-Pr	257-4149	anderson	Fnce	PHD	74	Alabama	1979
Darrat, Ali F.	Prof	257-3874	darrat	EG	PHD	81	Indiana	1987
Premier Bank Professor								
Gilley, Otis W.	Prof	257-3768	gilley	D	PHD	79	Purdue	1988
Smith, Lawrence C.	Prof	257-2112	lcsmith		PHD	68	Miss	1970
Chopin, Marc	Assoc	257-3701	chopin	DL	PHD	92	Tx A&M	1992
O'Boyle, Edward John	Assoc	257-3804	oboyle		PHD	72	St Louis	1977
Bisping, T.	Asst	257-4464		DJL	PHD	97	Oklahoma	2000

University of Louisville — Louisville, KY 40292-0001 (502) 852-7836 — gwise.louisville.edu
Department of Economics — Col Business & Pub Adm Fax=852-7672 — Charlotte Ford

Taylor, Robert L.	Dean	852-7684	rltaylo1	Mgt	DBA	72	Indiana	8-84
Davidson, Audrey	C-Ac	852-4839	abdavi01	L	PHD	93	Auburn	1993
Coomes, Paul A.	Prof	852-4841	pacoom01	R	PHD	85	Tx-Austin	1985
Gohmann, Stephan F.	Prof	852-4844	sfgohm01	J	PHD	84	N Car St	1988
Nahata, Babu L.	Prof	852-4864	b0naha01	D	PHD	77	N Illinois	8-78
Nelson, John P.	Prof	852-7901	jpnelso01	H	PHD	68	Kentucky	
Chou, Nan-Ting	Assoc	852-4840	ntchou01	E	PHD	86	Ohio St	1991
Vahaly, John	Assoc	852-4863	j0vaha01	R	PHD	75	Vanderbilt	1975
Haworth, Barry	Asst	852-4845	bmhawo01	L	PHD	94	Ca-Davis	1995
Izyumov, Alexei	Asst	852-4842	a0izyu01	F	PHD	85	USSR	8-97

Loyola College in Maryland — Baltimore, MD 21210-2699 (410) 617-2357 — loyola.edu
Department of Economics — Sellinger Sch Bus & Mgt Fax=617-2118 — Bonnie Nauman

Gray, John A.	Dean$	617-2301	jag	Mgt	STD	70	Catholic	1978
Williams, Nancy A.	C-Ac	617-2825	nwilliams	QH	PHD	84	Berkeley	1987
Derrick, Frederick W.	Prof	617-2712	fderrick	CI	PHD	76	N Car St	1982
DiLorenzo, Thomas J.	Prof	617-2755		KLH	PHD	80	Va Tech	1992
Larson, John C.	Prof	617-2476	jlarson	E	PHD	77	Minnesota	1974
Scott, Charles E.	Prof	617-2618	cscott	MJH	PHD	79	Vanderbilt	1985
Walters, Stephen J. K.	Prof	617-2313	swalters	KL	PHD	82	UCLA	1981
Burger, John	Asst	617-2357	jburger	FE	PHD	99	N Carol	1999
Hilton S.J., F. G.	Asst	617-2544	fhilton	QF	PHD	96	Wisconsin	1996
Sedgley, Norman	Asst	617-2848	nsedgley	EO	PHD	98	NewHamp	2000
Ward, Marianne	Asst	617-5557	mward3	EN	PHD	00	U Miami	2000

Loyola University - Chicago — Chicago, IL 60611-2196 (312) 915-6062 — luc.edu
Department of Economics — School of Business Adm Fax=915-8508 — Amanda Krars

Cain, Louis P.	C-Pr	915-6075	lcain	ADNR	PHD	69	Nrthwstrn	1968
Cinar, E. Mine	Prof	915-6066	mcinar	ACDO	PHD	76	Tx A&M	1983
Malliaris, Tassos	Prof	915-6063	tmallia	ACG	PHD	72	Oklahoma	1972
Gabriel, Paul E.	Assoc	915-6070	pgabrie	ADJ	PHD	87	Kentucky	1990
Gobin, Roy T.	Assoc	915-6074	tgobin	AEHO	PHD	78	Illinois	1978
Hayford, Marc D.	Assoc	915-6073	mhayfor	AE	PHD	87	Brown	1986
Merriman, David F.	Assoc	915-6071	dmerrim	ADHO	PHD	83	Wisconsin	1987
Mirza, David B.	Assoc	915-6062	dmirza	AF	PHD	73	Nrthwstrn	1969
Vanderporten, Bruce S.	Assoc	915-6076	bvander	ACD	PHD	73	Wayne St	1978

Loyola Univ-New Orleans New Orleans, LA 70118 (504) 865-3544 beta.loyno.edu
Department of Economics College of Business Adm Fax=865-3496
Did Not Respond--1999-2000 Listing

O'Brien, J. Patrick	Dean	865-3547		AEHR	PHD	77	Okla St	1995
Walker, Deborah L.	C-Ac	865-3924		ABDJ	PHD	87	GeoMason	1987
Barnett, William	Assoc	865-2165		DEFK	PHD	74	Mich St	1974
Dauterive, Jerry W. Associate Dean	Assoc	865-3545		ADH	PHD	76	Tx Tech	1979
Mundell, Cyril Lee	Assoc	865-2549		AC	PHD	76	N Carol	1981
Saliba, Michael T.	Assoc	865-2681		ADM	PHD	72	Oklahoma	1973
Wood, J. Stuart	Assoc	865-2171		GM	PHD	80	NYU	1984

Loyola Marymount Univ Los Angeles, CA 90045-8410 (310) 338-7373 lmumail.lmu.edu
Department of Economics College of Liberal Arts Fax=338-1950 M. Edwards/B. Bernard

Chan, Kenyon	Dean	338-2716	kchan		PHD	74	UCLA	1998
Singleton, Robert	C-As	338-7373	rsinglet	AJR	PHD	83	UCLA	1982
Devine, James N.	Prof	338-2948	jdevine	AEJN	PHD	81	Berkeley	1985
Earley, Joseph E.	Assoc	338-4572	jearley	AC	PHD	74	Fordham	1974
Konow, James D.	Assoc	338-2956	jkonow	ACD	PHD	93	UCLA	1989
Shoukry, Kamal	Assoc	338-8215	kshoukry	ABCE	PHD	72	S Calif	1980
Thimester, Renate	Assoc	338-2817	rthimest	ABKM	PHD	67	Alabama	1971
Zekavat, Seid M.	Assoc	338-7372	szekavat	ACG	PHD	64	S Calif	1964
Barkley, Daniel	Asst	338-5956	dbarkley	AJR	PHD	01	Ca-Irvine	2001
Eusufzai, Zaki	Asst	338-2822	zeusufza	ACFD	PHD	94	UCLA	1989

Luther College Decorah, IA 52101-1045 (563) 387-1340 luther.edu
Dept of Economics & Business Div of Social Sciences Fax=387-1088 Dodi Bernatz

Wee, Liang Chee	H-Pr	287-1338	weeliang	Mis	PHD	92	Arizona	1992
Kaschins, Edward A.	Prof	387-1130	kaschins		PHD	73	Iowa	1961
Lund, Mark	Prof	387-1275	marklund		PHD	75	Iowa St	1978
Gomersall, C. Nicholas	Assoc	387-1133	gomersni		PHD	91	Cornell	1991
Leake, Richard S.	Assoc	387-1812	leakeric		MBA	84	Wi-LaCros	1975
Shitts, Wade	Asst	387-1714	shittswa		PHD	99	Iowa	1997

Lycoming College Williamsport, PA 17701-5192 (570) 321-4100 lycoming.edu
Economics Faculty Dept of Economics Fax=321-4161 Carolyn Vander Weide

Bolander, Steven F.	Dean	862-1983	steve.bolander	Mgt	DBA	72	Kent St	7-00
Madresehee, Mehrdad	C-Ac	321-4179	madreseh	FKLR	PHD	85	Wash St	1986
Sprunger, Philip W.	Asst	321-4178	sprunger	AJQH	PHD	93	Indiana	1993
Yerger, David B.	Asst	321-4154	yerger	JFTN	PHD	94	Penn St	1996

Lynchburg College Lynchburg, VA 24501-3199 (434) 544-8256 lynchburg.edu
Dept of Economics Sch of Business & Econ Fax=544-8639 Virginia Kern
Homepage: lynchburg.edu/schools/business.htm

Husted, Stewart W.	Dean	544-8621		Mgt	PHD	77	Mich St	9-89
Turek, Joseph H.	C-Pr	544-8542			PHD	87	SUNY-Alb	1986
Messerschmidt, Daniel C.	Prof	544-8359			PHD	84	Iowa St	1985
Prinzinger, Joseph M.	Prof	544-8329			PHD	74	Geo St	1987

Lyndon State College Lyndonville, VT 05851 (802) 626-6200 queen.lsc.vsc.edu
Economics Faculty Business Adm Department Fax=626-9770

Fishbein, Michael	Dean	626-6406			PHD	81	Clark	9-00
Hilton, Mark	C-As	626-6339	hiltonm		MBA	93	Plymouth	1-00
Siegel, Rachel S.	Assoc	626-9371	siegelr	CGQN	MBA	89	Yale	9-90
Mitchell, Linda M.	Asst	626-9371	mitchelll		MBA	79	Columbia	1-89

Lyon College Batesville, AR 72501-2317 (870) 698-4258 lyon.edu
Department of Economics Business & Econ Div Fax=698-4622 Peggy Weaver
Did Not Respond--1999-2000 Listing

Cooper, Thomas E. Anne J. Stewart Professor of Economics	C-Ac	698-4364	tcooper	DGHL	PHD	84	Princeton	1987
Cohen, Richard H.	Asst	793-1740	rcohen	EG	PHD	92	Indiana	1998

Macalester College St. Paul, MN 55105-1899 (651) 696-6227 macalester.edu
Economics Faculty Economics Department Fax=696-6746 Jane Kollasch
Homepage: www.macalester.edu/~economic/

Sukhatme, Vasant A. Edward J. Noble Professor of Economics	C-Pr	696-6744	sukhatme	ADO	PHD	77	Chicago	1978
Egge, Karl A. F. R. Bigelow Professor of Economics	Prof	696-6743	egge	AGM	PHD	73	Ohio St	1970
Ferderer, J. Peter	Assoc	696-6093	ferderer	EFN	PHD	89	Wash U	1996
Krueger, Gary J.	Assoc	696-6222	krueger	ACP	PHD	89	Wisconsin	1989
Moe, Karine S.	Assoc	696-6793	moe	AJ	PHD	95	Minnesota	1995
Robertson, Raymond	Asst	696-6739	robertson	AEF	PHD	97	Texas	1999
West, Sarah	Asst	696-6482	west	HQ	PHD	99	Texas	2000

Univ of Maine Orono, ME 04469-5774 (207) 581-1850 umit.maine.edu
Department of Economics Col Liberal Arts & Sci Fax=581-1851 Rebecca Nadeau-Oliver

Wihry, David F.	C-Ac	581-1850	david.wihry	HIA	PHD	72	Syracuse	1969
Burke, Melvin	Prof	581-1853	melvin.burke	O	PHD	67	Pittsburgh	1966
Duchesneau, Thomas D.	Prof	581-1858	tom.duchesneau	AO	PHD	69	Boston C	1967
Hunt, Gary	Prof	581-1861	gary.hunt	AR	PHD	84	Colorado	1993
Lutz, Mark A.	Prof	581-1859		AB	PHD	72	Berkeley	1970
Townsend, Ralph E.	Prof	581-1852	ralph.townsend	CHQA	PHD	83	Wisconsin	1980
Breece, James H.	Assoc	581-1863	james.breece	AEF	PHD	82	Boston C	1983
Montgomery, Michael	Assoc	581-1857	michael.mont+	AE	PHD	88	Florida	1991
Trostel, Philip	Assoc	581-1822		AHJ	PHD	91	Tx A&M	1987
Kearney, Adrienne	Asst	581-1854	adrienne.kearney	AF	PHD	92	Penn St	1997
Tanguay, Georges	Asst	581-1820	georges.tanguay	AHQ	PHD	98	Laval	1993

Manchester College N Manchester, IN 46962 (219) 982-5000 manchester.edu
Economics Faculty Department of Economics Fax=982-5043
Homepage: www.manchester.edu/academic/programs/departments/

Peterson, Brian J.	C-As	982-5205	bjpeterson	ADH	PHD	00	Indiana	1997
Monaco, Diane K.	Asst	982-5301	dkmonaco	EFJ	PHD	98	Wayne St	1999

Manhattan College Riverdale, NY 10471 (718) 862-7220 manhattan.edu
Dept of Economics & Finance School of Business Fax=862-8032

Suarez, James M.	Dean	862-7440			PHD	72	Columbia	1984
Abdulahad, Faraj	C-Ac	862-7220	fabdulah	F	PHD	68	Boston C	1970
Geisst, Charles R.	Prof	862-7242	cgeisst@a	N	PHD	72	LondonEc	1985
Tomer, John F.	Prof	862-7462	jtomer@juno.com		PHD	73	Rutgers	1983
Maclachlan, Fiona C.	Assoc	862-7466			PHD	91	NYU	1992
Topyan, Kudret	Assoc	862-7887			PHD	92	CUNY	1991
Guirguis, Hany	Asst	862-7455			PHD	95	Oregon	2001
Murphy, Albert	Asst	862-7181			PHD	01	CUNY	2000
Sadler, Thomas	Asst	862-7468			PHD	98	Tennessee	2001

Mansfield University of PA Mansfield, PA 16933 (717) 662-4510 mnsfld.edu
Economics Faculty Business & Economics Fax=662-4111
Did Not Respond--1999-2000 Listing

Welch, Paula	C-Ac	662-4512	pwelch		MBA	80	Syracuse	1976
Yacovissi, William A.	Prof	662-4764	wyacoviss		PHD	89	SUNY-Bin	1976
Carpenter, Bruce E.	Assoc	662-4761	bcarrpent		PHD	90	Conn	1987

Marian College Indianapolis, IN 46222-1997 (317) 955-6045 marian.edu
Economics Faculty Business Fax=955-6448

Hoogerwert, Richard	C-Ac	955-6045	mtprof		MS	77	Butler	1988
Truesdell, Marie K.	Asst	955-6035	mtrue		PHD	99	Georgia	2000
Schuttler, Robert D.	Inst	955-6038	robert		MBA	80	Evansville	1985

Marietta College Marietta, OH 45750-4029 (740) 376-4633 marietta.edu
Brachman Dp Econ, Mgt & Atg College of Business Fax=376-7501 Paula Lewis

Potash, Sidney	C-Pr	376-4633	potashs	Mgt	PHD	79	SUNY-Buf	1974
Delemeester, Gregory	Assoc	376-4630	delemeeg	DJK	PHD	89	Tx A&M	1986
Milton Friedman Chair in Economics								
Khorassani, Jacqueline	Asst	376-4621	khorassj	AEFH	PHD	97	W Virginia	1994

Marist College Poughkeepsie, NY 12601-1387 (845) 575-3225 marist.edu
Economic Faculty School of Management Fax=575-3640 Debbie Smith

Badovick, Gordon J.	Dean	575-3225	gordon.badovick	Mktg	PHD	88	Oregon	1997
Walsh, Rob	C-As	575-3000	robert.walsh	Atg	PHD	94	Notre Dm	1997
Davis, Ann E.	Asst	575-3000	ann.davis	RT	PHD	83	Boston C	1981
Sue, Della	Asst	575-3000	della.lee.sue	HN	PHD	96	Columbia	2000

Marquette University Milwaukee, WI 53201-1881 (414) 288-7377 marquette.edu
Department of Economics College of Business Adm Fax=288-5757 Sue Fligor

Shrock, David L.	Dean	288-7141	david.shrock	Tran	DBA	74	Indiana	1999
Brush, Brian C.	C-Pr	288-3367	brian.brush	DL	PHD	73	N Carol	1968
Davis, John B.	Prof	288-5438	john.davis	BI	PHD	85	Mich St	1987
Smiley, William G.	Prof	288-5664	william.smiley	DN	PHD	73	Iowa	1973
Booth, Douglas E.	Assoc	288-7310	douglas.booth	DQ	PHD	72	U Wash	1976
Breeden, Charles H.	Assoc	288-3370	charles.breeden	DHK	PHD	77	Va Tech	1979
Chowdhury, Abdur R.	Assoc	288-3417	abdur.chowdhury	EFO	PHD	83	Kentucky	1989
Clark, David E.	Assoc	288-3339	david.clark	DR	PHD	86	SUNY-Bin	1985
Crane, Steven E.	Assoc	288-1450	steven.crane	DHLR	PHD	81	Colorado	1980
Daniels, Joseph P.	Assoc	288-3368	joseph.daniels	EFG	PHD	92	Indiana	1989
McGibany, James M.	Assoc	288-7187	james.mcgibany	CER	PHD	83	Mich St	1983
Nourzad, Farrokh	Assoc	288-3570	farrokh.nourzad	CEO	PHD	82	Kansas	1981
Toumanoff, Peter	Assoc	288-7523	peter.toumanoff	DOPC	PHD	77	U Wash	1995

Marshall University — Huntington, WV 25755-2320 (304) 696-4330 — marshall.edu
Div of Finance & Economics — Lewis College of Bus Fax=696-4344

Kent, Calvin A.	Dean	696-2614	kent		PHD	67	Missouri	1993
Shao, Lawrence P.	H-Ac	696-4330	shao	Fnce	PHD	89	Tennessee	2000
Adkins, Roger L.	Prof	696-2609	adkinsr		PHD	81	Kansas St	1981
Akkihal, Ramchandra G.	Prof	696-2613	akkihal		PHD	69	Tennessee	1970
Shuklian, Steve	Assoc	696-2605	shuklian		PHD	88	Utah	1988
Smith, Harlan II	Assoc	696-3233	smithh		PHD	89	Yale	1991
Wilkins, Allen J.	Assoc	696-3351	wilkins		PHD	84	Wisconsin	1985
Zapalska, Alina	Assoc	696-3234	zapalska		PHD	91	Kentucky	1991
Agesa, Jacqueline	Asst	696-2607	agesaj		PHD	96	Wi-Milwa	2000
Agesa, Richard	Asst	696-2606	agesa		PHD	96	Wi-Milwa	2000
Burton, Mark L.	Asst	696-2382	burtonm		PHD	91	Tennessee	1999
Hicks, Michael	Asst	696-3125	hicksm		PHD	97	Tennessee	2000
Newsome, Mike	Asst	696-2709	newsome		PHD	97	Kentucky	1999

University of Mary — Bismarck, ND 58504-9652 (701) 255-7500 — umary.edu
Economics Faculty — Division of Business Fax=255-7687
phone 255-7500

Borgelt, Marvin	C-Ac	Ext 439	mborgelt	Mgt	MBA	82	Maryland	9-82
Boor, Randy	Assoc	Ext 438			MS		N Dak St	

Mary Baldwin College — Staunton, VA 24401 (540) 887-7053 — cit.mbc.edu
Economics Faculty — Department of Economics Fax=887-7137
Did Not Respond Again--1997-98 Listing

Klein, Judy L.	C-Ac	887-7053	jklein	BC	PHD	86	London	1982
Diduch, Amy	Asst	887-7114	adiduch	J	PHD	95	Harvard	1995

Univ of Mary Hardin-Baylor — Belton, TX 76513 (254) 295-4644 — umbh.edu
Dept Atg, Economics & Fnce — School of Business Fax=295-4535
Did Not Respond Again--1997-98 Listing

Baldwin, Lee E.	Dean	295-4644	lbaldwin	Mgt	PHD	80	North Tx	1992
Fabritius, Michael	Prof	295-4655	mfabriti	ABDE	PHD	87	Tx-Austin	1987

Claude McBryde Professor of Finance-Economics

Mary Washington College — FredericksburgVA 22401-5358 (540) 654-1483 — mwu.edu
Economics Faculty — Department of Economics Fax=654-1074 — Jane Clark 654-1066

Greenlaw, Steven A.	C-Pr	654-1483	greenla	EFA	PHD	87	SUNY-Bin	1982
Rycroft, Robert S.	Prof	654-1500	rrycroft	CHJG	PHD	78	Maryland	1977
Ray, Margaret A.	Assoc	654-1485	mray	LQRA	PHD	88	Tennessee	
Stageberg, Stephen P.	Assoc	654-1486	sstagebe	CFN	PHD	84	Geotown	1982
Hansen, Bradley	Asst	654-1484	bhansen	N	PHD	95	Wash U	1995

Univ Maryland-Baltimore Co — Baltimore, MD 21228-5398 (410) 455-2137 — umbc2.umbc.edu
Department of Economics — Col of Arts & Sciences Fax= — Iris Bachelor
Did Not Respond Again--1995-96 Listing

Burchard, Robert	Dean$	455-2386		Biol	PHD	65	Minnesota	
Sorkin, Alan L.	C-Pr	455-2173			PHD	66	J Hopkins	1974
Bradley, Michael E.	Prof	455-2170			PHD	67	Cornell	
Goldfarb, Marsha G.	Prof	455-2171			PHD	68	Nrthwstrn	1973
Gindling, Thomas H.	Assoc	455-3629	gindling	O	PHD	87	Cornell	
Lord, William A.	Assoc	455-2498			PHD	84	Indiana	1987
McConnell, Virginia D.	Assoc	455-2068			PHD	78	Maryland	
Mitch, David F.	Assoc	455-2157			PHD	82	Chicago	1983
Peake, Charles F.	Assoc	455-2168			PHD	68	Maryland	1967
Takacs, Wendy E.	Assoc	455-2174			PHD	76	J Hopkins	1981
Wu, Roland Y.	Assoc	455-2176			PHD	71	Stanford	
Carroll, Kathleen A.	Asst	455-2169			PHD	76	J Hopkins	1980
Knapp, Kimberly A.	Asst	455-3243			PHD	88	Brown	
Lamdin, Douglas J.	Asst	455-2672			PHD	91	Maryland	1989
Humphreys, Brad	Inst	455-2177			MA	91	J Hopkins	
Davis, Mary	Lect	455-3177			MBA	78	Maryland	

University of Maryland — College Park, MD 20742-7211 (301) 405-3266 — umd.edu
Department of Economics — Col Behav & Social Sci Fax=405-3542 — Martha Best 405-3506

Goldstein, Irwin	Dean	405-1679	PHD	64	Maryland	1991
Straszheim, Mahlon R.	C-Pr	405-3266	PHD	66	Harvard	
Almon, Clopper Jr.	Prof	405-4604	PHD	62	Harvard	1966
Ausubel, Lawrence M.	Prof	405-3495	PHD	84	Stanford	1992
Betancourt, Roger R.	Prof	405-3479	PHD	69	Wisconsin	1980
Calvo, Guillermo	Prof	405-3553	PHD	74	Yale	1994
Cramton, Peter C.	Prof	405-6987	PHD	84	Stanford	1993
Cropper, Maureen L.	Prof	405-3266	PHD	73	Cornell	1980
Evans, William N.	Prof	405-3486	PHD	87	Duke	1987

Haltiwanger, John C.	Prof	405-3490			PHD	81	J Hopkins	1987
Hulten, Charles R.	Prof	405-3549			PHD	73	Berkeley	1985
Kelejian, Harry	Prof	405-3492			PHD	68	Wisconsin	1968
Montgomery, Edward B.	Prof	405-3498			PHD	82	Harvard	1990
Murrell, Peter	Prof	405-3476			PHD	77	Penn	1977
Oates, Wallace	Prof	405-3496			PHD	65	Stanford	1979
Panagariya, Arvind	Prof	405-3546			PHD	78	Princeton	1978
Prucha, Ingmar R.	Prof	405-3499			PHD	77	Vienna	1981
Schelling, Thomas	Prof	405-3494			PHD	51	Harvard	1991
Schwab, Robert M.	Prof	405-3478			PHD	80	J Hopkins	1980
Wallis, John J.	Prof	405-3552			PHD	81	U Wash	1983
Coughlin, Peter J.	Assoc	405-3482			PHD	76	SUNY-Alb	1982
Lyon, Andrew B.	Assoc	405-3493			PHD	86	Princeton	1987
on leave								
Sakellaris, Plutarchos	Assoc	405-3509			PHD	92	Harvard	1992
Sanders, Seth	Assoc	405-3497			PHD	93	Chicago	1999
Shea, John	Assoc	405-3491			PHD	90	MIT	1996
Vincent, Daniel	Assoc	405-3485			PHD	87	Princeton	1998
Binder, Michael	Asst	405-3466			PHD	95	Penn	1995
Chao, John	Asst	405-4366			PHD	95	Yale	1995
Gelbach, Jonah	Asst	405-3512			PHD	98	MIT	1998
on leave								
Hellerstein, Judith	Asst	405-3545			PHD	94	Harvard	1996
Kranton, Rachel E.	Asst	405-3487			PHD	93	Berkeley	1993
on leave								
Pries, Michael	Asst	405-3515			PHD	99	Stanford	1999
Rodriguez, Francisco	Asst	405-3480			PHD	98	Harvard	1998
on leave								

Marymount University Arlington, VA 22207-4299 (703) 284-5910 marymount.edu
Economics Faculty School of Business Adm Fax=527-3830 Sara Caltrider/Anne Horne

Sigethy, Robert	Dean	284-5910	rsigethy	Mgt	PHD	80	American	1983
England, Catherine	C-Pr	284-5976	cengland	Mgt	PHD	88	Tx A&M	1997
Hassanein, Saad A.	Prof	234-5938	shassanein		PHD	88	Catholic	1988
Long, Teresa M.	Prof	284-5918	tlong		PHD	80	Iowa St	1981
on sabbatical								
Marshall, Louise	Prof	284-5932	lmarshall		PHD	89	Maryland	1976

Marywood University Scranton, PA 18509-1598 (570) 348-6288 ac.marywood.edu
Economics Faculty Social Science Dept Fax=340-6012 Mrs. Jean Yeselevage
Homepage: ac.marywood.edu

Allesio, John	Dean				PHD	70	Geotown	
Munley, Kathleen	C	348-6288						
Fagal, Frederick F. Jr.	Assoc				PHD	81	Syracuse	1987

University of Massachusetts Amherst, MA 01003-7510 (413) 545-2590 econs.umass.edu
Department of Economics Col of Arts & Science Fax=545-2921 Judy Dietel

Flaherty, Diane P.	C-Pr	545-4703	chair		PHD	78	NYU	
Bausor, Randall S.	Prof	545-0595	bausor		PHD	78	Duke	1979
Bowles, Samuel S.	Prof	545-1373	bowles		PHD	65	Harvard	1973
Boyce, James K.	Prof	545-3815	boyce		PHD	85	Oxford	1985
Brimmer, Andrew F.	VProf				PHD	57	Harvard	
Costrell, Robert M.	Prof	545-1374	costrell		PHD	78	Harvard	1978
Crotty, James R.	Prof	545-2768	crotty		PHD	73	Car Mellon	1974
Deere, Carmen D.	Prof	545-0455	deere		PHD	78	Berkeley	1977
Epstein, Gerald A.	Prof	545-6355	gepstein		PHD	81	Princeton	1987
Folbre, Nancy	Prof	545-3283	folbre		PHD	79	Mass	1985
Gintis, Herbert M.	Prof	545-6363	gintis		PHD	69	Harvard	1975
Katzner, Donald W.	Prof	545-6350			PHD	65	Minnesota	1975
Kotz, David M.	Prof	545-4536	dmkotz		PHD	75	Berkeley	
Pollin, Robert N.	Prof	577-0126	pollin		PHD	82	New Sch	1998
Rao, J. Mohan	Prof	545-4808	rao@mit.edu		PHD	82	Harvard	1989
Resnick, Stephen A.	Prof	545-0947			PHD	64	MIT	
Wolff, Richard D.	Prof	545-6351		ABNP	PHD	69	Yale	9-73
Ballou, Dale	Assoc	545-6358	rdballou		PHD	89	Yale	
Friedman, Gerald	Assoc	545-6357	gfriedma		PHD	86	Harvard	1984
Heim, Carol E.	Assoc	545-0854	cheim	NRE	PHD	82	Yale	1-81
Ash, Michael	Asst	545-6329	mash		PHD	99	Berkeley	1999
Badgett, Lee	Asst	545-0159	lbadgett		PHD	90	Berkeley	1997
Levenstein, Margaret C.	Asst	545-6361			PHD	91	Yale	2000
on leave 2001-2002 at University of Michigan								
Ndikumana, Leonce	Asst	545-6359	ndiku		PHD	96	Wash U	1996
Saunders, Lisa F.	Asst	545-0546	saunders		PHD	87	Berkeley	1987

U Massachusetts at Boston Boston, MA 02125-3393 (617) 287-6950 umb.edu
Department of Economics Col of Arts & Sciences Fax=287-6976 Ms. Yvonne Ceurvels
Homepage: omega.cc.umb.edu/~economics

Albelda, Randy P.	Prof	287-6963	randy.albelda	JI	PHD	83	Mass	1988
Chiong, Winston R.	Prof	287-6957	winston.chiong	E	PHD	74	Boston C	1982
MacEwan, Arthur	Prof	287-6956	arthur.macewan	FOI	PHD	69	Harvard	1975
Stevenson, Mary H.	Prof	287-6958	mary.stevenson	JIR	PHD	74	Michigan	1972
Terkla, David G.	Prof	287-6952	david.terkla	QRH	PHD	79	Berkeley	1987
Wolozin, Harold	Prof	287-6961	harold.wolozin	B	PHD	55	Columbia	1966
Campen, James T.	Assoc	287-6962		EG	PHD	76	Harvard	1976
email: jimcampen@mediaone.net								
Cotton, Jeremiah	Assoc	287-6965	jeremiah.cotton	IJ	PHD	83	Michigan	1985
Kapler, Janis	Assoc	287-6955	jk.kapler	FL	PHD	93	American	1993
Lynde, Catherine	Assoc	287-6959	catherine.lynde	EIO	PHD	85	Ca-Davis	1983
Kim, Marlene	Asst	287-6954	marlene.kim	DJ	PHD	90	Berkeley	2000
Marcelli, Enrico	Asst		enrico.marcelli	DH	PHD	96	S Calif	2000
McDonald, Tammy	Asst		tammy.mcdonald	QR	ABD		Mass	2001

U Massachusetts-Dartmouth No Dartmouth MA 02747-2300 (508) 999-8347 umassd.edu
Department of Economics Col of Arts & Sciences Fax=999-9125

Steinman, Michael	Dean	999-8268	msteinman					
Hogan, William V.	C-Pr	999-8257	whogan		PHD	76	Cornell	1976
Berger, David E.	Prof	999-8256	dberger	IJOR	PHD	72	Wash U	1972
Georgianna, Daniel L.	Prof	999-8414	dgeorgianna		PHD	77	Mass	1977
Ohly, John H.	Assoc	999-8518		A	PHD	76	Boston U	1977
Jones, Robert	Asst	910-6436	rjones					
Shadbegian, Ronald	Asst	999-8337	rshadbegian	HKQ	PHD	91	Clark	1993
Walgreen, Sonia	VLect	999-8337	swalgreen		MA	63	Boston C	1984

U of Massachusetts at Lowell Lowell, MA 01854-2881 (978) 934-2780 uml.edu
Department of Economics Col of Arts & Sciences Fax=934-3071 Judy 934-2820
Did Not Respond--1999-2000 Listing

Kleniewski, Nancy	Dean	934-3847		Soc	PHD			
Sanz, Ernesto	C-Pr	934-2780	ernesto.sanz	FNP	PHD	75	Boston C	
Cederlund, Albert M.	Prof	934-2783		HL	PHD	75	Clark	
MacBeth, Thomas G.	Prof	934-2790		AC	PHD	62	S Calif	
McDonough, Carol C.	Prof	934-2784		DN	PHD	69	Boston C	1970
Sihag, Balbir S.	Prof	934-2786		CI	PHD	78	MIT	1980
Carter, Michael J.	Assoc	934-2794		CEQ	PHD	81	Stanford	
Dery, George C.	Assoc	934-2788		CD	MA		Boston C	
Goodwin, Susan A.	Assoc	934-3450		G	PHD	75	Tufts	
Vice Chancellor of Administration & Finance								
Lahiri, Supriya	Assoc	934-2789	lahiris	CQ	PHD	75	Delhi	
Snoonian, Paul E.	Assoc	934-2793		EQ	PHD	71	Mich St	

Mass College of Liberal Arts North Adams, MA 01247-4100 (413) 662-5311 mecn.mass.edu
Economics Faculty Business Adm & Econ Pgm Fax=662-5306 Barbara P. Sunskis

Ovitsky, Nancy L.	C-As	Ext 5307	novitsky		PHD	82	Illinois	8-84
Hajizadeh, Avaz	Assoc	Ext 5329			PHD	85	Rensselaer	
Kahn, Abraham Ben	Assoc	Ext 5306			MA	79	SUNY-Alb	
Zomorrodian, Reza	Asst	Ext 5303			EDD	90	Mass	

Massachusetts Inst of Tech Cambridge, MA 02142-1347 (617) 253-3361 mit.edu
Department of Economics Sch Humanities &Soc Sci Fax=253-1330 John Arditi

Schmalensee, Richard L.	Dean	253-2957	rschmal	O	PHD	70	MIT	1977
Goldon Y. Billard Professor Economics & Management								
Blanchard, Olivier J.	H-Pr	253-8891	blanchar	G	PHD	77	MIT	1985
Class of 1941 Professor of Economics								
Angrist, Joshua D.	Prof	253-8909	angrist	J	PHD	89	Princeton	1996
Banerjee, Abhijit V.	Prof	253-8855	banerjee	G	PHD	88	Harvard	1993
Basu, Kaushik	VProf			DHLO	PHD	76	LondonEc	2001
visiting from Cornell University								
Caballero, Ricardo	Prof	253-0489	caball	E	PHD	88	MIT	1992
Diamond, Peter A.	Prof	253-3363	pdiamond	E	PHD	63	MIT	1966
Institute Professor								
Dornbusch, Rudiger	Prof	253-3648	rudi	F	PHD	71	Chicago	1975
Ford International Professor of Economics								
Ellison, Glenn D.	Prof	253-8702	gellison	L	PHD	92	MIT	1994
Fisher, Franklin M.	Prof	253-3373	ffisher	P	PHD	60	Harvard	1960
Gruber, Jonathan H.	Prof	253-8892	gruberj	G	PHD	92	Harvard	1992
Harris, Jeffrey E.	Prof	253-2677	jeffrey	I	PHD	75	Penn	1976
Hausman, Jerry A.	Prof	253-3644	jhausman	C	DPHI	73	Oxford	1973
John and Jennie S. MacDonald Professor of Economics								
Holmstrom, Bengt	Prof	253-0506	bengt	L	PHD	78	Stanford	1995
Paul A. Samuelson Professor of Economics								

Joskow, Paul L.	Prof	253-6664	pjoskow	O	PHD	72	Yale	1972
Mitsui Professor of Economics and Management								
Kleiman, Ephraim	VProf				PHD	58	LondonEc	2001
Machin, Steve	VProf				PHD	98	Warwick	2001
Newey, Whitney K.	Prof	253-6420	wnewey	CDH	PHD	83	MIT	6-90
Piore, Michael J.	Prof	253-3377	mpiore	J	PHD	66	Harvard	1966
David W. Skinner Professor of Political Economy								
Poterba, James M.	Prof	253-6673	poterba	H	DPHI	83	Oxford	1983
Mitsui Professor of Economics								
Rose, Nancy E.	Prof	253-8956	nrose@sloan	L	PHD	85	MIT	1985
Ross, Stephen A.	Prof	258-8371	scross	G	PHD	69	Harvard	1998
Franco Modiglani Professor of Finance and Economics								
Snyder, James M. Jr.	Prof	253-2669	millett		PHD	85	Cal Tech	
Temin, Peter	Prof	253-3126	ptemin	N	PHD	64	MIT	1965
Elish Gray II Professor								
Thurow, Lester C.	Prof	253-2932	lthurow	F	PHD	64	Harvard	1968
Jerome and Dorothy Lemelson Professor of Economics and Management								
Tirole, Jean	VProf	253-8884	tirolecict.fr	O	PHD	81	MIT	1984
Voth, Hans-Joachim	VProf				DPHL	96	Oxford	2001
Wheaton, William C.	Prof	253-1723	wheaton	R	PHD	72	Penn	1972
Acemoglu, Daron	Assoc	253-1927	daron	J	PHD	92	LondonEc	1993
Costa, Dora L.	Assoc	253-2989	costa	N	PHD	93	Chicago	1993
Ford Career Development Associate Professor of Economics								
Ventura, Jaume	Assoc	253-6878	jaume	E	PHD	95	Harvard	1995
Angeletos, George-Marios	Asst	452-3859			PHD	01	Harvard	2001
Autor, David	Asst			J	PHD	99	Harvard	1999
Duflo, Ester	Asst		eduflo	O	PHD	99	MIT	1999
Castle Krob Career Development Assistant Professor of Economics								
Duggan, Mark	VAsst				PHD	99	Harvard	2001
Gabaix, Xavier	Asst		xgabaiz	G	PHD	99	Harvard	1999
Kuersteiner, Guido	Asst	253-2118	gkuerste	E	PHD	92	Princeton	1997
Mullainathan, Sendhlil	Asst	258-8047	mullain		PHD	98	Harvard	1998
mark K. Kyman Jr. Career Development Assistant Professor of Economics								
Spector, David	Asst	258-9268	spector	E	PHD	96	LondonEc	1996
Ellison, Sara	Lect	253-3821	sellison	L	PHD	93	MIT	1997

McMurry University	Abilene, TX		79697	(915) 691-6396				
Economic Faculty	School of Business		Fax=691-6268					
Valentine, John	Dean	793-3850			MBA		Abilene	1980
Williams, Eugene	Prof	793-3860			PHD	71	Arkansas	1988

McNeese State University	Lake Charles, LA		70609-1415	(337) 475-5522			ucsvm.mcneese.edu	
Dept Atg, Fnce & Econ 91415	College of Business		Fax=475-5010					
Burckel, Daryl V.	H-Pr	475-5522		Atg	DBA	86	Miss St	1992
Foshee, Andrew W.	Prof	475-5562			PHD	80	LSU	1978
Kurth, Michael M.	Prof	475-5558			PHD	82	Va Tech	1984
McNiel, Douglas W.	Prof	475-5560	dmcniel		PHD	77	Okla St	1984

University of Memphis	Memphis, TN		38152-6460	(901) 678-2432			memphis.edu	
Department of Economics	Fogelman Col Bus & Econ		Fax=678-2685					
Pepin, John J.	Dean	678-2432	jjpepin	Mktg	PHD	69	Miss	1965
Heath, Julia A.	C-Pr	678-2785	jheath	JI	PHD	86	S Carol	1986
Chang, Cyril F.	Prof	678-3565	cchang	IM	PHD	79	Virginia	1981
Ciscel, David H.	Prof	678-2281	dhciscel	LM	PHD	71	Houston	1973
Daniel, Coldwell III	Prof	678-2473	cdaniel1	IL	PHD	68	Virginia	1970
Evans, Richard D.	Prof	678-3632	revans1	CM	PHD	70	Harvard	1978
Fung, Kwok-Kwan	Prof	678-4626	kkfung	OP	PHD	70	Harvard	1975
Gnuschke, John E.	Prof	678-2281	jgnuschk	MR	PHD	75	Missouri	1976
Director, Ctr for Manpower Studies and Bureau of Business & Economic Research								
Gootzeit, Michael J.	Prof	678-4625	mgoot	BE	PHD	66	Purdue	1975
Kemme, David M.	Prof	678-5408	dmkemme	FCP	PHD	80	Ohio St	1994
Morris Chair of Excellence in International Econ								
Okunade, Albert A.	Prof	678-2672	aokunade	JI	PHD	86	Arkansas	1987
Rubin, Rose M.	Prof	678-4622	rmrubin	JI	PHD	68	Kansas St	1994
White-Means, Shelley L.	Prof	678-2456	swhitmns	DJI	PHD	83	Nrthwstrn	1988
Bose, Pinaki	Assoc	678-5528	psbose	LD	PHD	90	NYU	9-95
Smith, William	Assoc	678-3675	wtsmith	EF	PHD	87	Virginia	1993
Zhang, Richard	Asst	678-2432			PHD		Ohio St	2001

Mercer University-Atlanta	Atlanta, GA		30341-4415	(678) 547-6199			mercer.edu	
Economics Faculty	Stetson Sch Bus & Econ		Fax=547-6337					
Joiner, W. Carl	Dean	547-6438	joiner_wc		PHD	78	Alabama	1974
Jalili, Reza	Assoc	547-6325	jalili_ar		PHD	94	NewHamp	1993
Yu, Tie-Liu	Assoc	547-6368	yu_tl		PHD	90	Miss St	1990
Connell, James A.	Asst	547-6195	connell_ja		DBA	92	La Tech	1996

Mercer University-Macon Macon, GA 31207-0001 (478) 301-2832 mercer.edu
Economic Faculty Stetson Sch Bus & Econ Fax=301-2635 Mamye Rogers

Joiner, W. Carl	Dean	301-2832	joiner_wc	Mgt	PHD	78	Alabama	1974
Andrews, Charles Haynes	Prof	301-2834			PHD	67	Vanderbilt	1973
Stetson Professor of Economics								
Mounts, William S. Jr.	Prof	301-2837			PHD	77	Georgia	1978
Barber, G. Russell Jr.	Assoc	301-2162			PHD	90	Miss	1973
Lynch, Allen K.	Asst	301-4055		FAC	PHD	99	Fla St	2000

Meredith College Raleigh, NC 27607-5298 (919) 760-8487 meredith.edu
Economic Faculty School of Business Fax=760-8470

Adkins, Sidney	Dean	760-8487		Ed	EDD	70	Virginia	2001
Ammann, Alan I.	Assoc	760-8472			DBA	78	Miss St	1990
Chappell, Glenn	Assoc	760-8473			PHD		Tennessee	1991
Wakeman, Douglas J.	Assoc	760-8482			PHD	86	N Carol	1987
York, Anne	Asst	760-8483			PHD		N Car St	1999

Merrimack College North Andover MA 01845 (978) Ext 4245 merrimack.edu
Dept of Economics Div of Liberal Arts Fax=837-5078 Jacqueline P. McLeod
phone 837-5000

Rossi, Michael	Dean	837-5244			PHD		Illinois	
Charos, Evangelos N.	C-Pr	Ext 4247			PHD	84	NewHamp	1983
Laramie, Anthony J.	C-Pr	837-4552			PHD	86	Clark	
Amariglio, Jack	Prof	Ext 4313			PHD	84	Mass	
Donovan, Elaine M.	Assoc	837-5445			PHD	81	Houston	
Looney, Lawrence J.	Assoc	Ext 5246			MA		Boston C	
Tontar, Charles F.	Assoc	Ext 4163			MA		New Sch	

Mesa State College Grand JunctionCO 81502 (970) 248-1656 mesastate.edu
Business Administration Professional Studies Fax=248-1730 Joy Donofrio, Ellin ALstatt

Rogers, Dave	Dean$	248-1656						
Bridge, Morgan K.	C-Ac$				PHD	94	Wyoming	1995
Rees, David M.	Prof	248-2656			PHD	73	Oregon	1983

Metropolitan St Coll Denver Denver, CO 80217-3362 (303) 556-3217 mscd.edu
Department of Economics School of Business Fax=556-3966 Teddy Podschun
Homepage: http://clem.mscd.edu/~econ/

Robertson, James W.	Dean	556-3245	robertsoj	Atg	PHD	63	U Wash	9-98
Cochran, John	C-Pr	556-3218	cochranj	ABEN	PHD	85	Colorado	1984
Akacemn, Mohammed	Prof	556-4649	akacemm	AOP	PHD	84	Colorado	1991
Call, Stephen T.	Prof	556-3916	calls	ADE	PHD	77	Indiana	1979
Erickson, Erick Lee	Prof	556-3038	ericksoe	ACDQ	PHD		New Mex	1984
Fleisher, Arthur A. III	Prof	556-4079	fleishet	ADHK	PHD	87	GeoMason	1990
Kulkarni, Kishore G.	Prof	556-2675	kulkarnk	AEF	PHD	82	Pittsburgh	1989
Gilliam, Lynde O.	Assoc	556-3037	gilliaml	ADE	PHD	80	Colo St	1986

University of Miami Coral Gables, FL 33124-6550 (305) 284-5540 exchange.sba.miami.edu
Department of Economics Sch of Business Admin Fax=284-2985 Ms. Denise Eutsey

Sugrue, Paul K.	Dean	284-4643	psugrue	Mas	PHD	77	Mass	1977
Connolly, Michael B.	C-Pr	284-4098	mconnolly	F	PHD	69	Chicago	1987
Fishe, Raymond P. H.	Prof	284-4397	rfishe	CD	PHD	79	Florida	1981
Holtmann, Alphonse G.	Prof	284-1721	hholtmann	DI	PHD	63	Wash U	1981
Robins, Philip K.	Prof	284-5664	pkrobins	IJ	PHD	72	Wisconsin	1982
Foley, James W.	Assoc	284-4641	jfoley	O	PHD	69	Mich St	1968
Hirano, Keisuke	Assoc	284-5540	khirano	CD	PHD		Harvard	1998
Locay, Luis	Assoc	284-1502	llocay	DJOT	PHD	83	Chicago	1989
Streeter, Lanny E.	Assoc	284-1627	lstreeter	C	PHD	70	Illinois	1967
Austin, Adrian	Asst	284-3338	aaustin	CG	PHD	98	Duke	1998
Bajona, Claustre	Asst	284-1777	cbajona	EF	PHD		Minnesota	2000
Ederington, William	Asst	284-1626	wedering	F	PHD	98	Wisconsin	1998
Gomis-Porqueras, Pedro	Asst	284-5540		CEG	PHD		Tx-Austin	2001
Julien, Benoit	Asst	284-3736	bjuilien		PHD		W Ontario	1997
Katzman, Brett E.	Asst	284-1654	bkatzman	DL	PHD	96	Duke	1996
Kelly, David	Asst	284-3725	dkelly	E	PHD	95	Car Mellon	1998
Minier, Jenny	Asst	284-1628	jminier	EO	PHD	98	Wisconsin	1998

Miami University Oxford, OH 45056-1675 (513) 529-2836 muohio.edu
Department of Economics R.T. Farmer Sch Bus Adm Fax=529-6992 Sandra Richardson

Short, Daniel G.	Dean	529-3631	dshort	Atg	PHD	77	Michigan	7-95
Ferguson, J. David	C-Pr	529-2836	fergusjd	EF	PHD	74	Brown	1970
Brock, James W.	Prof	529-2846	brockj	AK	PHD	81	Mich St	1979
Bill R. Moeckel Professor of Business								
Davis, George K.	Prof	529-2842	davisgk	EO	PHD	84	So Meth	1985
Dunlevy, James A.	Prof	529-5333	dunlevja	JF	PHD	74	Nrthwstrn	1980

Erekson, O. Homer	Prof	529-2836	ereksooh	HR	PHD	80	N Carol	1978
Associate Dean								
Even, William E.	Prof	529-2865	evenwe	JC	PHD	84	Iowa	1983
Hall, Thomas E.	Prof	529-2862	hallte	EC	PHD	82	Ca-SnBarb	1982
Hart, William R.	Prof	529-4352	hartwr	EA	PHD	76	Wash U	1974
McBride, Mark E.	Prof	529-2864	mcbridme		PHD	79	Wash U	1983
Miller, Norman C.	Prof	529-2854	millergm	EF	PHD	66	Pittsburgh	1985
Julian G. Lange Professor of Economics & American Enterprise								
Noble, Nicholas R.	Prof	529-6288	noblenr	EC	PHD	78	Cincinnati	1976
Seiver, Daniel A.	Prof	529-2863	seiverda	TG	PHD	74	Yale	1978
Sullivan, Dennis H.	Prof	529-2867	sullivdh	HI	PHD	75	Princeton	1973
Williamson, Samuel H.	Prof	529-2851	williash	NI	PHD	68	Purdue	1983
Curme, Michael A.	Assoc	529-6215	curmema	JD	PHD	89	Illinois	1988
Granderson, Gerald	Assoc	529-2841	grandegd	DG	PHD	93	N Carol	1993
Gupta, Barnali	Assoc	529-4116	guptab	DR	PHD	90	Florida	1993
Mehdizadeh, Mostafa	Assoc	727-3311	mehdizm	A	PHD	80	Oklahoma	1982
Middleton Campus								
Platt, Glenn	Assoc	529-2869	plattgj	CR	PHD	93	Car Mellon	1993
Raynold, Prosper	Assoc	529-4348	raynolp	EG	PHD	89	LSU	1989
Elliott, Steven R.	Asst	529-4932	elliotsr	DQ	PHD	91	Colorado	2000
Lyons, John S.	Asst	529-2853	lyonsjs	NO	PHD	77	Berkeley	1985
Thomasson, Melissa	Asst	529-2858	thomasma	IN	PHD	98	Arizona	1998
Miller, Gerald M.	SInst	529-2838	millergm	DC	MA	73	Brown	1971
Assistant Chairperson								

University of Michigan Ann Arbor, MI 48109-1220 (734) 764-2355 umich.edu
Department of Economics Col Lit,Science, & Arts Fax=764-2769 Carolyn Dymond
Did Not Respond--1999-2000 Listing; email @1=econ.lsa.umich.edu

Goldenberg, Edie	Dean	764-0322		PolS	PHD	74	Stanford	
Solon, Gary R.	C-Pr	763-1306	gsolon		PHD	83	Princeton	1983
Adams, William James	Prof	764-5273	jimadams		PHD	73	Harvard	1973
Bound, John	Prof	747-2319	jbound@psc.lsa.		PHD	87	Harvard	
Brown, Charles C.	Prof	763-6867	charlieb		PHD	74	Harvard	1985
Courant, Paul N.	Prof	763-2499	pnc		PHD	74	Princeton	1973
Cross, John D.	Prof	763-3479	jcross		PHD	65	Princeton	1965
Deardorff, Alan V.	Prof	764-6817	alandear		PHD	71	Cornell	1970
Gramlich, Edward M.	Prof	764-3490			PHD	65	Yale	1976
Holbrook, Robert S.	Prof	763-1282	rsh		PHD	65	Berkeley	1965
Howrey, E. Philip	Prof	763-1087	eph	CE	PHD	64	N Carol	9-73
Hymans, Saul H.	Prof	764-3299	shymans		PHD	64	Berkeley	1964
Johnson, George	Prof	764-2374	gjohnson		PHD	66	Berkeley	
Juster, F. Thomas	Prof	764-4207			PHD	56	Columbia	1973
Laitner, John	Prof	763-9620	jlaitner@1		PHD	76	Harvard	1975
Lam, David A.	Prof	764-2355	davidl@1		PHD	83	Berkeley	1983
Lillard, Lee	Prof	647-5609	lillard@isr.		PHD	72	N Car St	
Porter, Richard C.	Prof	769-9419	rporter		PHD	57	Yale	1964
Salant, Stephen W.	Prof	764-2370	ssalant		PHD	73	Penn	1981
Saxonhouse, Gary R.	Prof	764-3296	grsaxon		PHD	71	Yale	1970
Shapiro, Matthew D.	Prof	764-5419	shapiro		PHD	84	MIT	1989
Simon, Carl P.	Prof	763-3074	cpsimon	CDT	PHD	70	Nrthwstrn	7-72
Slemrod, Joel B.	Prof	936-3914	joel.slemrod		PHD	80	Harvard	1987
Stachetti, Ennio	Prof	764-8022	ennio		PHD	83	Wisconsin	1992
Stafford, Frank P.	Prof	936-0323	fstaffor		PHD	68	Chicago	1974
Stern, Robert M.	Prof	764-2373	rmstern		PHD	58	Columbia	1961
Weisskopf, Thomas E.	Prof	763-3037	tomw		PHD	66	MIT	1972
Whatley, Warren	Prof	764-5256	wwhatley	NJOR	PHD	82	Stanford	1981
Barsky, Robert	Assoc	764-9476	barsky@1		PHD	86	MIT	
Basu, Susanto	Assoc	764-5359	sbasu		PHD	92	Harvard	1992
Hanson, Gordon H.	Assoc		gohanson	FO	PHD	92	MIT	
Kimball, Miles S.	Assoc	764-2375	mkimball		PHD	87	Harvard	1987
Kuhn, Kai-uwe	Assoc	763-5317	kukuhn@1					
Levinsohn, James A.	Assoc	763-2319	jamesl		PHD	88	Princeton	1987
Mackie-Mason, Jeffrey K.	Assoc	764-7438	jmm		PHD	86	MIT	1986
Smith, Lones A.	Assoc	764-2357	lones	D	PHD	91	Chicago	
Tesar, Linda L.	Assoc	763-2254	ltesar	FGE	PHD	90	Rochester	
Charles, Kerwin	Asst	764-8075	kcharles		PHD	95	Cornell	1995
Chen, Yan	Asst	763-9619	yanchen@1		PHD	94	Cal Tech	1994
Cullie, Julie	Asst	764-2367	jbcullie					
Kilian, Lutz	Asst	764-2320	lkilian					
Kossoudji, Sherrie A.	Asst	764-2381	kossoudj		PHD	84	Michigan	1987
Sakata, Shinichi	Asst	764-2368	ssakata@1					
Sonanathan, Rohini	Asst	647-5611	rohinis@1					
Sonmez, Tayfun O.	Asst	763-9238	tsonmez@1	CDH	PHD	95	Rochester	1995
Van't Veld, Klaas	Asst	763-5319	kvtveld					
Gerson, Janet	Lect	764-2355	jgerson	AD	PHD	81	Michigan	
Thompson, Frank W.	Lect	763-2392	fthom		PHD	73	Harvard	1990
Wolfe, Janet C.	Lect	763-2515	janwolfe		MPP	80	Michigan	1987

Univ of Michigan-Dearborn Dearborn, MI 48128-1491 (313) 593-5096 umd.umich.edu
Dept of Social Sciences Col of Arts, Sci & Ltrs Fax=593-5645 Betty Greco/Gerri Habitz

Anderson, Donald F.	C	593-5096						
Hull, Brooks B.	Prof	593-5304	bhull	LQ	PHD	82	U Wash	1981
Pietrykowski, Bruce	Prof	593-9970	bpie	BJNR	PHD	90	New Sch	1988
Assistant Dean								
Roehl, Richard	Prof	593-5155	rroehl	BJNR	PHD	68	Berkeley	1976
Associate Dean								
Twomey, Michael J.	Prof	593-5176	mtwomey	FNO	PHD	74	Cornell	1977
Crowell, Elizabeth	Assoc	436-9183	bcrowell	DHIJ	PHD	71	Indiana	1978
Smith, Patricia	Assoc	593-5205	sksmith	IJK	PHD	86	Va Tech	1988
Bergeron, Suzanne	VAsst	593-4591	sbergero	BENO	PHD	98	Notre Dm	1998
Kim, Grace	Asst	436-9180	gracekim		PHD	01	Vanderbilt	2000
Miteza, Ilir	Asst	593-5096			ABD		Wisconsin	2001

Univ of Michigan-Flint Flint, MI 48502-1950 (810) 762-3280 umflint.edu
Department of Economics Col of Arts & Sciences Fax=762-3281 Judy J. Bedore
Homepage: www.flint.umich.edu/econ

Trela, D. J.	Dean	762-3234	djtrela	Engr	PHD		Edinburgh	1999
Nas, Tevfik F.	C-Pr	762-3280	tnas		PHD	77	Fla St	1982
Reddy, Nallapu N.	Prof	762-3280	nreddy		PHD	67	Penn St	1974
Lutzker, Adam	Asst	762-3280	alutzker	EB	PHD	99	Michigan	1999
Perry, Mark J.	Asst	762-3280	mjperry		PHD	93	GeoMason	1996

Michigan State University East Lansing, MI 48824-1038 (517) 355-7583 msu.edu
Department of Economics College of Social Sci Fax=432-1068 Terie Snyder 355-5238
Did Not Respond to Three Requests--1999-2000 Listing

Baba, Marietta	Dean	355-6675						
Goddeeris, John H.	C-Pr	355-5238	goddeeri		PHD	80	Wisconsin	1980
Allen, Bruce T.	Prof	355-7739	allenb		PHD	65	Cornell	1965
Baillie, Richard T.	Prof	355-1864	baillie	CFG	PHD	78	LondonEc	8-86
Pasant Chair of Economics & Finance								
Ballard, Charles L.	Prof	353-2961	ballard		PHD	83	Stanford	1983
Biddle, Jeff E.	Prof	353-7862	biddle		PHD	85	Duke	1985
Boyer, Kenneth D.	Prof	353-9088	boyerkd		PHD	75	Michigan	1984
Brown, Byron W.	Prof	355-2364	brownb		PHD	66	J Hopkins	1978
Davidson, Carl	Prof	355-7756	davidso4		PHD	87	Wisconsin	1982
Fisher, Ronald C.	Prof	353-4582	fisherr1		PHD	77	Brown	1976
Kreinin, Mordechai E.	Prof	355-6579	kreinin		PHD	54	Michigan	1959
University Distinguished Professor								
Liedholm, Carl E.	Prof	355-1812	liedhol1		PHD	65	Michigan	1967
Linz, Susan	Prof	355-7280	linz		PHD	80	Illinois	1988
Mackey, M. Cecil	Prof	355-8306	mackey		PHD	55	Illinois	1980
Martin, Lawrence W.	Prof	353-3528	martinl3		PHD	81	Maryland	1982
Matusz, Steven J.	Prof	353-8719	matusz		PHD	83	Penn	1983
Menchik, Paul L.	Prof	355-4553	menchik		PHD	76	Penn	1979
Meyer, Jack	Prof	355-7749	jmeyer		PHD	74	Stanford	1983
Neumark, David B.	Prof	353-7275	nuemarkd		PHD	87	Harvard	1995
Obst, Norman P.	Prof	353-5252	obst		PHD	70	Purdue	1973
Pecchenino, Rowena A.	Prof	353-6621	rowenap		PHD	85	Wisconsin	1985
Schmidt, Peter J.	Prof	355-8381	schmidtp		PHD	70	Mich St	1977
University Distinguished Professor								
Strauss, John A.	Prof	355-1863	jstrauss		PHD	81	Mich St	1992
Wilson, John D.	Prof	432-3116	wilsonjd		PHD	79	MIT	1998
Woodbury, Stephen A.	Prof	355-4587	woodbur2		PHD	81	Wisconsin	1982
Wooldridge, Jeffrey	Prof	353-5972	wooldri1	C	PHD	06	Ca-SnDgo	9-91
Amsler, Christine E.	Assoc	355-3774	amsler		PHD	80	Penn	1980
Choi, Jay Pil	Assoc	353-7281	choijay	LFE	PHD	90	Harvard	
Creane, Anthony J.	Assoc	355-4667	creane		PHD	91	Virginia	1990
Irvine, F. Owen	Assoc	353-9008	irvinef		PHD	76	MIT	1982
Papke, Leslie E.	Assoc	355-3773	papke		PHD	87	MIT	1990
deJong, Robert	Asst	353-9933	dejongr		PHD	93	Free	1997
Giles, John T.	Asst	355-7755	gilesj		PHD	99	Berkeley	1999
Mullin, Wallace P.	Asst	353-9934	wpmullin		PHD	92	MIT	1992
Herrear, Ana Marie		355-8320	herrer20					
Shevchenko, Andrei		353-5007	shevchen					
Simon, Kosali		355-9647	simonko					

Michigan Technological Univ Houghton, MI 49931-1295 (906) 487-2669 mtu.edu
Economics Faculty School of Bus & Eng Adm Fax=487-1863 Judy Chapman
Homepage: www.sbe.mtu.edu

Klippel, R. Eugene	Dean	487-2669	reklippe	Mktg	PHD	91	Penn St	1994
Campbell, Gary A.	Prof	487-2803	gcampbe	Q	PHD	82	Penn St	1982
Gale, James R.	Prof	487-2674	jrgale	E	PHD	72	Iowa	1971
Joyce, B. Patrick	Prof	487-2677	pjoyce	D	PHD	74	Missouri	1972
Merz, Thomas E.	Prof	487-2805	temerz	E	PHD	80	Pittsburgh	1980
Monson, Terry D.	Prof	487-3124	tmonson	F	PHD	72	Minnesota	1977
Associate Dean								
Roberts, Mark C.	Prof	487-2771	mroberts	Q	PHD	85	Arizona	1985
Nelson, Paul A.	Assoc	487-2809	pnelson	M	PHD	74	Wisconsin	1972

Middle Tennessee State Univ Murfreesboro, TN 37132 (615) 898-2520 frank.mtsu.edu
Dept of Economics & Finance College of Business Fax=898-5596 Thenartis Ellis

Burton, E. James	Dean			Atg	PHD	76	Illinois	
Lee, John T.	C-Pr	898-2520	jtlee		PHD	77	Georgia	1984
DePrince, Albert E. Jr.	Prof	898-5995	deprince	GM	PHD	78	NYU	1991
Fayissa, Bichaka	Prof	898-2385	bfayissa	D	PHD	82	Tennessee	1980
Ford, William F.	Prof	898-2889	wfford	GHM	PHD	66	Michigan	1991
Weatherford Chair								
Graddy, Duane B.	Prof	898-2525	dgraddy	GHA	PHD	74	Lehigh	1972
Hannah, Richard	Prof	898-2228	rhannah	J	PHD	81	Utah	1992
Kawahito, Kiyoshi	Prof	898-5751	kkawah;ito	FE	PHD	71	Maryland	1971
Kyle, Reuben	Prof	898-5617	rkyle	L	PHD	72	Tennessee	1972
Director, Bureau of Business & Economic Research								
Naqvi, Nadeem	Prof	898-2520	nnaqvi	DF	PHD	84	So Meth	2001
Zietz, Joachim	Prof	898-5619	jzietz	EC	PHD	81	Gottingen	1989
Eff, E. Anthon	Assoc	898-2387	aeff	RB	PHD	89	Tx-Austin	1990
Nguyen, Nghiep H.	Assoc	898-5117	nnguyen	L	PHD	81	Tennessee	1981
Norman-Zietz, Emily J.	Assoc	898-5497	enorman	M	PHD	94	Fla St	1993
Sarver, F. Lee	Assoc	898-5919	lsarver	M	PHD	87	Tennessee	1991
Baum, Charles	Asst	898-2527	cbaum	J	PHD	99	N Carol	1999
Deme, Mamit	Asst	898-5750	mdeme	FE	PHD	90	Tx-Austin	1990
Fowler, Stuart	Asst	898-2383	sfowler	E	PHD	99	So Meth	2000

Middlebury College Middlebury, VT 05753-6125 (802) 443-5327 middlebury.edu
Economics Faculty Department of Economics Fax=443-2084 Amy Holbrook
phone: 443-5000

Ramaswamy, Sunder	C-As	Ext 5322	ramaswam	DFO	PHD	90	Purdue	1990
Claudon, Michael Paul	Prof	Ext 5324	claudon	FLMP	PHD	71	J Hopkins	1970
Colander, David C.	Prof	Ext 5302	colander	ABE	PHD	76	Columbia	1982
Christian A. Johnson Distinguished Professor of Economics								
Pardee, Scott	Prof	Ext 5640	spardee	G	PHD	62	MIT	2000
Alan R. Holmes Visiting Professor in Monetary Economics								
Sommers, Paul M.	Prof	Ext 5325	psommers	CDT	PHD	76	Ca-SnDgo	1976
Wunnava, Phanindra V.	Prof	Ext 5024	wunnava	ACIJ	PHD	86	SUNY-Bin	1985
Carpenter, Jeffrey	Asst	Ext 3241	jcarpent	DC	PHD	99	Mass	1999
Holmes, Jessica	Asst	Ext 3439	jholmes	DHI	PHD	98	Yale	2001
Isham, Jonathan T. Jr.	Asst	Ext 3238	jisham	DOQ	PHD	00	Maryland	1999
Kelly, Thomas	Asst	Ext 2432	tkelly	OQ	PHD	97	Ca-Rivers	1997
Matthews, Peter H.	Asst	Ext 5591	pmatthew	BCEJ	PHD	95	Yale	1995
Pyle, William	Asst	Ext 3240	wpyle	P	PHD	97	Duke	1999
Warin, Thierry	Asst	Ext 3475	twarin	EF	PHD	00	Essec	2001

Midwestern State University Wichita Falls TX 76308-2099 (940) 397-4248 nexus.mwsu.edu
Department of Economics Div of Business Admin Fax=397-4280 Ms. Karin Patterson
Did Not Respond--1999-2000 Listing

Fukasawa, Yoshi	Dean	397-4360		EF	PHD	79	Kansas St	1978
Welch, Robert G.	H-Pr	397-4290		ADP	PHD	62	Oregon St	1966
Krienke, Albert B.	Prof	397-4722		DP	PHD	67	Tx A&M	1965
Martinez, John	Prof	397-4662		ABCO	PHD	84	Oklahoma	1997
Rodriguez, Louis J.	Prof	397-4211		EF	PHD	63	LSU	1981
President								
Harmel, Robert	Assoc	397-4365		DL	PHD	74	Iowa St	1989

Millersville Univ of PA Millersville, PA 17551-0302 (717) 872-3679 millersv.edu
Dept of Economics Sch of Human & Soc Sci Fax=871-2326 Ms. Beth A. Crumling

Marinho, Rita	Dean	872-3553			PHD	66	Brown	2001
Suliman, Osman	C-Pr	872-3679			PHD	84	Indiana	1993
Hamid, M. Khalil	Prof	872-3560			PHD	66	Iowa	1968
Margolis, Marvin S.	Prof	872-3561			PHD	69	Purdue	1981
Gumpper, Michael R.	Asst	872-3944			PHD	97	Kentucky	1995
Madden, Kirsten K.	Asst	872-3576			PHD	95	N Carol	1996
Smith, Kenneth	Asst	872-3582			PHD	93	Wisconsin	2000

Millikin University Decatur, IL 62522-2084 (217) 424-6284 mail.millikin.edu
Dept of Economics & Finance Tabor Sch of Business Fax=424-6286 Pamela J. Goodman
Homepage: http://www.millikin.edu/academics/tabor/
Did Not Respond--1999-2000 Listing

Zemke, Douglas	Dean	424-6284						
Liberatore, Anthony F.	Assoc	546-6446	aliberat		PHD	78	Conn	1984
Watson, James O.	Assoc	424-6380	jwatson		PHD	76	Purdue	1979
Cohn, Cheryl L.	Asst	827-8478	ccohn		DA	85	Illin St	1984
area code (309)								

Millsaps College Jackson, MS 39210-0001 (601) 974-1274 millsaps.edu
Economic Faculty Esle Sch of Management Fax=974-1260 Ms. Carol Heatherly

Boxx, W. Randy	Dean	974-1270	boxxwr	Mgt	PHD	71	Arkansas	1999
Taylor, Patrick A.	C-Ac	974-1274	taylorpa	AD	PHD	85	Alabama	1984
Director of BBA Program								
Brooking, Carl G.	Prof	974-1261	brookcg	CDK	PHD	74	Penn	1981
Taylor, Susan W.	Assoc	974-1278	taylorsw	AFH	PHD	89	LSU	1992
The J. A. Brown Chair of Business Administration								
Fox, M. Blakely	Asst	974-1269	foxmb	CDJ	PHD	00	Tennessee	2000

University of Minnesota Minneapolis, MN 55455-0413 (612) 625-6353 econ.umn.edu
Department of Economics College of Liberal Arts Fax=624-0209 Sara Shuford
Homepage: www.econ.unm.edu
Told me to go to their website to update this list--since the website is not updated, I did not bother

Rosenstone, Steven	Dean				PHD	79	Berkeley	1996
Chari, V. V.	C-Pr	626-7151	chari		PHD	81	Car Mellon	1994
Allen, Beth Elaine	Prof	625-8213			PHD	78	Berkeley	1992
Chipman, John S.	Prof	625-2816	jchipman		PHD	51	J Hopkins	1955
Regents' Professor								
Coen, Edward	Emer				PHD	53	London	
Feldman, Roger D.	Prof	624-5669			PHD	76	Rochester	1985
Foster, Edward M.	Prof	624-6567	foster		PHD	61	MIT	1961
Director Graduate Studies								
Geweke, John F.	Prof	625-7563	geweke		PHD	75	Minnesota	1990
Hurwicz, Leo	Prof	625-5808	hurwicz		LLM	38	Warsaw	1951
Kehoe, Timothy J.	Prof	625-1589	tkehoe		PHD	79	Yale	1987
Mohring, Herbert D.	Emer	625-6520	mohring		PHD	59	MIT	1961
Prescott, Edward C.	Prof	625-3810	prescott		PHD	67	Car Mellon	1980
Regent's Professor								
Richter, Marcel K.	Prof	625-7832			PHD	59	MIT	1959
Ruttan, Vernon W.	Emer	625-4707			PHD	52	Chicago	1976
Regents' Professor								
Schuh, G. Edward	Prof	625-0669			PHD	61	Chicago	1979
Smith, Harlan	Emer	625-8035			PHD	49	Chicago	
Swan, Craig E.	Prof	625-6353	cswan		PHD	70	Yale	1969
Holmes, Thomas J.	Assoc	625-4512	holmes		PHD	85	Nrthwstrn	1995
McLennan, Andrew M.	Assoc	625-7504	mclennan		PHD	82	Princeton	1987
Ohanian, Lee E.	Assoc	624-4060	ohanian		PHD	93	Rochester	1995
Werner, Jan	Assoc	625-0708	jwerner		PHD	85	Bonn	1987
Gownsaukaran, Gautam	Asst	625-8310	gautam		PHD	95	Yale	1995

U of Minnesota - Duluth Duluth, MN 55812-2496 (218) 726-7284 ub.d.umn.edu
Department of Economics Sch of Business & Econ Fax=726-6509 Becky Skurla
Did Not Respond--1999-2000 Listing

Knudsen, Kjell R.	Dean	726-7288	kknudsen	Mgt	PHD	73	Minnesota	1974
Jesswein, Wayne A.	H-Pr	726-7297	wjesswei	FA	PHD	69	Illinois	1968
Anderson, Curtis L.	Prof	726-7568	canderso	QA	PHD	81	Wyoming	1980
Lichty, Richard W.	Prof	726-7219	rlichty	R	PHD	71	Kansas St	1971
Peterson, Jerrold M.	Prof	726-7256	jpeterson	HE	PHD	70	Illinois	1969
Raab, Raymond L.	Prof	726-8508	rraab1	L	PHD	71	Colo St	1970
Steinnes, Donald N.	Prof	726-8243	dsteinne	C	PHD	72	Nrthwstrn	1975
O'Brien, A. Maureen	Assoc	726-7981	mobrien	J	PHD	83	W Virginia	1982
Vose, David	Assoc	726-8756	dvose	QA	PHD	66	Wisconsin	1966

Minnesota State U, Mankato Mankato, MN 56001 (507) 389-2969 msus.edu
Department of Economics Col of Social & Beh Sci Fax=389-6377 Barbara Lutz

Coultrap-McQuin, Susan	Dean	389-5717	susan.coutrap-+		PHD		Iowa	1995
Sharma, Ved P.	C-Pr	389-2711	ved.sharma	CDT	PHD	77	Wash U	1976
Chowdhury, Ashok K.	Prof	389-6614	ashok.chowd+	AC	PHD	80	Iowa St	1980
Hickerson, Steven	Prof	389-5330	steven.hicker+	ABK	PHD	80	Nebraska	1980
Renner, Donald E.	Prof	389-5249	donald.renner	ACHR	PHD	78	Cincinnati	1979
Schiming, Richard C.	Prof	389-5323	richard.schim+	AE	PHD	74	Ohio St	1981
Simonson, Robert D.	Prof	389-5324	robert.simonson	AJ	PHD	79	Nebraska	1981
Skorr, Arlen J.	Prof	389-2712	arlen.skorr	AE	PHD	70	Nebraska	1965
Smith, Gerald A.	Prof	389-5325	gerald.smith	AOQ	PHD	79	LSU	1979
Wells, Arnold R.	Prof	389-5248	arnold.wells	ADM	PHD	66	Minnesota	1966
Abel, David R.	Asst	389-2969	david.abel	AE	ABD		Minnesota	1969
Ghosh, Roy Attrayee	Asst						Nebraska	2001

Minnesota State U, Moorhead Moorhead, MN 56563 (218) 236-2842 mnstate.edu
Economics Department Business & Industry Fax=236-2168 Brenda Shoemaker

Dobitz, Carol	Dean	236-2076	dobitz	Atg	PHD	89	N Dakota	9-78
Flores, Oscar	C-Pr	236-3489	flores		PHD	90	Cincinnati	1989
Dobis, Vernon J.	Prof	236-4029	dobis		PHD	94	Manitoba	1981
Greenley, Douglas A.	Prof	236-4031	greenley		PHD	79	Colo St	1978
Bolduc, Steven	Asst	236-4683	bolduc		MA	93	Indiana	2000
Cooper, John M.	Asst	236-4030			MA	75	Oregon	1972
Stutes, Gregory	Asst	236-4027	stutes		MA	99	Nebraska	2000

Minot State University Minot, ND 58707 (701) 858-3130 minotstateu.edu
Div Social Sci-Dept of Econ Col of Arts & Sciences Fax=839-6933 Ms. Deborah Brothrs
Homepage: www.misu.nodak.edu/artsnsci/socsci.html

Rabe, Gary	Dean	858-3159	rabe		PHD	93	Deleware	1993
Lomire, Patricia M.	C-Pr	858-3130	lomire		PHD	86	Notre Dm	
Huenneke, Steve	Assoc	858-3135	huenneke	AR	PHD	92	Kansas St	1991
Chiu, I-Ming	Asst	858-3151			PHD	00	Wi-Milwa	2001

Mississippi College Clinton, MS 39058 (601) 925-3214 mc.edu
Dept Business Adm-Economics School of Business Fax=925-3954 Shea Elkins
Homepage: www.mc.edu

Eduardo, Marcelo	Dean	925-3420	eduardo	AG	PHD	95	Miss	1997
Hood, Frank	Prof	925-3413			PHD	72	Miss	1972
Lee, Gerald R.	Prof	925-3220			PHD	73	Miss	1970
Roberts, Lloyd	Prof	925-3419			PHD	74	Miss	1982

University of Mississippi University, MS 38677-1848 (662) 915-7076 bus.olemiss.edu
Economics School of Business Adm Fax=915-5087 Ms. Cynthia Jeffries

Womer, N. Keith	Dean$	915-5820			PHD	70	Penn St	1986
Shughart, William F. II	C-Pr	915-7579	wshugart	DHL	PHD	78	Tx A&M	1988
FAP Barnard Distinguished Professor & Robert M. Hearin Chair								
Belongia, Michael T.	Prof	915-7785	mbelonngia	E	PHD	82	N Car St	1993
Ingene, Chuck	Prof	915-6778			PHD	75	Brown	2001
Smith, Lewis	Prof	915-5924	lsmith	J	PHD	71	Tennessee	1971
Terasawa, Katsuaki	Prof	915-7291			PHD	98	Kansas	1999
Tollison, Robert D.	Prof	915-5041	btollison	DHL	PHD	69	Virginia	1999
Robert M. Hearin Professor								
Boylan, Richard	Assoc	915-5912	rboylan	DHK	PHD	91	Cal Tech	1999
Chappell, William	Assoc	915-5835		AM	PHD	83	S Carol	1987
Conlon, John	Assoc	915-5708	jconlon	CEF	PHD	78	Chicago	1987
Hanes, Christopher L.	Assoc	915-5829	chanes	EN	PHD	90	Harvard	1999
Johnson, John	Assoc	915-5492			PHD	88	Tx A&M	1988
Mayer, Walt	Assoc	915-5980	wmayer	C	PHD	86	Florida	1987
Moen, Jon R.	Assoc	915-5467	jmoen	JN	PHD	87	Chicago	1990
Razzolini, Laura	Assoc	915-7530	lrazzolini	D	PHD	94	So Meth	1994
on leave NSF								
Van Boening, Mark V.	Assoc	915-5841	mvanboening	DL	PHD	91	Arizona	1990
Wolcott, Susan	Assoc	915-5700	swolcott	NO	PHD	88	Stanford	1999
Archibald, Glenn S.	Asst	915-5845	garchibald	D	PHD	91	Houston	2001
Kamazawa, Risa	Asst	915-5820			PHD	01	Tx-Austin	2001
Karahan, Gokhan	Asst	915-1579			PHD	01	Miss	2000

Mississippi State Univ Miss St, MS 39762-9580 (662) 325-2341 cobilan.msstate.edu
Dept Finance & Economics Col of Business & Indus Fax=325-1977 Beverly Poole

Freedman, Sara M.	Dean	325-2580	sfreedman	Mgt	PHD	76	N Carol	1998
Grimes, Paul W.	C-Pr	325-1987	pgrimes	JA	PHD	84	Okla St	1987
Campbell, Charles A.	Prof	325-7477	ccampell	RON	PHD	85	Tennessee	1985
Blair, Benjamin	Assoc	325-1980	bblair	DL	PHD	92	Florida	1997
Rogers, Kevin	Assoc	325-1982	krogers	CE	PHD	96	Georgia	1996
Sanderson, Patricia L.	Assoc	325-1970	psanderson	F	PHD	77	Oklahoma	1979
Verrall, George	Assoc	325-1978	gveeerrall	A	DBA	72	Miss St	1965
Millea, Meghan	Asst	325-7476	mmillea	HE	PHD	98	Nebraska	1998
Phelps, Janie	Asst	325-2561	jphelps	PM	PHD	98	Kansas	1998
Rezek, Jon	Asst	325-1976	jrezek	QF	PHD	00	Nebraska	2000

Mississippi Valley St Univ Itta Bena, MS 38941-1400 (601) 254-3601 mvsu.edu
Economics Faculty Department of Business Fax=254-3600 Mrs. Mary Carter
Homepage: www.mvsu.edu

Lee, Dae Sung	Dean	254-3801	dslee	ADEC	PHD	69	Mass	1999
Chowdhury, A. A. Farhad	Prof	254-3606	achowdhu		PHD	93	Miss St	1993
Kim, Juho	Prof	254-3604			PHD	73	Oklahoma	1973
Rajanikauth, N.	Inst	254-3609			MBA		Miss St	1987

Univ of Missouri-Columbia Columbia, MO 65211 (573) 882-4574 missouri.edu
Department of Economics Col of Arts & Sciences Fax=882-2697 Melanie Himmelberg
Homepage: web.missouri.edu/~econwww/

Podgursky, Michael J.	C-Pr	882-4574	podgurskym	IJ	PHD	80	Wisconsin	1995
Menezes, Carmen F.	Prof	882-6094	menezesc	DF	PHD	66	Nrthwstrn	1965
Ratti, Ronald A.	Prof	882-6474	rattir	EFG	PHD	75	So Meth	1975
Wallace, Richard L.	Prof	882-3387	wallacer		PHD	65	Vanderbilt	1967
Chancellor								
Geiss, Charles G.	Assoc	882-6073	geissc	C	PHD	74	N Carol	1972
Liu, Ming	Assoc	882-0063		CG	PHD	96	Duke	2001
Mandy, David M.	Assoc	882-1763	mandyd	CD	PHD	87	Illinois	1994
Mueser, Peter R.	Assoc	882-6427	mueserp	DJT	PHD	83	Chicago	1985

Raymon, Neil A.	Assoc	882-3072	raymonn	CDEF	PHD	77	Colorado	1983
Gao, Ting	Asst	884-8005	gao	FJ	PHD	98	Michigan	1998
Gladden, Tricia	Asst	884-9793	gladdenp	JC	PHD	00	Nrthwstrn	2001
Haslag, Joseph H.	Asst	882-3483	haslagj	OGE	PHD	87	So Meth	2000
McCracken, Michael	Asst	882-7282	mccrackenm	CE	PHD	98	Wisconsin	2001
Ni, Xiagoguang	Asst	882-6878	ni	EH	PHD	91	Minnesota	1990
Pham, Van	Asst	882-3161	pham	FL	PHD	98	Cornell	1998
Troske, Kenneth	Asst	882-4229	troskek	J	PHD	92	Chicago	1997
Wang, Xinghe	Asst	882-4954	wangx	CDO	PHD	90	Iowa	1990

U Missouri--Kansas City Kansas City, MO 64110-2499 (816) 235-1314 umkc.edu
Department of Economics Col of Arts & Sciences Fax=235-2834 Ms. Jennifer Harris
Homepage: www.umkc.edu/economics

Bubacz, Bruce	Dean$			Phil	PHD			
Ward, John O.	C-Pr	235-1309	wardjo	KIO	PHD	70	Oklahoma	1969
Brazelton, W. Robert	Emer	235-2831		EP	PHD	61	Oklahoma	1963
Hubbell, L. Kenneth	Emer	235-2835		GHM	PHD	70	Nebraska	1968
Lee, Frederick S.	Prof	235-2543		ADN	PHD		Rutgers	
Olson, Gerald W.	Prof	235-1317		CGH	PHD	73	Rutgers	1971
Shepherd, A. Ross	Emer	235-2836		DF	PHD	63	Syracuse	1967
Sturgeon, James I.	Prof	235-3837		BO	PHD	74	Oklahoma	1977
Vorst, Karen S.	Prof	235-2838		EC	PHD	80	Indiana	1980
Wagner, F. Eugene	Prof	235-2840		AJO	PHD	67	Syracuse	1967
Wray, Randall	Prof	235-5687			PHD	88	U Wash	1999
Eaton, Peter J.	Assoc	235-2832		CIT	PHD	76	Florida	1979
Bell, Stephanie	Asst	233-5700		AFG	PHD	01	New Sch	2001
Forstater, Mathew B.	Asst	235-5687		ABF	PHD	96	New Sch	1999
Kelsy, Michael	Lect	235-5105		CQ	PHD	91	Tennessee	1996
Young, Ben	Lect	235-1314		A	PHD	73	Oklahoma	1993

University Missouri - Rolla Rolla, MO 65409-1250 (573) 341-4800 umr.edu
Department of Economics Col of Arts & Sciences Fax=341-4866 Leatta Nichols
Homepage: http://www.umr.edu/~econ
Did Not Respond--1999-2000 Listing

Johnson, Walter D.	C-Pr	341-4809	wjohnson	Ecol	PHD	71	Oklahoma	1988
Gelles, Gregory	C-Ac	341-4825	gelles		PHD	89	W Virginia	1989
Hentzel, David	Prof	341-4827	hentzel		PHD	67	S Illinois	1969
Bryant, Richard R.	Assoc	341-4823	rrbryant		PHD	84	Ca-Davis	1977
Manning, Linda M.	Assoc	341-4828	lindam		PHD	90	Il-Chicago	1989
Sen, Amit	Asst	341-6688	samit		PHD	97	N Carol	1997
Thompson, Philip B.	Asst	341-4893	philthom		PHD	88	Arizona	1994

U Missouri--St. Louis St. Louis, MO 63121-4499 (314) 516-5351 umslvma.umsl.edu
Department of Economics Col of Arts & Sciences Fax=516-5352 Gloria Axe

Young, David	Dean	516-5501						
Feigenbaum, Susan K.	C-Pr	516-5554		DHKP	PHD	80	Wisconsin	1988
Ireland, Thomas R.	Prof	516-5558	strirel		PHD	68	Virginia	1972
Levin, Sharon G.	Prof	516-5560	c4876	DJ	PHD	73	Michigan	1974
Phares, Donald	Prof	516-5551	c1706	HR	PHD	70	Syracuse	1969
Rose, David C.	Prof	516-5307	srose	CDIJ	PHD	87	Virginia	1985
Sorensen, Robert L.	Prof	516-5562	c1752	KMAO	PHD	71	Va Tech	1970
Graduate Coordinator								
Greene, Clinton	Assoc	516-5565		CE	PHD	92	Ca-Davis	1994
Kridel, Donald	Assoc	516-5553		CD	PHD	87	Arizona	1993
McBride, Timothy	Assoc	516-5530	stdmcbr	IH	PHD	87	Wisconsin	1991
Winkler, Anne E.	Assoc	516-5563	c4934	JT	PHD	89	Illinois	1989
McCorkle, Sarapage	Asst	516-5248	ssmccor	A	EDD	87	Mo-StLou	1970
Director, Center for Economic Education								
Allison, Michael	Lect	516-5306	smallis	CE	ABD		Virginia	1993
Phares, Kathleen	Lect	516-5570	skphare	A	MA	76	Mo-StLou	1977
Sulter, Mary	Lect	516-5248	smsuite	A	MIEE		Delaware	
Associate Director, Center for Economic Education								

Missouri Southern St Col Joplin, MO 64801-1595 (417) 625-9319 vm.mssc.edu
Economics Faculty Sch of Business Admin Fax=625-9604

Gray, James W.	Dean	625-9319			MBA	69	Arkansas	1969
La Near, Richard E.	Prof	625-9530		ADGN	PHD	79	Miss	1987
Dr. J. R. Kuhn Chair in Finance								
Miller, Robert J.	Prof	625-9345	miller-b		MA	67	Cen Mo St	1968
Adrahams, Niradete	Asst	625-9536			PHD			
Rawlins, Richard B.	Asst	625-9716			PHD	98	Arkansas	1988

Missouri Western St College Saint Joseph, MO 64507-2294 (816) 271-5870 griffon.mwsc.edu
Department of Economics Liberal Arts & Sciences Fax=271-5871 Jan Yardley
Homepage: www.mwsc.edu/economics/

Johnson, Martin	Dean	271-4272	mjohnson	SocP	PHD	73	Brighm Yg	
Lawson, Catherine L.	C-Ac	271-5826	lawsonc	A	PHD	88	Colorado	1995
Hamzaee, Reza G.	Prof	271-4262	hamzaee	E	PHD	85	Ariz St	1984
McMurry, Patrick H.	Prof	271-4276	mcmurray	J	PHD	81	Arkansas	1978
Vargha, Nader	Assoc	271-4339	vargha	A	MA	76	Oklahoma	1980

Molloy College Rockville Cn, NY 11570-5002 (516) Ext 6342
Economics Faculty Business Management Dp Fax=256-2288
Did Not Respond--1999-2000 Listing; phone 678-5000

O'Donoghue, Joseph	C-Pr	Ext 6342			PHD	75	Catholic	1997
Butler, Sister Agnes	Asst	Ext 6275			ABD		Indiana	

Monmouth University W Lg Branch NJ 07764 (732) 263-5531 monmouth.edu
Dept of Economics & Finance Sch of Business Admin Fax=263-5516 Beth Boyington

Kelly, Frederick J.	Dean	571-3423	fkelly	Fnce	PHD	74	Columbia	2001
Christofi, Andreas C.	C-Pr	263-5540	achristo	CFG	PHD	84	Penn St	9-97
Pressman, Steven	Prof	571-3658	pressman	HJN	PHD	83	New Sch	1981
Aslanbeigui, Nahid	Assoc	571-3642	naslanbe	E	PHD	84	Michigan	1988
Mahajan, Y. Lal	Assoc	571-3647	ymahajan	CDEG	PHD	95	N Illinois	1979
Moliver, Donald M.	Assoc	571-3660	dmoliver	DE	PHD	78	Va Tech	9-68
Nag, Raja	Asst	263-5344	rnag	G	PHD	98	Michigan	1998
Panayides, Alex	Asst	571-3641	apanayid	CFR	PHD	00	SUNY-Bin	2000

University of Montana Missoula, MT 59812-1012 (406) 243-2925 selway.umt.edu
Department of Economics Col of Arts & Sciences Fax= Becky Hofstad

Flightner, James A.	Dean	243-2632		Lang	PHD	72	SUNY-Buf	
Power, Thomas M.	C-Pr	243-2925	tmpower	HQR	PHD	71	Princeton	
Barrett, Richard	Prof	243-4497	rbarrett	EOJQ	PHD	72	Wisconsin	
O'Donnell, Dennis J.	Prof	243-2926	dennisl	OJR	PHD	74	Penn St	
Photiades, John G.	Prof	243-5612	johnp	BOH	PHD	72	Illinois	
Unger, Kay C.	Prof	243-4655	kunger	IDEC	PHD	74	J Hopkins	
Wicks, John H.	Prof	243-4122	jwicks	DH	PHD	62	Illinois	
Dalenberg, Douglas R.	Assoc	243-4406	ecdrd	CRL	PHD	87	Oregon	1990
Kupilik, Michael H.	Assoc	243-4575	radmatt	PHBN	PHD	76	Colorado	1976

Montana State University Bozeman, MT 59717-2920 (406) 994-3701 montana.edu
Department of Economics Col Letters & Sci/C Agr Fax=994-4838 Rebecca Gwin, Adm Asst

Watts, Myles	H	994-3701						
Antle, John M.	Prof	994-3701			PHD	80	Chicago	1987
Stroup, Richard L.	Prof	994-3701			PHD	70	U Wash	1969
Young, Douglas J.	Prof	994-3701			PHD	78	Wisconsin	1977
Atwood, Joseph A.	Assoc	994-3701			PHD	87	Nebraska	1987
Brester, Gary	Assoc	994-3701			PHD	90	N Car St	1997
Capalbo, Susan M.	Assoc	994-3710			PHD	82	Ca-Davis	1991
Lueck, Dean L.	Assoc	994-3701			PHD	87	U Wash	1997
Rucker, Randal R.	Assoc	994-3701			PHD	84	U Wash	1991
Smith, Vincent H.	Assoc	994-3701			PHD	87	N Car St	1988
Stock, Wendy A.	Assoc	994-7984	wstock	JCQ	PHD	96	Mich St	8-00
Buschena, David E.	Asst	994-3701			PHD	93	Berkeley	1992
Fleck, Robert K.	Asst	994-3701			PHD	94	Stanford	1995
Hanssen, F. Andrew	Asst	994-3701			PHD	95	Chicago	1995

Montana State Univ-Billings Billings, MT 59101-0298 (406) 657-2295 msubillings.edu
Dept of Bus Academic Prog College of Business Fax=657-2237
Did Not Respond--1999-2000 Listing

Nemacek, Barbara H.	Dean	657-1630	bnemecek	Mktg	PHD	87	Minnesota	1997
Lynch, Daniel	C-Ac	657-2035	mm_lynch	Mktg	PHD	98	Arkansas	1989
Farsio, Farzad	Prof	657-2033	econ_farsio		PHD	89	Claremont	1987
Harris, R. Scott	Assoc	657-1653	econ_harris		PHD	85	UCLA	1988

Montclair State University U Montclair, NJ 07043 (973) 655-5255 mail.montclair.edu
Dept of Economics & Finance Sch of Business Admin Fax=655-7629 Ms. Ida S. Fazio

Oppenheim, Alan J.	Dean	655-4304	oppenheima	Stat	PHD	73	NYU	1973
Leveen, Serpil S.	C-Pr	655-7402	leveen	ADEG	PHD	73	NYU	1974
Baytas, Ahmet	Prof	655-7633	baytasa		PHD	86	Illinois	1988
Desai, Suresh	Prof	655-4370	desais		PHD	68	UCLA	1973
Flint, Harold	Prof	655-7403	flinth	AEGP	PHD	72	S Illinois	1971
LeBel, Phillip	Prof	655-7778	lebelp	DOQH	PHD	77	Boston U	1981
Rawlins, Glenville W.	Prof	655-4339	rawlingsg	AGOQ	PHD	83	NYU	1984
Chakraborty, Chandana	Assoc	655-4125	chankrabortyc	ACDO	PHD	87	Rensselaer	9-89
Rezvani, Farahmand	Assoc	655-7568	rezvanif	ACGH	PHD	83	CUNY	1984
Pirouz, Kamrouz	Asst	655-5124	pirouzk	ADGN	PHD	73	Hawaii	1980
Zamanian, Zaman	Asst	655-7399	zammanianz	ACEF	PHD	83	Indiana	1984

University of Montevallo Montevallo, AL 35115-6000 (205) 665-6540 montevallo.edu
Economics Faculty Michael E. Stephens COB Fax=665-6560 Jonathan Fancher
Homepage: www.cob.montevallo.edu

Bell, Nancy Sutton	Dean	665-6540	belln	Insr	PHD	85	Georgia	1999
Blevins, Dallas R.	Prof	665-6542	blevins		DBA	76	Fla St	1983
MacPherson, Roderick S.	Assoc	665-6535	macpherson		DBA	77	Miss St	1977
Motii, Brian	Asst	665-6533	motii		PHD	98	Oklahoma	2001

Moravian College Bethlehem, PA 18018-6650 (610) 861-1571 moravian.edu
Economic Faculty Economics & Bus Dept Fax=625-7919 Mrs. Maryann Weaver

von Allmen, Peter	C-Ac	861-1413	mepva01	CDL	PHD	90	Temple	1990
West, James P.	Prof	861-1381	mejpw01	FM	PHD	87	Lehigh	1989
Brower, George D.	Assoc	861-1379	megdb01	COM	PHD	85	SUNY-Buf	1989
Ravelle, Linda J.	Assoc	861-1453	meljr01	AG	PHD	90	Lehigh	1989
Leeds, Eva Masikeva	Asst	861-1446	meedl01	BFP	PHD	83	Princeton	1999

Morehead State University Morehead, KY 40351-1689 (606) 783-2152 morehead-st.edu
Dept of Atg, Econ & Finance Sch of Business & Econ Fax=783-5025 Mary Howard

Miller, Green	C-Pr	783-2721	g.miller		PHD	85	Kentucky	1979
Buck, Roland	Prof	783-2722	r.buck		PHD	79	Tx A&M	1983
Ahmadi, Ali	Assoc	783-2749	a.ahmadi		PHD	97	Oklahoma	1995
Yasin, Mesghena	Assoc	783-2758	m.yasin		PHD	86	Cincinnati	1986
Creahan, Thomas	Asst	783-2740	t.creahan		PHD	95	Cincinnati	1996
Ghirmay, Teame	Asst	783-2152	t.ghirmay		PHD	97	S Illinois	2001

Morehouse College Atlanta, GA 30314-3773 (404) 215-2618 morehouse.edu
Economics Faculty Div Economics & Bus Ad Fax=215-2719 Mrs. Patricia Allen/Jackson

Williams, John E.	Dean	215-2618		Fnce	PHD	86	Geo St	1976
Mills Bee Lane Professor of Finance								
Handy, John	C-Pr	215-2618			PHD	85	Geo St	1978
Sheftall, Willis B. Jr.	Prof	215-2618			PHD	81	Geo St	1986
Charles E. Merrill Professor of Economics								
Eagan, J. Vincent	Assoc	215-2618			PHD	86	Geo St	1993
Gissy, William G.	Asst	215-2618			PHD	87	Geo St	1988
Ross, Glenwood	Asst	215-2618			PHD		Geo St	
Williams, Roger C.	Asst	215-2618			PHD		SUNY-SBr	

Morgan State University Baltimore, MD 21239 (443) 319-3438 morgan.edu
Department of Economics Col of Arts & Sciences Fax=319-3358 Jo Ann McCready
Did Not Respond Again--1995-96 Listing

Hollis, Burney	Dean	319-3090						
Fessiehatzen, Tekie	C-Pr	319-3438			PHD		Pittsburgh	
Favor, Homer	Prof	319-3558			PHD	60	Pittsburgh	
Whittaker, Victor A.	Prof	319-3440			PHD	71	Illinois	1974
Amegbe, Annan	Assoc	319-3531			PHD	77	Catholic	1978
Evans, Bernice	Asst	319-3446			MBA		Baruch	
Karangu, Mwangi	Asst	319-3440		CDEG	PHD	81	Walden	9-71
Bagheri, Rashid	Inst	319-3099			MA		Howard	
Kimani, Joseph	Inst	319-3099			MBA		Atlanta	

Morningside College Sioux City, IA 51106-1751 (712) 274-5131 alpha.morningside.edu
Economics Faculty Dept of Economics Fax=274-5101 Deb Protexter
Did Not Respond--1999-2000 Listing

Ghoshroy, Atrayee	Asst	274-5318	agoooz	HF	PHD	97	Nebraska	1999

Morris Brown College Atlanta, GA 30314-4140 (404) 220-0233 morrisbrown.edu
Economics Faculty Dept of Econ & Bus Adm Fax=220-3683 Marilyn Judge
phone 222-0270

Nwaokovo, Amechi	C	Ext 1478	nwaokovo.amechi		PHD	96	Okla St	2001
Obi, Emmanuel	Asst	Ext 1463	emmanuel.obi		PHD	97	Clark Atl	1998

Mount Holyoke College South Hadley, MA 01075-1481 (413) 538-2432 mtholyoke.edu
Economics Faculty Department of Economics Fax=538-2323 Dawn Larder
Homepage: www.mtholyoke.edu/acad/econ

Robinson, Michael D.	C-Ac	538-2215	mirobins		PHD	87	Tx-Austin	1988
Moseley, Fred B.	Prof	538-2517	fmoseley		PHD	82	Mass	1989
Rapoport, John	Prof	538-2818	rapoport		PHD	70	Penn	1970
Christiansen, Jens	Assoc	538-2750	jchristi		PHD	82	Stanford	1986
Paus, Eva	Assoc	538-2518	epaus		PHD	83	Pittsburgh	1987
Gabriel, Satyananda Jordan	Asst	538-2043	sgabriel		PHD	89	Mass	1989
Hartley, James E.	Asst	538-2566	jhartley		PHD	94	Ca-Davis	1994
Higino-Schneider, Patricia	Asst	538-2752	pschnneid		PHD	00	Ca-SnCruz	1994
Wilson, Lucas	Asst	538-2751	lbwilson		PHD	95	Mass	1995

Mount Saint Mary's College Los Angeles, CA 90049 (310) 954-4155 msmc.la.edu
Economics Faculty Dept Business & Econ Fax=954-4159 Tanya White
Chalon Campus

Slopper, Mary	C-Ac	954-4155	msloper		MBA		CS-Domin	1976
Whitman, Katherine	Assoc	954-4152	kwhitman	ANF	MA		UCLA	1980

Mount St. Mary's College-MD Emmitsburg, MD 21727 (301) 447-6122 msmary.edu
Economics Faculty Dept of Bus, Atg & Econ Fax=447-5335

Zarnowski, C. Frank	Prof	447-6122	zarnowsk	AE	DA	78	Lehigh	1967
Stanton, Timothy J.	Assoc	447-6122	stanton	CD	PHD	88	Kentucky	1988
Einolf, Karl	Asst	447-6122	einolf	BFC	PHD	98	Lehigh	1998

Muhlenberg College Allentown, PA 18104-5586 (484) 664-3280 muhlenberg.edu
Economics Faculty Department of Economics Fax=664-3536 Justine Frantz

Heitmann, George	C-Pr	664-3278	heitmann		PHD	63	Princeton	1-94
Marshall, James N.	Prof	664-3284			PHD	82	Lehigh	1975
Sinha, Rohini P.	Prof	664-3282			PHD	65	New Sch	1965
Dale, Donald	Asst	664-3580			PHD	01	Princeton	2000
Kish-Goodling, Donna M.	Asst	664-3479			PHD	92	Lehigh	1990
Raymond, Arthur J.	Asst	664-3278			PHD	90	Tufts	1991
Walsh, Vivian	Lect	664-3290			PHD	53	Trinity	1989
Zumas, Susan	Lect	664-3507			PHD	94	Lehigh	1992

Murray State University Murray, KY 42071-0009 (270) 762-4188 murraystate.edu
Dept of Economics & Finance Col Bus & Public Affair Fax=762-5478 Marion Elkins

Harrison, Dannie	Dean	762-4181	dannie.harrison	EPO	PHD	74	S Illinois	1969
Guin, Larry D.	C-Ac	762-4188	lguin	Fnce	DBA	79	Miss St	1978
Brasfield, David	Prof	762-4324	david.brasfield	EGC	PHD	89	N Carol	1986
Mathis, Gilbert L.	Prof	762-4283	gilbert.mathis	DFKQ	PHD	66	Ohio St	1966
McCoy, James P.	Prof	762-4274	jim.mccoy	DFOP	PHD	86	N Carol	1985
Milkman, Martin	Prof	762-4282	martin.milkman	CJH	PHD	89	Oregon	1988
Hassan, Seid	Assoc	762-4284	seid.hassan	CEFR	PHD	93	Tx A&M	1992
Eaton, David	Asst	762-4290	david.eaton	HCL	PHD	95	Michigan	1996
Brown, Barry	Lect	762-4277	barry.brown	EOF	MS	77	Murray St	1991
Reed, Mary Tripp	Lect	762-3932	mary-tripp.reed	ADFJ	MA	95	American	1995

Naval Postgraduate School Monterey, CA 93943-5000 (831) 656-2161 nps.navy.mil
Economics Faculty Dept of Systems Mgt Fax=656-3068
Did Not Respond--1999-2000 Listing

Euske, Kenneth J.	Dean	656-2860	0123p	Atg	PHD	78	Ariz St	1978
Boger, Dan C.	Prof	656-2607	dboger	C	PHD	79	Berkeley	1979
Frederiksen, Peter C.	Prof	656-2661	pcfreder	AOR	PHD	74	Wash St	7-74
Jones, Carl R.	Prof	656-2995	crjones	D	PHD	65	Claremont	1965
LaCivita, Charles J.	Prof	656-2445	clacivita	DM	PHD	81	Ca-SnBarb	1985
Looney, Robert	Prof	656-3484	relooney	OF	PHD	69	Berkeley	1977
Mehay, Stephen L.	Prof	656-2643	smehay	IJ	PHD	73	UCLA	1985
Parker, Patrick J.	Prof	656-2097	p.parker@stl.	AH	MBA	55	Chicago	9-74
Thomas, George W.	Prof	656-2741	gwthomas	J	PHD	71	Purdue	1978
Gates, William R.	Assoc	656-2754	brgates	D	PHD	74	Yale	1988
Henderson, David R.	Assoc	656-2524	drhender	D	PHD	76	UCLA	1984
Hildebrandt, Gregory G.	Assoc	656-2767	ghildebrandt	D	PHD	76	Princeton	1992
Melese, Francois	Assoc	656-2009	fmelese	C	PHD	82	Belgium	1987
Cook, Michael D.	Asst	656-3508	mdcook	J	PHD	96	Maryland	1996
Webb, Natalie J.	Asst	656-2013	njwebb	H	PHD	92	Duke	1992

Nazareth Coll of Rochester Rochester, NY 14618-3790 (716) Ext 558 naz.edu
Economics Faculty Dept Bus, Econ, & Mgt Fax=586-2452 Joan Van du Zer
Did Not Respond Again--1995-96 Listing; phone 586-2525

Zappia, Gerard	C-Ac	Ext 561			MSED		Nazareth	
Aerni, April Laskey	Assoc	Ext 549			PHD	87	Cincinnati	
DaBoll-Lavoie, Joseph T.	Assoc	Ext 592	jtdaboll	BHJ	PHD	89	SUNY-Bin	9-88
Maley, Leonard A.	Assoc	Ext 550			MBA	62	Cincinnati	
Schroeder, Edward A.	Assoc				PHD	80	UCLA	1988

University of Nebraska Lincoln, NE 68588-0489 (402) 472-2319 unlnotes.unl.edu
Department of Economics College of Business Adm Fax=472-9700 Carol Nelson

Milligan, Cynthia	Dean	472-9500			JD	67	Geo Wash	1988
Schmidt, James R.	C-Pr	472-2315	jschmidt2	CR	PHD	78	Rice	1977
Dr. James W. and Helen A. Hanson Professor of Economics								
Anderson, John E.	Prof	472-1190	janderson	H	PHD	77	Claremont	1991
Director of Graduate Program								
Bodvarsson, Orn B.	Prof	472-3372	obodvars	DJL	PHD	86	Simon Fr	2001
visiting from St Cloud University								
Hayden, F. Gregory	Prof	472-2332	ghayden	HQI	PHD	68	Tx-Austin	1967

Lamphear, F. Charles	Prof	472-7928		OR	PHD	67	Kansas St	1966
Director, Bureau of Business Research								
MacPhee, Craig R.	Prof	472-2319	cmacphee	EF	PHD	70	Mich St	1969
Paul C. Burnmeister College Professor								
Riefler, Roger F.	Prof	472-2327	rriefler	R	PHD	66	U Wash	1973
Rosenbaum, David I.	Prof	472-2318	dir	L	PHD	85	Wisconsin	1985
Walstad, William B.	Prof	472-2333	wwalstad	I	PHD	78	Minnesota	1982
John and Mabel Hay Professorship								
Cushing, Matthew J.	Assoc	472-2323	mcushing	EJ	PHD	85	Virginia	1992
Fuess, Scott M.	Assoc	472-6281	sfuess	J	PHD	86	Purdue	1986
Kim, Benjamin J. C.	Assoc	472-3083	kimjc	EF	PHD	83	UCLA	1983
May, Ann Mari	Assoc	472-3369	amay	BE	PHD	87	Colo St	1987
McGarvey, Mary G.	Assoc	472-9415	mcgarvey	E	PHD	83	Virginia	1992
Van den Berg, Hendrik F.	Assoc	472-3004	hvan-den-berg	F	PHD	89	Wisconsin	1989
Allgood, Sam	Asst	472-3367	sallgood	DJG	PHD	93	Georgia	
Klaus, Bettina	Asst	472-2129	bklaus	D	PHD	98	Maastricht	1998
Univ of Nebraska at Kearney	Kearney, NE		68849-4570 (308) 865-8530				platte.unk.edu	
Department of Economics	Col of Business & Tech		Fax=865-8459				Connie J. Fie	
Hadley, Galen D.	Dean	865-8342		Atg	PHD	75	Nebraska	8-91
Kotcherlakota, V. V.	C-Pr	865-8785			PHD	77	India	1986
Eshleman, Tom	Assoc	865-8458			PHD	94	Okla St	1993
Jenkins, Allan	Assoc	865-8461			PHD	87	Nebraska	1987
Marxsen, Craig S.	Assoc	865-8043			PHD	76	Geo St	1987
Bridges, Deborah	Asst	865-8044			PHD	94	Wash St	1997
Johannsson, Hannes	Asst	865-8148			PHD	99	Colo St	1999
Univ of Nebraska at Omaha	Omaha, NE		68182-0048 (402) 554-2570				mail.unomaha.edu	
Department of Economics	College of Business Adm		Fax=554-3747				Scott Hays	
Hille, Stanley J.	Dean	554-2599	shille	Mgt	PHD	66	Minnesota	1996
Sosin, Kim	C-Pr	554-2570	ksosin	ECO	PHD	70	Nebraska	1981
Diamond, Arthur M.	Prof	554-3657	adiamond	BJ	PHD	78	Chicago	1986
Nielsen, Donald A.	Prof	554-2453	dnielsen	AR	PHD	70	Syracuse	1972
Sindt, Roger	Prof	554-2802	rsindt	AR	PHD	72	Tx-Austin	1979
Wohar, Mark	Prof	554-4342	mwohar	ECGF	PHD	85	Illinois	1988
Baum, Donald N.	Assoc		dbaum	HD	PHD	79	Claremont	1987
Corcoran, William J.	Assoc	554-2915	wcorcora	LQD	PHD	75	Rutgers	1980
Lin, Shuanglin	Assoc	554-2815	slin	CDEO	PHD	89	Purdue	1989
Co, Catherine	Asst	554-2570	cco	FLO	PHD	95	Rutgers	2001
Decker, Christopher	Asst	554-2570	cdecker	LDM	PHD	00	Indiana	2001
West, Janet Mason	Asst	554-2806	jwest	AJ	MA	64	Mich St	1967
Nebraska Wesleyan Univ	Lincoln, NE		68504-2796 (402) 465-2213				nebrwesleyan.edu	
Div Economics-Social Science	Dept Bus Admin & Econ		Fax=465-2179					
Fairchild, Loretta	Prof	465-2204	llf		PHD	72	Cornell	1975
Gleason, Joyce G.	Assoc	465-2444	jgg		PHD	86	Nebraska	1990
Univ of Nevada, Las Vegas	Las Vegas, NV		89154-6005 (702) 895-3776				ccmail.nevada.edu	
Department of Economics	College of Business		Fax=895-1354				Katherine Melcic	
Miller, Stephen M.	C-Pr	895-3969	stephen.miller	E	PHD	72	SUNY-Buf	2001
Carroll, Thomas M.	Prof	895-3652	carroll	D	PHD	73	Syracuse	1986
Daneshvary, Nasser	Prof	895-3362	daneshvary	R	PHD	84	Tennessee	1990
Associate Dean								
Hoppe, Hans Hermann	Prof	895-3227	hoppe	B	PHD		Goethe	1986
Malamud, Bernard	Prof	895-3294	malamud	E	PHD	71	New Sch	1968
Ray, Clarence G.	Prof	895-0817	ray	K	PHD	72	S Carol	1971
Schlottmann, Alan M.	Prof	895-0817	aschlott	R	PHD	75	Wash U	2000
Schwer, Keith	Prof	895-3191	schwer	R	PHD	73	Maryland	1986
Chen, Lein-Lein	Assoc	895-3950	chen	F	PHD	92	U Miami	1993
Cronovich, Ron	Assoc	895-3015	cronovich	E	PHD	95	Michigan	1994
Karstensson, Lewis	Assoc	895-3653	karstensson	B	PHD	74	Ohio U	1979
Waddoups, C. Jeffrey	Assoc	895-3497	waddoups	J	PHD	89	Utah	1989
Assane, Djeto	Asst	895-3284	assane	O	PHD	88	Colorado	1988
Bold, Frederick	Asst	895-3376		D	PHD		U Wash	1995
Riddle, Mary	Asst	895-3191	mriddle	Q	PHD	98	Colo St	1999
Robinson, William J.	Asst	895-3769	robinson	A	PHD	83	Colorado	1980
Wimmer, Bradley	Asst	895-3018	wimmer	L	PHD	92	Kentucky	1998
Yamashita, Takashi	Asst	895-2467	tyamashi	E	PHD	99	Ca-SnDgo	2000
University of Nevada, Reno	Reno, NV		89557-0016 (775) 784-6850				unr.edu	
Department of Economics	Col of Business Admin		Fax=784-4728				Theresa E. Moser	
Reed, Howard M.	Dean	784-4912	cioreed@1		PHD	75	Utah	1972
Pingle, Mark	C-Ac	784-6634	pingle		PHD	88	S Calif	1990
Atkinson, Glendel W.	Prof	784-6678	atkinson		PHD	68	Oklahoma	1967
Cargill, Thomas F.	Prof	784-6812	cargill		PHD	68	Ca-Davis	1973

Eadington, William R.	Prof	784-6887	eading		PHD	73	Claremont	1969
Raffiee, Kambiz	Prof	784-6864	raffiee		PHD	83	Oregon	1983
Wendel, Jeanne L.	Prof	784-6695	wendel		PHD	77	So Meth	1985
Dobra, John L.	Assoc	784-6859	drjohn		PHD	80	Va Tech	1980
Metts, Robert Lyle	Assoc	784-1115	metts		PHD	85	Berkeley	1984
Mitchell, Mike	Assoc	784-1112	mikem		PHD	88	Oregon	1988
Nichols, Mark W.	Asst	784-6936	mnichols	LKJ	PHD	94	Fla St	1996
Parker, Elliott	Asst	784-6408	elliott		PHD	92	U Wash	1992
Song, Shunfeng	Asst	784-6860	song		PHD	92	Ca-Irvine	1992

University of New Hampshire Durham, NH 03824-3593 (603) 862-3457 christa.unh.edu
Department of Economics Whittemore Sch Bus & Ec Fax=862-3383 Sinthy Kounlasa
email @1=oribt.umh.edu

Wible, James R.	C-Pr	862-3324	jrwible	BE	PHD	80	Penn St	1984
England, Richard W.	Prof	662-3335	rwe	OQ	PHD	74	Michigan	1976
Simos, Evangelos O.	Prof	862-3363	eos	EF	PHD	77	N Illinois	1977
Conway, Karen Smith	Assoc	862-3386	ksconway	HJ	PHD	87	N Carol	1990
Graduate Program Coordinator								
Elmslie, Bruce T.	Assoc	862-3347	bte	BF	PHD	88	Utah	1989
Goldberg, Michael	Assoc	862-3385	michaelg	EF	PHD	91	NYU	1991
Herold, Marc W.	Assoc	862-3375	mwherold	O	PHD	77	Berkeley	1975
Huang, Ju-Chin	Assoc	862-3279	jehuang	CQ	PHD	94	N Car St	1998
Mills, Richard L.	Assoc	862-3350	rmills	CD	PHD	67	Indiana	1967
Niman, Neil B.	Assoc	862-3336	neil@1	BL	PHD	85	Tx-Austin	1987
Schmidt, Torsten	Assoc	862-3349	ts	DL	PHD	90	Florida	1988
Thompson, Allen R.	Assoc	862-2771	art	GM	PHD	73	Tx-Austin	1974
Choi, Chi-Young	Asst	862-3457			PHD	00	Ohio St	2001
Mohr, Robert	Asst	862-3457			PHD	01	Tx-Austin	2001

New Hampshire College Manchester, NH 03104-1394 (603) 645-9691 nhc.edu
Economic & Finance Dept School of Business Fax=645-9603 Polly Popek
Did Not Respond--1999-2000 Listing

Doucette, Francis G.	Dean	668-2211		EDD	78	Vanderbilt	8-94
Hall, Yvonne C.	C-Pr	668-2211		PHD	81	Colo St	
Johnson, R. Larry	Prof			DBA	82	Geo Wash	
Hassan, Mahboubul	Assoc			MAPE	82	Boston U	
White, Charles V.	Assoc			PHD	73	Ohio St	
Widener, Steven	Assoc	668-2211		PHD	88	NewHamp	

University of New Haven West Haven, CT 06516-1999 (203) 932-7355 charger.newhaven.edu
Department of Economics School of Business Fax=931-6076 Patricia Skinner

Martin, Linda R.	Dean	932-7120	lmartin		PHD	81	S Carol	8-95
Shapiro, Steven J.	C-Pr	932-7496		GKLM	PHD	88	Geotown	9-87
Kaplan, Phillip	Prof	932-7419		NL	PHD	64	J Hopkins	
Phelan, John	Assoc	932-7350		HI	PHD		Geo Wash	9-95
Parker, Joseph A.	Prof	932-7349		JR	PHD	68	Oklahoma	9-69
Suster, Zeljan	Assoc	932-7115	zsuster	FNOP	PHD	88	Belgrade	9-90
Associate Dean								
Upadhyaya, Kamal	Assoc	932-7487			PHD		Auburn	
Rodriguez, Armando		932-7372						
Sencicek, Mehmet		932-7487						

The College of New Jersey Ewing, NJ 08628-0718 (609) 771-2566 tcnj.edu
Economics Program School of Business Fax=637-5143 Diane Perry

Vandegrift, Donald	C-Ac	771-2294	PHD	93	Conn	
Breslia, Thomas	Prof	771-2891	PHD	76	W Virginia	
Liu, Chao-Nan	Prof	771-2240	PHD	76	Tx A&M	
Leven, Bozen	Assoc	771-3140	PHD	91	Cornell	
Naples, Michele I.	Assoc	771-2896	PHD	82	Mass	
Samanta, Subarna K.	Assoc	771-3496	PHD	85	So Meth	1987
Cerf, G.		771-3220	MA	65	Syracuse	

New Jersey City University Jersey City, NJ 07305-1597 (201) 200-3272 njcu.edu
Economics Department Sch of Arts & Science Fax=200-2072 Ms. Rita Lange
Homepage: http://ellserver3.njcu.edu/economics

Hordon, Harris	C-Pr	200-3272	hhordon	AG	PHD	68	NYU	
Ghebrat, Ezra	Prof	200-3390	eghebrat	ADEF	PHD	82	New Sch	
Steinberg, Ivan	Assoc	200-3462	isteinberg	LA	ABD	71	New Sch	
Anderson, Richard T.	Asst	200-2285	randerson	AI	PHD	91	CUNY	
Vohra, Rubina A.	Asst	200-3074	rvohra	AJO	PHD	93	Northeas	9-94

New Jersey Inst Technology Newark, NJ 07102-1982 (973) 596-3248 njit.edu
Economics Faculty Sch of Industrial Mgt Fax=596-3074 Essie Richardson
Did Not Respond--1999-2000 Listing

Chakrabarti, Alok K.	Dean	596-3256		Mgt	PHD	72	Nrthwstrn	1989
Distinguished Professor of Management; Sponsored Chair in Management of Tech								
Hasan, Iftekhar	Prof	596-8238			PHD	87	Houston	1994
Anyanwu, Lenard C.	Asst	596-6426			PHD	90	Tx-Dallas	1990
Bonitsis, T. Homer	Asst	596-3263			PHD	84	CUNY	1990
Sau, Ranjit	Visit	596-4281			PHD	64	Wayne St	1995

University of New Mexico Albuquerque, NM 87131-1101 (505) 277-5304 unm.edu
Department of Economics Col of Arts & Sciences Fax=277-9445 Lourdes McKenna

Allen, Fritz	Dean$	277-3046	fallen		PHD			
Santos, Richard	C-Ac	277-2107	santos	IJ	PHD	77	Mich St	1989
Bohara, Alok	Prof	277-5903	bohara	CQ	PHD	86	Colorado	1987
Brookshire, David S.	Prof	277-1964	brookshi	Q	PHD	76	New Mex	1989
Burness, H. Stuart	Prof	277-1952	burness	CDQ	PHD	70	Kansas	1978
Coes, Donald V.	Prof	277-3145	dcoes		PHD	77	Princeton	
Gisser, Micha	Prof	277-2420	gisser	DLQ	PHD	62	Chicago	1973
McKee, Michael	Prof	277-1960	mckee	HKQL	PHD	85	Carleton	1991
Berrens, Robert	Assoc	277-9004	rberrens	DQ	PHD	93	Oregon St	1994
Chermak, Janie	Assoc	277-4906	jchermak	DQ	PHD	91	Co Mines	1995
Ganderton, Philip	Assoc	277-1962	gandini	DH	PHD	89	Ca-SnBarb	1989
Gawande, Kishore	Assoc	277-1965	gawande	CEFP	PHD	91	UCLA	1991
Sauer, Christine	Assoc	277-1963	sauer	EF	PHD	87	Brown	1985
Anderson, Deborah	Asst	277-5560	andersod	CHJ	PHD	98	Cornell	1998
Binder, Melissa	Asst	277-3548	mbinder	FJO	PHD	95	Columbia	1995
Krause, Kate	Asst	277-3429	kkrause	HK	PHD	96	Wisconsin	1996

New Mexico Highlands Univ Las Vegas, NM 87701-4211 (505) 454-3344 crux.nmhu.edu
Economics Faculty School of Business Fax=454-3334 Gloria Brown-Lopez

Young, Margaret	D-Pr	454-3344	youngm	Mktg	PHD	97	N Mex St	1993
Ferran, Manuel A.	Assoc	454-3575	m_ferran	ADEG	PHD	69	Oklahoma	1993

New Mexico State Univ Las Cruces, NM 88003-8001 (505) 646-2113 nmsu.edu
Dept of Econ & Internl Bus Col Business Adm & Econ Fax=646-1915 Stella Barrio
Did Not Respond--1999-2000 Listing

Arnold, Daniel R.	Dean	646-4083	darnold		DBA	76	La Tech	7-94
Nowotny, Kenneth	H-Pr	646-2113	knowotny	HN	PHD	77	Tx-Austin	1976
Ellis, Michael	Prof	646-4101	mellis	I	PHD	75	Ca-Rivers	1973
Nordyke, James W.	Emer	646-5688		FE	PHD	59	Princeton	1964
Orton, Eliot S.	Emer	646-3800	eorton	N	PHD	71	Cornell	1970
Peach, James T.	Prof	646-3113	jpeach	T	PHD	78	Tx-Austin	1980
Smith, David B	Prof	646-5879	dbsmith	H	PHD	71	Nebraska	1970
Willman, Elliott	Prof	646-1005	ewiillman	EF	PHD	77	Indiana	1979
Brook, Kathleen	Assoc	646-4905	kbrook	E	PHD	76	Tx-Austin	1980
Associate Dean								
Cabe, Richard	Assoc	646-5909	rcabe	K	PHD	83	Wyoming	1988
Enomoto, Carl E.	Assoc	646-1992	cenomote	FE	PHD	82	Tx A&M	1983
Gegax, Douglas A.	Assoc	646-1903	dgegax	HD	PHD	84	Wyoming	1984
Ghosh, Soumendra	Assoc	646-2340	sghosh	O	PHD	87	Utah St	1988
Matta, Benjamin N.	Assoc	646-4085		IJ	PHD	79	Tx-Austin	1972
McGuckin, J. T.	Assoc	646-6302		Q	PHD	90	Wisconsin	1989
Popp, Anthony V.	Assoc	646-5198	apopp	H	PHD	80	N Illinois	1981
Tanski, Janet M.	Assoc	646-1905	jtanski	OI	PHD	91	SUNY-Buf	1989
Adrisson, Rick	Asst	646-4988	radkisso	FH	PHD	94	Nebraska	8-94
Erickson, Christopher A.	Asst	646-5715	chericks	EF	PHD	89	Ariz St	1987
Mora, Marie T.	Asst	646-1595	mmora	JI	PHD	95	Tx A&M	8-95

University of New Orleans New Orleans, LA 70148-1555 (504) 280-6485 uno.edu
Dept of Economics & Finance College of Business Adm Fax=280-6397 Russel Holliday 280-6487

Ryan, Timothy P.	Dean	280-6241			PHD	78	Ohio St	1978
Hibernia Professor of Economics								
Lane, Walter J.	C-Ac	280-7145			PHD	78	Ca-SnDgo	1986
Altazan, John E.	Prof	280-6434			PHD	54	Illinois	1958
Davis, J. Ronnie	Prof	280-7148			PHD	67	Virginia	1989
Miller, Edward M.	Prof	280-6913			PHD	70	MIT	1984
Mukherjee, Tarun K.	Prof	280-7146		Fnce	DBA	77	Tx Tech	
Speyrer, Janet F.	Prof	280-6981			PHD	82	J Hopkins	1987
Director, Division of Business & Economic Research								
Turunen-Red, Arja H.	Prof	280-6912			PHD	85	Brit Colum	1995
Whitney, Gerald A.	Prof	280-6903			PHD	77	Tulane	1979
Abdel-Rahman, Hesham M.	Assoc	280-7343			PHD	87	Penn	1987
Naka, Atsuyuki	Assoc	280-6896			PHD	89	Arizona	1989
Daal, Elton	Asst	280-6270			PHD	99	Maryland	1999
Maroney, Neal C.	Asst	280-6908			PHD	96	Claremont	1997
Xiao, W.	Asst	280-7147			PHD	01	Pittsburgh	2001

New York University New York, NY 10012-1126 (212) 998-0860 stern.nyu.edu
Department of Economics Stern Sch of Business Fax=995-4218 Ms. Felicia B. Shutter
Homepage: http://www.stern.nyu.edu/econ/

Daly, George G.	Dean	998-0900	gdale	D	PHD	67	Nrthwstrn	1993
Greene, William H.	C-Pr	998-0876	wgreene	CDE	PHD	76	Wisconsin	1982
Backus, David	Prof	998-0873	dbackus	EFG	PHD	81	Yale	1990
Cabral, Luis M. B.	Prof	998-0858	lcabral	DL	PHD	89	Stanford	2000
Cooley, Thomas F.	Prof	998-0870	tcooley	EG	PHD	71	Penn	1999
Paganelli-Bull Professor of Economics								
Diamond, Daniel E.	Prof	998-0887	ddiamond	DEN	PHD	58	NYU	1958
Economides, Nicholas S.	Prof	998-0864	neconomi	DKL	PHD	81	Berkeley	1990
Guilfoil, John D.	Prof	998-0045	jguilfoi	DKN	PHD	64	NYU	1964
Katz, Barbara G.	Prof	998-0865	bkatz	CDP	PHD	73	Penn	1974
Kavesh, Robert A.	Prof	998-0863	rkavesh	B	PHD	54	Harvard	1958
Marcus Nadler Professor of Finance & Economics								
Pugel, Thomas A.	Prof	998-0404	tpugel	DEF	PHD	78	Harvard	1978
Ramachandran, Rama	Prof	998-0759	rramacha	DEH	PHD	75	Brown	1987
Sato, Ryuzo	Prof	998-0707	rsato	CO	PHD	62	J Hopkins	1985
C. V. Starr Professor of Economics								
Smith, George	Prof	998-0878	gsmith	N	PHD	76	Harvard	1988
Sylla, Richard	Prof	998-0869	rsylla	DN	PHD	69	Harvard	1990
Henry Kaufman Professor of the History of Financial Institutions & Markets								
Wachtel, Paul A.	Prof	998-4030	pwachtel	EG	PHD	71	Rochester	1972
Research Professor								
Walter, Ingo	Prof	998-0707	iwalter	FG	PHD	66	NYU	1970
Charles Simon Professor of Applied Financial Economics								
White, Lawrence	Prof	998-0880	lwhite	DGKL	PHD	69	Harvard	1976
Arthur E. Imperitore Professor of Economics								
Roubini, Nouriel	Assoc	998-0886	nroubini	EF	PHD	88	Harvard	1995
Ferri, Fabrizio	Asst	998-0251	fperri	EFG	PHD	99	Penn	1998
Fogli, Alessandra	Asst	998-0872	afogli	EFJ	PHD	00	Penn	2000
Quadrini, Vincenzo	Asst	998-0874	vquadrin	EF	PHD	96	Penn	2000

New York University New York, NY 10012 (212) 998-8900 nyu.edu
Department of Economics Faculty Arts & Sciences Fax=995-4186 Emily Rizzo
Homepage: www.nyu.edu/econ/

Gale, Douglas	C-Pr	998-8900	douglas.gale	D	PHD	75	Cambridge	1996
Baumol, William J.	Prof	998-8943	william.baumol	D	PHD	49	London	1971
Benhabib, Jess	Prof	998-8971	jess.benhabib	EO	PHD	76	Columbia	1980
Benoit, Jean-Pierre	Prof	998-8934	jeanpierre.be+	D	PHD	83	Stanford	1989
Caplin, Andrew	Prof	998-8950	andrew.caplin	D	PHD	83	Yale	1995
Fernandez, Raquel	Prof	998-8908	raquel.fernandez	F	PHD	87	Columbia	1995
Flinn, Christopher	Prof	998-8909	christopher.f+	J	PHD	84	Chicago	1987
Frydman, Roman	Prof	998-8967	roman.frydman	E	PHD	78	Columbia	1978
Gately, Dermot	Prof	998-8955	dermot.gately	Q	PHD	73	Princeton	1973
Gertler, Mark	Prof	998-8931	mark.gertler	D	PHD	78	Stanford	1990
Jovanovic, Boyan	Prof	998-8953	boyan.jovanovic	L	PHD	78	Chicago	1983
Keane, Michael P.	Prof	998-8992	michael.keane	D	PHD	90	Brown	1998
Nadiri, M. Ishaq	Prof	998-8968	m.ishaq.nadiri	O	PHD	65	Berkeley	1971
Nyarko, Yaw	Prof	998-8928	yaw.nyarko	D	PHD	86	Cornell	1992
Ok, Efe	Prof	998-8920	efe.ok	H	PHD	95	Cornell	1995
Ordover, Janusz A.	Prof	998-8956	janusz.ordover	G	PHD	73	Columbia	1982
Prager, Jonas	Prof	998-8911	jonas.prager	G	PHD	64	Columbia	1962
Ramsey, James B.	Prof	998-8947	james.ramsey	C	PHD	68	Wisconsin	1976
Ray, Debraj	Prof	998-8900	debraj.ray	D	PHD	83	Cornell	1999
Rizzo, Mario J.	Prof	998-8932	mario.rizzo	K	PHD	77	Chicago	1979
Wilson, Charles A.	Prof	998-8954	charles.wilson	D	PHD	76	Rochester	1983
Wolff, Edward N.	Prof	998-8917	edward.wolff	J	PHD	74	Yale	1974
Lizzeri, Alessandro	Assoc	998-8907	alessandro.l+	L	PHD	95	Nrthwstrn	2000
Bisin, Alberto	Asst	998-8916	alberto.bisin	D	PHD	93	Chicago	1997
Comin, Diego	Asst	998-8926	diego.comin	E	PHD	00	Harvard	2000
Eliaz, Kfir	Asst	998-8912	kfir.eliaz	D	PHD	00	Tel Aviv	2001
Lagos, Ricardo	Asst	998-8937	ricardo.lagos	J	PHD	97	Penn	2000
Lee, Donghoon	Asst	998-8938	donghoon.lee	DE	PHD	01	Penn	2001
Ludvigson, Sydney	Asst	998-8927	sydney.ludvigson	E	PHD	96	Princeton	2001
Razin, Ronny	Asst	9998-890	4ronny.razin	D	PHD	00	Princeton	2000
Topa, Giorgio	Asst	998-8957	mario.topa	C	PHD	96	Chicago	1996

New York Institute of Tech New York, NY 11568-8000 (516) 686-7754 student.nyit.edu
Department of Economics School of Management Fax=484-8328 Trudy Waser
Did Not Respond--1999-2000 Listing; 261- exchange have 212 area code

Decker, David R.	Dean	686-7423		Intl	PHD	77	Kansas	2000
Chandrasekar, Krishnamurti	Prof	261-1602			PHD	69	New Sch	1969
Lawrence, William	Prof	261-1706			PHD	75	NYU	1971
Schwartz, Carol H.	Prof	686-7739			PHD	63	Columbia	1987
Kutasovic, Paul R.	Assoc	686-7709			PHD	83	Rutgers	1988
Afxentiou, Diamando	Asst	348-3065	afxentiou:jl		PHD	90	W Virginia	1990

Niagara University Niagara Univ, NY 14109 (716) 286-8160 eagle.niagara.edu
Department of Commerce Col of Business Admin Fax=286-8206 Melissa Heidt

Miller, Keith T.	Dean	286-8050	ktm	Mgt	PHD	83	Arizona	1994
Peek, William A.	C-Ac	286-8171	wap		PHD	85	Syracuse	1980
Lee, Tenpao	Prof	286-8177	jhn		PHD	84	Iowa St	1987
Neimanis, George J.	Prof	286-8169	genne		MA	65	NYU	1970
Scherer, Philip M.	Prof	286-8165	pscherer		PHD	72	Missouri	1980
Warren, Stanton A.	Prof	286-8173	warren		PHD	73	SUNY-Buf	1981

Nicholls State University Thibodaux, LA 70310 (985) 448-4232 nicholls.edu
Dept of Economics & Finance Col of Business Admin Fax=448-4922 Bobbie Taylor
Homepage: www.nicholls.edu/busadmin/finance.htm

Gros, Ridley J. Jr.	Dean	448-4170	ba-rjg		PHD	71	LSU	1971
McManis, Bruce L.	H-Pr	448-4188	ecfi-blm	G	PHD	81	LSU	1978
Boyet, Wayne E.	Prof	448-4231	ecfi-web	G	PHD	65	N Car St	1985
Chotigeat, Tosporn	Prof	448-4189	ecfi-tc	FO	PHD	78	S Illinois	1988
Coats, R. Morris	Prof	448-4237	ecfi-rmc	HIRQ	PHD	83	Va Tech	1985
Kooros, Syrous	Prof	448-4407	ecfi-skk	EFOC	PHD	80	Rensselaer	1991
Stanley, Thomas O.	Prof	448-4194	ecfi-tos	FG	PHD	82	Nebraska	1988
Lejaunie, John	Assoc	448-4210	ecfi-jpl	FG	PHD	92	N Orleans	1991

Nichols College Dudley, MA 01571-5000 (508) 213-2256 nichols.edu
Dept of Atg, Fnce & Econ College of Business Adm Fax=213-2225

Reinhardt, Alan J.	Dean	213-2201	reinhardta		PHD	83	Ind-Penn	9-98
Armstrong, John A.	C-Ac	213-2124	john.armstrong	Atg	MBA	76	Pace	1986
Corkum, Keith H.	Prof	213-2256			PHD	76	Lehigh	1972
Nordstrom, Louise J.	Prof	213-2259		ADFH	PHD	71	Clark	9-74

Norfolk State University Norfolk, VA 23504-2954 (757) 823-8955 vger.nsu.edu
Entrepreneurial Studies School of Business Fax=823-2506 Francine Hightower

Achampong, Francis	Dean$	823-8920	fachampong	Mgt	PHD	81	London	1985
Shiau, Liang-rong	C-Pr	683-9581	lshiau	CAR	PHD	72	S Miss	1972
Sissoko, Macki	Asst	823-2583			PHD	91	Auburn	1999

University of North Alabama Florence, AL 35632-0001 (256) unanov.edu
Dept of Economics & Finance School of Business Fax=765-4811 Debbie Westmoreland

Gatlin, Kerry P.	Dean	765-4261	kgatlin	Mgt	PHD	82	Oklahoma	1987
Morris, Barry K.	C-Pr	765-4411			PHD	74	Arkansas	1974
Copeland, Joe B.	Prof	765-4270			PHD	74	Arkansas	1983
Couch, Jim	Asst	765-4412			PHD		Miss	1991
Williams, P.	Asst	765-4315			PHD		Miss	1997

North Carolina at Asheville Asheville, NC 28804-3299 (828) 251-6550 unca.edu
Economics Faculty Department of Economics Fax=251-6572 Ms. Kim Moore
Homepage: www.unca.edu/econ/
email @1=bulldog.unca.edu

Larson, Bruce D.	C-Pr	251-6562	blarson	ABCD	PHD	83	N Carol	1983
Browning, Shirley C.	Prof	251-6549	sbrowning	AEPQ	PHD	71	Conn	1970
Nickless, Pamela J.	Prof	251-6563	nickless	AJN	PHD	76	Purdue	1983
Sulock, Joseph M.	Prof	251-6568	jsulock	AGH	PHD	76	Virginia	1975
Bell, Christopher Ross	Assoc	251-6552	bell	AGHL	PHD	87	Penn	1989
Konz, Jeffery M.	Asst	251-6570	jkonz	BEFO	PHD	94	N Carol	1996
Mathews, Leah Greden	Asst	251-6561	lmathews@1	HDQO	PHD	97	Minnesota	1997
Bumgarner, Sarah J.	Lect	251-6569	sbumgarner	A	MBA	82	Appalach	1990

University of North Carolina Chapel Hill, NC 27599-3305 (919) 966-2383 unc.edu
Div Soc Sci-Dept Economics Col of Arts & Sciences Fax=966-4986 Mrs. Page LoRe'
email @1=email.unc.edu

Akin, John S.	C-Pr	966-5335	john_akin	IGH	PHD	71	Michigan	1973
Benavie, Arthur	Prof	966-5326		AE	PHD	63	Michigan	1967
Biglaiser, Gary	Prof	966-4884	gbiglais@1	EL	PHD	88	Berkeley	1988
Black, Stanley W.	Prof	966-5926	sblack@1	F	PHD	65	Yale	1983
Lurcy Professor								
Blau, David M.	Prof	966-3962	david_blau	J	PHD	80	Wisconsin	1992
Conway, Patrick	Prof	966-5376	patrick_conway	F	PHD	84	Princeton	1983
Darity, William A. Jr.	Prof	966-5392	sandy_darity	E	PHD	78	MIT	1983
Boshamer Professor								
Field, Alfred J. Jr.	Prof	843-9451	afield@1	F	PHD	67	Iowa St	1967
Associate Chairperson; Director, Undergraduate Studies								
Friedman, James W.	Emer	966-3669	friedman@1	DL	PHD	63	Yale	1985
Froyen, Richard T.	Prof	966-5375	froyen@1	E	PHD	72	Maryland	1971
Gallant, A. Ronald	Prof	966-5338	ron_gallant	C	PHD	71	Iowa St	1993
Latane' Professor								

Ghysels, Eric	Prof	962-9810	ghysels		PHD	86	Nrthwstrn	1-00
Edward M. Bernstein Distinguished Professor								
Guilkey, David K.	Prof	843-9452	david_guilkey	C	PHD	73	N Carol	1983
Ingram, James C.	Emer		jcingram@1		PHD	52	Cornell	1952
McFarland, David	Prof	966-5342		BDL	PHD	63	Vanderbilt	1964
Mezzetti, Claudio	Prof	966-5377	mezzetti@1	D	PHD	88	Oxford	1990
Mroz, Thomas A.	Prof	966-5395	tom_mroz	J	PHD	84	Stanford	1989
Murphy, James L.	Prof	966-5346	jlmurphy@1	C	PHD	64	Purdue	1964
Dean, UNC Summer School								
Pfouts, William	Emer				PHD	52	N Carol	1947
Rhode, Paul	Prof	843-9842	prhode@1	N	PHD	90	Stanford	1990
Rosefielde, Steven	Prof	966-5371	stevern@1	P	PHD	72	Harvard	1970
Salemi, Michael K.	Prof	966-5391	michael_salemi	E	PHD	76	Minnesota	1976
Stewart, John F.	Prof	966-5345	jstewar@1	L	PHD	76	Wisconsin	1975
Tarascio, Vincent J.	Prof	966-5374	vtarasci@1	N	PHD	66	Rice	1964
Tauchen, Helen	Prof	966-5394	tauchen@1	D	PHD	77	Minnesota	1977
Director of Graduate Studies								
Gilleskie, Donna	Assoc	966-5372	donna_gilleskie	IJ	PHD	94	Minnesota	1994
Orsagh, Thomas	Emer				PHD	64	Penn	1965
Parke, William	Assoc	843-9453	parke@1	C	PHD	80	Yale	1988
Strumpf, Koleman	Assoc	966-4485	cigar	GH	PHD	95	MIT	1995
Turchi, Boone A.	Assoc	966-5348	turchi@1	AT	PHD	73	Michigan	1971
Vanderklaauw, H. Wilbert	Assoc	966-2383	vanderkl	J	PHD	92	Brown	1999
Wilde, James A.	Assoc	966-5328	jwilde@1	GH	PHD	68	Princeton	1965
Anderson, Evan	Asst	966-4886	ewanders@1	E	PHD	98	Chicago	1998
Kovalenkov, Alexander	Asst	966-5327	akovalen@1	D	PHD	98	Automoma	1998
Wu, Xiaodong	Asst	966-2383	wux@1		PHD	99	Princeton	1999
Willis, Rachel A.	Adj	966-3710	rawillis@1	J	PHD	90	Nrthwstrn	1982

North Carolina at Charlotte	Charlotte, NC		28223-0001 (704) 687-2186				email.uncc.edu	
Department of Economics	Col of Business Admin		Fax=687-6442		Jackie Harper, Sabra Reece			
Lilly, Claude C. III	Dean	687-2165	cclilly	Insu	PHD	73	Geo St	8-97
Gandar, John Maxim	C-Pr	687-4133	jmgandar		PHD	82	Missouri	1982
Amato, Louis	Prof	687-4130	ltamato		PHD	80	S Carol	1980
Connaughton, John E.	Prof	687-4134	jec		PHD	81	Northeas	1978
Director, UNC-Charlotte Economic "Forecast"								
Davis, W. Young Jr.	Prof	687-2187	wydavis		PHD	70	Georgia	1970
Madsen, Ron	Prof	687-4127	ramadsen					
Neel, Richard E.	Prof	687-4122	reneel		PHD	60	Ohio St	1969
Schwarz, Peter M.	Prof	687-4126	pschwarz		PHD	80	Ohio St	1978
Zuber, Richard A.	Prof	687-4129	razuber		PHD	78	Kentucky	1978
Lin, Hwan-Chyang	Assoc	687-3796	hclin		PHD	90	Illinois	1993
Liner, Gaines Howard	Assoc	687-4128	ghliner		PHD	71	Clemson	1971
McGregor, Rob R.	Assoc	687-4121	rrmcgreg		PHD	91	S Carol	1991
Russo, Benjamin	Assoc	687-4137	brusso		PHD	85	Iowa	1984
Tseng, Hui-Kuan	Assoc	687-4123	hktseng		PHD	88	Illinois	1988
Tucker, Irvin B. III	Assoc	687-4136	ibtucker		PHD	82	S Carol	1981
Sewell, Ellen M.	Asst	687-4132	esewell		PHD	83	Florida	1982
Troyer, Jennifer	Asst	687-2185	jtroyer		PHD	99	Florida	1999

North Carolina at Greensboro	Greensboro, NC		27402-6165 (336) 334-5463				uncg.edu	
Department of Economics	Bryan Sch of Bus & Econ		Fax=334-4089				Ms. Judy Tuttle	
Weeks, James K.	Dean	334-5338	jim_weeks	Mgt	PHD	74	S Carol	1976
Allen, Stuart D.	H-Pr	334-3166	stuart_allen	E	PHD	77	Virginia	1976
Caldwell, Bruce J.	Prof	334-4865	bruce_caldwell	B	PHD	79	N Carol	1978
Link, Albert N.	Prof	334-5146	al_link	O	PHD	76	Tulane	1982
Neufeld, John L.	Prof	334-4869	john_neufeld	ND	PHD	75	Michigan	1974
Ruhm, Christopher J.	Prof	334-5148	c_ruhm	JI	PHD	84	Berkeley	1991
Seaks, Terry G.	Emer	228-9048	tgseaks	C	PHD	72	Duke	1972
Layson, Steve	Assoc	334-4868	layson	D	PHD	83	Chicago	1978
Leyden, Dennis P.	Assoc	334-3904	leyden	H	PHD	87	Car Mellon	1984
McCrickard, Donald L.	Assoc	334-5338	don_mccrickard	EF	PHD	76	N Carol	1975
Snowden, Kenneth A.	Assoc	334-4870	snowden	NG	PHD	83	Wisconsin	1983
Bearse, Peter	Asst	334-4871	pmbearse	CH	PHD	95	Virginia	1998
Dawsey, Amanda	Asst	883-3910		H	PHD	01	Maryland	2001
Rosenbaum, Dan	Asst	334-4872	dtrosenb	JI	PHD	98	Nrthwstrn	1998
Sheran, Michelle	Asst	334-5463		J	PHD	01	Virginia	2001
Brod, Andrew C.	Inst	334-4867	andrew_brod	Q	PHD	92	Minnesota	1989

North Carolina at Wilmington	Wilmington, NC		28403-3297 (910) 395-3510				ecn.uncwil.edu	
Dept of Economics & Finance	Cameron Sch of Bus Adm		Fax=395-3815					
Clark, Lawrence	Dean	395-3501						
Lawson, Luther Drew	C-Pr		lawson	AJL	PHD	81	Tennessee	
Farrell, Claude H. III	Prof	395-3510	farrell	EGR	PHD	74	N Car St	
Hall, William Woodward Jr.	Prof		hallw	QR	PHD	72	Clemson	
Director, Center for Business & Economics Services								
Hill, Roger Post	Prof	395-3510	hillr	G	PHD	68	Mich St	

Howell, Kristen K.	Assoc		howellk	F	PHD	89	Kentucky	
Robinson, Ned Stephen	Assoc		robinsonn	A	PHD	73	Oklahoma	
Wadman, William Morgan	Assoc		wadmanw	CDH	PHD	76	Claremont	
Burrus, Robert T.	Asst		busserr	D	PHD	97	Virginia	
Dumas, Christopher	Asst		dumusc	Q	PHD	97	Berkeley	
Schuhmann, Peter	Asst		schuhp	Q	PHD	96	N Car St	
Whitehead, John C.	Asst	395-3510	whitehs	Q	PHD	90	Kentucky	

U North Carolina at Pembroke Pembroke, NC 28372-1510 (910) 521-6214 sassette.uncp.edu
Economics Faculty School of Business Fax=521-6162 Rena Hill

Clow, Kenneth E.	C-Pr	521-6214		Mktg	PHD	92	Arkansas	1998
Ashiaf, Mohammad	Asst	521-6464			PHD		N Illinois	1999
Frederick, James R.	Asst	521-6592			PHD	83	Wayne St	1988

North Carolina A&T State Un Greensboro, NC 27411 (336) 334-7746 ncat.edu
Dept Econ & Trans Logistics Sch of Business & Econ Fax=334-7093 Ms. Cathy Dalton
phone 334-7744

Craig, Quiester	Dean	334-7632	craigq	Atg	PHD	72	Missouri	8-72
Simmons, Michael	C-As	Ext 2000	simmonsm		PHD	79	Wash St	8-70
Benjamin, Julian	Prof	Ext 2020	benjaminm		PHD	77	SUNY-Buf	
Coley, Basil G.	Prof	334-7744	coleyb		PHD	71	Illinois	1966
Khan, Anwar S.	Prof	Ext 2007	khana		PHD	72	Wisconsin	
Obeng, Kofi	Prof	Ext 2018	obengk		PHD	81	Penn	1982
UPS Chair								
Addus, Abdussalam A.	Assoc	Ext 2009	addusa		PHD	82	Penn St	1980
Chen, David Y.	Assoc	Ext 2014	chend		PHD	71	Wisconsin	
Jeong, Dong K.	Assoc	Ext 2013	jeongd		PHD	74	Wayne St	
King, Vereda J.	Assoc	Ext 2008	kingv		PHD	84	Duke	
Morse, Lawrence B.	Assoc	Ext 2003	morsel		PHD	68	Minnesota	1976
Cloud, Darrell	Asst	Ext 2011	darrellc		PHD	00	Wi-Milwa	2000
Granger, Maury	Asst	Ext 2015	grangerm		PHD	95	Kentucky	1993
Price, Gregory N.	Asst	Ext 2011	priceg		PHD	93	Wi-Milwa	
Sakano, Ryoichi	Asst	Ext 2015	sakanor		PHD	90	Alabama	1992
Simkins, Scott P.	Asst	Ext 2001	simkinss		PHD	88	Iowa	
Bunkey, Mark	AdjAs	Ext 4036	bunkeym		PHD		Duke	2000

North Carolina Central Univ Durham, NC 27707 (919) 530-7393 wpo.nccu.edu
Department of Economic School of Business Fax=530-6163

Williams, H. James	Dean	560-6175		Atg	PHD	82	Georgia	1999
Gokcekus, Omer	H-As	530-7393	ogokceku		PHD	95	Duke	1996
Amoateng, Kofi A. D.	Prof	530-7384	amoakng		PHD	86	Tx-Austin	1990
Dutton, Marilyn M.	Assoc	530-7390	mdutton		PHD	89	Duke	1991
Hakeem, Salih	Asst	560-6131	shakeem		PHD	87	N Car St	1988
Nasir, Abm	Asst	530-6138			PHD	01	Wi-Milwa	2001

North Carolina State Univ Raleigh, NC 27695-8110 (919) 515-3274 ncsu.edu
Department of Economics College of Management Fax=515-7873 Carolyn Smith

Margolis, Stephen E.	H-Pr	515-3274	steve_margolis	LKD	PHD	78	UCLA	1982
Allen, Steven G.	Prof	515-6941	steve_allen	JD	PHD	78	Harvard	1978
Clark, Robert L.	Prof	515-4568	robert_clark	JD	PHD	74	Duke	1975
Craig, Lee A.	Prof	515-2887	lee_craig	NJD	PHD	89	Indiana	1989
Erickson, Edward W.	Prof	515-3201	ed_erickson	LQD	PHD	86	Vanderbilt	1965
Fearn, Robert M.	Emer	515-4616	fearn	JDP	PHD	68	Chicago	1965
Fisher, Douglas	Prof	515-2887	doug_fisher	EN	PHD	65	Chicago	1977
Flath, David	Prof	515-2472	david_flath	LDP	PHD	76	UCLA	1976
Grennes, Thomas	Prof	515-3274	tom_grennes	FD	MA	65	Wisconsin	1968
Hall, Alastair R.	Prof	515-2887	alastair_hall	C	PHD	85	Warwick	1985
Holthausen, Duncan M. Jr.	Prof	515-7680	duncan_holtha+	DC	PHD	76	Nrthwstrn	1974
Hyman, David Neil	Prof	515-2472	hyman_david	HA	PHD	69	Princeton	1969
Knoeber, Charles R.	Prof	515-7680	charles_knoeber	LKDG	PHD	76	UCLA	1976
Lapp, John S.	Prof	515-7680	john_lapp	EGF	PHD	74	Princeton	1974
Palmquist, Raymond B.	Prof	515-3274	palmquist	QDR	PHD	78	U Wash	1979
Pearce, Douglas K.	Prof	515-2472	doug_pearce	EG	PHD	74	Wisconsin	1985
Seater, John J.	Prof	515-2472	john_seater	EH	PHD	75	Brown	1981
Thurman, Walter N.	Prof	515-4545	wally_thurman	QCD	PHD	84	Chicago	1984
Wessels, Walter J.	Prof	515-2472	walt_wessels	JD	PHD	76	Chicago	1975
Ball, David Stafford	Assoc	515-3274	david_bell	FND	PHD	67	N Carol	1966
Headen, Alvin E.	Assoc	515-2887	al_headen	IJD	PHD	81	MIT	1986
McElroy, Michael B.	Assoc	515-7680	mike_mcelroy	E	PHD	70	Nrthwstrn	1970
Newmark, Craig M.	Assoc	515-7680	craig_newmark	LD	PHD	84	UCLA	1984
Tsoulouhas, Theofanis	Assoc	515-7680	fanis_tsoulouhas	CD	PHD	93	Illinois	1993
Levy, Armando	Asst	515-3274	armando	C	PHD	96	Berkeley	1996

North Central College Naperville, IL 60566-7063 (630) 637-5240 noctrt.edu
Economic Department Div Economic & Bus Adm Fax=637-5121
Homepage: http://172.16.50.2/intrhome.htm

Barger, Peter S.	C-Ac	637-5246	psb	G	PHD	89	Illinois	1989
Love, Thomas M.	Prof	637-5245	tml	F	PHD	67	Wisconsin	1972
Whitaker, Andrew L.	Prof	637-5241	alw	G	PHD	88	Illinois	1988
Bogart, Marti S.	Assoc	637-5243	msb	J	PHD	86	Purdue	1982
Anstine, Diane	Asst	637-5242	dianstin	D	PHD	97	Kentucky	1997

University of North Dakota Grand Forks, ND 58202-8369 (701) 777-2637 und.nodak.edu
Div of Econ & Public Affairs Col of Bus & Pub Admin Fax=777-5099 Ruth Holweger

Elbert, Dennis J.	Dean	777-2135	dennis_elbert	Mktg	PHD	76	Missouri	8-80
O'Neill, Patrick B.	C-Pr	777-3358	patrick_oneill	ADL	PHD	87	Boston C	1987
Blackwell, J. Lloyd III	Prof	777-3357	joseph_blackwell	C	PHD	73	Geo St	1980
Ramsett, David E.	Prof	777-3349	david_ramsett	AHQ	PHD	68	Oklahoma	1968
Bagheri, Fathollah	Assoc	777-3350	fathollah_bag+	AJ	PHD	78	Penn	1990
Biederman, Daniel K.	Assoc	777-3347	daniel_biederman	CGI	PHD	87	Kansas	1987
Flynn, David	Asst	777-2637	david_flynn		ABD		Indiana	2001
Goenner, Cullen	Asst	777-2637	cullen_goenner		PHD	01	Wisconsin	2001
Kara, Orhan	Asst	777-2637	orhan_kara		ABD		Wi-Milwa	2001
Owens, Daniel	Asst	777-2637	daniel_owens		ABD		Kentucky	2000
Snaith, Sean	Asst	777-2637	sean_snaith		PHD	96	Penn St	2001

University of North Florida Jacksonville, FL 32224-2645 (904) 620-2640 unf.edu
Dept Economics & Geography College of Business Adm Fax=620-1300 Vicki Gipe

Traynham, Earle C. Jr.	Dean	646-2590	traynham		PHD	73	S Carol	1973
Perry, Joseph M.	C-Pr	646-2640	jperry	NOR	PHD	66	Nrthwstrn	1971
Borg, Mary O.	Prof	646-2640	mborg	HT	PHD	85	N Carol	1984
Director of University Scholar Programs								
Mason, Paul M.	Prof	646-2641	pmason	HE	PHD	84	Tx-Austin	1985
Woods, Louis A.	Prof	646-2641		OQR	PHD	72	N Carol	1972
Shapiro, Stephen L.	Assoc	646-2641	sshapiro	AH	PHD	72	S Carol	1972
Director, Center for Economic Education								
Steagall, Jeffrey W.	Assoc	646-260j	steagal	FAC	PHD	90	Wisconsin	1990
Stranahan, Harriett	Assoc	646-2641	hstranah	JGD	PHD	95	Wash	1994
Baliamoune, Mina	Asst	620-2640	mbaliamo		PHD	95	Northeas	2001
Cobb, Sharon	Asst	620-2640	scobb	AC	PHD	98	Florida	1998
Salazar, Natalia	Asst	620-2640	nsinyars		PHD	00	Ohio St	2000

North Georgia Col & St Univ Dahlonega, GA 30597 (706) 864-1610 nugget.ngc.peachnet.edu
Economic Faculty Dept of Business Admin Fax=864-1668 Christy Waters

Skelly, Gerald U.	Dean	864-1609	gskelly	Mkgt	PHD	78	Fla St	1993
Grant, Clayton	H-Pr	864-1620	cgrant	K	PHD	71	Clemson	1985
Campbell, Noel	Asst	864-1610	ndcampbell	H	PHD	97	GeoMason	1998

University of North Texas Denton, TX 76203-5457 (940) 565-2573 econ.unt.edu
Department of Economics Col of Arts & Sciences Fax=565-4426 Nancy L. Boyd, Adm Asst
Homepage: http://www.econ.unt.edu
Did Not Respond--1999-2000 Listing

Burggrew, Warren	Dean							
Cobb, Steven Lee	C-Ac	565-2184	cobb	AFOP	PHD	87	N Carol	1987
Abernathy, Lewis M.	Prof	565-4322	lewis	J	PHD	67	Oklahoma	1963
Director, Labor & Industrial Relations Institute								
Koelln, Kenneth	Assoc	565-4542	koelln	LI	PHD	91	Florida	1991
Nieswiadomy, Michael L.	Assoc	565-2244	mike	HRIQ	PHD	83	Tx A&M	1985
Jewell, R. Todd	Asst	565-3337	tjewell	HJ	PHD	92	Ca-SnBarb	1996
Redfearn, Michael	Asst	565-2220	redfearn	EG	PHD	92	Mich St	1992
Tieslau, Margie	Asst	565-3442	tieslau	EC	PHD	92	Mich St	1992
Werger, Jennie	Asst	565-4544	jennie	HJ	PHD	96	N Carol	1996

Northeastern University Boston, MA 02115 (617) 373-2882 neu.edu
Department of Economics Col of Arts & Sciences Fax=373-3640
Did Not Respond--1999-2000 Listing; email @1=lynx.neu.edu @2=nuhub.neu.edu

Morrison, Steven A.	C-Pr$	373-3646	sam1		PHD	79	Berkeley	1982
Alam, M. Shahid	Prof	373-2849	salam@1		PHD	79	W Ontario	1988
Fraumeni, Barbara M.	Prof	373-2252			PHD	80	Boston C	1982
Hellman, Daryl A.	Prof	373-7517	dhellman@2		PHD	70	Rutgers	1972
Graduate Coordinator								
Kim, Sungwoo	Prof	373-2893	kim		PHD	57	Berkeley	1972
Schachter, Gustav	Prof	373-2886	gschacte@1		PHD	62	NYU	1965
Sum, Andrew M.	Prof	373-2242			MA	71	MIT	1971
Alper, Neil O.	Assoc	373-2839	alper		PHD	77	Pittsburgh	1979
Brookins, Oscar T.	Assoc	373-2251	otbrookins@2		PHD	76	SUNY-Buf	1983
Dadkhah, Kamran N.	Assoc	373-2297	kdadkhah@1		PHD	75	Indiana	1981
Dyer, Alan W.	Assoc	373-2610	dyer		PHD	82	Maryland	1983
Undergraduate Coordinator								
Wassall, Gregory H.	Assoc	373-2196	wassall		PHD	78	Rutgers	1979

Northeastern Illinois Univ — Chicago, IL 60625-4699 (773) 442-5690 — neiu.edu
Department of Economics — Col of Arts & Sciences Fax=442-5650 — Anita Oxley

Pastors, Charles	Dean$	442-5700	c-pastors		PHD		Loyol-Chgo	
Easton, Robert F.	C-As	442-5648	r-easton		MA		Nrthwstrn	
Freiberg, Lewis	Prof	442-5688	l-freiberg	DHI	PHD	72	Kentucky	1982
Stuart, Edward F.	Prof	442-5695	e-stuarat1	FP	PHD	78	Oklahoma	1986
Bergan, Daniel J.	Assoc	442-5697	d-bergan	ADEG	PHD	85	Tx Tech	
Brewton, Audie R.	Assoc	442-5693	a-brewton	CBDN	PHD	79	Utah	1984
Stehman, Diane	Assoc	442-5699	d-stehman	CL	PHD	86	Il-Chicago	1978
Collum, Thomas E.	Asst	442-5694	t-collum	LDHP	MA	75	Nrthwstrn	1977
Rothstein, Sheldon H.	Asst	442-5656	s-rothstein	ADGJ	MA		Chicago	

Northeastern State Univ — Tahlequah, OK 74464-2399 (918) 458-2091 — cherokee.nsuok.edu
Dept of Economics & Mgt — Col of Business & Indus Fax=458-2337 — Linda

Dotson, Penny C.	Dean	456-2091	dotson	Mktg	EDD	94	Arkansas	1977
Hileman, A. Eugene	C-Pr	456-5511	hileman	AGM	PHD	71	Tennessee	1988
Greubel, Robert T.	Prof		greubel	AEF	PHD	72	Arkansas	1965
Wier, Thomas	Asst	456-5511	weir	RCB	PHD	89	Tennessee	1998

Northern Arizona University — Flagstaff, AZ 86011-5066 (928) 523-3657 — nau.edu
Dept of Business Admin-Econ — Col of Business Admin Fax=523-7331 — Kay Pinto
Homepage: www.cba.nau.edu/pinto-j/economics

Gerety, Mason S.	Dean$	523-2345	mason.gerety	Fnce	PHD	86	U Wash	8-93
Gunderson, Ronald J.	C-Pr	523-7358	ronald.gunderson	DR	PHD	77	Nebraska	1977
Brown, Douglas	Prof	523-7394	douglas.brown	OP	PHD	85	Colo St	1985
Jerrell, Max E.	Prof	523-7405	max.jerrell	EC	PHD	84	Ariz St	1981
Pinto, James V.	Prof	523-7356	jim.pinto	DC	PHD	75	Oklahoma	1981
Campione, Wendy A.	Assoc	523-7360	wendy.campione	HJ	PHD	84	Illinois	1981
Duncan, Wallace H.	Assoc	523-7366	wallace.duncan	EG	PHD	76	Wyoming	1978
Smith, Dean G.	Assoc	523-7396	dean.smith	RC	PHD	85	Tx A&M	1989
Ng, Pin T.	Asst	523-3657	pin.ng	CF	PHD	89	Illinois	2001
Foster, Dennis	Inst	523-8178	dennis.foster	AM	PHD	91	Hawaii	1990
Eastwood, John D.	Lect	523-7353	john.eastwood	CD	MS	80	Wyoming	1990

Univ of Northern Colorado — Greeley, CO 80639 (970) 351-2739 — bentley.univnorthco.edu
Department of Economics — Col of Arts & Sciences Fax=351-4296 — Linda Jack

Flake, Sandra	Dean	351-2707		Eng	PHD	74	Wisconsin	1997
McDaniel, Bruce A.	C-Ac	351-1163		OGMQ	PHD	79	Colo St	1992
Livingston, Marie L.	Prof	351-2739	mllivin	FHOQ	PHD	84	Colo St	1985
Kallon, Kelfala M.	Assoc	351-2134	kmkallo	EFHO	PHD	83	Virginia	1993
Aske, David	Asst	351-1564		AITR	PHD	92	Nebraska	1992
Connolly, Laura	Asst	351-1158		HL	PHD		Nrthwstrn	2000
Graham, Patricia E.	Asst	351-1559		IJOQ	PHD	88	Colo St	1988

Northern Illinois Univ — Dekalb, IL 60115-2854 (815) 753-1031 — niu.edu
Department of Economics — Col Liberal Arts & Sci Fax=752-1019 — Ms. Connie Rumer

Kitterle, Frederick	Dean	753-1061						7-95
Katz, Eliakim	C-Pr	753-6970	elik	CD	PHD	76	London	1976
Dalal, Ardeshir J.	Prof	753-6971	adalal	D	PHD	77	Iowa	1977
Kim, Young Chin	Prof	753-6972	ykim	O	PHD	68	Columbia	1970
Kwon, Jene K.	Prof	753-6977	jkwon	E	PHD	68	Iowa	1968
Mohabbat, Khan A.	Prof	753-6973	kmohabbat	E	PHD	64	SUNY-Buf	1968
Nord, Steven	Prof	753-6976	sen	R	PHD	76	Illinois	1979
Scaperlanda, Anthony E.	Emer		tonyscap	F	PHD	64	Tx-Austin	1964
Williams, Martin	Prof	753-6960	mwilliams	R	PHD	76	SUNY-Bin	1976
Karlson, Stephen	Assoc	753-6980	skarlson	D	PHD	80	Wisconsin	1986
Porter-Hudak, Susan	Assoc	753-6983	sphudak	C	PHD	82	Wisconsin	1982
Slotsve, George A.	Assoc	753-6966	gslotsve	JD	PHD	89	Wisconsin	1996
Temple, Judy A.	Assoc	753-6962	jtemple	H	PHD	90	Mich St	1989
Wilcox-Gok, Virginia L.	Assoc	753-6957	vlw	J	PHD	84	Wash U	1994
Campbell, Carl M. III	Asst	753-6974	carlcamp	E	PHD	88	Princeton	1999
Assistant Chair								
Lee, Woojin	Asst	753-6383	woojinlee	H	PHD	98	Ca-Davis	2001

University of Northern Iowa — Cedar Falls, IA 50614-0129 (319) 273-2412 — uni.edu
Department of Economics — Col of Business Admin Fax=273-2922 — Beverly Barber
Homepage: http://www.cba.uni.edu/economics/

Moussavi, Farzad	Dean$	273-6240	farzad.moussavi	Mgt	PHD	85	Arkansas	1985
Abraham, Fred J.	H-Pr	273-2412	abrahamf	AEHK	PHD	73	Oregon	1973
Hakes, David R.	Prof	273-3597	hakes	BEFG	PHD	85	Iowa St	1992
Isakson, Hans R.	Prof	273-2950	hans.isakson		PHD	78	Wisconsin	1990
McCormick, Kenneth J.	Prof	273-6051	mccormick	BEA	PHD	82	Iowa St	1982
Rives, Janet M.	Prof	273-6368	rives	ADJM	PHD	71	Duke	1984
Brown, Ken	Assoc	273-3087	ken.brown	CR	PHD	94	Illinois	1994
Uyar, Bulent	Assoc	273-6343	uyar	ACH	PHD	77	Pittsburgh	1991

Alam, M. Imam	Asst	273-7339	alam	CFO	PHD	95	Illinois	1996
Amin, Shahina	Asst	273-2637	amin		PHD	97	Illinois	2000
Jepsen, Lisa	Asst	273-2592	lisa.jepsen		PHD	98	Vanderbilt	2000
Kanago, Bryce	Asst	273-2951	bryce.kanago	E	PHD	88	Iowa	2000
Shin, Dongsoo	Asst	273-2412	dongsoo.shin		PHD	01	Wash	2001
Thorpe, Steven G.	Asst	273-2103	thorpe	HQ	PHD	95	Colorado	1996
Lindell, Lois A.	Inst	273-2952	lindell		BA	80	Wi-White	1996
Associate Director of UNI Center for Economic Education								
Mardis, Barbara K.	Inst	273-3062	mardis	C	MBA	81	N Iowa	1981
Northern Kentucky Univ	Highland Hght KY	41099-0503	(859) 572-6581					nku.edu
Economics Department	College of Business		Fax=572-6627		Marilyn McGinley/Ruth Griffin			
Carrell, Michael R.	Dean	572-5165	carrellm	Mgt	DBA	76	Kentucky	7-98
Lang, Nancy A.	C-Ac	572-5155	lang		EDD	83	Georgia	1983
Director Center for Economic Education								
Cate, Thomas H.	Prof	572-5799	cate		PHD	79	Fla St	1975
Clayton, Gary E.	Prof	572-6542	clayton		PHD	74	Utah	1980
Giesbrecht, Martin G.	Prof	572-5153			PHD	58	Munich	1987
Noyd, Louis E.	Assoc	572-5160	noyd		PHD	73	Oregon	1972
Snyder, Richard S.	Assoc	572-5651	snyderr		PHD	76	Indiana	1978
Simkonis, Carl	Inst	572-5979	simkonisca		MPA	91	N Kentucky	2000
Northern Michigan Univ	Marquette, MI		49855	(906) 227-2220				nmu.edu
Department of Economics	Arts & Sciences		Fax=227-2229					Alice McKinney
Homepage: www.nmu.edu/departments/econ.htm								
Prychitko, David L.	H-Pr	227-2220	dprychit	ABP	PHD	89	GeoMason	1997
Swaine, Howard R.	Prof	227-1214	hswaine	AKDH	PHD	65	UCLA	1966
Ferrarini, Tawni	Asst	227-1218	tferrari	ANO	PHD	95	Wash U	1997
Quinn, Robert	Asst	227-1215	rquinn	AIJ	PHD	95	U Miami	2001
Steffens, Karin	Asst	227-1217	ksteffen	AFQ	PHD	99	Mich St	1999
Northern State University	Aberdeen, SD		57401-7198	(605) 626-2400				wolf.northern.edu
Dept of Business & Economics	Sch of Business & Tech		Fax=626-3022					
Arnold, Clyde L.	Dean	626-2400			PHD	82	Oklahoma	1988
Trierweiler, John	C-Pr	626-2576			PHD	70	Nebraska	1985
Neumann, Hillar Jr.	Assoc	626-7719			PHD	86	Rutgers	1983
Chaudhrey, Mukesh	Asst	626-3001			PHD	94	Clev St	1995
Peterson, John E.	Asst	626-2434	petersoj		PHD	97	Kansas	1992
Savitski, David	Asst	626-3002			PHD	97	UCLA	1997
Northwest Missouri St Univ	Maryville, MO		64468-6001	(660) 562-1835				mail.nwmissouri.edu
Dept of Atg, Econ & Finance	Col Prof & Applied Sci		Fax=562-1750					Alisa Meyer
DeYoung, Ronald C.	Dean	562-1277	deyoung	BEd	EDD	71	N Illinois	1984
McLaughlin, Patrick	C-Ac	562-1291	jpat	K	JD	78	Mo-Ks Cty	1978
Jelavich, Mark S.	Prof	562-1763	mjelav	FR	PHD	80	J Hopkins	1981
Kharadia, Virabhai C.	Prof	562-1284	vkharad	AED	PHD	73	Illinois	1973
Collier, Ben	Assoc	562-1762	collier	ADFK	PHD	84	Purdue	1981
White, Jason T.	Inst	562-1764	jwhite	AGHM	ABD		Mo-Ks Cty	1999
Northwestern University	Evanston, IL		60208-2600	(847) 491-5140				nwu.edu
Department of Economics	Weinberg Col Arts & Sci		Fax=491-7001					Ethel McKay King
Sunquist, Eric	Dean	491-5697			PHD			1997
Mokyr, Joel	C-Pr	491-5693	j-mokyr		PHD	74	Yale	1974
Robert H. Strotz Professor of Arts & Sciences								
Alexis, Marcus	Prof	467-1318	m-alexis		PHD	59	Minnesota	1985
Daniel F. and Ada L. Rice Professor of Economics								
Altonji, Joseph G.	Prof	491-8218	altonji		PHD	81	Princeton	1990
Braeutigam, Ronald R.	Prof	491-8243	braeutigam		PHD	76	Stanford	1975
Harvey Kapnick Professor of Business Institutions & Transportation Center								
Christiano, Lawrence	Prof	491-8231	l-christiano		PHD	82	Columbia	
Coen, Robert M.	Prof	491-8207	rcoen		PHD	67	Nrthwstrn	1971
Dekel, Eddie	Prof	491-4414	dekel		PHD	86	Harvard	
Eichenbaum, Martin	Prof	491-8232	eich		PHD	81	Minnesota	1988
Gordon, Robert J.	Prof	491-5697	rjg		PHD	67	MIT	1973
Stanley G. Harris Professor of the Social Sciences								
Horowitz, Joel	Prof	491-8253			PHD	67	Cornell	2001
Kamien, Morton I.	Prof	491-5167	m-kamien		PHD	64	Purdue	1970
Manski, Charles F.	Prof	491-8223	cfmanski		PHD	73	MIT	1997
Board of Trustees Professor								
Matsuyama, Kiminori	Prof	491-8490	kmatsu		PHD	87	Harvard	
Matzkin, Rosa L.	Prof	491-8220	matzkin		PHD	86	Minnesota	
Household International, Inc. Professorship								
Meyer, Bruce	Prof	491-8226	bmeyer		PHD	87	MIT	1987
Mortensen, Dale T.	Prof	491-8230	d-mortensen		PHD	67	Car Mellon	1965
Ida C. Cook Professor of Consumer Economics								

Moses, Leon N.	Prof	491-8209	leon1		PHD	52	Harvard	1959
Panzar, John C.	Prof	491-8242	jpanzar		PHD	75	Stanford	1983
Louis W. Menk Professor								
Porter, Robert H.	Prof	491-3491	r-porter		PHD	81	Princeton	1987
William R. Kenan Jr. Professor								
Reiter, Stanley	Prof	491-3527	s-reiter		PHD	55	Chicago	
Charles E. and Emma H. Morrison Professor of Economics								
Rogerson, William P.	Prof	491-8484	wrogerson		PHD	81	Cal Tech	
Satterthwaite, Mark A.	Prof	491-5482	m-satterthwaite		PHD	73	Wisconsin	1973
Weisbrod, Burton A.	Prof	491-8704	b-weisbrod		PHD	58	Nrthwstrn	
John Evans Professor of Economic, Director,Ctr for Urban Affairs & Policy Rec								
Whinston, Michael D.	Prof	491-8260	mwhinston	DL	PHD	84	MIT	1996
Robert & Emily King Professor of Business Institutions								
Wolinsky, Asher	Prof	491-4415	wolinsky		PHD	80	Stanford	
Alfred W. Chase Professor in Business Administration								
Barlevy, Gadi	Asst	491-5395	barley		PHD	97	Harvard	1997
Ely, Jeffrey	Asst	491-8219	ely		PHD	96	Berkeley	1996
Ferrie, Joseph	Asst	491-8210	j-ferrie		PHD	92	Chicago	
Hu, Luojia	Asst	491-8224	luojiahu		PHD	97	Princeton	2000
Lam, Ricky	Asst	491-8233	rickylam		PHD	00	Yale	2000
Monge, Alexander	Asst	491-8234	a-mongel		PHD	99	Chicago	1999
Moriguchi, Chiaki	Asst	491-8237			PHD	98	Stanford	2001
Olszewski, Wojciech	Asst	491-4842			PHD	98	Princeton	2001
Pavan, Alejandro	Asst	491-8266			PHD	01	MIT	2001
Taber, Christopher	Asst	491-8229	ctaber		PHD	95	Chicago	1995
Zheng, Charles	Asst	491-8213	dzheng		PHD	99	Minnesota	1999
Savage, Ian P.	SLect	491-5140	ipsavage		PHD	84	Leeds	
Assistant Chairperson								

Northwestern State U of LA — Natchitoches, LA 71497 (318) 357-5161 — alpha.nsula.edu
Economics Faculty — Division of Business Fax=357-5990 — Penny O'Bryan

Worley, Joel	Dean	357-5162	worley	Mgt	PHD	83	Va Tech	
Elliott, Stephen	Prof	357-5700	elliott	GM	PHD	83	La Tech	
Jones, Robert C. III	Assoc	357-4581	jonesrc		PHD	91	UCLA	

Northwood University — Midland, MI 48640-2398 (517) — northwood.edu
Economics Faculty — Business Fax=
Did Not Respond--1999-2000 Listing

Chen, Catherine W.	Dean	837-4371		Lit	PHD	75	Minnesota	1974
Amin, R. John	H-Pr	837-4431		BDFM	PHD	78	Cincinnati	9-86
Haywood, Dale M.	Prof	837-4291			PHD	80	North Tx	
Luptowski, Thomas S.	Prof	837-4263			BS			
Matcheck, Dale C.	Asst	837-4256	matchek_d	Q	PHD	93	Cornell	1995

Norwich University — Northfield, VT 05663 (802) 485-2210 — norwich.edu
Dept of Economics & Finance — Div of Business & Mgt Fax=485-2087 — Sandra Kingsley
Did Not Respond Again--1997-98 Listing

Rotondi, Robert T.	C-Pr	485-2221	rrotondi	Atg	MBA	71	Fordham	9-77
Murtaugh, Frank M. Jr.	H-Ac	485-2216			PHD	81	Emory	1982
Hurd, John II	Prof	485-2217			PHD	69	Penn	1978
Mohaghegh, Mehdi	Assoc	485-2224			PHD	86	Clark	1986

University of Notre Dame — Notre Dame, IN 46556-0783 (219) 631-6335 — nd.edu
Department of Economics — Col of Arts & Sciences Fax=631-8809 — Ms. Juli Tate

Jensen, Richard A.	C-Pr	631-9382	rjensen	DL	PHD	80	Nrthwstrn	2000
Bartell, Ernest J.	Prof	631-6580	ernest.j.bartell	O	PHD	66	Princeton	1977
Dutt, Amitava K.	Prof	631-6335	amitava.k.dutt	EFOC	PHD	83	MIT	1988
Goulet, Denis A.	Prof	631-5250	denis.a.goulet	O	PHD	63	SaoPaulo	1979
Kim, Kwan S.	Prof	631-5179	kwan.s.kim	OF	PHD	67	Minnesota	1975
Leahy, William H.	Prof	631-7238	william.h.leahy	JR	PHD	66	Notre Dm	1963
Mirowski, Philip E.	Prof	631-7580	philip.e.mirowsk	B	PHD	79	Michigan	1990
Ros, Jaime	Prof	631-7009	jaime.ros	OE	PHD	78	Cambridge	1990
Skurski, Roger B.	Prof	631-7016	roger.b.skurski	P	PHD	70	Wisconsin	1974
Swartz, Thomas R.	Prof	631-7737	thomas.r.swartz	HA	PHD	65	Indiana	1965
Betson, David M.	Assoc	631-5068	david.m.betson	HI	PHD	80	Wisconsin	1979
Bonello, Frank J.	Assoc	631-7229	frank.j.bonello	EA	PHD	68	Mich St	1968
Ghilarducci, Teresa	Assoc	631-7581	teresa.ghilarduc	J	PHD	84	Berkeley	1983
Lee, Byung	Assoc	631-6837	byungjoo.lee	CD	PHD	88	Wisconsin	1996
Marsh, Lawrence C.	Assoc	631-6210	lawrence.c.marsh	CD	PHD	76	Mich St	1975
Mui, Vai-Lam	Assoc	631-7570	vailam.mui.1	DL	PHD	92	Berkeley	1999
Rakowski, James J.	Assoc	631-6644	james.j.rakowski	DF	PHD	68	Minnesota	1967
Rath, Kali P.	Assoc	631-6954	kali.p.rath	CD	PHD	92	J Hopkins	1990
Ruccio, David F.	Assoc	631-6434	david.f.ruccio	BO	PHD	84	Mass	1982
Sent, Esther-Mirjam	Assoc	631-6979	esther-mirjamsen	BE	PHD	94	Stanford	1994
Warlick, Jennifer L.	Assoc	631-7531	jennifer.l.warli	HI	PHD	79	Wisconsin	1981
Wolfson, Martin H.	Assoc	631-8093	martin.h.wolfson	EG	PHD	84	American	1990

University of Notre Dame Notre Dame, IN 46556-0399 (219) 631-6370 nd.edu
Dept of Finance & Bus Econ College of Business Fax=631-5255 Sharon Duram

Woo, Carolyn Y.	Dean	631-7236	carolyn.y.woo.5	Mgt	PHD	79	Purdue	1997
Cosimano, Thomas	Prof	631-5178	thomas.f.cos+.1	EF	PHD	79	SUNY-Buf	1987
Gresik, Thomas A.	Prof	631-9341	thomas.a.gr+.1	D	PHD	87	Penn	2000
Keating, Barry P.	Prof	631-9127	barry.p.kea+.1	R	PHD	74	Notre Dm	1978
Jesse H. Jones Professor								
Sheehan, Richard G.	Prof	631-5212	richard.g.s+.1	R	PHD	78	Boston C	1987
Bergstrand, Jeffrey	Assoc	631-6761	jeffrey.h.b+.1	EF	PHD	81	Wisconsin	1986
Trubac, Edward R.	Assoc	631-6404	edward.r.t+.1	R	PHD	65	Syracuse	1971
Saito, Mika	Asst	631-6139	mika.saito.3	F	PHD	00	Cornell	2000
Zambrano, Eduardo	Asst	631-4597	eduardo.zam+.1	D	PHD	99	Cornell	1999

Oakland University Rochester, MI 48309-4401 (248) 370-3523 oakland.edu
Department of Economics School of Business Adm Fax=370-4275 Sally Galloway 370-3283

Gardner, John C.	Dean	370-3286	jcgard	Atg	PHD	83	Mich St	8-96
Stano, Miron	C-Pr	370-3291	stano	IL	PHD	71	Cornell	1977
Esposito, Louis	Prof	370-4975	esposito	IL	PHD	68	Boston C	1999
Fosu, Augustin K.	Prof	370-3523	fosu	JOC	PHD	79	Nrthwstrn	1979
Izraeli, Oded	Prof	370-3524	izraeli	RHA	PHD	73	Chicago	1978
Murphy, Kevin J.	Prof	370-3294	murphy	JC	PHD	81	Mich St	1985
Sahu, Anandi P.	Prof	370-3537	sahu	EG	PHD	85	Wash U	1985
Coppin, Addington M.	Assoc	370-3541	coppin	FO	PHD	87	Illinois	1989
Folland, Sherman T.	Assoc	370-4086	folland	IB	PHD	74	Iowa	1986
Tracy, Ronald L.	Assoc	370-3514	tracy	CE	PHD	75	Mich St	1983
Kalist, David E.	Asst	370-2505	kalist	IJ	PHD	01	Wayne St	2001
Mukherji, Nivedita	Asst	370-4087	mukherji	EF	PHD	92	Va Tech	1992

Oberlin College Oberlin, OH 44074-1095 (216) 775-8483 oberlin.edu
Department of Economics Col of Arts & Sciences Fax=775-6978 Terri D. Pleska

Craig, Barbara	C-Pr	775-8766	barbara.craig	CFQ	PHD	88	Minnesota	1989
Cleeton, David L.	Prof	775-8449	david.cleeton	DGIM	PHD	80	Wash U	1980
Fernandez, Luis	Prof	775-8486	luis.fernandez	CDGL	PHD	83	Berkeley	1980
Hess, Gregory	Prof	775-8592	gregory.hess	E	PHD	89	J Hopkins	1993
Kasper, Hirshel	Prof	775-8489	hirshel.kasper	DJ	PHD	63	Minnesota	1963
Piron, Robert	Prof	775-8485	robert.piron	BD	PHD	66	Nrthwstrn	1961
Zinser, James E.	Prof	775-8484	james.zinser	KLO	PHD	67	Oregon	1967
Gaudin, Sylvestre	Asst	775-6716	sylvestre.gaudin	HQ	PHD	99	Rice	2001

Occidental College Los Angeles, CA 90041-3314 (323) 259-2775
Economics Faculty Department of Economics Fax=341-4990 Nancy Grubb

Studenmund, A. H.	C-Pr	259-2776		C	PHD	70	Cornell	1970
Richard W. Millar Professor of Economics & Director of Institutional Planning								
Halstead, James F.	Prof	259-2778		A	PHD	72	Stanford	1977
Moore, Robert L.	Prof	259-2779		J	PHD	77	Harvard	1978
Whitney, James D.	Prof	259-2750		F	PHD	83	Wisconsin	1982
Hirschfeld, Mary L.	Assoc	259-2932		N	PHD	89	Harvard	1988
Secondi, Giorgio	Asst	259-2582		O	PHD	96	Michigan	1998

Oglethorpe University Atlanta, GA 30319 (404) facstaff.oglethorpe.edu
Department of Economics Div Economics & Bus Adm Fax=364-8500

Hetherington, Bruce W.	C-Pr	364-8348	bhetherington	NE	PHD	82	Va Tech	1980
Shropshire, William O.	Prof	364-8347	wshropshire	EO	PHD	63	Duke	1979
Callaway Professor of Economics								
Tucker, Dean	Prof	364-8352	dtucker	HMQ	PHD	79	Mich St	1-88
Rikard Chaired Professor								
Copeland, Cassandra	Asst	364-8464	ccopeland		PHD		Auburn	2000
Hunger, David	Asst	364-3464	dhunger	LDC	PHD	98	Oregon	1993

Ohio University Athens, OH 45701-2979 (740) 593-2040 ohiou.edu
Department of Economics Col of Arts & Sciences Fax=593-0181

Palmer, Jan S.	C-Ac	593-2032		A	PHD	74	Mich St	1979
Adie, Douglas K.	Prof	260-2033		BGM	PHD	68	Chicago	1968
Boyd, Roy G.	Prof	593-2050		QH	PHD	81	Duke	1984
Doroodian, Khosrow	Prof	593-2046		QAF	PHD	81	Oregon	1982
Gallaway, Lowell	Prof	593-2036			PHD	59	Ohio St	1967
Distinguished Professor								
Ghazalah, Ismail A.	Prof	593-2034		DFHI	PHD	69	Berkeley	1969
Jung, Chulho	Prof	593-2041		CDFQ	PHD	89	Michigan	1989
Klingaman, David C.	Prof	593-2047		DE	PHD	67	Virginia	1967
Koshal, Rajindar K.	Prof	593-2038		TACQ	PHD	68	Rochester	1970
Rossiter, Rosemary D.	Prof	593-2043			PHD	80	Wi-Milwa	1983
Caporale, Tony	Assoc	593-2051			PHD	92	GeoMason	1992
Winter, Harold	Assoc	593-2048		KL	PHD	90	Rochester	1992
Caporale, Barbara	Asst	593-2049		EGN	PHD	94	GeoMason	1994
Lacombe, Donald J.	Asst	593-2040			PHD	00	Fla St	2001
Paxton, Julia	Asst	593-2042			PHD	96	Ohio St	2000
Shambora, William E.	Asst	593-1845			PHD	00	Kentucky	9-00

Ohio Northern University Ada, OH 45810 (419) 772-2082 onu.edu
Department of Economics Col of Business Admin Fax=772-1932 Diane Thede 772-2082
Did Not Respond--1999-2000 Listing

Maris, Terry L.	Dean	772-2070	t-maris	Mgt	PHD	79	Nebraska	1990
Goldberg, Roger H.	Prof	772-2076	r-goldberg		PHD	81	Indiana	1969
Associate Vice President Academic Affairs								
Meininger, Richard P.	Prof	772-2083	r-meininger		PHD	87	Ohio U	1973
Associate Dean								
Meenakshi, Rishi	Assoc	772-2072	m-rishi		PHD	93	Mass	1993
Kloft, Leonard	Asst	772-2080	l-kloft		PHD	95	Iowa	1995

Ohio State University Columbus, OH 43210-1172 (614) 292-6701 osu.edu
Department of Economics Col of Social & Beh Sci Fax=
Homepage: www.econ.ohio-state.edu

Hashimoto, Masanori	C-Pr	292-4196	hashimoto.1	J	PHD	71	Columbia	1987
Cecchetti, Stephen G.	Prof	292-9339	cecchetti.1	E	PHD	82	Berkeley	1991
Cosslett, Stephen R.	Prof	292-4106	cosslett.1		PHD	79	Berkeley	1987
Dunn, Lucia	Prof	292-8071	dunn.4	J	PHD	74	Berkeley	1987
Evans, Paul D.	Prof	292-0072	evans.21	E	PHD	76	Chicago	1987
Fleisher, Belton M.	Prof	292-6429	fleisher.1	J	PHD	61	Stanford	1965
Gonzalez-Vega, Claudio	Prof	292-0387	gonzalez.4	O	PHD	76	Stanford	
Haurin, Donald R.	Prof	292-8448	haurin.2	R	PHD	78	Chicago	1975
Associate Dean								
Ichiishi, Tatsuro	Prof	292-0762	ichiishi.1	C	PHD	74	Berkeley	1987
Kagel, John H.	Prof	292-4812	kagel.r	L	PHD	70	Purdue	1999
University Chaired Professor								
Lee, Lung-fei	Prof	292-5508	lee.1777	C	PHD	77	Rochester	1999
University Chaired Professor								
Levin, Dan	Prof	688-4239	levin.36	MI	PHD	82	MIT	1995
Mark, Nelson C.	Prof	192-0413	mark.1	FG	PHD	83	Chicago	1983
Marvel, Howard P.	Prof	422-1020	marvel.2	L	PHD	75	Chicago	1973
Honors Director								
McCafferty, Stephen A.	Prof	292-7122	mccafferty.1	EF	PHD	77	Brown	1982
McCulloch, J. Huston	Prof	292-0382	mcculloch.2	E	PHD	73	Chicago	1979
Miyazaki, Hajime	Prof	292-7939	miyazaki.1	LJ	PHD	77	Berkeley	1984
Director of Graduate Studies								
Olsen, Randall J.	Prof	442-7348	olsen.6	J	PHD	77	Chicago	1982
Director Center for Human Resource Research								
Ray, Edward J.	Prof	292-5881	ray.1	F	PHD	71	Stanford	1970
Senior Vice Provost								
Reagan, Patricia B.	Prof	292-0192	reagan.3	LJ	PHD	80	MIT	1989
Schmeidler, David	Prof	292-1148	schmeidler.1		PHD	69	Hebrew	1987
Steckel, Richard H.	Prof	422-5008	steckel.1	N	PHD	77	Chicago	1977
Aly, Hassan	Assoc	292-9133	aly.1		PHD	86	S Illinois	1989
Baack, Bennett D.	Assoc	292-2489	baack.1	N	PHD	72	U Wash	1988
Fisher, Eric O.	Assoc	292-2009	fisher.244	F	PHD	85	Berkeley	1993
Lam, Pok-sang	Assoc	292-6567	lam.1	E	PHD	86	Harvard	1985
Mumy, Gene E.	Assoc	292-0376	mumy.1	D	PHD	74	J Hopkins	1978
Director of Undergraduate Studies								
Ogaki, Masao	Assoc	292-5842	ogaki.1	E	PHD	88	Chicago	1994
Peck, James D.	Assoc	292-0182	peck.33	D	PHD	85	Penn	1992
Sharma, V. V.	Assoc	292-9108	sharma.3		PHD	68	Illinois	1970
Weinberg, Bruce	Assoc	292-5642	weinberg.27	J	PHD	96	Chicago	1996
Kaboski, Joseph	Asst	292-5588		EF	PHD	01	Chicago	2001
Light, Audrey	Asst	292-0493	light.20	J	PHD	87	UCLA	1995
Ye, Lixin	Asst	292-6883		CD	PHD	01	Stanford	2001
Zhang, Qiang	Asst	292-4094	zhang.100	EF	PHD	98	Ohio St	1998
Gill, Leroy	Lect	292-8863						
Marshall, Kathryn G.	Lect	292-8863	marshall.220	HQ	PHD	90	Berkeley	
McCulloch, Laurence	Lect	292-8863	mcculloch.1					
Mirzaie, Ida	Lect	292-6110	mirazie.1		PHD	99	Wisconsin	2000
Osman, Alan	Lect	292-2670	osman.1					
Parsons, Deborah	Lect	292-8863	parsons.5					

Ohio Wesleyan University Delaware, OH 43015-2370 (740) 368-3535 cc.owu.edu
Economics Faculty Department of Economics Fax=368-3551 Patti Krebehenne

Harvey, Joann P.	C-Pr	368-3541	jpharvey	Atg	MBA	82	Ohio St	1981
Gharrity, Norman J.	Prof	368-3538	njgharri		PHD	66	J Hopkins	1962
Gitter, Robert J.	Prof	368-3536	rjgitter		PHD	78	Wisconsin	1976
Simon, Alice E.	Prof	368-3540	aesimon		PHD	84	Ohio St	1985
Rahmon, Saif	Asst	368-3549	msrahmon		PHD	98	N Carol	2000
Yazar, Julide	Asst	368-3538	jjyazar		PHD		Ohio St	1999

University of Oklahoma Norman, OK 73019-2103 (405) 325-2861 ou.edu
Department of Economics Col of Arts & Sciences Fax=325-5842 Tami Kinsey
Homepage: ou.edu/cas/econ

Dunne, Timothy	C-Pr	325-2861		DLJ	PHD	87	Penn St	1992
Dauffenbach, Robert C.	Prof	744-5125		J	PHD	73	Illinois	
Grier, Kevin B.	Prof	325-3748		E	PHD	84	Wash U	1999
Hartigan, James C.	Prof	325-2358		FL	PHD	79	Duke	1988
Holmes, Alexander B.	Prof			RD	PHD	74	SUNY-Bin	
Kondonassis, Alexander J.	Prof	325-5234		NO	PHD	61	Indiana	1979
David Ross Boyd Professor of Economics								
Reed, Robert	Prof	325-2861		JD	PHD	85	Nrthwstrn	1992
Clark, William M.	Assoc			O	PHD	81	Virginia	1977
Ju, Jiandong	Assoc	325-2861		D	PHD	95	Penn St	1995
Chakraborty, Indranil	Asst	325-5846			PHD	97	Illinois	1999
Grier, Robin	Asst	325-0581		O	PHD	95	GeoMason	1999
Kosmopoulou, Georgia	Asst	325-2861		D	PHD	96	Illinois	1997
Okediji, Tade	Asst	325-4353		O	PHD	96	Oklahoma	1997
Rogers, Cynthia	Asst	325-2861		JR	PHD	94	Pittsburgh	1997
Smallwood, Aaron	Asst	325-2861			PHD	01	Fla St	2001
Sutter, Dan	Asst	325-5448		H	PHD	93	GeoMason	1995

Oklahoma Baptist University Shawnee, OK 74804-2590 (405) 878-3254 mail.okbu.edu
Economics Faculty Dickinson Sch Business Fax=878-3253
phone 878-3254

Reeder, Danny B.	Deam	878-3254	dan_reeder		PHD	93	Okla St	8-91
Walker, G. Craig	Assoc	Ext 3272		ACFG	PHD	96	So Meth	8-00

Oklahoma Christian Univ Oklahoma Cy OK 73136-1100 (405) 425-5560 oc.edu
Economics Faculty College of Business Fax=425-5574 Wanda Neel

Lewis, Phillip V.	Dean	425-5561		Mgt	EDD	70	Houston	7-99
Miller, Ken	C	425-5569		Fnce				

Oklahoma City University Oklahoma City OK 73106-1493 (405) 521-5357 okcu.edu
Economics Faculty Meinders Sch Business Fax=521-5098 Ms. Jean Kobs
Homepage: www.okcu.edu/economics

Ward, Bart H.	Dean	521-5276	bward	Atg	PHD	73	Nrthwstrn	1-00
Carter, Thomas J.	C-Ac	521-5418	tcarter	FJ	PHD	87	Wisconsin	1994
Alli, Ali M.	Prof	521-5132	aalli	CIP	PHD	68	Okla St	1985
Moini, Mostafa	Prof	521-5357	mmoini		PHD	70	Oklahoma	1985
May, David	Assoc	521-5817	dlmay	QC	PHD	96	Fla St	1996
Shandiz, Mohmood	Assoc	521-5130	mshandiz		PHD	81	Okla St	1985
Associate Dean								
Willner, Jonathan	Assoc	521-5133	jwillner	FO	PHD	94	Purdue	1995
Simmons, Kevin	Asst	521-5357	ksimmons		PHD	99	Tx Tech	1999

Oklahoma State University Stillwater, OK 74078-4011 (405) 744-5195 okstate.edu
Dept Econ & Legal Sds in Bus Col of Business Admin Fax=744-5180 Ruby Ladd
Homepage: www2.bus.okstate.edu/ecls/dept/index.html

Lumpkin, James R.	Dean	744-5064	jrlcba	Mktg	PHD	80	Arkansas	2000
Willett, Keith D.	H-Pr	744-5195	kwillet	Q	PHD	82	New Mex	9-81
Adkins, Lee C.	Prof	744-8637	ladkins	C	PHD	88	LSU	1988
Amos, Orley M. Jr.	Prof	744-8657	amos	R	PHD	79	Iowa St	1979
Applegate, Michael J.	Prof	744-8656	mja1701	O	PHD	73	Iowa St	1974
Fain, James R.	Prof	744-8651	jrfain	J	PHD	86	Purdue	1986
Jadlow, Joseph M. Jr.	Prof	744-5195	jad1942	L	PHD	70	Virginia	1968
Lage, Gerald M.	Prof	744-5064	glage	FD	PHD	67	Minnesota	1966
Regents Service Professor; Associate Dean for Graduate Studies & Research								
Moomaw, Ronald L.	Prof	744-7359	rmoomaw	R	PHD	76	Princeton	1972
Regents Professor and CBA Associates Chair								
Olson, Kent W.	Prof	744-8655	kolson	HI	PHD	69	Oregon	1974
Rickman, Dan S.	Prof	744-8662	rdan	RC	PHD	87	Wyoming	1996
OG&E Chair in Regional Economic Analysis								
Steindl, Frank G.	Prof	744-5091	steindl	E	PHD	63	Iowa	1962
Regents' Professor and Ardmore Chair								
Currier, Kevin M.	Assoc	744-8658	kmcur	C	PHD	85	SUNY-Alb	1984
Gade, Mary N.	Assoc	744-8652	mgade	H	PHD	86	Mich St	1986
Price, Edward O. III	Assoc	744-7669	edprice	B	PHD	80	Tx A&M	1979
Savvides, Andreas	Assoc	744-5110	asavvid	FO	PHD	83	Florida	1985

Old Dominion University Norfolk, VA 23529-0221 (757) 683-3567 odu.edu
Department of Economics Col of Bus & Pub Admin Fax=683-5639 Vicky Curtis

Agarwal, Vinod	C-Pr	683-3526	jagarwal		PHD	86	Ca-SnBarb	
Graduate Program Director								
Koch, James V.	Prof	683-3458			PHD	68	Nrthwstrn	1990

Talley, Wayne K.	Prof	683-3534	wtalley		PHD	72	Kentucky	1972
Eminent Professor								
Yochum, Gilbert R.	Prof	683-3535	gyochum		PHD	74	W Virginia	1975
Anderson, Eric E.	Assoc	683-3512	eanderson		PHD	84	U Wash	1984
Colburn, Christopher B.	Assoc	683-4341	ccolburn	R	PHD	88	Tx A&M	1987
Schwarz-Miller, Ann V.	Assoc	683-3572	asmiller	DJKM	PHD	74	Nrthwstrn	1978
Turner, Charlie G.	Assoc	683-3576	cgturner		PHD	81	Harvard	1984
Bezmen, Trisha	Asst	683-3571	tbezmen	F	PHD	98	Georgia	1999
Filer, Larry	Asst		lfiler		PHD	99	Kentucky	1999
Selover, David D.	Asst	683-3541	dselover	F	PHD	91	Ca-SnDgo	1999
Carter, Melanie	Inst	683-3548	mcarter		MA		Old Dom	1997
Hofler, Martha	Inst	683-3543	mhofler	F	MA		Old Dom	
Director, CEE								

Olivet College — Olivet, MI 49076 (616) 749-7650 — olivetcollege.edu
Economics Faculty — Dept of Bus Adm & Econ Fax=749-7178

Hubbel, Michael R.	C-Pr	749-7626	mhubbel		MBA	94	Insurance	1985
Homer, John S.	Prof	749-7662	jhomer		PHD	91	Hawaii	1979
Stover, Stewart	Asst	749-7663	sstover		MBA			1999

Olivet Nazarene University — Bourbonnais, IL 60914-2271 (815) 939-5133 — olivet.edu
Economics Faculty — Business Department Fax=928-5454 — Mindy Nelson
Homepage: business.olivet.edu

Rewerts, Glen	C-Pr	939-5133	grewerts	K	JD	87	S Illinois	1993
Koch, Paul R.	Prof	939-5100	pkoch	AFHP	EDD	94	Illin St	1992

University of Oregon — Eugene, OR 97403-1285 (541) 346-6027 — oregon.uoregon.edu
Department of Economics — Col of Arts & Sciences Fax=346-1243 — Linda M. Steller 346-1263

Stone, Joe A.	Dean	346-4663	jstone	JFE	PHD	77	Mich St	1970
W. E. Miner Professor of Economics								
Kolpin, Van W.	C-Pr	346-3011	vkolpin	C	PHD	86	Iowa	1986
Cameron, Trudy A.	Prof	346-6027		OQ	PHD	82	Princeton	D-01
Drazen, Allen	Prof	405-3477			PHD	76	MIT	1990
on leave								
Ellis, Christopher J.	Prof	346-4657	cjellis	E	PHD	83	Warwick	1983
Evans, George	Prof	346-6027	gevans	E	PHD	80	Berkeley	1994
John B. Hamacher Professor of Economics								
Gray, Jo Anna	Prof	346-4667	jgray	E	PHD	76	Chicago	1989
Haynes, Stephen E.	Prof	346-4665	shaynes	FE	PHD	76	Ca-SnBarb	1978
Singell, Larry D. Jr.	Prof	346-4672	lsingell	J	PHD	88	Ca-SnBarb	1988
Wilson, Wesley W.	Prof	346-4690	wwilson	CD	PHD	86	Wash St	1989
Blonigen, Bruce A.	Assoc	346-4680	bruceb	FL	PHD	95	Ca-Davis	1995
Harbaugh, William T.	Assoc	346-1244	harbaugh	HQ	PHD	95	Wisconsin	1995
Van den Nouweland, Anne	Assoc	346-1267	annev	CL	PHD	93	Tilburg	1996
Ziliak, James P.	Assoc	346-4681	jziliak	J	PHD	93	Indiana	1993
Chakraborty, Shakha	Asst	346-6027		EO	PHD	99	UCLA	1999
Davies, Ronald B.	Asst	346-6027		FL	PHD	99	Penn St	1999
Waddell, Glen	Asst	346-1259	gwadell	FL	PHD	00	Purdue	2001

Oregon State University — Corvallis, OR 97331-3612 (541) 737-2321 — ccmail.orst.edu
Department of Economics — College of Liberal Arts Fax=737-5917 — Eric Dickey
email @1=ucs.orst.edu

Schaffer, Kay	Dean	737-4580			PHD	72	Ohio St	9-94
Tremblay, Victor J.	C-Pr	737-2321	v.tremblay	DLC	PHD	83	Wash St	9-90
Fare, Rolf	Prof	737-8184	rolf.fare	CD	DOC	76	Lund	9-98
Farrell, John P.	Prof	737-1479	john.p.farrell	BO	PHD	73	Wisconsin	9-72
Grosskopf, Shawna	Prof	737-8185	shawna.grosskopf	CHJ	PHD	77	Syracuse	9-98
McMullen, B. Starr	Prof	737-1480	s.mcmullen	LE	PHD	79	Berkeley	9-80
Fraundorf, Martha	Assoc	737-1477	martha.n.frau+	J	PHD	76	Cornell	9-76
Kerkvliet, Joe R.	Assoc	737-1482	kerkvlij@1	L	PHD	86	Wyoming	9-88
Martins, Carlos	Assoc	737-1476	carlos.martins	DCL	PHD	92	Tennessee	9-92
Tremblay, Carol	Assoc	737-1468	carol.h.tremblay	CJ	PHD	84	Wash St	9-92
McGough, Bruce	Asst	737-1429	bruce.mcgough	ED	PHD	00	Oregon	9-00
Stivers, Andrew	Asst	737-2321	andrew.stivers	DL	PHD	01	Tx-Austin	9-01
Waldkirch, Andreas	Asst	737-2371	andreas.wald+	FD	PHD	01	Boston C	9-01

Otterbein College — Westerville, OH 43081 (614) 823-1310 — otterbein.edu
Economics Faculty — Dept Bus, Atg & Econ Fax=898-1014 — Ms. Donna bowers
Homepage: ocfrontpage.otterbein.edu/businessdept/home.htm

Smith, Charles G.	C-Pr	823-1892	csmith	Mgt	PHD	89	Ohio St	2000
Aristotelous, Kyriacos	Assoc	823-1611	karistotelous	EFO	PHD	93	Ohio St	1993
Prindle, Allen M.	Assoc	823-1481	amprindle	DQ	PHD	77	Penn St	1988
Smith, Stephanie	Assoc	823-1310	sasmith	G	PHD	95	Va Comm	2001

Pace University New York, NY 10038-1502 (212) 346-1469 pace.edu
Economics Department Dyson Col of Arts & Sci Fax=346-1467 Margaret Pawluszko

Masiello, Charles	Dean	346-1710		Math	PHD	68	CUNY	
Lott, Elizabeth J.	C-Ac	346-1469		ACNR	PHD		Columbia	1990
Bynoe, Ann	Assoc	346-1466			PHD	79	NYU	1997
Colman, Gregory	Assoc	346-1102			PHD			2001
Shostya, Anna	Assoc	346-1469			MA			
Weinstock, Maek	Assoc	346-1468			MA			

University of the Pacific Stockton, CA 95211 (209) 946-2258 uop.edu
Department of Economics College of the Pacific Fax=946-2577 Suzanne B. Westphal
Homepage: www1.ucp.edu/ccp/economics

Benedetti, Robert R.	Dean	946-2141	rbenedet	PolS	PHD	75		
Herrin, William E.	C-Ac	946-2259	bherrin	RC	PHD	85	SUNY-Bin	1985
Flynn, Dennis O.	Prof	946-2913	doflynn	DNO	PHD	77	Utah	1979
Keefe, David E.	Assoc	946-2257	dkeefe	FT	PHD	80	Berkeley	1978
Meyer, Peter J.	Assoc	946-2906	pmeyer	BJL	PHD	79	Berkeley	1985
OrdovenskyStaniel, J. Farley	Assoc	946-2910	jfarley	HJ	PHD	92	Duke	1993
Warner, Lori	Assoc	946-2907	lwarner	ENQ	PHD	86	Utah	1987
Dennis, Benjamin	Asst	946-2817	bdennis	EO	PHD	96	Harvard	1996
King, Sharmila	Asst	946-2293	sking	EF	PHD	01	Ca-Davis	2001

Pacific Lutheran University Tacoma, WA 98447-0003 (253) 535-7598 plu.edu
Department of Economics Div of Social Sciences Fax=535-8305 Ms. Peggy Jobe
Did Not Respond--1999-2000 Listing

Kelleher, Ann	Dean			PolS	PHD			
Reiman, Mark A.	C-Ac	535-8875	reimanma	FPQ	PHD	88	U Wash	1988
Brue, Stanley L.	Prof	535-7634		ABJ	PHD	71	Nebraska	1971
Peterson, Norris A.	Prof	535-7645	petersna	J	PHD	81	Minnesota	1981
Vinje, David L.	Prof	535-7144	vinjedl	O	PHD	64	Wisconsin	1970
Wentworth, Donald R.	Prof	535-7644	wentwodr	A	PHD	65	Minnesota	1972
Jensen, Robert J.	Assoc	535-7594	jensenrj		MA	67	Nebraska	1968
Nugent, Rachel A.	Asst	535-7684	nugentra	DFQH	PHD	94	Geo Wash	1991
Travis, Karen M.	Asst	535-7684	traviskm	I	PHD	95	U Wash	1999

Pacific Union College Angwin, CA 94508-9797 (707) 965-6238 puc.edu
Economics Faculty Dept of Bus Adm & Econ Fax=965-6237

Voth, Richard T.	C-Pr	965-6525	rvoth	Mgt	PHD	73	Ariz St	1968
Hardcastle, Rodney	Prof	965-6530	rhardcastle		MBA	89	Golden Gt	1989
Neergaard, Keith	Prof	965-6523	kneergaa		PHD	94	Ca-Irvine	1988
Taylor, Lary	Assoc	965-6238	ltaylor		MBA	76	Maryland	1978

University of Pennsylvania Philadelphia, PA 19104-6297 (215) 898-7701 econ.sas.upenn.edu
Department of Economics Sch of Arts & Sciences Fax=573-2057
Did Not Respond Again--1997-98 Listing; email: @1=penndrls.upenn.edu

Stevens, Rosemary	Dean	898-2327						
Rosenzweig, Mark R.	C-Pr	898-7408		OJL	PHD	73	Columbia	1990
email markr@markr2.pop.upenn.edu								
Adams, F. Gerard	Prof	898-4477	adams		PHD	56	Michigan	1961
Director, Economic Research Unit								
Ando, Albert K.	Prof	898-7712	aando		PHD	59	Car Mellon	1963
Behrman, Jere R.	Prof	898-7712	jbehrman	OJL	PHD	66	MIT	1965
William R. Kenan Jr. Professor of Economics								
Bloomfield, Arthur I.	Emer				PHD	42	Chicago	1958
Cass, David	Prof	898-5735	dcass	DCG	PHD	65	Stanford	1974
Paul F. & E. Warren Shafer Miller Professor of Economics								
Diebold, Francis X.	Prof	898-1507	diebold		PHD	86	Penn	1989
Undergraduate Chair								
Ethier, Wilfred J.	Prof	898-5105	ethier	F	PHD	70	Rochester	1969
Hess, Arleigh P. Jr.	Emer	898-8473	ahess		PHD	49	Penn	1949
Associate Undergraduate Chair for Advising								
Heston, Alan W.	Prof	898-8485	aheston		PHD	62	Yale	
Inman, Robert R.	Prof	898-8299	inman@wharton		PHD	72	Harvard	
Kehoe, Patrick J.	Prof	898-7409	pkehoe	POF	PHD	86	Harvard	1992
Ronald S. Lauder Term Associate Professor of Economics								
Kihlstrom, Richard E.	Prof	898-4378	kihlstro@wharton		PHD	64	Minnesota	
Miller-Friedman Professor of Finance & Professor of Economics								
Klein, Lawrence R.	Emer	898-7713	lrk		PHD	44	MIT	1958
Benjamin Franklin Professor of Economics & Finance								
Levine, Herbert S.	Prof	898-7706	hlevine	P	PHD	61	Harvard	1960
Mailath, George J.	Prof	898-7908	gmailath	CDH	PHD	85	Princeton	1985
Graduate Chair								
Mansfield, Edwin	Prof	898-7788			PHD	55	Duke	1963
Mariano, Roberto S.	Prof	898-6771	mariano		PHD	70	Stanford	1971
Matthews, Steven A.	Prof	898-7701			PHD	78	Cal Tech	1997
Phillips, Almarin	Emer	896-5017	phillipa		PHD	53	Harvard	1953

Postlewaite, Andrew W.	Prof	898-7350	apostlew	DH	PHD	74	Nrthwstrn	9-80
Pacific Term Professor in the Social Studies								
Rob, Rafael	Prof	898-6775	rrob		PHD	81	UCLA	1984
Summers, Robert	Emer	898-7717			PHD	56	Stanford	1959
Wolpin, Kenneth I.	Prof	898-7708	wolpink		PHD	74	CUNY	1995
Wright, Randall	Prof	898-7194	rwright	JE	PHD	86	Minnesota	1987
Atkeson, Andrew G.	Asst	898-6691	atkeson	PF	PHD	88	Stanford	1993
Chang, Yongsung	Asst	898-7701			PHD	97	Rochester	1997
Corradi, Valentina	Asst	898-1505	corradi		PHD	94	Ca-SnDgo	1994
Cres, Herve	Asst	898-6260	hres		PHD	94	Geneva	1994
Kajii, Atsushi	Asst	898-1875	akajii	G	PHD	91	Harvard	1991
Matsui, Akihiko	Asst	898-7749	amatsui	CDE	PHD	90	Nrthwstrn	1990
William P. Carey Term Assistant Professor of Economics								
Perli, Roberto	Asst	898-1504	perlir	E	PHD	95	NYU	1995
Persico, Nicola	Asst	898-7701			PHD	96	Nrthwstrn	1997
Rios-Rull, Jose-Victor	Asst	898-7767		O	PHD	90	Minnesota	1990
Simon Kuznets Term Assistant Profess of Econ; email vr0j@anaga.sas.upenn.edu								
Todd, Petra	Asst	898-4084	ptodd		PHD	96	Chicago	1996
Zhou, Ruilin	Asst	898-6774	ruilin	FDE	PHD	93	Pittsburgh	1993

Penn State University	Univ Park, PA		16802-3306 (814) 865-1456					psu.edu
Department of Economics	College of Liberal Arts		Fax=863-4775		Janette Moore/Naomi McNulty			
Fox, Thomas G.	H-Pr$	863-2650	tgf	A	PHD	66	Syracuse	1966
Marshall, Robert C.	H-Pr	865-1456	rcm10		PHD	83	Ca-SnDgo	1995
on sabbatical 7/1/01 to 6/30/02								
Bierens, Herman	Prof	865-4921	hbierens		PHD	80	Amsterdm	1996
Bond, Eric W.	Prof	863-0315	ewb1	F	PHD	79	Rochester	1981
Chatterjee, Kalyan	Prof	865-6050	kchatterjee	D	PHD	79	Harvard	1998
Jordan, James S.	Prof	865-2201	jxj13	E	PHD	75	Nrthwstrn	1998
Klein, Philip A.	Prof	865-5781	pak11	E	PHD	58	Berkeley	1955
Krishna, Kala	Prof	865-1106	kmk4	F	PHD	84	Princeton	1993
Krishna, Vijay	Prof	863-8543	vxk5	D	PHD	83	Princeton	1993
Lombra, Raymond E.	Prof	865-5452	rl3	E	PHD	71	Penn St	1969
Nelson, Jon P.	Prof	865-8871	jpn	QD	PHD	70	Wisconsin	1969
Ravikumar, B.	Prof	865-8929	ravikumar		PHD	89	Iowa	2000
Roberts, Bee-Yan	Prof	863-1996	byr	O	PHD	80	Wisconsin	1981
Roberts, Mark J.	Prof	863-1535	m7r	D	PHD	80	Wisconsin	1980
Wallace, Neil	Prof	863-3805	neilw	E	PHD	64	Chicago	1997
Coulson, N. Edward	Assoc	863-0625	fyj	R	PHD	83	Ca-SnDgo	1984
Ickes, Barry W.	Assoc	863-2652	bwickes	P	PHD	84	Berkeley	1983
Laing, Derek	Assoc	863-2656	dxl8	E	PHD	89	Essex	1989
Shapiro, David	Assoc	863-1533	dshapiro	J	PHD	72	Princeton	1980
Sjostrom, J. Tomas	Assoc	863-1295	jts10	E	PHD	91	Rochester	1998
Terza, Joseph V.	Assoc	863-3743	jvt	C	PHD	81	Pittsburgh	1986
Esteban, Susanna	Asst	865-1456			PHD	99	Rochester	2001
Guner, Nezih	Asst	865-1456			PHD	99	Rochester	2001
Li, Jenny	Asst	865-5452	li@math	C	PHD	93	Cornell	1997
Ventura, Gustavo	Asst	865-1456			PHD	97	Illinois	2001

Penn State Univ - Erie	Erie, PA		16563-1400 (814) 898-6107					psu.edu
School of Business	Behrend College		Fax=898-6223					
Did Not Respond--1999-2000 Listing								
Magenau, John M. III	D-Ac	898-6173	owc	JM	PHD	88	SUNY-Buf	1985
Weller, Barry R.	H-Ac	898-6326	brw	ACE	PHD	71	Penn St	1971
Fizel, John L.	Prof	898-6266	fzk	ALC	PHD	81	Mich St	1985
Kurre, James A.	Assoc	898-6266	k12	RA	PHD	82	Penn St	1977
Louie, Kenneth K. T.	Assoc	898-6265	obr	AFJ	PHD	87	Penn St	1984

Penn State Univ-Harrisburg	Middleton, PA		17057-4898 (717) 948-6141					psu.edu
Finance/Economics Program	School of Business		Fax=948-6456					Becky Dolan
Homepage: www.hbg.psu.edu								
Kulkarni, Mukund S.	D-Ac	948-6141	msk5	Fnce	PHD	82	Kentucky	1985
DeRooy, Jacob	C-Ac	948-6155	jxd5		PHD	69	Rutgers	1975
Ahmed, Parvez	Asst	948-6162	pxa13		PHD	96	Tx-Arlin	1998
Murti, Vedula N.	Asst	948-6164	vm3		PHD	66	Penn	1969
Sinisi, John	Asst	385-3634			PHD	76	Mass	1982
Tawatnuntachai, Oranee	Asst	948-6160	oxy4		PHD	99	N Orleans	1999
Vora, Premal	Asst	948-6148	fpv		PHD	91	Penn St	2001

Pepperdine Univ-Malibu	Malibu, CA		90263-4372 (310) 456-4372					pepperdine.edu
Social Science Division	Seaver College		Fax=317-7271					Mr. Randy Kitchen
Baird, David	Dean	456-4280	dbaird	Hist	PHD		Oklahoma	1988
Soper, Chris	C-Pr	506-4792	csoper		PHD		Yale	1992
Batchelder, Ronald W.	Prof	456-4544	rbatch	DEFK	PHD	75	UCLA	1984
Sexton, Robert L.	Prof	456-4345	rsexton	ADNQ	PHD	80	Colorado	1979
Galles, Gary M.	Assoc	456-4250	ggalles	AHLR	PHD	88	UCLA	1982
Carter, Tanja	Asst		tcarter		PHD	99	Ca-SnBarb	1999

Pfeiffer University Misenheimer, NC 28109-0960 (704) pfieffer.edu
Economics Program College of Arts & Sci Fax=463-1363
Did Not Respond Again--1997-98 Listing

Starr, Bettie C.	Dean	463-1360	bstarr		PHD	76	Duke	1974
Poplin, Toby L.	C-Ac				MA	68	Appalach	1976
Jozsa, Frank P. Jr.	Assoc				PHD	77	Geo St	1991

Piedmont College Demorest, GA 30535-0010 (706) Ext 1250 piedmont.edu
Economics Faculty School of Business Fax=776-9608 Ms. Joyce Webb
phone: 778-8500

Gardner, Mark L.	C-Pr	Ext 1250	mgardner		PHD	85	Geo St	1979
Wolfe, Edward	Asst	548-6190	ewolfe		MA		SUNY-SBr	2001

Pittsburg State University Pittsburg, KS 66762-7500 (620) 235-4547 mail.pittstate.edu
Dept Econ, Finance & Banking Kelch Col of Bus & Econ Fax=232-4572 Mrs. Kathy Bernard
Homepage: www.pittstate.edu/econ/dephom.htm/

Clement, Ron W.	Dean	235-4590		Mgt	PHD	78	Mich St	
Fischer, Charles C.	C-Pr	235-4547		BJ	PHD	75	Wash St	1974
Cortes, Bienvenido S.	Prof	235-4547		F	PHD	87	Okla St	
Smith, Kenneth L.	Prof	235-4547		G	PHD	81	Ca-Rivers	
Lal, Anil K.	Asst	235-4547		A	PHD	95	Wash St	
Crough, B. Jane	Lect	235-4547		A	MBA	84	Pittsburgh	

University of Pittsburgh Pittsburgh, PA 15260 (412) 648-1760 pitt.edu
Department of Economics Col of Arts & Sciences Fax=648-1793 Irene Petrovich/Donna Yorko
Homepage: www.pitt.edu/~econdept/

Cooper, N. John	Dean	624-6090	cooper@fas.		DPHL	76	Oxford	1998
Richard, Jean Francois	C-Pr	648-1750	fantin	C	PHD	73	Louvain	1991
Blume, Andreas	Prof	648-7088			PHD	87	Ca-SnDgo	2000
Cassing, James H.	Prof	648-8746	jcassing	F	PHD	75	Iowa	1985
Giarratani, Frank	Prof	648-7378	frankg	R	PHD	75	W Virginia	1979
Gruver, Gene W.	Prof	648-1731	gruver	O	PHD	72	Iowa St	1970
Husted, Steven L.	Prof	648-1757	husted1	F	PHD	80	Mich St	1980
Ochs, Jack N.	Prof	624-5711	jochs	H	PHD	66	Indiana	1968
Rawski, Thomas G.	Prof	648-7062	tgrawski	O	PHD	72	Harvard	1985
Wells, Jerome C.	Prof	648-1749	wells01	O	PHD	64	Michigan	1964
Beeson, Patricia E.	Assoc	648-1754	beeson	R	PHD	83	Oregon	1983
Chesler, Herbert	Assoc	648-1706	chesler	J	PHD	64	MIT	1963
DeJong, David	Assoc	648-2242	dejong	E	PHD	89	Iowa	1989
Kenkel, James L.	Assoc	648-1767	kenkel	C	PHD	69	Purdue	1969
Sontheimer, Kevin C.	Assoc	648-7071	sontheim	D	PHD	69	Minnesota	1979
Berkowitz, Daniel	Asst	648-7072	dmberk	GH	PHD	88	Columbia	1992
Caner, Mehmet	Asst	648-1762		C	PHD	96	Brown	2000
Duffy, John	Asst	648-1733	jduffy	E	PHD	92	UCLA	1992
Kim, Minseong	Asst	648-2823	mkim	E	PHD	96	Brown	1996
Park, In-uck	Asst	648-1137			PHD	93	Minnesota	2000
Ripoll, Marla	Asst	648-2243		F	PHD	00	Rochester	2000
Vesterlund, Lise	Asst	648-1794		H	PHD	97	Wisconsin	2001
Cassing, Shirley	Lect	648-1729	cassing	R	PHD	76	Iowa	1985

U of Pittsburgh at Johnstown Johnstown, PA 15904 (814) 269-2990 pitt.edu
Div of Social Sci-Economics Col of Arts & Sciences Fax=269-7255
Did Not Respond--1999-2000 Listing

Berger, George	C-Ac	269-2982	berger	EJK	PHD	87	Ca-Davis	1989
Yates, Michael Daniel	Prof	269-2986	mikey	JP	PHD	76	Pittsburgh	1969
Long, Stanley G.	Emer		sglong	D-95	PHD	69	Iowa	1973
McGahagan, Thomas A.	Assoc	269-2985	mgahagan	FN	PHD	76	Penn	1982
Strausser, Clark W.	Assoc	269-2980	cstrauss	CG	PHD	70	Minnesota	1973
Lavine, Jeffrey A.	Asst	269-7000	jlavine		MA	68	Pittsburgh	1970

Director of Administration and Budget

Plymouth State College Plymouth, NH 03264-1600 (603) 535-2610 plymouth.edu
Economics Faculty Department of Business Fax=535-2611

Buck, Paul M.	C-Pr	535-2208		Atg	MS	68	Northeas	9-72
Boggess, Trent E.	Prof	535-2414			PHD	80	Kansas	1983
Jang, Soo M.	Prof	535-2413		E	PHD	78	Cincinnati	1983
Couvillion, L. Michael	Assoc	536-2205		I	PHD	82	La Tech	1980
Brickley, Colleen	Inst	535-2278		D	ABD	78	NewHamp	1993

Point Loma Nazarene Univ San Diego, CA 92106-2899 (619) 849-2305 ptloma.edu
Economics Faculty Dept of Acc, Bus & Econ Fax=849-2691 Aurora Brown

Shea, Gene A.	C	849-2305						
Adjibolosoo, Senyo	Prof	849-2622	sadjibol	AFO	PHD	87	Simon Fr	2000
Havens, Rebecca A.	Prof	849-2293	beckyhavens	CT	PHD	87	Ca-SnDgo	1990
McEliece, James H.	Prof	849-2307	jamesmceliece	AC	PHD	86	Co Mines	1994

University of Portland Portland, OR 97203-5798 (503) 943-7224 uofport.edu
Economics Faculty School of Business Adm Fax=943-8041 Elise Petersen

Lewis, Lawrence D.	Dean	943-7224	lewis	Atg	PHD	84	Nebraska	2001
Adrangi, Bahram	Prof	943-7220	adrangi	CDFR	PHD	82	Oregon	1982
Allender, Mary E.	Assoc	943-7154	allender	LC	PHD	90	Oregon	1985
Easton, Todd E.	Assoc	943-7209	easton	JR	PHD	84	Berkeley	1981
Seal, James W.	Assoc	943-7272	seal	HRE	PHD	77	Illinois	1977
Barnes, William F.	Asst	943-7456	barnesw	GJP	PHD	01	Notre Dm	2000

Portland State University Portland, OR 97207-0751 (503) 725-3915 pdx.edu
Department of Economics Col Liberal Arts & Sci Fax=725-3945 Rita Spears
Homepage: econ.pdx.edu

Kaiser, Marvin	Dean	725-3514	kaiserm		PHD			1993
King, Mary C.	C-Ac	725-3915	kingm	J	PHD	91	Berkeley	1992
Hall, John B.	Prof	725-3939	hallj	P	PHD	84	New Sch	1985
Lin, Kuan-Pin	Prof	725-3931	link	C	PHD	77	SUNY-SBr	1979
Qayum, Abdul	Prof	725-3936	abdul	O	DSC	59	Netherld	1970
Walker, John F.	Prof	725-3934	walkerj	H	PHD	72	Utah	1966
Potiowsky, Thomas P.	Assoc	725-3929	thomasp	E	PHD	81	Colorado	1982
Evrensel, Ayse	Asst	725-3942	evrensela	E	PHD	99	Clemson	2001
Koss, Patricia	Asst	725-3938	kossp	D	PHD	93	Simon Fr	1997
Rodriguez, Leopoldo	Asst	725-3929	rodriguezl	F	PHD	99	Tx-Austin	2001
Schmidt, Martin	Asst	725-3940	schmidtm	E	PHD	94	Colo St	1997
Sharma, Rajiv	Asst	725-3933		I	PHD	98	Florida	1998

Prairie View A&M University Prairie View, TX 77446-0638 (936) 857-2122 pvamu.edu
Dept of Mgt & Marketing College of Business Fax=857-2243 Yolanda Kesee

Quddus, Munir	Dean	857-4310	munir_quddus		PHD	85	Vanderbilt	2001
Pointer, Lucille V.	C-Ac	857-4010	lucille_pointer	Mktg	PHD	00	Tx A&M	1982
Khan, M. Moosa	Assoc	857-2122	moosa_khan	FEM	PHD	86	Simon Fr	1989
Soliman, Mostafa A.	Assoc	857-2122	mostafa_soliman	DHQ	PHD	67	Iowa St	1971
Thiagarajan, K. R.	Asst	857-2122		DE	MA	55	Annamali	1967
Nazemzadeh, Nasrin	Inst	857-2122	nasrin_nazemz+		MBA	88	SW La	

Presbyterian College Clinton, SC 29325 (864) 833-8370 cs1.presby.edu
Economics Faculty Dept of Econ & Bus Adm Fax=833-8481 Robin Dover

Slice, Jerry Kibler	C-Pr	833-8274	jkslice	QFD	PHD	86	Miss St	1989
Lipford, Jody W.	Assoc	833-8353	jlipford	HEFI	PHD	90	Clemson	1991

Princeton University Princeton, NJ 08544-1021 (609) 258-4000 princeton.edu
Economics Faculty Department of Economics Fax=258-6419 Uta Runyan, Dept Adm
email @1=phoenix.princeton.edu

Bernanke, Ben S.	C-Pr	258-4000	bernanke@wws.		PHD	79	MIT	1985
Ashenfelter, Orley C.	Prof	452-4040	c6789@alfa.		PHD	70	Princeton	1968
Blinder, Alan S.	Prof	258-3358	blinder@pucc.		PHD	71	MIT	1971
Bogan, Elizabeth C.	Prof	258-4035	ebogan		PHD	71	Columbia	
Bradford, David F.	Prof	258-1856	bradford@wws.		PHD	66	Stanford	1966
Branson, William H.	Prof	258-4828	wbranson@wws.		PHD	67	MIT	1967
Chow, Gregory C.	Prof	258-4030	gcnow	CDEP	PHD	55	Chicago	7-70
Deaton, Angus S.	Prof	258-5967	deaton@wws.		PHD	74	Cambridge	1983
Dixit, Avinash K.	Prof	258-4013	dixitak		PHD	68	MIT	1981
Farber, Henry S.	Prof	258-4044	farber@trumph.		PHD	77	Princeton	
Grossman, Gene M.	Prof	258-4823	grossman@wws.		PHD	80	MIT	1980
Gul, Faruk	Prof	258-4009	fgul@phoenix.		PHD	86	Princeton	1995
Kenen, Peter B.	Prof	258-4051	pbkenen@pucc.		PHD	58	Harvard	1971
Walker Professor Economics & International Finance								
Krueger, Alan B.	Prof	258-4046	akrueger@wws.	JH	PHD	87	Harvard	6-87
Malkiel, Burton G.	Prof	258-6445	bmalkiel@pucc.		PHD	64	Princeton	1966
Quandt, Richard E.	Prof	258-4005	quandt@pucc.		PHD	57	Harvard	1959
Reinhardt, Uwe E.	Prof	258-4781	reinhard@wws.		PHD	70	Yale	1967
Rosen, Harvey S.	Prof	258-4022	hsr@pucc.		PHD	74	Harvard	1974
Rubinstein, Ariel	Prof	258-4000	ariel		PHD	79	Hebrew	
Shapiro, Harold T.	Prof	258-6100	hts		PHD	64	Princeton	1988
Trussell, T. James	Prof	258-4801	trussell@opr.	CIT	PHD	75	Princeton	O-74
Watson, Mark W.	Prof	258-4811	mwatson@wws.		PHD	80	Ca-SnDgo	
Willig, Robert D.	Prof	258-4843	willig@wws.		PHD	73	Stanford	1978
Woodford, Michael	Prof	258-4003	woodford@1		PHD	83	MIT	
Paxson, Christina H.	Assoc	258-6474	cpaxson@wws.		PHD	86	Columbia	1986
Case, Anne C.	Asst	258-2177	accase@wws.		PHD	88	Princeton	1991
Honore, Bo Erno		258-4014	honore		PHD	87	Chicago	
Maggi, Giovanni		258-4016	maggi					
Morgan, John		258-4842	rjmorgan					
Rouse, Cecilia		258-6478	rouse					
Shimer, Robert		258-4031	shimer					

Providence College Providence, RI 02918-0001 (401) 865-2194 providence.edu
Department of Economics Economics Fax=865-1264
Homepage: www.providence.edu/admiss/ecn.htm

Marquis O.P., Fr. William	C-Ac	865-2875	wmarquis	JEI	PHD	96	Ohio St	1998
Kessler, Alan L.	Assoc	865-2248	akessler	DH	PHD	84	Boston C	1985
Latif-Zaman, Nazma	Assoc	865-2572	nzaman	OFC	PHD		Northeas	
O'Brien, Francis T.	Assoc	865-2156	fobrien	JK	MA	57	Boston C	1958
Simeone, William J.	Assoc	865-2567	wjsim	JEI	PHD	85	Boston C	1959
Lenon, Mary Jane	Asst	865-2566	mjlenon	REI	PHD	89	Conn	1986
Sawdy, George F.	Asst	865-2570	gsawdy	QEH	PHD	83	Brown	
Kaparakis, Emmanuel	Inst	865-2568	ekap	EGF	ABD		Conn	1990
Palumbo, Edwin P.	Inst	865-2189	epalumbo	RJ	MA		Boston C	

University of Puget Sound Tacoma, WA 98416-0140 (253) 756-3136 ups.edu
Economics Faculty Department of Economics Fax=756-3500 Reggie Tison
Did Not Respond--1999-2000 Listing

Stirling, Kathleen J.	C-Pr	756-3590	stirling	AEIT	PHD	87	Notre Dm	
Goodman, Douglas	Prof	756-3596	goodman	AE	PHD	78	Illinois	1977
Hands, Wade	Prof	756-3592	hands	ABC	PHD	65	U Wash	
Mann, Bruce D.	Prof	756-3593	mann	ADJK	PHD	76	Indiana	1975
Singleton, Ross	Prof	756-3591	singleton	ADKO	PHD	77	Oregon	
Veseth, Michael	Prof	756-3720	veseth	AFH	PHD	76	Purdue	1975
Sable, Karin	Asst	756-3136	sable	AHQ	PHD	97	Colo St	1997
Warning, Matt	Asst	756-3136	warning	ACO	PHD	97	Berkeley	1997

Purdue University W Lafayette, IN 47907-1310 (765) 494-4449 mgm.purdue.edu
Economics Krannert Grad Sch Mgt Fax=494-9658 Marsha Lowery
Homepage: http://www.mgmt.purdue.edu/departments/economics

Barron, John M.	C-Pr	494-4451	barron		PHD	76	Brown	1976
Umbeck, John R.	C-Pr	494-4447	umbeck		PHD	76	U Wash	1975
Aliprantis, C. D. Roko	Prof	494-4404	aliprantis		PHD	73	Cal Tech	1998
Carlson, John A.	Prof	494-4450	carlson		PHD	61	J Hopkins	1962
Loeb Professor of Economics								
Cason, Timothy	Prof	494-1737	cason		PHD	91	Berkeley	1998
Horwich, George	Prof	494-4443	ghorwich		PHD	54	Chicago	1956
Kadiyala, K. Rao	Prof	494-4476	kadiyala		PHD	66	Wisconsin	1970
Kovenock, Dan J.	Prof	494-4468	kovenock		PHD	83	Wisconsin	1983
Moore, James C.	Prof	494-4430	duke		PHD	68	Minnesota	1969
Papke, James A.	Prof	494-4442	papke		PHD	59	Cornell	1962
Thursby, Jerry G.	Prof	494-4462	jgt		PHD	75	N Carol	1988
Thursby, Marie C.	Prof	494-4463	mct		PHD	74	N Carol	1988
Burton D. Morgan Chair of Intl Mgt Policy; Dir Cntr of Intl Busines Education								
Watts, Michael W.	Prof	494-8543	bfp		PHD	78	LSU	1981
Director, Purdue Center for Economic Education								
Hueckel, Glenn R.	Assoc	494-4402	hueckel		PHD	72	Wisconsin	1972
Lynch, Gerald J.	Assoc	494-4388	lynch		PHD	75	Kentucky	1983
Noussair, Charles N.	Assoc	494-4416	noussair		PHD	93	Cal Tech	1994
Novshek, William	Assoc	494-4418	novshek		PHD	79	Nrthwstrn	1986
Pomery, John D.	Assoc	494-4515	pomery		PHD	77	Rochester	1982
Camera, Gabriele	Asst	494-4456	gcamera		PHD	97	Iowa	1997
Dahl, Christian	Asst	494-4503	dahlc		PHD	00	Aarhus	2000
Delacroix, Alain	Asst	496-6695	delacdroixa		PHD	99	Penn	1999
Hjummels, David	Asst	494-4495	hummelsd		PHD	95	Michigan	2000
Netz, Janet S.	Asst	494-4452	netz		PHD	92	Michigan	1994

Purdue University-Calumet Hammond, IN 46323-2904 (219) 989-2388 mgmt.calumet.purdue.edu
Department of Management School of Management Fax=989-3158 Nancy Sorrick

Sil, Shomir	Dean	989-2606	sil	Fnce	DBA	83	Tx Tech	1983
Furdek, Jonathan M.	Assoc	989-2426			PHD	74	Purdue	1974
Jennings, E. James	Assoc	989-2381			PHD	79	So Meth	1978
McGrath, Paul T.	Assoc	989-2425			PHD	88	N Illinois	1986
Mitra, Anilau	Asst	989-2313			PHD	98	N Illinois	1998
Tsoukalas, Dimitrios	Asst	989-2440			PHD	96	Illinois	1998

Quinnipiac College Hamden, CT 06518-1908 (203) Ext 8367 quinnipiac.edu
Department of Economics School of Business Fax=582-8664 Gail Retzer
phone 582-8576

Frese, Philip B.	Dean	280-8720		Atg	PHD	93	Drexel	1993
Gius, Mark P.	C-Pr	582-8576		ACDJ	PHD	91	Penn St	1994
DeAndrea, Vincent F.	Prof	582-8367		CDEN	PHD	72	Mass	1968
Driscoll, Vincent R.	Prof	582-8788		AEG	PHD	75	New Sch	1967
Johnson, Donn M.	Assoc	Ext 8205		AHQR	PHD	89	Colo St	1996
Kelly, Trish	Assoc	Ext 8318		EFO	PHD	94	Mass	1995
Everett, Michael	Asst	Ext 8256		ADBP	PHD	96	Conn	1996
Rafferty, Matt	Asst	Ext 3396		ENC	PHD	97	Ca-Davis	2000

Radford University Radford, VA 24142 (540) 831-5100 radford.edu
Dept of Economics Col of Business & Econ Fax=831-6209 Ms. Teresa Grubb
Homepage: www.radfor.edu/~econ-web

Dempsey, William A.	Dean	831-5300	wdempsey	Mktg	DBA	73	Maryland	1999
Hashemzadeh, Nozar	C-Pr	831-5888	nhashemz	CJG	PHD	74	Va Tech	1983
Kasturi, Prahlad	Prof	831-5884	pkasturi	DOQ	PHD	83	Hawaii	1985
Roufagalas, John	Prof	831-5892	jroufaga	DGE	PHD	83	Florida	1985
Santopietro, George D.	Prof	831-5891	gsantopi	QDK	PHD	86	Va Tech	1987
Woolley, Douglas C.	Prof	831-5885	dwoolley	HP	PHD	76	Conn	1975
Orlov, Alexei	Asst	831-5889	aorlov	FE	PHD	01	Virginia	2001
Wilson, Loretta S.	Asst	831-6225	lwilson	FN	PHD	86	Mass	1987
Wade, Ernie	Inst	831-5890	ewwade	AQ	MS	86	Va Tech	1997

Randolph-Macon College Ashland, VA 23005-5005 (804) 752-7204 rmc.edu
Economics Faculty Dept of Economics & Bus Fax=752-7231

Staples, Catherine L.	C-Ac	752-7204		Atg	PHD	90	N Carol	1995
Lowry, George S.	Prof	752-7306	glowry	G	PHD	92	Va Comm	1984
Pfitzner, C. Barry	Prof	752-7307	bpfitzner	DFC	PHD	83	Catholic	1982
Edward W. Seese Professor of Economics and Business								
Lang, Steven D.	Assoc	752-7356	slang	ECR	PHD	90	Pittsburgh	1987
Schmidt, Edward J.	Assoc	752-7333	eschmidt	E	MA	67	Maryland	1967
Brat, David	Asst	752-7353	dbrat	DBO	PHD	95	American	1996

University of Redlands Redlands, CA 92373-0999 (909) 335-4068 uor.edu
Economics Faculty Dept of Mgt & Business Fax=335-5125
Did Not Respond Again--1997-98 Listing

Pick, James	C-Pr	335-4068	pick	RT	PHD	74	Ca-Irvine	1991
Halvorsen, Marcia L.	Prof	793-2121			PHD	78	Geo St	1975
Segur, W. Hubbard	Prof	335-4068		Busi	PHD	80	Ca-Davis	1989
Bandzak, Ruth Anne	Asst				MA		Notre Dm	1988
Fazeli, Rafat R.	Asst	793-2121			PHD	92	New Sch	1989

Reed College Portland, OR 97202-8199 (503) 771-1112 reed.edu
Department of Economics Div History & Soc Sci Fax=777-7776 Lois Hobbs
Homepage: //web .reed.edu/academic/departments/economics

Netusil, Noelwah R.	C-Ac	771-1112	netusil	AQDH	PHD	92	Illinois	1990
Parker, Jeffrey A.	Prof	771-1112	parker	AECF	PHD	81	Stanford	1988
George Hay Professor of Economics								
Hare, Denise	Assoc	771-1112	dhare	AJOD	PHD	92	Stanford	1992
Clausing, Kimberly	Asst	771-1112	kclausing	ADFH	PHD	97	Harvard	1997

Regent University Virginia Bch, VA 23464-9850 (757) 579-4302 regent.edu
Economics Faculty Robertson Sch of Govt Fax=226-4369 Mrs. Sherry Hansen
Did Not Respond Again--1997-98 Listing

James, Kay C.	Dean	579-4530	kjames	I	BA			1996
Bom, Philip C.	Prof	579-4303	philbom	FOP	PHD		Free	1983

Regis College - MA Weston, MA 02193-1571 (617) 768-7418
Economics Div of Social Sciences Fax-768-8339
Did Not Respond--1999-2000 Listing

Hewins, Dana C.	C-Ac	768-7418			PHD	75	Illinois	
Oates, Mary J.	Prof	768-7420		N	PHD	69	Yale	1970

Regis College of Regis Univ Denver, CO 80221-1099 (303) 458-4170
Economics Program Div of Business Fax=964-5485 Sharon Hershfeldt

Muth, John	D-Ac	458-3584		AGNM	PHD	78	Colorado	9-83
Richard, James S.	Assoc	458-4185			PHD	80	Tx-Austin	1979
Shannon, Lee R.	Assoc	458-4175			PHD	70	N Colo	1978

Rensselaer Poly Institute Troy, NY 12180-3590 (518) 276-6387 rpi.edu
Department of Economics Sch of Human & Soc Sci Fax=276-2235 Betty Jean Kaufmann
Homepage: rpi.edu.economics

Duchin, Faye	Dean	276-6575	duchin					1996
Gowdy, John M.	Prof	276-8094	gowdyj		PHD	80	W Virginia	1983
Hughes, Greg	Prof	276-2590	hughesg		PHD	72	Princeton	1997
Vitaliano, Donald F.	Prof	276-8093	vitald		PHD	69	CUNY	1969
Erickson, Jon	Asst	276-2523	erick		PHD	97	Cornell	1997
Goldfarb, Brent	Asst	276-6387	goldfb		PHD	01	Stanford	2001
Gustanski, Julie Ann	Asst	276-6387	gustaj		PHD	99	Edinburgh	2001
Heim, John	Asst	276-8092	heimj		PHD	72	SUNY-Alb	1997

University of Rhode Island Kingston, RI 02881-0808 (401) 874-2212 uri.edu
Department of Economics Col of Arts & Sciences Fax=874-2588 Linda Gray

Ramstad, Yngve	C-Pr	874-4113	yramstad	BA	PHD	81	Berkeley	1982
Barnett, Harold C.	Prof	874-2070	hbarnett	EKQ	PHD	73	MIT	1970
Burkett, John P.	Prof	874-4122	burkett	CDFI	PHD	81	Berkeley	1981
Lardard, Leonard P.	Prof	874-4128	lardaro	CE	PHD	79	Indiana	1981
McIntyre, Richard	Prof	874-4126	rmc8875u	FJN	PHD	89	Mass	1989
Mead, Arthur C.	Prof	874-4123	acmead	A	PHD	78	Boston C	1976
Miller, Carole F.	Prof	874-4111	cmi6707u	ACDJ	PHD	88	Syracuse	1986
Ramsay, Glenworth A.	Prof	874-4129	ramsay	L	PHD	74	Boston C	1973
Sharif, Mohammed	Prof	874-4119	sharif	O	PHD	83	Boston U	1984
Starkey, James L.	Prof	874-4117	starkey	Q	PHD	71	Boston C	1967
Suzawa, Gilbert S.	Assoc	874-4125	gilsuzawa@cs.com	AD	PHD	73	Brown	1971

Rhode Island College Providence RI 02908-1991 (401) 456-8036 ric.edu
Dept of Econ & Finance Center for Mgt & Tech Fax=456-8379 Ms. Pamela Santos

Karim, Alema	C-Ac	456-9538			PHD	86	Boston U	
Moore, Peter R.	Prof	456-8037			PHD	75	Illinois	
Blais, Jeffrey	Assoc	456-8037			PHD	75	Pittsburgh	1986
Harman, Peter	Assoc	456-9518			PHD	76	N Carol	
Kazemi, Abbas A.	Assoc	456-9557			PHD	88	SUNY-SBr	
Marks, Peter A.	Assoc	456-9529			PHD	78	N Carol	

Rhodes College Memphis, TN 38112-1690 (901) 843-3863 rhodes.edu
Dept of Economics & Business Div Social Sciences Fax=843-3798 Amy Radford
Did Not Respond--1999-2000 Listing

Orvis, Charles C.	H-Ac	843-3922	orvis		PHD	75	Minnesota	1973
Bolch, Ben W.	Prof	843-3995	bolch		PHD	66	N Carol	1987
Iskander, Wasfy B.	Prof	843-3983	iskander		PHD	73	Indiana	
McMahon, Marshall E.	Prof	843-3863	mcmahon		PHD	72	Vanderbilt	1972
Rollosson, Michael	Inst	843-3566	rollesoon		ABD			1993

Rice University Houston, TX 77251-1892 (713) 527-4875 rice.edu
Economics Faculty POBox 1894 Dept of Economics MS-22 Fax=285-5278 Elizabeth Powell
Homepage: http://www.ruf.rice.edu/~econ/

Stein, Robert	Dean	384-4824		PolS				
Hartley, Peter R.	C-Pr	348-2534	hartley		PHD	80	Chicago	1986
Brito, Dagobert L.	Prof	348-5792	brito		PHD	70	Rice	1984
George A. Peterkin Professor of Political Economy								
Brown, Bryan W.	Prof	348-2345	bwbwn		PHD	77	Penn	1983
Hargrove Professor of Economics								
Brown, James	Prof	348-3343	jbrown		PHD	80	Chicago	1992
Bryant, John B.	Prof	348-3341	jbb		PHD	75	Car Mellon	1981
Henry S. Fox, Sr. Professor of Economics								
Gillis, Malcolm	Prof	348-4041			PHD	68	Illinois	1993
President								
Mieszkowski, Peter	Prof	348-3453	mieszko		PHD	63	J Hopkins	1981
Cline Professor of Economics & Finance								
Moulin, Herve	Prof	348-3312	moulin	CD	PHD	75	Paris	7-99
Peterkin Professor of Economics								
Sickles, Robin C.	Prof	348-3322	rsickles		PHD	76	N Carol	1985
Smith, Gordon W.	Prof	348-3332	gsmith		PHD	66	Harvard	1968
Soligo, Ronald	Prof	348-3354	soligo		PHD	64	Yale	1967
Zodrow, George R.	Prof	348-4891	zodrdow		PHD	80	Princeton	1979
Chae, Suchan	Assoc	348-5752	chae		PHD	85	Penn	1985
Dudey, Marc Peter	Assoc	348-3270	dudey		PHD	84	Princeton	1990
Barut, Yasar	Asst	348-3323	ybarut		PHD	98	Purdue	7-98
Chang, Yoosoon	Asst	348-2796	yoosoon		PHD	95	Yale	1995
Hasker, Kevin	Asst	348-3414	hasker		PHD	98	Nrthwstrn	7-98
Ohno, Yuka	Asst	348-2354	yuka	FL	PHD	93	U Wash	9-94

University of Richmond Richmond, VA 23173 (804) 289-8587 richmond.edu
Department of Economics Robins Sch of Business Fax=289-8878 Sue Hopfensperger

Newman, Karen L.	Dean	289-8550	knewman	Mgt	PHD	78	Chicago	1999
Schmidt, Robert M.	C-Pr	289-8587	rschmidt		PHD	81	Duke	1981
Dolan, Robert C.	Prof	289-8562	rdolan		PHD	82	Rutgers	1980
Raines, J. Patrick	Prof	289-8566	praines		PHD	83	Alabama	1982
Cook, Robert W. Jr.	Assoc	289-8561	rcook		PHD	81	Va Tech	1980
Dean, David H.	Assoc	289-8559	ddean		PHD	88	Rutgers	1987
McGoldrick, Kim Marie	Assoc	289-8575	kmcgoldr		PHD	93	SUNY-Bin	1992
Nicholson, Robert H.	Assoc	298-8565	rnichols		PHD	72	N Carol	1972
Wight, Jonathan B.	Assoc	289-8570	jwight		PHD	82	Vanderbilt	1982
Craft, Erik D.	Asst	287-6573	ecraft		PHD	95	Chicago	1994
Monks, James W.	Asst	289-8587	jmonks		PHD	95	Boston C	2001
Pasernak, Jacob I.	Visit	289-8571	jpastern		ABD		N Carol	1999
Taylor, Travis K.	Visit	287-1928	ttaylor		PHD	01	Conn	2000
Voeks, Lisa Ford	Visit	287-6645	lvoeks		PHD	00	Georgia	1999

Rider University Lawrenceville NJ 08648-3099 (609) 895-5562 rider.edu
Department of Economics College of Business Adm Fax=896-5304 Diana Cook
Did Not Respond--1999-2000 Listing

Sandberg, Mark E.	Dean$	896-5152		Mgt	PHD	71	Cornell	1970
McCall, Charles W.	C-Ac	895-5562		AL	PHD	82	Temple	1979
Corman, Hope	Prof	895-5559		IJKT	PHD	78	CUNY	1988
Gishlick, Herbert E.	Prof	895-5564		ER	PHD	73	Penn	1964
Bentley, Jerome T.	Assoc	895-5563		D	PHD	74	Pittsburgh	1974
Taga, Leonore S.	Assoc	895-5531		P	PHD	79	Berkeley	1986

University of Rio Grande Rio Grande, OH 45674 (740) 245-7267 rio.edu
Department of Economics E.E. Evans Col Bus Mgt Fax=245-7123 Shari Wootan

Lloyd, Paul	Dean	245-7373	plloyd		MA	66	Marshall	1966
Sebastian, Paul	C-Pr	245-7292	pauls	Mgt	PHD	94	Kent St	1995
Kool, Krishna L.	Prof	245-7268	kkool		PHD	76	Tennessee	1970
Koirala, Govinda	Asst	245-7284	gkoirala		PHD	95	NYU	1996

Roanoke College Salem, VA 24153-3794 (540) 375-2426 roanoke.edu
Economics Faculty Dept of Bus Adm & Econ Fax=375-2577 Nan Watson

Lynch, Larry A.	C-Pr	375-2413	llynch	Mgt	PHD	87	Va Tech	1978
Fleming, Garry A.	Assoc	375-2509	fleming		PHD	79	Kentucky	1987
Lowry, Darryl W.	Assoc	375-2428	dlowry		PHD	72	Berkeley	1981
Stauffer, Robert F.	Assoc	375-2427	stauffer		PHD	74	Va Tech	1978

Robert Morris College Coraopolis, PA 15108-1189 (412) 227-6859 robert-morris.edu
Dept of Social Science Sch of Appl Sci & Educ Fax=391-3329
Did Not Respond Again--1997-98 Listing

Shank, Jon	Dean	262-8279			EDD		Pittsburgh	
Norberg, Robert W.	C-As	227-6859			MA		Ind-Penn	1968
Litzinger, Patrick J.	Prof	262-8438			PHD	75	Pittsburgh	1977
Eschenfelder, Mark J.	Assoc	262-8491			PHD	93	W Illinois	
Holstein, Adora	Assoc				PHD	87	Penn St	
Lynch, James W.	Assoc	262-8439			MA	72	Pittsburgh	1974
Reiland, Ralph R.	Assoc	227-4055			MBA		Duquesne	
Zeman, Allan H.	Assoc	227-6844			PHD	78	Pittsburgh	1964

University of Rochester Rochester, NY 14627-0156 (716) 275-7221 troi.cc.rochester.edu
Department of Economics Col of Arts & Science Fax=256-2309 Lynn Enright
Homepage: www.rochester.edu

Plosser, Charles I.	Dean	275-3316	plosser		PHD	76	Chicago	1978
John M. Olin Distinguished Professor of Economics								
Jones, Ronald W.	C-Pr	275-7221	jonr		PHD	56	MIT	1958
Xerox Professor of Economics								
Bils, Mark J.	Prof	275-0488	bils	D	PHD	85	MIT	1985
Engerman, Stanley L.	Prof	275-3165	enge		PHD	62	J Hopkins	1963
John Munro Professor of Economics								
Epstein, Larry G.	Prof	275-4320	lepn		PHD	77	Brit Colum	1998
Greenwood, Jeremy	Prof	275-1871	gree	D	PHD	83	Rochester	1992
Hanushek, Eric A.	Prof	275-5059	hanu		PHD	68	MIT	1978
Director, W.A. Wallis Institute of Political Economy								
Hopenhayn, Hugo	Prof	275-4081	huho		PHD	89	Minnesota	1994
Krusell, Per	Prof	275-4903	pekr	O	PHD	92	Minnesota	1994
Director, Center for the Study of Economic Growth and Cycles								
McKenzie, Lionel W.	Emer	275-3096	mcke		PHD	42	Princeton	1957
Oi, Walter Y.	Prof	275-4991	oiwa		PHD	61	Chicago	1967
Elmer B. Milliman Professor of Economics								
Phelps, Charles E.	Prof	275-5149			PHD	73	Chicago	1984
Provost								
Ploberger, Werner	Prof	275-4196	wplo		HAB	93	Vienna T	1997
Stockman, Alan C.	Prof	275-7221	stoc		PHD	78	Chicago	1979
Wilson Professor of Economics								
Thomson, William L.	Prof	275-2236	wth2	CDH	PHD	76	Stanford	9-83
Landsburg, Steven E.	Assoc	275-4971	landsbur		PHD	79	Chicago	
Alonso, Irasema	Asst	275-4980	iral		PHD	93	Minnesota	1994
Carrasco, Marine	Asst	275-7307	csco		PHD	95	Toulouse	2000
Caucutt, Elizabeth	Asst	275-0093	ecau		PHD	97	Minnesota	1997
Dahl, Gordon B.	Asst	275-6279	dahl		PHD	98	Princeton	1998
Guvenen, Muhammet Fatih	Asst	275-3968			PHD	01	Car Mellon	2001
Khan, Shakeeb	Asst	275-2180	skhan		PHD	97	Princeton	1998
Lochner, Lance	Asst	275-4239	lance		PHD	98	Chicago	1998
Squintani, Francesco	Asst	275-4821	sqnt		PHD	00	Nrthwstrn	2000
Wolkoff, Michael	Lect	275-5279	wolk		PHD	81	Michigan	1980
Deputy Chairperson, Department of Economics								

Rochester Inst of Technology	Rochester, NY	14623-5604 (716)					ritvax.isc.rit.edu	
Div Soc Sci-Dept of Econ	Col of Liberal Arts	Fax=475-7120						
Vernarelli, Michael J.	C-Pr	475-2455			PHD	78	SUNY-Bin	1976
Batabyal, Amitjatreet	Prof	475-2805		FOQ	PHD	94	Berkeley	2000
Arthur J. Gosnell Professor of Economics								
Lee, Hoyoung	Prof	475-2406		ABDE	PHD	70	Maryland	1970
Dumangane, Constantino Sr.	Assoc	475-2807	econ.dwelop	GLDM	PHD	88	SUNY-Buf	1986
Mitchell, Jeannette C.	Asst	475-6077	jcmgsm	FOB	PHD	95	Utah	1985
Wagner, M. Jeffrey	Asst				PHD	97	Illinois	2001

Rockhurst University	Kansas City, MO	64110-2561 (816) 501-4200					rockhurst.edu	
Department of Economics	School of Management	Fax=501-4650						
Homepage: www.rockhurst.edu								
Walker, Earl	Dean	501-4201	e_walker		PHD	80	MIT	1998
Tansey, Michael M.	Prof	273-3061			PHD	78	Wisconsin	1982
Miller, Gerald	Assoc	501-4016			PHD	75	Notre Dm	1982
Stellern, Michael J.	Asst	501-4153			PHD	83	Arizona	1979
Rabbitt, Michael T.	Lect				MA	75	Wash U	1988

Rollins College	Winter Park, FL	32789-4499 (407) 646-2569					rollins.edu	
Economics Faculty	Department of Economics	Fax=646-2485					Sharon Miller	
Rock, Charles Patrick	C-Pr	646-2152	crock	BJOP	PHD	86	Cornell	1984
Taylor, Kenna C.	Prof	646-2312	ktaylor		PHD	79	Florida	1974
Kypralos, Harry N.	Assoc	646-2510	hkypralos		PHD	87	Virginia	1983
Schutz, Eric A.	Assoc	646-2509	eschutz		PHD	82	N Carol	1987
Skelley, A. Chris	Assoc	646-2489	cskelley		PHD	85	Brown	1987
Steen, Robert C.	Assoc	646-2614	rsteen	RHN	PHD	82	Princeton	1987

Roosevelt University	Chicago, IL	60605-1394 (847) 341-3695					roosevelt.edu	
Dept Econ/Sch Policy Studies	Col of Arts & Sciences	Fax=341-3680						
Did Not Respond--1999-2000 Listing								
Tallman, Ronald	Dean	341-3670	rtallman					
Langer, Gary F.	D-Ac	341-3767	glander		PHD	80	Ca-Rivers	1983
Balkin, Steven M.	Prof	341-3696			PHD	76	Wayne St	1984
email=eco@interaccess.com								
Rosenberg, Sam	Prof	341-3697	srosenbe		PHD	75	Berkeley	1982
Stein, Howard	Prof	341-3692	hstein		PHD	83	Ca-Rivers	1983
Lapidus, June	Assoc	341-3765	jlapidus		PHD	88	Mass	1990
Baiman, Ron	Asst	341-3879	rbaiman		PHD	89	New Sch	1994

Rowan University	Glassboro, NJ	08028-1748 (856) 256-4060					rowan.edu	
Department of Economics	School of Liberal Arts	Fax=256-4921					Patricia Jenkins	
phone 256-4500								
Harper, Jay	Dean	256-4850		Psy	PHD			
Kressler, Peter	C-Pr	Ext 3321	kressler		PHD	68	Penn	1972
Hamer, Thomas P.	Prof	256-4062	hamer		PHD	75	Claremont	1974
Mukhoti, Bela	Prof	Ext 3322	mukhoti		PHD	64	London	1974
Jam, Habib O. E.	Assoc	Ext 4061	jam		PHD	75	S Illinois	1979
Reaves, Natalie	Asst	Ext 3320	reaves		PHD	95	Wayne St	1998

The Sage Colleges	Troy, NY	12180-4115 (518) 270-2235					sage.edu	
Social & Global Studies	Russell Sage College	Fax=271-4545					Pam McKee	
Did Not Respond--1999-2000 Listing								
Melero, Francisco	D-Ac	270-2241	melerf	DCF	PHD	83	Rensselaer	1982
DiMambro, Carol	Assoc	462-8629	dimamc	AKP	MA	89	SUNY-Alb	1989
Tribble, John A.	Assoc	270-2296	tribbj		PHD	75	Utah St	1976
Lawrence Professor of Economics								
Sabi, Manijeh	Adj	270-2397	sabim	EGO	MA	86	Northeas	1988

Rutgers University-Camden	Camden, NJ	08102 (856) 225-6136					camden.rutgers.edu	
Department of Economics	Col of Arts & Sciences	Fax=225-6495					Dee Jonczak	
Homepage: www.camden.rutgers.edu/dept-pages/economics								
Marsh, Margaret	Dean				PHD	74	Rutgers	
Worrall, John D.	C-Pr	225-6290			PHD	75	Rutgers	1983
Seplaki, Les	Prof	225-6319			PHD	70	Ca-Rivers	
Yamada, Tetsuji	Prof	225-6025			PHD	87	CUNY	1987
Ma, Jinpeng	Assoc	225-6025			PHD	93	SUNY-SBr	
Chen, Baolin	Asst	225-6025			PHD	94	Indiana	

Rutgers University-Newark	Newark, NJ	07102 (973) 353-5259					andromeda.rutgers.edu	
Department of Economics	Faculty of Arts & Sci	Fax=353-5819					Marilyn Johnson	
Diner, Steven	Dean							
Loeb, Peter D.	C-Pr	353-5259	ploeb		PHD	73	Rutgers	1973

Coate, Douglas C.	Prof	353-5164	dcoate		PHD	74	CUNY	1971
Graham, John W. III	Prof	353-5354	jwgraham		PHD	78	Nrthwstrn	1986
Troy, Leo	Prof	353-5529	leotroy		PHD	58	Columbia	
VanderHoff, James H.	Prof	353-5256	jhv		PHD	79	N Carol	1980
Rodriguez, Alvaro	Assoc	353-5809	alvaror		PHD	82	Columbia	1994
Seiglie, Carlos C.	Assoc	353-5914	seiglie		PHD	91	Chicago	1986
Goldbaum, David	Asst	353-5164	goldbaum		PHD	96	Wisconsin	1998
Markowtiz, Sara	Asst	353-5835	smarkow		PHD	98	CUNY	2000
Tournas, Ioannis	Asst	353-1320	itournas		PHD	95	Nrthwstrn	1996

Rutgers Univ-New Brunswick	New BrunswickNJ 08901-1248 (908) 932-7363						fas-econ.rutgers.edu	
Department of Economics	Faculty of Arts & Sci Fax=942-7416						Laura Ford	
Falk, Richard S.	Dean	932-7896						
Killingworth, Mark R.	C-Pr	932-7794	killings	J	DPHI	77	Oxford	1978
Blair, Douglas H.	Prof	932-7858	blair	D	PHD	76	Yale	1981
Bordo, Michael D.	Prof	932-7069	bordo	N	PHD	72	Chicago	1981
Dutta, Manoranjan	Prof	932-7054	dutta	E	PHD	62	Penn	1989
Gang, Ira N.	Prof	932-7405	gang	O	PHD	83	Cornell	1986
Gigliotti, Gary A.	Prof	932-7466	gag@rci	D	PHD	78	Columbia	1978
Klein, Roger W.	Prof	932-7543	klein	C	PHD	70	Yale	1994
Marcus, Matityahu	Prof	932-7344	marcus	G	PHD	63	Brown	1962
McLean, Richard P.	Prof	932-7709	mclean	D	PHD	79	SUNY-SBr	1986
Perry, Martin K.	Prof	932-7572	perry	L	PHD	76	Stanford	1989
Prusa, Thomas	Prof	932-7670	prusa	F	PHD	88	Stanford	1994
Rockoff, Hugh T.	Prof	932-7857	rockoff	N	PHD	72	Chicago	1971
Rubin, Jeffrey I.	Prof	932-7452	rubin	H	PHD	75	Duke	1973
Undergraduate Director								
Russell, Louise B.	Prof	932-6507	lrussell@rci.	I	PHD	71	Harvard	1987
Sato, Kazuo	Prof	932-7077		E	PHD	60	Yale	1984
Seneca, Joseph J.	Prof	932-7821	seneca.oldqueens	H	PHD	68	Penn	1967
Stuart, Robert C.	Prof	932-8841	stuart	P	PHD	69	Wisconsin	1968
Tsurumi, Hiroki	Prof	932-7932	tsurumi	C	PHD	67	Penn	1974
White, Eugene N.	Prof	932-7486	white	N	PHD	80	Illinois	1980
Altshuler, Rosanne	Assoc	932-7783	altshule	H	PHD	88	Penn	1992
Chang, Roberto J.	Assoc	932-7269	chang	E	PHD	89	Penn	2000
Hartline, Jessie C.	Assoc	932-7951	hartline	G	PHD	68	Rutgers	1968
Hughes, Joseph P.	Assoc	932-7517	hughes	D	PHD	74	N Carol	1975
Mizrach, Bruce	Assoc	932-8261	mizrach	E	PHD	87	Penn	1995
Schmitt-Grobe, Stephanie	Assoc	932-2960	grohe	E	PHD	94	Chicago	1998
Sheflin, Neil	Assoc	932-7834	sheflin	C	PHD	79	Rutgers	1975
Sigman, Hilary	Assoc	932-7594	sigman	I	PHD	93	MIT	1999
Sopher, Barry	Assoc	932-7197	sopher	D	PHD	88	Iowa	1987
Graduate Director								
Vella, Francis G. M.	Assoc	932-7691	vella	C	PHD	90	Rochester	1997
Campbell, Colin	Asst	932-8259	campblell	D	PHD	95	Nrthwstrn	1999
Evenett, Simon	Asst		evenett	F	PHD	95	Yale	1997
Friedman, Eric J.	Asst	932-7797	friedman	D	PHD	93	Berkeley	1996
Landon-Lane, John	Asst	932-7363		C	PHD	98	Minnesota	2001
Occhino, Filippo	Asst	932-7491	occhino	E	PHD	00	Chicago	2000
Sbordone, Argia	Asst	932-8271	sbordone	E	PHD	93	Chicago	1998

Sacred Heart University	Fairfield, CT 06432-1000 (203) 371-7953						sacredheart.edu	
Economics Program	Fac Fin Stds,Govt & Law Fax=396-6543							
Did Not Respond--1999-2000 Listing								
Orlowski, Lucjan T.	Prof		orlowskil	EFGP	PHD	79	Poland	1983
Corrigan, Tom D.	Assoc		corrigant	AFG	PHD	69	Maryland	1986
Frangul, Ramzi N.	Assoc		frangulr	G	PHD	73	NYU	1977
Lim, Ralph	Assoc		limr	GLM	MBA		Penn	1981
Mangiero, Susan M.	Asst	396-6580	mangieros	ACDG	PHD	97	Conn	1990

Saginaw Valley State Univ	Univ Center, MI 48710 (517) 790-4084						svsu.edu	
Department of Economics	Col of Business & Mgt Fax=249-4699							
Uselding, Paul J.	Dean	790-4064		N	PHD	70	Nrthwstrn	1999
Kanthi, Mahendra S.	Prof	790-4379	msk	FO	PHD	80	Kentucky	1984
Novey, Donald F.	Prof	790-4352	dfn	DE	MS		S Dak St	1969
Park, Hong Youl	Prof	790-4084	hyp	KMEL	PHD	75	Utah St	1975
Sarkar, Shyamalendu S.	Prof	790-4367	ssarkar		PHD	69	Mich St	1969
Welch, William P.	Assoc	790-5605	welch	CJL	PHD	86	U Wash	1986

St. Ambrose University	Davenport, IA 52803 (319) 333-6382						sau.edu	
Dept of Finance & Economics	College of Business Fax=333-6268						Caryl S. Altemus	
Collis, John W.	Dean	333-6272	jcollis		PHD	84	Iowa	1984
Bereskin, C. Gregory	Prof	333-6140	gbereskn		PHD	83	Missouri	1991
Lee, Christopher	Prof	333-6120	clee		PHD	90	GeoMason	1995
Oberle, Wayne H.	Prof	333-6120	woberle		PHD	69	Missouri	1977
Woodruff, Theodore S.	Prof	333-6420	twoodruf	DEHL	PHD	76	Columbia	8-95
Lynn, Billy	Assoc	333-6383	blynn		PHD	94	Illinois	1994
Moreau, Arthur	Assoc	333-6436	amoreau		PHD			1999

Saint Anselm College Manchester, NH 03102-1310 (603)
Economics Faculty Dept of Economics & Bus Fax=641-7116
Did Not Respond Again--1995-96 Listing

Romps, John F.	C-Ac	641-7140		ABEH	MA	68	Fordham	1968
Kenison, Arthur M.	Prof	641-7138		ACG	PHD	80	Boston U	1980
Kenison, Jeanne H.	Assoc	669-1030		C	EDD	86	Vanderbilt	1988
Minor, Frank J.	Assoc	641-7125			PHD	58	Ohio St	
Moses, Anthony T.	Assoc	641-7139			PHD			
Becker, Gilbert B.	Asst	641-7134		AD	PHD	83	Boston C	1987

College of Saint Benedict St Joseph, MN 56374 (612) 363-5383 csbsju.edu
Economics Faculty Department of Economics Fax= Judy Eggeret
Homepage: www.csbsju.edu/economics/
share faculty with Saint John's Univ, Collegeville MN

Olson, John F.	C-Ac	363-5406	jolson	NE	PHD	84	Rochester	1985
Diedrich, Ernest R.	Prof	363-3518	ediedrich	GR	PHD	83	Colo St	1980
Finn, Daniel Rush	Prof	363-3048	dfinn	B	PHD	77	Chicago	1977
Clemens Chair in Economics and the Liberal Arts-Dean, School of Theology								
Friedrich, Joseph	Prof	363-3045	jfriedrich	DHI	MA	70	Wisconsin	1967
Lewis, Margaret	Assoc	363-5977	mlewis	CBJL	PHD	89	Maryland	1989
Litterst, Lawrence J.	Assoc	363-5917	llitterst	EGJ	PHD	81	N Illinois	1979
Rambeck, Charles	Assoc	363-3524	crambeck	CDF	PHD	79	Minnesota	1975
Johnston, Lewis	Asst	363-2574	ljohnston	ENO	PHD	90	Berkeley	1997

Saint Bonaventure Univ S Bonaventure NY 14778 (716) 375-2082 sbu.edu
Finance and Economics Sch of Business Admin Fax=375-2191

Fischer, Michael J.	Dean	375-2200	mfischer	Atg	PHD	93	Penn St	1985
Peterson, Jeffrey H.	C-Ac	375-2082	peterson	G	PHD	91	Alabama	1984
Florence, Robert	Asst	375-2082		HD	PHD	97	Purdue	2000
Paul, Rodney	Asst	375-2082		E	PHD	00	Clemson	2001
Bachstein, Kristen	Lect	375-2082		E	MA	93	Alabama	2001

College of St. Catherine St Paul, MN 55105 (651) 690-8717 stkate.edu
Economics Faculty Department of Economics Fax=690-6024

Jewell, Nasrin	Prof	690-6830		OA	PHD	81	Wisconsin	1981
Ashley, James R.	Assoc	690-6852	jrashley	AL	PHD	84	Wisconsin	1984
Shikha, Deep	Assoc	690-6577	dshikha	FA	PHD	85	LSU	1985

St. Cloud State University Saint Cloud, MN 56301-4498 (320) 255-2227 stcloudstate.edu
Department of Economics Col of Social Sciences Fax=255-2228 Melanie Tighe

Luksetich, William A.	C-Pr	255-4291	a00001		PHD	73	N Illinois	1972
Banaian, King	Prof	255-4797	kbanaian		PHD	86	Claremont	1984
Bodvarsson, Orn B.	Prof	255-2968	i00002		PHD	86	Simon Fr	1988
Edwards, Mary E.	Prof	255-3742	edwards		PHD	88	Tx A&M	1985
Gallagher, Daniel J.	Prof	255-3051	dgallagher		PHD	76	Maryland	1982
Gleisner, Richard F.	Prof	255-3052	b00001		PHD	72	Geotown	1968
Larkin, L. Andrew	Prof	229-5628	larkin		PHD	82	Nebraska	1982
Lofgreen, Harold A.	Prof	255-4250	lofgreen		PHD	72	Iowa	1972
Director, Social Science Research Institute								
Moghaddam, Masoud	Prof	255-4209	masoud		PHD	82	Iowa St	1983
White, Michael D.	Prof	255-3163	mdwhite		PHD	78	Tx Tech	1978
Hampton, Nathan E.	Assoc	255-3825	h00003		PHD	89	Ca-SnBarb	1987
Hughes, Patricia A. Nold	Assoc	255-2076	nold		PHD	91	Ca-SnBarb	1988
Kang, Eungmin B.	Assoc	654-5223	kang		PHD	90	Geo St	1990
Patridge, Mark	Assoc	255-2072	mpartridge		PHD	91	Illinois	1995
Grossman, Philip J.	Asst	255-4232	pgrossman		PHD	84	Virginia	9-99
MacDonald, Richard A.	Asst	255-4781	macdonald		PHD	92	SUNY-Bin	1989
Director, Center for Economic Education								

St. Edward's University Austin, TX 78704-6489 (512) 448-8696 admin.stedwards.edu
Department of Economics School of Business Fax=416-5819
Did Not Respond Again--1997-98 Listing

Kelliher, Marsha	Dean	448-8658	marshak		LLM	94	Ca-SnDgo	1993
Tombe, Wani Luan	C-As	448-8599			PHD	85	Tx-Austin	1990
Pluta, Joseph E.	Prof	448-8645			PHD	72	Tx-Austin	1984
Koch, James C.	Assoc	448-8453			MSIR	59	Loyl-Chgo	1960

St. Francis College-NY Brooklyn Hght NY 11201-4398 (718) 489-5266 stfranciscollege.edu
Economics Faculty Department of Economics Fax=522-1274 Ms. Johnnie Cheatham

Tabrizi, Behrouz	C-As	489-5445	btabrizi		PHD	84	Jawahar	9-97
Quick, Paddy	Prof	489-5266	pquick	ABN	PHD	75	Harvard	9-85
Assistant Dean								

St. John Fisher College	Rochester, NY	14618	(716) 385-8099					sjfc.edu
Economics Faculty	Department of Economics	Fax=385-8129						
Linsley, Colin A.	C-Acc	385-8099	linsley	N	PHD	86	Essex	1987
Maggs, Gary E.	Prof	385-8432	maggs	E	PHD	86	W Virginia	1986
Maley, Jean E.	Prof	385-8097	maley	D	PHD	72	Rochester	1968
Roche, John T.	Assoc	385-8119	roche	BP	PHD	81	Mass	1981
Cherry, Monica	Asst	385-8101	cherry	J	PHD	98	SUNY-Bin	1996
Hovey, Craig	VInst	385-8099	hovey	M	PHD		Union In	1998

St. John's University	Jamaica, NY	11439	(718) 990-6419					stjohns.edu
Dept of Economics & Finance	Col of Business Admin	Fax=990-1868						
Tobin, Peter	Dean	990-6477						1998
Angelini, Anthony L. P.	C-Ac	990-6420			MA	51	Temple	
Liaw, K. Thomas	C-Pr	990-6161	liawt		PHD	88	Nrthwstrn	9-88
Chen, Thomas P.	Prof	990-7347			PHD	76	CUNY	
Clark, Charles	Prof	990-6161			PHD	90	New Sch	1985
Gokturk, S. Sadik	Prof				PHD	72	Columbia	
Gordon, Sara L.	Prof	969-6161			PHD	71	Stanford	1978
Jain, Chaman Lal	Prof				PHD	65	American	
Lawson, Stanley J.	Prof	990-6161			PHD	73	NYU	1978
Lees, Francis A.	Prof	990-6161			PHD	61	NYU	1961
Mauer, Laurence J.	Prof	990-6161			PHD	67	Tennessee	1983
Rider, Christine	Prof	969-6161			PHD	79	New Sch	1976
Shapiro, Aharon H.	Prof	969-6161			PHD	66	New Sch	1967
Bansal, Vipul K.	Assoc				PHD	88	Miss	
Buechner, M. Northup	Assoc	990-6161			PHD	71	Virginia	1970
Choi, Young Back	Assoc	876-6161			PHD	86	Michigan	
Ellis, Mary E.	Assoc				PHD	83	S Carol	
Englander, Valerie	Assoc	390-4545			PHD	75	Rutgers	1982
Flowers, Edward B.	Assoc				PHD	75	Geo St	
Furfero, Arlene J.	Assoc				PHD	80	Rutgers	
Giacalone, Joseph A.	Assoc	990-6161			PHD	71	Columbia	1962
Maran, Michael J.	Assoc				PHD	94	Penn	
Mongiovi, Gary	Assoc	990-7380			PHD	88	New Sch	1985
Moy, Ronald L.	Assoc				PHD	90	Rutgers	
Pappas, Anthony	Assoc				PHD	71	Yale	
Terregrossa, Ralph A.	Assoc				PHD	91	SUNY-Bin	
Tomic, Igor M.	Assoc				PHD	85	CUNY	
Wong, Kwok-Fai Matthew	Assoc	Ext 7313	wongk@sjuvm.	GM	PHD	91	Miss	1990
Eng, Maximo	Adj	990-6161			PHD	66	NYU	1985
Pizzigno, Gregory D.	Adj				MBA		St Johns	
Assistant Dean & Director of Graduate Program								

Saint Joseph's University	Philadelphia, PA	19131-1395	(610) 660-1593					sju.edu
Department of Economics	Col of Arts & Sciences	Fax=660-3300						Mrs. Dori Pappas
Chapman, Judith G.	Dean	660-1282	jchapman	Psy	PHD	87	Syracuse	1988
Prendergast, George A.	C-Pr	660-1592	gprender	EN	PHD	72	Penn	1956
Bookman, Milica Z.	Assoc	660-1590	mbookman	OP	PHD	83	Temple	1983
Dragonette, Joseph E.	Assoc	660-1594	jdragone	CE	PHD	74	Penn	1967
Fox, Nancy R.	Assoc	660-1596	nfox	DJL	PHD	89	Penn	1986
Burke, Thomas F.	VAsst	660-3355	tburke		PHD	99	Temple	1995
Sullivan, Edward J.	VInst	660-1595	wmc1998@a	EF	ABD	81	Fordham	1998

St. Lawrence University	Canton, NY	13617-1475	(315) 229-5430					stlawu.edu
Economics Faculty	Department of Economics	Fax=229-5819						Judith Van Kennen
Blewett, Robert A.	C-Pr	229-5429	blewett	OR	PHD	80	Va Tech	1983
Richardson, David H.	Prof	229-5431	drichardson	CJEF	PHD	66	Purdue	1979
Charles A. Dana Professor of Economics								
Young, Jeffrey T.	Prof	229-5427	jyoung	BQ	PHD	75	Colorado	1980
FitzRandolph, Peter Winfield	Assoc	229-5425	pfitzrandolph	FN	PHD	79	Tufts	1973
Horwitz, Steven G.	Assoc	229-5731	shorwitz	EPB	PHD	90	GeoMason	1989
Chezum, Brian	Asst	229-5426	bchezum	JL	PHD	92	Kentucky	1995
Delrossi, Alison	Asst	229-5449	adelrossi	HK	PHD	93	Penn	1999
Gottschall, Tiffani	VAsst	229-5430	tgottschall	JR	PHD	00	SUNY-Bin	2001
Jenkins, M.	Asst	229-5525	mjenkins	FE	PHD	95	Penn St	2000
Kroll, Stephen	Asst	229-5428	skroll	QC	PHD	99	Wyoming	1999

Saint Louis University	St. Louis, MO	63108	(314) 977-3848					slu.edu
Department of Economics	John Cook School of Bus	Fax=977-1478						Nancy Young
Seitz, Neil E.	Dean	977-3833		Fnce	PHD	73	Ohio St	1975
Islam, Muhammad Q.	C-Ac	977-3822			PHD	89	Indiana	1988
Grossman, Leroy J.	Prof	977-3830			PHD	63	Vanderbilt	1964
Welch, Patrick J.	Prof	977-3814			PHD	73	Pittsburgh	1983
Strauss, Jack K.	Assoc	977-3813			PHD	89	Duke	
Bednarek, Heather L.	Asst	977-3848			PHD	99	Mich St	2001

Chaney, Rick L.	Asst				PHD	84	Illinois	1986
Dean St Louis-Madrid								
Funk, Mark	Asst	977-3844			PHD	98	Ca-Davis	1998
Qian, Hailong	Asst	977-3866			PHD	95	Mich St	1999
Varghese, Adel	Asst	977-3629			PHD	96	Penn	1995
Yigit, Taner	Asst	977-3604			PHD	99	N Carol	2000

Saint Martin's College Lacey, WA 98503-1297 (360) 438-4512 crcstmartin.edu
Economics Faculty Div Business & Econ Fax=438-4522 Linda Newman
Did Not Respond--1999-2000 Listing

Knutson, Jerry L.	Dean	438-4512	jknutson		MBA	83	Puget Sd	1987
Wallace, Don	Assoc	438-4329	dwallace		PHD	63	U Wash	

Saint Mary's College-CA Moraga, CA 94575-4230 (925) 631-4607 stmarys-ca.edu
Economics Faculty Sch of Econ & Bus Adm Fax=376-5625

Allen, Roy E.	Dean	631-4595	rallen		PHD	83	Berkeley	1985
Hannon, Joan U.	C-Pr	631-4588	jhannon		PHD	78	Wisconsin	1987
Bodily, Jerry J.	Prof	631-4607	jbodily		PHD	74	Purdue	1978
Chase, Kristine L.	Prof	631-4590	kchase		PHD	87	Maryland	1985
Vice President, Finance								
Lee, William C.	Prof	631-4589	wlee		PHD	77	Ca-SnBarb	1982
Moseldjord, Asbjorn	Assoc	631-4596	amoseidj		PHD		Ca-SnBarb	1991
Katz, Elizabeth	Asst	631-4583	ekatz	O	PHD	92	Wisconsin	1999

Saint Marys College-IN Notre Dame, IN 46556-5001 (219) 284-4501 saintmarys.edu
Economics Faculty Dept Bus Admin & Econ Fax=284-4716 Vivian Vargo
Homepage: http://www.saint-marys.edu/~buec/

McElroy, Jerome L.	C-Pr	284-4488	jmcelroy	AEFO	PHD	71	Colorado	8-82
Measell, Richard F.	Asst	284-4525	rmeasell	ADHJ	PHD	85	Maryland	8-83

St. Mary's University-TX San Antonio, TX 78284 (210) 436-3112 stmarytx.edu
Department of Economics Sch of Human & Soc Sci Fax=431-4211

Dizimno, Janet	Dean	436-3737		Psy	PHD	82	Fla St	
Robbins, Roy E.	C-As	436-3112	rrobins		MA	75	St MryTX	1983
Velez, Alejandro	Prof	436-3142	econal		PHD	77	Florida	
Scott, Gary J.	Asst	436-3111	gscott		PHD	93	Notre Dm	1994

Saint Michael's College Colchester, VT 05439-0125 (802) 654-2298 smcvax.smvt.educ
Economics Faculty Department of Economics Fax=655-3680 Carol Martin

Kessel, Herbert	C-Pr	654-2460	kessel	AJDC	PHD	81	Boston U	1977
Carvellas, John N.	Prof	654-2365	carvellas	ACER	PHD	81	Syracuse	1974
Ramazani, M. Reza	Prof	654-2360	ramazani	AFEC	PHD	90	Colorado	1986
Natarajan-Marsh, Tara	Asst	654-2298		AOPB	PHD	01	Nebraska	1996

St. Norbert College DePere, WI 54115-2099 (920) 403-3224 mail.snc.edu
Department of Economics Div of Social Sciences Fax=403-4098
Did Not Respond--1999-2000 Listing

Elfner, Eliot S.	C-Pr	403-3233	elfnes	BAdm	PHD	77	Wisconsin	1971
Odorzynski, Sandra J.	C-Pr	403-3224	odorsj		PHD	76	Purdue	1978
Paul, Sanjay	Asst	403-3889	paulsa		PHD	92	SUNY-Buf	1992
Quinn, Kevin G.	Asst	403-3447	quinkg		PHD	95	Il-Chicago	1994
vonderRuhr, Marc	Asst		vondma		PHD	99	Indiana	1999

St. Olaf College Northfield, MN 55057-1098 (507) 646-3149 stolaf.edu
Economics Faculty Department of Economics Fax=646-3523 Pat Hall

Carlson, William L.	C-Pr	646-3152	carlson	C	PHD	70	Michigan	1973
Dalgaard, Bruce R.	Prof	646-3567	dalgaard	EPA	PHD	76	Illinois	1992
Husby-Johnson Professor in Business & Economics								
Emery, E. David	Prof	646-3139	emeryd	DIA	PHD	69	Minnesota	1969
Schodt, David W.	Prof	646-3156	schodt	OAH	PHD	80	Wisconsin	1977
Becker, Anthony D.	Assoc	437-2882	becker	DLC	PHD	86	Duke	1987
Chadwick, Kathy	Assoc	646-3154	chadwick	M	PHD	83	Nrthwstrn	1985
Emery, Mary Ann	Assoc	646-3139	emerym	M	MA	65	Minnesota	1969
Geodde, Richard	Assoc	646-3126	goedde	M	MBA		Wisconsin	1988
Judge, Rebecca P.	Assoc	646-3151	judge	ADQ	PHD	76	Duke	1987
Pernecky, Mark L.	Assoc	646-3432	pernecky	EJA	PHD	90	Notre Dm	1990
Pomponio, Xun	Assoc	646-3151	pomponio	FP	PHD	91	Penn St	1991
Soderlind, Steven D.	Assoc	646-3153	soderlin	RA	PHD	80	Mass	1982
Wojick, Paul P.	Assoc	646-3152	wojick	AE	PHD	89	Colorado	1988

Saint Peter's College	Jersey City, NJ	07306	(201) 915-9250				spcvxa.spc.edu	
Economics Faculty	Department of Economics	Fax=					Nancy Carbone	
Did Not Respond--1999-2000 Listing								
D'Amico, Thomas F.	C-Pr	915-9250	damico_t	EJT	PHD	83	NYU	1982
Shapiro, Nina	Assoc			DEL	PHD		New Sch	1999
Biolsi, Robert	Asst	915-9251		FG	PHD		CUNY	6-97
Gorcau, Suleyman	Asst			FG	PHD		CUNY	1998

The College of Saint Rose	Albany, NY	12203	(518) 458-5272				mail.strose.edu	
Economics Faculty	School of Business	Fax=458-5449					Maria Freund	
Carlson, Severin C.	Dean	454-2122	scarlson	Fnce	DBA	79	Indiana	1999
Mehtabdin, Khalid R.	C-Ac	458-5467	mehtabd	AEFM	PHD	79	Pittsburgh	1986
Sung, Simona	Assoc	458-5869	sungs	CDEL	PHD	90	Rensselaer	8-90

College of St. Scholastica	Duluth, MN	55811-4199	(218) 723-6415				css.edu	
Economic Faculty	Economics	Fax=723-6150					Mary E. Lee	
Tarnowski, Susan	Dean	723-6012			PHD		Minnesota	7-01
Barrett, Anthony	C-Pr	723-6471	tbarrett		PHD	84	Geo Wash	
Hoffman, Robert	Asst	723-6715	rhoffman	E	PHD	92	Boston C	

St. Thomas University-FL	Miami, FL	33054	(305) 628-6627				stu.edu	
Department of Business Adm	School of Business Adm	Fax=628-6504						
Mitchell, Lloyd A.	C-As	628-6622	lmitchel		MBA	81	U Miami	1984
Carrillo, Raul J.	Assoc	628-6534	rcarril		DA		U Miami	1972
Espino, Dolores	Assoc	628-6791	mespino		PHD		Fla St	1999
Flax, Stanley	Asst	628-6635	sflax		MBA		NYU	1986

University of St. Thomas-MN	St. Paul, MN	55105-1096	(651) 962-5675				stthomas.edu	
Economics Faculty	Div of Social Sciences	Fax=962-6360					Mary Rudolph	
phone 962-5000								
Connery, Thomas	Dean	962-6000						
Langan, Terence G.	C-Acc	962-5684	t9langan	L	PHD	88	Minnesota	
Blumenthal, Marsha A.	Prof	962-5678	mablumenthal	JH	PHD	85	Minnesota	1984
Gray, Charles M.	Prof	962-4301	cmgray	K	PHD	78	Wash U	1976
Kreitzer, Joseph L.	Prof	962-5683	jlkreitzer	C	PHD	83	Iowa	1981
Alexander, Susan L.	Assoc	962-5677	slalexander	F	PHD	77	So Meth	1981
Fairchild, Daniel R.	Assoc	962-5676	drfairchild	F	PHD	78	St Louis	1976
Marcott, Craig S.	Assoc	962-5685	csmarcott	C	PHD	83	Purdue	1982
Papagapitos, Agapipos	Assoc	962-5686	a9papagapitos	OP	PHD	92	Ohio St	
Riley, Robert	Assoc	962-5687	rjriley	F	PHD	91	Wisconsin	
Selim, Mohamed Ali	Assoc	962-5180	maselim	A	PHD	81	Minnesota	1959
Vincent, James W.	Assoc	962-5689	jwvincent	Q	PHD	82	Wisconsin	1988
Walsh, William J.	Assoc	962-5690	wjwalsh	E	PHD	70	Notre Dm	1970
Fenn, Aju	Asst	962-5675	ajfenn	HQ	PHD	98	Iowa St	1999
Harmann, Monica	Asst	962-5681	mehartmann	CKL	PHD	00	Virginia	2000
Kim, Jaebeom	Asst	962-5675	jbkim	CF	PHD	00	Ohio St	2001
Saavedra, Luz A.	Asst	962-5675	lasaavedra	HR	PHD	98	Illinois	2001
Supel, Mary R.	Asst	962-5688	m9supel	L	BA		Denison	1976

University of St. Thomas-TX	Houston, TX	77006-4696	(713) 525-2100				basil.stthom.edu	
Department of Economics	Cameron Sch of Business	Fax=525-2110						
Ho, Yhi-Min	Dean	522-7911		OQ	PHD	65	Vanderbilt	8-70
Hugh Roy and Lillie Cullen Professor of Economics								
Wilbratte, Barry J.	C-Pr	522-7911		FG	PHD	71	Tulane	1971
Canac, Pierre	Assoc	522-7911		F	PHD	87	Houston	1990
Morefield, Roger D.	Assoc	522-7911		I	PHD	77	Duke	1980
Shirvani, Hassan M.	Assoc	522-7911		FG	PHD	79	Harvard	1986
Ueng, C. Joe	Assoc	522-7911		GM	PHD	95	St Louis	1996
Williams, Michael	Asst	522-7911		H	PHD	96	Rice	2000

Saint Vincent College	Latrobe, PA	15650-2690	(724) 537-4597				stvincent.edu	
Economics Faculty	Department of Economics	Fax=537-4599						
Quinlivan, Gary M.	C-Pr	537-4597	gq	CDF	PHD	83	SUNY-Alb	1981
Herr, Andy	Assoc	537-4597	herr	HEQ	PHD	96	Indiana	1991

Salem State College	Salem, MA	01970-4589	(978)				mecn.mass.edu	
Department of Economics	Sch of Business & Econ	Fax=542-6027						
Did Not Respond Again--1995-96 Listing								
Meadow, H. Lee	Dean	542-6640		Mktg	PHD	83	Va Tech	2001
Wesolowski, Karl A.	C-Ac	542-6636			MA		Boston C	
Calabro, Eugene A.	Prof	542-6653			MA		Boston C	
Lucas, Henry A. Jr.	Assoc	542-6683			JD		Suffolk	
Crofts, Robert D.	Asst	542-6615			MA		Northeas	
Pawlak, Andrew T.	Asst	542-6682			MA		Tufts	
Siden, Dorothy R.	Asst	542-6681			PHD	90	Northeas	

Salisbury University Salisbury, MD 21801-6860 (410) 543-6315 salisbury.edu
Department of Economics Perdue Sch of Business Fax=546-6208 Ellen Fykes

Rubenson, George	Dean$	543-6316	gcrubenson	Mktg	PHD	89	Maryland	8-87
Manakyan, Herman	C-Pr	543-6315	hxmanakyan		PHD	89	Alabama	8-99
Khazeh, Kashi	Prof	543-6315	kxkhazeh		PHD	85	Tennessee	O-85
Greene, Benjamin B. Jr.	Assoc	543-6315	bbgreene		PHD	74	Boston C	8-78
Caviglia-Harris, Jill	Asst	543-6315	jlcaviglia		PHD	97	Tennessee	8-98
Cheng, Ping	Asst	543-6315	pxcheng		PHD	97	Geo St	8-98
Ervin, Danny	Asst	543-6315	dservin		PHD	96	Kentucky	1-99
Wu, Ying	Asst	543-6315	yxwu		PHD	92	Oregon	8-98
Kincard, Joel	Lect	543-6315	jkincard		PHD	99	N Car St	8-97

Salve Regina University Newport, RI 02840-4192 (401) Ext 3130 salve.edu
Economics Faculty Department of Economics Fax=
phone 847-6650 Ext 3130

Tonn, Victor Lux	C-Pr	847-6650	tonnv	AGOP	PHD	94	Utah St	1984
Lawber, Harold E. Jr.	Assoc	847-6650		ABEN	PHD	89	Conn	1988
Coughlan, Carmel	PLect	847-6650		M	MBA	90	Salve Rg	1990

Sam Houston State Univ Huntsville, TX 77341-2118 (409) 294-1265 shsu.edu
Dept Economics & Intl Bus College of Business Adm Fax=294-3488 Ms. Sally Kundig

Lewis, R. Dean	Dean	294-1254	bed rdl	Mktg	PHD	72	Arkansas	1980
Green, William B.	C-Pr	294-1265	eco¯wbg		PHD	74	LSU	1974
Samuels, George E.	Prof	294-1269	eco¯ges		PHD	72	Oregon	1975
Bumpass, Donald L.	Assoc	294-1268	eco¯dlb		PHD	76	Okla St	1992
Berg, Milo Douglas	Asst	294-1243	eco¯mdb		PHD	95	Tx A&M	1995
Blackburne, Edward	Asst	294-3934	eco¯efb		PHD	98	Tx A&M	1997
Freeman, Donald	Asst	294-1264	eco¯dgf		PHD	88	So Meth	1998
Muehsam, Mitchell J.	Asst	294-1243	eco¯mjm		PHD	89	Tx A&M	1989
Muehsam, Valerie P.	Asst	294-3712	eco¯vpm		PHD	98	Tx A&M	1993
Miller, John	Lect	294-1293	eco¯jmm		MS	65	Rice	1998

Samford University Birmingham, AL 35229-2306 (205) 726-2364 mailbox.samford.edu
Economics Faculty School of Business Fax=726-2464 M. J. Niesen
Did Not Respond--1999-2000 Listing

Bellas, Carl J.	Dean	726-2308		Mgt	PHD	69	Oregon	1996
Hendon, Fred N.	Prof	726-2549		FN	PHD	68	Alabama	1968
Marshall, Jennings B.	Prof	726-2539		CD	PHD	77	Kentucky	1986

University of San Diego San Diego, CA 92110-2492 (619) 260-4877 sandiego.edu
Department of Economics Sch of Business Admin Fax=260-4891 Dorene Deturi
Homepage: http://usdbusiness.sandiego.edu

Cook, Curtis	Dean	260-4886		Mgt	DBA	74	S Calif	1997
Allen, Andrew T.	Prof	260-4832	andrewt		PHD	83	Illinois	1984
Anderson, Joan B.	Prof	260-4857	joana		PHD	71	Ca-SnDgo	1981
Dimon, Denise	Prof	260-4836	dimon		PHD	86	Illinois	1983
Doshi, Kokila	Prof	260-4843	kdoshi		PHD		Rochester	1990
Johnson, Robert	Prof	260-4849	johnson		PHD		Oregon	1978
Narwold, Andrew	Prof	260-4875	drew		PHD	91	Ca-SnBarb	1991
O'Neil, Robert F.	Emer	260-4855	roneil		PHD	75	Fordham	
Sandy, Jonathan G.	Prof	260-4880	sandy		PHD	86	Ca-SnBarb	1986
Yandell, Dirk	Prof	260-4835	yandell		PHD	81	Purdue	1981
Gin, Alan	Assoc	260-4883	agin		PHD	87	Ca-SnBarb	1988
Holt, Charles F.	Assoc	291-6480	cholt		PHD	70	Purdue	1973

San Diego State University San Diego, CA 92182-4485 (619) 594-1675 mail.sdsu.edu
Department of Economics Col of Arts & Letters Fax=594-5062 Marie Butler 594-5530

Strand, Paul J.	Dean			PolS	PHD	75	Ohio St	1977
Thayer, Mark A.	C-Pr	594-5510	mthayer		PHD	79	New Mex	1981
Adler, Renatte K.	Prof	594-1662	radler	Q	PHD	79	New Mex	1982
Boddy, Raford D.	Prof	594-6239	rboddy		PHD	68	Michigan	1980
Frantz, Roger S.	Prof	594-3718	rfrantz		PHD	78	Wash St	1978
Gerber, James B.	Prof	594-5532	jgerber		PHD	86	Ca-Davis	1985
Green, Louis C.	Prof	594-5680	lgreen		PHD	75	Berkeley	1976
Grossbard-Shechtman, Shoshan	Prof	594-5468	shosh		PHD	78	Chicago	1981
Kartman, Arthur E.	Prof	594-5539	akartman		PHD	69	U Wash	1968
Madhavan, Murugappa C.	Prof	594-5492	madhavan		PHD	69	Wisconsin	1968
Nam, Woo Hyun	Prof	594-5478	wnam		PHD	68	U Wash	1968
Stewart, Douglas B.	Prof	594-5502	dstewart		PHD	70	Oregon	1971
Venieris, Yiannis P.	Prof	594-5503	venieris		PHD	69	Oregon	1967
Hambleton, John W.	Assoc	594-5458	jhamble		PHD	71	Wisconsin	1969
Amuedo-Dorantes, Catalina	Asst	594-1663			PHD	98	W Mich	1999
Bansak, Cynthia	Asst	594-1675			PHD	00	Ca-SnDgo	2001
Brunner, Eric	Asst	594-5601	brunner		PHD	95	Ca-SnBarb	1998
Mundra, Kusum	Asst	594-1675			PHD	01	Ca-Rivers	2001

University of San Francisco San Francisco CA 94117-1080 (415) 422-6784 usfca.edu
Department of Economics Col of Arts & Sciences Fax=422-2632 Cheryl Czekala

Nel, Stanley D.	Dean	422-6172	nel	Fnce	PHD	80	Capetown	1983
Veitch, John	C-Ac	422-6271	veitchj	EG	PHD	85	Nrthwstrn	1985
Fischer, Hartmut	Prof	422-6453	fischer	FA	PHD	73	Berkeley	1970
Kofi, Tetteh A.	Prof	422-6670	kofi	OA	PHD	70	Berkeley	1981
Lehmann, Michael B.	Prof	422-6631	lehmannm	NB	PHD	69	Cornell	1966
Lau, Man-Lui	Assoc	422-6730	laum	CD	PHD	86	Cornell	1992
N'Chu-Oguie, Charles	Assoc	422-6189	nchooguie	CO	PHD	84	Stanford	1984
Garcia, Marilyn	Asst	422-2257	garciam	EO	PHD	97	Berkeley	1997
Wydick, W. Bruce	Asst	422-5863	wydickb	DO	PHD	96	Berkeley	1996

San Francisco State Univ San Francisco CA 94132-4155 (415) 338-1839 sfsu.edu
Department of Economics Col of Behav & Soc Sci Fax=338-1057 Tammie McGee
Homepage: bss.sfsu.edu/economics

Kasiola, Joel	Dean	338-1846		PolS	PHD	74	Princeton	1995
Potepan, Michael J.	C-Ac	338-2648			PHD	85	Ca-Davis	1991
Anspach, Ralph	Prof	338-7513			PHD	63	Berkeley	1963
Spring Semester only								
Blecha, Betty J.	Prof	338-7516			PHD	76	Iowa	1983
Gemello, John M.	Prof	338-1839			PHD	74	Stanford	1975
Associate Vice President for Academic Resources								
Mason, William J.	Prof	338-7513			PHD	58	Iowa	1958
Moss, Joanna	Prof	338-3026			PHD	78	New Sch	1981
Osman, Jack W.	Prof	338-1116			PHD	66	Rutgers	1967
Fall semesters only								
Schweitzer, Robert N.	Prof	338-1839			PHD	63	Berkeley	1962
Fall semesters only								
Sisk, David E.	Prof	338-1715			PHD	76	UCLA	1978
Vencill, C. Daniel	Prof	338-7514			PHD	71	Stanford	1974
King, Philip G.	Assoc	338-2108			PHD	87	Cornell	1987
Mar, Donald W.	Assoc	338-2499			PHD	85	Berkeley	1987
Chattopadhyay, Sudip	Asst	338-1447			PHD	95	Illinois	1999
Hasse, Charles	Asst	338-1839			PHD	96	Ca-Davis	1997
Xu, Peng	Asst	338-7512			PHD	94	Iowa	1994

San Jose State University San Jose, CA 95192-0114 (408) 924-5400 sjsu.edu
Department of Economics Sch of Social Sciences Fax=924-5406 Janiece Fister

Noble, Lela G.	Dean	924-5300		Poly	PHD	70	Fletcher	1965
Ortega, Lydia	C-Pr	924-5400			PHD	87	GeoMason	1989
Cheng, Doris	Prof	924-5423			PHD	76	Notre Dm	1988
Garnel, Donald	Prof	924-5407			PHD	66	Berkeley	1958
Gonzalez, Rodolfo	Prof	924-5400			PHD	90	Ca-Davis	1990
Greer, Douglas F.	Prof	924-5409			PHD	68	Cornell	1975
Means, Tom S.	Prof	924-5414			PHD	83	UCLA	1986
Pogodzinski, Joseph Michael	Prof	924-5421			PHD	80	SUNY-SBr	1987
Saurman, David	Prof	924-1371			PHD	79	Tx A&M	1991
Shieh, Yeung-Nan	Prof	924-5413			PHD	80	Tx A&M	1989
Snowbarger, Marvin R.	Prof	924-5422			PHD	66	Michigan	1966
Watkins, Thayer H.	Prof	924-5420			PHD	65	Colorado	1957

Santa Clara University Santa Clara, CA 95050-0385 (408) 554-4341 scu.edu
Department of Economics Leavey Sch of Bus & Adm Fax=554-2331 Sharon Squyres
Homepage: http://lsb.scu.edu/economics

Posner, Barry Z.	Dean	554-4523	bposner	Mgt	PHD	76	Mass	1976
Sundstrom, William A.	C-Ac	554-6892	wsundstrom		PHD	86	Stanford	1987
Belotti, Mario L.	Prof	554-4086	mbelotti		PHD	69	Tx-Austin	1959
Donnelly, William F.	Prof	554-4948	wdonnelly		PHD	69	NYU	1969
Field, Alexander J.	Prof	554-4348	afield		PHD	74	Berkeley	1982
Heineke, John M.	Prof	554-4346	jheineke		PHD	68	Iowa	1968
Iannaccone, Laurence R.	Prof	554-4345	liannaccone		PHD	84	Chicago	1982
Whalen, Thaddeus J. Jr.	Prof	554-4791	twhalen		PHD	64	Berkeley	1962
Demmert, Henry G.	Assoc	554-4344	hdemmert		PHD	72	Stanford	1968
Associate Dean for Undergraduate Programs								
Kamas, Linda	Assoc	554-6950	lkamas		PHD	82	Berkeley	1988
Klein, Daniel B.	Assoc	554-6951	dklein		PHD	90	NYU	1996
Popper, Helen A.	Assoc	554-6952	hpopper		PHD	90	Berkeley	1991
Russell, Thomas R.	Assoc	554-6953	trussell		PHD	73	Cambridge	1978
Kevane, Michael	Asst	554-4574	mkevane		PHD	94	Berkeley	1995
Mitchener, Kris J.	Asst	554-4341	kmitchener		PHD	01	Berkeley	2001

Sarah Lawrence College Bronxville, NY 10708-5999 (914) 337-0700 mail.slc.edu
Economics Faculty Department of Economics Fax=395-2663

Power, Marilyn	C-Pr	395-2658	mpower	ABJ	PHD	77	Berkeley	1990
Price, Charlotte A.	Prof	395-2404	cprice	AENQ	PHD	67	Columbia	1971
Roosevelt, Frank	Prof	395-2491	froos	ABDP	PHD	76	New Sch	1977
Moudud, Jamee	Guest	395-2623	jmoudud	EFO	PHD	98	New Sch	2000

University of Scranton Scranton, PA 18510-4602 (570) 941-4048 uofs.edu
Dept of Economics & Finance Kania School of Mgt Fax=941-4825 Ms. Susan Moir

Johnson, Ronald D.	Dean	941-4208	johnsonr2		DBA	70	Indiana	1997
Ghosh, Satyajit	C-Pr	941-6197	ghoshs1		PHD	85	SUNY-Buf	1986
Bose, Mrigen	Assoc	941-7727	mb353		PHD	72	Utah	1968
Corcione, Frank P.	Assoc	941-7760	corcionef1		PHD	75	Lehigh	1978
Hussain, Riaz	Assoc	941-7497	hussain		PHD	90	Lehigh	1967
Kallianiotis, John	Assoc	941-7577	jnk353		PHD	85	CUNY	1990
Murli, Rajan	Assoc	941-6240	mr353		PHD	92	Temple	1989
Nguyen, Hong V.	Assoc	941-7475	jnk353		PHD	81	SUNY-Bin	1979
Scahill, Edward M.	Assoc	941-4187	ems343		PHD	83	SUNY-Bin	1989
Trussler, Susan	Assoc	941-6122	trussler		PHD	89	Penn St	1985

Seattle University Seattle, WA 98122-4340 (206) 296-2540 seattleu.edu
Dept of Economics & Finance Albers Sch Bus & Econ Fax=296-2486 Ms. Peggy Allende

Phillips, Joseph M. Jr.	Dean	296-5700	phillipsj	FOR	PHD	82	Notre Dm	2001
Yates, Barbara M.	C-Pr	296-2540	bmyates	AEGH	PHD	69	Michigan	1970
Rivers, Mary J.	Assoc	296-5717	rivers	CDM	PHD	82	Pittsburgh	1978
Sorenson, Timothy L.	Assoc	296-5738	tsore	MDF	PHD	91	Harvard	1991
Green, Gareth P.	Asst	296-2536	greeng	DEQ	PHD	95	Berkeley	2001
Hiedemann, Bridget G.	Asst	296-2803	bgh	DJT	PHD	92	Duke	1994
Peterson, Dean J.	Asst	296-2538	dean	B	PHD	94	Illinois	1991
Weber, Christian E.	Asst	296-5725	cweber	EO	PHD	92	Duke	1993

Seattle Pacific University Seattle, WA 98119-1997 (206) 281-2700 spu.edu
Department of Economics Sch of Business & Econ Fax=281-2733 Ruth Myers
Homepage: www.spu.edu/depts/sbe/

VanDuzer, Jeffrey B.	Dean	281-2087	vandj	Law	JD	79	Yale	9-98
Downing, Douglas A.	C-Ac	281-2890	ddowning	ACH	PHD	87	Yale	1983
Deming, Jonathan C.	Assoc	281-2181	jdeming	BR	PHD	79	Oregon	1977
Surdyk, Lisa	Assoc	281-2709	lsurdyk	G	PHD	91	U Wash	1991

Seton Hall University South Orange, NJ 07079-2692 (973) 761-7723 lanmail.shu.edu
Department of Economics Stillman School of Bus Fax=761-9217 Ms. Alliya Cunningham
Did Not Respond--1999-2000 Listing

Martin, Dolores	Dean	761-9013			PHD	76	Va Tech	
Dall, John J. Jr.	C-Pr	761-9356	dalljohn		PHD	68	Penn	
Jordan, W. John	Prof	761-9236	jordanja		PHD	77	SUNY-Alb	1977
Ketkar, Kusum	Prof	761-9102	ketkarku		PHD	80	Vanderbilt	1983
Tinari, Frank D.	Prof	761-9125	tinarifr		PHD	76	Fordham	
Tzannetakis, George	Prof	761-9211	tzannege		PHD	64	NYU	
Ikpoh, Andrew	Assoc	761-9799	ikpohand		PHD	88	Columbia	
Kant, Chander	Assoc	761-9281	kantchan		PHD	80	So Meth	1987
Loviscek, Anthony	Asst	761-9127	lovisclo		PHD	80	W Virginia	1992

Shenandoah University Winchester, VA 22601-5195 (540) 665-4572 su.edu
Economics Faculty Byrd School of Business Fax=665-5437

Harrison, Stanley E.	Dean	665-4572	sharriso		PHD	89	OSU	1999
Pavsek, Daniel A.	Prof	665-4526	dpavsek		PHD	81	Case Wes	1992
Thies, Clifford F.	Prof	665-5450	cthies		PHD	82	Boston C	1992
Honeycutt, Theresa	Assoc	665-4572	tspencer		PHD	89	N Car St	1997

Shepherd College Shepherdstwn WV 25443-1569 (304) 876-5241 shepherd.wvnet.edu
Department of Economics Business & Soc Sciences Fax=876-5193 Arlene Stevens

Reid, Kathleen A.	C-Pr	876-5306	kreid		PHD	86	Penn St	1983
Johnson, E. William	Prof	876-5432	bjohnson		PHD	74	Virginia	1971
Phillips, Edward S.	Prof	876-5353	sphillips		PHD	70	Colorado	1974
Kinney, Kinney	Assoc	876-5434	lkinney		PHD	85	Maryland	1994
Schultz, John A.	Assoc	876-5352	jschultz		PHD	85	S Carol	1988

Shippensburg University Shippensburg, PA 17257-2299 (717) 477-1437 ark.ship.edu
Department of Economics College of Business Fax=477-4003 Vicki Shaak
Did Not Respond--1999-2000 Listing

Finucane, Brendan P.	C-Pr	477-1437			PHD	82	Pittsburgh	1982
Bastin, Hamid	Prof	477-1679			PHD	89	Geo St	1989
Eggleston, Robert C.	Prof	477-1675			PHD	84	Pittsburgh	1965
Lee, Daniel Y.	Prof	477-1556			PHD	86	Pittsburgh	1986
Mathis, Stephen A.	Prof	477-1696			PHD	79	Iowa St	1979
Posatko, Robert C.	Prof	477-1138			PHD	75	Penn St	1981
Reinwald, Thomas P.	Prof	477-1437			PHD	73	Illinois	1974
Koscianski, Janet	Assoc	477-1174			PHD	90	S Illinois	1990

Siena College Loundonville, NY 12211-1462 (518) 783-2398 siena.edu
Department of Economics Business Division Fax=783-4293

Conway, Thomas E. Jr.	Dean	783-2321	tconway	Atg	PHD	98	Maryland	1999
Trees, W. Scott	C-As		trees		PHD	94	Notre Dm	9-85
Howe, Edward T.	Prof		howe		PHD	73	SUNY-Alb	
Reinhart, Blaise F.	Prof				PHD	62	Catholic	
Shirey, Richard L.	Assoc	783-2398	shirey		PHD	94	SUNY-Alb	9-79

Simmons College Boston, MA 02115-5898 (617) 521-2594 vmsvax.simmons.edu
Economics Faculty Col Arts & Sci & Prof S Fax=521-3199 Jaye Smith
Did Not Respond--1999-2000 Listing

Kenyon, Daphne A.	C-Pr	521-2587	dkenyon	HI	PHD	80	Michigan	1989
Basch, Donald L.	Prof	521-2584	dbasch	D	PHD	77	Yale	1980
Sawtelle, Barbara A.	Prof	521-2582	bsawtelle	E	PHD	76	MIT	1970
Biewener, Carole	Assoc	521-2583	cbiewener	FB	PHD	89	Mass	1987
Aoki, Masato	VAsst	521-2580	maoki	A	PHD	95	Mass	1994

Simpson College Indianola, IA 50125 (515) 961-1652 storm.simpson.edu
Dept Mgt, Atg & Economics Div of Policy Studies Fax=961-1498 Cindy Hamilton

Mueller, Marilyn	C-Pr	961-1574	mueller	Law	JD	81	Drake	1986
Colella, Francis J.	Prof	961-1513	colella	BEFN	PHD	73	Fordham	1977
Palmieri, James	Asst	961-1801	palmieri	DHIJ	PHD	95	Indiana	1997

Skidmore College Saratoga Sprg NY 12866-1632 (518) Ext 5090 skidmore.edu
Economics Faculty Department of Economics Fax=580-5099 Amelia Clarke
Homepage: skidmore.edu/academics/economics/econhome.html

Baum, Sandra R.	C-Pr	580-5092	sbaum		PHD	81	Columbia	1987
Rotheim, Roy J.	Prof	580-5115	rrotheim		PHD	77	Rutgers	1980
Jones, Robert J.	Assoc	580-5094	rjones		PHD	78	Columbia	1973
on leave Spring 2002								
Koechlin, Tim	Assoc	580-5095	tkoechli		PHD	89	Mass	1988
on leave Fall 2001								
Odekon, Mehmet A.	Assoc	580-5097	modekon		PHD	77	SUNY-Alb	1983
Chiteji, Ngina	Asst	580-5073	nchiteji		PHD	99	N Carol	1999
Flores-Guri, Daniel	Asst	580-5090	dflores		PHD	01	Boston	2001
Haynes, Curtis Jr.	Asst	580-5097	chaynes		PHD	93	Mass	2001
Vargha, Linda	Asst	580-5098	lvargha		PHD	99	Wisconsin	1999

Slippery Rock University Slippery Rock PA 16057-1326 (724) 738-2008 sru.edu
School of Business Col Bus, Info & Soc Sci Fax=738-2959 Carrie Kerr 738-2223

Mastrianna, Frank V.	Dean	738-2008	un3600		PHD	68	Cincinnati	3-87
Orvis, Bruce	C-As	738-2013		Mktg	PHD	96	Oklahoma	8-95
Culp, David B.	Assoc	738-2971	david.culp	AEN	PHD	96	S Illinois	1978
Tannery, Frederick J.	Assoc	738-2579	frederick.tan+	ACDJ	PHD	80	Pittsburgh	1981
Valencia, Jesus M.	Asst	738-2577	jesus.valencia	ACFJ	PHD	88	Pittsburgh	1983

Smith College Northampton, MA 01063 (413) 585-3600 email.smith.edu
Economics Faculty Department of Economics Fax=585-3389 Judy Fountain

Kaufman, Roger T.	C-Pr	585-3612	rtkaufman	CEJP	PHD	78	MIT	1983
Aldrich, Mark	Prof	585-3603	maldrich	JLN	PHD	69	Tx-Austin	1968
Averitt, Robert T.	Prof	585-3604	raveritt	ABE	PHD	61	Tx-Austin	1961
Bartlett, Randall	Prof	585-3605	rbartlett	AHR	PHD	71	Stanford	1979
Buchele, Robert	Prof	585-3607	rbuchele	CAJP	PHD	76	Harvard	1977
Haas-Wilson, Deborah	Prof	585-3636	dhwilson	DIL	PHD	83	Berkeley	1984
Leonard, Frederick H.	Prof	585-3614	fleonard	AEG	PHD	66	Michigan	1966
Pfeifer, Karen	Prof	585-3623	kpfeifer	BNOP	PHD	81	American	1979
Savoca, Elizabeth A.	Prof	585-3615	esavoca	CEIT	PHD	82	Berkeley	1982
Zimbalist, Andrew	Prof	585-3622	zimbalis	CJLP	PHD	74	Harvard	1974
Mahdavi, Mahnaz	Assoc	585-3629	mmahdavi	FGM	PHD	86	Michigan	1985
Reinhardt, Nola	Assoc	585-3617	nreinhar	OPQ	PHD	81	Berkeley	1981
Riddell, Thomas A.	Assoc	585-4910	triddell	AHNO	PHD	75	American	1980
Staelin, Charles P.	Assoc	585-3621	cstaelin	ACDF	PHD	71	Michigan	1981
Davis, Lewis	Asst	585-2792		AFO	PHD	99	N Carol	
Miller, James	Asst	585-3613	jdmiller		PHD	97	Chicago	1996
Spence, Ardith	Asst	585-3606	aspence					

Sonoma State University Rohnert Park, CA 94928-3609 (707) 664-2377 sonoma.edu
Department of Economics Sch of Business & Econ Fax=664-4009 Sheila Mackintosh
Homepage: www.sonoma.edu/econ

Hosseini, Ahmad	Dean	664-2220	ahmad.hosseini	Atg	PHD	72	Missouri	1999
Lewis, Stephen D.	C-Pr	664-2305	steve.lewis	CD	PHD	69	Ca-SnBarb	1983
Ben-Zion, Barry	Emer			2000	PHD	73	Oregon	1969
Benito, Carlos	Prof	664-2410	benito	O	PHD	73	Ca-Davis	1990
Garlin, Victor A.	Emer			2001	PHD	65	Berkeley	1970
Hayes, Sue E.	Prof	664-3070	sue.hayes	Q	PHD	75	Berkeley	1974
Cuellar, Steven	Asst	664-2366	steven.cuellar	D	PHD	98	Tx A&M	2001
Eyler, Robert	Asst	664-4256	robert.eyler	E	PHD	98	Ca-Davis	1998

University of the South Sewanee, TN 37383-1000 (931) 598-1000 sewanee.edu
Department of Economics Col of Arts & Sciences Fax=598-1145
Did Not Respond--1999-2000 Listing

Keele, Robert	Dean	598-1248	bkeele	PolS	PHD	60		
Mohiuddin, Yasmeen	C-Pr	598-1462	ymohiudd	FOE	PHD	83	Vanderbilt	
Gottfried, Robert Richard	Prof	598-1243	rgottri	OQR	PHD	81	N Carol	
Ingles, Jerry Lee	Prof	598-1235	jingles	BL	PHD	75	Cornell	
Schaefer, Arthur McCluny	Prof	598-1146	aschaefer	CD	PHD	67	Penn	
Hendrickson, Jill K.	Asst	598-1805	jhendric	EGC	PHD		Notre Dm	1995

University of South Alabama Mobile, AL 36688-0002 (334) 460-7171 usouthal.edu
Dept of Econ & Finance College of Business Fax=460-6408 Ms. Lissa Williams
Did Not Respond--1999-2000 Listing

Moore, Carl C.	Dean	460-6902		Mgt	PHD	70	Alabama	1971
Moak, Donald L.	C-Pr	460-7171		Fnce	PHD	74	Miss	9-93
Bobo, James R.	Emer				PHD	61	LSU	1978
Chang, Semoon	Prof	460-6156		M	PHD	71	Fla St	1972
Swofford, James L.	Prof	460-6705	jswoffor@jaguar1	E	PHD	81	Florida	1984
Forbus, Philip R.	Assoc	460-6708		AD	PHD	78	Arkansas	1978
Stutsman, A. Douglas	Emer	460-6706		AB	PHD	70	Miss	1968

Univ So Carolina at Aiken Aiken, SC 29801 (803) 641-3340 aiken.sc.edu
Economics Faculty School Bus Adm & Econ Fax=641-3445 Gina Buckley
Did Not Respond--1999-2000 Listing; phone 648-6851

Vyas, Niren M.	H-Ac	648-6851	nirenv	Mktg	PHD	81	S Carol	1981
Shelburn, Marsha	Prof	648-6851	marshas		PHD	80	N Carol	1980
Folsom, Davis	Assoc	648-6851	davisf		PHD	79	Conn	1979

Univ of South Carolina Columbia, SC 29208 (803) 777-7400 darla.badm.sc.edu
Department of Economics Darla Moore Sch of Bus Fax=777-6876 Georgene Dance
Homepage: econ.badm.sc.edu

Wilder, Ronald P.	C-Pr	777-7400			PHD	69	Vanderbilt	1987
Addison, John T.	Prof	777-4608			PHD	71	London	
Blackburn, McKinley L.	Prof	777-4931			PHD	87	Harvard	1987
Breger, Gerald E.	Emer	777-4780			PHD	64	Arkansas	
Carlsson, Robert J.	Prof	777-6044			PHD	64	Rutgers	
Clower, Robert W.	Emer	777-5919			DLIT	78	Oxford	1986
Hugh C. Lane Professor of Economics								
Cohn, Elchanan	Prof	777-2714			PHD	68	Iowa St	
Harrison, Glenn W.	Prof	777-4943			PHD	82	UCLA	
Dewey H. Johnson Professor of Economics								
Kiker, B. F.	Prof	777-4904			PHD	65	Tulane	1971
Jeff B. Bates Professor of Public Administration & Finance								
Liles, W. Pierce	Prof	777-2306			PHD	72	S Carol	
Martin, Randolph C.	Prof	777-3176			PHD	71	Wash U	1970
Putnam, William F.	Emer	777-7602			MS	57	S Carol	
Boucher-Breuer, Janice L.	Assoc	777-7419			PHD	87	N Carol	1987
Chappell, Henry W.	Assoc	777-4940			PHD	79	Yale	1980
McDermott, John H.	Assoc	777-4939			PHD	79	Brown	1983
Phillips, William H.	Assoc	777-4930			PHD	80	MIT	1979
Director Undergraduate Studies								
Rawson, William S.	Emer	777-3865			PHD	67	Duke	1967
Rutstrom, Lisa	Assoc	777-4932	lisar	DFQ	PHD	90	Stockholm	8-91
Johnson, Eric	Asst	777-2583			PHD	97	Ca-SnDgo	8-98
McInnes, Melayne	Asst				PHD	98	Yale	8-97
Woodward, Doug P.	Asst	777-2510			PHD	86	Tx-Austin	
Director, Division of Research								
Balch, Donald C.	Lect	777-6828	sxabalch	AD	MA	88	S Carol	8-84
Bradley, James Jr.	DLect	777-2786	jbradley	AHM	CHPL	70	N Carol	9-74

U South Carolina at Spartanb Spartanburg, SC 29303 (864) 503-5581 gw.uscs.edu
Department of Economics Sch of Bus Admin & Econ Fax=503-5583 Elda Rattie

Word, William R.	Dean	503-5549	bword	ADEJ	PHD	70	Tennessee	1998
Tanyel, Faruk I.	C-Pr	503-5587	ftanyel	Mktg	PHD	83	Tennessee	1981
Jilling, Michael	Prof	503-5586	mjilling	ACMF	PHD	76	S Carol	1975
Reese, James W.	Assoc	503-5585	jreese	AFPH	PHD	73	Tennessee	1982
Rook, Sarah P.	Assoc	503-5584	srook	ADEQ	PHD	80	N Car St	1980
Jolly, Eric S.	Asst	503-5288		A	MA		Ohio U	1968
Connelly, Robert A. Jr.	Inst	503-5230		A	MA		Appalach	1972

South Carolina St University Orangeburg, SC 29117 (803) 536-8070 scsi.edu
Dept Agribusiness & Econ School of Business Fax=536-3639 Ms. Patricia McDonald
Did Not Respond--1999-2000 Listing

Reuben, Lucy J.	Dean	536-8086	lreuben	BusA	PHD	81	Michigan	1995
Modeste, Nelson C.	C-Ac	536-8076	nmodeste		PHD	76	Florida	1994

Londhe, Suresh R.	Prof	536-8449	londhe	PHD	65	LSU	1969
Onunkwo, Emmanuel N.	Prof	536-8843	emonunkwo	PHD	73	Geotown	1978
Karemera, David	Assoc	536-7136	kdaremera	PHD	89	Nebraska	1997
Kyereme, Stephen	Assoc	536-8448	skyereme	PHD	84	Cornell	1984
Mustafa, Muhammad	Assoc	536-8459	mmustafa	PHD	88	Wayne St	1989
Selassie, Haile G.	Assoc	536-8456	selassie	PHD	83	Okla St	1984
Sureshwaran, S.	Asst	536-8456	ssuresh	PHD	89	Clemson	1990

University of South Dakota — Vermillion, SD 57069-2390 (605) 677-5455 — usd.edu
Dept of Econ, Dec Sci & MIS — School of Business Fax=677-5427 — Ann Ward

Hoadley, Diane	Dean	677-5567	dhoadley		JD	82		1983
Powell, John	C	677-5455	jpowell	Mis	DBA	72	Indiana	1962
Brown, Ralph J.	Prof	677-5620	rbrown		PHD	70	Colorado	1977
Johnson, Jerry W.	Prof	677-5455	jerryj		PHD	71	Iowa St	1967
Reinke, Robert W.	Prof	677-5540	rreinke		PHD	82	Minnesota	1987
Ring, Raymond J. Jr.	Prof	677-6861	rring		PHD	73	Kansas	1978
Tosternd, Robert	Prof	677-5565	btostern		PHD	73	Manitoba	1991
Waldron, Randall	Asst	677-6643	rwaldron		PHD	94	Vanderbilt	1994

South Dakota State Univ — Brookings, SD 57007-0895 (605) 688-4141 — sdstate.edu
Economics Department — Col of Agri & Biol Sci Fax=688-6386 — June Larkin

Cholick, Fred	Dean	668-4148	fred_cholick		PHD	77	Colo St	1998
Shane, Richard C.	H-Pr	688-4141	richard_shane	Q	PHD	78	Wash St	1977
Beutler, Martin K.	Prof	394-2236		Q	PHD	86	Purdue	1986
Dobbs, Thomas L.	Prof	688-4874	thomas_dobbs	Q	PHD	69	Maryland	1978
Fausti, Scott W.	Prof	688-4868	scott_fausti	F	PHD	91	Illinois	1991
Gilbert, Howard A.	Prof	688-4844	howard_gilbert	A	PHD	67	Oregon St	1966
Janssen, Larry L.	Prof	688-4871	larry_janssen	Q	PHD	78	Nebraska	1978
Kim, Han J.	Prof	688-4848	han_kim	C	PHD	69	Oregon St	1967
Lamberton, Charles E.	Prof	688-4865	charles_lamb+	G	PHD	75	Iowa St	1974
Lyons, Patrick A.	Prof	688-4842	patrick_lyons	M	JD	74	S Dakota	1975
O'Brien, Jamie L.	Prof	688-4144	jamie_obrien	K	MPA	84	S Dakota	1984
Peterson, Donald L.	Prof	688-4859	donald_peterson	Q	PHD	73	Nebraska	1974
Pflueger, Burton W.	Prof	688-4141	burton_pflueger	Q	PHD	85	Illinois	1985
Sondey, John A.	Prof	688-4873	john_sondey	H	PHD	89	Wash St	1990
Adamson, Dwight W. (Bill)	Assoc	688-4105	bill.adamson	E	PHD	88	Wash St	1989
Cumber, Carol J.	Assoc	688-4849	carol_cumber	M	PHD	94	S Dak St	1990
Franklin, Douglas R.	Assoc	688-4861	douglas_franklin	Q	PHD	82	Utah	1988
Klein, Nicole L.	Assoc	688-4847	nicole_klein	Q	PHD	96	Kansas St	1997
Qasmi, Bashir A.	Assoc	688-4870	bashir_hasmi	Q	PHD	86	Iowa St	1987
VanderSluis, Evert	Assoc	688-4872	evert_vanders+	FO	PHD	93	Minnesota	1997
Diersen, Matthew	Asst	688-4141	matthew_diersen	Q	PHD	99	Illinois	1999
Santos, Joseph	Asst	668-4846	joseph_santos	E	PHD	96	Rutgers	1997
Taylor, Gary	Asst	688-4851	gary-taylor	Q	PHD	95	Okla St	2000
Zimmerman, Jason	Asst	688-4141	jason_zimmerman		MA	PHD		98
Purdue								1999
Ellingson, Wayne D.	Inst	688-4869	wayne_ellingson	C	BS	70	Iowa St	1980
Gustafson, Curtis O.	Inst	688-4850	curtis_gustafson	M	MPA	86	S Dakota	1989
Rasmussen, Chris H.	Inst	688-4145	chris_rasmussen	M	BA	75	SW State	1978

University of South Florida — Tampa, FL 33620-5500 (813) 974-4252 — coba.usf.edu
Department of Economics — Col of Business Admin Fax=974-6510 — Mary L. Bennett
Homepage: http://www.coba.usf.usf.edu/departments/economics

Anderson, Robert L.	Dean	974-3229	randerso		PHD	70	North Tx	1971
DeSalvo, Joseph S.	C-Pr	974-6388	jdesalvo	R	PHD	68	Nrthwstrn	1983
Bellante, Donald M.	Prof	974-6386	dbellant	J	PHD	71	Fla St	1985
Gyimah-Brempong, Kwabena	Prof	974-6520	kgyimah	O	PHD	81	Wayne St	1994
Herander, Mark G.	Prof	974-6540	mherande	F	PHD	80	N Carol	1979
Porter, Philip K.	Prof	974-6539	pporer	H	PHD	78	Tx A&M	1985
Rowe, John W.	Prof	974-6543	jrowe	D	PHD	66	Illinois	1979
Ford, Edward J. Jr.	Assoc	974-6559	eford	R	PHD	71	Boston C	1971
Green-Weishaupt, Carole A.	Assoc	974-6521	cgreen	J	PHD	82	Illinois	1982
Kamp, Bradley P.	Assoc	974-6549	bkamp	L	PHD	93	Ca-SnDgo	1992
Loewy, Michael	Assoc	974-6532	mloewy	E	PHD	86	Minnesota	1998
Picone, Gabriel A.	Assoc	974-6537	gpicone	C	PHD	93	Vanderbilt	1993
Racine, Jeffrey S.	Assoc	974-6555	jracine	C	PHD	91	W Ontario	1993
Spence, James G.	Assoc	432-5524		A	PHD	79	Oklahoma	1975
email=jspence2@stpt.usf.edu								
Thomas, Christopher R.	Assoc	974-6546	cthomas	L	PHD	80	Tx A&M	1982
Wilson, R. Mark	Assoc	974-6514	mwilson	I	PHD	77	Nrthwstrn	1978
Swinton, John R.	Asst	974-4363	jswinton	Q	PHD	96	Wisconsin	1995
Bartlett, Sue A.	Lect	974-6547	sbartlet	A	MA	93	S Fla	1994

Southeast Missouri St Univ C Girardeau, MO 63701-4799 (573) 651-2181 semovm.semo.edu
Department of Economics Harrison Coll Business Fax=651-2947 Ms. Debbie McKee
Homepage: economics.semo.edu/economics/index.html

McDougall, Gerald S.	Dean	651-2112	c476bux	HL	PHD	74	Claremont	1993
Summary, Rebecca M.	C-Pr	651-2945	rsummary	FA	PHD	83	Illinois	1983
Domazlicky, Bruce R.	Prof	651-2013	c819sse	AK	PHD	76	Wyoming	1986
Kerr, Peter M.	Prof	651-2012	c446ssb	AEBF	PHD	79	Kansas	1980
Park, Kang Hoon	Prof	651-2942	c382bue	CF	PHD	81	S Illinois	1979
Sutton, Terry	Prof	651-2944	c721bue	B	PHD	70	Kansas St	1972
Weber, William L.	Prof	651-2946	c645sse	GHI	PHD	86	S Illinois	1986
Primont, Diane F.	Assoc	651-2819	c794sse	JDE	PHD	87	N Carol	1990
Redmond, Willie	Asst	651-2181	wredmond	AFL	PHD	99	S Carol	1999

Southeastern Louisiana Univ Hammond, LA 70402 (985) 549-2086 selu.edu
Dept of General Business College of Bus & Tech Fax=549-2881 Lou Salisbury

Budden, Michael C.	Dean	549-2258	mbudden	Mktg	PHD	82	Arkansas	1999
Hsing, Yu	H-Pr	549-2086	yhsing	EJOR	PHD	83	Tennessee	1987
Gibson, Jo Anne	Assoc	549-3098	jgibson	EF	PHD	72	Miss	
Lee, Sang H.	Asst	549-2086	shyup	E	PHD	99	Florida	
Leonard, John	Asst	549-2086	jleonard		PHD	81	Ca-SnBarb	
Lin, Tin-Chun	Asst	549-2086	ltin	E	PHD	01	Penn St	
Quayes, M. Shakil	Asst	549-2086	squayes	E	PHD	00	Illinois	2001
Taylor, Leon E.	Asst	549-2086	ltaylor	E	PHD	90	Maryland	
Thomasson, Henry E.	Asst	549-3068	htomasson	AJ	MS		LSU	
Wang, Xuejun	Inst	549-2086	xwang	E	PHD	97	Purdue	

Southeastern Oklahoma State Durant, OK 74701-0609 (580) Ext 2713 sosu.edu
Dept of Economics & Finance Sch of Arts & Sciences Fax=920-7479
phone 924-0121

Chinn, Kenneth L.	C-Ac	924-0121	kchinn	EC	PHD	91	Colo St	1982
Collier, George A. Jr.	Emer	Ext 2821		ARM	PHD	78	Okla St	1972
Tengesdal, Mark O.	Asst	Ext 2707	mtengesdal		PHD	95	Ca-Rivers	1997

Southern Adventist Univ Collegedale, TN 37315-0370 (423) 238-2751 southern.edu
Economics Faculty Dept of Business & Mgt Fax=238-3151 Linda Wilhelm

VanOrnam, Don	Dean	238-2750			PHD	95	Claremont	1997
Erickson, Richard J.	Assoc	238-2755		A	MBA	81	Aust Pea	1984

Southern University Baton Rouge, LA 70813-9723 (225) 771-2992 subrvm.subr.edu
Department of Economics College of Business Fax=771-5262 Marilyn Doherty

Andrews, Donald R.	Dean$	771-5641		QR	PHD	80	Tx A&M	1995
Yigletu, Ashagre	C-Ac	771-2992		AE	PHD	72	Belgrade	1972
Jindia, Jaswant R.	Prof	771-2992	jaswant	AO	PHD	70	Illinois	1970
Agnihotri, Krisna	Asst	771-2992		A	MA	57	Punjab	1969
Lokhande, Vineeta	Asst	771-2992		G	PHD	94	N Orleans	1994
Osagie, Emmanuel I.	Asst	771-2992			PHD	85	LSU	1985
Smyser, Michael W.	Asst	771-2992		G	PHD	91	Fla Intl	1991

Southern Arkansas Univ Magnolia, AR 71753-5000 (870) 235-4304 saumag.edu
Dept of Economics & Finance Sch of Business Admin Fax=235-4800 Mrs. Gaye Calhoun
Did Not Respond--1999-2000 Listing

Rankin, David F.	Dean	235-4300	dfrankin	Fnce	PHD	70	Miss	1968
Ashby, David J.	C-Ac	235-4304	jdasby	Fnce	DBA	96	La Tech	1992
Bellamy, D. Scott	Assoc	235-5162	scbellamy	I	PHD		Kentucky	1993

Univ of Southern California Los Angeles, CA 90089-0253 (213) 740-8335 usc.edu
Department of Economics Col of Ltrs, Arts & Sci Fax=740-8543 Sheila Williams
email @1=almaak.usc.edu

Schapiro, Morton Owen	Dean	740-8218	schapiro@rcf.		PHD	79	Penn	1991
Vuong, Quang	C-Pr	740-3528	qvuong@mizar		PHD	82	Nrthwstrn	1987
Cvitanic, Jaksa	Prof	740-3794	cvitanic@math.		PHD	92	Columbia	1999
Day, Richard H.	Prof	740-2432	rday@rcf.		PHD	61	Harvard	1976
Easterlin, Richard A.	Prof	743-6993	easterl@rcf.		PHD	53	Penn	1982
Elliott, John E.	Prof	740-3510	jeelliot@rcf.		PHD	56	Harvard	1966
Gordon, Peter	Prof	743-2770	pgordon@1		PHD	71	Penn	1971
Hsiao, Cheng	Prof	740-2103	chsiao@1		PHD	72	Stanford	1985
Imrohoroglu, Ayse	Prof	740-6518	ayse@marshall.		PHD	88	Minnesota	1989
Imrohoroglu, Selo	Prof	740-6546	simr+u@marshall.		PHD	88	Minnesota	1989
Kalaba, Robert E.	Prof	740-2109	kalaba@rcf.		PHD	58	NYU	1969
Kuran, Timur	Prof	740-7432	kuran@rcf.		PHD	82	Stanford	1982
Laffont, Jean-Jacques	Prof	740-2511	laffont@1		PHD	75	Harvard	2001
MacLeod, Bentley	Prof	740-3517	wmacleon@1		PHD	84	Brit Colum	1997
Magill, Michael J. P.	Prof	740-2104	magill@1		PHD	70	Brown	1979

Nugent, Jeffrey B.	Prof	740-2107	nugent@1		PHD	65	New Sch	1973
Richardson, Harry W.	Prof	740-3954	hrichard@rfc.		MA	61	Manchester	1975
Ridder, Geert	Prof	740-2110	ridder@1		PHD	87	Amsterdm	2000
Sandler, Todd M.	Prof	740-3526	tsardler@1	HD	PHD	71	SUNY-Bin	2000
Yett, Donald E.	Prof	740-3514	yett@rcf.		PHD	68	Berkeley	1966
Betts, Caroline	Assoc	740-2430	cbetts@rcf.		PHD	94	Brit Colum	1994
Cheng, Harrison C.	Assoc	740-2105	hacheng@mizar.		PHD	77	Berkeley	1978
Dawid, Herbert	Assoc	740-8842	dherbert@1		PHD	95	Vienne	1999
Dekle, Robert	Assoc	740-2134	dekle@1		PHD	88	Yale	1998
DePrano, Michael E.	Assoc	740-3525	deprano@rcf.		PHD	63	Illinois	1963
Rosendorff, Peter	Assoc	740-3529	bpeter@1		PHD	93	Columbia	1992
Heong, Hyeok	Asst	740-3512	hyeong@1		PHD	00	Chicago	2000
Moon, Roger	Asst	740-2108	moon@1		PHD	88	Yale	2000
Perrigne, Isabelle	Asst	740-3528	perrigne@rcf		PHD	91	Toulouse	1997
Kamrany, Nake M.	SLect	740-6997	kamrany@rcf.		PHD	62	S Calif	1976
Univ of Southern Colorado	Pueblo, CO		81001-4901	(719) 549-2142			uscolo.edu	
Business Adm Department	Hasan Sch of Business		Fax=549-2909					
Fuller, Rex D.	Dean	549-2142	rfuller	JLH	PHD	82	Utah	2100
Hanks, Sue	C-Ac	549-2882	hanks	Mgt	EDD	83	Arkansas	1992
Duncan, Kevin C.	Prof	549-2228	duncan	JR	PHD	87	Utah	1994
Goodman, D. Jay	Asst	549-2155	goodman	FQ	PHD	95	Colorado	1998
Whited, Ida	Asst	549-3843	whited	GEF	PHD	00	Claremont	2001
Southern Connecticut St Un	New Haven, CT		06515	(203) 392-5629			scsud.ctstate.edu	
Dept of Economics & Finance	School of Business		Fax=392-5863				Gloria Nichols	
Kraft, Kenneth	Dean	392-5631	kraft		DBA	82	Maryland	1999
Andoh, Samuel Kojo	C-Pr	392-5616	andoh	EO	PHD	86	NYU	
Crakes, Gary M.	Prof	392-5619	crakes	AI	PHD	84	Conn	1980
Morgan, Alfred D.	Prof	392-5624		G	PHD	51	Harvard	
Mostaghimi, Mehdi	Prof	392-5625	mostaghimi	CEM	PHD	87	Virginia	8-84
Bodo, Peter	Assoc	392-5617	bodo	CL	PHD	91	Conn	
Eldridge, Robert M.	Assoc	392-5628	eldridge_r	G	DBA	87	Geo Wash	
Gebremariam, Yilma	Assoc	392-5620	gebremariam	FO	PHD	89	S Calif	1990
Mills, Judith W.	Assoc	392-5623	mills	CNT	PHD	94	SUNY-SBr	1991
Thorson, James A.	Assoc	392-5626	thorson	R	PHD	91	Il-Chicago	1992
Savage, Deborah A.	Asst	392-5627	savage	I	PHD	93	Conn	
Southern Illinois Univ	Carbondale, IL		62901-4515	(618) 536-7746			siu.edu	
Department of Economics	College of Liberal Arts		Fax=453-2717				Mrs. Nancy Mallett	
Homepage: www.siu.edu/~econ/								
Clay Scott, Shirley	Dean	453-2466			PHD	73	Kent St	1999
Grabowski, Richard L.	C-Pr	453-5082	ricardo	OF	PHD	77	Utah	1979
Edelman, Milton	Emer	453-5063			PHD	51	Illinois	1950
Laumas, G. S.	Prof	453-5740	gslaumas	EC	PHD	66	Wayne St	1990
Layer, Robert	Emer				PHD	52	Harvard	1955
Myers, John G.	Emer	453-5073			PHD	61	Columbia	1977
Primont, Daniel A.	Prof	453-5066	primo	DC	PHD	70	Ca-SnBarb	1978
Sharma, Subhash	Prof	453-5070	sharma	C	PHD	83	Kentucky	1983
Trescott, Paul B.	Emer	453-5095		EB	PHD	54	Princeton	1976
Ellis, Robert J. Jr.	Emer	453-5063			PHD	66	Virginia	1965
Foran, Terry G.	Emer			J	PHD	71	Penn St	1970
Mitchell, Thomas M.	Assoc	453-5072	tmitch	DC	PHD	84	Brown	1983
Dibooglu, Selhattin	Asst	453-5346	dibo	F	PHD	93	Iowa St	1993
Gilbert, Scott	Asst	453-5065	gilberts	C	PHD	96	Ca-SnDgo	1999
Sylwester, Kevin	Asst	453-5347	ksylwest	EO	PHD	97	Wisconsin	1998
Watts, Alison	Asst	453-5072	wattsa	DKL	PHD	93	Duke	2001
Zemcik, Petr	Asst	453-5062	petrz	EG	PHD	97	Pittsburgh	1998
So Illinois, Edwardsville	Edwardsville, IL		62026-1102	(618) 650-2542			siue.edu	
Dept of Economics & Finance	School of Business		Fax=650-3047				Sally Moonier	
Carver, M. Robert Jr.	Dean	650-3823	bcarver	Atg	PHD	80	Missouri	1974
Hafer, Rik W.	C-Pr	650-2747	rhafer	EG	PHD	79	Va Tech	
Ault, David E.	Prof	650-2578	dault	AFJK	PHD	69	Illinois	1969
Elliott, Donald S. Jr.	Prof	650-2599	delliot	AHMR	PHD	76	Minnesota	1976
Kutan, Ali M.	Prof	650-3473	akutan	EFG	PHD	90	Ariz St	1991
Levin, Stanford L.	Prof	650-2592	slevin	DL	PHD	74	Michigan	1972
Meisel, John B.	Prof	650-2581	jmeisel	ADL	PHD	78	Boston C	1977
Edmonds, Radcliff G. Jr.	Assoc	650-2598	redmond	ACF	PHD	79	Michigan	1977
Navin, John	Assoc	650-3423	jnavin	HIJ	PHD	92	Mich St	
Jones, Garett	Asst	650-2892	garjone	EG	PHD	00	Ca-SnDgo	2000
Sullivan, Timothy	Asst	650-3469	tsulliv	IJT	PHD	95	Maryland	1995
Pettit, Mary Ann	Inst	650-2583	mpettit	A	MA	77	Tennessee	1989
Richards, Warren	Inst	650-2162	wrichar	A	MS	90	S Il-Edw	2000
Wolff, Laura	Inst	650-2875	lwolff	AO	MS	88	Missouri	1990

Univ of Southern Indiana Evansvillle, IN 47712-3597 (812) 464-1979 usi.edu
Dept of Economics & Finance School of Business Fax=465-1044
Homepage: business.usi.edu/dept_econ_fin.htm

Fisher, Philip C.	Dean	464-1718	pfisher	Mgt	PHD	79	Stanford	1991
Khayum, Mohammed	C-Pr	464-7034	mkhayum		PHD	90	Temple	1991
Cox, Steven R.	Prof	464-1983	scox		PHD	71	Michigan	1989
Schibik, Timothy J.	Prof	464-1880	tschibik		PHD	89	W Virginia	1988
Cashel-Cordo, Peter	Assoc	465-7033	cashel		PHD	88	Houston	1994
Friesner, Daniel	Asst	465-7145	dfriesne		PHD	00	Wash St	2000
Mujumdar, Sudesh	Asst	465-7147	smujumda		PHD	00	Cincinnati	2001
Mahoney, Timothy B.	Inst	464-1947	tmahoney		MS	65	Illinois	1987

Univ of Southern Maine Portland, ME 04104-9300 (207) 780-4020 usm.maine.edu
Department of Economics College of Arts & Sci Fax=780-5507

Medley, Joseph E.	C-Ac	780-4293	medley	BO	PHD	81	Mass	1983
Bay, John W.	Prof	780-4445	jbay	E	PHD	66	Boston C	1965
Executive Director Off Campus Instruction								
Roberts, Bruce B.	Prof	780-5503	broberts	BE	PHD	81	Mass	1995
Feiner, Susan F.	Assoc	780-4966	sffein	BN	PHD	81	Mass	1995
Goldstein, Nance	Assoc	780-4602	nance	IJ	PHD	88	ThamesPoly	1987
Hillard, Michael	Assoc	780-4416	mhillard	EJ	PHD	88	Mass	1987
Phillips, William A.	Assoc	780-4313	phillips	ACDF	PHD	79	Fla St	1980
Mamgain, Vaishali	Asst	780-5807		CO	PHD	79	N Carol	1997

Southern Methodist Univ Dallas, TX 75275-0496 (214) 768-4335 mail.smu.edu
Department of Economics Dedman College Fax=768-1821 Pontip Vattakavanich
Homepage: www.smu.edu/economics

Neel, Jasper	Dean	768-3212	jneel		PHD	75	Tennessee	1997
Dean and Vice Provost, Dedman College								
Balke, Nathan S.	C-Pr	768-2693	nblake	EG	PHD	86	Nrthwstrn	1986
Batra, Raveendra N.	Prof	768-2707	rbaatra	F	PHD	69	S Illinois	1973
Deb, Rajat	Prof	768-3556	rdeb	D	PHD	75	LondonEc	1976
Fomby, Thomas	Prof	768-2559	tfomby	CD	PHD	75	Missouri	1975
Hayes, Kathy J.	Prof	768-4485	khayes	HIL	PHD	80	Syracuse	1989
Associate Dean for Academic Affairs, Dedman College								
Maasoumi, Esfandiar	Prof	768-4298	maasoumi	C	PHD	77	LondonEc	1976
Robert H. & Nancy Dedman Professor								
Russell, William R.	Prof	768-2715	wrussell	D	PHD	64	U Wash	1971
Seo, Tae Kun	Prof	768-3547	tseo	D	PHD	73	Tx A&M	1973
Slottje, Daniel J.	Prof	768-2715	dslottje	DJK	PHD	83	Tx A&M	1989
Weber, Shlomo	Prof	768-3577	sweber	DHL	PHD	79	Hebrew	1993
Robert H. & Nancy Dedman Trustee Professor; Dir R.B. Johnson Economic Studies								
Saggi, Kamal	Assoc	768-3274	ksaggi	FLO	PHD	95	Penn	1995
Director Graduate Studies								
Bogomolnaia, Anna	Asst	868-4050		DC	PHD		Barcelonia	1999
Fredriksson, Per	Asst	768-3520		DF	PHD	94	Penn	1999
Millimet, Daniel	Asst	768-3269		CJO	PHD	99	Brown	1999
Osang, Thomas	Asst	768-4398	tosang	FO	PHD	94	Ca-SnDgo	1994
Director Undergraduate Studies								
Ozertwrk, Saltuk	Asst	868-4335		ELG	PHD	01	NYU	2001

U of Southern Mississippi Hattiesburg, MS 39406-5072 (601) 266-4648 cba.usm.edu
Dept Economics & Intl Bus Col of Business Adm Fax=266-4920 Ms. Janet McKee

Gunther, William D.	Dean	266-4659		R	PHD	69	Kentucky	1998
Black, Tyrone	Prof	266-6580		E	PHD	70	Tulane	1969
Carter, George H. III	Prof	266-4651		R	PHD	77	Tx A&M	1979
Klinedinst, Mark A.	Prof	266-4649		P	PHD	87	Cornell	1986
Lewis, Eddie Miley Jr.	Prof	266-4652		F	DBA	74	Miss St	1970
Niroomand, Farhang	Prof	266-5028		F	PHD	83	Mich St	1984
Associate Dean								
Nissan, Edward	Prof	266-4656		R	PHD	69	Tx A&M	1969
Sawyer, W. Charles	Prof	266-4489		F	PHD	83	Arkansas	1983
Green, Trellis Garnett	Assoc	266-4662		Q	PHD	84	Fla St	1983
Mixon, Frank	Assoc	266-4648		J	PHD	92	Auburn	1994
Trevino, Len	Assoc	266-6094		F	PHD	91	Indiana	1999
Whitesell, Frank Cook	Assoc	266-4366		A	PHD	71	Tulane	1968
Lo, Melody	Asst	266-4648		F	PHD	01	Purdue	2001

Southern Nazarene Univ Bethany, OK 73008 (405) 491-6359 snu.edu
Economics Faculty School of Business Fax=491-6384

Mills, Larry W.	C-Pr	491-6392	lmills	Mgt	PHD	78	Oklahoma	1969
Seyfert, Jeff	Asst	491-6671	jseyfert		MBA	89	Tulsa	1990

Southern Oregon University Ashland, OR 97520-5082 (541) 552-6787 sou.edu
Department of Economics Social Science Area Fax=552-6439 Terry Knowles
Homepage: www.sou.edu/economics

Kempner, Ken	Dean	562-6417	kempner		PHD	79	Oregon	2001
Young, Linda Wilcox	C-Pr	552-6787	lwyoung	JOF	PHD	87	Berkeley	1994
Pirasteh, Hassan	Prof	552-6434	pirasteh	CEG	PHD	85	Oregon	1982
Rubenson, Daniel L.	Prof	552-6437	drube	CEG	PHD	85	Car Mellon	1986
Holt, Richard P. F.	Assoc	552-6784	rholt	ABDM	PHD	87	Utah	1996

Southern Utah University Cedar City, UT 84720 (435) 865-8167 suu.edu
Dept of Business-Economics Sch of Bus, Tech & Comm Fax=586-5493
Did Not Respond--1999-2000 Listing

Groesbeck, John D.	C-Ac	586-7784			PHD	93	Utah St	1993
Bowman, Rhead S.	Assoc	586-5412			PHD	75	Utah	1978
Chen, Heiwei	Asst	586-5405			PHD	97	Emory	1998
Craft, Kim	Asst	586-5414			PHD	96	Ca-Davis	1996

Southwest Baptist Univ Bolivar, MO 65613-2496 (417) 326-1951 sbuniv.edu
Business Administration College of Business Fax=326-1887 Ms. Theresa Treacy
Homepage: sbuniv.edu/business

Whitlock, David W.	Dean	328-1759	dwhitloc	Mgt	PHD	95	Oklahoma	1999
DeBauche, Susan	C-As	328-1958	sdebauch	Bus	EDD	90	Arkansas	1985
Ellis, Barry	Assoc	328-1753	bellis		PHD		Texas	2001
Credille, Ronda	Asst	328-1750			MBA		Drury	1990
Jones, James G.	Asst	328-1757		ECO	MBA		Arkansas	1988
Skinreich, Dale	Asst	328-1751	dskinch		PHD		Auburn	2001
Smith, Angie	Inst	328-1754	asmith		MBA		SW Bapt	2001

Southwest Missouri St Univ Springfield, MO 65804-0094 (417) 836-5516 smsu.edu
Department of Economics Col Humanity & Pub Aff Fax=836-4236 Ms. Sandra K. Wilkins

Stone, Lorene	Dean	836-5529		Soc				
Bell, Joe A.	Prof	836-5140	jab856f		PHD	80	Okla St	1971
Hoftyzer, John	Prof	836-5347	joh689f		PHD	74	Indiana	1987
Hoppes, Robert B.	Prof	836-5352	rbh018f		PHD	75	Nebraska	1980
Stone, Allan D.	Emer	836-5350	ads98lf		PHD	73	Oklahoma	1972
Wasson, E. Dale	Prof	836-5349	edw389f		PHD	80	Okla St	1969
Wyrick, Thomas L.	Prof	836-5060	tlw918f		PHD	79	Va Tech	1978
email=twyrick@earthlink.net								
Olsen, Reed N.	Assoc	836-5379	rno174f		PHD	89	Illinois	1990
Sheets, Doris Files	Assoc	836-5351	def230f		PHD	81	Missouri	1974
Barari, Mahua	Asst	836-5171	mab953f		PHD	92	Iowa St	1993
Cox, Larry G.	Asst	836-5551			MA	70	Kansas St	1970
email=econ99@earthlink.net								
Topping, Elizabeth E.	Asst	836-5615	eet326f		PHD	85	Missouri	1979
Geile, Gerald L.	Inst	836-5740	glg138f		MA	91	St Louis	1991

Southwest State University Marshall, MN 56258 (507) southwest.msus.edu
Economics Faculty Dept of Business Adm Fax=537-6577
Did Not Respond Again--1997-98 Listing

Ramos, Melba	Dean	537-6218		Anth	PHD	82	Mass	1993
Mitchell, George	C-Pr	537-6223		Mgt	ABD			
Blitstein, Allen	Prof			DFN	PHD	72	Minnesota	1976
Cameron, John S.	Assoc	537-6560		EFJ	PHD	79	Nebraska	1986

Southwest Texas State Univ San Marcos, TX 78666-4616 (512) 245-2547 academia.swt.edu
Dept Finance & Economics College of Business Adm Fax=245-3089 Patty Aranda
Homepage: www.business.swt.edu.fin_eco

Holland, A. Steven	C-Pr	245-2547	sh20	E	PHD	83	Mich St	1998
Blankmeyer, Eric	Prof	245-3253	eb01	F	PHD	71	Princeton	1982
Gowens, Paul R.	Prof	245-2311	pg01	M	PHD	73	Miss	1980
Mogab, John William	Prof	245-3244	jm12	O	PHD	81	Tennessee	1981
Charles, Joni S.	Assoc	245-3243	jc18	D	PHD	87	Purdue	1984
Kishan, Ruby Pandey	Assoc	245-3248	rk02	E	PHD	86	Tx A&M	1986
Showalter, Dean	Assoc	245-3194	ds29	L	PHD	94	Kentucky	1995
Campbell, Rebecca	Asst	245-3251	rc17	H	PHD	98	LSU	1998
on leave 2001-2002								
Carbacho-Burgos, Andres	Asst	215-2463	ac12	O	PHD	99	Mass	1999
McClung, Bruce Alan	Asst	245-3220	bm03	J	PHD	88	Tx A&M	1988

Southwestern University Georgetown, TX 78627-0770 (512) 863-1574 southwestern.edu
Economic & Business Dept Brown Col of Arts & Sci Fax=863-1535 Kathy Buchhorn
Homepage: southwestern.edu/~econbus/

Hunt, James W.	Dean$	863-1567	huntj	Edu	EDD	87	NW St La	1988
Sellers, Fred E.	C-Ac	863-1574	sellerf	Atg	PHD	84	Kansas	1987

Roberts, Kenneth D.	Prof	863-1993	robertsk	GEOT	PHD	80	Wisconsin	1981
Young, Mary E.	Prof	863-1994	youngm	CDJQ	PHD	89	Tx-Austin	1990
Early, Dirk W.	Assoc	863-1592	earlyd	DEHR	PHD	95	Virginia	1994
Northrop, Emily M.	Assoc	863-1591	northroe	ENQR	PHD	88	Tx-Austin	1994

Southwestern Oklahoma St U Weatherford, OK 73096-3098 (580) 774-3066 swosu.edu
Department of Business Adm School of Business Fax=774-7067

May, Ralph	Dean$	774-3282	mayr		PHD	75	Purdue	1989
Crall, Les	C-Pr	774-3751			JD	83	Oklahoma	2001
Nowka, Harry E.	Prof	774-3754			EDD		Okla St	1963
Russell, R. K.	Prof	774-3081			PHD	82	Okla St	1973
Hankins, Marvin	Asst	774-3750			EDD		Okla St	1979

Stanford University Stanford, CA 94305-6072 (650) 725-3266 leland.edu
Department of Economics Sch of Humanities & Sci Fax=725-5702 Janet Weitz 723-3712

Wright, Gavin	C-Pr	723-3712	write		PHD	69	Yale	1982
William Robertson Coe Professor of American Economic History								
Amemiya, Takeshi	Prof	723-3986	amemiya		PHD	64	J Hopkins	1968
Edward Ames Edmonds Professor of Economics								
Aoki, Masahiko	Prof	723-3975	aoki		PHD	67	Minnesota	1984
Henri and Tomoye Takahashi Professor of Japanese Studies								
Bernheim, B. Douglas	Prof	725-8732	bernheim		PHD	82	MIT	1994
Lewis and Virginia Eaton Professor in Economics								
Boskin, Michael J.	Prof	723-3864	boskin		PHD	71	Berkeley	1970
Tully Friedman Professor in Economics								
Bresnahan, Timothy F.	Prof	723-9471	tbres		PHD	80	Princeton	1979
David, Paul A.	Prof	723-3710			PHD	73	Harvard	1969
Goulder, Lawrence	Prof	723-3706	goulder		PHD	82	Stanford	1989
Greif, Avner	Prof	725-8936	avner		PHD	89	Nrthwstrn	1993
Hall, Robert E.	Prof	723-2215	hall@hoover		PHD	67	MIT	1978
Hammond, Peter J.	Prof	723-3987	hammond		PHD	74	Cambridge	1979
Krueger, Anne O.	Prof	723-0188	akrueger		PHD	58	Wisconsin	
Herald L. and Caroline L. Reitch Professor in Humanities and Sciences								
Kurz, Mordecai	Prof	723-2220	mordecai		PHD	61	Yale	1966
Joan Kenney Professor of Economics								
Lau, Lawrence J.	Prof	723-3708	ljlau		PHD	69	Berkeley	1966
Kwoh-Ting Li Professor of Economic Development								
MaCurdy, Thomas E.	Prof	723-3983	tmac		PHD	78	Chicago	1983
McKinnon, Ronald I.	Prof	723-3721	mckinnon		PHD	61	Minnesota	1961
William D. Eberle Professor of Economics								
Milgrom, Paul R.	Prof	723-3397	milgrom		PHD	79	Stanford	1987
Shirley R. and Leonard W. Ely, Jr. Professor in Humanities and Sciences								
Noll, Roger G.	Prof	723-2297	rnoll		PHD	67	Harvard	1984
Morris M. Doyle Centennial Professor								
Pencavel, John H.	Prof	723-3981	pencavel		PHD	69	Princeton	1979
Rosenberg, Nathan	Prof	723-1902	ib.nat@forsythe		PHD	55	Wisconsin	
Fairleigh S. Dickinson, Jr., Professor of Public Policy								
Sargent, Thomas	Prof	725-8161			PHD	68	Harvard	
Shoven, John B.	Prof	326-5377			PHD	73	Yale	1978
Charles R. Schwab Professor of Economics								
Taylor, John B.	Prof	723-9677	johntayl		PHD	73	Stanford	
Mary and Robert Raymond Professor of Economics								
Wolak, Frank A.	Prof	723-3944	wolak@zia		PHD	85	Harvard	1986
Athey, Susan	Assoc	725-8696	athey	L	PHD	95	Stanford	2001
McClellan, Mark	Assoc	723-3982	markm@texas		PHD	93	Harvard	9-95
Segal, Ilya	Assoc	724-4905	isegal		PHD	95	Harvard	1999
Bajari, Patrick	Asst	725-8856	bajari		PHD	97	Minnesota	
Kochar, Anjini	Asst	723-9766	anjini		PHD	91	Chicago	1990
Krueger, Dirk	Asst	724-4901	dkrueger		PHD	99	Minnesota	1999
Kubler, Felix	Asst	724-4902	fkubler		PHD	99	Yale	1999
Kumhof, Michael	Asst	725-6120	kumhof					
Levin, Jonathan	Asst	723-5962	jdlevin		PHD	99	MIT	1999
McKenzie, David	Asst	723-9276			PHD	01	Yale	2001
Paal, Beatrix	Asst	724-4903	beatrix.paal		PHD	99	Cornell	1999
Pistaferri, Luigi	Asst	724-4904	pista		PHD	99	London	1999
Rangel, Antonio	Asst	723-0533	rangel					
Tadelis, Steven	Asst	723-3544	725-8169		PHD		Harvard	
Vytlacil, Ed	Asst	725-7836	vytlacil		PHD	00	Chicago	2000
Rothwell, Geoffrey S.	SLect	725-3456	rothwell		PHD	85	Berkeley	1986

SUNY at Fredonia Fredonia, NY 14063-1198 (716) 673-3509 fredonia.edu
Economics Faculty Department of Economics Fax=673-3332 Amy Dorler
Homepage: fredonia.edu/department/econ/index.htm

Foeller, William H.	C-Pr	673-3403	foeller	AJ	PHD	72	Iowa St	1984
El Nasser, Marwan M.	Prof	673-3827	elnasser	EG	PHD	70	Ohio St	1970
Hefner, Dennis L.	Prof	673-3456	hefner	IL	PHD	71	Wash St	1996
Parai, Amar K.	Prof	673-3289	parai	AF	PHD	79	So Meth	1988

Sarkar, Amin U.	Prof	673-3509	sarkar	DO	PHD	88	Berkeley	1989
on leave to Georgia College								
Choudhary, Munir A. S.	Assoc	673-3830	choudhary	CE	PHD	85	Fla St	1987
Peterson, Janice L.	Assoc	673-3522	peterson	BA	PHD	87	Nebraska	1990
on leave								
Miah, Solaiman	VAsst	673-3509	miah	AC	PHD	01	N Illinois	2001
Reinelt, Peter	VAsst	673-3509	reinelt	QR	PHD	99	Berkeley	2001

SUNY Col at Cortland Cortland, NY 13045-0900 (607) 753-4109 syncorva.cortland.edu
Department of Economics College of Arts & Sci Fax=753-5983 Denise Riley
Homepage: www.cortland.edu/economics/

Prus, Mark J.	C-Pr	753-5758	prus	JN	PHD	85	Utah	1990
Botwinick, Howard I.	Assoc	753-2435		BJ	PHD	88	New Sch	1985
Krall, Mary Elyse	Assoc	753-2438	krallm	AIJQ	PHD	89	Utah	8-90
Phillips, Timothy P.	Assoc	753-2437		M	MBA	83	Clarkson	1983
Burke, Kathleen	Asst			CD	PHD		SUNY-SBr	1999
Maxcy, Joel	Asst			KJ	PHD	96	Wash St	1998
Polley, Susanne M.	Asst	753-2469	pollys	EHM	PHD	94	Penn St	8-94
Spencer, Deborah	Asst			KFP	PHD		Notre Dm	1999
Zariar-Hayos, German	Asst			FOP	PHD		Ca-Rivers	2001
Graham, Katherine	Lect	753-4110			MS		Cornell	
Keller, Ric	Lect				MBA		Geo St	2001
Quick, R. C.	Lect							
Shirley, John	Lect	753-2190						
VonDonsel, Richard	Lect	753-2469						

State Un College at Geneseo Geneseo, NY 14454-1401 (716) 245-5367 geneseo.edu
Department of Economics Jones Sch of Business Fax=245-5467 Kathleen Ackerman

Zuckerman, Mary Ellen	H-Pr	245-5367	waller	Mktg	PHD	86	Columbia	9-85
Strang, Daniel R.	Prof	245-5365	strang	CQ	PHD	75	Cornell	1992
Annala, Christopher	Asst	245-5424	annala	E	PHD	00	Wash St	2000
Asgary, Nader	Asst	245-5366	nader	FJ	PHD	91	Houston	1996
Gu, Anthony	Asst	245-5368	gu	D	PHD	99	Illinois	1999
Stone, Leonie L.	Asst	245-4365	stone	OD	PHD	93	Ohio St	1993

SUNY at Old Westbury Old Westbury, NY 11568 (516) 876-3292 oldwestbury.edu
Economics Faculty School of Business Fax=876-3360 Laura Gallagher
Homepage: www.oldwestbury.edu

O'Sullivan, Patrick J.	D-Pr	876-3292	osullivan	Fnce	PHD	82	Fordham	9-75
Forti, Annette D.	Prof	876-3277	fortea		PHD	75	Fordham	
Geyikdagi, Yasar	Prof	876-3316			PHD		Bath	
Tabriztchi, Sirousse	Assoc	876-3318	cyrus1314@a		PHD	70	Columbia	
Keefe, Maureen	VInst	876-3309						

SUNY College at Oneonta Oneonta, NY 13820-4015 (607) 436-3458 oneonta.edu
Dept of Economics & Business Behavioral & Applied Sc Fax=436-2543 Ms. Dawn Tompkins
Homepage: http://www.oneonta.edu/economics

Lubell, Alfred M.	Dean$	436-3458		ADF	PHD	74	NYU	1974
Thomas, Wade L.	C-Ac	436-3458	thomaswl	DEJ	PHD	82	Nebraska	1989
O'Dea, William P.	Assoc	436-2127	odeawp	DEP	PHD	88	SUNY-Alb	1979
Ring, David W.	Assoc	436-3145	ringdw	DEPR	PHD	82	SUNY-SBr	1981
Beck, Edward J.	Asst	436-3695	beckei	DE	MBA	82	Syracuse	1977
McAvoy, Michael	Asst	436-4287	mcavoym		PHD	01	Illinois	2000

SUNY College at Oswego Oswego, NY 13126 (315) 312-2175 oswego.edu
Economics Faculty Col of Arts & Sciences Fax=312-5444 Sandi Cotter

Kane, John C.	C-Pr	312-2581	kane	ACJ	PHD	86	SUNY-SBr	1983
Atri, Said	Prof	312-3954	atri	AFI	PHD	82	SUNY-Alb	1981
Jhun, U-Jin	Prof	312-3455	jhun	EH	PHD	73	SUNY-Alb	1972
Spizman, Lawrence	Prof	312-3479	spizman	AJK	PHD	77	SUNY-Alb	1977
Goffe, William L.	Assoc	312-3480	goffe	ACE	PHD	90	N Carol	2000
Graham, Glenn	Assoc	312-3482	graham	AIL	PHD	95	SUNY-Bin	1992
Cooper, Brian	Asst	312-3484	bcooper1	ABJ	PHD	97	Harvard	1998
Dighe, Ranjit S.	Asst	312-3480	dighe	AEN	PHD	98	Yale	1997
Schmitt, Elizabeth Dunne	Asst	312-3488	edunne	AEG	ABD		Iowa	1990

SUNY at Stony Brook Stony Brook, NY 11794-4384 (631) 632-7540 sunysb.edu
Department of Economics College of Arts & Sci Fax=632-7516 Janice Byron/Barbara Lawrence
email @1=ms.cc.sunysb.edu

Dawes, William	C	632-7556	wdawes		PHD	72	Purdue	1969
Sanderson, Warren	C-Pr	632-7530	wsanderson		PHD	74	Stanford	1989
Dubey, Pradeep	Prof	632-7549	pdubey		PHD	75	Cornell	1989
Hause, John C.	Prof	632-7547	jhause		PHD	62	Chicago	1978
Hool, Bryce	Prof	632-7537	bhool		PHD	74	Berkeley	1979

Montgomery, Mark	Prof	632-7529	mmontgomery		PHD	82	Michigan	1988
Muench, Thomas	Prof	632-7544	tmuench		PHD	65	Purdue	1975
Director of Graduate Studies								
Neuberger, Egon	Prof	632-7545	eneuberger		PHD	58	Harvard	1967
Tauman, Yair	Prof	632-7557	ytauman		PHD	79	Hebrew	1989
Zweig, Michael	Prof	632-7536	mzweig		PHD	67	Michigan	1967
Director of Undergraduate Studies								
Kamihigashi, Takashi	Assoc	632-7548	tkamihigashi		PHD	94	Wisconsin	1994
Armantier, Olivier	Asst	632-1334	oarmantier		PHD	98	Pittsburgh	1998
Benitez-Silva, Hugo	Asst	632-7551	hbenitezsilv@1		PHD			
Carceles-Poveda, Eva	Asst	632-7533	ecarceles		PHD			
Dwyer, Debra	Asst	632-7532	debradwyer		PHD	96	Cornell	1998
Park, Sangin	Asst	632-7559	spark		PHD	96	Yale	1996
Swann, Christopher	Asst	632-7526	cswann@1		PHD	97	Virginia	1999

Univ at Albany, SUNY Albany, NY 12222 (518) 442-4735 cnsvax.albany.edu
Department of Economics Col of Arts & Sciences Fax=442-4736 Sue Phillips
Did Not Respond--1999-2000 Listing; email @1=cnsunix.albany.edu @2=csc.alban

Hoffmann, Richard	Dean	442-4654	rjh@2					
Kinal, Terrence	C-Pr	442-4744	twk58	CD	PHD	76	Minnesota	1980
Daniel, Betty C.	Prof	442-4747	bd892	EF	PHD	76	N Carol	1983
Jerison, Michael	Prof	442-4287	mi770	DC	PHD	77	Wisconsin	1977
Lahiri, Kajal	Prof	442-4758	kl758	E	PHD	75	Rochester	1977
Reeb, Donald J.	Prof	442-4738	dreeb	RG	PHD	63	Syracuse	1965
Sattinger, Michael	Prof	442-4761	ms339@3	J	PHD	73	Car Mellon	1981
Uppal, Jogindar S.	Prof	442-4748	jsull	OH	PHD	65	Minnesota	1971
Yun, Kwan Koo	Prof	442-4741	ky948	CD	PHD	74	Stanford	1974
Dieffenbach, Bruce C.	Assoc	442-4750	bd455	E	PHD	72	Harvard	1978
Lankford, R. Hamilton	Assoc	442-4743	rh104	HD	PHD	81	N Carol	1981
Mirer, Thad W.	Assoc	442-4755	mirer@3	H	PHD	71	Yale	1973
Joh, Sung-Wook	Asst	442-4737	joh	DL	PHD	94	Harvard	1994
Jones, John	Asst	442-4926	jbjones@2	E	PHD	98	Wisconsin	1998
Kim, Jae-Young	Asst	442-4926	jykim@1	CE	PHD	95	Minnesota	1994
Kranich, Laurence J.	Asst	442-4741	l.kranich	DH	PHD	89	Rochester	1998
Marschke, Gerald	Asst	447-3755	marschke@2	DJL	PHD	98	Chicago	1998

SUNY at Binghamton Binghamton, NY 13902-6000 (607) 777-2572 binghamton.edu
Div Soc Sci - Dept Economics Harpur Col Arts & Sci Fax=777-2681 Joanne F. Ardune

Kokkelenberg, Edward C.	C-Pr	777-2550	kokkele	EO	PHD	81	Nrthwstrn	1980
Basmann, Robert L.	Prof	777-2660		C	PHD	66	Iowa St	1988
Bischoff, Charles W.	Prof	777-4351	cbischo	EC	PHD	68	MIT	1977
Britto, Ronald	Prof	777-2660	rbritto	FE	PHD	66	Brown	1974
Clark, Clifford D.	Prof	777-6415	cclark	OF	PHD	53	Chicago	1973
Cowing, Thomas G.	Prof	777-4480	tcowing	LD	PHD	70	Berkeley	1969
Greene, Kenneth V.	Prof	777-2944	kgreene	HK	PHD	68	Virginia	1968
Director of Undergraduate Studies								
Kumbhakar, Subal C.	Prof	777-4762	kkar	C	PHD	86	S Calif	2001
Masters, Stanley H.	Prof	777-2660	masterssj@a	J	PHD	65	Princeton	1981
Ofek, Haim	Prof	777-4351	hofek	J	PHD	71	Columbia	1981
Polachek, Solomon W.	Prof	777-6866	polachek	J	PHD	73	Columbia	1983
Sorensen, Bent	Prof	777-2572	sorensen	E	PHD	90	Copenhag	2001
Kern, Clifford R.	Assoc	777-2228	ckern	R	PHD	74	Harvard	1971
Director of Graduate Studies								
Leighton, Richard I.	Assoc	777-2339	rleight	F	PHD	61	Duke	1964
Yoon, Bong J.	Assoc	777-2987	yoon	JC	PHD	78	Illinois	1983
Jones, Barry	Asst	777-4353	bjones	EC	PHD	99	Wash U	1999
Kang, Inbong	Asst	777-2339	inbkang	EO	PHD	95	Rochester	1995
Khanna, Neha	Asst	777-2689	nkhanna	QD	PHD	97	Cornell	1998
Plassmann, Florenz	Asst	777-4304	fplass	HRF	PHD	97	Va Tech	1999
Wong, Linda	Asst	777-4351	lwong	JD	PHD	98	Iowa	1999
Zheng, Mingmei	VAsst	777-4755	mjones	HD	PHD	99	Wash U	1999

SUNY at Buffalo Buffalo, NY 14260-1520 (716) 645-2121 acsu.buffalo.edu
Department of Economics College of Arts & Sci Fax=645-2127 Betty C. Baker
Homepage: www.economics.buffalo.edu

Stinger, Charles	Dean	645-2711	cas-dean	Hst	PHD			
Ehrlich, Isaac	C-Pr	645-2121	mgtehrl	OLK	PHD	70	Columbia	1977
Anas, Alex	Prof	645-2121	alexanas	DR	PHD	75	Penn	1991
Chang, Winston W.	Prof	645-2121	ecowwc	DF	PHD	68	Rochester	1967
Gort, Michael	Prof	645-2121	gort	O	PHD	54	Columbia	1964
Holmes, James M.	Prof	645-2121	ecoholme	EF	PHD	67	Chicago	1967
Revankar, Nagesh S.	Prof	645-2121	ecorevan	DC	PHD	67	Wisconsin	1967
Zarembka, Paul	Prof	645-2121	zarembka	BO	PHD	67	Wisconsin	1976
Harwitz, Mitchell	Assoc	645-2121	harwitz	COTR	PHD	59	MIT	1958
Morgan, Peter B.	Assoc	645-2121	pbmorgan	D	PHD	78	Canterbu	1989
Kim, Jinyoung	Asst	645-2121	jinkim	OJ	PHD	94	Chicago	
Liu, Zhiqiany	Asst	645-2121	zqliu	DECO	PHD	93	SUNY-Buf	2001

Mendoza, Juan	Asst	645-2121	mendozaj	ED	PHD	99	Brown	1999
Park, Jungsoo	Asst	645-2121	jungsoo	OF	PHD	99	Stanford	1998
Plehn-Dujowich, Jose	Asst	645-2121		LICD	PHD	01	Chicago	2001
Subramanian, Chetan	Asst	645-2121	chetan	ECF	PHD	00	S Calif	2001
Yin, Yong	Asst	645-2121	yyin	CDE	PHD	95	Ohio St	1995

SUNY Empire State College Saratoga Spr, NY 12866-4391 (518) 587-2100 esc.edu
Economics Faculty Business Mgt & Econ Fax=587-2660 Ddoreen DeCrescenzo
area codes 598=(212) 587=(518) 358&948=(914) 360&997=(516) 394&886&244=(716)

Elliott, Joyce	VPAA				PHD			1989
RyanMann, Duncan	Assoc	587-2100	dryanman	I	PHD	84	Penn	1994
Cobb, Anne	Asst	244-3884	acobb	I	PHD	69	N Carol	1990
Angiello, Joseph		358-3990	jangiello	A	PHD	77	Tx-Austin	1983
Coffey, Sergia		587-2190	sergia.coffey		PHD			
DuBois, David		244-3884	ddubois	M	PHD	90	Union In	1976
Fortunato, Michael		587-2100	mfortuna	OMF	PHD	84	Harvard	1990
Fulk, David		997-4700	david.falk		ABD			
Giordano, Justin		598-0640	jgiordan	M	MBA		St Johns	1992
Hartley, William		673-3575	william.hartley		PHD			
Herdendorf, Phyllis		886-8020	pherdend	F	PHD	81	SUNY	1987
Hunt, Alan		647-7800	alan.hunt					
Jarvis, Leslie		997-4700	ljarvis	A	PHD	82	New Sch	1986
Jones, Otolorin		587-2100	ojones	A	PHD	83	Ohio U	1985
Lill, Lloyd		394-1110	llill	BO	PHD	77	Walden	1973
Mendelsohn, Frieda		853-7700	frieda.mendels+		ABD			
Musoke, Moses		948-6206	mmusoke	NM	PHD	78	Wisconsin	1985
Pauszek, Ruffin		587-2100	rpauszek	A	MBA		SUNY-Buf	1992
Saueracher, Ed		997-4700	ed.saueracher		PHD			
Sussman, Jeffrey		997-4700	jsussman	G	PHD	75	CUNY	1975
Todd, Edward		360-1215	etodd	A	PHD	69	Chicago	1985
Weiss, Jeffrey		948-6206	jweiss	A	PHD	67	Harvard	1986

SUNY at New Paltz New Paltz, NY 12561-2499 (845) 257-2969 npvm.newpaltz.edu
Department of Economics Economics Fax=257-3693 Jannette Carcich
Did Not Respond--1999-2000 Listing

Seshu, Chigurupati R.	Assoc	257-3559		AEO	PHD	60	New Sch	1967
Azari-Rad, Hamid	Asst				PHD	96	Utah	1999
Mozayeni, Simin B.	Asst	257-2919	mozayens	ALH	PHD	89	Columbia	1990

SUNY, Col at Plattsburgh Plattsburgh, NY 12901-2697 (518) 564-4185 plattsburgh.edu
Department of Economics Sch of Business & Econ Fax=564-3183 Beverly Cross
Homepage: www.plattsburgh.edu/academics
www.plattsburgh.edu

Shojai, Siamack	Dean	564-4185	siamack.shojai	GQ	PHD	84	Fordham	2001
Christopherson, Robert L.	C-Ac	564-4195	christrl	GH	PHD	90	Wayne St	1990
Dixon, Warren R.	Prof	564-4196	dixonwr	BP	PHD	71	Colorado	1968
Jang, Young S.	Prof	564-4193	jangys	CD	PHD	69	SUNY-Alb	1968
Page, Walter	Prof	564-3182	pagewp	DE	PHD	68	Kansas	1983
Duffy, Neal E.	Assoc	564-4194	duffyne	CR	PHD	82	W Virginia	1982
Withington, Robert P.	Assoc	564-4200	withinpr	NJ	PHD	76	Penn	1972
Fitzpatrick, Ellen	Asst	564-4217	fitzpae	FOQ	PHD	97	Mich St	1994

SUNY Col at Potsdam Potsdam, NY 13676-2294 (315) 267-2206 sunypotsdam.edu
Department of Economics Sch of Arts & Sciences Fax=267-2797 Colleen Wheaton
Did Not Respond--1999-2000 Listing

Pletcher, Galen K.	Dean	267-2231	pletchgk	Phil	PHD	71	Michigan	
Baktari, Paul	C-Ac	267-2204	baktarp		PHD		W Virginia	
Chugh, Ram L.	Prof	267-2206	chughrl		PHD	70	Wayne St	1970
Cliff, Lee	Assoc	267-2295	clliffh		MBA		Clarkson	
Nuwer, Michael J.	Assoc	267-2077	nuwermj		PHD	85	Utah	1986
Shu, Florence P.	Assoc	267-2221	shufp		PHD	86	Mich St	1986
Campbell, Martha	Asst				PHD	91	New Sch	1999
Mosier, Donna	Asst	267-2238	mosierdj		PHD	95	Clarkson	1997
Portugal, Edwin	Asst	267-2212	portugej		PHD	93	SUNY-Alb	

SUNY College at Purchase Purchase, NY 10577-1400 (914) 251-6601
Division of Social Science Coll Arts & Letters Fax=251-6603 Valencia Wallace

Bell, Peter F.	C-Ac	251-6633			PHD	68	Wisconsin	1971
O'Cleireacain, Seamus	Prof	251-6600			PHD	71	Michigan	1974
Christensen, Kimberly	Assoc	251-6622			PHD	86	Mass	1985
Ikeda, Sanford	Assoc	251-6614			PHD	88	NYU	1990

Stephen F. Austin St Univ — Nacogdoches, TX 75962-3009 (936) 468-4301 — sfasu.edu
Dept of Economics & Finance — College of Business Fax=468-1447 — Barbara Roos
Homepage: www.cob.sfasu.edu/eco-fin

Young, Marlin C.	Dean	468-3101	myoung	BEd	EDD	74	Ariz St	1967
Jones, Clifton T.	C-Pr	468-4301	ctjones	CD	PHD	85	Tx A&M	1995
Howard, James E.	Assoc	468-1752	jhoward	AC	PHD	77	Georgia	1976
Stroup, Michael	Assoc	468-1557	mstroup	DH	PHD	93	Fla St	1999
Ballinger, T. Parker	Asst	468-1442	pballinger	CE	PHD	99	Houston	1999
Halvorson, Jon	Asst	468-1501	jhalvorson	CDH	PHD	00	Alabama	2001
Ishwaran, Jayvanth	Asst	468-1457	chaos	EF	PHD	97	Purdue	1997
Rummery, Sarah	Asst	468-1783	srummery	J	PHD	94	Austr Natl	1998

Stetson University — Deland, FL 32720-3756 (904) 822-7570 — stetson.edu
Department of Economics — Col of Arts & Sciences Fax=822-7569 — Divina Bungard
Homepage: http://www.stetson.edu/~econ

Ballenger, Grady	Dean	822-7515	gballeng	Eng	PHD	83	N Carol	1998
Long, Neal B.	C-Pr	822-7571	nlong	ACP	PHD	64	Indiana	1974
Wood, Richard H. Jr.	Prof	822-7572	rwood	AFO	PHD	72	Wisconsin	1970
Aldrich, Carole	Visit	822-7542	quakermac@a	ACD	PHD	72	Car Mellon	1998
Thaver, Ranjini L.	Assoc	822-7573	rthaver	AHP	PHD	95	Notre Dm	1992

Richard Stockton College — Pomona, NJ 08240-0195 (609) 652-1776 — stockton.edu
Department of Economics — Social & Behavioral Sci Fax=748-5559
Did Not Respond--1999-2000 Listing

Carr, David	Dean	652-1776		PolS	PHD	75	SUNY-Bin	1978
Ghorashi, Gholam-Reza	C-Ac	652-1776			PHD	86	Fordham	1981
Elmore, Elizabeth A.	Prof	652-1776			PHD	76	Notre Dm	1972
Figort, Debb	Assoc	652-1776			PHD	95	American	1989
Harrison, Kenneth	Assoc	652-1776	laprod2556		PHD	76	SUNY-Alb	1976
Lakew, Melaku	Assoc	652-1776			PHD	81	Ca-Rivers	1982
Alpan, Erkan	Asst	652-1776			PHD	84	Ca-Rivers	1980

Stonehill College — North Easton, MA 02357-1135 (508) 565-1276 — stonehill.edu
Economics Faculty — Dept of Economics Fax=565-1444

Kazemi, Hossein S.	C-Ac	565-1276	kazemi	GE	PHD	83	Clark	1982
Pepin, Raymond A.	Prof	565-1042		AD	PHD	71	Clark	1969
Rosenthal, Robert A.	Prof	565-1230		AI	PHD	78	Boston U	1975
Wiles, James L.	Emer	565-1327		KN	PHD	76	Harvard	1955
Kazarosian, Mark	Assoc	565-1249		CG	PHD	90	Boston C	1997
Motomura, Akira	Assoc	565-1241		KN	PHD	85	Nrthwstrn	1995
Hammerle, Nancy E.	Asst	565-1257		A	MA		Temple	1980

Suffolk University — Boston, MA 02108-2770 (617) 573-8259 — suffolk.edu
Department of Economics — College of Arts & Sci Fax=994-4216 — Alyssa M. Truong
Homepage: www.cas.suffolk.edu/economics
email @1=beaconhill.org

Ronayne, Michael R.	Dean			Chem	PHD	63	Notre Dm	
Tuerck, David G.	C-Pr	573-8259			PHD	66	Virginia	1982
email=dtuerck@beaconhill.org								
Jaggia, Sanjiv	Prof	573-8023	sjaggia@1		PHD	90	Indiana	
Chisholm, Darlene C.	Assoc	305-1932	dchishol	LD	PHD	91	U Wash	2001
Kelly-Hawke, Alison	Assoc	573-8069	akelly		PHD	93	Boston C	
Mohtadi, Shahruz	Assoc	573-8670	smohtadi		PHD	84	LSU	1983
Baek, In-Mee	Asst	573-8376	ibaek		PHD	90	Indiana	
Haughton, Jonathan H.	Asst	573-8127	jhaughto@1		PHD	83	Harvard	1997

Susquehanna University — Selinsgrove, PA 17870-1001 (570) 372-4186 — susqu.edu
Department of Economics — Sigmund Weis Sch Bus Fax=372-4491

Brock, James L.	Dean	372-4455	brock	Mktg	PHD	80	Mich St	9-96
Zadeh, Ali Haji-Mohamad	H-Pr	372-4189	azadeh	CEGO	PHD	82	Mich St	1987
Fisher, Warren L.	Prof	372-4186	fisherw	ABQ	PHD	73	Conn	1988
Onafowora, Olugbenga A.	Assoc	372-4187	onafowor	CDOQ	PHD	89	W Virginia	1989
Rusek, Antonin	Assoc	372-4182	rusek	EFP	PHD	84	SUNY-SBr	1986

Swarthmore College — Swarthmore, PA 19081-1397 (610) 328-8125 — swarthmore.edu
Department of Economics — Div of Social Sciences Fax=328-7352 — Mary Anne Stewart

Kuperberg, Mark J.	C-Pr	328-8123	mkuperb1	EK	PHD	81	MIT	1977
Caskey, John P.	Prof	328-8128	jcaskey1	EG	PHD	84	Stanford	1988
Golub, Stephen S.	Prof	328-8103	sgolub1	AE	PHD	83	Yale	1981
Hollister, Robinson G. Jr.	Prof	328-8105	rhollis1	IJ	PHD	65	Stanford	1971
Joseph Wharton Professor of Economics								
O'Connell, Stephen A.	Prof	328-8107	soconne1	EO	PHD	86	MIT	1990
Pryor, Frederic	Emer	328-8130	fpryor1	OP	PHD	57	Yale	1972

Saffran, Bernard	Prof	328-8124	bsaffra1	AH	PHD	63	Minnesota	1973
Franklin and Betty Barr Professor of Economics								
Westphal, Larry E.	Prof	328-8096	lwestph1	DO	PHD	69	Harvard	1985
J. Archer & Helen C. Turner Professor of Economics								
Bayer, Amanda	Assoc	328-7821	abayer1	DJ	PHD	95	Yale	1992
Jefferson, Philip N.	Assoc	690-6856	pjeffer1	CE	PHD	87	Virginia	1999
Magenheim, Ellen B.	Assoc	328-8140	emagen1	DI	PHD	86	Maryland	1986
Dee, Thomas S.	Asst	690-5767	tdee1	CI	PHD	97	Maryland	1999

Syracuse University Syracuse, NY 13244-1090 (315) 443-3843 maxwell.syr.edu
Department of Economics Maxwell S Citznship &PA Fax=443-3717 Patty Stach 443-3612
Homepage: www.maxwell.syr.edu/econ
email @1=syr.edu

Palmer, John L.	Dean	443-2252		I	PHD	70	Stanford	1988
Black, Dan A.	C-Pr	443-3114	dablac01	DJI	PHD	83	Purdue	1999
Dutkowsky, Donald H.	Prof	443-1918	dondutk	E	PHD	82	SUNY-Buf	1985
Holtz-Eakin, Douglas	Prof	443-9050	djheakin	H	PHD	85	Princeton	1990
Kao, C. H.	Prof	443-3233	ckao	C	PHD	83	SUNY-SBr	1985
Kelly, Jerry S.	Prof	443-2345	jskelly@1	D	PHD	69	Harvard	1971
Kniesner, Thomas J.	Prof	443-3114	tkniesne	J	PHD	74	Ohio St	1999
Ondrich, Jan Ivar	Prof	443-9052	jondrich	C	PHD	83	Wisconsin	1982
Richardson, J. David	Prof	443-4339	jdrichar	F	PHD	70	Michigan	1991
Rosenthal, Stuart S.	Prof	443-3114	ssrosent	RHG	PHD	86	Wisconsin	1999
Smeeding, Timothy M.	Prof	443-9045	tmsmeed	I	PHD	75	Wisconsin	1990
Tussing, A. Dale	Prof	443-2642	tussing	I	PHD	64	Syracuse	1966
Wasylenko, Michael J.	Prof	443-3612	mjwasyle	H	PHD	75	Syracuse	1989
Yinger, John M.	Prof	443-9062	jyinger	RI	PHD	74	Princeton	1986
Engelhardt, Gary	Assoc	443-3114	gvengelh		PHD	93	MIT	1999
Evensky, Jerry	Assoc	443-5863	jevensky	B	PHD	84	Syracuse	1985
Gensemer, Susan H.	Assoc	443-2294	gensemer	D	PHD	84	Purdue	1984
Lovely, Mary E.	Assoc	443-9048	melovely	F	PHD	89	Michigan	1986
Conlin, Michael	Asst	44301354	meconlin	LD	PHD	95	Wisconsin	
Dickert-Conlin, Stacy	Asst	443-3232	sdickert	GHJ	PHD	95	Wisconsin	1998
Kubik, Jeff	Asst	443-9063	jdkubik	HJ	PHD	97	MIT	1997
Moran, John	Asst	443-3114	jmoran	DIL	PHD	97	Penn St	1999
Sinclair, Robert	Asst	443-4079	rdsincla	EF	PHD	99	Stanford	1999
Trindade, Vitor	Asst	443-3802	vmtrinda	F	PHD	00	Ca-SnDgo	2000

University of Tampa Tampa, FL 33606-1490 (813) Ext 3336 alpha.utampa.edu
Dept of Finance & Economics College of Business Fax=258-7408
phone: 253-6221

McCann, Joseph E. III	Dean	253-6221	jmccann	Mgt	PHD	80	Penn	2000
Truscott, Michael H.	C-Pr	253-6221	mhtruscott@a	AEF	PHD	71	LSU	1971
Fesmire, James M.	Prof	253-6221		DKL	PHD	73	Florida	1973
Dana Professor of Economics								
Hoke, Leon R. Jr.	Prof	253-6221		ADJ	PHD	79	Pittsburgh	1981
Brust, Peter J.	Assoc	253-6221		EF	PHD	80	Indiana	1981
Crummett, Maria	Assoc	253-6221		AEO	PHD	85	New Sch	1999

Tarleton State University Stephenville, TX 76402 (254) 968-9047 tarleton.edu
Dept of Business Systems College of Business Adm Fax=968-9345 Mrs. Sharon Iley

Collins, Dan	Dean	968-9350	Cis	PHD	83	North Tx	1975
Brocato, Joe M.	Prof	968-9047	CEG	PHD	81	Tennessee	1989
Jafri, Syed Hussain Ali	Prof	968-9633	AFG	PHD	86	Wisconsin	1989
Zelman, Patricia G.	Prof	968-9629	N	PHD	80	Ohio St	1982
Beaty, William L.	Asst	968-9622	ADR	MS	73	Utah St	1985

Taylor University Upland, IN 46989-1001 (765) 998-5135 tayloru.edu
Dept of Business, Atg & Econ Division of Business Fax=998-4930 Nancy Gillespie

Bennett, Christopher P.	C-Ac	998-5137	chbennett	PHD	98	Union In	1988
Associate Dean							
Erickson, Lee E.	Prof	998-5138	leerickso	PHD	75	Michigan	1979
Mitchell, Hadley T.	Assoc	998-4948	hdmitchel	PHD	85	Tennessee	1993

Teikyo Post University Waterbury, CT 06723-2540 (203) 596-4656 teikyopost.edu
Economic Faculty School of Business Adm Fax=575-9691 Patricia Jennings

Sanders, Patricia	VP $	596-4652	PHD			
Philippides, Andreas	Prof	596-4661	PHD	94	Conn	1988

Temple University Philadelphia, PA 19122 (215) 204-8880 foxmail.sbm.temple.edu
Department of Economics Sch of Business & Mgt Fax=204-8173 Ms. Karen Robinson
Homepage: www/sbm.temple.edu/~econdept/

Porat, Moshe	Dean	204-1836	Risk	PHD	81	Temple	1981
Stull, William J.	C-Pr	204-5022	IR	PHD	72	MIT	1976

Bandera, Vladimir N.	Prof	204-5039		FP	PHD	60	Berkeley	1972
Blackstone, Erwin A.	Prof	204-5027		L	PHD	68	Michigan	1976
Buck, Andrew J.	Prof	204-1985		C	PHD	77	Illinois	1977
Dunkelberg, William C.	Prof	204-6686		M	PHD	69	Michigan	1987
Hakim, Simon	Prof	204-5037		R	PHD	76	Penn	1976
Kushnirsky, Fyodor I.	Prof	204-5021		P	PHD	68	Moscow	1980
Lady, George	Prof	204-8174		CD	PHD	67	J Hopkins	1981
Raphaelson, Arnold H.	Prof	204-8165		H	PHD	60	Clark	1970
Rima, Ingrid H.	Prof	204-8190		B	PHD	51	Penn	1946
Bernstein, Richard E.	Assoc	204-8182		MG	PHD	73	Brown	1972
Bognanno, Michael	Assoc	204-1680		J	PHD	90	Cornell	1990
Bowman, Gary W.	Assoc	204-5026		D	PHD	71	Car Mellon	1973
Diamantaras, Dimitrios	Assoc	204-8169		CD	PHD	88	Rochester	1988
Fardmanesh, Mohsen	Assoc	204-5043		OF	PHD	85	Yale	1985
Goetz, Michael	Assoc	204-1762		MH	PHD	77	Minnesota	1978
Holmes, William L.	Assoc	204-8175		CD	PHD	66	Illinois	1966
Klotz, Benjamin P.	Emer	204-8452		E	PHD	69	Minnesota	1975
Leeds, Michael A.	Assoc	204-8030		J	PHD	82	Princeton	1982
Phelps, Charlotte D.	Emer	204-1677		TI	PHD	61	Yale	1967
Rappoport, Paul N.	Assoc	204-5025		C	PHD	74	Ohio St	1977
Seidenstat, Paul	Assoc	204-8893		H	PHD	64	Nrthwstrn	1967
Sorrentino, John A. Jr.	Assoc	204-8164		Q	PHD	73	Purdue	1979
Swanson, Charles	Assoc	204-8168		E	PHD	91	Minnesota	1993
Weiss, Merle	Assoc	204-5029		IJ	PHD	67	Columbia	1972

University of Tennessee	Knoxville, TN		37996-0550 (865) 974-3303				utk.edu	
Department of Economics	Col of Business Admin		Fax=974-4601				Donna Kemper 974-1697	
email @1=utkux.utcc.utk.edu								
Neel, C. Warren	Dean	974-5061	cneel	Mgt	PHD	69	Alabama	9-69
Murray, Matthew N.	C-Ac	974-5441	mmurray@1		PHD	86	Syracuse	1986
Bohm, Robert A.	Prof	974-1687	rbohm		PHD	71	Wash U	1968
Chang, Hui-Shyong	Prof	974-1692	hchang		PHD	73	Vanderbilt	1971
Clark, Don P.	Prof	974-1706	dclark3		PHD	78	Mich St	1978
Fox, William F.	Prof	974-1697	billfox		PHD	75	Ohio St	1979
Herzog, Henry W. Jr.	Prof	974-1701	pb55978@utkvm1.		PHD	74		
Maryland								1974
Gauger, Jean A.	Assoc	974-1702	jgaugher		PHD	84	Iowa St	1985
Glustoff, Errol	Assoc	974-1705	eglustof@1		PHD	69	Stanford	1970
Barkoulas, John	Asst	974-1699		EGF	PHD	95	Boston C	2001
Bruce, Donald	Asst	974-3303					Syracuse	1999
Mohsin, Mohammed	Asst	974-6081			PHD	01	York	2001
Munkin, Murat	Asst	974-1695			PHD	01	Indiana	2001
Santore, Rudy	Asst	974-3303			PHD	98	Ohio St	1999

Tennessee at Chattanooga	Chattanooga, TN		37403-2598 (423) 755-4360				utc.edu	
Department of Economics	Col of Arts & Sciences		Fax=785-2385				Jewell Chason	
Homepage: www.utc.edu								
Burhenn, Herbert	Dean	755-4635			PHD			
Keilany, Ziad Guerry Professor	H-Pr	755-4116	ziad-keilany	EO	PHD	68	Indiana	1968
Clark, J. R. Probasco Chair in Free Enterprise	Prof	755-4118	j-clark	M	PHD	70	Va Tech	1993
Garrett, John R. UC Foundation Associate Professor	Prof	755-4080	john-garrett	EFG	PHD	85	Mass	1984
Giffin, Phillip E.	Prof	755-4129	phillip-giffin	DBLN	PHD	72	Tennessee	1977
Hutchinson, E. Bruce	Prof	755-4180	bruce-hutchinson	DFLR	PHD	79	Virginia	1982
Pratt, Leila J. Hart Professor	Prof	755-4138	leila-pratt	DC	PHD	75	Va Tech	1974
Rabin, Alan UC Foundation Professor	Prof	755-4154	alan-rabin	E	PHD	77	Virginia	1977
Efaw, Fritz W.	Assoc	755-4688	fritz-efaw	CJ	PHD	87	Rutgers	1988

Univ of Tennessee at Martin	Martin, TN		38238-5015 (731) 587-7226				utm.edu	
Dept of Atg, Fnce & Econ	Col of Bus & Public Aff		Fax=587-7241				Mary Prather	
Moser, Ernest C.	Dean	587-7225	emoser	BM	PHD	73	Tx A&M	8-01
Figgins, Bob G.	C-Pr	587-7232			PHD	73	Arkansas	1973
Cashdollar, Parker D.	Prof	587-7242			PHD	71	Tennessee	
Davis, William L.	Assoc	587-7239			PHD	90	Okla St	
Kowalsky, Stan	Inst	587-7244			MA	61	Rutgers	8-01

Tennessee State University	Nashville, TN		37203-3401 (615) 963-7145				tnstate.edu	
Economics Faculty	School of Business		Fax=963-7139				Ms. C. Brown	
Curry, Tilden J.	Dean	963-7124		Plan	PHD	78	Fla St	1976
Hartmann, G. Bruce MBA Coordinator	H-Pr	963-7146	bhartman		PHD	74	SUNY-Alb	1974
Hasty, John M. Jr.	Prof	963-7145			PHD	73	Geo St	
Wahid, Abu	Prof	963-7145			PHD	89	Manitoba	
Weis, Charles E.	Prof	963-7145			DBA	74	Ariz St	

Tennessee Technological Un	Cookeville, TN	38505	(931) 372-3745					tntech.edu
Dept of Econ, Fnce & Mktg	Col of Business Admin	Fax=372-6249						Hilda McDowell
Niebuhr, Robert E.	Dean	372-3372	niebuhr	Mgt	PHD	77	Ohio St	2001
Stephens, Mark A.	C-Pr$	372-3745	mstephens	FO	PHD	85	Tennessee	1980
Cho, Whewon	Prof	372-3839	wcho	CD	PHD	71	Vanderbilt	1983
Rappl, Magdalena	Prof	372-3369	mrappl	GN	PHD	85	S Carol	1985
Throckmorton, H. Bruce	Prof	372-3781	bthrockmor	EN	PHD	72	Arkansas	1971
Isbell, Steven	Assoc	372-3794	steve_isbell	EJ	PHD	85	Miss	1985
Jonokin, Jon	Assoc	372-3767	jjonakin		PHD	94	Tennessee	1989

U of Texas at Arlington	Arlington, TX	76019-0479	(817) 272-3061					uta.edu
Department of Economics	College of Business Adm	Fax=272-3145						Barbara Sellers, Adm Asst
Himarios, Daniel	Dean	272-2881	himarios	FE	PHD	84	Va Tech	1983
Amacher, Ryan C.	Prof	272-3888	amacher	FH	PHD	71	Virginia	1992
Hayashi, Paul M.	Prof	272-3257	hayashi	D	PHD	69	So Meth	1965
Meiners, Roger E.	Prof	272-3116	meiners	KJ	PHD	76	Va Tech	1993
Mullendore, Walter	Prof	272-3397	mullendor	R	PHD	68	Iowa St	1969
Crowder, William J.	Assoc	272-3147	crowder	EF	PHD	93	Arizona	1992
Duwaji, Ghazi	Assoc	272-3148	duwaji	F	PHD	66	Duke	1966
Depken, Craig	Asst	272-3290	depken	DL	PHD	96	Geo St	1996
Sonora, Robert	Asst	272-3062	sonora	F	PHD	98	Ohio St	1998
Wilson, Dennis	VAsst	272-3284	dpwilson	DL	PHD	99	Kentucky	1999
Wilson, Richard C.	Asst	272-3383	rwilson	AH	MA	66	Georgia	1966
Himarios, Jane	SLect	272-3293	jhimarios	J	PHD	87	Va Tech	1986
Kelly, Kathy	Lect	272-3330	kkelly	DE	MA	89	So Meth	1996
Liggett, Ron	Lect	272-2635	liggett	R	MBA	89	Tx-Arlin	1989
Wehr, Roger	Lect	272-3287	wehr	DE	MA	96	Tx-Arlin	1993
Wilson, Linda	Lect	272-3282	l.wilson	DB	MS	92	North Tx	1993

Univ of Texas at Austin	Austin, TX	78712-1173	(512) 471-3211					mundo.eco.utexas.edu
Department of Economics	College of Liberal Arts	Fax=471-3510						Kathy Slade, Exec Asst
Lariviere, Richard	Dean	471-4141						
Bronars, Stephen G.	C-Ac	471-3211		JD	PHD	83	Chicago	9-92
Dacy, Douglas C.	Prof	471-3211		EO	PHD	64	Harvard	1-65
Dusansky, Richard	Prof	471-3211		DH	PHD	69	Brown	9-89
Richard J. Gonzales Regents Chair in Economic Progress								
Fullerton, Don	Prof	471-3211		HQ	PHD	78	Berkeley	9-94
Addison Baker Duncan Centennial Professor in Economics								
Geraci, Vincent J.	Prof	471-3211		CI	PHD	74	Wisconsin	9-73
Sue Killam Professorship in the Foundations of Economics								
Glade, William P. Jr.	Prof	471-3211		OR	PHD	55	Tx-Austin	9-70
Hamermesh, Daniel S.	Prof	471-3211		J	PHD	69	Yale	9-73
Eedward Everett Hale Centennial Professor in Economics								
Hansen, Niles M.	Prof	471-3211		RP	PHD	63	Indiana	1-63
Leroy G. Denmann, Jr. Regents Professor in Economics								
Kendrick, David A.	Prof	471-3211		CE	PHD	66	MIT	7-70
Ralph W. Yarborough Centennial Professor of Liberal Arts								
McAfee, R. Preston	Prof	471-3211		D	PHD	80	Purdue	9-90
Murray S. Johnson Chair in Economics								
Norman, Alfred L.	Prof	471-3211		C	PHD	71	Minnesota	7-72
Sibley, David S.	Prof	471-3211		D	PHD	73	Yale	1-91
John Michael Stuart Centennial Professor of Economics								
Slesnick, Daniel T.	Prof	471-3211		CH	PHD	82	Harvard	9-82
Rex G. Baker, Jr., Professorship in Political Economy								
Smith, Bruce D.	Prof	471-3211		E	PHD	81	MIT	9-96
Fred Hofheinz Professor in Economics								
Stahl, Dale O. III	Prof	471-3211		DC	PHD	81	Berkeley	7-88
Malcolm Forsman Centennial Professorship								
Cleaver, Harry	Assoc	471-3211		P	PHD	75	Stanford	9-76
Freeman, Scott	Assoc	471-3211		E	PHD	83	Minnesota	9-91
Stinchcombe, Maxwell B.	Assoc	471-3211		DC	PHD	86	Berkeley	1-94
Trejo, Stephen J.	Assoc	471-3211		J	PHD	88	Chicago	9-99
Wilson, Paul W.	Assoc	471-3211		RC	PHD	86	Brown	9-90
Debaere, Peter	Asst	471-3211		F	PHD	98	Michigan	9-98
Gan, Li	Asst	471-3211		C	PHD	98	Berkeley	9-98
Keller, Wolfgang	Asst	471-3211		FO	PHD	95	Yale	9-98
Minicozzi, Alexandra	Asst	471-3211		E	PHD	97	Wisconsin	9-97
Oettinger, Gerald	Asst	471-3211		JC	PHD	93	MIT	9-92
Wilcoxen, Peter J.	Asst	471-3211		QD	PHD	89	Harvard	9-91
Williams, Roberton III	Asst	471-3211		H	PHD	99	Stanford	9-99
Shiue, Carol	Inst	471-3211		ON	PHD	99	Yale	9-98

Univ Texas at Brownsville	Brownsville, TX	78520	(956) 548-8707					utb.edu
Business Adm Department	School of Business	Fax=982-0159						Magie Arriaga
Boze, Betsy V.	Dean	982-0231	bboze	Mktg	PHD	84	Arkansas	1994
Hardebeck, Suzanne	C-Ac	982-0230	shardebeck	Mgt	PHD	80	North Tx	1994
Lackey, Charles W. Jr.	Assoc	548-8707	clackey	AFL	PHD	84	S Carol	1995
Banerjee, Guarango	Asst	544-8992	gbanerjee	AE	PHD	97	Al-Birm	1997
Estrada, Joselito K.	Asst	982-0230	jestrada	AQR	PHD	92	Miss St	2000

Univ of Texas at Dallas Richardson, TX 75083-0688 (972) 883-2920 utdallas.edu
Dept of Economics & Finance Sch of Social Sciences Fax=883-2735 Sheila Rollerson

Stewart, Marianne	Dean	883-2935			PHD	86	Duke	1988
Amin-Gutierrez de Pineres, S	H-Ac	883-6228	pineres		PHD	92	Duke	1996
Berry, Brian J. L.	Prof	883-2041	berry		PHD	58	U Wash	
L. V. Berkner Professor								
Dumas, Lloyd J.	Prof	883-2010	ljdumas		PHD	72	Columbia	1979
Hicks, Donald A.	Prof	883-2733	dahicks		PHD	76	N Carol	
Hoch, Irving J.	Prof	883-2928	hoch		PHD	57	Chicago	1985
Kain, John F.	Prof	883-6227	kain		PHD	61	Berkeley	1996
Murdoch, James	Prof	883-2280	murdoch		PHD	82	Wyoming	
Seldon, Barry	Prof	883-2043	seldon		PHD	85	Duke	
Vijverberg, Wim P. M.	Prof	883-2042	vijver		PHD	81	Pittsburgh	1986
Beron, Kurt J.	Assoc	883-2929	kberon		PHD	85	N Carol	1985
Jargowky, Paul	Assoc	883-2992	jargo		PHD	91	Harvard	
Berg, Nathan	Asst	883-2920			PHD	01	Kansas	2001
DeFavia, Joao	Asst	883-2920			PHD	98	Kent	2001
O'Brien, Dan	Asst	883-4700			PHD	99	Tx-Dallas	2001

Univ of Texas at El Paso El Paso, TX 79968-0543 (915) 747-5245 mail.utep.edu
Dept of Economics & Finance Col of Business Admin Fax=747-6282 Gloria Armistead

Hoy, Frank	Dean	747-5241		Mgt	PHD	79	Tx A&M	9-91
Roth, Timothy P.	C-Pr	747-5245		AD	PHD	70	Tx A&M	1970
A.B. Templeton Professor								
Herendeen, James B.	Prof	747-5245		AQ	PHD	63	Penn St	1992
James, Dilmus Delano	Prof	747-5245		AFO	PHD	70	Mich St	1958
Frank & Mary Hanley Professor								
Brannon, Jeffery T.	Assoc	747-5245		JNO	PHD	80	Alabama	1982
Holcomb, James H. Jr.	Assoc	747-5245		CDL	PHD	85	Tx A&M	1985
Schauer, David A.	Assoc	747-5245		P	PHD	75	Notre Dm	1975
Smith, William Doyle	Assoc	747-5245		AEC	PHD	81	Tx Tech	1981
Sprinkle, Richard L.	Assoc	747-5245		ABCF	PHD	82	Arkansas	1982
Tollen, Robert D.	Assoc	747-5245		D	PHD	72	Tx-Austin	1972
Fullerton, Thomas	Asst	747-5245		RC	PHD	96	Florida	1996

Univ of Texas-Pan American Edinburg, TX 78539-2999 (956) 381-3354 panam1.panam.edu
Dept of Economics & Finance College of Business Adm Fax=384-5020 Nora Herrera

Emery, John T.	Dean	384-5087	emery	Fnce	PHD	69	U Wash	1-01
Davila, Alberto	C-Pr	326-7136	adavila		PHD	82	Iowa St	1996
Cardenas, Gilbert	Prof	381-3369	gcardenas		PHD	77	Illinois	1975
Ellard, Charles J.	Prof	381-3391	cjeb12b		PHD	74	Houston	1976
Pagan, Jose	Assoc	381-3383	jpagan		PHD	95	New Mex	1995
Soydemir, Gokoe	Asst	381-3368	soydemir		PHD	97	Claremont	1998

U Texas of the Permian Basin Odessa, TX 79762-0001 (915) 552-2170 utpb.edu
Dept of Economics School of Business Fax=552-2174 Carolyn Jennings

Franklin, Geralyn M.	Dean	552-2194	fanklin_g	Mgt	PHD	89	North Tx	7-99
Hodges, Paul E.	Prof	552-2193	hodges_p	CHRT	PHD	74	Stanford	
Carson, Scott	Asst	552-2195	carson_s	NBJK	PHD	98	Utah	8-99

Un of Texas at San Antonio San Antonio, TX 78249-0633 (210) 458-4315 utsa.edu
Department of Economics College of Business Fax=458-5837

Bublitz, Bruce O.	Dean	458-4313		Atg	PHD	82	Illinois	8-00
Flory-Truett, Lila J.	C-Pr	458-4315	ltruett	DFMO	PHD	72	Iowa	1975
Collinge, Robert A.	Prof	458-5312	rcollinge	FHKQ	PHD	83	Maryland	1987
de la Vina, Lynda	Prof	458-4317			PHD	82	Rice	1979
Hollas, Daniel R.	Prof	458-4313			PHD	77	Illinois	1988
Associate Dean								
Lien, Da-Hsiang D.	Prof	458-4315	dlien	O	PHD	86	Cal Tech	2001
Merrifield, John D.	Prof	458-5310	jmerrifi	HQR	PHD	84	Wyoming	1987
Truett, Dale B.	Prof	458-5313	dtruett	DFMO	PHD	67	Tx-Austin	1973
Asbel Smith Professor								
Ayers, Ronald M.	Assoc	458-5302	rayers	GJM	PHD	78	Tulane	1979
Firoozi, Fathall K.	Assoc	458-5395	ffiroozi	CF	PHD	87	Oklahoma	1988
Mahdavi, Saeid	Assoc	458-5301	smahdavi	EFO	PHD	85	Ca-SnBarb	1984
Weiher, Kenneth E.	Assoc	458-5315	kweiher	BEN	PHD	75	Indiana	1975
Zhou, Su	Assoc	458-5398	szhou	CEFP	PHD	91	Ariz St	1991
De La Cruz, Justino	Asst	458-5303	jdcruz	CEFH	PHD	94	Iowa St	1996

Univ of Texas at Tyler Tyler, TX 75799 (903) 566-7371 mail.uttyl.edu
Social Sciences Department School of Liberal Arts Fax=566-7377 Charlotte Chambers

Dickerson, Donna L.	Dean	566-7368	ddickers	Jou	PHD	77	S Illinois	1998
Hart, Barbara	C-Pr	566-7426	bhart	CRIJ	PHD		Sam Hous	
Kane, Tim D.	Prof	566-7430	tkane		PHD	72	Tx-Austin	1981

Texas A&M University Coll Station, TX 77843-4228 (409) 845-7351 tamu.edu
Department of Economics College of Liberal Arts Fax=847-8757 Tricia Kelm
email @1=econ.tamu.edu @2=acs.tamu.edu

Jones, Woodrow	Dean$	845-5141	woodyj	PolS	PHD	74	Oregon	1988
Jansen, Dennis W.	H-Pr	845-7358	d-jansen	EG	PHD	83	N Carol	1983
Allen, John William	Prof	845-7397	jwa@1	D	PHD	67	Illinois	1967
Anderson, Richard K.	Prof	845-4547	rka3591@2	CF	PHD	76	Purdue	1975
Auernheimer, Leonardo J. A.	Prof	845-7302	leonardo@3	EF	PHD	73	Chicago	1973
Baltagi, Badi H.	Prof	845-7380	badi@1	C	PHD	79	Penn	1988
George Summey Jr. Professor in Liberal Arts								
Battalio, Ray	Prof	845-7309	rcb@1	C	PHD	69	Purdue	1969
Mary Tucker Currie Professorship in Liberal Arts								
Browning, Edgar K.	Prof	845-7355	1	H	PHD	71	Princeton	1984
Alfred F. Chalk Professor of Economics								
Greenhut, Melvin L.	Emer	845-7351			PHD	51	Wash U	1966
Distinguished Professor of Economics								
Griffin, James M.	Prof	845-9950	jmgrif@2	C	PHD	70	Penn	1982
Hugh Roy Cullen Professor in Liberal Arts								
Gronberg, Timothy J.	Prof	845-8849	tjg@1	H	PHD	78	Nrthwstrn	1977
Hanson, John R. II	Prof	845-4593	hanson@1	N	PHD	72	Penn	1974
Hwang, Hae-Shin	Prof	845-7301	hwang@1	C	PHD	76	Minnesota	1977
Li, Qi	Prof	862-8859	qi@1	C	PHD	91	Tx A&M	1999
Moroney, John R.	Prof	845-1363	jmoroney@1	C	PHD	64	Duke	1981
Pejovich, Svetozar	Emer	845-7347	s-pejovich	P	PHD	63	Geotown	1975
Reynolds, Morgan O.	Prof	845-7307		J	PHD	71	Wisconsin	1974
Saving, Thomas R.	Prof	845-7559	t-saving	DE	PHD	60	Chicago	1968
Distinguished Professor, Jeff Montgomery Prof; Dir Private Enterprise Rsch								
Tian, Guoqiang	Prof	845-7393	gtian	C	PHD	87	Minnesota	1987
Van Huyck, John B.	Prof	845-7392	john.vanhuyck	CD	PHD	86	Brown	1985
Private Enterprise Research Center Rex B. Grey Professor								
Welch, Finis R.	Prof	847-8648	bbc@1	J	PHD	66	Chicago	1991
Distinguished Professor and George T. & Gladys H. Abell Prof of Liberal Arts								
Wiggins, Steven N.	Prof	845-7383	snw	L	PHD	79	MIT	1979
Deere, Donald R.	Assoc	845-2059	deere	J	PHD	83	MIT	1983
Neilson, William S.	Assoc	845-9954	wsn@1	CD	PHD	88	Ca-SnDgo	1988
Sarin, Rajiv	Assoc	845-7382	r-sarin@1	CD	PHD	94	Ca-SnDgo	9-94
Swanson, Norman	Assoc	845-9345	nswanson@1		PHD	94	Ca-SnDgo	1999
Ureta, Manuelita	Assoc	847-9449	manuelita-ureta	J	PHD	87	UCLA	1991
Jeitschko, Thomas	Asst	845-6929	thosd@1	L	PHD	95	Virginia	1995
Strayer, Wayne	Asst	845-8508	strayer@1	J	PHD	97	Ohio St	1997
Tam, Henry	Asst	845-0676	htam@1	E	PHD	99	Harvard	1999

Texas A&M Univ-Commerce Commerce, TX 75429-3011 (903) 886-5681 tamu-commerce.edu
Dept of Economics & Finance College of Business Fax=886-5601 Debra Thode

Langford, Harold P.	Dean	886-5189	hal.langford	Mgt	PHD	86	Geo St	2001
Avard, Stephen L.	H-Ac	886-5681	steve_avard	GFDE	PHD	83	North Tx	1983
Funderburk, Dale R.	Prof	886-5675	dale_funderburk	IEKJ	PHD	71	Okla St	1968
Shwiff, Steven S.	Assoc	886-5679	steve_shwiff	CROD	PHD	77	Tx A&M	1987
Washer, Kenneth	Asst	886-5678	ken_washer	CEG	DBA	98	La Tech	1996

Texas A&M Un- Corpus Christi Corpus Chr, TX 78412 (361) 825-2665 cob.tamucc.edu
Finance, Economics & Dec Sci College of Business Fax=825-2725

Abdelsamad, Moustafa H.	Dean	825-6045	moustafa	Fnce	DBA	70	Geo Wash	7-91
Vokurka, Robert	C-Pr	825-2458	vokurka	AO	PHD	97	Tx A&M	9-01
Benavides, Adolfo	Assoc	825-2769	abenavides	AO	PHD	82	Wash St	9-96
Assistant Dean								
Crowley, Patrick	Assoc	825-6011	pcrowley	AO	PHD	90	McGill	9-00
Lee, Jim	Assoc	825-5831	jlee	AO	PHD	91	Penn St	7-99

Texas A&M Univ-Kingsville Kingsville, TX 78363 (361) 593-4174 tamuk.edu
Economics Faculty Cl Business Adm Box 186 Fax=593-3912
Homepage: www.cba.tamuk.edu

Diersing, Robert J.	Dean	593-3801	r-diersing		PHD	91	Tx A&M	1990
Bigbee, Dalton L.	C-Pr$	593-4174	dbigbee	Fnce	DBA	81	Tx Tech	1985
Rossman, Joseph E.	Assoc	593-2506	j-rossman		PHD	75	Iowa St	1976
Harun, Syed	VAsst	593-3938	syed.harum		ABD		N Orleans	2000

Texas A&M International Univ Laredo, TX 78041-1900 (956) 326-2490 tamiu.edu
Dept of Economics & Finance College of Business Adm Fax=326-2494 Gabriela Gamez
Homepage: tamui.edu/coba/depart/eflindex.html

Kohl, John P.	Dean	32602480	jkohl	Mgt	PHD	82	Penn St	6-99
Rodriguez, Antonio J.	C-Ac	326-2517	rodriguez	Fnce	PHD	85	Alabama	9-93
Patrick, J. Michael	Prof	326-2547	jmpatrick	FR	PHD	77	Mich St	9-93
Joskowitz, David	Asst	326-2509	yosko	Q	PHD	97	Tx Tech	9-98
Pisani, Michael	VAsst	326-2531	mpisani	R	PHD	00	Tx-Pan Am	9-98

Texas Christian University Fort Worth, TX 76129-8510 (817) 257-7230 tcu.edu
Dept of Economics Box 298510 AddRan Col/Arts & Sci Fax= Ms. Suzanne B. Powell
Did Not Respond--1999-2000 Listing

McCracken, Michael D.	Dean	257-7160		Biol	PHD	69	Indiana	1971
McNertney, Edward M.	C-Ac	257-7230			PHD	77	Mass	1977
Becker, Charles McVey	Assoc	257-7230			PHD	66	Arizona	1967
Butler, Michael R.	Assoc	257-7230			PHD	86	N Carol	1986
Harvey, John T.	Assoc	257-7230			PHD	87	Tennessee	1987
Elliott, Dawn Richards	Asst	257-7230			PHD	94	New Sch	1995
Klopfenstein, Kristin	Asst	257-7230			PHD	99	Colorado	1999
Quinn, Stephen F.	Asst	257-7230			PHD	94	Illinois	1995

Texas Lutheran University Seguin, TX 78155-5999 (830) 372-6073 tlu.edu
Economics Faculty Dept Econ & P Sci & Soc Fax=372-8188

Walsh, Germaine	C	372-6073						
Giesber, Frank W.	Prof	379-6071	fgiesber	A	PHD	78	Tx-Austin	1966
Vaughan, Ben F.	Asst	372-6567	bvaughan		PHD	97	Berkeley	1998

Texas Southern University Houston, TX 77004 (713) 313-7210 tsu.edu
Dept Hst, Geography & Econ College of Arts & Sci Fax=
Did Not Respond Again--1995-96 Listing

Sapp, John	Dean							
Akalou, Woldie-Michael	H	313-7429			PHD		UCLA	
Horwitz, Sigmund	Prof	313-7735			PHD		Houston	
Keleta, Ethiopia	Assoc	313-7702			PHD	84	Rice	
Norman, Emlyn A.	Asst	313-7892			AM		Harvard	
Norris, Hodge	Asst	313-7814			MS		Tx A&I	
Batie, Clarence	Inst	313-7815			MA		Prairie	

Texas Tech University Lubbock, TX 79409-1014 (806) 742-2201 ttu.edu
Dept of Economics & Geog Col of Arts & Sciences Fax=742-1137 Karen Davis
Homepage: ttu.edu/~ecogeog/

King, Joseph E.	C-Pr	742-2201			PHD	71	Illinois	1970
Steinmeier, Thomas L.	Prof	742-2201			PHD	75	Yale	1982
Becker, Klaus G.	Assoc	742-2201			PHD	87	Kansas	1989
Ewing, Bradley T.	Assoc	742-2201			PHD	94	Purdue	1998
Gilbert, Ronald D.	Assoc	742-2201			PHD	70	Okla St	1977
Kruse, Jamie I.	Assoc	742-2201			PHD	88	Arizona	1996
McComb, Robert P.	Assoc	742-2201			PHD	89	Illinois	1991
Rahnama, Masha	Assoc	742-2201			PHD	88	Iowa St	1996
Al-Hmoud, Rashid	Asst	742-2201			PHD	94	Tx Tech	1995
Carton, Joel	Asst	742-2201			PHD	99	Oregon	1999
Crooker, Skip	Asst	742-2201			PHD	98	Iowa St	1999
Von Ende, Eleanor Theresa	Asst	742-2201			PHD	90	Kansas	1990

Texas Wesleyan University Fort Worth, TX 76105-1536 (817) 531-4840 txwes.edu
Economics Faculty School of Business Fax=531-4268 JoAnn Moore

McLain, Louis P.	Dean$	531-4840	lmclain		MBA	74	So Meth	1976
Klaasen, Thomas A.	Prof		klaasent		PHD	69	Mich St	1989
Ellis, Charles Michael	Assoc		ellism		PHD	73	Alabama	1983

Texas Woman's University Denton, TX 76204-5738 (940) 898-2111 twu.edu
Dept of Business & Economics Col of Arts & Sciences Fax=898-2120 Betty Hodge
Did Not Respond--1999-2000 Listing

Griffin, Adelaide	C-Pr	898-2111	f_griffin	Mgt	PHD	79	North Tx	1979
Hersh-Cochran, Mona S.	Prof				PHD	66	So Meth	

Conaro Professor of Business and Economics

University of Toledo Toledo, OH 43606-3390 (419) 530-2572 utoledo.edu
Department of Economics Col of Arts & Sciences Fax=530-7844 Jeannie Stambaugh
Homepage: www.econ.utoledo.edu
email: @1=uoft02.utoledo.edu

Stern, David	Dean	530-2164			PHD			
Dowd, Michael R.	C-Ac	530-4603	mdowd	E	PHD	90	SUNY-Buf	1989
Lesage, James P.	Prof	530-4754	jpl@jpl.	RC	PHD	83	Boston C	1988
Magura, Michael	Emer	530-4631	mm@mm.	RL	PHD	72	Boston C	1969
Roy, Raj	Prof	530-4430		F	PHD	68	Wayne St	1963
Weiss, Steven J.	Emer	530-4124	sweiss@1	HI	PHD	71	Colorado	1968
Black, David C.	Assoc	530-4153	dcb@dcb.	E	PHD	92	SUNY-Buf	1990
Chang, Hsin	Assoc	530-4677		OP	PHD	89	Michigan	1989
Keith, Kristen	Assoc	530-4132	kkeith@1	J	PHD	89	Ohio St	1994
Murray, John E.	Assoc	530-4148	jmurray@1	B	PHD	92	Ohio St	1994
Tank, Frederick E.	Emer	530-2562	fet@fet.	KQ	PHD	72	Wayne St	1970
Yurgin, Nicole	Asst	530-2572						

Towson University Towson, MD 21252-7097 (410) 704-2959 towson.edu
Department of Economics Col of Business & Econ Fax=704-3424 C. F. Eifert

Leberknight, Alan M.	Dean	704-3342	leberknight	MBA		Loyola	1995
Georgiou, George C.	C-Pr	704-2146	georgiou	PHD	79	Geo Wash	1980
Dorn, James A.	Prof	704-2956	dorn	PHD	76	Virginia	1973
Fenstermaker, J. Van	Prof	704-2145	fenstermaker	PHD	63	Illinois	1988
Kong, Chang Min	Prof	704-2191	kong	PHD	77	Wi-Milwa	1978
Paul, Harvey	Prof	704-2954	paul	PHD	72	SUNY-Buf	1966
Shin, Bong Ju	Prof	704-2951	shin	PHD	69	Ohio St	1966
Woroby, Tamara	Prof	704-3575	woroby	PHD	81	Queens	1978
Egger, John B.	Assoc	704-3576	egger	PHD	85	NYU	1987
Laurence, Louise	Assoc	704-3275	laurence	PHD	87	Maryland	1987
Lee, Kangoh	Assoc	704-3551	lee	PHD	87	Illinois	1990
Sullivan, Timothy	Assoc	704-2338	sullivan	PHD	87	Illinois	1989
Weintraub, Irvin	Assoc	704-2952	weintraub	MS	51	Columbia	1966
Lee, J. J.	Asst	704-2675	jjlee	PHD	00	Stanford	2000
Li, Ling	Asst	704-2675	li	PHD	94	Pittsburgh	1994
McPerson, Sandra	Asst	704-3576	mcpherson	PHD	98	Indiana	2000
Michael, Jeffery	Asst	704-2959	michael	PHD	99	N Carol	1999
Osborne, Melissa	Asst	704-3781	osborne	PHD	00	Mass	2000
Rhoads, Thomas	Asst	704-2959	rhoads	PHD	99	Wyoming	1999

Transylvania University Lexington, KY 40508-1797 (859) 233-8104 transy.edu
Economics Faculty Div of Bus Adm & Econ Fax=233-8749 Faye Pepperl
Did Not Respond--1999-2000 Listing

Pepper, Michael R.	C-Pr	233-8249	MS	69	NewHamp	1989
Erfani, G. Rod	Prof	233-8196	PHD	84	Fla St	1986
Lynch, Lawrence K.	Emer	233-8157	PHD	66	Kentucky	1979
Shearer, Charles L.	Prof	233-8100	PHD	81	Mich St	
President Transylvania University						
Bartley, Alan	Asst		PHD	99	Vanderbilt	1999

Tri-State University Angola, IN 46703-0307 (219) 665-4243 tristate.edu
Dept of Social Sciences Sch of Arts & Sciences Fax=665-4292
Did Not Respond Again--1997-98 Listing

Tichenor, Delores	Dean	665-4242				
Morin, John E.	C-Pr	665-4206	SocS	MS	Ind St	1966
Moore, Derald L.	Assoc	665-4207		MA	Mich St	1968
Scheffer, Ronald E.	Assoc	665-4202		MA	Ohio	1967
Dobbert, Duane	Asst	665-4862		MA	Mich St	1995

Trinity College Hartford, CT 06106-3100 (860) 297-2485
Economics Faculty Department of Economics Fax=297-2257
Did Not Respond--1999-2000 Listing

Butos, William N.	C-Pr	297-2485	PHD	83	Penn St	1981
Curran, Ward S.	Prof		PHD	61	Columbia	1960
Ramirez, Miguel	Prof		PHD	84	Illinois	1985
Zannoni, Diane C.	Prof		PHD	76	SUNY-SBr	1975
Clark, Carol	Assoc		PHD	91	Cornell	1990
Egan, Francis J.	Assoc		PHD	73	Fordham	1967
Gold, Andrew J.	Assoc		PHD	67	Nrthwstrn	1971
Grossberg, Adam J.	Assoc		PHD	86	Illinois	1986
Setterfield, Mark	Assoc		PHD	92	Dalhousie	1992
Wen, G. James	Assoc		PHD	89	Chicago	1994
Zavareei, Manijeh	VAsoc		PHD	82	SUNY-Buf	1991
Fongemie, Claude A.	Lect		PHD	79	Conn	1977
Jacobs, Cindy	VLect		PHD	89	Illinois	1991
O'Connor, F. William	Lect		JD	78	Conn	1984

Trinity University San Antonio, TX 78212-7200 (210) 999-7221 trinity.edu
Department of Economics Economics Fax=999-7255 Susie DuBose

Gonzalez, Jorge G.	C-Pr	999-7224	jorge.gonzalez	F	PHD	89	Mich St	1989
Breit, William L.	Prof	999-8492	wbreit	B	PHD	61	Mich St	1982
Vernon F. Taylor Distinguished Professor of Economics								
Butler, Richard V.	Prof	999-7256	rbutler	H	PHD	77	MIT	1982
Hirsch, Barry T.	Prof	999-8112	barry.hirsch	J	PHD	77	Virginia	2000
E.M. Stevens Distinguished Professor of Economics								
Huston, John H.	Prof	999-8471	jhuston	D	PHD	83	Wisconsin	1983
Salvucci, Richard	Prof	999-8494	rsalvucc	N	PHD	82	Princeton	
Spencer, Roger W.	Prof	999-7222	rspencer	E	PHD	69	Virginia	1980
Kamdar, Nipoli	Assoc	999-7441	nkamdar	H	PHD	93	Syracuse	1993
DeCourcy, Julie	Asst	999-7226	julie.decourcy	L	PHD	01	Mich St	2001
Smith, Julie K.	Asst	999-7223	julie.smith	E	PHD	01	J Hopkins	2001

Troy State University Troy, AL 36082 (334) 670-3459 troyst.edu
Dept Mktg, Mgt & Economics Sorrell Col of Business Fax=670-3599
Homepage: http://spectrum.troyst.edu/~sorrell/mme/mme.html

Ratcliffe, Thomas A.	Dean	670-3137	tratclif	Atg	PHD	78	Alabama	1986
Eminent Scholar in Accounting and Finance								
Kirkland, Jack	Prof	670-3579	jkirk	ADEH	PHD	82	Wash St	1995
Merkel, Edward T.	Prof	670-3194	emerkel	AFH	PHD	74	N Illinois	1978
Thompson, Charles L.	Asst	670-3195	cthompsn	ADE	MS	82	Auburn	1984

Truman State University Kirksville, MO 63501-4221 (660) 785-4636 truman.edu
Department of Economics Div of Social Science Fax=785-4337 Kay Anderson

Patterson, Seymour	H-Pr	785-4360	spatters		PHD	80	Oklahoma	1980
Sawani, Mustafa A.	Prof	785-4659	msawani		PHD	85	Missouri	1985
Sublette, Werner Johann	Prof	785-4651	wsublett		PHD	74	Arizona	1974
Sung, Jane C.	Prof	785-4658	jsung		PHD	85	Wayne St	1987
Gillette, David H.	Assoc	785-4334	dgillette		PHD	90	Wash St	1990
Nnadozie, Emmanuel U.	Assoc	785-4099	ennadozi		PHD	87	Sorbonne	1989
Olson, Terry L.	Assoc	785-4503	tolson		PHD	86	Illinois	1990
Coggins, Bruce	Asst	785-4656	bcoggins		PHD	95	Ca-Rivers	1998

Tufts University Medford, MA 02155 (617) 627-3560 tufts.edu
Department of Economics Col of Liberal Arts Fax=627-3917

Ernst, Susan	Dean	627-3864	sernst	Bio	PHD	79	Mass	1979
Garman, David M.	C-Ac	627-2683	dgarman	C	PHD	84	Michigan	1983
Ioannides, Yannis M.	Prof	627-3294	jannis.ionnides	O	PHD	74	Stanford	1995
Neubauer Chair Holder								
Norman, George	Prof	627-3663	george.norman	L	PHD	77	Cambridge	1995
Cummings Chair Holder								
Bianconi, Marcello	Assoc	627-2677	mbiancon	E	PHD	88	Illinois	1989
Brown, Drusilla K.	Assoc	627-3096	drusilla.brown	F	PHD	84	Michigan	1983
Dapice, David O.	Assoc	627-5947		O	PHD	73	Harvard	1973
email: david_dapice@harvard.edu								
Loury, Linda D.	Assoc	627-3348	lloury	J	PHD	78	MIT	1984
Metcalf, Gilbert	Assoc	627-3685	gilbert.metcalf		PHD	88	Harvard	1994
Pepall, Lynne	Assoc	627-5477	lynne.pepall	L	PHD	83	Cambridge	1987
Richards, Daniel J.	Assoc	627-2679	dan.richards	E	PHD	81	Yale	1985
Rothenberg, Winnie	Assoc	627-5221	wrothenb	N	PHD	85	Brandeis	1986
Zabel, Jeffrey	Assoc	627-2318	feff.zabel	C	PHD	87	Ca-SnDgo	1989
Downes, Thomas A.	Asst	627-2687	thomas.downes	H	PHD	88	Stanford	1994
Eggleston, Karen	Asst	627-5948	karen.eggleston		PHD	99	Harvard	1999
Kim, Henry	Asst	627-3662	kenry.kim	F	PHD	97	Yale	2001
Kutsoati, Edward	Asst	627-2688	edward.kutsoati	G	PHD	98	Queens	1998
McMillan, Margaret	Asst	627-3560	mmcmilla	O	PHD	97	Columbia	1997
Mukand, Sharun	Asst	627-3560	smukand	F	PHD	97	Boston U	1997
Yamarik, Steven	Asst	627-2701	steven.yamarik	E	PHD	96	N Carol	2001
Yu, David	Asst	627-3138	dyu01	G	PHD	97	Princeton	1998

Tulane University New Orleans, LA 70118-5698 (504) 865-5321 tulane.edu
Department of Economics Col of Arts & Sciences Fax=865-5869

Horiba, Yutaka	Prof	862-8346			PHD	69	Purdue	1971
Malueg, David A.	Prof	862-8344			PHD	83	Nrthwstrn	1991
Nelson, Douglas R.	Prof	865-5317			PHD	81	N Carol	1993
Oakland, William H.	Prof	862-8343			PHD	65	MIT	1979
Edwards, John H.	Assoc	862-8357			PHD	85	Maryland	1985
Pritchett, Jonathan B.	Assoc	862-8359			PHD	86	Chicago	1985
Silver, Emilson	Assoc	862-8354			PHD	93	Illinois	1999
Brasington, David	Asst	862-8348			PHD	99	Ohio St	1998
Dix, Manfred	Asst	862-8353			PHD	98	Illinois	2001
Semenick Alam, Ila	Asst	862-8354			PHD	94	Rice	1994
Wheeler, Christopher	Asst	862-8358			PHD	98	Wisconsin	1999
Yates, Andrew J.	Asst	862-8345			PHD	92	Stanford	1998

University of Tulsa Tulsa, OK 74104-3189 (918) 631-2219 utulsa.edu
Department of Economics Kendall Col Arts & Sci Fax=
Did Not Respond Again--1997-98 Listing

Horne, Thomas	Dean							
Ray, Cadwell L.	C-Ac	631-2221			PHD	67	Tx-Austin	
Dugger, William M.	Prof	631-2951			PHD	74	Tx-Austin	
Steib, Steve B.	Prof	631-2219			PHD	72	Iowa St	1972
Horn, Bobbie L.	Assoc	631-2219			PHD	86	Iowa St	
Karikari, John A.	Assoc	631-3157		AFMO	PHD	85	Queen's	
Soltow, Allen R.	Assoc	631-2335			PHD	69	Iowa St	1973

Tuskegee University Tuskegee, AL 36088 (334) 727-8116 acd.tusk.edu
Department of Economics Col of Bus, Org & Mgt Fax=727-8604 Susie Stenson
Homepage: www.tusk.edu/bus/main.htm

Jackson, Alicia J.	Dean$	727-8707	ajjackson	Atg	PHD	97	Tx-Austin	6-99
Duncan, Jerome L. Jr.	C-Ac	727-8296	jduncan		PHD	80	Florida	1991
Sara, Tejinder S.	Prof	727-8705	tsara		PHD	75	Mass	1973
Cheng, William I.	Assoc	727-6307	chengw		PHD	90	SUNY-Bin	1990
Upchurch, Leo	Assoc	727-8732	upchurch		PHD	82	Michigan	1990
Fuller, M. Elaine	Asst	727-2673	efuller		PHD	98	New Sch	2000
Suh, Jingyo	Asst	727-2673	jsuh		PHD	00	Alabama	2000

Union College-NY Schenectady, NY 12308-3163 (518) 388-6200 union.edu
Department of Economics Div of Social Sciences Fax=388-6988 Kathleen Basirico
Homepage: www.union.edu/public/ecodept/index.html

McCarty, Therese A.	C-Acc	388-6045	mccartyt	GI	PHD	87	Michigan	1987
Fried, Harold O.	Prof	388-6368	friedh	CIL	PHD	78	N Carol	1983
Kenney, James M.	Prof	388-6018	kennyj	QDMG	PHD	72	Stanford	1972
Klein, J. Douglass	Prof	388-6056	kleind	LQD	PHD	75	Wisconsin	1979
Reynolds, Bruce L.	Prof	388-6217	reynoldb	ODP	PHD	75	Michigan	1974
Schmidt, Shelton S.	Prof	388-6218	schmidts	LCA	PHD	77	Virginia	1974
Motahar, Eshragh	Assoc	388-6065	motahare	EFG	PHD	89	J Hopkins	1984
Schmidt, Stephen J.	Assoc	388-6078	schmidsj	LCH	PHD	95	Stanford	1994
Yaisawarng, Suthathip	Assoc	388-6606	yaisawas	CD	PHD	89	S Illinois	1989
Billger, Sherrilyn	VAsst	388-8016	billgers	IO	PHD	00	Illinois	2000
Crocker, J. Kevin	VAsst	388-6493	crockerj	BFO	ABD		Mass	2000
Duttaray, Mousumi	VAsst	388-8068	duttaram	FO	PHD	01	Indiana	2001
Freed, Marc	VAsst	388-8043	freedm	G	ABD		NYU	2001
Santelli, Anthony	VAsst	388-6505	santella	G	PHD	97	GeoMason	2001
Sener, Mehmet F.	Asst	388-7093	senerm	FOEJ	PHD	99	Florida	1999

Union University Jackson, TN 38305-3697 (901) 661-5360 uu.edu
Department of Economics Sch of Business Admin Fax=661-5366 Judy Leforgee

Padelford, Walton M.	Dean$	661-5362	wpadelfo	ABFO	PHD	75	LSU	1980
Newell, Howard	Prof	661-5471	hewell		PHD	74	Indiana	1982
Holt, Kenneth	Assoc	661-5365	kholt		ABD		Memphis	1987
Pray, Bwalee	Assoc	661-5109	bpray		PHD	92	Memphis	1991

U.S. Air Force Academy Colorado Spr, CO 80840-6238 (719) 333-3080 usafa.af.mil
Department of Economics Social Science Division Fax=333-7137 Ms. Isabel Witt

Slate, Stephen	H-Ac	333-3080	slatest.dfeg		PHD	94	Colorado	1992
Linster, Bruce G.	Prof	333-3080	linsterbg.dfeg		PHD	90	Michigan	1990
Shambert, Vladimir M.	Prof	333-3080	shambergvm.dfeg		PHD	52	Moscow	1992
Rappaport, Neal J.	Assoc	333-3080	rappaportnj.dfeg	DC	PHD	94	MIT	1998
Waller, Robert L.	Assoc	333-3080	wallerrl.dfeg	AF	PHD	86	Boston U	1998
Carson, Katherine S.	Asst	333-3080	carsonks.dfeg	ACO	PHD	97	Colorado	1997
Lucchesi, Michael S.	Asst	333-3080	lucchesims.dfeg		MA	86	U Wash	1993
Mullin, R. David	Asst	333-3080	mullinrd.dfeg	AD	PHD	93	Virginia	1998
Prosseda, Phil D.	Asst	333-3080	prossedapd.dfeg		ABD	97	Colorado	1997
Sohan, Gerald	Asst	333-3080	sohange.dfeg		ABD		Tx A&M	1999
West, James E.	Asst	333-3080	westje.dfeg	AD	PHD	94	Michigan	1997
Breisch, Rob	Inst	333-3080	rob.breisch		MA	99	Utah	2000
Paik, Seung	Inst	333-3080	seung.paik		MA	92	Penn St	2000

U.S. Military Academy West Point, NY 10996-1798 (845) 938-3795 usma.edu
Economics Faculty Dept of Social Sciences Fax=938-4563

Messe, Michael J.	D	938-4002	jm6695	HE	PHD	77	Princeton	1990
Gujarati, Damodar N.	Prof	938-3236		CE	PHD	65	Chicago	1990
Smallwood, Dennis	Prof	938-2879		DHL	PHD	66	Yale	1996
Dudley, Dean	Asst	938-3144		DHL	PHD	93	Indiana	1993
Lofgren, Stephanie	Asst	938-2899	js4617	DHF	PHD	96	Nrthwstrn	1995

U.S. Naval Academy Annapolis, MD 21402-5042 (410) 293-6880 nadn.navy.mil
Economics Department Div Humanities & Soc Sc Fax=293-6899 Ms. Lou Ellen Hazel

Bowman, William R.	C-Pr	293-6881	bowman		PHD	79	Maryland	1980
Fredland, John E.	Prof	293-6897	fredland		PHD	70	Michigan	1974
Goodman, Rae Jean B.	Prof	293-6891	goodman		PHD	76	Wash U	1973
Little, Roger D.	Prof	293-6889	little		PHD	70	Houston	1970
Thierfelder, Karen	Assoc	293-6887	thier		PHD	92	Wisconsin	1992
Zak, Thomas A.	Assoc	293-6895	zakt		PHD	80	Vanderbilt	1981
Baker, Matthew	Asst	293-6890	mbaker		PHD	00	Conn	
Cunningham, Brendan	Asst	293-6880	bcunning		PHD	00	Columbia	
Li, Victor	Asst	293-6880	li	E	PHD	85	Nrthwstrn	
McCoskey, Suzanne K.	Asst	298-6893	mccoskey		PHD	97	Syracuse	1997
Schmitt, Pamela	Asst	293-6888	schmitt		PHD	00	Indiana	
Swope, Kortis	Asst	293-5382	swope		PHD	00	Indiana	

University of Utah — Salt Lake CY, UT 84112 (801) 581-7481 — econ.sbs.utah.edu
Department of Economics — Col of Soc & Behav Sci Fax=585-5649 — Ginger Head Adm Officer

Ott, J. Steven	Dean	581-8820		PolS	PHD			
Hunt, E. K.	C-Pr	581-7656	hunt		PHD	68	Utah	1978
Gander, James P.	Prof	581-5670	gander		PHD	66	Berkeley	1965
Girton, Lance	Prof	581-7622	girton		PHD	76	Chicago	1978
Glick, Mark	Prof	581-7464	glick		PHD	85	New Sch	1985
Jameson, Kenneth P.	Prof	581-8620	jameson		PHD	70	Wisconsin	1989
Kiefer, David M.	Prof	581-4308	kiefer		PHD	74	Michigan	1981
Phillips, Peter W.	Prof	585-6465	phillips		PHD	80	Stanford	1978
Rock, James M.	Prof	581-7481	rock		PHD	66	Nrthwstrn	1967
Berik, Gunseli	Assoc	581-7435	berik		PHD	86	Mass	1994
Cagatay, Nilufer	Assoc	581-7667	cagatay		PHD	86	Stanford	1991
Carlisle, William T.	Assoc	581-8511	carlisle		PHD	75	Cornell	1971
Ehrbar, Hans G.	Assoc	581-7797	ehrbar		PHD	85	Michigan	1986
Erturk, Korkut	Assoc	581-4576	korkut		PHD	92	New Sch	1992
Fowles, Richard G.	Assoc	581-4577	fowles		PHD	85	Utah	1990
Lozada, Gabriel A.	Assoc	581-7650	lozada		PHD	87	Stanford	1993
Maloney, Tom	Assoc	581-7704	maloney		PHD	93	Michigan	1992
Reynolds, Stephen E.	Assoc	581-7603	reynolds		PHD	69	Wisconsin	1969
Waltzman, Norman J.	Assoc	581-7600	waltzman		PHD	88	American	1988
Linebarger, Laura	Visit	581-7697	linebarg		PHD	97	Utah	

Utah State University — Logan, UT 84322-3530 (435) 797-2310 — econ.usu.edu
Department of Economics — College of Business Fax=797-2701 — Suzette Alder, Staff Asst
Homepage: http://www.econ.usu.edu

Stephens, David B.	Dean	797-2272	dstephens	Mgt	PHD	75	Tx-Austin	6-87
Criddle, Keith R.	H-Pr	797-2180	kcriddle	CQ	PHD	89	Ca-Davis	1998
Bailey, DeeVon	Prof	797-2316	dbailey	Q	PHD	83	Tx A&M	1983
Biswas, Basudeb	Prof	797-2304	biswas	CFO	PHD	76	Chicago	1976
Fawson, Christopher	Prof	797-2296	cfawson	CGMO	PHD	86	Tx A&M	1990
Glover, Terrence F.	Prof	797-2297	tglover	DCQ	PHD	71	Purdue	1974
Godfrey, E. Bruce	Prof	797-2294	bruceg	Q	PHD	71	Oregon St	1977
Israelsen, L. Dwight	Prof	797-2298	disraelsen	ABDE	PHD	73	MIT	1980
Keith, John E.	Prof	797-2303	jkeith	DEQR	PHD	73	Utah St	1972
Lewis, W. Cris	Prof	797-2327	clewis	MCR	PHD	69	Iowa St	1972
Lyon, Kenneth S.	Prof	797-2292	klyon	CDEQ	PHD	70	Chicago	1966
Petersen, Harold Craig	Prof	797-1167		GM	PHD	73	Stanford	1973
Chief of Staff; craigp@champ.usu.edu								
Snyder, Donald L.	Prof	797-2383	dsnyder	CQ	PHD	79	Utah St	1981
Jakus, Paul	Assoc	797-2309	pjakus	OQ	PHD	92	N Car St	2001
Aadland, David	Asst	797-2322	aadland	CE	PHD	97	Oregon	1997
Bowles, Tyler	Asst	797-2378	tbowles	AF	PHD	91	N Carol	1994
Caplan, Arthur	Asst	797-0775	acaplan	CQ	PHD	96	Oregon	2001
Dickinson, David	Asst	797-2287	ddickinson	JL	PHD	97	Arizona	1999
Gilbert, John	Asst	797-2314	jgilbert	FOC	PHD	98	Auckland	2001
Huang, Kevin	Asst	797-2320	khuang	EFG	PHD	98	Minnesota	1998
Hunnicutt, Lynn	Asst	797-2317	hunnicut	DLM	PHD	97	Tx-Austin	1998
Shiptssova, Rimma	Asst	797-2324		CO	PHD	98	Ohio St	2002
Ward, Ruby	Asst	797-2323	rward	Q	PHD	98	Tx A&M	1999
Bentley, Marion	ExtSp	797-2284	mbentley	H	MPA	70	NYU	1975

Utica College — Utica, NY 13502-4892 (315) 792-3055 — utica.ucsu.edu
Economics Department — Div of Social Sci & Mgt Fax=792-3173 — Susan Cox

Neun, Stephen P.	Dean	792-3055	sneun	IJ	PHD	88	Conn	1982
Blanchfield, William C.	D-Pr	792-3109		Educ	PHD	70	SUNY-Alb	1966
Fenner, Richard G.	Assoc	792-3112	rfenner	AIR	PHD	92	Syracuse	1989

Valdosta State University — Valdosta, GA 31698-0075 (229) 245-2234 — valdosta.edu
Dept of Mktg & Economics — College of Business Adm Fax=245-2248 — Bonnie Ely
Homepage: www.valdosta.edu/mktg

Stanley, Kenneth L.	Dean	333-5991	kstanley		PHD	78	Purdue	1984
Allen, Ralph C.	H-Pr	245-2243	rcallen	FDK	PHD	81	Geo St	1982
Plumly, L. Wayne Jr.	Prof	245-3815	lwplumly	JA	PHD	83	Geo St	1980
Mitchell, David	Asst	245-2234	dmitchel	DQ	PHD	01	Okla St	2001
Tori, Cynthia R.	Asst	245-2246	crtori	EF	PHD	92	Kentucky	1998

Valparaiso University — Valparaiso, IN 46383-6493 (219) 464-5696 — valpo.edu
Department of Economics — Col of Arts & Sciences Fax=464-5381 — Suzanna L. Tudor

Trost, Albert R.	Dean	464-5314	albert.trost	PolS	PHD	71	Wash U	1963
Shingleton, Virginia	C-Ac	464-5405	virginia.shin+	CJIA	PHD	94	Notre Dm	1992
Henderson, James P.	Prof	464-5404	james.henderson	NBA	PHD	77	N Illinois	1975
Bernard, James A. Jr.	Assoc	464-5045	james.bernard	AOP	PHD	72	Notre Dm	1968
Raman, Jaishankar	Asst	464-6814	jaishankar.raman	OFA	PHD	97	Notre Dm	1996

Vanderbilt University — Nashville, TN 37235 (615) 322-2871 — vanderbilt.edu
Department of Economics — Col of Arts & Science Fax=343-8495 — Kelly Degnan
Homepage: www.vandaerbilt.edu/econ/index.html

Atack, Jeremy	C-Pr	343-2871	jeremy.atack	N	PHD	76	Indiana	1993
Damon, William W.	Prof	322-3427	william.w.damon	DGM	PHD	70	Cornell	1976
Daughety, Andrew F.	Prof	322-3453	andrew.f.daug+	LK	PHD	72	Case Wes	1995
Driskill, Robert A.	Prof	343-1516	robert.a.dris+	EFM	PHD	78	J Hopkins	1992
Fan, Yanquin	Prof	322-3796	yanquin.fan	C	PHD	90	W Ontario	2001
Finegan, T. Aldrich	Prof	343-0461	t.aldrich.fin+	J	PHD	60	Chicago	1970
Foster, James E.	Prof	322-2192	james.e.foster	DG	PHD	82	Cornell	1990
Getz, Malcolm	Prof	322-3425	getz	HR	PHD	73	Yale	1973
Huffman, Gregory W.	Prof	343-2468	gregory.w.hu+	EG	PHD	83	Minnesota	2001
Maneschi, Andrea	Prof	322-2993	andrrea.maneschi	FO	PHD	64	J Hopkins	1969
Margo, Robert A.	Prof	322-2189	robert.a.margo	NJ	PHD	82	Harvard	1989
Reinganum, Jennifer F.	Prof	322-2937	jennifer.f.r+	LK	PHD	79	Nrthwstrn	1995
Bronson Ingram Professor of Economics								
Russell, Clifford S.	Prof	322-8512	cliff.russell	HQ	PHD	68	Harvard	1986
Siegfried, John J.	Prof	322-2429	john.siegfried	LJ	PHD	72	Wisconsin	1972
Wang, Ping	Prof	322-2388	ping.wang	E	PHD	87	Rochester	1999
Weymark, John A.	Prof	322-1437	john.weymark	D	PHD	77	Penn	1999
Anderson, Kathryn H.	Assoc	322-0263	kathryn.anderson	JO	PHD	78	N Car St	1980
Senior Fellow, Inst for Public Policy Studies								
Crucini, Mario J.	Assoc	322-7357	mario.j.crucini	E	PHD	91	Rochester	1999
Sweeney, George H.	Assoc	322-2845	george.h.sweeney	DL	PHD	77	Nrthwstrn	1976
Associate Dean								
Ahlin, Christian	Asst	322-2482		E	PHD	01	Chicago	2001
Jiang, Neville Nien-Huei	Asst	322-0715	nien-huei.jiang	E	PHD	00	Chicago	2000
Mullin, Charles H.	Asst	322-2128	charles.h.mullin	JC	PHD	98	Chicago	1998
Rousseau, Peter L.	Asst	322-2466	peter.l.rouss+	EM	PHD	95	NYU	1995
Schwartz, Jesse	Asst	322-3339	jesse.schwartz	DLQ	PHD	99	Maryland	1999
Shintani, Mototsugu	Asst	322-2196	mototsugu.sh+	CE	PHD	00	Yale	2000
Wen, Quan	Asst	322-3445	quan.wen	F	PHD	91	W Ontario	1999
Weymark, Diana N.	Asst	322-3445	diana.weymark	EG	PHD	90	Brit Colum	1999

Vassar College — Poughkeepsie, NY 12604-0708 (914) 437-7395 — vassar.edu
Economics Faculty — Department of Economics Fax=437-7576 — Susan M. Conger

Johnson, Paul A.	C-Ac	437-5213	pajohnson	E	PHD	84	Stanford	1995
Jehle, Geoffrey A.	Prof	437-5210	jehle	D	PHD	83	Princeton	1981
Kennett, David A.	Prof	437-7000	kennett	F	PHD	76	Columbia	1976
Thompson, Alexander M.	Prof	437-5257	thompson	BH	PHD	79	Stanford	1977
Herbst, Lawrence A.	Assoc	437-7398		N	PHD	74	Penn	1970
Johnson-Lars, Shirley B.	Assoc	437-5214	sjlans	I	PHD	66	Columbia	1967
Lunt, William E.	Assoc	437-7396	lunt	C	PHD	77	Stanford	1974
Jones, Patricia	Asst	437-5209		JO	PHD	98	Oxford	1999
Kilby, Christopher P.	Asst	437-5212	chkilby	O	PHD	94	Stanford	1993
Marco, Alan	Asst	437-5209	marco	KL	PHD	00	Berkeley	2000
Rork, Jonathan	Asst	437-7398	rork	DR	PHD	99	Stanford	2000

University of Vermont — Burlington, VT 05405-4160 (802) 656-3064 — uvm.edu
Department of Economics — Col of Arts & Sciences Fax=656-8405
Homepage: www.uvm.edu/necon

Smith, Joan	Dean	656-3166	joan.smith					
Knodell, Jane E.	C-Ac	656-0189	jane.knodell	EN	PHD	84	Stanford	1986
Alnasrawi, Abbas	Prof	656-3064	abbas.alnasrawi	AFOQ	PHD	65	Harvard	1963
Gibson, William A.	Prof	656-3064	william.gibson	CFOQ	PHD	77	Berkeley	1986
Gedeon, Shirley J.	Assoc	656-0188	shirley.gedeon	EP	PHD	82	Mass	1981
McCrate, Elaine D.	Assoc	656-3064	elaine.mccrate	JIT	PHD	85	Mass	1985
Rizvi, Saiyid A.	Assoc	656-3064	saiyid.rizvi	BDF	PHD	90	New Sch	1987
Thomson, Ross	Assoc	656-3064	ross.thomson	NDB	PHD	76	Yale	1991
Woolf, Arthur G.	Assoc	656-3064	arthur.woolf	HNR	PHD	80	Wisconsin	1980
Brooks, Nancy	Asst	656-0946	nancy.brooks	DHQR	PHD	94	Penn	1994
Seguino, Stephanie	Asst	656-0187	stephanie.seg+	EFOP	PHD	94	American	1995
Solnick, Sara J.	Asst	656-0183	ssolnick	DI	PHD	96	Penn	2000

Villanova University — Villanova, PA 19085-1678 (610) 519-4370 — email.vill.edu
Department of Economics — Col of Commerce & Fnce Fax=519-6054 — Caroly Mitchell 519-4360

Monahan, Thomas F.	Dean$	519-4354	thomas.monahan	Atg	PHD	81	Temple	1981
Mathis, Edward J.	C-Pr	519-4387	edward.mathis		PHD	71	SUNY-Buf	1966
DeFina, Robert H.	Prof	519-4482	robert.defina		PHD	79	Wash U	1989
Thanawala, Kishor H.	Prof	519-4385	kishor.thanawala		PHD	61	Bombay	1967
Zech, Charles E.	Prof	519-4371	charles.zech		PHD	73	Notre Dm	1974
Clain, Suzanne H.	Assoc	519-6556	suzanne.clain		PHD	84	Princeton	1987
Donziger, Alan J.	Assoc	519-4315	alan.donziger		PHD	72	Bryn Mawr	1967
Giordano, James N.	Assoc	519-4167	james.giordano		PHD	82	Indiana	1983
Kroch, Eugene A.	Assoc	519-6428	eugene.kroch		PHD	78	Harvard	1991
Wolnicki, Miron J.	Assoc	519-4384	miron.wolnicki		PHD	80	Lodz	1984

Zaleski, Peter A.	Assoc	519-4378	peter.zaleski		PHD	88	Maryland	1987
Alexandrin, Glen	Asst	519-6101	glen.alexandrin		PHD	67	Clark	1970
Asher, Cheryl	Asst	519-4159	cheryl.asher		PHD	81	Penn	1984
Casario, Michelle	Asst	519-4362	michelle.casario		PHD	91	Northeas	1991
Farrell, Rev. John	Asst	519-4324	john.farrell		PHD	72	Catholic	1993
Mao, Wen	Asst	519-4370	wen.mao		PHD	94	Va Tech	1995
Taylor, Kenneth B.	Asst	519-6430	kenneth.taylor		PHD	80	SUNY-SBr	1985

University of Virginia Charlottesvil VA 22904-4182 (434) 924-3177 virginia.edu
J. Wilson Dept of Economics Grad Sch of Arts & Sci Fax=982-2904 Bunny Stinnett
Homepage: http://www.virginia.edu/~econ

Mills, David E.	C-Pr	924-3061	mills	LD	PHD	75	Stanford	1975
Anderson, Simon P.	Prof	924-3861	sa9w	LDR	PHD	85	Queen's	1987
Elzinga, Kenneth G.	Prof	924-6752	kge8z	LDR	PHD	67	Mich St	1967
Engers, Maxim P.	Prof	924-3130	mpe2m	ACDQ	PHD	84	UCLA	1982
Epps, Thomas W.	Prof	924-7947	twe	GC	PHD	69	Duke	1972
Holt, Charles A.	Prof	924-7894	cah2k	CDL	PHD	77	Car Mellon	1983
Merrill Bankard Professor of Economics								
James, John A.	Prof	924-3525	jaj8y	NO	PHD	74	MIT	1973
Johnson, William R.	Prof	924-3251	wjohnson	JH	PHD	75	MIT	1974
McLaren, John	Prof	924-3994	jem6x	F	PHD	92	Princeton	2000
Mirman, Leonard J.	Prof	924-6756	lm8h	ACDQ	PHD	70	Rochester	1986
Paul Goodloe McIntire Professor of Economics								
Olsen, Edgar O.	Prof	924-3443	eoo	HI	PHD	68	Rice	1970
Stern, Steven N.	Prof	924-6754	sns5r	JCI	PHD	85	Yale	1985
Graduate Director								
van Wincoop, Jan Eric	Prof	924-3177		F	PHD	89	Harvard	2001
Whitaker, John K.	Prof	924-3459	jw9s	BC	PHD	62	Cambridge	1969
Georgia S. Bankard Professor of Economics								
Goeree, Jacob	Assoc	924-7649	jg2n	CDL	PHD	97	Amsterdm	1996
Michener, Ronald W.	Assoc	924-7113	rwm3n	EN	PHD	81	Chicago	1979
Cagetti, Marco	Asst	924-6751	cacio	E	PHD	00	Chicago	2000
Choi, Albert	Asst	924-3177		K	PHD	01	MIT	2001
Cohen, Andrew	Asst	924-6747	ac6m	LD	PHD	00	Nrthwstrn	2000
Friedberg, Leora	Asst	924-3225	lfriedberg	HJ	PHD	96	MIT	2000
Jain, Sanjay	Asst	924-3177		OF	PHD	94	Princeton	2001
Kim, Jinill	Asst	924-7581	jk9n	EF	PHD	96	Yale	1998
Lo, Ming	Asst	924-3997	ml8z	FE	PHD	00	U Wash	2000
Otrok, Christopher	Asst	924-3692	cmo3h	EC	PHD	99	Iowa	1999
Pepper, John	Asst	924-3402	jvp3m	HD	PHD	96	Wisconsin	1996
Ramezzaua, Paolo	Asst	924-3177		FL	PHD	01	LondonEc	2001
Taylor, Jason	Asst	924-3811	jet9b	NO	PHD	98	Georgia	1998
Turner, Sarah	Asst	924-7857	sturner	IJ	PHD	97	Michigan	1997

Virginia Commonwealth Univ Richmond, VA 23284-4000 (804) 828-1717 vcu.edu
Department of Economics School of Business Fax=828-1719 Dvora Baldwin
Homepage: www.bus.vcu.edu/economics/

Sesnowitz, Michael L.	Dean	827-0072	msesnowi	HG	PHD	71	Pittsburgh	2000
Millner, Edward L.	C-Pr	828-1717	elmillne		PHD	82	N Carol	1983
Bowman, John H.	Prof	828-1717	jhbowman		PHD	73	Ohio St	1981
Davis, Douglas D.	Prof	828-7110	dddavis		PHD	84	Indiana	1987
Hoffer, George E.	Prof	828-7089	gehoffer		PHD	72	Virginia	1970
Pratt, Michael D.	Prof	828-1835	mdpratt		PHD	77	Kansas	1979
Reilly, Robert J.	Prof	828-3184	rjreilly		PHD	78	Tennessee	1978
Gallagher, Charles J.	Assoc	828-1745	cjgallag		PHD	70	W Virginia	1971
Associate Dean External Affairs								
Harless, David W.	Assoc	828-7190	dwharles		PHD	88	Indiana	8-93
Mitchell, Shannon K.	Assoc	828-7142	skmitche		PHD	89	Virginia	1990
O'Toole, Dennis M.	Assoc	828-3185	dmotoole		PHD	71	Ohio U	1967
Peterson, Steven P.	Assoc	828-3186	sppeters		PHD	89	Indiana	1989
Wetzel, James N.	Assoc	828-7145	jnwetzel		PHD	74	N Carol	1974
Lehr, Carol A.	Asst	828-7148	cslehr		PHD	91	Penn St	1997
Stratton, Leslie A.	Asst	828-7141	lsstratt		PHD	89	MIT	1997

Virginia Military Institute Lexington, VA 24450-0304 (540) 464-7234 mail.vmi.edu
Dept of Economics & Business Liberal Arts Division Fax=464-7005 Beverley Clements

Daley, Edward V.	H-Pr	464-7234	daleyev		PHD	74	Missouri	1981
Bush, H. Francis	Prof	464-7234	bushhf		PHD	89	Florida	1994
Duncan, Floyd H.	Prof	464-7234	duncanfh		PHD	72	S Carol	1978
Fraley, Charles E.	Prof	464-7234	fraleyce		PHD	78	Oklahoma	1980
Sexton, Edwin A.	Prof	464-7234	sextonea		PHD	87	Illinois	1992
West, Clifford T.	Prof	464-7234	westct		PHD	92	Indiana	1996
Greenwade, George D.	Assoc	464-7234	greenwadegd		PHD	88	Tx Tech	2001
Basu, Atin	Asst	464-7234	basua		PHD	98	Miss	1999
Gutermuth, Karen	Asst	464-7234	gutermuthk		PHD	96	LSU	1997
Sen, Tinni	Asst	464-7234	sensb		PHD	99	Miss	2000
Schwartz, William T.	Lect	464-7234	schwartzwt		MBA	70	Penn	2001

Virginia Poly Inst & St Un Blacksburg, VA 24061-0316 (540) 231-5688 vt.edu
Department of Economics Col of Arts & Sciences Fax=231-5097 Ms. Sherry Williams
Homepage: //www.econ.vt.edu

Bates, Robert C.	Dean	231-5421	bates					
Spanos, Aris	C-Pr	231-7981	aris	CB	PHD	82	LondonEc	1988
Ashley, Richard A.	Prof	231-6220	ashleyr	CE	PHD	82	Ca-SnDgo	1981
Buchanan, James M.	Emer	231-4348	jmbuchanan	H	PHD	48	Chicago	1969
Eckel, Catherine C.	Prof	231-7707	eckelc	P	PHD	83	Virginia	1983
Feltenstein, Andrew	Prof	231-7958	afeltens	DHO	PHD	76	Yale	1993
Haller, Hans H.	Prof	231-7591	haller	D	PHD	78	Erlangen	1985
Kats, Amoz	Prof	231-6289	amoz	CDL	PHD	72	Minnesota	1974
Mandelstamm, Allen B.	Emer	552-6869	amandel	A	PHD	62	Michigan	1974
Meiselman, David I.	Emer			D	PHD	61	Chicago	1971
Salehi-Isfahani, Djavad	Prof	231-7697	salehi	OT	PHD	77	Harvard	1984
Tideman, T. Nicolaus	Prof	231-7592	ntideman	H	PHD	69	Chicago	1975
Baik, Kyung H.	Assoc	231-4378	khbaik	LD	PHD	89	Va Tech	2001
Ball, Sheryl B.	Assoc	231-4349	sball	DMH	PHD	91	Nrthwstrn	1992
Cothren, Richard D.	Assoc	231-6980	rcothren	E	PHD	81	N Carol	1985
Gilles, Robert P.	Assoc	231-4069	rgilles	DH	PHD	90	Tilburg	1991
Lutz, Nancy A.	Assoc	231-7353	nlutz	DLM	PHD	87	Stanford	1992
Stegeman, Mark W.	Assoc	231-4923	stegeman	DL	PHD	87	MIT	1994
Yang, Dennis T.	Assoc	231-7474	deyang	DJOT	PHD	94	Michigan	2001
Kourtellos, Andros	Asst	231-7958	akourtel	CEO	PHD	01	Wisconsin	2001
Murphy, Russell D. Jr.	Asst	231-4537	rdmurphy	D	PHD	97	Boston U	1997
Snyder, Susan	Asst	231-4431	sksnyder	HDC	PHD	96	Stanford	8-95
McLeod, Mark A.	Inst	231-5942	markmc					1998
Cremer, Jacques	Adj				PHD	78	MIT	1983

Virginia State University Petersburg, VA 23806-9398 (804) 524-5335 vsu.edu
Dept of Economics & Finance School of Business Fax=524-6512 Mrs. Shirley Lewis
Did Not Respond--1999-2000 Listing

Gregory, Sadie R.	Dean	524-5166	sgregory		PHD	87	Howard	1-79
Badu, Yaw Agyeman	C-Ac	524-5363	abadu		PHD	80	S Carol	1984
Khan, Agha Nisar	Prof	524-5872	akhan		PHD	70	Va Tech	1972
Meeks, Thomas J.	Prof	524-5364	tmeeks		PHD	71	Duke	1969
Bawuah, Kwado	Assoc	524-5881	kbawuah		PHD	83	Va Tech	1987
Eseonu, Maxwell O.	Assoc	524-5882	meseonu		PHD	83	Howard	1982
Ohn, Jonathan	Asst	524-5324	john		PHD	98	Lehigh	1999
Trainor, William J.	Asst	524-5365	wtrainor		PHD	94	Va Tech	1996

Wake Forest University Winston-SalemNC 27109 (336) 758-5334 wfu.edu
Department of Economics 7505 Reynolda Station Fax=758-6028 Laura Covington

Cottrell, Allin F.	C-Pr	758-5762	cottrell		PHD	81	Edinburgh	1989
Brown, David G.	Prof	758-4878			PHD	61	Princeton	1990
email david_brown@mail.mba.wfu.edu								
Frey, Donald E.	Prof	758-5618	frey		PHD	72	Princeton	1972
Hammond, Claire Holton	Prof	758-5292	hammonc		PHD	82	Virginia	1978
Hammond, J. Daniel	Prof	758-5335	hammond		PHD	79	Virginia	1978
Lawlor, Michael S.	Prof	758-5564	lawlor		PHD	86	Iowa St	1986
Moorhouse, John C.	Prof	758-5130	moorhous		PHD	69	Nrthwstrn	1969
Archie Carroll Professor of Ethical Leadership								
Patterson, Perry L.	Prof	758-5528	patterso		PHD	86	Nrthwstrn	1906
Wood, John H.	Prof	758-5250	jw		PHD	64	Purdue	1985
Reynolds Professor of Economics								
Boko, Sylvain	Asst	758-4461	bokosh		PHD	96	Iowa St	1997
Chen, Frederick H.	Asst	758-5231	chenfh		ABD		Chicago	2000
Heckelman, Jac C.	Asst	758-5923	heckeljc		PHD	94	Maryland	1996
Whaples, Robert M.	Asst	758-4916	whaples		PHD	90	Penn	1991

Walla Walla College College Place,WA 99324-3000 (509) 527-2951 wwc.edu
Economics Faculty Department of Business Fax=527-2962 Ms. Cheri Windemuth

Anderson, Clarence	C-Ac	527-2951	andecl		PHD	91		1993
Thompson, Dana	Prof	527-2645	thomda		EDD	89	LLU	1998

Wartburg College Waverly, IA 50677-0903 (319) 352-8415 wartburg.edu
Economics Faculty Dept of Bus Adm & Econ Fax=352-8581 Ann Killion

Magnall, Paul	C-Ac	352-8428	magnall	Atg	MBA	82	N Iowa	1983
Campbell, Gloria L.	Assoc	352-8229	campbell		MBA	84	N Iowa	1979
Folkers, Kim	Assoc	352-8424	folkers		MIM	89	St Thomas	1989
Yee, Janice G.	Assoc	352-8485	yee		PHD	90	Clark	1991
Fullwiler, Scott	Asst	352-8452	fullwiler		PHD	01	Nebraska	2001
Lengan, Patrick	Asst	352-8416	langan		PHD	97	Iowa	2000
Mehanna, Rock-Antoine	Asst	352-8315	mehanna		PHD	00	Southern	2001

Washburn Univ of Topeka — Topeka, KS 66621 (785) Ext 1308 — acc.wuacc.edu
Department of Economics — School of Business Fax=231-1063 — Phyllis Sanderson
phone: 231-1010 Ext 1309

Mazachek, Juliann	Dean	Ext 1309	zzmaza	Atg	PHD	93	Kansas	8-92
Gustavson, Robert L.	Prof	231-1010	zzgust		PHD	76	Colorado	1976
Olson, Richard	Prof	231-1010	zzolso		PHD	65	Nebraska	1980
Kerchner, Robert B.	Assoc	231-1010	zzkerc		PHD	73	Missouri	1976
Smith, Russell E.	Assoc	231-1010	zzsmith		PHD	84	Illinois	1984
Ball, Jennifer	Asst	231-1010			PHD	01	S Calif	2001
Mizovtsev, Dmitri	Asst	231-1010			PHD	01	Purdue	2001
Dickes, Allen L.	Inst				MA	70	Toledo	1978
Director, Institutional Research								

University of Washington — Seattle, WA 98195-3200 (206) 543-4773 — u.washington.edu
Dept of Finance & Bus Econ — Sch of Business Adm Fax=221-6856 — Andrew Anderson, Adm Asst

Gupta, Yash P.	Dean	543-4752		Mgt	PHD	76	Brunel	1999
Schall, Lawrence D.	C-Pr	543-7689	lschall		PHD	69	Chicago	1967
Alberts, William W.	Emer	543-6579			PHD	61	Chicago	1987
Frost, Peter S.	Prof	543-0992	pfrost		PHD	66	UCLA	1969
Haley, Charles W.	Prof	543-7697	chiph		PHD	68	Stanford	1966
Hess, Alan C.	Prof	543-4579	hess		PHD	69	Car Mellon	1967
Higgins, Robert C.	Prof	543-4379	rhiggins		PHD	69	Stanford	1967
Kamara, Avraham	Prof	543-0652	kamara		PHD	86	Columbia	1984
Karpoff, Jonathan M.	Prof	685-4954	karpoff		PHD	82	UCLA	1983
Malatesta, Paul H.	Prof	685-1987	phmalat		PHD	81	Rochester	1980
Roley, V. Vance	Prof	543-7476	vroley		PHD	77	Harvard	1983
Siegel, Andrew F.	Prof	543-4476	asiegel		PHD	83	MIT	1990
Dewenter, Kathryn L.	Assoc	685-7893	dewe		PHD	93	Chicago	1992
Koski, Jennifer L.	Assoc	543-7975	jkoski		PHD	91	Stanford	1991
Pontiff, Jeffrey	Assoc	543-3021	pontiff		PHD	94	Rochester	1992
Rice, Edward M.	Assoc	543-4480	erice		PHD	78	UCLA	1979
Lin, Parsy	Asst	543-8780	pclin		PHD	00	UCLA	2000
Novaes, Walter	Asst	543-4435	novaes		PHD	93	MIT	1993
Glassman, Debra	SLect	543-8738	dg2854		PHD	80	Wisconsin	1992
Hadjimichalakis, Karma	SLect	685-8044	karmah		PHD	74	Rochester	1970
Tarhouni, Ali	SLect	543-4577	tarhouni		PHD	84	Mich St	1985

University of Washington — Seattle, WA 98195 (206) 543-5955 — u.washington.edu
Dept of Economics Box 353330 — Col of Arts & Sciences Fax=685-7477 — Karen Russell

Barzel, Yoram	Prof	543-2510	yoramb		PHD	61	Chicago	1961
Brown, Gardner	Prof	543-5744	gbrown	QDH	PHD	64	Berkeley	1965
Bruce, Neil	Prof	543-5874	brucen		PHD	75	Chicago	1990
Deolalikar, Anil B.	Prof	543-6145	anil		PHD	81	Stanford	1989
Halvorsen, Robert F.	Prof	543-5546	halvor		PHD	73	Harvard	1972
Hartman, Richard C.	Prof	685-1630	rhartman		PHD	71	Berkeley	1971
Lundberg, Shelly J.	Prof	543-6149	lundberg		PHD	81	Nrthwstrn	1984
Nelson, Charles R.	Prof	685-1382	cnelson	EGC	PHD	69	Wisconsin	1975
Parks, Richard	Prof	543-4493	rwparks		PHD	66	Berkeley	1970
Siberberg, Eugene	Prof	543-8664	silber		PHD	64	Purdue	1967
Startz, Richard	Prof	543-5955	startz		PHD	78	MIT	1984
Thornton, Judith Ann	Prof	543-5784	thornj		PHD	60	Harvard	1961
Turnovsky, Stephen J.	Prof	685-8028	sturn		PHD	68	Harvard	1987
Wong, Kar-yiu	Prof	543-1859	karyiu		PHD	83	Columbia	1983
Brock, Philip L.	Assoc	543-5796	plbrock		PHD	82	Stanford	1991
Eicher, Theo S.	Assoc	685-8082	te		PHD	94	Columbia	1994
Hadjimichalakis, Michael	Assoc	543-5835	mhadjimi		PHD	69	Rochester	1969
Khalil, Fahad A.	Assoc	543-5836	khalil		PHD	91	Va Tech	1991
Kochin, Levis A.	Assoc	543-5845	lakochin		PHD	75	Chicago	1972
Lawarree, Jacques P.	Assoc	543-5632	lawarree		PHD	90	Berkeley	1990
Leffler, Keith B.	Assoc	543-5795			PHD	77	UCLA	1978
Rose, Elaina	Assoc	543-5237	erose		PHD	93	Penn	1993
Thomas, Robert P.	Assoc	543-5842	rthomas		PHD	64	Nrthwstrn	1968
Zivot, Eric W.	Assoc	543-6715	ezivot		PHD	92	Yale	1993
Liu, Wen-Fang	Asst	543-8983	linwf		PHD	98	Chicago	1998
Salehi-Esfahani, Haideh	SLect	543-7463	haideh		PHD	85	Penn	1990
Turnovsky, Michelle H. L.	SLect	543-1967	mturn		PHD	78	Austr Natl	1987

Washington University — St. Louis, MO 63130-4899 (314) 935-5670 — wueconc.wustl.edu
Department of Economics — Col of Arts & Sciences Fax=935-4156 — Karen Rensing
Homepage: economics.wustl.edu

Macias, Edward	Dean	935-6820	macias@hilltop		PHD	70	MIT	1970
Fazzari, Steven M.	C-Pr	935-5632	fazz	E	PHD	82	Stanford	1982
Barnett, William A.	Prof	935-4236	barnett	E	PHD	74	Car Mellon	1990
Benham, Lee K.	Prof	935-4535	benham	LP	PHD	70	Stanford	1974
Berliant, Marcus C.	Prof	935-8486	berliant	DHR	PHD	82	Berkeley	1994
Felix, David	Emer	935-5639	felix	O	PHD	55	Berkeley	1964
Greenberg, Edward	Prof	935-5641	edg	DE	PHD	61	Wisconsin	1963

Leven, Charles L.	Emer	935-5836	leven	IR	PHD	58	Nrthwstrn	1964
Meyer, Laurence H.	Prof	935-5648		E	PHD	70	MIT	1969
on leave 2001-2002								
Neuefeind, Wilhelm	Prof	935-5615	wilhelm@neue+	D	PHD	72	Bonn	1978
North, Douglass C.	Prof	935-5809	north	NO	PHD	52	Berkeley	1983
Spencer T. Olin Professor of Arts & Sciences/1993 Nobel Prize in Economics								
Parks, Robert P.	Prof	935-5665	bparks	H	PHD	71	Purdue	1971
Petersen, Bruce C.	Prof	935-5643	petersen	L	PHD	81	Harvard	1991
Pollak, Robert A.	Prof	935-4918	pollak	DJT	PHD	64	MIT	1995
Hernreich Distinguished Professor of Economics								
Schofield, Norman J.	Prof	935-4774	schofld	DH	PHD	76	Essex	1986
William Taussig Professor of Political Economy								
Weidenbaum, Murray L.	Prof	935-5662	moseley@wc	HM	PHD	58	Princeton	1961
Edward Mallinckrodt Distinguished University Professor								
Kim, Sukkoo	Assoc	935-4961	soks	NR	PHD	93	UCLA	1993
Nachbar, John	Assoc	935-5612	nachbar	CD	PHD	88	Harvard	1990
Nye, John V. C.	Assoc	935-6736	nye	N	PHD	85	Nrthwstrn	1985
Raines, Fredric Q.	Assoc	935-5636	raines	J	PHD	67	Wisconsin	1964
Rothstein, Paul	Assoc	935-4352	rstein	H	PHD	88	Berkeley	1988
Antinolfi, Gaetano	Asst	935-7335	gaetano	E	PHD	97	Cornell	1997
Ginther, Donna	Asst	935-6607	dginther	J	PHD	95	Wisconsin	1997
Morley, James	Asst	935-4437	morley	E	PHD	99	U Wash	1999
Moul, Charles	Asst	935-5836	moul	L	PHD	00	Nrthwstrn	2000

Washington & Jefferson Col Washington, PA 15301-4801 (412) washjeff.edu
Economics Faculty Dept of Economics & Bus Fax=223-5271
Homepage: www.washjeff.edu/deartments/economics/

Gregor, John J.	C-Pr	223-6150	jgregor	PHD	76	Penn St	1989
Robison, K. Wayne	Prof	223-6253	wrobison	MBA	79	Ohio St	1979
West, James S.	Prof	223-6154	jwest	PHD	97	Nebraska	1997
Kuhn, Stephen D.	Assoc		skuhn	MACC	91	Bowl Gr	
Moschetta, Judith K.	Assoc	223-6152	jmoschetta	MS	78	W Virginia	1978
Swint, Kenneth J.	Assoc	223-6156	kswint	PHD	89	Pittsburgh	1988
Gidas, Sam	Asst	223-6157	sgidas	JD		Yale	1998
Lyon, William R.	Asst	223-6516	wlyon	MBA	89	Morehead	1988
Yalcindag, Selin	Asst	223-6151	syalcindag	PHD		Brit Colum	1998

Washington and Lee Univ Lexington, VA 24450-0303 (540) 463-8604 fs.commerce.wlu.edu
Department of Economics Sch Comm, Econ & Pol Fax=463-8639 Carol Ruley

Peppers, Larry C.	Dean	463-8602	peppers.l.c		PHD	70	Vanderbilt	1986
Goldsmith, Arthur H.	C-Pr	463-8970	goldsmith.a.h	EJ	PHD	79	Illinois	1990
Jackson T. Stephens Professor of Economics								
Cline, Philip L.	Prof	463-8622	cline.p.l	C	PHD	75	Okla St	1975
Lewis Whitabker Adams Professor of Economics								
Gunn, John McKenzie	Emer	463-8616	gunn.j.m	E	MA	54	Princeton	1957
Lewis Whitaker Adams Professor of Economics Emeritus								
Herrick, Bruce H.	Emer	463-8615	herrick.b.h	OP	PHD	64	MIT	1980
John F. Hendon Professor of Economics, Emeritus								
Kahn, James A.	Prof	463-8036	kahn.j	QO	PHD	86	MIT	
Kaiser, Carl P.	Prof	463-8617	kaiser.c.p	JC	PHD	80	Wash U	1979
Lowry, Stanley T.	Emer	463-8614	lowry.s.t	BK	PHD	58	LSU	1959
Phillips, Charles F. Jr.	Prof	463-8618	phillips.c.f	L	PHD	60	Harvard	1959
Robert C. Brown Professor of Economics								
Winfrey, John C.	Prof	463-8606	winfrey.j.c	DH	PHD	65	Duke	1965
Anderson, Michael A.	Assoc	463-8971	anderson.m.a	F	PHD	90	Wisconsin	1990
Hooks, Linda M.	Assoc	463-8621	hooks.l.m	E	PHD	91	UCLA	1993
Smitka, Michael J.	Assoc	463-8625	smitka.m.j.	FL	PHD	89	Yale	1986
Capra, C. Monica	Asst	463-8604	capra.c.m	D	PHD	98	Virginia	1999
Casey, James	Asst	463-8102	casey.j	QO	PHD		N Car St	2001

Washington State University Pullman, WA 99164-4741 (509) 335-6651 wsu.edu
Department of Economics Col of Business & Econ Fax=335-4362 Ms. Jan Musick
email @1=mail.wsu.edu @2=wsuvm1.csc.wsu.edu @3=tricity.wsu.edu

Johnson, Glenn L.	Dean	335-3596	glennl	Atg	PHD	65	Berkeley	1979
Leigh, Duane E.	C-Pr	335-4441	leighd		PHD	69	Mich St	1968
Batina, Raymond	Prof	335-8057	juliab@1		PHD	85	Minnesota	1985
Fort, Rodney D.	Prof	335-6468	fort@1		PHD	85	Cal Tech	1984
Joerdling, Wayne H.	Prof	335-6468	joerd@1		PHD	79	Nrthwstrn	1979
Krautkraemer, Jeffrey A.	Prof	335-3420	krautkra@2		PHD	82	Stanford	1981
Lowinger, Thomas C.	Prof	335-4913			PHD	70	Mich St	1978
Roseman, Robert E.	Prof	335-1193	yakama@1		PHD	82	Minnesota	1983
Stromsdorfer, Ernst W.	Prof	335-4471	stroms		PHD	62	Wash U	1983
Associate Dean								
Hallagan, William S.	Assoc	335-6651	hallagan		PHD	77	Ca-Davis	1984
Inaba, Frederick S.	Assoc	335-6651	inaba		PHD	74	Berkeley	1977
Nziramasanga, Mudziviri T.	Assoc	335-6651	nziramasangam		PHD	74	Stanford	1973
Chaudhuri, Ananish	Asst	372-7238	achaudh@3		PHD	97	Rutgers	1998
He, Susan	Asst	335-5314	yhe		PHD	00	Wash St	
Morshed, Mahbub	Asst				PHD	01	U Wash	

Wayne State College Wayne, NE 68787 (402) 375-7243 wsc.edu
Dept of Business & Economics School of Bus & Tech Fax=375-7458 L. Teach
Homepage: www.wsc.edu/academic/socialsci/eco.htm

Benson, Vaughn L.	Dean	375-7245	vabenso1	Atg	PHD	85	Nebraska	1974
Nelson, Jeryl	C	375-7251	jenelso1		PHD	00	Nebraska	1986
Dalal, Meenakshi N.	Prof	375-7509	medala1	OE	PHD	84	Northeas	1985
Parker, Charles	Assoc	375-7036	chparke1	ADKL	PHD	94	Cincinnati	8-95

Wayne State University Detroit, MI 48202 (313) 577-3345 econ.wayne.edu
Department of Economics Col of Liberal Arts Fax=577-0149 Cheri Miller/Delores Tennille

Levin, Jay H.	C-Pr	577-3344	jlevin	F	PHD	68	Michigan	1976
Braid, Ralph M.	Prof	577-2540	rbraid	R	PHD	79	MIT	1988
Goodman, Allen C.	Prof	577-3235	agoodman	IR	PHD	76	Yale	1986
Jensen, Gail A.	Prof	577-3345		I	PHD	86	Minnesota	1989
Lee, Li Way	Prof	577-2256		L	PHD	76	Columbia	1981
Rossana, Robert J.	Prof	577-3760	rossana	E	PHD	80	J Hopkins	1991
Spurr, Stephen J.	Assoc	577-3232	sspurr	JK	PHD	86	Chicago	1987
Bekdache, Basma	Asst	577-3231	bbekdac	E	PHD	94	Boston C	1994
Cotter, Kevin D.	Asst	577-3233	kcotter	D	PHD	84	Minnesota	1989
Hunsaker, Julie	Asst	577-0603	jhunsake	L	PHD	93	Purdue	1993
Komagai, Tomomi	Asst	577-3345		C	PHD	01	MIT	2001

Weber State University Ogden, UT 84408-3807 (801) 626-6066 cobe.weber.edu
Department of Economics Col of Business & Econ Fax=626-7423 Elaine Thomas

Vaughan, Michael B.	Dean	626-6084		AMK	PHD	80	Nebraska	1981
Nowell, Clifford	C-Pr	626-6488	cnowell	ADQ	PHD	88	Wyoming	1988
Alston, Richard M.	Prof	626-6061	ralston	ABNQ	PHD	70	Cornell	1969
Chi, Wan Fu	Prof	626-6792	wchi	AC	PHD	69	S Illinois	1969
Fuller, Dan A.	Prof	626-6794	dfuller	ADH	PHD	82	N Carol	1981
Mbaku, John M.	Prof	626-7442	jmbaku	AHOP	PHD	85	Georgia	1991
Neal, Cora	VAsst	626-6407	cneal		PHD	01	Utah St	
Grijalva, Therese	Assoc	626-7567	tcavloovic		PHD	00	New Mex	1995
Geide-Stevenson, Doris	Asst	626-7634	dgsteven	AF	PHD	95	SUNY-Buf	1996

Webster University St. Louis, MO 63119-3194 (314) 968-7021 webster.edu
Business Department Sch of Business & Mgt Fax=968-7077 Nancy Wilson

Akande, Benjamin Ola	Dean	968-5950	akandeb		PHD	95	Oklahoma	2000
Hinson, Steven Y.	C-Ac	968-7017	hinsonsy	AFDH	PHD	93	Kentucky	1993
Westerfield, Donald	Prof	968-7021		DIMC	PHD	84	St Louis	1985
MacNeill, Alan	Assoc	968-7489			PHD		Mass	1994
Rishe, Patrick	Asst				PHD	97	SUNY-Bin	1998

Wellesley College Wellesley, MA 02481-8260 (781) 283-2154 wellesley.edu
Economics Faculty Department of Economics Fax=283-2177 Patricia Sjostedt
Homepage: www.wellesley.edu/Economics

Skeath, Susan E.	C-Ac	283-2180	sskeath	DFL	PHD	89	Princeton	1989
Case, Karl E.	Prof	283-2178	kcase	RHD	PHD	77	Harvard	1976
Joyce, Joseph P.	Prof	283-2160	jjoyce	EF	PHD	84	Boston U	1982
Lindauer, David	Prof	283-2159	dlindauer	OFD	PHD	79	Harvard	1981
Matthaei, Julie Ann	Prof	283-2181	jmatthaei	B	PHD	78	Yale	1978
Witte, Ann D.	Prof	283-2163	awitte	DHK	PHD	71	N Car St	1985
Blomberg, Brock	Assoc	283-2382	sblomber	E	PHD	94	J Hopkins	1995
Kauffman, Kyle	Assoc	283-2153	kkauffman	DN	PHD	93	Illinois	1993
Levine, Philip	Assoc	283-2163	plevine	JD	PHD	91	Princeton	1991
Velenchik, Ann D.	Assoc	283-2183	avelenchik	OFD	PHD	89	Stanford	1989
Ardagna, Silvia	Asst	283-2165	sardagna	EF	PHD	00	Boston C	2000
Coile, Courtney	Asst	283-2408	ccoile	DHI	PHD	99	MIT	2000
Johnson, Dan	Asst	283-2236	djohnson	AD	PHD	98	Yale	1997
Weerapana, Akila	Asst	283-2300	aweerapa	EF	PHD	99	Stanford	1999

Wesleyan University Middletown, CT 06459-0007 (860) 685-2340 mail.wesleyan.edu
Economics Faculty Department of Economics Fax=685-2781 Gloria Cone

Bonin, John P.	C-Pr	685-2353	jbonin	P	PHD	73	Rochester	1970
Andrews Professor of Economics								
Adelstein, Richard P.	Prof	685-2366	radelstein	K	PHD	75	Penn	1975
Barber, William J.	Emer	685-2362	wbarber	B	DPHI	57	Oxford	1957
Grossman, Richard	Prof	685-2356	rgrossman	N	PHD	88	Harvard	1990
Jacobsen, Joyce P.	Prof	685-2357	jjacobson	J	PHD	91	Stanford	1993
Kilby, Peter	Prof	685-2365	pkilby	O	DPHI	67	Oxford	1965
Lebergott, Stanley	Emer	685-2364	slebergott	N	MA	39	Michigan	1962
University Professor								
Lovell, Michael C.	Prof	685-2355	mlovell	E	PHD	59	Harvard	1969
Chester D. Hubbard Professor of Economics & Social Science								
Miller, Richard A.	Prof	685-2354	ramiller	L	PHD	62	Yale	1960
Moore, Basil J.	Prof	685-2363	bmoore	E	PHD	58	J Hopkins	1958

Whitin, Thomson M.	Emer	685-2347	twhitin	C	PHD	52	Princeton	1963
Yohe, Gary W.	Prof	685-3658	gyohe	D	PHD	75	Yale	1977
Rayack, Wendy	Assoc	685-2358	wrayack	J	PHD	84	Wisconsin	1983
Skillman, Gilbert L.	Assoc	685-2359	gskillman	D	PHD	85	Michigan	1993
Hanson, Michael S.	Asst	685-2348	mhanson	E	PHD	99	Michigan	1999
Hogendorn, Christiaan P.	Asst	685-2348	chogendorn	L	PHD	00	Penn	2001
Rosenblat, Tanya S.	Asst	685-2348	trosenblat	E	PHD	99	MIT	1999

University of West Alabama Livingston, AL 35470 (205) 652-3471 uwamail.westal.edu
Dept of Adm & Management College of Business Fax=652-3576 Sieglinde Fleming

Peper, Merle J.	Dean	652-3471	mjp		PHD	86	LSU	9-95
Carr, Linda A.	C-Pr	652-3476			EDD	68	Alabama	1965
Sheffield, Howell	Inst	652-3473			MBA		Alabama	1998

West Chester Univ of PA West Chester, PA 19383-2220 (610) 436-3460 wcupa.edu
Dept of Economics & Finance Sch of Bus & Public Aff Fax=436-2592 Pat Zellman

Fiorentino, Christopher M.	Dean	436-2930	cfiorentino	DQ	PHD	89	Temple	9-85
Tolin, Thomas	C-As	436-2217	ttolin	JD	PHD	92	Houston	1992
Benzing, Cynthia D.	Prof	738-0433	cbenzing	AEG	PHD	87	Drexel	1988
Naggar, Tahany	Prof	436-2834	tnaggar	ADTN	PHD	76	Oklahoma	1977
Sylvester, Patrick J.	Prof	436-2964	psylvester	AE	PHD	73	Bryn Mawr	1968
Bove, Roger E.	Assoc	436-2134	rbove	FP	PHD	73	Harvard	1984
DeMoss, Philip M.	Assoc	436-2964	pdemoss	AGM	PHD	69	Kansas St	1973
Mohan, Daniel F.	Assoc	436-3468	dmohan	GM	PHD	75	Rutgers	1980
Andrews, Thomas	Asst	436-1082	tandrews	DHQL	PHD	96	Temple	1997
Dunleavy, Kevin C.	Asst	436-3422	kdunleavy	ACE	PHD	79	Duke	1979

University of West Florida Pensacola, FL 32514-5752 (850) 474-2652 uwf.edu
Dept of Mktg & Economics College of Business Fax=474-3069 Marianne Baker
Did Not Respond--1999-2000 Listing

Ranelli, Edward	Dean	474-2348	eranelli		PHD	69	Alabama	2000
Sjolander, Richard J.	C-Pr	474-2663		Mktg	PHD	84	Mich St	1985
Ashraf, Javed	Prof	474-2664		AJ	PHD	86	N Illinois	1990
Huth, William L.	Prof	474-2652		AMG	PHD	80	Arkansas	1989
Arguea, Nestor M.	Assoc	474-3071		ACD	PHD	90	S Calif	1990
Harper, Richard K.	Assoc	474-3072		AFM	PHD	89	Duke	1989
Conroy, Stephen	Asst	474-3072		ACJ	PHD	98	S Calif	1999
Hawkins, Richard R.	Asst	474-2656		ACR	PHD	96	Geo St	1996

State Univ of West Georgia Carrollton, GA 30118-3020 (770) 836-6477 westga.edu
Department of Economics Richards College of Bus Fax=836-6774 Ms. Elizabeth Key
Homepage: www.westga.edu/~econ/

Johnson, Jack E.	Dean	836-6467	jjohnnson	Mgt				
Boldt, David John	C-Ac	836-6477	dboldt	AR	PHD	87	New Mex	1988
Fryman, Richard F.	Prof	836-6477	rfryman	AH	PHD	67	Illinois	1986
Gustafson, Leland Verne	Prof	836-6477	lgustafs	AC	PHD	74	Fla St	
Schaniel, William C.	Prof	836-6477	wschanie	BP	PHD	85	Tennessee	
Dutt, Swarna D.	Assoc	836-6477	sdutt	F	PHD	93	Wayne St	1994
Raper, Michael Dennis	Assoc	836-6477	mraper	AR	PHD	88	Geo St	
Dole, Carol	Asst	836-6477	edole	E	PHD	92	Florida	2001
Kassis, Mary C.	Asst	836-6477	mkassis	HJ	PHD	99	Geo St	1-02

West Liberty State College West Liberty, WV 26074-0295 (304) 336-8053
Dept of Financial Systems School of Business Adm Fax= Sharon Rinderer

Holcombe, Douglas	Dean	336-8055			PHD	82	Ohio St	2001
Turrentine, S. Michael	C-As	336-8164			JD	96	Duquesne	1999
Mullin, Marian V.	Assoc	336-8054		DE	MS	85	Rbt Morr	1975
Reuther, Carol J.	Assoc	336-8156		CDGH	MS	73	Fla St	1991

West Texas A&M University Canyon, TX 79016-0001 (806) 651-2525 mail.wtamu.edu
Dept of Atg, Econ & Finance Pickens Col of Business Fax=651-2514 Betsey Tonne

Duman, Barry L.	H-Pr	651-2519	bduman	BDP	PHD	71	S Calif	1969
Rosa, Duane J.	Assoc	651-2276	drosa	EOQ	PHD	89	Tx Tech	1984
Lewer, Joshua J.	Asst	651-2508	jlewer	EHN	PHD	00	Nebraska	2000
Terry, Neil W.	Asst	651-2512	nterry	EOQ	PHD	97	Tx Tech	1997

West Virginia University Morgantown, WV 26506-6025 (304) 293-7859 mail.wvu.edu
Department of Economics Col of Business & Econ Fax=293-7061 Barbara Michniak
Homepage: www.be.wvu.edu/div/econ

Dahringer, Lee D.	Dean	293-7800	lee.dahringer	Mktg	DBA	78	Colorado	1999
Trumbull, William N.	C-Ac	293-7860	william.trumbull	HKD	PHD	85	N Carol	1983
Adams, Donald R. Jr.	Prof	293-7861	donald.adams	N	PHD	67	Penn	1981
Hawley, Clifford B.	Prof	293-7865	clifford.hawley	JD	PHD	77	Duke	1978

Hwang, Ming-jeng	Prof	293-7866	ming.hwang	DRC	PHD	73	Tx A&M	1974
Kymn, Kern O.	Prof	293-7867	kern.kymn	EC	PHD	64	Chicago	1976
Labys, Walter C.	Prof	293-6253	walter.labys	Q	PHD	68	Nottinghm	1975
Mann, Patrick C.	Prof	293-7872	patrick.mann	DH	PHD	67	Indiana	1967
Mitchell, Douglas W.	Prof	293-7868	douglas.mitchell	E	PHD	78	Princeton	1984
Reece, William S.	Prof	293-4092	william.reece	CH	PHD	75	Wash U	1990
Witt, Tom S.	Prof	293-7835	tom.witt	CR	PHD	74	Wash U	1970
Balvers, Ronald J.	Assoc	293-7880	ronald.balvers	EG	PHD	84	Pittsburgh	1991
Cushing, Brian J.	Assoc	293-7881	brian.cushing	RCH	PHD	81	Maryland	1981
Douglas, Stratford M.	Assoc	293-7863	douglas.strat+	CHD	PHD	87	N Carol	990
Fletcher, Jerald J.	Assoc	293-6253	jerald.fletcher	Q	PHD	82	Berkeley	1989
Phipps, Tim	Assoc	293-6353	tim.phipps	Q	PHD	82	Berkeley	1989
Bandyopadhyay, Subhayu	Asst	293-7879	subhayu.band+	F	PHD	94	Maryland	1993
Bandyopadhyay, Sudeshna	Asst	293-7869	sudeshna.band+	J	PHD	92	Maryland	1992
Chow, C. Victor	Asst	293-7888	victor.chow	G	PHD	89	Alabama	1989
Sobel, Russell S.	Asst	293-7864	russell.sobel	H	PHD	94	Fla St	1994
Vilasuso, Jon R.	Asst	293-7871	jon.vilasuso	EFG	PHD	94	Conn	1999
Watts, Royce J.	Asst	293-5695	royce.watts	C	MS	61	W Virginia	1955

West Virginia State College — Institute, WV 25112-1000 (304) 766-3065 — ernie.wvsc.edu
Department of Economics — Sch of Bus Admin & Econ Fax=766-3089 — Carolyn Wilkinson

Islam, Mahmood	C-Ac	766-3057			PHD	85	Wayne St	1987
Fazio, John	Inst	766-3065			MBA	76	W Virginia	2001
Yousefsibdari, Soheil	Inst	766-3065			MA	01	Va Tech	2001

Western Carolina University — Cullowhee, NC 28723-9033 (828) 227-3053 — wcuvax1.wcu.edu
Bus Cpt Systems & Economics — School of Business Fax=227-7414 — Kathy Brashear
Homepage: www.wcu.edu/cob/departments/cise/cise.html

Shiffler, Ronald E.	Dean	227-3008	rshiffler	Mgt	PHD	80	Florida	7-96
Hunter, Jennie L.	H	227-3704	jhunter	Cis	MA	66	W Carol	1972
Jarrell, Stephen B.	Prof	227-3294	jarrell	C	PHD	78	Purdue	1988
Jones, Royal Maurice	Prof	227-3300		P	PHD	67	Maryland	1971
Spencer, Austin Harvey	Prof	227-3356	aspence	G	PHD	72	Indiana	1980
Allen, Grace C.	Assoc	227-3189	alleng	G	PHD	91	S Carol	1992
Hays, Patrick A.	Assoc	227-3227	hays	G	PHD	77	N Carol	1985
Schreiber, Max M.	Assoc	227-3295	schreibr	C	PHD	78	S Carol	1977
Mulligan, Richard	Asst	227-3329	mulligan	E	PHD	93	SUNY-Bin	1997
Murphy, James H.	Asst	227-7074	jmurphy	F	PHD	00	Geo St	1998
Ullmer, James H.	Asst	227-3762	ullmer	N	PHD	96	Tennessee	1999

Western Conn State Univ — Danbury, CT 06810 (203) 837-8484 — wcsub.ctstateu.edu
Economics Faculty — Sch of Arts & Sciences Fax=837-8525 — A. Strucky
Did Not Respond--1999-2000 Listing; email address: wcsu.edu

Hawkes, Carol A.	Dean		hawkes	Lang	PHD	53	Columbia	
Bannister, Jerry	C-Pr	837-8454	bannisterj	Soci	MA		Syracuse	
Owoye, Oluwole	Prof	837-8456	owoye	EFHJ	PHD	89	N Illinois	
Skinner, Steven P.	Prof	837-8457	skinner	BJQR	PHD	80	Conn	
Pan, Zuohong	Asst		panz	CJLO	PHD	95	Mich St	

Western Illinois University — Macomb, IL 61455-1390 (309) 298-1153 — wiu.edu
Department of Economics — Col of Business & Tech Fax=298-1020 — Mary Sherwood, Esther Grimes

Walzer, Norman C.	D-Pr	298-1031	n-walzer	ADHR	PHD	70	Illinois	1970
Director, Illinois Institute for Rural Affairs								
Jones, Warren	C-Ac	298-1477	w-jones	AEHN	PHD	82	Iowa	1983
Andrianacos, Dimitri	Prof	298-2331	d-andrianacos	ACE	PHD	89	Chicago	1990
Hattwick, Richard E.	Prof	298-1594	r-hattwick	AM	PHD	65	Vanderbilt	1969
Pledge, Michael T.	Prof	298-1637	m-pledge	AEG	PHD	68	Houston	1968
Rao, Vaman	Prof	298-1321	v-rao	ACEO	PHD	73	Missouri	1979
Rock, Steven M.	Prof	298-1343	s-rock	AJM	PHD	75	Nrthwstrn	1990
Straub, LaVonne	Prof	298-1413	l-straub	AIJR	PHD	83	Utah	1982
Yunker, James A.	Prof	298-1639	j-yunker	ACDP	PHD	71	Nrthwstrn	1968
Fosu, Joseph	Assoc	298-2265	j-fosu	ADEO	PHD	87	Iowa St	1987
Westerhold, Tara D.	Asst	298-1313	twesterhold	ADH	PHD	98	S Carol	1998

Western Kentucky University — Bowling Green KY 42101-3576 (270) 745-2249 — wku.edu
Dept of Economics & Mktg — College of Business Adm Fax=745-3190 — Karen Braun

Jefferson, Robert M.	Dean	745-6311	robert.jeff+	Mktg	PHD	69	Iowa	1996
Wassom, John C.	H-Pr	745-2249		G	PHD	70	Indiana	1971
Borland, Melvin V.	Prof	745-3112		BDA	PHD	72	Wash U	1978
Goff, Brian L.	Prof	745-3855		GHK	PHD	86	GeoMason	1986
Kim, Hak Youn	Prof	745-3187		CDO	PHD	82	Cincinnati	1983
Lile, Stephen E.	Prof	745-3115		H	PHD	72	Kentucky	1973
Pulsinelli, Robert W.	Prof	745-3118		DK	PHD	74	Rutgers	1967
Wisley, Thomas O.	Prof	745-3127		GHK	PHD	79	Purdue	1985
Brown, J. Michael	Assoc	745-3893		G	PHD	71	Kentucky	1988

Cantrell, Richard P.	Assoc	745-3146		C	MA	63	S Illinois	1967
Davis, William W.	Assoc	745-3123		F	PHD	65	Kentucky	1970
Howsen, Roy M.	Assoc	745-3172		D	PHD	80	Arkansas	1981
Myers, Daniel A.	Assoc	745-3684		R	PHD	86	Vanderbilt	1986
Noser, Thomas C.	Assoc	745-3642		CA	PHD	86	Alabama	1984
Carey, Cathrine	Asst	745-6401		F	PHD	92	Kentucky	1992
Strow, Brian	Asst	745-7082			PHD		Vanderbilt	
Strow, Claudia	Asst	745-3627			ABD		Vanderbilt	
Trawick, Michelle	Asst	745-8803			PHD	96	N Car St	

Western Maryland College Westminster, MD 21157-4390 (410) 857-2450 wmdc.edu
Economics Faculty Dept of Econ & Bus Adm Fax=857-2729 Pat Holford
Did Not Respond--1999-2000 Listing

Law, Alton D.	C-Pr	848-7000	ns1		PHD	68	Rutgers	1966
Claycombe, Richard J.	Prof	848-7000	rclaycom		PHD	80	Geo Wash	1981
Milstein, Susan Matz	Prof	848-7000	smilstei		MBA		MtStMary	1983
Olsh, John Lindsay	Prof	848-7000			PHD	74	Ca-Davis	1980
Seidel, Ethan A.	Prof	848-7000	eseidel		PHD	77	J Hopkins	1969
Singer, Diana Sue	Prof	848-7000	ssinger		MBA		Loyola	1983

Western Michigan University Kalamazoo, MI 49008-5023 (616) 387-5535 wmich.edu
Department of Economics Col of Arts & Sciences Fax=387-3999 Mrs. Becky Ryder

Sichel, Werner	C-Pr	387-5539	werner.sichel	D	PHD	64	Nrthwstrn	1960
Asefa, Sisay	Prof	387-5540	sisay.asefa	O	PHD	80	Iowa St	1980
Hoffman, Emily P.	Prof	387-5546	emily.hoffman	J	PHD	75	Mass	1981
Huang, Wei-Chiao	Prof	387-5547	wei-chiao.huang	J	PHD	84	Ca-SnBarb	1985
Pozo, Susan	Prof	387-5553	susan.pozo	F	PHD	80	Mich St	1982
Alexander, Donald L.	Assoc	387-5526	donald.alexander	D	PHD	83	Penn St	9900
Alvi, Eskander	Assoc	387-5547	eskander.alvi	E	PHD	85	J Hopkins	1994
Harik, Bassam	Assoc	387-5554	bassam.harik	E	PHD	78	Wayne St	1979
Higgins, Matthew L.	Assoc	387-5543	matthew.higgins	C	PHD	89	Illinois	1995
Kern, William	Assoc	387-5549	william.kern	B	PHD	82	Colo St	1987
Kimmel, Jean	Assoc	387-5541	jean.kimmel	J	PHD	90	N Carol	2001
Meyer, Donald J.	Assoc	387-5531	donald.meyer	D	PHD	83	Tx A&M	1991
Neill, Jon R.	Assoc	387-5551	jon.neill	H	PHD	83	Pittsburgh	1980
Wheeler, Mark V.	Assoc	387-5563	mark.wheeler	E	PHD	85	Kentucky	1990
Zhou, Huizhong	Assoc	387-5550	huizhong.zhou	C	PHD	86	Nrthwstrn	1990
Ryan, Michael	Asst	387-5545	michael.ryan	F	PHD	00	Indiana	2000

Western New England Coll Springfield, MA 01119-2684 (413) 782-1252 wnec.edu
Department of Economics Sch of Arts & Sciences Fax=782-1746 Donna Utter 782-1480
Homepage: mars.wnec.edu/~econ

Ghahramani, Saeed	Dean			Math	PHD		Calif	2000
Meeropol, Michael A.	C-Pr	782-1252			PHD	73	Wisconsin	1970
Andrulis, John A.	Prof	782-1601			PHD	75	Purdue	1981
Mannur, Hanumant G.	Prof		hmannur		PHD	72	Indiana	2001
Casimir, Schiller	Asst	782-1741	scasimir		PHD	97	SUNY-Bin	1997
Eskot, Herbert J.	Asst	782-1743	heskot		PHD	84	Tufts	1984

Western Oregon University Monmouth, OR 97361 (503) 838-8421 wou.edu
Division of Business & Econ Sch Liberal Arts & Sci Fax=838-8723 Dianna Hewell
Did Not Respond--1999-2000 Listing

Minahan, John P.	Dean				PHD	69	Geotown	1986
Bahari-Kashani, Hamid	C-Pr	838-8354	baharih		PHD	83	Wash St	1988
Leadley, John C.	Assoc	838-8719	leadlej		PHD	85	Wisconsin	1991
Zygmont, Zenon X.	Asst	838-8244	zygmouz	APLF	PHD	94	GeoMason	1998

Western State College of CO Gunnison, CO 81231 (970) 943-7011 western.edu
Economics Faculty Dept of Business & Atg Fax=943-3380
Did Not Respond--1999-2000 Listing

Axelson, David J.	C-Ac	943-3081			EDD	76	Colorado	1982
Plante, David	Asst	943-2207			ABD		Utah	1997

Western Washington Univ Bellingham, WA 98225-9074 (360) 650-3910 wwu.edu
Department of Economics Col of Business & Econ Fax=650-4844 Theresa Gresley
Homepage: http://www.wwu.edu/~econ/econ.html

Murphy, Dennis R.	Dean	650-3896	dennis.murphy	FM	PHD	74	Indiana	1979
Nelson, David M.	C-Pr	650-4804	david.nelson	EGI	PHD	75	Oregon	1977
Ghali, Moheb A.	Prof	650-2284	moheb.ghali	CDEF	PHD	67	U Wash	1993
Dean of Graduate School								
Globerman, Steven	Prof	650-7708	steven.globerman	DFIL	PHD	71	NYU	1994
Hansen, Julia L.	Prof	650-3204	julie.hansen	DR	PHD	84	Berkeley	1988
Harder, K. Peter	Prof	650-3920	peter.harder	BNP	PHD	68	Nebraska	1970
Hagen, Daniel A.	Assoc	650-3964	dan.hagen	JEFQ	PHD	83	Berkeley	1988

Henson, Steven E.	Assoc	650-4843	steve.henson	QD	PHD	82	Oregon	1985
Sleeman, Allan G.	Assoc	650-3910	allan.sleeman	CD	PHD	83	Simon Fr	1977
Storer, Paul	Assoc	650-6531	paul.storer	EJ	PHD	92	W Ontario	1996
Durham, Yvonne	Asst	650-2794	durham	A	PHD	94	Arizona	2000
Roelofs, Matthew	Asst	650-3910	matthew.roelofs	DL	PHD	96	Purdue	1997
Hendryson, Mary Ann	Lect	650-4799	mary.ann.hend+	DOF	ABD		Wash St	1989
Hodges, L. Hart	Lect	650-7560	hart.hodges	OQR	PHD	94	U Wash	2000
Whalley, Pamela	Lect	650-4823	pam.whally	DG	ABD		Indiana	1989

Westfield State College Westfield, MA 01086 (413) 572-5590 foma.wsc.mass.edu
Economics Faculty Dept of Econ & Bus Mgt Fax=562-3613 Danielle S. Bramucci

Knipes, Bradford J.	C-Pr	572-5574	b_knipes	Mgt	PHD	88	Mass	1988
Bellico, Russell P.	Prof	572-5312			EDD		Mass	1970
Darrow, John J.	Prof	572-5715			PHD	72	Conn	1971
Gural, Michael L.	Assoc	572-5591			MA		Rutgers	1982
Wagner, John R.	Assoc	572-5697			PHD	77	Temple	1986

Westminster College-PA NewWilmingtonPA 16172-0001 (412) 946-7160 westminster.edu
Economics Faculty Dept of Business & Econ Fax=946-7171 Mrs. Kathleen A. Proctor
Did Not Respond--1999-2000 Listing

Miller, Gail L.	C-Pr	946-7160		Bus	DBA		Kentucky	1983
Fischmar, Daniel E.	Prof	946-7162			PHD	75	S Illinois	1975
Groothuis, Peter A.	Assoc	946-7163			PHD	89	Kentucky	1989

Westminster Cl of Salt Lk Ct Salt Lk City, UT 84105-3697 (801) 488-4220 wcslc.edu
Economics Program Gore School of Business Fax=466-6916
Did Not Respond--1999-2000 Listing

Seidelman, James E.	Dean	488-4222	c.seidel		PHD	86	Utah	1980
Watkins, John P.	C-Pr	488-4221	j-watkin	BNQ	PHD	85	Utah	1984
Chapman, Richard	Prof	488-4228	d-chapma	JNB	PHD	92	Utah	1985
Hansen, Ann	Prof	488-4146	a-hansen	CHL	PHD	81	Utah	1990
Wrotniak, Maria	Assoc	488-4155	m-wrotni	BCO	PHD	80	Lodz	1989

Wheaton College-IL Wheaton, IL 60187-5593 (630) 752-5035 wheaton.edu
Economics Faculty Dept of Business & Econ Fax=752-7037 Mrs. Pat Unander

Howard, Bruce	C-Pr	752-5313	bruce.howard	ABM	PHD	89	N Illinois	1980
Halteman, James	Prof	752-5312	james.halteman	AB	PHD	74	Penn St	1979
Hendrickson Chair								
Hill, Peter J.	Prof	752-5033	p.j.hill	ANPQ	PHD	70	Chicago	1986
George F. Bennett Professor of Economics								
Norton, Seth	Prof	752-5310	seth.norton	GJLM	PHD	82	Chicago	1995
Aldeen Chair								
Ewert, Norman J.	Assoc	752-5311	norman.j.ewert	AF	PHD	76	S Illinois	1973
Tomal, Annette	Assoc	752-7058	annette.tomal	AIM	PHD	95	Illinois	1995

Wheaton College-MA Norton, MA 02766 (508) 285-8200 wheatonma.edu
Economics Faculty Department of Economics Fax=
Did Not Respond--1999-2000 Listing; phone 285-8200

Miller, John A.	C-Pr	Ext 3667	jmiller		PHD	82	Pittsburgh	1979
Gildea, John A.	Prof	Ext 3663	jgildea	EG	PHD	85	Duke	1985
Walgreen, John A.	Prof	Ext 3668	jwalgree		PHD	65	Boston C	1967
Weil, Gordon	Prof	Ext 3666	gweil	FOP	PHD	81	Tufts	1981
Wyss, Brenda	Asst	Ext 3665	bwyss	JTO	PHD	95	Mass	1992

Whitman College Walla Walla, WA 99362 (509) 527-5125 whitman.edu
Economics Faculty Social Sciences Div Fax=527-5026

Hazlett, Denise J.	C-Ac	527-5155	hazlett	EG	PHD	92	Minnesota	1992
Shepherd, James F.	Prof	527-5149	shepherd	HN	PHD	66	U Wash	1971
Crouter, Jan P.	Assoc	527-5174	crouter	KLQ	PHD	85	Illinois	1985
Parcells, R. J. "Pete"	Assoc	527-5267	parcells	CR	PHD	83	SUNY-Bin	1982
Belay, Halefom	Asst	522-6431	belayh	CEO	PHD	96	SUNY-Bin	1996

Whitworth College Spokane, WA 99251 (509) 466-3283 whitworth.edu
Economics Faculty Dept of Economics & Bus Fax=466-3720 Patricia Parker

Schatz, Richard E.	C-Pr	777-4454	rschatz	DEFO	PHD	74	Hawaii	1989
Hagen, Elizabeth	Asst	777-4675	ehagen	AN	ABD		Utah	2000

Wichita State University Wichita, KS 67260-0078 (316) 978-3220 wichita.edu
Department of Economics Barton Sch of Business Fax=978-3308 Mrs. Brenda Lehman

Cheng, Jen-Chi	C-Ac	978-3220	jenchi.cheng		PHD	89	Vanderbilt	1989
Cho, Dong Woo	Prof	978-7089	dong.cho		PHD	73	Illinois	1972
Haydon, Randall B.	Prof	978-3220			PHD	62	Illinois	1970

Hersch, Philip L.	Prof	978-7096	philip.hersch		PHD	82	Ohio St	1983
Perline, Martin M.	Prof	978-7088			PHD	65	Ohio St	1965
Webb, Samuel C.	Prof	978-3220			PHD	68	Kansas	1966
Clark, James E.	Assoc	978-7097	jeclark		PHD	77	Nrthwstrn	1976
Director Center for Economic Education								
Duell, Dennis	Assoc	978-3220			PHD	69	Illinois	1967
Pfannestiel, Maurice	Assoc	978-7093			PHD	67	Okla St	1966
Terrell, William T.	Assoc	978-3220			PHD	70	Vanderbilt	1967
Im, Kyung So	Asst	978-7094			PHD	95	Mich St	1998
Li, Qing	Asst	978-3220			PHD	95	Houston	1995
Messer, Jodi	Asst	978-7092			PHD	00	Kentucky	2000
Miles, William	Asst	978-7085			PHD	98	Illinois	1999
Dimmen, Janet L.	Inst	978-7090			ABD	78	Ohio St	1981

Widener University Chester, PA 19013-5792 (610) 499-4306 widener.edu
Department of Economics School of Business Adm Fax=499-4614 Mrs. Marilyn Lehman
Did Not Respond--1999-2000 Listing

DiAngelo, Joseph A. Jr.	Dean	499-4301		Mgt	EDD	87	Temple	1980
Saltzman, Cynthia J.	H-Ac	499-4326	cynthia.saltz+	EFGO	PHD	86	Maryland	1980
Duggal, Vijaya G.	Prof	499-1176		CEDQ	PHD	67	Harvard	1983
Fuhr, Joseph P.	Prof	499-1172		DIKQ	PHD	81	Temple	1979
Waldauer, Charles	Prof	499-4329		DEHR	PHD	69	Syracuse	1968
Williams, Mary L.	Prof	499-4324		BOMQ	PHD	84	Temple	1982
Zangeneh, Hamid	Prof	499-1140		EFGP	PHD	84	Missouri	1985
Leppel, Karen	Assoc	499-1170		JCT	PHD	80	Princeton	1985

Wilkes University Wilkes-Barre, PA 18766 (570) 408-4725 wilkes1.wilkes.edu
Dept of Business & Economics Sch Bus,Society &PubPol Fax=408-7874 Ms. Sandra L. Rybak
Did Not Respond Again--1997-98 Listing

Bedford, Bonnie C.	Dean	408-4600	bedford	Engl	PHD		SUNY-Bin	8-90
Alves, Jeffrey R.	C-Ac	408-4725	alves	Fnce	PHD	87	Mass	9-97
Taylor, Wagiha A.	Prof	831-4712		EFO	PHD	66	Clark	1969
Seeley, Robert D.	Assoc	831-4717	rseeley	AIJH	PHD	86	Maryland	9-89
Latzko, David	Asst	831-4718	dlatzko	BEFQ	PHD	92	Maryland	9-93

Willamette University Salem, OR 97301-3922 (503) 370-6060 willamette.edu
Department of Economics College of Liberal Arts Fax=375-5398 Fran Wolfe

Cress, Lawrence	Dean	370-6285		Hst	PHD	76	Virginia	
Gray, Jerry	C-Ac	370-6307			PHD	89	Utah	1990
Beaton, C. Russell	Prof	370-6306			PHD	68	Claremont	1971
Hanson, James S.	Prof	370-6316			PHD	71	Stanford	1976
Hibbard, Thomas H.	Prof	370-6317			PHD	67	Claremont	1973
Frew, James R.	Assoc	370-6232			PHD	79	Purdue	1984
Negri, Donald H.	Assoc	370-6326			PHD	86	Michigan	1990
Whiting, Cathleen L.	Assoc	370-6075			PHD	86	U Wash	1986
Boyce, Nathan	Asst	370-6060			PHD	01	Stanford	2001

College of William & Mary Williamsburg, VA 23187-8795 (757) 221-4311 wm.edu
Department of Economics Faculty Arts & Sciences Fax=221-1175 Pat Luke

Moody, Carlisle E.	C-Pr	221-2373	cemood		PHD	70	Conn	1970
Archibald, Robert B.	Prof	221-2366	rbarch		PHD	74	Purdue	1976
Baker, Samuel H. III	Prof	221-2371	shbake		PHD	70	Virginia	1969
Campbell, Donald E.	Prof	221-2383	decamp		PHD	72	Princeton	1989
CSX Professor of Economics Public Policy								
Finifter, David H.	Prof	221-2370	dhfini		PHD	74	Pittsburgh	1973
Garrett, Martin A.	Prof	221-2375	mcgarr		PHD	66	Vanderbilt	1963
Haulman, Clyde A.	Prof	221-1276	ahaul		PHD	69	Fla St	1969
Hausman, William J.	Prof	221-2381	wjhaus		PHD	76	Illinois	1981
Chancellor Professor								
Pereira, Alfredo M.	Prof				PHD	88	Stanford	1995
Abegaz, Berhanu	Assoc	221-2379	bxabeg		PHD	82	Penn	1982
Feldman, David H.	Assoc	221-2372	dhfeld		PHD	82	Duke	1988
Jensen, Eric R.	Assoc	221-2365	erjens		PHD	82	Michigan	1982
Rodgers, William	Assoc	221-2398	wmrodg		PHD	93	Harvard	1993
Edwin L. & Frances L. Cummings Associate Professor								
Anderson, Lisa	Asst	221-2354	lrande		PHD	94	Virginia	1997
Basu, Arnab	Asst	221-1318	akbasu		PHD	97	J Hopkins	1998
Branch, William	Asst	221-2232	wabran		PHD	01	Oregon	2001
Gerlach, Jeff	Asst	221-1379	grgerl		ABD		Indiana	2001
Jaeger, David	Asst	221-2375	djaeger		PHD	95	Michigan	2001
Mellor, Jennifer	Asst	221-2852	jkmell		PHD	96	Maryland	1998
Rodgers, Yana	Asst	221-1276	yvrodg		PHD	93	Harvard	1993
Stafford, Sarah	Asst	221-1317			PHD	98	J Hopkins	1998

William Jewell College	Liberty, MO		64068-1896 (816) 781-7700				william.jewell.edu	
Economics Faculty	Dept of Bus Adm & Econ Fax=415-5027							
Did Not Respond--1999-2000 Listing; phone 781-7700								
Cook, Michael T.	C-Pr	Ext 5699		EF	PHD	83	Vanderbilt	1978
John W. Boatwright Professor of Economics								
William Paterson University	Wayne, NJ		07470-2103 (973) 720-2434				wpunj.edu	
Dept of Economics & Finance	School of Business		Fax=720-2809				Mrs. Angela Mazza	
Leung, Cho Kin	Dean$	720-2650	leungc		PHD	68	NYU	1974
Haroian, Berch	C-Pr	720-2411	harorianb		PHD	72	NYU	1978
Boronico, Jess	Prof	720-2964			PHD	92	Penn	2001
Swanson, Paul	Prof	720-2784	swansonp		PHD	84	Columbia	1982
Ramin, Taghi	Assoc	720-2781	ramint		PHD	86	NYU	1984
Coxwell, Tricia	Asst	720-2958	coxwellt		PHD	00	Tennessee	2000
Gritsch, Martin	Asst	720-2958	gritschm		PHD	00	Tx A&M	2000
Williams College	Williamstown, MA		01267 (413) 597-2476				williams.edu	
Economics Faculty	Department of Economics Fax=597-4045						Kathy Butterfield	
Did Not Respond--1999-2000 Listing								
Winston, Gordon C.	C-Pr	597-2254			PHD	64	Stanford	1963
Orrin Sage Professor of Political Economy								
Hill, Catharine Bond	C-Ac	597-3143			PHD	85	Yale	1985
Bolton, Roger E.	Prof	597-2393			PHD	64	Harvard	1966
William Brough Professor of Economics								
Bradburd, Ralph M.	Prof	597-2300			PHD	76	Columbia	1976
David A. Wells Professor of Political Economy								
Bruton, Henry J.	Emer	597-2357			PHD	52	Harvard	1962
Montiel, Peter J.	Prof	597-2103		EF	PHD	78	MIT	1995
Chair, Center for Development Economics								
Sabot, Richard	Prof	597-3082			DPHI	73	Oxford	
John J. Gibson Emeritus Professor of Economics								
Husbands, Kaye G.	Assoc	597-2469			PHD	90	Harvard	
Brainerd, Elizabeth	Asst	597-2300			PHD	96	Harvard	1996
Conning, Jonathan	Asst	597-2101			PHD	96	Yale	1996
Constantine, Jill M.	Asst	597-2995			PHD	94	Penn	
Frankl, Jennifer	Asst				PHD	96	Berkeley	1997
Gollin, Doug	Asst	597-2449			PHD	96	Minnesota	1996
Samson, Mike	Asst	597-2325			PHD	94	Stanford	
Schulz, Eric	Asst	597-2270			PHD	93	Nrthwstrn	
Siegler, Mark	Asst				PHD	96	Ca-Davis	1997
Zimmerman, David J.	Asst	597-3184			PHD	92	Princeton	1991
Wingate University	Wingate, NC		28174-0157 (704) 233-8148				wingate.edu	
Economics Program	School Business & Econ Fax=233-8146						Ms. Kathryn Rowell	
Pitts, Hampton	Dean				PHD		Miss	1984
Calcagno, Peter	Asst	233-8136			PHD	97	Auburn	1999
Winona State University	Winona, MN		55987-0838 (507) 457-5014				vax2.winona.msus.edu	
Dept of Economics & Finance	College of Business		Fax=457-5697				Jan Tollefson	
Gorman, Kenneth L.	Dean	457-5014	kgorman	BusE	EDD	80	N Illinois	1980
Manrique, Gabriel G.	C-Pr	457-5193	manrique		PHD	82	Notre Dm	1989
Gallegos, Alejandro	Prof	457-5469	agallegos		PHD	86	Wi-Milwa	1988
Gieske, Michael	Prof	457-5171	wngieske		BS		Iowa St	1972
Hyle, Matthew R.	Prof	457-5496	mhyle		PHD	85	Maryland	1988
Kauffman, Daniel E.	Prof	457-5195	kdauffman		PHD	80	Nebraska	1983
Pevas, Mary Ann	Prof	457-5183	mapevas		PHD	90	Notre Dm	1990
Rieder, Mary	Prof				PHD	72		
Salyards, Donald M.	Prof	457-5622	wenonak		PHD	75	Kansas St	1975
Winston-Salem State Univ	Winston-SalemNC		27110 (336) 750-2342				wssu.edu	
Economics Faculty	Div of Business & Econ Fax=750-2335						Sandra L. McCracken	
Did Not Respond--1999-2000 Listing								
King, Arthur T.	D-Pr	750-2330		D	PHD	77	Colorado	8-95
Elassar, Sammy E.	Prof	750-2339			PHD	68	Maryland	1968
Winthrop University	Rock Hill, SC		29733 (803) 323-2186				mail.winthrop.edu	
Dept of Atg, Fin & Econ	College of Business Adm Fax=323-3960							
Weikle, Roger D.	Dean	323-2185	weikler	Mgt	PHD	85	S Carol	1974
Letourneau, C. Angela	C-Pr	323-2679	letournneaua	Atc	DBA	87	La Tech	9-88
Stone, Gary L.	Prof		stoneg	ACD	PHD	80	N Carol	9-75
Seyfried, William L.	Assoc	323-4824	seyfriedw	AMF	PHD	90	Purdue	9-00
Vo, Han X.	Assoc		voh	EF	PHD	79	Tennessee	9-79
Pantuosco, Louis J.	Asst		pantuoscol	EHIJ	PHD	92	Northeas	9-97

U of Wisconsin-Eau Claire Eau Claire, WI 54702-4004 (715) 836-5743 uwec.edu
Department of Economics Sch of Arts & Sciences Fax=836-5071 Mrs. Janna Johnson

Young, Edward G.	C-Pr	836-5743	youngeg	J	PHD	77	Wash St	1977
Carroll, Wayne D.	Prof	836-3388	carrolwd	QE	PHD	84	Minnesota	1986
Hansen, Jan M.	Prof	836-2150	hansenjm	J	PHD	74	Missouri	1985
Kolb, Fredric	Prof	836-3518	kolbfr	ACG	PHD	71	Utah	1971
Oyen, Duane B.	Prof	836-3507	oyend	E	PHD	73	Iowa	1976
Avin, Rose Marie	Assoc	836-4513	avinr	FO	PHD	86	Maryland	1987
DaCosta, Maria N.	Assoc	836-4511	dacostmn	RO	PHD	87	Northeas	1989
Schaffer, David	Asst	836-3513	schaffdl	JEH	PHD	90	MIT	1998
Benesh, Diann	Lect	836-3527	beneshdg	A	ABD		Va Tech	1976

Univ of Wisconsin-Green Bay Green Bay, WI 54311-7001 (920) 465-2355 uwgb.edu
Economics Faculty Department of Economics Fax=465-2791

Pollis, Carol	Dean	465-2476			PHD		Okla St	
Shariff, Ismail	C-Pr	465-2355			PHD	65	Wisconsin	
Kangayappan, Kumaraswamy	Prof	465-2308			PHD	69	Wisconsin	
Murray, James M.	Prof	465-2426			PHD	62	Oregon	1969
Stoll, John R.	Prof	465-2358			PHD	80	Kentucky	
Smith, Larry J.	Assoc	465-2161			PHD	73	Chicago	
Troyer, Michael D.	Assoc	465-2434			PHD	75	Duke	
Nesslein, Thomas S.	Asst	465-2099	nessleit		PHD	92	U Wash	1996

U of Wisconsin-La Crosse La Crosse, WI 54601 (608) 785-8099 mail.uwlax.edu
Department of Economics College of Business Fax=785-6700 Jean M.E. Bonde, Prog Asst
Did Not Respond--1999-2000 Listing

Haupert, Michael J.	C-Pr	785-6863	haupert	AEN	PHD	89	Wash U	1989
Clark, Barry S.	Prof	785-6860	clark_bs	BHOP	PHD	80	Mass	1978
Daellenbach, Lawrence A.	Prof	785-8108	daell_la	ADR	PHD	69	Iowa St	1969
Hampton, Mary B.	Prof	785-6867	hampton	GHIJ	PHD	91	Wi-Milwa	1991
Khandker, A. Wahhab	Prof	785-6862	khandker	ACF	PHD	80	So Meth	1983
Nyatepe-Coo, Akorlie A.	Prof	785-6865	nyatepec	FHO	PHD	89	N Illinois	1989
Sherony, Deith R.	Prof	785-8101	sherony	ACE	PHD	82	Wi-Milwa	1983
Anderson, Donna M.	Assoc	785-6864	ander_dm	DIJ	PHD	93	Mich St	1994
Knowles, Glenn J.	Assoc	785-6861	knowles	CQR	PHD	80	Minnesota	1985
Brooks, T. J.	Asst			CF	PHD	99	Wi-Milwa	1999

Univ of Wisconsin-Madison Madison, WI 53706-1393 (608) 263-2989 ssc.wisc.edu
Department of Economics Col of Letters & Sci Fax=262-2033 Mary Anne Clarke
email: @1=facstaff.wisc.edu @2=lafollette.wisc.edu

Certain, Phillip	Dean	262-2644		Chem				
Durlauf, Steven N.	C-Pr	263-3859	sdurlauf		PHD	86	Yale	1993
Andreoni, James R.	Prof	263-3864	andrdeoni@1		PHD	86	Michigan	1986
Brock, William Allen	Prof	263-6665	wbrock		PHD	69	Berkeley	1981
F. P. Ramsey Professor of Economics								
Che, Yeon-Koo	Prof	262-2819	yche@1		PHD	91	Stanford	1991
Deneckere, Raymond	Prof	263-6724	rideneck@1		PHD	83	Wisconsin	1993
Engel, Charles M.	Prof	262-3697	cengel		PHD	83	Berkeley	2000
Hansen, Bruce	Prof	263-3880	bhansen	CE	PHD	89	Yale	1998
Haveman, Robert H.	Prof	263-7398	haveman@2		PHD	63	Vanderbilt	1970
John Bascom Professor of Economics								
Kennan, John F.	Prof	262-5393	jkennan		PHD	73	Nrthwstrn	1992
Lipman, Barton L.	Prof	262-5373	blipman		PHD	85	Michigan	1998
Lyall, Katharine C.	Prof	262-4048			PHD	69	Cornell	1982
President								
Manuelli, Rodolfo	Prof	263-3877	manuelli		PHD	86	Minnesota	1993
Nichols, Donald A.	Prof	263-2327	nichols@2		PHD	68	Yale	1983
Samuelson, Larry W.	Prof	263-7791	larrysam		PHD	78	Illinois	1990
Staiger, Robert W.	Prof	262-2265	rstaiger@1		PHD	85	Michigan	1993
Taylor, M. Scott	Prof	263-2515	staylor		PHD	91	Queen's	1998
Walker, James R.	Prof	263-3863	walker		PHD	86	Chicago	1987
West, Kenneth D.	Prof	262-0033	kdwest@1		PHD	83	MIT	1988
Wolfe, Barbara L.	Prof	262-0030	bwolfe@1		PHD	73	Penn	1976
Hendel, Igal	Assoc	262-9890	igal		PHD	94	Harvard	2000
Kitamura, Yuichi	Assoc	262-8910	ykitamur		PHD	93	Yale	1998
on leave to University of Pennysylvania								
Montgomery, James D.	Assoc	265-4475	jmontgom		PHD	89	MIT	2000
Neal, Derek A.	Assoc	263-3854	dneal		PHD	92	Virginia	1998
on leave to University of Chicago								
Scholz, J. Karl	Assoc	262-5380	jkscholz@1		PHD	88	Stanford	1988
Brown, Meta	Asst	262-8789			PHD	01	NYU	2001
Haile, Philip	Asst	263-3867	phaile		PHD	96	Nrthwstrn	1996
on leave to University of Chicago								
Keely, Louise	Asst	262-6723	lkeely		PHD	00	LondonEc	2000
Mazzocco, Maurizio	Asst	262-3906			PHD	01	Chicago	2001
Norman, Peter	Asst	263-3886	pnorman@1		PHD	96	Penn	1996
Sandholm, William	Asst	263-3858	whs		PHD	98	Nrthwstrn	1998

Seshadri, Ananth	Asst	262-6196	aseshadr		PHD	00	Rochester	2000
Severinov, Sergei	Asst	262-9891	sseverin		PHD	98	Stanford	1998
Tripathi, Gautam	Asst	262-3804	gtripath		PHD	97	Nrthwstrn	1997
Wallace, Geoffrey	Asst	262-0488	wallace@2		PHD	99	Nrthwstrn	1999

Univ of Wisconsin-Milwaukee Milwaukee, WI 53201 (414) 229-4811 csd.uwm.edu
Department of Economics Col of Letters & Sci Fax=229-3860
Homepage: www.uwm.edu/Dept/Economics

Holahan, William L.	C-Pr	963-5759			PHD	74	Brown	1972
Bahmani-Oskooee, Mohsen	Prof	229-4334			PHD	81	Mich St	1981
Heywood, John S.	Prof	229-4437			PHD	86	Michigan	1986
Kandil, Magda	Prof	229-6493			PHD	88	Wash St	1992
Lee, Tong Hun	Emer	229-4429			PHD	61	Wisconsin	1967
Mamalakis, Markos J.	Prof	229-4449			PHD	62	Berkeley	1967
Niho, Yoshio	Prof	229-4811			PHD	73	Brown	1970
Peoples, James A.	Prof	229-4482			PHD	84	Berkeley	1990
Perlman, Richard W.	Emer	229-4212			PHD	53	Columbia	1964
Schenker, Eric	Emer	229-4235			PHD	57	Florida	1959
Schur, Leon M.	Emer	963-4678			PHD	55	Wisconsin	1964
Arora, Swarnjit S.	Assoc	229-6617			PHD	71	SUNY-Buf	1978
Kim, Sunwoong	Assoc	229-6924			PHD	85	MIT	1989
Meadows, G. Richard	Assoc	229-5883			PHD	72	Wash U	1971
Mohtadi, Hamid	Assoc	229-5334			PHD	82	Michigan	1983
Bender, Keith	Asst	229-4811			PHD	94	Duke	1999
Chakrabarti, Avik	Asst	229-4860			PHD	98	Michigan	1998
Drewianka, Scott	Asst	229-6278			PHD	99	Chicago	2001
Holman, Jill Ann	Asst	229-6536		EF	PHD	97	Colorado	2001
Lei, Vivian	Asst	229-6494			PHD	00	Purdue	2000
Murshid, Antu	Asst	229-4402			PHD	01	Rutgers	2001
Newmann, Rebecca	Asst	229-4347			PHD	00	Colorado	2000
Tahmiscioglu, Kamil	Asst	229-4429			PHD	96	USC	1997

Univ of Wisconsin-Oshkosh Oshkosh, WI 54901-8634 (920) 424-1441 uwosh.edu
Department of Economics Col Letters & Sciences Fax=424-1734

Zimmerman, Michael	Dean	424-1210	mz	Biol	PHD			1992
Gunderson, Ralph O.	C-Pr	424-1473	gundrson	OR	PHD	78	Arkansas	1987
Grunloh, James J.	Prof	424-2441	grunloh	A	PHD	79	Wash U	1969
Lee, Hy Sang	Emer	424-7150	leehs	O	PHD	65	Wisconsin	1962
Brannon, J. Isaac	Assoc	424-7154	brannon	J	PHD	93	Indiana	1994
Burnett, Nancy J.	Assoc	424-1471	burnett	E	PHD	88	UCLA	1994
Hussain, Syed Bashir	Assoc	424-7149	hussain	F	PHD	83	Ca-Rivers	1982
McGee, M. Kevin	Assoc	424-7155	mcgee	H	PHD	83	Ohio St	1982
Robson, Denise A.	Assoc	424-7152	robson	AF	PHD	93	Nebraska	1994
Vanscyoc, Lee	Assoc	424-7153	vanscyoc	AL	PHD	87	Nebraska	1987
Johnson, Marianne	Asst	424-1441		D	PHD	99	Mich St	2001
Mitchell, Milt	Asst	424-1473	mitchell	Q	MA	65	Wisconsin	1967

Univ of Wisconsin-Parkside Kenosha, WI 53141-2000 (414) 595-2316 uwp.edu
Department of Economics College of Arts & Sci Fax=595-2206 Luella Vines

Khan, Farida C.	C-Ac	595-2662	farida.kahn	FO	PHD	90	Maryland	1990
Cloutier, Norman R.	Prof	595-2572	norman.cloutier	DJR	PHD	81	W Virginia	1981
Duetsch, Larry L.	Prof	595-2483	larry.duetsch	DKL	PHD	70	Wisconsin	1969
Keehn, Richard	Prof	595-2259	richard.keehn	EGN	PHD	72	Wisconsin	1969
Kaufman, Dennis A.	Assoc	595-2192	dennis.kaufman	CH	PHD	87	Kansas	1987
Rosenberg, Richard E.	Assoc	595-2268	richard.rosen+	FOP	PHD	70	Wisconsin	1969

U of Wisconsin-Platteville Platteville, WI 53818-3099 (608) 342-1550 uwplatt.edu
Department of Economics C of Liberal Arts & Edu Fax=342-1036 Carol Gill

Ifediora, John O.	C-Ac	342-1051	ifediora		PHD	88	Il-Chicago	1988
Al Yasiri, Kahtan A.	Prof	342-1822	alyasiri		PHD	65	Iowa St	1965
Liska, Terrence L.	Prof	342-1550	liska		PHD	82	Wisconsin	1980
Simonson, John C.	Prof	342-1560	simonson		PHD	72	Wisconsin	1966
Soofi, Abdollah S.	Assoc	342-1570	soofi		PHD	81	Ca-Rivers	1980
Dehghan, Farhad	Asst	342-1755	dehghan		PHD	84	Illinois	1985
Peckham, Brian W.	Asst	342-1752	peckham		PHD	79	Wisconsin	1987

U of Wisconsin-River Falls River Falls, WI 54022-5001 (715) 425-3991 uwrf.edu
Department of Economics School of Bus & Econ Fax=425-3536 Ms. Eunice Filkins

Nemecek, Barbara	Dean	425-3335	busad	Mktg	PHD	87	Minnesota	2001
Potts, Glenn T.	C-Pr	425-3125	glenn.t.potts	E	PHD	76	Iowa St	1976
Brux, Jacqueline M.	Prof	425-3991	jacqueline.m.b+	O	PHD	83	Michigan	1986
Cowen, Janna L.	Prof	425-3519	janna.l.cowen	JL	PHD	79	Nebraska	1979
Eftekhari, Hossein	Prof	425-3158	hossein.eftakari	DC	PHD	85	Nebraska	1985
Schultz, Brian L.	Prof	425-3125	brian.l.schultz	C	PHD	80	Notre Dm	1979
Tabesh, Hamid	Prof	425-3158	hamid.tabesh	EF	PHD	87	Iowa St	1988
Walker, John	Prof	425-3519	john.r.walker	JB	PHD	89	Utah	1990
Ngoboka, Pascal	Assoc	425-3158	pascal.t.ngoboka	HP	PHD	87	Wi-Milwa	1990

U of Wisconsin-Stevens Point — Stevens Point WI 54481-3897 (715) 346-2728 — uwsp.edu
Div of Business & Economics — Col Letters & Sciences Fax=346-4215 — J. Cayo

Paul, Justus F.	Dean	346-4224		Hist	PHD	66	Nebraska	1966
Mullins, Gary	C-As	436-3906		Mgt	PHD	94	Wash U	8-94
Cray, Randy F.	Prof	346-2537			PHD	86	Kansas St	8-86
Palmini, Dennis J.	Prof	346-3875			PHD	75	Illinois	1980
Weiser, Lawrence A.	Prof	346-3310			PHD	67	Wisconsin	1972
Christie, Darrell A.	Assoc	346-2018			MS		Illinois	1964
Hofer, Tracy	Asst	346-2728			PHD	97	Texas	1999
Wallace, H. Scott	Asst	346-4358			PHD	99	Conn	2000

Univ of Wisconsin-Superior — Superior, WI 54880-4500 (715) 394-8209 — uwsuper.edu
Economics Faculty — Dept of Bus & Economics Fax=394-8180 — Sharon McCusker

Trudeau, Gregory P.	C-Pr	394-8209	gtrudeau	Atg	EDD	01	Minnesota	1988
Beam, Robert D.	Prof	394-8302			PHD	80	Cincinnati	1980

U of Wisconsin-Whitewater — Whitewater, WI 53190-1790 (262) 472-1361 — mail.uww.edu
Department of Economics — Col of Business & Econ Fax=472-4863 — Christie Kornhoff

Bhargava, Ashok	C-Pr	472-4704	bhargava		PHD	75	Wisconsin	1970
Dominguez, John R.	Prof	472-5586	dominguj		PHD	71	MIT	1988
Domitrz, Joseph S.	Prof		domitzj		PHD	71	S Illinois	1976
Kim, Kirk Y.	Prof	472-5576	kimk		PHD	70	Utah	1969
Laurent, Jerome K.	Prof	472-4715	laurentj		PHD	73	Indiana	1965
Marks, Denton	Prof	472-5576	marksd		PHD	81	Princeton	1990
Parks, Susan	Prof	472-1747	parkss		PHD	82	Purdue	1980
Director, Center for Economic Education								
Snow, Sandra L.	Prof	472-1361	snows		PHD	76	Missouri	1981
Glosser, Stuart M.	Assoc	472-5580	glossers		PHD	85	Tx-Austin	1985
Schweigert, Thomas E.	Assoc	472-5582	schweigt		PHD	90	Wisconsin	1984
Anstine, Jeffrey	Asst	472-5583	anstinej		PHD	96	Kentucky	1999
Heinrich, Jeffery	Asst	472-4046	heinricj					
Skidmore, Mark	Asst	472-1354	skidmorm	H	PHD	94	Colorado	1998

Wittenberg University — Springfield, OH 45501-0720 (937) 327-7928 — wittenberg.edu
Economics Faculty — Department of Economics Fax=327-6340 — Norma Kettler

Wishart, David M.	C-Pr	327-7303	dwishart	ABN	PHD	85	Illinois	1983
Ankrom, Jeff A.	Prof	327-7930	jankrom	AEG	PHD	82	Notre Dm	1982
Goulet, Janet C.	Prof	327-7929		AJM	PHD	75	Notre Dm	1975
Gwinn, Lawrence	Assoc	327-7934	lgwinn	ACEF	PHD	83	Kansas	1988
Tiffany, Frederick G.	Assoc	327-7933	ftiffany	ACDL	PHD	88	Penn	1987
Frost, Marcia J.	Asst	327-7935	mfrost	AJMO	PHD	95	Penn	2001

Wofford College — Spartanburg, SC 29303-3663 (864) 597-4570 — wofford.edu
Economics Faculty — Department of Economics Fax=597-4019
Did Not Respond--1999-2000 Listing

Stephenson, Matthew A.	C-Pr	597-4570		DI N	PHD	65	Tulane	1970
T. B. Stackhouse Professor of Economics								
Wallace, Richard M.	Prof	597-4572	wallacerm	ABK	PHD	81	S Carol	1982
Machovec, Frank M.	Assoc	597-4586		EFP	PHD	86	NYU	1988
McArthur, John R.	Assoc	597-4571	mcarthurjr	EHKQ	PHD	91	Claremont	1990

Woodbury University — Burbank, CA 91510-7846 (818) 767-0888 — woodbury.edu
Economics Faculty — Sch of Business and Mgt Fax=504-9320 — Vera Hernandez
Homepage: www.woodbury.edu/faculty/ebgendel

Gendel, Eugene B.	Prof	767-0888	eb.gendel	AJDE	PHD	79	Boston U	7-94
Afshar, Tahmoures A.	Asst	767-0888	ted.afshar	FGM	PHD	94	Indiana	1-95

The College of Wooster — Wooster, OH 44691-2263 (330) 263-2302 — acs.wooster.edu
Economics Faculty — Department of Economics Fax=263-2614

Burnell, James D.	C-Pr	263-2308	burnell		PHD	77	Illinois	1977
Burnell, Barbara S.	Prof	263-2417	bburnell		PHD	77	Illinois	1977
Sell, John W.	Prof	263-2383	jwsell		PHD	81	UCLA	1981
Wellington, Alison J.	Asst	263-2407	awellington	J	PHD	90	Michigan	1997
Werner, James M.	Asst	263-2309	jwerner		PHD	96	Utah	1999

Worcester State College — Worcester, MA 01602-2597 (508) 929-8091 — worcester.edu
Economics Faculty — Dept of Bus Adm & Econ Fax=929-8048 — Esther Golub 793-8091

Jain, Renuka	C-Pr	793-8091	rjain		PHD	85	McGill	1985
Lee, Wei Pang	Assoc	793-8101			PHD	87	Georgia	
Trimby, F. Stephen	Assoc	793-8093	strimby		ABD			1970
O'Brien, William F. Jr.	Asst	793-8093	wobrien		PHD	89	Northeas	1997

Wright State University Dayton, OH 45435-0001 (937) 775-3070 wright.edu
Department of Economics Col of Business & Admin Fax=775-2441 Penny Stacy, Fern Freeman
Homepage: www.wright.edu/coba/econ/

Farmer, Berkwood M.	Dean	775-2377		Q	PHD	70	N Car St	7-01
Traynor, Thomas L.	C-Ac	775-3070	thomas.traynor	CL	PHD	88	Purdue	1988
Blair, John	Prof	775-3484	john.blair	HR	PHD	74	W Virginia	1981
Fichtenbaum, Rudy H.	Prof	775-3085	rudy.fichten+	CIJ	PHD	80	Missouri	1980
Premus, Robert	Prof	775-3069	robert.premus	EOR	PHD	75	Lehigh	1975
Renas, Stephen M.	Prof	775-3030	stephen.renas	EM	PHD	71	Geo St	1971
Sav, Thomas G.	Prof	775-3306	tom.sav	DH	PHD	81	Geo Wash	1985
Swaney, James A.	Prof	775-2769	james.swaney	BPQ	PHD	79	Colo St	1979
Dung, Tran H.	Assoc	775-2295	tran.dung	DF	PHD	78	Syracuse	1982
Hopkins, Barbara	Assoc	775-2080	barbara.hopkins	FOP	PHD	92	Maryland	1995
Olson, Paulette I.	Assoc	775-2409	paulette.olson	BJN	PHD	89	Utah	1988
Osborne, Evan	Assoc	775-4599	evan.osborne	FK	PHD	93	UCLA	1995
Endres, Carole R.	Lect	775-2823	carole.endres	AFG	MS	87	Wright St	

University of Wyoming Laramie, WY 82071-3985 (307) 766-2178 uwyo.edu
Dept of Economics & Finance College of Business Fax=766-5090 Jane H. Scheurman

Griffin, Kenyon	Dean$							
Phillips, Owen R.	C-Pr	766-2195	exper	DK	PHD	80	Stanford	1985
Barber, Edward	Prof	766-2358	ebarber		PHD	86	Birkbeck	2000
Birch, John W.	Emer	766-4215	birch	1995	PHD	62	J Hopkins	1964
Cramer, Curtis A.	Prof	766-3384	ccramer	BK	PHD	66	Maryland	1966
Crocker, Thomas D.	Prof	766-6423	tcrocker	Q	PHD	67	Missouri	1975
D'Arge, Ralph C.	Emer	766-6425		1996	PHD	69	Cornell	1975
Mason, Charles F.	Prof	766-5336	bambuzlr	DK	PHD	83	Berkeley	1982
Morgan, William E.	Prof	766-6315	wemorgan	H	PHD	64	Colorado	1968
Shogren, Jason F.	Prof	766-5430	jramses	Q	PHD	86	Wyoming	1995
Tschirhart, John T.	Prof	766-2356	jtsch	DK	PHD	75	Purdue	1985
Sterbenz, Frederic P.	Assoc	766-2201	sterbenz	EG	PHD	81	Penn	1981
Godby, Robert	Asst	766-3843	rgodby		PHD	97	McMaster	1997
Hultberg, Patrik	Asst	766-3143	hultberg		PHD	98	Rice	1998

Xavier University Cincinnati, OH 45207-3212 (513) 745-3075 xu.edu
Dpt Econ & Human Resources Col of Business Admin Fax=745-3692 Ms. Izola White

Webb, Michael A.	Dean	745-3528		FO	PHD	80	Illinois	1997
Rashed, Jamal A.	C-Pr	745-2938		ACFO	PHD	88	So Meth	1989
Bertaux, Nancy E.	Prof	745-2930		ABJN	PHD	87	Michigan	1985
Donnelly, Lawrence I.	Prof	745-3054		AJM	PHD	64	Cincinnati	1956
Marmo, Michael	Prof	745-3056		J	PHD	71	Illinois	1970
Zimmerman, Robert O.	Prof	745-3075		ADEF	PHD	69	SUNY-Buf	1970
Blackwell, Melanie A.	Assoc	745-2037		ACQ	PHD	88	Kentucky	1987
Cobb, Steven A.	Assoc	745-3053		AEHR	PHD	74	Brown	1984
Rankin, Carol A.	Assoc	745-2932		ADJ	PHD	80	Houston	1984
Weinberg, David R.	Assoc	745-3052		ARP	PHD	73	Berkeley	1980
Queneau, Herve'	Asst	745-3062			PHD	96	ParisDaup	1996
Shahinpoor, Nasrin	Asst	745-3058			PHD	01	Cincinnati	2001
D'Angelo, James		745-3000			MA			2001

Yale University New Haven, CT 06520-8268 (203) 432-3576 yale.edu
Economics Faculty Department of Economics Fax=432-5779 Pam Warner
Did Not Respond--1999-2000 Listing; email: @1=econ.yale.edu

Srinivasan, T. N.	C-Pr	436-3630	t.srinivasan	FO	PHD	62	Yale	1980
Andrews, Donald W. K.	Prof	432-3698	dandrews@1	C	PHD	82	Berkeley	1982
Berry, Steven T.	Prof	432-3556	steveb@1		PHD	89	Wisconsin	1988
Bewley, Truman F.	Prof	432-3719	truman.bewley	D	PHD	70	Berkeley	1983
Director of Graduate Studies								
Brainard, William C.	Prof	432-3571	william.brainard	DE	PHD	63	Yale	1981
Broude, Henry W.	Prof	432-0556		N	PHD	54	Harvard	1978
Brown, Donald J.	Prof	432-6934	donald.brown					
Director of Undergraduate Studies								
Evenson, Robert E.	Prof	432-3626	robert.everson	DO	PHD	68	Chicago	1977
Fair, Ray C.'	Prof	432-3715	fair@1	E	PHD	68	MIT	1974
Geanakoplos, John	Prof	432-3397	john.geanakoplos	CD	PHD	80	Harvard	
Hamada, Koichi	Prof	432-3610	koichi.hamada	F	PHD	65	Yale	1986
Jaynes, Gerald D.	Prof	432-3586	gerald.jaynes	N	PHD	76	Illinois	
Klevorick, Alvin K.	Prof	432-3705	alvin.klevorick	K	PHD	67	Princeton	1975
Levin, Richard C.	Prof	432-2550	richard.levin	O	PHD	74	Yale	1974
President Yale University								
Linton, Oliver	Prof	432-3699	linton@1	C	PHD	91	Berkeley	
Mendelsohn, Robert	Prof	432-5128	robert.mendels+		PHD	78	Yale	1984
Montias, J. Michael	Emer	432-3247		N	PHD	58	Columbia	1963
Morris, Stephen	Prof	432-6903	stephen.morris	D	PHD	91	Yale	1998
Nalebuff, Barry J.	Prof	432-5968	barry.nalebuff	D	DPH	82	Oxford	1989
Nordhaus, William D.	Prof	432-3587	nordhaus@1	E	PHD	67	MIT	1967
Pearce, David G.	Prof	432-3583	pearce@1	D	PHD	83	Princeton	

Peck, Merton J.	Prof	432-3558	mjpeck@1	LO	PHD	54	Harvard	1978
Phillips, Peter C. B.	Prof	432-3695	peter.phillips	C	PHD	74	London	
Ranis, Gustav	Prof	432-3632	gustav.ranis	O	PHD	56	Yale	1960
Rust, John P.	Prof	432-3569	john.rust		PHD	83	MIT	
Scarf, Herbert E.	Prof	432-3693	herbert.scarf	C	PHD	54	Princeton	1963
Schultz, T. Paul	Prof	432-3620	paul.schultz	J	PHD	66	MIT	1975
Shiller, Robert J.	Prof	432-3708	shiller@1	D	PHD	72	MIT	1982
Shubik, Martin	Prof	432-3704	martin.shubik	G	PHD	53	Princeton	
Sims, Christopher A.	Prof	432-3560	sims@1	D	PHD	68	Harvard	
Udry, Christopher R.	Prof	432-3637	udry	O	PHD	91	Yale	1998
Guinnane, Timothy J.	Assoc	432-3616	timothy.guinn+	N	PHD	87	Stanford	
Hunt, Jennifer A.	Assoc	432-3714	jennifer.hunt	J	PHD	92	Harvard	1992
Lanjouw, Jean Olson	Assoc	432-3568	lanjouw@1	CO	PHD	92	LondonEc	
Polak, Benjamin	Assoc	432-3590	polak@1	N	PHD	92	Harvard	
Bergemann, Dirk	Asst	432-3592	dirk@1		PHD	94	Penn	
Boozer, Michael A.	Asst	432-3623	maboozer@1	DJ	PHD	94	Princeton	1993
Corsetti, Giancurlo	Asst	432-3562	corsetti@1	F	PHD	92	Yale	1998
Hall, George	Asst	432-3566	george.hall	E	PHD	96	Chicago	1996
Krieger, Stefan	Asst		stefan.krieger	E	PHD	99	Chicago	1997
Levy, Philip I.	Asst	432-3638	levy@1	DF	PHD	94	Stanford	
Moscarini, Giuseppe	Asst	432-3596	giuseppe.mosc+	E	PHD	96	MIT	1996
Pesendorfer, Martin	Asst	432-3549	martionp@1	L	PHD	95	Nrthwstrn	9-95
Stevens, Ann Huff	Asst	432-3628	ann.stevens	J	PHD	95	Michigan	1995
Timmins, Christopher	Asst	432-9901	christopher.ti+	LH	PHD	97	Stanford	1997

Yeshiva University New York, NY 10033-3299 (212) 960-5214 yu1.yu.edu
Department of Economics Yeshiva College Fax=960-5245 Cecell Levinson
Did Not Respond Again--1997-98 Listing

Adler, Norman	Dean	960-5214	Psyc	PHD	58	Wisconsin	
Levine, Aaron	C-Pr	960-5214		PHD	81	NYU	
Samson and Halina Bitensky Professor of Economics							
Kanovsky, Eliyahu	Prof	960-5214		PHD	61	Columbia	
Ludwig Jesselson Chair in Economics; spring only							
Horowitz, Avery M.	Assoc	960-5214		PHD	84	CUNY	1986
Assistant Dean							
Arluck, Gregory M.	Asst	960-5214		PHD	87	CUNY	
Gutman, Nancy	Adjln	960-5214		BA	82	Barnard	

York College of Pennsylvania York, PA 17405-7199 (717) 815-1423 ycp.edu
Economic Faculty Dept of Business Adm Fax=849-1619 Julie Sterner

Meisenhelter, Mary C.	C-As			Mgt	PHD		Geo Wash	1996
Landis, Brook I.	Assoc	815-1416	blandis		PHD	74	Cornell	
Scalet, Kenneth G.	Assoc	815-1415	kscalet		MBA		St Johns	1970
Slaysman, Kenneth	Assoc	815-1708	kslaysma		PHD		Penn St	

Youngstown State University Youngstown, OH 44555-0001 (330) cc.ysu.edu
Department of Economics Col of Arts & Sciences Fax= Dena Kay Crissman

Brothers, Barbara	Dean			Engl	PHD	73	Kent St	
Porter, Tod S.	C-Pr	742-3431	tsporter		PHD	84	Syracuse	1984
Bee, Richard H.	Prof	742-1677	rhbee		DBA	76	Kent St	1966
Liu, Yih-Wu	Prof	742-1674	ywliu		PHD	68	S Illinois	1968
Mehra, Jadish C.	Prof	742-1681			PHD	68	SUNY-Buf	1965
Milley, Donald J.	Prof	742-1676			PHD	74	SUNY-Buf	1969
Petruska, Dennis A.	Prof	742-1679			PHD	84	Ohio St	1984
Morris, Clyde D.	Assoc	742-3434			PHD	87	Case Wes	1970
Riley, Teresa M.	Assoc	742-1675	triley		PHD	84	Syracuse	1984
Usip, Ebenge E.	Assoc	742-1682	eeusip		PHD	84	Conn	1985
Ruffer, Rochelle L.	Asst	742-1673	rlruffer	DH	PHD	94	Wisconsin	1995

McMaster University Hamilton Canada ON L8S 4M4 (905) Ext24630 mcmaster.ca
Finance & Bus Econ Area DeGroote Sch of Bus Fax=521-8995 Ms. Kathy Matthews
Did Not Respond Again--1997-98 Listing; phone: 525-9140 Ext 24630

Mountain, Dean C.	C-Pr	Ext23988	mountain	CD	PHD	79	W Ontario	1987
Chamberlain, Trevor W.	Prof	Ext23980	chambert	G	PHD	86	Toronto	1985
Chan, M. W. Luke	Prof	Ext29648	chanmwl	DE	PHD	78	McMaster	1981
Cheung, C. Sherman	Prof	Ext23968	scheung	G	PHD	81	Illinois	1981
Krinsky, Itzhak	Prof	Ext23984	krinsky	G	PHD	83	McMaster	1982
Kwan, Clarence C. Y.	Prof	Ext23797	kwanc	CG	PHD	79	Toronto	1979
Deaves, Richard W.	Assoc	Ext23976	deaves	EG	PHD	87	Toronto	1987
Lee, Jason	Assoc	Ext23987	jasonlee	G	PHD	91	Alberta	1990
Thomas, Hugh A.	Assoc	Ext23983	thomas	G	PHD	91	NYU	1991

Bogazici University Bebek, Instanbul Turkey 90212 287-2453 boun.edu.tr
Economics Faculty Department of Economics Fax=287-2453
Did Not Respond Again--1997-98 Listing; phone 90 212 263 1540

Ozmucur, Suleyman	C-Pr	Ext 1505	ozmucur	CEL	PHD	76	Istanbul	1976
Aleskerov, Fuad	Prof	Ext 1803	aleskero	C	PHD	81	Moscow	1995
Balcim, Metin	Prof	Ext 1807	balcim	EH	PHD	73	NYU	1973
Behar, Cem	Prof	Ext 1809	behar	BJT	PHD	72	Paris	1977
Bubik, Osman	Prof	Ext 1508	bubik	QR	PHD	73	Ca-Rivers	1974
Bugray, Ayse	Prof	Ext 1803	bugray	BO	PHD	80	McGill	1985
Cizakca, Murat	Prof	Ext 1807	cizak	N	PHD	79	Penn	1975
Karatas, Cevat	Prof	Ext 1518	karatas	ACDH	PHD	70	Glasgow	1985
Kayalir, Resad	Prof	Ext 1803	kayalir	BE	PHD	76	Istanbul	1972
Kaytaz, Mehmet	Prof	Ext 1808	kaytaz	CE	PHD	78	Nottinghm	1978
Koymen, Oya	Prof	Ext 1524	koymen	NQ	PHD	67	Strathcl	1976
Onis, Ziya	Prof	Ext 1804	onis	AEO	PHD	83	Manchester	1984
Sertel, Murat	Prof	Ext 1522	sertel	AC	PHD	71	MIT	1979
Adaman, Fikret	Assoc	Ext 1809	adaman	BDPQ	PHD	93	Manchester	1993
Erzan, Refik	Assoc	Ext 1809	erzan	F	PHD	83	Stockholm	1992
Evcimen, Gunar	Assoc	Ext 1808	evcimen	FO	PHD	79	Istanbul	1980
Akcay, Cevdet	Asst	Ext 1802	akcay	CE	PHD	92	CUNY	1992
Alper, Emre	Asst	Ext 1526	alper	CEFG	PHD	95	Geotown	1995
Bayazitoglu, Berna	Asst	Ext 1505	bernab	CDO	PHD	96	Cornell	1996
Ercan, Hakan	Asst	Ext 1591	ercanh	CHJ	PHD	94	Iowa	1994
Karasulu, Meral	Asst	Ext 1800	karasulu	CEF	PHD	95	Boston C	1995
Ozar, Semsa	Asst	Ext 1519	ozar	J	PHD	90	Wirtschaf	1990
Sari, Osman	Asst	Ext 1804	sario	FG	PHD	93	CUNY	1993
Zenginobuz, Unal	Asst	Ext 1505	zengin	AHLP	PHD	96	Penn	1996

INSEAD Fontainebleau France 33-1 60724212 insead.fr
Economic & Political Sc Area Business School 77305 Fax=60745500 Brigette Pernet
Homepage: www.insead.fr/facultyresearch/economics
email @1=econ.insead.fr @2=cedep.inseaf.fr @3=insead.edu.fr

Borges, Antonio	Dean			EQA	PHD	80	Stanford	9-93
Gabel, H. Landis	Dean$	60724033	landis.gabel	DHU	PHD	77	Penn	9-82
MBA Dean								
Ayres, Robert	Emer	60724011	robert.ayres	OU	PHD	58	London	9-92
Chairman Sandoz Chair on Environment								
Kapstein, Ethan	Prof	60724521	ethan.kapstein	V	PHD	86	Medford	2001
Michaud, Claude	Prof	64224805	michaud@2	O	D		Bordeaux	8-70
CEDEP Director								
Roller, Lars-Hendrik	Prof	60724251		L	PHD	87	Penn	9-87
Story, Jonathan	Prof	60724435	jonathan.story		PHD	73	J Hopkins	7-74
Van Zandt, Timothy	Prof	60724981	tvz@1	DP	PHD	89	Penn	9-98
Vives, Xavier	Prof		xavier.vives	DGL	PHD	83	Berkeley	2001
Walter, Ingo	Prof	60724393	ingo.walter	LEFG	PHD	66	NYU	1999
Cadot, Olivier	Assoc	60724452	cadot		PHD	89	Princeton	9-89
Fatas, Antonio	Assoc	60724419	fatas@1	EF	PHD	93	Harvard	1-94
Mihov, Ilian	Assoc	60724434	mihov@1	DE	PHD	96	Princeton	9-96
Webber, Douglas	Assoc	7995332	webber	V	PHD	85	Essex	1-91
Perrotti, Liesa	Asst	60724478	luisa.perrotti	V				9-97
Sarafidis, Yianis	Asst		yianis.sarafidis	DF	PHD	01	Yale	2001
Strauss-Kahn, Vanessa	Asst		v+.strauskahn	FJ	PHD	00	NYU	2001
Traca, Daniel	Asst	7995340	traca@3		PHD	96	Columbia	9-96
Veldkamp, Laura	Asst		laura.veldkamp	EGV	PHD	01	Stanford	2001

University of Lancaster LancasterLA1 4YX England 01524 594230 lancaster.ac.uk
Economics The Management School Fax=594244

Fildes, Robert A.	Dean$		r.fildes	Mgt	PHD		Calif	
Kirby, Maurice W.	H-Pr				PHD		Sheffield	
Balasubramanyam, V. N.	Prof				PHD	70	Illinois	
Johnes, Geraint	Prof				PHD	87	Lancaster	

Sapsford, David	Prof				PHD		Leeds	
Taylor, James	Prof				PHD		Lancaster	
Rothschild, Robert	Read				MA		Capetown	
Bradley, Steven	SLect				PHD		Lancaster	
Rose, Mary B.	SLect				PHD		Manchest	
Snowden, Peter N.	SLect				PHD		Leeds	
Westall, Oliver M.	SLect				BSC		London	
Whittenlas, John	SLect				PHD		Capetown	
Ingham, Hilary C.	SLect			JCD	PHD		Glasgow	
Read, Robert A.	Lect				PHD		Reading	
Steele, Gerald R.	Lect				MA		Sheffield	
Elliott, Caroline	Lect				PHD		Manchester	

Manchester Inst Sci & Tech Manchester, UK M60 1QD 44-61 200-3438 umist.ac.uk
Economics Department Manchester Sch of Mgt Fax=200-3505 Mrs. June Hall
Did Not Respond Again--1997-98 Listing

Little, Dale	H	200-3465	dale.little	Mktg				
Bosworth, Derek L.	Prof	200-3438	bosworth	JOD	PHD		Warwick	1992
Bowe, Michael A.	Lect	200-3407	bowe	EFG	PHD	89	Carleton	1993
Duffy, Martyn H.	Lect	200-3483	duffy	EC	PHD	95	Manchest	1972
Eliot, Stuart J.	Lect	200-3480	eliot	DMA	MA		Manchest	1974
Harrald, Paul D.	Lect	200-3488	harrard	BCDL	PHD		Simon Fr	1994
Jones, Trefor T.	Lect	200-3484	jones	HLR	PHD		Dundee	1976
Simpson, Paul	Lect	200-3485	simpson	LC	MA		Newcastle	1984

ALPHABETICAL BY INDIVIDUAL

Name	Rank	Location	Area	Degree			Start
A'Hearn, Brian	Asst	Frank & Mars		PHD	94	Berkeley	1999
Aadland, David	Asst	Utah State	CE	PHD	97	Oregon	1997
Abadeer, Adel	Assoc	Calvin		PHD	92	Boston U	1999
Abdel-Rahman, Hesham M.	Assoc	New Orleans		PHD	87	Penn	1987
Abdulahad, Faraj	C-Ac	Manhattan	F	PHD	68	Boston C	1970
Abdulkadiroglu, Atila	Asst	Columbia		PHD	01	Rochester	2001
Abdullah, Dewan A.	Prof	E Michigan		PHD	84	Kentucky	1988
Abegaz, Berhanu	Assoc	Wm & Mary		PHD	82	Penn	1982
Abel, David R.	Asst	Mankato St	AE	ABD		Minnesota	1969
Abernathy, Lewis M.	Prof	North Texas	J	PHD	67	Oklahoma	1963
Abraham, Elizabeth	Asst	Gustavus Ado		ABD		Arizona	1997
Abraham, Fred J.	H-Pr	No Iowa	AEHK	PHD	73	Oregon	1973
Abrahamsson, Bernhard J.	Retir	Wis-Superior		PHD	66	Wisconsin	1989
Abrams, Burton A.	Prof	Delaware	EH	PHD	74	Ohio St	1974
Abrams, Eric	Assoc	Hawaii Pacif		PHD	97	Iowa	1997
Aburachis, Abdelrahman E.	Prof	Gannon	G	PHD	72	Pittsburgh	
Acemoglu, Daron	Assoc	MIT	J	PHD	92	LondonEc	1993
Ackert, Lucy F.	Prof	Kennesaw St	GM	PHD	90	Emory	2000
Acs, Zoltan J.	Prof	Baltimore		PHD	80	New Sch	1989
Adaman, Fikret	Assoc	Bogazici	BDPQ	PHD	93	Manchester	1993
Adamovich, Ljubisa S.	Prof	Florida St	E	PHD	61	Belgrade	1967
Adams, Donald R. Jr.	Prof	W Virginia	N	PHD	67	Penn	1981
Adams, Earl W. Jr.	C-Pr	Allegheny	AEGH	PHD	71	MIT	1972
Andrew Wells Robertson Professor of Economics							
Adams, F. Gerard	Prof	Pennsylvania		PHD	56	Michigan	1961
Adams, Jack E.	Retir	Ark-Ltl Rock		PHD	75	Okla St	1980
Adams, James D.	Prof	Florida	OJ	PHD	76	Chicago	1979
Adams, Jean W.	Prof	Iowa State	L	PHD	73	Illinois	1972
Adams, John	Retir	Northeastern		PHD	68	Tx-Austin	1990
Adams, John P.	Retir	Cal Poly-SLO		PHD	72	Claremont	1970
Adams, Robert J.	Assoc	Edinboro		PHD	71	Penn St	1977
Adams, Ronald G.	Prof	CS-Chico	ACKR	PHD	75	Kansas St	1971
Adams, Roy Dean	Prof	Iowa State	HE	PHD	72	Illinois	1972
Adams, Walter	Retir	Michigan St		PHD	47	Yale	1947
Distinguished Professor; President Emeritus							
Adams, William James	Prof	Michigan		PHD	73	Harvard	1973
Adamson, Dwight W. (Bill)	Assoc	So Dakota St	E	PHD	88	Wash St	1989
Adcock, Marvin	Inst	Alabama A&M					
Addison, John T.	Prof	So Carolina		PHD	71	London	
Addus, Abdussalam A.	Assoc	N Carol A&T		PHD	82	Penn St	1980
Adelman, Irma	Retir	Cal-Berkeley		PHD	55	Berkeley	1979
Adelstein, Richard P.	Prof	Wesleyan-CT	K	PHD	75	Penn	1975
Adibi, Esmael	Prof	Chapman	AEFC	PHD	80	Claremont	1978
Director, A. Gary Anderson Center for Economic Research; Anderson Chair							
Adie, Douglas K.	Prof	Ohio Univ	BGM	PHD	68	Chicago	1968
Adjibolosoo, Senyo	Prof	Pt Loma Naz	AFO	PHD	87	Simon Fr	2000
Adkins, Lee C.	Prof	Oklahoma St	C	PHD	88	LSU	1988
Adkins, Roger L.	Prof	Marshall		PHD	81	Kansas St	1981
Adler, Michael	Retir	Columbia		DBA	68	Harvard	1968
Adler, Renatte K.	Prof	San Diego St	Q	PHD	79	New Mex	1982
Adrahams, Niradete	Asst	Missouri So		PHD			
Adrangi, Bahram	Prof	Portland	CDFR	PHD	82	Orogon	1982
Adrisson, Rick	Asst	New Mex St	FH	PHD	94	Nebraska	8-94
Adsera, Alicia	Asst	Ill-Chicago	EF	PHD	96	Boston U	1999
Aduddell, Robert M.	Retir	Loyola-Chicg		PHD	71	Nrthwstrn	1965
Adusei, Edward O.	Assoc	Longwood		PHD	88	Va Tech	1992
Aerni, April Laskey	Assoc	Nazareth		PHD	87	Cincinnati	
Afifi, Ashraf S.	Prof	Ferris State	ADH	PHD	83	Kansas	1980
Afrasiabi, Ahmad	Assoc	Allegheny	BCQR	PHD	85	W Virginia	1985
Afshar, Tahmoures A.	Asst	Woodbury	FGM	PHD	94	Indiana	1-95
Afxentiou, Diamando	Asst	NY Inst Tech		PHD	90	W Virginia	1990
Agahro, Steve B.	Deces	Jackson St		PHD	91	Denver	1988
Agarwal, Vinod	C-Pr	Old Dominion		PHD	86	Ca-SnBarb	
Agbetsiafa, Douglas K.	Prof	Ind-So Bend	AGO	PHD	80	Notre Dm	1980
Agbeyegbe, Terence	Prof	CUNY-Hunter		PHD	83	Essex	1994
Agesa, Jacqueline	Asst	Marshall		PHD	96	Wi-Milwa	2000
Agesa, Richard	Asst	Marshall		PHD	96	Wi-Milwa	2000
Aghion, Philippe	Prof	Harvard		PHD		Harvard	
Agnello, Richard J.	Assoc	Delaware	C	PHD	70	J Hopkins	1968
Agnihotri, Krisna	Asst	Southern	A	MA	57	Punjab	1969
Aguirre, Sophia	Assoc	Catholic	FG	PHD	92	Notre Dm	1993
Ahene, Rexford A.	Assoc	Lafayette	OR	PHD	83	Wisconsin	1982
Ahking, Francis W.	Assoc	Connecticut	EF	PHD	81	Va Tech	1980
Ahlin, Christian	Asst	Vanderbilt	E	PHD	01	Chicago	2001
Ahmadi, Ali	Assoc	Morehead St		PHD	97	Oklahoma	1995
Ahmed, Ehsan	D-Pr	Jms Madison	EC	PHD	83	Mich St	1984

Ahmed, Parvez	Asst	Penn St-Harr		PHD	96	Tx-Arlin	1998
Ahn, Seung C.	Assoc	Arizona St		PHD	90	Mich St	1990
Ahrens, Ashley	Asst	Alaska SE		PHD			
Ai, Chunrong	Asst	Florida	CT	PHD	90	MIT	1994
Aitken, Hugh G. J.	Retir	Amherst		PHD	51	Harvard	1965
Aiyegoro, Ademola	Asst	Howard		PHD	90	GeoMason	
Aizeuman, Joshua	Prof	Ca-Santa Crz	EFH	PHD	81	Chicago	2001
Aka, Arsene A.	Asst	Catholic		PHD		Pittsburgh	8-00
Akacemn, Mohammed	Prof	Metro St-CO	AOP	PHD	84	Colorado	1991
Akalou, Woldie-Michael	H	Txs Southern		PHD		UCLA	
Akande, Benjamin Ola	Dean	Webster		PHD	95	Oklahoma	2000
Akarca, Ali	Lect	Ill-Chicago	E	MS	72	Nrthwstrn	1985
Akbari, Ali	Prof	Calif Luther		PHD	85	S Calif	1984
Akcay, Cevdet	Asst	Bogazici	CE	PHD	92	CUNY	1992
Akerlof, George A.	Prof	Cal-Berkeley		PHD	66	MIT	1966
Akhavi-Pour, Hossein	Assoc	Hamline	FO	PHD	79	Kansas	1988
Akin, John S.	C-Pr	No Carolina	IGH	PHD	71	Michigan	1973
Akkihal, Ramchandra G.	Prof	Marshall		PHD	69	Tennessee	1970
Akkina, Krishna Rao	Assoc	Kansas State	ECO	PHD	72	Minnesota	1972
Al Yasiri, Kahtan A.	Prof	Wis-Plattev		PHD	65	Iowa St	1965
Al-Hmoud, Rashid	Asst	Texas Tech		PHD	94	Tx Tech	1995
Al-Sabea, Taha H.	Prof	CS-Pomona		PHD	68	S Calif	1968
Alam, M. Imam	Asst	No Iowa	CFO	PHD	95	Illinois	1996
Alam, M. Shahid	Prof	Northeastern		PHD	79	W Ontario	1988
Alavi, Jafar	C-Pr	East Tenn St		PHD	86	Tennessee	1985
Albelda, Randy P.	Prof	Mass-Boston	JI	PHD	83	Mass	1988
Alberts, William W.	Emer	U Washington		PHD	61	Chicago	1987
Albrecht, James W.	Prof	Georgetown	DJ	PHD	76	Berkeley	1992
Albrecht, William P.	Prof	Iowa		PHD	65	Yale	1965
Aldana, Carolyn	Assoc	CS-San Bern	E	PHD	95	Ca-Rivers	1995
Aldrich, Carole	Visit	Stetson	ACD	PHD	72	Car Mellon	1998
Aldrich, Mark	Prof	Smith	JLN	PHD	69	Tx-Austin	1968
Alesina, Alberto F.	Prof	Harvard		PHD	86	Harvard	1988
Paul Sack Associate Professor of Political Economy							
Aleskerov, Fuad	Prof	Bogazici	C	PHD	81	Moscow	1995
Alexander, Donald L.	Assoc	W Michigan	D	PHD	83	Penn St	9900
Alexander, James	Prof	Alabama A&M	EAOH	PHD	89	Tx-Austin	1983
Alexander, McKinley	Retir	Jackson St		PHD	86	Illinois	1975
Alexander, Peter	Assoc	Hartwick	ACDL	PHD	90	Mass	1997
Alexander, Susan L.	Assoc	St Thomas-MN	F	PHD	77	So Meth	1981
Alexanderson, Peter	Asst	CUNY-Lehman		JD			
Alexandrin, Glen	Asst	Villanova		PHD	67	Clark	1970
Alexeev, Michael	Prof	Indiana		PHD	84	Duke	1992
Alexis, Marcus	Prof	Northwestern		PHD	59	Minnesota	1985
Daniel F. and Ada L. Rice Professor of Economics							
Alger, I.	Asst	Boston Coll	DL	PHD	97	Toulouse	1999
Ali, Mukhtar M.	Prof	Kentucky	C	PHD	69	Wisconsin	1969
Aliprantis, C. D. Roko	Prof	Purdue		PHD	73	Cal Tech	1998
Allen, Andrew T.	Prof	San Diego		PHD	83	Illinois	1984
Allen, Beth Elaine	Prof	Minnesota		PHD	78	Berkeley	1992
Allen, Bruce T.	Prof	Michigan St		PHD	65	Cornell	1965
Allen, Charles L.	Prof	Lamar	RC	PHD	78	Arkansas	1979
Allen, Grace C.	Assoc	W Carolina	G	PHD	91	S Carol	1992
Allen, John William	Prof	Texas A&M	D	PHD	67	Illinois	1967
Allen, Polly R.	Prof	Connecticut	FE	PHD	70	Brown	1976
Allen, Ralph C.	H-Pr	Valdosta St	FDK	PHD	81	Geo St	1982
Allen, Robert F.	Prof	Creighton	DKL	PHD	69	Mich St	1986
Allen, Roy E.	Dean	St Marys-Cal		PHD	83	Berkeley	1985
Allen, Steven G.	Prof	N Carol St	JD	PHD	78	Harvard	1978
Allen, Stuart D.	H-Pr	N Car-Greens	E	PHD	77	Virginia	1976
Allen, W. David	Assoc	Alabama-Hunt	J	PHD	94	Arkansas	1994
Allender, Mary E.	Assoc	Portland	LC	PHD	90	Oregon	1985
Allgood, Sam	Asst	Nebraska	DJG	PHD	93	Georgia	
Alli, Ali M.	Prof	Okla City	CIP	PHD	68	Okla St	1985
Allison, Michael	Lect	Mo-St Louis	CE	ABD		Virginia	1993
Allison, Robert J.	Prof	CS-Fresno	B	PHD	66	Colorado	1967
Alm, James R.	C-Pr	Georgia St	DHO	PHD	80	Wisconsin	1999
Almon, Clopper Jr.	Prof	Maryland		PHD	62	Harvard	1966
Alnasrawi, Abbas	Prof	Vermont	AFOQ	PHD	65	Harvard	1963
Alonso, Irasema	Asst	Rochester		PHD	93	Minnesota	1994
Alonso, Irma T. de	Prof	Fla Internat	OCFI	PHD	69	York-Eng	1981
Alpan, Erkan	Asst	R Stockton		PHD	84	Ca-Rivers	1980
Alper, Emre	Asst	Bogazici	CEFG	PHD	95	Geotown	1995
Alper, Neil O.	Assoc	Northeastern		PHD	77	Pittsburgh	1979
Alpert, William T.	Assoc	Connecticut	J	PHD	79	Columbia	1983
Alse, Jahardhanan	Asst	Indiana SE	FE	PHD	93	Wisconsin	1992
Alshallah, Mohamed	Assoc	Fairmont St	AD	MBA		Bridgepr	1988
Alston, Lee	Prof	Illinois	NQ	PHD	78	U Wash	1988
Alston, Richard M.	Prof	Weber State	ABNQ	PHD	70	Cornell	1969
Altazan, John E.	Prof	New Orleans		PHD	54	Illinois	1958

Altieri, Paul L.	Prof	Central Conn	E	PHD	76	Boston C	1975
Altmann, James L.	Prof	Indiana SE	DM	PHD	78	Wisconsin	1978
Altonji, Joseph G.	Prof	Northwestern		PHD	81	Princeton	1990
Altshuler, Rosanne	Assoc	Rutgers-N Br	H	PHD	88	Penn	1992
Alvarez, Fernando	Assoc	Chicago		PHD	94	Minnesota	1996
Alvi, Eskander	Assoc	W Michigan	E	PHD	85	J Hopkins	1994
Aly, Hassan	Assoc	Ohio State		PHD	86	S Illinois	1989
Amacher, Ryan C.	Prof	Tx-Arlington	FH	PHD	71	Virginia	1992
Amarante, Massimiliano	Asst	Columbia	C	PHD	99	MIT	1999
Amariglio, Jack	Prof	Merrimack		PHD	84	Mass	
Amato, Louis	Prof	N Car-Charl		PHD	80	S Carol	1980
Amegbe, Annan	Assoc	Morgan State		PHD	77	Catholic	1978
Amemiya, Takeshi	Prof	Stanford		PHD	64	J Hopkins	1968
Edward Ames Edmonds Professor of Economics							
Amin, R. John	H-Pr	Northwood	BDFM	PHD	78	Cincinnati	9-86
Amin, Shahina	Asst	No Iowa		PHD	97	Illinois	2000
Amin-Gutierrez de Pineres, S	H-Ac	Texas-Dallas		PHD	92	Duke	1996
Ammann, Alan I.	Assoc	Meredith		DBA	78	Miss St	1990
Amoateng, Kofi A. D.	Prof	N Carol Cen		PHD	86	Tx-Austin	1990
Amoo, Taiwoo	Asst	CUNY-Brookly		PHD	92	Exeter	1999
Amos, Orley M. Jr.	Prof	Oklahoma St	R	PHD	79	Iowa St	1979
Amrhein, Joseph	Retir	St Michael's		PHD	58	NYU	
Amsler, Christine E.	Assoc	Michigan St		PHD	80	Penn	1980
Amuedo-Dorantes, Catalina	Asst	San Diego St		PHD	98	W Mich	1999
Anas, Alex	Prof	SUNY-Buffalo	DR	PHD	75	Penn	1991
Anastasopoulos, Petros	Assoc	F Dick-Teane	ADE	PHD	84	New Sch	1986
Anbarci, Nejat M.	Assoc	Fla Internat	DC	PHD	88	Iowa	1995
Anderlini, Luca	Prof	Georgetown	D	PHD	97	Cambridge	2001
Anders, Steven L.	C-Pr	Graceland	ARD	PHD	88	Kansas St	1978
Anderson, B. Wylie	Retir	No Iowa	AEGJ	PHD	73	Iowa	1966
Anderson, Charles E.	Dean	Kean		PHD	75	Stanford	7-88
Anderson, Curtis L.	Prof	Minn-Duluth	QA	PHD	81	Wyoming	1980
Anderson, David A.	C-Ac	Centre	ACHK	PHD	92	Duke	1992
Blazer Associate Professor of Economics							
Anderson, Deborah	Asst	New Mexico	CHJ	PHD	98	Cornell	1998
Anderson, Donna M.	Assoc	Wis-La Cross	DIJ	PHD	93	Mich St	1994
Anderson, Eric E.	Assoc	Old Dominion		PHD	84	U Wash	1984
Anderson, Evan	Asst	No Carolina	E	PHD	98	Chicago	1998
Anderson, Gary M.	Prof	CS-Northrdge	GLTR	PHD	87	GeoMason	1987
Anderson, James E.	Prof	Boston Coll	DFN	PHD	69	Wisconsin	1969
Anderson, Joan B.	Prof	San Diego		PHD	71	Ca-SnDgo	1981
Anderson, John E.	Prof	Nebraska	H	PHD	77	Claremont	1991
Anderson, John Whiting	Retir	Bucknell		PHD	67	Penn	1961
Anderson, Kathryn H.	Assoc	Vanderbilt	JO	PHD	78	N Car St	1980
Anderson, Lee G.	Prof	Delaware	Q	PHD	70	U Wash	1974
Anderson, Lisa	Asst	Wm & Mary		PHD	94	Virginia	1997
Anderson, Michael A.	Assoc	Wash & Lee	F	PHD	90	Wisconsin	1990
Anderson, Patricia Mary	Assoc	Dartmouth		PHD	91	Princeton	1991
Anderson, Richard K.	Prof	Texas A&M	CF	PHD	76	Purdue	1975
Anderson, Richard T.	Asst	NewJerseyCty	AI	PHD	91	CUNY	
Anderson, Robert M.	Prof	Cal-Berkeley		PHD	77	Yale	
Anderson, Roy C.	Prof	CS-Long Bch		PHD	65	Tulane	1965
Anderson, Simon P.	Prof	Virginia	LDR	PHD	85	Queen's	1987
Anderson, Thomas C.	Retir	Kennesaw St	ADM	PHD	72	Berkeley	1985
Anderton, Charles H.	C-Pr	Holy Cross	ACDF	PHD	86	Cornell	1986
Ando, Albert K.	Prof	Pennsylvania		PHD	59	Car Mellon	1963
Andoh, Samuel Kojo	C-Pr	So Conn St	EO	PHD	86	NYU	
Andreoni, James R.	Prof	Wisconsin		PHD	86	Michigan	1986
Andrews, Charles Haynes	Prof	Mercer-Macon		PHD	67	Vanderbilt	1973
Stetson Professor of Economics							
Andrews, Donald W. K.	Prof	Yale	C	PHD	82	Berkeley	1982
Andrews, Kim	Assoc	Cen Missouri		PHD	94	Okla St	1990
Andrews, Thomas	Asst	West Chester	DHQL	PHD	96	Temple	1997
Andrianacos, Dimitri	Prof	W Illinois	ACE	PHD	89	Chicago	1990
Andrulis, John A.	Prof	W New Eng		PHD	75	Purdue	1981
Angeletos, George-Marios	Asst	MIT		PHD	01	Harvard	2001
Angelini, Anthony L. P.	C-Ac	St John's		MA	51	Temple	
Angiello, Joseph		SUNY-Empire	A	PHD	77	Tx-Austin	1983
Angkatavanich, Virote	Retir	F Dick-Teane	AEFG	PHD	67	New Sch	1963
Angrist, Joshua D.	Prof	MIT	J	PHD	89	Princeton	1996
Ankrom, Jeff A.	Prof	Wittenberg	AEG	PHD	82	Notre Dm	1982
Anna, Alexandra	Assoc	Colorado Col		PHD	95	Utah	2001
Annala, Christopher	Asst	SUNY-Geneseo	E	PHD	00	Wash St	2000
Ansari, Mohammed	Assoc	Albany State	F	PHD	89	Simon Fr	8-01
Anspach, Ralph	Prof	San Fran St		PHD	63	Berkeley	1963
Anstine, Diane	Asst	No Central	D	PHD	97	Kentucky	1997
Anstine, Jeffrey	Asst	Wis-Whitewat		PHD	96	Kentucky	1999
Antecol, Heather	Asst	Claremont	JIG	PHD	99	McMaster	
Antel, John J.	C-Pr	Houston	J	PHD	82	UCLA	1981
Antinolfi, Gaetano	Asst	Wash Univ	E	PHD	97	Cornell	1997

Antle, John M.	Prof	Montana St		PHD	80	Chicago	1987
Anton, Wilma	Asst	Cen Florida	Q	PHD	01	Illinois	2001
Antonovics, Kate	Asst	Ca-San Diego	JIH	PHD	00	Wisconsin	2000
Anyamele, Dennis	Asst	Jackson St		PHD	92	Howard	
Anyanwu, Lenard C.	Asst	NJ Inst Tech		PHD	90	Tx-Dallas	1990
Aoki, Masahiko	Prof	Stanford		PHD	67	Minnesota	1984
Henri and Tomoye Takahashi Professor of Japanese Studies							
Aoki, Masanao	Emer	UCLA		PHD	65	Tokyo In	1983
Aoki, Masato	VAsst	Simmons	A	PHD	95	Mass	1994
Applegate, Michael J.	Prof	Oklahoma St	O	PHD	73	Iowa St	1974
Appleyard, Dennis R.	C-Pr	Davidson	F	PHD	66	Michigan	1990
James B. Duke Professor of International Studies							
Arabian, Ghodratollah	Asst	Lincoln-MO		PHD	85	Indiana	1984
Aranson, Peter H.	Prof	Emory	HKL	PHD	72	Rochester	1981
Arbatskaya, Maria	Asst	Emory	DL	ABD		Indiana	9-99
Arcadi, Antony	C-Ac	CUNY-Brookly		MA	86	CUNY	1985
Archer, Stephen H.	Retir	Willamette		PHD	58	Minnesota	1973
Archibald, Glenn S.	Asst	Mississippi	D	PHD	91	Houston	2001
Archibald, Robert B.	Prof	Wm & Mary		PHD	74	Purdue	1976
Ardagna, Silvia	Asst	Wellesley	EF	PHD	00	Boston C	2000
Arenberg, Yuri	Assoc	CUNY-Brookly	D	PHD	86	NYU	1985
Arguea, Nestor M.	Assoc	West Florida	ACD	PHD	90	S Calif	1990
Argys, Laura M.	Assoc	Colo-Denver	IOCD	PHD	93	Colorado	1990
Arias, James J.		Georgia Col	E	PHD	96	Tx A&M	
Aristotelous, Kyriacos	Assoc	Otterbein	EFO	PHD	93	Ohio St	1993
Arjomand, H. Lari	Prof	Clayton St		PHD	80	Oklahoma	1980
Arluck, Gregory M.	Asst	Yeshiva		PHD	87	CUNY	
Armantier, Olivier	Asst	SUNY-Stony B		PHD	98	Pittsburgh	1998
Armentano, Dominick T.	Retir	Hartford		PHD	66	Conn	1966
Armstrong, Ken D.	Dean	Anderson U		PHD	85	Nrthwstrn	1990
Arndt, Sven W.	Prof	Claremont		PHD	64	Berkeley	1990
Charles M. Stone Professor of Money, Credit & Trade							
Arnold, Michael	Assoc	Delaware	LD	PHD	92	UCLA	1992
Arnold, Roger A.	Prof	CS-S Marcos		PHD	79	Va Tech	
Arnold, Thomas R.	Retir	King's Col		PHD	70	Syracuse	6-60
Arnott, Richard J.	Prof	Boston Coll	DHR	PHD	75	Yale	1988
Arnould, Richard J.	H-Pr	Illinois	DIKL	PHD	68	Iowa St	1967
Aronson, J. Richard	Prof	Lehigh	HG	PHD	64	Clark	1965
William L. Clayton Professor of Business and Economics							
Arora, Harjit K.	Prof	LeMoyne	EFH	PHD	84	Wi-Milwa	1987
Arora, Swarnjit S.	Assoc	Wis-Milwauke		PHD	71	SUNY-Buf	1978
Arvan, Lanny D.	Assoc	Illinois	CD	PHD	81	Nrthwstrn	1980
Arzac, Enrique R.	Retir	Columbia		PHD	68	Columbia	1971
Asamoah, Yaw	Prof	Indiana U-PA	FO	PHD	85	Wash U	1984
Aschauer, David Alan	Prof	Bates	E	PHD	84	Rochester	1990
Elmer W. Campbell Professor of Economics							
Aschheim, Joseph	Retir	George Wash	E	PHD	54	Harvard	1964
Asea, Patrick	Asst	UCLA		PHD	93	J Hopkins	
Asefa, Sally Ann	C-Pr	Brescia		PHD	78	Iowa St	8-80
Asefa, Sisay	Prof	W Michigan	O	PHD	80	Iowa St	1980
Asgary, Nader	Asst	SUNY-Geneseo	FJ	PHD	91	Houston	1996
Ash, Michael	Asst	Massachusett		PHD	99	Berkeley	1999
Asheghian, Par	Prof	CS-San Bern	F	PHD	80	Geo St	1991
Ashenfelter, Orley C.	Prof	Princeton		PHD	70	Princeton	1968
Asher, Cheryl	Asst	Villanova		PHD	81	Penn	1984
Ashiaf, Mohammad	Asst	NC-Pembroke		PHD		N Illinois	1999
Ashley, James R.	Assoc	St Catherine	AL	PHD	84	Wisconsin	1984
Ashley, Richard A.	Prof	Virg Tech	CE	PHD	82	Ca-SnDgo	1981
Ashman, H. Lowell	Prof	Lenoir-Rhyne		PHD	73	Utah	1975
Ashraf, Javed	Prof	West Florida	AJ	PHD	86	N Illinois	1990
Asiedu, Elizabeth	Asst	Kansas	F	PHD	98	Illinois	1998
Askalani, Mohamed H.	Retir	Mankato St	AC	PHD	70	Iowa St	1969
Askari, Ammar	Lect	Ind-Purdue/I		PHD	95	Indiana	1989
Aske, David	Asst	No Colorado	AITR	PHD	92	Nebraska	1992
Aslanbeigui, Nahid	Assoc	Monmouth	E	PHD	84	Michigan	1988
Assad, Jean-Claud	Asst	Jackson St		PHD	87	Howard	1991
Assane, Djeto	Asst	Nev-L Vegas	O	PHD	88	Colorado	1988
Assibey-Mensah, Albert	Asst	Kentucky St	AG	PHD	94	Cincinnati	1994
Assumpta, Sister Virginia A	C-Ac	Immaculata		MA		Catholic	9-68
Atack, Jeremy	C-Pr	Vanderbilt	N	PHD	76	Indiana	1993
Atencio, Leonard D.	Prof	Fort Lewis		PHD	69	Kansas St	1968
Atesoglu, H. Sonmez	Prof	Clarkson	EFO	PHD	72	Pittsburgh	1977
Athey, Susan	Assoc	Stanford	L	PHD	95	Stanford	2001
Atkeson, Andrew G.	Asst	Pennsylvania	PF	PHD	88	Stanford	1993
Atkinson, Glendel W.	Prof	Nevada-Reno		PHD	68	Oklahoma	1967
Atkinson, Scott E.	Prof	Georgia	CQK	PHD	72	Colorado	1985
Atri, Said	Prof	SUNY Oswego	AFI	PHD	82	SUNY-Alb	1981
Attiyeh, Richard E.	Prof	Ca-San Diego	EI	PHD	66	Yale	1982
Atwood, Edward Charles Jr.	Retir	Wash & Lee		PHD	59	Princeton	1969
Atwood, Joseph A.	Assoc	Montana St		PHD	87	Nebraska	1987

Auerbach, Alan J.	C-Pr	Cal-Berkeley	GEH	PHD	78	Harvard	1994
Auernheimer, Leonardo J. A.	Prof	Texas A&M	EF	PHD	73	Chicago	1973
Ault, David E.	Prof	S Ill-Edward	AFJK	PHD	69	Illinois	1969
Ault, Richard W.	Assoc	Auburn		PHD	83	Virginia	1983
Austin, Adrian	Asst	U Miami	CG	PHD	98	Duke	1998
Austin, Ellis T.	Deces			PHD	55	Mich St	
Austin, John A.	Prof	La St-Shreve		PHD	72	Ariz St	1983
Ausubel, Lawrence M.	Prof	Maryland		PHD	84	Stanford	1992
Autor, David	Asst	MIT	J	PHD	99	Harvard	1999
Auzenne, George R.	Lect	Florida A&M	LM	MS	63	Boston	1976
Avard, Stephen L.	H-Ac	Tx A&M-Comm	GFDE	PHD	83	North Tx	1983
Averett, Susan	Assoc	Lafayette	CJI	PHD	91	Colorado	1991
Averitt, Robert T.	Prof	Smith	ABE	PHD	61	Tx-Austin	1961
Avin, Rose Marie	Assoc	Wis-Eau Clar	FO	PHD	86	Maryland	1987
Awh, Robert Y.	Retir	Miss State		PHD	60	Florida	1968
Axarloglou, Kostas	Asst	Babson	F	PHD	93	Michigan	1994
Axelson, David J.	C-Ac	Western St		EDD	76	Colorado	1982
Ayal, Eliezer B.	Emer	Ill-Chicago	O	PHD	61	Cornell	1970
Ayanian, Robert L.	Retir	CS-Fullerton		PHD	74	UCLA	1977
Ayers, Michael	Retir	Il-Springfld	HR	PHD	73	Oklahoma	1971
Ayers, Ronald M.	Assoc	Tx-S Antonio	GJM	PHD	78	Tulane	1979
Ayittey, George B. N.	VAsoc	American U		PHD	81	Manitoba	1994
Ayres, Robert	Emer	INSEAD	OU	PHD	58	London	9-92
Chairman Sandoz Chair on Environment							
Azari-Rad, Hamid	Asst	SUNY-N Paltz		PHD	96	Utah	1999
Azariadis, Constantine C.	Prof	UCLA		PHD	75	Car Mellon	
Aziz, Fahima	C-As	Hamline	DJ	PHD	95	Minnesota	1994
Baack, Bennett D.	Assoc	Ohio State	N	PHD	72	U Wash	1988
Baba, Marietta	Dean	Michigan St					
Babcock, Michael W.	Prof	Kansas State	RQ	PHD	73	Illinois	1972
Babilot, George	Retir	San Diego St		PHD	58	Oregon	1956
Bacdayan, Andrew W.	Prof	Lamar	AE	PHD	73	Utah St	
Bachstein, Kristen	Lect	St Bonaventu	E	MA	93	Alabama	2001
Backus, David	Prof	New York U	EFG	PHD	81	Yale	1990
Badgett, Lee	Asst	Massachusett		PHD	90	Berkeley	1997
Badu, Yaw Agyeman	C-Ac	Virginia St		PHD	80	S Carol	1984
Bae, Jay	Asst	Georgia St	I	PHD	93	UCLA	2000
Baek, In-Mee	Asst	Suffolk		PHD	90	Indiana	
Baer, Werner	Prof	Illinois	EFO	PHD	58	Harvard	1974
Bagheri, Fathollah	Assoc	North Dakota	AJ	PHD	78	Penn	1990
Bagheri, Rashid	Inst	Morgan State		MA		Howard	
Bagi, Sukhwinder	Asst	Bloomsburg		PHD	87	Vanderbilt	
Bagwell, Kyle W.	Prof	Columbia	LF	PHD	86	Stanford	1996
Bahatiuk, Nicholas G.	Retir	LeMoyne		PHD		Ukranian	1962
Bahl, Roy W. Jr.	Dean	Georgia St	HR	PHD	65	Kentucky	1988
Bahmani-Oskooee, Mohsen	Prof	Wis-Milwauke		PHD	81	Mich St	1981
Bai, Jushan J.	Prof	Boston Coll	CE	PHD	92	Berkeley	1998
Baicker, Katherine	Asst	Dartmouth		PHD	98	Harvard	1998
Baier, Scott L.	Asst	Clemson	FED	PHD	96	Mich St	2001
Baik, Kyung H.	Assoc	Virg Tech	LD	PHD	89	Va Tech	2001
Bailey BVM, Mary P. F.	Retir	Loyola-Chicg		MA	69	Notre Dm	1991
Bailey, DeeVon	Prof	Utah State	Q	PHD	83	Tx A&M	1983
Bailey, Duncan	Retir	SC-Spartanbu	AEOR	PHD	70	Va Tech	1984
Bailey, Martin J.	Deces	Emory	E	PHD	56	J Hopkins	1989
Bailey, Mary Ann	Adj	George Wash	I	PHD	74	MIT	1983
Baillie, Richard T.	Prof	Michigan St	CFG	PHD	78	LondonEc	8-86
Pasant Chair of Economics & Finance							
Bails, Dale G.	Assoc	Christian Br		PHD	78	S Dakota	1995
Baiman, Ron	Asst	Roosevelt		PHD	89	New Sch	1994
Baird, Charles W.	C-Pr	CS-Hayward	BHJ	PHD	68	Berkeley	1972
Baird, Robert N.	Retir	Case Western	A	PHD	65	Kentucky	1965
Bajari, Patrick	Asst	Stanford		PHD	97	Minnesota	
Bajona, Claustre	Asst	U Miami	EF	PHD		Minnesota	2000
Baker, Ben	Assoc	Davidson	G	MA	83	S Carol	1997
Baker, Matthew	Asst	USN Academy		PHD	00	Conn	
Baker, Samuel H. III	Prof	Wm & Mary		PHD	70	Virginia	1969
Baker, Stephen A.	Prof	Capital		PHD	82	York UK	1987
Bakir, Saad T.	Assoc	Alabama St	CM	PHD	77	Va Tech	1-93
Baktari, Paul	C-Ac	SUNY-Potsdam		PHD		W Virginia	
Balaban, Rita	Asst	Charleston	AI	PHD	00	Pittsburgh	2000
Balabkins, Nicholas W.	Retir	Lehigh		PHD	56	Rutgers	1966
Balasubramanyam, V. N.	Prof	U Lancaster		PHD	70	Illinois	
Balch, Billy W.	Retir	Mid Tenn St		PHD	68	Alabama	1964
Balch, Donald C.	Lect	So Carolina	AD	MA	88	S Carol	8-84
Balch, Michael S.	Assoc	Iowa		PHD	65	NYU	1971
Balcim, Metin	Prof	Bogazici	EH	PHD	73	NYU	1973
Baldani, Jeffrey P.	Assoc	Colgate	CD	PHD	83	Cornell	1982
Baldwin, Marjorie L.	Prof	East Carol	DIJ	PHD	88	Syracuse	1989
Baldwin, Robert E.	Retir	Wisconsin		PHD	50	Harvard	1964
Baldwin, William Lee	Retir	Dartmouth		PHD	58	Princeton	1956

Baliamoune, Mina	Asst	North Fla		PHD	95	Northeas	2001
Balkan, Erol M.	C-Pr	Hamilton	OF	PHD	88	SUNY-Bin	1987
Balke, Nathan S.	C-Pr	So Methodist	EG	PHD	86	Nrthwstrn	1986
Balkin, Steven M.	Prof	Roosevelt		PHD	76	Wayne St	1984
Ball, David Stafford	Assoc	N Carol St	FND	PHD	67	N Carol	1966
Ball, Jennifer	Asst	Washburn		PHD	01	S Calif	2001
Ball, Laurence M.	Prof	J Hopkins		PHD	86	MIT	1994
Ball, Sheryl B.	Assoc	Virg Tech	DMH	PHD	91	Nrthwstrn	1992
Ballantyne, A. Paul	Prof	Colorado Spr	ABEO	PHD	65	Stanford	1967
Ballard, Charles L.	Prof	Michigan St		PHD	83	Stanford	1983
Ballinger, T. Parker	Asst	S F Austin	CE	PHD	99	Houston	1999
Ballman, Richard J. Jr.	C-Pr	Augustana IL	ABDE	PHD	77	Iowa	1972
Ballou, Dale	Assoc	Massachusett		PHD	89	Yale	
Balough, Robert S.	C-Pr	Clarion		PHD	81	N Illinois	1981
Baltagi, Badi H.	Prof	Texas A&M	C	PHD	79	Penn	1988
George Summey Jr. Professor in Liberal Arts							
Balvers, Ronald J.	Assoc	W Virginia	EG	PHD	84	Pittsburgh	1991
Banaian, King	Prof	St Cloud St		PHD	86	Claremont	1984
Bandera, Vladimir N.	Prof	Temple	FP	PHD	60	Berkeley	1972
Bandyopadhayay, Taradas	Prof	Cal-Riversid	AD	PHD	80	So Meth	1987
Bandyopadhyay, Subhayu	Asst	W Virginia	F	PHD	94	Maryland	1993
Bandyopadhyay, Sudeshna	Asst	W Virginia	J	PHD	92	Maryland	1992
Bandzak, Ruth Anne	Asst	Redlands		MA		Notre Dm	1988
Banerjee, Abhijit V.	Prof	MIT	G	PHD	88	Harvard	1993
Banerjee, Guarango	Asst	Tx-Brownsvil	AE	PHD	97	Al-Birm	1997
Banks, Nina	Asst	Bucknell	JNR	PHD	99	Mass	9-01
Bansak, Cynthia	Asst	San Diego St		PHD	00	Ca-SnDgo	2001
Bansal, Vipul K.	Assoc	St John's		PHD	88	Miss	
Baqir, Ghalib M.	Retir	Alabama St	1995	PHD	67	St Louis	1973
Barakeh, A. K.	Retir	So Alabama	F	PHD	68	Indiana	1968
Barari, Mahua	Asst	SW Missouri		PHD	92	Iowa St	1993
Barber, Edward	Prof	Wyoming		PHD	86	Birkbeck	2000
Barber, G. Russell Jr.	Assoc	Mercer-Macon		PHD	90	Miss	1973
Barber, William J.	Emer	Wesleyan-CT	B	DPHI	57	Oxford	1957
Barbezat, Daniel P.	Prof	Amherst	ANO	PHD	88	Illinois	1988
Barbezat, Debra A.	Assoc	Colby	JIA	PHD	85	Michigan	1992
Barbour, G. Jeffrey	Asst	Cen Michigan		PHD	73	Fla St	1971
Barbour, James L.	Assoc	Elon	AB	PHD	87	Kentucky	1990
Bardhan, Pranab K.	Prof	Cal-Berkeley		PHD		Cambridge	
Barger, Peter S.	C-Ac	No Central	G	PHD	89	Illinois	1989
Barilla, Anthony	Asst	Geo Southern		PHD	01	Kansas St	2001
Barkley, Daniel	Asst	Loyola Marym	AJR	PHD	01	Ca-Irvine	2001
Barkoulas, John	Asst	Tennessee	EGF	PHD	95	Boston C	2001
Barlevy, Gadi	Asst	Northwestern		PHD	97	Harvard	1997
Barnes, Clarence H.	Dean	Gonzaga		PHD	73	Tennessee	9-73
Barnes, Robert R.	Retir	Millersville		MA	67	Penn	1963
Barnes, William F.	Asst	Portland	GJP	PHD	01	Notre Dm	2000
Barnett, Harold C.	Prof	Rhode Island	EKQ	PHD	73	MIT	1970
Barnett, William	Assoc	Loyola-N Orl	DEFK	PHD	74	Mich St	1974
Barnett, William A.	Prof	Wash Univ	E	PHD	74	Car Mellon	1990
Barone, Charles A.	Assoc	Dickinson Cl	AO	PHD	78	American	1975
Baroutsis, A. Paul	Retir	Slippery Roc	ADP	PHD	72	Purdue	1972
Barrett, Anthony	C-Pr	St Scholasti		PHD	84	Geo Wash	
Barrett, Richard	Prof	Montana	EOJQ	PHD	72	Wisconsin	
Barro, Robert J.	Prof	Harvard		PHD	70	Harvard	1987
Barron, John M.	C-Pr	Purdue		PHD	76	Brown	1976
Barsky, Robert	Assoc	Michigan		PHD	86	MIT	
Bartel, Ann	Prof	Columbia		PHD	74	Columbia	1976
A. Barton Hepburn Professor of Economics							
Bartell, Ernest J.	Prof	Notre Dame	O	PHD	66	Princeton	1977
Bartell, H. Robert Jr.	Retir	East Tenn St		PHD	63	Columbia	1989
Barth, Peter S.	Prof	Connecticut	J	PHD	65	Michigan	1973
Bartholomew, A. Wayne	Prof	Ind-So Bend	AET	PHD	72	Cornell	1972
Bartlett, Randall	Prof	Smith	AHR	PHD	71	Stanford	1979
Bartlett, Robin L.	Prof	Denison	AJ	PHD	74	Mich St	1973
Laura C. Harris Chair							
Bartlett, Sue A.	Lect	South Fla	A	MA	93	S Fla	1994
Bartley, Alan	Asst	Transylvania		PHD	99	Vanderbilt	1999
Barton, William E.	Retir	Colorado Col		PHD	70	Missouri	1958
Barut, Yasar	Asst	Rice		PHD	98	Purdue	7-98
Barzel, Yoram	Prof	U Washington		PHD	61	Chicago	1961
Basch, Donald L.	Prof	Simmons	D	PHD	77	Yale	1980
Bashir, Abdel H.	H-As	Grambling St		PHD	90	Wisconsin	1990
Baskan, Asuman	Assoc	Allegheny	CDFE	PHD	88	Lehigh	1987
Basmann, Robert L.	Prof	SUNY-Bingham	C	PHD	66	Iowa St	1988
Bassett, Gilbert W.	Prof	Ill-Chicago	C	PHD	73	Michigan	1973
Bastin, Hamid	Prof	Shippensburg		PHD	89	Geo St	1989
Basu, Arnab	Asst	Wm & Mary		PHD	97	J Hopkins	1998
Basu, Atin	Asst	Va Military		PHD	98	Miss	1999
Basu, Bharati	Prof	Cen Michigan	FODJ	PHD	82	Rochester	1990

Basu, Kaushik	Prof	Cornell	DHLO	PHD	76	LondonEc	
on leave to MIT							
Basu, Parantap	Assoc	Fordham		PHD	85	Ca-SnBarb	1988
Basu, Susanto	Assoc	Michigan		PHD	92	Harvard	1992
Batabyal, Amitjatreet	Prof	Rochest Tech	FOQ	PHD	94	Berkeley	2000
Arthur J. Gosnell Professor of Economics							
Batavia, Bala	Prof	DePaul	CD	PHD	74	N Car St	1976
Batchelder, Ronald W.	Prof	Pepper-Malib	DEFK	PHD	75	UCLA	1984
Bateman, Bradley W.	Prof	Grinnell	B	PHD	84	Kentucky	1987
Bateman, Fred	Prof	Georgia	N	PHD	65	Tulane	1991
Nicholas A. Beadles Professor							
Bates, Laurie	Assoc	Bryant	HD	PHD	89	Conn	
Bates, Lawrence W.	Assoc	E Illinois		PHD	75	Tx-Austin	1970
Bathgate, James	VAsst	Linfield		PHD	01	Conn	2001
Batie, Clarence	Inst	Txs Southern		MA		Prairie	
Batina, Raymond	Prof	Wash State		PHD	85	Minnesota	1985
Batra, Raveendra N.	Prof	So Methodist	F	PHD	69	S Illinois	1973
Battacharya, Radha S.	Asst	CS-Fullerton	E	PHD	90	Penn St	1990
Battalio, Ray	Prof	Texas A&M	C	PHD	69	Purdue	1969
Mary Tucker Currie Professorship in Liberal Arts							
Battigalli, Pierpaolo	Prof	European U		DE	92	Italian M	1999
European University Institute; Fiesole, Italy; battigal@iue.it							
Baum, Charles	Asst	Mid Tenn St	J	PHD	99	N Carol	1999
Baum, Christopher F.	Assoc	Boston Coll	CE	PHD	77	Michigan	1977
Baum, Donald N.	Assoc	Neb-Omaha	HD	PHD	79	Claremont	1987
Baum, Sandra R.	C-Pr	Skidmore		PHD	81	Columbia	1987
Baumol, William J.	Prof	New York U	D	PHD	49	London	1971
Bausor, Randall S.	Prof	Massachusett		PHD	78	Duke	1979
Bawuah, Kwado	Assoc	Virginia St		PHD	83	Va Tech	1987
Bay, John W.	Prof	So Maine	E	PHD	66	Boston C	1965
Bayazitoglu, Berna	Asst	Bogazici	CDO	PHD	96	Cornell	1996
Baye, Michael R.	Prof	Indiana	DIO	PHD	83	Purdue	1997
Bayer, Amanda	Assoc	Swarthmore	DJ	PHD	95	Yale	1992
Bayer, Arthur A.	Prof	Babson	AH	PHD	68	Mich St	1978
Bays, Carson W.	C-Pr	East Carol	IKL	PHD	74	Michigan	1982
Baytas, Ahmet	Prof	Montclair St		PHD	86	Illinois	1988
Beall, Larry G.	Retir	Virg Comm		PHD	73	Duke	1970
Beals, Ralph E.	Prof	Amherst	ACO	PHD	70	MIT	1966
Clarence Francis Professor of Economics							
Beam, Robert D.	Prof	Wis-Superior		PHD	80	Cincinnati	1980
Bean, Richard N.	Assoc	Houston	N	PHD	71	U Wash	1970
Bear, Donald V. T.	Emer	Ca-San Diego	AE	PHD	63	Stanford	1965
Beard, Thomas R.	Emer	Louisiana St	E	PHD	63	Duke	1961
LSU Alumni Professor Emeritus							
Beard, Thomas Randolph	Assoc	Auburn		PHD	88	Vanderbilt	1988
Beardsley, George L.	Prof	Cal Poly-SLO		PHD	74	Penn	1975
Bearse, Peter	Asst	N Car-Greens	CH	PHD	95	Virginia	1998
Beasley, Christine Daughtry	Retir	Campbell		MA		E Carol	1969
Beaton, C. Russell	Prof	Willamette		PHD	68	Claremont	1971
Beaty, William L.	Asst	Tarleton St	ADR	MS	73	Utah St	1985
Beaumont, Marion S.	Prof	CS-Long Bch		PHD	67	Claremont	1967
Beaumont, Paul M.	Assoc	Florida St	C	PHD	84	Penn	1988
Bechdolt, Burley V.	Retir	No Illinois	C	PHD	70	S Calif	1970
Beck, Edward J.	Asst	SUNY-Oneonta	DE	MBA	82	Syracuse	1977
Beck, John H.	D-Ac	Gonzaga	BH	PHD	76	Mich St	1988
Beck, Paul	Assoc	Graceland	AFJE	PHD	94	Missouri	1992
Beck, Stacie E.	Assoc	Delaware	GEF	PHD	87	Penn	1986
Beck, William C. II	Retir	USAF Academy		MA		Michigan	
Becker, Anthony D.	Assoc	St Olaf	DLC	PHD	86	Duke	1987
Becker, Charles McVey	Assoc	Tx Christian		PHD	66	Arizona	1967
Becker, Gary S.	Prof	Chicago		PHD	55	Chicago	1970
Becker, Gilbert B.	Asst	St Anselm	AD	PHD	83	Boston C	1987
Becker, Klaus G.	Assoc	Texas Tech		PHD	87	Kansas	1989
Becker, Robert	C-Pr	Indiana		PHD	78	Rochester	1978
Becker, William	Prof	Indiana		PHD	73	Pittsburgh	1979
Becker, William S.	Retir	Colorado Col		PHD	70	LSU	1970
Beckert, W.	Asst	Florida	C	PHD	00	Berkeley	2000
Beckman, Mary P.	Assoc	Lafayette	OP	PHD	86	Notre Dm	1985
Beckman, Steven R.	Assoc	Colo-Denver	F	PHD	82	Ca-Davis	1988
Bedard, Kelly	Asst	Cal-Santa Br		PHD	96	Queen's	
Bednarek, Heather L.	Asst	St Louis		PHD	99	Mich St	2001
Bee, Richard H.	Prof	Youngstown		DBA	76	Kent St	1966
Beelders, Owen	Asst	Emory	CG	PHD	98	Rochester	1997
Beeson, Bennie E. Jr.	Retir	Radford		PHD	71	Tennessee	
Beeson, Patricia E.	Assoc	Pittsburgh	R	PHD	83	Oregon	1983
Behar, Cem	Prof	Bogazici	BJT	PHD	72	Paris	1977
Behdad, Sohrab	Prof	Denison	BF	PHD	73	Mich St	1985
Behr, Todd	Asst	E Stroudsbur	EH	MBA	78	Lehigh	1989
Behrman, Jere R.	Prof	Pennsylvania	OJL	PHD	66	MIT	1965
William R. Kenan Jr. Professor of Economics							

Beil, Richard O.	Assoc	Auburn		PHD	88	Tx A&M	1988
Bej, Emil	Retir	Shippensburg		DR	70	Ukranian	1969
Bekar, Clifford T.	Asst	Lewis & Clrk	HPIL	ABD		Simon Fr	1998
Bekdache, Basma	Asst	Wayne State	E	PHD	94	Boston C	1994
Beladi, Hamid	Prof	Dayton	F	PHD	83	Utah St	1988
Belay, Halefom	Asst	Whitman	CEO	PHD	96	SUNY-Bin	1996
Bell, Christine A.	C-As	Albright		MBA	77	Temple	1989
Bell, Christopher Ross	Assoc	N Car-Ashvil	AGHL	PHD	87	Penn	1989
Bell, Duran	Prof	Calif-Irvine		PHD	65	Berkeley	1965
Bell, Edward B.	Assoc	Cleveland St	DHJ	PHD	73	Ohio St	1971
Bell, Frederick W.	Retir	Florida St	7-97	PHD	64	Wayne St	1962
Bell, Jim	Prof	Cen Arkansas					
Bell, Joe A.	Prof	SW Missouri		PHD	80	Okla St	1971
Bell, Peter F.	C-Ac	SUNY-Purchas		PHD	68	Wisconsin	1971
Bell, Robert	Prof	CUNY-Brookly	M	PHD	72	Brunel	1986
Bell, Stephanie	Asst	Mo-Kansas Ct	AFG	PHD	01	New Sch	2001
Bellamy, D. Scott	Assoc	Southern Ark	I	PHD		Kentucky	1993
Bellante, Donald M.	Prof	South Fla	J	PHD	71	Fla St	1985
Bellico, Russell P.	Prof	Westfield St		EDD		Mass	1970
Bellinger, William K.	Asst	Dickinson Cl	JE	PHD	85	Nrthwstrn	1981
Belongia, Michael T.	Prof	Mississippi	E	PHD	82	N Car St	1993
Belotti, Mario L.	Prof	Santa Clara		PHD	69	Tx-Austin	1959
Belsley, David A.	Prof	Boston Coll	CD	PHD	65	MIT	1966
Belton, Willie J. Jr.	Assoc	Georgia Tech	E	PHD	86	Penn St	1987
Ben-Zion, Barry	Emer	Sonoma State	2000	PHD	73	Oregon	1969
Benavides, Adolfo	Assoc	Tx A&M-C Chr	AO	PHD	82	Wash St	9-96
Benavie, Arthur	Prof	No Carolina	AE	PHD	63	Michigan	1967
Benchekroun, Hassan	Asst	Fla Atlantic	DL	PHD	98	Laval	1999
Bender, Keith	Asst	Wis-Milwauke		PHD	94	Duke	1999
Benedict, Mary Ellen	Assoc	Bowling Gr		PHD	91	Car Mellon	1991
Benefield, Michael E.	Asst	Ark Tech		PHD	89	Purdue	1995
Benesh, Diann	Lect	Wis-Eau Clar	A	ABD		Va Tech	1976
Benhabib, Jess	Prof	New York U	EO	PHD	76	Columbia	1980
Benham, Lee K.	Prof	Wash Univ	LP	PHD	70	Stanford	1974
Benitez-Silva, Hugo	Asst	SUNY-Stony B		PHD			
Benito, Carlos	Prof	Sonoma State	O	PHD	73	Ca-Davis	1990
Benjamin, Daniel K.	Prof	Clemson	DEGJ	PHD	75	UCLA	1985
Benjamin, Julian	Prof	N Carol A&T		PHD	77	SUNY-Buf	
Bennett, Charles A.	Asst	Gannon	A	MA	68	Fordham	1968
Bennett, Doris S.	Prof	Jacksonvl St		PHD	79	Alabama	1986
Bennett, James T.	Prof	George Mason		PHD	70	Case Wes	1975
William P. Snavely Professor of Economics							
Bennett, R. J.	Retir	Aquinas		PHD		St Louis	1969
Bennett, Randall W.	Prof	Gonzaga	HL	PHD	84	Mich St	1988
Bennett, Richard E.	Retir	Kent State	C	PHD	70	Ohio St	1968
Bennett, Robert L.	Retir	Maryland		PHD	63	Tx-Austin	1966
Benoit, Jean-Pierre	Prof	New York U	D	PHD	83	Stanford	1989
Benson, Bruce L.	Prof	Florida St	K	PHD	78	Tx A&M	1987
VeDoe Moore Distinguished Research Professor							
Benson, C. Scott	Assoc	Idaho State	ABEF	PHD	88	Ca-Davis	1990
Benston, George J.	Prof	Emory	GKLM	PHD	63	Chicago	9-87
John H. Harland Professor of Finance, Economics, and Accounting							
Bentley, Jerome T.	Assoc	Rider	D	PHD	74	Pittsburgh	1974
Bentley, Marion	ExtSp	Utah State	H	MPA	70	NYU	1975
Benz, George A.	Retir	St Marys-Txs		PHD	69	Oklahoma	1985
Benzing, Cynthia D.	Prof	West Chester	AEG	PHD	87	Drexel	1988
Bera, Anil K.	Prof	Illinois	C	PHD	83	Austr Natl	1983
Berdell, John	Assoc	DePaul	NE	PHD	91	Cambridge	1991
Bereskin, C. Gregory	Prof	St Ambrose		PHD	83	Missouri	1991
Berg, Milo Douglas	Asst	Sam Houston		PHD	95	Tx A&M	1995
Berg, Nathan	Asst	Texas-Dallas		PHD	01	Kansas	2001
Berg, Sanford V.	Prof	Florida	T	PHD	70	Yale	1971
Exec Dir Public Utility Research Ctr;Public Utilities & Distinguished Serv Pr							
Bergan, Daniel J.	Assoc	NE Illinois	ADEG	PHD	85	Tx Tech	
Bergemann, Dirk	Asst	Yale		PHD	94	Penn	
Berger, David E.	Prof	Mass-Dartmou	IJOR	PHD	72	Wash U	1972
Berger, George	C-Ac	Pitts-Johnst	EJK	PHD	87	Ca-Davis	1989
Berger, Mark C.	Prof	Kentucky	J	PHD	81	Ohio St	1981
Stugill Professor							
Bergeron, Suzanne	VAsst	Mich-Dearbor	BENO	PHD	98	Notre Dm	1998
Bergin, Paul	Asst	Cal-Davis	EF	PHD	96	Yale	1996
Bergman, Lila	Retir	CUNY-Hunter		MBA	79	Fordham	9-85
Bergmann, Barbara R.	Retir	American U		PHD	59	Harvard	1988
Bergsten, Gordon S.	Assoc	Dickinson Cl	BNDE	PHD	77	Berkeley	1984
Bergstrand, Jeffrey	Assoc	Notre Dame	EF	PHD	81	Wisconsin	1986
Bergstrom, Theodore C.	Prof	Cal-Santa Br		PHD	67	Stanford	
Berik, Gunseli	Assoc	Utah		PHD	86	Mass	1994
Berkowitz, Daniel	Asst	Pittsburgh	GH	PHD	88	Columbia	1992
Berliant, Marcus C.	Prof	Wash Univ	DHR	PHD	82	Berkeley	1994
Berman, Eli	Asst	Boston Univ	CJ	PHD	93	Harvard	1993

Bernanke, Ben S.	C-Pr	Princeton		PHD	79	MIT	1985
Bernard, James A. Jr.	Assoc	Valparaiso	AOP	PHD	72	Notre Dm	1968
Bernasek, Alexandra	Assoc	Colorado St	DA	PHD	92	Michigan	1992
Berney, Robert E.	Retir	Wash State		PHD	63	Wisconsin	1966
Bernhardt, Dan	Prof	Illinois	DGJL	PHD	86	Car Mellon	1998
Bernheim, B. Douglas	Prof	Stanford		PHD	82	MIT	1994
Lewis and Virginia Eaton Professor in Economics							
Bernhofen, Daniel	Assoc	Clark		PHD	94	Syracuse	1994
Bernstein, Richard E.	Assoc	Temple	MG	PHD	73	Brown	1972
Beron, Kurt J.	Assoc	Texas-Dallas		PHD	85	N Carol	1985
Berrens, Robert	Assoc	New Mexico	DQ	PHD	93	Oregon St	1994
Berri, David	Asst	Coe	BD	PHD	97	Colo St	1998
Berry, Brian J. L.	Prof	Texas-Dallas		PHD	58	U Wash	
L. V. Berkner Professor							
Berry, Charles A.	Prof	Cincinnati	O	PHD	68	Cincinnati	1961
Berry, Dale A.	Retir	Drake		PHD	66	Indiana	1962
Berry, Stanley Keith	Assoc	Hendrix	DL	PHD	79	Vanderbilt	1989
Berry, Steven T.	Prof	Yale		PHD	89	Wisconsin	1988
Bertaux, Nancy E.	Prof	Xavier	ABJN	PHD	87	Michigan	1985
Best, Michael	Asst	Berea		PHD	94	Kentucky	1996
Betancourt, Roger R.	Prof	Maryland		PHD	69	Wisconsin	1980
Bethune, John J.	Dean	Barton		PHD	87	Fla St	8-00
Betsey, Charles L.	Prof	Howard	J	PHD	76	Michigan	1990
Betson, David M.	Assoc	Notre Dame	HI	PHD	80	Wisconsin	1979
Bettinger, Eric	Asst	Case Western	IS	PHD	00	MIT	2000
Betts, Caroline	Assoc	So Calif		PHD	94	Brit Colum	1994
Betts, Julian R.	Prof	Ca-San Diego	CJ	PHD	90	Queen's	1990
Beutler, Martin K.	Prof	So Dakota St	Q	PHD	86	Purdue	1986
Beuttenmuller, Doris Henle	Retir	Webster	AIJN	PHD	52	St Louis	1974
Beversluis, Eric H.	C-Ac	Aquinas		PHD	70	Nrthwstrn	1988
Bewley, Truman F.	Prof	Yale	D	PHD	70	Berkeley	1983
Bezmen, Trisha	Asst	Old Dominion	F	PHD	98	Georgia	1999
Bezuneh, Mesfin	C-Ac	Clark Atlant		PHD	85	Va Tech	
Bhagwati, Jagdish	Prof	Columbia	F	PHD	67	MIT	1980
Bhandari, Ravi	Asst	Hawaii-Hilo		PHD	01	Amherst	2001
Bhargava, Alok	Prof	Houston	C	PHD	82	London	1989
Bhargava, Ashok	C-Pr	Wis-Whitewat		PHD	75	Wisconsin	1970
Bhat, Mahadev G.	Assoc	Fla Internat	Q	PHD	91	Tennessee	1994
Bhatacharya, Joydeep	Asst	Iowa State	E	PHD	96	Cornell	1999
Bhatia, Shyam L.	Assoc	Indiana NW	FDEL	PHD	76	Indiana	1976
Bhattacharya, Anindya	Asst	CUNY-Brookly		PHD	71	Columbia	1998
Bhattacharya, Gautam	Assoc	Kansas	LDO	PHD	80	Rochester	1980
Bianconi, Marcello	Assoc	Tufts	E	PHD	88	Illinois	1989
Bias, Peter V.	Assoc	Fla Southern	ER	PHD	89	Cincinnati	1988
Bice, Douglas	Asst	E New Mexico		PHD	96	Kentucky	1997
Bidarkota, Prasad V.	Asst	Kansas State	CEG	PHD	96	Ohio St	1999
Biddle, Jeff E.	Prof	Michigan St		PHD	85	Duke	1985
Biederman, Daniel K.	Assoc	North Dakota	CGI	PHD	87	Kansas	1987
Bieker, Richard F.	Prof	Delaware St		PHD	70	Kentucky	
Bierens, Herman	Prof	Penn State		PHD	80	Amsterdm	1996
Bierhanzl, Elwood	Assoc	Florida A&M					
Bierman, H. Scott	Prof	Carleton	DHL	PHD	85	Virginia	1982
Ada M. Harrison Professor of Social Sciences							
Biewener, Carole	Assoc	Simmons	EB	PHD	89	Mass	1987
Biglaiser, Gary	Prof	No Carolina	EL	PHD	88	Berkeley	1988
Billes, Frank V.	C-Pr	CS-Dominguez	AENP	PHD	74	UCLA	1972
Billger, Sherrilyn	VAsst	Union	IO	PHD	00	Illinois	2000
Billings, C. David	Dean	Alabama-Hunt	H	PHD	69	Missouri	1981
Bilodeau, Marc	Assoc	Ind-Purdue/I	HL	PHD	90	W Ontario	1996
Bils, Mark J.	Prof	Rochester	D	PHD	85	MIT	1985
Bin, Oxmuung	Asst	East Carol	CQ	PHD	98	Oregon St	2001
Binder, Melissa	Asst	New Mexico	FJO	PHD	95	Columbia	1995
Binder, Michael	Asst	Maryland		PHD	95	Penn	1995
Biolsi, Robert	Asst	St Peters	FG	PHD		CUNY	6-97
Birch, John W.	Emer	Wyoming	1995	PHD	62	J Hopkins	1964
Birckmayer, H. Peter	Retir	SUNY-Empire	O	MBA	56	Cornell	1983
Bird, Michael C.	Prof	Colorado Col		PHD	68	Colorado	1968
Bisakha, Sen	Asst	Cen Florida	J	PHD	98	Ohio St	1998
Bischoff, Charles W.	Prof	SUNY-Bingham	EC	PHD	68	MIT	1977
Bishop, John A.	Prof	East Carol	DHI	PHD	87	Alabama	1988
Bisin, Alberto	Asst	New York U	D	PHD	93	Chicago	1997
Bisping, T.	Asst	Louisiana Te	DJL	PHD	97	Oklahoma	2000
Biswas, Basudeb	Prof	Utah State	CFO	PHD	76	Chicago	1976
Biven, W. Carl	Prof	Georgia Tech	EB	PHD	56	St Louis	1958
Bivin, David	Assoc	Ind-Purdue/I	E	PHD	80	Purdue	1985
Bjork, Gordon C.	Prof	Claremont		PHD	63	U Wash	1975
Jonathan B. Lovelace Professor							
Black, Dan A.	C-Pr	Syracuse	DJI	PHD	83	Purdue	1999
Black, David C.	Assoc	Toledo	E	PHD	92	SUNY-Buf	1990
Black, David E.	Assoc	Delaware	HO	PHD	69	MIT	1975

Black, Duncan	Asst	Calif-Irvine		PHD	99	Brown	1999
Black, Fischer	Deces	Goldman Sach	1995	PHD	64	Harvard	1984
Black, Stanley W.	Prof	No Carolina	F	PHD	65	Yale	1983
Lurcy Professor							
Black, Tyrone	Prof	So Miss	E	PHD	70	Tulane	1969
Blackburn, McKinley L.	Prof	So Carolina		PHD	87	Harvard	1987
Blackburne, Edward	Asst	Sam Houston		PHD	98	Tx A&M	1997
Blackley, Dixie M.	Prof	LeMoyne	DRC	PHD	84	Syracuse	1982
Blackley, Paul R.	Prof	LeMoyne	HR	PHD	82	Syracuse	1982
Blackstone, Erwin A.	Prof	Temple	L	PHD	68	Michigan	1976
Blackwell, Calvin	Asst	Charleston		PHD	01	New Mex	2001
Blackwell, J. Lloyd III	Prof	North Dakota	C	PHD	73	Geo St	1980
Blackwell, Melanie A.	Assoc	Xavier	ACQ	PHD	88	Kentucky	1987
Blair, Benjamin	Assoc	Miss State	DL	PHD	92	Florida	1997
Blair, Douglas H.	Prof	Rutgers-N Br	D	PHD	76	Yale	1981
Blair, John	Prof	Wright State	HR	PHD	74	W Virginia	1981
Blair, Roger Duncan	Prof	Florida	KT	PHD	68	Mich St	1970
Huber Hurst Professor of Business and Legal Studies							
Blais, Jeffrey	Assoc	Rhode Isl Cl		PHD	75	Pittsburgh	1986
Blake, Daniel R.	Prof	CS-Northrdge		PHD	71	Oregon	1971
Blake, Gordon	Retir	Neb-Kearney		PHD	70	Nebraska	1963
Blakemore, Arthur E.	C-Pr	Arizona St		PHD	77	S Illinois	1979
Blalock, M. Gale	C-Ac	Evansville		PHD	80	Okla St	1977
Blanchard, Olivier J.	H-Pr	MIT	G	PHD	77	MIT	1985
Class of 1941 Professor of Economics							
Blanchflower, David Graham	Prof	Dartmouth		PHD	85	London	1989
Blank, Emily	Assoc	Howard	J	PHD	85	Boston C	1985
Blankenau, William F.	Asst	Kansas State	EC	PHD	97	Iowa	2001
Blankmeyer, Eric	Prof	SW Texas St	F	PHD	71	Princeton	1982
Blattenberger, Gail R.	Retir	Utah		PHD	77	Michigan	1981
Blau, David M.	Prof	No Carolina	J	PHD	80	Wisconsin	1992
Blecha, Betty J.	Prof	San Fran St		PHD	76	Iowa	1983
Blecker, Robert A.	Prof	American U		PHD	87	Stanford	1985
Blevins, Dallas R.	Prof	Montevallo		DBA	76	Fla St	1983
Blewett, Robert A.	C-Pr	St Lawrence	OR	PHD	80	Va Tech	1983
Blinder, Alan S.	Prof	Princeton		PHD	71	MIT	1971
Blitstein, Allen	Prof	SW State	DFN	PHD	72	Minnesota	1976
Bloch, Howard Ruben	Retir	George Mason		PHD	64	Princeton	
Block, Michael K.	Prof	Arizona		PHD	72	Stanford	1981
Block, Walter	Prof	Loyola-NO		PHD	72	Columbia	5-01
Harold E. Wirth Eminent Scholar Endowed Chair in Economics							
Blomberg, Brock	Assoc	Wellesley	E	PHD	94	J Hopkins	1995
Blomquist, Glenn C.	C-Pr	Kentucky	IHQ	PHD	77	Chicago	1980
Pollard Professor							
Blonigen, Bruce A.	Assoc	Oregon	FL	PHD	95	Ca-Davis	1995
Bloom, Jay D.	Retir	SUNY-N Paltz	ADJ	MA	58	Chicago	1965
Bloomfield, Arthur I.	Emer	Pennsylvania		PHD	42	Chicago	1958
Bloss, Richard J.	Retir	Chicago St		PHD		Penn	1968
Blume, Andreas	Prof	Pittsburgh		PHD	87	Ca-SnDgo	2000
Blume, Lawrence E.	Prof	Cornell		PHD	77	Berkeley	
Blumenthal, Marsha A.	Prof	St Thomas-MN	JH	PHD	85	Minnesota	1984
Blumner, Sidney M.	Retir	CS-Pomona		PHD	68	Arizona	1967
Blush, Lawrence D.	Retir	West Liberty		MA	59	Ohio St	1963
Boal, William M.	Assoc	Drake		PHD	85	Stanford	1995
Bober, Stanley	Prof	Duquesne		PHD	62	NYU	1964
Bobo, James R.	Emer	So Alabama		PHD	61	LSU	1978
Bochnak, Mary	Assoc	Hamline	M	PHD	82	Minnesota	1990
Boddy, Raford D.	Prof	San Diego St		PHD	68	Michigan	1980
Bodenhorn, Howard	Assoc	Lafayette	AN	PHD	90	Rutgers	1993
Bodily, Jerry J.	Prof	St Marys-Cal		PHD	74	Purdue	1978
Bodo, Peter	Assoc	So Conn St	CL	PHD	91	Conn	
Bodvarsson, Orn B.	Prof	St Cloud St		PHD	86	Simon Fr	1988
Boeh, Jeanne	C-Ac	Augsburg	I	PHD	89	Il-Chicago	1990
Bogan, Elizabeth C.	Prof	Princeton		PHD	71	Columbia	
Bogart, Marti S.	Assoc	No Central	J	PHD	86	Purdue	1982
Bogart, William T.	C-Ac	Case Western	HRDA	PHD	90	Princeton	1990
Boger, Dan C.	Prof	Naval Postgr	C	PHD	79	Berkeley	1979
Boggess, Trent E.	Prof	Plymouth St		PHD	80	Kansas	1983
Bognanno, Michael	Asst	Temple	J	PHD	90	Cornell	1990
Bogomolnaia, Anna	Asst	So Methodist	DC	PHD		Barcelonia	1999
Bohanon, Cecil E.	Prof	Ball State	H	PHD	81	Va Tech	1980
Bohara, Alok	Prof	New Mexico	CQ	PHD	86	Colorado	1987
Bohling, Peter H.	Prof	Bloomsburg		PHD	77	Mass	1978
Bohm, Robert A.	Prof	Tennessee		PHD	71	Wash U	1968
Bohmer, Peter G.		Evergreen St		PHD	85	Mass	1987
Bohn, Henning	Prof	Cal-Santa Br	EF	PHD	86	Stanford	1992
Boileau, Martin	Asst	Colorado		PHD	94	Queen's	1998
Boivin, Jean	Asst	Columbia		PHD	99	Princeton	1999
Boko, Sylvain	Asst	Wake Forest		PHD	96	Iowa St	1997
Boland, Dennis	Assoc	Univ of D C	BA	PHD	70	Illinois	1976

Bolch, Ben W.	Prof	Rhodes		PHD	66	N Carol	1987
Bold, Frederick	Asst	Nev-L Vegas	D	PHD		U Wash	1995
Boldt, David John	C-Ac	West Georgia	AR	PHD	87	New Mex	1988
Bolduc, Steven	Asst	Mn-Moorhead		MA	93	Indiana	2000
Bolino, August C.	Retir	Catholic		PHD	57	St Louis	
Bollerslev, Tim	Prof	Duke	CG	PHD	86	Ca-SnDgo	1999
Bollinger, Christopher R.	Assoc	Kentucky	CDJ	PHD	93	Wisconsin	1998
Bolton, Roger E.	Prof	Williams		PHD	64	Harvard	1966
William Brough Professor of Economics							
Bom, Philip C.	Prof	Regent	FOP	PHD		Free	1983
Bombelles, Joseph T.	Retir	John Carroll	ABOP	PHD	65	Case Wes	1963
Bomberger, William A.	Assoc	Florida		PHD	73	Brown	1977
Bonanno, Giacomo F.	Prof	Cal-Davis	CD	PHD	75	LondonEc	1987
Bond, Eric W.	Prof	Penn State	F	PHD	79	Rochester	1981
Bond, Larry Keith	Retir	Utah State	Q	PHD	72	Utah St	1972
Bond, Richard E.	Assoc	Duquesne		PHD	69	Maryland	1969
Bondreaux, Donald	C-Pr	George Mason		PHD	86	Auburn	
Bonello, Frank J.	Assoc	Notre Dame	EA	PHD	68	Mich St	1968
Bonham, Carl S.	Assoc	Hawaii-Manoa		PHD	89	Tx-Austin	1989
Bonhan, John M.	Retir	Tulsa		PHD	65	Okla St	
Bonin, John P.	C-Pr	Wesleyan-CT	P	PHD	73	Rochester	1970
Andrews Professor of Economics							
Bonitsis, T. Homer	Asst	NJ Inst Tech		PHD	84	CUNY	1990
Bonsor, Thomas W.	Deces	East Wash		MA	55	Tufts	1958
Bonutti, Karl	Retir	Cleveland St		PHD		Fribourg	1965
Booker, H. Marshall	Prof	Chris Newpor	AFMO	PHD	65	Virginia	1971
Booker, James F.	C-Ac	Alfred		PHD	90	Colo St	1993
Bookman, Milica Z.	Assoc	St Joseph	OP	PHD	83	Temple	1983
Boor, Randy	Assoc	Mary		MS		N Dak St	
Booth, Donald R.	Prof	Chapman	AD	PHD	70	UCLA	1959
Booth, Douglas E.	Assoc	Marquette	DQ	PHD	72	U Wash	1976
Booth, John M.	Retir	Stetson		PHD		Penn	1973
Boozer, Michael A.	Asst	Yale	DJ	PHD	94	Princeton	1993
Border, Kim Christian	Assoc	Cal Tech	C	PHD	79	Minnesota	1979
Bordo, Michael D.	Prof	Rutgers-N Br	N	PHD	72	Chicago	1981
Borg, Mary O.	Prof	North Fla	HT	PHD	85	N Carol	1984
Borges, Antonio	Dean	INSEAD	EQA	PHD	80	Stanford	9-93
Borland, Melvin V.	Prof	W Kentucky	BDA	PHD	72	Wash U	1978
Boronico, Jess	Prof	Wm Paterson		PHD	92	Penn	2001
Borts, George H.	Prof	Brown		PHD	53	Chicago	1964
George S. and Nancy B. Parker Professor of Economics							
Bos, Theodore	Prof	Alabama-Birm	CG	PHD	82	Illinois	1982
Bose, Mrigen	Assoc	Scranton		PHD	72	Utah	1968
Bose, Pinaki	Assoc	Memphis	LD	PHD	90	NYU	9-95
Bose, Subir	Asst	Iowa State	D	PHD	96	Yale	1996
Boskin, Michael J.	Prof	Stanford		PHD	71	Berkeley	1970
Tully Friedman Professor in Economics							
Bossaerts, Peter	Assoc	Cal Tech	G	PHD	86	UCLA	1990
Bosshardt, William D.	Assoc	Fla Atlantic	F	PHD	91	Purdue	1995
Bostaph, Samuel H.	C-Ac	Dallas	BNP	PHD	76	S Illinois	1981
Boston, Thomas D.	Prof	Georgia Tech	JN	PHD	76	Cornell	1985
Bosworth, Derek L.	Prof	Manches Inst	JOD	PHD		Warwick	1992
Botana, Joseph D.	Asst	Lakeland	AFND	MBA		Roosevelt	1990
Botsas, Eleftherios N.	Retir	Oakland	FA	PHD	65	Wayne St	1976
Botticini, Maristella	Asst	Boston Univ	N	ABD		Nrthwstrn	1997
Bottoms, I. Glenn	Prof	Gardner-Webb		PHD	81	Geo St	1983
Botwinick, Howard I.	Assoc	SUNY-Cortlan	BJ	PHD	88	New Sch	1985
Boucher-Breuer, Janice L.	Assoc	So Carolina		PHD	87	N Carol	1987
Boulier, Bryan L.	Prof	George Wash	JT	PHD	74	Princeton	1981
Bound, John	Prof	Michigan		PHD	87	Harvard	
Bourque, Philip J.	Retir	U Washington		PHD	56	Penn	1957
Bove, Roger E.	Assoc	West Chester	FP	PHD	73	Harvard	1984
Bowe, Michael A.	Lect	Manches Inst	EFG	PHD	89	Carleton	1993
Bowen, Freddie R. Jr.	Retir	Norfolk St	CHA	MA	70	Wash U	1970
Bowerman, Priscilla V.		Evergreen St		MPHI	71	Yale	1973
Bowers, Patricia F.	Retir	CUNY-Brookly	G	PHD	65	NYU	1964
Bowlby, Roger L.	Retir	Tennessee		PHD	58	Tx-Austin	1965
Bowles, Samuel S.	Prof	Massachusett		PHD	65	Harvard	1973
Bowles, Tyler	Asst	Utah State	AF	PHD	91	N Carol	1994
Bowles, W. Donald	Retir	American U	1994	PHD	58	Columbia	1957
Bowling, James	Retir	Jackson St		PHD	85	Miss	1975
Bowman, Gary W.	Assoc	Temple	D	PHD	71	Car Mellon	1973
Bowman, John H.	Prof	Virg Comm		PHD	73	Ohio St	1981
Bowman, Judy C.	Lect	Baylor		MS	74	Baylor	1974
Bowman, Mary Jean	Emer	Chicago		PHD	38	Harvard	1958
Bowman, Rhead S.	Assoc	So Utah		PHD	75	Utah	1978
Bowman, William R.	C-Pr	USN Academy		PHD	79	Maryland	1980
Bown, Chad B.	Asst	Brandeis		PHD	99	Wisconsin	1999
Bownds, Lynne	Asst	East Wash		PHD	98	Tennessee	1999
Boyce, James K.	Prof	Massachusett		PHD	85	Oxford	1985

Boyce, Nathan	Asst	Willamette		PHD	01	Stanford	2001
Boyd, David W.	Assoc	Denison	KLD	PHD	91	Ohio St	1991
Boyd, John H. III	Assoc	Fla Internat	DC	PHD	86	Indiana	1998
Boyd, Laura A.	Assoc	Denison	JI	PHD	91	Ohio St	1991
Boyd, Roy G.	Prof	Ohio Univ	QH	PHD	81	Duke	1984
Boyer, Carol	Asst	Clarkson	GM	PHD	00	Fla St	2000
Boyer, Kenneth D.	Prof	Michigan St		PHD	75	Michigan	1984
Boyes, William J.	Prof	Arizona St		PHD	74	Claremont	1969
Boyet, Wayne E.	Prof	Nicholls St	G	PHD	65	N Car St	1985
Boylan, Richard	Assoc	Mississippi	DHK	PHD	91	Cal Tech	1999
Brada, Josef C.	Prof	Arizona St		PHD	71	Minnesota	1978
Bradburd, Ralph M.	Prof	Williams		PHD	76	Columbia	1976
David A. Wells Professor of Political Economy							
Bradfield, James	Prof	Hamilton	GD	PHD	73	Rochester	1976
Bradford, Colin	Prof	American U		PHD	70	Columbia	1998
Bradford, David F.	Prof	Princeton		PHD	66	Stanford	1966
Bradford, Scott	Asst	Brigham Yg	F	PHD	98	Harvard	1998
Bradley, James Jr.	DLect	So Carolina	AHM	CHPL	70	N Carol	9-74
Bradley, Michael D.	Prof	George Wash	E	PHD	82	N Carol	1987
Bradley, Michael E.	Prof	MD-Baltim Co		PHD	67	Cornell	
Bradley, Steven	SLect	U Lancaster		PHD		Lancaster	
Brady, James J.	Prof	Jacksonvil U		PHD	69	Notre Dm	
Jessie Ball duPont Professor of Economics							
Braeutigam, Ronald R.	Prof	Northwestern		PHD	76	Stanford	1975
Harvey Kapnick Professor of Business Institutions & Transportation Center							
Braid, Ralph M.	Prof	Wayne State	R	PHD	79	MIT	1988
Brainard, William C.	Prof	Yale	DE	PHD	63	Yale	1981
Brainerd, Elizabeth	Asst	Williams		PHD	96	Harvard	1996
Brajer, Victor	Assoc	CS-Fullerton	DQ	PHD	83	New Mex	1987
Bramhall, David F.	Emer	Colo-Denver		PHD	61	Penn	
Branch, William	Asst	Wm & Mary		PHD	01	Oregon	2001
Brannon, J. Isaac	Assoc	Wis-Oshkosh	J	PHD	93	Indiana	1994
Brannon, Jeffery T.	Assoc	Txs-El Paso	JNO	PHD	80	Alabama	1982
Branson, William H.	Prof	Princeton		PHD	67	MIT	1967
Branstetter, Lee	Asst	Cal-Davis	FL	PH	96	Harvard	1996
Brasfield, David	Prof	Murray State	EGC	PHD	89	N Carol	1986
Brasington, David	Asst	Tulane		PHD	99	Ohio St	1998
Brastow, Raymond T.	Assoc	Longwood	J	PHD	87	U Wash	1987
Brat, David	Asst	Randolph-Mac	DBO	PHD	95	American	1996
Bratsberg, Bernt	Prof	Kansas State	JD	PHD	91	Ca-SnBarb	1991
Brauer, Jurgen	Assoc	Augusta	AFIT	PHD	89	Notre Dm	1991
Braun, Bradley M.	Assoc	Cen Florida	D	PHD	86	Tulane	1986
Bray, Robert T.	Prof	CS-Pomona		PHD	72	UCLA	1965
Brazelton, W. Robert	Emer	Mo-Kansas Ct	EP	PHD	61	Oklahoma	1963
Brechling, Frank P.	Retir	Maryland		PHD	55	Trinity	1979
Breece, James H.	Assoc	Maine	AEF	PHD	82	Boston C	1983
Breeden, Charles H.	Assoc	Marquette	DHK	PHD	77	Va Tech	1979
Breger, Gerald E.	Emer	So Carolina		PHD	64	Arkansas	
Breisch, Rob	Inst	USAF Academy		MA	99	Utah	2000
Breit, William L.	Prof	Trinity	B	PHD	61	Mich St	1982
Vernon F. Taylor Distinguished Professor of Economics							
Brendler, Michael D.	Prof	La St-Shreve		PHD	77	Tx A&M	1977
Brennan, David	Asst	Frank & Mars		PHD	00	Notre Dm	1998
Brennan, Michael J.	Retir	Wesleyan-CT	J	PHD	56	Chicago	1974
Brent, Robert J.	Assoc	Fordham		PHD	76	Manchest	1980
Breslia, Thomas	Prof	C New Jersey		PHD	76	W Virginia	
Bresnahan, Timothy F.	Prof	Stanford		PHD	80	Princeton	1979
Bresnock, Anne E.	Prof	CS-Pomona		PHD	81	Colorado	1990
Brester, Gary	Assoc	Montana St		PHD	90	N Car St	1997
Brewer, Stephanie M.	Asst	Indiana U-PA	DHF	PHD	99	Indiana	1999
Brewton, Audie R.	Assoc	NE Illinois	CBDN	PHD	79	Utah	1984
Brickley, Colleen	Inst	Plymouth St	D	ABD	78	NewHamp	1993
Bridges, Deborah	Asst	Neb-Kearney		PHD	94	Wash St	1997
Briefs, Henry W.	Retir	Georgetown		PHD	54	Geotown	1973
Briggs, Charles	Inst	Alabama A&M	A	MS	90	Alab A&M	1990
Briley, James	Asst	Cumberland		PHD	98	Tx Tech	1985
Brimmer, Andrew F.	VProf	Massachusett		PHD	57	Harvard	
Brinkman, Richard L.	Retir	Portland St		PHD	65	Rutgers	1961
Brite, Robert L.	Retir	New Orleans		PHD	69	Rutgers	1970
Brito, Dagobert L.	Prof	Rice		PHD	70	Rice	1984
George A. Peterkin Professor of Political Economy							
Britt, Robert D.	Retir	W Virginia	BN	PHD	66	Colorado	1968
Brittingham, Robert L.	Prof	Christian Br	AD	PHD	73	St Louis	1989
Britto, Ronald	Prof	SUNY-Bingham	FE	PHD	66	Brown	1974
Britton, Charles R.	Prof	Arkansas	E	PHD	71	Iowa	1978
Brocato, Joe M.	Prof	Tarleton St	CEG	PHD	81	Tennessee	1989
Brock, Baird A.	Prof	Cen Missouri		PHD	77	Arkansas	1969
Brock, Gerald W.	Prof	George Wash	L	PHD	73	Harvard	1990
Brock, Greg J.	Asst	Geo Southern	PO	PHD	89	Ohio St	1999

Brock, James W.	Prof	Miami U-Ohio	AK	PHD	81	Mich St	1979
Bill R. Moeckel Professor of Business							
Brock, John R. Jr.	VAsoc	Colorado Spr	DHKL	PHD	88	Cornell	1998
Brock, Philip L.	Assoc	U Washington		PHD	82	Stanford	1991
Brock, William Allen	Prof	Wisconsin		PHD	69	Berkeley	1981
F. P. Ramsey Professor of Economics							
Brod, Andrew C.	Inst	N Car-Greens	Q	PHD	92	Minnesota	1989
Broder, Ivy E.	Prof	American U		PHD	74	SUNY-SBr	1975
Brodsky, Noel	Assoc	E Illinois		PHD	88	Illinois	1988
Bronars, Stephen G.	C-Ac	Texas-Austin	JD	PHD	83	Chicago	9-92
Brook, Kathleen	Assoc	New Mex St	E	PHD	76	Tx-Austin	1980
Brooker, Robert F.	Assoc	Gannon	C	PHD	85	N Car St	1982
Brooking, Carl G.	Prof	Millsaps	CDK	PHD	74	Penn	1981
Brookins, Oscar T.	Assoc	Northeastern		PHD	76	SUNY-Buf	1983
Brooks, Eileen	Asst	Ca-Santa Crz	FL	PHD	01	Harvard	2001
Brooks, Nancy	Asst	Vermont	DHQR	PHD	94	Penn	1994
Brooks, Rickey A.	Asst	Freed Hardem	DEF	MBA	91	Miss	8-92
Brooks, Samuel W. III	Deces	Valdosta St		MBA		Georgia	1965
Brooks, T. J.	Asst	Wis-La Cross	CF	PHD	99	Wi-Milwa	1999
Brookshire, David S.	Prof	New Mexico	Q	PHD	76	New Mex	1989
Brorby, Bruce M.	Asst	Detroit Merc		MA	67	Detroit	1971
Brotman, Billie Ann	Prof	Kennesaw St	AGIM	PHD	78	Notre Dm	1989
Broude, Henry W.	Prof	Yale	N	PHD	54	Harvard	1978
Broughton, John B.	Prof	Chapman	G	PHD	89	Va Tech	1993
Brower, George D.	Assoc	Moravian	COM	PHD	85	SUNY-Buf	1989
Brown, Barry	Lect	Murray State	EOF	MS	77	Murray St	1991
Brown, Bruce	Asst	CS-Pomona		PHD		UCLA	
Brown, Bryan W.	Prof	Rice		PHD	77	Penn	1983
Hargrove Professor of Economics							
Brown, Byron B.	Retir	So Oregon St	FNOP	PHD	64	Houston	1968
Brown, Byron W.	Prof	Michigan St		PHD	66	J Hopkins	1978
Brown, Carl C.	C-Pr	Fla Southern	EFHL	PHD	79	Okla St	1980
William F. Chatlos Professorship in Business & Economics							
Brown, Charles C.	Prof	Michigan		PHD	74	Harvard	1985
Brown, Christopher R.	C-Ac	Arkansas St	AEKM	PHD	89	Tennessee	1990
Brown, David G.	Prof	Wake Forest		PHD	61	Princeton	1990
Brown, Donald J.	Prof	Yale					
Brown, Douglas	Prof	No Arizona	OP	PHD	85	Colo St	1985
Brown, Douglas M.	Assoc	Georgetown	DIR	PHD	69	W Virginia	1972
Brown, Drusilla K.	Assoc	Tufts	F	PHD	84	Michigan	1983
Brown, Gardner	Prof	U Washington	QDH	PHD	64	Berkeley	1965
Brown, J. Michael	Assoc	W Kentucky	G	PHD	71	Kentucky	1988
Brown, James	Prof	Rice		PHD	80	Chicago	1992
Brown, James D.	Retir	So Conn St		PHD		Wisconsin	
Brown, John C.	Assoc	Clark		PHD	86	Michigan	1986
Brown, John H.	Asst	Geo Southern		PHD	89	Mich St	1994
Brown, Ken	Assoc	No Iowa	CR	PHD	94	Illinois	1994
Brown, Lisa Jo	Assoc	East Wash		PHD	86	Colorado	1981
Brown, Meta	Asst	Wisconsin		PHD	01	NYU	2001
Brown, Murray	Retir	SUNY-Buffalo	CD	PHD	56	New Sch	1967
Brown, R. Clair	Prof	Cal-Berkeley	J	PHD	73	Maryland	9-73
Brown, Ralph J.	Prof	South Dakota		PHD	70	Colorado	1977
Brown, Robert E.	Deces	NW Missouri	1994	MA	56	Tx A&I	1971
Brown, Robert W.	Assoc	CS-S Marcos	GIKH	PHD	91	Ca-SnBarb	1997
Brown, William O.	Assoc	Claremont		PHD	93	Clemson	1994
Brown, William W.	Prof	CS-Northrdge		MA	66	UCLA	1975
Browne, M. Neil	Prof	Bowling Gr		PHD	69	Tx-Austin	1968
Distinguished Teaching Professor							
Browning, Edgar K.	Prof	Texas A&M	H	PHD	71	Princeton	1984
Alfred F. Chalk Professor of Economics							
Browning, Shirley C.	Prof	N Car-Ashvil	AEPQ	PHD	71	Conn	1970
Brownlee, Robert J.	Prof	Centre	AER	PHD	73	Syracuse	1978
Brownstein, Barry	Assoc	Baltimore		PHD	77	Rutgers	
Brownstone, David	Prof	Calif-Irvine		PHD	80	Berkeley	1984
Bruce, Donald	Asst	Tennessee				Syracuse	1999
Bruce, Neil	Prof	U Washington		PHD	75	Chicago	1990
Brue, Stanley L.	Prof	Pacific Luth	ABJ	PHD	71	Nebraska	1971
Brueckner, Jan K.	Prof	Illinois	DHR	PHD	76	Stanford	1976
Bruehler, James	Assoc	E Illinois		PHD	93	Illinois	1993
Bruggink, Thomas H.	Assoc	Lafayette	CQ	PHD	79	Illinois	1978
Bruner, Bill		Evergreen St		BA	67	W Wash	1981
Brunner, Eric	Asst	San Diego St		PHD	95	Ca-SnBarb	1998
Brunner, Lawrence P.	Assoc	Cen Michigan		PHD	81	J Hopkins	1982
Brunsen, William H.	C-Pr	E New Mexico	GHMA	PHD	76	Virginia	1987
Brunton, Bruce G.	Asst	Jms Madison	FNO	PHD	89	Utah	1984
Bruschke, Heinrich H.	Retir	St Louis		MA	63	Minnesota	1973
Brush, Brian C.	C-Pr	Marquette	DL	PHD	73	N Carol	1968
Brust, Peter J.	Assoc	Tampa	EF	PHD	80	Indiana	1981
Bruton, Henry J.	Emer	Williams		PHD	52	Harvard	1962
Brux, Jacqueline M.	Prof	Wis-Rvr Fall	O	PHD	83	Michigan	1986

Bryant, Harold L.	Retir	Xavier	AF	PHD	67	Cincinnati	1967
Bryant, John B.	Prof	Rice		PHD	75	Car Mellon	1981
Henry S. Fox, Sr. Professor of Economics							
Bryant, Richard R.	Assoc	Mo-Rolla		PHD	84	Ca-Davis	1977
Brzeski, Andrzej	Emer	Cal-Davis	AP	PHD	64	Berkeley	1963
Bubik, Osman	Prof	Bogazici	QR	PHD	73	Ca-Rivers	1974
Bucci, Gabriella A.	Assoc	DePaul	DH	PHD	88	J Hopkins	1989
Buccino, Joan G.	Prof	Fla Southern	A	PHD	90	S Fla	1980
Dorotha Tanner Chair in Ethics in Business & Economics							
Buchanan, James M.	Emer	George Mason		PHD	48	Chicago	1983
University Professor of Economics Emeritus							
Buchele, Robert	Prof	Smith	CAJP	PHD	76	Harvard	1977
Buchinsky, Moshe	Prof	Brown	CJ	PHD	91	Harvard	
Buck, Andrew J.	Prof	Temple	C	PHD	77	Illinois	1977
Buck, Donald T.	Retir	So Conn St	G	MA	61	NewHamp	1965
Buck, John	Asst	Jacksonvil U		PHD	89	Wisconsin	1994
Buck, Roland	Prof	Morehead St		PHD	79	Tx A&M	1983
Buechner, M. Northup	Assoc	St John's		PHD	71	Virginia	1970
Buehler, John E.	Retir	Arizona		PHD	67	SUNY-Buf	1968
Buettgen, Elise	Retir	Tx-Brownsvil	AFG	PHD	53	Kiel	1979
Buffie, Edward F.	Prof	Indiana		PHD	82	Yale	1992
Bugray, Ayse	Prof	Bogazici	BO	PHD	80	McGill	1985
Bui, Linda T.	Asst	Boston Univ	HLQ	PHD	93	MIT	1993
Bulan, Laarni	Asst	Brandeis		PHD	01	Columbia	2001
Bull, Jacqueline Henry	Asst	Immaculata		MA		Cen Mich	1998
Bull, Vivian A.	Prof	Linfield		PHD	74	NYU	1992
Bumgarner, Mary	Prof	Kennesaw St	AERH	PHD	84	Geo St	1985
Bumgarner, Sarah J.	Lect	N Car-Ashvil	A	MBA	82	Appalach	1990
Bumpass, Donald L.	Assoc	Sam Houston		PHD	76	Okla St	1992
Bungum, John L.	Assoc	Gustavus Ado		PHD	77	Nebraska	1979
Bunjun, Seewoonundun	Prof	E Stroudsbur	D	PHD	79	Penn St	1979
Bunkey, Mark	AdjAs	N Carol A&T		PHD		Duke	2000
Bunting, David C.	Prof	East Wash		PHD	72	Oregon	1971
Bunzel, Helle	Asst	Iowa State	C	PHD	99	Cornell	1999
Burczak, Ted A.	Asst	Dickinson Cl	ELF	PHD	94	Mass	
Burdekin, Richard C. K.	Prof	Claremont		PHD	85	Houston	1989
Burford, William E.	Retir	Denver	D-99	PHD	70	Ohio St	1969
Burger, John	Asst	Loyola-Maryl	FE	PHD	99	N Carol	1999
Burgess, Paul L.	Prof	Arizona St		PHD	69	Colorado	1969
Burggraf, Shirley	Prof	Florida A&M	CE	PHD	68	Case Wes	1968
Burgstaller, Andre C.	Prof	Barnard	EOBF	PHD	79	Columbia	1977
Burke, John F. Jr.	Retir	Cleveland St		PHD		Notre Dm	1967
Burke, John T.	Retir	W Michigan	Atg	PHD	58	Mich St	1962
Burke, Jonathan L.	Assoc	Ind-Purdue/I	C	PHD	85	MIT	1998
Burke, Kathleen	Asst	SUNY-Cortlan	CD	PHD		SUNY-SBr	1999
Burke, Mary A.	Asst	Florida St	D	PHD	98	J Hopkins	1997
Burke, Melvin	Prof	Maine	O	PHD	67	Pittsburgh	1966
Burke, Ronald L.	Prof	Chadron St	MQE	PHD	70	Minnesota	1987
Burke, Thomas F.	VAsst	St Joseph		PHD	99	Temple	1995
Burkett, Evelyn	Asst	Ark-Pine Blf		MA		Houston	
Burkett, John P.	Prof	Rhode Island	CDFI	PHD	81	Berkeley	1981
Burkett, Paul G.	Prof	Indiana St	EO	PHD	84	Syracuse	1991
Burmeister, Edwin	Resr	Duke	GC	PHD	65	MIT	
Burnell, Barbara S.	Prof	Wooster		PHD	77	Illinois	1977
Burnell, James D.	C-Pr	Wooster		PHD	77	Illinois	1977
Burness, H. Stuart	Prof	New Mexico	CDQ	PHD	70	Kansas	1978
Burnett, Nancy J.	Assoc	Wis-Oshkosh	E	PHD	88	UCLA	1994
Burnside, A. Craig	Retir	Pittsburgh	4-95	PHD	91	Nrthwstrn	1992
Burrus, Robert T.	Asst	N Car-Wilmin	D	PHD	97	Virginia	
Burton, Mark L.	Asst	Marshall		PHD	91	Tennessee	1999
Burton, Maureen	Prof	CS-Pomona		PHD	86	Ca-Rivers	1988
Burton, Robert C.	Deces	Frostburg St		PHD	62	Virginia	
Buschena, David E.	Asst	Montana St		PHD	93	Berkeley	1992
Bush, H. Francis	Prof	Va Military		PHD	89	Florida	1994
Bush, Paul D.	Retir	CS-Fresno	AL	PHD	64	Claremont	1961
Buss, James A.	Prof	Fairfield	EOP	PHD	72	Conn	1975
Butcher, Kristin F.	Asst	Boston Coll	DJ	PHD	93	Princeton	1995
Butkiewicz, James L.	Prof	Delaware	E	PHD	77	Virginia	1976
Butler, Alison	Assoc	Kent State	FEO	PHD	89	Oregon	1999
Butler, Donald T.	Retir	Central Iowa		PHD	60	Wisconsin	1953
Butler, Doug		Georgia Col		ABD			
Butler, James F.	Retir	Ark-Ltl Rock		PHD	68	LSU	1963
Butler, Michael R.	Assoc	Tx Christian		PHD	86	N Carol	1986
Butler, Michael W.	Dean	Angelo State	P	PHD	74	Iowa	2001
Butler, Richard J.	Prof	Brigham Yg	J	PHD	79	Chicago	1982
Butler, Richard V.	Prof	Trinity	H	PHD	77	MIT	1982
Butler, Sister Agnes	Asst	Molloy		ABD		Indiana	
Butos, William N.	C-Pr	Trinity-CT		PHD	83	Penn St	1981
Bynoe, Ann	Assoc	Pace		PHD	79	NYU	1997
Byrne, Dennis	Retir	Akron	AJL	PHD	75	Notre Dm	1975

Byrne, Donald R.	Prof	Detroit Merc		PHD	71	Notre Dm	1966
Caballero, Ricardo	Prof	MIT	E	PHD	88	MIT	1992
Cabe, Richard	Assoc	New Mex St	K	PHD	83	Wyoming	1988
Cabral, Luis M. B.	Prof	New York U	DL	PHD	89	Stanford	2000
Cabrera, Glenn	Asst	Bethel-MN	CF	PHD	98	Rice	2001
Cadet, Marc	Assoc	Grambling St		PHD	91	Kansas St	9-68
Cadot, Olivier	Assoc	INSEAD		PHD	89	Princeton	9-89
Cagatay, Nilufer	Assoc	Utah		PHD	86	Stanford	1991
Cagetti, Marco	Asst	Virginia	E	PHD	00	Chicago	2000
Cagliesi, Gabriella	Asst	Rutgers-Newk		PHD	93	Penn	
Cahill, Gerard	Assoc	Fla Inst Tec	AG	PHD	73	NYU	1987
Cahill, Miles B.	Asst	Holy Cross	AEJ	PHD	95	Purdue	1995
Cahill, Neil S.J.	Deces	Creighton	1-01	MA	47	St Louis	1962
Cain, Louis P.	C-Pr	Loyola-Chicg	ADNR	PHD	69	Nrthwstrn	1968
Caines, W. Royce	Prof	Lander	ALPQ	PHD	88	Clemson	1988
Cairo, Joseph P.	Asst	LaSalle	BE	MA		Penn	1963
Cakici, Nusret	Assoc	CUNY-City C	G	PHD	89	Baruch	1997
Calabro, Eugene A.	Prof	Salem State		MA		Boston C	
Calandri, Kevin	Prof	CS-Sacrament		PHD	85	Ca-Davis	1986
Calcagno, Peter	Asst	Wingate		PHD	97	Auburn	1999
Caldwell, Bruce J.	Prof	N Car-Greens	B	PHD	79	N Carol	1978
Calgaard, Ronald K.	Retir	Trinity		PHD	63	Iowa	1979
Calkins, Lindsay Noble	Assoc	John Carroll	ADH	PHD	86	Michigan	1986
Call, Stephen T.	Prof	Metro St-CO	ADE	PHD	77	Indiana	1979
Callan, Scott J.	Prof	Bentley	CDQ	PHD	85	Tx A&M	1987
Callari, Antonio	C-Pr	Frank & Mars		PHD	81	Mass	1979
Calvet, Laurent E.	Asst	Harvard		PHD		Yale	
Calvo, Guillermo	Prof	Maryland		PHD	74	Yale	1994
Camacho, Antonio	Prof	Ill-Chicago	D	PHD	65	Minnesota	1973
Cambronero, Alfredo	C-As	Fisk	DOE	PHD	92	Vanderbilt	1992
Camera, Gabriele	Asst	Purdue		PHD	97	Iowa	1997
Camerer, Colin	Prof	Cal Tech		PHD	81	Chicago	1994
Rea A. & Lela G. Axline Professor of Business Economics							
Cameron, Colin	Asst	Cal-Davis	CIJ	PHD	88	Stanford	1989
Cameron, John S.	Assoc	SW State	EFJ	PHD	79	Nebraska	1986
Cameron, Ottamise C. W.	Retir	So Miss	F	DBA	69	Indiana	1962
Cameron, Rondo	Retir	Emory		PHD	52	Chicago	
Cameron, Stephen	Asst	Columbia	JC	PHD	93	Chicago	1994
Cameron, Trudy A.	Prof	Oregon	OQ	PHD	82	Princeton	D-01
Cammarosano, Joseph R.	Prof	Fordham		PHD	56	Fordham	1955
Campagna, Anthony S.	Retir	Vermont	EH	PHD	66	Rutgers	1965
Campbell, Burnham O.	Retir	Hawaii-Manoa		PHD	61	Stanford	1967
Campbell, Carl M. III	Asst	No Illinois	E	PHD	88	Princeton	1999
Campbell, Charles A.	Prof	Miss State	RON	PHD	85	Tennessee	1985
Campbell, Charles W. III	Retir	Centre	AEHF	PHD	66	Virginia	1968
Campbell, Colin	Asst	Rutgers-N Br	D	PHD	95	Nrthwstrn	1999
Campbell, Donald E.	Prof	Wm & Mary		PHD	72	Princeton	1989
CSX Professor of Economics Public Policy							
Campbell, Everett	Retir	Pt Loma Naz	1997	PHD	76	Temple	1989
Campbell, Gary A.	Prof	Mich Tech	Q	PHD	82	Penn St	1982
Campbell, Gloria L.	Assoc	Wartburg		MBA	84	N Iowa	1979
Campbell, Jeffrey	Asst	Chicago		PHD	95	Nrthwstrn	1999
Campbell, John	Prof	Harvard	GE	PHD	84	Yale	7-94
Otto Eckstein Professor of Applied Economics							
Campbell, Martha	Asst	SUNY-Potsdam		PHD	91	New Sch	1999
Campbell, Noel	Asst	No Georgia	H	PHD	97	GeoMason	1998
Campbell, Rebecca	Asst	SW Texas St	H	PHD	98	LSU	1998
Campbell, Thomas C.	Retir	Virg Comm		PHD	47	Pittsburgh	1980
Campbell, William F.	Retir	Louisiana St	N	PHD	66	Virginia	
Campen, James T.	Assoc	Mass-Boston	EG	PHD	76	Harvard	1976
Campione, Wendy A.	Assoc	No Arizona	HJ	PHD	84	Illinois	1981
Canac, Pierre	Assoc	St Thomas-TX	F	PHD	87	Houston	1990
Canals-Cerda, Jose	Asst	Colorado		PHD	98	Virginia	
Canarella, Giorgio	Prof	CS-L Angeles		PHD	73	Virginia	1973
Candley, William	Prof	Benedict Col		PHD	76	Pittsburgh	1999
Caner, Mehmet	Asst	Pittsburgh	C	PHD	96	Brown	2000
Caniglia, Alan S.	Prof	Frank & Mars		PHD	83	Virginia	1982
The Sigmund M. and Mary B. Hyman Professor of Economics							
Canterbery, E. Ray	Prof	Florida St	F	PHD	66	Wash U	1970
Cantrell, Pat	C-Ac	Cen Arkansas		PHD	83	So Meth	8-84
Cantrell, Richard P.	Assoc	W Kentucky	C	MA	63	S Illinois	1967
Canzoneri, Matthew B.	Prof	Georgetown	EFG	PHD	75	Minnesota	1985
Capalbo, Susan M.	Assoc	Montana St		PHD	82	Ca-Davis	1991
Caplan, Arthur	Asst	Utah State	CQ	PHD	96	Oregon	2001
Caplan, Bryan	Asst	George Mason		PHD	97	Princeton	1997
Caplin, Andrew	Prof	New York U	D	PHD	83	Yale	1995
Caporale, Barbara	Asst	Ohio Univ	EGN	PHD	94	GeoMason	1994
Caporale, Tony	Assoc	Ohio Univ		PHD	92	GeoMason	1992
Capps, Cory	Asst	Illinois	IL	ABD		Nrthwstrn	1998
Capra, C. Monica	Asst	Wash & Lee	D	PHD	98	Virginia	1999

Carbacho-Burgos, Andres	Asst	SW Texas St	O	PHD	99	Mass	1999
Carbaugh, Robert John	Prof	Central Wash	AFEK	PHD	74	Colo St	1985
Carceles-Poveda, Eva	Asst	SUNY-Stony B		PHD			
Card, David E.	Prof	Cal-Berkeley		PHD	83	Princeton	
Cardenas, Gilbert	Prof	Tx-Pan Amer		PHD	77	Illinois	1975
Cardon, James H.	Asst	Brigham Yg	LC	PHD	96	Princeton	1996
Carey, Cathrine	Asst	W Kentucky	F	PHD	92	Kentucky	1992
Carey, Kevin	Asst	American U	E	PHD	95	Princeton	1997
Cargill, Thomas F.	Prof	Nevada-Reno		PHD	68	Ca-Davis	1973
Carlin, Paul S.	Assoc	Ind-Purdue/I	J	PHD	85	Pittsburgh	1985
Carliner, Geoffrey	VAsoc	Babson	F				
Carlisle, William T.	Assoc	Utah		PHD	75	Cornell	1971
Carlos, Ann M.	Prof	Colorado		PHD	80	W Ontario	1990
Carlson, J. Lon	Assoc	Illinois St	PQ	PHD	84	Illinois	1986
Carlson, John A.	Prof	Purdue		PHD	61	J Hopkins	1962
Loeb Professor of Economics							
Carlson, Leonard	Assoc	Emory	DJN	PHD	77	Stanford	1975
Carlson, William L.	C-Pr	St Olaf	C	PHD	70	Michigan	1973
Carlsson, Bo A.	Prof	Case Western	DFMO	PHD	72	Stanford	1984
DeWindt Professor of Industrial Economics; Assoc Dean							
Carlsson, Robert J.	Prof	So Carolina		PHD	64	Rutgers	
Carney, Kim	Retir	Tx-Arlington	I	PHD	68	So Meth	1967
Carpenter, Bruce E.	Assoc	Mansfield		PHD	90	Conn	1987
Carpenter, Jeffrey	Asst	Middlebury	DC	PHD	99	Mass	1999
Carpenter, Robert	Asst	Emory	EL	PHD	92	Wash U	1992
Carr, Linda A.	C-Pr	West Alabama		EDD	68	Alabama	1965
Carrasco, Marine	Asst	Rochester		PHD	95	Toulouse	2000
Carreno, Eufronio	Assoc	Kean	DEFO	PHD	80	Rutgers	9-88
Carrier, Ronald E.	Prof	Jms Madison	A	PHD	60	Illinois	1971
Carrillo, Juan	Asst	Columbia		PHD			2001
Carrillo, Raul J.	Assoc	St Thomas-FL		DA		U Miami	1972
Carrington, Samantha	Assoc	CS-L Angeles		PHD	85	Ca-SnBarb	1986
Carroll, Christopher D.	Prof	J Hopkins		PHD	90	MIT	1995
Carroll, Kathleen A.	Asst	MD-Baltim Co		PHD	76	J Hopkins	1980
Carroll, Michael	Asst	Bowling Gr		PHD	97	Colo St	2001
Carroll, Richard R.	Prof	Lock Haven		PHD	73	Kentucky	1977
Carroll, Sidney L.	Retir	Tennessee		PHD	71	Harvard	1972
Carroll, Thomas M.	Prof	Nev-L Vegas	D	PHD	73	Syracuse	1986
Carroll, Wayne D.	Prof	Wis-Eau Clar	QE	PHD	84	Minnesota	1986
Carson, Katherine S.	Asst	USAF Academy	ACO	PHD	97	Colorado	1997
Carson, Leslie O.	Retir	Augustana SD	ABM	MS	63	Colorado	1958
Carson, Richard T.	Prof	Ca-San Diego	CQ	PHD	85	Berkeley	1985
Carson, Scott	Asst	Txs-Perm Bas	NBJK	PHD	98	Utah	8-99
Carstens, Pamela J.	C-Pr	Coe		PHD	93	Iowa	1985
Carstensen, Fred V.	Prof	Connecticut	N	PHD	76	Yale	1982
Carter, Anne P.	Prof	Brandeis		PHD	49	Harvard	1971
Fred C. Hecht Professor of Economics							
Carter, Charlie	Assoc	Clark Atlant		PHD	75	Illinois	
Carter, George H. III	Prof	So Miss	R	PHD	77	Tx A&M	1979
Carter, Jane	Assoc	Cumberland		MBA	85	Kentucky	1985
Carter, John R.	Prof	Holy Cross	CDL	PHD	76	Cornell	1976
Carter, Melanie	Inst	Old Dominion		MA		Old Dom	1997
Carter, Michael J.	Assoc	Mass-Lowell	CEQ	PHD	81	Stanford	
Carter, Shawn	Asst	Jacksonvl St		PHD	97	Tx A&M	1998
Carter, Susan B.	Prof	Cal-Riversid	AJNT	PHD	81	Stanford	1990
Carter, Tanja	Asst	Pepper-Malib		PHD	99	Ca-SnBarb	1999
Carter, Thomas J.	C-Ac	Okla City	FJ	PHD	87	Wisconsin	1994
Carton, Joel	Asst	Texas Tech		PHD	99	Oregon	1999
Carvajal, Manuel J.	Prof	Fla Internat	JITQ	PHD	74	Florida	1981
Carvellas, John N.	Prof	St Michael's	ACER	PHD	81	Syracuse	1974
Carvounis, Christos C.	Deces	St John's	D-95	PHD	79	New Sch	
Casario, Michelle	Asst	Villanova		PHD	91	Northeas	1991
Case, Anne C.	Asst	Princeton		PHD	88	Princeton	1991
Case, Karl E.	Prof	Wellesley	RHD	PHD	77	Harvard	1976
Casella, Alessandra	Prof	Columbia	EF	PHD	88	MIT	1983
Caselli, Franesco	Asst	Harvard		PHD		Harvard	
Casey, James	Asst	Wash & Lee	QO	PHD		N Car St	2001
Casey, William L. Jr.	Prof	Babson	F	PHD	63	Boston C	1964
Cashdollar, Parker D.	Prof	Tenn-Martin		PHD	71	Tennessee	
Cashel-Cordo, Peter	Assoc	So Indiana		PHD	88	Houston	1994
Casimir, Schiller	Asst	W New Eng		PHD	97	SUNY-Bin	1997
Caskey, John P.	Prof	Swarthmore	EG	PHD	84	Stanford	1988
Casler, Stephen D.	Prof	Allegheny	ACEQ	PHD	83	Illinois	1988
Cason, Timothy	Prof	Purdue		PHD	91	Berkeley	1998
Casper, Cheryl A.	Prof	Kent State	D	PHD	75	Case Wes	1973
Casperson, Luvonia J.	Retir	La St-Shreve		PHD	74	Oklahoma	1975
Cass, David	Prof	Pennsylvania	DCG	PHD	65	Stanford	1974
Paul F. & E. Warren Shafer Miller Professor of Economics							
Cassimatis, Peter J.	Retir	F Dick-Teane	ACDL	PHD	67	New Sch	1964
Cassing, James H.	Prof	Pittsburgh	F	PHD	75	Iowa	1985

Cassing, Shirley	Lect	Pittsburgh	R	PHD	76	Iowa	1985
Cassou, Steven P.	Assoc	Kansas State	EC	PHD	89	Minnesota	1996
Cassuto, Alexander E.	Prof	CS-Hayward	CEGM	PHD	73	UCLA	1971
Castaneda, Marco	Asst	Kentucky	LD	PHD	00	Wash U	2001
Catanese, Anthony V.	Prof	DePauw		PHD	72	S Illinois	1979
Cate, Thomas H.	Prof	No Kentucky		PHD	79	Fla St	1975
Cati, Regina C.	Asst	Boston Univ	C	PHD	95	Sao Paulo	1997
Catlett, Robert B.	Asst	Emporia St		MA	75	Nebraska	1976
Caucutt, Elizabeth	Asst	Rochester		PHD	97	Minnesota	1997
Caudill, Steven B.	Prof	Auburn		PHD	82	Florida	1981
Cauley, Jon	Prof	Hawaii-Hilo		PHD	71	Colorado	
Caveny, Regina	Retir	So Miss		PHD	92	Alabama	1979
Caves, Richard E.	Prof	Harvard		PHD	58	Harvard	1962
Nathaniel Ropes Professor of Political Economy							
Caviglia-Harris, Jill	Asst	Salisbury St		PHD	97	Tennessee	8-98
Cebula, Richard J.	Prof	Armstrong At	EDR	PHD	71	Geo St	1999
Eminent Scholar in Economics							
Cecchetti, Stephen G.	Prof	Ohio State	E	PHD	82	Berkeley	1991
Cecen, A. Aydin	Prof	Cen Michigan		PHD	86	Indiana	1987
Cederlund, Albert M.	Prof	Mass-Lowell	HL	PHD	75	Clark	
Ceglowski, Janet E.	Assoc	Bryn Mawr		PHD	86	Berkeley	1990
Cerf, G.		C New Jersey		MA	65	Syracuse	
Ceyhun, Fikret	Retir	North Dakota	AO	PHD	72	Wayne St	1970
Chade, Hector	Asst	Arizona St		PHD	96	Illinois	1997
Chadwick, Kathy	Assoc	St Olaf	M	PHD	83	Nrthwstrn	1985
Chae, Suchan	Assoc	Rice		PHD	85	Penn	1985
Chaffee, Donald M. Jr.	Prof	Aquinas		PHD	70	Ca-Davis	1992
Chaikind, Stephen B.	C-Pr	Gallaudet		PHD	78	CUNY	1989
Chaing, Alpha C.	Retir	Connecticut		PHD			
Chakrabarti, Avik	Asst	Wis-Milwauke		PHD	98	Michigan	1998
Chakrabarti, Subir	Prof	Ind-Purdue/I	C	PHD	85	Iowa	1985
Chakraborhy, L.	Asst	Emporia St		PHD	98	Utah St	2000
Chakraborty, Chandana	Assoc	Montclair St	ACDO	PHD	87	Rensselaer	9-89
Chakraborty, Debasish	Prof	Cen Michigan		PHD	87	Pittsburgh	1988
Chakraborty, Indranil	Asst	Oklahoma		PHD	97	Illinois	1999
Chakraborty, Shakha	Asst	Oregon	EO	PHD	99	UCLA	1999
Chakravorty, Ujjayant	Assoc	Emory	QRH	PHD	89	Hawaii	1999
Chaloupka, Frank J. IV	Prof	Ill-Chicago	I	PHD	88	CUNY	1988
Chamberlain, Gary	Prof	Harvard		PHD	75	Harvard	1987
Chamberlain, Trevor W.	Prof	McMaster U	G	PHD	86	Toronto	1985
Chambers, Catherine M.	Assoc	Cen Missouri		PHD	90	Kentucky	1990
Chambers, Donald R.	Prof	Lafayette	MG	PHD	81	N Carol	1992
Walter E. Hanson/KPMG Professor of Business & Finance							
Chambers, Paul	Prof	Cen Missouri		PHD	89	Kentucky	1990
Chamley, Christophe	Prof	Boston Univ	HEO	PHD	77	Harvard	
Champ, Bruce	Asst	Fordham		PHD	90	Minnesota	1994
Champlin, Dell	Assoc	E Illinois		PHD	90	Utah	1995
Chan, Jimmy	Asst	J Hopkins		PHD	98	Berkeley	1998
Chan, M. W. Luke	Prof	McMaster U	DE	PHD	78	McMaster	1981
Chandler, Clevelend	Retir	Howard	R	PHD	69	Maryland	1976
Chandra, Amitabh	Asst	Dartmouth		PHD	00	Kentucky	2000
Chandrasekar, Krishnamurti	Prof	NY Inst Tech		PHD	69	New Sch	1969
Chanoy, Rick L.	Asst	St Louis		PHD	84	Illinois	1986
Chang, Cyril F.	Prof	Memphis	IM	PHD	79	Virginia	1981
Chang, Fwu-Ranq	Assoc	Indiana		PHD	85	Chicago	1983
Chang, Hsin	Assoc	Toledo	OP	PHD	89	Michigan	1989
Chang, Hui-Shyong	Prof	Tennessee		PHD	73	Vanderbilt	1971
Chang, Myong-Hun	Assoc	Cleveland St	LDMN	PHD	89	J Hopkins	1988
Chang, Roberto J.	Assoc	Rutgers-N Br	E	PHD	89	Penn	2000
Chang, Semoon	Prof	So Alabama	M	PHD	71	Fla St	1972
Chang, Winston W.	Prof	SUNY-Buffalo	DF	PHD	68	Rochester	1967
Chang, Yang-Ming	Assoc	Kansas State	DCF	PHD	84	SUNY-Buf	1984
Chang, Yongsung	Asst	Pennsylvania		PHD	97	Rochester	1997
Chang, Yoosoon	Asst	Rice		PHD	95	Yale	1995
Chao, Ching Y.	Retir	Jackson St		PHD	64	Iowa St	1972
Chao, John	Asst	Maryland		PHD	95	Yale	1995
Chao, Kang	Retir	Wisconsin		PHD	62	Michigan	1967
Chapman, Janet G.	Retir	Pittsburgh		PHD	63	Columbia	1964
Chapman, Kenneth S.	Prof	CS-Northrdge	IG	PHD	86	Minnesota	1991
Chapman, Margaret L.	Prof	Ill Wesleyan	L	PHD	77	Illinois	1977
Chapman, Richard	Prof	Westminst-UT	JNB	PHD	92	Utah	1985
Chappell, Glenn	Assoc	Meredith		PHD		Tennessee	1991
Chappell, Henry W.	Assoc	So Carolina		PHD	79	Yale	1980
Chappell, William	Assoc	Mississippi	AM	PHD	83	S Carol	1987
Chari, V. V.	C-Pr	Minnesota		PHD	81	Car Mellon	1994
Charkins, Ralph James	Prof	CS-San Bern	A	PHD	70	N Carol	1976
Charle, Edwin G.	Retir	Ohio Univ		PHD	58	Indiana	
Charlebois, Cecile M.	Lect	Assumption	AHJ	ABD		Clark	1980
Charles, Joni S.	Assoc	SW Texas St	D	PHD	87	Purdue	1984
Charles, Kerwin	Asst	Michigan		PHD	95	Cornell	1995

Charness, Gary	Asst	Cal-Santa Br	D	PHD	96	Berkeley	2001
Charos, Evangelos N.	C-Pr	Merrimack		PHD	84	NewHamp	1983
Chase, Kristine L.	Prof	St Marys-Cal		PHD	87	Maryland	1985
Chase, Richard X.	Retir	Vermont	BE	PHD	66	Maryland	1966
Chaston, Kelly	Asst	Davidson	DL	PHD	97	Boston C	1997
Chatha, Jaspal	Asst	CUNY-Lehman		PHD	85	New Sch	
Chatterjee, Kalyan	Prof	Penn State	D	PHD	79	Harvard	1998
Chatterjee, Santanu	Asst	Georgia		PHD	01	U Wash	2001
Chatterton, R. Edward	Prof	Lock Haven		PHD	80	Wash St	1982
Chattopadhyay, Sudip	Asst	San Fran St		PHD	95	Illinois	1999
Chaudhrey, Mukesh	Asst	Northern St		PHD	94	Clev St	1995
Chaudhuri, Adhrp	Asst	Georgetown	IFB	PHD	79	Columbia	1979
Chaudhuri, Ananish	Asst	Wash State		PHD	97	Rutgers	1998
Chaudhuri, Shubham	Asst	Columbia	HOD	PHD	93	Princeton	1994
Chauvet, Marcelle	Asst	Cal-Riversid	AE	PHD	95	Penn	1995
Chawdhry, M. Arshad	Prof	Calif U-Penn		PHD	74	Illinois	1976
Che, Jiahua	Asst	Illinois	DG	PHD	96	Stanford	2001
Che, Yeon-Koo	Prof	Wisconsin		PHD	91	Stanford	1991
Cheema, Balwir Singh	Retir	Wittenberg		PHD		American	1966
Chen, Aimin	Assoc	Indiana St	PD	PHD	90	Penn St	1991
Chen, Baolin	Asst	Rutgers-Camd		PHD	94	Indiana	
Chen, David Y.	Assoc	N Carol A&T		PHD	71	Wisconsin	
Chen, Frederick H.	Asst	Wake Forest		ABD		Chicago	2000
Chen, Heiwei	Asst	So Utah		PHD	97	Emory	1998
Chen, Lein-Lein	Assoc	Nev-L Vegas	F	PHD	92	U Miami	1993
Chen, Li Hsueh	Asst	CS-L Angeles		PHD	98	Michigan	1998
Chen, Thomas P.	Prof	St John's		PHD	76	CUNY	
Chen, Yan	Asst	Michigan		PHD	94	Cal Tech	1994
Chen, Yongmin	Asst	Colorado		PHD	92	Boston U	1996
Cheng, Benjamin S.	Deces	Southern	AE	PHD	71	Oklahoma	1971
Cheng, Chu-Yuan	Prof	Ball State	OP	PHD	64	Geotown	1971
Cheng, David C.	Retir	Alabama		PHD	73	Yale	1974
Cheng, Doris	Prof	San Jose St		PHD	76	Notre Dm	1988
Cheng, Harrison C.	Assoc	So Calif		PHD	77	Berkeley	1978
Cheng, Jen-Chi	C-Ac	Wichita St		PHD	89	Vanderbilt	1989
Cheng, Juei Ming	Retir	Georgia St	CO	PHD	68	Purdue	1968
Cheng, Ping	Asst	Salisbury St		PHD	97	Geo St	8-98
Cheng, William I.	Assoc	Tuskegee		PHD	90	SUNY-Bin	1990
Cheng, Xu	Asst	Cal-Riversid	CFO	PHD	99	Columbia	1998
Cheong, Kwang-Soo	Asst	Hawaii-Manoa		PHD	94	Stanford	1994
Chermak, Janie	Assoc	New Mexico	DQ	PHD	91	Co Mines	1995
Chernick, Howard	Prof	CUNY-Hunter		PHD	76	Penn	1982
Cherry, Monica	Asst	St John Fshr	J	PHD	98	SUNY-Bin	1996
Cherry, Robert D.	Prof	CUNY-Brookly	AJ	PHD	69	Kansas	1977
Cherry, Todd	Asst	Appalach St	DQ	PHD	98	Wyoming	2001
Chesler, Herbert	Assoc	Pittsburgh	J	PHD	64	MIT	1963
Cheung, C. Sherman	Prof	McMaster U	G	PHD	81	Illinois	1981
Cheung, Kowk Hung (Francis)			DJR	PHD	89	Mich St	
Cheung, Yin-Wong	Assoc	Ca-Santa Crz	CFG	PHD	90	Penn	1990
Chezum, Brian	Asst	St Lawrence	JL	PHD	92	Kentucky	1995
Chhikara, Rajkumar	Retir	Iowa State		PHD	86	Illinois	1986
Chi, Wan Fu	Prof	Weber State	AC	PHD	69	S Illinois	1969
Chiappori, Pierre Andre	Prof	Chicago		PHD	81	Paris	1997
Chilcote, Ronald H.	Prof	Cal-Riversid	P	PHD	65	Stanford	1963
Chiles, Ted W.	Assoc	Auburn-Montg	ADJM	PHD	90	Penn St	1990
Chin, Aimee	Asst	Houston	OJ	PHD	01	MIT	2001
Chinn, Kenneth L.	C-Ac	SE Okla St	EC	PHD	91	Colo St	1982
Chinn, Menzie	Asst	Ca-Santa Crz	FCE	PHD	91	Berkeley	1991
Chiong, Winston R.	Prof	Mass-Boston	E	PHD	74	Boston C	1982
Chipman, John S. Regents' Professor	Prof	Minnesota		PHD	51	J Hopkins	1955
Chiremba, Daniel S.	Lect	CUNY-Queens	O	MA	69	New Sch	1969
Chirinko, Robert	C-Ac$	Emory	EGH	PHD	82	Nrthwstrn	1994
Chisholm, Darlene C.	Assoc	Suffolk	LD	PHD	91	U Wash	2001
Chisholm, Roger K.	Prof	Ark-Ltl Rock		PHD	67	Chicago	1985
Chisik, Richard	Asst	Fla Internat	DFL	PHD	97	Nrthwstrn	2000
Chiswick, Barry R.	H-Pr	Ill-Chicago	J	PHD	67	Columbia	1978
Chiswick, Carmel U.	Prof	Ill-Chicago	JT	PHD	72	Columbia	1978
Chiteji, Ngina	Asst	Skidmore		PHD	99	N Carol	1999
Chittle, Charles R.	Retir	Bowling Gr		PHD	69	Purdue	1965
Chiu, I-Ming	Asst	Minot State		PHD	00	Wi-Milwa	2001
Chizmar, John F.	Prof	Illinois St	CM	PHD	71	Boston C	1971
Cho, Dong Woo	Prof	Wichita St		PHD	73	Illinois	1972
Cho, In-Koo	Prof	Illinois	CDE	PHD	86	Princeton	1998
Cho, Whewon	Prof	Tenn Tech	CD	PHD	71	Vanderbilt	1983
Choate, G. Marc	Retir	Willamette		PHD	70	U Wash	1974
Choi, Albert	Asst	Virginia	K	PHD	01	MIT	2001
Choi, Chi-Young	Asst	New Hampshir		PHD	00	Ohio St	2001
Choi, In	Retir	Ohio State		PHD	90	Yale	1989
Choi, Jai-Young	Prof	Lamar	DF	PHD	82	Oklahoma	1982

Choi, Jay Pil	Assoc	Michigan St	LFE	PHD	90	Harvard	
Choi, Jin	Assoc	DePaul	GMC	PHD	82	Iowa St	8-88
Choi, Kee	Retir	Worcester St		PHD		Harvard	1970
Choi, Young Back	Assoc	St John's		PHD	86	Michigan	
Choksy, George Dorian	Assoc	Alma	DNRC	PHD	86	Tennessee	1989
Chopin, Marc	Assoc	Louisiana Te	DL	PHD	92	Tx A&M	1992
Chotigeat, Tosporn	Prof	Nicholls St	FO	PHD	78	S Illinois	1988
Chou, Nan-Ting	Assoc	Louisville	E	PHD	86	Ohio St	1991
Choudhary, Munir A. S.	Assoc	SUNY-Fredoni	CE	PHD	85	Fla St	1987
Chow, C. Victor	Asst	W Virginia	G	PHD	89	Alabama	1989
Chow, Gregory C.	Prof	Princeton	CDEP	PHD	55	Chicago	7-70
Chow, Peter	Prof	CUNY-City C	O	PHD	76	S Illinois	1986
Chowdhury, A. A. Farhad	Prof	Miss Vall St		PHD	93	Miss St	1993
Chowdhury, Abdur R.	Assoc	Marquette	EFO	PHD	83	Kentucky	1989
Chowdhury, Ashok K.	Prof	Mankato St	AC	PHD	80	Iowa St	1980
Christensen, Kimberly	Assoc	SUNY-Purchas		PHD	86	Mass	1985
Christensen, Paul P.	Assoc	Hofstra	B	PHD	76	Wisconsin	
Christiano, Lawrence	Prof	Northwestern		PHD	82	Columbia	
Christiansen, Daniel S.	C-Pr	Albion	CD	PHD	75	Stanford	1981
Christiansen, Gregory B.	Prof	CS-Hayward	BEHO	PHD	81	Wisconsin	1983
Christiansen, Jens	Assoc	Mt Holyoke		PHD	82	Stanford	1986
Christianson, Kenneth	Asst	Ithaca		ABD		Syracuse	2000
Christie, Darrell A.	Assoc	Wis-Stev Pt		MS		Illinois	1964
Christofi, Andreas C.	C-Pr	Monmouth	CFG	PHD	84	Penn St	9-97
Christofides, Constantinos A	Prof	E Stroudsbur	CRT	PHD	77	Lehigh	1971
Christopher, Jan E.	Assoc	Delaware St	CDMR	PHD	93	Howard	1994
Christopherson, Robert L.	C-Ac	SUNY-Plattsb	GH	PHD	90	Wayne St	1990
Chu, Betty Y.	Retir	San Jose St		PHD	73	Notre Dm	1974
Chu, Kong	Prof	Georgia Tech	OC	PHD	64	Tulane	1968
Chu, Kwang-Wen	Prof	CS-Fullerton	D	PHD	72	UCLA	1970
Chu, Shih-Fan	Retir	Nevada-Reno		PHD	68	Illinois	1967
Chuak, Sam	Prof	Andrews	CD	PHD	92	Wash St	1998
Chuderewicz, Russell	VLect	Fla Internat	AEFG	PHD	97	Penn St	2000
Chugh, Ram L.	Prof	SUNY-Potsdam		PHD	70	Wayne St	1970
Chung, Hyung C.	Retir	Bridgeport		PHD	70	Columbia	1970
Chung, Jae Wan	Retir	George Mason		PHD	72	NYU	
Chung, Kuk-Soo	Lect	CUNY-Lehman		MA		Yale	
Chung, Nae Hoon	Deces			PHD	63	Mich St	
Chung, Young-Iob	Prof	E Michigan		PHD	65	Columbia	1966
Church, John	SpLec	Boise State	ART	MS	80	Idaho	2000
Ciecka, James E.	Prof	DePaul	CD	PHD	70	Purdue	1970
Ciliberto, Federico	Asst	Fla Internat	DL	ABD		Nrthwstrn	2001
Cima, Lawrence R.	Assoc	John Carroll	ADEF	PHD	82	W Virginia	1971
Cinar, E. Mine	Prof	Loyola-Chicg	ACDO	PHD	76	Tx A&M	1983
Cirace, John	Prof	CUNY-Lehman		PHD	75	Columbia	
Ciscel, David H.	Prof	Memphis	LM	PHD	71	Houston	1973
Cizakca, Murat	Prof	Bogazici	N	PHD	79	Penn	1975
Clague, Christopher K.	Retir	Maryland		PHD	66	Harvard	1979
Claiborn, Edward L.	Retir	Va Military		PHD	64	Princeton	1981
Clain, Suzanne H.	Assoc	Villanova		PHD	84	Princeton	1987
Clarida, Richard	C-Pr	Columbia	FE	PHD	83	Harvard	1988
Clark, Barry S.	Prof	Wis-La Cross	BHOP	PHD	80	Mass	1978
Clark, Carol	Assoc	Trinity-CT		PHD	91	Cornell	1990
Clark, Carol M.	Retir	Guilford	5-99	PHD	79	Michigan	1981
Clark, Carolyn	Retir	Wash State		PHD	70	Berkeley	1973
Clark, Charles	Prof	St John's		PHD	90	New Sch	1985
Clark, Clifford D.	Prof	SUNY-Bingham	OF	PHD	53	Chicago	1973
Clark, David E.	Assoc	Marquette	DR	PHD	86	SUNY-Bin	1985
Clark, David H.	Retir	Maine	JOA	PHD	62	Wisconsin	1963
Clark, Don P.	Prof	Tennessee		PHD	78	Mich St	1978
Clark, Gregory	Prof	Cal-Davis	NO	PHD	85	Harvard	1990
Clark, J. R.	Prof	Tenn-Chattan	M	PHD	70	Va Tech	1993
Probasco Chair in Free Enterprise							
Clark, James E.	Assoc	Wichita St		PHD	77	Nrthwstrn	1976
Clark, Joy	Assoc	Auburn-Montg	APQB	PHD	88	Tx A&M	1988
Clark, Robert L.	Prof	N Carol St	JD	PHD	74	Duke	1975
Clark, Wayne Walter	Retir	Brigham Yg		PHD	60	Tx A&M	1962
Clark, William M.	Assoc	Oklahoma	O	PHD	81	Virginia	1977
Clarke, Jere W.	Retir	So Conn St		PHD		Virginia	
Clarke, William A.	C-Pr	Bentley	AD	PHD	73	Rutgers	1972
Clary, Betsy Jane	Prof	Charleston		PHD	81	Miss	1984
Claudon, Michael Paul	Prof	Middlebury	FLMP	PHD	71	J Hopkins	1970
Clausing, Kimberly	Asst	Reed	ADFH	PHD	97	Harvard	1997
Clay, James P.	Prof	Fort Lewis		PHD	74	Kansas St	1982
Claycombe, Richard J.	Prof	W Maryland		PHD	80	Geo Wash	1981
Clayton, Gary E.	Prof	No Kentucky		PHD	74	Utah	1980
Cleaver, Harry	Assoc	Texas	P	PHD	75	Stanford	9-76
Cleeton, David L.	Prof	Oberlin	DGIM	PHD	80	Wash U	1980
Clement, Meredith Owen	Retir	Dartmouth		PHD	58	Berkeley	1956
Clement, Norris C.	Retir	San Diego St		PHD	68	Colorado	1968

Cleminti, Gian Luca	Asst	Carnegie Mel		PHD	00	Rochester	2000
Clemmer, Richard B.	Assoc	Cen Michigan		PHD	81	Chicago	1982
Cleveland, Paul	Assoc	Birminghm So		PHD	85	Tx A&M	1995
Cliff, Lee	Assoc	SUNY-Potsdam		MBA		Clarkson	
Cline, Philip L.	Prof	Wash & Lee	C	PHD	75	Okla St	1975
Lewis Whitabker Adams Professor of Economics							
Cloninger, Dale O.	Prof	Houston-Cl L		DBA	73	Fla St	9-74
Cloud, Darrell	Asst	N Carol A&T		PHD	00	Wi-Milwa	2000
Cloutier, Norman R.	Prof	Wis-Parkside	DJR	PHD	81	W Virginia	1981
Clower, Robert W.	Emer	So Carolina		DLIT	78	Oxford	1986
Hugh C. Lane Professor of Economics							
Co, Catherine	Asst	Neb-Omaha	FLO	PHD	95	Rutgers	2001
Coate, Douglas C.	Prof	Rutgers-Newk		PHD	74	CUNY	1971
Coate, Stephen	Prof	Cornell		PHD	88	Nrthwstrn	
Coats, R. Morris	Prof	Nicholls St	HIRQ	PHD	83	Va Tech	1985
Cobb, Anne	Asst	SUNY-Empire	I	PHD	69	N Carol	1990
Cobb, Sharon	Asst	North Fla	AC	PHD	98	Florida	1998
Cobb, Steven A.	Assoc	Xavier	AEHR	PHD	74	Brown	1984
Cobb, Steven Lee	C-Ac	North Texas	AFOP	PHD	87	N Carol	1987
Cobbe, James H.	C-Pr	Florida St	O	PHD	77	Yale	1976
Cocheba, Donald John	Prof	Central Wash	QR	PHD	71	Wash St	1970
Distinguished Professor, Research (1992)							
Cochi Ficano, Carlena	Asst	Hartwick	ACDJ	PHD	97	Cornell	1997
Cochran, Howard H. Jr.	Assoc	Belmont	AFM	DA	94	Mid Tenn	1989
Cochran, John	C-Pr	Metro St-CO	ABEN	PHD	85	Colorado	1984
Cochrane, Harold	Prof	Colorado St	EA	PHD	75	Colorado	1975
Coehlo, Philip R. P.	Prof	Ball State	NT	PHD	69	U Wash	1986
Coen, Edward	Emer	Minnesota		PHD	53	London	
Coen, Robert M.	Prof	Northwestern		PHD	67	Nrthwstrn	1971
Coen-Pirani, Daniele	Asst	Carnegie Mel		PHD	00	Rochester	2000
Coes, Donald V.	Prof	New Mexico		PHD	77	Princeton	
Coffey, Sergia		SUNY-Empire		PHD			
Coffman, Richard B.	Assoc	Idaho	DL	PHD	72	U Wash	1978
Coggins, Bruce	Asst	Truman State		PHD	95	Ca-Rivers	1998
Cogley, Timothy	Assoc	Arizona St		PHD	88	Berkeley	1999
Cohen, Alvin	Retir	Lehigh	FO	PHD	62	Florida	1970
Cohen, Andrew	Asst	Virginia	LD	PHD	00	Nrthwstrn	2000
Cohen, Jeffrey P.	Asst	Hartford	CDER	PHD	98	Maryland	2000
Cohen, Linda	Prof	Calif-Irvine		PHD	79	Cal Tech	1988
Cohen, Richard H.	Asst	Lyon College	EG	PHD	92	Indiana	1998
Cohn, Cheryl L.	Asst	Millikin		DA	85	Illin St	1984
Cohn, Elchanan	Prof	So Carolina		PHD	68	Iowa St	
Cohn, Raymond L.	Prof	Illinois St	DN	PHD	77	Oregon	1983
Coile, Courtney	Asst	Wellesley	DHI	PHD	99	MIT	2000
Coiner, H. Michael	Assoc	Brandeis		PHD	79	Yale	1980
Colander, David C.	Prof	Middlebury	ABE	PHD	76	Columbia	1982
Christian A. Johnson Distinguished Professor of Economics							
Colburn, Christopher B.	Assoc	Old Dominion	R	PHD	88	Tx A&M	1987
Cole, Charles L.	Prof	CS-Long Bch		PHD	63	S Calif	1967
Cole, Donald P.	Prof	Drew	AH	PHD	68	Ohio St	1966
Cole, Ismail	Prof	Calif U-Penn		PHD	86	Pittsburgh	1984
Cole, Raymond E.	Prof	Ark Tech		PHD	76	Arkansas	1970
Cole, William E.	Retir	Tennessee		PHD	65	Tx-Austin	1965
Colella, Francis J.	Prof	Simpson	BEFN	PHD	73	Fordham	1977
Coley, Basil G.	Prof	N Carol A&T		PHD	71	Illinois	1966
Collier, Ben	Assoc	NW Missouri	ADFK	PHD	84	Purdue	1981
Collier, George A. Jr.	Emer	SE Okla St	ARM	PHD	78	Okla St	1972
Collinge, Robert A.	Prof	Tx-S Antonio	FHKQ	PHD	83	Maryland	1987
Collins, Susan M.	Assoc	Georgetown	FO	PHD	84	MIT	1992
Collum, Thomas E.	Asst	NE Illinois	LDHP	MA	75	Nrthwstrn	1977
Colman, Gregory	Assoc	Pace		PHD			2001
Colonna, Carl M.	Assoc	Chris Newpor	AEIR	MA		Old Dom	1970
Colton, Nora Ann	Assoc	Drew	FPT	DPHL	92	Oxford	1994
Comanor, William S.	Prof	Cal-Santa Br	LD	PHD	64	Harvard	1975
Combs, Ernest F.	Retir	Puget Sound	AOQ	PHD	71	U Wash	1967
Combs, J. Paul	Prof	Appalach St	MR	PHD	73	N Car St	1971
Comin, Diego	Asst	New York U	E	PHD	00	Harvard	2000
Comolli, Paul M.	Assoc	Kansas	QF	PHD	75	Purdue	1975
Conant, John L.	C-Pr	Indiana St	DJB	PHD	84	Tennessee	1981
Condon, Carol M.	Asst	Kean		PHD	78	Columbia	9-85
Condon, Clarence M. III	Dean	Charleston		PHD	78	S Carol	1980
Congleton, Roger D.	Prof	George Mason		PHD	78	Va Tech	1988
Conhaim, Louis E.	Retir	St John's		PHD	60	Columbia	1979
Conley, John	Prof	Illinois	DGH	PHD	90	Rochester	1990
Conlin, Michael	Asst	Syracuse	LD	PHD	95	Wisconsin	
Conlisk, John	Emer	Ca-San Diego	ET	PHD	65	Stanford	1968
Conlon, John	Assoc	Mississippi	CEF	PHD	78	Chicago	1987
Connaughton, John E.	Prof	N Car-Charl		PHD	81	Northeas	1978
Connell, Donald R.	Retir	Neb-Omaha	AF	MS	58	Ft Hays	1965
Connell, James A.	Asst	Mercer-Atlan		DBA	92	La Tech	1996

Connelly, Rachel E.	Assoc	Bowdoin	JT	PHD	85	Michigan	1985
Connelly, Robert A. Jr.	Inst	SC-Spartanbu	A	MA		Appalach	1972
Connery, Thomas	Dean	St Thomas-MN					
Conning, Jonathan	Asst	Williams		PHD	96	Yale	1996
Connolly, Laura	Asst	No Colorado	HL	PHD		Nrthwstrn	2000
Connolly, Michael B.	C-Pr	U Miami	F	PHD	69	Chicago	1987
Connolly, Michelle	Asst	Duke	FG	PHD	96	Yale	1997
Conover, Roger B.	C-As	Azusa Pacif		MA	82	Ca-SnDgo	9-90
Conrad, James M.	Dean	Indianapolis		PHD	70	Kentucky	1979
Conroy, Stephen	Asst	West Florida	ACJ	PHD	98	S Calif	1999
Constantine, Jill M.	Asst	Williams		PHD	94	Penn	
Conway, Karen Smith	Assoc	New Hampshir	HJ	PHD	87	N Carol	1990
Conway, Patrick	Prof	No Carolina	F	PHD	84	Princeton	1983
Conway, William B.	Retir	Augustana IL	AIJK	PHD	69	Minnesota	1970
Cook, John P. Jr.	Asst	Heidelberg	AG	PHD	94	Kentucky	1995
Cook, Laura	Fell	Gallaudet		MA	01		
Cook, Michael D.	Asst	Naval Postgr	J	PHD	96	Maryland	1996
Cook, Michael T.	C-Pr	Wm Jewell	EF	PHD	83	Vanderbilt	1978
John W. Boatwright Professor of Economics							
Cook, Robert W. Jr.	Assoc	Richmond		PHD	81	Va Tech	1980
Cooke, John P.	Retir	South Fla	H	PHD	67	Colorado	1968
Cookingham, Mary E.	Deces	Michigan St	3-01	PHD	80	Berkeley	1979
Cooley, Thomas F.	Prof	New York U	EG	PHD	71	Penn	1999
Paganelli-Bull Professor of Economics							
Coolidge, Cathleen J.	Assoc	CS-Chico	AHKL	PHD	83	Va Tech	1984
Coomes, Paul A.	Prof	Louisville	R	PHD	85	Tx-Austin	1985
Cooper, Brian	Asst	SUNY Oswego	ABJ	PHD	97	Harvard	1998
Cooper, David J.	Asst	Case Western	CD	PHD	92	Princeton	1999
Cooper, John M.	Asst	Mn-Moorhead		MA	75	Oregon	1972
Cooper, Richard N.	Prof	Harvard		PHD	62	Harvard	1981
Maurits C. Boas Professor ofInternational Economics							
Cooper, Russell W.	Prof	Boston Univ	CDE	PHD	79	Penn	
Cooper, Thomas E.	C-Ac	Lyon College	DGHL	PHD	84	Princeton	1987
Anne J. Stewart Professor of Economics							
Copeland, Cassandra	Asst	Oglethorpe		PHD		Auburn	2000
Copeland, Joe B.	Prof	No Alabama		PHD	74	Arkansas	1983
Coppejans, Mark	Asst	Duke	CG	PHD	96	Nrthwstrn	1996
Coppin, Addington M.	Assoc	Oakland	FO	PHD	87	Illinois	1989
Coppock, Lee	Asst	Hillsdale		PHD	94	GeoMason	1994
Corcione, Frank P.	Assoc	Scranton		PHD	75	Lehigh	1978
Corcoran, William J.	Assoc	Neb-Omaha	LQD	PHD	75	Rutgers	1980
Cordes, Joseph J.	Prof	George Wash	H	PHD	77	Wisconsin	1975
Corkum, Keith H.	Prof	Nichols Col		PHD	76	Lehigh	1972
Corley, Edward M.	Prof	E Illinois		PHD	64	Okla St	1967
Corman, Hope	Prof	Rider	IJKT	PHD	78	CUNY	1988
Cornwall, Richard R.	Retir	Middlebury		PHD	68	Berkeley	1977
Cornwell, Christopher M.	Assoc	Georgia	CHJ	PHD	85	Mich St	1988
Corradi, Valentina	Asst	Pennsylvania		PHD	94	Ca-SnDgo	1994
Corrigan, Tom D.	Assoc	Sacred Heart	AFG	PHD	69	Maryland	1986
Corsetti, Giancurlo	Asst	Yale	F	PHD	92	Yale	1998
Cortes, Bienvenido S.	Prof	Pittsburg St	F	PHD	87	Okla St	
Cosgel, Metin M.	Assoc	Connecticut	N	PHD	89	Iowa	1989
Cosimano, Thomas	Prof	Notre Dame	EF	PHD	79	SUNY-Buf	1987
Cosslett, Stephen R.	Prof	Ohio State		PHD	79	Berkeley	1987
Costa, Dora L.	Assoc	MIT	N	PHD	93	Chicago	1993
Ford Career Development Associate Professor of Economics							
Coston, Robert D.	Retir	Geo Southern		PHD	73	Arkansas	1970
Costrell, Robert M.	Prof	Massachusett		PHD	78	Harvard	1978
Cothren, Richard D.	Assoc	Virg Tech	E	PHD	81	N Carol	1985
Cotter, Kevin D.	Asst	Wayne State	D	PHD	84	Minnesota	1989
Cotton, Jeremiah	Assoc	Mass-Boston	IJ	PHD	83	Michigan	1985
Cottrell, Allin F.	C-Pr	Wake Forest		PHD	81	Edinburgh	1989
Couch, Jim	Asst	No Alabama		PHD		Miss	1991
Couch, Kenneth A.	Asst	Connecticut	J	PHD	92	Wisconsin	1995
Coughlan, Carmel	PLect	Salve Regina	M	MBA	90	Salve Rg	1990
Coughlin, Peter J.	Assoc	Maryland		PHD	76	SUNY-Alb	1982
Coulson, N. Edward	Assoc	Penn State	R	PHD	83	Ca-SnDgo	1984
Coultrap-McQuin, Susan	Dean	Mankato St		PHD		Iowa	1995
Coupe, John D.	Retir	Maine	ACD	PHD	60	Clark	1962
Courant, Paul N.	Prof	Michigan		PHD	74	Princeton	1973
Courbois, Jean-Pierre	Prof	Appalach St	F	PHD	68	American	1968
Courington, John M.	Prof	Cameron		PHD	87	Okla St	1979
Couvillion, L. Michael	Assoc	Plymouth St	I	PHD	82	La Tech	1980
Cover, James P.	Prof	Alabama		PHD	82	Virginia	1982
Cowen, Janna L.	Prof	Wis-Rvr Fall	JL	PHD	79	Nebraska	1979
Cowen, Tyler	Prof	George Mason		PHD	87	Harvard	
Cowing, Thomas G.	Prof	SUNY-Bingham	LD	PHD	70	Berkeley	1969
Cox, Donald C.	Prof	Boston Coll	DJ	PHD	80	Brown	1987
Cox, James C.	Prof	Arizona		PHD	71	Harvard	1977
Cox, Larry G.	Asst	SW Missouri		MA	70	Kansas St	1970

Cox, Steven R.	Prof	So Indiana		PHD	71	Michigan	1989
Coxwell, Tricia	Asst	Wm Paterson		PHD	00	Tennessee	2000
Coyle, Sister Ann	Assoc	Immaculata		MA		Temple	1978
Cracraft, Scott	Retir	Albion	1997	MS	60	Miss	1977
Craft, Erik D.	Asst	Richmond		PHD	95	Chicago	1994
Craft, Kim	Asst	So Utah		PHD	96	Ca-Davis	1996
Craft, Rolf	Retir	Wartburg		PHD	68	Iowa St	1996
Craig, Barbara	C-Pr	Oberlin	CFQ	PHD	88	Minnesota	1989
Craig, Eleanor D.	Assoc	Delaware	H	MA	61	Penn	1962
Craig, George	Retir	Okla City		PHD	68	Illinois	1982
Craig, Lee A.	Prof	N Carol St	NJD	PHD	89	Indiana	1989
Craig, Steven C.	Prof	Houston	HR	PHD	81	Penn	1989
Crain, W. Mark	Prof	George Mason		PHD	76	Tx A&M	
Craine, Roger	Prof	Cal-Berkeley		PHD	72	Maryland	1977
Crakes, Gary M.	Prof	So Conn St	AI	PHD	84	Conn	1980
Cramer, Curtis A.	Prof	Wyoming	BK	PHD	66	Maryland	1966
Cramton, Peter C.	Prof	Maryland		PHD	84	Stanford	1993
Crane, Steven E.	Assoc	Marquette	DHLR	PHD	81	Colorado	1980
Crary, David B.	Assoc	E Michigan		PHD	82	Maryland	1980
Crawford, Gregory	Asst	Duke	CL	PHD	98	Stanford	1996
Crawford, Jerry L.	Prof	Arkansas St	ADTM	PHD	69	Arkansas	1966
Crawford, Vincent	Prof	Ca-San Diego	D	PHD	76	MIT	1976
Cray, Randy F.	Prof	Wis-Stev Pt		PHD	86	Kansas St	8-86
Craycraft, Joseph L.	Retir	Cincinnati	L	PHD	64	Cincinnati	1962
Craypo, Charles	Retir	Notre Dame	J	PHD	66	Mich St	1978
Creahan, Thomas	Asst	Morehead St		PHD	95	Cincinnati	1996
Creane, Anthony J.	Assoc	Michigan St		PHD	91	Virginia	1990
Credille, Ronda	Asst	SW Baptist		MBA		Drury	1990
Cremer, Jacques	Adj	Virg Tech		PHD	78	MIT	1983
Cres, Herve	Asst	Pennsylvania		PHD	94	Geneva	1994
Cribari-Neto, Francisco		Brazil	E	PHD	94	Illinois	
Universidade Federal de Pernambuco; Brazil							
Crick, Nelson B.	Retir	Portland St		PHD	67	Colorado	1967
Criddle, Keith R.	H-Pr	Utah State	CQ	PHD	89	Ca-Davis	1998
Crist, William D.	Prof	CS-Stanislau		PHD	72	Nebraska	1969
Crocker, J. Kevin	VAsst	Union	BFO	ABD		Mass	2000
Crocker, Thomas D.	Prof	Wyoming	Q	PHD	67	Missouri	1975
Crofts, Robert D.	Asst	Salem State		MA		Northeas	
Cron, William R.	Prof	Cen Mich	Atg	PHD	73	Mich St	1982
Cronovich, Ron	Assoc	Nev-L Vegas	E	PHD	95	Michigan	1994
Crooker, Skip	Asst	Texas Tech		PHD	98	Iowa St	1999
Cropper, Maureen L.	Prof	Maryland		PHD	73	Cornell	1980
Cross, John D.	Prof	Michigan		PHD	65	Princeton	1965
Cross, John W.	Assoc	Indiana U-PA	EG	MA	68	Mass	1969
Cross, Phil	Asst	Georgetown	HD	PHD	01	Wisconsin	2001
Crotty, James R.	Prof	Massachusett		PHD	73	Car Mellon	1974
Crouch, Robert L.	Prof	Cal-Santa Br	A	PHD	67	Essex	1973
Crough, B. Jane	Lect	Pittsburg St	A	MBA	84	Pittsburgh	
Crouter, Jan P.	Assoc	Whitman	KLQ	PHD	85	Illinois	1985
Crowder, William J.	Assoc	Tx-Arlington	EF	PHD	93	Arizona	1992
Crowell, Elizabeth	Assoc	Mich-Dearbor	DHIJ	PHD	71	Indiana	1978
Crowley, Patrick	Assoc	Tx A&M-C Chr	AO	PHD	90	McGill	9-00
Crowther, Simeon J.	Prof	CS-Long Bch		PHD	70	Penn	1968
Crucini, Mario J.	Assoc	Vanderbilt	E	PHD	91	Rochester	1999
Crummett, Maria	Assoc	Tampa	AEO	PHD	85	New Sch	1999
Cruz, Robert D.	Assoc	Barry		PHD	85	Penn	1993
Cruz-Saco, Maria A.	C-Ac	Conn Coll	O	PHD	83	Pittsburgh	1990
Cuddington, John T.	C-Pr	Georgetown	FO	PHD	78	Wisconsin	1986
Cuellar, Steven	Asst	Sonoma State	D	PHD	98	Tx A&M	2001
Culbertson, W. Patton Jr.	Prof	Louisiana St	F	PHD	72	Tx-Austin	
Cullenberg, Stephen E.	C-Pr	Cal-Riversid	ABCP	PHD	87	Mass	1988
Cullie, Julie	Asst	Michigan					
Cullity, John P.	Retir	Rutgers-Newk		PHD	63	Columbia	1977
Culp, David B.	Assoc	Slippery Roc	AEN	PHD	96	S Illinois	1978
Culver, Sarah E.	Assoc	Alabama-Birm	CEFG	PHD	93	Houston	1993
Cumber, Carol J.	Assoc	So Dakota St	M	PHD	94	S Dak St	1990
Cumby, Robert	Prof	Georgetown	FG	PHD	82	MIT	1994
Cummingham, Robert	Asst	Alma		PHD		SUNY-Bin	1999
Cummings, Donald G.	Retir	No Iowa	AEH	PHD	75	Tulane	1963
Cummings, Ronald G.	Prof	Georgia St	Q	PHD	68	Kansas	1993
Noah Langdale Jr. Eminent Scholar Chair of Environmental Policy							
Cunningham, Brendan	Asst	USN Academy		PHD	00	Columbia	
Cunningham, Steven R.	Assoc	Connecticut	EB	PHD	89	Fla St	1989
Cupper, Robert Dean	Prof	Allegheny	ACD	PHD	74	Pittsburgh	1977
Curington, William P.	Prof	Arkansas	J	PHD	79	Syracuse	1989
Curley, Michael D.	Prof	Kennesaw St	ADMG	PHD	74	Kentucky	1984
Curme, Michael A.	Assoc	Miami U-Ohio	JD	PHD	89	Illinois	1988
Curran, Christopher	Assoc	Emory	CDK	PHD	72	Purdue	1970
Curran, Ward S.	Prof	Trinity-CT		PHD	61	Columbia	1960
Currie, Janet	Prof	UCLA		PHD	88	Princeton	1988

Currier, Kevin M.	Assoc	Oklahoma St	C	PHD	85	SUNY-Alb	1984
Curtis, Fred	Prof	Drew	BJO	PHD	83	Mass	1978
Curtis, Thomas D.	Retir	South Fla	B	PHD	65	Indiana	1974
Cushing, Brian J.	Assoc	W Virginia	RCH	PHD	81	Maryland	1981
Cushing, Matthew J.	Assoc	Nebraska	EJ	PHD	85	Virginia	1992
Cutler, David M.	Prof	Harvard		PHD	91	MIT	
Cutler, Harvey	Prof	Colorado St	EC	PHD	85	U Wash	1980
Cvitanic, Jaksa	Prof	So Calif		PHD	92	Columbia	1999
Cwik, Paul F.	Asst	Campbell		ABD		Auburn	1998
Cyert, Richard M.	Deces	Carnegie Mel		PHD	51	Columbia	1948
Cypher, James M.	Prof	CS-Fresno	OP	PHD	73	Ca-Rivers	1967
D'Ambrosio, Charles A.	Retir	U Washington		PHD	82	Illinois	1980
D'Amico, Thomas F.	C-Pr	St Peters	EJT	PHD	83	NYU	1982
D'Angelo, James		Xavier		MA			2001
D'Arge, Ralph C.	Emer	Wyoming	1996	PHD	69	Cornell	1975
Daal, Elton	Asst	New Orleans		PHD	99	Maryland	1999
DaBoll-Lavoie, Joseph T.	Assoc	Nazareth	BHJ	PHD	89	SUNY-Bin	9-88
DaCosta, Maria N.	Assoc	Wis-Eau Clar	RO	PHD	87	Northeas	1989
Dacy, Douglas C.	Prof	Texas	EO	PHD	64	Harvard	1-65
Dadkhah, Kamran N.	Assoc	Northeastern		PHD	75	Indiana	1981
Dadzie, Frank	Lect	Clark Atlant		MA			
Daellenbach, Lawrence A.	Prof	Wis-La Cross	ADR	PHD	69	Iowa St	1969
Daghestani, Eddie	Assoc	Barry		PHD	71	Colo St	1988
Dahl, Christian	Asst	Purdue		PHD	00	Aarhus	2000
Dahl, Gordon B.	Asst	Rochester		PHD	98	Princeton	1998
Dahms, Joseph E.	C-Ac	Hood	NOP	PHD	83	American	1978
Daigle, Ronald R.	Prof	Central Conn	EG	PHD	75	Clark	1976
Dakhlia, Sami F.	Asst	Alabama		PHD	98	Wash U	1999
Dalal, Ardeshir J.	Prof	No Illinois	D	PHD	77	Iowa	1977
Dalal, Meenakshi N.	Prof	Wayne St Col	OE	PHD	84	Northeas	1985
Dale, Donald	Asst	Muhlenberg		PHD	01	Princeton	2000
Dale, Lawrence Raymond	Prof	Arkansas St	ABPQ	PHD	79	Ohio U	1986
Dalenberg, Douglas R.	Assoc	Montana	CRL	PHD	87	Oregon	1990
Daley, Edward V.	H-Pr	Va Military		PHD	74	Missouri	1981
Dalgaard, Bruce R.	Prof	St Olaf	EPA	PHD	76	Illinois	1992
Husby-Johnson Professor in Business & Economics							
Dall, John J. Jr.	C-Pr	Seton Hall		PHD	68	Penn	
Dalmia, Sonia	Asst	Grand Valley		PHD	99	Iowa	1999
Dalton, George	Deces	Northwestern		PHD		Oregon	
Dalton, Margaret M.	Prof	Frostburg St		PHD	86	W Virginia	1981
Dalton, W. Robert	SrLec	Carnegie Mel		PHD	72	Missouri	1985
Daly, George G.	Dean	New York U	D	PHD	67	Nrthwstrn	1993
Dammon, Robert	Assoc	Carnegie Mel		PHD	84	Wisconsin	
Damon, William W.	Prof	Vanderbilt	DGM	PHD	70	Cornell	1976
Damooei, Jamshid	Assoc	Calif Luther		PHD		Surrey	1987
Dane, Andrew J.	Prof	Angelo State	P	PHD	75	Oklahoma	1973
Daneshvary, Nasser	Prof	Nev-L Vegas	R	PHD	84	Tennessee	1990
Daneshyar, Arifeen M.	Prof	Kutztown	AE	PHD	76	S Illinois	1984
Daniel, Betty C.	Prof	SUNY-Albany	EF	PHD	76	N Carol	1983
Daniel, Coldwell III	Prof	Memphis	IL	PHD	68	Virginia	1970
Daniel, Joseph	Assoc	Delaware	L	PHD	92	Minnesota	1991
Daniels, Joseph P.	Assoc	Marquette	EFG	PHD	92	Indiana	1989
Daniels, Michael J.	Prof	Columbus	JKR	PHD	79	Geo St	1980
Daniels, Rudolph	Prof	Florida A&M	DJQ	PHD	80	Fla St	1977
Danielsen, Albert L.	Prof	Georgia	MH	PHD	66	Duke	1963
Dao, Minh Quang	Prof	E Illinois		PHD	87	Illinois	1987
Dapice, David O.	Assoc	Tufts	O	PHD	73	Harvard	1973
Dardis, Rachel	Retir	Maryland		PHD	65	Minnesota	1992
Darity, William A. Jr.	Prof	No Carolina	E	PHD	78	MIT	1983
Boshamer Professor							
Darrat, Ali F.	Prof	Louisiana Te	EG	PHD	81	Indiana	1987
Premier Bank Professor							
Darrow, John J.	Prof	Westfield St		PHD	72	Conn	1971
Das, Jayoti	Asst	Elon	FL	PHD	93	Cincinnati	1996
Das, Mitali	Asst	Columbia	CIG	PHD	98	MIT	1998
Dasgupta, Manabendra	Assoc	Alabama-Birm	CDHL	PHD	89	So Meth	1992
Datta, Manjira	Asst	Arizona St		PHD	92	Cornell	1995
Dauffenbach, Robert C.	Prof	Oklahoma	J	PHD	73	Illinois	
Daughety, Andrew F.	Prof	Vanderbilt	LK	PHD	72	Case Wes	1995
Dauterive, Jerry W.	Assoc	Loyola-N Orl	ADH	PHD	76	Tx Tech	1979
David, Byron	Asst	CUNY-City C	LM	PHD	90	CUNY	1994
David, Martin H.	Retir	Wisconsin		PHD	60	Michigan	1962
David, Paul A.	Prof	Stanford		PHD	73	Harvard	1969
Davidoff, Howard	Assoc	CUNY-Brookly		LLM	87	NYU	1986
Davidson, Audrey	C-Ac	Louisville	L	PHD	93	Auburn	1993
Davidson, Carl	Prof	Michigan St		PHD	87	Wisconsin	1982
Davidson, Larry	Prof	Indiana		PHD	77	N Carol	1990
Davidson, Paul	Retir	Tennessee		PHD	59	Penn	1987
Davies, Ronald B.	Asst	Oregon	FL	PHD	99	Penn St	1999
Davila, Alberto	C-Pr	Tx-Pan Amer		PHD	82	Iowa St	1996

Davis, Ann E.	Asst	Marist	RT	PHD	83	Boston C	1981
Davis, Donald R.	Prof	Columbia	F	PHD	92	Columbia	1999
Davis, Douglas D.	Prof	Virg Comm		PHD	84	Indiana	1987
Davis, Elynor G.	Prof	Geo Southern		PHD	78	Tx A&M	1979
Davis, George K.	Prof	Miami U-Ohio	EO	PHD	84	So Meth	1985
Davis, J. Ronnie	Prof	New Orleans		PHD	67	Virginia	1989
Davis, Joe C.	Retir	Trinity	J	PHD	71	Tx-Austin	1969
Davis, John B.	Prof	Marquette	BI	PHD	85	Mich St	1987
Davis, Lance E.	Prof	Cal Tech	N	PHD	56	J Hopkins	1968
Mary Stillman Harkness Professor of Social Science							
Davis, Lewis	Asst	Smith	AFO	PHD	99	N Carol	
Davis, Mary	Lect	MD-Baltim Co		MBA	78	Maryland	
Davis, Tom E.	Prof	Cornell		PHD	56	J Hopkins	
Davis, W. Young Jr.	Prof	N Car-Charl		PHD	70	Georgia	1970
Davis, William L.	Assoc	Tenn-Martin		PHD	90	Okla St	
Davis, William W.	Assoc	W Kentucky	F	PHD	65	Kentucky	1970
Dawes, William	C	SUNY-Stony B		PHD	72	Purdue	1969
Dawid, Herbert	Assoc	So Calif		PHD	95	Vienne	1999
Dawsey, Amanda	Asst	N Car-Greens	H	PHD	01	Maryland	2001
Dawson, John	Asst	Appalach St	E	PHD	97	N Car St	2000
Dawson, John C.	Retir	Grinnell	1994	PHD	57	Cornell	1971
Day, A. Edward	Assoc	Cen Florida	D	PHD	76	Purdue	1983
Day, Richard H.	Prof	So Calif		PHD	61	Harvard	1976
De La Cruz, Justino	Asst	Tx-S Antonio	CEFH	PHD	94	Iowa St	1996
de la Vina, Lynda	Prof	Tx-S Antonio		PHD	82	Rice	1979
De los Santos, Tomas	Assoc	Central Okla	AEFO	PHD	88	Clark	1991
Deacon, Robert T.	Prof	Cal-Santa Br	QH	PHD	72	U Wash	1972
Deak, Edward J.	Prof	Fairfield	LRK	PHD	74	Conn	1970
Dean, David H.	Assoc	Richmond		PHD	88	Rutgers	1987
DeAndrea, Vincent F.	Prof	Quinnipiac	CDEN	PHD	72	Mass	1968
Dearden, James A.	Assoc	Lehigh	DH	PHD	87	Penn St	1989
Deardorff, Alan V.	Prof	Michigan		PHD	71	Cornell	1970
Deaton, Angus S.	Prof	Princeton		PHD	74	Cambridge	1983
Deaves, Richard W.	Assoc	McMaster U	EG	PHD	87	Toronto	1987
Deb, Partha	Assoc	Ind-Purdue/I	C	PHD	91	Rutgers	1991
Deb, Rajat	Prof	So Methodist	D	PHD	75	LondonEc	1976
Debaere, Peter	Asst	Texas	F	PHD	98	Michigan	9-98
deBartolome, Charles	Assoc	Colorado		PHD	85	Penn	1993
DeBoer, Dale	C-Ac	Colorado Spr	DFO	PHD	93	Ca-Davis	1993
Debrecht, Dennis M.	Asst	Carroll		PHD	81	Iowa St	1984
Debreu, Gerard	Emer	Cal-Berkeley		DSC	56	Paris	1962
DeBrock, Lawrence	Prof	Illinois	DIL	PHD	80	Cornell	1979
DeCanio, Stephen J.	Prof	Cal-Santa Br	NCD	PHD	72	MIT	1978
Dechert, W. Davis	Prof	Houston	C	PHD	77	Cornell	
Decker, Christopher	Asst	Neb-Omaha	LDM	PHD	00	Indiana	2001
DeCosmo, Michael C.	Assoc	E Stroudsbur		MBA	84	Lehigh	1984
DeCoster, Gregory Paul	Assoc	Bowdoin	ER	PHD	85	Tx-Austin	1985
DeCourcy, Julie	Asst	Trinity	L	PHD	01	Mich St	2001
Dee, Thomas S.	Asst	Swarthmore	CI	PHD	97	Maryland	1999
Deere, Carmen D.	Prof	Massachusett		PHD	78	Berkeley	1977
Deere, Donald R.	Assoc	Texas A&M	J	PHD	83	MIT	1983
DeFavia, Joao	Asst	Texas-Dallas		PHD	98	Kent	2001
DeFina, Robert H.	Prof	Villanova		PHD	79	Wash U	1989
DeFreitas, Gregory E.	Assoc	Hofstra	J	PHD	79	Columbia	
DeGraff, Deborah S.	Asst	Bowdoin	OT	PHD	89	Michigan	1991
DeGregori, Thomas R.	Prof	Houston	O	PHD	65	Tx-Austin	1967
Dehghan, Farhad	Asst	Wis-Plattev		PHD	84	Illinois	1985
Dehijia, Rajeev	Asst	Columbia	JCD	PHD	97	Harvard	1998
Deily, Mary E.	Assoc	Lehigh	LQ	PHD	85	Harvard	1991
Deitsch, Clarence R.	Prof	Ball State	J	PHD	74	NewHamp	1974
DeJong, David	Assoc	Pittsburgh	E	PHD	89	Iowa	1989
deJong, Robert	Asst	Michigan St		PHD	93	Free	1997
Dekel, Eddie	Prof	Northwestern		PHD	86	Harvard	
Dekle, Robert	Assoc	So Calif		PHD	88	Yale	1998
Delacroix, Alain	Asst	Purdue		PHD	99	Penn	1999
Delemeester, Gregory	Assoc	Marietta	DJK	PHD	89	Tx A&M	1986
Milton Friedman Chair in Economics							
DeLoach, Stephen B.	Asst	Elon	EF	PHD	93	Mich St	1996
DeLong, J. Bradford	Prof	Cal-Berkeley		PHD	87	Harvard	1995
DeLorme, Charles D. Jr.	H-Pr	Georgia	EH	PHD	66	LSU	1968
Delrossi, Alison	Asst	St Lawrence	HK	PHD	93	Penn	1999
Deltas, George M.	Asst	Illinois	CDKL	PHD	96	Yale	1995
DeMarchi, Neil B.	Prof	Duke	EB	PHD	70	Austr Natl	1983
Deme, Mamit	Asst	Mid Tenn St	FE	PHD	90	Tx-Austin	1990
Deming, Jonathan C.	Assoc	Seattle Pac	BR	PHD	79	Oregon	1977
Demmert, Henry G.	Assoc	Santa Clara		PHD	72	Stanford	1968
DeMoss, Philip M.	Assoc	West Chester	AGM	PHD	69	Kansas St	1973
Demsetz, Harold	Emer	UCLA		PHD	59	Nrthwstrn	1971
Deneckere, Raymond	Prof	Wisconsin		PHD	83	Wisconsin	1993
denHaan, Wouter	Prof	Ca-San Diego	AE	PHD	91	Car Mellon	1991

Dennis, Benjamin	Asst	Pacific	EO	PHD	96	Harvard	1996
Denslow, David A. Jr.	Prof	Florida	EH	PHD	74	Yale	1970
Distinguished Service Professor							
Denzer, Thomas F.	Retir	Rockhurst	1994	STB	62		1957
Deolalikar, Anil B.	Prof	U Washington		PHD	81	Stanford	1989
Depken, Craig	Asst	Tx-Arlington	DL	PHD	96	Geo St	1996
Depperschmidt, Thomas O.	Retir	Memphis	KH	PHD	65	Tx-Austin	1966
DePrano, Michael E.	Assoc	So Calif		PHD	63	Illinois	1963
DePrince, Albert E. Jr.	Prof	Mid Tenn St	GM	PHD	78	NYU	1991
Deravi, M. Keivan	Prof	Auburn-Montg	DFGJ	PHD	85	Okla St	1985
Dernburg, Thomas F.	Retir	American U		PHD	57	Yale	1975
DeRooy, Jacob	C-Ac	Penn St-Harr		PHD	69	Rutgers	1975
Derrick, Frederick W.	Prof	Loyola-Maryl	CI	PHD	76	N Car St	1982
Dery, George C.	Assoc	Mass-Lowell	CD	MA		Boston C	
Desai, Padma	Prof	Columbia	O	PHD	60	Harvard	1980
Desai, Suresh	Prof	Montclair St		PHD	68	UCLA	1973
DeSalvo, Joseph S.	C-Pr	South Fla	R	PHD	68	Nrthwstrn	1983
Deschenes, Olivier	Asst	Cal-Santa Br	JD	ABD			2001
DeSerpa, Allan C.	Prof	Arizona St		PHD	70	Ca-SnBarb	1975
DeSimone, Jeffrey	Asst	East Carol	DIJ	PHD	98	Yale	1999
DeVany, Arthur S.	Prof	Calif-Irvine		PHD	70	UCLA	1984
DeVault, James M.	Assoc	Lafayette	EFQ	PHD	90	Wisconsin	1989
Devereux, John J.	Assoc	CUNY-Queens	DFO	PHD	89	Chicago	1998
Devine, James N.	Prof	Loyola Marym	AEJN	PHD	81	Berkeley	1985
Devine, Robert	Asst	Framingham		MA		Northeas	
Devino, William S.	Retir	Maine		PHD	59	Mich St	1960
DeVries, Jan	Prof	Cal-Berkeley		PHD	70	Yale	
DeVries, Rick	Asst	Calvin		PHD	99	Notre Dm	1995
Dewenter, Kathryn L.	Assoc	U Washington		PHD	93	Chicago	1992
Dezhbakhsh, Hashem	Assoc	Emory	CG	PHD	89	Ohio St	1992
Dhrymes, Phoebus	Prof	Columbia	B	PHD	61	MIT	1973
Diagne, Assane	Asst	Ark-Pine Blf		PHD	96	LSU	
Diamantaras, Dimitrios	Assoc	Temple	CD	PHD	88	Rochester	1988
Diamond, Arthur M.	Prof	Neb-Omaha	BJ	PHD	78	Chicago	1986
Diamond, Daniel E.	Prof	New York U	DEN	PHD	58	NYU	1958
Diamond, James J.	Emer	DePaul	EC	PHD	62	Nrthwstrn	9-55
Diamond, Peter A.	Prof	MIT	E	PHD	63	MIT	1966
Institute Professor							
Diba, Behzad T.	Assoc	Georgetown	EFG	PHD	84	Brown	1988
Dibooglu, Selhattin	Asst	So Illinois	F	PHD	93	Iowa St	1993
Dickens, Edwin T.	Asst	Drew	EG	PHD	90	New Sch	1996
Dickert-Conlin, Stacy	Asst	Syracuse	GHJ	PHD	95	Wisconsin	1998
Dickes, Allen L.	Inst	Washburn		MA	70	Toledo	1978
Dickes, Lori	Asst	Lander		MA	96	Cen Fla	1998
Dickey, Steven W.	Assoc	E Kentucky		PHD	85	S Illinois	1983
Dickhaus, Elizabeth	Retir	Missouri	IN	PHD	74	Missouri	1974
Dickie, Mark T.	Prof	Cen Florida	Q	PHD	89	Wyoming	2001
Dickinson, David	Asst	Utah State	JL	PHD	97	Arizona	1999
Didia, Dal	Asst	Jackson St		PHD	93	LSU	1997
Diduch, Amy	Asst	Mary Baldwin	J	PHD	95	Harvard	1995
Diebold, Francis X.	Prof	Pennsylvania		PHD	86	Penn	1989
Diedrich, Ernest R.	Prof	St Benedict	GR	PHD	83	Colo St	1980
Dieffenbach, Bruce C.	Assoc	SUNY-Albany	E	PHD	72	Harvard	1978
Diersen, Matthew	Asst	So Dakota St	Q	PHD	99	Illinois	1999
Dietz, James L.	Prof	CS-Fullerton	O	PHD	74	Ca-Rivers	1973
Diffine, Donald P.	Prof	Harding		PHD	75	Miss	1971
Dighe, Ranjit S.	Asst	SUNY Oswego	AEN	PHD	98	Yale	1997
DiLiberto, Maryann	Asst	CUNY-Lehman		PHD	84	Columbia	
Dill, Floyd R.	Emer	DePaul	N	PHD	73	Cornell	1975
DiLorenzo, Thomas J.	Prof	Loyola-Maryl	KLH	PHD	80	Va Tech	1992
DiMambro, Carol	Assoc	Russell Sage	AKP	MA	89	SUNY-Alb	1989
Dimkpah, Young	Asst	Bethune-Cook		PHD	97	Howard	2001
Dimmen, Janet L.	Inst	Wichita St		ABD	78	Ohio St	1981
Dimon, Denise	Prof	San Diego		PHD	86	Illinois	1983
DiNardo, John	Prof	Calif-Irvine		PHD	90	Princeton	1991
Dinlersoz, Emin	Asst	Houston	L	PHD	00	Rochester	2000
Dinopoulos, Elias	Prof	Florida	FO	PHD	85	Columbia	1988
DiNoto, Michael J.	Prof	Idaho	JR	PHD	73	SUNY-Buf	1970
DiPrimio, Anthony	Dean	Holy Family		PHD			7-98
Diskin, Jonathan	C-Ac	Earlham		PHD	89	Mass	1988
Diulio, Eugene A.	Assoc	Fordham		PHD	66	Columbia	1963
Diwan, Romesh K.	Retir	Rensselaer		PHD	65	Birminghm	1967
Dix, Manfred	Asst	Tulane		PHD	98	Illinois	2001
Dixit, Avinash K.	Prof	Princeton		PHD	68	MIT	1981
Dixon, Bruce	Prof	Arkansas	TQ	PHD	76	Ca-Davis	1986
Dixon, Warren R.	Prof	SUNY-Plattsb	BP	PHD	71	Colorado	1968
Djimopoulos, Evangelos S.	Prof	F Dick-Teane	ADEF	PHD	69	Columbia	
Doak, Paul D.	Retir	Iowa State	1994	PHD	65	Iowa St	1961
Dobbert, Duane	Asst	Tri-State		MA		Mich St	1995
Dobbs, Thomas L.	Prof	So Dakota St	Q	PHD	69	Maryland	1978

Dobis, Vernon J.	Prof	Mn-Moorhead		PHD	94	Manitoba	1981
Dobitz, Clifford P.	Retir	N Dakota St	ABDL	PHD	71	Colo St	1970
Dobkins, Linda H.	Asst	Emory Henry	ROF	PHD	95	Va Tech	1996
Dobra, John L.	Assoc	Nevada-Reno		PHD	80	Va Tech	1980
Doeringer, Peter B.	Prof	Boston Univ	JL	PHD	66	Harvard	1974
Dohan, Michael R.	Assoc	CUNY-Queens	PQ	PHD	69	MIT	1971
Dolan, Robert C.	Prof	Richmond		PHD	82	Rutgers	1980
Dolbear, F. Treanery Jr.	Prof	Brandeis		PHD	63	Yale	1968
Dole, Carol	Asst	West Georgia	E	PHD	92	Florida	2001
Domazlicky, Bruce R.	Prof	SE Missouri	AK	PHD	76	Wyoming	1986
Dominguez, John R.	Prof	Wis-Whitewat		PHD	71	MIT	1988
Domitrz, Joseph S.	Prof	Wis-Whitewat		PHD	71	S Illinois	1976
Dompere, Kofi	Assoc	Howard	HEC	PHD	80	Temple	1977
Donaldson, John B.	Prof	Columbia		PHD	76	Car Mellon	1977
Mario J. Gabelli Professor of Finance							
Donihue, Michael R.	C-Ac	Colby	CEA	PHD	89	Michigan	1989
Donley, Thomas D.	Assoc	DePaul	C	PHD	93	Wisconsin	8-90
Donnelley, Lawrence P.	Assoc	Delaware	O	PHD	70	Brown	1968
Donnelly, Lawrence I.	Prof	Xavier	AJM	PHD	64	Cincinnati	1956
Donnelly, William F.	Prof	Santa Clara		PHD	69	NYU	1969
Donovan, Elaine M.	Assoc	Merrimack		PHD	81	Houston	
Donziger, Alan J.	Assoc	Villanova		PHD	72	Bryn Mawr	1967
Dooley, Michael	Prof	Ca-Santa Crz	F	PHD	71	Penn	1992
Dor, Avi	Assoc	Case Western	I	PHD	86	CUNY	1995
John R. Mannix Blue Cross & Blue Shield Professor of Health Care Economics							
Dorai, Gopal C.	Retir	Wm Patterson		PHD	67	Wayne St	1974
Doral, Murat	Inst	Kennesaw St	AHG	MBA	90	W Virginia	1999
Dorfman, Mark S.	Retir	Ark-Ltl Rock		PHD	70	Illinois	1987
Dorn, James A.	Prof	Towson		PHD	76	Virginia	1973
Dornbusch, Rudiger	Prof	MIT	F	PHD	71	Chicago	1975
Ford International Professor of Economics							
Doroodian, Khosrow	Prof	Ohio Univ	QAF	PHD	81	Oregon	1982
Dorsainvil, Kathleen	Asst	Howard	CEO	PHD	97	Penn St	1995
Dorsey, John W.	Retir	Maryland		PHD	65	Harvard	1989
Doshi, Kokila	Prof	San Diego		PHD		Rochester	1990
Doss, Veda	Retir	Wingate	BDJF	PHD	69	Syracuse	1984
Doti, James L.	Prof	Chapman	AEC	PHD	76	Chicago	1974
Dotterweich, Douglas P.	Prof	East Tenn St		PHD	78	Delaware	1984
Dougan, William R.	C-Pr	Clemson	HDEL	PHD	81	Chicago	1988
Douglas, Richard W. Jr.	Assoc	Bowling Gr		PHD	75	Iowa	1976
Douglas, Stratford M.	Assoc	W Virginia	CHD	PHD	87	N Carol	990
Dowd, Michael R.	C-Ac	Toledo	E	PHD	90	SUNY-Buf	1989
Dowling, Edward T.	Prof	Fordham		PHD	73	Cornell	1973
Downes, Thomas A.	Asst	Tufts	H	PHD	88	Stanford	1994
Downing, Douglas A.	C-Ac	Seattle Pac	ACH	PHD	87	Yale	1983
Downing, Paul B.	Retir	Florida St		PHD	67	Wisconsin	1980
Doyle, George A.	Emer	Assumption	FBOP	PHD	51	Fordham	1961
Doyle, Joanne M.	Asst	Jms Madison	DC	PHD	93	Boston C	1993
Doyle, Matthew	Asst	Iowa State	D	PHD	01	Brit Colum	2001
Doyle, William	Assoc	Dallas	GN	PHD	91	Tennessee	1991
Doyle-Burke, Christine	Assoc	Framingham		MA		Boston C	
Drabicki, John Z.	Assoc	Arizona		PHD	73	Purdue	1970
Drabkin, Eric	C-Ac	Hawaii Pacif	MCEF	PHD	93	UCLA	1994
Dragonette, Joseph E.	Assoc	St Joseph	CE	PHD	74	Penn	1967
Drazen, Allen	Prof	Maryland		PHD	76	MIT	1990
Drewianka, Scott	Asst	Wis-Milwauke		PHD	99	Chicago	2001
Driscoll, John	Asst	Brown		PHD	95	Harvard	1995
Driscoll, Vincent R.	Prof	Quinnipiac	AEG	PHD	75	New Sch	1967
Driskill, Robert A.	Prof	Vanderbilt	EFM	PHD	78	J Hopkins	1992
Dropsy, Vincent	Asst	CS-Fullerton	FE	PHD	90	S Calif	1989
Du Boff, Richard B.	Retir	Bryn Mawr		PHD	64	Penn	1964
Dube, Smile W.	Assoc	CS-Sacrament		PHD	89	Tx-Austin	1989
Dubey, Pradeep	Prof	SUNY-Stony B		PHD	75	Cornell	1989
Dubin, Jeffrey A.	Assoc	Cal Tech		PHD	82	MIT	1982
Dubin, Robin A.	Assoc	Case Western	RCD	PHD	82	J Hopkins	1988
DuBois, David		SUNY-Empire	M	PHD	90	Union In	1976
Duchatelet, Martine	Prof	Barry		PHD	77	Stanford	1989
Duchesneau, Thomas D.	Prof	Maine	AO	PHD	69	Boston C	1967
Dudey, Marc Peter	Assoc	Rice		PHD	84	Princeton	1990
Dudley, Dean	Asst	USM Academy	DHL	PHD	93	Indiana	1993
Duell, Dennis	Assoc	Wichita St		PHD	69	Illinois	1967
Duetsch, Larry L.	Prof	Wis-Parkside	DKL	PHD	70	Wisconsin	1969
Duffy, John	Asst	Pittsburgh	E	PHD	92	UCLA	1992
Duffy, John A.	Retir	LaSalle		PHD	71	Boston C	1964
Duffy, Martyn H.	Lect	Manches Inst	EC	PHD	95	Manchest	1972
Duffy, Neal E.	Assoc	SUNY-Plattsb	CR	PHD	82	W Virginia	1982
Duflo, Ester	Asst	MIT	O	PHD	99	MIT	1999
Castle Krob Career Development Assistant Professor of Economics							
Duggal, Vijaya G.	Prof	Widener	CEDQ	PHD	67	Harvard	1983
Duggan, Mark	VAsst	MIT		PHD	99	Harvard	2001

Duggar, Jan W.	Dean	Arkansas St		PHD	67	Fla St	2000
Dugger, William M.	Prof	Tulsa		PHD	74	Tx-Austin	
Dulaney, Ronald A.	Retir	Montana	DJ	PHD	73	Columbia	
Duman, Barry L.	H-Pr	West Tx A&M	BDP	PHD	71	S Calif	1969
Dumangane, Constantino Sr.	Assoc	Rochest Tech	GLDM	PHD	88	SUNY-Buf	1986
Dumas, Christopher	Asst	N Car-Wilmin	Q	PHD	97	Berkeley	
Dumas, Lloyd J.	Prof	Texas-Dallas		PHD	72	Columbia	1979
Dumont, David A.	Deces	Lander	ADJR	PHD	77	SUNY-Alb	1972
Duncan, Brian	Asst	Colo-Denver	HC	PHD	98	Ca-SnBarb	1998
Duncan, Floyd H.	Prof	Va Military		PHD	72	S Carol	1978
Duncan, Jerome L. Jr.	C-Ac	Tuskegee		PHD	80	Florida	1991
Duncan, Kevin C.	Prof	So Colorado	JR	PHD	87	Utah	1994
Duncan, Wallace H.	Assoc	No Arizona	EG	PHD	76	Wyoming	1978
Dung, Tran H.	Assoc	Wright State	DF	PHD	78	Syracuse	1982
Dunham, Heather	Prof	Centenary	ADEM	EDD	99	St Johns	8-84
Dunkelberg, William C.	Prof	Temple	M	PHD	69	Michigan	1987
Dunleavy, Kevin C.	Asst	West Chester	ACE	PHD	79	Duke	1979
Dunlevy, James A.	Prof	Miami U-Ohio	JF	PHD	74	Nrthwstrn	1980
Dunn, James R.	Prof	Edinboro		PHD	81	SUNY-Bin	1974
Dunn, Leroy	Retir	Trinity-CT	1990	PHD	56	LondonEc	1957
Dunn, Lucia	Prof	Ohio State	J	PHD	74	Berkeley	1987
Dunn, Robert M. Jr.	Prof	George Wash	F	PHD	67	Stanford	1978
Dunne, Maureen E.	Prof	Framingham		MBA		Detroit	
Dunne, Timothy	C-Pr	Oklahoma	DLJ	PHD	87	Penn St	1992
Dupree, Jill L.	Asst	Holy Cross	FNT	PHD	96	Colorado	1996
Durden, Gary C.	Prof	Appalach St	EH	PHD	71	Fla St	1982
Durell, Alan	Asst	Dartmouth		PHD	99	Harvard	1999
Durgin, Frank A. Jr.	Retir	So Maine	NPQ	DRD	56	France	1964
Durham, Yvonne	Asst	Western Wash	A	PHD	94	Arizona	2000
Durlauf, Steven N.	C-Pr	Wisconsin		PHD	86	Yale	1993
Durtschi, Reed R.	Retir	Utah State	AE	PHD	67	U Wash	1958
Dusansky, Richard	Prof	Texas	DH	PHD	69	Brown	9-89
Richard J. Gonzales Regents Chair in Economic Progress							
Duston, Thomas E.	Assoc	Keene State		PHD	72	Brown	1984
Dutkowsky, Donald H.	Prof	Syracuse	E	PHD	82	SUNY-Buf	1985
Dutt, Amitava K.	Prof	Notre Dame	EFOC	PHD	83	MIT	1988
Dutt, Swarna D.	Assoc	West Georgia	F	PHD	93	Wayne St	1994
Dutta, Manoranjan	Prof	Rutgers-N Br	E	PHD	62	Penn	1989
Dutta, Prajit	Prof	Columbia	DLG	PHD	87	Cornell	1992
Duttaray, Mousumi	VAsst	Union	FO	PHD	01	Indiana	2001
Dutton, Marilyn M.	Assoc	N Carol Cen		PHD	89	Duke	1991
Duwaji, Ghazi	Assoc	Tx-Arlington	F	PHD	66	Duke	1966
Dvorak, Eldon J.	Retir	CS-Long Bch	1994	PHD	62	U Wash	1961
Dwyer, Debra	Asst	SUNY-Stony B		PHD	96	Cornell	1998
Dyal, James A.	Prof	Indiana U-PA	JR	PHD	75	Illinois	1977
Dye, Alan	Asst	Barnard	NOL	PHD	91	Illinois	1995
Dye, Howard S.	Retir	0retirFla		PHD	49	Cornell	1973
Dyer, Alan W.	Assoc	Northeastern		PHD	82	Maryland	1983
Dykema, Eugene R.	Prof	George Fox		PHD	83	Notre Dm	
Dymski, Gary A.	Prof	Cal-Riversid	AEHP	PHD	87	Mass	1991
Eadington, William R.	Prof	Nevada-Reno		PHD	73	Claremont	1969
Eagan, J. Vincent	Assoc	Morehouse		PHD	86	Geo St	1993
Eapen, A. Thomas	Retir	SUNY-Bingham		PHD	61	Michigan	1966
Earley, Joseph E.	Assoc	Loyola Marym	AC	PHD	74	Fordham	1974
Early, Dirk W.	Assoc	Southwestern	DEHR	PHD	95	Virginia	1994
Earnhart, Dietrich	Asst	Kansas	QK	PHD	95	Wisconsin	8-97
Easley, David A.	Prof	Cornell	DGC	PHD	79	Nrthwstrn	9-79
Henry Scarborough Professor of Social Sciences							
Easterlin, Richard A.	Prof	So Calif		PHD	53	Penn	1982
Eastham, George M.	Retir	Cal Poly-SLO		PHD	78	Claremont	1966
Easton, Robert F.	C-As	NE Illinois		MA		Nrthwstrn	
Easton, Todd E.	Assoc	Portland	JR	PHD	84	Berkeley	1981
Eastwood, John D.	Lect	No Arizona	CD	MS	80	Wyoming	1990
Eaton, David	Asst	Murray State	HCL	PHD	95	Michigan	1996
Eaton, Jonathan	Prof	Boston Univ	FG	PHD	76	Yale	
Eaton, Peter J.	Assoc	Mo-Kansas Ct	CIT	PHD	76	Florida	1979
Ebeling, Richard M.	C-Ac	Hillsdale		MA	80	Rutgers	1988
Ludwig von Mises Chair							
Eberhardt, Duane O.	Retir	Missouri So		PHD	70	S Calif	1986
Ebert, Robert R.	Prof	Baldwin-Wal	DFP	PHD	74	Case Wes	1967
Eckalbar, John C.	Prof	CS-Chico	CE	PHD	75	Colorado	1978
Eckaus, Richard S.	Retir	MIT	O	PHD	54	MIT	1965
Eckel, Catherine C.	Prof	Virg Tech	P	PHD	83	Virginia	1983
Economides, Nicholas S.	Prof	New York U	DKL	PHD	81	Berkeley	1990
Edelman, Milton	Emer	So Illinois		PHD	51	Illinois	1950
Edelstein, Michael	Prof	CUNY-Queens	NOF	PHD	70	Penn	1974
Ederington, William	Asst	U Miami	F	PHD	98	Wisconsin	1998
Edgmand, Michael R.	Retir	Oklahoma St	E	PHD	68	Mich St	1983
Edgren, John A.	Prof	E Michigan		PHD	79	Michigan	1979
Edlin, Aaron	Prof	Cal-Berkeley		PHD	93	Stanford	1995

Edlund, Lena	Asst	Columbia	HIT	PHD	96	Stockholm	1999
Edmiston, Kelly D.	Asst	Georgia St	EGHR	PHD	98	Tennessee	1998
Edmonds, Eric V.	Asst	Dartmouth		PHD	99	Princeton	1999
Edmonds, Radcliff G. Jr.	Assoc	S Ill-Edward	ACF	PHD	79	Michigan	1977
Edmondson, Robert	Asst	Barton		MBA	87	Wake For	8-91
Eduardo, Marcelo	Dean	Miss College	AG	PHD	95	Miss	1997
Edwards, Alejandra C.	Prof	CS-Long Bch		PHD	84	Chicago	1966
Edwards, Bruce E.	Retir	Bowling Gr		PHD		Michigan	1966
Edwards, Dennis	VInst	Centre	AF	ABD		LSU	2000
Edwards, Franklin R.	C-Pr	Columbia		PHD	64	Harvard	1966
Arthur F. Burns Professor of Free and Competitive Enterprise							
Edwards, John H.	Assoc	Tulane		PHD	85	Maryland	1985
Edwards, Mary E.	Prof	St Cloud St		PHD	88	Tx A&M	1985
Edwards, N. Fayne	Retir	Richmond		PHD	68	Kentucky	1968
Edwards, Sebastian	Prof	UCLA		PHD	81	Chicago	1985
Efaw, Fritz W.	Assoc	Tenn-Chattan	CJ	PHD	87	Rutgers	1988
Eff, E. Anthon	Assoc	Mid Tenn St	RB	PHD	89	Tx-Austin	1990
Eftekhari, Hossein	Prof	Wis-Rvr Fall	DC	PHD	85	Nebraska	1985
Egan, Francis J.	Assoc	Trinity-CT		PHD	73	Fordham	1967
Egan, James P.	Retir	Wis-Eau Clar	E	PHD	82	Syracuse	1970
Egge, Karl A.	Prof	Macalester	AGM	PHD	73	Ohio St	1970
F. R. Bigelow Professor of Economics							
Egger, John B.	Assoc	Towson		PHD	85	NYU	1987
Eggleston, Brian D.	C-Ac	Augustana SD	ABQ	PHD	91	Wash St	1988
Eggleston, Karen	Asst	Tufts		PHD	99	Harvard	1999
Eggleston, Robert C.	Prof	Shippensburg		PHD	84	Pittsburgh	1965
Ehrbar, Hans G.	Assoc	Utah		PHD	85	Michigan	1986
Ehrenberg, Ronald G.	Prof	Cornell		PHD	70	Nrthwstrn	1985
Irving M. Ives Professor of Industrial & Labor Relations and Economics							
Ehrlich, Isaac	C-Pr	SUNY-Buffalo	OLK	PHD	70	Columbia	1977
Eichenbaum, Martin	Prof	Northwestern		PHD	81	Minnesota	1988
Eichengreen, Barry	Prof	Cal-Berkeley		PHD	79	Yale	1987
Eicher, Theo S.	Assoc	U Washington		PHD	94	Columbia	1994
Eichhorn, Richard	Asst	Coe	CE	PHD	99	Colo St	2000
Eide, Eric	Asst	Brigham Yg	JC	PHD	93	Ca-SnBarb	1993
Einolf, Karl	Asst	Mt St Mary's	BFC	PHD	98	Lehigh	1998
Eisenhauer, Joseph G.	Asst	Canisius	EI	PHD	91	SUNY-Buf	1986
Eisenstadt, Robert C.	H-Acc	La-Monroe	JI	PHD	91	Geo St	
Eisner, Robert	Retir	Northwestern		PHD	51	J Hopkins	1952
Eissa, Nada	Asst	Cal-Berkeley		PHD	95	Harvard	1995
Ekanem, Frank	Asst	Howard	EGHR	PHD	74	Geo Wash	1987
Ekelund, Robert B. Jr.	Prof	Auburn		PHD	67	LSU	1979
Lowder Eminent Scholar							
El Nasser, Marwan M.	Prof	SUNY-Fredoni	EG	PHD	70	Ohio St	1970
El-Hodiri, Mohamed A.	Prof	Kansas		PHD	66	Minnesota	1966
Elassar, Sammy E.	Prof	Winston-Sal		PHD	68	Maryland	1968
Elbaum, Bernard	Assoc	Ca-Santa Crz	N	PHD	82	Harvard	1986
Elder, Erick	Asst	Ark-Ltl Rock		PHD	97	Pittsburgh	8-96
Elder, Harold W.	Prof	Alabama		PHD	82	Va Tech	1981
Eldridge, Robert M.	Assoc	So Conn St	G	DBA	87	Geo Wash	
Eliaz, Kfir	Asst	New York U	D	PHD	00	Tel Aviv	2001
Elike, Uchenna I.	Asst	Alabama A&M	AOF	PHD	85	Alabama	1985
Eliot, Stuart J.	Lect	Manches Inst	DMA	MA		Manchest	1974
Elkins, Ron	Inst	Central Wash					1996
Ellard, Charles J.	Prof	Tx-Pan Amer		PHD	74	Houston	1976
Elledge, Barry	Prof	Appalach St	IM	PHD	70	N Car St	1969
Eller, Eric P.	Asst	Bellarmine	AEFO	PHD	98	Virginia	9-98
Ellickson, Bryan C.	C-Pr	UCLA		PHD	70	MIT	1973
Ellickson, Donald L.	Retir	Wis-Eau Clar		PHD	66	Wisconsin	1958
Ellingson, Wayne D.	Inst	So Dakota St	C	BS	70	Iowa St	1980
Elliott, Caroline	Lect	U Lancaster		PHD		Manchester	
Elliott, Dawn Richards	Asst	Tx Christian		PHD	94	New Sch	1995
Elliott, Donald S. Jr.	Prof	S Ill-Edward	AHMR	PHD	76	Minnesota	1976
Elliott, Graham	Assoc	Ca-San Diego	CEF	PHD	94	Harvard	1994
Elliott, John E.	Prof	So Calif		PHD	56	Harvard	1966
Elliott, Stephen	Prof	NW St of LA	GM	PHD	83	La Tech	
Elliott, Steven R.	Asst	Miami U-Ohio	DQ	PHD	91	Colorado	2000
Ellis, Barry	Assoc	SW Baptist		PHD		Texas	2001
Ellis, Charles M.	Retir	Dallas Bapt		PHD	73	Alabama	
Ellis, Charles Michael	Assoc	Txs Wesleyan		PHD	73	Alabama	1983
Ellis, Christopher J.	Prof	Oregon	E	PHD	83	Warwick	1983
Ellis, Larry V.	Prof	Appalach St	E	PHD	78	Missouri	1978
Ellis, Mary E.	Assoc	St John's		PHD	83	S Carol	
Ellis, Michael	Prof	New Mex St	I	PHD	75	Ca-Rivers	1973
Ellis, Michael A.	Assoc	Kent State	EF	PHD	91	Tx A&M	1990
Ellis, Randall P.	Prof	Boston Univ	CILQ	PHD	81	MIT	1981
Ellis, Robert J. Jr.	Emer	So Illinois		PHD	66	Virginia	1965
Ellis, Theodore	Prof	Adams State		PHD	72	Colo St	1967
Ellison, Glenn D.	Prof	MIT	L	PHD	92	MIT	1994
Ellison, Sara	Lect	MIT	L	PHD	93	MIT	1997

Elmore, Elizabeth A.	Prof	R Stockton		PHD	76	Notre Dm	1972
Elmslie, Bruce T.	Assoc	New Hampshir	BF	PHD	88	Utah	1989
Elston, Julie Ann	Asst	Cen Florida	G	PHD	92	U Wash	1998
Elul, Ronel	Asst	Brown		PHD	95	Yale	
Elwood, S. Kirk	Asst	Jms Madison	EFC	PHD	93	Ca-Davis	1992
Ely, Jeffrey	Asst	Northwestern		PHD	96	Berkeley	1996
Elzinga, Kenneth G.	Prof	Virginia	LDR	PHD	67	Mich St	1967
Emerson, Patrick	Asst	Colo-Denver		PHD	00	Cornell	
Emery, E. David	Prof	St Olaf	DIA	PHD	69	Minnesota	1969
Emery, Mary Ann	Assoc	St Olaf	M	MA	65	Minnesota	1969
Enders, Walter		Alabama	EF	PHD	75	Columbia	
Endres, Carole R.	Lect	Wright State	AFG	MS	87	Wright St	
Eng, Maximo	Adj	St John's		PHD	66	NYU	1985
Engel, Charles M.	Prof	Wisconsin		PHD	83	Berkeley	2000
Engelhardt, Gary	Assoc	Syracuse		PHD	93	MIT	1999
Engelmann, Paul H.	C-Pr	Cen Missouri		PHD	76	Okla St	1972
Engerman, Stanley L.	Prof	Rochester		PHD	62	J Hopkins	1963
John Munro Professor of Economics							
Engers, Maxim P.	Prof	Virginia	ACDQ	PHD	84	UCLA	1982
England, Richard W.	Prof	New Hampshir	OQ	PHD	74	Michigan	1976
Englander, Frederick	Prof	F Dick-Madis	DE	PHD	75	Rutgers	9-87
Englander, Valerie	Assoc	St John's		PHD	75	Rutgers	1982
Engle, Fred A. Jr.	Retir	E Kentucky		EDD	66	Kentucky	1959
Engle, Robert F.	Prof	Ca-San Diego	CGR	PHD	66	Cornell	1975
Chancellor's Associates Chair in Econometrics							
English, Mary P.	Assoc	DePauw		PHD	89	So Meth	1988
Enomoto, Carl E.	Assoc	New Mex St	FE	PHD	82	Tx A&M	1983
Epple, Dennis N.	Prof	Carnegie Mel		PHD	74	Princeton	1974
Epps, Thomas W.	Prof	Virginia	GC	PHD	69	Duke	1972
Epstein, Gerald A.	Prof	Massachusett		PHD	81	Princeton	1987
Epstein, Jose D.	Deces	American U		PHD	85	San Andres	
Epstein, Larry G.	Prof	Rochester		PHD	77	Brit Colum	1998
Epstein, Seth	Assoc	DePaul	D	PHD	88	Arizona	1992
Ercan, Hakan	Asst	Bogazici	CHJ	PHD	94	Iowa	1994
Erdilek, Asim	Prof	Case Western	F	PHD	72	Harvard	1971
Erekson, O. Homer	Prof	Miami U-Ohio	HR	PHD	80	N Carol	1978
Erenburg, Sharon J.	Prof	E Michigan		PHD	86	Illinois	1987
Erfani, G. Rod	Prof	Transylvania		PHD	84	Fla St	1986
Erickson, Christopher A.	Asst	New Mex St	EF	PHD	89	Ariz St	1987
Erickson, Edward C.	C-Pr	CS-Stanislau		PHD	70	S Calif	1970
Erickson, Edward W.	Prof	N Carol St	LQD	PHD	86	Vanderbilt	1965
Erickson, Elizabeth L.	Assoc	Akron	AOQ	PHD	72	Illinois	1969
Erickson, Erick Lee	Prof	Metro St-CO	ACDQ	PHD		New Mex	1984
Erickson, Jon	Asst	Rensselaer		PHD	97	Cornell	1997
Erickson, Lee E.	Prof	Taylor		PHD	75	Michigan	1979
Erickson, Richard J.	Assoc	So Adventist	A	MBA	81	Aust Pea	1984
Ericson, Richard	Prof	Columbia	O	PHD	79	Berkeley	1985
Erkkila, John	Prof	Lk Superior	ADEF	PHD	87	W Ontario	9-90
Erturk, Korkut	Assoc	Utah		PHD	92	New Sch	1992
Ervin, Danny	Asst	Salisbury St		PHD	96	Kentucky	1-99
Erzan, Refik	Assoc	Bogazici	F	PHD	83	Stockholm	1992
Eschenfelder, Mark J.	Assoc	Robt Morris		PHD	93	W Illinois	
Eschker, Erik	Asst	CS-Humboldt		PHD	97	Ca-Davis	1998
Escoe, Gisela Meyer	Assoc	Cincinnati	O	PHD	91	Ohio St	1991
Esensoy, Yilmaz	Retir	Alabama A&M	AOD	PHD	69	Ohio St	
Eseonu, Maxwell O.	Assoc	Virginia St		PHD	83	Howard	1982
Esfahani, Hadi S.	Assoc	Illinois	EFLO	PHD	84	Berkeley	1984
Eshleman, Tom	Assoc	Neb-Kearney		PHD	94	Okla St	1993
Eskot, Herbert J.	Asst	W New Eng		PHD	84	Tufts	1984
Espino, Dolores	Assoc	St Thomas-FL		PHD		Fla St	1999
Espiritu, Antonina	Asst	Hawaii Pacif		PHD	98	Nebraska	1998
Esposito, Frances F.	Retir	Mass-Dartmou		PHD	67	Boston C	1967
Esposito, Louis	Prof	Oakland	IL	PHD	68	Boston C	1999
Esposto, Alfredo G.	Prof	E Michigan		PHD	83	Temple	1990
Essenburg, Timothy J.	Prof	Bethel-MN	AI	PHD	91	Tennessee	1989
Esteban, Susanna	Asst	Penn State		PHD	99	Rochester	2001
Estenson, Paul	Asst	Gustavus Ado		PHD	86	Nebraska	1986
Estrada, Joselito K.	Asst	Tx-Brownsvil	AQR	PHD	92	Miss St	2000
Ethier, Wilfred J.	Prof	Pennsylvania	F	PHD	70	Rochester	1969
Eubank, Wayne F.	Retir	SE Missouri		PHD		Kentucky	1964
Eubanks, Larry S.	Assoc	Colorado Spr	DHQ	PHD	80	Wyoming	1986
Eusufzai, Zaki	Asst	Loyola Marym	ACFD	PHD	94	UCLA	1989
Euzent, Patricia	Inst	Cen Florida	A	MA	82	Clemson	1991
Evans, Bernice	Asst	Morgan State		MBA		Baruch	
Evans, Boyd	Retir	Mid Tenn St	A	MA	64	Auburn	1965
Evans, George	Prof	Oregon	E	PHD	80	Berkeley	1994
John B. Hamacher Professor of Economics							
Evans, Hugh G. Jr.	C-Ac	Elizabethtwn		MA	66	Penn St	1968
Evans, John S.	Retir	Alabama		PHD	71	Wisconsin	1968
Evans, Keith D.	Retir	CS-Northrdge		PHD	71	U Wash	1971

Evans, Mark O.	Prof	CS-Bakersf	AIQR	PHD	77	New Mex	1978
Evans, Martin D. D.	Prof	Georgetown	EFG	PHD	87	Princeton	1996
Evans, Paul D.	Prof	Ohio State	E	PHD	76	Chicago	1987
Evans, Richard D.	Prof	Memphis	CM	PHD	70	Harvard	1978
Evans, Robert Jr.	Retir	Brandeis		PHD	59	Chicago	1967
Evans, Stacey	VInst	Babson	AE				
Evans, William N.	Prof	Maryland		PHD	87	Duke	1987
Evcimen, Gunar	Assoc	Bogazici	FO	PHD	79	Istanbul	1980
Even, William E.	Prof	Miami U-Ohio	JC	PHD	84	Iowa	1983
Evenett, Simon	Asst	Rutgers-N Br	F	PHD	95	Yale	1997
Evensky, Jerry	Assoc	Syracuse	B	PHD	84	Syracuse	1985
Evenson, Robert E.	Prof	Yale	DO	PHD	68	Chicago	1977
Everett, Michael	Asst	Quinnipiac	ADBP	PHD	96	Conn	1996
Everett, Michael David	Assoc	East Tenn St		PHD	67	Wash U	1977
Evrensel, Ayse	Asst	Portland St	E	PHD	99	Clemson	2001
Ewert, Norman J.	Assoc	Wheaton-IL	AF	PHD	76	S Illinois	1973
Ewing, Bradley T.	Assoc	Texas Tech		PHD	94	Purdue	1998
Eyler, Robert	Asst	Sonoma State	E	PHD	98	Ca-Davis	1998
Ezeani, Eboh	Prof	Univ of D C	O	PHD	76	American	1976
Fabritius, Michael	Prof	Mary Hrdn-By	ABDE	PHD	87	Tx-Austin	1987
Claude McBryde Professor of Finance-Economics							
Fackler, James S.	Prof	Kentucky	E	PHD	77	Indiana	1982
Fagal, Frederick F. Jr.	Assoc	Marywood		PHD	81	Syracuse	1987
Fahy, Colleen A.	Assoc	Assumption	HLCD	PHD	89	SUNY-Bin	1994
Fahy, Paul R.	Assoc	E Illinois		PHD	76	Conn	1976
Fain, James R.	Prof	Oklahoma St	J	PHD	86	Purdue	1986
Fair, Ray C.	Prof	Yale	E	PHD	68	MIT	1974
Fairchild, Daniel R.	Assoc	St Thomas-MN	F	PHD	78	St Louis	1976
Fairchild, Loretta	Prof	Nebraska Wes		PHD	72	Cornell	1975
Fairlie, Robert	Asst	Ca-Santa Crz	J	PHD	94	Nrthwstrn	1994
Fairris, David H.	Assoc	Cal-Riversid	AJP	PHD	84	Duke	1989
Faith, Roger L.	Prof	Arizona St		PHD	73	UCLA	1981
Falaris, Evangelos M.	Assoc	Delaware	O	PHD	79	Minnesota	1986
Falero, Frank Jr.	Retir	CS-Bakersf	ADEG	PHD	67	Fla St	1972
Falk, Barry L.	Assoc	Iowa State	E	PHD	82	Minnesota	1980
Falkowski, Daniel C.	Assoc	Canisius	F	PHD	72	NYU	1975
Falls, Gregory A.	Prof	Cen Michigan		PHD	82	Purdue	1981
Fan, Chuen-mei	Prof	Colorado St	HD	PHD	72	Minnesota	1978
Fan, Liang-Shing	Prof	Colorado St	AOF	PHD	65	Minnesota	1968
Fan, Yanquin	Prof	Vanderbilt	C	PHD	90	W Ontario	2001
Fanchon, Phillip F.	Prof	Cal Poly-SLO		PHD	82	Ca-SnBarb	
Farber, Henry S.	Prof	Princeton		PHD	77	Princeton	
Fardmanesh, Mohsen	Assoc	Temple	OF	PHD	85	Yale	1985
Fare, Rolf	Prof	Oregon State	CD	DOC	76	Lund	9-98
Farley, Noel J. J.	Prof	Bryn Mawr		PHD	65	Yale	1971
Farmer, Amy F.	Assoc	Arkansas	DK	PHD	91	Duke	1999
Farmer, Berkwood M.	Dean	Wright State	Q	PHD	70	N Car St	7-01
Farmer, Roger E. A.	Prof	UCLA		PHD	82	W Ontario	1988
Farnham, Paul G.	Assoc	Georgia St	DHI	PHD	78	Berkeley	1977
Farr, William Kendrick	Assoc	Georgia Col	ADQ	PHD	85	Georgia	1985
Farrell, Claude H. III	Prof	N Car-Wilmin	EGR	PHD	74	N Car St	
Farrell, John P.	Prof	Oregon State	BO	PHD	73	Wisconsin	9-72
Farrell, Joseph V.	Prof	Cal-Berkeley		PHD	81	Oxford	
Farrell, Michael J.	Prof	CS-Long Bch		PHD	69	Stanford	1969
Farrell, Rev. John	Asst	Villanova		PHD	72	Catholic	1993
Farsio, Farzad	Prof	Mont St-Bill		PHD	89	Claremont	1987
Fatas, Antonio	Assoc	INSEAD	EF	PHD	93	Harvard	1-94
Faulk, Dagney	Asst	Indiana SE	R	PHD	99	Geo St	1999
Faurot, David J.	Assoc	Kansas	J	PHD	75	Nrthwstrn	1975
Fausti, Scott W.	Prof	So Dakota St	F	PHD	91	Illinois	1991
Favor, Homer	Prof	Morgan State		PHD	60	Pittsburgh	
Fawson, Christopher	Prof	Utah State	CGMO	PHD	86	Tx A&M	1990
Fayazmanesh, Sasan	Asst	CS-Fresno	BCE	PHD	84	Ca-Rivers	1990
Fayissa, Bichaka	Prof	Mid Tenn St	D	PHD	82	Tennessee	1980
Fazeli, Rafat R.	Asst	Redlands		PHD	92	New Sch	1989
Fazio, John	Inst	W Virg St		MBA	76	W Virginia	2001
Fazzari, Steven M.	C-Pr	Wash Univ	E	PHD	82	Stanford	1982
Fearn, Robert M.	Emer	N Carol St	JDP	PHD	68	Chicago	1965
Feenstra, Robert	Prof	Cal-Davis	F	PHD	81	MIT	1986
Feige, Edgar L.	Retir	Wisconsin		PHD	63	Chicago	1963
Feigenbaum, Susan K.	C-Pr	Mo-St Louis	DHKP	PHD	80	Wisconsin	1988
Feinberg, Robert M.	Prof	American U		PHD	76	Virginia	1989
Feiner, Susan F.	Assoc	So Maine	BN	PHD	81	Mass	1995
Felder, Joseph	Assoc	Bradley		PHD	79	UCLA	1981
Feldman, Allan M.	Assoc	Brown		PHD	72	J Hopkins	1977
Feldman, David H.	Assoc	Wm & Mary		PHD	82	Duke	1988
Feldman, Roger D.	Prof	Minnesota		PHD	76	Rochester	1985
Feldstein, Martin S.	Prof	Harvard		DPHL	67	Oxford	1969
George F. Baker Professor of Economics							
Feliciano, Zadia M.	Asst	CUNY-Queens	JFN	PHD	95	Harvard	1994

Felix, David	Emer	Wash Univ	O	PHD	55	Berkeley	1964
Feller, Irwin	Retir	Penn State	O	PHD	66	Minnesota	1963
Feltenstein, Andrew	Prof	Virg Tech	DHO	PHD	76	Yale	1993
Feltner, Richard L.	Retir	Bellarmine		PHD	65	N Car St	6-86
Fender, Ann Harper	Prof	Gettysburg	ADNL	PHD	76	J Hopkins	1978
Fenn, Aju	Asst	St Thomas-MN	HQ	PHD	98	Iowa St	1999
Fenner, Richard G.	Assoc	Utica	AIR	PHD	92	Syracuse	1989
Fenstermaker, J. Van	Prof	Towson		PHD	63	Illinois	1988
Fenton, Sister Helen M.	Retir	Regis-MA		PHD	73	Boston C	
Ferber, Marianne A.	Retir	Illinois		PHD	54	Chicago	1956
Ferderer, J. Peter	Assoc	Macalester	EFN	PHD	89	Wash U	1996
Ferdnance, Tyrone	Asst	Hampton	OCFN	PHD	94	Notre Dm	1998
Ferdowsi, Abdollah	Prof	Ferris State		PHD	82	Mich St	1984
Ferguson, J. David	C-Pr	Miami U-Ohio	EF	PHD	74	Brown	1970
Ferguson, William D.	Assoc	Grinnell	JE	PHD	89	Mass	1989
Fernandez, Luis	Prof	Oberlin	CDGL	PHD	83	Berkeley	1980
Fernandez, Raquel	Prof	New York U	F	PHD	87	Columbia	1995
Ferran, Manuel A.	Assoc	New Mex High	ADEG	PHD	69	Oklahoma	1993
Ferrarini, Tawni	Asst	No Michigan	ANO	PHD	95	Wash U	1997
Ferraro, Paul	Asst	Georgia St	C	PHD	01	Cornell	2001
Ferri, Fabrizio	Asst	New York U	EFG	PHD	99	Penn	1998
Ferrie, Joseph	Asst	Northwestern		PHD	92	Chicago	
Ferrier, Gary D.	Assoc	Arkansas	DC	PHD	88	N Carol	1993
Fesmire, James M.	Prof	Tampa	DKL	PHD	73	Florida	1973
Dana Professor of Economics							
Fessiehatzen, Tekie	C-Pr	Morgan State		PHD		Pittsburgh	
Fethke, Carol C.	Prof	Iowa		PHD	71	Iowa	1975
Feyrer, James	Asst	Dartmouth		PHD	01	Brown	2001
Fichtenbaum, Rudy H.	Prof	Wright State	CIJ	PHD	80	Missouri	1980
Field, Alexander J.	Prof	Santa Clara		PHD	74	Berkeley	1982
Field, Alfred J. Jr.	Prof	No Carolina	F	PHD	67	Iowa St	1967
Field, William J.	Prof	DePauw		PHD	80	Michigan	1979
Field, William P. Jr.	Retir	Nicholls St	E	PHD	71	N Carol	1973
Field-Hendrey, Elizabeth	Assoc	CUNY-Queens	NJC	PHD	85	Duke	1989
Fielding, Gordon J.	Emer	Calif-Irvine		PHD	62	UCLA	1965
Fielding, William T.	Dean	Jacksonvl St		PHD	76	S Carol	1968
Fields, Judith M.	Asst	CUNY-Lehman		PHD	84	NYU	1984
Fields, T. Windsor	Prof	Jms Madison	EC	PHD	78	Virginia	1990
Figgins, Bob G.	C-Pr	Tenn-Martin		PHD	73	Arkansas	1973
Figort, Debb	Assoc	R Stockton		PHD	95	American	1989
Filer, Larry	Asst	Old Dominion		PHD	99	Kentucky	1999
Filer, Randall K.	Assoc	CUNY-Hunter		PHD	79	Princeton	1986
Finch, Eugene B.	Retir	Kean		PHD		Syracuse	9-69
Fincher, Phillip E.	Retir	Louisiana Te		PHD	78	Miss	1964
Findlay, David W.	Prof	Colby	EGA	PHD	86	Purdue	1985
Dana Professor							
Findlay, Ronald	Prof	Columbia	FB	PHD	60	MIT	1970
Finegan, T. Aldrich	Prof	Vanderbilt	J	PHD	60	Chicago	1970
Finifter, David H.	Prof	Wm & Mary		PHD	74	Pittsburgh	1973
Finley, Henry E.	Retir	Florida A&M		PHD		Indiana	1959
Finn, Daniel Rush	Prof	St Benedict	B	PHD	77	Chicago	1977
Clemens Chair in Economics and the Liberal Arts-Dean, School of Theology							
Finn, Thomas J. Jr.	Retir	Wayne State		PHD	59	Harvard	1963
Finney, Miles	Assoc	CS-L Angeles		PHD	92	Houston	1991
Finoff, David	Asst	Con Florida	Q	PHD	91	Wyoming	2001
Finster, Ronald D.	Retir	W Oregon St		PHD	70	Arizona	1971
Finucane, Brendan P.	C-Pr	Shippensburg		PHD	82	Pittsburgh	1982
Fiorentino, Christopher M.	Dean	West Chester	DQ	PHD	89	Temple	9-85
Firoozi, Fathall K.	Assoc	Tx-S Antonio	CF	PHD	87	Oklahoma	1988
First, Ramona K.	Retir	San Fran St		PHD	49	Wisconsin	1956
Fischbaum, Marvin N.	Retir	Indiana St	DP	PHD	65	Columbia	1965
Fischel, William Alan	C-Pr	Dartmouth		PHD	73	Princeton	1973
Fischer, Charles C.	C-Pr	Pittsburg St	BJ	PHD	75	Wash St	1974
Fischer, Hartmut	Prof	San Francisc	FA	PHD	73	Berkeley	1970
Fischer, Stanley	Retir	MIT	G	PHD	69	MIT	1977
Fischmar, Daniel E.	Prof	Westminst-PA		PHD	75	S Illinois	1975
Fish, Mary	Retir	Alabama		PHD	63	Oklahoma	1965
Fishback, Price V.	H-Pr	Arizona		PHD	83	U Wash	1990
Fishbaugh, Charles P.	Retir	New Orleans	1995	PHD	66	Indiana	1967
Fishe, Raymond P. H.	Prof	U Miami	CD	PHD	79	Florida	1981
Fisher, Douglas	Prof	N Carol St	EN	PHD	65	Chicago	1977
Fisher, Eric O.	Assoc	Ohio State	F	PHD	85	Berkeley	1993
Fisher, Franklin M.	Prof	MIT	P	PHD	60	Harvard	1960
Fisher, Robert B.	Prof	CS-Chico	H	PHD		Oregon	1968
Fisher, Ronald C.	Prof	Michigan St		PHD	77	Brown	1976
Fisher, Warren L.	Prof	Susquehanna	ABQ	PHD	73	Conn	1988
Fisman, Raymond	Asst	Columbia		PHD	98	Harvard	1999
Fitzgerald, John M.	Prof	Bowdoin	HC	PHD	83	Wisconsin	1983
Fitzpatrick, Ellen	Asst	SUNY-Plattsb	FOQ	PHD	97	Mich St	1994
FitzRandolph, Peter Winfield	Assoc	St Lawrence	FN	PHD	79	Tufts	1973

Fitzsimmons, Edward L.	Assoc	Creighton	AD	PHD	84	Nebraska	1984
Fizel, John L.	Prof	Penn St-Erie	ALC	PHD	81	Mich St	1985
Flaherty, Diane P.	C-Pr	Massachusett		PHD	78	NYU	
Flaherty, Sean	Prof	Frank & Mars	J	PHD	81	Berkeley	1980
Flammang, Robert A.	Retir	SW Texas St		PHD	62	Iowa	1991
Flanagan, Edward J.	Retir	Bradley		PHD	69	Mich St	1963
Flath, David	Prof	N Carol St	LDP	PHD	76	UCLA	1976
Flavin, Marjorie A.	Assoc	Ca-San Diego	E	PHD	81	MIT	1992
Flax, Stanley	Asst	St Thomas-FL		MBA		NYU	1986
Fleck, Robert K.	Asst	Montana St		PHD	94	Stanford	1995
Fleisher, Arthur A. III	Prof	Metro St-CO	ADHK	PHD	87	GeoMason	1990
Fleisher, Belton M.	Prof	Ohio State	J	PHD	61	Stanford	1965
Fleming, Garry A.	Assoc	Roanoke		PHD	79	Kentucky	1987
Flessig, Adrian	Assoc	CS-Fullerton	EF	PHD	93	N Car St	1999
Fletcher, Daniel O.	Retir	Denison		PHD	60	Michigan	1966
Fletcher, Jean W.	C-Ac	Gettysburg	AJD	PHD	83	Wash U	1986
Fletcher, Jerald J.	Assoc	W Virginia	Q	PHD	82	Berkeley	1989
Fletcher, Lehman B.	Prof	Iowa State	O	PHD	69	Berkeley	1960
Flinn, Christopher	Prof	New York U	J	PHD	84	Chicago	1987
Flint, Harold	Prof	Montclair St	AEGP	PHD	72	S Illinois	1971
Florence, Robert	Asst	St Bonaventu	HD	PHD	97	Purdue	2000
Flores, Nicholas E.	Asst	Colorado		PHD	95	Ca-SnDgo	1995
Flores, Oscar	C-Pr	Mn-Moorhead		PHD	90	Cincinnati	1989
Flores-Guri, Daniel	Asst	Skidmore		PHD	01	Boston	2001
Flores-lagunes, Alfonso	Asst	Arizona		PHD	01	Ohio St	2001
Floro, Maria Sagrario	Assoc	American U	OGDQ	PHD	87	Stanford	1988
Flory-Truett, Lila J.	C-Pr	Tx-S Antonio	DFMO	PHD	72	Iowa	1975
Flowers, Edward B.	Assoc	St John's		PHD	75	Geo St	
Flowers, Marilyn	C-Pr	Ball State	H	PHD	74	Va Tech	1990
Flueckiger, Gerald E.	Deces	Miami U-Ohio	CD	PHD	70	Purdue	1968
Flynn, David	Asst	North Dakota		ABD		Indiana	2001
Flynn, Dennis O.	Prof	Pacific	DNO	PHD	77	Utah	1979
Foeller, William H.	C-Pr	SUNY-Fredoni	AJ	PHD	72	Iowa St	1984
Fogarty, Michael S.	Retir	Case Western	RO	PHD	75	Pittsburgh	1986
Fogel, Robert W.	Prof	Chicago		PHD	63	J Hopkins	1981
Charles R. Walgreen Professor/Director, Center for Population Economics							
Fogli, Alessandra	Asst	New York U	EFJ	PHD	00	Penn	2000
Fohlin, Caroline	Asst	Cal Tech	NFL	PHD	94	Berkeley	1994
Folbre, Nancy	Prof	Massachusett		PHD	79	Mass	1985
Foley, James W.	Assoc	U Miami	O	PHD	69	Mich St	1968
Foley, Mark	Asst	Davidson	JP	PHD	97	Yale	2000
Folkers, Kim	Assoc	Wartburg		MIM	89	St Thomas	1989
Folland, Sherman T.	Assoc	Oakland	IB	PHD	74	Iowa	1986
Folsom, Davis	Assoc	So Car-Aiken		PHD	79	Conn	1979
Folsom, Roger Nils	Retir	San Jose St		PHD	73	Claremont	1976
Fomby, Thomas	Prof	So Methodist	CD	PHD	75	Missouri	1975
Fon, Vincy	Asst	George Wash	CD	PHD	81	Kansas	1979
Fong, Tat P.	Asst	Geneva	F	PHD	91	Pittsburgh	1996
Fongemie, Claude A.	Lect	Trinity-CT		PHD	79	Conn	1977
Foote, Chris	Asst	Harvard		PHD	96	Michigan	
Foran, Terry G.	Emer	So Illinois	J	PHD	71	Penn St	1970
Forbes, Kevin F.	C-Ac	Catholic	DHLQ	PHD	82	Maryland	1983
Forbus, Philip R.	Assoc	So Alabama	AD	PHD	78	Arkansas	1978
Ford, Edward J. Jr.	Assoc	South Fla	R	PHD	71	Boston C	1971
Ford, Richard	Prof	Ark-Ltl Rock		PHD	79	Arkansas	1981
Ford, William F.	Prof	Mid Tenn St	GHM	PHD	66	Michigan	1991
Weatherford Chair							
Formby, John P.	Prof	Alabama		PHD	65	Colorado	1982
Hayes Professor of Economics							
Forstater, Mathew B.	Asst	Mo-Kansas Ct	ABF	PHD	96	New Sch	1999
Forsyth, Grant	Asst	East Wash		PHD	96	Wash St	1999
Forsythe, Robert	Prof	Iowa		PHD	75	Car Mellon	1981
Fort, Rodney D.	Prof	Wash State		PHD	85	Cal Tech	1984
Forti, Annette D.	Prof	SUNY Old Wes		PHD	75	Fordham	
Fortunato, Michael		SUNY-Empire	OMF	PHD	84	Harvard	1990
Foshee, Andrew W.	Prof	McNeese St		PHD	80	LSU	1978
Foster, Dennis	Inst	No Arizona	AM	PHD	91	Hawaii	1990
Foster, Edward M.	Prof	Minnesota		PHD	61	MIT	1983
Foster, James E.	Prof	Vanderbilt	DG	PHD	82	Cornell	1990
Foster, Kevin	Asst	CUNY-City C				Yale	1998
Fosu, Augustin K.	Prof	Oakland	JOC	PHD	79	Nrthwstrn	1979
Fosu, Joseph	Assoc	W Illinois	ADEO	PHD	87	Iowa St	1987
Fournier, Gary M.	Prof	Florida St	L	PHD	81	Virginia	1980
Fowler, Stuart	Asst	Mid Tenn St	E	PHD	99	So Meth	2000
Fowles, Richard G.	Assoc	Utah		PHD	85	Utah	1990
Fox, Eugene H.	Retir	NE Louisiana		PHD	62	Alabama	1965
Fox, M. Blakely	Asst	Millsaps	CDJ	PHD	00	Tennessee	2000
Fox, Mark	Assoc	CUNY-Brookly		PHD	98	Harvard	1989
Fox, Nancy R.	Assoc	St Joseph	DJL	PHD	89	Penn	1986
Fox, Thomas G.	H-Pr$	Penn State	A	PHD	66	Syracuse	1966

Fox, William F.	Prof	Tennessee		PHD	75	Ohio St	1979
Fraley, Charles E.	Prof	Va Military		PHD	78	Oklahoma	1980
France, Robert R.	Retir	Rochester		PHD	52	Princeton	
Franceschi, Dina	Asst	Fairfield	QPO	PHD		Tennessee	1999
Francis, Gary E.	Prof	CS-Chico	ABGH	PHD	72	Colorado	1967
Francis, Neville	Asst	Lehigh		PHD	01	Ca-SnDgo	2001
Franco, April	Asst	Iowa		PHD	99	Rochester	1999
Frangul, Ramzi N.	Assoc	Sacred Heart	G	PHD	73	NYU	1977
Frank, Robert H.	Retir	Cornell		PHD	72	Berkeley	1972
Frankl, Jennifer	Asst	Williams		PHD	96	Berkeley	1997
Franklin, Douglas R.	Assoc	So Dakota St	Q	PHD	82	Utah	1988
Franklin, Raymond S.	Emer	CUNY-Queens	JBP	PHD	66	Berkeley	1966
Franko, Patrice	Prof	Colby	FAO	PHD	86	Notre Dm	1986
Frantz, Roger S.	Prof	San Diego St		PHD	78	Wash St	1978
Franz, Wolfgang W.	Retir	Central Wash	HJK	PHD	70	Wash St	1969
Frasca, Ralph R.	Prof	Dayton	A	PHD	75	Indiana	1972
Frascatore, Mark	Assoc	Clarkson	DL	PHD	94	Va Tech	1994
Fratianni, Michele	C-Pr	Indiana		PHD	71	Ohio St	1971
Fraumeni, Barbara M.	Prof	Northeastern		PHD	80	Boston C	1982
Fraundorf, Martha	Assoc	Oregon State	J	PHD	76	Cornell	9-76
Frech, H. E. III	Prof	Cal-Santa Br	LAI	PHD	74	UCLA	1973
Frederick, James R.	Asst	NC-Pembroke		PHD	83	Wayne St	1988
Frederiksen, Peter C.	Prof	Naval Postgr	AOR	PHD	74	Wash St	7-74
Fredland, John E.	Prof	USN Academy		PHD	70	Michigan	1974
Fredriksson, Per	Asst	So Methodist	DF	PHD	94	Penn	1999
Free, Rhona C.	Assoc	Eastern Conn		PHD	83	Notre Dm	1983
Free, Veronica	Retir	No Alabama		PHD	70	Miss St	1984
Freed, Marc	VAsst	Union	G	ABD		NYU	2001
Freed, Rodney Alan	Prof	CS-Dominguez	ACR	PHD	77	Virginia	1979
Freeman, Albert Myrick III	Prof	Bowdoin	QD	PHD	65	U Wash	1965
William Shipman Professor of Economics							
Freeman, Donald	Asst	Sam Houston		PHD	88	So Meth	1998
Freeman, James	Retir	Columbia		MBA	70	Penn	1991
Freeman, Katherine	Assoc	Denver	AD	PHD	78	Fla St	1983
Freeman, Patricia A.	Assoc	Jackson St		PHD	88	LSU	1998
Freeman, Richard B.	Prof	Harvard		PHD	68	Harvard	
Herbert S. Ascherman Professor of Economics							
Freeman, Scott	Assoc	Texas	E	PHD	83	Minnesota	9-91
Freiberg, Lewis	Prof	NE Illinois	DHI	PHD	72	Kentucky	1982
Freudenberger, Herman	Retir	Tulane		PHD	57	Columbia	
Frevert, Peter	Retir	Kansas	DF	PHD	64	Purdue	1964
Frew, James R.	Assoc	Willamette		PHD	79	Purdue	1984
Frey, Donald E.	Prof	Wake Forest		PHD	72	Princeton	1972
Fried, Harold O.	Prof	Union	CIL	PHD	78	N Carol	1983
Friedberg, Leora	Asst	Virginia	HJ	PHD	96	MIT	2000
Friedberg, Rachel	Lect	Brown		PHD	93	MIT	
Friedlander, Stanley	C-Pr	CUNY-City C	DJ	PHD	64	MIT	1964
Friedman, Benjamin M.	Prof	Harvard		PHD	71	Harvard	1972
William Joseph Maier Professor of Political Economy							
Friedman, Daniel	Prof	Ca-Santa Crz	CDGL	PHD	77	Ca-SanCrz	1979
Friedman, Eric J.	Asst	Rutgers-N Br	D	PHD	93	Berkeley	1996
Friedman, Gerald	Assoc	Massachusett		PHD	86	Harvard	1984
Friedman, Hershey H.	Prof	CUNY-Brookly	M	PHD	77	CUNY	1986
Friedman, James W.	Emer	No Carolina	DL	PHD	63	Yale	1985
Friedman, Milton	Emer	Chicago		PHD	46	Columbia	1946
Paul Snowden Russell Distinguished Service Professor Emeritus							
Friedman, Richard	Retir	CS-Northrdge		ABD		CUNY	1961
Friedrich, Joseph	Prof	St Benedict	DHI	MA	70	Wisconsin	1967
Friesner, Daniel	Asst	So Indiana		PHD	00	Wash St	2000
Frost, Marcia J.	Asst	Wittenberg	AJMO	PHD	95	Penn	2001
Frost, Peter S.	Prof	U Washington		PHD	66	UCLA	1969
Froyen, Richard T.	Prof	No Carolina	E	PHD	72	Maryland	1971
Frydman, Roman	Prof	New York U	E	PHD	78	Columbia	1978
Fryman, Richard F.	Prof	West Georgia	AH	PHD	67	Illinois	1986
Fuchs, Victor R.	Retir	Stanford		PHD	55	Columbia	1974
Fudenberg, Drew D.	Prof	Harvard		PHD	81	MIT	1987
Fuerst, Timothy S.	Assoc	Bowling Gr		PHD	90	Chicago	1993
Fuess, Scott M.	Assoc	Nebraska	J	PHD	86	Purdue	1986
Fugar, Christian V.	C-Ac	Dillard		PHD	89	Howard	
Fuhr, Joseph P.	Prof	Widener	DIKQ	PHD	81	Temple	1979
Fujii, Edwin T.	Deces	Hawaii-Manoa		PHD	73	Stanford	
Fukasawa, Yoshi	Dean	Midwest St	EF	PHD	79	Kansas St	1978
Fulk, David		SUNY-Empire		ABD			
Fuller, Dan A.	Prof	Weber State	ADH	PHD	82	N Carol	1981
Fuller, John W.	Retir	Iowa		PHD	68	Wash St	1979
Fuller, M. Elaine	Asst	Tuskegee		PHD	98	New Sch	2000
Fuller, Rex D.	Dean	So Colorado	JLH	PHD	82	Utah	2100
Fullerton, Don	Prof	Texas	HQ	PHD	78	Berkeley	9-94
Addison Baker Duncan Centennial Professor in Economics							
Fullerton, Herbert H.	Retir	Utah State	OQR	PHD	71	Iowa St	1969

Fullerton, Thomas	Asst	Txs-El Paso	RC	PHD	96	Florida	1996
Fullwiler, Scott	Asst	Wartburg		PHD	01	Nebraska	2001
Fulton, Betty	Retir	SE Missouri	P	PHD	75	Missouri	1968
Funderburk, Dale R.	Prof	Tx A&M-Comm	IEKJ	PHD	71	Okla St	1968
Fung, Kwok-Chiu	Assoc	Ca-Santa Crz	F	PHD	70	Wisconsin	1989
Fung, Kwok-Kwan	Prof	Memphis	OP	PHD	70	Harvard	1975
Funk, Herbert J.	Emer	Creighton	AC	PHD	64	Iowa St	1967
Funk, Mark	Asst	St Louis		PHD	98	Ca-Davis	1998
Funkhouser, Ed	Lect	Cal-Santa Br	OJ	PHD	90	Harvard	1992
Furdek, Jonathan M.	Assoc	Purdue-Calmu		PHD	74	Purdue	1974
Furfero, Arlene J.	Assoc	St John's		PHD	80	Rutgers	
Furubotn, Eirik G.	Retir	Tx-Arlington	DNB	PHD	59	Columbia	1982
Futayyeh, Mohamed-Amin	Asst	La-Monroe		PHD	70	Oklahoma	
Futrell, Gene Allen	Deces	Iowa State	1994	PHD	64	Ohio St	1964
Gabaix, Xavier	Asst	MIT	G	PHD	99	Harvard	1999
Gabel, David J.	Assoc	CUNY-Queens	DNC	PHD	87	Wisconsin	1987
Gabel, H. Landis	Dean$	INSEAD	DHU	PHD	77	Penn	9-82
Gabriel, Albert H.	Retir	SW Okla St		PHD	65	Mich St	1956
Gabriel, Paul E.	Assoc	Loyola-Chicg	ADJ	PHD	87	Kentucky	1990
Gabriel, Satyananda Jordan	Asst	Mt Holyoke		PHD	89	Mass	1989
Gade, Mary N.	Assoc	Oklahoma St	H	PHD	86	Mich St	1986
Gaertner, Robert C.	Retir	Lk Superior	DM	MBA	65	Notre Dm	1-70
Gafar, John S.	C-Pr	Lg Isl-Post		PHD	79	W Indies	1980
Gaffney, Mason	Prof	Cal-Riversid	AHR	PHD	56	Berkeley	1976
Gahvari, Firouz	Prof	Illinois	DH	PHD	81	UCLA	1994
Galatin, Malcolm	Prof	CUNY-City C	CE	PHD	65	MIT	1967
Galbreath, George T.	Retir	CS-Pomona		MA	49	Stanford	1953
Galchus, Kenneth	Prof	Ark-Ltl Rock		PHD	70	Wash U	1976
Gale, Douglas	C-Pr	New York U	D	PHD	75	Cambridge	1996
Gale, Ian L.	Prof	Georgetown	L	PHD	86	Princeton	1995
Gale, James R.	Prof	Mich Tech	E	PHD	72	Iowa	1971
Gale, Louis	Asst	La-Lafayette		PHD	94	Ariz St	1995
Galenson, David W.	Prof	Chicago		PHD	79	Harvard	1978
Gallagher, Charles J.	Assoc	Virg Comm		PHD	70	W Virginia	1971
Gallagher, Daniel J.	Prof	St Cloud St		PHD	76	Maryland	1982
Gallant, A. Ronald	Prof	No Carolina	C	PHD	71	Iowa St	1993
Latane' Professor							
Gallaway, Lowell	Prof	Ohio Univ		PHD	59	Ohio St	1967
Distinguished Professor							
Gallegos, Alejandro	Prof	Winona State		PHD	86	Wi-Milwa	1988
Galles, Gary M.	Assoc	Pepper-Malib	AHLR	PHD	88	UCLA	1982
Gallet, Craig	Asst	CS-Sacrament	CDL	PHD	95	Iowa St	2001
Gallman, Robert E.	Deces	No Carolina		PHD	56	Penn	1962
Gallo, David E.	Prof	CS-Chico	AEHQ	PHD	74	Oregon	1970
Gallo, Joseph C.	Prof	Cincinnati	L	PHD	69	Missouri	1967
Gallup, Lanny W.	Retir	Okla City		MS	63	Okla St	1964
Gamba, Maria V.	Asst	Findlay	AD	MS		Wright St	1988
Gamber, Edward N.	Assoc	Lafayette	EC	PHD	86	Va Tech	1992
Gamble, Ralph C. Jr.	Prof	Fort Hays St	AEG	PHD	89	Okla St	1984
Gambles, Glenn C.	Retir	CS-Sacrament		PHD	70	Maryland	1969
Gan, Li	Asst	Texas	C	PHD	98	Berkeley	9-98
Gandar, John Maxim	C-Pr	N Car-Charl		PHD	82	Missouri	1982
Gander, James P.	Prof	Utah		PHD	66	Berkeley	1965
Ganderton, Philip	Assoc	New Mexico	DH	PHD	89	Ca-SnBarb	1989
Gang, Ira N.	Prof	Rutgers-N Br	O	PHD	83	Cornell	1986
Gangnes, Byron S.	Assoc	Hawaii-Manoa		PHD	90	Penn	1990
Gao, Ting	Asst	Missouri	FJ	PHD	98	Michigan	1998
Gapinski, James H.	Deces	Florida St	2001	PHD	71	SUNY-Buf	1979
Garcia, Javier F.	Assoc	Ashland		JD		Akron	1980
Garcia, Marilyn	Asst	San Francisc	EO	PHD	97	Berkeley	1997
Gardner, B. Delworth	Retir	Brigham Yg		PHD	60	Chicago	1986
Gardner, H. Stephen	Prof	Baylor	FP	PHD	78	Berkeley	1978
Herman Brown Professor of Economics							
Gardner, Mark L.	C-Pr	Piedmont		PHD	85	Geo St	1979
Gardner, Roy J.	Prof	Indiana		PHD	75	Cornell	1983
Chancellor Professor							
Gardner, Wayland D.	Retir	W Michigan	H	PHD	58	Wisconsin	1964
Garen, John E.	Prof	Kentucky	J	PHD	82	Ohio St	1982
Gatton Professor							
Garfinkel, Michelle	C-Ac	Calif-Irvine		PHD	88	Brown	1991
Garhart, Robert E. Jr.	Deces	St Thomas-MN	R	PHD	82	Pittsburgh	1981
Garlick, Peter C.	Retir	SUNY-N Paltz	BEHN	PHD	72	London	1967
Garlin, Victor A.	Emer	Sonoma State	2001	PHD	65	Berkeley	1970
Garman, David M.	C-Ac	Tufts	C	PHD	84	Michigan	1983
Garnel, Donald	Prof	San Jose St		PHD	66	Berkeley	1958
Garofalo, Gasper A.	Prof	Akron	ADR	PHD	74	Pittsburgh	1979
Garratt, Rodney J.	Asst	Cal-Santa Br	AEH	PHD	91	Cornell	1991
Garrett, John R.	Prof	Tenn-Chattan	EFG	PHD	85	Mass	1984
UC Foundation Associate Professor							
Garrett, Martin A.	Prof	Wm & Mary		PHD	66	Vanderbilt	1963

Garriga, Carlos	Asst	Florida St		PHD	99	Barcelona	2001
Garrison, Charles B.	Retir	Tennessee		PHD	68	Kentucky	1967
Garrison, Roger W.	Prof	Auburn		PHD	81	Virginia	1983
Garston, Neil H.	Prof	CS-L Angeles		PHD	73	Brown	1975
Garvin, Alexander	Retir	Indiana U-PA	CE	PHD	73	Tennessee	1969
Gashugi, Leonard K.	C-Pr	Andrews	CF	PHD	92	Boston U	1979
Gately, Dermot	Prof	New York U	Q	PHD	73	Princeton	1973
Gates, William R.	Assoc	Naval Postgr	D	PHD	74	Yale	1988
Gau, Carolina	Prof	Alcorn State		PHD		Missouri	
Gau, Paul K.	Prof	Alcorn State		PHD	71	Illinois	1972
Gaudin, Sylvestre	Asst	Oberlin	HQ	PHD	99	Rice	2001
Gauger, Jean A.	Assoc	Tennessee		PHD	84	Iowa St	1985
Gawande, Kishore	Assoc	New Mexico	CEFP	PHD	91	UCLA	1991
Gay, David E.	Prof	Arkansas	H	PHD	73	Tx A&M	1983
Gaynor, Patricia E.	Prof	Appalach St	C	PHD	73	U Miami	1976
Ge, Wei	Assoc	Bucknell	DFOR	PHD	93	Penn	9-95
Geanakoplos, John	Prof	Yale	CD	PHD	80	Harvard	
Gebremariam, Yilma	Assoc	So Conn St	FO	PHD	89	S Calif	1990
Gebremikael, Fesseha	Inst	Alabama A&M	A	MS	97	Alab A&M	1996
Geddes, Raymond R.	Asst	Fordham		PHD	91	Chicago	1991
Gedeon, Shirley J.	Assoc	Vermont	EP	PHD	82	Mass	1981
Gegax, Douglas A.	Assoc	New Mex St	HD	PHD	84	Wyoming	1984
Geide-Stevenson, Doris	Asst	Weber State	AF	PHD	95	SUNY-Buf	1996
Geile, Gerald L.	Inst	SW Missouri		MA	91	St Louis	1991
Geiss, Charles G.	Assoc	Missouri	C	PHD	74	N Carol	1972
Geisst, Charles R.	Prof	Manhattan	N	PHD	72	LondonEc	1985
Gelbach, Jonah	Asst	Maryland		PHD	98	MIT	1998
Gelles, Gregory	C-Ac	Mo-Rolla		PHD	89	W Virginia	1989
Gemello, John M.	Prof	San Fran St		PHD	74	Stanford	1975
Gemery, Henry A.	Prof	Colby	NAB	PHD	67	Penn	1961
Pugh Family Professor of Economics							
Gemmill, Robert M.	Retir	Gettysburg	AEG	ABD		Nrthwstrn	1958
Genc, Ismail H.	Asst	Idaho	ACG	PHD	99	Tx A&M	1999
Gendel, Eugene B.	Prof	Woodbury	AJDE	PHD	79	Boston U	7-94
Genicot, Garance	Asst	Calif-Irvine		PHD	99	Cornell	1999
Gensemer, Bruce L.	Prof	Kenyon	HPDI	PHD	66	Michigan	1966
Gensemer, Susan H.	Assoc	Syracuse	D	PHD	84	Purdue	1984
Gentenaar, Robert	Assoc	Hope	EC	PHD	77	Mich St	1977
Gentry, William M.	Assoc	Columbia		PHD	91	Princeton	1995
Geodde, Richard	Assoc	St Olaf	M	MBA		Wisconsin	1988
Geoghegan, Jacqueline	Asst	Clark		PHD	95	Berkeley	1996
George, David L.	Assoc	LaSalle	ABN	PHD	84	Temple	1979
Georges, Christophre	Assoc	Hamilton	EJB	PHD	89	Michigan	1989
Georgianna, Daniel L.	Prof	Mass-Dartmou		PHD	77	Mass	1977
Georgiou, George C.	C-Pr	Towson		PHD	79	Geo Wash	1980
Geraci, Vincent J.	Prof	Texas	CI	PHD	74	Wisconsin	9-73
Sue Killam Professorship in the Foundations of Economics							
Gerber, James B.	Prof	San Diego St		PHD	86	Ca-Davis	1985
Gerking, Shelby D.	Prof	Cen Florida	R	PHD	75	Indiana	2001
Gerlach, Jeff	Asst	Wm & Mary		ABD		Indiana	2001
Gerlowski, Daniel A.	Dean$	Baltimore	ALM	PHD	87	Pittsburgh	8-87
Gernant, Paul L.	Retir	Ferris State		PHD		Michigan	1979
Gershenberg, Irving	Retir	Mass-Boston	FOL	PHD	67	Berkeley	1982
Gerson, Janet	Lect	Michigan	AD	PHD	81	Michigan	
Gersovitz, Mark	Prof	J Hopkins		PHD	75	Yale	1994
Gertler, Mark	Prof	New York U	D	PHD	78	Stanford	1990
Geruson, Richard T.	Retir	LaSalle	TR	PHD	73	Penn	1958
Gery, Frank W.	Retir	St Olaf		PHD	57	Boston U	1962
Getz, Malcolm	Prof	Vanderbilt	HR	PHD	73	Yale	1973
Geweke, John F.	Prof	Minnesota		PHD	75	Minnesota	1990
Geyikdagi, Yasar	Prof	SUNY Old Wes		PHD		Bath	
Ghali, Moheb A.	Prof	Western Wash	CDEF	PHD	67	U Wash	1993
Gharrity, Norman J.	Prof	Ohio Wesley		PHD	66	J Hopkins	1962
Ghatak, Maintreesh	Asst	Chicago		PHD	96	Harvard	1996
Ghazalah, Ismail A.	Prof	Ohio Univ	DFHI	PHD	69	Berkeley	1969
Ghazanfar, Shaikh M.	H-Pr	Idaho	HOB	PHD	69	Wash St	1968
Ghebrat, Ezra	Prof	NewJerseyCty	ADEF	PHD	82	New Sch	
Ghebreyesus, Ghirmay	Assoc	Grambling St	EFJO	PHD	88	Strathcl	1990
Ghebreyohannes, Keleta	Assoc	Grambling St		PHD		Colo St	9-81
Ghent, Linda	Asst	E Illinois	DJ	PHD	94	N Car St	
Gherity, James A.	Retir	No Illinois	B	PHD	58	Illinois	1964
Ghiara, Ranjetta	C-Ac	CS-S Marcos		PHD	94	Ca-Rivers	1994
Ghilarducci, Teresa	Assoc	Notre Dame	J	PHD	84	Berkeley	1983
Ghirardato, Paolo	Asst	Cal Tech	D	PHD	95	Berkeley	1995
Ghirmay, Teame	Asst	Morehead St		PHD	97	S Illinois	2001
Ghironi, F.	Asst	Boston Coll	CE	PHD	99	Berkeley	2001
Ghorashi, Gholam-Reza	C-Ac	R Stockton		PHD	86	Fordham	1981
Ghosh, Dipak	Asst	Emporia St		PHD	94	Tulane	1997
Ghosh, Koushik	Assoc	Central Wash		PHD		Wash St	
Ghosh, Roy Attrayee	Asst	MN St-Mankat				Nebraska	2001

Ghosh, Satyajit	C-Pr	Scranton		PHD	85	SUNY-Buf	1986
Ghosh, Soumendra	Assoc	New Mex St	O	PHD	87	Utah St	1988
Ghosh, Sucharita	Asst	Akron	AEF	PHD	93	Kansas	1993
Ghosh, Sudeep	VAsst	Colgate	D	PHD	01	Iowa	2001
Ghoshal, Animesh	Prof	DePaul	DE	PHD	74	Michigan	1981
Ghoshroy, Atrayee	Asst	Morningside	HF	PHD	97	Nebraska	1999
Ghysels, Eric	Prof	No Carolina		PHD	86	Nrthwstrn	1-00
Edward M. Bernstein Distinguished Professor							
Giacalone, Joseph A.	Assoc	St John's		PHD	71	Columbia	1962
Giannakouros, George	Prof	Loras		PHD	74	Iowa	1966
Giannoros, Demetrios	Prof	Hartford	AEMP	PHD	81	Boston U	
Giarratani, Frank	Prof	Pittsburgh	R	PHD	75	W Virginia	1979
Gibb, Arthur Jr.	Retir	USN Academy		PHD	74	Michigan	1974
Gibbens, John M.	Retir	Wis-Whitewat		PHD	64	Iowa St	1961
Gibbons, Donna M.	Asst	Carleton	DOR	PHD	95	Brown	1993
Gibbs, W. Ernest	Assoc	Cen Florida	D	PHD	87	Rutgers	1987
Gibson, Jo Anne	Assoc	SE Louisiana	EF	PHD	72	Miss	
Gibson, William A.	Prof	Vermont	CFOQ	PHD	77	Berkeley	1986
Gidas, Sam	Asst	Wash & Jeff		JD		Yale	1998
Gidwani, Sushila J.	Retir	Manhattan		PHD	64	Minnesota	1965
Giertz, J. Fred	Prof	Illinois	HO	PHD	70	Nrthwstrn	1980
Giesber, Frank W.	Prof	Tx Lutheran	A	PHD	78	Tx-Austin	1966
Giesbrecht, Martin G.	Prof	No Kentucky		PHD	58	Munich	1987
Giesecke, Leonard F.	Deces	Southwestern		PHD	75	Tx-Austin	1968
Gieske, Michael	Prof	Winona State		BS		Iowa St	1972
Giffin, Phillip E.	Prof	Tenn-Chattan	DBLN	PHD	72	Tennessee	1977
Gifford, Adam Jr.	C-Pr	CS-Northrdge		PHD	72	Ca-SnDgo	1975
Gift, Richard E.	Prof	Kentucky	FB	PHD	65	Duke	1965
Gigliotti, Gary A.	Prof	Rutgers-N Br	D	PHD	78	Columbia	1978
Giladi, Kreindal C.	Asst	CUNY-Brookly		MA	81	CUNY	1981
Gilbert, Howard A.	Prof	So Dakota St	A	PHD	67	Oregon St	1966
Gilbert, John	Asst	Utah State	FOC	PHD	98	Auckland	2001
Gilbert, Richard J.	Prof	Cal-Berkeley		PHD	76	Stanford	1976
Gilbert, Ronald D.	Assoc	Texas Tech		PHD	70	Okla St	1977
Gilbert, Roy F.	Retir	Texas A&M	C	PHD	69	Mich St	1970
Gilbert, Scott	Asst	So Illinois	C	PHD	96	Ca-SnDgo	1999
Gilbreath, L. Kent	Prof	Baylor	GN	PHD	71	Florida	1973
Stevens Professor of Private Enterprise							
Gilchrist, Simon	Asst	Boston Univ	C	PHD	90	Wisconsin	1995
Gildea, John A.	Prof	Wheaton-MA	EG	PHD	85	Duke	1985
Giles, John T.	Asst	Michigan St		PHD	99	Berkeley	1999
Gill, Andrew M.	Prof	CS-Fullerton	J	PHD	85	Wash St	1984
Gill, Leroy	Lect	Ohio State					
Gilles, Robert P.	Assoc	Virg Tech	DH	PHD	90	Tilburg	1991
Gilles, William	Retir	Nebraska		EDE	73	Nebraska	1963
Gilleskie, Donna	Assoc	No Carolina	IJ	PHD	94	Minnesota	1994
Gillespie, Robert W.	Retir	Illinois		PHD	61	MIT	1960
Gillette, David H.	Assoc	Truman State		PHD	90	Wash St	1990
Gillette, J. Robert	Assoc	Kentucky	A	PHD	86	Tx A&M	1994
Gillette, Lynn G.	Dean	Houston Bapt		PHD	81	Tx A&M	1998
Gilley, Otis W.	Prof	Louisiana Te	D	PHD	79	Purdue	1988
Gilliam, Kenneth P.	Prof	Kennesaw St	ACD	PHD	76	Lehigh	1984
Gilliam, Lynde O.	Assoc	Metro St-CO	ADE	PHD	80	Colo St	1986
Gillis, Malcolm	Prof	Rice		PHD	68	Illinois	1993
Gilsdorf, Keith F.	Asst	Augsburg	FE	PHD	90	Nebraska	2001
Gilson, Preston	Assoc	Fort Hays St	F	PHD	93	St Louis	1988
Gin, Alan	Assoc	San Diego		PHD	87	Ca-SnBarb	1988
Gindling, Thomas H.	Assoc	MD-Baltim Co	O	PHD	87	Cornell	
Ginsburg, Helen	Retir	CUNY-Brookly	J	PHD	67	New Sch	1977
Ginther, Donna	Asst	Wash Univ	J	PHD	95	Wisconsin	1997
Gintis, Herbert M.	Prof	Massachusett		PHD	69	Harvard	1975
Giordano, James N.	Assoc	Villanova		PHD	82	Indiana	1983
Giordano, Justin		SUNY-Empire	M	MBA		St Johns	1992
Girton, Lance	Prof	Utah		PHD	76	Chicago	1978
Gishlick, Herbert E.	Prof	Rider	ER	PHD	73	Penn	1964
Gisser, Micha	Prof	New Mexico	DLQ	PHD	62	Chicago	1973
Gissy, William G.	Asst	Morehouse		PHD	87	Geo St	1988
Gitter, Robert J.	Prof	Ohio Wesley		PHD	78	Wisconsin	1976
Giunta, A. John	Retir	Scranton		PHD		Syracuse	1960
Gius, Mark P.	C-Pr	Quinnipiac	ACDJ	PHD	91	Penn St	1994
Gjerde, Kathy A. Paulson	Asst	Butler	LJ	PHD	93	Purdue	1997
Gladden, Tricia	Asst	Missouri	JC	PHD	00	Nrthwstrn	2001
Glade, William P. Jr.	Prof	Texas	OR	PHD	55	Tx-Austin	9-70
Glaeser, Edward L.	Assoc	Harvard		PHD	92	Chicago	
Glahe, Fred R.	Prof	Colorado		PHD	64	Purdue	1965
Glassman, Debra	SLect	U Washington		PHD	80	Wisconsin	1992
Glazer, Amihai	Prof	Calif-Irvine		PHD	78	Yale	1978
Gleason, Joyce G.	Assoc	Nebraska Wes		PHD	86	Nebraska	1990
Gleicher, David	Assoc	Adelphi	BJ	PHD	84	Columbia	1981
Gleisner, Richard F.	Prof	St Cloud St		PHD	72	Geotown	1968

Glendening, Richard N.	Prof	Central Iowa	EFHO	PHD	93	Iowa St	1966
Glezakos, Constantine	Prof	CS-Long Bch		PHD	70	S Calif	1968
Glick, Lee	Retir	Duquesne		PHD		Pittsburgh	
Glick, Mark	Prof	Utah		PHD	85	New Sch	1985
Globerman, Steven	Prof	Western Wash	DFIL	PHD	71	NYU	1994
Glomm, Gerhard	Prof	Indiana		PHD	88	Minnesota	2000
Glosser, Stuart M.	Assoc	Wis-Whitewat		PHD	85	Tx-Austin	1985
Glover, Terrence F.	Prof	Utah State	DCQ	PHD	71	Purdue	1974
Glustoff, Errol	Assoc	Tennessee		PHD	69	Stanford	1970
Gnuschke, John E.	Prof	Memphis	MR	PHD	75	Missouri	1976
Gobin, Roy T.	Assoc	Loyola-Chicg	AEHO	PHD	78	Illinois	1978
Godby, Robert	Asst	Wyoming		PHD	97	McMaster	1997
Goddard, Frederick O.	Retir	Florida		PHD	67	Duke	1966
Goddard, Haynes C.	Assoc	Cincinnati	H	PHD	70	Indiana	
Goddeeris, John H.	C-Pr	Michigan St		PHD	80	Wisconsin	1980
Godfrey, E. Bruce	Prof	Utah State	Q	PHD	71	Oregon St	1977
Goel, Rajeev Kumar	Assoc	Illinois St	CO	PHD	87	Houston	1989
Goenner, Cullen	Asst	North Dakota		PHD	01	Wisconsin	2001
Goeree, Jacob	Assoc	Virginia	CDL	PHD	97	Amsterdm	1996
Goering, Gregory	Assoc	Alaska-Fairb		PHD	90	Purdue	1990
Goettler, Ronald	Asst	Carnegie Mel		PHD	99	Yale	
Goetz, Michael	Assoc	Temple	MH	PHD	77	Minnesota	1978
Goff, Brian L.	Prof	W Kentucky	GHK	PHD	86	GeoMason	1986
Goffe, William L.	Assoc	SUNY Oswego	ACE	PHD	90	N Carol	2000
Gohmann, Stephan F.	Prof	Louisville	J	PHD	84	N Car St	1988
Gokcekus, Omer	H-As	N Carol Cen		PHD	95	Duke	1996
Gokturk, S. Sadik	Prof	St John's		PHD	72	Columbia	
Golan, Amos	Prof	American U		PHD	88	Berkeley	1996
Golbe, Devra L.	Assoc	CUNY-Hunter		PHD	79	NYU	1987
Gold, Andrew J.	Assoc	Trinity-CT		PHD	67	Nrthwstrn	1971
Goldbaum, David	Asst	Rutgers-Newk		PHD	96	Wisconsin	1998
Goldberg, Kalman	Prof	Bradley		PHD	54	Cornell	1952
Goldberg, Michael	Assoc	New Hampshir	EF	PHD	91	NYU	1991
Goldberg, Paul A.	Assoc	CUNY-Brookly	HP	PHD	84	Columbia	1978
Goldberg, Roger H.	Prof	Ohio Northrn		PHD	81	Indiana	1969
Goldberger, Arthur S.	Retir	Wisconsin		PHD	58	Michigan	1960
Goldfarb, Brent	Asst	Rensselaer		PHD	01	Stanford	2001
Goldfarb, Marsha G.	Prof	MD-Baltim Co		PHD	68	Nrthwstrn	1973
Goldfarb, Robert S.	Prof	George Wash	BJ	PHD	68	Yale	1980
Goldfeld, Stephen M.	Deces	Princeton		PHD	63	MIT	1969
Goldin, Claudia D.	Prof	Harvard		PHD	72	Chicago	1990
Goldman, Marshall I.	Retir	Wellesley		PHD	61	Harvard	1958
Goldman, Steven M.	Prof	Cal-Berkeley		PHD	66	Stanford	1979
Goldsmith, Arthur H.	C-Pr	Wash & Lee	EJ	PHD	79	Illinois	1990
Jackson T. Stephens Professor of Economics							
Goldsmith, O. Scott	Retir	Alaska-Ancho	CH	PHD	76	Wisconsin	1975
Goldstein, Donald	Assoc	Allegheny	ABG	PHD	91	Mass	1989
Goldstein, Harold M.	Retir	Northeastern		PHD	61	Clark	1961
Goldstein, Henry	Retir	Oregon	1997	PHD	67	J Hopkins	1967
Goldstein, Jonathan Paul	C-Pr$	Bowdoin	EC	PHD	82	Mass	1979
Goldstein, Nance	Assoc	So Maine	IJ	PHD	88	ThamesPoly	1987
Gollin, Doug	Asst	Williams		PHD	96	Minnesota	1996
Gollop, Frank M.	Prof	Boston Coll	DL	PHD	74	Harvard	1979
Golub, Stephen S.	Prof	Swarthmore	AE	PHD	83	Yale	1981
Goma, Ophelia		DePauw					
Gomersall, C. Nicholas	Assoc	Luther		PHD	91	Cornell	1991
Gomes-Casseres, Benjamin	Assoc	Brandeis		DBA	85	Harvard	1995
Gomis-Porqueras, Pedro	Asst	U Miami	CEG	PHD		Tx-Austin	2001
Gonce, Richard A.	Prof	Grand Valley	ABDK	PHD	66	Wisconsin	1972
Gondwe, Derrick K.	Prof	Gettysburg	ABEO	PHD	78	Manitoba	1977
Gonzalez, Jorge G.	C-Pr	Trinity	F	PHD	89	Mich St	1989
Gonzalez, Rodolfo	Prof	San Jose St		PHD	90	Ca-Davis	1990
Gonzalez-Rivera, Gloria	Assoc	Cal-Riversid	CG	PHD	91	Ca-SnDgo	1991
Gonzalez-Vega, Claudio	Prof	Ohio State	O	PHD	76	Stanford	
Good, Delmar	Prof	Goshen	AH	PHD	70	Illinois	2-67
Gooding, Elmer R.	Prof	Arizona St		PHD	69	Kansas	1988
Goodman, Allen C.	Prof	Wayne State	IR	PHD	76	Yale	1986
Goodman, D. Jay	Asst	So Colorado	FQ	PHD	95	Colorado	1998
Goodman, Douglas	Prof	Puget Sound	AE	PHD	78	Illinois	1977
Goodman, Rae Jean B.	Prof	USN Academy		PHD	76	Wash U	1973
Goodstein, Eban	C-Ac	Lewis & Clrk	QDGL	PHD	89	Michigan	1995
Goodwin, Craufurd	Prof	Duke	ABFN	PHD	58	Duke	9-62
James D. Duke Professor							
Goodwin, Randall B.	Assoc	Kennesaw St	ADM	PHD	82	Georgia	1982
Goodwin, Susan A.	Assoc	Mass-Lowell	G	PHD	75	Tufts	
Gootzeit, Michael J.	Prof	Memphis	BE	PHD	66	Purdue	1975
Gorcau, Suleyman	Asst	St Peters	FG	PHD		CUNY	1998
Gordon, Brunhild	Retir	South Fla		PHD	57	S Calif	1960
Gordon, David B.	Assoc	Clemson	DE	PHD	95	Chicago	1992
Gordon, Peter	Prof	So Calif		PHD	71	Penn	1971

Gordon, Robert J.	Prof	Northwestern		PHD	67	MIT	1973
Stanley G. Harris Professor of the Social Sciences							
Gordon, Roger H.	Prof	Ca-San Diego	H	PHD	76	MIT	2001
Gordon, Sara L.	Prof	St John's		PHD	71	Stanford	1978
Gormely, Patrick J.	Assoc	Kansas State	OF	PHD	67	Duke	1967
Gort, Michael	Prof	SUNY-Buffalo	O	PHD	54	Columbia	1964
Goss, Ernest P.	Prof	Creighton	RC	PHD	83	Tennessee	1992
MacAllister Chair in Regional Economics							
Gottfried, Robert Richard	Prof	Univ South	OQR	PHD	81	N Carol	
Gottheil, Fred	Prof	Illinois	AB	PHD	59	Duke	1959
Gottschalk, Peter	Prof	Boston Coll	DIJ	PHD	73	Penn	1987
Gottschall, Tiffani	VAsst	St Lawrence	JR	PHD	00	SUNY-Bin	2001
Gottschang, Thomas R.	Assoc	Holy Cross	AOP	PHD	82	Michigan	1979
Gouke, Cecil G.	Retir	Ohio State	M	PHD	67	NYU	1973
Goulder, Lawrence	Prof	Stanford		PHD	82	Stanford	1989
Goulet, Denis A.	Prof	Notre Dame	O	PHD	63	SaoPaulo	1979
Goulet, Janet C.	Prof	Wittenberg	AJM	PHD	75	Notre Dm	1975
Gowdy, John M.	Prof	Rensselaer		PHD	80	W Virginia	1983
Gowens, Paul R.	Prof	SW Texas St	M	PHD	73	Miss	1980
Gownsaukaran, Gautam	Asst	Minnesota		PHD	95	Yale	1995
Goyal, Tarsiam L.	C-Pr	Univ of D C		DSC	70	Geo Wash	1967
Grabowski, Henry G.	Prof	Duke		PHD	67	Princeton	1972
Grabowski, Richard L.	C-Pr	So Illinois	OF	PHD	77	Utah	1979
Graddy, Duane B.	Prof	Mid Tenn St	GHA	PHD	74	Lehigh	1972
Grady, John	Assoc	LaSalle	BE	MA		Temple	1960
Graeser, Paul	Deces	No Illinois	L	PHD	67	Columbia	1967
Graham, D. A.	Prof	Duke		PHD	69	Duke	1969
Graham, Fred C.	Assoc	American U		PHD	85	Virginia	1988
Graham, Glenn	Assoc	SUNY Oswego	AIL	PHD	95	SUNY-Bin	1992
Graham, John W. III	Prof	Rutgers-Newk		PHD	78	Nrthwstrn	1986
Graham, Katherine	Lect	SUNY-Cortlan		MS		Cornell	
Graham, Patricia E.	Asst	No Colorado	IJOQ	PHD	88	Colo St	1988
Graham, William R.	Retir	CS-L Angeles		PHD	69	Arizona	1969
Gram, Harvey H.	Prof	CUNY-Queens	FCE	PHD	73	Wisconsin	1974
Grambo, Ralph W. Jr.	Retir	Scranton		PHD	73	Penn	1973
Gramlich, Edward M.	Prof	Michigan		PHD	65	Yale	1976
Grammy, Abbas P.	C-Pr	CS-Bakersf	ACOR	PHD	82	Colorado	1989
Granderson, Gerald	Assoc	Miami U-Ohio	DG	PHD	93	N Carol	1993
Granger, Clive W. J.	Prof	Ca-San Diego	C	PHD	74	Nottinghm	1974
Chancellor's Associates Chair in Economics							
Granger, George L.	Retir	East Tenn St		PHD	71	Penn	1961
Granger, Maury	Asst	N Carol A&T		PHD	95	Kentucky	1993
Grant, Alan	Assoc	E Illinois		PHD	96	Kansas St	1997
Grant, Clayton	H-Pr	No Georgia	K	PHD	71	Clemson	1985
Grant, James H.	Asst	Lewis & Clrk	CDJA	PHD	79	Mich St	1987
Grant, Randy R.	C-Ac	Linfield		PHD	96	Nebraska	1993
Grant, Stephen K.	Retir	Mass Lib Art		PHD	74	Clark	
Grapard, Ulla A.	Assoc	Colgate	AB	PHD	90	Cornell	1985
Grass, R. Gail	Assoc	Jackson St		PHD	89	Harvard	1989
Grawe, Nathan	Asst	Carleton	IJ	PHD	01	Chicago	1999
Gray, Charles M.	Prof	St Thomas-MN	K	PHD	78	Wash U	1976
Gray, Jerry	C-Ac	Willamette		PHD	89	Utah	1990
Gray, Jo Anna	Prof	Oregon	E	PHD	76	Chicago	1989
Gray, Wayne B.	C-Ac	Clark		PHD	83	Harvard	1984
Greaney, Theresa M.	Asst	Hawaii-Manoa	F	PHD	94	Michigan	2000
Greckel, Fay E.	Retir	Indiana SE	OJR	PHD	69	Indiana	1967
Greco, Anthony J.	H-Pr	La-Lafayette	ADL	PHD	78	Tennessee	8-84
Green, Gareth P.	Asst	Seattle	DEQ	PHD	95	Berkeley	2001
Green, Gregory G.	Asst	Idaho State	ACEF	PHD	97	Temple	1997
Green, Jeffery	Assoc	Ball State	C	PHD	72	Cornell	1972
Green, Jeffery	Prof	Indiana		PHD	67	Illinois	1985
Green, Jerry R.	Prof	Harvard		PHD	70	Rochester	1973
David A. Wells Professor of Political Economy							
Green, Louis C.	Prof	San Diego St		PHD	75	Berkeley	1976
Green, Richard	Prof	Carnegie Mel		PHD	82	Wisconsin	
Richard M. and Margaret S. Cyert Professor of Economics and Management							
Green, Rodney D.	Prof	Howard	R	PHD	80	American	1977
Green, Steven L.	C-Pr	Baylor		PHD	84	Brown	1986
Green, Trellis Garnett	Assoc	So Miss	Q	PHD	84	Fla St	1983
Green, William B.	C-Pr	Sam Houston		PHD	74	LSU	1974
Green-Weishaupt, Carole A.	Assoc	South Fla	J	PHD	82	Illinois	1982
Greenbaum, Harry	Retir	So Dakota St	E	PHD	61	Ohio St	1961
Greenberg, Edward	Prof	Wash Univ	DE	PHD	61	Wisconsin	1963
Greene, Benjamin B. Jr.	Assoc	Salisbury St		PHD	74	Boston C	8-78
Greene, Clinton	Assoc	Mo-St Louis	CE	PHD	92	Ca-Davis	1994
Greene, Kenneth V.	Prof	SUNY-Bingham	HK	PHD	68	Virginia	1968
Greene, William H.	C-Pr	New York U	CDE	PHD	76	Wisconsin	1982
Greenfield, Robert L.	Prof	F Dick-Madis	GP	PHD	79	Rutgers	8-79
Greenhut, Melvin L.	Emer	Texas A&M		PHD	51	Wash U	1966
Distinguished Professor of Economics							

Greenlaw, Steven A.	C-Pr	Mary Wash	EFA	PHD	87	SUNY-Bin	1982
Greenley, Douglas A.	Prof	Mn-Moorhead		PHD	79	Colo St	1978
Greenwade, George D.	Assoc	Va Military		PHD	88	Tx Tech	2001
Greenwald, Bruce C. N.	Prof	Columbia		PHD	78	MIT	1991
Robert Heilbrunn Professo of Finance and Asset Management							
Greenwald, William	Prof	CUNY-City C	CE	PHD	50	NYU	1946
Greenwood, Daphne T.	Prof	Colorado Spr	HJT	PHD	80	Oklahoma	1980
Greenwood, Jeremy	Prof	Rochester	D	PHD	83	Rochester	1992
Greenwood, Michael J.	Prof	Colorado		PHD	67	Nrthwstrn	1980
Greer, Douglas F.	Prof	San Jose St		PHD	68	Cornell	1975
Greer, Mark	C-As	Dowling		PHD	90	Michigan	1994
Gregor, John J.	C-Pr	Wash & Jeff		PHD	76	Penn St	1989
Gregorowicz, Phillip	H-Pr	Auburn-Montg	EFGJ	PHD	82	N Illinois	1980
Gregory, Paul R.	Prof	Houston	P	PHD	69	Harvard	1972
Gregory, Sadie R.	Dean	Virginia St		PHD	87	Howard	1-79
Greif, Avner	Prof	Stanford		PHD	89	Nrthwstrn	1993
Grennes, Thomas	Prof	N Carol St	FD	MA	65	Wisconsin	1968
Gresik, Thomas A.	Prof	Notre Dame	D	PHD	87	Penn	2000
Grether, David M.	Prof	Cal Tech		PHD	69	Stanford	1970
Greubel, Robert T.	Prof	NE St-Okla	AEF	PHD	72	Arkansas	1965
Greytak, David	Retir	Syracuse	D	PHD	68	Wash U	
Grier, Kevin B.	Prof	Oklahoma	E	PHD	84	Wash U	1999
Grier, Robin	Asst	Oklahoma	O	PHD	95	GeoMason	1999
Grieson, Ronald E.	Prof	Ca-Santa Crz	RHD	PHD	72	Rochester	1980
Griffin, James M.	Prof	Texas A&M	C	PHD	70	Penn	1982
Hugh Roy Cullen Professor in Liberal Arts							
Griffin, Keith B.	Prof	Cal-Riversid	AOP	DPHI	65	Oxford	1988
Griffith, Jacqueline	Asst	Kean		MBA			
Griffith, Winston Harold	Prof	Bucknell	FOD	PHD	81	Howard	1987
Griffiths, L. Christopher	Prof	Colorado Col		PHD	70	Colorado	1967
Grigg, Vernon H.	Retir	South Fla		PHD	54	MIT	1981
Grijalva, Therese	Assoc	Weber State		PHD	00	New Mex	1995
Griliches, Zvi	Deces	Harvard		PHD	57	Chicago	1969
Paul M. Warburg Professor of Economics							
Grimes, Paul W.	C-Pr	Miss State	JA	PHD	84	Okla St	1987
Grinols, Earl L.	Prof	Illinois	DFO	PHD	77	MIT	1984
Gritsch, Martin	Asst	Wm Paterson		PHD	00	Tx A&M	2000
Grobar, Lisa M.	Prof	CS-Long Bch		PHD	89	Michigan	1989
Grobey, John H.	Retir	CS-Humboldt		PHD	75	U Wash	1967
Groesbeck, John D.	C-Ac	So Utah		PHD	93	Utah St	1993
Gronberg, Timothy J.	Prof	Texas A&M	H	PHD	78	Nrthwstrn	1977
Groothuis, Peter A.	Assoc	Westminst-PA		PHD	89	Kentucky	1989
Gropp, Jeffrey		DePauw					
Gropper, Daniel M.	Assoc	Auburn		PHD	89	Fla St	1988
Grossbard-Shechtman, Shoshan	Prof	San Diego St		PHD	78	Chicago	1981
Grossberg, Adam J.	Assoc	Trinity-CT		PHD	86	Illinois	1986
Grosskopf, Shawna	Prof	Oregon State	CHJ	PHD	77	Syracuse	9-98
Grossman, Gene M.	Prof	Princeton		PHD	80	MIT	1980
Grossman, Gregory	Emer	Cal-Berkeley		PHD	53	Harvard	1953
Grossman, Herschel I.	Prof	Brown		PHD	65	J Hopkins	1973
Merton P. Stolz Professor in the Social Sciences							
Grossman, Leroy J.	Prof	St Louis		PHD	63	Vanderbilt	1964
Grossman, Peter Z.	Assoc	Butler	NL	PHD	92	Wash U	1994
Efroymson Chair in Economics							
Grossman, Philip J.	Asst	St Cloud St		PHD	84	Virginia	9-99
Grossman, Richard	Prof	Wesleyan-CT	N	PHD	88	Harvard	1990
Groves, Theodore	Prof	Ca-San Diego	DHM	PHD	70	Berkeley	1978
Grubaugh, Stephen G.	Prof	Bentley	CF	PHD	82	Chicago	1981
Grubb, Farley	Prof	Delaware	N	PHD	84	Chicago	1983
Gruber, Jonathan H.	Prof	MIT	G	PHD	92	Harvard	1992
Grunloh, James J.	Prof	Wis-Oshkosh	A	PHD	79	Wash U	1969
Gruver, Gene W.	Prof	Pittsburgh	O	PHD	72	Iowa St	1970
Gu, Anthony	Asst	SUNY-Geneseo	D	PHD	99	Illinois	1999
Guell, Robert	Assoc	Indiana St	HC	PHD	91	Syracuse	1991
Guffey, Loren	Retir	Cen Arkansas		PHD	66	Arkansas	9-65
Guha, Gauri-Shankar	Asst	Arkansas St		PHD			
Guiler, Charles J.	Retir	Grove City		MED	66	Ind-Penn	1967
Guilfoil, John D.	Prof	New York U	DKN	PHD	64	NYU	1964
Guilkey, David K.	Prof	No Carolina	C	PHD	73	N Carol	1983
Guinnane, Timothy J.	Assoc	Yale	N	PHD	87	Stanford	
Guirguis, Hany	Asst	Manhattan		PHD	95	Oregon	2001
Gujarati, Damodar N.	Prof	USM Academy	CE	PHD	65	Chicago	1990
Gul, Faruk	Prof	Princeton		PHD	86	Princeton	1995
Gullason, Edward T.	Assoc	Dowling		PHD	86	Penn	
Gulley, O. David	Assoc	Bentley	EG	MA	89	Kentucky	1990
Gummerson, A.	Lect	Fla Internat	AEF	PHD	71	Wisconsin	1989
Gumpper, Michael R.	Asst	Millersville		PHD	97	Kentucky	1995
Gunden, Randal G.	Assoc	Goshen	EIO	ABD		Notre Dm	1984
Gunderson, Elizabeth W.	Assoc	Hamline	C	PHD	91	Union In	1980
Gunderson, Ralph O.	C-Pr	Wis-Oshkosh	OR	PHD	78	Arkansas	1987

Gunderson, Ronald J.	C-Pr	No Arizona	DR	PHD	77	Nebraska	1977
Guner, Nezih	Asst	Penn State		PHD	99	Rochester	2001
Gunn, John McKenzie	Emer	Wash & Lee	E	MA	54	Princeton	1957
Lewis Whitaker Adams Professor of Economics Emeritus							
Gunter, Frank R.	Assoc	Lehigh	FK	PHD	85	J Hopkins	1984
Gunther, William D.	Dean	So Miss	R	PHD	69	Kentucky	1998
Guo, Binbin	Asst	Ca-Santa Crz	CG	PHD	98	Yale	2000
Guo, Jang-Ting	Assoc	Cal-Riversid	AC	PHD	93	UCLA	1993
Gupta, Barnali	Assoc	Miami U-Ohio	DR	PHD	90	Florida	1993
Gupta, Harish C.	Retir	Nebraska	FO	PHD	69	Tennessee	1969
Gupta, Shiv K.	Prof	Findlay	AJ	DBA	83	London	1983
Gupta, Srabana	Asst	Fla Atlantic	DL	PHD	95	Florida	1995
Gural, Michael L.	Assoc	Westfield St		MA		Rutgers	1982
Gurmu, Shiferaw	Assoc	Georgia St	CI	PHD	92	Indiana	1998
Gurtunca, Esen Z.	Prof	Indianapolis		PHD	73	Purdue	1974
Donald W. Tanselle Professor of Economics							
Gustafson, Curtis O.	Inst	So Dakota St	M	MPA	86	S Dakota	1989
Gustafson, Elizabeth F.	C-Ac	Dayton	C	PHD	74	N Carol	1983
Gustafson, Leland Verne	Prof	West Georgia	AC	PHD	74	Fla St	
Gustafson, W. Eric	Emer	Cal-Davis	AO	PHD	59	Harvard	1978
Gustanski, Julie Ann	Asst	Rensselaer		PHD	99	Edinburgh	2001
Gustavson, Robert L.	Prof	Washburn		PHD	76	Colorado	1976
Gustman, Alan Leslie	Prof	Dartmouth		PHD	69	Michigan	1969
Loren M. Berry Professor							
Gutermuth, Karen	Asst	Va Military		PHD	96	LSU	1997
Gutman, Nancy	AdjIn	Yeshiva		BA	82	Barnard	
Gutmann, Peter M.	Prof	CUNY-Baruch	EF	PHD	57	Harvard	1963
Gutowsky, Albert R.	Prof	CS-Sacrament		PHD	65	Oregon	1967
Guttmann, Robert P.	Prof	Hofstra	F	PHD	79	London	
Guvenen, Muhammet Fatih	Asst	Rochester		PHD	01	Car Mellon	2001
Guynn, Richard Dickson	Retir	West Georgia	JA	PHD	71	Alabama	
Gwartney, James D.	Prof	Florida St	A	PHD	69	U Wash	1968
Gwin, Carl	Asst	Baylor	DL	PHD	97	Indiana	2001
Gwinn, Lawrence	Assoc	Wittenberg	ACEF	PHD	83	Kansas	1988
Gyimah-Brempong, Kwabena	Prof	South Fla	O	PHD	81	Wayne St	1994
Gylys, Julius A.	Retir	Toledo		PHD	69	Wayne St	1967
Haas, Paul F.	Prof	Bowling Gr		PHD	70	Boston C	1967
Haas-Wilson, Deborah	Prof	Smith	DIL	PHD	83	Berkeley	1984
Haberland, Chris	Asst	Clayton St		MBA	76	Geo St	1987
Habib, Ahsan M.	Prof	Adrian		PHD	80	McMaster	1981
Hackett, Steven C.	Assoc	CS-Humboldt		PHD	89	Tx A&M	1994
Hadjimichalakis, Karma	SLect	U Washington		PHD	74	Rochester	1970
Hadjimichalakis, Michael	Assoc	U Washington		PHD	69	Rochester	1969
Hadley, Lawrence H.	Assoc	Dayton	J	PHD	75	Conn	1977
Hafer, Rik W.	C-Pr	S Ill-Edward	EG	PHD	79	Va Tech	
Hagen, Daniel A.	Assoc	Western Wash	JEFQ	PHD	83	Berkeley	1988
Hagen, Elizabeth	Asst	Whitworth	AN	ABD		Utah	2000
Haggerty, Mark E.	Prof	Clarion		PHD	88	Wash St	1989
Hagstrom, Paul Alan	Assoc	Hamilton	JHI	PHD	91	Wisconsin	1991
Hahn, Jinyong	Assoc	Brown		PHD	93	Harvard	2000
Hahn, Youngki	Prof	Hawaii-Hilo		PHD	71	Ca-Rivers	
Hahnel, Robin E.	Prof	American U		PHD	79	American	1976
Hai, Wen	Asst	Fort Lewis		PHD	91	Ca-Davis	1992
Haight, Alan D.	Assoc	Bowling Gr		PHD	90	Wisconsin	1991
Haile, Philip	Asst	Wisconsin		PHD	96	Nrthwstrn	1996
Hailstones, Thomas J.	Deces	South Fla		PHD	51	St Louis	1988
Haines, Michael R.	Prof	Colgate	TN	PHD	71	Penn	1990
Banfi Vintners Professor of Economics							
Haj, Mahmound	Asst	Grambling St		PHD	00	N Orleans	8-99
Hajizadeh, Avaz	Assoc	Mass Lib Art		PHD	85	Rensselaer	
Hake, Eric	Asst	E Illinois		PHD	94	Tennessee	
Hakeem, Salih	Asst	N Carol Cen		PHD	87	N Car St	1988
Hakes, David R.	Prof	No Iowa	BEFG	PHD	85	Iowa St	1992
Hakes, Jahn K.	Asst	Clemson	HQC	PHD	96	Duke	1999
Hakim, Simon	Prof	Temple	R	PHD	76	Penn	1976
Halcoussis, Dennis	Assoc	CS-Northrdge	C	PHD	92	Penn	1991
Haley, Charles W.	Prof	U Washington		PHD	68	Stanford	1966
Halil, Kiymaz	Asst	Houston-Cl L		PHD	94	N Orleans	1-97
Hall, Alastair R.	Prof	N Carol St	C	PHD	85	Warwick	1985
Hall, Bernard	Retir	Kent State	BNH	PHD	55	Berkeley	1955
Hall, Bronwyn H.	Prof	Cal-Berkeley		PHD	88	Stanford	1987
Hall, Darwin C.	Prof	CS-Long Bch		PHD	77	Berkeley	1986
Hall, George	Asst	Yale	E	PHD	96	Chicago	1996
Hall, Jane V.	Prof	CS-Fullerton	Q	PHD	77	Berkeley	1981
Hall, John B.	Prof	Portland St	P	PHD	84	New Sch	1985
Hall, John R. Jr.	Asst	Ark-Ltl Rock		PHD	92	Indiana	
Hall, Robert E.	Prof	Stanford		PHD	67	MIT	1978
Hall, Thomas E.	Prof	Miami U-Ohio	EC	PHD	82	Ca-SnBarb	1982
Hall, W. Clayton	Retir	Illinois Tch		PHD	64	Illinois	
Hall, William Woodward Jr.	Prof	N Car-Wilmin	QR	PHD	72	Clemson	

Hall, Yvonne C.	C-Pr	New Hamp Col		PHD	81	Colo St	
Hallagan, William S.	Assoc	Wash State		PHD	77	Ca-Davis	1984
Hallam, Arne	C-Pr	Iowa State	D	PHD	83	Berkeley	1983
Haller, Hans H.	Prof	Virg Tech	D	PHD	78	Erlangen	1985
Hallock, Kevin F.	Assoc	Illinois	HJ	PHD	95	Princeton	1995
Hallwood, C. Paul	Prof	Connecticut	F	PHD	88	Aberdeen	1986
Halstead, James F.	Prof	Occidental	A	PHD	72	Stanford	1977
Halteman, James	Prof	Wheaton-IL	AB	PHD	74	Penn St	1979
Hendrickson Chair							
Haltiwanger, John C.	Prof	Maryland		PHD	81	J Hopkins	1987
Halvorsen, Marcia L.	Prof	Redlands		PHD	78	Geo St	1975
Halvorsen, Robert F.	Prof	U Washington		PHD	73	Harvard	1972
Halvorson, Jon	Asst	S F Austin	CDH	PHD	00	Alabama	2001
Ham, C. L.	Retir	CS-Northrdge	8-94	PHD	72	S Calif	1963
Hamada, Koichi	Prof	Yale	F	PHD	65	Yale	1986
Hambleton, John W.	Assoc	San Diego St		PHD	71	Wisconsin	1969
Hamer, Thomas P.	Prof	Rowan Col-NJ		PHD	75	Claremont	1974
Hamermesh, Daniel S.	Prof	Texas	J	PHD	69	Yale	9-73
Eedward Everett Hale Centennial Professor in Economics							
Hamid, M. Khalil	Prof	Millersville		PHD	66	Iowa	1968
Hamilton, Bruce W.	Prof	J Hopkins		PHD	72	Princeton	1973
Hamilton, James D.	C-Pr	Ca-San Diego	D	PHD	83	Berkeley	1992
Hamilton, Johnathan H.	Prof	Florida	HRD	PHD	82	MIT	1984
Hamilton, Steve	Assoc	Cen Florida	Q	PHD	96	Berkeley	2001
Hammack, Judd	Retir	CS-L Angeles		PHD	69	U Wash	1970
Hammerle, Nancy E.	Asst	Stonehill	A	MA		Temple	1980
Hammes, David L.	Prof	Hawaii-Hilo		PHD	85	Simon Fr	1988
Hammond, Claire Holton	Prof	Wake Forest		PHD	82	Virginia	1978
Hammond, J. Daniel	Prof	Wake Forest		PHD	79	Virginia	1978
Hammond, Peter J.	Prof	Stanford		PHD	74	Cambridge	1979
Hammoudeh, Shawka M.	Assoc	Drexel		PHD	80	Kansas	1990
Hampton, Mary B.	Prof	Wis-La Cross	GHIJ	PHD	91	Wi-Milwa	1991
Hampton, Nathan E.	Assoc	St Cloud St		PHD	89	Ca-SnBarb	1987
Hamzaee, Reza G.	Prof	Missouri Wes	E	PHD	85	Ariz St	1984
Han, Hsiang-Ling	Asst	Babson	CE	PHD	92	Rochester	1997
Hands, Wade	Prof	Puget Sound	ABC	PHD	65	U Wash	
Handy, John	C-Pr	Morehouse		PHD	85	Geo St	1978
Hanes, Christopher L.	Assoc	Mississippi	EN	PHD	90	Harvard	1999
Hankins, Marvin	Asst	SW Okla St		EDD		Okla St	1979
Hanna, Raouf S.	H-Pr	E Michigan		PHD	73	Indiana	1977
Hannah, Richard	Prof	Mid Tenn St	J	PHD	81	Utah	1992
Hannan, Michael J.	C-Pr	Edinboro		PHD	88	W Virginia	1988
Hannes, Lance E.	Assoc	Edinboro		MBA	87	SUNY-Buf	1978
Hanni, Eila A.	Retir	South Fla		PHD	70	Yale	1970
Hannon, Joan U.	C-Pr	St Marys-Cal		PHD	78	Wisconsin	1987
Hansen, Ann	Prof	Westminst-UT	CHL	PHD	81	Utah	1990
Hansen, Bradley	Asst	Mary Wash	N	PHD	95	Wash U	1995
Hansen, Bruce	Prof	Wisconsin	CE	PHD	89	Yale	1998
Hansen, David	Prof	Linfield		MS		Portland	1969
Hansen, Gary B.	Retir	Utah State	J	PHD	71	Cornell	1967
Hansen, Gary D.	Prof	UCLA		PHD	86	Minnesota	1987
Hansen, Jan M.	Prof	Wis-Eau Clar	J	PHD	74	Missouri	1985
Hansen, Julia L.	Prof	Western Wash	DR	PHD	84	Berkeley	1988
Hansen, Lars Peter	C-Pr	Chicago		PHD	78	Minnesota	1982
Homer J. Livingston Distinguished Service Professor							
Hansen, Niles M.	Prof	Texas	RP	PHD	63	Indiana	1-63
Leroy G. Denmann, Jr. Regents Professor in Economics							
Hansen, Peter	Asst	Brown		PHD	00	Ca-SnDgo	2000
Hansen, W. Lee	Retir	Wisconsin		PHD	58	J Hopkins	1965
Hanson, Gordon H.	Assoc	Michigan	FO	PHD	92	MIT	
Hanson, James S.	Prof	Willamette		PHD	71	Stanford	1976
Hanson, John R. II	Prof	Texas A&M	N	PHD	72	Penn	1974
Hanson, Michael S.	Asst	Wesleyan-CT	E	PHD	99	Michigan	1999
Hanson, Robin	Asst	George Mason		PHD	99	Cal Tech	1999
Hanssen, F. Andrew	Asst	Montana St		PHD	95	Chicago	1995
Hanushek, Eric A.	Prof	Rochester		PHD	68	MIT	1978
Happel, Stephen K.	Prof	Arizona St		PHD	76	Duke	1975
Harbaugh, Richard	Asst	Claremont		PHD	97	Pittsburgh	1999
Harbaugh, William T.	Assoc	Oregon	HQ	PHD	95	Wisconsin	1995
Harberger, Arnold C.	Prof	UCLA		PHD	50	Chicago	
Hardcastle, Rodney	Prof	Pacific Unio		MBA	89	Golden Gt	1989
Harder, K. Peter	Prof	Western Wash	BNP	PHD	68	Nebraska	1970
Hare, Denise	Assoc	Reed	AJOD	PHD	92	Stanford	1992
Harford, Jon D.	C-Ac	Cleveland St	DHKQ	PHD	74	Stanford	1982
Harger, Bruce T.	Prof	Lk Superior	A	PHD	91	Mich St	9-67
Harik, Bassam	Assoc	W Michigan	E	PHD	78	Wayne St	1979
Haririan, Mehdi	Prof	Bloomsburg		PHD	87	New Sch	1982
Harju, Melvin W.	Dean	La St-Shreve		PHD	72	Florida	8-77
Harl, Neil E.	Prof	Iowa State	QK	PHD	65	Iowa St	1964
Harless, David W.	Assoc	Virg Comm		PHD	88	Indiana	8-93

Harman, Peter	Assoc	Rhode Isl Cl		PHD	76	N Carol	
Harmann, Monica	Asst	St Thomas-MN	CKL	PHD	00	Virginia	2000
Harmel, Robert	Assoc	Midwest St	DL	PHD	74	Iowa St	1989
Harmon, Oskar R.	Assoc	Connecticut	H	PHD	80	Rutgers	1982
Haroian, Berch	C-Pr	Wm Patterson		PHD	72	NYU	1978
Harper, Richard K.	Assoc	West Florida	AFM	PHD	89	Duke	1989
Harraf, Abe	Prof	Embry-Riddle		PHD	84	Utah St	
Harrald, Paul D.	Lect	Manches Inst	BCDL	PHD		Simon Fr	1994
Harrington, David E.	Assoc	Kenyon	QRHC	PHD	84	Wisconsin	1986
Himmelright Associate Professor in Economics							
Harrington, Joseph E.	Prof	J Hopkins		PHD	84	Duke	1983
Harris, Donald J.	Retir	Stanford		PHD	66	Berkeley	1972
Harris, James G.	Prof	CS-Dominguez	AEDH	PHD	70	Oregon	1969
Harris, Jeffrey E.	Prof	MIT	I	PHD	75	Penn	1976
Harris, John R.	Prof	Boston Univ	ER	PHD	67	Nrthwstrn	1975
Harris, R. Scott	Assoc	Mont St-Bill		PHD	85	UCLA	1988
Harris, Robert	Prof	Ind-Purdue/I	A	PHD	79	Ohio St	1981
Harris, William	Assoc	Delaware	H	PHD	79	Va Tech	1983
Harris, William G.	Retir	Georgetown		PHD	67	Oregon	
Harrison, Dannie	Dean	Murray State	EPO	PHD	74	S Illinois	1969
Harrison, Glenn W.	Prof	So Carolina		PHD	82	UCLA	
Dewey H. Johnson Professor of Economics							
Harrison, Kenneth	Assoc	R Stockton		PHD	76	SUNY-Alb	1976
Harrison, Paul	Assoc	Brandeis		PHD	94	Duke	1995
Harrison, Sharon	Asst	Barnard	EC	PHD	97	Nrthwstrn	1997
Harrison, William B. III	Retir	Virg Comm		PHD	72	Maryland	1972
Hart, Barbara	C-Pr	Texas-Tyler	CRIJ	PHD		Sam Hous	
Hart, Oliver D'Arcy	C-Pr	Harvard		PHD	74	Princeton	1993
Hart, William R.	Prof	Miami U-Ohio	EA	PHD	76	Wash U	1974
Hart-Landsberg, Martin	Prof	Lewis & Clrk	POFA	PHD	74	Wisconsin	1978
Harter, John F. R.	Asst	E Kentucky		PHD	92	Purdue	1999
Hartigan, James C.	Prof	Oklahoma	FL	PHD	79	Duke	1988
Hartley, James E.	Asst	Mt Holyoke		PHD	94	Ca-Davis	1994
Hartley, Michael J.	Retir	New Orleans		PHD	70	Penn	
Hartley, Peter R.	C-Pr	Rice		PHD	80	Chicago	1986
Hartley, William		SUNY-Empire		PHD			
Hartline, Jessie C.	Assoc	Rutgers-N Br	G	PHD	68	Rutgers	1968
Hartman, Harrison G.	C-Pr	E Stroudsbur	J	PHD	76	NYU	1964
Hartman, Richard C.	Prof	U Washington		PHD	71	Berkeley	1971
Hartmann, G. Bruce	H-Pr	Tenn State		PHD	74	SUNY-Alb	1974
Harun, Syed	VAsst	Tx A&M-Kings		ABD		N Orleans	2000
Harvey, Curtis E.	Retir	Kentucky	P	PHD	63	S Calif	1963
Harvey, John T.	Assoc	Tx Christian		PHD	87	Tennessee	1987
Harwitz, Mitchell	Assoc	SUNY-Buffalo	COTR	PHD	59	MIT	1958
Hasan, Iftekhar	Prof	NJ Inst Tech		PHD	87	Houston	1994
Hashemzadeh, Nozar	C-Pr	Radford	CJG	PHD	74	Va Tech	1983
Hashimoto, Masanori	C-Pr	Ohio State	J	PHD	71	Columbia	1987
Hasker, Kevin	Asst	Rice		PHD	98	Nrthwstrn	7-98
Haslag, Joseph H.	Asst	Missouri	OGE	PHD	87	So Meth	2000
Hassan, Mahboubul	Assoc	New Hamp Col		MAPE	82	Boston U	
Hassan, Seid	Assoc	Murray State	CEFR	PHD	93	Tx A&M	1992
Hassanein, Saad A.	Prof	Marymount		PHD	88	Catholic	1988
Hasse, Charles	Asst	San Fran St		PHD	96	Ca-Davis	1997
Hastings, Justine	Asst	Dartmouth		PHD	01	Berkeley	2001
Hasty, John M. Jr.	Prof	Tenn State		PHD	73	Geo St	
Hattwick, Richard E.	Prof	W Illinois	AM	PHD	65	Vanderbilt	1969
Hau, Jong-Chol	Retir	Millersville		PHD	67	St Louis	1969
Haughton, Jonathan H.	Asst	Suffolk		PHD	83	Harvard	1997
Haulman, Clyde A.	Prof	Wm & Mary		PHD	69	Fla St	1969
Haupert, Michael J.	C-Pr	Wis-La Cross	AEN	PHD	89	Wash U	1989
Haurin, Donald R.	Prof	Ohio State	R	PHD	78	Chicago	1975
Hause, John C.	Prof	SUNY-Stony B		PHD	62	Chicago	1978
Hausman, Jerry A.	Prof	MIT	C	DPHI	73	Oxford	1973
John and Jennie S. MacDonald Professor of Economics							
Hausman, William J.	Prof	Wm & Mary		PHD	76	Illinois	1981
Chancellor Professor							
Haveman, Robert H.	Prof	Wisconsin		PHD	63	Vanderbilt	1970
John Bascom Professor of Economics							
Havens, Rebecca A.	Prof	Pt Loma Naz	CT	PHD	87	Ca-SnDgo	1990
Havrilesky, Thomas	Deces	Duke		PHD	66	Illinois	1969
Hawkins, Charles F.	C-Pr	Lamar	RK	PHD	80	LSU	1966
Regents' Professor of Economics							
Hawkins, Richard R.	Asst	West Florida	ACR	PHD	96	Geo St	1996
Hawley, Clifford B.	Prof	W Virginia	JD	PHD	77	Duke	1978
Haworth, Barry	Asst	Louisville	L	PHD	94	Ca-Davis	1995
Hay, George A.	Prof	Cornell		PHD	69	Nrthwstrn	1979
Edward Cornell Professor Law and Professor of Economics							
Hayashi, Paul M.	Prof	Tx-Arlington	D	PHD	69	So Meth	1965
Hayden, F. Gregory	Prof	Nebraska	HQI	PHD	68	Tx-Austin	1967
Haydon, Randall B.	Prof	Wichita St		PHD	62	Illinois	1970

Hayes, Kathy J.	Prof	So Methodist	HIL	PHD	80	Syracuse	1989
Hayes, Sue E.	Prof	Sonoma State	Q	PHD	75	Berkeley	1974
Hayford, Marc D.	Assoc	Loyola-Chicg	AE	PHD	87	Brown	1986
Haynes, C. Beth	Prof	Brighm Yg-Hl	DAO	PHD	81	Purdue	1994
Haynes, Curtis Jr.	Asst	Skidmore		PHD	93	Mass	2001
Haynes, Michael C.	Retir	So Oregon St	ADK	MS	64	Brighm Yg	1964
Haynes, Stephen E.	Prof	Oregon	FE	PHD	76	Ca-SnBarb	1978
Hays, Patrick A.	Assoc	W Carolina	G	PHD	77	N Carol	1985
Hays, Sally	Asst	CS-Fresno	QLC	PHD	99	Oregon	2000
Haywood, Dale M.	Prof	Northwood		PHD	80	North Tx	
Hayworth, Steve	Assoc	E Michigan		PHD	87	MIT	1977
Hazilla, Michael	Assoc	American U		PHD	78	SUNY-Bin	1988
Hazlett, Denise J.	C-Ac	Whitman	EG	PHD	92	Minnesota	1992
He, Susan	Asst	Wash State		PHD	00	Wash St	
Head, Tom	C-Pr	George Fox		MA	80	Berkeley	
Headen, Alvin E.	Assoc	N Carol St	IJD	PHD	81	MIT	1986
Heahigh, David J.	Assoc	King's Col		PHD	79	Geotown	9-90
Heal, Geoffrey M.	Prof	Columbia		PHD	68	Cambridge	1983
Paul Garett Professor of Public Policy and Business Responsibility							
Heath, Julia A.	C-Pr	Memphis	JI	PHD	86	S Carol	1986
Heath, W. Cary	Assoc	La-Lafayette		PHD	82	LSU	
Heavey, Jerome F.	C-Pr	Lafayette	DHP	PHD	76	Penn St	1973
Heberling, Gregory Dean	Assoc	Anderson U		MBA		Ball St	1978
Hebert, Robert F.	Retir	Auburn		PHD	70	LSU	1974
Heckelman, Jac C.	Asst	Wake Forest		PHD	94	Maryland	1996
Heckerman, Donald G.	Assoc	Arizona		PHD	67	MIT	1971
Heckman, James J.	Prof	Chicago		PHD	71	Princeton	1973
Henry Schultz Professor of Economics & Soc Sciences; 2000 Nobel Prize							
Hecox, Walter E.	Prof	Colorado Col		PHD	69	Syracuse	1970
Hedrick, David W.	Assoc	Central Wash	AIO	PHD	84	Oregon	1987
Heffley, Dennis R.	Prof	Connecticut	RI	PHD	75	Ca-SnBarb	193
Hefner, Dennis L.	Prof	SUNY-Fredoni	IL	PHD	71	Wash St	1996
Hefner, Frank L.	Assoc	Charleston		PHD	88	Kansas	1995
Hegji, Charles E.	Prof	Auburn-Montg	DFMJ	PHD	80	Wash U	1985
Heilbrun, James	Retir	Fordham		PHD	64	Columbia	1970
Heim, Carol E.	Assoc	Massachusett	NRE	PHD	82	Yale	1-81
Heim, John	Asst	Rensselaer		PHD	72	SUNY-Alb	1997
Heineke, John M.	Prof	Santa Clara		PHD	68	Iowa	1968
Heiner, Ronald A.	Prof	George Mason		PHD	75	UCLA	1989
Heiney, Joseph N.	D-Pr	Elmhurst		PHD	83	Chicago	1977
Coleman Foundation Distinguished Chair in Business							
Heinicke, Craig W.	Assoc	Baldwin-Wal	NOE	PHD	91	Toronto	1991
Heinrich, Jeffery	Asst	Wis-Whitewat					
Heins, A. James	Retir	Illinois		PHD	61	Wisconsin	1960
Heise, Paul A.	Assoc	Lebanon Val		PHD	91	New Sch	1991
Heisler, James B.	C-Pr	Hope	PD	PHD	75	Nebraska	1981
Heitmann, George	C-Pr	Muhlenberg		PHD	63	Princeton	1-94
Hekmat, Ali	C-Pr	Estrn Utah	E	PHD	93	Wi-Milwa	1994
Helburn, Suzanne W.	Emer	Colo-Denver	BI	PHD	61	Indiana	1970
Helfand, Steven	Asst	Cal-Riversid	AOQ	PHD	94	Berkeley	1995
Helland, Eric	Assoc	Claremont		PHD	95	U Wash	1998
Heller, Dana	Asst	Chicago		PHD	98	Stanford	1998
Hellerstein, Judith	Asst	Maryland		PHD	94	Harvard	1996
Hellman, Daryl A.	Prof	Northeastern		PHD	70	Rutgers	1972
Helms, L. Jay	Assoc	Cal-Davis	DHI	PHD	79	MIT	1985
Helper, Susan	Assoc	Case Western	ONM	PHD	87	Harvard	1990
Helpman, Elhanen	Prof	Harvard		PHD		Harvard	1974
Hemesath, Michael	C-Ac	Carleton	AFP	PHD	88	Harvard	1989
Hendel, Igal	Assoc	Wisconsin		PHD	94	Harvard	2000
Henderson, David R.	Assoc	Naval Postgr	D	PHD	76	UCLA	1984
Henderson, J. Vernon	Prof	Brown		PHD	72	Chicago	1974
Eastman Professor of Political Economy							
Henderson, James M.	Deces	Duke		PHD	55	Harvard	1986
Henderson, James P.	Prof	Valparaiso	NBA	PHD	77	N Illinois	1975
Henderson, James W.	Prof	Baylor	IJ	PHD	81	So Meth	1981
Ben H. Williams Professor of Economics							
Henderson, Sandra R.	Retir	W Virg St	AFR	MA	60	Pittsburgh	1968
Henderson, Upton B.	Retir	Central Okla		PHD	65	Missouri	1971
Hendon, Fred N.	Prof	Samford	FN	PHD	68	Alabama	1968
Hendricks, Lutz	Asst	Arizona St		PHD	96	Penn	1996
Hendrickson, Jill K.	Asst	Univ South	EGC	PHD		Notre Dm	1995
Hendryson, Mary Ann	Lect	Western Wash	DOF	ABD		Wash St	1989
Henowitz, Harvey	Asst	Adelphi		MBA		Adelphia	
Henry, John F.	Prof	CS-Sacrament		PHD	74	McGill	1970
Henry, Marc	Asst	Columbia	CIG	PHD	98	LondonEc	1998
Henson, Steven E.	Assoc	Western Wash	QD	PHD	82	Oregon	1985
Hentzel, David	Prof	Mo-Rolla		PHD	67	S Illinois	1969
Heong, Hyeok	Asst	So Calif		PHD	00	Chicago	2000
Hepner, Mickey A.	Asst	Central Okla	HDJI				
Herander, Mark G.	Prof	South Fla	F	PHD	80	N Carol	1979

Herbener, Jeffrey M.	Prof	Grove City		PHD	82	Okla St	1997
Herber, Bernard P.	Retir	Arizona		PHD	69	U Wash	1957
Herbst, Lawrence A.	Assoc	Vassar	N	PHD	74	Penn	1970
Herdendorf, Phyllis		SUNY-Empire	F	PHD	81	SUNY	1987
Herendeen, James B.	Prof	Txs-El Paso	AQ	PHD	63	Penn St	1992
Hermalin, Benjamin E.	Assoc	Cal-Berkeley		PHD	88	MIT	1988
Herman, E. Edward	H-Pr$	Cincinnati	J	PHD	65	McGill	1966
Herman, Walter J.	Retir	South Fla	E	PHD	65	Florida	1980
Hermann, Mark	Assoc	Alaska-Fairb		PHD	90	Wash St	1990
Herold, Marc W.	Assoc	New Hampshir	O	PHD	77	Berkeley	1975
Herr, Andy	Assoc	St Vincent	HEQ	PHD	96	Indiana	1991
Herrear, Ana Marie		Michigan St					
Herreiner, Dorothea K.	Asst	Bowdoin	L	PHD	00	Florence	2001
Herrick, Bruce H.	Emer	Wash & Lee	OP	PHD	64	MIT	1980
John F. Hendon Professor of Economics, Emeritus							
Herrin, William E.	C-Ac	Pacific	RC	PHD	85	SUNY-Bin	1985
Herrnstadt, Irwin L.	Retir	Northeastern		PHD	64	MIT	1960
Hersch, Philip L.	Prof	Wichita St		PHD	82	Ohio St	1983
Herschede, Alfred J.	Prof	Ind-So Bend	ADP	PHD	76	Illinois	1976
Hersh-Cochran, Mona S.	Prof	Txs Woman's		PHD	66	So Meth	
Conaro Professor of Business and Economics							
Hervitz, Hugo M.	Prof	Barry		PHD	83	Indiana	1982
Herzog, Henry W. Jr.	Prof	Tennessee		PHD	74	Maryland	1974
Hess, Alan C.	Prof	U Washington		PHD	69	Car Mellon	1967
Hess, Arleigh P. Jr.	Emer	Pennsylvania		PHD	49	Penn	1949
Associate Undergraduate Chair for Advising							
Hess, Gregory	Prof	Oberlin	E	PHD	89	J Hopkins	1993
Hess, Peter N.	Prof	Davidson	OT	PHD	82	N Carol	1980
Gail M. and Ernst G. Doe Professor of Economics							
Hester, Donald D.	Retir	Wisconsin		PHD	61	Yale	1968
Heston, Alan W.	Prof	Pennsylvania		PHD	62	Yale	
Hetherington, Bruce W.	C-Pr	Ogelthorpe	NE	PHD	82	Va Tech	1980
Hettich, Walter	Prof	CS-Fullerton	H	PHD	67	Yale	1983
Hettler, Paul	Asst	Duquesne		PHD	98	Pittsburgh	1999
Heung, C. James	Asst	Alabama		PHD	97	Wisconsin	1997
Hewett, Roger S.	Assoc	Drake		PHD	84	Illinois	1981
Hewins, Dana C.	C-Ac	Regis-MA		PHD	75	Illinois	
Heyne, Paul T.	Deces	U Washington		PHD	63	Chicago	1976
Heywood, John S.	Prof	Wis-Milwauke		PHD	86	Michigan	1986
Hibbard, Thomas H.	Prof	Willamette		PHD	67	Claremont	1973
Hickerson, Steven	Prof	Mankato St	ABK	PHD	80	Nebraska	1980
Hickey, Kevin L.	Assoc	Assumption		MLA	76	Harvard	1972
Hickman, Bert G.	Retir	Stanford		PHD	51	Berkeley	1966
Hicks, Donald A.	Prof	Texas-Dallas		PHD	76	N Carol	
Hicks, Michael	Asst	Marshall		PHD	97	Tennessee	2000
Hicks, W. Whitney	Retir	Missouri	O	PHD	65	Stanford	1965
Hiebert, L. Dean	Prof	Illinois St	ADE	PHD	72	Wisconsin	1973
Hiedemann, Bridget G.	Asst	Seattle	DJT	PHD	92	Duke	1994
Hiestand, Thomas W.	Assoc	Concordia C	CD	PHD	74	Kansas St	1972
Higgins, Matthew L.	Assoc	W Michigan	C	PHD	89	Illinois	1995
Higgins, Neal O.	Retir	Portland	RH	PHD	74	Nebraska	1976
Higgins, Robert C.	Prof	U Washington		PHD	69	Stanford	1967
Highfill, Jannett K.	Prof	Bradley		PHD	85	Kansas	1985
Hildebrandt, Gregory G.	Assoc	Naval Postgr	D	PHD	76	Princeton	1992
Hildred, William M.	Retir	No Arizona	HA	PHD	64	Colo St	1988
Hileman, A. Eugene	C-Pr	NE St-Okla	AGM	PHD	71	Tennessee	1988
Hill, Catharine Bond	C-Ac	Williams		PHD	85	Yale	1985
Hill, Cynthia D.	Asst	Idaho State	AIJQ	PHD	97	Wash St	1998
Hill, James Richard	Assoc	Cen Michigan		PHD	80	Kentucky	1981
Hill, John A.	Asst	Hardin-Simm		PHD	95	Tennessee	1998
Hill, Lewis E.	Retir	Texas Tech		PHD	57	Tx-Austin	1967
Hill, M. Anne	C-Pr	CUNY-Queens	JC	PHD	80	Duke	1989
Hill, Pershing J.	Assoc	Alaska-Ancho	EFH	PHD	76	Wash St	1975
Hill, Peter J.	Prof	Wheaton-IL	ANPQ	PHD	70	Chicago	1986
George F. Bennett Professor of Economics							
Hill, R. Carter	C-Pr	Louisiana St	C	PHD	75	Missouri	
Marjory B. Ourso Excellence in Teaching Professor							
Hill, Roger Post	Prof	N Car-Wilmin	G	PHD	68	Mich St	
Hillard, Michael	Assoc	So Maine	EJ	PHD	88	Mass	1987
Hilton S.J., F. G.	Asst	Loyola-Maryl	QF	PHD	96	Wisconsin	1996
Himarios, Daniel	Dean	Tx-Arlington	FE	PHD	84	Va Tech	1983
Himarios, Jane	SLect	Tx-Arlington	J	PHD	87	Va Tech	1986
Himmelberg, Charles P.	Assoc	Columbia	DEL	PHD	90	Nrthwstrn	1995
Hinderliter, Roger H.	Assoc	Ithaca	BE	PHD	70	Wash U	1986
Hinshaw, C. Elton	Retir	Vanderbilt	N	PHD	66	Vanderbilt	1966
Hinson, Steven Y.	C-Ac	Webster	AFDH	PHD	93	Kentucky	1993
Hippie, F. Steb	Prof	East Tenn St		PHD	72	So Meth	1982
Hirano, Keisuke	Assoc	U Miami	CD	PHD		Harvard	1998
Hirsch, Barry T.	Prof	Trinity	J	PHD	77	Virginia	2000
E.M. Stevens Distinguished Professor of Economics							

Hirschfeld, Mary L.	Assoc	Occidental	N	PHD	89	Harvard	1988
Hitchner, Benjamin	Retir	Rowan Col-NJ		MS		Penn	1964
Hjummels, David	Asst	Purdue		PHD	95	Michigan	2000
Ho, Franklin Y. H.	Prof	CS-Pomona		PHD	57	S Calif	1961
Ho, Peter S.	C-Ac	Denver	FO	PHD	89	Stanford	1987
Ho, Yhi-Min	Dean	St Thomas-TX	OQ	PHD	65	Vanderbilt	8-70
Hugh Roy and Lillie Cullen Professor of Economics							
Hoag, John H.	C-Pr	Bowling Gr		PHD	72	Kansas	1972
Hoch, Irving J.	Prof	Texas-Dallas		PHD	57	Chicago	1985
Hochman, Harold M.	Prof	Lafayette	HIK	PHD	65	Yale	1992
Wm. E. Simon Professor of Political Economics							
Hodges, L. Hart	Lect	Western Wash	OQR	PHD	94	U Wash	2000
Hodges, Paul E.	Prof	Txs-Perm Bas	CHRT	PHD	74	Stanford	
Hodgin, Gary L.	Assoc	Belmont		PHD	85	Tennessee	1983
Hodgin, Robert F.	Assoc	Houston-Cl L		DA	80	Illin St	9-81
Hodrick, Robert	Prof	Columbia		PHD	96	Chicago	1996
Nomure Professor of International Finance							
Hofer, Tracy	Asst	Wis-Stev Pt		PHD	97	Texas	1999
Hoffer, George E.	Prof	Virg Comm		PHD	72	Virginia	1970
Hoffman, Dennis L.	Prof	Arizona St		PHD	78	Mich St	1979
Hoffman, Emily P.	Prof	W Michigan	J	PHD	75	Mass	1981
Hoffman, Naphtali	C-Ac	Elmira		PHD	80	Case Wes	1976
Hoffman, Robert	Asst	St Scholasti	E	PHD	92	Boston C	
Hoffman, Saul D.	C-Pr	Delaware	TJ	PHD	77	Michigan	1977
Hofler, Martha	Inst	Old Dominion	F	MA		Old Dom	
Hofler, Richard A.	Prof	Cen Florida	CIJ	PHD	82	N Carol	1989
Hofman, Cornelius A.	Retir	Idaho State	5-97	PHD	64	Utah	1960
Hofrenning, Stella	Asst	Augsburg	I	PHD	92	Il-Chicago	2001
Hoftyzer, John	Prof	SW Missouri		PHD	74	Indiana	1987
Hogan, Timothy D.	Prof	Arizona St		PHD	71	Va Tech	1970
Hogan, William V.	C-Pr	Mass-Dartmou		PHD	76	Cornell	1976
Hogendorn, Christiaan P.	Asst	Wesleyan-CT	L	PHD	00	Penn	2001
Hogendorn, Jan S.	Prof	Colby	FOA	PHD	66	London	1966
Grossman Professor of Economics							
Hohenberg, Paul M.	Retir	Rensselaer		PHD	63	MIT	1977
Hoke, Leon R. Jr.	Prof	Tampa	ADJ	PHD	79	Pittsburgh	1981
Hoksbergen, Roland G.	C-Pr	Calvin		PHD	86	Notre Dm	1983
Holahan, William L.	C-Pr	Wis-Milwauke		PHD	74	Brown	1972
Holbrook, Robert S.	Prof	Michigan		PHD	65	Berkeley	1965
Holcomb, James H. Jr.	Assoc	Txs-El Paso	CDL	PHD	85	Tx A&M	1985
Holcombe, Randall G.	Prof	Florida St	H	PHD	76	Va Tech	1988
DeVoe Moore Professor							
Holland, A. Steven	C-Pr	SW Texas St	E	PHD	83	Mich St	1998
Holland, John J. Jr.	Retir	Monmouth	EN	PHD	72	NYU	9-97
Holland, Larry C.	Assoc	Ark-Ltl Rock		PHD	96	Okla St	1995
Holland, Thomas E.	Retir	Tx-Arlington	D	PHD	63	Duke	1970
Hollas, Daniel R.	Prof	Tx-S Antonio		PHD	77	Illinois	1988
Holley, Don	C-Vis	Boise State	DMR	PHD	71	Ca-Rivers	1999
Hollifield, Burton	Assoc	Carnegie Mel		PHD	92	Car Mellon	
Hollister, Robinson G. Jr.	Prof	Swarthmore	IJ	PHD	65	Stanford	1971
Joseph Wharton Professor of Economics							
Holman, Jill Ann	Asst	Wis-Milwauke	EF	PHD	97	Colorado	2001
Holman, Mary A.	Retir	George Wash	L	PHD	63	Geo Wash	1963
Holmes, Alexander B.	Prof	Oklahoma	RD	PHD	74	SUNY-Bin	
Holmes, George M.	Asst	East Carol	CIJ	PHD	99	N Carol	1999
Holmes, James M.	Prof	SUNY-Buffalo	EF	PHD	67	Chicago	1967
Holmes, Jessica	Asst	Middlebury	DHI	PHD	98	Yale	2001
Holmes, Thomas J.	Assoc	Minnesota		PHD	85	Nrthwstrn	1995
Holmes, William L.	Assoc	Temple	CD	PHD	66	Illinois	1966
Holmstrom, Bengt	Prof	MIT	L	PHD	78	Stanford	1995
Paul A. Samuelson Professor of Economics							
Holmstrom, Thomas K.	Retir	No Michigan	AEF	PHD	73	Okla St	1966
Holstein, Adora	Assoc	Robt Morris		PHD	87	Penn St	
Holt, Charles A.	Prof	Virginia	CDL	PHD	77	Car Mellon	1983
Merrill Bankard Professor of Economics							
Holt, Charles F.	Assoc	San Diego		PHD	70	Purdue	1973
Holt, Harry G.	Retir	Indiana U-PA	IP	MS	61	Bucknell	1968
Holt, Kenneth	Assoc	Union-TN		ABD		Memphis	1987
Holt, Richard P. F.	Assoc	So Oregon St	ABDM	PHD	87	Utah	1996
Holthausen, Duncan M. Jr.	Prof	N Carol St	DC	PHD	76	Nrthwstrn	1974
Holtmann, Alphonse G.	Prof	U Miami	DI	PHD	63	Wash U	1981
Holtz-Eakin, Douglas	Prof	Syracuse	H	PHD	85	Princeton	1990
Holzman, Franklyn Dunn	Retir	Tufts		PHD	52	Harvard	1961
Homer, John S.	Prof	Olivet		PHD	91	Hawaii	1979
Honeycutt, Theresa	Assoc	Shenandoah		PHD	89	N Car St	1997
Hong, Youngmaio	Prof	Cornell		PHD	93	Ca-SnDgo	7-93
Honig, Marjorie	C-Pr	CUNY-Hunter		PHD	71	Columbia	
Honig, Susan	Asst	CUNY-Lehman		MS		Pace	
Honkalehto, Oswald	Retir	Colgate	C	PHD	69	MIT	1962
Honore, Bo Erno		Princeton		PHD	87	Chicago	

Hood, Frank	Prof	Miss College		PHD	72	Miss	1972
Hooks, Donald L.	Assoc	Alabama		PHD	71	Tx A&M	1971
Hooks, Jon A.	Prof	Albion	G	PHD	89	Mich St	1989
Hooks, Linda M.	Assoc	Wash & Lee	E	PHD	91	UCLA	1993
Hool, Bryce	Prof	SUNY-Stony B		PHD	74	Berkeley	1979
Hoover, Gary A.	Asst	Alabama		PHD	98	Wash U	1998
Hoover, Kevin D.	C-Pr	Cal-Davis	BE	DPHI	85	Oxford	1985
Hope, Barney F.	Retir	CS-Chico	RFO	PHD	79	Ca-Rivers	1977
Hopenhayn, Hugo	Prof	Rochester		PHD	89	Minnesota	1994
Hopkins, Barbara	Assoc	Wright State	FOP	PHD	92	Maryland	1995
Hoppe, Hans Hermann	Prof	Nev-L Vegas	B	PHD		Goethe	1986
Hoppes, Robert B.	Prof	SW Missouri		PHD	75	Nebraska	1980
Hoppie, Maurice R.	Assoc	Elizabethtwn		PHD	85	Tennessee	1980
Hordon, Harris	C-Pr	NewJerseyCty	AG	PHD	68	NYU	
Horiba, Yutaka	Prof	Tulane		PHD	69	Purdue	1971
Horn, Bobbie L.	Assoc	Tulsa		PHD	86	Iowa St	
Horn, Robert N.	Prof	Jms Madison	JD	PHD	78	NewHamp	1978
Horner, James	Prof	Cameron		PHD	85	Tx-Dallas	1976
Horney, Mary Jean	Prof	Furman		PHD	77	Duke	1979
Frederick W. Symmes Professor of Economics							
Hornsten, James	Asst	Bowdoin	L	ABD		Nrthwstrn	1999
Horowitz, Andrew W.	Assoc	Arkansas	OFD	PHD	89	Wisconsin	1998
Horowitz, Ann R.	Retir	Florida		PHD	66	Indiana	1972
Horowitz, Avery M.	Assoc	Yeshiva		PHD	84	CUNY	1986
Horowitz, Joel	Prof	Northwestern		PHD	67	Cornell	2001
Horowitz, John B.	Assoc	Ball State	HJ	PHD	88	Tx A&M	1989
Horowtiz, Joel	Retir	Iowa		PHD	67	Cornell	1982
Horrace, William	Asst	Arizona		PHD	96	Mich St	1996
Hortascu, Ali	Asst	Chicago		PHD	01	Maryland	2001
Horton, Joseph J.	C-Pr	Cen Arkansas		PHD	68	So Meth	7-96
Horvath, Janos	Retir	Butler	FE	PHD	67	Columbia	
Horwich, George	Prof	Purdue		PHD	54	Chicago	1956
Horwitz, Sigmund	Prof	Txs Southern		PHD		Houston	
Horwitz, Steven G.	Assoc	St Lawrence	EPB	PHD	90	GeoMason	1989
Hoselitz, Bert F.	Retir	Chicago		JD	36	Vienna	1945
Hosni, Djehane	C-Ac	Cen Florida	O	PHD	78	Arkansas	1978
Hosseini, Hamid S.	Prof	King's Col	BEFO	PHD	77	Oregon	9-86
John S. Davis Distinguished Service Professor							
Hosseinzadeh, Esmail	Prof	Drake		PHD	87	New Sch	1988
Hotchkiss, Julie L.	Assoc	Georgia St	CJ	PHD	89	Cornell	1989
Hotelling, Harold	Assoc	Lawrence Tec	KL	PHD	82	Duke	9-89
Hou, Chi-Ming	Deces	Colgate	1994	PHD	54	Columbia	1956
Hou, Jack W.	Prof	CS-Long Bch		PHD	89	Yale	1989
Houser, Daniel	Asst	Arizona		PHD	97	Minnesota	1997
Houser, Scott	Assoc	CS-Fresno	HRI	PHD	96	Wisconsin	1996
Houston, A. Craig	Retir	Dickinson Cl		PHD	62	Penn St	1956
Houston, Robert G.	Asst	E Kentucky		ABD	99	Kentucky	1998
Houthakker, Hendrick S.	Retir	Harvard		ECD	49	Amsterdm	
Henry Lee Professor of Economics							
Hovey, Craig	VInst	St John Fshr	M	PHD		Union In	1998
Howard, Bruce	C-Pr	Wheaton-IL	ABM	PHD	89	N Illinois	1980
Howard, James E.	Assoc	S F Austin	AC	PHD	77	Georgia	1976
Howe, Charles W.	Prof	Colorado		PHD	59	Stanford	1970
Howe, Edward T.	Prof	Siena		PHD	73	SUNY-Alb	
Howell, Kristen K.	Assoc	N Car-Wilmin	F	PHD	89	Kentucky	
Howitt, Peter	Prof	Brown	E	PHD	73	Nrthwstrn	2000
Howrey, E. Philip	Prof	Michigan	CE	PHD	64	N Carol	9-73
Howsen, Roy M.	Assoc	W Kentucky	D	PHD	80	Arkansas	1981
Hoxby, Caroline Minter	Assoc	Harvard	JH	PHD	94	MIT	7-94
Hoynes, Hilary	Assoc	Cal-Davis	D	PHD	92	Stanford	
Hoyt, Gail Mitchell	Assoc	Kentucky	A	PHD	92	Kentucky	1994
Hoyt, William H.	Prof	Kentucky	RHG	PHD	86	Wisconsin	1986
Gatton Professor							
Hsia, Ke Ting	Retir	CS-L Angeles		PHD	66	Wisconsin	1963
Hsiao, Cheng	Prof	So Calif		PHD	72	Stanford	1985
Hsiao, Frank S. T.	Prof	Colorado		PHD	67	Rochester	1975
Hsiao, James C.	Retir	So Conn St		PHD		Conn	
Hsiao, Mei-chu W.	Prof	Colo-Denver	OC	PHD	67	Rochester	1981
Hsiao, Yu-Mong	Prof	Campbell		PHD	85	N Car St	1984
Hsieh, Chengho	Assoc	La St-Shreve		PHD		LSU	1989
Hsieh, Edward W.	C-Pr	CS-L Angeles		PHD	88	Houston	1989
Hsing, Yu	H-Pr	SE Louisiana	EJOR	PHD	83	Tennessee	1987
Hsu, Robert C.	Prof	Clark		PHD	70	Berkeley	1971
Hsu, Yu-Chu	Retir	So Conn St	HO	PHD	65	Cornell	
Hu, Luojia	Asst	Northwestern		PHD	97	Princeton	2000
Hu, Sheng C.	Retir	Purdue		PHD	70	Rochester	1968
Hu, Wei-Yin	Asst	UCLA		PHD	94	Stanford	
Huang, Cliff J.	Retir	Vanderbilt	C	PHD	68	N Carol	1969
Huang, Ju-Chin	Assoc	New Hampshir	CQ	PHD	94	N Car St	1998
Huang, Kevin	Asst	Utah State	EFG	PHD	98	Minnesota	1998

Huang, Lien-fu	Retir	Howard	I	PHD	71	Rochester	
Huang, Wei-Chiao	Prof	W Michigan	J	PHD	84	Ca-SnBarb	1985
Hubbard, R. Glenn	Prof	Columbia	HEG	PHD	83	Harvard	1988
Russell L. Carson Professor of Finance and Economics							
Hubbard, Thomas	Asst	UCLA		PHD	96	Stanford	
Hubbell, L. Kenneth	Emer	Mo-Kansas Ct	GHM	PHD	70	Nebraska	1968
Huckins, Larry E.	Asst	CUNY-Baruch		PHD	83	Chicago	1980
Huddle, Donald L.	Retir	Rice		PHD	64	Vanderbilt	1964
Huddleston, Kenneth M.	Asst	Georgia SW		MBA		Geo St	
Hueckel, Glenn R.	Assoc	Purdue		PHD	72	Wisconsin	1972
Huenneke, Steve	Assoc	Minot State	AR	PHD	92	Kansas St	1991
Huetter, David A.	Retir	Oklahoma	L	PHD	72	Case Wes	1974
Huffman, Gregory W.	Prof	Vanderbilt	EG	PHD	83	Minnesota	2001
Huffman, Wallace E.	Prof	Iowa State	J	PHD	72	Chicago	1974
Huggett, Mark	Asst	Georgetown	O	PHD	91	Minnesota	1999
Hughes, Greg	Prof	Rensselaer		PHD	72	Princeton	1997
Hughes, James W.	C-As	Bates	J	PHD	87	Michigan	1982
Hughes, Johnathan R. T.	Deces	Northwestern		PHIL		Oxford	
Hughes, Joseph P.	Assoc	Rutgers-N Br	D	PHD	74	N Carol	1975
Hughes, Patricia A. Nold	Assoc	St Cloud St		PHD	91	Ca-SnBarb	1988
Hughes, Woodrow W. Jr.	C-As	Converse		PHD	89	S Carol	1986
Hull, Brooks B.	Prof	Mich-Dearbor	LQ	PHD	82	U Wash	1981
Hull, Everson W.	Asst	Howard		PHD	77	Howard	
Hultberg, Patrik	Asst	Wyoming		PHD	98	Rice	1998
Hulten, Charles R.	Prof	Maryland		PHD	73	Berkeley	1985
Hultman, Charles W.	Retir	Kentucky	F	PHD	60	Iowa	1969
Humphreys, Brad	Inst	MD-Baltim Co		MA	91	J Hopkins	
Humphries, John	Retir	Rochest Tech		PHD	67	Syracuse	1962
Hung, Chao-shun	Prof	Fla Atlantic	D	PHD	82	Tx A&M	1982
Hung, Gregory	Prof	Howard	O	PHD	65	Virginia	
Hunger, David	Asst	Ogelthorpe	LDC	PHD	98	Oregon	1993
Hunnicutt, Lynn	Asst	Utah State	DLM	PHD	97	Tx-Austin	1998
Hunsaker, Julie	Asst	Wayne State	L	PHD	93	Purdue	1993
Hunt, Alan		SUNY-Empire					
Hunt, E. K.	C-Pr	Utah		PHD	68	Utah	1978
Hunt, Gary	Prof	Maine	AR	PHD	84	Colorado	1993
Hunt, Jennifer A.	Assoc	Yale	J	PHD	92	Harvard	1992
Hunt, Joseph W.	Retir	Shippensburg		PHD	66	Indiana	1980
Hunte, C. Kenrick	Asst	Howard	OF	PHD		Ohio St	
Hunter, Thomas Kenneth	Retir	S F Austin		PHD	68	Tennessee	1968
Hurd, John II	Prof	Norwich		PHD	69	Penn	1978
Hurd, Michael	Retir	SUNY-Stony B		PHD	71	Berkeley	1978
Hurley, John F.	C-Ac	Jackson St		PHD	71	Illinois	1972
Hurwicz, Leo	Prof	Minnesota		LLM	38	Warsaw	1951
Husbands, Kaye G.	Assoc	Williams		PHD	90	Harvard	
Husby, Ralph D.	Retir	Illinois	EJ	PHD	69	Cornell	1967
Huskey, Lee	Prof	Alaska-Ancho	AJR	PHD	77	Wash U	1977
Hussain, Riaz	Assoc	Scranton		PHD	90	Lehigh	1967
Hussain, Syed Bashir	Assoc	Wis-Oshkosh	F	PHD	83	Ca-Rivers	1982
Hussen, Ahmed M.	Prof	Kalamazoo	DQ	PHD	78	Oregon St	1985
Husted, Steven L.	Prof	Pittsburgh	F	PHD	80	Mich St	1980
Husted, Thomas A.	Assoc	American U		PHD	86	N Carol	1986
Huston, John H.	Prof	Trinity	D	PHD	83	Wisconsin	1983
Hutcheson, Aaron A.	Retir	Austin Peay	AQ	PHD	68	Clemson	1967
Hutchinson, E. Bruce	Prof	Tenn-Chattan	DFLR	PHD	79	Virginia	1982
Hutchinson, Gladstone	Assoc	Lafayette	AO	PHD	90	Clark	1992
Hutchinson, William K.	Retir	Miami U-Ohio	EF	PHD	75	Iowa	1972
Hutchison, Michael M.	C-Pr	Ca-Santa Crz	EFG	PHD	83	Oregon	1985
Huth, William L.	Prof	West Florida	AMG	PHD	80	Arkansas	1989
Huttman, John P.	Retir	San Fran St		PHD	69	London	1970
Hutton, Patricia A.	Prof	Canisius	EC	PHD	80	Wisconsin	1981
Hvidding, James M.	C-Pr	Kutztown	EB	PHD	76	Maryland	1986
Hwang, Hae-Shin	Prof	Texas A&M	C	PHD	76	Minnesota	1977
Hwang, Ming-jeng	Prof	W Virginia	DRC	PHD	73	Tx A&M	1974
Hyclak, Thomas J.	C-Pr	Lehigh	JR	PHD	76	Notre Dm	1979
Hyle, Matthew R.	Prof	Winona State		PHD	85	Maryland	1988
Hyman, David Neil	Prof	N Carol St	HA	PHD	69	Princeton	1969
Hymans, Saul H.	Prof	Michigan		PHD	64	Berkeley	1964
Hyslop, Dean	Asst	UCLA		PHD	95	Princeton	
Iannaccone, Laurence R.	Prof	Santa Clara		PHD	84	Chicago	1982
Ibister, John W.	Prof	Ca-Santa Crz	O	PHD	69	Princeton	1968
Ichiishi, Tatsuro	Prof	Ohio State	C	PHD	74	Berkeley	1987
Ickes, Barry W.	Assoc	Penn State	P	PHD	84	Berkeley	1983
Idson, Todd	Assoc	Columbia	CJ	PHD	86	Columbia	1990
Ierulli, Kathryn	Asst	Ill-Chicago	D	PHD	94	Chicago	1993
Ifediora, John O.	C-Ac	Wis-Plattev		PHD	88	Il-Chicago	1988
Ignatin, George	Assoc	Alabama-Birm	AJK	PHD	69	Tx-Austin	1969
Ihlanfeldt, Keith R.	Prof	Florida St	HR	PHD	78	Wash U	2000
DeVoe Moore Eminent Scholar Chair							
Ikeda, Sanford	Assoc	SUNY-Purchas		PHD	88	NYU	1990

Ikpoh, Andrew	Assoc	Seton Hall		PHD	88	Columbia	
Ilacqua, Joseph A.	Prof	Bryant	AJ	EDD	93	Boston U	1968
Im, Eric I.	Prof	Hawaii-Hilo		PHD	82	Hi-Manoa	
Im, Kyung So	Asst	Wichita St		PHD	95	Mich St	1998
Imrohoroglu, Ayse	Prof	So Calif		PHD	88	Minnesota	1989
Imrohoroglu, Selo	Prof	So Calif		PHD	88	Minnesota	1989
Inaba, Frederick S.	Assoc	Wash State		PHD	74	Berkeley	1977
Ingene, Chuck	Prof	Mississippi		PHD	75	Brown	2001
Ingham, Hilary C.	SLect	U Lancaster	JCD	PHD		Glasgow	
Ingles, Jerry Lee	Prof	Univ South	BL	PHD	75	Cornell	
Ingram, James C.	Emer	No Carolina		PHD	52	Cornell	1952
Ingram, Marlynne B. F.	Assoc	Iowa		PHD	86	Iowa	1988
Inman, Robert R.	Prof	Pennsylvania		PHD	72	Harvard	
Innes, Jon T.	Prof	Lehigh	EB	PHD	67	Oregon	1987
Intriligator, Michael D.	Emer	UCLA		PHD	63	MIT	1972
Ioannatos, Petros	Asst	Kettering		PHD	89	Wayne St	
Ioannides, Yannis M.	Prof	Tufts	O	PHD	74	Stanford	1995
Neubauer Chair Holder							
Ireland, Peter N.	C-Ac	Boston Coll	E	PHD	91	Chicago	1998
Ireland, Thomas R.	Prof	Mo-St Louis		PHD	68	Virginia	1972
Irons, John S.	Asst	Amherst	AEH	PHD	99	MIT	1999
Irvine, F. Owen	Assoc	Michigan St		PHD	76	MIT	1982
Irwin, Douglas A.	Prof	Dartmouth		PHD	88	Columbia	1997
Irwin, James R.	Asst	Cen Michigan		PHD	86	Rochester	1989
Isaac, Alan G.	Assoc	American U		PHD	86	Ca-Davis	1987
Isaac, R. Mark	Prof	Florida St		PHD	81	Cal Tech	2001
Quinn Eminent Scholar Chair							
Isaacs, Patricia	Assoc	Berea		DBA	94	Kentucky	1989
Isakson, Hans R.	Prof	No Iowa		PHD	78	Wisconsin	1990
Isbell, Steven	Assoc	Tenn Tech	EJ	PHD	85	Miss	1985
Isely, Paul N.	Asst	Grand Valley		PHD	95	Purdue	1997
Isenberg, Dorene L.	C-Pr	Drew	E	PHD	86	Ca-Rivers	1989
Isham, Jonathan T. Jr.	Asst	Middlebury	DOQ	PHD	00	Maryland	1999
Ishimine, Tomotaka	Prof	CS-Long Bch		PHD	71	Wisconsin	1967
Ishwaran, Jayvanth	Asst	S F Austin	EF	PHD	97	Purdue	1997
Iskander, Wasfy B.	Prof	Rhodes		PHD	73	Indiana	
Islam, Anisul	Prof	Houston-Down		PHD	84	Alberta	1990
Islam, Muhammad Q.	C-Ac	St Louis		PHD	89	Indiana	1988
Islam, Nazrul	Asst	Emory	ECO	PHD	93	Harvard	1997
Isley, Phyllis	Assoc	Geo Southern		PHD	86	NewHamp	1998
Ispahani, Ahmed S.	C-Pr	LaVerne		PHD	66	S Calif	1964
Israel, Debra	Asst	Indiana St		PHD	99	Wisconsin	2001
Israelsen, L. Dwight	Prof	Utah State	ABDE	PHD	73	MIT	1980
Ito, Harumi	Asst	Brown		PHD	97	Stanford	
Iwand, Thomas	Retir	Nebraska	D	PHD	59	Oregon	1967
Iwasa, Jeanette	Asst	CS-Fresno	E	ABD		Nebraska	2001
Iwata, Shigeru	Assoc	Kansas	EJ	PHD	88	UCLA	1988
Iwomi, Peter O.	Assoc	Cen St-Ohio		EDD		Cincinnati	1981
Iyigun, Murat	Asst	Colorado		PHD	95	Brown	2000
Izraeli, Oded	Prof	Oakland	RHA	PHD	73	Chicago	1978
Izyumov, Alexei	Asst	Louisville	F	PHD	85	USSR	8-97
Jackson, John D.	Prof	Auburn		PHD	77	Claremont	1984
Jackson, Marvin R. Jr.	Retir	Arizona St		PHD	67	Berkeley	1962
Jackson, Matthew O.	Prof	Cal Tech		PHD	88	Stanford	1997
Jackson, Peter	Assoc	Kean		PHD		Harvard	
Jackstadt, Stephen L.	Prof	Alaska-Ancho	AEH	EDD	81	Indiana	1985
Jacobs, Cindy	VLect	Trinity-CT		PHD	89	Illinois	1991
Jacobsen, Joyce P.	Prof	Wesleyan-CT	J	PHD	91	Stanford	1993
Jadlow, Joseph M. Jr.	Prof	Oklahoma St	L	PHD	70	Virginia	1968
Jaeger, David	Asst	Wm & Mary		PHD	95	Michigan	2001
Jaffe, Adam B.	C-Pr	Brandeis		PHD	85	Harvard	1994
Jaffee, Bruce	Prof	Indiana		PHD	71	J Hopkins	1971
Jafri, Syed Hussain Ali	Prof	Tarleton St	AFG	PHD	86	Wisconsin	1989
Jaggia, Sanjiv	Prof	Suffolk		PHD	90	Indiana	
Jain, Chaman Lal	Prof	St John's		PHD	65	American	
Jain, Sanjay	Asst	Virginia	OF	PHD	94	Princeton	2001
Jakus, Paul	Assoc	Utah State	OQ	PHD	92	N Car St	2001
Jalili, Reza	Assoc	Mercer-Atlan		PHD	94	NewHamp	1993
Jam, Habib O. E.	Assoc	Rowan Col-NJ		PHD	75	S Illinois	1979
James, Dilmus Delano	Prof	Txs-El Paso	AFO	PHD	70	Mich St	1958
Frank & Mary Hanley Professor							
James, Duncan	Asst	Fordham		PHD	98	Arizona	1999
James, John A.	Prof	Virginia	NO	PHD	74	MIT	1973
James, John B.	Retir	Mid Tenn St		PHD	70	Tx A&M	1969
James, Kay C.	Dean	Regent	I	BA			1996
James, Robert G.	Prof	CS-Chico	EFG	PHD	78	Oregon	1981
Jameson, Kenneth P.	Prof	Utah		PHD	70	Wisconsin	1989
Janeba, Eckhard	Asst	Colorado		PHD	94	Bonn	
Jang, Soo M.	Prof	Plymouth St	E	PHD	78	Cincinnati	1983
Jang, Young S.	Prof	SUNY-Plattsb	CD	PHD	69	SUNY-Alb	1968

Jannuzi, F. Tomasson	Retir	Texas	OR	PHD	58	LondonEc	9-68
Jansen, Dennis W.	H-Pr	Texas A&M	EG	PHD	83	N Carol	1983
Janssen, Arthur J.	Asst	Emporia St		MA		Missouri	1976
Janssen, Larry L.	Prof	So Dakota St	Q	PHD	78	Nebraska	1978
Jantzen, Robert H.	Prof	Iona	CIJ	PHD	82	Northeas	1982
Jaques, David G.	Prof	CS-Pomona		PHD	73	Claremont	1965
Jargowky, Paul	Assoc	Texas-Dallas		PHD	91	Harvard	
Jarrell, Stephen B.	Prof	W Carolina	C	PHD	78	Purdue	1988
Jarvis, Leslie		SUNY-Empire	A	PHD	82	New Sch	1986
Jasek-Rysdahl, Kelvin	Assoc	CS-Stanislau		PHD	96	Colo St	1996
Jaswal, Jasbir S.	Retir	Missouri So		PHD	76	Missouri	1977
Jaynes, Gerald D.	Prof	Yale	N	PHD	76	Illinois	
Jeannero, Marshall J.	Retir	Bentley	AGP	PHD	69	Fletcher	1966
Jefferson, Gary H.	Prof	Brandeis		PHD	86	Yale	1984
Jefferson, Philip N.	Assoc	Swarthmore	CE	PHD	87	Virginia	1999
Jeffress, Philip W.	Retir	New Orleans		PHD	69	Kentucky	1995
Jeffries, Christopher N.	Asst	Jackson St		PHD	88	Fla St	1992
Jehle, Geoffrey A.	Prof	Vassar	D	PHD	83	Princeton	1981
Jeitschko, Thomas	Asst	Texas A&M	L	PHD	95	Virginia	1995
Jelavich, Mark S.	Prof	NW Missouri	FR	PHD	80	J Hopkins	1981
Jelen, Jonathan	Adj	CUNY-City C	AM	PHD	92	PAU France	1977
Jenkins, Allan	Assoc	Neb-Kearney		PHD	87	Nebraska	1987
Jenkins, M.	Asst	St Lawrence	FE	PHD	95	Penn St	2000
Jenkins, Sidney L.	Retir	SE Okla St	AQ	MS	59	Okla St	1968
Jennings, Donna	Asst	East Tenn St		PHD	95	Vanderbilt	1994
Jennings, E. James	Assoc	Purdue-Calmu		PHD	79	So Meth	1978
Jensen, Elizabeth J.	Prof	Hamilton	LN	PHD	84	MIT	1983
Jensen, Eric R.	Assoc	Wm & Mary		PHD	82	Michigan	1982
Jensen, Farrell E.	Prof	Brigham Yg	QG	PHD	72	Kansas St	1982
Jensen, Gail A.	Prof	Wayne State	I	PHD	86	Minnesota	1989
Jensen, George	Retir	CS-L Angeles		PHD	68	U Wash	1962
Jensen, Hans E.	Retir	Tennessee	1993	PHD	61	Tx-Austin	1963
Jensen, Mark J.	Assoc	Brigham Yg	EC	PHD	94	Wash U	2001
Jensen, Paul	Asst	Drexel		PHD	97	Penn St	1997
Jensen, Richard A.	C-Pr	Notre Dame	DL	PHD	80	Nrthwstrn	2000
Jensen, Robert J.	Assoc	Pacific Luth		MA	67	Nebraska	1968
Jensen, Rolf W.	Assoc	Conn Coll	O	PHD	81	Mass	
Jeon, Bang Nam	Assoc	Drexel		PHD	87	Indiana	1988
Jeong, Dong K.	Assoc	N Carol A&T		PHD	74	Wayne St	
Jepsen, Lisa	Asst	No Iowa		PHD	98	Vanderbilt	2000
Jerison, Michael	Prof	SUNY-Albany	DC	PHD	77	Wisconsin	1977
Jerome, Robert T. Jr.	Assoc	Jms Madison	DF	PHD	82	Virginia	1981
Jerrell, Max E.	Prof	No Arizona	EC	PHD	84	Ariz St	1981
Jessup, Paul F.	Prof	Hamline	G	PHD	66	Nrthwstrn	1988
William Kahlert Professor							
Jesswein, Wayne A.	H-Pr	Minn-Duluth	FA	PHD	69	Illinois	1968
Jewell, Nasrin	Prof	St Catherine	OA	PHD	81	Wisconsin	1981
Jewell, R. Todd	Asst	North Texas	HJ	PHD	92	Ca-SnBarb	1996
Jhun, U-Jin	Prof	SUNY Oswego	EH	PHD	73	SUNY-Alb	1972
Jianakoplos, Nancy A.	Assoc	Colorado St	CE	PHD	83	Ohio St	1990
Jiang, Neville Nien-Huei	Asst	Vanderbilt	E	PHD	00	Chicago	2000
Jilling, Michael	Prof	SC Spartanbu	ACMF	PHD	76	S Carol	1975
Jin, Yi	Asst	Kansas	E	PHD	01	Iowa	2001
Jindia, Jaswant R.	Prof	Southern	AO	PHD	70	Illinois	1970
Joerdling, Wayne H.	Prof	Wash State		PHD	79	Nrthwstrn	1979
Joh, Sung-Wook	Asst	SUNY Albany	DL	PHD	94	Harvard	1994
Johannsson, Hannes	Asst	Neb-Kearney		PHD	99	Colo St	1999
Johansen, Thomas C.	Assoc	Fort Hays St	GE	PHD	90	Okla St	1989
Johnes, Geraint	Prof	U Lancaster		PHD	87	Lancaster	
Johnson, Bruce H.	C-Ac	Gustavus Ado		PHD	79	Houston	1986
Johnson, Bruce K.	Prof	Centre	AD	PHD	85	Virginia	1987
James Graham Brown Professor of Economics							
Johnson, Byron L.	Deces	Colo-Denver		PHD	47	Wisconsin	1947
Johnson, Colleen	Prof	E Oregon St	AEJM	PHD	88	Wash St	9-86
Johnson, D. Gale	Emer	Chicago		PHD	45	Iowa St	1944
Eliakim Hastings Moore Distinguished Service Professor							
Johnson, Dan	Asst	Wellesley	AD	PHD	98	Yale	1997
Johnson, David B.	Retir	Louisiana St	H	PHD	68	Virginia	
Johnson, Dennis A.	Retir	South Dakota		PHD	72	Iowa	1964
Johnson, Donn M.	Assoc	Quinnipiac	AHQR	PHD	89	Colo St	1996
Johnson, Dudley W.	Retir	U Washington		PHD	57	Nrthwstrn	1960
Johnson, E. William	Prof	Shepherd		PHD	74	Virginia	1971
Johnson, Eric	Asst	So Carolina		PHD	97	Ca-SnDgo	8-98
Johnson, George	Prof	Michigan		PHD	66	Berkeley	
Johnson, Ivan C.	Prof	CS-Northrdge		PHD	71	W Ontario	1973
Johnson, James A.	Retir	Colorado Col		MA	59	Stanford	1956
Johnson, Jeffery	C	E Oregon St		PHD	78	Ca-Rivers	9-82
Johnson, Jerry W.	Prof	South Dakota		PHD	71	Iowa St	1967
Johnson, John	Assoc	Mississippi		PHD	88	Tx A&M	1988
Johnson, Joseph T.	Asst	Central Okla	AMR	PHD	80	Chicago	1992

Johnson, Karen R.	Lect	Baylor		MIM		Baylor	1979
Johnson, Laurie	Asst	Denver	DHQ	PHD	98	U Wash	2000
Johnson, Lowell E.	Prof	Bemidji St		PHD	75	Cornell	1976
Johnson, M. Bruce	Retir	Cal-Santa Br		PHD	62	Nrthwstrn	1968
Johnson, Marianne	Asst	Wis-Oshkosh	D	PHD	99	Mich St	2001
Johnson, Mark A.	Assoc	Chicago St	J	PHD	85	Stanford	1995
Johnson, Paul A.	C-Ac	Vassar	E	PHD	84	Stanford	1995
Johnson, Paul R.	C-Ac	Alaska-Ancho		PHD	85	Rochester	1989
Johnson, R. Larry	Prof	New Hamp Col		DBA	82	Geo Wash	
Johnson, Robert	Prof	San Diego		PHD		Oregon	1978
Johnson, Robert S.	Dean	Columbus		PHD	64	Virginia	1993
Bill Heard Chair of Business Administration							
Johnson, W. Clint	Prof	Cen Arkansas		PHD	75	Tx Tech	1975
Johnson, Walter L.	Retir	Missouri	AEGH	PHD	63	Duke	1965
Johnson, William R.	Prof	Virginia	JH	PHD	75	MIT	1974
Johnson-Lars, Shirley B.	Assoc	Vassar	I	PHD	66	Columbia	1967
Johnston, John	Emer	Calif-Irvine		PHD	57	Wales	1978
Johnston, Lewis	Asst	St Benedict	ENO	PHD	90	Berkeley	1997
Johnstone, Robert L.	Retir	Berea		PHD	61	Illinois	1964
Jolly, Eric S.	Asst	SC-Spartanbu	A	MA		Ohio U	1968
Jones, Barbara A. P.	Dean	Alabama A&M	AP	PHD	73	Geo St	1997
Jones, Barry	Asst	SUNY-Bingham	EC	PHD	99	Wash U	1999
Jones, Bryce J.	Retir	Rockhurst	1994	PHD	55	St Louis	1964
Jones, Carl R.	Prof	Naval Postgr	D	PHD	65	Claremont	1965
Jones, Charlotte A.	Prof	La St-Shreve		DBA	85	La Tech	1984
Jones, Clifton T.	C-Pr	S F Austin	CD	PHD	85	Tx A&M	1995
Jones, David D.	Retir	St Thomas-MN	E	PHD	75	Indiana	1972
Jones, Derek C.	Prof	Hamilton	PJ	PHD	74	Cornell	1972
Jones, Ellis J.	Retir	Gustavus Ado		EDD	65	N Dakota	1958
Jones, Ethel B.	Retir	Auburn		PHD	61	Chicago	1975
Jones, Garett	Asst	S Ill-Edward	EG	PHD	00	Ca-SnDgo	2000
Jones, James G.	Asst	SW Baptist	ECO	MBA		Arkansas	1988
Jones, John	Asst	SUNY-Albany	E	PHD	98	Wisconsin	1998
Jones, Kenneth D.	Prof	Georgia Col		PHD	77	La Tech	1987
Jones, Kent A.	C-Pr	Babson	F	PHD	81	Geneva	1982
Jones, Lamar B.	Prof	Louisiana St	J	PHD	65	Tx-Austin	1967
Jones, Leroy P.	Prof	Boston Univ	HLO	PHD	74	Harvard	1976
Jones, Michael	Assoc	Bowdoin	F	PHD	79	Yale	1987
Jones, Otolorin		SUNY-Empire	A	PHD	83	Ohio U	1985
Jones, Patricia	Asst	Vassar	JO	PHD	98	Oxford	1999
Jones, Robert	Asst	Mass-Dartmou					
Jones, Robert C. III	Assoc	NW St of LA		PHD	91	UCLA	
Jones, Robert J.	Assoc	Skidmore		PHD	78	Columbia	1973
Jones, Ronald W.	C-Pr	Rochester		PHD	56	MIT	1958
Xerox Professor of Economics							
Jones, Royal Maurice	Prof	W Carolina	P	PHD	67	Maryland	1971
Jones, Trefor T.	Lect	Manches Inst	HLR	PHD		Dundee	1976
Jones, Warren	C-Ac	W Illinois	AEHN	PHD	82	Iowa	1983
Jonnard, Claude	Prof	F Dick-Madis	A	PHD	63	NYU	9-65
Jonokin, Jon	Assoc	Tenn Tech		PHD	94	Tennessee	1989
Jonsson, Petur O.	Prof	Fayetteville		PHD	86	Penn St	
Joray, Paul A.	Prof	Ind-So Bend	ADJ	PHD	71	Illinois	1971
Jorda, Oscar	Prof	Cal-Davis	E	PHD	97	Ca-SnDgo	1997
Jordan, James S.	Prof	Penn State	E	PHD	75	Nrthwstrn	1998
Jordan, W. John	Prof	Seton Hall		PHD	77	SUNY-Alb	1977
Jorge, Antonio	Prof	Fla Internat	BPO	PHD		Villanova	
Jorgenson, Dale W.	Prof	Harvard		PHD	59	Harvard	1969
Frederick E. Abbe Professor of Economics							
Joseph, Hyman	Prof	Iowa		PHD	69	Nrthwstrn	1966
Joshi, Sumit	Assoc	George Wash	CD	PHD	91	Indiana	1992
Joskow, Paul L.	Prof	MIT	O	PHD	72	Yale	1972
Mitsui Professor of Economics and Management							
Joskowitz, David	Asst	Tx A&M Intl	Q	PHD	97	Tx Tech	9-98
Joutz, Frederick L.	Assoc	George Wash	EC	PHD	87	U Wash	1988
Jovanovic, Boyan	Prof	New York U	L	PHD	78	Chicago	1983
Joyce, B. Patrick	Prof	Mich Tech	D	PHD	74	Missouri	1972
Joyce, Joseph P.	Prof	Wellesley	EF	PHD	84	Boston U	1982
Joyce, Theodore	Prof	CUNY-Baruch		PHD	85	CUNY	1986
Jozefowicz, James J.	Asst	Indiana U-PA	CEL	PHD	99	SUNY-Alb	1999
Jozsa, Frank P. Jr.	Assoc	Pfeiffer		PHD	77	Geo St	1991
Ju, Biung-Ghi	Asst	Kansas	D	PHD	01	Rochester	2001
Ju, Jiandong	Assoc	Oklahoma	D	PHD	95	Penn St	1995
Jubinski, Dan	Asst	Colgate	G	PHD	01	Virginia	2001
Judge, Rebecca P.	Assoc	St Olaf	ADQ	PHD	76	Duke	1987
Juhl, Ted	Asst	Kansas	E	PHD	99	Illinois	1999
Juhn, Chinhui	Assoc	Houston	J	PHD	91	Chicago	1992
Julien, Benoit	Asst	U Miami		PHD		W Ontario	1997
Jung, Chulho	Prof	Ohio Univ	CDFQ	PHD	89	Michigan	1989
Junk, Paul E.	Retir	Minn-Duluth	E	PHD	62	Nrthwstrn	1979
Jursa, Paul E.	Retir	Charleston		PHD	72	Tx-Austin	1976

Juster, F. Thomas	Prof	Michigan		PHD	56	Columbia	1973
Kabis, Zeinhom M.	Retir	St Ambrose		PHD	68	Illinois	1973
Kaboski, Joseph	Asst	Ohio State	EF	PHD	01	Chicago	2001
Kabot, Alvin A.	Retir	CUNY-Hunter	1-99	LLM	63	NYU	9-67
Kacapyr, Elia W.	C-Ac	Ithaca	CE	PHD	78	Geo St	1985
Kader, Ahmad A.	Retir	Carroll		PHD	74	W Virginia	1974
Kadiyala, K. Rao	Prof	Purdue		PHD	66	Wisconsin	1970
Kaempfer, William H.	Prof	Colorado		PHD	79	Duke	1981
Kafi, Farhoud	VInst	Babson	D	MA		Northeas	
Kafoglis, Milton Z.	Retir	Emory	LI	PHD	58	Ohio St	1979
Kaganovich, M.	Assoc	Indiana		PHD	85	USSR	1991
Kagel, John H.	Prof	Ohio State	L	PHD	70	Purdue	1999
University Chaired Professor							
Kahai, Simran K.	Asst	John Carroll	CDFL	PHD	95	Auburn	2001
Kahane, Leo H.	Assoc	CS-Hayward	CFL	PHD	91	Columbia	1991
Kahn, Abraham Ben	Assoc	Mass Lib Art		MA	79	SUNY-Alb	
Kahn, James A.	Prof	Wash & Lee	QO	PHD	86	MIT	
Kahwar, Mariam	Asst	Elmira		PHD	97	J Hopkins	1997
Kain, John F.	Prof	Texas-Dallas		PHD	61	Berkeley	1996
Kaiser, Brooks	Asst	Gettysburg	ADNQ	PHD	98	Nrthwstrn	2000
Kaiser, Carl P.	Prof	Wash & Lee	JC	PHD	80	Wash U	1979
Kajii, Atsushi	Asst	Pennsylvania	G	PHD	91	Harvard	1991
Kakoli, Philip	Asst	Dallas Bapt	F	PHD	01	Niarobi	1988
Kalaba, Robert E.	Prof	So Calif		PHD	58	NYU	1969
Kalemli-Ozcan, Sebnem	Asst	Houston	FO	PHD	00	Brown	2000
Kali, Raja	Asst	Arkansas	LOFD	PHD	96	Maryland	1999
Kalish, Richard J.	Retir	SUNY-Albany	N	PHD	63	Colorado	1969
Kalist, David E.	Asst	Oakland	IJ	PHD	01	Wayne St	2001
Kallianiotis, John	Assoc	Scranton		PHD	85	CUNY	1990
Kallon, Kelfala M.	Assoc	No Colorado	EFHO	PHD	83	Virginia	1993
Kamara, Avraham	Prof	U Washington		PHD	86	Columbia	1984
Kamas, Linda	Assoc	Santa Clara		PHD	82	Berkeley	1988
Kamath, Shyam J.	Prof	CS-Hayward	BFMO	PHD	87	Simon Fr	1986
Kamazawa, Risa	Asst	Mississippi		PHD	01	Tx-Austin	2001
Kamdar, Nipoli	Assoc	Trinity	H	PHD	93	Syracuse	1993
Kamen, Michelle	Asst	CUNY-Lehman		MBA		St Johns	
Kamerschen, David R.	Prof	Georgia	DK	PHD	64	Mich St	1974
Jasper N. Dorsey Professor							
Kamery, Rob H.	Prof	Christian Br	ABJ	MS	81	Arkansas	1987
Kamien, Morton I.	Prof	Northwestern		PHD	64	Purdue	1970
Kamihigashi, Takashi	Assoc	SUNY-Stony B		PHD	94	Wisconsin	1994
Kaminarides, John S.	Retir	Arkansas St	AFTO	PHD	68	Houston	1968
Kaminsky, Graciela	Prof	George Wash	F	PHD	83	MIT	1998
Kamm, Judy	Asst	Lindenwood		MS		Mo-StLou	8-96
Kamp, Bradley P.	Assoc	South Fla	L	PHD	93	Ca-SnDgo	1992
Kamps, William E.	Retir	So Dakota St	E	PHD	74	Wash St	1972
Kamrany, Nake M.	SLect	So Calif		PHD	62	S Calif	1976
Kanago, Bryce	Asst	No Iowa	E	PHD	88	Iowa	2000
Kanazawa, Mark T.	Assoc	Carleton	DKNQ	PHD	87	Stanford	1985
Kanbur, Sanjiv	Prof	Cornell		PHD	81	Oxford	
Lee Teng-hui Professor of World Arts							
Kandil, Magda	Prof	Wis-Milwauke		PHD	88	Wash St	1992
Kane, John C.	C-Pr	SUNY Oswego	ACJ	PHD	86	SUNY-SBr	1983
Kane, Joseph A.	Retir	LaSalle		PHD	72	Temple	1961
Kane, Mamadou	Assoc	E Stroudsbur	EFN	MA	72	NYU	1973
Kane, Tim D.	Prof	Texas-Tyler		PHD	72	Tx-Austin	1981
Kaneda, Hiromitsu	Emer	Cal-Davis	AFOQ	PHD	64	Stanford	1973
Kaneda, Mitch	Asst	Georgetown	F	PHD	94	Penn	1994
Kang, Eungmin B.	Assoc	St Cloud St		PHD	90	Geo St	1990
Kang, Inbong	Asst	SUNY-Bingham	EO	PHD	95	Rochester	1995
Kang, Keejoon	Prof	Indiana		PHD	80	U Wash	1980
Kangayappan, Kumaraswamy	Prof	WI-Green Bay		PHD	69	Wisconsin	
Kannappan, Subbiah	Retir	Michigan St		PHD	56	Tufts	1961
Kanovsky, Eliyahu	Prof	Yeshiva		PHD	61	Columbia	
Ludwig Jesselson Chair in Economics; spring only							
Kant, Chander	Assoc	Seton Hall		PHD	80	So Meth	1987
Kantarelis, Demetrius	Assoc	Assumption	DCKL	PHD	83	Clark	1983
Kanthi, Mahendra S.	Prof	Saginaw Vall	FO	PHD	80	Kentucky	1984
Kantor, Shawn E.	Prof	Arizona		PHD	90	Cal Tech	1990
Kao, C. H.	Prof	Syracuse	C	PHD	83	SUNY-SBr	1985
Kaparakis, Emmanuel	Inst	Providence	EGF	ABD		Conn	1990
Kaplan, Phillip	Prof	New Haven	NL	PHD	64	J Hopkins	
Kapler, Janis	Assoc	Mass-Boston	FL	PHD	93	American	1993
Kapstein, Ethan	Prof	INSEAD	V	PHD	86	Medford	2001
Kapuria-Foreman, Vibha	Assoc	Colorado Col		PHD	87	Pittsburgh	1989
Kara, Orhan	Asst	North Dakota		ABD		WI-Milwa	2001
Kara, S. Murat	Asst	Angelo State	PM	PHD	83	Tx Tech	2000
Karahan, Gokhan	Asst	Mississippi		PHD	01	Miss	2000
Karangu, Mwangi	Asst	Morgan State	CDEG	PHD	81	Walden	9-71
Karasulu, Meral	Asst	Bogazici	CEF	PHD	95	Boston C	1995

Karatas, Cevat	Prof	Bogazici	ACDH	PHD	70	Glasgow	1985
Karatjas, Nicholas	C-Pr	Indiana U-PA	ADI	PHD	76	SUNY-SBr	1978
Karayaicin, Ali Cem	Assoc	Fla Internat	EF	PHD	89	Columbia	1989
Karbassioon, Ebrahim	C-Pr	E Illinois		PHD	81	Nebraska	1980
Kareken, John H.	Retir	Minnesota		PHD	56	MIT	1958
Karemera, David	Assoc	So Carol St		PHD	89	Nebraska	1997
Karier, Thomas M.	Prof	East Wash		PHD	85	Berkeley	1981
Karikari, John A.	Assoc	Tulsa	AFMO	PHD	85	Queen's	
Karim, Alema	C-Ac	Rhode Isl Cl		PHD	86	Boston U	
Karlson, Stephen	Assoc	No Illinois	D	PHD	80	Wisconsin	1986
Karni, Edi	Prof	J Hopkins		PHD	71	Chicago	1981
Karns, James M.	Retir	E Kentucky		PHD	75	Oklahoma	1975
Karpoff, Jonathan M.	Prof	U Washington		PHD	82	UCLA	1983
Karras, Georgios	Prof	Ill-Chicago	E	PHD	90	Ohio St	1990
Karscig, Mark P.	Prof	Cen Missouri		PHD	87	Pittsburgh	1981
Karsten, Siegfried G.	Retir	West Georgia	8-94	PHD	70	Utah	1978
Karstensson, Lewis	Assoc	Nev-L Vegas	B	PHD	74	Ohio U	1979
Kartman, Arthur E.	Prof	San Diego St		PHD	69	U Wash	1968
Kaschins, Edward A.	Prof	Luther		PHD	73	Iowa	1961
Kaserman, David L.	Prof	Auburn		PHD	76	Florida	1986
Torchmark Professor							
Kasper, Hirshel	Prof	Oberlin	DJ	PHD	63	Minnesota	1963
Kassis, Mary C.	Asst	West Georgia	HJ	PHD	99	Geo St	1-02
Kassouf, Sheen T.	Emer	Calif-Irvine		PHD	65	Columbia	1965
Kasturi, Prahlad	Prof	Radford	DOQ	PHD	83	Hawaii	1985
Kasun, Jacqueline R.	Retir	CS-Humboldt		PHD	56	Columbia	1969
Kato, Takao	Prof	Colgate	J	PHD	86	Queen's	1986
Kats, Amoz	Prof	Virg Tech	CDL	PHD	72	Minnesota	1974
Katz, Arnold M.	Retir	Pittsburgh	J	PHD	61	Yale	
Katz, Barbara G.	Prof	New York U	CDP	PHD	73	Penn	1974
Katz, Eliakim	C-Pr	No Illinois	CD	PHD	76	London	1976
Katz, Elizabeth	Asst	St Marys-Cal	O	PHD	92	Wisconsin	1999
Katz, Lawrence F.	Prof	Harvard		PHD	85	MIT	1986
Katz, Michael	Prof	Cal-Berkeley		PHD		Oxford	
Katzman, Brett E.	Asst	U Miami	DL	PHD	96	Duke	1996
Katzner, Donald W.	Prof	Massachusett		PHD	65	Minnesota	1975
Kauffman, Daniel E.	Prof	Winona State		PHD	80	Nebraska	1983
Kauffman, Kyle	Assoc	Wellesley	DN	PHD	93	Illinois	1993
Kaufman, Bruce E.	Prof	Georgia St	JN	PHD	78	Wisconsin	1977
Kaufman, Dennis A.	Assoc	Wis-Parkside	CH	PHD	87	Kansas	1987
Kaufman, Roger T.	C-Pr	Smith	CEJP	PHD	78	MIT	1983
Kaufmann, Hugo M.	Prof	CUNY-Queens	FE	PHD	68	Columbia	1967
Kaun, David E.	Prof	Ca-Santa Crz	J	PHD	64	Stanford	1966
Kavesh, Robert A.	Prof	New York U	B	PHD	54	Harvard	1958
Marcus Nadler Professor of Finance & Economics							
Kaviani, Mohammad	Lect	Ind-Purdue/I		MA	85	Indiana	1986
Kawahito, Kiyoshi	Prof	Mid Tenn St	FE	PHD	71	Maryland	1971
Kayaalp, Orhan	Assoc	CUNY-Lehman		PHD	84	CUNY	1979
Kayalir, Resad	Prof	Bogazici	BE	PHD	76	Istanbul	1972
Kaytaz, Mehmet	Prof	Bogazici	CE	PHD	78	Nottinghm	1978
Kazarosian, Mark	Assoc	Stonehill	CG	PHD	90	Boston C	1997
Kazemi, Abbas A.	Assoc	Rhode Isl Cl		PHD	88	SUNY-SBr	
Kazemi, Hossein S.	C-Ac	Stonehill	GE	PHD	83	Clark	1982
Kazura, Martie	C-As	Berea		MBA	90	Montana	1991
Keane, Michael P.	Prof	New York U	D	PHD	90	Brown	1998
Kearl, James R.	Prof	Brigham Yg	KD	PHD	75	MIT	1975
Kearney, Adrienne	Asst	Maine	AF	PHD	92	Penn St	1997
Kearns, Robert W.	Retir	Carroll	1995	MBA		Miami	9-72
Keating, Barry P.	Prof	Notre Dame	R	PHD	74	Notre Dm	1978
Jesse H. Jones Professor							
Keating, John W.	Asst	Kansas	E	PHD	89	Nrthwstrn	8-97
Keefe, David E.	Assoc	Pacific	FT	PHD	80	Berkeley	1978
Keefe, Maureen	VInst	SUNY Old Wes					
Keehn, Richard	Prof	Wis-Parkside	EGN	PHD	72	Wisconsin	1969
Keeler, James	C-Pr	Kenyon	CEB	PHD	81	Indiana	1984
Keeler, Theodore E.	Prof	Cal-Berkeley		PHD	71	MIT	1977
Keely, Louise	Asst	Wisconsin		PHD	00	LondonEc	2000
Keenan, Donald C.	Prof	Georgia	CHR	DSC	78	Wash U	1978
Kehoe, Patrick J.	Prof	Pennsylvania	POF	PHD	86	Harvard	1992
Ronald S. Lauder Term Associate Professor of Economics							
Kehoe, Timothy J.	Prof	Minnesota		PHD	79	Yale	1987
Keil, Manfred W.	Assoc	Claremont	ECJA	PHD	85	LondonEc	7-95
Keil, Stanley R.	Assoc	Ball State	QR	PHD	73	Oregon	1973
Keilany, Ziad	H-Pr	Tenn-Chattan	EO	PHD	68	Indiana	1968
Guerry Professor							
Keiser, Kurt J.	Asst	Adams State		ABD		Colo St	
Keith, John E.	Prof	Utah State	DEQR	PHD	73	Utah St	1972
Keith, Kristen	Assoc	Toledo	J	PHD	89	Ohio St	1994
Kelejian, Harry	Prof	Maryland		PHD	68	Wisconsin	1968
Keleta, Ethiopia	Assoc	Txs Southern		PHD	84	Rice	

Keller, Anita	Inst	Ark-Ltl Rock		MBA	76	Ark St	1991
Keller, Ric	Lect	SUNY-Cortlan		MBA		Geo St	2001
Keller, Robert R.	Prof	Colorado St	EN	PHD	71	Wisconsin	1974
Keller, Wolfgang	Asst	Texas	FO	PHD	95	Yale	9-98
Kelley, Allen C.	Prof	Duke	O	PHD	64	Stanford	1972
James D. Duke Professor							
Kelley, George T.	Retir	Worcester St		PHD	71	Clark	1969
Kelley, Hugh E.	Asst	Indiana		PHD	98	Calif	2000
Kellman, Mitchell	Prof	CUNY-City C	DEF	PHD	72	Penn	1982
Kelly, David	Asst	U Miami	E	PHD	95	Car Mellon	1998
Kelly, Eamon M.	Retir	Tulane		PHD	65	Columbia	1981
Kelly, Jerry S.	Prof	Syracuse	D	PHD	69	Harvard	1971
Kelly, Kathy	Lect	Tx-Arlington	DE	MA	89	So Meth	1996
Kelly, Robert A.	Asst	Fairfield	HKC	PHD	71	Geotown	1978
Kelly, Thomas	Asst	Middlebury	OQ	PHD	97	Ca-Rivers	1997
Kelly, Thomas M.	Prof	Baylor	R	PHD	70	Okla St	1969
Kelly, Trish	Assoc	Quinnipiac	EFO	PHD	94	Mass	1995
Kelly-Hawke, Alison	Assoc	Suffolk		PHD	93	Boston C	
Kelso, Patrick R.	Retir	West Tx A&M	EHN	PHD	68	Tx-Austin	1967
Kelsy, Michael	Lect	Mo-Kansas Ct	CQ	PHD	91	Tennessee	1996
Kelton, Christina	Assoc	Cincinnati		PHD	79	Wisconsin	1996
Kemme, David M.	Prof	Memphis	FCP	PHD	80	Ohio St	1994
Morris Chair of Excellence in International Econ							
Kempey, William M.	C-Pr	Kean		PHD	70	NYU	9-78
Kendrick, David A.	Prof	Texas	CE	PHD	66	MIT	7-70
Ralph W. Yarborough Centennial Professor of Liberal Arts							
Kenen, Peter B.	Prof	Princeton		PHD	58	Harvard	1971
Walker Professor Economics & International Finance							
Kenison, Arthur M.	Prof	St Anselm	ACG	PHD	80	Boston U	1980
Kenison, Jeanne H.	Assoc	St Anselm	C	EDD	86	Vanderbilt	1988
Kenkel, James L.	Assoc	Pittsburgh	C	PHD	69	Purdue	1969
Kennan, John F.	Prof	Wisconsin		PHD	73	Nrthwstrn	1992
Kennett, David A.	Prof	Vassar	F	PHD	76	Columbia	1976
Kenney, James M.	Prof	Union	QDMG	PHD	72	Stanford	1972
Kenny, Lawrence W.	Prof	Florida	DHJ	PHD	77	Chicago	1975
Kent, Calvin A.	Dean	Marshall		PHD	67	Missouri	1993
Kent, Richard J.	C-Ac	Kent State	E	PHD	76	Berkeley	1983
Kenyon, Daphne A.	C-Pr	Simmons	HI	PHD	80	Michigan	1989
Kerby, William C.	Prof	CS-Sacrament		PHD	71	Oregon	1967
Kerchner, Robert B.	Assoc	Washburn		PHD	73	Missouri	1976
Kercsmar, John	Assoc	E Stroudsbur	M	PHD	85	Houston	
Kerkvliet, Joe R.	Assoc	Oregon State	L	PHD	86	Wyoming	9-88
Kermani, Taghi T.	Retir	Youngstown		PHD	59	Nebraska	1959
Kern, Clifford R.	Assoc	SUNY-Bingham	R	PHD	74	Harvard	1971
Kern, William	Assoc	W Michigan	B	PHD	82	Colo St	1987
Kerr, Peter M.	Prof	SE Missouri	AEBF	PHD	79	Kansas	1980
Kersten, Timothy W.	Prof	Cal Poly-SLO		PHD	73	Oregon	1971
Kessel, Herbert	C-Pr	St Michael's	AJDC	PHD	81	Boston U	1977
Kesselring, Randall G.	Prof	Arkansas St	ACJF	PHD	80	Oklahoma	1984
Kessler, Adam	Assoc	F Dick-Teane	ACDE	PHD	78	NYU	
Kessler, Alan L.	Assoc	Providence	DH	PHD	84	Boston C	1985
Ketkar, Kusum	Prof	Seton Hall		PHD	80	Vanderbilt	1983
Kevane, Michael	Asst	Santa Clara		PHD	94	Berkeley	1995
Key, Euell Dwyane	Retir	S F Austin	A	PHD	70	S Illinois	1970
Khactu, Dominique	Retir	North Dakota	FG	PHD	65	Minnesota	1966
Khalil, Fahad A.	Assoc	U Washington		PHD	91	Va Tech	1991
Khalil, Mohamad	C-Pr	Fairmont St	CF	PHD	88	W Virginia	1988
Khan, Agha Nisar	Prof	Virginia St		PHD	70	Va Tech	1972
Khan, Anwar S.	Prof	N Carol A&T		PHD	72	Wisconsin	
Khan, Azizur Rahman	Prof	Cal-Riversid	FOPR	PHD	66	Cambridge	1988
Khan, B. Zorina	Asst	Bowdoin	GN	PHD	91	UCLA	1996
Khan, Farida C.	C-Ac	Wis-Parkside	FO	PHD	90	Maryland	1990
Khan, M. Ali	Prof	J Hopkins		PHD	73	Yale	1988
Khan, M. Moosa	Assoc	Prairie View	FEM	PHD	86	Simon Fr	1989
Khan, Saleem M.	C-Pr	Bloomsburg	AEOP	PHD	67	J Gutenb	1-78
Khan, Shakeeb	Asst	Rochester		PHD	97	Princeton	1998
Khandke, Kailash	Assoc	Furman		PHD	93	Ca-Davis	1995
Khandker, A. Wahhab	Prof	Wis-La Cross	ACF	PHD	80	So Meth	1983
Khang, Chulsoon	Retir	Oregon	1997	PHD	65	Minnesota	1966
Khanna, Jyoti	Assoc	Colgate	H	PHD	90	Iowa	1992
Khanna, Neha	Asst	SUNY-Bingham	QD	PHD	97	Cornell	1998
Kharadia, Virabhai C.	Prof	NW Missouri	AED	PHD	73	Illinois	1973
Khayum, Mohammed	C-Pr	So Indiana		PHD	90	Temple	1991
Khazeh, Kashi	Prof	Salisbury St		PHD	85	Tennessee	O-85
Khe, Sriram	Lect	CS-Bakersf	RO	PHD	93	S Calif	2000
Khorassani, Jacqueline	Asst	Marietta	AEFH	PHD	97	W Virginia	1994
Kidane, Abraham Z.	Prof	CS-Dominguez	AFOI	PHD	71	UCLA	1971
Kidman, Peter N.	Prof	E Stroudsbur	K	PHD	71	W Virginia	1977
Kiefer, David M.	Prof	Utah		PHD	74	Michigan	1981

Kiefer, Nicholas M.	Prof	Cornell		PHD	76	Princeton	1980
Ta-Chung Liu Professor of Economics							
Kiel, Katherine A.	Asst	Holy Cross	CDQR	PHD	89	Ca-SnDgo	1998
Kiernan, Joseph J.	Asst	F Dick-Teane	AEG	PHD	80	Fordham	
Kiesling, Herbert J.	Retir	Indiana		PHD	65	Harvard	1965
Kihlstrom, Richard E.	Prof	Pennsylvania		PHD	64	Minnesota	
Miller-Friedman Professor of Finance & Professor of Economics							
Kiker, B. F.	Prof	So Carolina		PHD	65	Tulane	1971
Jeff B. Bates Professor of Public Administration & Finance							
Kilby, Christopher P.	Asst	Vassar	O	PHD	94	Stanford	1993
Kilby, Peter	Prof	Wesleyan-CT	O	DPHI	67	Oxford	1965
Kilian, Lutz	Asst	Michigan					
Killingworth, Mark R.	C-Pr	Rutgers-N Br	J	DPHI	77	Oxford	1978
Kim, Benjamin J. C.	Assoc	Nebraska	EF	PHD	83	UCLA	1983
Kim, Eungsuk	Asst	CS-Stanislau		PHD	99	Indiana	2000
Kim, Gew-Rae	Assoc	Bridgeport		PHD	92	CUNY	
Kim, Grace	Asst	Mich-Dearbor		PHD	01	Vanderbilt	2000
Kim, Hak Youn	Prof	W Kentucky	CDO	PHD	82	Cincinnati	1983
Kim, Han J.	Prof	So Dakota St	C	PHD	69	Oregon St	1967
Kim, Henry	Asst	Tufts	F	PHD	97	Yale	2001
Kim, Jae-Young	Asst	SUNY-Albany	CE	PHD	95	Minnesota	1994
Kim, Jaebeom	Asst	St Thomas-MN	CF	PHD	00	Ohio St	2001
Kim, Jinill	Asst	Virginia	EF	PHD	96	Yale	1998
Kim, Jinyoung	Asst	SUNY-Buffalo	OJ	PHD	94	Chicago	
Kim, Jongsung	Asst	Bryant	AJ	PHD	98	J Hopkins	1998
Kim, Juho	Prof	Miss Vall St		PHD	73	Oklahoma	1973
Kim, Ki Hoon	Prof	Central Conn	FO	PHD	68	Conn	1967
Kim, Kil-Joong	Prof	Austin Peay	FO	PHD	80	Cincinnati	1980
Kim, Kirk Y.	Prof	Wis-Whitewat		PHD	70	Utah	1969
Kim, Kwan S.	Prof	Notre Dame	OF	PHD	67	Minnesota	1975
Kim, Kyoo H.	Prof	Bowling Gr		PHD	78	Wisconsin	1978
Kim, Marlene	Asst	Mass-Boston	DJ	PHD	90	Berkeley	2000
Kim, Minseong	Asst	Pittsburgh	E	PHD	96	Brown	1996
Kim, Sang	Asst	Hood		PHD	95	Penn St	2001
Kim, Soyoung	Asst	Illinois	EF	PHD	96	Yale	1997
Kim, Sukkoo	Assoc	Wash Univ	NR	PHD	93	UCLA	1993
Kim, Sun K.	Prof	CS-L Angeles		PHD	66	S Calif	1964
Kim, Sungwoo	Prof	Northeastern		PHD	57	Berkeley	1972
Kim, Sunwoong	Assoc	Wis-Milwauke		PHD	85	MIT	1989
Kim, Yang H.	Retir	Alabama A&M	AOE	PHD	67	Utah	1965
Kim, Yoonbai	Assoc	Kentucky	EFG	PHD	87	Stanford	1991
Kim, Youn Suk	Prof	Kean		PHD	73	New Sch	9-74
Kim, Young Chin	Prof	No Illinois	O	PHD	68	Columbia	1970
Kimani, Joseph	Inst	Morgan State		MBA		Atlanta	
Kimball, Miles S.	Assoc	Michigan		PHD	87	Harvard	1987
Kimbrough, Kent P.	Prof	Duke	F	PHD	80	Chicago	1980
Kimenyi, Samson M.	Assoc	Connecticut	HI	PHD	86	GeoMason	1991
Kimmel, Jean	Assoc	W Michigan	J	PHD	90	N Carol	2001
Kimzey, Bruce W.	Prof	Brighm Yg-HI		PHD	70	Wash St	1989
Kinal, Terrence	C-Pr	SUNY-Albany	CD	PHD	76	Minnesota	1980
Kincard, Joel	Lect	Salisbury St		PHD	99	N Car St	8-97
Kindahl, James K.	Retir	Massachusett		PHD	58	Chicago	1967
King, Amanda	Asst	Elon	EJ	PHD	00	Vanderbilt	2000
King, Arthur E.	Prof	Lehigh	FP	PHD	76	Ohio St	1976
King, Arthur T.	D-Pr	Winston-Sal	D	PHD	77	Colorado	8-95
King, Clay B.	Retir	Minot State	A	PHD	72	Wash St	1975
King, Mary C.	C-Ac	Portland St	J	PHD	91	Berkeley	1992
King, Paul G.	Prof	Denison	OAQ	PHD	71	Illinois	1967
John Harris Chair							
King, Philip G.	Assoc	San Fran St		PHD	87	Cornell	1987
King, Randall H.	Assoc	Akron	ADJ	PHD	78	Ohio St	1978
King, Sharmila	Asst	Pacific	EF	PHD	01	Ca-Davis	2001
King, Vereda J.	Assoc	N Carol A&T		PHD	84	Duke	
Kingston, Christopher G.	Asst	Amherst	AFOP	PHD	01	Stanford	2001
Kingston, Jerry L.	Prof	Arizona St		PHD	69	Penn St	1969
Kinnaman, Thomas	Assoc	Bucknell	HQ	PHD	94	Virginia	9-94
Kinney, Kinney	Assoc	Shepherd		PHD	85	Maryland	1994
Kirby, Maurice W.	H-Pr	U Lancaster		PHD		Sheffield	
Kiriazis, David M.	Lect	Frostburg St		PHD	97	Wayne St	
Kirk, Robert	Retir	Ind-Purdue/I	HR	PHD	69	Iowa St	1972
Kirkland, Jack	Prof	Troy State	ADEH	PHD	82	Wash St	1995
Kirkpatrick, Rickey C.	Assoc	Appalach St	FM	PHD	78	Tulane	1980
Kiser, Larry L.	Prof	East Wash		PHD	73	Rutgers	1971
Kish-Goodling, Donna M.	Asst	Muhlenberg		PHD	92	Lehigh	1990
Kishan, Ruby Pandey	Assoc	SW Texas St	E	PHD	86	Tx A&M	1986
Kitamura, Yuichi	Assoc	Wisconsin		PHD	93	Yale	1998
Kjetsaa, Richard W.	Assoc	F Dick-Teane	AEG	PHD	85	Fordham	
Klaasen, Thomas A.	Prof	Txs Wesleyan		PHD	69	Mich St	1989
Klaus, Bettina	Asst	Nebraska	D	PHD	98	Maastricht	1998
Klay, Robin	Assoc	Hope	BO	PHD	73	Princeton	1979

Klebaner, Benjamim	Prof	CUNY-City C	E	PHD	52	Columbia	1947
Kleiman, Ephraim	VProf	MIT		PHD	58	LondonEc	2001
Klein, Benjamin	Prof	UCLA		PHD	70	Chicago	1978
Klein, Daniel B.	Assoc	Santa Clara		PHD	90	NYU	1996
Klein, J. Douglass	Prof	Union	LQD	PHD	75	Wisconsin	1979
Klein, Judy L.	C-Ac	Mary Baldwin	BC	PHD	86	London	1982
Klein, Lawrence R.	Emer	Pennsylvania		PHD	44	MIT	1958
Benjamin Franklin Professor of Economics & Finance							
Klein, Nicole L.	Assoc	So Dakota St	Q	PHD	96	Kansas St	1997
Klein, Peter G.	Asst	Georgia	GKL	PHD	95	Berkeley	1995
Klein, Philip A.	Prof	Penn State	E	PHD	58	Berkeley	1955
Klein, Roger W.	Prof	Rutgers-N Br	C	PHD	70	Yale	1994
Klein, Yehuda L.	Assoc	CUNY-Brookly	CDQ	PHD	85	Berkeley	1989
Kleinberg, Norman L.	Assoc	CUNY-Baruch		PHD	77	MIT	
Kleiner, William C.	Retir	W Illinois	AEF	PHD	74	Mich St	1971
Klepper, Steven I.	Prof	Carnegie Mel		PHD	75	Cornell	1980
Kletzer, Kenneth M.	Prof	Ca-Santa Crz	FDOH	PHD	82	Berkeley	1992
Kletzer, Lori Gladstein	Asst	Ca-Santa Crz	J	PHD	86	Berkeley	1993
Klevorick, Alvin K.	Prof	Yale	K	PHD	67	Princeton	1975
Klinedinst, Mark A.	Prof	So Miss	P	PHD	87	Cornell	1986
Kling, Robert W.	Assoc	Colorado St	DQ	PHD	85	Kansas	1984
Klingaman, David C.	Prof	Ohio Univ	DE	PHD	67	Virginia	1967
Kloft, Leonard	Asst	Ohio Northrn		PHD	95	Iowa	1995
Klopfenstein, Kristin	Asst	Tx Christian		PHD	99	Colorado	1999
Klose, Gilbert	Prof	Earlham		MA		Nrthwstrn	1960
Klotz, Benjamin P.	Assoc	Temple	E	PHD	69	Minnesota	1975
Knabb, Shawn	Asst	Colo-Denver		PHD	01	Ca-SnBarb	
Knabe, Rudolph	Assoc	Embry-Riddle		MA	76	Tennessee	
Knapp, Kimberly A.	Asst	MD-Baltim Co		PHD	88	Brown	
Kniesner, Thomas J.	Prof	Syracuse	J	PHD	74	Ohio St	1999
Knight, Robert E. L.	Retir	Maryland		PHD	58	Berkeley	1960
Knight, Tori H.	Asst	Carson-Newmn	CDHI	PHD			2000
Knodell, Jane E.	C-Ac	Vermont	EN	PHD	84	Stanford	1986
Knoeber, Charles R.	Prof	N Carol St	LKDG	PHD	76	UCLA	1976
Knoedler, Janet T.	Assoc	Bucknell	LNO	PHD	91	Tennessee	9-92
Knowles, Glenn J.	Assoc	Wis-La Cross	CQR	PHD	80	Minnesota	1985
Knox, Robert L.	Retir	Arizona St		PHD	63	N Carol	1963
Knudsen, James J.	Asst	Creighton	CHJ	PHD	89	Iowa St	1989
Knudsen, John W.	Retir	Idaho	EP	PHD	70	Minnesota	1972
Knusel, Jack L.	Retir	Wis-Whitewat		PHD		Colorado	1965
Koch, James C.	Assoc	St Edwards		MSIR	59	Loyl-Chgo	1960
Koch, James V.	Prof	Old Dominion		PHD	68	Nrthwstrn	1990
Koch, Paul D.	Prof	Kansas	Fnce	PHD	80	Mich St	1988
Koch, Paul R.	Prof	Olivet Nazar	AFHP	EDD	94	Illin St	1992
Koch, S.	Asst	Geo Southern		PHD	97	Penn St	1998
Kochanowski, Paul S.	Prof	Ind-So Bend	CDR	DBA	72	Indiana	1972
Kochar, Anjini	Asst	Stanford		PHD	91	Chicago	1990
Kochin, Levis A.	Assoc	U Washington		PHD	75	Chicago	1972
Kockesen, Levent	Asst	Columbia	DB	PHD	99	NYU	1999
Koechlin, Tim	Assoc	Skidmore		PHD	89	Mass	1988
Koelln, Kenneth	Assoc	North Texas	LI	PHD	91	Florida	1991
Koenker, Roger	Prof	Illinois	CL	PHD	74	Michigan	1983
Kofi, Tetteh A.	Prof	San Francisc	OA	PHD	70	Berkeley	1981
Koford, Kenneth	Prof	Delaware	H	PHD	77	UCLA	1979
Kogut, Carl A.	Assoc	La-Monroe	DLJ	PHD	84	Tx A&M	1992
Kohen, Andrew I.	Prof	Jms Madison	JD	PHD	73	Ohio St	1976
Kohler, Heinz	Emer	Amherst	APCD	PHD	61	Michigan	1961
Willard Long Thorp Professor of Economics							
Kohlhase, Janet E.	Assoc	Houston	RHD	PHD	80	Penn	1983
Kohn, Meir G.	Prof	Dartmouth		PHD	73	MIT	1978
Koirala, Govinda	Asst	Rio Grande		PHD	95	NYU	1996
Koizumi, Tetsunori	Retir	Ohio State	E	PHD	70	Brown	1970
Kokkelenberg, Edward C.	C-Pr	SUNY-Bingham	EO	PHD	81	Nrthwstrn	1980
Kolb, Fredric	Prof	Wis-Eau Clar	ACG	PHD	71	Utah	1971
Kolberg, William	Assoc	Ithaca	AQ	PHD	84	Rhode Isl	1984
Kolluri, Bharat R.	C-Pr	Hartford	CEGH	PHD	77	SUNY-Buf	1976
Kolmer, Lee Roy	Retir	Iowa State	1994	PHD	54	Iowa St	1973
Kolpin, Van W.	C-Pr	Oregon	C	PHD	86	Iowa	1986
Kolstad, Charles	Prof	Cal-Santa Br	QLD	PHD	82	Stanford	1992
Komagai, Tomomi	Asst	Wayne State	C	PHD	01	MIT	2001
Konan, Denise	Asst	Hawaii-Manoa		PHD	93	Colorado	1993
Kondeas, Alexander G.	Asst	Greensboro	EG	PHD	98	Auburn	1999
Kondonassis, Alexander J.	Prof	Oklahoma	NO	PHD	61	Indiana	1979
David Ross Boyd Professor of Economics							
Kong, Chang Min	Prof	Towson		PHD	77	Wi-Milwa	1978
Konishi, Hideo	Assoc	Boston Coll	DHL	PHD	94	Rochester	1999
Konow, James D.	Assoc	Loyola Marym	ACD	PHD	93	UCLA	1989
Konya, Istvan	Asst	Boston Coll	FJ	PHD	01	Nrthwstrn	2001
Konyar, Kazim	Assoc	CS-San Bern	CQ	PHD	85	Ca-Rivers	1991
Konz, Jeffery M.	Asst	N Car-Ashvil	BEFO	PHD	94	N Carol	1996

Konzelmann, Suzanne	Assoc	Ind-So Bend	ADJ	PHD	91	Notre Dm	1989
Koo, Anthony Y.	VProf	Florida St	F	PHD	46	Harvard	
Kool, Krishna L.	Prof	Rio Grande		PHD	76	Tennessee	1970
Koont, Sinan	C-As	Dickinson Cl	CFE	PHD	87	Mass	1986
Kooros, Syrous	Prof	Nicholls St	EFOC	PHD	80	Rensselaer	1991
Kopecky, Helen Pauline	Retir	Oklahoma St		PHD	72	Houston	1973
Koppl, Roger	Assoc	F Dick-Madis	BEG	PHD	88	Auburn	1988
Koray, Faik A.	Prof	Louisiana St	EF	PHD	84	Duke	1984
Korbach, Robert J.	Retir	North Dakota	AGH	PHD	73	Maryland	1970
Kordsmeier, William F.	Assoc	Cen Arkansas		PHD	86	Tx A&M	
Kornai, Janos	Prof	Harvard		DSC	66	Hungaria	1986
Kornecki, Lucyna	Asst	Embry-Riddle		PHD	80	Krakow	
Kortum, Sam	Asst	Boston Univ	ELO	PHD	92	Yale	1991
Koscianski, Janet	Assoc	Shippensburg		PHD	90	S Illinois	1990
Kose, Ayham	Asst	Brandeis		PHD	97	Iowa	1997
Koshal, Rajindar K.	Prof	Ohio Univ	TACQ	PHD	68	Rochester	1970
Koski, Jennifer L.	Assoc	U Washington		PHD	91	Stanford	1991
Kosmopoulou, Georgia	Asst	Oklahoma	D	PHD	96	Illinois	1997
Kosobud, Richard F.	Prof	Ill-Chicago	D	PHD	63	Penn	1966
Koss, Joseph J.	Retir	Youngstown		EDD	87	Akron	1967
Koss, Patricia	Asst	Portland St	D	PHD	93	Simon Fr	1997
Kossoudji, Sherrie A.	Asst	Michigan		PHD	84	Michigan	1987
Kotcherlakota, V. V.	C-Pr	Neb-Kearney		PHD	77	India	1986
Kotlikoff, Laurence J.	C-Pr	Boston Univ	EH	PHD	77	Harvard	
Kotz, David M.	Prof	Massachusett		PHD	75	Berkeley	
Kourtellos, Andros	Asst	Virg Tech	CEO	PHD	01	Wisconsin	2001
Kovalenkov, Alexander	Asst	No Carolina	D	PHD	98	Automoma	1998
Kovenock, Dan J.	Prof	Purdue		PHD	83	Wisconsin	1983
Kowal, Lubomyr M.	Retir	Mich-Flint		PHD	65	Illinois	1966
Kowalsky, Stan	Inst	Tenn-Martin		MA	61	Rutgers	8-01
Koymen, Oya	Prof	Bogazici	NQ	PHD	67	Strathcl	1976
Koziara, Edward C.	Prof	Drexel		PHD	65	Wisconsin	1966
Kozlov, Nicholas N.	Assoc	Hofstra	P	PHD	88	NewHamp	
Kozmetsky, George	Retir	Texas	O	PHD	57	Harvard	9-66
Kpakol, Mahnus L.	VAsst	Dallas	CFJO	PHD	88	Tx-Dallas	2000
Kraft, John L.	Dean	Florida		PHD	71	Pittsburgh	1990
Kraft, Kenneth	Dean	So Conn St		DBA	82	Maryland	1999
Krall, Mary Elyse	Assoc	SUNY-Cortlan	AIJQ	PHD	89	Utah	8-90
Kramer, Melvin L.	Retir	Wartburg		PHD	66	Iowa	1956
Kranich, Laurence J.	Asst	SUNY-Albany	DH	PHD	89	Rochester	1998
Kranton, Rachel E.	Asst	Maryland		PHD	93	Berkeley	1993
Krasa, Stefan	Prof	Illinois	DG	PHD	87	Vienna	1990
Kraus, James A.	Asst	CUNY-Lehman		JD		Columbia	
Kraus, Marvin C.	Prof	Boston Coll	DR	PHD	73	Minnesota	1972
Krause, Kate	Asst	New Mexico	HK	PHD	96	Wisconsin	1996
Krautkraemer, Jeffrey A.	Prof	Wash State		PHD	82	Stanford	1981
Krautmann, Anthony C.	Prof	DePaul	DL	PHD	85	Iowa	1985
Krebs, Tom	Asst	Brown		PHD	95	Columbia	1999
Kreider, Brent	Asst	Iowa State	J	PHD	94	Wisconsin	2001
Kreinin, Mordechai E.	Prof	Michigan St		PHD	54	Michigan	1959
University Distinguished Professor							
Kreitzer, Joseph L.	Prof	St Thomas-MN	C	PHD	83	Iowa	1981
Kremer, Michael R.	Prof	Harvard	E	PHD	92	Harvard	1985
Kresl, Peter K.	Prof	Bucknell	FO	PHD	70	Tx-Austin	1969
Kressler, Peter	C-Pr	Rowan Col-NJ		PHD	68	Penn	1972
Kreutzer, David W.	Assoc	Jms Madison	FH	PHD	84	GeoMason	1984
Kridel, Donald	Assoc	Mo-St Louis	CD	PHD	87	Arizona	1993
Krieger, Stefan	Asst	Yale	E	PHD	99	Chicago	1997
Krienke, Albert B.	Prof	Midwest St	DP	PHD	67	Tx A&M	1965
Krier, Donald F.	Prof	Framingham		PHD	69	Boston C	1973
Krinsky, Itzhak	Prof	McMaster U	G	PHD	83	McMaster	1982
Krishna, Kala	Prof	Penn State	F	PHD	84	Princeton	1993
Krishna, Pravin	Asst	Brown		PHD	95	Columbia	1995
Krishna, Vijay	Prof	Penn State	D	PHD	83	Princeton	1993
Krishnan, V. N.	Retir	Bowling Gr		PHD	68	Mich St	1965
Krislov, Joseph	Retir	Kentucky	JN	PHD	54	Wisconsin	1954
Kroch, Eugene A.	Assoc	Villanova		PHD	78	Harvard	1991
Krohn, Gregory A.	Assoc	Bucknell	EGA	PHD	85	Wisconsin	1983
Krol, Robert	Prof	CS-Northrdge	FGT	PHD	82	S Illinois	1983
Kroll, Stephen	Asst	St Lawrence	QC	PHD	99	Wyoming	1999
Krouse, Clement G.	Prof	Cal-Santa Br	D	PHD	69	UCLA	1979
Krueger, Alan B.	Prof	Princeton	JH	PHD	87	Harvard	6-87
Krueger, Anne O.	Prof	Stanford		PHD	58	Wisconsin	
Herald L. and Caroline L. Reitch Professor in Humanities and Sciences							
Krueger, Dirk	Asst	Stanford		PHD	99	Minnesota	1999
Krueger, Gary J.	Assoc	Macalester	ACP	PHD	89	Wisconsin	1989
Kruse, Jamie I.	Assoc	Texas Tech		PHD	88	Arizona	1996
Krusell, Per	Prof	Rochester	O	PHD	92	Minnesota	1994
Kuan, Chen I.	Retir	SUNY-Albany	OF	PHD		Berkeley	
Kubik, Jeff	Asst	Syracuse	HJ	PHD	97	MIT	1997

Kubler, Felix	Asst	Stanford		PHD	99	Yale	1999
Kudek, James F.	Assoc	Lakeland	ABCD	MBA		Wi-Milwa	1982
Kuenne, Robert E.	Retir	Princeton	6-97	PHD	53	Harvard	1969
Kuersteiner, Guido	Asst	MIT	E	PHD	92	Princeton	1997
Kuester, Dan	VAsst	Arkansas		PHD	00	Missouri	2000
Kuforiji, John	Asst	Albany State	J	PHD	87	Pittsburgh	8-00
Kugler, Penny L.	Inst	Cen Missouri		MA	88	Cen Mo St	1988
Kuhn, Kai-uwe	Assoc	Michigan					
Kuhn, Stephen D.	Assoc	Wash & Jeff		MACC	91	Bowl Gr	
Kulkarni, Kishore G.	Prof	Metro St-CO	AEF	PHD	82	Pittsburgh	1989
Kumar, Vikram	Assoc	Davidson	E	PHD	87	Vanderbilt	1986
Kumbhakar, Subal C.	Prof	SUNY-Bingham	C	PHD	86	S Calif	2001
Kumhof, Michael	Asst	Stanford					
Kuntz, Dale F.	Prof	Bentley	AEO	PHD	79	Conn	1975
Kuperberg, Mark J.	C-Pr	Swarthmore	EK	PHD	81	MIT	1977
Kupilik, Michael H.	Assoc	Montana	PHBN	PHD	76	Colorado	1976
Kuran, Timur	Prof	So Calif		PHD	82	Stanford	1982
Kurban, Haydar	Asst	Howard	R	PHD	99	Il-Chicago	2001
Kurre, James A.	Assoc	Penn St-Erie	RA	PHD	82	Penn St	1977
Kurth, Michael M.	Prof	McNeese St		PHD	82	Va Tech	1984
Kurz, Mordecai	Prof	Stanford		PHD	61	Yale	1966
Joan Kenney Professor of Economics							
Kushner, Joseph W.	Retir	Valdosta St	A	PHD	69	Tennessee	1969
Kushnirsky, Fyodor I.	Prof	Temple	P	PHD	68	Moscow	1980
Kutan, Ali M.	Prof	S Ill-Edward	EFG	PHD	90	Ariz St	1991
Kutasovic, Paul R.	Assoc	NY Inst Tech		PHD	83	Rutgers	1988
Kutsoati, Edward	Asst	Tufts	G	PHD	98	Queens	1998
Kuznets, Paul W.	Retir	Indiana		PHD	64	Yale	1964
Kwack, Sung Y.	Prof	Howard	E	PHD	68	Berkeley	
Kwak, Young-sik	Assoc	Delaware St		PHD	94	Miss	1993
Kwan, Clarence C. Y.	Prof	McMaster U	CG	PHD	79	Toronto	1979
Kwoka, John E. Jr.	Prof	George Wash	L	PHD	72	Penn	1981
Kwon, Jene K.	Prof	No Illinois	E	PHD	68	Iowa	1968
Kydland, Finn	Prof	Carnegie Mel		PHD	73	Car Mellon	1977
Kyer, Ben L.	Prof	Fran Marion		PHD	84	W Virginia	
Kyereme, Stephen	Assoc	So Carol St		PHD	84	Cornell	1984
Kyle, James T.	Retir	Indiana St	J	ABD	63	Indiana	1963
Kyle, Reuben	Prof	Mid Tenn St	L	PHD	72	Tennessee	1972
Kymn, Kern O.	Prof	W Virginia	EC	PHD	64	Chicago	1976
Kyn, Oldrich	Prof	Boston Univ	CEP	PHD		Charles	1971
Kynski, Kathy	Assoc	Kenyon	CDIJ	PHD	86	Wisconsin	7-86
Himmelright Associate Professor of Economics							
Kypralos, Harry N.	Assoc	Rollins		PHD	87	Virginia	1983
La Croix, Sumner J.	C-Pr	Hawaii-Manoa		PHD	81	U Wash	1981
La Near, Richard E.	Prof	Missouri So	ADGN	PHD	79	Miss	1987
Dr. J. R. Kuhn Chair in Finance							
La Point, James	Asst	La-Lafayette					
La Tourette, John E.	Retir	No Illinois	E	PHD	62	Rutgers	1979
Labadie, Pamela A.	Prof	George Wash	E	PHD	84	Chicago	1996
Labys, Walter C.	Prof	W Virginia	Q	PHD	68	Nottinghm	1975
Lachman, Teddy	Assoc	CUNY-Brookly		MBA	74	CUNY	1980
LaCivita, Charles J.	Prof	Naval Postgr	DM	PHD	81	Ca-SnBarb	1985
Lackey, Charles W. Jr.	Assoc	Tx-Brownsvil	AFL	PHD	84	S Carol	1995
Lacombe, Donald J.	Asst	Ohio Univ		PHD	00	Fla St	2001
Lacy, Allen W.	Emer	Auburn-Montg	ETIH	PHD	71	Iowa St	1976
Ladd, George W.	Retir	Iowa State	1994	PHD	55	Illinois	1955
Lady, George	Assoc	Temple	CD	PHD	67	J Hopkins	1981
Laffont, Jean-Jacques	Prof	So Calif		PHD	75	Harvard	2001
Lage, Gerald M.	Prof	Oklahoma St	FD	PHD	67	Minnesota	1966
Regents Service Professor; Associate Dean for Graduate Studies & Research							
Lages, John David	Deces	SW Missouri		PHD	67	Iowa St	1963
Lagos, Ricardo	Asst	New York U	J	PHD	97	Penn	2000
Lagunoff, Roger D.	Assoc	Georgetown	DLH	PHD	89	Minnesota	1996
Lahiri, Amartya	Asst	UCLA		PHD	95	Maryland	
Lahiri, Kajal	Prof	SUNY-Albany	E	PHD	75	Rochester	1977
Lahiri, Supriya	Assoc	Mass-Lowell	CQ	PHD	75	Delhi	
Lai, Kon Sun	Prof	CS-L Angeles		PHD	87	Penn	1987
Lai, T. H.	Assoc	Liberty	AEFG	PHD	84	Ohio St	9-85
Laibman, David	Prof	CUNY-Brookly	AP	PHD	73	New Sch	1967
Laibson, David	Asst	Harvard	DE	PHD	94	MIT	7-94
Laing, Derek	Assoc	Penn State	E	PHD	89	Essex	1989
Laird, William E.	Retir	Florida St	6-97	PHD	62	Virginia	1960
Laitner, John	Prof	Michigan		PHD	76	Harvard	1975
Lakew, Melaku	Assoc	R Stockton		PHD	81	Ca-Rivers	1982
Lal, Anil K.	Asst	Pittsburg St	A	PHD	95	Wash St	
Lal, Deepak	Prof	UCLA		PHD	65	Oxford	
Lam, David A.	Prof	Michigan		PHD	83	Berkeley	1983
Lam, Pok-sang	Assoc	Ohio State	E	PHD	86	Harvard	1985
Lam, Ricky	Asst	Northwestern		PHD	00	Yale	2000
Lambertini, Luisa	Asst	UCLA		PHD	95	Berkeley	

Lamberton, Charles E.	Prof	So Dakota St	G	PHD	75	Iowa St	1974
Lambson, Val E.	Prof	Brigham Yg	L	PHD	83	Rochester	1989
Lamdin, Douglas J.	Asst	MD-Baltim Co		PHD	91	Maryland	1989
Lamoreaux, Naomi	Prof	UCLA		PHD	79	J Hopkins	
Lamphear, F. Charles	Prof	Nebraska	OR	PHD	67	Kansas St	1966
Lamson, George H.	Prof	Carleton	EF	PHD	71	Nrthwstrn	1969
Wadsworth W. Williams Professor of Economics							
Lancaster, Anthony	C-Pr	Brown		PHD	64	Cambridge	1986
Herbert H. Goldberger Professor of Economics							
Lancaster, Kelvin	Deces	Columbia	B	PHD	58	London	1966
Landau, Daniel L.	Assoc	Connecticut	O	PHD	74	Chicago	1981
Landis, Brook I.	Assoc	York-Penn		PHD	74	Cornell	
Landon-Lane, John	Asst	Rutgers-N Br	C	PHD	98	Minnesota	2001
Landsburg, Steven E.	Assoc	Rochester		PHD	79	Chicago	
Lane, Julia I.	Prof	American U		PHD	82	Missouri	1990
Lane, Philip J.	C-Ac	Fairfield	EGR	PHD	83	Tufts	1981
Lane, Walter J.	C-Ac	New Orleans		PHD	78	Ca-SnDgo	1986
Lang, Kevin	Prof	Boston Univ	JC	PHD	82	MIT	1987
Lang, Nancy A.	C-Ac	No Kentucky		EDD	83	Georgia	1983
Lang, Steven D.	Assoc	Randolph-Mac	ECR	PHD	90	Pittsburgh	1987
Langan, Terence G.	C-Acc	St Thomas-MN	L	PHD	88	Minnesota	
Langbert, Mitchell	Asst	CUNY-Brookly		PHD	91	Columbia	1998
Lange, Ralph W.	Retir	SE Louisiana	AF	PHD	74	LSU	
Langer, Gary F.	D-Ac	Roosevelt		PHD	80	Ca-Rivers	1983
Langlois, Richard N.	Prof	Connecticut	B	PHD	81	Stanford	1983
Langston, Vicky	Assoc	Austin Peay	RM	PHD	83	Tx-Austin	1997
Lanjouw, Jean Olson	Assoc	Yale	CO	PHD	92	LondonEc	
Lankford, R. Hamilton	Assoc	SUNY-Albany	HD	PHD	81	N Carol	1981
Lanzillotti, Robert F.	Retir	Florida	T	PHD	53	Berkeley	1969
Laopodis, Nikiforos T.	Asst	Villa Julie	CFOG	PHD	91	Catholic	1994
f-laopod@mail.vjc.edu							
Lapan, Harvey E.	Prof	Iowa State	DF	PHD	71	MIT	1972
Lapidus, June	Assoc	Roosevelt		PHD	88	Mass	1990
LaPorta, Rafael	Asst	Harvard		PHD	94	Harvard	
Lapp, John S.	Prof	N Carol St	EGF	PHD	74	Princeton	1974
Laramie, Anthony J.	C-Pr	Merrimack		PHD	86	Clark	
Lardard, Leonard P.	Prof	Rhode Island	CE	PHD	79	Indiana	1981
Larkin, L. Andrew	Prof	St Cloud St		PHD	82	Nebraska	1982
LaRoe, Ross M.	C-Ac	Denison	AHQ	PHD	82	American	1985
Larson, Bruce D.	C-Pr	N Car-Ashvil	ABCD	PHD	83	N Carol	1983
Larson, David A.	Retir	New Orleans		PHD	68	Maryland	
Larson, John C.	Prof	Loyola-Maryl	E	PHD	77	Minnesota	1974
Larson, Marvin L.	Retir	Missouri So		MA	84	Mo-StLou	1990
Larson, Tom Edward	Prof	CS-L Angeles		PHD	86	Berkeley	1987
Larudee, Mehrene	Asst	Kansas	F	ABD		Mass	1984
Lastrapes, William D.	Assoc	Georgia	CEF	PHD	86	N Carol	1990
Latanich, Gary A.	Assoc	Arkansas St	AREM	PHD	78	Nebraska	1981
Latham, William R. III	Assoc	Delaware	RC	PHD	73	Illinois	1971
Latif-Zaman, Nazma	Assoc	Providence	OFC	PHD		Northeas	
Latzko, David	Asst	Wilkes	BEFQ	PHD	92	Maryland	9-93
Lau, Lawrence J.	Prof	Stanford		PHD	69	Berkeley	1966
Kwoh-Ting Li Professor of Economic Development							
Lau, Man-Lui	Assoc	San Francisc	CD	PHD	86	Cornell	1992
Laughlin, William	Assoc	Fairmont St	AE	MA		Cincinnati	1966
Laumas, G. S.	Prof	So Illinois	EC	PHD	66	Wayne St	1990
Laumas, Prem S.	Retir	No Illinois	1995	PHD	65	Wayne St	1971
Laurence, Louise	Assoc	Towson		PHD	87	Maryland	1987
Laurent, Jerome K.	Prof	Wis-Whitewat		PHD	73	Indiana	1965
Laury, Susan K.	Asst	Georgia St	HC	PHD	96	Indiana	1999
Lave, Charles	Emer	Calif-Irvine		PHD	68	Stanford	1964
Lave, Lester B.	Prof	Carnegie Mel		PHD	63	Harvard	1963
Harry B. & James H. Higgins University Professor of Economics							
Lavine, Jeffrey A.	Asst	Pitts-Johnst		MA	68	Pittsburgh	1970
Law, Alton D.	C-Pr	W Maryland		PHD	68	Rutgers	1966
Lawarree, Jacques P.	Assoc	U Washington		PHD	90	Berkeley	1990
Lawber, Harold E. Jr.	Assoc	Salve Regina	ABEN	PHD	89	Conn	1988
Lawlor, Michael S.	Prof	Wake Forest		PHD	86	Iowa St	1986
Lawrence, William	Prof	NY Inst Tech		PHD	75	NYU	1971
Lawson, Catherine L.	C-Ac	Missouri Wes	A	PHD	88	Colorado	1995
Lawson, Luther Drew	C-Pr	N Car-Wilmin	AJL	PHD	81	Tennessee	
Lawson, Robert	Asst	Capital		PHD		Fla St	1996
Lawson, Robert L.	Retir	Ball State		PHD	67	Iowa	1963
Lawson, Stanley J.	Prof	St John's		PHD	73	NYU	1978
Layer, Robert	Emer	So Illinois		PHD	52	Harvard	1955
Layson, Steve	Assoc	N Car-Greens	D	PHD	83	Chicago	1978
Lazarcik, Gregor	Retir	CUNY-Brookly	O	PHD	60	Columbia	1985
Lazonick, William H.	Retir	Barnard		PHD		Harvard	1985
Leach, Elroy M.	Prof	Chicago St		PHD	85	Il-Chicago	1985
Leadley, John C.	Assoc	W Oregon St		PHD	85	Wisconsin	1991
Leahy, John V.	Assoc	Boston Univ	E	PHD	90	Princeton	1997

Leahy, William H.	Prof	Notre Dame	JR	PHD	66	Notre Dm	1963
Leake, Richard S.	Assoc	Luther		MBA	84	Wi-LaCros	1975
Leamer, Edward E.	Prof	UCLA		PHD	70	Michigan	1975
Leathers, Charles G.	Prof	Alabama		PHD	68	Oklahoma	1968
LeBaron, Blake	Prof	Brandeis		PHD	88	Chicago	1999
LeBel, Phillip	Prof	Montclair St	DOQH	PHD	77	Boston U	1981
Lebergott, Stanley	Emer	Wesleyan-CT	N	MA	39	Michigan	1962
University Professor							
Lebrenz, Eugene R.	Prof	Fla Southern	J	EDD		N Illinois	1987
LeClair, Mark S.	Assoc	Fairfield	FGC	PHD	87	Rutgers	1988
Ledyard, John O.	C-Pr	Cal Tech		PHD	67	Purdue	1985
Lee, Albert Yin-Po	Emer	CS-Stanislau		PHD	70	S Illinois	1970
Lee, Byung	Assoc	Howard	CDH	PHD	73	Catholic	8-73
Lee, Byung	Assoc	Notre Dame	CD	PHD	88	Wisconsin	1996
Lee, Christopher	Prof	St Ambrose		PHD	90	GeoMason	1995
Lee, Chung H.	Prof	Hawaii-Manoa		PHD	66	Berkeley	1980
Lee, Dae Sung	Dean	Miss Vall St	ADEC	PHD	69	Mass	1999
Lee, Daniel Y.	Prof	Shippensburg		PHD	86	Pittsburgh	1986
Lee, Donghoon	Asst	New York U	DE	PHD	01	Penn	2001
Lee, Dwight R.	Prof	Georgia	DHM	PHD	72	Ca-SnDgo	1985
Bernard B. & Eugenia A. Ramsey Professor							
Lee, Eric Y.	Retir	F Dick-Madis	F	PHD	73	Columbia	
Lee, Feng-Yao	Retir	Tennessee		PHD	65	Mich St	1965
Lee, Frederick S.	Prof	Mo-Kansas Ct	ADN	PHD		Rutgers	
Lee, Gerald R.	Prof	Miss College		PHD	73	Miss	1970
Lee, Hoyoung	Prof	Rochest Tech	ABDE	PHD	70	Maryland	1970
Lee, Hy Sang	Emer	Wis-Oshkosh	O	PHD	65	Wisconsin	1962
Lee, J. J.	Asst	Towson		PHD	00	Stanford	2000
Lee, Jae Won	Assoc	CUNY-Baruch		PHD	69	CUNY	1972
Lee, Jason	Assoc	McMaster U	G	PHD	91	Alberta	1990
Lee, Jim	Assoc	Tx A&M-C Chr	AO	PHD	91	Penn St	7-99
Lee, Jin Man	ResSp	Ill-Chicago	C	PHD	00	Il-Chicago	2000
Lee, Joe W.	Retir	Howard		DBA		Indiana	
Lee, John T.	C-Pr	Mid Tenn St		PHD	77	Georgia	1984
Lee, Joseph S.	Retir	Mankato St	JK	PHD	70	Mass	1970
Lee, Junsoo	Asst	Cen Florida	E	PHD	91	Mich St	1998
Lee, Kangoh	Assoc	Towson		PHD	87	Illinois	1990
Lee, Kie Bok	Retir	Skidmore		PHD	67	Virginia	1963
Lee, Li Way	Prof	Wayne State	L	PHD	76	Columbia	1981
Lee, Lung-fei	Prof	Ohio State	C	PHD	77	Rochester	1999
University Chaired Professor							
Lee, Maw Lin	Retir	Missouri	C	PHD	61	Wisconsin	1968
Lee, Raymond	Prof	Benedict Col		PHD	95	Cincinnati	1998
Lee, Ronald D.	Prof	Cal-Berkeley		PHD	71	Harvard	1979
Lee, Sang H.	Asst	SE Louisiana	E	PHD	99	Florida	
Lee, Seung-Dong	Prof	Alabama-Birm	CDFQ	PHD	79	So Meth	1979
Lee, Soyon	Prof	Benedictn-IL	GO	PHD	77	N Illinois	1974
Lee, Susan		Florida St		PHD	00	Wisconsin	2000
Lee, Tae-Hwy	Assoc	Cal-Riversid	ACG	PHD	90	Ca-SnDgo	1995
Lee, Tenpao	Prof	Niagara		PHD	84	Iowa St	1987
Lee, Tong Hun	Emer	Wis-Milwauke		PHD	61	Wisconsin	1967
Lee, Wei Pang	Assoc	Worcester St		PHD	87	Georgia	
Lee, William C.	Prof	St Marys-Cal		PHD	77	Ca-SnBarb	1982
Lee, Woo Bong	Prof	Bloomsburg		PHD	72	Rutgers	1977
Lee, Woojin	Asst	No Illinois	H	PHD	98	Ca-Davis	2001
Leeds, Eva Masikeva	Asst	Moravian	BFP	PHD	83	Princeton	1999
Leeds, Michael A.	Assoc	Temple	J	PHD	82	Princeton	1982
Leekley, Robert M.	Assoc	Ill Wesleyan	H	PHD	74	Mich St	1974
Leeper, Eric M.	Assoc	Indiana		PHD	89	Minnesota	1995
Lees, Francis A.	Prof	St John's		PHD	61	NYU	1961
Leet, Don R.	Prof	CS-Fresno	TNA	PHD	72	Penn	1969
Leeth, John D.	Prof	Bentley	GCJ	PHD	83	N Carol	1987
Leffler, Keith B.	Assoc	U Washington		PHD	77	UCLA	1978
Lefgren, Lars	Asst	Brigham Yg		PHD	01	Chicago	2001
Leftwich, Howard M.	Prof	Cincinnati	J	PHD	65	Illinois	1964
Lehman, Dale E.	Assoc	Fort Lewis		PHD	81	Rochester	1983
Lehmann, Michael B.	Prof	San Francisc	NB	PHD	69	Cornell	1966
Lehr, Carol A.	Asst	Virg Comm		PHD	91	Penn St	1997
Lehrer, Evelyn L.	Prof	Ill-Chicago	T	PHD	78	Nrthwstrn	1980
Lei, Vivian	Asst	Wis-Milwauke		PHD	00	Purdue	2000
Leigh, Duane E.	C-Pr	Wash State		PHD	69	Mich St	1968
Leightner, Jonathan E.	Assoc	Augusta	DTOP	PHD	89	N Carol	1989
Leighton, Linda S.	Assoc	Fordham		PHD	78	Columbia	1979
Leighton, Richard I.	Assoc	SUNY-Bingham	F	PHD	61	Duke	1964
Leijonhufvud, Axel S. B.	Emer	UCLA		PHD	87	Nrthwstrn	
Leitner, Keith R.	Retir	Wis-Eau Clar	AMQ	PHD	74	Kansas St	1974
Lejaunie, John	Assoc	Nicholls St	FG	PHD	92	N Orleans	1991
Lemke, Robert J.	Asst	Fla Internat	DJ	PHD	97	Wisconsin	1997
Lemon, Gary D.	Prof	DePauw		PHD	82	Kansas	1976
Lengan, Patrick	Asst	Wartburg		PHD	97	Iowa	2000

Lenihan, Patrick M.	Retir	E Illinois		PHD	68	Wisconsin	1967
Lennson, Arik M.	Assoc	Georgetown	HQ	PHD	93	Columbia	2000
Lenon, Mary Jane	Asst	Providence	REI	PHD	89	Conn	1986
Leon, Jean-Claude	Asst	Catholic		PHD	87	Geo Wash	1987
Leonard, Frederick H.	Prof	Smith	AEG	PHD	66	Michigan	1966
Leonard, John	Asst	SE Louisiana		PHD	81	Ca-SnBarb	
Leonard, Kenneth	Asst	Columbia	9D	PHD	97	Berkeley	1997
Leonard, William J.	Retir	St Joseph		MA	69	Notre Dm	1957
Leontief, Wassily W.	Retir	New York U		PHD	28	Berlin	
LePage, James	Assoc	Lincoln-MO		PHD		Kansas	1984
Leppel, Karen	Assoc	Widener	JCT	PHD	80	Princeton	1985
Lerman, Robert I.	Prof	American U		PHD	70	MIT	1989
LeRoy, Stephen F.	Prof	Cal-Santa Br	GE	PHD	71	Penn	1997
Lerrick, Adam	SrLec	Carnegie Mel		PHD	81	MIT	
Friends of Allan H. Meltzer Chair							
Lesage, James P.	Prof	Toledo	RC	PHD	83	Boston C	1988
Lesser, Mary H.	Assoc	Iona	FG	PHD	82	Fordham	1982
Lester, Bijou	Assoc	Drexel		PHD	81	Penn	1988
Leube, Kurt R.	Prof	CS-Hayward	DBHK	DLE	71	Salzburg	1985
Leung, Cho Kin	Dean$	Wm Paterson		PHD	68	NYU	1974
Leuthold, Jane H.	Retir	Illinois	HO	PHD	68	Wisconsin	1967
Leveen, Serpil S.	C-Pr	Montclair St	ADEG	PHD	73	NYU	1974
Leven, Bozen	Assoc	C New Jersey		PHD	91	Cornell	
Leven, Charles L.	Emer	Wash Univ	IR	PHD	58	Nrthwstrn	1964
Levenson, Albert M.	Emer	CUNY-Queens	DFC	PHD	59	Columbia	1961
Levenstein, Margaret C.	Asst	Massachusett		PHD	91	Yale	2000
Lever, Jacqueline	Assoc	Albright		PHD	82	Pittsburgh	1990
Levernier, William B.	Assoc	Geo Southern		PHD	88	W Virginia	1989
Levin, Dan	Prof	Ohio State	MI	PHD	82	MIT	1995
Levin, Jay H.	C-Pr	Wayne State	F	PHD	68	Michigan	1976
Levin, Jonathan	Asst	Stanford		PHD	99	MIT	1999
Levin, Richard C.	Prof	Yale	O	PHD	74	Yale	1974
Levin, Sharon G.	Prof	Mo-St Louis	DJ	PHD	73	Michigan	1974
Levin, Stanford L.	Prof	S Ill-Edward	DL	PHD	74	Michigan	1972
Levine, Aaron	C-Pr	Yeshiva		PHD	81	NYU	
Samson and Halina Bitensky Professor of Economics							
Levine, David K.	Prof	UCLA		PHD	81	MIT	1981
Levine, Herbert S.	Prof	Pennsylvania	P	PHD	61	Harvard	1960
Levine, Philip	Assoc	Wellesley	JD	PHD	91	Princeton	1991
Levinsohn, James A.	Assoc	Michigan		PHD	88	Princeton	1987
Levinson, Marshall M.	Retir	Duquesne		MA	50	Columbia	1966
Levitt, Steven D.	Prof	Chicago		PHD	94	MIT	1997
Levy, Armando	Asst	N Carol St	C	PHD	96	Berkeley	1996
Levy, Daniel	Assoc	Emory	EC	PHD	90	Ca-Irvine	1992
Levy, David M.	Assoc	George Mason		PHD	79	Chicago	1983
Levy, David T.	Prof	Baltimore		PHD		N Carol	
Levy, Lester S.	Retir	No Illinois	N	PHD	56	Cornell	1964
Levy, Philip I.	Asst	Yale	DF	PHD	94	Stanford	
Lewbel, Arthur	Prof	Boston Coll	CD	PHD	84	MIT	1998
Lewer, Joshua J.	Asst	West Txs St	EHN	PHD	00	Nebraska	2000
Lewis, Carl	Retir	Neb-Kearney		PHD		Nebraska	1969
Lewis, David P.	Retir	Alabama-Birm	CER	PHD	68	Tennessee	1969
Lewis, Eddie Miley Jr.	Prof	So Miss	F	DBA	74	Miss St	1970
Lewis, J. Patrick	Retir	Otterbein	FO	PHD	74	Ohio St	1974
Lewis, Kenneth A.	Prof	Delaware	CE	PHD	69	Princeton	1973
Lewis, Lynne	Assoc	Bates		PHD	94	Colorado	2000
Lewis, Margaret	Assoc	St Benedict	CBJL	PHD	89	Maryland	1989
Lewis, Stephen D.	C-Pr	Sonoma State	CD	PHD	69	Ca-SnBarb	1983
Lewis, Stephen R. Jr.	Prof	Carleton	FO	PHD	63	Stanford	1987
Lewis, Tracy R.	Prof	Florida	TDQ	PHD	75	Ca-SnDgo	1991
James Walter Eminent Scholar in Economics							
Lewis, W. Cris	Prof	Utah State	MCR	PHD	69	Iowa St	1972
Ley, Robert D.	C-Pr	Bemidji St		PHD	77	Wash St	1977
Leyden, Dennis P.	Assoc	N Car-Greens	H	PHD	87	Car Mellon	1984
Li, Dong	Asst	East Carol	CDG	PHD	98	Tx A&M	1999
Li, Haizheng C.	Asst	Georgia Tech	C	PHD	97	Colorado	1997
Li, Hao	Asst	Toronto	DC	PHD	95	Chicago	1999
Li, Jenny	Asst	Penn State	C	PHD	93	Cornell	1997
Li, Judith	Asst	Harvard		PHD		Harvard	
Li, Ling	Asst	Towson		PHD	94	Pittsburgh	1994
Li, Qi	Prof	Texas A&M	C	PHD	91	Tx A&M	1999
Li, Qing	Asst	Wichita St		PHD	95	Houston	1995
Li, Tien En	Retir	Delaware St		PHD		Tx A&M	
Li, Tong	Asst	Indiana		PHD	93	Ca-SnDgo	1999
Li, Victor	Asst	USN Academy	E	PHD	85	Nrthwstrn	
Liang, Lan	Asst	Ill-Chicago	I	PHD	96	Duke	1999
Liaw, K. Thomas	C-Pr	St John's		PHD	88	Nrthwstrn	9-88
Libecap, Gary D.	Prof	Arizona		PHD	76	Penn	1984
Liberatore, Anthony F.	Assoc	Millikin		PHD	78	Conn	1984

Lichtenberg, Frank R.	Prof	Columbia		PHD	82	Penn	1983
Courtney C. Brown Professor of Business							
Lichtenstein, Larry	Assoc	Canisius	DRH	PHD	81	SUNY-Bin	1981
Lichtenstein, Peter M.	Prof	Boise State	PEF	PHD	74	Colorado	1975
Lichty, Richard W.	Prof	Minn-Duluth	R	PHD	71	Kansas St	1971
Lidman, Russell M.	Retir	Evergreen St		PHD	72	Wisconsin	1974
Lieberman, Sima	Retir	Utah		PHD	67	Berkeley	1967
Liechty, Elden E.	Retir	Weber State		PHD	72	Utah	1972
Liedholm, Carl E.	Prof	Michigan St		PHD	65	Michigan	1967
Lien, Da-Hsiang D.	Prof	Tx-S Antonio	O	PHD	86	Cal Tech	2001
Liew, Chong K.	Deces	Oklahoma		PHD	68	Berkeley	1969
Liggett, Ron	Lect	Tx-Arlington	R	MBA	89	Tx-Arlin	1989
Light, Audrey	Asst	Ohio State	J	PHD	87	UCLA	1995
Lile, Stephen E.	Prof	W Kentucky	H	PHD	72	Kentucky	1973
Liles, W. Pierce	Prof	So Carolina		PHD	72	S Carol	
Lilien, David M.	Prof	Calif-Irvine		PHD	77	MIT	1984
Lill, Lloyd		SUNY-Empire	BO	PHD	77	Walden	1973
Lillard, Lee	Prof	Michigan		PHD	72	N Car St	
Lilly, Gregory A.	C-Ac	Elon	CDA	PHD	88	Duke	1990
Lillydahl, Jane H.	Prof	Colorado		PHD	76	Duke	1976
Lim, Ralph	Assoc	Sacred Heart	GLM	MBA		Penn	1981
Lima, Anthony K.	Prof	CS-Hayward	CEGM	PHD	80	Stanford	1979
Lin, An-Yhi (Steven)	Retir	S Ill-Edward	CDFO	PHD	67	Iowa St	1968
Lin, Emily	Asst	Connecticut	HJ	PHD	98	Michigan	1998
Lin, Hwan-Chyang	Assoc	N Car-Charl		PHD	90	Illinois	1993
Lin, Kuan-Pin	Prof	Portland St	C	PHD	77	SUNY-SBr	1979
Lin, Lung-Ho	Deces	Akron	AE	PHD	74	Notre Dm	1978
Lin, Parsy	Asst	U Washington		PHD	00	UCLA	2000
Lin, Shuanglin	Assoc	Neb-Omaha	CDEO	PHD	89	Purdue	1989
Lin, Tin-Chun	Asst	SE Louisiana	E	PHD	01	Penn St	
Lindauer, David	Prof	Wellesley	OFD	PHD	79	Harvard	1981
Lindell, Lois A.	Inst	No Iowa		BA	80	Wi-White	1996
Lindeman, Bruce	Prof	Ark-Ltl Rock		PHD	68	Duke	1975
Lindert, Peter H.	Prof	Cal-Davis	FN	PHD	67	Cornell	1978
Lindgren, Jon G.	Retir	N Dakota St	ADH	PHD	68	Missouri	1968
Lindsay, Cotton M.	Prof	Clemson	DHJK	PHD	68	Virginia	1984
J. Wilson Newman Professor							
Lindsey, Debra A.	Assoc	Howard		PHD	83	Howard	
Linebarger, Laura	Visit	Utah		PHD	97	Utah	
Liner, Gaines Howard	Assoc	N Car-Charl		PHD	71	Clemson	1971
Link, Albert N.	Prof	N Car-Greens	O	PHD	76	Tulane	1982
Link, Charles R.	Prof	Delaware	J	PHD	71	Wisconsin	1701
Linsley, Colin A.	C-Acc	St John Fshr	N	PHD	86	Essex	1987
Linster, Bruce G.	Prof	USAF Academy		PHD	90	Michigan	1990
Linton, Oliver	Prof	Yale	C	PHD	91	Berkeley	
Linz, Susan	Prof	Michigan St		PHD	80	Illinois	1988
Liossatos, Panagis S.	C-Pr	Fla Internat	CODR	PHD	68	Penn	1981
Lipford, Jody W.	Assoc	Presbyterian	HEFI	PHD	90	Clemson	1991
Lipman, Barton L.	Prof	Wisconsin		PHD	85	Michigan	1998
Lipner, Kenneth	Assoc	Fla Internat	RJA	PHD	77	Rutgers	1981
Lippit, Victor D.	Prof	Cal-Riversid	AOP	PHD	71	Yale	1971
Lipsey, Robert E.	Emer	CUNY-Queens	FC	PHD	61	Columbia	1967
Liska, Terrence L.	Prof	Wis-Plattev		PHD	82	Wisconsin	1980
Litterst, Lawrence J.	Assoc	St Benedict	EGJ	PHD	81	N Illinois	1979
Little, Charles H.	Retir	St John's		PHD	65	Berkeley	
Little, Roger D.	Prof	USN Academy		PHD	70	Houston	1970
Litzinger, Patrick J.	Prof	Robt Morris		PHD	75	Pittsburgh	1977
Liu, Chao-Nan	Prof	C New Jersey		PHD	76	Tx A&M	
Liu, Jung-Chao	Deces	SUNY-Bingham		PHD	60	Michigan	1970
Liu, Ming	Assoc	Missouri	CG	PHD	96	Duke	2001
Liu, Tsung-Hua	Prof	East Wash		PHD	69	Toronto	1970
Liu, Tung	Assoc	Ball State	C	PHD	90	Ca-SnDgo	1990
Liu, Wen-Fang	Asst	U Washington		PHD	98	Chicago	1998
Liu, Yih-Wu	Prof	Youngstown		PHD	68	S Illinois	1968
Liu, Zhiqiany	Asst	SUNY-Buffalo	DECO	PHD	93	SUNY-Buf	2001
Liveson, Avi O.	Asst	CUNY-Hunter		LLM	75	NYU	9-86
Livingston, Marie L.	Prof	No Colorado	FHOQ	PHD	84	Colo St	1985
Lizzeri, Alessandro	Assoc	New York U	L	PHD	95	Nrthwstrn	2000
Lo, Melody	Asst	So Miss	F	PHD	01	Purdue	2001
Lo, Ming	Asst	Virginia	FE	PHD	00	U Wash	2000
Lobo, Isobel	Asst	Benedictn-IL	FAO	PHD	98	Notre Dm	2001
Locay, Luis	Assoc	U Miami	DJOT	PHD	83	Chicago	1989
Lochner, Lance	Asst	Rochester		PHD	98	Chicago	1998
Loeb, Peter D.	C-Pr	Rutgers-Newk		PHD	73	Rutgers	1973
Loewy, Michael	Assoc	South Fla	E	PHD	86	Minnesota	1998
Lofgreen, Harold A.	Prof	St Cloud St		PHD	72	Iowa	1972
Lofgren, Stephanie	Asst	USM Academy	DHF	PHD	96	Nrthwstrn	1995
Logan, Robert	Assoc	Alaska-Fairb		PHD	86	Iowa	1986
Lokhande, Vineeta	Asst	Southern	G	PHD	94	N Orleans	1994
Lombard, John	Prof	Eastern Conn		PHD	78	Conn	

Lombardi, Waldo J.	Prof	Lg Isl-Brook	ACD	PHD	70	Columbia	
Lombra, Raymond E.	Prof	Penn State	E	PHD	71	Penn St	1969
Londhe, Suresh R.	Prof	So Carol St		PHD	65	LSU	1969
Long, C. Richard	Retir	Georgia St	BE	PHD	68	Vanderbilt	1968
Long, Cheryl	Asst	Colgate	K	PHD	01	Wash U	2001
Long, James E.	H-Pr$	Auburn		PHD	74	Fla St	1974
Long, Neal B.	C-Pr	Stetson	ACP	PHD	64	Indiana	1974
Long, Stanley G.	Emer	Pitts-Johnst	D-95	PHD	69	Iowa	1973
Long, Stewart L.	Prof	CS-Fullerton	N	PHD	74	Illinois	1973
Long, Teresa M.	Prof	Marymount		PHD	80	Iowa St	1981
Loomis, David	Asst	Illinois St	OE	PHD	95	Temple	8-96
Looney, Lawrence J.	Assoc	Merrimack		MA		Boston C	
Looney, Robert	Prof	Naval Postgr	OF	PHD	69	Berkeley	1977
Lopus, Jane S.	Assoc	CS-Hayward	AEH	PHD	90	Ca-Davis	1979
Lord, William A.	Assoc	MD-Baltim Co		PHD	84	Indiana	1987
Loschky, David J.	Retir	Missouri	TN	PHD	62	Harvard	1967
Lotspeich, Richard	Assoc	Indiana St	PQ	PHD	86	New Mex	1990
Lott, Elizabeth J.	C-Ac	Pace	ACNR	PHD		Columbia	1990
Lott, William F.	Assoc	Connecticut	C	PHD	69	N Car St	1969
Loucks, Christine	Prof	Boise State	ELH	PHD	83	Wash St	1989
Loughlin, James C.	Prof	Central Conn	DH	PHD	65	Clark	1968
Louie, Kenneth K. T.	Assoc	Penn St-Erie	AFJ	PHD	87	Penn St	1984
Louisy-Louis, Valerie	Asst	CUNY-City C	MG	PHD	97	CUNY	
Loury, Glenn C.	Prof	Boston Univ	DJ	PHD	76	MIT	1991
Loury, Linda D.	Assoc	Tufts	J	PHD	78	MIT	1984
Love, Barry A.	C-Ac	Emory Henry		PHD	78	Virginia	1984

Holbert L. Harris Professorship in Free Enterprise

Love, Thomas M.	Prof	No Central	F	PHD	67	Wisconsin	1972
Lovejoy, Robert M.	Retir	SUNY-Bingham	E	PHD	63	Michigan	1965
Lovell, Hugh G.	Retir	Portland St		PHD	51	MIT	1964
Lovell, Knox	Prof	Georgia	D	PHD	66	Duke	1994

Herman & Mary Virginia Terry Professor

Lovell, Michael C.	Prof	Wesleyan-CT	E	PHD	59	Harvard	1969

Chester D. Hubbard Professor of Economics & Social Science

Lovely, Mary E.	Assoc	Syracuse	F	PHD	89	Michigan	1986
Loviscek, Anthony	Asst	Seton Hall		PHD	80	W Virginia	1992
Low, Stuart A.	Prof	Arizona St		PHD	79	Illinois	1979
Lowenberg, Tony	Prof	CS-Northrdge	GH	PHD	84	Simon Fr	1984
Lowinger, Thomas C.	Prof	Wash State		PHD	70	Mich St	1978
Lowry, Darryl W.	Assoc	Roanoke		PHD	72	Berkeley	1981
Lowry, George S.	Prof	Randolph-Mac	G	PHD	92	Va Comm	1984
Lowry, Stanley T.	Emer	Wash & Lee	BK	PHD	58	LSU	1959
Lozada, Gabriel A.	Assoc	Utah		PHD	87	Stanford	1993
Lu, Laura	Asst	Lg Isl-Post		PHD	89	SUNY-SBr	
Lu, Xiaohua	Asst	Kansas State	LDC	PHD	95	Tx-Austin	1997
Lubell, Alfred M.	Dean$	SUNY-Oneonta	ADF	PHD	74	NYU	1974
Lubik, Thomas	Asst	J Hopkins					
Lucas, Eruesto	Asst	Hawaii Pacif		PHD	69	Hi-Manoa	1993
Lucas, Henry A. Jr.	Assoc	Salem State		JD		Suffolk	
Lucas, Robert E. B.	Prof	Boston Univ	CFJO	PHD	72	MIT	1976
Lucas, Robert E. Jr.	D-Pr	Chicago		PHD	64	Chicago	1974

John Dewey Distinguished Service Professor; 1995 Nobel Prize

Lucas, Terry	Inst	Kennesaw St	AF	MS	69	USCG	1999
Lucchesi, Michael S.	Asst	USAF Academy		MA	86	U Wash	1993
Luce, Ducan	Emer	Calif-Irvine		PHD	50	MIT	1988
Lucier, Richard L.	Prof	Denison	ADF	PHD	72	Claremont	1971
Luckett, Dudley G.	Retir	Iowa State	EN	PHD	58	Tx-Austin	1957
Lucking-Reiley, David	Assoc	Arizona		PHD	96	MIT	2001
Lucy-Bouler, Tink	Inst	Auburn-Montg					
Ludema, Rodney	Asst	Georgetown	F	PHD	90	Columbia	1995
Ludolf, Gordon W.	Retir	East Tenn St		PHD	64	Ohio St	1961
Ludvigson, Sydney	Asst	New York U	E	PHD	96	Princeton	2001
Lueck, Dean L.	Assoc	Montana St		PHD	87	U Wash	1997
Luizer, James C.	Assoc	Kutztown	JC	PHD	84	Lehigh	1984
Luksetich, William A.	C-Pr	St Cloud St		PHD	73	N Illinois	1972
Lumsdaine, Robin	Prof	Brown		PHD	91	Harvard	
Lund, Mark	Prof	Luther		PHD	75	Iowa St	1978
Lund, Peter B.	Prof	CS-Sacrament		PHD	67	Berkeley	1970
Lundberg, Shelly J.	Prof	U Washington		PHD	81	Nrthwstrn	1984
Lunn, John E.	Prof	Hope	LD	PHD	80	UCLA	1992
Lunt, William E.	Assoc	Vassar	C	PHD	77	Stanford	1974
Luptowski, Thomas S.	Prof	Northwood		BS			
Lusardi, Annamaria	Assoc	Dartmouth		PHD	92	Princeton	1993
Lustgarten, Steven	Prof	CUNY-Baruch		PHD	71	UCLA	
Lutz, Mark A.	Prof	Maine	AB	PHD	72	Berkeley	1970
Lutz, Nancy A.	Assoc	Virg Tech	DLM	PHD	87	Stanford	1992
Lutzker, Adam	Asst	Mich-Flint	EB	PHD	99	Michigan	1999
Lwamugira, Pirudas L.	Assoc	Fitchburg St		PHD	90	Temple	1991
Lyall, Katharine C.	Prof	Wisconsin		PHD	69	Cornell	1982
Lybecker, Kristina	Asst	Drexel		PHD	00	Berkeley	2000

Lyell, Ed	Asst	Adams State		PHD		Colorado	
Lyman, R. Ashley	Assoc	Idaho	DC	PHD	72	Nrthwstrn	1976
Lynch, Allen K.	Asst	Mercer-Macon	FAC	PHD	99	Fla St	2000
Lynch, Gary	Prof	Indiana NW	RTE	PHD	70	Wash St	1981
Lynch, Gerald J.	Assoc	Purdue		PHD	75	Kentucky	1983
Lynch, James W.	Assoc	Robt Morris		MA	72	Pittsburgh	1974
Lynch, Lawrence K.	Emer	Transylvania		PHD	66	Kentucky	1979
Lynch, Vernon E. Jr.	Prof	Fort Lewis		PHD	76	Arizona	1972
Lynde, Catherine	Assoc	Mass-Boston	EIO	PHD	85	Ca-Davis	1983
Lynn, Billy	Assoc	St Ambrose		PHD	94	Illinois	1994
Lynn, Stuart R.	C-Ac	Assumption	DBFO	PHD	71	N Carol	1987
Lyon, Andrew B.	Assoc	Maryland		PHD	86	Princeton	1987
Lyon, Kenneth S.	Prof	Utah State	CDEQ	PHD	70	Chicago	1966
Lyon, Tom	Assoc	Indiana		PHD	89	Stanford	1989
Lyon, William R.	Asst	Wash & Jeff		MBA	89	Morehead	1988
Lyons, John S.	Asst	Miami U-Ohio	NO	PHD	77	Berkeley	1985
Lyons, Patrick A.	Prof	So Dakota St	M	JD	74	S Dakota	1975
Lyons, Thomas P.	Prof	Cornell		PHD	83	Cornell	1988
Ma, Barry K.	Asst	CUNY-Baruch		PHD	86	Stanford	1989
Ma, Ching-to Albert	Assoc	Boston Univ	DIL	PHD	88	LondonEc	1987
Ma, Jinpeng	Assoc	Rutgers-Camd		PHD	93	SUNY-SBr	
Maasoumi, Esfandiar	Prof	So Methodist	C	PHD	77	LondonEc	1976
Robert H. & Nancy Dedman Professor							
MacBeth, Thomas G.	Prof	Mass-Lowell	AC	PHD	62	S Calif	
Maccini, Louis J.	C-Pr	J Hopkins		PHD	70	Nrthwstrn	1969
MacDonald, John A.	Asst	Clarkson	GM	PHD	87	Va Tech	1995
MacDonald, Richard A.	Asst	St Cloud St		PHD	92	SUNY-Bin	1989
Macesich, George	Prof	Florida St	E	PHD	58	Chicago	1959
MacEwan, Arthur	Prof	Mass-Boston	FOI	PHD	69	Harvard	1975
Machin, Steve	VProf	MIT		PHD	98	Warwick	2001
Machina, Mark J.	Prof	Ca-San Diego	D	PHD	79	MIT	1979
Machlis, David	Assoc	Adelphi	E	PHD	71	Rutgers	1968
Machovec, Frank M.	Assoc	Wofford	EFP	PHD	86	NYU	1988
Mack, Richard Stanley	Prof	Central Wash	RQP	PHD	72	Colo St	1972
Distinguished Professor, Research (1988)							
Mackara, W. Frederick	Assoc	East Tenn St		PHD	76	Tx A&M	1975
Mackay, Bret P.	Asst	Brigham Yg	CG	PHD	99	U Wash	2001
Mackey, M. Cecil	Prof	Michigan St		PHD	55	Illinois	1980
Mackie-Mason, Jeffrey K.	Assoc	Michigan		PHD	86	MIT	1986
Maclachlan, Fiona C.	Assoc	Manhattan		PHD	91	NYU	1992
MacLeod, Bentley	Prof	So Calif		PHD	84	Brit Colum	1997
MacNeill, Alan	Assoc	Webster		PHD		Mass	1994
MacPhee, Craig R.	Prof	Nebraska	EF	PHD	70	Mich St	1969
Paul C. Burnmeister College Professor							
Macpherson, David A.	Prof	Florida St	J	PHD	87	Penn St	1992
MacPherson, Roderick S.	Assoc	Montevallo		DBA	77	Miss St	1977
MacRitchie, Donald R.	Assoc	Framingham		MA	85	Boston C	1987
Macunovich, Diane J.	Prof	Barnard	JT	PHD	89	S Calif	1999
MaCurdy, Thomas E.	Prof	Stanford		PHD	78	Chicago	1983
Madajewicz, Margaret	Asst	Columbia	BOM	PHD	99	Harvard	1999
Madan, Vibhas	C-Ac	Drexel		PHD	89	Mich St	1989
Maddala, G. S.	Retir	Ohio State		PHD	63	Chicago	1975
Madden, John L.	Retir	Kentucky	N	PHD	68	Kansas St	1968
Madden, Kirsten K.	Asst	Millersville		PHD	95	N Carol	1996
Maddox, D. Pat	Assoc	Angelo State	PI	PHD	82	Tx Tech	1988
Madhavan, Murugappa C.	Prof	San Diego St		PHD	60	Wisconsin	1968
Madresehee, Mehrdad	C-Ac	Lycoming	FKLR	PHD	85	Wash St	1986
Madsen, Ron	Prof	N Car-Charl					
Maeshiro, Asatoshi	Retir	Pittsburgh	C	PHD	65	Michigan	1979
Magaddino, Joseph P.	C-Pr	CS-Long Bch		PHD	72	Va Tech	1973
Magee, Chris	Asst	Bucknell	F	PHD	98	Wisconsin	9-01
Magenau, John M. III	D-Ac	Penn St-Erie	JM	PHD	88	SUNY-Buf	1985
Magenheim, Ellen B.	Assoc	Swarthmore	DI	PHD	86	Maryland	1986
Maggi, Giovanni		Princeton					
Maggs, Gary E.	Prof	St John Fshr	E	PHD	86	W Virginia	1986
Magill, Michael J. P.	Prof	So Calif		PHD	70	Brown	1979
Magura, Michael	Emer	Toledo	RL	PHD	72	Boston C	1969
Mahajan, Y. Lal	Assoc	Monmouth	CDEG	PHD	95	N Illinois	1979
Mahan, Gary P.	Assoc	Gannon		PHD	78	N Car St	1977
Mahdavi, Mahnaz	Assoc	Smith	FGM	PHD	86	Michigan	1985
Mahdavi, Saeid	Assoc	Tx-S Antonio	EFO	PHD	85	Ca-SnBarb	1984
Mahdi, Syed I.	C-Pr	Benedict Col		PHD	76	Mass	1975
Maher, William F. X.	Retir	St Peters		PHD	71	Boston C	1965
Mahoney, Timothy B.	Inst	So Indiana		MS	65	Illinois	1987
Mailath, George J.	Prof	Pennsylvania	CDH	PHD	85	Princeton	1985
Main, Robert S.	C-Pr	Butler	HQ	PHD	73	UCLA	1981
Maine, Robert	Asst	Bridgeport		PHD	78	Conn	1996
Majumdar, Mukul K.	Prof	Cornell		PHD	70	Berkeley	
H.T. & R.I. Warshow Professor of Economics							
Mak, James	Prof	Hawaii-Manoa		PHD	70	Purdue	1970

Makowski, Louis	Prof	Cal-Davis	DE	PHD	75	UCLA	1985
Malamud, Bernard	Prof	Nev-L Vegas	E	PHD	71	New Sch	1968
Malatesta, Paul H.	Prof	U Washington		PHD	81	Rochester	1980
Malenbaum, Wilfred	Retir	Pennsylvania		PHD	41	Harvard	1959
Maley, Jean E.	Prof	St John Fshr	D	PHD	72	Rochester	1968
Maley, Leonard A.	Assoc	Nazareth		MBA	62	Cincinnati	
Malhotra, Devinder	Prof	Akron	ADR	PHD	79	Kansas St	1979
Malik, Arun	Assoc	George Wash	Q	PHD	84	J Hopkins	1992
Malixi, Margaret M.	Prof	CS-Bakersf	ACFP	PHD	88	Wisconsin	1988
Malkiel, Burton G.	Prof	Princeton		PHD	64	Princeton	1966
Mallela, Parthasaradhi	Retir	No Illinois	C	PHD	70	Rochester	1976
Malliaris, Tassos	Prof	Loyola-Chicg	ACG	PHD	72	Oklahoma	1972
Malone, Laurence J.	C-Ac	Hartwick	ABFN	PHD	91	New Sch	1986
Maloney, Michael T.	Prof	Clemson	DGKL	PHD	78	LSU	1974
Maloney, Tom	Assoc	Utah		PHD	93	Michigan	1992
Maltsev, Yuri N.	Assoc	Carthage	DFJP	PHD	80	Inst Labor	1991
Malueg, David A.	Prof	Tulane		PHD	83	Nrthwstrn	1991
Mamalakis, Markos J.	Prof	Wis-Milwauke		PHD	62	Berkeley	1967
Mamgain, Vaishali	Asst	So Maine	CO	PHD	79	N Carol	1997
Mammen, Thampy	Retir	St Norbert		PHD	67	Penn	1968
Manage, Neela D.	Assoc	Fla Atlantic	FE	PHD	81	Geo Wash	1981
Mandelstamm, Allen B.	Emer	Virg Tech	A	PHD	62	Michigan	1974
Mandle, Jay R.	Prof	Colgate	ON	PHD	69	Penn	
W. Bradford Wiley Professor of Economics							
Mandy, David M.	Assoc	Missouri	CD	PHD	87	Illinois	1994
Manelli, Alejandro	Prof	Arizona St		PHD	88	Berkeley	1997
Maneschi, Andrea	Prof	Vanderbilt	FO	PHD	64	J Hopkins	1969
Mangiero, Susan M.	Asst	Sacred Heart	ACDG	PHD	97	Conn	1990
Mangum, Garth L.	Retir	Utah		PHD	60	Harvard	1969
Mangum, James M.	Retir	Louisiana Te		PHD	72	Okla St	1970
Manion, Thomas A.	Retir	St Norbert		PHD	74	Clark	1983
Mankiw, N. Gregory	Prof	Harvard		PHD	84	MIT	1985
Mann, Bruce D.	Prof	Puget Sound	ADJK	PHD	76	Indiana	1975
Mann, Patrick C.	Prof	W Virginia	DH	PHD	67	Indiana	1967
Mann, Prem S.	Assoc	Eastern Conn		PHD	88	UCLA	1986
Manning, Linda M.	Assoc	Mo-Rolla		PHD	90	Il-Chicago	1989
Mannur, Hanumant G.	Prof	W New Eng		PHD	72	Indiana	2001
Manove, Michael	Prof	Boston Univ	D	PHD	70	MIT	1975
Manrique, Gabriel G.	C-Pr	Winona State		PHD	82	Notre Dm	1989
Mansfield, Edwin	Prof	Pennsylvania		PHD	55	Duke	1963
Mansfield, Jon	Assoc	Georgia St	AM	PHD	92	Geo St	1996
Manski, Charles F.	Prof	Northwestern		PHD	73	MIT	1997
Board of Trustees Professor							
Mansori, Kashif	Asst	Colby	EF	PHD	97	Princeton	1997
Manuelli, Rodolfo	Prof	Wisconsin		PHD	86	Minnesota	1993
Manuszak, Mark	Asst	Carnegie Mel		PHD	00	Nrthwstrn	
Mao, Wen	Asst	Villanova		PHD	94	Va Tech	1995
Mapalad, Claret	Asst	Alfred		PHD	94	Ca-Rivers	7-99
Mar, Donald W.	Assoc	San Fran St		PHD	85	Berkeley	1987
Maran, Michael J.	Assoc	St John's		PHD	94	Penn	
Marburger, Daniel R.	Assoc	Arkansas St	AJMD	PHD	89	Ariz St	1989
Marcal, Leah	Asst	CS-Northrdge		PHD	96	Wisconsin	1996
Marcelli, Enrico	Asst	Mass-Boston	DH	PHD	96	S Calif	2000
Marcis, John G.	Assoc	Fran Marion		PHD		Missouri	
Marco, Alan	Asst	Vassar	KL	PHD	00	Berkeley	2000
Marcott, Craig S.	Assoc	St Thomas-MN	C	PHD	83	Purdue	1982
Marcouiller, Douglas	Assoc	Boston Coll	FO	PHD	94	Tx-Austin	1994
Marcus, Matityahu	Prof	Rutgers-N Br	G	PHD	63	Brown	1962
Marcus, Morton	Lect	Indiana		MA	63	Wash U	1973
Mardfin, Ward	Assoc	Hawaii Pacif		PHD	79	Hi-Manoa	1992
Mardis, Barbara K.	Inst	No Iowa	C	MBA	81	N Iowa	1981
Marett, Pamela	Asst	Embry-Riddle		PHD	82	Tennessee	
Marglin, Stephen A.	Prof	Harvard		PHD	65	Harvard	
Walter S. Barker Professor of Economics							
Margo, Robert A.	Prof	Vanderbilt	NJ	PHD	82	Harvard	1989
Margolis, H. Albert	Prof	Kutztown	NC	PHD	69	Purdue	1976
Margolis, Julius	Emer	Calif-Irvine		PHD	49	Harvard	1976
Margolis, Marvin S.	Prof	Millersville		PHD	69	Purdue	1981
Margolis, Stephen E.	H-Pr	N Carol St	LKD	PHD	78	UCLA	1982
Mariano, Roberto S.	Prof	Pennsylvania		PHD	70	Stanford	1971
Marion, Nancy P.	Prof	Dartmouth		PHD	77	Princeton	1976
Mark, Adolph E.	Emer	DePaul	A	PHD	63	Illinois	9-61
Mark, Nelson C.	Prof	Ohio State	FG	PHD	83	Chicago	1983
Market, Donald R.	Retir	Arkansas	E	PHD	67	LSU	1975
Markowtiz, Sara	Asst	Rutgers-Newk		PHD	98	CUNY	2000
Marks, Denton	Prof	Wis-Whitewat		PHD	81	Princeton	1990
Marks, Melanie B.	Assoc	Longwood		PHD	93	Tx A&M	1993
Marks, Peter A.	Assoc	Rhode Isl Cl		PHD	78	N Carol	
Markusen, James R.	Prof	Colorado		PHD	73	Boston C	1990
Marlin, Matthew R.	Assoc	Duquesne		PHD	81	Fla St	1987

Marlow, Michael L.	Prof	Cal Poly-SLO		PHD	78	Va Tech	1988
Marme, Christopher B.	Asst	Augustana IL	ACEO	PHD	94	Illinois	1988
Marmo, Michael	Prof	Xavier	J	PHD	71	Illinois	1970
Maroney, Neal C.	Asst	New Orleans		PHD	96	Claremont	1997
Marquis O.P., Fr. William	C-Ac	Providence	JEI	PHD	96	Ohio St	1998
Marquis, Milton H.	Prof	Florida St	E	PHD	85	Indiana	1986
Marschke, Gerald	Asst	SUNY-Albany	DJL	PHD	98	Chicago	1998
Marsh, Lawrence C.	Assoc	Notre Dame	CD	PHD	76	Mich St	1975
Marshall, James N.	Prof	Muhlenberg		PHD	82	Lehigh	1975
Marshall, Jennings B.	Prof	Samford	CD	PHD	77	Kentucky	1986
Marshall, John M.	Prof	Cal-Santa Br	A	PHD	69	MIT	1972
Marshall, Kathryn G.	Lect	Ohio State	HQ	PHD	90	Berkeley	
Marshall, Louise	Prof	Marymount		PHD	89	Maryland	1976
Marshall, Robert C.	H-Pr	Penn State		PHD	83	Ca-SnDgo	1995
Marshall, Robert H.	Emer	Arizona		PHD	57	Ohio St	1957
Martel, Arthur H.	Prof	Indiana U-PA	JK	PHD	74	Mass	1970
Martellaro, Joseph A.	Retir	No Illinois		PHD	62	Notre Dm	
Marthinsen, John E.	Prof	Babson	FD	PHD	74	Conn	1974
Martin, David A.	Prof	Albright		DA	80	Lehigh	1983
Martin, David A.	Retir	SUNY-Geneseo	BA	PHD	64	Syracuse	1966
Martin, David W.	Prof	Davidson	GQ	PHD	84	Illinois	1984
Martin, Dolores	Dean	Seton Hall		PHD	76	Va Tech	
Martin, Lawrence W.	Prof	Michigan St		PHD	81	Maryland	1982
Martin, Linda R.	Dean	New Haven		PHD	81	S Carol	8-95
Martin, Randolph C.	Prof	So Carolina		PHD	71	Wash U	1970
Martin, Richard S.	Retir	Hartford		PHD		Cornell	1968
Martin, Robert E.	Prof	Centre	CD	PHD	79	So Meth	1996
Ewing T. Boles Professor of Economics							
Martin, Thomas L.	Assoc	Cen Florida	B	PHD	81	Rice	1983
Martinez, John	Prof	Midwest St	ABCO	PHD	84	Oklahoma	1997
Martinez, Jorge L.	Prof	Georgia St	DF	PHD	78	Wash U	1977
Martins, Carlos	Assoc	Oregon State	DCL	PHD	92	Tennessee	9-92
Marty, Alvin L.	Prof	CUNY-Baruch		PHD	55	Berkeley	1960
Marvasti, Akbar B.	Assoc	Houston-Down		PHD	85	LSU	1990
Marvel, Howard P.	Prof	Ohio State	L	PHD	75	Chicago	1973
Marx, Karl B.	Retir	W Illinois	ADH	PHD	61	Illinois	1961
Marxsen, Craig S.	Assoc	Neb-Kearney		PHD	76	Geo St	1987
Masih, Nolin	Retir	St Cloud St		PHD	88	Kansas	1964
Maske, Kellie	Asst	Appalach St	DF	PHD	98	N Carol	2000
Maskin, Eric S.	Prof	Harvard		PHD	76	Harvard	
Maskus, Keith E.	C-Pr	Colorado		PHD	81	Michigan	1981
Mason, Andrew	Prof	Hawaii-Manoa		PHD	75	Michigan	1975
Mason, Charles F.	Prof	Wyoming	DK	PHD	83	Berkeley	1982
Mason, John D.	Prof	Gordon	AJR	PHD	69	Mich St	1968
Mason, Patrick L.	Assoc	Florida St	J	PHD	91	New Sch	1999
Mason, Paul M.	Prof	North Fla	HE	PHD	84	Tx-Austin	1985
Mason, Timothy I.	Assoc	E Illinois		PHD	87	Indiana	1989
Mason, William J.	Prof	San Fran St		PHD	58	Iowa	1958
Masson, Robert T.	Prof	Cornell		PHD	69	Berkeley	1976
Masten, John T.	Retir	Tenn State		PHD	67	S Illinois	
Masters, Stanley H.	Prof	SUNY-Bingham	J	PHD	65	Princeton	1981
Mastrianna, Frank V.	Dean	Slippery Roc		PHD	68	Cincinnati	3-87
Matcheck, Dale C.	Asst	Northwood	Q	PHD	93	Cornell	1995
Mateer, Robert N.	C-Pr	Liberty		MBA	64	Tulane	1984
Mathews, Leah Gredcn	Asst	N Car-Ashvil	HDQO	PHD	97	Minnesota	1997
Mathis, Edward J.	C-Pr	Villanova		PHD	71	SUNY-Buf	1966
Mathis, Gilbert L.	Prof	Murray State	DFKQ	PHD	66	Ohio St	1966
Mathis, Stephen A.	Prof	Shippensburg		PHD	79	Iowa St	1979
Mathur, Vijay K.	Prof	Cleveland St	DR	PHD	69	Wayne St	1968
Matsui, Akihiko	Asst	Pennsylvania	CDE	PHD	90	Nrthwstrn	1990
William P. Carey Term Assistant Professor of Economics							
Matsumoto, Keishiro	Retir	So Conn St		PHD		Minnesota	
Matsuyama, Kiminori	Prof	Northwestern		PHD	87	Harvard	
Matta, Benjamin N.	Assoc	New Mex St	IJ	PHD	79	Tx-Austin	1972
Matthaei, Julie Ann	Prof	Wellesley	B	PHD	78	Yale	1978
Matthews, Michelle	Inst	Delta State		ABD		Miss	8-01
Matthews, Peter H.	Asst	Middlebury	BCEJ	PHD	95	Yale	1995
Matthews, Steven A.	Prof	Pennsylvania		PHD	78	Cal Tech	1997
Mattila, John Peter	Prof	Iowa State	J	PHD	69	Wisconsin	1973
Mattox, Bruce W. Sr.	Retir	NC-Pembroke		PHD	71	Oregon St	1988
Matusz, Steven J.	Prof	Michigan St		PHD	83	Penn	1983
Matzkin, Rosa L.	Prof	Northwestern		PHD	86	Minnesota	
Household International, Inc. Professorship							
Mauer, Laurence J.	Prof	St John's		PHD	67	Tennessee	1983
Mauney, William M.	C-Pr	Lenoir-Rhyne	AE	MA	76	Appalach	1967
Centennial Professor of Economics - Director Broyhill Institute							
Maurer-Fazio, Margaret	Assoc	Bates	O	PHD	94	Pittsburgh	1994
Maurice, S. Charles	Deces	Texas A&M		PHD	67	Georgia	1967
Maxcy, Joel	Asst	SUNY-Cortlan	KJ	PHD	96	Wash St	1998
Maxwell, Don P.	Prof	Central Okla	ADEH	PHD	82	Okla St	1981

Maxwell, John	Asst	Indiana		PHD	93	Queen's	1992
Maxwell, Nan L.	Prof	CS-Hayward	ADJT	PHD	83	Fla St	1985
May, Ann Mari	Assoc	Nebraska	BE	PHD	87	Colo St	1987
May, David	Assoc	Okla City	QC	PHD	96	Fla St	1996
Mayer, Thomas	Emer	Cal-Davis	BE	PHD	53	Columbia	1962
Mayer, Walt	Assoc	Mississippi	C	PHD	86	Florida	1987
Mayer, Wolfgang	Prof	Cincinnati	FD	PHD	71	SUNY-Buf	1970
David Sinton Professor							
Mayhew, Anne	Retir	Tennessee		PHD	66	Tx-Austin	1968
Maynard, Raymond	Asst	Frank & Mars		PHD	00	Tennessee	2000
Mayor, Thomas H.	Prof	Houston	AK	PHD	65	Maryland	1969
Mazumdar, Joy	Asst	Emory	FEO	PHD	96	Michigan	1996
Mazzarella, James	Asst	Holy Family		PHD	87	Columbia	
Mazzocco, Maurizio	Asst	Wisconsin		PHD	01	Chicago	2001
Mbaku, John M.	Prof	Weber State	AHOP	PHD	85	Georgia	1991
McAfee, R. Preston	Prof	Texas	D	PHD	80	Purdue	9-90
Murray S. Johnson Chair in Economics							
McArthur, John R.	Assoc	Wofford	EHKQ	PHD	91	Claremont	1990
McAuliffe, Robert E. Jr.	Assoc	Babson	EL	PHD	82	Virginia	1982
McAusland, Carol	Asst	Cal-Santa Br		PHD		Michigan	
McAvoy, Michael	Asst	SUNY-Oneonta		PHD	01	Illinois	2000
McBearty, James C.	Assoc	Arizona		PHD	68	Illinois	1968
McBride, Howard	Retir	Cincinnati		PHD	59	Illinois	
McBride, Mark E.	Prof	Miami U-Ohio		PHD	79	Wash U	1983
McBride, Timothy	Assoc	Mo-St Louis	IH	PHD	87	Wisconsin	1991
McCabe, Mark J.	Asst	Georgia Tech	L	PHD	91	MIT	1998
McCafferty, Stephen A.	Prof	Ohio State	EF	PHD	77	Brown	1982
McCain, Roger A. III	Prof	Drexel		PHD	71	LSU	1988
McCaleb, Thomas S.	Assoc	Florida St		PHD	75	N Carol	1980
McCall, Charles W.	C-Ac	Rider	AL	PHD	82	Temple	1979
McCall, John B.	Retir	Tx-Arlington	OQ	PHD	68	Okla St	1964
McCall, John J.	Emer	UCLA		PHD	59	Chicago	
McCallum, Bennett T.	Prof	Carnegie Mel		PHD	69	Rice	1981
H. J. Heinz Professor of Economics							
McCallum, George E.	Retir	St Norbert		PHD		Calif	1967
McCalman, Philip	Asst	Ca-Santa Crz	FL	PHD	98	Wisconsin	2000
McCarl, Henry N.	Retir	Alabama-Birm	AR	PHD	69	Penn St	1969
McCarley, James F.	Prof	Albion	J	PHD	70	Mich St	1965
McCarty, Cynthia S.	Assoc	Jacksonvl St		PHD	94	N Carol	1990
McCarty, Marilu H.	Assoc	Georgia Tech	EH	PHD	72	Geo St	1972
McCarty, Therese A.	C-Ac	Union	GI	PHD	87	Michigan	1987
McClellan, Mark	Assoc	Stanford		PHD	93	Harvard	9-95
McClelland, Peter D.	Prof	Cornell		PHD	67	Harvard	1968
McClintock, Brent	Assoc	Carthage	EFG	PHD	90	Colo St	1991
McCloskey, Deirdre N.	Prof	Ill-Chicago	B	PHD	70	Harvard	2000
McClung, Bruce Alan	Asst	SW Texas St	J	PHD	88	Tx A&M	1988
McClure, James Edward	Assoc	Ball State	J	PHD	83	Purdue	1982
McCollum, James B.	Retir	Columbus		PHD	68	Tulane	1976
McComb, Robert P.	Assoc	Texas Tech		PHD	89	Illinois	1991
McConnell, Virginia D.	Assoc	MD-Baltim Co		PHD	78	Maryland	
McCorkle, Sarapage	Asst	Mo-St Louis	A	EDD	87	Mo-StLou	1970
McCormack, Edward	Asst	Berea		MBA	80	Estrn Ky	1985
McCormick, Kenneth J.	Prof	No Iowa	BEA	PHD	82	Iowa St	1982
McCormick, Robert E.	Prof	Clemson	DGKH	PHD	78	Tx A&M	1982
McCoskey, Suzanne K.	Asst	USN Academy		PHD	97	Syracuse	1997
McCown, James	Asst	Fla Atlantic	FE	PHD	97	Ohio St	1997
McCoy, James P.	Prof	Murray State	DFOP	PHD	86	N Carol	1985
McCracken, Michael	Asst	Missouri	CE	PHD	98	Wisconsin	2001
McCrate, Elaine D.	Assoc	Vermont	JIT	PHD	85	Mass	1985
McCrickard, Donald L.	Assoc	N Car-Greens	EF	PHD	76	N Carol	1975
McCrickard, Myra J.	C-Pr	Bellarmine	AL	PHD	89	N Car St	1989
McCulloch, J. Huston	Prof	Ohio State	E	PHD	73	Chicago	1979
McCulloch, Laurence	Lect	Ohio State					
McCulloch, Rachel	Prof	Brandeis		PHD	73	Chicago	1987
McDaniel, Bruce A.	C-Ac	No Colorado	OGMQ	PHD	79	Colo St	1992
McDermott, John H.	Assoc	So Carolina		PHD	79	Brown	1983
McDevitt, Catherine L.	Asst	Cen Michigan		PHD	86	Rochester	1989
McDonald, James B.	C-Pr	Brigham Yg	C	PHD	70	Purdue	1972
McDonald, John F.	Prof	Ill-Chicago	R	PHD	71	Yale	1971
McDonald, Judith Ann	Assoc	Lehigh	FE	PHD	86	Princeton	1990
McDonald, Stephen L.	Retir	Texas	HQ	PHD	51	Tx-Austin	9-61
McDonald, Tammy	Asst	Mass-Boston	QR	ABD		Mass	2001
McDonald, Vincent R.	Prof	Howard		PHD	68	Maryland	
McDonough, Carol C.	Prof	Mass-Lowell	DN	PHD	69	Boston C	1970
McDougall, Gerald S.	Dean	SE Missouri	HL	PHD	74	Claremont	1993
McDowell, John M.	Prof	Arizona St		PHD	79	UCLA	1978
McEachern, William A.	Prof	Connecticut	H	PHD	75	Virginia	1978
McEliece, James H.	Prof	Pt Loma Naz	AC	PHD	86	Co Mines	1994
McElroy, F. William	Retir	Georgetown		PHD	67	Geotown	1968
McElroy, Jerome L.	C-Pr	St Marys-Ind	AEFO	PHD	71	Colorado	8-82

McElroy, Marjorie B.	C-Pr	Duke	J	PHD	69	Nrthwstrn	1976
McElroy, Michael B.	Assoc	N Carol St	E	PHD	70	Nrthwstrn	1970
McFadden, Daniel L.	Prof	Cal-Berkeley		PHD	62	Minnesota	1963
McFarland, David	Prof	No Carolina	BDL	PHD	63	Vanderbilt	1964
McFarland, Earl L. Jr.	Retir	Williams		PHD	73	Columbia	1968
McFerrin, Randy	Asst	E New Mexico		PHD	95	Tx A&M	1995
McGahagan, Thomas A.	Assoc	Pitts-Johnst	FN	PHD	76	Penn	1982
McGarrity, Joseph	Assoc	Cen Arkansas		PHD	94	GeoMason	8-95
McGarry, Kathleen	Asst	UCLA		PHD	92	SUNY-SBr	
McGarvey, Mary G.	Assoc	Nebraska	E	PHD	83	Virginia	1992
McGee, L. Randolph	Retir	Kentucky	MG	PHD	63	Tulane	1963
McGee, M. Kevin	Assoc	Wis-Oshkosh	H	PHD	83	Ohio St	1982
McGibany, James M.	Assoc	Marquette	CER	PHD	83	Mich St	1983
McGill-Tillman, Patricia	Inst	Jackson St		MA	65	Atlanta	1968
McGoldrick, Kim Marie	Assoc	Richmond		PHD	93	SUNY-Bin	1992
McGough, Bruce	Asst	Oregon State	ED	PHD	00	Oregon	9-00
McGowan, Susan	Prof	CS-Sacrament		PHD	77	Ca-Davis	1974
McGrath, Paul T.	Assoc	Purdue-Calmu		PHD	88	N Illinois	1986
McGrath, Richard	Asst	Armstrong At	DHG	PHD	97	Virginia	1997
McGregor, Rob R.	Assoc	N Car-Charl		PHD	91	S Carol	1991
McGuckin, J. T.	Assoc	New Mex St	Q	PHD	90	Wisconsin	1989
McGuire, Martin C.	Prof	Calif-Irvine		PHD	64	Harvard	1992
McGuire, Robert A.	Prof	Akron	AKN	PHD	78	U Wash	1990
McGuire, Wanda	Exec	Alabama A&M					
McHone, W. Warren	Prof	Cen Florida	R	PHD	80	Penn	1982
McInnes, Melayne	Asst	So Carolina		PHD	98	Yale	8-97
McIntyre, Richard	Prof	Rhode Island	FJN	PHD	89	Mass	1989
McKee, David L.	Prof	Kent State	OR	PHD	66	Notre Dm	1967
McKee, Michael	Prof	New Mexico	HKQL	PHD	85	Carleton	1991
McKenna, Edward J.	Assoc	Conn Coll	E	PHD	81	SUNY-SBr	
McKenzie, David	Asst	Stanford		PHD	01	Yale	2001
McKenzie, Lionel W.	Emer	Rochester		PHD	42	Princeton	1957
McKinney, Charles W.	Retir	Whitworth	DE	PHD	73	Wash St	1985
McKinney, Hannah J.	C-As	Kalamazoo	HJR	PHD	84	Penn	1988
McKinney, Joseph A.	Prof	Baylor	F	PHD	70	Mich St	1976
McKinney, Marie M.	Prof	Framingham		PHD	83	SUNY-Bin	1985
McKinnon, Ronald I.	Prof	Stanford		PHD	61	Minnesota	1961
William D. Eberle Professor of Economics							
McKinnon, Thomas	Prof	Arkansas	NA	PHD	72	Miss	1981
McLain, James J.	Retir	New Orleans		PHD	72	Pittsburgh	1972
McLain, Louis P.	Dean$	Txs Wesleyan		MBA	74	So Meth	1976
McLaren, John	Prof	Virginia	F	PHD	92	Princeton	2000
McLaughlin, Francis M.	Assoc	Boston Coll	JN	PHD	64	MIT	1961
McLaughlin, Kenneth J.	Assoc	CUNY-Hunter		PHD	87	Chicago	9-94
McLaughlin, Patrick	C-Ac	NW Missouri	K	JD	78	Mo-Ks Cty	1978
McLean, Richard P.	Prof	Rutgers-N Br	D	PHD	79	SUNY-SBr	1986
McLean, Thomas A.	Retir	Portland St		PHD	66	Utah	1962
McLellan, Jacquelynne W.	Assoc	Frostburg St		PHD	93	Wayne St	1994
McLennan, Andrew M.	Assoc	Minnesota		PHD	82	Princeton	1987
McLeod, Darryl L.	Asst	Fordham		PHD	82	Berkeley	1984
McLeod, Mark A.	Inst	Virg Tech					1998
McMahon, Marshall E.	Prof	Rhodes		PHD	72	Vanderbilt	1972
McMahon, Robert C.	Retir	So Maine	R	PHD	70	Lehigh	1969
McMahon, Walter W.	Retir	Illinois		PHD	57	Iowa	1957
McManis, Bruce L.	H-Pr	Nicholls St	G	PHD	81	LSU	1978
McMillan, Margaret	Asst	Tufts	O	PHD	97	Columbia	1997
McMillen, Daniel P.	Prof	Ill-Chicago	R	PHD	87	Nrthwstrn	1999
McMillin, W. Douglas	Prof	Louisiana St	E	PHD	79	LSU	1985
South Central Bell Business Partnership Professor							
McMinn, Jim Thomas	Retir	Austin Peay	GM	DBA	75	Miss St	1977
McMinn, Robert D.	Retir	Tx A&M-C Chr	A	PHD	73	Oklahoma	9-74
McMullen, B. Starr	Prof	Oregon State	LE	PHD	79	Berkeley	9-80
McMurry, Patrick H.	Prof	Missouri Wes	J	PHD	81	Arkansas	1978
McNamara, John R.	Retir	Lehigh	MO	PHD	71	Rensselaer	1973
McNelis, Paul D.	Prof	Georgetown	EFG	PHD	74	J Hopkins	1977
McNertney, Edward M.	C-Ac	Tx Christian		PHD	77	Mass	1977
McNiel, Douglas W.	Prof	McNeese St		PHD	77	Okla St	1984
McNown, Robert F.	Prof	Colorado		PHD	71	Ca-SnDgo	1971
McPerson, Sandra	Asst	Towson		PHD	98	Indiana	2000
McPheters, Lee R.	Prof	Arizona St		PHD	72	Va Tech	1976
McQuiston, James M. Jr.	Retir	So Miss		BS	56	S Miss	1960
McRae, Larry T.	Assoc	Appalach St	CDE	PHD	78	N Carol	1977
McRostie, Clair M.	Retir	Gustavus Ado		PHD	64	Wisconsin	1957
McTague, Edward	Assoc	CUNY-Brookly		MBA	75	Fairl Dick	1982
Mead, Arthur C.	Prof	Rhode Island	A	PHD	78	Boston C	1976
Meadows, G. Richard	Assoc	Wis-Milwauke		PHD	72	Wash U	1971
Meadows, Tommy C.	C-Pr	Austin Peay	HJ	PHD	79	Clemson	1977
Meaney, Martha M.	Prof	Framingham		MA		Boston C	
Means, Tom S.	Prof	San Jose St		PHD	83	UCLA	1986
Measell, Richard F.	Asst	St Marys-Ind	ADHJ	PHD	85	Maryland	8-83

Mechnet, Emily	Asst	Bates		PHD	98	Harvard	1998
Medema, Steven G.	Prof	Colo-Denver	BHDK	PHD	89	Mich St	1989
Medley, Joseph E.	C-Ac	So Maine	BO	PHD	81	Mass	1983
Medoff, James L.	Prof	Harvard		PHD	75	Harvard	
Meyer Kestnbaum Professor of Labor & Industry							
Medoff, Marshall H.	Prof	CS-Long Bch		PHD	73	Berkeley	1979
Meehan, James P.	Retir	Edinboro		MA	61	Notre Dm	1966
Meehan, James W.	Prof	Colby	DM	PHD	67	Boston C	1973
Herbert E. Wadsworth Professor of Economics							
Meeks, Thomas J.	Prof	Virginia St		PHD	71	Duke	1969
Meenakshi, Rishi	Assoc	Ohio Northrn		PHD	93	Mass	1993
Meepagala, Gaminie	Asst	Howard	C	PHD	86	SUNY-Alb	1988
Meeropol, Michael A.	C-Pr	W New Eng		PHD	73	Wisconsin	1970
Mehanna, Rock-Antoine	Asst	Wartburg		PHD	00	Southern	2001
Mehay, Stephen L.	Prof	Naval Postgr	IJ	PHD	73	UCLA	1985
Mehdizadeh, Mostafa	Assoc	Miami U-Ohio	A	PHD	80	Oklahoma	1982
Mehra, Jadish C.	Prof	Youngstown		PHD	68	SUNY-Buf	1965
Mehra, Rajnish	C-Pr	Cal-Santa Br	GF	PHD	78	Car Mellon	1988
Mehrling, Perry G.	C-Pr	Barnard	EGB	PHD	88	Harvard	1987
Mehtabdin, Khalid R.	C-Ac	St Rose	AEFM	PHD	79	Pittsburgh	1986
Meiners, Roger E.	Prof	Tx-Arlington	KJ	PHD	76	Va Tech	1993
Meininger, Richard P.	Prof	Ohio Northrn		PHD	87	Ohio U	1973
Meisel, John B.	Prof	S Ill-Edward	ADL	PHD	78	Boston C	1977
Meiselman, David I.	Emer	Virg Tech	D	PHD	61	Chicago	1971
Meister, J. Patrick	VAsst	Butler	L	PHD	92	Michigan	1996
Melero, Francisco	D-Ac	Russell Sage	DCF	PHD	83	Rensselaer	1982
Melese, Francois	Assoc	Naval Postgr	C	PHD	82	Belgium	1987
Melick, William R.	Assoc	Kenyon	EGCF	PHD	87	Ohio St	7-98
Melitz, Marc J.	Asst	Harvard		PHD		Michigan	
Melkoneam, Martin	Asst	Hofstra		MA	64	New Sch	
Mellor, Jennifer	Asst	Wm & Mary		PHD	96	Maryland	1998
Melnikov, Oleg	Asst	Cornell		PHD	00	Yale	7-01
Meltzer, Allan H.	Prof	Carnegie Mel		PHD	58	UCLA	1957
The Allan H. Meltzer University Professor of Political Economy							
Meltzer, Yale L.	Asst	CUNY-Stn Isl	EG	MBA	66	NYU	1983
Melvin, Michael T.	Prof	Arizona St		PHD	80	UCLA	1980
Menchik, Paul L.	Prof	Michigan St		PHD	76	Penn	1979
Mendelsohn, Frieda		SUNY-Empire		ABD			
Mendelsohn, Robert	Prof	Yale		PHD	78	Yale	1984
Mendez, Jose A.	Prof	Arizona St		PHD	80	So Meth	1980
Mendez-Carbajo, Diego	Asst	Ill Wesleyan	E	PHD	00	Fla Intl	2000
Mendoza, Enrique	Prof	Duke	FO	PHD	89	W Ontario	1997
Mendoza, Juan	Asst	SUNY-Buffalo	ED	PHD	99	Brown	1999
Menes, Rebecca	Asst	George Mason		PHD	97	Harvard	1999
Menezes, Carmen F.	Prof	Missouri	DF	PHD	66	Nrthwstrn	1965
Menge, John A.	Retir	Dartmouth		PHD	59	MIT	1956
Mengistu, Tadessa	Assoc	Dillard		PHD	86	Indiana	
Menon, Nidhiya	Asst	Brandeis		PHD	01	Brown	2001
Menz, Fredric C.	Prof	Clarkson	HQD	PHD	70	Virginia	1974
Mercer, Lloyd J.	Prof	Cal-Santa Br	ND	PHD	67	U Wash	1966
Mercuro, Nicholas	Retir	New Orleans		PHD	77	Mich St	1977
Merkel, Edward T.	Prof	Troy State	AFH	PHD	74	N Illinois	1978
Merkle, Paul E.	Retir	La St-Shreve		PHD	77	La Tech	1976
Merrifield, David E.	Deces	Western Wash	M	PHD	82	Claremont	1983
Merrifield, John D.	Prof	Tx-S Antonio	HQR	PHD	84	Wyoming	1987
Merrill, William C.	Retir	Iowa State	O	PHD	64	Berkeley	1964
Merriman, David F.	Assoc	Loyola-Chicg	ADHO	PHD	83	Wisconsin	1987
Merz, Thomas E.	Prof	Mich Tech	E	PHD	80	Pittsburgh	1980
Mesa-Lago, Carmelo	Retir	Pittsburgh	P	PHD	68	Cornell	1968
Mescon, Timothy S.	Dean	Kennesaw St		PHD	79	Georgia	1990
Messe, Michael J.	D	USM Academy	HE	PHD	77	Princeton	1990
Messer, Jodi	Asst	Wichita St		PHD	00	Kentucky	2000
Messerschmidt, Daniel C.	Prof	Lynchburg		PHD	84	Iowa St	1985
Metcalf, Gilbert	Assoc	Tufts		PHD	88	Harvard	1994
Metrick, Andrew P.	Asst	Harvard		PHD	94	Harvard	
Metts, Robert Lyle	Assoc	Nevada-Reno		PHD	85	Berkeley	1984
Metzgar, Matthew	Asst	Kent State	H	ABD		Tennessee	2001
Metzger, Michael R.	C-Pr	Central Okla	DIL	PHD	78	Stanford	1991
Meurs, Mieke E.	Assoc	American U		PHD	88	Mass	1989
Meyer, Bruce	Prof	Northwestern		PHD	87	MIT	1987
Meyer, Carrie A.	Assoc	George Mason		PHD	88	Illinois	1988
Meyer, Charles W.	Retir	Iowa State	G	PHD	61	J Hopkins	1961
Meyer, Donald J.	Assoc	W Michigan	D	PHD	83	Tx A&M	1991
Meyer, Jack	Prof	Michigan St		PHD	74	Stanford	1983
Meyer, Laurence H.	Prof	Wash Univ	E	PHD	70	MIT	1969
Meyer, Peter	Retir	Louisville		PHD	70	Wisconsin	
Meyer, Peter J.	Assoc	Pacific	BJL	PHD	79	Berkeley	1985
Mezzetti, Claudio	Prof	No Carolina	D	PHD	88	Oxford	1990
Miah, Solaiman	VAsst	SUNY-Fredoni	AC	PHD	01	N Illinois	2001
Miceli, Thomas J.	Prof	Connecticut	KR	PHD	88	Brown	1987

Michael, Jeffery	Asst	Towson		PHD	99	N Carol	1999
Michaels, Robert J.	Prof	CS-Fullerton	L	PHD	72	UCLA	1968
Michalik, Benjamin A.	Retir	St Peters	1987	PHD	57	Fordham	1947
Michaud, Claude	Prof	INSEAD	O	D		Bordeaux	8-70
Michener, Ronald W.	Assoc	Virginia	EN	PHD	81	Chicago	1979
Michl, Thomas R.	Prof	Colgate	EJ	PHD	84	New Sch	1983
Michos, Leon	VAsst	Centre		PHD	00	Clemson	2001
Mieczkowski, Bogdan	Retir	Ithaca	AF	PHD	54	Illinois	1954
Mieszkowski, Peter	Prof	Rice		PHD	63	J Hopkins	1981
Cline Professor of Economics & Finance							
Mihov, Ilian	Assoc	INSEAD	DE	PHD	96	Princeton	9-96
Mikhail, Ossama	Asst	Cen Florida	E	ABD		McGill	2001
Miklius, Walter	Retir	Hawaii-Manoa		PHD	64	UCLA	
Milener, Eugene D. III	Retir	Hartwick		PHD		NYU	1960
Miles, William	Asst	Wichita St		PHD	98	Illinois	1999
Milgrom, Paul R.	Prof	Stanford		PHD	79	Stanford	1987
Shirley R. and Leonard W. Ely, Jr. Professor in Humanities and Sciences							
Milkman, Martin	Prof	Murray State	CJH	PHD	89	Oregon	1988
Millar, James R.	Prof	George Wash	P	PHD	65	Cornell	1989
Millea, Meghan	Asst	Miss State	HE	PHD	98	Nebraska	1998
Miller, Carole F.	Prof	Rhode Island	ACDJ	PHD	88	Syracuse	1986
Miller, Dennis D.	Assoc	Baldwin-Wal	OQ	PHD	85	Colorado	1987
Miller, Edward M.	Prof	New Orleans		PHD	70	MIT	1984
Miller, Gerald	Assoc	Rockhurst		PHD	75	Notre Dm	1982
Miller, Gerald M.	SInst	Miami U-Ohio	DC	MA	73	Brown	1971
Miller, Green	C-Pr	Morehead St		PHD	85	Kentucky	1979
Miller, James	Asst	Smith		PHD	97	Chicago	1996
Miller, Jeffrey B.	Prof	Delaware	EP	PHD	76	Penn	1976
Miller, John	Lect	Sam Houston		MS	65	Rice	1998
Miller, John A.	C-Pr	Wheaton-MA		PHD	82	Pittsburgh	1979
Miller, Jon R.	Prof	Idaho	BQ	PHD	74	Wash U	1989
Miller, Michael S.	C-Ac	DePaul	E	PHD	80	Pittsburgh	1980
Miller, Norman C.	Prof	Miami U-Ohio	EF	PHD	66	Pittsburgh	1985
Julian G. Lange Professor of Economics & American Enterprise							
Miller, Oscar	Emer	Ill-Chicago	A	MA	46	Chicago	1948
Miller, Otis E.	Retir	Wm Jewell		PHD	62	Missouri	1978
Miller, Richard A.	Prof	Wesleyan-CT	L	PHD	62	Yale	1960
Miller, Robert A.	Assoc	Carnegie Mel		PHD	82	Chicago	1982
Miller, Robert J.	Prof	Missouri So		MA	67	Cen Mo St	1968
Miller, Ronald	Asst	Columbia	EO	PHD	94	Princeton	1994
Miller, Stephen M.	C-Pr	Nev-L Vegas	E	PHD	72	SUNY-Buf	2001
Miller, Timothy I.	Prof	Denison	CE	PHD	79	S Illinois	1978
Miller, Tracy C.	Assoc	Grove City		PHD	86	Chicago	1995
Milley, Donald J.	Prof	Youngstown		PHD	74	SUNY-Buf	1969
Milliman, Scott R.	Assoc	Jms Madison	DQ	PHD	85	Wisconsin	1986
Millimet, Daniel	Asst	So Methodist	CJO	PHD	99	Brown	1999
Millner, Edward L.	C-Pr	Virg Comm		PHD	82	N Carol	1983
Mills, David E.	C-Pr	Virginia	LD	PHD	75	Stanford	1975
Mills, Jeffrey A.	Assoc	Cincinnati	C	PHD	89	Wash U	1992
Mills, Judith W.	Assoc	So Conn St	CNT	PHD	94	SUNY-SBr	1991
Mills, Richard L.	Assoc	New Hampshir	CD	PHD	67	Indiana	1967
Millsaps, Steven	Prof	Appalach St	CDQ	PHD	73	N Car St	1973
Milon, J. Witter	Prof	Cen Florida	Q	PHD	78	Fla St	2000
Milstein, Susan Matz	Prof	W Maryland		MBA		MtStMary	1983
Minars, David	Prof	CUNY-Brookly		JD	70	NYU	1971
Minehart, Deborah	Asst	Boston Univ	CDL	PHD	94	Berkeley	1994
Miner, Jerry	Retir	Syracuse		PHD	58	Michigan	
Miners, Cathy	VAsst	Fairfield	EG	PHD	81	N Carol	1998
Miners, Laurence A.	Assoc	Fairfield	CIJA	PHD	79	N Carol	1981
Minet, Lawrence J.	Retir	Canisius		PHD	53	Columbia	1958
Ming, Xing	Asst	Indiana		PHD	95	Rice	1995
Mini, Peter S.	Assoc	Bryant	BN	PHD	65	Tulane	
Minick, Robert A.	Retir	CS-Fresno		PHD	67	Tx-Austin	1962
Minicozzi, Alexandra	Asst	Texas	E	PHD	97	Wisconsin	9-97
Minier, Jenny	Asst	U Miami	EO	PHD	98	Wisconsin	1998
Minisian, Jora	Retir	CS-Northrdge		PHD	60	Chicago	1972
Minkler, Alanson P.	Assoc	Connecticut	DK	PHD	88	Ca-Davis	1989
Minniti, Maria	Asst	Babson	E	PHD	97	NYU	1997
Minor, Frank J.	Assoc	St Anselm		PHD	58	Ohio St	
Minsky, Hyman P.	Retir	Wash Univ		PHD	54	Harvard	1965
Miranne, Martha	Retir	Pace		MA		Pace	1977
Mirer, Thad W.	Assoc	SUNY-Albany	H	PHD	71	Yale	1973
Mirman, Leonard J.	Prof	Virginia	ACDQ	PHD	70	Rochester	1986
Paul Goodloe McIntire Professor of Economics							
Mirmirani, Sam	C-Pr	Bryant	IMO	PHD	85	Clark	1982
Miron, Jeffrey A.	Prof	Boston Univ	EKN	PHD	84	MIT	1990
Mirowski, Philip E.	Prof	Notre Dame	B	PHD	79	Michigan	1990
Mirza, David B.	Assoc	Loyola-Chicg	AF	PHD	73	Nrthwstrn	1969
Mirzaie, Ida	Lect	Ohio State		PHD	99	Wisconsin	2000
Misdzar, Sujetlana	Asst	Gustavus Ado		PHD	96	Minnesota	1994

Mishkin, Frederic S.	Prof	Columbia		PHD	76	MIT	1983
Alfred Lerner Professor of Banking and Financial Institutions							
Misiolek, Walter S.	Prof	Alabama		PHD	76	Cornell	1975
Mitch, David F.	Assoc	MD-Baltim Co		PHD	82	Chicago	1983
Mitchell, David	Asst	Valdosta St	DQ	PHD	01	Okla St	2001
Mitchell, Douglas W.	Prof	W Virginia	E	PHD	78	Princeton	1984
Mitchell, Hadley T.	Assoc	Taylor		PHD	85	Tennessee	1993
Mitchell, Jeannette C.	Asst	Rochest Tech	FOB	PHD	95	Utah	1985
Mitchell, Lloyd A.	C-As	St Thomas-FL		MBA	81	U Miami	1984
Mitchell, Mike	Assoc	Nevada-Reno		PHD	88	Oregon	1988
Mitchell, Milt	Asst	Wis-Oshkosh	Q	MA	65	Wisconsin	1967
Mitchell, Shannon K.	Assoc	Virg Comm		PHD	89	Virginia	1990
Mitchell, Thomas M.	Assoc	So Illinois	DC	PHD	84	Brown	1983
Mitchell, William E.	Retir	Mo-St Louis	EG	PHD	67	Duke	1965
Mitchener, Kris J.	Asst	Santa Clara		PHD	01	Berkeley	2001
Miteza, Ilir	Asst	Mich-Dearbor		ABD		Wisconsin	2001
Mitra, Anilau	Asst	Purdue-Calmu		PHD	98	N Illinois	1998
Mitra, Devashish	Asst	Fla Internat	FLO	PHD	96	Columbia	1996
Mitra, Tapan	C-Pr	Cornell		PHD	75	Rochester	
Mixon, Frank	Assoc	So Miss	J	PHD	92	Auburn	1994
Mixon, J. Wilson	Prof	Berry	N	PHD	74	U Wash	1986
Miyagawa, Eiichi	Asst	Columbia	DH	PHD	92	Rochester	1998
Miyagiwa, Kaz	Assoc	Louisiana St	FO	PHD	85	Tx-Austin	8-95
Miyazaki, Hajime	Prof	Ohio State	LJ	PHD	77	Berkeley	1984
Mizak, Daniel A.	Prof	Frostburg St		PHD	84	Pittsburgh	1977
Mizak, Patrick	Asst	Armstrong At		MA	98	Clev St	2000
Mizovtsev, Dmitri	Asst	Washburn		PHD	01	Purdue	2001
Mizrach, Bruce	Assoc	Rutgers-N Br	E	PHD	87	Penn	1995
Moberly, H. Dean	Retir	Auburn-Montg	ADIQ	PHD	68	Tx A&M	1970
Mobius, M.	Asst	Harvard		PHD		MIT	
Mocan, Naci H.	C-Pr	Colo-Denver	CJI	PHD	89	CUNY	1990
Modeste, Nelson C.	C-Ac	So Carol St		PHD	76	Florida	1994
Modigliani, Franco	Retir	MIT		PHD	44	New Sch	1960
Moe, Karine S.	Assoc	Macalester	AJ	PHD	95	Minnesota	1995
Moen, Jon R.	Assoc	Mississippi	JN	PHD	87	Chicago	1990
Moewes, David S.	Prof	Concordia C	EH	PHD	82	Utah	1968
Moffett, Russell E.	Retir	Ferris State		PHD	61	Ca-Davis	1965
Moffit, Tim	Asst	Kalamazoo	M	MBA	84	Dartmouth	1994
Moffitt, Robert A.	Prof	J Hopkins		PHD	75	Brown	1995
Mogab, John William	Prof	SW Texas St	O	PHD	81	Tennessee	1981
Moghadam, Fatemeh	Prof	Hofstra	NOQ	PHD	79	Oxford	
Moghaddam, Masoud	Prof	St Cloud St		PHD	82	Iowa St	1983
Mohabbat, Khan A.	Prof	No Illinois	E	PHD	64	SUNY-Buf	1968
Mohaghegh, Mehdi	Assoc	Norwich		PHD	86	Clark	1986
Mohammadi, Hassan	Assoc	Illinois St	E	PHD	88	Wash St	1988
Mohan, Daniel F.	Assoc	West Chester	GM	PHD	75	Rutgers	1980
Mohanty, Madhu	Prof	CS-L Angeles		PHD	90	Wi-Milwa	1990
Mohindru, Rajesh K.	Prof	Bloomsburg		PHD	69	Penn	
Mohiuddin, Yasmeen	C-Pr	Univ South	FOE	PHD	83	Vanderbilt	
Mohr, Robert	Asst	New Hampshir		PHD	01	Tx-Austin	2001
Mohring, Herbert D.	Emer	Minnesota		PHD	59	MIT	1961
Mohsin, Mohammed	Asst	Tennessee		PHD	01	York	2001
Mohtadi, Hamid	Assoc	Wis-Milwauke		PHD	82	Michigan	1983
Mohtadi, Shahruz	Assoc	Suffolk		PHD	84	LSU	1983
Moini, Mostafa	Prof	Okla City		PHD	70	Oklahoma	1985
Moite, Leonard M.	Assoc	CS-Dominguez	AEDJ	PHD	84	UCLA	1980
Mokyr, Joel	C-Pr	Northwestern		PHD	74	Yale	1974
Robert H. Strotz Professor of Arts & Sciences							
Moliver, Donald M.	Assoc	Monmouth	DE	PHD	78	Va Tech	9-68
Monacelli, T.	Asst	Boston Coll	EF	PHD	99	NYU	1999
Monaco, Diane K.	Asst	Manchester	EFJ	PHD	98	Wayne St	1999
Monaco, Kristen	Assoc	CS-Long Bch	LJ	PHD	98	Wi-Milwa	1998
Moncur, James E. T.	Prof	Hawaii-Manoa		PHD	71	Wash St	1969
Mondschean, Thomas H.	Prof	DePaul	EG	PHD	89	Wisconsin	1987
Monge, Alexander	Asst	Northwestern		PHD	99	Chicago	1999
Mongell, Susan	Assoc	Calif U-Penn		PHD		Pittsburgh	1990
Mongiovi, Gary	Assoc	St John's		PHD	88	New Sch	1985
Monhollon, Jimmie R.	Dean	Hardin-Simm		PHD	61	Vanderbilt	1995
Distinguished Professor							
Monhollon, Michael	VAsst	Hardin-Simm		JD	84	Virginia	1998
Monks, James W.	Asst	Richmond		PHD	95	Boston C	2001
Monsma, George N. Jr.	Prof	Calvin		PHD	69	Princeton	1969
Monson, Terry D.	Prof	Mich Tech	F	PHD	72	Minnesota	1977
Montano, Carl B.	Prof	Lamar	OQ	PHD	82	Mich St	1981
Monteith, Chalmers A.	Retir	Kent State	N	PHD	58	Ohio St	1958
Montgomery, Edward B.	Prof	Maryland		PHD	82	Harvard	1990
Montgomery, James D.	Assoc	Wisconsin		PHD	89	MIT	2000
Montgomery, Mark	C-Pr	Grinnell	JQH	PHD	82	Wisconsin	1989
Montgomery, Mark	Prof	SUNY-Stony B		PHD	82	Michigan	1988
Montgomery, Michael	Assoc	Maine	AE	PHD	88	Florida	1991

Montias, J. Michael	Emer	Yale	N	PHD	58	Columbia	1963
Montiel, Peter J.	Prof	Williams	EF	PHD	78	MIT	1995
Moody, Carlisle E.	C-Pr	Wm & Mary		PHD	70	Conn	1970
Moohr, Michael	Assoc	Bucknell	FNO	PHD	71	Cambridge	1975
Mookherjee, Dilip M.	Prof	Boston Univ	HLO	PHD	82	LondonEc	1995
Moomaw, Ronald L.	Prof	Oklahoma St	R	PHD	76	Princeton	1972
Regents Professor and CBA Associates Chair							
Moon, Roger	Asst	So Calif		PHD	88	Yale	2000
Moore, Barbara	Inst	Cen Florida	A	MAAE	97	Cen Fla	1988
Moore, Basil J.	Prof	Wesleyan-CT	E	PHD	58	J Hopkins	1958
Moore, Billy C.	C-Pr	Delta State	AG	PHD	95	Miss	8-86
Moore, Derald L.	Assoc	Tri-State		MA		Mich St	1968
Moore, Donald A.	Retir			PHD	56	Mich St	
Moore, Gary A.	Dean$	Lamar	J	PHD	74	Nebraska	1998
Moore, James C.	Prof	Purdue		PHD	68	Minnesota	1969
Moore, Joseph L.	Prof	Ark Tech		PHD	75	Arkansas	1988
Moore, M.	Asst	Calif-Irvine		PHD	97	MIT	1997
Moore, Mack A.	Retir	Georgia Tech	J	PHD	63	Wisconsin	1963
Moore, Margaret D.	Retir	Franklin		PHD	86	Ohio St	
Moore, Michael Owen	Assoc	George Wash	F	PHD	88	Wisconsin	1988
Moore, Peter R.	Prof	Rhode Isl Cl		PHD	75	Illinois	
Moore, Robert E.	Assoc	Georgia St	FO	PHD	88	Cornell	1989
Moore, Robert L.	Prof	Occidental	J	PHD	77	Harvard	1978
Moore, William J.	Prof	Louisiana St	IJ	PHD	70	Tx-Austin	
Gulf Coast Coca Cola Business Partnership Professor							
Moorhouse, John C.	Prof	Wake Forest		PHD	69	Nrthwstrn	1969
Archie Carroll Professor of Ethical Leadership							
Mora, Marie T.	Asst	New Mex St	JI	PHD	95	Tx A&M	8-95
Moran, John	Asst	Syracuse	DIL	PHD	97	Penn St	1999
Morand, Oliver	Asst	Connecticut	DO	PHD	97	Ariz St	1997
Moreau, Arthur	Assoc	St Ambrose		PHD			1999
Morefield, Roger D.	Assoc	St Thomas-TX	I	PHD	77	Duke	1980
Morehouse, Thomas	Retir	Alaska-Ancho		PHD	68	Minnesota	
Moreland, Kemper W.	Prof	E Michigan		PHD	80	Wisconsin	1980
Morelli, Massimo		Ohio State	D	PHD	96	Harvard	
Morey, Edward R.	Prof	Colorado		PHD	78	Brit Colum	1980
Morgan, Alfred D.	Prof	So Conn St	G	PHD	51	Harvard	
Morgan, Celia A.	Retir	SW Texas St		PHD	71	Houston	1971
Morgan, Daniel C. Jr.	Retir	Texas	H	PHD	62	Wisconsin	7-76
Morgan, J. Michael	C-Pr	Charleston		PHD	77	S Carol	1967
Morgan, John		Princeton					
Morgan, Peter B.	Assoc	SUNY-Buffalo	D	PHD	78	Canterbu	1989
Morgan, W. Douglas	Prof	Cal-Santa Br	HDE	PHD	69	Berkeley	1973
Morgan, William E.	Prof	Wyoming	H	PHD	64	Colorado	1968
Moriguchi, Chiaki	Asst	Northwestern		PHD	98	Stanford	2001
Morley, James	Asst	Wash Univ	E	PHD	99	U Wash	1999
Morlock, Mark J.	Prof	CS-Chico	J	PHD	78	Wash St	1980
Moroney, John R.	Prof	Texas A&M	C	PHD	64	Duke	1981
Morra, Wayne A.	Assoc	Arcadia	ALR	PHD	84	Temple	8-81
Morrell, Stephen O.	Prof	Barry		PHD	77	Va Tech	1990
Morris, Barry K.	C-Pr	No Alabama		PHD	74	Arkansas	1974
Morris, Clair E. Jr.	Retir	USN Academy		PHD	72	Wisconsin	1966
Morris, Clyde D.	Assoc	Youngstown		PHD	87	Case Wes	1970
Morris, Cynthia T.	Retir	Smith	BNOP	PHD	59	Yale	1983
Morris, Gayle A.	Asst	Edinboro	FGOQ	PHD	81	Penn St	1999
Morris, John R. Jr.	Emer	Colo-Denver	BI	PHD	66	Purdue	1970
Morris, Stephen	Prof	Yale	D	PHD	91	Yale	1990
Morrison, Clarence C.	Retir	Indiana		PHD	64	N Carol	1970
Morrison, Gwendolyn	Asst	Ind-Purdue/I	I	PHD	96	York	2001
Morrison, Rodney J.	Retir	Wellesley		PHD	65	Wisconsin	1965
Morrison, Steven A.	C-Pr$	Northeastern		PHD	79	Berkeley	1982
Morrow, Bert	Asst	Birminghm So		PHD		Tx A&M	2001
Morrow, William R.	Retir	E Kentucky		PHD	68	Tennessee	1968
Morse, Lawrence B.	Assoc	N Carol A&T		PHD	68	Minnesota	1976
Morshed, Mahbub	Asst	Wash State		PHD	01	U Wash	
Mortensen, Dale T.	Prof	Northwestern		PHD	67	Car Mellon	1965
Ida C. Cook Professor of Consumer Economics							
Mortimer, Julie	Asst	Harvard		PHD	01	UCLA	2001
Mosby, James B.	Asst	Detroit Merc		MA	70	Detroit	1972
Moscarini, Giuseppe	Asst	Yale	E	PHD	96	MIT	1996
Moschetta, Judith K.	Assoc	Wash & Jeff		MS	78	W Virginia	1978
Moseldjord, Asbjorn	Assoc	St Marys-Cal		PHD		Ca-SnBarb	1991
Moseley, Fred B.	Prof	Mt Holyoke		PHD	82	Mass	1989
Moser, Ernest C.	Dean	Tenn-Martin	BM	PHD	73	Tx A&M	8-01
Moser, William	Lect	Assumption		ABD		Clark	
Moses, Anthony T.	Assoc	St Anselm		PHD			
Moses, Leon N.	Prof	Northwestern		PHD	52	Harvard	1959
Moses, Ronald P.	Retir	Ill-Chicago	F	PHD	69	Chicago	1964
Moshtagh, Ali R.	Assoc	E Illinois		PHD	88	Arkansas	1987
Mosier, Donna	Asst	SUNY-Potsdam		PHD	95	Clarkson	1997

Moskwa, Antoni	Assoc	Allegheny	AFCP	PHD	75	Warsaw	1982
Moss, Joanna	Prof	San Fran St		PHD	78	New Sch	1981
Moss, Laurence S.	Prof	Babson	K	PHD	71	Columbia	1977
Moss, Richard L.	Retir	CS-San Bern	A	PHD	73	New Mex	1973
Mostaghimi, Mehdi	Prof	So Conn St	CEM	PHD	87	Virginia	8-84
Mostashari, Shahriar	C-Pr	Campbell		PHD	78	N Car St	1982
Motahar, Eshragh	Assoc	Union	EFG	PHD	89	J Hopkins	1984
Motii, Brian	Asst	Montevallo		PHD	98	Oklahoma	2001
Motomura, Akira	Assoc	Stonehill	KN	PHD	85	Nrthwstrn	1995
Mott, Tracy L.	Assoc	Denver	BE	PHD	82	Stanford	1991
Moudud, Jamee	Guest	Sarah Lawr	EFO	PHD	98	New Sch	2000
Mouhammed, Adil	Assoc	Il-Springfld	FP	PHD	85	Nebraska	1988
Moul, Charles	Asst	Wash Univ	L	PHD	00	Nrthwstrn	2000
Moulin, Herve	Prof	Rice	CD	PHD	75	Paris	7-99
Peterkin Professor of Economics							
Mount, Randall I.	Prof	Kent State	CD	PHD	69	Purdue	1966
Mountain, Dean C.	C-Pr	McMaster U	CD	PHD	79	W Ontario	1987
Mounts, William S. Jr.	Prof	Mercer-Macon		PHD	77	Georgia	1978
Mourdoukoutas, Panos	Prof	Lg Isl-Post		PHD	83	SUNY-SBr	1984
Moy, Ronald L.	Assoc	St John's		PHD	90	Rutgers	
Moyer, James T.	Prof	Albright		PHD	76	Lehigh	9-68
Mozayeni, Simin B.	Asst	SUNY-N Paltz	ALH	PHD	89	Columbia	1990
Mroz, Thomas A.	Prof	No Carolina	J	PHD	84	Stanford	1989
Mshomba, Richard	Asst	LaSalle	FO	PHD	92	Illinois	1991
Muehsam, Mitchell J.	Asst	Sam Houston		PHD	89	Tx A&M	1989
Muehsam, Valerie P.	Asst	Sam Houston		PHD	98	Tx A&M	1993
Mueller, Hans G.	Retir	Mid Tenn St		PHD	68	Vanderbilt	1961
Mueller, James V.	C-Ac	Alma	ABEH	ABD		Ca-Irvine	1976
Muench, Thomas	Prof	SUNY-Stony B		PHD	65	Purdue	1975
Mueser, Peter R.	Assoc	Missouri	DJT	PHD	83	Chicago	1985
Mui, Vai-Lam	Assoc	Notre Dame	DL	PHD	92	Berkeley	1999
Mujumdar, Sudesh	Asst	So Indiana		PHD	00	Cincinnati	2001
Mukand, Sharun	Asst	Tufts	F	PHD	97	Boston U	1997
Mukerjee, Swati	Assoc	Bentley	DFI	PHD	86	Boston U	1989
Mukherji, Nivedita	Asst	Oakland	EF	PHD	92	Va Tech	1992
Mukhoti, Bela	Prof	Rowan Col-NJ		PHD	64	London	1974
Mulder, Cathy	Inst	Frank & Mars		ABD		Mass	1999
Mulherin, Harold	Prof	Claremont		PHD	84	UCLA	2001
Mullainathan, Sendhlil	Asst	MIT		PHD	98	Harvard	1998
mark K. Kyman Jr. Career Development Assistant Professor of Economics							
Mullen, John K.	Prof	Clarkson	GHR	PHD	78	SUNY-Bin	1977
Mullendore, Walter	Prof	Tx-Arlington	R	PHD	68	Iowa St	1969
Muller, Herman J.	Retir	Detroit Merc		PHD		Loyola	1956
Muller, Ronald E.	Prof	American U		PHD		American	1970
Mulligan, Casey	Assoc	Chicago		PHD	93	Chicago	1993
Mulligan, James G.	Prof	Delaware	L	PHD	80	Minnesota	1980
Mulligan, Richard	Asst	W Carolina	E	PHD	93	SUNY-Bin	1997
Mulligan, Robert M.	Retir	Providence	EK	MA	61	Boston C	1965
Mullin, Charles H.	Asst	Vanderbilt	JC	PHD	98	Chicago	1998
Mullin, Marian V.	Assoc	West Liberty	DE	MS	85	Rbt Morr	1975
Mullin, R. David	Asst	USAF Academy	AD	PHD	93	Virginia	1998
Mullin, Wallace P.	Asst	Michigan St		PHD	92	MIT	1992
Mullings, Llewellyn M.	Retir	Bridgeport		PHD	64	Clark	
Mullins, Steven	Assoc	Drury		PHD	83	Okla St	1982
Mumy, Gene E.	Assoc	Ohio State	D	PHD	74	J Hopkins	1978
Munasinghe, Lalith	Asst	Barnard	JC	PHD	95	Columbia	1997
Mundell, Cyril Lee	Assoc	Loyola-N Orl	AC	PHD	76	N Carol	1981
Mundell, Robert	Prof	Columbia	EF	PHD	56	MIT	1974
Mundra, Kusum	Asst	San Diego St		PHD	01	Ca-Rivers	2001
Munkin, Murat	Asst	Tennessee		PHD	01	Indiana	2001
Munley, Vincent G.	Prof	Lehigh	HI	PHD	79	SUNY-Bin	1980
Lee Iacocca Professor of Business & Economics							
Munyon, Paul G.	Assoc	Grinnell	L	PHD	75	Harvard	1982
Murans, Frank	Retir			PHD	57	Mich St	
Muraoka, Dennis D.	Prof	CS-Long Bch		PHD	81	Ca-SnBarb	1982
Murat, Kara S.	Asst	Angelo State	PM	PHD	93	Tx Tech	2000
Murdoch, James	Prof	Texas-Dallas		PHD	82	Wyoming	
Murdock, E. Wayne	Retir	S F Austin	AR	PHD	71	Oklahoma	1972
Murli, Rajan	Assoc	Scranton		PHD	92	Temple	1989
Murphy, Albert	Asst	Manhattan		PHD	01	CUNY	2000
Murphy, Caroline	Retir	Fitchburg St		PHD	71	Clark	1971
Murphy, Dennis R.	Dean	Western Wash	FM	PHD	74	Indiana	1979
Murphy, George G. S.	Emer	UCLA		PHD	57	U Wash	
Murphy, James H.	Asst	W Carolina	F	PHD	00	Geo St	1998
Murphy, James L.	Prof	No Carolina	C	PHD	64	Purdue	1964
Murphy, John J.	Retir	Catholic		PHD	61	Yale	1967
Murphy, Kevin J.	Prof	Oakland	JC	PHD	81	Mich St	1985
Murphy, Robert G.	Assoc	Boston Coll	EF	PHD	84	MIT	1984
Murphy, Russell D. Jr.	Asst	Virg Tech	D	PHD	97	Boston U	1997
Murra, Gene E.	Retir	So Dakota St	Q	PHD	63	Ohio St	1959

Murray, Chris	Asst	Houston	E	PHD	98	U Wash	1998
Murray, Jack W.	Retir	Tarleton St	1995	PHD	66	Tx-Arlin	1968
Murray, James M.	Prof	WI-Green Bay		PHD	62	Oregon	1969
Murray, John E.	Assoc	Toledo	B	PHD	92	Ohio St	1994
Murray, Matthew N.	C-Ac	Tennessee		PHD	86	Syracuse	1986
Murray, Michael P.	Prof	Bates	RH	PHD	74	Iowa St	1986
Phillips Professor of Economics							
Murray, Tracy W.	Prof	Arkansas	F	PHD	69	Mich St	1978
Distinguished Professor & Chairholder, Phillips Petroleum Company Chair/IEB							
Murrell, Peter	Prof	Maryland		PHD	77	Penn	1977
Murry, Donald A.	Retir	Oklahoma	L	PHD	66	Missouri	
Murshid, Antu	Asst	Wis-Milwauke		PHD	01	Rutgers	2001
Murtaugh, Frank M. Jr.	H-Ac	Norwich		PHD	81	Emory	1982
Murthy, N. R. Vasudeva	Prof	Creighton	CDH	PHD	75	SUNY-Bin	1979
Murti, Vedula N.	Asst	Penn St-Harr		PHD	66	Penn	1969
Musgrave, Frank W.	Prof	Ithaca	IJ	PHD	68	Rutgers	1968
Mushinski, David	Asst	Colorado St	CHO	PHD	96	Wisconsin	1997
Musoke, Moses		SUNY-Empire	NM	PHD	78	Wisconsin	1985
Musser, Thomas		DePauw					
Mustafa, Muhammad	Assoc	So Carol St		PHD	88	Wayne St	1989
Mustard, David B.	Asst	Georgia	DJK	PHD	97	Chicago	1997
Muth, John	D-Ac	Regis-CO	AGNM	PHD	78	Colorado	9-83
Muth, Richard F.	Prof	Emory	N	PHD	58	Chicago	1983
Fuller E. Callaway Professor of Economics							
Mutti, John	Prof	Grinnell	FHQ	PHD	74	Wisconsin	1987
Sydney Meyer Professor of International Economics							
Myers, Daniel A.	Assoc	W Kentucky	R	PHD	86	Vanderbilt	1986
Myers, George G.	Retir	East Tenn St		EDD	65	Tennessee	1957
Myers, John G.	Emer	So Illinois		PHD	61	Columbia	1977
Myers, Steven	Assoc	Akron	ACJ	PHD	80	Ohio St	1979
Myerson, Roger B.	Prof	Chicago		PHD	76	Harvard	2001
N'Chu-Oguie, Charles	Assoc	San Francisc	CO	PHD	84	Stanford	1984
Nachbar, John	Assoc	Wash Univ	CD	PHD	88	Harvard	1990
Nadenichek, Jon	Asst	CS-Northrdge		PHD	96	Rochester	1996
Nadiri, M. Ishaq	Prof	New York U	O	PHD	65	Berkeley	1971
Nadler, Mark A.	C-Ac	Ashland		PHD	83	Iowa St	1989
A. L. Garber Family Chair of Economics							
Nafziger, E. Wayne	Prof	Kansas State	OPF	PHD	67	Illinois	1966
Nag, Raja	Asst	Monmouth	G	PHD	98	Michigan	1998
Naggar, Tahany	Prof	West Chester	ADTN	PHD	76	Oklahoma	1977
Nahata, Babu L.	Prof	Louisville	D	PHD	77	N Illinois	8-78
Nair, Usha C.	Asst	Georgia Tech	F	PHD	95	Purdue	1996
Naish, Howard F.	Prof	CS-Fullerton	E	PHD	83	S Calif	1988
Naito, Hisahiro	Asst	Calif-Irvine		PHD	98	Michigan	1999
Najjar, Annette	Asst	Lindenwood		MBA	95	Millsaps	4-01
Naka, Atsuyuki	Assoc	New Orleans		PHD	89	Arizona	1989
Nakajami, Tomoyuki	Asst	Brown		PHD	99	Chicago	1999
Nalebuff, Barry J.	Prof	Yale	D	DPH	82	Oxford	1989
Nam, Woo Hyun	Prof	San Diego St		PHD	68	U Wash	1968
Nantz, Kathryn A.	Assoc	Fairfield	JDPA	PHD	87	Purdue	1986
Naples, Michele I.	Assoc	C New Jersey		PHD	82	Mass	
Naqvi, Nadeem	Prof	Mid Tenn St	DF	PHD	84	So Meth	2001
Narwold, Andrew	Prof	San Diego		PHD	91	Ca-SnBarb	1991
Nas, Tevfik F.	C-Pr	Mich-Flint		PHD	77	Fla St	1982
Nash, Robert T.	Retir	Tx A&M-Kings		PHD	71	Tx A&M	1971
Nasir, Abm	Asst	N Carol Cen		PHD	01	Wi-Milwa	2001
Nasser, Alan		Evergreen St		PHD	71	Indiana	1975
Natarajan-Marsh, Tara	Asst	St Michael's	AOPB	PHD	01	Nebraska	1996
Natke, Paul A.	Prof	Cen Michigan		PHD	82	Notre Dm	1981
Navin, John	Assoc	S Ill-Edward	HIJ	PHD	92	Mich St	
Navin, Leo J.	Retir	Bowling Gr		PHD	68	Mich St	
Navratil, Frank J.	Dean	John Carroll	G	PHD	74	Notre Dm	1973
Naya, Seiji	Prof	Hawaii-Manoa		PHD	66	Wisconsin	1961
Nazemzadah, Asghar	C-Pr	Houston-Down		PHD	83	Fla St	1989
Nazemzadeh, Nasrin	Inst	Prairie View		MBA	88	SW La	
Ndikumana, Leonce	Asst	Massachusett		PHD	96	Wash U	1996
Neal, Cora	VAsst	Weber State		PHD	01	Utah St	
Neal, Derek A.	Assoc	Wisconsin		PHD	92	Virginia	1998
Neal, Larry	Prof	Illinois	EGN	PHD	68	Berkeley	1967
Neale, Walter C.	Retir	Tennessee		PHD		LondonEc	1968
Neel, Richard E.	Prof	N Car-Charl		PHD	60	Ohio St	1969
Neelakantan, P.	Asst	E Stroudsbur	D	PHD	92	SUNY-Buf	1992
Neeman, Zvika	Asst	Boston Univ	CD	PHD	95	Nrthwstrn	1995
Neenan, William B.	Retir	Boston Coll	HR	PHD	66	Michigan	1980
Neergaard, Keith	Prof	Pacific Unio		PHD	94	Ca-Irvine	1988
Negbenebor, Anthony I.	Prof	Gardner-Webb		PHD	88	Miss St	1989
Negri, Donald H.	Assoc	Willamette		PHD	86	Michigan	1990
Nehman, Gerlad	Retir	Tx-Arlington	Q	PHD	73	Ohio St	1993
Nehring, Klaus D.	Assoc	Cal-Davis	DG	PHD	91	Harvard	1992
Neill, Jon R.	Assoc	W Michigan	H	PHD	83	Pittsburgh	1980

Neils, Allan E.	Retir	East Wash		JD		Gonzaga	1969
Neilson, William S.	Assoc	Texas A&M	CD	PHD	88	Ca-SnDgo	1988
Neimanis, George J.	Prof	Niagara		MA	65	NYU	1970
Nelson, Charles R.	Prof	U Washington	EGC	PHD	69	Wisconsin	1975
Nelson, David M.	C-Pr	Western Wash	EGI	PHD	75	Oregon	1977
Nelson, Dennis L.	Retir	Minn-Duluth	A	PHD	70	Minnesota	1964
Nelson, Douglas R.	Prof	Tulane		PHD	81	N Carol	1993
Nelson, Forrest D.	Prof	Iowa		PHD	75	Rochester	1980
Nelson, John P.	Prof	Louisville	H	PHD	68	Kentucky	
Nelson, Jon P.	Prof	Penn State	QD	PHD	70	Wisconsin	1969
Nelson, Michael A.	C-Pr	Akron	AH	PHD	80	Purdue	2000
Nelson, Paul A.	Assoc	Mich Tech	M	PHD	74	Wisconsin	1972
Nelson, Paul S.	Assoc	La-Monroe	DL	PHD	85	Tx A&M	1989
Nelson, Phillip J.	Retir	SUNY-Bingham	L	PHD	67	Columbia	1969
Nelson, Ralph L.	Retir	CUNY-Queens	MG	PHD	55	Columbia	1964
Nelson, Randy A.	Prof	Colby	GM	PHD	79	Illinois	1987
Douglas Professor of Economics							
Nelson, Richard R.	Retir	Columbia		PHD	56	Yale	1986
Nemec, Richard W.	Retir	Tx A&M-Kings		PHD	97	Kentucky	1981
Neral, John A.	Assoc	Frostburg St		PHD	89	Pittsburgh	1986
Nesiba, Reynold F.	Asst	Augustana SD	EG	PHD	95	Notre Dm	1995
Nesslein, Thomas S.	Asst	WI-Green Bay		PHD	92	U Wash	1996
Netusil, Noelwah R.	C-Ac	Reed	AQDH	PHD	92	Illinois	1990
Netz, Janet S.	Asst	Purdue		PHD	92	Michigan	1994
Neuberger, Egon	Prof	SUNY-Stony B		PHD	58	Harvard	1967
Neuefeind, Wilhelm	Prof	Wash Univ	D	PHD	72	Bonn	1978
Neufeld, John L.	Prof	N Car-Greens	ND	PHD	75	Michigan	1974
Neumann, George R.	Prof	Iowa		PHD	74	Nrthwstrn	1984
Neumann, Hillar Jr.	Assoc	Northern St		PHD	86	Rutgers	1983
Neumark, David B.	Prof	Michigan St		PHD	87	Harvard	1995
Neun, Stephen P.	Dean	Utica	IJ	PHD	88	Conn	1982
Neville, Howard R.	Deces			PHD	56	Mich St	
Newburger, Harriet B.	Assoc	Bryn Mawr		PHD	84	Wisconsin	1987
Newell, Barbara W.	Retir	Florida St	1996	PHD	58	Wisconsin	1987
Newell, Howard	Prof	Union-TN		PHD	74	Indiana	1982
Newey, Whitney K.	Prof	MIT	CDH	PHD	83	MIT	6-90
Newkirk, Wayne	Retir	Drake		PHD	65	LSU	1967
Newlon, Elizabeth H.	Asst	Kentucky	H	PHD	01	Car Mellon	2000
Newman, Robert J.	Prof	Louisiana St	IJ	PHD	80	UCLA	1983
South Central Bell Business Partnership Professor							
Newmann, Rebecca	Asst	Wis-Milwauke		PHD	00	Colorado	2000
Newmark, Craig M.	Assoc	N Carol St	LD	PHD	84	UCLA	1984
Newsome, Heather	Lect	Baylor		MS	96	Baylor	1996
Newsome, Mike	Asst	Marshall		PHD	97	Kentucky	1999
Newton, James E.	C-Pr	Franklin		PHD	97	Ohio St	
Ng, Kenneth	Assoc	CS-Northrdge	N	PHD	88	Rochester	1986
Ng, Pin T.	Asst	No Arizona	CF	PHD	89	Illinois	2001
Ng, Serena	Assoc	Boston Coll	CE	PHD	93	Princeton	1996
Ngoboka, Pascal	Assoc	Wis-Rvr Fall	HP	PHD	87	Wi-Milwa	1990
Nguyen, Hong V.	Assoc	Scranton		PHD	81	SUNY-Bin	1979
Nguyen, Nghiep H.	Assoc	Mid Tenn St	L	PHD	81	Tennessee	1981
Ni, Xiagoguang	Asst	Missouri	EH	PHD	91	Minnesota	1990
Nichols, Archie J.	Retir	Butler	B	PHD	61	Penn	1957
Nichols, Donald A.	Prof	Wisconsin		PHD	68	Yale	1983
Nichols, Mark W.	Asst	Nevada-Reno	LKJ	PHD	94	Fla St	1996
Nicholson, Robert H.	Assoc	Richmond		PHD	72	N Carol	1972
Nicholson, Walter E.	Prof	Amherst	ACDK	PHD	70	MIT	1968
Ward H. Patton, Jr. Professor of Economics							
Nickerson, David	Assoc	Colorado St	G	PHD	81	Nrthwstrn	2001
Nickless, Pamela J.	Prof	N Car-Ashvil	AJN	PHD	76	Purdue	1983
Nielsen, Darwin B.	Retir	Utah State	Q	PHD	64	Oregon St	1965
Nielsen, Donald A.	Prof	Neb-Omaha	AR	PHD	70	Syracuse	1972
Nieswiadomy, Michael L.	Assoc	North Texas	HRIQ	PHD	83	Tx A&M	1985
Niho, Yoshio	Prof	Wis-Milwauke		PHD	73	Brown	1970
Nijhawan, Inder P.	C-Pr	Fayetteville		PHD	71	N Carol	
Nilsson, Eric A.	Prof	CS-San Bern	FJ	PHD	89	Mass	1989
Niman, Neil B.	Assoc	New Hampshir	BL	PHD	85	Tx-Austin	1987
Niroomand, Farhang	Prof	So Miss	F	PHD	83	Mich St	1984
Nirro, Katsuyuki	Assoc	Gettysburg	AC	PHD	75	Pittsburgh	1972
Nisbet, Charles T.	Retir	Evergreen St		PHD	67	Oregon	1971
Nisbet, Mary J.	SLect	Cal-Santa Br	G	PHD	91	Glasgow	1991
Niss, James F.	Retir	W Illinois	1994	PHD		Illinois	1968
Nissan, Edward	Prof	So Miss	R	PHD	69	Tx A&M	1969
Nitsch, Thomas O.	Emer	Creighton	ENP	PHD	63	Ohio St	1969
Nix, Joan	Assoc	CUNY-Queens	DG	PHD	89	NYU	1988
Njoku, Anthanasius O.	Prof	Benedict Col		PHD	71	Illinois	1971
Nnadozie, Emmanuel U.	Assoc	Truman State		PHD	87	Sorbonne	1989
Noam, Eli	Prof	Columbia		PHD	75	Harvard	1976
Noble, Nicholas R.	Prof	Miami U-Ohio	EC	PHD	78	Cincinnati	1976

Noll, Roger G.	Prof	Stanford		PHD	67	Harvard	1984
Morris M. Doyle Centennial Professor							
Nonnenmacher, Tomas	Asst	Allegheny	DKLN	PHD	96	Illinois	1996
Norberg, Robert W.	C-As	Robt Morris		MA		Ind-Penn	1968
Nord, Steven	Prof	No Illinois	R	PHD	76	Illinois	1979
Nordhaus, William D.	Prof	Yale	E	PHD	67	MIT	1967
Nordin, Harold D.	Retir	E Illinois		PHD	76	Illinois	1967
Nordquist, Gerald L.	Emer	Iowa		PHD	60	Iowa	1968
Nordstrom, Louise J.	Prof	Nichols Col	ADFH	PHD	71	Clark	9-74
Nordyke, James W.	Emer	New Mex St	FE	PHD	59	Princeton	1964
Norman, Alfred L.	Prof	Texas	C	PHD	71	Minnesota	7-72
Norman, Emlyn A.	Asst	Txs Southern		AM		Harvard	
Norman, George	Prof	Tufts	L	PHD	77	Cambridge	1995
Cummings Chair Holder							
Norman, Lee	Prof	Idaho State	ALN	PHD	80	Utah	1981
Norman, Peter	Asst	Wisconsin		PHD	96	Penn	1996
Norman-Zietz, Emily J.	Assoc	Mid Tenn St	M	PHD	94	Fla St	1993
Norrbin, Stefan C.	Prof	Florida St	F	PHD	86	Ariz St	1990
Norris, Hodge	Asst	Txs Southern		MS		Tx A&I	
North, Charles	Asst	Baylor	K	PHD	99	Tx-Austin	1998
North, Douglass C.	Prof	Wash Univ	NO	PHD	52	Berkeley	1983
Spencer T. Olin Professor of Arts & Sciences/1993 Nobel Prize in Economics							
Northrop, Emily M.	Assoc	Southwestern	ENQR	PHD	88	Tx-Austin	1994
Norton, Nancy	Assoc	Albany State	Q	PHD	94	W Virginia	1-01
Norton, Seth	Prof	Wheaton-IL	GJLM	PHD	82	Chicago	1995
Aldeen Chair							
Norton, Virgil	Prof	Albany State	QI	PHD	63	Oregon St	1-01
Norwood, Dwight Lamar	Retir	Campbell		PHD	74	Arkansas	1973
Noser, Thomas C.	Assoc	W Kentucky	CA	PHD	86	Alabama	1984
Nourzad, Farrokh	Assoc	Marquette	CEO	PHD	82	Kansas	1981
Noussair, Charles N.	Assoc	Purdue		PHD	93	Cal Tech	1994
Novaes, Walter	Asst	U Washington		PHD	93	MIT	1993
Novey, Donald F.	Prof	Saginaw Vall	DE	MS		S Dak St	1969
Novshek, William	Assoc	Purdue		PHD	79	Nrthwstrn	1986
Nowell, Clifford	C-Pr	Weber State	ADQ	PHD	88	Wyoming	1988
Nowka, Harry E.	Prof	SW Okla St		EDD		Okla St	1963
Nowotny, Kenneth	H-Pr	New Mex St	HN	PHD	77	Tx-Austin	1976
Noyd, Louis E.	Assoc	No Kentucky		PHD	73	Oregon	1972
Nugent, Jeffrey B.	Prof	So Calif		PHD	65	New Sch	1973
Nugent, Rachel A.	Asst	Pacific Luth	DFQH	PHD	94	Geo Wash	1991
Nunn, Geoffrey E.	Retir	San Jose St		PHD	73	Virginia	1974
Nuwer, Michael J.	Assoc	SUNY-Potsdam		PHD	85	Utah	1986
Nwaokovo, Amechi	C	Morris Brown		PHD	96	Okla St	2001
Nyamwange, Richard	Assoc	E Stroudsbur	D	MBA	82	Long Isl	1987
Nyarko, Yaw	Prof	New York U	D	PHD	86	Cornell	1992
Nyatepe-Coo, Akorlie A.	Prof	Wis-La Cross	FHO	PHD	89	N Illinois	1989
Nye, John V. C.	Assoc	Wash Univ	N	PHD	85	Nrthwstrn	1985
Nyomba, Ajamu	Asst	Clark Atlant		PHD	91	Tx-Austin	
Nziramasanga, Mudziviri T.	Assoc	Wash State		PHD	74	Stanford	1973
O'Boyle, Edward John	Assoc	Louisiana Te		PHD	72	St Louis	1977
O'Brien, A. Maureen	Assoc	Minn-Duluth	J	PHD	83	W Virginia	1982
O'Brien, Anthony P.	Assoc	Lehigh	NE	PHD	86	Berkeley	1987
O'Brien, Dan	Asst	Texas-Dallas		PHD	99	Tx-Dallas	2001
O'Brien, Francis T.	Assoc	Providence	JK	MA	57	Boston C	1958
O'Brien, J. Patrick	Dean	Loyola-N Orl	AEHR	PHD	77	Okla St	1995
O'Brien, Jamie L.	Prof	So Dakota St	K	MPA	84	S Dakota	1984
O'Brien, Kevin M.	Assoc	Bradley		PHD	88	Illinois	1992
O'Brien, M. Barry	Assoc	Fran Marion		PHD	86	S Carol	
O'Brien, Peter A. Jr.	Retir	Pace		MBA	57	Rutgers	1964
O'Brien, William F. Jr.	Asst	Worcester St		PHD	89	Northeas	1997
O'Cleiracain, Seamus	Prof	SUNY-Purchas		PHD	71	Michigan	1974
O'Connell, John F.	Prof	Holy Cross	CDIJ	PHD	70	Wisconsin	1974
O'Connell, Stephen A.	Prof	Swarthmore	EO	PHD	86	MIT	1990
O'Connor, Catherine	Asst	Bucknell	DJC	PHD	96	Virginia	9-96
O'Connor, Dennis A.	Prof	Loras		PHD	84	Notre Dm	1983
O'Connor, F. William	Lect	Trinity-CT		JD	78	Conn	1984
O'Connor, J. Francis	Prof	E Kentucky		PHD	74	Minnesota	1989
O'Dea, William P.	Assoc	SUNY-Oneonta	DEP	PHD	88	SUNY-Alb	1979
O'Donnell, Dennis J.	Prof	Montana	OJR	PHD	74	Penn St	
O'Donnell, Margaret G.	Deces	SW Louisiana		PHD	76	Tx A&M	
O'Donoghue, Joseph	C-Pr	Molloy		PHD	75	Catholic	1997
O'Donoghue, Ted	Asst	Cornell		PHD	96	Berkeley	
O'Flaherty, Brendan	Assoc	Columbia	RA	PHD	80	Harvard	1987
O'Keefe, Suzanne	Asst	CS-Sacrament		PHD	00	Berkeley	2001
O'Neil, Robert F.	Emer	San Diego		PHD	75	Fordham	
O'Neill, James B.	Prof	Delaware	A	PHD	71	Purdue	1971
O'Neill, June E.	Prof	CUNY-Baruch		PHD	70	Columbia	1987
O'Neill, Patrick B.	C-Pr	North Dakota	ADL	PHD	87	Boston C	1987
O'Sullivan, Arthur M.	Prof	Lewis & Clrk	RKHQ	PHD	81	Princeton	2001
O'Toole, Dennis M.	Assoc	Virg Comm		PHD	71	Ohio U	1967

O'Toole, James K.	Prof	CS-Chico	ADR	PHD	83	Va Tech	1984
Oakland, William H.	Prof	Tulane		PHD	65	MIT	1979
Oates, Mary J.	Prof	Regis-MA	N	PHD	69	Yale	1970
Oates, Wallace	Prof	Maryland		PHD	65	Stanford	1979
Oaxaca, Ronald L.	Prof	Arizona		PHD	71	Princeton	1976
Obeng, Kofi	Prof	N Carol A&T		PHD	81	Penn	1982
UPS Chair							
Oberle, Wayne H.	Prof	St Ambrose		PHD	69	Missouri	1977
Obi, Emmanuel	Asst	Morris Brown		PHD	97	Clark Atl	1998
Obst, Norman P.	Prof	Michigan St		PHD	70	Purdue	1973
Obstfeld, Maurice	Prof	Cal-Berkeley		PHD	79	MIT	
Obutelewicz, Robert S.	Assoc	Bloomsburg		PHD	71	Mass	
Occhino, Filippo	Asst	Rutgers-N Br	E	PHD	00	Chicago	2000
Ochs, Jack N.	Prof	Pittsburgh	H	PHD	66	Indiana	1968
Odegaard, Thomas A.	Lect	Baylor		MA	70	Rice	1985
Odekon, Mehmet A.	Assoc	Skidmore		PHD	77	SUNY-Alb	1983
Odoom, Charles	Adj	CUNY-City C	AM			New Sch	1998
Odorzynski, Sandra J.	C-Pr	St Norbert		PHD	76	Purdue	1978
Oerther, Frederick J.	Prof	Greensboro	EH	PHD	89	GeoMason	1990
Oettinger, Gerald	Asst	Texas	JC	PHD	93	MIT	9-92
Ofek, Haim	Prof	SUNY-Bingham	J	PHD	71	Columbia	1981
Officer, Lawrence H.	Prof	Ill-Chicago	F	PHD	65	Harvard	1987
Ogaki, Masao	Assoc	Ohio State	E	PHD	88	Chicago	1994
Ogloblin, Constantin	Asst	Geo Southern		PHD	99	Kent	2000
Oguledo, Victor I.	C-Pr	Florida A&M	FL	PHD	89	Nebraska	1990
Ogum, George	Assoc	LaSierra	CFGM	DBA	90	Memphis	1997
Ohanian, Lee E.	Assoc	Minnesota		PHD	93	Rochester	1995
Ohly, John H.	Assoc	Mass-Dartmou	A	PHD	76	Boston U	1977
Ohn, Jonathan	Asst	Virginia St		PHD	98	Lehigh	1999
Ohno, Yuka	Asst	Rice	FL	PHD	93	U Wash	9-94
Oi, Walter Y.	Prof	Rochester		PHD	61	Chicago	1967
Elmer B. Milliman Professor of Economics							
Ojemakinde, Abiodun	Dean	Albany State	M	PHD	89	LSU	9-89
Ok, Efe	Prof	New York U	H	PHD	95	Cornell	1995
Okediji, Tade	Asst	Oklahoma	O	PHD	96	Oklahoma	1997
Okonkwo, C. Valentine	Dean	Kentucky St		PHD	85	Fla St	2000
Okpala, Amon O.	Prof	Fayetteville		PHD	84	LSU	1984
Okten, Cagla	Asst	Louisiana St	L	PHD	99	Nrthwstrn	8-99
Okun, Bernard	Retir	CUNY-Brookly	CO	PHD	57	J Hopkins	1966
Okunade, Albert A.	Prof	Memphis	JI	PHD	86	Arkansas	1987
Oladi, Gholamreza	Asst	Dayton	D	PHD	00	McGill	2000
Oldfather, Michael	Assoc	Kansas State	EJ	PHD	80	Ohio	1983
Oliver, Michael	Assoc	Bates		PHD	95	Manchest	2001
Olley, G. Steven	Asst	Georgetown	L	PHD	92	Wisconsin	1997
Olmstead, Alan L.	Prof	Cal-Davis	HN	PHD	70	Wisconsin	1969
Olnetti, Claudia	Asst	Boston Univ	CJ	PHD	01	Penn	2001
Olsen, Edgar O.	Prof	Virginia	HI	PHD	68	Rice	1970
Olsen, Randall J.	Prof	Ohio State	J	PHD	77	Chicago	1982
Olsen, Reed N.	Assoc	SW Missouri		PHD	89	Illinois	1990
Olsh, John Lindsay	Prof	W Maryland		PHD	74	Ca-Davis	1980
Olson, Edwin G.	Retir	Kansas State	HBM	PHD	71	U Wash	1968
Olson, Gerald W.	Prof	Mo-Kansas Ct	CGH	PHD	73	Rutgers	1971
Olson, John F.	C-Ac	St Benedict	NE	PHD	84	Rochester	1985
Olson, Kent W.	Prof	Oklahoma St	HI	PHD	69	Oregon	1974
Olson, Mancur	Deces	Maryland		PHD	60	Harvard	1969
Olson, Paulette I.	Assoc	Wright State	BJN	PHD	89	Utah	1988
Olson, Richard	Prof	Washburn		PHD	65	Nebraska	1980
Olson, Terry L.	Assoc	Truman State		PHD	86	Illinois	1990
Olszewski, Wojciech	Asst	Northwestern		PHD	98	Princeton	2001
Omar, Hanai	Assoc	Univ of D C	AH	PHD	96	Am World	1976
Omarzai, Mahmood	Prof	Calif U-Penn		PHD	76	Indiana	1979
Onafowora, Olugbenga A.	Assoc	Susquehanna	CDOQ	PHD	89	W Virginia	1989
Onatski, Alexei	Asst	Columbia		PHD	01	Harvard	2001
Ondrich, Jan Ivar	Prof	Syracuse	C	PHD	83	Wisconsin	1982
Onis, Ziya	Prof	Bogazici	AEO	PHD	83	Manchester	1984
Onunkwo, Emmanuel N.	Prof	So Carol St		PHD	73	Geotown	1978
Onyeiwu, Stephen Z.	Asst	Allegheny	ADLM	PHD	97	Conn	2001
Opara-Nadi, Gregory	Inst	Jackson St		MBA	77	Rust	
Opdahl, Roger W.	Retir	Lycoming	AENR	DED	70	Penn St	1962
Opiela, Timothy P.	Assoc	DePaul	EG	PHD	87	Tx A&M	2000
Oppenheimer, Margaret M.	Prof	DePaul	JDK	PHD	74	Nrthwstrn	9-76
Orazem, Peter F.	Prof	Iowa State	J	PHD	83	Yale	1982
Orcutt, Bonnie	C-As	American Int	ADJH	PHD	93	Clark	1992
OrdovenskyStaniel, J. Farley	Assoc	Pacific	HJ	PHD	92	Duke	1993
Ordover, Janusz A.	Prof	New York U	G	PHD	73	Columbia	1982
Orlov, Alexei	Asst	Radford	FE	PHD	01	Virginia	2001
Orlowski, Lucjan T.	Prof	Sacred Heart	EFGP	PHD	79	Poland	1983
Ormiston, Michael B.	Prof	Arizona St		PHD	77	J Hopkins	1984
Orr, Daniel	Retir	Illinois		PHD	60	Princeton	1989
Orr, Douglas V.	Assoc	East Wash		PHD	82	Colorado	1991

Orr, Lloyd D.	Retir	Indiana		PHD	64	Nrthwstrn	1964
Orsagh, Thomas	Emer	No Carolina		PHD	64	Penn	1965
Ortega, Lydia	C-Pr	San Jose St		PHD	87	GeoMason	1989
Orton, Eliot S.	Emer	New Mex St	N	PHD	71	Cornell	1970
Orvis, Charles C.	H-Ac	Rhodes		PHD	75	Minnesota	1973
Osagie, Emmanuel I.	Asst	Southern		PHD	85	LSU	1985
Osakue, John U.	Asst	CUNY-Stn Isl	FO	PHD	80	Nebraska	1991
Osang, Thomas	Asst	So Methodist	FO	PHD	94	Ca-SnDgo	1994
Osborne, Evan	Assoc	Wright State	FK	PHD	93	UCLA	1995
Osborne, Melissa	Asst	Towson		PHD	00	Mass	2000
Osborne, Theresa	Asst	CUNY-Hunter		PHD	97	Princeton	9-97
Oseghale, Braimoh	C-Ac	F Dick-Teane	F	PHD	89	Temple	1994
Osili, Una O.	Asst	Ind-Purdue/I	O	PHD	97	Nrthwstrn	1999
Osman, Alan	Lect	Ohio State					
Osman, Jack W.	Prof	San Fran St		PHD	66	Rutgers	1967
Ossella-Durbal, Ilaria	Asst	Ill Wesleyan	O	PHD	99	Cornell	1999
Ostas, James R.	Retir	Bowling Gr		PHD		Indiana	1969
Ostrosky, Anthony L. Jr.	Prof	Illinois St	ADEC	PHD	73	Pittsburgh	1973
Ostroy, Joseph M.	Prof	UCLA		PHD	70	Nrthwstrn	
Oswald, Donald J.	Assoc	CS-Bakersf	ABKN	PHD	74	Wash St	1961
Otrok, Christopher	Asst	Virginia	EC	PHD	99	Iowa	1999
Ott, Attiat F.	Prof	Clark		PHD	62	Michigan	1969
Ovitsky, Nancy L.	C-As	Mass Lib Art		PHD	82	Illinois	8-84
Oweiss, Ibrahim M.	Assoc	Georgetown	OF	PHD	69	Minnesota	1967
Owen, Ann	Asst	Hamilton	EO	PHD	95	Brown	1997
Owen, Jeff	Asst	Indiana St		PHD	00	Iowa	2000
Owen, John D.	Retir	Wayne State		PHD	64	Columbia	1975
Owen, Laura J.	Assoc	DePaul	NJ	PHD	91	Yale	1990
Owens, Daniel	Asst	North Dakota		ABD		Kentucky	2000
Owens, Gerald P.	Assoc	Angelo State	PI	PHD	65	Ohio St	1996
Owoye, Oluwole	Prof	Western Conn	EFHJ	PHD	89	N Illinois	
Oyen, Duane B.	Prof	Wis-Eau Clar	E	PHD	73	Iowa	1976
Ozaki, Robert S.	Retir	CS-Hayward	EFNO	PHD	60	Harvard	1960
Ozar, Semsa	Asst	Bogazici	J	PHD	90	Wirtschaf	1990
Ozawa, Terutomo	Prof	Colorado St	FO	PHD	66	Columbia	1974
Ozden, Caglar	Asst	Emory	FL	PHD	98	Stanford	1998
Ozertwrk, Saltuk	Asst	So Methodist	ELG	PHD	01	NYU	2001
Ozler, Sule	Assoc	UCLA		PHD	86	Stanford	1985
Ozmucur, Suleyman	C-Pr	Bogazici	CEL	PHD	76	Istanbul	1976
Ozsoy, Onur	VAsst	Alfred		PHD	98	SUNY-Bin	2000
Paal, Beatrix	Asst	Stanford		PHD	99	Cornell	1999
Paarsch, Harry	Assoc	Iowa		PHD	87	Stanford	1996
Paas, Martha W.	Prof	Carleton	BNO	PHD	79	Bryn Mawr	1975
Pachis, Dimitrios S.	Assoc	Eastern Conn		PHD	82	Mass	
Pack, Spencer J.	Prof	Conn Coll	B	PHD	83	NewHamp	1981
Padelford, Walton M.	Dean$	Union-TN	ABFO	PHD	75	LSU	1980
Pae, Ki-Tai	C-Pr	Central Conn	C	PHD	71	Conn	1971
Pagan, Jose	Assoc	Tx-Pan Amer		PHD	95	New Mex	1995
Page, Marianne E.	Asst	Cal-Davis	HJ	PHD	95	Michigan	1996
Page, Talbot	Prof	Brown		PHD	72	Cornell	
Page, Walter	Prof	SUNY-Plattsb	DE	PHD	68	Kansas	1983
Paglin, Morton	Retir	Portland St		PHD	56	Berkeley	1961
Paik, Seung	Inst	USAF Academy		MA	92	Penn St	2000
Pakes, Ariel	Prof	Harvard	CL	PHD	79	Harvard	
Pal, Debashis	Assoc	Cincinnati	L	PHD	90	Florida	1994
Palacios-Huercta, Ignacid	Asst	Brown		PHD	95	Chicago	
Paleisek, Karen Y.	Inst	Campbell		PHD		GeoMason	1993
Palfrey, Thomas R.	Prof	Cal Tech		PHD	81	Cal Tech	1986
Palivos, Theodore	Assoc	Louisiana St	F	PHD	92	Penn St	1992
Mack Hornbeak Business Partnership Professor							
Palm, Thomas	Retir	Portland St		PHD	67	Michigan	1967
Palmer, Jan S.	C-Ac	Ohio Univ	A	PHD	74	Mich St	1979
Palmer, Ransford W.	C-Pr	Howard	HO	PHD	66	Clark	1973
Palmieri, James	Asst	Simpson	DHIJ	PHD	95	Indiana	1997
Palmini, Dennis J.	Prof	Wis-Stev Pt		PHD	75	Illinois	1980
Palmquist, Raymond B.	Prof	N Carol St	QDR	PHD	78	U Wash	1979
Palomba, Neil A.	Retir	Ball State	2001	PHD	66	Minnesota	8-84
Palugod, Paul	Asst	Arcadia	AFM	PHD	93	Pittsburgh	9-99
Palumbo, Edwin P.	Inst	Providence	RJ	MA		Boston C	
Palumbo, George M.	C-Pr	Canisius	RT	PHD	77	Syracuse	1978
Pan, Zuohong	Asst	Western Conn	CJLO	PHD	95	Mich St	
Panagariya, Arvind	Prof	Maryland		PHD	78	Princeton	1978
Panayides, Alex	Asst	Monmouth	CFR	PHD	00	SUNY-Bin	2000
Pande, Rohini	Asst	Columbia	OH	PHD	99	London	1999
Panik, Michael J.	Prof	Hartford	CDHO	PHD	70	Boston C	1968
Pannell, Kerry E.	Asst	Bowdoin	NOF	PHD	88	Colorado	2000
Pantuosco, Louis J.	Asst	Winthrop	EHIJ	PHD	92	Northeas	9-97
Panzar, John C.	Prof	Northwestern		PHD	75	Stanford	1983
Louis W. Menk Professor							
Papachristou, Patricia T.	Prof	Christian Br	TI	MBA	79	Memphis	1980

Papagapitos, Agapipos	Assoc	St Thomas-MN	OP	PHD	92	Ohio St	
Papageorgio, Chris	Asst	Louisiana St	E	PHD	96	Pittsburgh	8-97
Papakyriazis, Panagiotis A.	Prof	Cal Poly-SLO		PHD	74	Ca-SnDgo	1971
Papathanasis, Anastasios	Prof	Central Conn	LK	PHD	79	Ca-Davis	1984
Papell, David H.	Prof	Houston	E	PHD	81	Columbia	1984
Papke, James A.	Prof	Purdue		PHD	59	Cornell	1962
Papke, Leslie E.	Assoc	Michigan St		PHD	87	MIT	1990
Pappas, Anthony	Assoc	St John's		PHD	71	Yale	
Parai, Amar K.	Prof	SUNY-Fredoni	AF	PHD	79	So Meth	1988
Parcells, R. J. "Pete"	Assoc	Whitman	CR	PHD	83	SUNY-Bin	1982
Pardee, Scott	Prof	Middlebury	G	PHD	62	MIT	2000
Alan R. Holmes Visiting Professor in Monetary Economics							
Parente, Stephen	Assoc	Illinois	DG	PHD	90	Minnesota	1999
Parigi, Sam F.	Retir	Lamar	J	PHD	64	Tx-Austin	1961
Paringer, Lynn C.	Prof	CS-Hayward	CDI	PHD	78	Wisconsin	1981
Park, David J.	Retir	CS-Pomona		PHD	62	S Calif	1965
Park, Gon Yung	Prof	LaVerne		PHD	93	Brown	1995
Park, Hong Youl	Prof	Saginaw Vall	KMEL	PHD	75	Utah St	1975
Park, In-uck	Asst	Pittsburgh		PHD	93	Minnesota	2000
Park, Jong-Heum	Prof	Kennesaw St	ADFO	PHD	74	Okla St	1988
Park, Jungsoo	Asst	SUNY-Buffalo	OF	PHD	99	Stanford	1998
Park, K.	Asst	Cornell		PHD	01	UCLA	7-01
Park, Kang Hoon	Prof	SE Missouri	CF	PHD	81	S Illinois	1979
Park, Sang O.	Prof	Chris Newpor	DFOR	PHD	63	N Carol	1982
Park, Sangin	Asst	SUNY-Stony B		PHD	96	Yale	1996
Park, Walter G.	Assoc	American U		PHD	91	Yale	1991
Park, William Laird	Retir	Brigham Yg		PHD	63	Cornell	1977
Park, Young J.	Prof	Calif U-Penn		PHD	74	Temple	1977
Parke, William	Assoc	No Carolina	C	PHD	80	Yale	1988
Parker, Carl D.	C-Pr	Fort Hays St	DIJM	PHD	71	Okla St	1976
Parker, Charles	Assoc	Wayne St Col	ADKL	PHD	94	Cincinnati	8-95
Parker, Elliott	Asst	Nevada-Reno		PHD	92	U Wash	1992
Parker, Jeffrey A.	Prof	Reed	AECF	PHD	81	Stanford	1988
George Hay Professor of Economics							
Parker, Joseph A.	Prof	New Haven	JR	PHD	68	Oklahoma	9-69
Parker, Patrick J.	Prof	Naval Postgr	AH	MBA	55	Chicago	9-74
Parker, Randall E.	Assoc	East Carol	EN	PHD	86	Kentucky	1986
Parker, Tommy R.	Asst	La-Monroe					
Parkison, Kathy	Assoc	Ind-Kokomo		PHD	83	Purdue	1993
Parks, Richard	Prof	U Washington		PHD	66	Berkeley	1970
Parks, Robert P.	Prof	Wash Univ	H	PHD	71	Purdue	1971
Parks, Susan	Prof	Wis-Whitewat		PHD	82	Purdue	1980
Parks, Terrance C.	Prof	Indiana St	OED	PHD	74	Illinois	1966
Parlour, Christine	Asst	Carnegie Mel		PHD	95	Queen's	1995
Parsons, Deborah	Lect	Ohio State					
Parsons, Donald O.	Prof	Geo Wash	J	PHD	70	Chicago	1997
Parsons, George R.	Asst	Delaware	Q	PHD	85	Wisconsin	1985
Parvin, Manoucher	Retir	Akron	ACP	PHD	79	Columbia	1978
Parzych, Kenneth M.	C-Pr	Eastern Conn		PHD	70	Conn	
Pasernak, Jacob I.	Visit	Richmond		ABD		N Carol	1999
Pasternak, Richard E.	Retir	Metro St-CO		PHD	62	Alabama	1968
Pasupathy, Meenakshi	Asst	CUNY-Baruch		PHD	96	Wash U	1996
Patch, Elizabeth P.	Assoc	Bloomsburg		PHD	90	Lehigh	
Patrick, Hugh T.	Prof	Columbia		PHD	60	Michigan	1984
R. D. Calkins Professor of International Business							
Patrick, J. Michael	Prof	Tx A&M Intl	FR	PHD	77	Mich St	9-93
Patridge, Mark	Assoc	St Cloud St		PHD	91	Illinois	1995
Pattanaik, Prasanta	Prof	Cal-Riversid	AO	PHD	68	Delhi	1991
Patterson, Braxton I.	Retir	Wis-Oshkosh		PHD	61	Mich St	1967
Patterson, Perry L.	Prof	Wake Forest		PHD	86	Nrthwstrn	1986
Patterson, Seymour	H-Pr	Truman State		PHD	80	Oklahoma	1980
Paul, Chris W.	C-Pr	Geo Southern	K	PHD	79	Tx A&M	2000
Paul, Harvey	Prof	Towson		PHD	72	SUNY-Buf	1966
Paul, Rodney	Asst	St Bonaventu	E	PHD	00	Clemson	2001
Paul, Sanjay	Asst	St Norbert		PHD	92	SUNY-Buf	1992
Paulin, Elizabeth	Assoc	LaSalle	J	PHD	87	Tx-Austin	1988
Paus, Eva	Assoc	Mt Holyoke		PHD	83	Pittsburgh	1987
Pauszek, Ruffin		SUNY-Empire	A	MBA		SUNY-Buf	1992
Pavan, Alejandro	Asst	Northwestern		PHD	01	MIT	2001
Pavcnik, Nina	Asst	Dartmouth		PHD	99	Princeton	1999
Pavsek, Daniel A.	Prof	Shenandoah		PHD	81	Case Wes	1992
Pawlak, Andrew T.	Asst	Salem State		MA		Tufts	
Paxson, Christina H.	Assoc	Princeton		PHD	86	Columbia	1986
Paxton, Donald	Retir	Jacksonvl St		PHD	71	Tulane	1977
Paxton, Julia	Asst	Ohio Univ		PHD	96	Ohio St	2000
Payne, Bill	Retir	Murray State	DFMQ	PHD	70	Oregon St	1975
Payne, Bruce C.	Prof	Barry		PHD	77	LSU	8-98
Payne, Richard D.	Prof	Boise State	HEA	PHD	70	S Calif	1970
Peach, James T.	Prof	New Mex St	T	PHD	78	Tx-Austin	1980
Peake, Charles F.	Assoc	MD-Baltim Co		PHD	68	Maryland	1967

Pearce, David G.	Prof	Yale	D	PHD	83	Princeton	
Pearce, Douglas K.	Prof	N Carol St	EG	PHD	74	Wisconsin	1985
Pearce, John F.	Retir	No Georgia		PHD	66	Alabama	1970
Pearson, Donald W.	Prof	E Michigan		PHD	70	Tx-Austin	1969
Peart, Sandra Joan	Assoc	Baldwin-Wal	BD	PHD	89	Toronto	1989
Pecchenino, Rowena A.	Prof	Michigan St		PHD	85	Wisconsin	1985
Peck, Cary	Asst	Arkansas		PHD	01	Arizona	2001
Peck, James D.	Assoc	Ohio State	D	PHD	85	Penn	1992
Peck, Merton J.	Prof	Yale	LO	PHD	54	Harvard	1978
Peck, Richard M.	Assoc	Ill-Chicago	D	PHD	83	Princeton	1981
Peckham, Brian W.	Asst	Wis-Plattev		PHD	79	Wisconsin	1987
Pecorino, Paul	Prof	Alabama		PHD	90	Duke	1994
Pedroni, Peter	Asst	Indiana		PHD	93	Columbia	1993
Peek, William A.	C-Ac	Niagara		PHD	85	Syracuse	1980
Peirce, William S.	Prof	Case Western	HOQ	PHD	66	Princeton	1966
Pejovich, Svetozar	Emer	Texas A&M	P	PHD	63	Geotown	1975
Pelzman, Joseph	Prof	George Wash	F	PHD	76	Boston C	1980
Pemberton, Donald K.	Prof	Detroit Merc		PHD	70	Kansas	1969
Pencavel, John H.	Prof	Stanford		PHD	69	Princeton	1979
Pendse, Dilip C.	Assoc	Ind-Kokomo		PHD	71	Oregon St	
Penn, William M.	Prof	Belhaven	AM	PHD	68	Duke	1981
Pennington, Robert L.	Assoc	Cen Florida	D	PHD	77	Tx A&M	1983
Peoples, James A.	Prof	Wis-Milwauke		PHD	84	Berkeley	1990
Pepall, Lynne	Assoc	Tufts	L	PHD	83	Cambridge	1987
Peper, Merle J.	Dean	West Alabama		PHD	86	LSU	9-95
Pepin, Raymond A.	Prof	Stonehill	AD	PHD	71	Clark	1969
Peppard, Donald M. Jr.	Prof	Conn Coll	R	PHD	75	Mich St	
Pepper, John	Asst	Virginia	HD	PHD	96	Wisconsin	1996
Peppers, Larry C.	Dean	Wash & Lee		PHD	70	Vanderbilt	1986
Peregon, Michael	Asst	Bentley	AJ	MA	76	Wayne St	2001
Pereira, Alfredo M.	Prof	Wm & Mary		PHD	88	Stanford	1995
Perelman, Michael A.	Prof	CS-Chico	N	PHD	71	Berkeley	1971
Peretto, Pietro	Assoc	Duke	EFLM	PHD	94	Yale	9-94
Perez, Stephen J.	Asst	CS-Sacrament		PHD	95	Ca-Davis	2001
Perkins, Dwight H.	Prof	Harvard		PHD	64	Harvard	1963
Harold Hitchings Burbank Professor of Political Economy							
Perkins, Garey B.	Assoc	Freed Hardem	DEQ	PHD	71	Tennessee	8-98
Perkins, George M.	Assoc	Holy Cross	AH	PHD	76	Boston C	2000
Perkins, Mary	Assoc	Howard	D	PHD	82	American	
Perli, Roberto	Asst	Pennsylvania	E	PHD	95	NYU	1995
Perline, Martin M.	Prof	Wichita St		PHD	65	Ohio St	1965
Perlman, Mark	Retir	Pittsburgh		PHD	50	Columbia	1963
Perlman, Richard W.	Emer	Wis-Milwauke		PHD	53	Columbia	1964
Pernecky, Mark L.	Assoc	St Olaf	EJA	PHD	90	Notre Dm	1990
Perri, Timothy J.	Prof	Appalach St	DJ	PHD	78	Ohio St	1980
Perrigne, Isabelle	Asst	So Calif		PHD	91	Toulouse	1997
Perron, Pierre	Prof	Boston Univ	C	PHD	86	Yale	1997
Perrotti, Liesa	Asst	INSEAD	V				9-97
Perry, Joseph M.	C-Pr	North Fla	NOR	PHD	66	Nrthwstrn	1971
Perry, Mark J.	Asst	Mich-Flint		PHD	93	GeoMason	1996
Perry, Martin K.	Prof	Rutgers-N Br	L	PHD	76	Stanford	1989
Persico, Nicola	Asst	Pennsylvania		PHD	96	Nrthwstrn	1997
Persky, Joseph J.	Prof	Ill-Chicago	R	PHD	71	Harvard	1974
Pescatrice, Donn R.	C-Pr	Iona	CDE	PHD	75	Purdue	1983
Pesek, Boris P.	Retir	Wis-Milwauke		PHD	56	Chicago	1967
Pesendorfer, Martin	Asst	Yale	L	PHD	95	Nrthwstrn	9-95
Petersen, Bruce C.	Prof	Wash Univ	L	PHD	81	Harvard	1991
Petersen, Harold A.	Assoc	Boston Coll	G	PHD	63	Brown	1960
Petersen, Harold Craig	Prof	Utah State	GM	PHD	73	Stanford	1973
Peterson, Brian J.	C-As	Manchester	ADH	PHD	00	Indiana	1997
Peterson, Dean J.	Asst	Seattle	B	PHD	94	Illinois	1991
Peterson, Donald L.	Prof	So Dakota St	Q	PHD	73	Nebraska	1974
Peterson, Elaine J.	Asst	CS-Stanislau		PHD	96	Wisconsin	1996
Peterson, Janice L.	Assoc	SUNY-Fredoni	BA	PHD	87	Nebraska	1990
Peterson, Jeffrey H.	C-Ac	St Bonaventu	G	PHD	91	Alabama	1984
Peterson, Jerrold M.	Prof	Minn-Duluth	HE	PHD	70	Illinois	1969
Peterson, John E.	Asst	Northern St		PHD	97	Kansas	1992
Peterson, Kenneth D.	Assoc	Furman		PHD	91	SUNY-SBr	1990
Peterson, Norris A.	Prof	Pacific Luth	J	PHD	81	Minnesota	1981
Peterson, Rodney	Retir	Colorado St	1994	PHD		Nebraska	
Peterson, Steven P.	Assoc	Virg Comm		PHD	89	Indiana	1989
Peterson, Thomas C.	Retir	Cen Michigan		PHD	70	UCLA	1972
Petr, Jerry L.	Retir	Nebraska	P	PHD	67	Indiana	1966
Petrakis, John T.	Retir	Lg Isl-Post		PHD		American	
Petratos, Vasilios	C-Ac	CUNY-Stn Isl	BF	PHD	70	NYU	1974
Petree, Daniel L.	C-Pr	Embry-Riddle	JT	PHD	00	Kansas	2001
Petruska, Dennis A.	Prof	Youngstown		PHD	84	Ohio St	1984
Pettit, Mary Ann	Inst	S Ill-Edward	A	MA	77	Tennessee	1989
Pevas, Mary Ann	Prof	Winona State		PHD	90	Notre Dm	1990
Pfaff, Alexander	Asst	Columbia	DQ	PHD	95	MIT	1995

Pfaff, Philip	Prof	Canisius	G	PHD	73	Mich St	1979
Pfannestiel, Maurice	Assoc	Wichita St		PHD	67	Okla St	1966
Pfeifer, Karen	Prof	Smith	BNOP	PHD	81	American	1979
Pfitzner, C. Barry	Prof	Randolph-Mac	DFC	PHD	83	Catholic	1982
Edward W. Seese Professor of Economics and Business							
Pflueger, Burton W.	Prof	So Dakota St	Q	PHD	85	Illinois	1985
Pfouts, William	Emer	No Carolina		PHD	52	N Carol	1947
Pham, Chung	Retir	New Mexico	CEGO	PHD	62	Penn	1963
Pham, Van	Asst	Missouri	FL	PHD	98	Cornell	1998
Phares, Donald	Prof	Mo-St Louis	HR	PHD	70	Syracuse	1969
Phares, Kathleen	Lect	Mo-St Louis	A	MA	76	Mo-StLou	1977
Phelan, John	Assoc	New Haven	HI	PHD		Geo Wash	9-95
Phelps, Charles E.	Prof	Rochester		PHD	73	Chicago	1984
Phelps, Charlotte D.	Assoc	Temple	TI	PHD	61	Yale	1967
Phelps, Edmund	Prof	Columbia	EG	PHD	59	Yale	1971
Phelps, Janie	Asst	Miss State	PM	PHD	98	Kansas	1998
Philippides, Andreas	Prof	Teikyo Post		PHD	94	Conn	1988
Philipps, Eugene A.	Retir	Moorhead St		PHD		Illinois	1966
Philipson, Tomas J.	Assoc	Chicago		PHD	89	Penn	1996
Phillips, Almarin	Emer	Pennsylvania		PHD	53	Harvard	1953
Phillips, Charles F. Jr.	Prof	Wash & Lee	L	PHD	60	Harvard	1959
Robert C. Brown Professor of Economics							
Phillips, Edward S.	Prof	Shepherd		PHD	70	Colorado	1974
Phillips, Joseph M. Jr.	Dean	Seattle	FOR	PHD	82	Notre Dm	2001
Phillips, K. E.	Retir	Tennessee		PHD		U Wash	
Phillips, Kerk	Assoc	Brigham Yg	EFO	PHD	91	Rochester	1992
Phillips, Llad	Prof	Cal-Santa Br	JC	PHD	69	Harvard	1972
Phillips, Owen R.	C-Pr	Wyoming	DK	PHD	80	Stanford	1985
Phillips, Peter C. B.	Prof	Yale	C	PHD	74	London	
Phillips, Peter W.	Prof	Utah		PHD	80	Stanford	1978
Phillips, Robert F.	Assoc	George Wash	C	PHD	85	Columbia	1985
Phillips, Ronnie J.	C-Pr	Colorado St	GB	PHD	80	Tx-Austin	1983
Phillips, Timothy P.	Assoc	SUNY-Cortlan	M	MBA	83	Clarkson	1983
Phillips, William A.	Assoc	So Maine	ACDF	PHD	79	Fla St	1980
Phillips, William H.	Assoc	So Carolina		PHD	80	MIT	1979
Phipps, Tim	Assoc	W Virginia	Q	PHD	82	Berkeley	1989
Photiades, John G.	Prof	Montana	BOH	PHD	72	Illinois	
Pickett, John C.	Prof	Ark-Ltl Rock		PHD	70	Missouri	1986
Picone, Gabriel A.	Assoc	South Fla	C	PHD	93	Vanderbilt	1993
Piedra, Alberto M.	Prof	Catholic	BNO	PHD	62	Geotown	
Pieger, Jim	Asst	Cal-Davis	LD	PHD	99	Ca-SnBarb	1993
Pieper, Paul J.	Assoc	Ill-Chicago	E	PHD	84	Nrthwstrn	1982
Pierce, James L.	Emer	Cal-Berkeley		PHD	64	Berkeley	1976
Pierce, Thomas J.	Prof	CS-San Bern	E	PHD	76	Notre Dm	1976
Pierson, Lynne M.	Prof	Chapman	NE	PHD	78	Ca-Rivers	1972
Pietrykowski, Bruce	Prof	Mich-Dearbor	BJNR	PHD	90	New Sch	1988
Pillsbury, Warren A.	Retir	Lehigh		PHD	63	Virginia	1962
Pinchin, Hugh M.	Prof	Colgate	F	PHD	70	Yale	1965
Pingkarawat, Nampeang	Prof	Chicago St		PHD	83	Il-Chicago	1982
Pingle, Mark	C-Ac	Nevada-Reno		PHD	88	S Calif	1990
Pinto, James V.	Prof	No Arizona	DC	PHD	75	Oklahoma	1981
Piore, Michael J.	Prof	MIT	J	PHD	66	Harvard	1966
David W. Skinner Professor of Political Economy							
Pippenger, John E.	Retir	Cal-Santa Br		PHD	66	UCLA	1965
Pippenger, Michael	H-As	Alaska-Fairb		PHD	90	Purdue	1991
Pirasteh, Hassan	Prof	So Oregon St	CEG	PHD	85	Oregon	1982
Piron, Robert	Prof	Oberlin	BD	PHD	66	Nrthwstrn	1961
Pirouz, Kamrouz	Asst	Montclair St	ADGN	PHD	73	Hawaii	1980
Pisani, Michael	VAsst	Tx A&M Intl	R	PHD	00	Tx-Pan Am	9-98
Pisciotta, John L.	Assoc	Baylor		PHD	71	Tx-Austin	1980
Pisciottoli, Louis F.	Retir	CS-Fresno		PHD	72	Duke	1967
Pistaferri, Luigi	Asst	Stanford		PHD	99	London	1999
Pitt, Mark M.	Prof	Brown		PHD	77	Berkeley	
Pitts, M. Melinda	Asst	Georgia St	IJ	PHD	97	N Car St	1998
Pizzi, Robert	Deces	Colorado Col		PHD	82	Wash	1990
Pizzigno, Gregory D.	Adj	St John's		MBA		St Johns	
Placone, Dennis L.	Assoc	Clemson	FPH	PHD	82	Pittsburgh	1976
Plagens, Les	Dean	Howard Payne		EDD	86	Tx A&M	1997
Plante, David	Asst	Western St		ABD		Utah	1997
Plassmann, Florenz	Asst	SUNY-Bingham	HRF	PHD	97	Va Tech	1999
Platt, Glenn	Assoc	Miami U-Ohio	CR	PHD	93	Car Mellon	1993
Platt, Henry M.	Retir	Pace		PHD		Columbia	1966
Pledge, Michael T.	Prof	W Illinois	AEG	PHD	68	Houston	1968
Plehn-Dujowich, Jose	Asst	SUNY-Buffalo	LICD	PHD	01	Chicago	2001
Pliskin, Jeffrey L.	Assoc	Hamilton	CF	PHD	85	Michigan	1982
Ploberger, Werner	Prof	Rochester		HAB	93	Vienna T	1997
Plosser, Charles I.	Dean	Rochester		PHD	76	Chicago	1978
John M. Olin Distinguished Professor of Economics							
Plott, Charles R.	Prof	Cal Tech		PHD	65	Virginia	1971
Edward S. Harkness Professor of Economics and Political Science							

Plumly, L. Wayne Jr.	Prof	Valdosta St	JA	PHD	83	Geo St	1980
Pluta, Joseph E.	Prof	St Edwards		PHD	72	Tx-Austin	1984
Pluta, Joseph E.	Retir	SW Texas St		PHD	72	Tx-Austin	1991
Podgursky, Michael J.	C-Pr	Missouri	IJ	PHD	80	Wisconsin	1995
Pogodzinski, Joseph Michael	Prof	San Jose St		PHD	80	SUNY-SBr	1987
Pogue, Thomas F.	Prof	Iowa		PHD	68	Yale	1965
Poirier, Dale	Prof	Calif-Irvine		PHD	73	Wisconsin	1999
Poirier, J. Eugene	Retir	Georgetown		PHD	66	Yale	
Poitras, Marc	Asst	Dayton	A	PHD	95	GeoMason	1998
Polachek, Solomon W.	Prof	SUNY-Bingham	J	PHD	73	Columbia	1983
Polak, Benjamin	Assoc	Yale	N	PHD	92	Harvard	
Polemarchakis, Hereakles	Prof	Brown		PHD	78	Harvard	2000
Polkinghorn, Bette A.	Prof	CS-Sacrament		PHD	72	Ca-Davis	1971
Pollak, Robert A.	Prof	Wash Univ	DJT	PHD	64	MIT	1995
Hernreich Distinguished Professor of Economics							
Polley, Susanne M.	Asst	SUNY-Cortlan	EHM	PHD	94	Penn St	8-94
Polley, William	Asst	Bradley		PHD	99	Iowa	1999
Pollin, Robert N.	Prof	Massachusett		PHD	82	New Sch	1998
Pollock, Gene Edward	Retir	Wooster		PHD	71	Ohio St	1961
Pollock, Richard L.	Deces	Hawaii-Manoa		PHD	67	Wisconsin	1968
Polutnik, Lidija	Asst	Babson	HJ	PHD	94	Geo St	1991
Pomery, John D.	Assoc	Purdue		PHD	77	Rochester	1982
Pompe, Jeffrey	Assoc	Fran Marion		PHD	90	Fla St	
Pomponio, Xun	Assoc	St Olaf	FP	PHD	91	Penn St	1991
Pongracic, Ivan	C-As	Indiana Wesl	AEFP	MA	68	Zagreb	1987
Pontiff, Jeffrey	Assoc	U Washington		PHD	94	Rochester	1992
Poole, Richard W.	Retir	Oklahoma St		PHD	60	Okla St	1965
Poole, William	Retir	Brown		PHD	66	Chicago	1974
Pope, C. Arden III	Prof	Brigham Yg		PHD	81	Iowa St	1984
Pope, Clayne L.	Prof	Brigham Yg	N	PHD	72	Chicago	1970
Pope, Rulon D.	Prof	Brigham Yg	QD	PHD	76	Berkeley	1982
Poper, Frank J.	Retir	Christian Br		PHD		NYU	1995
Poplin, Toby L.	C-Ac	Pfeiffer		MA	68	Appalach	1976
Popp, Anthony V.	Assoc	New Mex St	H	PHD	80	N Illinois	1981
Popper, Helen A.	Assoc	Santa Clara		PHD	90	Berkeley	1991
Pordeli, Hassan	Prof	Jacksonvil U		PHD	83	Nebraska	1983
Hugh F. Culverhouse Professor of Economics							
Porter, Jack	Asst	Harvard		PHD	96	MIT	
Porter, Philip K.	Prof	South Fla	H	PHD	78	Tx A&M	1985
Porter, Richard C.	Prof	Michigan		PHD	57	Yale	1964
Porter, Robert H.	Prof	Northwestern		PHD	81	Princeton	1987
William R. Kenan Jr. Professor							
Porter, Tod S.	C-Pr	Youngstown		PHD	84	Syracuse	1984
Porter-Hudak, Susan	Assoc	No Illinois	C	PHD	82	Wisconsin	1982
Portera, Kenneth	Adj	CUNY-City C	AM			Pace	1979
Portugal, Edwin	Asst	SUNY-Potsdam		PHD	93	SUNY-Alb	
Posatko, Robert C.	Prof	Shippensburg		PHD	75	Penn St	1981
Possen, Uri M.	Prof	Cornell		PHD	71	Yale	1971
Postlewaite, Andrew W.	Prof	Pennsylvania	DH	PHD	74	Nrthwstrn	9-80
Pacific Term Professor in the Social Studies							
Potepan, Michael J.	C-Ac	San Fran St		PHD	85	Ca-Davis	1991
Poterba, James M.	Prof	MIT	H	DPHI	83	Oxford	1983
Mitsui Professor of Economics							
Potiowsky, Thomas P.	Assoc	Portland St	E	PHD	81	Colorado	1982
Potter, Gordon Alwyn	Retir	Pace		MDIV		Gen Theo	1969
Potter, Simon M.	Asst	UCLA		PHD	90	Wisconsin	1990
Potter, William	Assoc	Fairmont St	AJ	MA		Memphis	1970
Potts, Glenn T.	C-Pr	Wis-Rvr Fall	E	PHD	76	Iowa St	1976
Poulson, Barry W.	Prof	Colorado		PHD	65	Ohio St	1965
Powell, Irene	Assoc	Grinnell	IL	PHD	85	Wisconsin	1989
Powelson, John P.	Retir	Colorado		PHD	51	Harvard	1966
Power, James	Prof	Cal-Berkeley		PHD	82	Stanford	1995
Power, Marilyn	C-Pr	Sarah Lawr	ABJ	PHD	77	Berkeley	1990
Power, Thomas M.	C-Pr	Montana	HQR	PHD	71	Princeton	
Powers, Elizabeth	Asst	Illinois	IJR	PHD	94	Penn	1996
Powers, John A.	Assoc	Cincinnati	C	PHD	66	Purdue	1965
Pozo, Susan	Prof	W Michigan	F	PHD	80	Mich St	1982
Prager, Jonas	Prof	New York U	G	PHD	64	Columbia	1962
Prasad, Kislaya	Assoc	Florida St	D	PHD	88	Syracuse	1988
Pratt, Leila J.	Prof	Tenn-Chattan	DC	PHD	75	Va Tech	1974
Hart Professor							
Pratt, Michael D.	Prof	Virg Comm		PHD	77	Kansas	1979
Pray, Bwalee	Assoc	Union-TN		PHD	92	Memphis	1991
Premus, Robert	Prof	Wright State	EOR	PHD	75	Lehigh	1975
Prendergast, George A.	C-Pr	St Joseph	EN	PHD	72	Penn	1956
Prescott, Edward C.	Prof	Minnesota		PHD	67	Car Mellon	1980
Regent's Professor							
Prescott, James R.	Retir	Iowa State	R	PHD	64	Harvard	1973
Pressman, Steven	Prof	Monmouth	HJN	PHD	83	New Sch	1981
Price, Charlotte A.	Prof	Sarah Lawr	AENQ	PHD	67	Columbia	1971

Price, Edward O. III	Assoc	Oklahoma St	B	PHD	80	Tx A&M	1979
Price, Gregory N.	Asst	N Carol A&T		PHD	93	Wi-Milwa	
Price, Hollis F. Jr.	Retir	U Miami	HR	PHD	72	Colorado	1971
Pries, Michael	Asst	Maryland		PHD	99	Stanford	1999
Prime, Penelope B.	Prof	Kennesaw St	ADFO	PHD	87	Michigan	1991
Primont, Daniel A.	Prof	So Illinois	DC	PHD	70	Ca-SnBarb	1978
Primont, Diane F.	Assoc	SE Missouri	JDE	PHD	87	N Carol	1990
Prindle, Allen M.	Assoc	Otterbein	DQ	PHD	77	Penn St	1988
Prinzinger, Joseph M.	Prof	Lynchburg		PHD	74	Geo St	1987
Pritchett, Jonathan B.	Assoc	Tulane		PHD	86	Chicago	1985
Prosper, Peter A. Jr.	Retir	Union	JA	PHD	70	Cornell	1964
Prosseda, Phil D.	Asst	USAF Academy		ABD	97	Colorado	1997
Proulx, Christopher	Asst	Cal-Santa Br	D	PHD	98	Michigan	1998
Prucha, Ingmar R.	Prof	Maryland		PHD	77	Vienna	1981
Prus, Mark J.	C-Pr	SUNY-Cortlan	JN	PHD	85	Utah	1990
Prusa, Thomas	Prof	Rutgers-N Br	F	PHD	88	Stanford	1994
Prychitko, David L.	H-Pr	No Michigan	ABP	PHD	89	GeoMason	1997
Pryor, Frederic	Emer	Swarthmore	OP	PHD	57	Yale	1972
Puffer, Frank W.	Prof	Clark		PHD	68	Brown	1968
Pugel, Thomas A.	Prof	New York U	DEF	PHD	78	Harvard	1978
Pugh, Joseph	Inst	Immaculata		MBA		Averett	
Pulchritudoff, Nikolai	Assoc	CS-L Angeles		PHD	71	Ca-Davis	1972
Pulikonda, Naga	Assoc	Ind-Kokomo		PHD	77	Illinois	
Pulsinelli, Robert W.	Prof	W Kentucky	DK	PHD	74	Rutgers	1967
Puri, Anil K.	Dean	CS-Fullerton	HR	PHD	77	Minnesota	1977
Purkayastha, Dipankar	Assoc	CS-Fullerton	O	PHD	90	Wash St	1990
Puth, Robert C.	Retir	New Hampshir	N	PHD	67	Nrthwstrn	1967
Putnam, William F.	Emer	So Carolina		MS	57	S Carol	
Putterman, Louis G.	Prof	Brown		PHD	80	Yale	1980
Pyle, William	Asst	Middlebury	P	PHD	97	Duke	1999
Qasmi, Bashir A.	Assoc	So Dakota St	Q	PHD	86	Iowa St	1987
Qastin, Abdul Masesh	Assoc	Lakeland	DGNP	PHD		Kennedy W	1985
Qayum, Abdul	Prof	Portland St	O	DSC	59	Netherld	1970
Qi, Min	Asst	Kent State	CDFG	PHD	96	Ohio St	1996
Qian, Hailong	Asst	St Louis		PHD	95	Mich St	1999
Qin, Cheng-Zhong	Assoc	Cal-Santa Br	D	PHD	89	Iowa	1989
Quade, Ane M.	Retir	CS-Sacrament		PHD	88	Illinois	1989
Quadrini, Vincenzo	Asst	New York U	EF	PHD	96	Penn	2000
Quandt, Richard E.	Prof	Princeton		PHD	57	Harvard	1959
Quayes, M. Shakil	Asst	SE Louisiana	E	PHD	00	Illinois	2001
Quddus, Munir	Dean	Prairie View		PHD	85	Vanderbilt	2001
Queneau, Herve'	Asst	Xavier		PHD	96	ParisDaup	1996
Quick, Paddy	Prof	St Fran-NY	ABN	PHD	75	Harvard	9-85
Quick, R. C.	Lect	SUNY-Cortlan					
Quigley, Herbert G.	Dean	Univ of D C		DBA	77	Geo Wash	1969
Quigley, John M.	Prof	Cal-Berkeley		PHD	72	Harvard	1979
Quinlivan, Gary M.	C-Pr	St Vincent	CDF	PHD	83	SUNY-Alb	1981
Quinn, J. Kevin	Assoc	Bowling Gr		PHD	89	American	1990
Quinn, Joseph F.	Dean	Boston Coll	DJ	PHD	75	MIT	1975
Quinn, Kevin G.	Asst	St Norbert		PHD	95	Il-Chicago	1994
Quinn, Robert	Asst	No Michigan	AIJ	PHD	95	U Miami	2001
Quinn, Stephen F.	Asst	Tx Christian		PHD	94	Illinois	1995
Quinzii, Martine	Prof	Cal-Davis	CDG	PHD	74	U Paris	1991
Quirmbach, Herman C.	Assoc	Iowa State	L	PHD	83	Princeton	1990
Qunjian, Daniel	Deces	Tufts		PHD		Harvard	1962
Raab, Raymond L.	Prof	Minn-Duluth	L	PHD	71	Colo St	1970
Rabbitt, Michael T.	Lect	Rockhurst		MA	75	Wash U	1988
Rabin, Alan UC Foundation Professor	Prof	Tenn-Chattan	E	PHD	77	Virginia	1977
Rabin, Matthew J.	Prof	Cal-Berkeley		PHD	89	MIT	
Racine, Jeffrey S.	Assoc	South Fla	C	PHD	91	W Ontario	1993
Radakovic, George	Assoc	Indiana U-PA	JR	PHD	79	Pittsburgh	1986
Radell, Willard W.	Prof	Indiana U-PA	NP	PHD	80	Illinois	1981
Radsich, Aleksander	Asst	CS-Long Bch		PHD	99	Princeton	1999
Raehsler, Rod D.	Assoc	Clarion		PHD	93	Iowa	
Rafeld, Frederick J.	Prof	Ashland		PHD	68	Ohio St	9-70
Raffa, Frederick A.	Retir	Cen Florida	E	PHD	69	Fla St	1969
Rafferty, Matt	Asst	Quinnipiac	ENC	PHD	97	Ca-Davis	2000
Raffiee, Kambiz	Prof	Nevada-Reno		PHD	83	Oregon	1983
Ragan, James F. Jr.	H-Pr	Kansas State	JA	PHD	75	Wash U	1977
Rahim, Niazur	Assoc	Chris Newpor		PHD	94	Va Comm	1998
Rahimian, Eric N.	C-Pr	Alabama A&M	ADOF	PHD	75	Indiana	1975
Rahmatian, Morteza	Prof	CS-Fullerton	Q	PHD	82	Wyoming	1988
Rahmon, Saif	Asst	Ohio Wesley		PHD	98	N Carol	2000
Rahnama, Masha	Assoc	Texas Tech		PHD	88	Iowa St	1996
Railing, William F.	Prof	Gettysburg	AHP	PHD	58	Cornell	1964
Raines, Fredric Q.	Assoc	Wash Univ	J	PHD	67	Wisconsin	1964
Raines, J. Patrick	Prof	Richmond		PHD	83	Alabama	1982
Rajan, Uday	Assoc	Carnegie Mel		PHD	95	Stanford	1995
Rajanikauth, N.	Inst	Miss Vall St		MBA		Miss St	1987

Raji, Seyed	Prof	Dowling		PHD	72	NYU	
Rakowski, James J.	Assoc	Notre Dame	DF	PHD	68	Minnesota	1967
Ram, Rati	Prof	Illinois St		PHD	76	Chicago	1982
Distinguished Professor							
Ramachandran, Rama	Prof	New York U	DEH	PHD	75	Brown	1987
Ramakomud, Sriprinya	Deces	Howard		PHD		Indiana	
Raman, Jaishankar	Asst	Valparaiso	OFA	PHD	97	Notre Dm	1996
Ramanathan, Ramu	Emer	Ca-San Diego	CFO	PHD	67	Minnesota	1967
Ramaswamy, Sunder	C-As	Middlebury	DFO	PHD	90	Purdue	1990
Ramazani, M. Reza	Prof	St Michael's	AFEC	PHD	90	Colorado	1986
Rambeck, Charles	Assoc	St Benedict	CDF	PHD	79	Minnesota	1975
Ramdas, Ganga P.	Asst	Lincoln-PA		PHD	87	Temple	
Ramey, Garey	Prof	Ca-San Diego	D	PHD	87	Stanford	1987
Ramey, James	Prof	N Carolina	GH	PHD	80	Kentucky	
Ramey, Valerie	Prof	Ca-San Diego	E	PHD	87	Stanford	1987
Ramezzaua, Paolo	Asst	Virginia	FL	PHD	01	LondonEc	2001
Ramin, Taghi	Assoc	Wm Patterson		PHD	86	NYU	1984
Ramirez, Carlos D.	Asst	George Mason		PHD	93	Harvard	
Ramirez, Miguel	Prof	Trinity-CT		PHD	84	Illinois	1985
Ramsay, Glenworth A.	Prof	Rhode Island	L	PHD	74	Boston C	1973
Ramsett, David E.	Prof	North Dakota	AHQ	PHD	68	Oklahoma	1968
Ramsey, David D.	C-Ac	Illinois St	DEH	PHD	67	Minnesota	1973
Ramsey, James B.	Prof	New York U	C	PHD	68	Wisconsin	1976
Ramstad, Yngve	C-Pr	Rhode Island	BA	PHD	81	Berkeley	1982
Randall, Laura	Retir	CUNY-Hunter		PHD	62	Columbia	
Randolph, Susan M.	Assoc	Connecticut	O	PHD	83	Cornell	1984
Ranelli, Edward	Dean	West Florida		PHD	69	Alabama	2000
Rangazas, Peter	Prof	Ind-Purdue/I	EH	PHD	83	Indiana	1989
Rangel, Antonio	Asst	Stanford					
Ranis, Gustav	Prof	Yale	O	PHD	56	Yale	1960
Ranjan, Priya	Asst	Calif-Irvine		PHD	97	Columbia	1997
Rankin, Carol A.	Assoc	Xavier	ADJ	PHD	80	Houston	1984
Ransom, Michael R.	Prof	Brigham Yg	J	PHD	83	Princeton	1988
Rao, J. Mohan	Prof	Massachusett		PHD	82	Harvard	1989
Rao, Vaman	Prof	W Illinois	ACEO	PHD	73	Missouri	1979
Raper, Michael Dennis	Assoc	West Georgia	AR	PHD	88	Geo St	
Raphaelson, Arnold H.	Prof	Temple	H	PHD	60	Clark	1970
Rapoport, John	Prof	Mt Holyoke		PHD	70	Penn	1970
Rappaport, Neal J.	Assoc	USAF Academy	DC	PHD	94	MIT	1998
Rapping, Leonard A.	Deces	Massachusett		PHD	60	Chicago	1972
Rappl, Magdalena	Prof	Tenn Tech	GN	PHD	85	S Carol	1985
Rappoport, Paul N.	Assoc	Temple	C	PHD	74	Ohio St	1977
Rasche, Robert H.	Retir	Michigan St		PHD	66	Michigan	1975
Rashed, Jamal A.	C-Pr	Xavier	ACFO	PHD	88	So Meth	1989
Rashid, Salim	Prof	Illinois	BGO	PHD	76	Yale	1981
Rask, Kevin N.	Assoc	Colgate	QI	PHD	91	Duke	1991
Rask, Kolleen J.	Assoc	Holy Cross	EFOP	PHD	89	Yale	1989
Rasmusen, Eric	Prof	Indiana		PHD	84	MIT	1992
Rasmussen, Chris H.	Inst	So Dakota St	M	BA	75	SW State	1978
Rasmussen, David W.	Prof	Florida St	K	PHD	69	Wash U	1968
Rassekh, Farhad	Prof	Hartford	ADFO	PHD	83	Houston	1989
Ratajczak, Donald	Retir	Georgia St	MN	PHD	72	MIT	1973
Rath, Kali P.	Assoc	Notre Dame	CD	PHD	92	J Hopkins	1990
Ratkus, Mark J.	C-As	LaSalle	O	PHD	76	Notre Dm	1973
Ratowsky, Henry	Asst	CUNY-Lehman		PHD	76	CUNY	1988
Ratti, Ronald A.	Prof	Missouri	EFG	PHD	75	So Meth	1975
Rauch, James	Asst	Gustavus Ado		PHD	94	Nebraska	1998
Rauch, James E.	Prof	Ca-San Diego	FO	PHD	85	Yale	1986
Ravelle, James J.	Retir	Moravian	KB	DA		Lehigh	1978
Ravelle, Linda J.	Assoc	Moravian	AG	PHD	90	Lehigh	1989
Ravenna, Federico	Asst	Ca-Santa Crz	EFG	PHD	01	NYU	2001
Ravikumar, B.	Prof	Penn State		PHD	89	Iowa	2000
Rawlins, Glenville W.	Prof	Montclair St	AGOQ	PHD	83	NYU	1984
Rawlins, Richard B.	Asst	Missouri So		PHD	98	Arkansas	1988
Rawski, Thomas G.	Prof	Pittsburgh	O	PHD	72	Harvard	1985
Rawson, William S.	Emer	So Carolina		PHD	67	Duke	1967
Ray, Cadwell L.	C-Ac	Tulsa		PHD	67	Tx-Austin	
Ray, Clarence G.	Prof	Nev-L Vegas	K	PHD	72	S Carol	1971
Ray, Debraj	Prof	New York U	D	PHD	83	Cornell	1999
Ray, Edward J.	Prof	Ohio State	F	PHD	71	Stanford	1970
Ray, Margaret A.	Assoc	Mary Wash	LQRA	PHD	88	Tennessee	
Ray, Subhash C.	Prof	Connecticut	CD	PHD	81	Ca-SnBarb	1982
Rayack, Wendy	Assoc	Wesleyan-CT	J	PHD	84	Wisconsin	1983
Raymon, Neil A.	Assoc	Missouri	CDEF	PHD	77	Colorado	1983
Raymond, Arthur J.	Asst	Muhlenberg		PHD	90	Tufts	1991
Raymond, Frank	Asst	Bellarmine	AFOR	PHD	97	Indiana	2000
Raymond, Richard D.	Retir	Kent State	DR	PHD	63	Brown	1970
Raynold, Prosper	Assoc	Miami U-Ohio	EG	PHD	89	LSU	1989
Razin, Assaf	Prof	Cornell		PHD	69	Chicago	7-01
Friedman Professor of International Economics							

Razin, Ronny	Asst	New York U	D	PHD	00	Princeton	2000
Razzolini, Laura	Assoc	Mississippi	D	PHD	94	So Meth	1994
Read, Colin	Assoc	Alaska-Fairb		PHD	88	Queen's	1989
Read, Robert A.	Lect	U Lancaster		PHD		Reading	
Reagan, Patricia B.	Prof	Ohio State	LJ	PHD	80	MIT	1989
Reagle, Derrick	Asst	Fordham		PHD	98	Vanderbilt	1998
Reaves, Natalie	Asst	Rowan Col-NJ		PHD	95	Wayne St	1998
Rebitzer, James B.	Prof	Case Western	J	PHD	85	Mass	1997
Reddy, Nallapu N.	Prof	Mich-Flint		PHD	67	Penn St	1974
Reddy, Sanjay	Asst	Barnard	NO	PHD	00	Harvard	2001
Redenius, Scott	Lect	Bryn Mawr		PHD	01	Yale	2000
Redfearn, Michael	Asst	North Texas	EG	PHD	92	Mich St	1992
Redington, Douglas B.	Asst	Elon	Q	PHD	89	Wyoming	1995
Redmond, Willie	Asst	SE Missouri	AFL	PHD	99	S Carol	1999
Redmount, Esther R.	C-Ac	Colorado Col		PHD	85	Virginia	1987
Reeb, Donald J.	Prof	SUNY-Albany	RG	PHD	63	Syracuse	1965
Reece, William S.	Prof	W Virginia	CH	PHD	75	Wash U	1990
Reed, J. David	Emer	Bowling Gr		PHD	70	Kansas St	1968
Reed, Mary Tripp	Lect	Murray State	ADFJ	MA	95	American	1995
Reed, Morris D.	Retir	East Central		MBA	70	Hawaii	1975
Reed, Robert	Prof	Oklahoma	JD	PHD	85	Nrthwstrn	1992
Reed, Robert R. III	Asst	Kentucky	E	PHD	98	Penn St	2000
Reeder, Danny B.	Deam	Okla Baptist		PHD	93	Okla St	8-91
Rees, Daniel I.	Assoc	Colo-Denver	J	PHD	92	Cornell	1993
Rees, David M.	Prof	Mesa State		PHD	73	Oregon	1983
Reese, David A.	Assoc	Gustavus Ado		PHD	80	Va Tech	1979
Reese, James W.	Assoc	SC-Spartanbu	AFPH	PHD	73	Tennessee	1982
Reffett, Kevin	Assoc	Arizona St		PHD	90	Purdue	1995
Register, Charles A.	C-Pr	Fla Atlantic	JL	PHD	84	Okla St	1997
Reiber, Ronald R.	Assoc	Canisius	G	PHD	74	Arizona	1971
Reich, Michael	Prof	Cal-Berkeley		PHD	74	Harvard	1974
Reid, Clifford E.	Prof	Colby	DCHR	PHD	73	Princeton	1987
Dana Professor							
Reid, John Joseph	Retir	Memphis	EF	PHD	62	Virginia	1966
Reid, Joseph D.	Assoc	George Mason		PHD	74	Chicago	1983
Reid, Kathleen A.	C-Pr	Shepherd		PHD	86	Penn St	1983
Reifel, John W.	Prof	Grand Valley	AHOR	PHD	72	Mich St	1971
Reiland, Ralph R.	Assoc	Robt Morris		MBA		Duquesne	
Reilly, Robert J.	Prof	Virg Comm		PHD	78	Tennessee	1978
Reiman, Mark A.	C-Ac	Pacific Luth	FPQ	PHD	88	U Wash	1988
Reimers, Cordelia W.	Prof	CUNY-Hunter		PHD	77	Columbia	1982
Reinelt, Peter	VAsst	SUNY-Fredoni	QR	PHD	99	Berkeley	2001
Reinganum, Jennifer F.	Prof	Vanderbilt	LK	PHD	79	Nrthwstrn	1995
Bronson Ingram Professor of Economics							
Reinhardt, Nola	Assoc	Smith	OPQ	PHD	81	Berkeley	1981
Reinhardt, Uwe E.	Prof	Princeton		PHD	70	Yale	1967
Reinhart, Blaise F.	Prof	Siena		PHD	62	Catholic	
Reinke, Robert W.	Prof	South Dakota		PHD	82	Minnesota	1987
Reinwald, Thomas P.	Prof	Shippensburg		PHD	73	Illinois	1974
Reiter, Stanley	Prof	Northwestern		PHD	55	Chicago	
Charles E. and Emma H. Morrison Professor of Economics							
Renas, Stephen M.	Prof	Wright State	EM	PHD	71	Geo St	1971
Rencher, Robert	Assoc	Liberty		MBA	81	Fairl Dick	1991
Renner, Donald E.	Prof	Mankato St	ACHR	PHD	78	Cincinnati	1979
Rennie, Henry	Prof	Heidelberg	CFG	PHD	73	Ohio St	9-92
Renning, H. Dieter	Emer	CS-Stanislau		DR	61	Freiburg	1970
Renshaw, Edward F.	Retir	SUNY-Albany	H	PHD	58	Chicago	
Renshaw, Robert H.	Retir	No Illinois	A	PHD	64	Mich St	1965
Resek, Robert W.	Prof	Illinois	CR	PHD	61	Harvard	1961
Resnick, Stephen A.	Prof	Massachusett		PHD	64	MIT	
Ressler, Rand W.	Asst	La-Lafayette	DJ	PHD	93	Auburn	8-93
Rethwisch, Kurt	Retir	Duquesne		PHD	69	Maryland	1967
Reuther, Carol J.	Assoc	West Liberty	CDGH	MS	73	Fla St	1991
Revankar, Nagesh S.	Prof	SUNY-Buffalo	DC	PHD	67	Wisconsin	1967
Revier, Charles F.	Assoc	Colorado St	EH	PHD	78	MIT	1974
Rewerts, Glen	C-Pr	Olivet Nazar	K	JD	87	S Illinois	1993
Reynolds, Bruce L.	Prof	Union	ODP	PHD	75	Michigan	1974
Reynolds, Douglas	Asst	Alaska-Fairb		PHD			
Reynolds, Morgan O.	Prof	Texas A&M	J	PHD	71	Wisconsin	1974
Reynolds, R. Larry	Prof	Boise State	BID	PHD	77	Wash St	1979
Reynolds, Stanley	Prof	Arizona		PHD	83	Nrthwstrn	1982
Reynolds, Stephen E.	Assoc	Utah		PHD	69	Wisconsin	1969
Rezek, Jon	Asst	Miss State	QF	PHD	00	Nebraska	2000
Rezvani, Farahmand	Assoc	Montclair St	ACGH	PHD	83	CUNY	1984
Rhoads, Thomas	Asst	Towson		PHD	99	Wyoming	1999
Rhodd, Rupert	Assoc	Fla Atlantic	FO	PHD	84	Fordham	1985
Rhode, Paul	Prof	No Carolina	N	PHD	90	Stanford	1990
Rhodes, George F.	Retir	Colorado St	LC	PHD	74	Tx A&M	1978
Rhodus, W. Gregory	Asst	Bentley	ACG	MA	75	Conn	1992
Ribar, David	Assoc	George Wash	J	PHD	93	Brown	1996

Ricciardi, Joseph M.	Assoc	Babson	EO	PHD	85	Tx-Austin	1985
Rice, Edward M.	Assoc	U Washington		PHD	78	UCLA	1979
Rice, G. Randolph	Emer	Louisiana St		PHD	70	Kentucky	1969
Rice, Walter E.	Retir	Cal Poly-SLO		PHD	73	Claremont	1964
Rich, Daniel P.	Assoc	Illinois St	DJ	PHD	87	Houston	1987
Rich, Stuart	Retir	Wis-Whitewat		DBA	60	Indiana	1959
Richard, James S.	Assoc	Regis-CO		PHD	80	Tx-Austin	1979
Richard, Jean Francois	C-Pr	Pittsburgh	C	PHD	73	Louvain	1991
Richards, Alan	Retir	Ca-Santa Crz	ONQ	PHD	75	Wisconsin	1976
Richards, Daniel J.	Assoc	Tufts	E	PHD	81	Yale	1985
Richards, Donald G.	Prof	Indiana St	FO	PHD	83	Conn	1985
Richards, Warren	Inst	S Ill-Edward	A	MS	90	S Il-Edw	2000
Richardson, David H.	Prof	St Lawrence	CJEF	PHD	66	Purdue	1979
Charles A. Dana Professor of Economics							
Richardson, Gary	Asst	Calif-Irvine		PHD	99	Berkeley	1999
Richardson, Harry W.	Prof	So Calif		MA	61	Manchester	1975
Richardson, J. David	Prof	Syracuse	F	PHD	70	Michigan	1991
Richardson, James A.	Prof	Louisiana St	H	PHD	71	Michigan	1970
Alumni Professor of Economics; Director Public Administration Institute							
Richter, Marcel K.	Prof	Minnesota		PHD	59	MIT	1959
Rickman, Bill D.	Prof	Fort Hays St	DEJ	PHD	82	Okla St	1972
Rickman, Dan S.	Prof	Oklahoma St	RC	PHD	87	Wyoming	1996
OG&E Chair in Regional Economic Analysis							
Riddell, Thomas A.	Assoc	Smith	AHNO	PHD	75	American	1980
Ridder, Geert	Prof	So Calif		PHD	87	Amsterdm	2000
Riddle, Mary	Asst	Nev-L Vegas	Q	PHD	98	Colo St	1999
Rider, Christine	Prof	St John's		PHD	79	New Sch	1976
Rider, Mark	Assoc	Kennesaw St	CDHJ	PHD	92	Geo St	1999
Rider, Robert L.	Assoc	CS-S Marcos	CDHK	PHD	89	S Calif	1992
Ridgway, Terry R.	Retir	Nev-L Vegas	D	PHD	74	Arizona	1968
Rieber, Michael	Prof	Arizona		PHD	63	MIT	1978
Rieber, William J.	Prof	Butler	F	PHD	79	Pittsburgh	1989
Rieder, Mary	Prof	Winona State		PHD	72		
Riefler, Roger F.	Prof	Nebraska	R	PHD	66	U Wash	1973
Ries, Christine P.	C-Pr	Georgia Tech		PHD	77	Chicago	1997
Riezman, Raymond G.	Prof	Iowa		PHD	77	Minnesota	
Riley, John G.	Prof	UCLA		PHD	72	MIT	1973
Riley, Robert	Assoc	St Thomas-MN	F	PHD	91	Wisconsin	
Riley, Teresa M.	Assoc	Youngstown		PHD	84	Syracuse	1984
Rima, Ingrid H.	Prof	Temple	B	PHD	51	Penn	1946
Rinehart, James R.	C-Pr	Fran Marion		PHD	62	Virginia	
Phillip N. Truluck Professor of Economics and Public Policy							
Ring, David W.	Assoc	SUNY-Oneonta	DEPR	PHD	82	SUNY-SBr	1981
Ring, Raymond J. Jr.	Prof	South Dakota		PHD	73	Kansas	1978
Rioja, Felix K.	Asst	Georgia St	EFG	PHD	97	Ariz St	1997
Riordan, Michael H.	Prof	Columbia	DLG	PHD	81	Berkeley	1999
Rios, Roberto J.	Asst	CUNY-Lehman		PHD	87	Columbia	1979
Rios-Rull, Jose-Victor	Asst	Pennsylvania	O	PHD	90	Minnesota	1990
Simon Kuznets Term Assistant Profess of Econ; email vr0j@anaga.sas.upenn.edu							
Ripoll, Marla	Asst	Pittsburgh	F	PHD	00	Rochester	2000
Rishe, Patrick	Asst	Webster		PHD	97	SUNY-Bin	1998
Riskin, Carl A.	Prof	CUNY-Queens	POQ	PHD	69	Berkeley	1974
Ritchey, Barry	Prof	Anderson U	DHR	PHD	88	Syracuse	1991
Ritenour, Shawn	Asst	Grove City		PHD	98	Auburn	2001
Rittenberg, Libby T.	Prof	Colorado Col		PHD	80	Rutgers	1989
Rittenoure, R. Lynn	Deces	Tulsa		PHD	70	Tx-Austin	1977
Rivera-Batiz, Francisco L.	Assoc	Columbia	FOJ	PHD	79	MIT	1991
Rivers, Mary J.	Assoc	Seattle	CDM	PHD	82	Pittsburgh	1978
Rives, Janet M.	Prof	No Iowa	ADJM	PHD	71	Duke	1984
Rivkin, Steven G.	Assoc	Amherst	AIJ	PHD	91	UCLA	1993
Rizvi, Saiyid A.	Assoc	Vermont	BDF	PHD	90	New Sch	1987
Rizzo, Mario J.	Prof	New York U	K	PHD	77	Chicago	1979
Roayaei, A. Jean	Prof	Fayetteville		PHD	84	Fla St	
Rob, Rafael	Prof	Pennsylvania		PHD	81	UCLA	1984
Robbani, Mohammad G.	Asst	Alabama A&M	GO	PHD	94	Fla Intl	9-94
Robbins, Roy E.	C-As	St Marys-Txs		MA	75	St MryTX	1983
Roberts, Bee-Yan	Prof	Penn State	O	PHD	80	Wisconsin	1981
Roberts, Bruce B.	Prof	So Maine	BE	PHD	81	Mass	1995
Roberts, Charles A.	Retir	W Kentucky	BN	PHD	79	Georgia	1969
Roberts, Helen	Asst	Ill-Chicago	E	PHD	95	Chicago	1995
Roberts, Kenneth D.	Prof	Southwestern	GEOT	PHD	80	Wisconsin	1981
Roberts, Mark C.	Prof	Mich Tech	Q	PHD	85	Arizona	1985
Roberts, Mark J.	Prof	Penn State	D	PHD	80	Wisconsin	1980
Roberts, Ray C. Jr.	Retir	Furman		PHD	61	N Carol	1969
Roberts, William W.	Prof	CS-Northrdge		PHD	74	Ca-SnDgo	1973
Robertson, Gary L.	Assoc	Aquinas		MA		Detroit	1969
Robertson, Marvin H.	Prof	Harding	EDK	JD	73	Arkansas	8-79
Robertson, Raymond	Asst	Macalester	AEF	PHD	97	Texas	1999
Robertson, Robert L. Jr.	Retir	Mt Holyoke		PHD	60	Wisconsin	1962
Robins, Philip K.	Prof	U Miami	IJ	PHD	72	Wisconsin	1982

Robinson, Michael D.	C-Ac	Mt Holyoke		PHD	87	Tx-Austin	1988
Robinson, Ned Stephen	Assoc	N Car-Wilmin	A	PHD	73	Oklahoma	
Robinson, William J.	Asst	Nev-L Vegas	A	PHD	83	Colorado	1980
Robison, H. David	Assoc	LaSalle	LQC	PHD	83	Maryland	1988
Robison, K. Wayne	Prof	Wash & Jeff		MBA	79	Ohio St	1979
Robles, Jack	Asst	Colorado		PHD	96	Ca-SnDgo	1996
Robson, Denise A.	Assoc	Wis-Oshkosh	AF	PHD	93	Nebraska	1994
Roca, Sergio G.	Deces	Adelphi		PHD	75	Rutgers	1971
Roche, John T.	Assoc	St John Fshr	BP	PHD	81	Mass	1981
Rochon, Louis-Phillip	Asst	Kalamazoo		PHD	98	New Sch	1999
Rock, Charles Patrick	C-Pr	Rollins	BJOP	PHD	86	Cornell	1984
Rock, James M.	Prof	Utah		PHD	66	Nrthwstrn	1967
Rock, Steven M.	Prof	W Illinois	AJM	PHD	75	Nrthwstrn	1990
Rockoff, Hugh T.	Prof	Rutgers-N Br	N	PHD	72	Chicago	1971
Rockwood, Charles E.	Retir	Florida St	O	PHD	63	Indiana	1960
Rodgers, James D.	Retir	Penn State	HK	PHD	70	Virginia	1969
Rodgers, William	Assoc	Wm & Mary		PHD	93	Harvard	1993
Edwin L. & Frances L. Cummings Associate Professor							
Rodgers, Yana	Asst	Wm & Mary		PHD	93	Harvard	1993
Rodriguez, Ada	Lect	CUNY-Lehman		MBA			
Rodriguez, Alvaro	Assoc	Rutgers-Newk		PHD	82	Columbia	1994
Rodriguez, Armando		New Haven					
Rodriguez, Francisco	Asst	Maryland		PHD	98	Harvard	1998
Rodriguez, Gustavo	VAsst	Kenyon	DCL	PHD	94	NYU	7-01
Rodriguez, Leopoldo	Asst	Portland St	F	PHD	99	Tx-Austin	2001
Rodriguez, Louis J.	Prof	Midwest St	EF	PHD	63	LSU	1981
Roe, R. David	Prof	Furman		PHD	78	Duke	1977
Roehl, Richard	Prof	Mich-Dearbor	BJNR	PHD	68	Berkeley	1976
Roelofs, Matthew	Asst	Western Wash	DL	PHD	96	Purdue	1997
Roemer, Michael	Deces	Harvard		PHD	68	MIT	1974
Rogers, Augustus J.	Deces			PHD	69	Mich St	
Rogers, Carol Ann	Prof	Georgetown	EH	PHD	83	Princeton	1984
Rogers, Craig	Asst	Canisius	RT	MA	94	SUNY-Buf	1998
Rogers, Cynthia	Asst	Oklahoma	JR	PHD	94	Pittsburgh	1997
Rogers, Kevin	Assoc	Miss State	CE	PHD	96	Georgia	1996
Rogers, Michael	Prof	Albany State	L	PHD	88	Tennessee	9-89
Rogers, Robert P.	Assoc	Ashland		PHD	83	Geo Wash	1993
Rogers, Walter B.	Retir	Mid Tenn St		PHD	69	Okla St	1981
Rogerson, Richard D.	Prof	Arizona St		PHD	84	Minnesota	2001
Edward Rondthaler Professor							
Rogerson, William P.	Prof	Northwestern		PHD	81	Cal Tech	
Rogoff, Kenneth S.	Prof	Harvard		PHD	80	MIT	2001
Rohacek, Jerry K.	Retir	Alaska-Ancho	DEN	MA	69	Ca-SnBarb	1973
Rohlf, William D. Jr.	Prof	Drury		PHD	72	Kansas St	1972
Roistacher, Elizabeth A.	Prof	CUNY-Queens	RH	PHD	72	Penn	1974
Roley, V. Vance	Prof	U Washington		PHD	77	Harvard	1983
Rolle, JoAnn	C-Ac	Hampton		PHD		Howard	1996
Roller, Lars-Hendrik	Prof	INSEAD	L	PHD	87	Penn	9-87
Rolleston, Barbara Sherman	C-Ac	Baldwin-Wal	HR	PHD	83	Cornell	1983
Rollosson, Michael	Inst	Rhodes		ABD			1993
Roman, Paul D.	Retir	St Louis		PHD	67	St Louis	1966
Romano, Richard E.	Prof	Florida	THOD	PHD	82	Pittsburgh	1982
Gerald L. Gunter Professor							
Romans, Thomas J.	Retir	SUNY-Buffalo	HR	PHD	63	Brown	1967
Romer, Christina D.	Prof	Cal-Berkeley		PHD	85	MIT	1988
Romer, David H.	Prof	Cal-Berkeley		PHD	85	MIT	1988
Romig, Rodney	Dean	Hawaii Pacif		PHD	75	Nebraska	8-87
Romps, John F.	C-Ac	St Anselm	ABEH	MA	68	Fordham	1968
Ronaghy, Hassan A.	Retir	Youngstown		PHD	69	Wisconsin	
Rook, Sarah P.	Assoc	SC-Spartanbu	ADEQ	PHD	80	N Car St	1980
Rooney, Patrick	Assoc	Ind-Purdue/I	JH	PHD	87	Notre Dm	1987
Rooney, Robert F.	Prof	CS-Long Bch		PHD	65	Stanford	1970
Roosevelt, Frank	Prof	Sarah Lawr	ABDP	PHD	76	New Sch	1977
Roper, Don E.	Prof	Colorado		PHD	70	Chicago	1985
Rork, Jonathan	Asst	Vassar	DR	PHD	99	Stanford	2000
Ros, Jaime	Prof	Notre Dame	OE	PHD	78	Cambridge	1990
Rosa, Duane J.	Assoc	West Tx A&M	EOQ	PHD	89	Tx Tech	1984
Rose, David C.	Prof	Mo-St Louis	CDIJ	PHD	87	Virginia	1985
Rose, Elaina	Assoc	U Washington		PHD	93	Penn	1993
Rose, Louis	Retir	Hawaii-Manoa		PHD	70	UCLA	1969
Rose, Margarita M.	Assoc	King's Col	AO	PHD	89	Notre Dm	9-90
Rose, Mary B.	SLect	U Lancaster		PHD		Manchest	
Rose, Nancy E.	C-Pr	CS-San Bern	IN	PHD	85	Miss	1985
Rosefielde, Steven	Prof	No Carolina	P	PHD	72	Harvard	1970
Rosegger, Gerhard	Emer	Case Western	OFND	DIUR	53	Austria	1965
Frank Tracy Carlton Professor Emeritus of Economics							
Roseman, Gary	Asst	Berry	G	PHD	97	Emory	2000
Roseman, Robert E.	Prof	Wash State		PHD	82	Minnesota	1983
Rosen, George	Retir	Ill-Chicago		PHD	49	Princeton	
Rosen, Harvey S.	Prof	Princeton		PHD	74	Harvard	1974

Rosen, Harvey S.	Retir	Cleveland St		PHD	69	Case Wes	1967
Rosen, Sherwin	Deces	Chicago	2001	PHD	66	Chicago	1977
Rosenbaum, Dan	Asst	N Car-Greens	JI	PHD	98	Nrthwstrn	1998
Rosenbaum, David I.	Prof	Nebraska	L	PHD	85	Wisconsin	1985
Rosenberg, Nathan	Prof	Stanford		PHD	55	Wisconsin	
Fairleigh S. Dickinson, Jr., Professor of Public Policy							
Rosenberg, Richard	Retir	Penn State	A	PHD	69	Minnesota	1965
Rosenberg, Richard E.	Assoc	Wis-Parkside	FOP	PHD	70	Wisconsin	1969
Rosenberg, Sam	Prof	Roosevelt		PHD	75	Berkeley	1982
Rosenblat, Tanya S.	Asst	Wesleyan-CT	E	PHD	99	MIT	1999
Rosenbloom, Joshua L.	Prof	Kansas	NJ	PHD	88	Stanford	1988
Rosendorff, Peter	Assoc	So Calif		PHD	93	Columbia	1992
Rosenthal, Jean-Laurent	Prof	UCLA		PHD	88	Cal Tech	1988
Rosenthal, Robert A.	Prof	Stonehill	AI	PHD	78	Boston U	1975
Rosenthal, Robert W.	Prof	Boston Univ	CD	PHD	71	Stanford	1987
Rosenthal, Stuart S.	Prof	Syracuse	RHG	PHD	86	Wisconsin	1999
Rosenzweig, Mark R.	C-Pr	Pennsylvania	OJL	PHD	73	Columbia	1990
Rosovsky, Henry	Emer	Harvard		PHD	59	Harvard	1965
Lewis P. and Linda L. Geyser University Professor, Emeritus							
Ross, Clark G.	Prof	Davidson	P	PHD	76	Boston C	1979
Frontis Johnston Professor of Economics							
Ross, David R.	C-Ac$	Bryn Mawr		PHD	84	Nrthwstrn	1992
Ross, Glenwood	Asst	Morehouse		PHD		Geo St	
Ross, Howard N.	Prof	CUNY-Baruch		PHD	64	Columbia	1964
Ross, Larry L.	Prof	Alaska-Ancho	ADE	MS	71	Oregon	1971
Ross, Robert P.	Assoc	Bloomsburg		MA	58	Wash U	1967
Ross, Stephen	Asst	Connecticut	R	PHD	94	Syracuse	1994
Ross, Stephen A.	Prof	MIT	G	PHD	69	Harvard	1998
Franco Modiglani Professor of Finance and Economics							
Ross, Thomas A.	Assoc	Baldwin-Wal	CG	MS		Bowl Gr	
Ross, William N.	Retir	Clarion		PHD	71	Kansas St	1972
Rossana, Robert J.	Prof	Wayne State	E	PHD	80	J Hopkins	1991
Rosser, J. Barkley Jr.	Prof	Jms Madison	R	PHD	76	Wisconsin	1977
Rosser, Marina V.	Assoc	Jms Madison	FP	PHD	79	MoscowSt	1987
Rossi, Armond A.	Asst	Frostburg St		PHD	93	W Virginia	1988
Rossiter, Rosemary D.	Prof	Ohio Univ		PHD	80	Wi-Milwa	1983
Rossman, Joseph E.	Assoc	Tx A&M-Kings		PHD	75	Iowa St	1976
Rossman, Kathleen	Asst	Birminghm So		PHD	99	Colorado	1999
Rotella, Elyce J.	Assoc	Indiana		PHD	77	Penn	1981
Roth, Alvin E.	Prof	Harvard		PHD	74	Stanford	
Roth, Margarete P.	Retir	Benedictn-IL	FA	PHD	67	Cologne	1970
Roth, Timothy P.	C-Pr	Txs-El Paso	AD	PHD	70	Tx A&M	1970
A.B. Templeton Professor							
Rotheim, Roy J.	Prof	Skidmore		PHD	77	Rutgers	1980
Rothenberg, Jerome	Retir	MIT	R	PHD	54	Columbia	1966
Rothenberg, Winnie	Assoc	Tufts	N	PHD	85	Brandeis	1986
Rothenburg, Thomas J.	Prof	Cal-Berkeley		PHD	66	MIT	1966
Rothman, Philip	Assoc	East Carol	CE	PHD	90	NYU	1992
Rothschild, Robert	Read	U Lancaster		MA		Capetown	
Rothstein, Paul	Assoc	Wash Univ	H	PHD	88	Berkeley	1988
Rothstein, Sheldon H.	Asst	NE Illinois	ADGJ	MA		Chicago	
Rothwell, Geoffrey S.	SLect	Stanford		PHD	85	Berkeley	1986
Rottenberg, Simon	Retir	Massachusett		PHD	50	Harvard	1971
Roubini, Nouriel	Assoc	New York U	EF	PHD	88	Harvard	1995
Roufagalas, John	Prof	Radford	DGE	PHD	83	Florida	1985
Roumasset, James A.	Prof	Hawaii-Manoa		PHD	73	Wisconsin	1976
Rouse, Cecilia		Princeton					
Rousseau, Peter L.	Asst	Vanderbilt	EM	PHD	95	NYU	1995
Routledge, Bryan	Asst	Carnegie Mel		PHD	95	Brit Colum	1995
Rowe, John W.	Prof	South Fla	D	PHD	66	Illinois	1979
Rowland, Patrick	Asst	Fordham		PHD	98	Ca-SnBarb	1996
Rowley, Charles K.	Prof	George Mason		PHD	64	Nottinghm	1984
Roy, Raj	Prof	Toledo	F	PHD	68	Wayne St	1963
Roy, Santanu	Assoc	Fla Internat	DLQF	PHD	91	Cornell	1998
Roy, Suddhasatwa	Asst	CS-Fullerton	LF	PHD	96	Purdue	1998
Roy, Tapan K.	Assoc	Eastern Conn		PHD	80	Temple	1977
Roy, Udayan	Assoc	Lg Isl-Post		PHD	91	SUNY-SBr	
Royalty, Anne B.	Asst	Ind-Purdue/I	J	PHD	93	Yale	1999
Rubenson, Daniel L.	Prof	So Oregon St	CEG	PHD	85	Car Mellon	1986
Rubin, Jeffrey I.	Prof	Rutgers-N Br	H	PHD	75	Duke	1973
Rubin, Paul	Prof	Emory	K	PHD	70	Purdue	1991
Rubin, Rose M.	Prof	Memphis	JI	PHD	68	Kansas St	1994
Rubinchik-Pessarh, Anna	Asst	Colorado		PHD	01	Penn	2001
Rubinfeld, Daniel L.	Prof	Cal-Berkeley		PHD	72	MIT	1983
Rubinstein, Ariel	Prof	Princeton		PHD	79	Hebrew	
Ruccio, David F.	Assoc	Notre Dame	BO	PHD	84	Mass	1982
Rucker, Randal R.	Assoc	Montana St		PHD	84	U Wash	1991
Ruffer, Rochelle L.	Asst	Youngstown	DH	PHD	94	Wisconsin	1995
Ruffin, Roy J.	Prof	Houston	F	PHD	67	Nrthwstrn	1976
Ruggiero, John	Assoc	Dayton	R	PHD	95	Syracuse	1995

Name	Rank	Institution	Fields	Degree	Year	Degree School	Since
Ruhm, Christopher J.	Prof	N Car-Greens	JI	PHD	84	Berkeley	1991
Ruiz, Nestor M.	Assoc	CS-Pomona		PHD	89	Ca-Davis	1990
Rummery, Sarah	Asst	S F Austin	J	PHD	94	Austr Natl	1998
Rumore, Nancy C.	Inst	La-Lafayette		MS	80	LSU	
Rundle, Steve	Asst	Biola	DEFN	PHD	97	Claremont	1998
Rungeling, Brian S.	Prof	Cen Florida	J	PHD	69	Kentucky	1981
Rupert, Lyle M.	C-Ac	Hendrix	G	MBA	85	Chicago	1987
Rupp, Daniel G.	Deces	Fort Hays St	AFH	PHD	81	Kansas St	1968
Rupp, Nicholas	Asst	East Carol	LQ	PHD	98	Tx A&M	2001
Ruppel, Fred J.	Assoc	E Kentucky		PHD	84	Maryland	1997
Ruprecht, Theodore K.	Retir	CS-Humboldt		PHD		Berkeley	1958
Rusek, Antonin	Assoc	Susquehanna	EFP	PHD	84	SUNY-SBr	1986
Rush, Lynda M.	C-Pr	CS-Pomona		PHD	84	Ca-Davis	1986
Rush, Mark	Prof	Florida	EF	PHD	82	Rochester	1982
Rushing, Francis W.	Retir	Georgia St	ANP	PHD	67	N Carol	1974
Russell, Clifford S.	Prof	Vanderbilt	HQ	PHD	68	Harvard	1986
Russell, Louise B.	Prof	Rutgers-N Br	I	PHD	71	Harvard	1987
Russell, Malcolm B.	Prof	Andrews	EN	PHD	78	J Hopkins	1979
Russell, Milton	Retir	Tennessee		PHD	63	Oklahoma	1987
Russell, Paul	Retir	Buena Vista		EDD	65	N Colo	9-67
Russell, R. K.	Prof	SW Okla St		PHD	82	Okla St	1973
Russell, R. Robert	Prof	Cal-Riversid	ADH	PHD	65	Harvard	1986
Russell, Steven	Assoc	Ind-Purdue/I		PHD	89	Minnesota	1993
Russell, Thomas R.	Assoc	Santa Clara		PHD	73	Cambridge	1978
Russell, William R.	Prof	So Methodist	D	PHD	64	U Wash	1971
Russo, Benjamin	Assoc	N Car-Charl		PHD	85	Iowa	1984
Russo, Daniel M.	Retir	East Tenn St		BA	61	Rutgers	1967
Russo, Gerard G.	Assoc	Hawaii-Manoa		PHD	89	Nrthwstrn	1987
Rust, John P.	Prof	Yale		PHD	83	MIT	
Rutherford, Thomas F.	Assoc	Colorado		PHD	87	Stanford	1995
Rutman, Gilbert L.	Retir	S Ill-Edward	JKD	PHD	65	Duke	1969
Rutstrom, Lisa	Assoc	So Carolina	DFQ	PHD	90	Stockholm	8-91
Ruttan, Vernon W.	Emer	Minnesota		PHD	52	Chicago	1976
Regents' Professor							
Ruud, Paul A.	Prof	Cal-Berkeley		PHD	81	MIT	1981
Ryan, Daniel	Asst	Temple	PL	PHD	90	Berkeley	1990
Ryan, Julie	Asst	Immaculata		PHD			1999
Ryan, Michael	Asst	W Michigan	F	PHD	00	Indiana	2000
Ryan, Peter C.	Asst	Framingham		PHD	77	Mass	
Ryan, Timothy P.	Dean	New Orleans		PHD	78	Ohio St	1978
Hibernia Professor of Economics							
RyanMann, Duncan	Assoc	SUNY-Empire	I	PHD	84	Penn	1994
Rycroft, Robert S.	Prof	Mary Wash	CHJG	PHD	78	Maryland	1977
Ryder, Harl E.	Prof	Brown		PHD	67	Stanford	1965
Saadatmand, Yassaman	H-Ac	Armstrong At	FO	PHD	88	NewHamp	1989
Saavedra, Luz A.	Asst	St Thomas-MN	HR	PHD	98	Illinois	2001
Saba, Richard P.	Assoc	Auburn		PHD	74	Tx A&M	1974
Sabbarese, Donald M.	Assoc	Kennesaw St	AEM	PHD	84	Geo St	1978
Sabella, Edward M.	Retir	Augsburg		PHD	71	Minnesota	1961
Sabi, Manijeh	Adj	Russell Sage	EGO	MA	86	Northeas	1988
Sable, Karin	Asst	Puget Sound	AHQ	PHD	97	Colo St	1997
Saboori, Farhad	Assoc	Albright		PHD	85	Indiana	1986
Sabot, Richard	Prof	Williams		DPHI	73	Oxford	
John J. Gibson Emeritus Professor of Economics							
Sacerdote, Bruce I.	Asst	Dartmouth		PHD	98	Harvard	1998
Sachs, Jeffrey D.	Prof	Harvard		PHD	80	Harvard	1983
Galen L. Stone Professor of International Trade							
Sackrey, Charles Melvin	C-Ac	Bucknell	A	PHD	65	Tx-Austin	1980
Sacks, Stephen R.	Prof	Connecticut	H	PHD	71	Berkeley	1971
Sadler, Thomas	Asst	Manhattan		PHD	98	Tennessee	2001
Saez, Emmanuel	Asst	Harvard		PHD		MIT	
Safarzadeh, Mohammad R.	Prof	CS-Pomona		PHD	84	Claremont	1987
Saffer, Henry	Assoc	Kean		PHD	77	CUNY	9-85
Saffran, Bernard	Prof	Swarthmore	AH	PHD	63	Minnesota	1973
Franklin and Betty Barr Professor of Economics							
Saft, Lester F.	Retir	CS-Northrdge		PHD	76	UCLA	1971
Sage, Lewis C.	Assoc	Baldwin-Wal	CIJ	PHD	85	Maryland	1985
Saggi, Kamal	Assoc	So Methodist	FLO	PHD	95	Penn	1995
Sahu, Anandi P.	Prof	Oakland	EG	PHD	85	Wash U	1985
Saito, Mika	Asst	Notre Dame	F	PHD	00	Cornell	2000
Sakai, Marcia	C-Pr	Hawaii-Hilo		PHD	85	Hi-Manoa	1991
Sakano, Ryoichi	Asst	N Carol A&T		PHD	90	Alabama	1992
Sakata, Shinichi	Asst	Michigan					
Sakellaris, Plutarchos	Assoc	Maryland		PHD	92	Harvard	1992
Sala-i-Martin, Xavier	Prof	Columbia	OE	PHD	90	Harvard	1996
Salant, Stephen W.	Prof	Michigan		PHD	73	Penn	1981
Salazar, Natalia	Asst	North Fla		PHD	00	Ohio St	2000
Salazar-Carrillo, Jorge	Prof	Fla Internat	OFA	PHD	67	Berkeley	
Sale, Tom S. III	Retir	Louisiana Te		PHD	72	LSU	1965
Salehi-Esfahani, Haideh	SLect	U Washington		PHD	85	Penn	1990

Salehi-Isfahani, Djavad	Prof	Virg Tech	OT	PHD	77	Harvard	1984
Salemi, Michael K.	Prof	No Carolina	E	PHD	76	Minnesota	1976
Salib, Anis B.	Retir	Alabama A&M	AI	PHD	72	Vanderbilt	1982
Saliba, Michael T.	Assoc	Loyola-N Orl	ADM	PHD	72	Oklahoma	1973
Salmon, Tim		Florida St		PHD	99	J Hopkins	2000
Saltzman, Cynthia J.	H-Ac	Widener	EFGO	PHD	86	Maryland	1980
Saltzman, Gregory M.	Prof	Albion	J	PHD	82	Wisconsin	1982
Salvatore, Dominick	C-Pr	Fordham		PHD	71	CUNY	1970
Salvucci, Richard	Prof	Trinity	N	PHD	82	Princeton	
Salyards, Donald M.	Prof	Winona State		PHD	75	Kansas St	1975
Salyer, Kevin D.	Assoc	Cal-Davis	EG	PHD	85	Ca-SnBarb	1990
Samanta, Subarna K.	Assoc	C New Jersey		PHD	85	So Meth	1987
Samhan, Muhammad	Assoc	Univ of D C	OP	PHD	82	American	1976
Samprone, Joseph C. Jr.	Prof	Georgia Col	AD	PHD	75	Ca-SnBarb	1983
Samson, Mike	Asst	Williams		PHD	94	Stanford	
Samuels, George E.	Prof	Sam Houston		PHD	72	Oregon	1975
Samuels, Warren J.	Retir	Michigan St		PHD	57	Wisconsin	1968
Samuelson, Larry W.	Prof	Wisconsin		PHD	78	Illinois	1990
Samuelson, Paul A.	Retir	MIT	D	PHD	41	Harvard	1940
Samwick, Andrew A.	Prof	Dartmouth		PHD	93	MIT	1994
Sanchez, Nicolas	Assoc	Holy Cross	DENO	PHD	72	S Calif	1977
Sandberg, Lars G.	Retir	Ohio State	NO	PHD	64	Harvard	
Sander, William III	Prof	DePaul	RD	PHD	78	Cornell	1989
Sanders, Seth	Assoc	Maryland		PHD	93	Chicago	1999
Sanders, William V.	Prof	Clarion		PHD	81	Penn St	1981
Sanderson, Allen	SLect	Chicago		MA	70	Chicago	
Sanderson, Patricia L.	Assoc	Miss State	F	PHD	77	Oklahoma	1979
Sanderson, Warren	C-Pr	SUNY-Stony B		PHD	74	Stanford	1989
Sandholm, William	Asst	Wisconsin		PHD	98	Nrthwstrn	1998
Sandler, Todd M.	Prof	So Calif	HD	PHD	71	SUNY-Bin	2000
Sands, Barbara N.	Assoc	Arizona		PHD	85	U Wash	1985
Sandy, Jonathan G.	Prof	San Diego		PHD	86	Ca-SnBarb	1986
Sandy, Robert	C-Ac	Ind-Purdue/I	J	PHD	77	Mich St	1974
Santelli, Anthony	VAsst	Union	G	PHD	97	GeoMason	2001
Santerre, Rexford E.	Prof	Bentley	DHI	PHD	83	Conn	1983
Santoni, Gary J.	Prof	Ball State	E	PHD	72	New Mex	1988
Santopietro, George D.	Prof	Radford	QDK	PHD	86	Va Tech	1987
Santore, Rudy	Asst	Tennessee		PHD	98	Ohio St	1999
Santos, Joseph	Asst	So Dakota St	E	PHD	96	Rutgers	1997
Santos, Manuel	Prof	Arizona St		PHD	84	Chicago	1999
Bank One Professor							
Santos, Richard	C-Ac	New Mexico	IJ	PHD	77	Mich St	1989
Sanyal, Paroma	Asst	Brandeis		PHD	01	Ca-Irvine	2001
Sanz, Ernesto	C-Pr	Mass-Lowell	FNP	PHD	75	Boston C	
Saposnik, Rubin	Retir	Georgia St	D	PHD	59	Minnesota	1970
Sappington, David A.	Prof	Florida	TD	PHD	80	Princeton	1989
Lanzillotti-McKethan Eminent Scholar; Dir Public Policy Research Center							
Sapra, Sunil	Prof	CS-L Angeles		PHD	83	Columbia	1991
Sapsford, David	Prof	U Lancaster		PHD		Leeds	
Sara, Tejinder S.	Prof	Tuskegee		PHD	75	Mass	1973
Sarafidis, Yianis	Asst	INSEAD	DF	PHD	01	Yale	2001
Sarangi, Sudipta	Asst	Louisiana St	L	PHD	00	Virginia	8 00
Saraniti, Brett	Assoc	Hawaii Pacif		PHD	97	Nrthwstrn	1997
Sardy, Hyman	Prof	CUNY-Brookly	C	PHD	63	New Sch	1957
Sargent, Thomas	Prof	Stanford		PHD	68	Harvard	
Sari, Osman	Asst	Bogazici	FG	PHD	93	CUNY	1993
Sarin, Rajiv	Assoc	Texas A&M	CD	PHD	94	Ca-SnDgo	9-94
Sarkar, Amin U.	C-Pr	Georgia Col	OQ	PHD	88	Berkeley	
Sarkar, Shyamalendu S.	Prof	Saginaw Vall		PHD	69	Mich St	1969
Sarki, Ayuba J.	Assoc	Hampton		PHD	84	Georgia	1982
Sarver, F. Lee	Assoc	Mid Tenn St	M	PHD	87	Tennessee	1991
Sass, Tim R.	Assoc	Florida St	L	PHD	84	U Wash	1990
Sassone, Peter G.	Deces	Georgia Tech	DH	PHD	73	Purdue	1972
Sato, Kazuo	Prof	Rutgers-N Br	E	PHD	60	Yale	1984
Sato, Ryuzo	Prof	New York U	CO	PHD	62	J Hopkins	1985
C. V. Starr Professor of Economics							
Satterthwaite, Mark A.	Prof	Northwestern		PHD	73	Wisconsin	1973
Sattinger, Michael	Prof	SUNY-Albany	J	PHD	73	Car Mellon	1981
Sattler, Edward L.	Prof	Bradley		PHD	79	Illinois	1977
Sau, Ranjit	Visit	NJ Inst Tech		PHD	64	Wayne St	1995
Sauer, Christine	Assoc	New Mexico	EF	PHD	87	Brown	1985
Saueracher, Ed		SUNY-Empire		PHD			
Saunders, Kent T.	Asst	LeMoyne	ADG	PHD	95	Clemson	1998
Saunders, Lisa F.	Asst	Massachusett		PHD	87	Berkeley	1987
Saunders, Peter J.	Prof	Central Wash	EHQ	PHD	81	Colorado	1988
Saunders, Phillip	Retir	Indiana		PHD	64	MIT	1970
Saurman, David	Prof	San Jose St		PHD	79	Tx A&M	1991
Saussy, Gordon A.	Retir	New Orleans		PHD	72	Yale	1970
Sav, Thomas G.	Prof	Wright State	DH	PHD	81	Geo Wash	1985
Savage, Deborah A.	Asst	So Conn St	I	PHD	93	Conn	

Savage, Ian P.	SLect	Northwestern		PHD	84	Leeds	
Savage, Vernon H.	Retir	SW Texas St		PHD	72	Tx-Austin	1971
Savin, Nathan E.	Prof	Iowa		PHD	69	Berkeley	1986
Saving, Thomas R.	Prof	Texas A&M	DE	PHD	60	Chicago	1968
Distinguished Professor, Jeff Montgomery Prof; Dir Private Enterprise Rsch							
Savitski, David	Asst	Northern St		PHD	97	UCLA	1997
Savoca, Elizabeth A.	Prof	Smith	CEIT	PHD	82	Berkeley	1982
Savvides, Andreas	Assoc	Oklahoma St	FO	PHD	83	Florida	1985
Sawani, Mustafa A.	Prof	Truman State		PHD	85	Missouri	1985
Sawdy, George F.	Asst	Providence	QEH	PHD	83	Brown	
Sawers, Larry	C-Pr	American U		PHD	69	Michigan	1969
Sawhney, Bansi L.	Prof	Baltimore		PHD	75	Geo Wash	1971
Sawtelle, Barbara A.	Prof	Simmons	E	PHD	76	MIT	1970
Sawyer, W. Charles	Prof	So Miss	F	PHD	83	Arkansas	1983
Saxonhouse, Gary R.	Prof	Michigan		PHD	71	Yale	1970
Sazama, Gerald W.	Assoc	Connecticut	H	PHD	67	Wisconsin	1966
Sbordone, Argia	Asst	Rutgers-N Br	E	PHD	93	Chicago	1998
Scafidi, Benjamin P.	Asst	Georgia St	HIR	PHD	97	Virginia	1998
Scahill, Edward M.	Assoc	Scranton		PHD	83	SUNY-Bin	1989
Scalet, Kenneth G.	Assoc	York-Penn		MBA		St Johns	1970
Scannell, Nancy J.	Asst	Il-Springfld	AG	PHD	92	Il-Chicago	1996
Scaperlanda, Anthony E.	Emer	No Illinois	F	PHD	64	Tx-Austin	1964
Scarf, Herbert E.	Prof	Yale	C	PHD	54	Princeton	1963
Schachter, Gustav	Prof	Northeastern		PHD	62	NYU	1965
Schad, Tom	Asst	Detroit Merc					
Schaefer, Arthur McCluny	Prof	Univ South	CD	PHD	67	Penn	
Schaefer, Donald F.	Retir	Wash State		PHD	67	N Carol	1982
Schaefer, Kurt C.	Prof	Calvin		PHD	84	Michigan	1987
Schaffer, Beverly K.	Prof	Emory	D	PHD	67	Duke	1965
Schaffer, David	Asst	Wis-Eau Clar	JEH	PHD	90	MIT	1998
Schaffer, William A.	Prof	Georgia Tech	R	PHD	63	Duke	1963
Schall, Lawrence D.	C-Pr	U Washington		PHD	69	Chicago	1967
Schaniel, William C.	Prof	West Georgia	BP	PHD	85	Tennessee	
Schansberg, D. Eric	Asst	Indiana SE	HJC	PHD	91	Tx A&M	1992
Schap, David J.	Prof	Holy Cross	CDK	PHD	82	Wash U	1981
Schatz, Richard E.	C-Pr	Whitworth	DEFO	PHD	74	Hawaii	1989
Schauer, David A.	Assoc	Txs-El Paso	P	PHD	75	Notre Dm	1975
Scheel, Daniel Curtis	Retir	CS-Sacrament		PHD	70	Oregon	1969
Scheffer, Ronald E.	Assoc	Tri-State		MA		Ohio	1967
Scheinkman, Jose	Retir	Chicago		PHD	74	Rochester	1973
Schelling, Thomas	Prof	Maryland		PHD	51	Harvard	1991
Schenker, Eric	Emer	Wis-Milwauke		PHD	57	Florida	1959
Scher, Frances	Retir	Montclair St	AHIT	MA		Columbia	1975
Scherer, Philip M.	Prof	Niagara		PHD	72	Missouri	1980
Scheuch, Richard	Retir	Trinity-CT	1989	PHD	52	Princeton	1950
Schhwalberg, Barney K.	Retir	Brandeis		PHD	66	Harvard	
Schiantarelli, Fabio	Prof	Boston Coll	CEF	PHD	81	LondonEc	1992
Schibik, Timothy J.	Prof	So Indiana		PHD	89	W Virginia	1988
Schieren, George A.	C-Pr	Appalach St	CDE	PHD	75	N Carol	1977
Schifrin, Leonard	Retir	Wm & Mary		PHD	64	Michigan	1964
Schilcutt, J. Garland	C-Pr	Lakeland	M	LLD		Marian	1958
Schilling, Donald J.	Retir	Missouri	EF	PHD	67	N Carol	1964
Schiming, Richard C.	Prof	Mankato St	AE	PHD	74	Ohio St	1981
Schlack, Robert F.	C-Pr	Carthage	FPRC	PHD	77	Wayne St	1975
Schlagenhauf, Don E.	Prof	Florida St	E	PHD	77	Illinois	1998
Brim Eminent Scholar Chair							
Schlee, Edward E.	Prof	Arizona St		PHD	88	Illinois	1990
Schlesinger, Harris	Prof	Alabama		PHD	80	Illinois	1987
Schlottmann, Alan M.	Prof	Nev-L Vegas	R	PHD	75	Wash U	2000
Schmalensee, Richard L.	Dean	MIT	O	PHD	70	MIT	1977
Goldon Y. Billard Professor Economics & Management							
Schmeidler, David	Prof	Ohio State		PHD	69	Hebrew	1987
Schmertmann, Carl P.	Assoc	Florida St	C	PHD	88	Berkeley	1990
Schmidt, Edward J.	Assoc	Randolph-Mac	E	MA	67	Maryland	1967
Schmidt, James R.	C-Pr	Nebraska	CR	PHD	78	Rice	1977
Dr. James W. and Helen A. Hanson Professor of Economics							
Schmidt, Martin	Asst	Portland St	E	PHD	94	Colo St	1997
Schmidt, Peter J.	Prof	Michigan St		PHD	70	Mich St	1977
University Distinguished Professor							
Schmidt, Robert M.	C-Pr	Richmond		PHD	81	Duke	1981
Schmidt, Shelton S.	Prof	Union	LCA	PHD	77	Virginia	1974
Schmidt, Stephen J.	Assoc	Union	LCH	PHD	95	Stanford	1994
Schmidt, Torsten	Assoc	New Hampshir	DL	PHD	90	Florida	1988
Schmitt, Elizabeth Dunne	Asst	SUNY Oswego	AEG	ABD		Iowa	1990
Schmitt, Pamela	Asst	USN Academy		PHD	00	Indiana	
Schmitt-Grobe, Stephanie	Assoc	Rutgers-N Br	E	PHD	94	Chicago	1998
Schmitz, Suzanne	Asst	Elmhurst		PHD	89	Kentucky	1990
Schneider, Geoffrey	Asst	Bucknell	NOBA	ABD	97	N Carol	9-96
Schneider, Lynn	Asst	Auburn-Montg		PHD	96	Houston	1998
Schnell, John F.	Prof	Alabama-Hunt	J	PHD	84	Illinois	1990

Schodt, David W.	Prof	St Olaf	OAH	PHD	80	Wisconsin	1977
Schoening, Niles C.	Prof	Alabama-Hunt	R	PHD	83	Tennessee	1983
Schofield, Norman J.	Prof	Wash Univ	DH	PHD	76	Essex	1986
William Taussig Professor of Political Economy							
Scholland, Ken	Assoc	Hawaii Pacif	MLFB	MSFB		Geotown	1991
Scholz, J. Karl	Assoc	Wisconsin		PHD	88	Stanford	1988
Schomaker, Charles	Asst	Centenary	ADEM	MSBA		Indiana	8-00
Schrag, Joel	Asst	Emory	DKL	PHD	93	Berkeley	1993
Schran, Peter	Retir	Illinois		PHD	61	Berkeley	1965
Schreiber, Max M.	Assoc	W Carolina	C	PHD	78	S Carol	1977
Schroeder, Edward A.	Assoc	Nazareth		PHD	80	UCLA	1988
Schroeter, John R.	Assoc	Iowa State	L	PHD	81	Minnesota	1983
Schuh, G. Edward	Prof	Minnesota		PHD	61	Chicago	1979
Schuhmann, Peter	Asst	N Car-Wilmin	Q	PHD	96	N Car St	
Schultz, Brian L.	Prof	Wis-Rvr Fall	C	PHD	80	Notre Dm	1979
Schultz, John A.	Assoc	Shepherd		PHD	85	S Carol	1988
Schultz, T. Paul	Prof	Yale	J	PHD	66	MIT	1975
Schultz, Theodore	Retir	Chicago		PHD	39	Wisconsin	1943
Schulz, Eric	Asst	Williams		PHD	93	Nrthwstrn	
Schumacher, Edward	Asst	East Carol	DIJ	PHD	94	Fla St	1994
Schumacher, Howard	Retir	Kean		MA		Columbia	9-56
Schupack, Mark B.	Emer	Brown		PHD	60	Princeton	1970
Schur, Leon M.	Emer	Wis-Milwauke		PHD	55	Wisconsin	1964
Schuttler, Robert D.	Inst	Marian		MBA	80	Evansville	1985
Schutz, Eric A.	Assoc	Rollins		PHD	82	N Carol	1987
Schwab, Robert M.	Prof	Maryland		PHD	80	J Hopkins	1980
Schwalbenberg, Henry M.	Asst	Fordham		PHD	88	Columbia	1988
Schwartz, Adina Tzur	Assoc	Lakeland	AEFG	MA		Wi-Milwa	1986
Schwartz, Carol H.	Prof	NY Inst Tech		PHD	63	Columbia	1987
Schwartz, David Lamar	Retir	Albright		MA	64	Mich St	1965
Schwartz, Jesse	Asst	Vanderbilt	DLQ	PHD	99	Maryland	1999
Schwartz, Marius	Prof	Georgetown	DL	PHD	82	UCLA	1982
Schwartz, William T.	Lect	Va Military		MBA	70	Penn	2001
Schwarz, Michael	Asst	Harvard		PHD		Stanford	
Schwarz, Peter M.	Prof	N Car-Charl		PHD	80	Ohio St	1978
Schwarz, Samuel	Prof	CUNY-Stn Isl	KC	PHD	78	Columbia	1986
Schwarz-Miller, Ann V.	Assoc	Old Dominion	DJKM	PHD	74	Nrthwstrn	1978
Schweigert, Thomas E.	Assoc	Wis-Whitewat		PHD	90	Wisconsin	1984
Schweitzer, Robert N.	Prof	San Fran St		PHD	63	Berkeley	1962
Schwer, Keith	Prof	Nev-L Vegas	R	PHD	73	Maryland	1986
Schwinn, Carl R.	Assoc	Bates	IO	PHD	78	Cornell	1975
Schydlowsky, Daniel M.	Prof	American U		PHD	66	Harvard	1990
Scott, Carole Elizabeth	Retir	West Georgia	NO	PHD	69	Geo St	
Scott, Charles E.	Prof	Loyola-Maryl	MJH	PHD	79	Vanderbilt	1985
Scott, Frank A. Jr.	Prof	Kentucky	GH	PHD	79	Virginia	1979
Gatton Professor							
Scott, Gary J.	Asst	St Marys-Txs		PHD	93	Notre Dm	1994
Scott, Gerald E.	Assoc	Fla Atlantic	DF	PHD	87	Maryland	1993
Scott, J. T.	Retir	Iowa State		PHD	57	Iowa St	1955
Scott, John L.	Assoc	La-Monroe	DC	PHD	90	S Carol	1989
Scott, John T.	Prof	Dartmouth		PHD	76	Harvard	1977
Scott, Loren C.	Emer	Louisiana St	J	PHD	69	Okla St	1969
Scott, Ralph D.	Prof	Hendrix	EF	PHD	83	Tulane	1979
Scott, Robert C.	C-Pr	Bradley		PHD	75	Iowa	1975
Scrogin, David	Asst	Cen Florida	Q	PHD	99	New Mex	2000
Seaks, Terry G.	Emer	N Car-Greens	C	PHD	72	Duke	1972
Seal, James W.	Assoc	Portland	HRE	PHD	77	Illinois	1977
Seaman, Bruce A.	Assoc	Georgia St	DL	PHD	78	Chicago	1978
Seater, John J.	Prof	N Carol St	EH	PHD	75	Brown	1981
Sebestyen, Zoltan H.	Retir	SUNY-N Paltz	DFA	PHD	68	Columbia	1969
Sechtem, Everett A.	Retir	Neb-Kearney		PHD	86	Nebraska	1970
Secondi, Giorgio	Asst	Occidental	O	PHD	96	Michigan	1998
Sedgley, Norman	Asst	Loyola-Maryl	EO	PHD	98	NewHamp	2000
Seeborg, Michael C.	C-Pr	Ill Wesleyan	J	PHD	76	Utah	1989
Robert S. Eckley Distinguished Professor of Economics							
Seeley, Robert D.	Assoc	Wilkes	AIJH	PHD	86	Maryland	9-89
Segal, Ilya	Assoc	Stanford		PHD	95	Harvard	1999
Segelhorst, Elbert W.	Retir	CS-Long Bch	1994	PHD	63	Columbia	1964
Segerson, Kathleen	Prof	Connecticut	QD	PHD	84	Cornell	1986
Seguino, Stephanie	Asst	Vermont	EFOP	PHD	94	American	1995
Seidel, Ethan A.	Prof	W Maryland		PHD	77	J Hopkins	1969
Seidelman, James E.	Dean	Westminst-UT		PHD	86	Utah	1980
Seidenstat, Paul	Assoc	Temple	H	PHD	64	Nrthwstrn	1967
Seldenstricker, Kenneth C.	Retir	Regis-CO		MA		Marquette	
Seidman, Laurence S.	Prof	Delaware	H	PHD	74	Berkeley	1982
Seifried, Edmond J.	Prof	Lafayette	JM	PHD	71	W Virginia	1978
Seiglie, Carlos C.	Assoc	Rutgers-Newk		PHD	91	Chicago	1986
Seiver, Daniel A.	Prof	Miami U-Ohio	TG	PHD	74	Yale	1978
Seiz, Janet A.	Assoc	Grinnell	BO	PHD	85	Duke	1989
Selassie, Haile G.	Assoc	So Carol St		PHD	83	Okla St	1984

Seldon, Barry	Prof	Texas-Dallas		PHD	85	Duke	
Selgin, George A.	Assoc	Georgia	EN	PHD	86	NYU	1989
Selim, Mohamed Ali	Assoc	St Thomas-MN	A	PHD	81	Minnesota	1959
Selivanoff, George A.	C-Pr	LaSierra	AFM	PHD	64	American	1984
Sell, John W.	Prof	Wooster		PHD	81	UCLA	1981
Sellers, Gary	Retir	Akron	AKL	PHD	77	Cincinnati	1976
Selover, David D.	Asst	Old Dominion	F	PHD	91	Ca-SnDgo	1999
Semenick Alam, Ila	Asst	Tulane		PHD	94	Rice	1994
Sen, Amartya K.	Retir	Harvard		PHD	59	Cambridge	1988
Sen, Amit	Asst	Mo-Rolla		PHD	97	N Carol	1997
Sen, Swapan	Assoc	Chris Newpor		PHD	91	Nebraska	1998
Sen, Tinni	Asst	Va Military		PHD	99	Miss	2000
Sencicek, Mehmet		New Haven					
Seneca, Joseph J.	Prof	Rutgers-N Br	H	PHD	68	Penn	1967
Seneca, Rosalind S.	Prof	Drew	DL	PHD	71	Penn	1981
Sener, Mehmet F.	Asst	Union	FOEJ	PHD	99	Florida	1999
Sengupta, Jati K.	Prof	Cal-Santa Br	CO	PHD	62	Iowa St	1976
Sent, Esther-Mirjam	Assoc	Notre Dame	BE	PHD	94	Stanford	1994
Seo, Tae Kun	Prof	So Methodist	D	PHD	73	Tx A&M	1973
Seplaki, Les	Prof	Rutgers-Camd		PHD	70	Ca-Rivers	
Seppala, Juhh	Asst	Illinois	DG	PHD	00	Chicago	2000
Seppi, Duane J.	Prof	Carnegie Mel		PHD	88	Chicago	1986
Serow, William J.	Prof	Florida St	T	PHD	72	Duke	1981
Serrano, Roberto	Prof	Brown		PHD	92	Harvard	
Sertel, Murat	Prof	Bogazici	AC	PHD	71	MIT	1979
Seshadri, Ananth	Asst	Wisconsin		PHD	00	Rochester	2000
Seshu, Chigurupati R.	Assoc	SUNY-N Paltz	AEO	PHD	60	New Sch	1967
Sesnowitz, Michael L.	Dean	Virg Comm	HG	PHD	71	Pittsburgh	2000
Sethi, Rajiv	Assoc	Barnard	DQ	PHD	93	New Sch	1995
Setterfield, Mark	Assoc	Trinity-CT		PHD	92	Dalhousie	1992
Settle, Russell F.	Prof	Delaware	H	PHD	74	Wisconsin	1974
Severinov, Sergei	Asst	Wisconsin		PHD	98	Stanford	1998
Sewell, Ellen M.	Asst	N Car-Charl		PHD	83	Florida	1982
Sexton, Edwin A.	Prof	Va Military		PHD	87	Illinois	1992
Sexton, Robert L.	Prof	Pepper-Malib	ADNQ	PHD	80	Colorado	1979
Sexton, Terri A.	C-Pr	CS-Sacrament		PHD	81	Minnesota	1987
Seyfert, Jeff	Asst	S Nazarene		MBA	89	Tulsa	1990
Seyfried, William L.	Assoc	Winthrop	AMF	PHD	90	Purdue	9-00
Sfeir, Raymond	Prof	Chapman	AC	PHD	82	Ca-SnBarb	1985
Sgontz, Larry G.	Emer	Iowa		PHD	64	Illinois	1964
Shaaf, Mohammad	Prof	Central Okla	BDEG	PHD	82	Tx Tech	1980
Shaanan, Joseph	Prof	Bryant	FL	PHD	79	Cornell	
Shachmurove, Yochanan	Assoc	CUNY-City C	CEFG	PHD	83	Minnesota	1997
Shackelford, Jean A.	Prof	Bucknell	ABE	PHD	74	Kentucky	1975
Shadbegian, Ronald	Asst	Mass-Dartmou	HKQ	PHD	91	Clark	1993
Shadoan, Donald	Retir	E Kentucky		PHD		Kentucky	1962
Shafer, Wayne	Prof	Illinois	CD	PHD	72	Ca-SnBarb	1990
Shaffer, Linda J.	C-Pr	CS-Fresno	JIC	PHD	78	Nrthwstrn	1984
Shah, Umanglal G.	Retir	Albany State		MA	64	Houston	9-66
Shahinpoor, Nasrin	Asst	Xavier		PHD	01	Cincinnati	2001
Shahjahan, Mirza	C-Pr	Ark-Pine Blf		PHD		Bonn	
Shambert, Vladimir M.	Prof	USAF Academy		PHD	52	Moscow	1992
Shambora, William E.	Asst	Ohio Univ		PHD	00	Kentucky	9-00
Shandiz, Mohmood	Assoc	Okla City		PHD	81	Okla St	1985
Shane, Richard C.	H-Pr	So Dakota St	Q	PHD	78	Wash St	1977
Shannon, Lee R.	Assoc	Regis-CO		PHD	70	N Colo	1978
Shapiro, Aharon H.	Prof	St John's		PHD	66	New Sch	1967
Shapiro, David	Assoc	Penn State	J	PHD	72	Princeton	1980
Shapiro, Edward	Retir	Toledo	1994	PHD		Harvard	1967
Shapiro, Harold T.	Prof	Princeton		PHD	64	Princeton	1988
Shapiro, Matthew D.	Prof	Michigan		PHD	84	MIT	1989
Shapiro, Nina	Assoc	St Peters	DEL	PHD		New Sch	1999
Shapiro, Perry	Prof	Cal-Santa Br	DH	PHD	67	Berkeley	1969
Shapiro, Stephen L.	Assoc	North Fla	AH	PHD	72	S Carol	1972
Shapiro, Steven J.	C-Ac	New Haven	GKLM	PHD	88	Geotown	9-87
Shapley, Lloyd S.	Prof	UCLA		PHD	53	Princeton	
Sharav, Itzhak	Prof	CUNY-Lehman		PHD	71	CUNY	9-67
Sharif, Mohammed	Prof	Rhode Island	O	PHD	83	Boston U	1984
Shariff, Ismail	C-Pr	WI-Green Bay		PHD	65	Wisconsin	
Sharma, Rajiv	Asst	Portland St	I	PHD	98	Florida	1998
Sharma, Subhash	Prof	So Illinois	C	PHD	83	Kentucky	1983
Sharma, V. V.	Assoc	Ohio State		PHD	68	Illinois	1970
Sharma, Ved P.	C-Pr	Mankato St	CDT	PHD	77	Wash U	1976
Sharp, Ansel M.	Retir	Univ South		PHD	56	LSU	1985
Sharp, Robert R.	Retir	E Kentucky		PHD	69	Kentucky	1969
Shatten, Richard	Prof	Case Western	HR	MBA	80	Harvard	1997
Shatto, Gloria M.	Deces	Berry		PHD	66	Rice	1979
Shaw, John A. Jr.	Prof	CS-Fresno	DNF	PHD	69	Purdue	1965
Shaw, Sue O.	Prof	Longwood		PHD	67	Harvard	1986
Shea, John	Assoc	Maryland		PHD	90	MIT	1996

Sheahan, John B.	Retir	Williams		PHD	54	Harvard	1954
Shearer, Charles L.	Prof	Transylvania		PHD	81	Mich St	
President Transylvania University							
Sheehan, Richard G.	Prof	Notre Dame	R	PHD	78	Boston C	1987
Sheets, Doris Files	Assoc	SW Missouri		PHD	81	Missouri	1974
Sheffield, Howell	Inst	West Alabama		MBA		Alabama	1998
Sheffrin, Steven M.	Dean	Cal-Davis	EH	PHD	76	MIT	1976
Sheflin, Neil	Assoc	Rutgers-N Br	C	PHD	79	Rutgers	1975
Sheftall, Willis B. Jr.	Prof	Morehouse		PHD	81	Geo St	1986
Charles E. Merrill Professor of Economics							
Shelburn, Marsha	Prof	So Car-Aiken		PHD	80	N Carol	1980
Shell, Karl	Prof	Cornell		PHD	65	Stanford	1986
Robert Julius Thorne Professor of Economics							
Shelton, David H.	Retir	N Car-Greens		PHD	58	Ohio St	1965
Shen, Raphael	Prof	Detroit Merc		PHD	75	Mich St	1977
Shen, Ruth R.	Retir	San Fran St		PHD	61	J Hopkins	1964
Shen, T. Y.	Emer	Cal-Davis	L	PHD	56	Yale	7-63
Shepard, Delynne	Asst	Andrews	EJ	PHD	95	Purdue	1995
Shepard, Edward M.	C-Ac	LeMoyne	HJL	PHD	87	Boston C	1990
Shepherd, A. Ross	Emer	Mo-Kansas Ct	DF	PHD	63	Syracuse	1967
Shepherd, James F.	Prof	Whitman	HN	PHD	66	U Wash	1971
Shepherd, Robert J.	Lect	Ca-Santa Crz	M	MSA	70	S Calif	1990
Shepherd, William G.	Retir	Massachusett		PHD	63	Yale	1986
Sheran, Michelle	Asst	N Car-Greens	J	PHD	01	Virginia	2001
Sheriff, Mohamed A.	Assoc	Dillard		PHD	91	Howard	
Sherman, Howard J.	Retir	Cal-Riversid	EK	PHD	60	S Calif	1966
Sherman, Robert P.	Asst	Cal Tech		PHD	91	Yale	1996
Sherman, Roger	Retir	Virginia	LD	PHD	66	Car Mellon	1971
Brown-Forman Professor of Economics							
Sherony, Deith R.	Prof	Wis-La Cross	ACE	PHD	82	Wi-Milwa	1983
Sherry, Robert L.	Assoc	Keene State		PHD	79	Yale	1984
Sherstyuk, Ekaterina	Assoc	Hawaii-Manoa		PHD	95	Cal Tech	2000
Shevchenko, Andrei		Michigan St					
Shi, Shouyong	Prof	Indiana		PHD	91	Toronto	2000
Shiau, Liang-rong	C-Pr	Norfolk St	CAR	PHD	72	S Miss	1972
Shick, Richard A.	Dean	Canisius	G	PHD	73	SUNY-Buf	1978
Shieh, John T.	Retir	CS-Pomona		DBA	81	S Calif	1967
Shieh, Yeung-Nan	Prof	San Jose St		PHD	80	Tx A&M	1989
Shields, Michael P.	C-Pr	Cen Michigan	OJR	PHD	75	Utah	1993
Shiers, Alden F.	C-Prc	Cal Poly-SLO		PHD	77	Ca-SnBarb	1975
Shih-Fen, Chen	Asst	Brandeis		PHD	96	Illinois	1999
Shikha, Deep	Assoc	St Catherine	FA	PHD	85	LSU	1985
Shiller, Robert J.	Prof	Yale	D	PHD	72	MIT	1982
Shimer, Robert		Princeton					
Shin, Bong Ju	Prof	Towson		PHD	69	Ohio St	1966
Shin, Dongsoo	Asst	No Iowa		PHD	01	Wash	2001
Shingleton, Virginia	C-Ac	Valparaiso	CJIA	PHD	94	Notre Dm	1992
Shintani, Mototsugu	Asst	Vanderbilt	CE	PHD	00	Yale	2000
Shiptssova, Rimma	Asst	Utah State	CO	PHD	98	Ohio St	2002
Shirey, Richard L.	Assoc	Siena		PHD	94	SUNY-Alb	9-79
Shirley, John	Lect	SUNY-Cortlan					
Shirvani, Hassan M.	Assoc	St Thomas-TX	FG	PHD	79	Harvard	1986
Shitts, Wade	Asst	Luther		PHD	99	Iowa	1997
Shiue, Carol	Inst	Texas	ON	PHD	99	Yale	9-98
Shively, Philip	Asst	Lafayette	CG	PHD	97	Michigan	1997
Shleifer, Andrei	Prof	Harvard		PHD	86	MIT	1991
Shmanske, Steven	Prof	CS-Hayward	CDHL	PHD	82	UCLA	1979
Shockley, Frederica	Prof	CS-Chico	HMOR	PHD	78	Geo St	1978
Shoenthal, Edward R.	Prof	CUNY-Brookly		PHD	85	NYU	1973
Shogren, Jason F.	Prof	Wyoming	Q	PHD	86	Wyoming	1995
Shojai, Siamack	Dean	SUNY-Plattsb	GQ	PHD	84	Fordham	2001
Short, Joanna	Inst	Augustana IL	ANHD	ABD		Indiana	2001
Shostya, Anna	Assoc	Pace		MA			
Shoukry, Kamal	Assoc	Loyola Marym	ABCE	PHD	72	S Calif	1980
Shoven, John B.	Prof	Stanford		PHD	73	Yale	1978
Charles R. Schwab Professor of Economics							
Showalter, Dean	Assoc	SW Texas St	L	PHD	94	Kentucky	1995
Showalter, Mark H.	Assoc	Brigham Yg	LC	PHD	91	MIT	1991
Shows, E. Warren	Retir	South Fla	L	PHD	68	Geo St	1964
Shreiber, Chanoch	C-Pr	CUNY-Lehman		PHD	73	Columbia	
Shropshire, William O.	Prof	Ogelthorpe	EO	PHD	63	Duke	1979
Callaway Professor of Economics							
Shu, Florence P.	Assoc	SUNY-Potsdam		PHD	86	Mich St	1986
Shubik, Martin	Prof	Yale	G	PHD	53	Princeton	
Shughart, William F. II	C-Pr	Mississippi	DHL	PHD	78	Tx A&M	1988
FAP Barnard Distinguished Professor & Robert M. Hearin Chair							
Shukla, Vishwa S.	Retir	Ohio Univ		PHD	72	Wisconsin	1966
Shuklian, Steve	Assoc	Marshall		PHD	88	Utah	1988
Shull, Bernard Jr.	Retir	CUNY-Hunter		PHD	57	Wisconsin	1970
Shull, Ralph B.	Retir	Ark-Ltl Rock		PHD	72	Arkansas	1971

Shulman, Steven J.	Prof	Colorado St	JKEI	PHD	84	Mass	1984
Shum, Matthew	Asst	J Hopkins					
Shupp, Franklin R.	Retir	Illinois		PHD	59	Princeton	1960
Shupp, Robert	Asst	Ball State					
Shute, Laurence	Prof	CS-Pomona		PHD	73	Columbia	1988
Shwiff, Steven S.	Assoc	Tx A&M-Comm	CROD	PHD	77	Tx A&M	1987
Siberberg, Eugene	Prof	U Washington		PHD	64	Purdue	1967
Sibley, David S.	Prof	Texas	D	PHD	73	Yale	1-91
John Michael Stuart Centennial Professor of Economics							
Sichel, Werner	C-Pr	W Michigan	D	PHD	64	Nrthwstrn	1960
Sicherman, Nachum	Prof	Columbia		PHD	87	Columbia	1991
Sicilian, Joseph M.	C-Ac	Kansas	D	PHD	77	Purdue	1977
Sicilian, Paul	Asst	Grand Valley	ACDJ	PHD	91	Illinois	1987
Sickles, Robin C.	Prof	Rice		PHD	76	N Carol	1985
Siconolfi, Paolo	Prof	Columbia		PHD	87	Penn	1989
Siddiquee, Baker A.	H-Ac	Il-Springfld	EFO	PHD	88	Manitoba	1987
Siden, Dorothy R.	Asst	Salem State		PHD	90	Northeas	
Sidwell, Richard J.	Retir	E Illinois		PHD	72	Utah	1970
Siebert, Calvin D.	Emer	Iowa		PHD	66	Berkeley	1965
Sieg, Holger	Assoc	Carnegie Mel		PHD	96	Car Mellon	
Siegel, Abraham J.	Retir	MIT		PHD	61	Berkeley	
Siegel, Andrew F.	Prof	U Washington		PHD	83	MIT	1990
Siegel, Rachel S.	Assoc	Lyndon State	CGQN	MBA	89	Yale	9-90
Siegfried, John J.	Prof	Vanderbilt	LJ	PHD	72	Wisconsin	1972
Siegler, Mark	Asst	Williams		PHD	96	Ca-Davis	1997
Sievers, Allen M.	Retir	Utah		PHD	48	Columbia	1968
Sigman, Hilary	Assoc	Rutgers-N Br	I	PHD	93	MIT	1999
Sihag, Balbir S.	Prof	Mass-Lowell	CI	PHD	78	MIT	1980
Sikes, Ellen	Assoc	Campbell		MS		N Carol	1966
Sileo, Patrick	SrLec	Carnegie Mel		PHD	94	Car Mellon	
Silva, Donald H.	Retir	Wis-Whitewat		PHD	64	Missouri	1964
Silver, Emilson	Assoc	Tulane		PHD	93	Illinois	1999
Silver, J. Lew	Assoc	Alabama		PHD	80	Duke	1990
Silver, Morris	Adj	CUNY-City C	E	PHD	64	Columbia	1961
Silver, Stephen J.	Assoc	Citadel		PHD	83	Maryland	8-90
Silvestre, Joaquim	Prof	Cal-Davis	D	PHD	73	Minnesota	1983
Simeone, William J.	Assoc	Providence	JEI	PHD	85	Boston C	1959
Simkins, Scott P.	Asst	N Carol A&T		PHD	88	Iowa	
Simkonis, Carl	Inst	No Kentucky		MPA	91	N Kentucky	2000
Simler, Norman J.	Retir	Macalester	AE	PHD	59	Minnesota	1991
Simmons, Kevin	Asst	Okla City		PHD	99	Tx Tech	1999
Simmons, Michael	C-As	N Carol A&T		PHD	79	Wash St	8-70
Simmons, Walter O.	Asst	John Carroll	JKNO	PHD	94	Wayne St	1995
Simon, Alice E.	Prof	Ohio Wesley		PHD	84	Ohio St	1985
Simon, Carl P.	Prof	Michigan	CDT	PHD	70	Nrthwstrn	7-72
Simon, Curtis J.	Assoc	Clemson	JOR	PHD	85	SUNY-Bin	1985
Simon, Kosali		Michigan St					
Simon, Peter J.	C-Ac	Loras		PHD	89	N Illinois	1989
Simons, Gerald P.	Asst	Grand Valley		PHD	95	Kansas	1995
Simonson, John C.	Prof	Wis-Plattev		PHD	72	Wisconsin	1966
Simonson, Robert D.	Prof	Mankato St	AJ	PHD	79	Nebraska	1981
Simos, Evangelos O.	Prof	New Hampshir	EF	PHD	77	N Illinois	1977
Simpson, Nicole B.	Asst	Colgate	E	PHD	01	Iowa	2001
Simpson, Paul	Lect	Manches Inst	LC	MA		Newcastle	1984
Sims, Christopher A.	Prof	Yale	D	PHD	68	Harvard	
Sinclair, Robert	Asst	Syracuse	EF	PHD	99	Stanford	1999
Sindt, Roger	Prof	Neb-Omaha	AR	PHD	72	Tx-Austin	1979
Singamsetti, Nageswara Rao	Assoc	Hartford	CDLM	PHD	73	SUNY-Buf	1974
Singell, Larry D.	Prof	Colorado		PHD	65	Wayne St	1968
Singell, Larry D. Jr.	Prof	Oregon	J	PHD	88	Ca-SnBarb	1988
Singer, Diana Sue	Prof	W Maryland		MBA		Loyola	1983
Singer, Les	Retir	Indiana NW	RTE	PHD	58	Indiana	1958
Singer, Russell	C-As$	King's Col		BS	58	Wilkes	9-67
Singh, Ajmer	Retir	W Oregon St		PHD	64	Oregon St	1965
Singh, Davinder	Prof	CS-Long Bch		PHD	78	S Carol	1983
Singh, Harinder	C-Pr	Grand Valley		PHD	85	Il-Chicago	1995
Singh, Nirvikar	Prof	Ca-Santa Crz	DLOM	PHD	82	Berkeley	1982
Singh, Rajesh	Asst	Iowa State	F	PHD	01	UCLA	2001
Singh, Ram Das	Retir	Illinois St	TIO	PHD	70	N Delhi	1981
Singh, Sarjit	Retir	Clarion		PHD		Okla St	1964
Singleton, Robert	C-As	Loyola Marym	AJR	PHD	83	UCLA	1982
Singleton, Ross	Prof	Puget Sound	ADKO	PHD	77	Oregon	
Sinha, Rohini P.	Prof	Muhlenberg		PHD	65	New Sch	1965
Sinisi, John	Asst	Penn St-Harr		PHD	76	Mass	1982
Siqueira, Kevin	Asst	Clarkson	HD	PHD	98	Iowa St	1999
Sisk, David E.	Prof	San Fran St		PHD	76	UCLA	1978
Sissoko, Macki	Asst	Norfolk St		PHD	91	Auburn	1999
Sites, Millicent M.	C-Ac	Carson-Newmn	EFGO	PHD	85	Tennessee	8-95
Sjaastad, Larry A.	Prof	Chicago		PHD	61	Chicago	1965
Sjoquist, David L.	Prof	Georgia St	DR	PHD	71	Minnesota	1970

Sjostrom, J. Tomas	Assoc	Penn State	E	PHD	91	Rochester	1998
Skaggs, Jimmy M.	Retir	Wichita St		PHD	70	Tx Tech	1970
Skaggs, Neil T.	Prof	Illinois St	BDE	PHD	80	Duke	1979
Skaperdas, Stergios	Assoc	Calif-Irvine		PHD	88	J Hopkins	1988
Skeath, Susan E.	C-Ac	Wellesley	DFL	PHD	89	Princeton	1989
Skeels, Jack W.	Retir	No Illinois	J	PHD	57	Wisconsin	1963
Skelley, A. Chris	Assoc	Rollins		PHD	85	Brown	1987
Skidmore, Mark	Asst	Wis-Whitewat	H	PHD	94	Colorado	1998
Skillman, Gilbert L.	Assoc	Wesleyan-CT	D	PHD	85	Michigan	1993
Skinner, Gordon S.	Retir	Cincinnati		PHD	53	Wisconsin	
Skinner, Jonathan	Prof	Dartmouth		PHD	83	UCLA	1995
John French Professor							
Skinner, Steven P.	Prof	Western Conn	BJQR	PHD	80	Conn	
Skinreich, Dale	Asst	SW Baptist		PHD		Auburn	2001
Skogstad, Samuel L.	Retir	Georgia St	EFO	PHD	65	Wash U	1994
Skoorka, Bruce	Asst	Kean		PHD	92	NYU	
Skorr, Arlen J.	Prof	Mankato St	AE	PHD	70	Nebraska	1965
Skov, Iva L.	Prof	CS-Long Bch		PHD	76	S Calif	1972
Skrabis, Kristin	Asst	Dickinson Cl	QD				
Skurski, Roger B.	Prof	Notre Dame	P	PHD	70	Wisconsin	1974
Slate, Stephen	H-Ac	USAF Academy		PHD	94	Colorado	1992
Slaughter, Matthew J.	Assoc	Dartmouth		PHD	94	MIT	1994
Slaysman, Kenneth	Assoc	York-Penn		PHD		Penn St	
Sleeman, Allan G.	Assoc	Western Wash	CD	PHD	83	Simon Fr	1977
Sleet, Christopher	Asst	Iowa	E	PHD	98	Stanford	2000
Slemrod, Joel B.	Prof	Michigan		PHD	80	Harvard	1987
Slesnick, Daniel T.	Prof	Texas	CH	PHD	82	Harvard	9-82
Rex G. Baker, Jr., Professorship in Political Economy							
Slesnick, Frank L.	Prof	Bellarmine	AIKJ	PHD	72	Minnesota	1975
Slice, Jerry Kibler	C-Pr	Presbyterian	QFD	PHD	86	Miss St	1989
Sliger, Bernard F.	Prof	Florida St	A	PHD	55	Mich St	1972
Sloan, Frank A.	Prof	Duke	I	PHD	69	Harvard	1993
Alexander McMahon Professor							
Slonim, Robert L.	Asst	Case Western	CD	PHD	95	Duke	1998
Slotkin, M.	Asst	Fla Inst Tec	AFQ	PHD	95	N Carol	1996
Slotsve, George A.	Assoc	No Illinois	JD	PHD	89	Wisconsin	1996
Slottje, Daniel J.	Prof	So Methodist	DJK	PHD	83	Tx A&M	1989
Slutsky, Steven M.	Prof	Florida	DH	PHD	75	Yale	1984
Smale, Stephen	Emer	Cal-Berkeley		PHD	57	Michigan	
Small, Kenneth A.	Prof	Calif-Irvine		PHD	76	Berkeley	1983
Smallwood, Aaron	Asst	Oklahoma		PHD	01	Fla St	2001
Smallwood, Dennis	Prof	USM Academy	DHL	PHD	66	Yale	1996
Smeeding, Timothy M.	Prof	Syracuse	I	PHD	75	Wisconsin	1990
Smiles, Ronald	C-Pr	Dallas Bapt	R	PHD	87	Tx-Arlin	1987
Smiley, Barry A.	Deces	NW St of LA		DBA	75	La Tech	
Smiley, William G.	Prof	Marquette	DN	PHD	73	Iowa	1973
Smith, Allen W.	Retir	E Illinois		PHD	70	Indiana	1970
Smith, Angie	Inst	SW Baptist		MBA		SW Bapt	2001
Smith, Anthony A.	Assoc	Carnegie Mel		PHD	91	Duke	1992
Smith, Barton A.	Prof	Houston	ADR	PHD	74	Chicago	1973
Smith, Bernard	Assoc	Drew	HOP	PHD	89	Yale	1986
Smith, Bruce D.	Prof	Texas	E	PHD	81	MIT	9-96
Fred Hofheinz Professor in Economics							
Smith, David B	Prof	New Mex St	H	PHD	71	Nebraska	1970
Smith, Dean G.	Assoc	No Arizona	RC	PHD	85	Tx A&M	1989
Smith, Fred	Asst	Davidson	RN	PHD	01	Vanderbilt	2000
Smith, Galen	Prof	Cedarville	ABFH	DMIN	98	Trinity	1981
Smith, George	Prof	New York U	N	PHD	76	Harvard	1988
Smith, Gerald A.	Prof	Mankato St	AOQ	PHD	79	LSU	1979
Smith, Gordon W.	Prof	Rice		PHD	66	Harvard	1968
Smith, Harlan	Emer	Minnesota		PHD	49	Chicago	
Smith, Harlan II	Assoc	Marshall		PHD	89	Yale	1991
Smith, Janet K.	C-Pr	Claremont		PHD	80	UCLA	1996
Smith, Jon L.	Assoc	East Tenn St		PHD	82	S Carol	1980
Smith, Julie K.	Asst	Trinity	E	PHD	01	J Hopkins	2001
Smith, Kenneth	Asst	Millersville		PHD	93	Wisconsin	2000
Smith, Kenneth L.	Prof	Pittsburg St	G	PHD	81	Ca-Rivers	
Smith, Kenneth R.	Prof	Arizona		PHD	68	Nrthwstrn	1980
Smith, Larry J.	Assoc	WI-Green Bay		PHD	73	Chicago	
Smith, Lawrence C.	Prof	Louisiana Te		PHD	68	Miss	1970
Smith, Lewis	Prof	Mississippi	J	PHD	71	Tennessee	1971
Smith, Lones A.	Assoc	Michigan	D	PHD	91	Chicago	
Smith, Lynn A.	Assoc	Clarion		PHD	85	Pittsburgh	1989
Smith, Mark G.	Assoc	Colorado Col		PHD	87	Duke	1988
Smith, Patricia	Assoc	Mich-Dearbor	IJK	PHD	86	Va Tech	1988
Smith, Richard S.	Assoc	Ark Tech		PHD	74	Tx-Austin	1991
Smith, Ronald G. E.	Retir	CUNY-Hunter	1-99	DBA	68	LSU	
Smith, Russell E.	Assoc	Washburn		PHD	84	Illinois	1984
Smith, Stanley K.	Prof	Florida	J	PHD	76	Michigan	1976
Smith, Stephanie	Assoc	Otterbein	G	PHD	95	Va Comm	2001

Smith, Stephen C.	Assoc	George Wash	O	PHD	83	Cornell	1983
Smith, Stephen L. S.	Prof	Gordon	FO	PHD	88	Stanford	1987
Smith, Vardaman Russell	Assoc	Jms Madison	B	PHD	80	Penn St	1979
Smith, Vernon L.	Emer	Arizona		PHD	55	Harvard	1975
Smith, Vincent H.	Assoc	Montana St		PHD	87	N Car St	1988
Smith, W. James	Dean	Colo-Denver		PHD	76	Colorado	
Smith, William	Assoc	Memphis	EF	PHD	87	Virginia	1993
Smith, William Doyle	Assoc	Txs-El Paso	AEC	PHD	81	Tx Tech	1981
Smitka, Michael J.	Assoc	Wash & Lee	FL	PHD	89	Yale	1986
Smolowitz, Ira E.	Prof	American Int		PHD	84	Rensselaer	1988
Smyser, Michael W.	Asst	Southern	G	PHD	91	Fla Intl	1991
Smyth, David J.	Retir	Louisiana St	E	PHD	68	Birminghm	1987
Smyth, John W.	Retir	Youngstown		PHD	73	Nebraska	
Snaith, Sean	Asst	North Dakota		PHD	96	Penn St	2001
Snoonian, Paul E.	Assoc	Mass-Lowell	EQ	PHD	71	Mich St	
Snow, Arthur	Assoc	Georgia	DH	PHD	79	Wisconsin	1989
Snow, Marcellus S.	Retir	Hawaii-Manoa		PHD	74	Berkeley	1974
Snow, Sandra L.	Prof	Wis-Whitewat		PHD	76	Missouri	1981
Snowbarger, Marvin R.	Prof	San Jose St		PHD	66	Michigan	1966
Snowden, Kenneth A.	Assoc	N Car-Greens	NG	PHD	83	Wisconsin	1983
Snowden, Peter N.	SLect	U Lancaster		PHD		Leeds	
Snyder, Christopher	Assoc	George Wash	L	PHD	94	MIT	1994
Snyder, Donald L.	Prof	Utah State	CQ	PHD	79	Utah St	1981
Snyder, James M. Jr.	Prof	MIT		PHD	85	Cal Tech	
Snyder, Marcia	Inst	Charleston		MA	95	London	1999
Snyder, Richard S.	Assoc	No Kentucky		PHD	76	Indiana	1978
Snyder, Susan	Asst	Virg Tech	HDC	PHD	96	Stanford	8-95
Soares, Jorge	Asst	George Wash	E	PHD	96	Rochester	1998
Sobel, Joel	Prof	Ca-San Diego	D	PHD	78	Berkeley	1978
Sobel, Russell S.	Asst	W Virginia	H	PHD	94	Fla St	1994
Sockwell, William D.	Assoc	Berry	B	PHD	89	Vanderbilt	1988
Soderlind, Steven D.	Assoc	St Olaf	RA	PHD	80	Mass	1982
Sohan, Gerald	Asst	USAF Academy		ABD		Tx A&M	1999
Sohng, Soong Nark	Prof	Clarion		PHD	82	Wayne St	1981
Sokoloff, Joel J.	Asst	Kentucky St	ACE	MA	67	Mass	1974
Sokoloff, Kenneth L.	Prof	UCLA		PHD	82	Harvard	1980
Solar, Donald	Prof	Lg Isl-Post		PHD	63	Columbia	1965
Solberg, Eric J.	Prof	CS-Fullerton	J	PHD	74	Claremont	1973
Soligo, Ronald	Prof	Rice		PHD	64	Yale	1967
Soliman, Mostafa A.	Assoc	Prairie View	DHQ	PHD	67	Iowa St	1971
Sollars, David L.	Assoc	Auburn-Montg	KHAE	PHD	91	Fla St	1990
Soller, Elizabeth	Asst	Drexel		PHD	97	Indiana	1997
Solnick, Sara J.	Asst	Vermont	DI	PHD	96	Penn	2000
Solomon, Elinor H.	Adj	George Wash	E	PHD	48	Harvard	1982
Solomon, Henry	Retir	George Wash	I	PHD	59	NYU	
Solomon, Howard	Prof	CUNY-Brookly		LLM	67	Brooklyn	1967
Solomon, Lynnette K.	Retir	S F Austin		PHD	70	Arkansas	1979
Solon, Babette S.	Emer	CUNY-Queens	DJ	PHD	58	MIT	1961
Solon, Gary R.	C-Pr	Michigan		PHD	83	Princeton	1983
Solow, John L.	Assoc	Iowa		PHD	83	Stanford	1981
Solow, Robert M.	Retir	MIT	E	PHD	51	Harvard	1958
Soltow, Allen R.	Assoc	Tulsa		PHD	69	Iowa St	1973
Sommers, Paul M.	Prof	Middlebury	CDT	PHD	76	Ca-SnDgo	1976
Sonanathan, Rohini	Asst	Michigan					
Sondey, John A.	Prof	So Dakota St	H	PHD	89	Wash St	1990
Song, Inbum	Retir	Louisville		PHD		Oklahoma	
Song, Shunfeng	Asst	Nevada-Reno		PHD	92	Ca-Irvine	1992
Song, Yoon K.	Prof	Detroit Merc		PHD	69	Illinois	1969
Sonmez, Tayfun O.	Asst	Michigan	CDH	PHD	95	Rochester	1995
Sonnenschein, Hugo F.	Prof	Chicago		PHD	64	Purdue	
Charles L. Hutchinson Distringushed Service Professor							
Sonny, Jacob	Assoc	Dowling		PHD	71	New Sch	
Sonora, Robert	Asst	Tx-Arlington	F	PHD	98	Ohio St	1998
Sonstelie, Jon C.	Prof	Cal-Santa Br	HR	PHD	75	Nrthwstrn	1977
Sontheimer, Kevin C.	Assoc	Pittsburgh	D	PHD	69	Minnesota	1979
Soofi, Abdollah S.	Assoc	Wis-Plattev		PHD	81	Ca-Rivers	1980
Soper, John C.	Prof	John Carroll	ENA	PHD	70	Mass	1982
Sopher, Barry	Assoc	Rutgers-N Br	D	PHD	88	Iowa	1987
Sorensen, Alan	Asst	Ca-San Diego	LH	PHD	99	MIT	1999
Sorensen, Bent	Prof	SUNY-Bingham	E	PHD	90	Copenhag	2001
Sorensen, Duane L.	Retir	Indiana St	R	MS	61	Iowa St	1968
Sorensen, Phillip E.	Retir	Florida St	Q	PHD	66	Berkeley	1971
Sorensen, Robert L.	Prof	Mo-St Louis	KMAO	PHD	71	Va Tech	1970
Sorenson, David	Asst	Augustana SD	RG	PHD	97	W Virginia	1997
Sorenson, Timothy L.	Assoc	Seattle	MDF	PHD	91	Harvard	1991
Sorkin, Alan L.	C-Pr	MD-Baltim Co		PHD	66	J Hopkins	1974
Sorrentino, John A. Jr.	Assoc	Temple	Q	PHD	73	Purdue	1979
Sosin, Kim	C-Pr	Neb-Omaha	ECO	PHD	70	Nebraska	1981
Soskin, Mark D.	Assoc	Cen Florida	C	PHD	79	Penn St	1988
Sowell, Clifford	Prof	Berea		PHD	78	Georgia	1981

Sowell, Fallaw B.	Assoc	Carnegie Mel		PHD	86	Duke	1988
Soydemir, Gokoe	Asst	Tx-Pan Amer		PHD	97	Claremont	1998
Spagnolo, John A.	Assoc	Iona	R	PHD	82	Fordham	1978
Spanos, Aris	C-Pr	Virg Tech	CB	PHD	82	LondonEc	1988
Sparks, Donald L.	Prof	Citadel		PHD	85	London	8-86
Spatt, Chester S.	Prof	Carnegie Mel		PHD	79	Penn	1979
Mellon Bank Professor of Finance							
Spear, Stephen E.	Prof	Carnegie Mel		PHD	82	Penn	1982
Spears, Philip V.	Prof	Berea		PHD	71	Kentucky	1968
Spechler, Martin	Prof	Ind-Purdue/I	BFNP	PHD	71	Harvard	1986
Spector, David	Asst	MIT	E	PHD	96	LondonEc	1996
Spector, Lee C.	Assoc	Ball State	E	PHD	85	Iowa	1985
Spence, Ardith	Asst	Smith					
Spence, James G.	Assoc	South Fla	A	PHD	79	Oklahoma	1975
Spencer, Austin Harvey	Prof	W Carolina	G	PHD	72	Indiana	1980
Spencer, David E.	Prof	Brigham Yg	EC	PHD	74	Tx A&M	1986
Spencer, Deborah	Asst	SUNY-Cortlan	KFP	PHD		Notre Dm	1999
Spencer, Roger W.	Prof	Trinity	E	PHD	69	Virginia	1980
Speyrer, Janet F.	Prof	New Orleans		PHD	82	J Hopkins	1987
Spiva, George A. Jr.	Retir	Tennessee		PHD	58	Tx-Austin	1958
Spizman, Lawrence	Prof	SUNY Oswego	AJK	PHD	77	SUNY-Alb	1977
Spolaore, Enrico	Asst	Brown		PHD	93	Harvard	
Spraberry, Hubert O.	Prof	Howard Payne		PHD	85	Tx Tech	1986
Sprenkle, Case	Retir	Illinois		PHD	60	Yale	1960
Sprinkle, Richard L.	Assoc	Txs-El Paso	ABCF	PHD	82	Arkansas	1982
Sprunger, Philip W.	Asst	Lycoming	AJQH	PHD	93	Indiana	1993
Spurr, Stephen J.	Assoc	Wayne State	JK	PHD	86	Chicago	1987
Squintani, Francesco	Asst	Rochester		PHD	00	Nrthwstrn	2000
Sraiheen, Abdulwahab	Assoc	Kutztown	CM	PHD	86	Penn St	1990
Srinivasan, T. N.	C-Pr	Yale	FO	PHD	62	Yale	1980
Srivastava, Sanjay	Prof	Carnegie Mel		PHD	82	MIT	1982
Alumni Professor of Economics and Finance							
St. Clair, David J.	Prof	CS-Hayward	BENP	PHD	79	Utah	1979
Stachetti, Ennio	Prof	Michigan		PHD	83	Wisconsin	1992
Staelin, Charles P.	Assoc	Smith	ACDF	PHD	71	Michigan	1981
Stafford, Frank P.	Prof	Michigan		PHD	68	Chicago	1974
Stafford, Sarah	Asst	Wm & Mary		PHD	98	J Hopkins	1998
Stageberg, Stephen P.	Assoc	Mary Wash	CFN	PHD	84	Geotown	1982
Stahl, Dale O. III	Prof	Texas	DC	PHD	81	Berkeley	7-88
Malcolm Forsman Centennial Professorship							
Staiger, Douglas O.	Assoc	Dartmouth		PHD	90	MIT	1998
Staiger, Robert W.	Prof	Wisconsin		PHD	85	Michigan	1993
Stair, Anthony G.	C-Ac	Frostburg St		PHD	93	W Virginia	1984
Staller, George J.	Prof	Cornell		PHD	59	Cornell	1960
Stallings, Dale G.	Retir	CS-Pomona	1994	PHD	62	Minnesota	1964
Stanfield, James Ronald	Prof	Colorado St	BA	PHD	72	Oklahoma	1976
Stanford, Richard A.	Prof	Furman		PHD	71	Georgia	1968
David C Garrett Jr. Professor of Economics							
Stanford, Robert	Prof	Alabama-Birm	C	PHD	71	Berkeley	1982
Stanford, William G.	Assoc	Ill-Chicago	C	PHD	84	Nrthwstrn	1983
Stanky, Marius	Asst	Case Western	IS	PHD	00	Harvard	2000
Stanley, Thomas O.	Prof	Nicholls St	FG	PHD	82	Nebraska	1988
Stanley, Tom D.	Assoc	Hendrix	CN	PHD	82	Purdue	1986
Stano, Miron	C-Pr	Oakland	IL	PHD	71	Cornell	1977
Stanton, Timothy J.	Assoc	Mt St Mary's	CD	PHD	88	Kentucky	1988
Stapp, Robert	VAsst	Arkansas		PHD		Okla St	1996
Starkey, James L.	Prof	Rhode Island	Q	PHD	71	Boston C	1967
Starleaf, Dennis R.	Retir	Iowa State	E	PHD	67	Vanderbilt	1963
Starr, Ross	Prof	Ca-San Diego	DE	PHD	72	Stanford	1980
Starrett, David A.	Retir	Stanford		PHD	68	Stanford	1973
Startz, Richard	Prof	U Washington		PHD	78	MIT	1984
Stauffer, Robert F.	Assoc	Roanoke		PHD	74	Va Tech	1978
Steagall, Jeffrey W.	Assoc	North Fla	FAC	PHD	90	Wisconsin	1990
Steckel, Richard H.	Prof	Ohio State	N	PHD	77	Chicago	1977
Steele, Gerald R.	Lect	U Lancaster		MA		Sheffield	
Steele, Henry B.	Prof	Houston	A	PHD	57	MIT	
Steen, Robert C.	Assoc	Rollins	RHN	PHD	82	Princeton	1987
Steen, Todd P.	Assoc	Hope	JT	PHD	93	Harvard	1988
Steenstra, Alex	Asst	E Oregon St	ABDQ	PHD	97	Utah	9-97
Steffens, Karin	Asst	No Michigan	AFQ	PHD	99	Mich St	1999
Stegeman, Mark W.	Assoc	Virg Tech	DL	PHD	87	MIT	1994
Steger, Eric K.	Prof	East Central		PHD	80	La Tech	1970
Stegner, Tesa	C-Ac	Idaho State	AHQ	PHD	89	Wash St	1992
Stehman, Diane	Assoc	NE Illinois	CL	PHD	86	Il-Chicago	1978
Steib, Steve B.	Prof	Tulsa		PHD	72	Iowa St	1972
Steigerwald, Douglas G.	Assoc	Cal-Santa Br	C	PHD	89	Berkeley	1988
Stein, Bruno	Retir	New York U		PHD	59	NYU	1959
Stein, Howard	Prof	Roosevelt		PHD	83	Ca-Rivers	1983
Stein, Jeremy	Prof	Harvard		PHD	86	MIT	
Stein, Jerome L.	Retir	Brown		PHD	55	Yale	1956

Stein, Sheldon H.	Assoc	Cleveland St	CER	PHD	78	J Hopkins	1976
Steinberg, Ivan	Assoc	NewJerseyCty	LA	ABD	71	New Sch	
Steinberg, Richard	Prof	Ind-Purdue/I	HL	PHD	84	Penn	1991
Steindl, Frank G.	Prof	Oklahoma St	E	PHD	63	Iowa	1962
Regents' Professor and Ardmore Chair							
Steiner, Peter	Retir	Michigan					
Steinhauer, Larry	Prof	Albion	E	PHD	74	Chicago	1968
Steinkamp, Stanley W.	Retir	Illinois		PHD	58	Michigan	1958
Steinmeier, Thomas L.	Prof	Texas Tech		PHD	75	Yale	1982
Steinnes, Donald N.	Prof	Minn-Duluth	C	PHD	72	Nrthwstrn	1975
Stellern, Michael J.	Asst	Rockhurst		PHD	83	Arizona	1979
Stephan, Paula E.	Prof	Georgia St	JO	PHD	71	Michigan	1971
Stephens, Mark A.	C-Pr$	Tenn Tech	FO	PHD	85	Tennessee	1980
Stephenson, E. Frank	Asst	Berry	EH	PHD	97	N Carol	1997
Stephenson, James A.	Retir	Iowa State		PHD	65	Berkeley	1964
Stephenson, Matthew A.	C-Pr	Wofford	DLN	PHD	65	Tulane	1970
T. B. Stackhouse Professor of Economics							
Sterbenz, Frederic P.	Assoc	Wyoming	EG	PHD	81	Penn	1981
Stern, Andrew	Prof	CS-Long Bch		PHD	67	Columbia	1967
Stern, Robert M.	Prof	Michigan		PHD	58	Columbia	1961
Stern, Steven N.	Prof	Virginia	JCI	PHD	85	Yale	1985
Stevens, Ann Huff	Asst	Yale	J	PHD	95	Michigan	1995
Stevens, David W.	Prof	Baltimore		PHD	65	Colorado	
Stevens, Flumo Y.	Prof	Lawrence Tec	G	PHD	74	Nebraska	1987
Stevens, George E.	Dean	Kent State	ADMS	DBA	79	Kent St	1995
Stevenson, Mary H.	Prof	Mass-Boston	JIR	PHD	74	Michigan	1972
Stevenson, Thomas M. Jr.	Retir	St Louis		PHD	64	Illinois	1965
Stewart, Douglas B.	Prof	San Diego St		PHD	70	Oregon	1971
Stewart, Douglas O.	Assoc	Cleveland St	DH	PHD	74	Michigan	1972
Stewart, John F.	Prof	No Carolina	L	PHD	76	Wisconsin	1975
Stewart, Max D.	Retir			PHD	60	Mich St	
Stewart, Milton D. Jr.	Retir	S F Austin		PHD	72	Tx-Austin	1966
Stieber, Jack	Retir	Michigan St		PHD	56	Harvard	1956
Stillwaggon, Eileen	Asst	Gettysburg	AFQO	PHD	79	American	1995
Stinchcombe, Maxwell B.	Assoc	Texas	DC	PHD	86	Berkeley	1-94
Stine, William F.	Prof	Clarion		PHD	83	Fordham	1981
Stirling, Kathleen J.	C-Pr	Puget Sound	AEIT	PHD	87	Notre Dm	
Stivers, Andrew	Asst	Oregon State	DL	PHD	01	Tx-Austin	9-01
Stober, William J.	Retir	Kentucky	D	PHD	65	Duke	1965
Stock, Wendy A.	Assoc	Montana St	JCQ	PHD	96	Mich St	8-00
Stockhausen, Gerard L. S.J.	Prov	Detroit Merc	AEFN	PHD	85	Michigan	2001
Stockman, Alan C.	Prof	Rochester		PHD	78	Chicago	1979
Wilson Professor of Economics							
Stockman, David	Asst	Delaware	CE	PHD	97	Chicago	1998
Stocks, Anthony H.	Retir	Youngstown		PHD	63	SUNY-Buf	1968
Stokes, Houston H.	Prof	Ill-Chicago	D	PHD	69	Chicago	1967
Stokey, Nancy	Prof	Chicago		PHD	78	Harvard	1990
Frederick Henry Prince Professor							
Stoll, John R.	Prof	WI-Green Bay		PHD	80	Kentucky	
Stollar, Andrew J.	Prof	Bentley	CFP	PHD	73	Boston C	1976
Stolnitz, George J.	Retir	Indiana		PHD	52	Princeton	
Stolte, William F.	Retir	Berea		PHD	71	Syracuse	1970
Stone, Allan D.	Emer	SW Missouri		PHD	73	Oklahoma	1972
Stone, Courtney C.	Prof	Ball State	EM	PHD	73	UCLA	1991
Stone, Gary L.	Prof	Winthrop	ACD	PHD	80	N Carol	9-75
Stone, Gerald W. Jr.	Retir	Metro St-CO		PHD	73	Rice	1975
Stone, Irving	Prof	CUNY-Baruch		PHD	62	Columbia	1962
Stone, Joe A.	Dean	Oregon	JFE	PHD	77	Mich St	1970
W. E. Miner Professor of Economics							
Stone, Leonie L.	Asst	SUNY-Geneseo	OD	PHD	93	Ohio St	1993
Stonebraker, Robert J.	Retir	Indiana U-PA	EK	PHD	73	Princeton	1971
Storer, Paul	Assoc	Western Wash	EJ	PHD	92	W Ontario	1996
Story, Jonathan	Prof	INSEAD		PHD	73	J Hopkins	7-74
Stout, Eric	Lect	Brandeis		PHD		Stanford	1999
Stover, Stewart	Asst	Olivet		MBA			1999
Stradley, Scot A.	C-Pr	Concordia C	NAB	PHD	77	Utah	2001
Straight, Ronald L.	Asst	Howard		DBA	79	Geo Wash	1988
Strait, Roger H.	Retir	F Dick-Teane	BN	STB		Harvard	
Stranahan, Harriett	Assoc	North Fla	JGD	PHD	95	Wash	1994
Strand, Larry D.	Dean	Biola		MBA	69	S Calif	1986
Strand, Stephen H.	Prof	Carleton	DL	PHD	76	Vanderbilt	1981
Raymond Plank Professor of Economics							
Strang, Daniel R.	Prof	SUNY-Geneseo	CQ	PHD	75	Cornell	1992
Strangways, Raymond S.	Retir	Old Dominion		PHD	66	Tulane	1962
Strasma, John D.	Retir	Wisconsin		PHD	60	Harvard	1966
Strassmann, W. Paul	Retir	Michigan St		PHD	56	Maryland	
Straszheim, Mahlon R.	C-Pr	Maryland		PHD	66	Harvard	
Stratton, Leslie A.	Asst	Virg Comm		PHD	89	MIT	1997
Stratton, Peter J.	Retir	W Illinois	AD	PHD	70	N Illinois	1970
Stratton, Richard	Assoc	Akron	ADJ	PHD	77	Conn	1978

Straub, LaVonne	Prof	W Illinois	AIJR	PHD	83	Utah	1982
Strauss, Jack K.	Assoc	St Louis		PHD	89	Duke	
Strauss, John A.	Prof	Michigan St		PHD	81	Mich St	1992
Strauss-Kahn, Vanessa	Asst	INSEAD	FJ	PHD	00	NYU	2001
Strausser, Clark W.	Assoc	Pitts-Johnst	CG	PHD	70	Minnesota	1973
Strayer, Wayne	Asst	Texas A&M	J	PHD	97	Ohio St	1997
Street, Barbara P.	Prof	Chaminade	ACEI	PHD	86	Virginia	1981
Street, Donald R.	Retir	Auburn		PHD	65	Penn St	1965
Streeter, Lanny E.	Assoc	U Miami	C	PHD	70	Illinois	1967
Strein, Charles T.	Retir	No Iowa	DLMR	PHD	77	Illinois	1970
Stromsdorfer, Ernst W.	Prof	Wash State		PHD	62	Wash U	1983
Strong, Jerome C.	Retir	Hartwick		PHD		Columbia	1965
Stronge, William B.	Prof	Fla Atlantic		PHD	71	Iowa St	1971
Stroup, Michael	Assoc	S F Austin	DH	PHD	93	Fla St	1999
Stroup, Richard L.	Prof	Montana St		PHD	70	U Wash	1969
Strow, Brian	Asst	W Kentucky		PHD		Vanderbilt	
Strow, Claudia	Asst	W Kentucky		ABD		Vanderbilt	
Strumpf, Koleman	Assoc	No Carolina	GH	PHD	95	MIT	1995
Stuart, Charles	Prof	Cal-Santa Br	HKD	PHD	75	Lunds	1980
Stuart, Edward F.	Prof	NE Illinois	FP	PHD	78	Oklahoma	1986
Stuart, Robert C.	Prof	Rutgers-N Br	P	PHD	69	Wisconsin	1968
Stubblebine, William Craig	Prof	Claremont		PHD	63	Virginia	1966
Studenmund, A. H.	C-Pr	Occidental	C	PHD	70	Cornell	1970
Richard W. Millar Professor of Economics & Director of Institutional Planning							
Stuligross, John D.	Retir	Hartwick	AEGR	PHD	71	Oklahoma	1980
Stull, Charles	Inst	Kalamazoo		ABD		Wisconsin	
Stull, William J.	C-Pr	Temple	IR	PHD	72	MIT	1976
Sturgeon, James I.	Prof	Mo-Kansas Ct	BO	PHD	74	Oklahoma	1977
Sturges, David M.	Asst	Colgate	EG	PHD	94	Yale	1995
Stutes, Gregory	Asst	Mn-Moorhead		MA	99	Nebraska	2000
Stutsman, A. Douglas	Emer	So Alabama	AB	PHD	70	Miss	1968
Su, Vincent	Prof	CUNY-Baruch		PHD	70	Rutgers	1971
Suarez, James M.	Dean	Manhattan		PHD	72	Columbia	1984
Sublette, Werner Johann	Prof	Truman State		PHD	74	Arizona	1974
Subramanian, Chetan	Asst	SUNY-Buffalo	ECF	PHD	00	S Calif	2001
Subramanian, Narayanan	Asst	Brandeis		PHD	99	Brown	1999
Subramanian, Shankar	Asst	Cornell	OQ	PHD	88	Berkeley	8-93
Sue, Della	Asst	Marist	HN	PHD	96	Columbia	2000
Suh, Jingyo	Asst	Tuskegee		PHD	00	Alabama	2000
Sukar, Abdul Hamid	Prof	Cameron		PHD	89	Tx Tech	1987
Sukhatme, Vasant A.	C-Pr	Macalester	ADO	PHD	77	Chicago	1978
Edward J. Noble Professor of Economics							
Sula, Laddie J.	Prof	Loras		PHD	76	Geo St	1983
Suliman, Osman	C-Pr	Millersville		PHD	84	Indiana	1993
Sullivan, Dennis H.	Prof	Miami U-Ohio	HI	PHD	75	Princeton	1973
Sullivan, Edward J.	VInst	St Joseph	EF	ABD	81	Fordham	1998
Sullivan, John J.	Retir	Hartford		PHD	67	Conn	
Sullivan, Timothy	Asst	S Ill-Edward	IJT	PHD	95	Maryland	1995
Sullivan, Timothy	Assoc	Towson		PHD	87	Illinois	1989
Sulock, Joseph M.	Prof	N Car-Ashvil	AGH	PHD	76	Virginia	1975
Sulter, Mary	Lect	Mo-St Louis	A	MIEE		Delaware	
Sum, Andrew M.	Prof	Northeastern		MA	71	MIT	1971
Summary, Rebecca M.	C-Pr	SE Missouri	FA	PHD	83	Illinois	1983
Summers, Jeffrey A.	Assoc	Linfield		PHD	87	Purdue	1992
Summers, Robert	Emer	Pennsylvania		PHD	56	Stanford	1959
Sumner, Scott B.	Prof	Bentley	EN	PHD	84	Chicago	1982
Sundaram, Ramya	Asst	Arizona		PHD	01	Penn	2001
Sundstrom, William A.	C-Ac	Santa Clara		PHD	86	Stanford	1987
Sung, Jane C.	Prof	Truman State		PHD	85	Wayne St	1987
Sung, Simona	Assoc	St Rose	CDEL	PHD	90	Rensselaer	8-90
Supel, Mary R.	Asst	St Thomas-MN	L	BA		Denison	1976
Suranovic, Steven M.	Assoc	George Wash	F	PHD	87	Cornell	1988
Surdyk, Lisa	Assoc	Seattle Pac	G	PHD	91	U Wash	1991
Sureshwaran, S.	Asst	So Carol St		PHD	89	Clemson	1990
Sussman, Jeffrey		SUNY-Empire	G	PHD	75	CUNY	1975
Suster, Zeljan	Assoc	New Haven	FNOP	PHD	88	Belgrade	9-90
Sutch, Richard C.	Prof	Cal-Riversid	AN	PHD	68	MIT	1998
Sutliffe, James S.	Deces	SUNY-Potsdam		PHD		Fla St	
Sutter, Dan	Asst	Oklahoma	H	PHD	93	GeoMason	1995
Sutton, James E.	Prof	CS-Pomona		BS	55	Wisconsin	1964
Sutton, Terry	Prof	SE Missouri	B	PHD	70	Kansas St	1972
Suwanakul, Sontachai	Assoc	Alabama St		PHD	86	Arkansas	1989
Suzawa, Gilbert S.	Assoc	Rhode Island	AD	PHD	73	Brown	1971
Svorny, Shirley V.	Prof	CS-Northrdge	IG	PHD	79	UCLA	1978
Swaino, Howard R.	Prof	No Michigan	AKDH	PHD	65	UCLA	1966
Swan, Craig E.	Prof	Minnesota		PHD	70	Yale	1969
Swaney, James A.	Prof	Wright State	BPQ	PHD	79	Colo St	1979
Swanke, Thomas A.	Asst	Chadron St	B	PHD	93	Colorado	2001
Swann, Christopher	Asst	SUNY-Stony B		PHD	97	Virginia	1999
Swanson, Charles	Asst	Temple	E	PHD	91	Minnesota	1993

Swanson, Gerald	Assoc	Arizona		PHD	72	Illinois	1970
Swanson, James A.	Assoc	Cen Missouri		PHD	87	Wash St	1986
Swanson, Norman	Assoc	Texas A&M		PHD	94	Ca-SnDgo	1999
Swanson, Paul	Prof	Wm Patterson		PHD	84	Columbia	1982
Swartz, Thomas R.	Prof	Notre Dame	HA	PHD	65	Indiana	1965
Sweeney, George H.	Assoc	Vanderbilt	DL	PHD	77	Nrthwstrn	1976
Sweeney, Vernon E.	Retir	Sam Houston		PHD	68	Tx-Austin	1971
Sweeney, William B. Jr.	Prof	Bryant	AE	PHD	73	Sarasota	
Swenson, Deborah	Assoc	Cal-Davis	FH	PHD	91	MIT	1993
Swint, Kenneth J.	Assoc	Wash & Jeff		PHD	89	Pittsburgh	1988
Swinton, John R.	Asst	South Fla	Q	PHD	96	Wisconsin	1995
Swofford, James L.	Prof	So Alabama	E	PHD	81	Florida	1984
Swope, Kortis	Asst	USN Academy		PHD	00	Indiana	
Sylla, Richard	Prof	New York U	DN	PHD	69	Harvard	1990
Henry Kaufman Professor of the History of Financial Institutions & Markets							
Sylvester, Patrick J.	Prof	West Chester	AE	PHD	73	Bryn Mawr	1968
Sylwester, Kevin	Asst	So Illinois	EO	PHD	97	Wisconsin	1998
Syropoulos, Constantinos	Assoc	Fla Internat	FLO	PHD	89	Yale	1996
Syvelson, Chad	Asst	Chicago		PHD	01	Stanford	2001
Tabb, William K.	Prof	CUNY-Queens	RO	PHD	68	Wisconsin	1971
Taber, Christopher	Asst	Northwestern		PHD	95	Chicago	1995
Tabesh, Hamid	Prof	Wis-Rvr Fall	EF	PHD	87	Iowa St	1988
Tabrizi, Behrouz	C-As	St Fran-NY		PHD	84	Jawahar	9-97
Tabriztchi, Sirousse	Assoc	SUNY Old Wes		PHD	70	Columbia	
Tacker, Thomas L.	Assoc	Embry-Riddle		PHD	87	N Carol	
Tadelis, Steven	Asst	Stanford		PHD		Harvard	
Taga, Leonore S.	Assoc	Rider	P	PHD	79	Berkeley	1986
Tahmiscioglu, Kamil	Asst	Wis-Milwauke		PHD	96	USC	1997
Tailby, Don	Retir	New Mexico	ABNO	PHD	61	Rutgers	1967
Taira, Koji	Retir	Illinois		PHD	61	Stanford	1970
Takacs, Wendy E.	Assoc	MD-Baltim Co		PHD	76	J Hopkins	1981
Takayama, Akira	Deces	So Illinois	FEDC	PHD	62	Rochester	1983
Takeyama, Lisa N.	Asst	Amherst	ADLQ	PHD	92	Stanford	1994
Talarico, Joseph F.	Retir	Rider	F	PHD	58	Rutgers	1967
Talbert, Lonnie E.	Retir	Arkansas St	AQMT	PHD	64	N Car St	1966
Tallarini, Thomas	Asst	Carnegie Mel		PHD	95	Chicago	1995
Talley, Wayne K.	Prof	Old Dominion		PHD	72	Kentucky	1972
Eminent Professor							
Tam, Henry	Asst	Texas A&M	E	PHD	99	Harvard	1999
Tam, Mo-Yin S.	Prof	Ill-Chicago	P	PHD	74	SUNY-SBr	1974
Tamura, Robert F.	Assoc	Clemson	IJO	PHD	88	Chicago	1996
Tan, Chinteck	Assoc	Cumberland		MBA	88	Tenn Tech	1988
Tandon, Pankaj	Assoc	Boston Univ	DO	PHD	79	Harvard	1978
Tang, Linghui	Asst	Drexel		PHD	98	Syracuse	1998
Tangri, Shanti S.	Retir	Rutgers-N Br	O	PHD	61	Berkeley	1970
Tanguay, Georges	Asst	Maine	AHQ	PHD	98	Laval	1993
Tank, Frederick E.	Emer	Toledo	KQ	PHD	72	Wayne St	1970
Tanner, J. Ernest	Retir	Tulane		PHD	68	Brown	1971
Tannery, Frederick J.	Assoc	Slippery Roc	ACDJ	PHD	80	Pittsburgh	1981
Tansey, Francis B.	Lect	CUNY-Baruch		MBA	65	CUNY	1967
Tansey, Michael M.	Prof	Rockhurst		PHD	78	Wisconsin	1982
Tanski, Janet M.	Assoc	New Mex St	OI	PHD	91	SUNY-Buf	1989
Tarascio, Vincent J.	Prof	No Carolina	N	PHD	66	Rice	1964
Tarhouni, Ali	SLect	U Washington		PHD	84	Mich St	1985
Tarpley, Fred A. Jr.	Retir	Georgia Tech	D	PHD	67	Tulane	1962
Tarullo, P. Ronald	Prof	Calif U-Penn		PHD	76	Pittsburgh	1978
Taub, Allan J.	Assoc	Cleveland St	CD	PHD	73	Nrthwstrn	1971
Taub, Bart	Prof	Illinois	E	PHD	81	Chicago	1989
Tauber, Linda	Asst	CUNY-Lehman		MBA			
Tauchen, George	Prof	Duke	CG	PHD	78	Minnesota	1977
Tauchen, Helen	Prof	No Carolina	D	PHD	77	Minnesota	1977
Tauman, Yair	Prof	SUNY-Stony B		PHD	79	Hebrew	1989
Tauras, John M.	Asst	Ill-Chicago	I	PHD	98	Il-Chicago	2000
Taussig, Michael K.	Retir	Rutgers-N Br	H	PHD	66	MIT	1967
Tawatnuntachai, Oranee	Asst	Penn St-Harr		PHD	99	N Orleans	1999
Tay, Abigail	Asst	Columbia	LI	PHD	99	Stanford	1999
Taylor, Alan M.	Assoc	Cal-Davis	FNO	PHD	92	Harvard	1987
Taylor, Arthur M.	Retir			PHD	54	Mich St	
Taylor, Beck	Asst	Baylor	D	PHD	97	Purdue	1997
Taylor, Donald C.	Retir	So Dakota St	O	PHD	65	Minnesota	1980
Taylor, Gary	Asst	So Dakota St	Q	PHD	95	Okla St	2000
Taylor, James	Prof	U Lancaster		PHD		Lancaster	
Taylor, Jason	Asst	Virginia	NO	PHD	98	Georgia	1998
Taylor, John B.	Prof	Stanford		PHD	73	Stanford	
Mary and Robert Raymond Professor of Economics							
Taylor, Kenna C.	Prof	Rollins		PHD	79	Florida	1974
Taylor, Kenneth B.	Asst	Villanova		PHD	80	SUNY-SBr	1985
Taylor, Larry W.	Assoc	Lehigh	CE	PHD	84	N Carol	1984
Taylor, Lary	Assoc	Pacific Unio		MBA	76	Maryland	1978
Taylor, Laura L.	Assoc	Georgia St	C	PHD	94	N Car St	1994

Taylor, Leon E.	Asst	SE Louisiana	E	PHD	90	Maryland	
Taylor, Lester D.	Prof	Arizona		PHD	63	Harvard	1972
Taylor, M. Scott	Prof	Wisconsin		PHD	91	Queen's	1998
Taylor, Patrick A.	C-Ac	Millsaps	AD	PHD	85	Alabama	1984
Taylor, Susan W.	Assoc	Millsaps	AFH	PHD	89	LSU	1992
The J. A. Brown Chair of Business Administration							
Taylor, Travis K.	Visit	Richmond		PHD	01	Conn	2000
Taylor, Wagiha A.	Prof	Wilkes	EFO	PHD	66	Clark	1969
Tchakerian, Viken	Assoc	CS-Northrdge	N	PHD	91	UCLA	1991
Teeples, Ronald K.	Prof	Claremont		PHD	70	UCLA	1969
Boswell Professor of Economics							
Teferra, Daniel	Prof	Ferris State		PHD	79	Wisconsin	1980
Tekin, Erdal	Asst	Georgia St	I	PHD	01	N Carol	2001
Tellew, Fuad H.	Retir	Cal Poly-SLO		PHD	59	S Calif	1960
Telmer, Chris I.	Assoc	Carnegie Mel		PHD	92	Queen's	1992
Telser, Lester G.	Emer	Chicago	1-98	PHD	56	Chicago	1958
Temimi, Akram	Asst	Alabama		PHD	96	Illinois	1996
Temin, Peter	Prof	MIT	N	PHD	64	MIT	1965
Elish Gray II Professor							
Temple, Frederick C.	Retir	Southern		PHD		Wisconsin	1950
Temple, Judy A.	Assoc	No Illinois	H	PHD	90	Mich St	1989
Temzelides, Ted	Asst	Iowa		PHD	95	Minnesota	1997
Tenenbaum, Marcel	Retir	Hofstra		PHD	69	Columbia	1964
Tengesdal, Mark O.	Asst	SE Okla St		PHD	95	Ca-Rivers	1997
Tenorio, Rafael	Assoc	DePaul	EDA	PHD	88	J Hopkins	1999
Terasawa, Katsuaki	Prof	Mississippi		PHD	98	Kansas	1999
Terkla, David G.	Prof	Mass-Boston	QRH	PHD	79	Berkeley	1987
Terrebonne, Peter	Assoc	Kennesaw St	DMQ	PHD	92	Emory	2000
Terregrossa, Ralph A.	Assoc	St John's		PHD	91	SUNY-Bin	
Terrell, Dek	Assoc	Louisiana St	C	PHD	91	Duke	8-96
Freeport McMoran Endowed Chair; Director Center for Econ Dev & Forecasting							
Terrell, Timothy	Asst	Liberty	ACPQ	PHD	98	Auburn	1998
Terrell, William T.	Assoc	Wichita St		PHD	70	Vanderbilt	1967
Terry, Andy	C-Ac	Ark-Ltl Rock		PHD	89	Michigan	1989
Terry, Neil W.	Asst	West Txs St	EOQ	PHD	97	Tx Tech	1997
Terry, Rory L.	Asst	Fort Hays St	GE	PHD	92	Utah	1997
Terza, Joseph V.	Assoc	Penn State	C	PHD	81	Pittsburgh	1986
Tesar, Linda L.	Assoc	Michigan	FGE	PHD	90	Rochester	
Tesfatsion, Leigh S.	Prof	Iowa State	E	PHD	75	Minnesota	1990
Testa, Gary	Assoc	CUNY-Brookly		MBA	78	St Johns	1978
Thakur, Rita	Prof	LaVerne		MBA		NW Mo St	1978
Thanawala, Kishor H.	Prof	Villanova		PHD	61	Bombay	1967
Thaver, Ranjini L.	Assoc	Stetson	AHP	PHD	95	Notre Dm	1992
Thayer, Mark A.	C-Pr	San Diego St		PHD	79	New Mex	1981
Thewell, Raphael R.	Retir	Howard		PHD		Geo Wash	
Thiagarajan, K. R.	Asst	Prairie View	DE	MA	55	Annamali	1967
Thierfelder, Karen	Assoc	USN Academy		PHD	92	Wisconsin	1992
Thies, Clifford F.	Prof	Shenandoah		PHD	82	Boston C	1992
Thimester, Renate	Assoc	Loyola Marym	ABKM	PHD	67	Alabama	1971
Thoma, George A. Jr.	Prof	Elmhurst		PHD	73	N Illinois	1970
Thomadsen, Raphael	Asst	Columbia		PHD		Stanford	2000
Thomakos, Dimitrios	Asst	Fla Internat	CEO	PHD	98	Columbia	1998
Thomas, Christopher R.	Assoc	South Fla	L	PHD	80	Tx A&M	1982
Thomas, Duncan	Prof	UCLA		PHD	86	Princeton	
Thomas, George W.	Prof	Naval Postgr	J	PHD	71	Purdue	1978
Thomas, Hugh A.	Assoc	McMaster U	G	PHD	91	NYU	1991
Thomas, Janet M.	Prof	Bentley	DHQ	PHD	87	Boston C	1987
Thomas, Johnny	Dean	LaSierra	C	PHD	01	Claremont	1989
Thomas, Lloyd B. Jr.	Prof	Kansas State	EA	PHD	70	Nrthwstrn	1968
Thomas, Philip S.	Retir	Kalamazoo	FO	PHD	61	Michigan	1965
Thomas, Robert P.	Assoc	U Washington		PHD	64	Nrthwstrn	1968
Thomas, Robert W. Jr.	Deces	Iowa State	1994	PHD	62	Iowa St	1957
Thomas, Wade L.	C-Ac	SUNY-Oneonta	DEJ	PHD	82	Nebraska	1989
Thomas, William J.	Deces			PHD	57	Mich St	
Thomasson, Henry E.	Asst	SE Louisiana	AJ	MS		LSU	
Thomasson, Melissa	Asst	Miami U-Ohio	IN	PHD	98	Arizona	1998
Thompson, Alexander M.	Prof	Vassar	BH	PHD	79	Stanford	1977
Thompson, Allen R.	Assoc	New Hampshir	GM	PHD	73	Tx-Austin	1974
Thompson, Charles L.	Asst	Troy State	ADE	MS	82	Auburn	1984
Thompson, Dana	Prof	Walla Walla		EDD	89	LLU	1998
Thompson, Earl A.	Prof	UCLA		PHD	61	Harvard	1965
Thompson, Eric	Assoc	Kentucky	R	PHD	92	Wisconsin	1995
Thompson, Frank W.	Lect	Michigan		PHD	73	Harvard	1990
Thompson, G. Richard	Prof	Clemson	HLM	PHD	72	Virginia	1983
Thompson, Gerald E.	Retir	Nebraska		PHD	53	Iowa	1954
Thompson, Mary M.	Asst	Belmont		MA		Notre Dm	1983
Thompson, Paul J.	Retir	Mankato St	AI	PHD	68	Iowa	1963
Thompson, Paul W.	Retir	Jacksonvl St		PHD	70	Duke	1974
Thompson, Peter	Asst	Houston		PHD	94	Florida	1996
Thompson, Philip B.	Asst	Mo-Rolla		PHD	88	Arizona	1994

Thompson, Samuel	Asst	Harvard		PHD		Berkeley	
Thompson, William F.	Prof	E Illinois		PHD	79	Arkansas	1981
Thomson, Ross	Assoc	Vermont	NDB	PHD	76	Yale	1991
Thomson, William L.	Prof	Rochester	CDH	PHD	76	Stanford	9-83
Thorbecke, Erik	Retir	Cornell		PHD	57	Berkeley	1974
Thorbecke, Willem	Assoc	George Mason		PHD	88	Berkeley	
Thorne, Emanuel D.	Asst	CUNY-Brookly	A	PHD	94	Yale	1989
Thornton, James	Prof	E Michigan		PHD	91	Oregon	1991
Thornton, James R.	Assoc	Delaware	P	PHD	74	Cornell	1973
Thornton, Judith Ann	Prof	U Washington		PHD	60	Harvard	1961
Thornton, Richard M.	Retir	DePaul		PHD	76	N Illinois	1974
Thornton, Robert J.	Prof	Lehigh	JI	PHD	70	Illinois	1970
Charles W. MacFarlane Professor of Economics							
Thorpe, Steven G.	Asst	No Iowa	HQ	PHD	95	Colorado	1996
Thorsnes, Paul E.	Asst	Grand Valley		PHD	94	Oregon	1995
Thorson, Douglas Y.	Retir	Bradley		PHD	62	Wisconsin	1960
Thorson, James A.	Assoc	So Conn St	R	PHD	91	Il-Chicago	1992
Throckmorton, H. Bruce	Prof	Tenn Tech	EN	PHD	72	Arkansas	1971
Thurman, Walter N.	Prof	N Carol St	QCD	PHD	84	Chicago	1984
Thurow, Lester C.	Prof	MIT	F	PHD	64	Harvard	1968
Jerome and Dorothy Lemelson Professor of Economics and Management							
Thursby, Jerry G.	Prof	Purdue		PHD	75	N Carol	1988
Thursby, Marie C.	Prof	Purdue		PHD	74	N Carol	1988
Burton D. Morgan Chair of Intl Mgt Policy; Dir Cntr of Intl Busines Education							
Thurston, Norman K.	Asst	Brigham Yg	HIJ	PHD	95	Princeton	1995
Thurston, Thom B.	Prof	CUNY-Queens	EC	PHD	70	Berkeley	1971
Thweatt, William O.	Retir	Vanderbilt		BPHI	55	Oxford	1963
Tian, Guoqiang	Prof	Texas A&M	C	PHD	87	Minnesota	1987
Tideman, T. Nicolaus	Prof	Virg Tech	H	PHD	69	Chicago	1975
Tiefenthaler, Jill M.	C-Ac	Colgate	TO	PHD	91	Duke	1991
Tiemann, Thomas K.	Prof	Elon	RC	PHD	75	Vanderbilt	1984
Tiemstra, John P.	Prof	Calvin		PHD	75	MIT	1975
Tieslau, Margie	Asst	North Texas	EC	PHD	92	Mich St	1992
Tietenberg, Thomas H.	Prof	Colby	QK	PHD	71	Wisconsin	1977
Mitchell Family Professor of Economics							
Tiffany, Frederick G.	Assoc	Wittenberg	ACDL	PHD	88	Penn	1987
Timmer, C. Peter	Retir	Harvard		PHD	69	Harvard	1980
Timmermann, Allan	Prof	Ca-San Diego	CG	PHD	92	Cambridge	1994
Timmins, Christopher	Asst	Yale	LH	PHD	97	Stanford	1997
Tinari, Frank D.	Prof	Seton Hall		PHD	76	Fordham	
Tirole, Jean	VProf	MIT	O	PHD	81	MIT	1984
Tiwari, Kashi N.	Assoc	Kennesaw St	CEG	PHD	81	So Meth	1988
Tobias, Justin	Asst	Calif-Irvine		PHD	99	Chicago	1999
Toda, Yasushi	Retir	Florida	RP	PHD	69	Harvard	1974
Todd, Edward		SUNY-Empire	A	PHD	69	Chicago	1985
Todd, Petra	Asst	Pennsylvania		PHD	96	Chicago	1996
Tohamy, Soumaya	Asst	Berry	FH	PHD	94	Emory	1997
Tokar, Bette L.	Prof	Holy Family	AFED	EDD	93	Temple	9-75
Tokle, Robert J.	Prof	Idaho State	AGL	PHD	86	Iowa St	1986
Tolin, Thomas	C-As	West Chester	JD	PHD	92	Houston	1992
Tollen, Robert D.	Assoc	Txs-El Paso	D	PHD	72	Tx-Austin	1972
Tolley, George S.	Emer	Chicago		PHD	55	Chicago	1966
Tollison, Robert D.	Prof	Mississippi	DHL	PHD	69	Virginia	1999
Robert M. Hearin Professor							
Tolliver, R. Wayne	Assoc	Berea		DBA	87	Kentucky	1975
Tolpin, Harriet G.	Retir	Simmons	I	PHD	73	Boston C	1974
Toma, Mark	Assoc	Kentucky	E	PHD	77	Va Tech	1989
Toma, Michael	Asst	Armstrong At	RE	PHD	96	GeoMason	1997
Tomal, Annette	Assoc	Wheaton-IL	AIM	PHD	95	Illinois	1995
Tomaske, John A.	Retir	CS-L Angeles		PHD	68	U Wash	1965
Tombe, Wani Luan	C-As	St Edwards		PHD	85	Tx-Austin	1990
Tomer, John F.	Prof	Manhattan		PHD	73	Rutgers	1983
Tomic, Igor M.	Assoc	St John's		PHD	85	CUNY	
Tomlin, KaSaundra	Asst	Cen Florida	F	PHD	98	Oregon	1998
Tomljanovich, Marc	Asst	Colgate	E	PHD	00	Cornell	2000
Toniolo, Gianni	Resr	Duke	FB	LAUR	66	Venice	
Tonn, Victor Lux	C-Pr	Salve Regina	AGOP	PHD	94	Utah St	1984
Tontar, Charles F.	Assoc	Merrimack		MA		New Sch	
Tontz, Jay L.	Dean	CS-Hayward	EGM	PHD	66	N Carol	9-69
Toole, Andrew	Asst	Illinois St	CILO	PHD	98	Michigan	8-01
Topa, Giorgio	Asst	New York U	C	PHD	96	Chicago	1996
Toporovsky, Rinaldo	Retir	F Dick-Teane	AEG	PHD	72	Columbia	1969
Topping, Elizabeth E.	Asst	SW Missouri		PHD	85	Missouri	1979
Topyan, Kudret	Assoc	Manhattan		PHD	92	CUNY	1991
Tori, Cynthia R.	Asst	Valdosta St	EF	PHD	92	Kentucky	1998
Torras, Mariano	Asst	Adelphi	FOP	PHD		Mass	
Toruno, Mayo C.	Prof	CS-San Bern	B	PHD	83	Ca-Rivers	1983
Tosternd, Robert	Prof	South Dakota		PHD	73	Manitoba	1991
Toulaboe, Dosse	Asst	Fort Hays St	DEFL	PHD	98	Okla St	2000
Toumanoff, Peter	Assoc	Marquette	DOPC	PHD	77	U Wash	1995

Tourk, Khairy A.	Assoc	Illinois Tch		PHD	71	Berkeley	
Tournas, Ioannis	Asst	Rutgers-Newk		PHD	95	Nrthwstrn	1996
Tower, Edward	Prof	Duke	EF	PHD	71	Harvard	1974
Townsend, David C.	Retir	Sam Houston		PHD	53	LSU	1982
Townsend, Ralph E.	Prof	Maine	CHQA	PHD	83	Wisconsin	1980
Townsend, Robert M.	Prof	Chicago		PHD	75	Minnesota	1985
Charles E. Merriam Professor							
Traca, Daniel	Asst	INSEAD		PHD	96	Columbia	9-96
Tracy, Ronald L.	Assoc	Oakland	CE	PHD	75	Mich St	1983
Trainor, William J.	Asst	Virginia St		PHD	94	Va Tech	1996
Tran, Dang	Prof	CS-L Angeles		PHD	77	Syracuse	1987
Trandel, Gregory A.	Assoc	Georgia	GK	PHD	92	Princeton	1989
Trask, Kathleen	Asst	Kentucky	FO	PHD	98	Penn St	1998
Travis, Karen M.	Asst	Pacific Luth	I	PHD	95	U Wash	1999
Trawick, Michelle	Asst	W Kentucky		PHD	96	N Car St	
Traynham, Earle C. Jr.	Dean	North Fla		PHD	73	S Carol	1973
Traynor, Thomas L.	C-Ac	Wright State	CL	PHD	88	Purdue	1988
Treacy, John J.	Retir	Wright State		PHD	64	Tulane	1967
Trebing, Harry M.	Retir	Michigan St		PHD	58	Wisconsin	1966
Trees, W. Scott	C-As	Siena		PHD	94	Notre Dm	9-85
Tregarthen, Timothy D.	Retir	Colorado Spr	DEHR	PHD	72	Ca-Davis	1971
Trejo, Stephen J.	Assoc	Texas	J	PHD	88	Chicago	9-99
Tremblay, Carol	Assoc	Oregon State	CJ	PHD	84	Wash St	9-92
Tremblay, Victor J.	C-Pr	Oregon State	DLC	PHD	83	Wash St	9-90
Treml, Vladimir G.	Emer	Duke		PHD	63	N Carol	1967
Trenary, Roger C.	Inst	Kansas State	A	MA	72	Wayne St	1977
Tresch, Richard W.	Assoc	Boston Coll	H	PHD	73	MIT	1969
Trescott, Paul B.	Emer	So Illinois	EB	PHD	54	Princeton	1976
Trethewey, Richard L.	Prof	Kenyon	NFKB	PHD	71	U Wash	1969
Trevino, Len	Assoc	So Miss	F	PHD	91	Indiana	1999
Treyz, George I.	Retir	Massachusett	1995	PHD	67	Cornell	1969
Tribble, John A.	Assoc	Russell Sage		PHD	75	Utah St	1976
Lawrence Professor of Economics							
Trierweiler, John	C-Pr	Northern St		PHD	70	Nebraska	1985
Trimby, F. Stephen	Assoc	Worcester St		ABD			1970
Trimm, John M.	Deces			PHD	67	Mich St	
Trindade, Vitor	Asst	Syracuse	F	PHD	00	Ca-SnDgo	2000
Tripathi, Gautam	Asst	Wisconsin		PHD	97	Nrthwstrn	1997
Trivedi, Pravin K.	Prof	Indiana		PHD	70	LondonEc	1987
Rudy Professor of Economics							
Trogen, Paul	Asst	East Tenn St		PHD	95	Fla St	1995
Troger, Thomas	Asst	Cal-Santa Br	D	PHD	99	Bonn	2001
Troske, Kenneth	Asst	Missouri	J	PHD	92	Chicago	1997
Trost, Robert P.	Prof	George Wash	C	PHD	77	Florida	1981
Trostel, Philip	Assoc	Maine	AHJ	PHD	91	Tx A&M	1987
Troy, Leo	Prof	Rutgers-Newk		PHD	58	Columbia	
Troyer, Jennifer	Asst	N Car-Charl		PHD	99	Florida	1999
Troyer, Michael D.	Assoc	WI-Green Bay		PHD	75	Duke	
Trubac, Edward R.	Assoc	Notre Dame	R	PHD	65	Syracuse	1971
Truesdell, Marie K.	Asst	Marian		PHD	99	Georgia	2000
Truett, Dale B.	Prof	Tx-S Antonio	DFMO	PHD	67	Tx-Austin	1973
Asbel Smith Professor							
Truitt, Terry C.	Assoc	Anderson U	G	PHD	96	Miss St	1995
Truitt, W. James	Prof	Baylor	D	PHD	68	Illinois	1968
Trulove, William T.	C-Pr	East Wash		PHD	73	Oregon	1969
Trumbull, William N.	C-Ac	W Virginia	HKD	PHD	85	N Carol	1983
Truscott, Michael H.	C-Pr	Tampa	AEF	PHD	71	LSU	1971
Trussell, T. James	Prof	Princeton	CIT	PHD	75	Princeton	O-74
Trussler, Susan	Assoc	Scranton		PHD	89	Penn St	1985
Tryon, Joseph L.	Retir	Georgetown		PHD	61	Harvard	
Tsai, Mau-Sung	Retir	Evansville		PHD	66	S Illinois	1964
Tschirhart, John T.	Prof	Wyoming	DK	PHD	75	Purdue	1985
Tseng, Hui-Kuan	Assoc	N Car-Charl		PHD	88	Illinois	1988
Tseng, S. C.	Prof	Catawba		PHD	72	Oklahoma	
Tsiang, Grace	SLect	Chicago		PHD	91	Chicago	1990
Tsoukalas, Dimitrios	Asst	Purdue-Calmu		PHD	96	Illinois	1998
Tsoulouhas, Theofanis	Assoc	N Carol St	CD	PHD	93	Illinois	1993
Tsurumi, Hiroki	Prof	Rutgers-N Br	C	PHD	67	Penn	1974
Tu, Yien-I	Retir	Arkansas	C	PHD	61	Iowa St	1981
Tuck, Bradford H.	Retir	Alaska-Ancho	CDL	PHD	73	Boston U	1977
Tucker, Dean	Prof	Ogelthorpe	HMQ	PHD	79	Mich St	1-88
Rikard Chaired Professor							
Tucker, Irvin B. III	Assoc	N Car-Charl		PHD	82	S Carol	1981
Tuerck, David G.	C-Pr	Suffolk		PHD	66	Virginia	1982
Tullock, Gordon	Emer	Arizona		JD	47	Chicago	1987
Tully, Cathyann	Asst	Kean					
Tuma, Elias H.	Emer	Cal-Davis	ANO	PHD	62	Berkeley	1967
Turchi, Boone A.	Assoc	No Carolina	AT	PHD	73	Michigan	1971
Turek, Joseph H.	C-Pr	Lynchburg		PHD	87	SUNY-Alb	1986
Turk, Michael	Assoc	Fitchburg St		PHD	76	Harvard	1982

Turnbull, Geoffrey K.	Prof	Georgia St	R	PHD	83	Wi-Milwa	2001
Turner, Charlie G.	Assoc	Old Dominion		PHD	81	Harvard	1984
Turner, Keith K.	Retir	Neb-Omaha	EM	PHD	68	Nebraska	1969
Turner, Robert W.	Prof	Colgate	CH	PHD	84	MIT	1983
Turner, Sarah	Asst	Virginia	IJ	PHD	97	Michigan	1997
Turner, Tracy M.	Asst	Kansas State	HD	PHD	00	Ca-Davis	2000
Turnovsky, Michelle H. L.	SLect	U Washington		PHD	78	Austr Natl	1987
Turnovsky, Stephen J.	Prof	U Washington		PHD	68	Harvard	1987
Turunen-Red, Arja H.	Prof	New Orleans		PHD	85	Brit Colum	1995
Tussing, A. Dale	Prof	Syracuse	I	PHD	64	Syracuse	1966
Tutterow, Roger C.	C-Pr	Kennesaw St	CDGM	PHD	90	Geo St	1991
Twight, Charlotte	Prof	Boise State	HKN	PHD	83	U Wash	1986
Twomey, Michael J.	Prof	Mich-Dearbor	FNO	PHD	74	Cornell	1977
Tyler, Thomas P.	Dean	Ark Tech		PHD	80	Arkansas	1967
Tyson, Laura D.	Dean	Cal-Berkeley		PHD	74	MIT	1977
Tzannetakis, George	Prof	Seton Hall		PHD	64	NYU	
Uctum, Merih	Asst	CUNY-Brookly		PHD	89	Queens	1996
Udis, Bernard	Retir	Colorado		PHD	59	Princeton	1965
Udry, Christopher R.	Prof	Yale	O	PHD	91	Yale	1998
Ueng, C. Joe	Assoc	St Thomas-TX	GM	PHD	95	St Louis	1996
Ullah, Aman	Prof	Cal-Riversid	C	PHD	71	Delhi	1989
Ullerich, Stan	Prof	Buena Vista	AQMA	PHD	95	Purdue	9-94
Ullmer, James H.	Asst	W Carolina	N	PHD	96	Tennessee	1999
Ulveling, Edwin F.	Retir	Georgia St	AO	PHD	81	Iowa St	1967
Umbeck, John R.	C-Pr	Purdue		PHD	76	U Wash	1975
Unger, Kay C.	Prof	Montana	IDEC	PHD	74	J Hopkins	
Upadhyay, Mukti	Asst	E Illinois		PHD	95	J Hopkins	
Upadhyaya, Kamal	Assoc	New Haven		PHD	93	Auburn	
Upchurch, Leo	Assoc	Tuskegee		PHD	82	Michigan	1990
Uppal, Jogindar S.	Prof	SUNY-Albany	OH	PHD	65	Minnesota	1971
Upton, Charles W.	Prof	Kent State	EQ	PHD	69	Car Mellon	8-89
Ureta, Manuelita	Assoc	Texas A&M	J	PHD	87	UCLA	1991
Urquhart, Robert	Assoc	Denver	BN	PHD	88	New Sch	1988
Uselding, Paul J.	Dean	Saginaw Vall	N	PHD	70	Nrthwstrn	1999
Usip, Ebenge E.	Assoc	Youngstown		PHD	84	Conn	1985
Uyar, Bulent	Assoc	No Iowa	ACH	PHD	77	Pittsburgh	1991
Vachris, Michelle A.	Assoc	Chris Newpor	DFHK	PHD	92	GeoMason	1994
Vafaie, Massie S.	C-As	Cen St-Ohio		PHD	79	Cincinnati	1991
Vahaly, John	Assoc	Louisville	R	PHD	75	Vanderbilt	1975
Vaidya, Ashish K.	Assoc	CS-L Angeles		PHD	90	Ca-Davis	1991
Vail, David Jeremiah	Prof	Bowdoin	OQ	PHD	71	Yale	1970
Adams-Catlin Professor of Economics							
Vaitheswaran, Ramakrishna	Retir	Coe	AFOP	PHD	77	Iowa St	1973
Valencia, Jesus M.	Asst	Slippery Roc	ACFJ	PHD	88	Pittsburgh	1983
Valentine, John	Dean	McMurry		MBA		Abilene	1980
Valentine, Lloyd M.	Retir	Cincinnati		MA	51	UCLA	1954
Valentino, Salvatore	Retir	Creighton	A	PHD	54	Nebraska	1961
Valev, Neven T.	Asst	Georgia St	EF	PHD	97	Purdue	1998
Vamosi, Alexander R.	Asst	Fla Inst Tec	AEC	PHD	95	N Carol	2001
Van Boening, Mark V.	Assoc	Mississippi	DL	PHD	91	Arizona	1990
Van Cott, T. Norman	Prof	Ball State	FH	PHD	69	U Wash	1977
Van den Berg, Hendrik F.	Assoc	Nebraska	F	PHD	89	Wisconsin	1989
Van den Nouweland, Anne	Assoc	Oregon	CL	PHD	93	Tilburg	1996
Van Der Heide, Evert M.	Prof	Calvin		PHD	82	Wayne St	1982
Van Huyck, John B.	Prof	Texas A&M	CD	PHD	86	Brown	1985
Private Enterprise Research Center Rex B. Grey Professor							
van Wincoop, Jan Eric	Prof	Virginia	F	PHD	89	Harvard	2001
Van Zandt, Timothy	Prof	INSEAD	DP	PHD	89	Penn	9-98
Van't Veld, Klaas	Asst	Michigan					
Vandegrift, Donald	C-Ac	C New Jersey		PHD	93	Conn	
Vander Linde, Scott H.	Prof	Calvin		PHD	89	Notre Dm	
Vander Meulen, Allen Jr.	Retir	No Central		PHD	75	Brown	1978
Vanderhart, Peter G.	Assoc	Bowling Gr		PHD	91	Wisconsin	1991
VanderHoff, James H.	Prof	Rutgers-Newk		PHD	79	N Carol	1980
Vanderklaauw, H. Wilbert	Assoc	No Carolina	J	PHD	92	Brown	1999
Vanderporten, Bruce S.	Assoc	Loyola-Chicg	ACD	PHD	73	Wayne St	1978
VanderSluis, Evert	Assoc	So Dakota St	FO	PHD	93	Minnesota	1997
Vandewetering, Hylke	Prof	Iowa State	O	PHD	64	Iowa St	1964
VanEaton, Charles D.	Retir	Hillsdale		PHD	74	Tulane	1978
Vanek, Jaroslav	Retir	Cornell		PHD	58	MIT	
VanGilder, Jennifer A.	Asst	CS-Bakersf	JDT	PHD	00	SUNY-Bin	2000
VanHoose, David D.	Prof	Baylor	EF	PHD	84	N Carol	2001
Herman W. Lay Professor of Private Enterprise							
VanMatre, Joe G.	Prof	Alabama-Birm	C	PHD	70	Alabama	1971
Vanscyoc, Lee	Assoc	Wis-Oshkosh	AL	PHD	87	Nebraska	1987
Vargha, Linda	Asst	Skidmore		PHD	99	Wisconsin	1999
Vargha, Nader	Assoc	Missouri Wes	A	MA	76	Oklahoma	1980
Varghese, Adel	Asst	St Louis		PHD	96	Penn	1995
Varghese, K. Thomas	Prof	Jms Madison	E	PHD	71	Wayne St	1970
Varma, Ranbir	C-Pr	Lg Isl-Brook	AFOP	PHD	57	New Sch	1959

Vasigh, Bijan	Prof	Embry-Riddle		PHD	84	SUNY-Bin	
Vaughan, Ben F.	Asst	Tx Lutheran		PHD	97	Berkeley	1998
Vaughan, Michael B.	Dean	Weber State	AMK	PHD	80	Nebraska	1981
Vaughn, Karen I.	Prof	George Mason		PHD	71	Duke	1978
Vedder, Richard K.	Retir	Ohio Univ		PHD	65	Illinois	1965
Veendorp, Emiel C.	Prof	Clark		PHD	63	Rice	1976
Vegh, Carlos	Assoc	UCLA		PHD	87	Chicago	
Veitch, John	C-Ac	San Franciscc	EG	PHD	85	Nrthwstrn	1985
Veldkamp, Laura	Asst	INSEAD	EGV	PHD	01	Stanford	2001
Velenchik, Ann D.	Assoc	Wellesley	OFD	PHD	89	Stanford	1989
Velez, Alejandro	Prof	St Marys-Txs		PHD	77	Florida	
Vella, Francis G. M.	Assoc	Rutgers-N Br	C	PHD	90	Rochester	1997
Vencill, C. Daniel	Prof	San Fran St		PHD	71	Stanford	1974
Venieris, Yiannis P.	Prof	San Diego St		PHD	69	Oregon	1967
Venti, Steven F.	Prof	Dartmouth		PHD	82	Harvard	1982
Ventocilla, Antonio A.	Retir	Ferris State		MA		American	1967
Ventura, Gustavo	Asst	Penn State		PHD	97	Illinois	2001
Ventura, Jaume	Assoc	MIT	E	PHD	95	Harvard	1995
Vercella, Kit J.	Retir	Alaska-Ancho	ADEO	MA	72	Ca-SnDgo	1974
Verdugo, Paul R.	Asst	Azusa Pacif		MA	76	Ca Poly	9-80
Vernarelli, Michael J.	C-Pr	Rochest Tech		PHD	78	SUNY-Bin	1976
Vernengo, Matias	Asst	Kalamazoo		PHD		New Sch	2001
Vernon, Jack R.	Retir	Florida	E	PHD	61	Nrthwstrn	1967
Vernon, John M.	Prof	Duke	L	PHD	66	MIT	1969
Vernon, Thomas T.	Retir	Clarion		PHD	71	Kansas St	1969
Verrall, George	Assoc	Miss State	A	DBA	72	Miss St	1965
Veseth, Michael	Prof	Puget Sound	AFH	PHD	76	Purdue	1975
Vesterlund, Lise	Asst	Pittsburgh	H	PHD	97	Wisconsin	2001
Vickers, Douglas W.	Retir	Massachusett	1995	PHD	56	London	1977
Vijverberg, Wim P. M.	Prof	Texas-Dallas		PHD	81	Pittsburgh	1986
Viksnins, George J.	Prof	Georgetown	GP	PHD	64	Geotown	1968
Vilasuso, Jon R.	Asst	W Virginia	EFG	PHD	94	Conn	1999
Villamil, Anne P.	Prof	Illinois	EG	PHD	88	Minnesota	1988
Villanueva, Miguel	Asst	Brandeis		PHD	99	Ohio St	1999
Villegas, Daniel J.	Assoc	Cal Poly-SLO		PHD	79	Stanford	1987
Villinski, Michele		DePauw					
Vincent, Daniel	Assoc	Maryland		PHD	87	Princeton	1998
Vincent, James W.	Assoc	St Thomas-MN	Q	PHD	82	Wisconsin	1988
Vinje, David L.	Prof	Pacific Luth	O	PHD	64	Wisconsin	1970
Vinod, Hrishinesh D.	Prof	Fordham		PHD	65	Harvard	1982
Virts, Nancy L.	Assoc	CS-Northrdge	N	PHD	85	UCLA	1985
Visgilio, Gerald R.	Prof	Conn Coll	K	PHD	73	Rhode Isl	
Vishwasrao, Sharmila	Asst	Fla Atlantic	F	PHD	94	Purdue	1995
Vissing-Jorgensen,	Asst	Chicago		PHD		MIT	1998
Vitallano, Donald F.	Prof	Rensselaer		PHD	69	CUNY	1969
Vives, Xavier	Prof	INSEAD	DGL	PHD	83	Berkeley	2001
Vo, Han X.	Assoc	Winthrop	EF	PHD	79	Tennessee	9-79
Voeks, Lisa Ford	Visit	Richmond		PHD	00	Georgia	1999
Voelker, Keith E.	Retir	Wis-Oshkosh	J	PHD	69	Wisconsin	1970
Vogelsang, Ingo	Prof	Boston Univ	HL	PHD	69	Heidelbe	1981
Vogelsang, Timothy	Assoc	Cornell		PHD	93	Princeton	9-83
Vogt, Michael G.	Prof	E Michigan		PHD	76	Wisconsin	1978
Vogt, Walter H.	Retir	San Diego St		PHD		Syracuse	1974
Vohra, Rajiv	Prof	Brown		PHD	83	J Hopkins	
Vohra, Rubina A.	Asst	NewJerseyCty	AJO	PHD	93	Northeas	9-94
Vokurka, Robert	C-Pr	Tx A&M-C Chr	AO	PHD	97	Tx A&M	9-01
Volij, Oscar	Assoc	Iowa State	H	PHD	94	Hebrew	2001
von Allmen, Peter	C-Ac	Moravian	CDL	PHD	90	Temple	1990
Von Ende, Eleanor Theresa	Asst	Texas Tech		PHD	90	Kansas	1990
von Furstenberg, George	Prof	Indiana		PHD	66	Princeton	1970
vonderRuhr, Marc	Asst	St Norbert		PHD	99	Indiana	1999
VonDonsel, Richard	Lect	SUNY-Cortlan					
VonHagen, Jurgen	Prof	Indiana		PHD	86	Bonn	1987
Vonortas, Nicholas S.	Assoc	George Wash	OL	PHD	89	NYU	
Vora, Premal	Asst	Penn St-Harr		PHD	91	Penn St	2001
Vorst, Karen S.	Prof	Mo-Kansas Ct	EC	PHD	80	Indiana	1980
Vose, David	Assoc	Minn-Duluth	QA	PHD	66	Wisconsin	1966
Votey, Harold L. Jr.	Retir	Cal-Santa Br		PHD	68	Berkeley	1976
Voth, Hans-Joachim	VProf	MIT		DPHL	96	Oxford	2001
Vowels, Robert C.	Retir	Tenn State		PHD	64	American	
Vredeveld, George	Prof	Cincinnati		PHD	73	Indiana	1977
Vroman, Susan	Prof	Georgetown	DJ	PHD	77	J Hopkins	1978
Vrooman, David H. Jr.	Retir	St Lawrence	GE	PHD	76	SUNY-Alb	1965
Vruwink, Carol J.	C-Pr	Central Iowa		MS	82	Drake	1979
Vuolteenaho, Tuomo	Asst	Harvard		PHD		Chicago	
Vuong, Quang	C-Pr	So Calif		PHD	82	Nrthwstrn	1987
Vytlacil, Ed	Asst	Stanford		PHD	00	Chicago	2000
Wachtel, Howard M.	Prof	American U		PHD	69	Michigan	1969
Wachtel, Paul A. Research Professor	Prof	New York U	EG	PHD	71	Rochester	1972

Wachter, Daniel R.	C-Ac	DePauw		PHD	82	Purdue	1979
Waddell, Glen	Asst	Oregon	FL	PHD	00	Purdue	2001
Waddoups, C. Jeffrey	Assoc	Nev-L Vegas	J	PHD	89	Utah	1989
Wade, Ernie	Inst	Radford	AQ	MS	86	Va Tech	1997
Wade, John A.	C-Ac	E Kentucky		PHD	82	Purdue	2000
Wadhawan, Satish C.	Prof	Howard	FO	PHD		Nehru	
Wadman, William Morgan	Assoc	N Car-Wilmin	CDH	PHD	76	Claremont	
Wagner, F. Eugene	Prof	Mo-Kansas Ct	AJO	PHD	67	Syracuse	1967
Wagner, Gary	Asst	Duquesne		PHD	99	W Virginia	2001
Wagner, John R.	Assoc	Westfield St		PHD	77	Temple	1986
Wagner, M. Jeffrey	Asst	Rochest Tech		PHD	97	Illinois	2001
Wagner, Richard E.	Prof	George Mason		PHD	66	Virginia	1988
Holbert I. Harris Professor of Economics							
Wagoner, Charles B.	Asst	Delta State	ACFG	PHD	93	Tulane	8-95
Wahid, Abu	Prof	Tenn State		PHD	89	Manitoba	
Wahl, Jenny Bourne	Asst	Carleton	JKN	PHD	86	Chicago	1998
Wakeman, Douglas J.	Assoc	Meredith		PHD	86	N Carol	1987
Walbert, Mark S.	Assoc	Illinois St	CDE	PHD	84	New Mex	1984
Waldauer, Charles	Prof	Widener	DEHR	PHD	69	Syracuse	1968
Waldkirch, Andreas	Asst	Oregon State	FD	PHD	01	Boston C	9-01
Waldman, Don E.	Prof	Colgate	L	PHD	76	Cornell	1981
Richard M. Kessler Professor of Economic Studies							
Waldman, Donald M.	Prof	Colorado		PHD	79	Wisconsin	1984
Waldo, Douglas G.	Assoc	Florida	EFO	PHD	80	N Carol	1981
Waldron, Randall	Asst	South Dakota		PHD	94	Vanderbilt	1994
Walgreen, John A.	Prof	Wheaton-MA		PHD	65	Boston C	1967
Walgreen, Sonia	VLect	Mass-Dartmou		MA	63	Boston C	1984
Walka, Joseph J.	Retir	No Arizona	HI	PHD	69	Harvard	1986
Walker, Deborah L.	C-Ac	Loyola-N Orl	ABDJ	PHD	87	GeoMason	1987
Walker, Donald A.	Retir	Indiana U-PA	BD	PHD	61	Harvard	1969
Walker, Doug		Georgia Col		PHD			
Walker, Franklin V.	Retir	SUNY-Albany	FE	PHD	58	Harvard	1966
Walker, G. Craig	Assoc	Okla Baptist	ACFG	PHD	96	So Meth	8-00
Walker, James M.	Prof	Indiana		PHD	78	Tx A&M	1984
Walker, James R.	Prof	Wisconsin		PHD	86	Chicago	1987
Walker, John	Prof	Wis-Rvr Fall	JB	PHD	89	Utah	1990
Walker, John F.	Prof	Portland St	H	PHD	72	Utah	1966
Walker, Mark A.	Prof	Arizona		PHD	70	Purdue	1990
Walker, Mary Beth	Assoc	Georgia St	DC	PHD	86	Rice	1991
Walker, Roger	Deces	Hamline	J	PHD	59	Cornell	1969
Wall, Richard A.	Prof	Canisius	EG	PHD	84	SUNY-Buf	1980
Wallace, Don	Assoc	St Martin		PHD	63	U Wash	
Wallace, Geoffrey	Asst	Wisconsin		PHD	99	Nrthwstrn	1999
Wallace, H. Scott	Asst	Wis-Stev Pt		PHD	99	Conn	2000
Wallace, Myles S.	Prof	Clemson	EFC	PHD	76	Colorado	1980
Wallace, Neil	Prof	Penn State	E	PHD	64	Chicago	1997
Wallace, Richard L.	Prof	Missouri		PHD	65	Vanderbilt	1967
Wallace, Richard M.	Prof	Wofford	ABK	PHD	81	S Carol	1982
Wallace, Robert	Prof	Framingham		PHD	72	Nrthwstrn	
Wallace, Sally	Assoc	Georgia St	GH	PHD	88	Syracuse	1991
Wallace, Suzanne	Assoc	Central Iowa	DJE	PHD	91	Georgia	1991
Wallace, T. Dudley	Emer	Duke					
James D. Duke Professor							
Waller, Christopher J.	Prof	Kentucky	E	PHD	86	Wash St	1998
Gatton Chair							
Waller, Robert L.	Assoc	USAF Academy	AF	PHD	86	Boston U	1998
Wallis, John J.	Prof	Maryland		PHD	81	U Wash	1983
Walsh, C. Gerald	Retir	Villanova		MA	60	Detroit	1960
Walsh, Carl E.	Prof	Ca-Santa Crz	E	PHD	76	Berkeley	1987
Walsh, Randall	Asst	Colorado		PHD	01	Duke	2001
Walsh, Vivian	Lect	Muhlenberg		PHD	53	Trinity	1989
Walsh, William J.	Assoc	St Thomas-MN	E	PHD	70	Notre Dm	1970
Walstad, William B.	Prof	Nebraska	I	PHD	78	Minnesota	1982
John and Mabel Hay Professorship							
Walter, Ingo	Prof	New York U	FG	PHD	66	NYU	1970
Charles Simon Professor of Applied Financial Economics							
Walters, Joan G.	Retir	Fairfield	EF	PHD	52	Harvard	1963
Walters, Stephen J. K.	Prof	Loyola-Maryl	KL	PHD	82	UCLA	1981
Walther, Theodore	Prof	Bates	FG	PHD	64	New Sch	1958
Walton, Gary M.	Prof	Cal-Davis	ADN	PHD	66	U Wash	1981
Waltzman, Norman J.	Assoc	Utah		PHD	88	American	1988
Walzer, Norman C.	D-Pr	W Illinois	ADHR	PHD	70	Illinois	1970
Wan, Henry Y. Jr.	Prof	Cornell		PHD	61	MIT	
Wan, Siaw-Peng	Asst	Elmhurst		PHD	94	Illinois	1995
Wang, Chena	Assoc	Iowa State	E	PHD	94	W Ontario	2001
Wang, Cheng	Assoc	Carnegie Mel		PHD	94	W Ontario	1994
Wang, Ping	Prof	Vanderbilt	E	PHD	87	Rochester	1999
Wang, Sivan	Asst	Delaware	CF	PHD	01	S Calif	2001
Wang, Tao	Asst	Fla Internat	EFG	PHD	00	J Hopkins	1999
Wang, Xiaojun	Asst	Hawaii-Manoa		PHD	01	Ohio St	2001

Wang, Xinghe	Asst	Missouri	CDO	PHD	90	Iowa	1990
Wang, Xuejun	Inst	SE Louisiana	E	PHD	97	Purdue	
Ward, Benjamin N.	Retir	Cal-Berkeley		PHD		Berkeley	
Ward, John O.	C-Pr	Mo-Kansas Ct	KIO	PHD	70	Oklahoma	1969
Ward, Marianne	Asst	Loyola-Maryl	EN	PHD	00	U Miami	2000
Ward, Ruby	Asst	Utah State	Q	PHD	98	Tx A&M	1999
Ward-Batts, Jennifer	Asst	Claremont		PHD	99	U Wash	
Ware, Stephen B.	Retir	Indiana U-PA	BE	BA	61	Ohio Wes	1969
Warin, Thierry	Asst	Middlebury	EF	PHD	00	Essec	2001
Warlick, Jennifer L.	Assoc	Notre Dame	HI	PHD	79	Wisconsin	1981
Warner, Geoffrey	Asst	Ind-Purdue/I	I	PHD	94	CUNY	1998
Warner, John T.	Prof	Clemson	DJE	PHD	76	N Car St	1980
Warner, Larkin B.	Retir	Oklahoma St		PHD	61	Indiana	1960
Warner, Lori	Assoc	Pacific	ENQ	PHD	86	Utah	1987
Warning, Matt	Asst	Puget Sound	ACO	PHD	97	Berkeley	1997
Warren, J. Harold	Assoc	East Tenn St		PHD	69	Okla St	1969
Warren, Ronald S.	Assoc	Georgia	JC	PHD	76	N Carol	1985
Warren, Shainne	Asst	Ithaca		PHD		Utah	2000
Warren, Stanton A.	Prof	Niagara		PHD	73	SUNY-Buf	1981
Washer, Kenneth	Asst	Tx A&M-Comm	CEG	DBA	98	La Tech	1996
Wasnich, Wendy S.	Asst	Ashland		MA		Ohio St	1985
Wassall, Gregory H.	Assoc	Northeastern		PHD	78	Rutgers	1979
Wassink, Darwin	Retir	Wis-Eau Clar	FO	PHD	68	Stanford	1976
Wassmer, Robert W.				PHD	89	Mich St	
Wassom, John C.	H-Pr	W Kentucky	G	PHD	70	Indiana	1971
Wasson, E. Dale	Prof	SW Missouri		PHD	80	Okla St	1969
Wasylenko, Michael J.	Prof	Syracuse	H	PHD	75	Syracuse	1989
Waters, Melissa S.	Asst	La-Lafayette	CJT	PHD	89	LSU	8-90
Watkins, John P.	C-Pr	Westminst-UT	BNQ	PHD	85	Utah	1984
Watkins, Thayer H.	Prof	San Jose St		PHD	65	Colorado	1957
Watkins, Thomas G.	Prof	E Kentucky		PHD	79	Iowa St	1984
Watkins, Todd A.	Asst	Lehigh	LO	PHD	95	Harvard	1992
Watson, Harry S.	C-Pr	George Wash	H	PHD	81	Indiana	1980
Watson, J. Keith	Asst	La-Lafayette		PHD	83	Tx A&M	
Watson, James O.	Assoc	Millikin		PHD	76	Purdue	1979
Watson, Joel	Assoc	Ca-San Diego	CF	PHD	92	Stanford	1994
Watson, Mark W.	Prof	Princeton		PHD	80	Ca-SnDgo	
Watters, Francis M.	Retir	CS-Chico		PHD	66	Berkeley	1966
Watts, Alison	Asst	So Illinois	DKL	PHD	93	Duke	2001
Watts, Harold	Retir	Columbia	P	PHD	57	Yale	1976
Watts, Michael W.	Prof	Purdue		PHD	78	LSU	1981
Watts, Royce J.	Asst	W Virginia	C	MS	61	W Virginia	1955
Waud, Roger N.	Retir	No Carolina		PHD	65	Berkeley	1969
Way, Philip K.	Assoc	Cincinnati	J	PHD	86	Warwick	1985
Weathers, Milledge W.	Retir	Adrian		PHD	61	Munich	1968
Weaver, James H.	Retir	American U		PHD	63	Oklahoma	1963
Weaver, Janice E.	Assoc	Drake		PHD	76	Illinois	1983
Webb, Bruce G.	C-Pr	Gordon	BGE	PHD	78	Clark	1977
Webb, Michael A.	Dean	Xavier	FO	PHD	80	Illinois	1997
Webb, Natalie J.	Asst	Naval Postgr	H	PHD	92	Duke	1992
Webb, Samuel C.	Prof	Wichita St		PHD	68	Kansas	1966
Webber, Douglas	Assoc	INSEAD	V	PHD	85	Essex	1-91
Weber, Arnold R.	Retir	Northwestern	1994	PHD		MIT	
Weber, Charles T.	Retir	Mich-Flint		PHD	77	Wayne St	1977
Weber, Christian E.	Asst	Seattle	EO	PHD	92	Duke	1993
Weber, Richard E.	Retir	Monmouth		PHD	74	Rutgers	9-79
Weber, Shlomo	Prof	So Methodist	DHL	PHD	79	Hebrew	1993
Robert H. & Nancy Dedman Trustee Professor; Dir R.B. Johnson Economic Studies							
Weber, William L.	Prof	SE Missouri	GHI	PHD	86	S Illinois	1986
Weckstein, Richard S.	Retir	Brandeis		PHD	53	Yale	1962
Weeks, Gregory C.		Evergreen St		PHD	78	Wash St	1981
Weerapana, Akila	Asst	Wellesley	EF	PHD	99	Stanford	1999
Wegge, Leon L.	Emer	Cal-Davis	F	PHD	63	MIT	1966
Wegge, Simone	Asst	CUNY-Stn Isl	JN	PHD	97	Nrthwstrn	
Wehr, Roger	Lect	Tx-Arlington	DE	MA	96	Tx-Arlin	1993
Weida, William J.	Prof	Colorado Col		DBA	75	Colorado	1985
Weidenbaum, Murray L.	Prof	Wash Univ	HM	PHD	58	Princeton	1961
Edward Mallinckrodt Distinguished University Professor							
Weidenmier, Marc	Asst	Claremont		PHD	99	Illinois	1999
Weiher, Kenneth E.	Assoc	Tx-S Antonio	BEN	PHD	75	Indiana	1975
Weil, David	Prof	Brown		PHD	90	Harvard	
Weil, Gordon	Prof	Wheaton-MA	FOP	PHD	81	Tufts	1981
Weiler, John E.	Retir	Dayton	H	PHD	73	Cincinnati	1967
Weiler, Stephan	Assoc	Colorado St	RO	PHD	94	Berkeley	1996
Weiman, David F.	Prof	Barnard	NL	PHD	84	Stanford	2001
Weinberg, Bruce	Assoc	Ohio State	J	PHD	96	Chicago	1996
Weinberg, David R.	Assoc	Xavier	ARP	PHD	73	Berkeley	1980
Weiner, Ross	Asst	CUNY-City C	ADJL	PHD	99	Mass	1999
Weinrobe, Maurice D.	Prof	Clark		PHD	69	Cornell	1976
Weinstein, David E.	Prof	Columbia	F	PHD	91	Michigan	1999

Weinstein, Paul A.	Deces	Maryland		PHD	61	Nrthwstrn	1965
Weinstock, Maek	Assoc	Pace		MA			
Weintraub, Andrew R.	Retir	Temple	A	PHD	66	Rutgers	1973
Weintraub, E. Roy	Prof	Duke	N	PHD	69	Penn	1970
Weintraub, Irvin	Assoc	Towson		MS	51	Columbia	1966
Weis, Charles E.	Prof	Tenn State		DBA	74	Ariz St	
Weisbrod, Burton A.	Prof	Northwestern		PHD	58	Nrthwstrn	
John Evans Professor of Economic, Director,Ctr for Urban Affairs & Policy Rec							
Weise, Charles	Asst	Gettysburg	ABEF	PHD	93	Wisconsin	2000
Weisenborn, David E.	Retir	Geo Southern		PHD	68	Florida	1976
Weiser, Lawrence A.	Prof	Wis-Stev Pt		PHD	67	Wisconsin	1972
Weisman, Dennis	Prof	Kansas State	LKD	PHD	93	Florida	1993
Weiss, Andrew M.	Prof	Boston Univ	DGJ	PHD	76	Stanford	1987
Weiss, Jeffrey		SUNY-Empire	A	PHD	67	Harvard	1986
Weiss, Jeffrey H.	Assoc	CUNY-Baruch		PHD	81	Wisconsin	1981
Weiss, Merle	Assoc	Temple	IJ	PHD	67	Columbia	1972
Weiss, Steven J.	Emer	Toledo	HI	PHD	71	Colorado	1968
Weiss, Thomas J.	Prof	Kansas	NF	PHD	67	N Carol	1967
Weisskopf, Thomas E.	Prof	Michigan		PHD	66	MIT	1972
Weistock, Mark	Adj	CUNY-City C	AM				
Weitzman, Martin L.	Prof	Harvard		PHD	67	MIT	1989
Ernest E. Monrad Professor of Economics							
Welch, Finis R.	Prof	Texas A&M	J	PHD	66	Chicago	1991
Distinguished Professor and George T. & Gladys H. Abell Prof of Liberal Arts							
Welch, Patrick J.	Prof	St Louis		PHD	73	Pittsburgh	1983
Welch, Robert G.	H-Pr	Midwest St	ADP	PHD	62	Oregon St	1966
Welch, William P.	Assoc	Saginaw Vall	CJL	PHD	86	U Wash	1986
Welki, Andrew M.	Asst	John Carroll	HR	PHD	83	Penn St	1982
Welle, Patrick G.	Prof	Bemidji St		PHD	86	Wisconsin	1982
Weller, Barry R.	H-Ac	Penn St-Erie	ACE	PHD	71	Penn St	1971
Weller, Jim	Asst	Cen Arkansas					
Wellington, Alison J.	Asst	Wooster	J	PHD	90	Michigan	1997
Wellington, Donald C.	Prof	Cincinnati	D	PHD	66	Chicago	
Wellisz, Stanislaw	Prof	Columbia	O	PHD	54	Harvard	1964
Wells, Arnold R.	Prof	Mankato St	ADM	PHD	66	Minnesota	1966
Wells, Donald A.	Emer	Arizona		PHD	61	Oregon	1969
Wells, Donald R.	Retir	Memphis		PHD	65	S Calif	1967
Wells, Jerome C.	Prof	Pittsburgh	O	PHD	64	Michigan	1964
Welsh, Arthur	Retir	Penn State	A	PHD	63	Illinois	1986
Wen, G. James	Assoc	Trinity-CT		PHD	89	Chicago	1994
Wen, Quan	Asst	Vanderbilt	F	PHD	91	W Ontario	1999
Wen, Yi	Asst	Cornell		PHD	96	Iowa	9-99
Wendel, Jeanne L.	Prof	Nevada-Reno		PHD	77	So Meth	1985
Wenders, John T.	Retir	Idaho	DL	PHD	67	Nrthwstrn	1981
Weng, Wenlong	Asst	Lehigh		PHD	01	Stanford	2001
Wentworth, Donald R.	Prof	Pacific Luth	A	PHD	65	Minnesota	1972
Werger, Jennie	Asst	North Texas	HJ	PHD	96	N Carol	1996
Werner, James M.	Asst	Wooster		PHD	96	Utah	1999
Werner, Jan	Assoc	Minnesota		PHD		Bonn	1987
Werner, Megan	Asst	Florida	CHQ	PHD	94	Ca-SnDgo	1994
Wesolowski, Karl A.	C-Ac	Salem State		MA		Boston C	
Wessel, Robert H.	Retir	Cincinnati		PHD	53	Cincinnati	1957
Wessels, Walter J.	Prof	N Carol St	JD	PHD	76	Chicago	1975
West, Carol Taylor	C-Pr	Florida	RQC	PHD	74	Michigan	1989
West, Clifford T.	Prof	Va Military		PHD	92	Indiana	1996
West, James E.	Asst	USAF Academy	AD	PHD	94	Michigan	1997
West, James P.	Prof	Moravian	FM	PHD	87	Lehigh	1989
West, James S.	Prof	Wash & Jeff		PHD	97	Nebraska	1997
West, Janet Mason	Asst	Neb-Omaha	AJ	MA	64	Mich St	1967
West, Kenneth D.	Prof	Wisconsin		PHD	83	MIT	1988
West, Sarah	Asst	Macalester	HQ	PHD	99	Texas	2000
Westall, Oliver M.	SLect	U Lancaster		BSC		London	
Westbrook, M. Daniel	Asst	Georgetown	D	PHD	78	Ohio St	1978
Westerfield, Donald	Prof	Webster	DIMC	PHD	84	St Louis	1985
Westerhold, Tara D.	Asst	W Illinois	ADH	PHD	98	S Carol	1998
Westfield, Fred M.	Retir	Vanderbilt	D	PHD	57	MIT	1965
Westhoff, Frank H.	Prof	Amherst	ADHC	PHD	74	Yale	1973
Weston, Gerald A.	Deces	Wis-Whitewat	2-99	PHD	65	Wash St	1968
Weston, Rafael R.	Dean	Adams State		PHD	72	Harvard	1988
Weston, Samuel C.	Asst	Dallas	B	PHD	87	Pittsburgh	1987
Westphal, Larry E.	Prof	Swarthmore	DO	PHD	69	Harvard	1985
J. Archer & Helen C. Turner Professor of Economics							
Wetzel, James N.	Assoc	Virg Comm		PHD	74	N Carol	1974
Wexler, Imanuel	Retir	Connecticut		PHD	59	Harvard	1961
Weymark, Diana N.	Asst	Vanderbilt	EG	PHD	90	Brit Colum	1999
Weymark, John A.	Prof	Vanderbilt	D	PHD	77	Penn	1999
Whalen, Thaddeus J. Jr.	Prof	Santa Clara		PHD	64	Berkeley	1962
Whalley, Pamela	Lect	Western Wash	DG	ABD		Indiana	1989
Whaples, Robert M.	Asst	Wake Forest		PHD	90	Penn	1991
Whatley, Warren	Prof	Michigan	NJOR	PHD	82	Stanford	1981

Wheaton, William C.	Prof	MIT	R	PHD	72	Penn	1972
Wheeler, Bert	Assoc	Cedarville	AFOP	PHD	85	Tennessee	1992
Wheeler, Christopher	Asst	Tulane		PHD	98	Wisconsin	1999
Wheeler, Clifford	Retir	NE St-Okla	1995	PHD		Missouri	1971
Wheeler, Mark V.	Assoc	W Michigan	E	PHD	85	Kentucky	1990
Whinston, Michael D.	Prof	Northwestern	DL	PHD	84	MIT	1996
Robert & Emily King Professor of Business Institutions							
Whitaker, Andrew L.	Prof	No Central	G	PHD	88	Illinois	1988
Whitaker, David A.	Retir	Richmond		PHD	71	Florida	1969
Whitaker, John K.	Prof	Virginia	BC	PHD	62	Cambridge	1969
Georgia S. Bankard Professor of Economics							
Whitaker, Morris D.	Retir	Utah State	FO	PHD	70	Purdue	1970
Whitaker, William M.	Retir	Geo Southern		PHD	68	Kentucky	1989
White, Charles E.	C-Pr	Framingham		PHD	81	Chicago	9-85
White, Charles V.	Assoc	New Hamp Col		PHD	73	Ohio St	
White, Eugene N.	Prof	Rutgers-N Br	N	PHD	80	Illinois	1980
White, Halbert L.	Prof	Ca-San Diego	C	PHD	76	MIT	1979
White, Harry Ruff	Retir	W Carolina		PHD	66	Kentucky	1968
White, Jason T.	Inst	NW Missouri	AGHM	ABD		Mo-Ks Cty	1999
White, Kenneth R.	Assoc	Cen Florida	C	PHD	71	Oklahoma	1968
White, Lawrence	Prof	New York U	DGKL	PHD	69	Harvard	1976
Arthur E. Imperitore Professor of Economics							
White, Leonard A.	Retir	Arkansas	D	PHD	63	St Louis	1971
White, Mark D.	Asst	CUNY-Stn Isl	C	PHD	97	Cincinnati	1993
White, Michael D.	Prof	St Cloud St		PHD	78	Tx Tech	1978
White, Michelle J.	Prof	Ca-San Diego	RK	PHD	73	Princeton	2001
White, Nancy E.	Assoc	Bucknell	RH	PHD	87	Colorado	1986
White, Thomas J.	Assoc	Assumption	EGQ	PHD	89	SUNY-Bin	1995
White-Means, Shelley L.	Prof	Memphis	DJI	PHD	83	Nrthwstrn	1988
Whited, Ida	Asst	So Colorado	GEF	PHD	00	Claremont	2001
Whitehead, John C.	Asst	N Car-Wilmin	Q	PHD	90	Kentucky	
Whiteman, Charles H.	Prof	Iowa		PHD	81	Minnesota	1980
Whitesell, Frank Cook	Assoc	So Miss	A	PHD	71	Tulane	1968
Whitesell, William E.	Prof	Frank & Mars		PHD	63	Tx-Austin	1965
Henry P. & Mary B. Stager Professor of Economics							
Whitin, Thomson M.	Emer	Wesleyan-CT	C	PHD	52	Princeton	1963
Whiting, Cathleen L.	Assoc	Willamette		PHD	86	U Wash	1986
Whitman, D. Glen	Asst	CS-Northrdge		PHD	00	Wyoming	2000
Whitman, Katherine	Assoc	Mt St Mary's	ANF	MA		UCLA	1980
Whitmore, Harland W. Jr.	Prof	Cincinnati	E	PHD	69	Mich St	1967
Whitney, Chet	Retir	Augustana SD	C	PHD	65	Kansas	1960
Whitney, Gerald A.	Prof	New Orleans		PHD	77	Tulane	1979
Whitney, James D.	Prof	Occidental	F	PHD	83	Wisconsin	1982
Whittaker, Victor A.	Prof	Morgan State		PHD	71	Illinois	1974
Whitten, David O.	Prof	Auburn		PHD	70	Tulane	1968
Whittenlas, John	SLect	U Lancaster		PHD		Capetown	
Whyte, Charles D.	Retir	Virginia St		PHD	69	Ohio St	1974
Wible, James R.	C-Pr	New Hampshir	BE	PHD	80	Penn St	1984
Wichers, C. Robert	Retir	Pittsburgh	C	PHD	68	Amsterdm	1976
Wicker, Elmus R.	Retir	Indiana		PHD	56	Duke	
Wickman, Kenneth P.	Retir	SUNY-Cortlan		PHD	62	Syracuse	1968
Wicks, John H.	Prof	Montana	DH	PHD	62	Illinois	
Widener, Steven	Assoc	New Hamp Col		PHD	88	NewHamp	
Widman, Robert	Assoc	CUNY-Brookly		MBA	73	Rutgers	1978
Wiegersma, Nancy A.	Prof	Fitchburg St		PHD	76	Maryland	1979
Wier, Thomas	Asst	NE St-Okla	RCB	PHD	89	Tennessee	1998
Wiest, Philip Ray	Assoc	George Mason		PHD	76	Pittsburgh	
Wiggins, Steven N.	Prof	Texas A&M	L	PHD	79	MIT	1979
Wight, Jonathan B.	Assoc	Richmond		PHD	82	Vanderbilt	1982
Wightman, James W.	Retir	SUNY-Potsdam		PHD	67	Clark	
Wihry, David F.	C-Ac	Maine	HIA	PHD	72	Syracuse	1969
Wilber, Charles K.	Retir	Notre Dame	BOP	PHD	66	Maryland	1975
Wilbratte, Barry J.	C-Pr	St Thomas-TX	FG	PHD	71	Tulane	1971
Wilcox, Nathaniel	Assoc	Houston	D	PHD	92	Chicago	1991
Wilcox-Gok, Virginia L.	Assoc	No Illinois	J	PHD	84	Wash U	1994
Wilcoxen, Peter J.	Asst	Texas	QD	PHD	89	Harvard	9-91
Wildasin, David E.	Retir	Vanderbilt	G	PHD	76	Iowa	1993
Wilde, James A.	Assoc	No Carolina	GH	PHD	68	Princeton	1965
Wilder, Lisa A.	Asst	Albright		PHD	95	Va Tech	2001
Wilder, Ronald P.	C-Pr	So Carolina		PHD	69	Vanderbilt	1987
Wiles, James L.	Emer	Stonehill	KN	PHD	76	Harvard	1955
Wilford, W. Terry	Deces	New Orleans	4-94	PHD	64	So Meth	1968
Wilhelm, Mark	Assoc	Ind-Purdue/I	CH	PHD	90	NYU	1998
Wilhite, Allen W.	C-Pr	Alabama-Hunt	DK	PHD	81	Illinois	1988
Wilkes, William	Asst	Athens State	AF	DA	98	Mid Tenn	1996
Wilkie, Simon	Asst	Cal Tech	L	PHD	90	Rochester	1995
Wilkins, Allen J.	Assoc	Marshall		PHD	84	Wisconsin	1985
Wilkins, Mira	Prof	Fla Internat	NF	PHD	57	Cambridge	1974
Wilkinson, Maurice	Prof	Columbia		PHD	65	Harvard	1965
Willard, Kristen L.	Asst	Columbia	DFH	PHD	94	Princeton	9-94

Willett, Keith D.	H-Pr	Oklahoma St	Q	PHD	82	New Mex	9-81
Willett, Thomas D.	Prof	Claremont		PHD	67	Virginia	1977
Horton Professor of Economics							
Williams, Anne D.	Prof	Bates	O	PHD	76	Chicago	1981
Williams, Arlington W.	Prof	Indiana		PHD	78	Arizona	1979
Williams, C. Glyn	Retir	So Carolina		PHD	60	Virginia	
Williams, D. C. Jr.	Retir	So Miss		PHD		LSU	
Williams, Darrell L.	Asst	UCLA	GKL	PHD	91	Wash U	F-90
Williams, Donald R.	Prof	Kent State	J	PHD	84	Nrthwstrn	1983
Williams, Eugene	Prof	McMurry		PHD	71	Arkansas	1988
Williams, Harold R.	Retir	Kent State	EF	PHD	65	Nebraska	1966
Williams, Martin	Prof	No Illinois	R	PHD	76	SUNY-Bin	1976
Williams, Mary L.	Prof	Widener	BOMQ	PHD	84	Temple	1982
Williams, Michael	Asst	St Thomas-TX	H	PHD	96	Rice	2000
Williams, Mike M.	Retir	Bethune-Cook		PHD	70	Ohio U	1991
Williams, Nancy A.	C-Ac	Loyola-Maryl	QH	PHD	84	Berkeley	1987
Williams, Nicolas	Assoc	Cincinnati	J	PHD	89	Nrthwstrn	1990
Williams, Norman C.	Retir	Tenn Tech		PHD	72	Arkansas	1972
Williams, P.	Asst	No Alabama		PHD		Miss	1997
Williams, Raburn M.	Retir	Hawaii-Manoa		PHD	70	Chicago	1969
Williams, Robert B.	Assoc	Guilford	HQRL	PHD	84	N Carol	1987
Williams, Robert G.	C-Pr	Guilford	POFE	PHD	78	Stanford	1978
Williams, Roberton III	Asst	Texas	H	PHD	99	Stanford	9-99
Williams, Roger C.	Asst	Morehouse		PHD		SUNY-SBr	
Williams, Steven R.	Prof	Illinois	CD	PHD	82	Nrthwstrn	1992
Williams, Walter E.	Prof	George Mason		PHD	72	UCLA	1981
John M. Olin Distinguished Professor of Economics							
Williams, William V.	Retir	Hamline	1994	PHD	61	Colorado	1961
Williamson, Daniel P.	Prof	Cal Poly-SLO		PHD	73	Ca-SnDgo	1970
Williamson, H. F. Jr.	Assoc	Illinois	AR	PHD	69	Yale	1964
Williamson, Jeffrey G.	Prof	Harvard		PHD	61	Stanford	1983
Laird Bell Professor of Economics							
Williamson, Oliver E.	Prof	Cal-Berkeley		PHD	63	Car Mellon	1988
Williamson, Samuel H.	Prof	Miami U-Ohio	NI	PHD	68	Purdue	1983
Williamson, Stephen D.	C-Pr	Iowa		PHD	84	Wisconsin	1992
Willig, Robert D.	Prof	Princeton		PHD	73	Stanford	1978
Willis, James F.	Retir	San Jose St		PHD	66	So Meth	1966
Willis, Rachel A.	Adj	No Carolina	J	PHD	90	Nrthwstrn	1982
Willman, Elliott	Prof	New Mex St	EF	PHD	77	Indiana	1979
Willner, Jonathan	Assoc	Okla City	FO	PHD	94	Purdue	1995
Willoughby, John A.	Assoc	American U		PHD	79	Berkeley	1979
Willumsen, Maria Jose	Assoc	Fla Internat	RO	PHD	84	Cornell	1984
Wilson, Beth	Asst	CS-Humboldt		PHD	95	Oregon	2001
Wilson, Bradley	Asst	Alabama-Birm	CEF	PHD	97	Kansas	1997
Wilson, Charles A.	Prof	New York U	D	PHD	76	Rochester	1983
Wilson, Dennis	VAsst	Tx-Arlington	DL	PHD	99	Kentucky	1999
Wilson, Dwayne H.	Dean	Freed Hardem	CDEQ	PHD	91	Miss	8-75
Wilson, Erika G.	Retir	CS-L Angeles		PHD	79	S Calif	1968
Wilson, F. Scott	Prof	Canisius	C	PHD	76	Minnesota	1977
Wilson, George W.	Dean	Cen Missouri		PHD	76	Okla St	1972
Wilson, John D.	Prof	Michigan St		PHD	79	MIT	1998
Wilson, Kathryn S.	Asst	Kent State	DHIJ	PHD	96	Wisconsin	1996
Wilson, Linda	Lect	Tx-Arlington	DB	MS	92	North Tx	1993
Wilson, Loretta S.	Asst	Radford	FN	PHD	86	Mass	1987
Wilson, Lucas	Asst	Mt Holyoke		PHD	95	Mass	1995
Wilson, Matthew	Asst	Denver	HR	PHD	00	Tx-Austin	2001
Wilson, Paul W.	Assoc	Texas	RC	PHD	86	Brown	9-90
Wilson, R. Mark	Assoc	South Fla	I	PHD	77	Nrthwstrn	1978
Wilson, Richard C.	Asst	Tx-Arlington	AH	MA	66	Georgia	1966
Wilson, Wesley W.	Prof	Oregon	CD	PHD	86	Wash St	1989
Wiltgen, Richard J.	Prof	DePaul	B	PHD	74	Illinois	1973
Wimberly, Jack Cook	Retir	So Miss		PHD		LSU	
Wimmer, Bradley	Asst	Nev-L Vegas	L	PHD	92	Kentucky	1998
Wimmer, Larry T.	Prof	Brigham Yg	NT	PHD	68	Chicago	1963
Winczewski, Greg A.	Asst	Fordham		PHD	92	Fordham	1995
Winder, Robert C.	Assoc	Chris Newpor		PHD	81	Rutgers	1991
Winfrey, John C.	Prof	Wash & Lee	DH	PHD	65	Duke	1965
Wing, Martin M.	Asst	Kettering		PHD	89	Wayne St	
Winkelman, Richard D.	Assoc	Arizona St		PHD	66	Illinois	1965
Winkler, Anne E.	Assoc	Mo-St Louis	JT	PHD	89	Illinois	1989
Winrich, J. Steven	Prof	Centre	APN	PHD	78	Kentucky	1981
Winston, Barbara	Retir	NE Illinois		PHD	74	Nrthwstrn	1974
Winston, Gordon C.	C-Pr	Williams		PHD	64	Stanford	1963
Orrin Sage Professor of Political Economy							
Winter, Harold	Assoc	Ohio Univ	KL	PHD	90	Rochester	1992
Wion, Douglas A.	Assoc	Lock Haven		PHD	80	Penn St	1980
Wiseman, A. Clark	Prof	Gonzaga	AFQ	PHD	68	U Wash	1981
Wishart, David M.	C-Pr	Wittenberg	ABN	PHD	85	Illinois	1983
Wisley, Thomas O.	Prof	W Kentucky	GHK	PHD	79	Purdue	1985
Wisman, Jon D.	Prof	American U		PHD	74	American	1971

Withington, Robert P.	Assoc	SUNY-Plattsb	NJ	PHD	76	Penn	1972
Witt, Tom S.	Prof	W Virginia	CR	PHD	74	Wash U	1970
Witte, Ann D.	Prof	Wellesley	DHK	PHD	71	N Car St	1985
Witte, Willard E.	Assoc	Indiana		PHD	75	Wisconsin	1981
Wittman, Donald A.	Prof	Ca-Santa Crz	KD	PHD	70	Berkeley	1969
Woglom, Geoffrey R.	C-Pr	Amherst	AEG	PHD	74	Yale	1978
Richard S. Volpergt '56 Professor in Economics							
Wohar, Mark	Prof	Neb-Omaha	ECGF	PHD	85	Illinois	1988
Wojcikewych, Raymond	Prof	Bradley		PHD	80	Penn St	1977
Wojick, Paul P.	Assoc	St Olaf	AE	PHD	89	Colorado	1988
Wolak, Frank A.	Prof	Stanford		PHD	85	Harvard	1986
Wolaver, Amy	Asst	Bucknell	IJH	PHD	98	Wisconsin	9-98
Wolcott, Susan	Assoc	Mississippi	NO	PHD	88	Stanford	1999
Wolcowitz, Jeffrey	SLect	Harvard	HDRJ	PHD	82	Harvard	7-78
Wolf, Avner S.	C-Pr	CUNY-Baruch		PHD	83	Columbia	
Wolfe, Barbara L.	Prof	Wisconsin		PHD	73	Penn	1976
Wolfe, Edward	Asst	Piedmont		MA		SUNY-SBr	2001
Wolfe, Janet C.	Lect	Michigan		MPP	80	Michigan	1987
Wolff, Edward N.	Prof	New York U	J	PHD	74	Yale	1974
Wolff, Laura	Inst	S Ill-Edward	AO	MS	88	Missouri	1990
Wolff, Richard D.	Prof	Massachusett	ABNP	PHD	69	Yale	9-73
Wolfram, Gary	Assoc	Hillsdale		PHD	76	Berkeley	1989
Wolfson, Martin H.	Assoc	Notre Dame	EG	PHD	84	American	1990
Wolfson, Melville Z.	Retir	New Orleans		PHD	71	Illinois	
Wolfson, Murray	Prof	CS-Fullerton	BC	PHD	63	Wisconsin	1986
Wolinsky, Asher	Prof	Northwestern		PHD	80	Stanford	
Alfred W. Chase Professor in Business Administration							
Wolkoff, Michael	Lect	Rochester		PHD	81	Michigan	1980
Wolnicki, Miron J.	Assoc	Villanova		PHD	80	Lodz	1984
Wolozin, Harold	Prof	Mass-Boston	B	PHD	55	Columbia	1966
Wolpin, Kenneth I.	Prof	Pennsylvania		PHD	74	CUNY	1995
Womeldorf, Thomas		Evergreen St		PHD	89	American	1991
Womer, N. Keith	Dean$	Mississippi		PHD	70	Penn St	1986
Wong, David C.	C-Pr	CS-Fullerton	CO	PHD	84	Ca-SnBarb	1981
Wong, Kar-yiu	Prof	U Washington		PHD	83	Columbia	1983
Wong, Kwok-Fai Matthew	Assoc	St John's	GM	PHD	91	Miss	1990
Wong, Linda	Asst	SUNY-Bingham	JD	PHD	98	Iowa	1999
Woo, Jaejoon	Asst	DePaul	EC	PHD	97	Harvard	2000
Woo, Wing T.	Prof	Cal-Davis	EFOP	PHD	82	Harvard	1985
Wood, Edgar	Retir	Mississippi		PHD	67	LSU	1967
Wood, J. Stuart	Assoc	Loyola-N Orl	GM	PHD	80	NYU	1984
Wood, John H.	Prof	Wake Forest		PHD	64	Purdue	1985
Reynolds Professor of Economics							
Wood, Richard H. Jr.	Prof	Stetson	AFO	PHD	72	Wisconsin	1970
Wood, William C.	Prof	Jms Madison	DA	PHD	80	Virginia	1989
Woodburne, Paul	Asst	Clarion		PHD	99	Ca-Rivers	1998
Woodbury, Stephen A.	Prof	Michigan St		PHD	81	Wisconsin	1982
Wooders, John C.	Assoc	Arizona		PHD	91	Cornell	1991
Woodford, Michael	Prof	Princeton		PHD	83	MIT	
Woodland, Bill M.	Prof	E Michigan		PHD	81	Purdue	1981
Woodruff, Theodore S.	Prof	St Ambrose	DEHL	PHD	76	Columbia	8-95
Woodruff, William D.	Retir	Florida	N	PHD	52	Nottinghm	1966
Woods, Louis A.	Prof	North Fla	OQR	PHD	72	N Carol	1972
Woodward, Doug P.	Asst	So Carolina		PHD	86	Tx-Austin	
Wooldridge, Jeffrey	Prof	Michigan St	C	PHD	86	Ca-SnDgo	9-91
Woolf, Arthur G.	Assoc	Vermont	HNR	PHD	80	Wisconsin	1980
Woolf, Linda L.	Retir	Washburn		PHD	70	Kansas St	1969
Woolley, Douglas C.	Prof	Radford	HP	PHD	76	Conn	1975
Woolley, Peter J.	C	F Dick-Madis	DS	PHD	89	Pittsburgh	1987
Woolsey, W. William	Assoc	Citadel		PHD	86	GeoMason	8-86
Word, William R.	Dean	SC-Spartanbu	ADEJ	PHD	70	Tennessee	1998
Worden, Debra	Asst	George Fox		PHD	84	Purdue	
Woroby, Tamara	Prof	Towson		PHD	81	Queens	1978
Worrall, John D.	C-Pr	Rutgers-Camd		PHD	75	Rutgers	1983
Woudenberg, Henry W. Jr.	Retir	Kent State	E	PHD	68	Mich St	1967
Wray, Randall	Prof	Mo-Kansas Ct		PHD	88	U Wash	1999
Wright, Arthur W.	Prof	Connecticut	KD	PHD	69	MIT	1979
Wright, Colin	Prof	Claremont		PHD	66	Chicago	1977
Norwood and Frances Berger Professor of Business & Soc							
Wright, Gavin	C-Pr	Stanford		PHD	69	Yale	1982
William Robertson Coe Professor of American Economic History							
Wright, Jeffrey J.	Prof	Lenoir-Rhyne	AFK	PHD	87	Conn	1989
Wright, Randall	Prof	Pennsylvania	JE	PHD	86	Minnesota	1987
Wright, Virginia B.	Retir	E Kentucky		PHD	71	Geo Wash	1982
Wrightsman, Dwayne E.	Retir	New Hampshir	Fnce	PHD	64	Mich St	1964
Wrotniak, Maria	Assoc	Westminst-UT	BCO	PHD	80	Lodz	1989
Wu, De-Min	Retir	Kansas		PHD	63	Wisconsin	1964
Wu, Mickey Tai Chuen	Prof	Coe	ACEF	PHD	79	Kentucky	1979
George R. Baker Professor of Economics and Business Administration							
Wu, Roland Y.	Assoc	MD-Baltim Co		PHD	71	Stanford	

Wu, Shih-Yen	Emer	Iowa		PHD	60	Nrthwstrn	1964
Wu, Shu	Asst	Kansas	EG	PHD	00	Stanford	2000
Wu, Stephen	Asst	Hamilton	IJ	PHD	00	Princeton	2000
Wu, Xiaodong	Asst	No Carolina		PHD	99	Princeton	1999
Wu, Ying	Asst	Salisbury St		PHD	92	Oregon	8-98
Wunnava, Phanindra V.	Prof	Middlebury	ACIJ	PHD	86	SUNY-Bin	1985
Wydick, W. Bruce	Asst	San Francisc	DO	PHD	96	Berkeley	1996
Wymar, Benno	Retir	South Dakota		PHD	73	Nebraska	1968
Wyrick, Thomas L.	Prof	SW Missouri		PHD	79	Va Tech	1978
Wyss, Brenda	Asst	Wheaton-MA	JTO	PHD	95	Mass	1992
Xander, James A.	Assoc	Cen Florida	D	PHD	74	Georgia	1969
Xiao, W.	Asst	New Orleans		PHD	01	Pittsburgh	2001
Xiao, Zhijie	Asst	Illinois	CL	PHD	97	Yale	1997
Xu, Bin	Asst	Florida	FO	PHD	95	Columbia	1995
Xu, Jian	VAsst	Kenyon	FEC	PHD	99	U Wash	7-01
Xu, Peng	Asst	San Fran St		PHD	94	Iowa	1994
Xu, Yongsheng	Assoc	Georgia St	DHC	PHD	92	Tulane	1999
Xu, Zhenhui		Georgia Col		PHD	93	Virginia	
Yacovissi, William A.	Prof	Mansfield		PHD	89	SUNY-Bin	1976
Yalcindag, Selin	Asst	Wash & Jeff		PHD		Brit Colum	1998
Yalsawarng, Suthathip	Assoc	Union	CD	PHD	89	S Illinois	1989
Yamada, Tetsuji	Prof	Rutgers-Camd		PHD	87	CUNY	1987
Yamarik, Steven	Asst	Tufts	E	PHD	96	N Carol	2001
Yamashiro, Guy	Asst	CS-Long Bch		PHD	01	Ca-SnDgo	2001
Yamashita, Takashi	Asst	Nev-L Vegas	E	PHD	99	Ca-SnDgo	2000
Yamazaki, Masato	Asst	Aquinas		PHD	84	Duke	1987
Yamoah, David A.	Assoc	Kean		PHD	90	Rutgers	9-87
Yan, Chiou-shuang	Prof	Drexel		PHD	66	Purdue	1967
Yan, Huibih	Asst	Ca-Santa Crz	CD	PHD	01	Wash U	2001
Yandell, Dirk	Prof	San Diego		PHD	81	Purdue	1981
Yandle, T. Bruce Jr.	Retir	Clemson	QKH	PHD	70	Geo St	1969
Yang, Bill	Asst	Geo Southern	LG	PHD	93	Iowa	2000
Yang, Chin-Wei	Prof	Clarion	DFHR	PHD	79	W Virginia	1981
Yang, Dennis T.	Assoc	Virg Tech	DJOT	PHD	94	Michigan	2001
Yang, Wei-Hsein	Deces	Ark-Pine Blf		PHD		Nebraska	
Yang, Yung Y.	Prof	CS-Sacrament		PHD	74	Oregon	1974
Yannelis, Nicholas C.	Prof	Illinois	D	PHD	83	Rochester	1988
Yanochik, Mark	Asst	Geo Southern		PHD	97	Auburn	2000
Yarbrough, Beth V.	Prof	Amherst	ADF	PHD	83	U Wash	1982
Willard Long Thorp Professor of Economics							
Yasin, Jehad	Assoc	Ft Valley St	ETAC	PHD	87	Fla St	9-88
Yasin, Mesghena	Assoc	Morehead St		PHD	86	Cincinnati	1986
Yatawara, Ravi	Asst	Delaware	FO	PHD	01	Columbia	2000
Yates, Andrew J.	Asst	Tulane		PHD	92	Stanford	1998
Yates, Barbara M.	C-Pr	Seattle	AEGH	PHD	69	Michigan	1970
Yates, Michael Daniel	Prof	Pitts-Johnst	JP	PHD	76	Pittsburgh	1969
Yazar, Julide	Asst	Ohio Wesley		PHD		Ohio St	1999
Ye, Lixin	Asst	Ohio State	CD	PHD	01	Stanford	2001
Yee, Janice G.	Assoc	Wartburg		PHD	90	Clark	1991
Yeh, Chiou-Nan	C-Pr	Alabama St		PHD	74	Mass	1974
Yeh, Yeong-Her	Prof	Hawaii-Manoa		PHD	66	Minnesota	1965
Yellen, Janet L.	Prof	Cal-Berkeley		PHD	71	Yale	1980
Yelowitz, Aaron	Assoc	Kentucky	HI	PHD	94	MIT	2001
Yerger, David B.	Asst	Lycoming	JFTN	PHD	94	Penn St	1996
Yett, Donald E.	Prof	So Calif		PHD	68	Berkeley	1966
Yezer, Anthony M.	Prof	George Wash	R	PHD	74	MIT	1972
Yigit, Taner	Asst	St Louis		PHD	99	N Carol	2000
Yigletu, Ashagre	C-Ac	Southern	AE	PHD	72	Belgrade	1972
Yiheyis, Zelealm	Asst	Clark Atlant		PHD			
Yin, Yong	Asst	SUNY-Buffalo	CDE	PHD	95	Ohio St	1995
Ying, John S.	Assoc	Delaware	L	PHD	87	Berkeley	1987
Yinger, John M.	Prof	Syracuse	RI	PHD	74	Princeton	1986
Yochum, Gilbert R.	Prof	Old Dominion		PHD	74	W Virginia	1975
Yohe, Gary W.	Prof	Wesleyan-CT	D	PHD	75	Yale	1977
Yohe, William P.	Emer	Duke		PHD	59	Michigan	1958
Yoho, Devon L.	Assoc	Ball State	A	PHD	74	Missouri	1978
Yoon, Bong J.	Assoc	SUNY-Bingham	JC	PHD	78	Illinois	1983
Yoon, Iee	Retir	Wichita St	5-95	PHD	67	Minnesota	1968
Yoon, Mann	Assoc	CS-L Angeles		PHD	91	Illinois	1991
Yordon, Wesley J.	Retir	Colorado		PHD		Harvard	
York, Anne	Asst	Meredith		PHD		N Car St	1999
Yorukoglu, Mehmet	Asst	Chicago		PHD	96	Rochester	1996
Young, Ben	Lect	Mo-Kansas Ct	A	PHD	73	Oklahoma	1993
Young, Douglas J.	Prof	Montana St		PHD	78	Wisconsin	1977
Young, Edward G.	C-Pr	Wis-Eau Clar	J	PHD	77	Wash St	1977
Young, Eric		Florida St		PHD	01	Car Mellon	2001
Young, Gary F.	Dean	Carson-Newmn	LMQR	PHD	77	La Tech	2000
Young, H. Peyton	Prof	J Hopkins		PHD	70	Michigan	1994
Young, Jeffrey T.	Prof	St Lawrence	BQ	PHD	75	Colorado	1980
Young, Linda Wilcox	C-Pr	So Oregon St	JOF	PHD	87	Berkeley	1994

Young, Madelyn V.	Asst	Converse		PHD	91	Geo St	1991
Young, Mary E.	Prof	Southwestern	CDJQ	PHD	89	Tx-Austin	1990
Young, Richard D.	Retir	Rice		PHD	65	Car Mellon	1965
Young, Shik C.	Retir	East Wash		PHD	69	Wash St	1966
Youngelson-Neal, Helen L.	Retir	Portland St		PHD	66	Columbia	1967
Youngil, Seon	Asst	Cen Michigan		PHD		Ca-SnDgo	2000
Yousef, Tarek M.	Asst	Georgetown	OB	PHD	97	Harvard	1999
Yousefsibdari, Soheil	Inst	W Virg St		MA	01	Va Tech	2001
Yousif, Salah A.	Asst	Alabama A&M	AJ	MA		Howard	1976
Yu, Ben T.	Prof	CS-Northrdge		PHD	78	U Wash	1984
Yu, David	Asst	Tufts	G	PHD	97	Princeton	1998
Yu, Tie-Liu	Assoc	Mercer-Atlan		PHD	90	Miss St	1990
Yuhn, Ky-hyang	Assoc	Fla Atlantic	ECG	PHD	85	N Illinois	8-93
Yun, Kwan Koo	Prof	SUNY-Albany	CD	PHD	74	Stanford	1974
Yunker, James A.	Prof	W Illinois	ACDP	PHD	71	Nrthwstrn	1968
Yurgin, Nicole	Asst	Toledo					
Zabel, Edward	Retir	Florida	D	PHD	56	Princeton	1981
Zabel, Jeffrey	Assoc	Tufts	C	PHD	87	Ca-SnDgo	1989
Zachariadis, Marios	Asst	Louisiana St	E	PHD	00	Ohio St	8-00
Zadeh, Ali Haji-Mohamad	H-Pr	Susquehanna	CEGO	PHD	82	Mich St	1987
Zahka, William J.	Retir	Widener	ABNO	ABD		Bryn Mawr	1959
Zahn, Frank	Retir	Neb-Omaha	E	PHD	69	Ca-SnBarb	1979
Zahrt Geib, Elizabeth	Asst	Lewis & Clrk	GEBJ	PHD	97	Calif	1997
Zajac, Edward E.	Emer	Arizona		PHD	54	Stanford	1983
Zak, Thomas A.	Assoc	USN Academy		PHD	80	Vanderbilt	1981
Zaki, Mokhlis Y.	Retir	No Michigan	ACDO	PHD	69	Berkeley	1969
Zaleski, Peter A.	Assoc	Villanova		PHD	88	Maryland	1987
Zamanian, Zaman	Asst	Montclair St	ACEF	PHD	83	Indiana	1984
Zambrano, Eduardo	Asst	Notre Dame	D	PHD	99	Cornell	1999
Zame, William	Prof	UCLA		PHD	70	Tulane	
Zampelli, Ernest M.	Assoc	Catholic	DHQ	PHD	82	Maryland	9-85
Zampieron, Alexander Alg	Prof	Bentley	ABF	PHD	72	Fletcher	1965
Zandvakili, Sourushe	Assoc	Cincinnati	J	PHD	87	Indiana	1987
Zangeneh, Hamid	Prof	Widener	EFGP	PHD	84	Missouri	1985
Zannoni, Diane C.	Prof	Trinity-CT		PHD	76	SUNY-SBr	1975
Zapalska, Alina	Assoc	Marshall		PHD	91	Kentucky	1991
Zaporowski, Mark P.	Prof	Canisius	EC	PHD	85	SUNY-Alb	1983
Zappia, Gerard	C-Ac	Nazareth		MSED		Nazareth	
Zarembka, Paul	Prof	SUNY-Buffalo	BO	PHD	67	Wisconsin	1976
Zariar-Hayos, German	Asst	SUNY-Cortlan	FOP	PHD		Ca-Rivers	2001
Zarinnia, Abdullah	Retir	Wis-Whitewat		PHD	66	Nebraska	1967
Zarnowski, C. Frank	Prof	Mt St Mary's	AE	DA	78	Lehigh	1967
Zavareei, Manijeh	VAsoc	Trinity-CT		PHD	82	SUNY-Buf	1991
Zax, Jeffrey S.	Prof	Colorado		PHD	84	Harvard	1990
Zeager, Lester A.	Assoc	East Carol	DIJ	PHD	87	Pittsburgh	1986
Zech, Charles E.	Prof	Villanova		PHD	73	Notre Dm	1974
Zegeye, Abera	Assoc	Ball State	A	PHD	77	Indiana	1974
Zein-Elabdin, Eiman	Assoc	Frank & Mars		PHD	93	Tennessee	1995
Zeineldin, Aly	Assoc	Lg Isl-Post		PHD	79	NYU	
Zekavat, Seid M.	Assoc	Loyola Marym	ACG	PHD	64	S Calif	1964
Zelcer, Moishe	Assoc	CUNY-Brookly	G	PHD	91	Baruch	1977
Zeldes, Stephen P.	Prof	Columbia		PHD	84	Brown	1996
Benjamin Rosen Professor of Finance and Economics							
Zelleke, Girma	Assoc	Kutztown	FO	PHD	84	Colorado	1986
Zelman, Patricia G.	Prof	Tarleton St	N	PHD	80	Ohio St	1982
Zeman, Allan H.	Assoc	Robt Morris		PHD	78	Pittsburgh	1964
Zemcik, Petr	Asst	So Illinois	EG	PHD	97	Pittsburgh	1998
Zenginobuz, Unal	Asst	Bogazici	AHLP	PHD	96	Penn	1996
Zestos, George K.	Assoc	Chris Newpor	CFHO	PHD	91	Indiana	1993
Zewail, Amin A.	Assoc	Lg Isl-Brook	AEHR	PHD	75	Fordham	
Zhang, Jianbo	Assoc	Kansas	D	PHD	90	Penn St	1990
Zhang, Kevin	Asst	Illinois St	F	PHD	96	Colorado	8-97
Zhang, Qiang	Asst	Ohio State	EF	PHD	98	Ohio St	1998
Zhang, Richard	Asst	Memphis		PHD		Ohio St	2001
Zheng, Buhong	Assoc	Colo-Denver	O	PHD	93	W Virginia	1995
Zheng, Charles	Asst	Northwestern		PHD	99	Minnesota	1999
Zheng, Mingmei	VAsst	SUNY-Bingham	HD	PHD	99	Wash U	1999
Zhou, Huizhong	Assoc	W Michigan	C	PHD	86	Nrthwstrn	1990
Zhou, Lin	Prof	Arizona St	CF	PHD	89	Princeton	2001
Lincoln Professor							
Zhou, Ruilin	Asst	Pennsylvania	FDE	PHD	93	Pittsburgh	1993
Zhou, Su	Assoc	Tx-S Antonio	CEFP	PHD	91	Ariz St	1991
Zhu, Zhen	Asst	Central Okla	CFG	PHD	94	Michigan	1994
Ziegert, Andrea	Asst	Denison		PHD	85	N Carol	1997
Ziegler, Joseph A.	H-Pr	Arkansas	R	PHD	71	Notre Dm	1980
Zietz, Joachim	Prof	Mid Tenn St	EC	PHD	81	Gottingen	1989
Ziliak, James P.	Assoc	Oregon	J	PHD	93	Indiana	1993
Ziliak, Stephen T.	Asst	Bowling Gr		PHD	96	Iowa	1996
Zimbalist, Andrew	Prof	Smith	CJLP	PHD	74	Harvard	1974
Zimmer, Basil G.	Asst	Cen Michigan		PHD	72	Rutgers	1969

Zimmer, Michael A.	Prof	Evansville		PHD	77	Tennessee	1976
Zimmerman, David J.	Asst	Williams		PHD	92	Princeton	1991
Zimmerman, Jason	Asst	So Dakota St	MA	PHD	98	Purdue	1999
Zimmerman, Robert O.	Prof	Xavier	ADEF	PHD	69	SUNY-Buf	1970
Zin, Stanley E.	H-Pr	Carnegie Mel		PHD	87	Toronto	1988
Richard M. Cyert and Morris H. DeGroot Professor of Economics and Finance							
Zinam, Oleg	Retir	Cincinnati		PHD	63	Cincinnati	
Zinkhan, F. Christian	Dean	Campbell		DBA	86	Miss St	1987
Zinn, Gary	VAsst	East Carol	A	PHD	77	Syracuse	2000
Zinser, James E.	Prof	Oberlin	KLO	PHD	67	Oregon	1967
Zivot, Eric W.	Assoc	U Washington		PHD	92	Yale	1993
Zlatoper, Thomas J.	C-Pr	John Carroll	ACD	PHD	80	Nrthwstrn	1984
Zodrow, George R.	Prof	Rice		PHD	80	Princeton	1979
Zomorrodian, Reza	Asst	Mass Lib Art		EDD	90	Mass	
Zottola, Armand J.	Prof	Central Conn	JRT	PHD	70	Catholic	1970
Zschock, Dieter	Retir	SUNY-Stony B		PHD	67	Tufts	1966
Zuber, Richard A.	Prof	N Car-Charl		PHD	78	Kentucky	1978
Zuberi, Habib A.	Prof	Cen Michigan		PHD	71	S Illinois	1971
Zuehlke, Thomas W.	Assoc	Florida St	C	PHD	83	Florida	1983
Zumas, Susan	Lect	Muhlenberg		PHD	94	Lehigh	1992
Zupan, Mark	Dean	Arizona		PHD	87	MIT	1996
Zwaan, Thomas	Inst	Immaculata		MBA		Delaware	
Zweig, Michael	Prof	SUNY-Stony B		PHD	67	Michigan	1967
Zygmont, Zenon X.	Asst	W Oregon St	APLF	PHD	94	GeoMason	1998